THE JEW IN ENGLISH DRAMA

An Annotated Bibliography

❦

Compiled by EDWARD D. COLEMAN

With a Preface by JOSHUA BLOCH

THE JEW IN WESTERN DRAMA:
AN ESSAY AND A CHECK LIST
(1968)
By EDGAR ROSENBERG

NEW YORK
THE NEW YORK PUBLIC LIBRARY
and
KTAV PUBLISHING HOUSE, INC.

The Jew in English Drama was originally published in the *Bulletin of The New York Public Library,* November 1938-November 1940, and it was reprinted, with revisions and additions, in book form by The New York Public Library in 1943.

This new printing, by offset, is jointly published by The New York Public Library and Ktav Publishing House, Inc., with the addition of "The Jew in Western Drama: An Essay and A Checklist"(the Essay is reprinted from the September 1968 *Bulletin of The New York Public Library*) by Edgar Rosenberg, and the "Addenda to The Jew in English Drama" by Flola L. Shepard.

Copyright © 1968, 1970 The New York Public Library,
Astor, Lenox & Tilden Foundations

SBN 87068-011-0

MANUFACTURED IN THE UNITED STATES OF AMERICA
LIBRARY OF CONGRESS CATALOG CARD NUMBER: 67-11901

TABLE OF CONTENTS

The Jew in Western Drama: An Essay (1968)
by Edgar Rosenberg 1

The Jew in English Drama (1943) by Edward D. Coleman

    Preface by Joshua Bloch v

    Introduction vii

    Bibliography 1

    General Works 2

    Collections 6

    Individual Plays

        Earliest Times to 1837 8

        1838–1914 53

        1915–1938 116

    Index of Authors (1943) 193

    Index of Titles (1943) 221

Appendix I: The Jew in Western Drama:
A Check List (1968) by Edgar Rosenberg 239

Appendix II: Addenda to The Jew in English
Drama (1968) by Flola L. Shepard 255

Index to The Jew in Western Drama and the Appendices 259

The Jew in Western Drama
By EDGAR ROSENBERG
Cornell University

EDWARD COLEMAN'S bibliography is the sort of work which can at best be updated but hardly improved upon, and its reissuance twenty-five years after its original publication is a tribute to Coleman's immense assiduity and learning. Almost the whole of Coleman's professional life — he was only forty-seven when he died — was devoted to that branch of Anglo-Judaic studies which deals with the appearance of the Jew in English literature. Although virtually all the work which he lived to complete confined itself to the field of English drama, he had planned at the time of his death to extend his research to other media, including not only poetry and fiction but eventually the film. His two major works, *The Jew in English Drama* and the earlier volume, *The Bible in English Drama*, first published in 1931 (and also about to be reissued) reveal not only the capacity for taking pains — or call it the collector's mania — which is the bibliographer's *sine qua non* and which assumes that only the truly exhaustive is truly interesting, but a relaxed willingness, too, to immerse himself in the sub-literary, the tabloid, and the fake. Anyone who has ever sat down and endeavoured to trace a single literary theme or figure through the centuries is bound to be struck almost at once by the mass of debris that has to be swept into his card-indexed pantechnicon. Great works are rare at the best of times, and where the literary figure, like the stage-Jew's, is of an essentially popular cast, deeply rooted in folk superstitions, the yield of triviality is apt to be disheartening. As Coleman's memorialist, Mr Abraham Berger, reminds us in his little monograph, Coleman felt it to be his duty "to buy the many vulgar and inane monologues for 'Hebrew Ladies,' 'Hebrew and Dutch Comedians,' 'Hebrews and straights,' . . . to dig out the less known and less formally dramatic pieces," in an effort to "illustrate the ramifications of Jewish interest throughout the whole range of English literature." A work such as *The Jew in English Drama* is therefore of value not only to the literary historian, the student of thematics, and the student of stage-history, but equally to the sociologist and cultural historian.

It is, I think, to Coleman's credit that *The Jew in English Drama* bears the subtitle "An Annotated Bibliography," not "A Critical Bibliography." Coleman's notes, though they compress an enormous amount of factual information, rest on the bibliographer's modest presumption that his own critical judgments are — his own, and irrelevant to the task of compilation. Instead of obtruding opinions which we can either take or leave, the notes offer meticulous records of performances, often in countries other than England and America, of translations and adaptations, of production dates; generally also an epitome of the Jewish character in a given drama and perhaps the briefest synopsis — but again Coleman tells us only as much as we need to know in order to identify the character and his role within the larger framework of the play. The book, in other words, bears on every page the imprint of its author's tact.

Since Coleman himself, in his own introduction, has already traced the general course of his subject by giving a — necessarily somewhat sketchy — outline of the Jew's portrayal in English drama, I may refrain from going over the same ground in this conversation. It may be useful, on the other hand, to supplement Coleman's introductory comments by focusing the discussion on a very few of the more important plays, "with special reference" (as they say) to the Elizabethans. In trying to discover the elements which go into the typical or stereotypical stage-Jew, one may be forgiven for concentrating on the biggest English stage-Jews of them all, Marlowe's and Shakespeare's, and, without becoming unwarrantably clinical, put them to such laboratory purposes as they may serve. Perhaps my bias in favor of the earlier plays has the practical advantage of serving as a kind of corrective: since Coleman's bibliography is necessarily enumerative and so guided by quantitative considerations alone, he devotes four times as much space to dramas after 1837 (his own slightly arbitrary dividing line) as he does to the dramas preceding. But I reserve the right to talk about some plays other than Marlowe's and Shakespeare's in passing if I can find an excuse to talk about them; and since M. J. Landa's sufficiently assertive book on *The Jew in Drama* is, I will not say silent, but reticent, on the subject of Continental plays, his restraint will provide me with the additional excuse of bagging writers like Zola and Chekhov into, at least, a parenthesis or two.

I

Whoever wrote *The Croxton Play of the Sacrament* in the second half of the fifteenth century displayed a certain degree of independence and wit in treating his Jews as crudely historical individuals instead of moral categories.

The writer worked — lived, rather — with a handful of assumptions about them; for example, he "knew," more or less, that Jews were deicidal, treacherous, hypocritical, and acquisitive; that their forefather and historical archtype, Judas, acting in collusion with Caiaphas, had contrived the arrest and crucifixion of the son of God in exchange for petty cash, that he had coupled his betrayal with an outward gesture of love, and that, in a fit of remorse, he had rid himself of his blood money and hanged himself. To assume that Jews were god-loving, upright, and indifferent to property would have been not simply double-talk but literally nonsense. We may say that the playwright (or anybody else) must have been brainwashed to believe such stuff, but in that case we had better admit that a modern playwright has been brainwashed if he believes in the operations of the unconscious or the reality of the libido. Of course, we may deplore the fact that a writer, who is a supposedly civilized human being, should acquiesce in a belief which is grounded on his hatred toward another group of human beings; none the less, where the possibility of an alternative has never occurred to him, it is idle to call him dirty names. For that matter, it is doubtful whether the author of the *Croxton Play* "hated" the Jews in any affectively meaningful way — the chances are that he didn't know any; and, if anything, the play tends rather to demonstrate the opposite — but it's hardly doubtful that he knew the Jews to be the *race maudite*. Only the criminal (or psychopathic) mind fails to make at least elementary distinctions between certain norms of good and certain norms of evil; and the medieval playwright didn't have to be a more-than-ordinarily moral citizen to accept the terrible truth that the Jews were in cahoots with Satan. This, as I say, doesn't necessarily mean that he felt any strong personal animus against them. It would take a fantastic distortion of perspective to imagine him saying: "some of my worst enemies are Jews." Every so often, had it even remotely occurred to him to weaken in his assumptions, he might have been brought up short by a piece of ecclesiastical propaganda, just as those of us Free Spirits who refuse to believe in the reality of the unconscious and even resolutely refuse to have dreams, discover yet another textbook on the subject, supplying still another demonstration, providing one more case-history. Occasionally, too, the medieval man's faith in the wickedness of the Jews might be invigorated by this and that local incident, which brought the actuality a little closer to home: rumors of ritual murder, ritual desecrations, poisoning of water-wells.

For all that — and in spite of his freedom from personal hatreds — the medieval writer no doubt shared the shadowy and deep-seated dread of the Jews, the kind which lies at the bottom of superstitions and fosters them, which is all the deeper because these reputedly (and irrefutably) sinister figures were somehow elemented of a different and alien nature — not merely of a different race or religion or (least important of all) nationality, but made of different stuff. Everybody knows that our own humanitarian sentiments and our belief in freedom of association, strong as they are, won't keep us from going to pieces by the news that the moon people are on the move. Why, as recently as twenty-five years ago, did the Japanese inspire so much more dread among us than the Germans? Why, at about the same time, did the advance of the Russians provoke waves of suicide among Germans who felt at worst ripples of disquiet at the approach of the British? Guilt about the atrocities in the East? Perhaps some. But chiefly the conviction that the Russians were Tartars, barbarians, Genghis Khans, whereas the British were Field Marshall Montgomery and Viscount Alexander, and the worst you could say of the Americans was General Patton. In looking at the medieval sources of the stage-Jew, in other words, we aren't dealing with a social phenomenon, subject to legislative amendment, but with an instinctual one, a prelogical cliché. From this point of view, the author of the *Croxton Play* reveals himself as a comparatively emancipated spirit.

Although no less an authority than Pollard has dismissed the *Play of the Sacrament* as having "absolutely nothing to recommend it," and Landa, who quotes Pollard's phrase with approval, takes a similarly dim view of it, the play nevertheless departs from the run-of-the-mill mystery dramas in certain interesting ways. Its full title reads *The Play of the Conversyon of Ser Jonathas the Jewe by Myracle of the Blyssed Sacrament* and it was probably performed shortly after 1461. Its protagonist is a wealthy Sicilian merchant, Aristorius, whose connections stretch from Denmark to Alexandria — a conventionally pious Christian to all appearances, who opens the play with the customary invocation to Christ and is about to proceed to church and render thanks to God, from Whom all blessings flow. In his absence, the merchant's clerk is sent off to be on the look-out for any foreign traders who may have arrived and with whom Aristorius might do business. At this point, a Jewish merchant, the Jonathas of the title, enters, attended by four lesser Jews: their entrance is preceded by the direction "Now ... the Jewe Jonathas shall make hys bost."

Jonathas' "boast," like the opening soliloquy in Marlowe's *Jew of Malta* a century afterwards, turns into an affirmation of his wealth, a sensuous recital of his material property, his "gold, syluer and presyous stonys," his "abu[n]ddance of spycis," his "long peper, and Indas lycorys":

> I have dyamantis derewourthy so to dresse,
>> And emerawdis, ryche I trow they be,
> Onyx and achatis both more and lesse,
>> Topazyons, smaragdis of grete degree,
>> Perlys precyous grete plente;
> Of rubes ryche I have grete renown;
>> Crepawdis [toadstones] and calcedonyes semely to se
> And curyous carbunclys here ye fynd moren.

The scheme which Jonathas now broaches, in complicity with his four underlings, is to get hold of the consecrated wafer in the church next-door. The Jewish underlings, it may be added, are of no particular importance in themselves; their presence helps to underline Jonathas' primacy and his self-conceit ("Jazun and Jazdun they waytyn on my wyll, / Masfat and Malchus they do the same"), just as those "base slaves," First Jew, Second Jew, and Third Jew emphasize, by contrast, Barabas' preeminence; and besides the playwright requires them to provide both the sense of conspiracy and the weird sense of movement in the spectacular farce to follow. Jonathas' ostensible motives for the theft of the Host are rather instructive:

> The beleve of thes Crysten men ys false, as I wene
> For the[y] beleve in a cake, — my thynk yt ys onkynde, —

"I think it's *unnatural*." Jonathas, one notes, is incapable of swallowing the symbolic substance of Christianity; as he fondles his precious gems, the idea of the transubstantiation dissolves into revolting nonsense. For that matter, he suspects the whole business about the Host to be a put-up job, a fairy-tale concocted by the Christians as proof of the crucifixion — an event which he also denies as a malicious fabrication. Once he has gotten hold of the wafer and been able to test it, he'll have his proof: thus I refute it.

The Jews are then taken to the house of Aristorius by that busy scout, his clerk, and Jonathas, coming to the point at once, asks Aristorius to steal the wafer, for which he is prepared to pay the merchant twenty pounds. Without waiting for Aristorius to ask him what he could possibly want with *that* merchandise, Jonathas quite candidly informs him that he wants to discover whether the Sacrament is in fact what the Christians claim it to be, adding that if he finds the claim to be bona fide, he will confess his mistake and turn Christian — but this last may be an improvised lie, an appeal to Aristorius' charitable desire to bring a stray sheep into the fold. Aristorius finds the Jew's request a little shocking — shockingly little; he temporizes; finally, in view of the risk he runs of being discovered in the act by the chaplain, he settles for a hundred pounds. Jonathas counts out the money then and there, and Aristorius, after making sure that the coast is clear, procures the Host for him.

The five Jews, left to themselves, place the Host on the table and in a series of responsive speeches recapitulate the narrative of the Gospels: this serves the double purpose of alerting the spectators to the enormity of the Jews' crime and of foreshadowing the scenes which follow. At this point, the action proper begins, and with it the play degenerates into a kind of weird Jews' Witches' Sabbath, not perhaps essentially different in quality from lurid episodes like it in other plays of the period; the plot can be put away in a paragraph. The Jews, in a transparent re-enactment of the Crucifixion, begin by savagely hacking away at the Host with their daggers, first piercing it in the four places which symbolize the wounds in Christ's hands and feet, Jonathas reserving to himself the right to inflict the final stroke — the spear-thrust into Christ's side:

> Now I am bold with batayle hym to bleyke [make pale],
>   This mydle part alle for to prene;
> A stowte stroke also for to stryke, —
>   In the myddys yt shalbe sene!

The Host begins to bleed; Jonathas, horrified, picks it up to toss it into a cauldron of oil, finds that the Sacrament clings to his hand, and runs (literally) mad with pain. The others catch hold of him, nail the Sacrament to a post, but in process of being pried loose from the Host, Jonathas is unable to disengage his hand, which is severed from his arm. Eventually (I omit a comic intermezzo involving a medical leech and his factotum) one of the Jews plucks the nails from the doorpost and — using a pair of pincers this time to avoid electric shock — flings the Host into the boiling cauldron, whose water turns blood-red. Jonathas, goaded into frenzy by the experience, instructs the others to prepare a fire and cast the Thing into an oven. This brings on the final shock, the reversal, and the miracle: the oven bursts, blood seeping through its crevices, and the image of the crucified Christ appears out of the fire. He lectures the Jews — but more in sorrow than in anger — on their faithlessness; and the Jews, humbled, convinced (or "outwitted" if you like), kneel before Him and ask His forgiveness:

> And mekely I aske mercy, amendys to make.

Jonathas' hand is restored; the image of Christ disappears and reverts to symbol; the double-dealing Aristorius seeks, and receives, absolution; and in the penultimate tableau the Jews submit to formal baptism:

> And therfor all we with on[e] consent
> Knele unto yower hygh souereynte;
> For to be crystenyd ys ower intent.
> Now all ower dedys to yow shewyd haue we.

It can be seen that the crimes at the heart of the play are the crimes of physical mutilation — blood sacrifice — and commercial malpractice. Though Jonathas is not greedy in the ordinary sense, as later stage-Jews are greedy, the playwright presents him initially in terms of his mammon-worship and leaves no doubt that the Jew puts his money to perverted uses — to "buy Christ's body." And though in this instance — not a typical one — the act of betrayal devolves on the Sicilian as much as on the Jews, Jonathas is clearly meant to play the role of the Tempter; compared with him Aristorius appears as an innocent. What gives the drama it uniqueness, apart from the duplicity of the Christian, are the intermittent resonance of its language, the attempt to humanize the Jews just enough to bring them out from the dark places where the devil squats, and the note of friendliness, of grace, on which it ends. "Here shall the bysshope crysten the Jewys with great solempnyte." If this is to be interpreted as a penalty, the implication is singularly absent. The play is most clearly within the tradition, and closest to the New Testament source of the stage-Jew, in the lurid re-creation of the deicide and the ruthless enjoyment that goes with it. Among the later playwrights the mutilation of Christ will be translated into human mutilation, cannibalism, the pound of flesh. For the rest, one is made to feel that the writer is very much aware of his audience, very conscious, too, of the festive and ceremonial character of his presentation. To say that he is "playing up to" their convictions would be to cheapen his motives; the convictions are deeply his own. As ritual, the thing conforms to certain unalterable patterns implicit in the Gospel narratives and the mysteries which are the *fons et origo* of drama, though — again as ritual — these plays invite incidental and improvised embellishments in tune with the times. One isn't surprised to read that in one of the passion plays performed in the Swiss Alps in 1923, Jesus rose to heaven waving the flag of Switzerland.

II

The image of the Jew as mutilator, usurer, and implacable alien reaches its apogee among the Renaissance writers. In line with the established conventions and the historical actualities, Elizabethan and Jacobean stage-Jews (and it is easy to exaggerate their number) axiomatically operate outside of England; they have no business among the cold nations of the moral North;

and though these geographical substitutions are frequently of little more than nominal importance in Shakespearean and post-Shakespearean romantic comedy, the presentation of the Jews as figures wholly beyond the reach of English life deepens the air of exoticism at which the playwright is aiming. In nine cases out of ten, you find them in Italy, the habitation of Machiavelli; but Lisbon, Turkey, and North Africa, too, provide an appropriate backdrop to these swarthy and blood-thirsty sons of Judas. So firmly is this tradition of the alien — the Southern — Jew fixed in the minds of the playwright, that the one London-based drama with a Jew in it, Robert Wilson's archaic and slightly incoherent allegory, *The Three Ladies of London,* which precedes *The Jew of Malta* by half a decade, needlessly adds to the confusion. by wrenching its geographical bearings from London to Turkey for its Jew-scene. In the later playwrights, the presence of the Jew-poisoner in a foreign milieu (or of the non-Jew disguising himself as Jew-poisoner, or Jew-cheat, or Jew-pander) is exploited in order to underline the general corruption of the Italianated world: in this — always slightly cheerful, slightly innocent — hail-horrors-hail atmosphere, the playwright turns the screw of horror another turn by bringing on the Jew as metaphor for putrescence in the state. In Webster's *The Devil's Law-Case,* for example, a more or less typical specimen of Jacobean "decadence," and not a bad one, a Neapolitan merchant, Romelio, dresses up as a Jewish doctor in order to inflict a lethal wound on his antagonist (this assumption of the Jewish disguise is simply another one of the Games People Play on the stage; it persists, as an increasingly pointless gag, through Holberg's *Diderich Menschenskraek* and Dumas Senior's *Monte Cristo*); Romelio dwells on his disguise in a soliloquy which, though obviously cribbed from Marlowe, defines itself so sharply from the pure indulgent Marlovian impudence, from those "heiteren Regionen / wo die schoenen Geister wohnen," that the two speeches, side by side, might almost be used as a class-room exercise in contrast between Elizabethan and Jacobean — and if not quite that, at least between Marlovian and Websterian:

> Excellently well habited! — why, me thinks
> That I could play with mine own shadow now,
> And be a rare Italianated Jew;
> To have as many several change of faces,
> As I have seen carv'd upon one Cherrystone;
> To wind about a man like rotten Ivy,
> Eat into him like Quicksilver, poison a friend
> With pulling but a loose hair from's beard, or give a drench,
> He should linger oft nine years, and ne'er complain,

> But in the Spring and Fall, and so the cause
> Imputed to the disease natural; for slight villanies,
> As to coin money, corrupt Ladies' Honours,
> Betray a Town to th' Turk, or make a Bonfire
> A' th' Christian Navy, I could settle to't,
> As if I had eat a Politician,
> And digested him to nothing but pure blood.

What we get in a passage such as this is a fairly elementary identification of *Jew* with political depravity, specifically "Italian" depravity, in the sense that Romelio — himself all along nefarious, homicidal, *politic* — reaches his moral nadir at the moment of "becoming" a Jew. The phrase "Italianated Jew" (unless Webster, quite improbably, intends it in the sense of "assimilated Jew") rather gives the whole show away, of course: Webster momentarily forgets that it isn't he talking but his character who, as an Italian himself, would hardly make an issue of his Italianate qualities: Romelio, for the moment, slips back into the guise of his fabricant, viewing the whole poisonous spectacle from Albion's shores.

In no work of the period (though fiction, not drama) is this element of the Italianated Jew more pronounced than it is in Thomas Nashe's *Unfortunate Traveller*. Since the book has been largely ignored by Anglo-Judaic historians, I shall say a word about it here. The book, which is almost precisely contemporary with *The Merchant of Venice*, is one of the great grotesque works of English narrative prose, the first halfway modern English novel in the sense of paying more attention to the disasters of its hero than to the triumphs of its rhetoric. Nashe's language is still enormously opaque: a passage in which the half-raised nails in a toenail torture are compared to "a Tailor's shop window half open on a holiday" naturally keeps the object (which is ghastly) at a consoling distance: Nashe invites you to enjoy the artifice while watching him at his Jew-baiting. Joyce might have modelled his vocabulary on Nashe's: "Why should I goe gadding and fisgigging after firking flantado amphibologies, wit is wit, and good will is good will;" and some of the extreme scaled-down situations in the novel (the rape of a Roman matron, the description of the sweating sickness, Jack Wilton waiting to be cut up by the Jewish anatomist) may be considered enjoyable bedtime reading by novelists like Wyndham Lewis and Djuna Barnes. Apart from its stylistic inflation, *The Unfortunate Traveller* sometimes reads very much like a novel by Defoe: it has its monolithic middle-class hero (Wilton), puts him through a dozen incidents of just sufficiently graduated intensity to suggest the rudiments of "structure;" and concludes with the hero's moral reformation and his withdrawal from the scenes of mundane experience. (Stripped of its puritanism, *Robinson Crusoe*, isn't in fact terribly different from *The Unfortunate Traveller* in some of its broader ethical premises). For Nashe does give you this sense of progression: the book begins with a series of disconnected jests (Wilton gulling a cider-merchant, a Switzer captain, and so on); the middle portion takes Jack on his "unfortunate" travels in Holland and Germany and presents some of the more brutal descriptions of physical violence and death to be found in Tudor fiction, along with some brilliantly improvised passages of inkhorn burlesque and sectarian critique; lastly Jack accompanies the Earl of Surrey to Italy, where the physical horror encountered earlier is deepened and finally checked by the moral and religious impulses which accelerate Jack's return to England and fortify his decision to make his peace with the world. In the course of the narrative, largely because so much of it is based on topical issues, we get a good picture of Jack's social and political attitudes, which are xenophobic, anti-Catholic, anti-Puritan, anti-Semitic, and anti-feminist, which is another way of saying that our young man is the one hundred percent normative Englishman of his day. Where there is so much leisure for prejudice, one may be tempted to dismiss Jack's Jew-hatred as no more and no less important than any of his other biasses. On the other hand, Nashe brings on his Jews to provide the climax of the book, as if to point his moral by their last-minute intrusion; as cannibalists they pose the most immediate physical threat to the hero; and by all but rounding out his story with one of the Jews' execution, Nashe somehow gives you the impression that of all the available monsters, the Jews are on the whole the worst of the lot.

Movement is the essence of *The Unfortunate Traveller*, and the title itself drives home Nashe's moral almost to the point of redundancy. For at the bottom of the book lies the conviction, so widely shared by Tudor moralists, that travel invites disaster — a conviction which is rooted in the more general suspicion towards "experience" as the thorniest road to wisdom. "Learning teacheth more in one yeare, than experience in twentie," Roger Ascham wrote (in at least twenty different ways) in *The Scholemaster*; and to travel is to go out of one's way to look for trouble. Only look at the Jews, says Nashe: "The first traveler was *Cain*, and he was called a vagabond runnagate on the face of the earth. Travel . . . is good for nothing but to tame and bring men under. God had no greater curse to lay upon the *Israelites*, than by leading them out of their own country to live as slaves in a strange land." But if travel corrupts, travel to Rome corrupts absolutely. "What men call gallantry and Gods adultery / Is much more common where the climate's sultry," jokes

Byron; and 250 years earlier the moral Ascham noted with pious spite: "I was once in *Italie* myselfe: but I thanke God, my abode there was but ix dayes: And yet I saw in that litle time, in one citie, more libertie to sinne than ever I heard tell of in our noble citie of *London* in ix yeares." Jack's Italian journey thus provides the appropriate climax to his apprenticeship; this is where the real *diablerie* is to be found, the types of greed and lust and brutality which the English are so foolish to seek out. His initial Italian adventure plunges him into a series of savage plots involving harlots, pimps, cheats, murderers: this, says Nashe, is the "real" Italy, which is accessible to satire and critique; and as if to contrast it with the dream-world of Belmont, Nashe precedes his description of the Roman plague and the Jew-villains with a wonderfully sustained reverie in a Roman garden, which drifts by degrees into a vision of the Golden Age, a time when "the rose had no cankers, the leaves no caterpillars, the sea no Sirens, the earth no usurers." But that is merely the dream-vision; the earth is full of usurers, and Italy is the place to look for them.

This is a rather roundabout way of getting the Jews into context — as Nashe would say, "my principal subject plucks me by the elbow." Toward the end of the novel, Jack is arrested on a false rape-murder charge and barely escapes hanging; and as he is making his way through the streets of Rome to look for his mistress, he stumbles on her making love to a Jew's apprentice. The Jew — Zadoch — first locks him up as a housebreaker and then sells him to a fellow-Jew, the Pope's private physician, Zachary, who is on the lookout for live anatomy subjects and willing to pay a good price for Jack as one of the few healthy specimens left in plague-infested Rome. Nashe hardly distinguishes the two Jews, and though Zachary is perhaps just a trifle more enterprising than Zadoch and a little more sharply pictured both in his miserly and his homicidal energies, the two might be interchangeable — the fact that at the end of the book Nashe rather arbitrarily imposes a death-sentence on the (comparatively) more harmless Zadoch and allows Zachary to escape merely suggests that judicious — and judicial — distinctions among Jews are less than pertinent. Zachary's avarice (but it could just as easily be Zadoch's) turns into a series of brilliant improvisations on Avaritia: one has got to piece the conceits together before anything like a coherent picture begins to emerge, and even then one is apt to ignore the whole for the parts:

> Miserable is that Mouse that lives in a Physician's house, *Tantalus* lives not so hunger starved in hell, as she doth there. Not the very crumbs that fall from his table, but Zachary sweeps together, and of them moulds up

a Manna. Of the ashy parings of his bread, he would make conserve of chippings. Out of bones after the meat was eaten off, he would alchemize an oil, that he sold for a shilling a dram. His snot and spittle a hundred times he hath put over to his apothecary for snow water. Any spider he would temper to perfect Mithridate. His rheumatic eyes when he went in the wind, or rose early in a morning, dropt as cool alum water as you would request. He was Dame Niggardize sole heir & executor.

En route to the Jew-anatomist's, Jack attracts the attention, and instant lust, of one of the Pope's concubines; and while Jack is waiting for Zachary to cut him up, she petitions Zachary to sell Jack to her as a lover. Zachary "Jewishly and churlishly" refusing her offer, she persuades the Pope of Zachary's complicity in a plot to poison him (to support her lie she herself administers poison to the Pope's "grand-sublimity-taster"); and though the Pope's immediate response is to murder all the Jews in Rome then and there, his Lucrezia prevails on him to mitigate the sentence to one of expulsion. "This request at the first was sealed with a kiss, and the Pope's edict without delay proclaimed throughout Rome, namely, that all foreskin clippers, whether male or female, belonging to the Old Jewry, should depart and avoid upon pain of hanging within twenty days after the date thereof." Jack, stretched out on Zachary's table and on the point of being butchered, is kidnapped by the concubine's henchmen and delivered to her boudoir; and the intrigue shifts back to Zachary and Zadock, whose reaction to the papal edict provokes one of the most hilariously sinister physical "descriptions" of the Jew in Rennaissance literature.

Descriptions, stand by [Nashe's breezy *Musa Mihil*]: here is to be expressed the fury of Lucifer when he was turned over heaven bar for a wrangler. There is a toad fish, which taken out of the water swells more than one would think his skin could hold, and bursts in his face that toucheth him. So swelled Zadoch, and was ready to burst out of his skin and shoot his bowels like chain-shot full at Zachary's face for bringing him such baleful tidings, his eyes glared & burnt blue like brimstone and *aqua vitae* set on fire in an eggshell, his very nose lightened glow-worms, his teeth crashed and grated together, like the joints of a high building cracking and rocking like a cradle, when as a tempest takes her full butt against his broad side.

The Jews are left to devise means of revenge; the poison-motif reappears momentarily with a characteristically obscene twist: "If thou wilt [Zadoch is speaking], I'll go to a house that is infected, where, catching the plague and having got a running sore upon me, I'll come and deliver [to the concubine] a supplication and breathe upon her. I know my breath stinks so already that it is within half a degree of poison: I'll pay her home if I perfect it with any more putrefaction." Zachary, more practically the clinician, suggests a more effective way of poisoning her food, but his commissionaire, Jack's sweetheart, betrays the scheme; and that is the end of that. One has somewhat to spell out these moves and countermoves, tedious as they sound without Nashe's prose to bounce you along, because the point of all this is to get Jack increasingly to see the vanity of "experience," of movement, of motion. In the end, Jack gets the point and repents: "I married my courtesan, performed many alms deeds; and hasted so fast out of the *Sodom* of *Italy*, that within forty days I arrived at the King of *England's* camp;" the Jew-doctor finds sanctuary with the Duke of Bourbon "and there practised with his bastardship all the mischief against the Pope & *Rome* that envy could put into his mind;" and the Jew-miser is butchered in a scene of such weirdly circumstantial detail that by comparison Barabas' "But now begins the extremity of heat" seems to pass into the void with the peremptory swiftness of a scream — but that is the difference between novel and play.

> To the execution place was he brought, where first and foremost he was stripped, then on a sharp iron stake fastened in the ground, he had his fundament pitched, which stake ran up along into a body like a spit; under his arm-holes, two of like sort; a great bonfire they made round about him, wherewith his flesh roasted, not burned: and ever as with the heat his skin blistered, the fire was drawn aside, and they basted him with a mixture of Aqua fortis, alum water, and Mercury sublimatum, which smarted to the very soul of him and searched him to the marrow. Then did they scourge his back parts so blistered and basted, with burning whips of red hot wire: his head they anointed over with pitch and tar, and so inflamed it. To his privy members they tied streaming fire-works: the skin from the crest of the shoulder, as also from his elbows, his huckle bones, his knees, his ankles, they plucked and gnawed off with sparkling pincers: his breast and his belly with seal-skins they grated over, which as fast as they grated and rawed, one stood over and laved with smith's cindery water & Aqua vitae: his nails they half raised up, and then underpropped them with sharp pricks, like a Tailor's shop window half open on a holiday: every one of his fingers they rent up to the wrist: his toes they brake off by the roots, and let them still hang by a little skin. In conclusion they had a small oil fire, such as men blow light bubbles of glass with, and beginning at his feet, they let him lingeringly burn up, limb by limb, till his heart was consumed, and then he died.

There are moments (Zadoch's death is one of them) when one is made to feel that Italy is really no explanation, and the Israelites are none at all; that what Nashe is saying — here and there, increasingly toward the end, when he himself has grown from an anthologist of jokes into a fine novelist

— is really (to paraphrase the vocabulary of American Gothic) that "the horror of which I write is not of Italy but of the soul." Still, Italy is horrible, too, and the Jews there roast babies and Englishmen.

And then also, of course (for this too needs to be said) Nashe is plainly enjoying the spectacle he reports and fascinated by it. For one of the lingering sensations one brings away from a scene such as this is the sense that for Nashe and for Marlowe and Shakespeare Jew-baiting, like bull-baiting, is a sport — a brutal sport, but a sport all the same. Naturally the animal had better be fierce enough to insure a lively game, or the groundlings are going to grumble. One thus needn't be surprised to find in so many of these writers a sense, finally, of *gloating* once the Jew has been brought to bay. In a more sophisticated writer like Shakespeare, this sense may be tempered by a sense of pity, of course (the two aren't mutually exclusive, provided only the beast is big enough or crafty enough and gives you a hard enough time), but the attitude which describes the Jew's downfall in Marlowe and Nashe and Shakespeare is just this sense of *Schadenfreude*. It's surely a mistake to assume, simplistically, that characters like Barabas and Shylock are intended to perish in an atmosphere strictly of horror or laughter or (least likely of all) pity; their exit takes place rather in an aura of vindictive, derisive relief. A student of mine once remarked that *The Merchant of Venice* is one of those plays which leaves a sour taste in your mouth. He didn't mean by this, I believe, what the lachrymose little girl in Heinrich Heine's anecdote meant when she began to yell at a performance of *The Merchant:* "The poor man has been wronged!" What I think he meant was: "The great author gloats too much. Leave Shylock alone already, will you. I don't much like him either. But all this mirth in funerals and baptisms.... It's unseemly."

III

Nashe is in a way closer to bull's eye than writers like Marlowe and Shakespeare, who enjoyed a relatively avant-garde position on the subject of the Jew. For example, they could exert their creative efforts towards allowing their Jews a limited measure of freedom as well as a patently self-conscious sense of their antagonists, which enabled characters like Barabas and Shylock to project their situations ethically: "Preach me not out of my possessions;" "Is theft the ground of your religion?" "You call me misbeliever, cutthroat dog, / And spit upon my Jewish gaberdine, / And all for use of that which is mine own," and so forth. Indeed these playwrights often surprise one by the liberties they took with their materials and their Jewish personnel — departures from the dead center which are striking enough when one compares their Jews with the half-dozen run-of-the-mill poisoners who perform their concise and ugly businesses in the plays of the Jacobeans. Still, the notion of a "good Jew" would have struck all these people as a fundamental absurdity, as much as to say: "he was the mildest-mannered Jew / That ever scuttled ship or cut a throat."

As the two great Jew-dramas of the period (or, for that matter, of English literature), *The Jew of Malta* and *The Merchant of Venice* have inevitably been lumped together in discussion, generally with the aim of showing up Shylock's superior virtues, and of praising Shakespeare's fine flashes of humanity at the expense of Marlowe's blatant and obtrusive crudeness. If you want to find a really wicked Jew, so runs the formula, not this man but Barabas. Since Shakespeare is obviously a weightier article than Marlowe, this distinction is of importance to commentators not only of the Calisch-Philipson generation but to the more recent historians, who find a certain boozy moral uplift in marshalling excuses for Shylock by dwelling in fear and trembling on the atrocious vices of our man from Malta.

Admittedly the two plays have enough in common to justify their being linked conversationally, and they are sometimes performed in one and the same program series. Evidently a number of elements in Shakespeare's play are borrowed from Marlowe's (but since authors have a habit of keeping what they borrow, the term may as well be expunged from the lexicon of scholarship hereafter: other languages are more scrupulous in this than ours). The resemblances are all fairly out in the open, and we may refrain from dwelling on them too emphatically. Both Marlowe and Shakespeare, as has been said, locate their Jews outside of England — Marlowe of course having the added stimulus of an historical or quasi-historical model in back of him in the Duke of Naxos. Both Barabas and Shylock engage in the two activities thrust upon them by superstition and long usage, those of usurer and mutilator. In Shylock the role of mutilator is of course the fact on which the whole play is predicated; in Barabas, more fastidiously the poisoner, the disciple and protégé of the Borgias, the motif of cannibalism is touched on in more incidental ways. In both plays, the Jew's initial appearance turns at once, and without hedging the issue, on his money-making function, though in *The Merchant* it is of course Antonio, not Shylock, who, like Barabas, is waiting for his ships to come in. (I find it difficult to associate Shylock with ships at all). Both bear an inveterate hatred toward the Christians, and on rather the same grounds, those of economic rivalry and religious oppression; and both rather plume themselves on their talent for disguising their hatred by assuming a stance of servility as the occasion requires. Both are crudely speaking "individualists," in that they operate virtually on their own resources and disparage communal allegiances of any sort; their individualism, even without the cristophobia, would be enough to damn them in the eyes of the average Elizabethan, who could be expected to enjoy the antics of the unsociable Outsider just so far but would find him morally objectionable in the end. In a world governed by austere ordinances and a rigid table of organization, the spectacle of the displaced person is apt to provoke a certain amount of slightly comic revulsion; in Shakespeare's day the "individualist" is necessarily of the devil's party. Beyond this, Shylock and Barabas alike are attended by just enough auxiliary Jews to impress you with at least the rudiments of a tight little Jewish community in back of them, Shylock conniving with Tubal and the invisible Chus, Barabas surrounding himself with his small-time Job's comforters, whose function in the play, however, is choric rather than dramatic, parody instead of the genuine article. As between the two, Shylock's convivial strolls to synagogue suggest a more effective and dangerous Jewish communal life, a "Jewish conspiracy," than the collection of weepy cronies who keep Barabas tea-time company at home — one may recall that Luther, surely as vulgar and rabble-rousing an anti-Semite as you can be without quite surrendering your magisterial intelligence, in his distasteful tract *Von den Juden und Ihren Luegen* (the great Reformator's "Protocols of the Elders of Zion") describes the synagogue literally as "ein Teuffels Nest." In keeping a rendez-vous in that dark domicile, Shylock and Tubal may thus be suspected of hammering out more alarming projects than an increase in the local usance rates.

Even so, Tubal and company remain a shadowy crew, born minor characters, consciously kept out of sight, lest they deflect from the Jew's purposefully going it alone and so threaten to undermine his frightening social dislocatedness. That leaves the Jew's daughter. Marlowe is the first playwright, and Shakespeare the second, to introduce the figure, so important as to be almost inseparable from the stereotype hereafter, of *la belle juive*, the Jew's pet, the gorgeous and generally blameless daughter, of whom Chateaubriand later made the fantastic comment that, unlike her father, she retained her pristine innocence *ex alto* for the simple reason that she hadn't taken part in the Crucifixion. The daughters function somewhat similarly in both plays: both run away from the father, though in response to rather different stimuli; Gentiles woo them both; both are formally baptised. In both plays the coexistence of daughters and ducats, girls and gold, generates a certain confusion, or perversion, in values, which persists through *Ivanhoe*. From one point of view, the daughter's desertion may be regarded as the ultimate judgment on the barbarian conduct of that ogre, the father, who places so high a price-tag on her; but again one's impulse to generalize is checked by the sharp temperamental and notional differences in the two girls. As Cardozo concisely formulates the distinction: "Abigail deserved a better father, Shylock a better daughter." Jessica is a nice worldly little tart, highly sexed, dying to get on with it, who turns her defection into an escapade; Abigail, who is Virginia (or Clarissa Harlowe) revolted into sanctity, turns it into a retreat. If Abigail were to claim that she is more an antique Roman than a Jew, Jessica (who is of no denominational significance whatsoever) would simply make sure that there's still some liquor left.

Either way, the presence of the Jew's daughter requires at least the factitious existence of the Jew's wife, but the playwright has no use for her and kills her before the curtain goes up. Evidently, any affective interference by her would at once shatter the illusion of the Jew's solitary and nasty self-sufficiency in a resolutely monosexual, professionally homogeneous world. Where the man spends the whole day in bargaining on the Rialto and his evenings in supping with the devil, what is there for Madame Jew to do? Very little, except to domesticate her husband, who *will not* be tamed. So there now trot onstage for the next two-hundred-fifty years an unbroken procession of Jewish widowers, as if, really, it were one of the rock-bottom conditions of Jewishness to outlive one's wife. Again, the widowerhood of Barabas and Shylock aren't given quite the same weight — or, to put it another way, Shylock is a trifle more clearly the widower than Barabas, whose wife is so thoroughly out of it that it would never occur to anyone to speculate on the domestic habits of the late Mrs B, whereas Shylock's Leah appears at least by allusion and so evokes the merest flash of pathos, which is extinguished the next moment in funny business, in "a wilderness of monkeys." The emergence in literature of the squat old Jewess, fit mate to the squat old Jew, is to all intents an invention of the nineteenth century. By then, of course, the Jew has been excused from his supernatural engagements and, along with it, divested of his Baroque triumphs, if not his squalid capitulations. Among the dramas of Shakespeare's younger contemporaries, Fletcher's *Custom of the Country*, which is based on Cervantes's last novel *Persiles y Sigismunda* and which Cardozo calls "one of the coarsest plays in existence," is unique in presenting an eligible Jew, the frightful Zabulon, who, in the final processionals of he's-and-she's, walks downstage holding hands with the madam of a male brothel. But this is hardly more than a curtain call, gesture rather than action; and when Colley Cibber, who, as

Dr Johnson said, "mutilated the plays of two generations," rewrote Fletcher's comedy under the title *Love Makes a Man,* the Jew-role was dropped.

There remain then a number of verbal echoes which Shakespeare picks up from Marlowe (these have been catalogued by Ward and Landa), and the unappetizing metaphors sanctified by tradition. Both playwrights very freely indulge in name-calling: the patent association with the devil, naturally — infused into the figure of Machiavel, he virtually presides over *The Jew of Malta* as Marlowe's prolocutor and nimble master of ceremonies; and both writers freely avail themselves of the customary allusions to repulsive or predatory animals. (One may find them equally congested in *Richard III* to describe another quite bad individualist, though their application in the history play is entirely local, of course, not toxic, and to that extent inoffensive to anybody except the nominee). In *The Merchant of Venice,* as Mark Van Doren has noted, the impression of Shylock's proximity to a world of subhuman categories is deepened finally by Shylock's own habit — in that dry, cracked, rasping, jarring voice of his — of bringing together one beast-analogy after another in his quarrels: "there be land-rats and water-rats, water-thieves and land-thieves;" "you call me misbeliever, cut-throat dog;" "is it possible a cur can lend three thousand ducats?"

> What if my house be troubled with a rat,
> And I be pleas'd to give ten thousand ducats
> To have it ban'd? what, are you answer'd yet?
> Some men there are love not a gaping pig!
> Some that are mad if they behold a cat!
> And others when the bagpipe sings i' th' nose,
> Cannot contain their urine....

"The wound," as Van Doren says, "is animal, self-inflicted, and self-licked."

But whatever else he may be — spider, wolf, hog, rat, vulture, weasel, fox, serpent, wasp — the Jew is chiefly and most consistently the *dog* — the ferocious cur in one aspect, the fawning spaniel in another — at least down to the days of good Queen Anne when, as Leslie Fiedler once wryly pointed out, the word *dog* as a pejorative term for *Jew* went momentarily underground, not because the value of Jews had gone up since Shakespeare's day, but because the value of dogs had. In that urbane, effeminate, snob-ridden society, with its polished insults and pernicious gossip, it paid to be careful. A writer like Pope, for example, to guard himself against the imputation of slandering such-and-such-a-one's expensive lap-dog, will therefore shift the metaphor to that of the toad:

> And every child hates Shylock, though his soul
> Still sits at squat, and peers not from its hole

— the image, as Fiedler reminds us, picked up two hundred years afterwards by Eliot in the opening passage of *Gerontion:*

> And the Jew squats on the window sill, the owner,
> Spawned in some estaminet of Antwerp....

After Pope, the picture of the Jew-dog is mounted once more by the sentimental writers of Cumberland's generation, but it no longer looks the same. The Jew is now readmitted (through the servant's entrance) as the "good Jew," "good little fellow," to be petted and patronized, answerable to such unmistakably dogged purposes as docility, submissiveness, loyalty, domestic vigilance, and the like. Walter Scott, for example, among novelists our foremost zoophile, who prefigures in a major way the whole literary tradition (if it is one) behind *Bob, Son of Battle* and *Lassie, Come Home*, consistently presents Isaac of York as a harmless dog, a toothless Shylock — though Scott also does this with greater acrimony than the purely oleaginous sentimentalizers of Cumberland's ilk.

IV

The historian of literature, who is more or less committed to an evolutionary view of his subject, has forever got to buck the temptation to sacrifice the autonomy and integrity of a play (or poem or novel) to such things as common patterns, influences, communities of ideas, and so on. After a certain point, the discovery of tendentious and thematic resemblances turns into a sort of academic tic. It sometimes takes a conscious effort of the will therefore to remind yourself that in sitting down to write *The Jew of Malta* and *The Merchant of Venice* Marlowe and Shakespeare were not urgently aware of writing Elizabethan plays, or of working in the post-medieval tradition, or (as we like to think) of living in a bawdy lusty riotous age: it is we who think of them as Renaissance, not they. It is all right for us to make these assumptions for them afterwards, as long as we keep the distance steadily in mind and allow them their own share of obliviousness. Very likely Marlowe and Shakespeare did not have very much in common temperamentally: as much, let us suppose, as Mailer and Styron. Of Shakespeare we know very little except what the plays reveal about him and what Sir Edmund Chambers has pieced together. Marlowe has been brought a little closer to us by the interesting circumstances of his death and the sensational allegations of atheism which were brought against him; but this information does not necessarily clarify our view of the plays, and may in fact obstruct or distort it. Whatever may be said of these two dramas, therefore, should be qualified by the small *caveat* that the appearance of Barabas in the one and of Shylock in the other provides little more than a pleasant excuse to talk about them, and that two stage-Jews do not make a Literature.

One may begin with the innocent suggestion that Marlowe's play is entitled *The Jew of Malta*, and that Shakespeare's play is not entitled *The Jew of Venice* — though later adaptations and perversions (like the German *Komoedia* of 1608 and Granville's grubby farce which dominated the English stage for forty years after 1701) gave it this title. In the cast of charcters, Shakespeare's man is simply listed as "Shylock, a Jew." It is just as well to bear in mind that for the next two hundred years, until Cumberland trotted out Shylock's antitype in his well-meant comedy at the end of the eighteenth century, Marlowe's remained the only English drama in which the Jew commands the leading role. (On the Continent, Lessing had stolen a fifty year's march on Cumberland with his little preliminary exercise to *Nathan the Wise*, the one-act comedy-of-errors-and-of-appearances entitled *Die Juden*.) Unlike Shylock, Barabas dominates his play from beginning to end: it is difficult in retrospect to think of scenes from which the Jew is excluded — the zany love-passages between Bellamira and Ithamore, say, or the secret alliances and double-crossings which go on the moment his back is turned. Marlowe, who presents him as his monolithic hero-villain, hardly bothers to characterize the opposition in more than a few elementary strokes — though he can probably trust his audience to draw their own morally meaningful distinctions among Spaniards, Maltese, Turks, and Jews, and grade them accordingly. Even though Del Bosco, Ferneze, and Selim Calymath are roughly again as powerful as the Jew is, and though they'll naturally have to outwit him in the end, Marlowe doesn't finally give them very much to do except to engage in their glib conspiracies, a little boring after a while. Like other Marlovian heroes, Barabas is adequately defined by his cheerful and narcissistic ambitiousness, by his commercial megalomania, and by the self-regarding, even rather complacent, pleasure he takes in his craftiness. He has his grounds for revenge, naturally: Ferneze, as unmitigated a cynic as the rest, has expropriated him without even the pretense of an excuse, as if theft were not merely the grounds of his religion but the natural basis of commerce; but Marlowe refrains from making too much of the motive, gives you the sense, rather, that even without Ferneze's barbarian conduct, Barabas would put as much time and energy into his scheming and politicking. Marlowe is not finally interested, as Shakespeare is, in questions which touch deeply on the nature of justice, is even less interested in legalistic quibbles; he enjoys the spectacle of these depraved noblemen of passion trying to cut each other's throats. If Barabas is vindictive, as he has every reason to be, one is also made to feel that a good deal of this is gratuitous, not adequately explained by the activities of his opponents. Ask Shylock why he wants his pound of flesh, and the answer lies simply in a binding legal agreement: because "I'll have my bond . . . I'll have my bond . . . I'll have no speaking, I will have my bond." Ask Barabas why he wants to poison wells and kill sick people groaning under walls (if he's really being serious), and the only halfway sensible answer would be: "because it is my nature." His mind is not resolutely bent, as Shylock's is, on the pursuit of an idée fixe, but adapts itself to situations as they arise, maliciously cocksure of itself and its endless capacity for cunning.

Protagonist that he is, Barabas even exacts a certain amount of amiable solicitude from Marlowe — though this notion may be rejected as frivolous by nine tenths of the critics. Hardly anybody, I suppose, would waste much breath in denying that Barabas has a lot more in common with the other Marlovian heroes, with Tamburlaine and Faustus, than Shylock has with any other Shakespearean figure — or, to put it another way, whereas we can attach a fairly specific meaning to the term "Marlovian" to describe particular norms of speech, of dramatic structure, of characterisation, the term "Shakespearean" is clearly much less restrictive and, instead of encouraging definition, is apt to generate cosmic flimflam. Compared with Shakespeare's, Marlowe's heroes are very much of a piece — if only because there are so many fewer of them, perhaps also because all of them came out of the same gestative period in Marlowe's brief career. Youthful writer that he is, Marlowe is apt to put a good deal of himself into his principals, to project himself more directly than Shakespeare does, even to empathize with them a little. In reading these plays, it is difficult to resist the inference — some may consider it obvious — that Marlowe was a far more "subjective" writer than Shakespeare ever was even in his earliest most immediately Marlovian phase (but the Marlovianism of Shakespeare is verbal as much as anything else; where the influence rubs off on the conception of the character — in *Titus Andronicus*, say, or even *Richard III* — the hero-villain is never quite so clearly the monolith as his analogue in Marlowe; Shakespeare allows him to be compromised by a number of complex antagonists and to that extent deflects attention from Number One, shades the glaring quality of the focal point). Marlowe's attitude toward Barabas can sometimes be measured, I think, by his refusal, or inability, to keep very much distance from his leading man, especially at moments when Barabas is left to speak for himself. Very often, in this soliloquy or that boast, Marlowe's own voice seems to insinuate itself easily, as it were unconsciously, into the voice of Barabas, merging with it, vibrating with the same pleasurable arrogance, the same slightly put-on outrage:

> Who hateth me but for my happiness?
> Or who is honoured now but for his wealth?
> Rather had I, a Jew, be hated thus,
> Than pitied in a Christian poverty,
> For I can see no fruits in all their faith
> But malice, falsehood, and excessive pride,
> Which methinks fits not their profession.
> Haply some hapless man hath conscience
> And for his conscience lives in beggary,

and so on: Barabas talks in this strain during much of the play when he is not engaged in witty repartee — and he can be as witty as anybody when he chooses, again unlike Shylock, whose humor has been petrified by his puritan hatred of the humor that is in other men. One feels that Marlowe reveals his sympathy, is most nearly at one with his character, whenever the Jew's voice betrays just this mingling of the passionate and the civilized. Quite how seriously he takes Barabas the moment he steps back from the scene and disengages himself from the character is perhaps difficult to say; the attitude, not necessarily consistent, oscillates between admiration and derisiveness; Marlowe cheers on now Barabas, now Ferneze, now Ithamore; he has his fun with them one by one. But it's the Jew finally who dwarfs all the others, from the moment he steps onstage, capturing and enlarging our imagination with his recital of Persian ships, of Samnit clients, Spanish oils and wines of Greece, taking a merchant's pride in the assurance that his

> argosy from Alexandria,
> Loaden with spice and silks, now under sail,
> Are smoothly gliding down by Candy shore
> To Malta, through our Mediterranean sea.

Definitely, here and now, "our" Mediterranean sea; *mare nostrum*, which nurtures Jew and non-Jew alike. Barabas flourishes wonderfully, at ease in his Zion, in touch with his prosperous merchant-leaguers the world over, naturally scornful of your small businessmen with their paltry silverlings. By the time the play begins, he takes his fortune for granted — always a mistake, doubly a mistake when you have had to implicate the slippery Machiavel in building up your commercial empire. Everybody knows that the wages of sin are death and that nobody survives in the Mafia. If the opening scene presents him on the spectacular heights, the obvious inference is that there is only one direction in which to go — down again, spectacularly.

In the Prologue to the play, our host from Florence invites us to watch "the tragedy of a Jew"; and when the play was performed by the Lord Admiral's Men, it was the celebrated tragedian Edward Alleyn who starred in the role. The structure of *The Jew of Malta* obeys the old tragic formula — the great man's fall from prosperity — without radical departures or innovations. Like *Faustus*, *The Jew of Malta* keeps provoking the objection, legitimate or no, that after the great beginnings, the later episodes fall off maddeningly (Acts III and IV in *Faustus*; III, IV, and V in *The Jew*), that in *The Jew* in particular Marlowe switches his ground-rules midway, and that in both plays the hero's grandly conceived projects dwindle into silly pranks, practical jokes suited to the mentality of a schoolboy, a terrible insult to the Einstein and the Rothschild of his age. The tonal integrity of the play has been upheld in Eliot's enormously influential essay on Marlowe (but which of his essays has not been enormously influential? which, for all its fecund speculations and concise assertions, has not left one with the sense of its seeming to say more than it does, as if the great man felt it to be a little ungentlemanly to press the issue and were mortally afraid of betraying bad table-manners by inquiring too scrupulously?). In a sentence which has passed into a critical commonplace, Eliot refers the coherence of the play to Marlowe's humor, "the terribly serious, even savage comic humour . . . which spent its last breath in the decadent genius of Dickens." This sounds good, and Eliot may be perfectly right. Likewise he may be perfectly wrong; or perhaps his statement has merely the virtue of its intuited suggestiveness and is not meant to be argued. One may wonder, out loud, whether even the most genially precocious writer in his mid-twenties goes in much for "terribly serious, savage comic humour"; he postures and mimics, throws himself into this exaggerated attitude and that, inflates his vocabulary, parades his erudition while he mocks at erudition, and makes faces at the audience without being always aware of making them. Our difficulty in quite knowing how to take Barabas involves, I think, our related difficulty in quite recapturing, with all the scholarly aids in the world, our sense of an audience who would have found nothing particularly weird or inconsistent in the spectacle of a "tragic" Jew who behaves like a mountebank, whose comedown is all the more blatant because of his superb self-conceit and amour-propre, and whose decline into silliness might illustrate, on the simplest level of comprehension, the total bankruptcy of policy. In a lot of ways Barabas has in fact a good deal in common with the figures drawn, at a comparable age, in the first flush of authorship, by "the decadent genius of Dickens" — figures on the order of Fagin, Squeers, Quilp, who move in rather the same atmosphere of sensational and cheerful criminality, buoyed up by their good healthy appetite for sinister wheeler-dealing, who impress you by their loudmouthed — or just wicked — bragging, their instinct (this has been noted by Douglas Bush) for self-dramatization, their extraordinary capacity for congratulating themselves on being as bad as you can get.

For that matter one might note that up to a point every stage-Jew (or every stagey Jew, for Fagin fits this bill as well as anybody) shares somewhat this delight in self-applause, plumes himself, openly or in stealth, on his surpassing talent for deceit; of all the dogs going, he himself is the sharpest by far — just wait. That little runt Isaac Mendoza in Sheridan's *Duenna* (whom Sheridan hit off in what is probably the best-known aphorism about Jews in all of eighteenth-century English literature — that "he stands like a dead wall between Church and Synagogue, or like the blank leaves between the Old and New Testament"), though he is obviously small potatoes by any standards, bubbles over with self-infatuation every time he reflects on his slyness — it is practically all he does: "Ah! this little brain is never at a loss — cunning Isaac, cunning rogue! . . . Oh, cunning rogue, Isaac! aye, aye, let this little brain alone! . . . Oh, this cunning little head! I'm a Machiavel — a very Machiavel. . . . Ha! ha! ha! I'm a cunning dog, an't I? a sly little villain, eh?" and so on, nauseatingly. With this compare:

> We Jews can fawn like spaniels when we please,
> And when we grin, we bite; yet are our looks
> As innocent and harmless as a lamb's.
> I learned in Florence how to kiss my hand,
> Heave up my shoulders when they call me dog,
> And duck as low as any barefoot friar,
> Hoping to see them starve upon a stall,
> Or else be gathered for in our synagogue,
> That when the offering-basin comes to me,
> Even for charity I may spit into't.

Allowing for the difference in resonance, the sentiments are alike enough; the amplifier has been turned down between Marlowe's day and Sheridan's, naturally, and one may shrink from comparing a lion with a rat; but the tune is familiar, familial. Whether there is any "terribly serious, savage humour" in this, I am not prepared to say.

With Shylock, after much philanthropic *pro* and much hard-nosed *con*, we are on safer ground.

V

Granville-Barker calls *The Merchant of Venice* "a fairy tale," with "no more reality in Shylock's bond and the Lord of Belmont's will than in Jack and the Beanstalk"; Auden calls it "among other things, as much of a 'problem' play as one by Ibsen or Shaw." No reason why both can't be right.

Unlike Barabas, with whom the play begins and all but ends, Shylock is present in only five scenes out of twenty (I 3; II 5; III 1 and 3; IV 1); but by any strictly quantitative measure all of the scenes, except III 3, are very substantial things (IV 1, of course, virtually spans the entire act) and in all of them Shylock crowds out the rest. Moreover, as Granville-Barker reminds us in his essay (which remains one of the best and sanest things written on the play, in its freedom from intrusive cant and its leisurely concentration on the show), Shylock is never very far out of the minds of the other characters; we see him as it were out of the corner of our eyes even when he is not onstage. Where Barabas is first discovered in his counting-house, Shylock appears in "A street in Venice," in front of his "sober" house — the appropriate mileu of comedy. By the time he appears at the beginning of Scene 3, Shakespeare has already mapped out the opposition and defined their values, has mobilized the two forces that are going to fight Shylock — one by pitiless raillery and outright slander; the other, less explicitly, by opposing to his narrow material claims the claims of friendliness, of generosity, and spiritual graciousness. Scene 1: the carnival world of Venice, dominated here by Antonio but more essentially defined by those two nimble dandies and nitwits, Salerio and Solanio; Scene 2: the graceful world of Belmont, presided over by Portia, and in a sense equally foreign to Antonio and Shylock, the two loneliest men in the entire play. Lastly, the Rialto. Shakespeare thus really contrives three different playgrounds, not two, and three corresponding norms of conduct; and though Bassanio and his crew may inhabit all three and move freely from one to the other, the distinctions are nonetheless observed. Characteristically, Portia, on the one important occasion when she has to leave her fairy-tale world for the courtroom realities of the city, submerges her own person in the fake personality of our learned friend from Padua; Jessica is as it were "converted" to the religion of Belmont after moving — again in male disguise — through the intermediate world of the masqueraders. Very likely the torchlight world of Gratiano and Lorenzo and the moonlit world of Belmont have more in common with each other than either has with the atmosphere of the Rialto: lavish and animated dominions, both of them, in contrast to Shylock's claustrophobic citadel. (Though Shakespeare is notoriously free and easy with his geography, Belmont is almost certainly outside of Italy, to judge from the distance Bassanio has to travel, and from Portia's dismissive remark — I 2, 70 — that her foolish English suitor must have "bought his doublet in Italy, his round hose in France, his bonnet in Germany").

As if to counterpoint these operative values at once, Shakespeare springs them in the opening lines of the first three scenes:

Scene 1, Antonio: "In sooth I know not why I am so sad";

Scene 2, Portia: "By my troth Nerissa, my little body is aweary of this great world."

Scene 3, Shylock: "Three thousand ducats, well."

Shylock comes to the point at once, turns over Antonio's offer in his mind before he quite commits himself. Then he sets Bassanio straight on a little semantic confusion in which that careless young person has involved himself in getting hung up on the word *good:* "Ho, no, no, no, no: my meaning in saying he is a good man, is to have you understand me that he is sufficient" — a distinction picked up two scenes later in Lancelot's pun to Bassanio: "The old proverb is very well parted between my master Shylock and you, sir — you have 'the grace of God,' sir, and he hath 'enough.'" The difference in interpretation, by which one party assumes "a good man" to mean "an honest man, a kind man," and the other party assumes it to mean "a good risk," defines the essential area of antagonism cleanly and unmistakably; it is all managed with wonderful economy by that good man, Shakespeare. How different, too, this dry, cautious, tentative "Three thousand ducats, well" from Barabas's opening speech as he fondles his infinite riches and luxuriates in sensuous reveries of

>   fiery opals, sapphires, amethysts,
> Jacinths, hard topaz, grass-green emeralds,
> Beateous rubies, sparkling diamonds;

and so forth — the whole difference between magnifico and miser; and how different again, say, from the bustling, mirthful, predatory "Good morning to the day; and, next: my gold" with which Volpone rises to the occasion.

Shylock's first line not only establishes his characteristic attitude and, beyond it, the Rialto mentality and the dialectic associated with the stage-Jew; as a piece of stage logistics, it sets the pace for dozens of dramas in which the Jew's entrance binds him at once, without fuss, to his cash-nexus: this, paradigmatically, is how the Jew comes onstage for the next two hundred years. The same coming-to-the-point, the same no-nonsense self-confidence, the same candour, combined sometimes with a certain wary patience, a willingness to wait and see it out. Skip ahead for a moment to a play like Zola's *Les héritiers Rabourdin*, a situation-farce modelled, as Zola points out in his Preface (with a sneer at his critics who were too dumb to notice the resemblance) on *Volpone* — a Volpone in the Provinces, really. The Jew's name is Isaac — most stage-Jews are Isaac, unless they are Moses, and the chances are about five to one that the Moseses are more to be trusted than the Isaacses are. Here is his first appearance — as the title suggests, his interlocutor, Rabourdin, is the Fox of the ensemble. *Heirs of Rabourdin*, Act I, Scene 12. Enter Isaac.

> *Rabourdin.* Ah, ah, ah, that excellent monsieur Isaac. But dear dear dear, this won't do, this won't do, my poor monsieur Isaac.... You look healthy as a Turc, upon my word, you do.
> *Isaac.* You're very kind. I'm well enough. I came about a little note.
> *Rabourdin.* A little note....
> *Isaac.* An old account, 272 francs, for a wooden chest....
> *Rabourdin.* What! No! What's that you're saying! You really mean to say the chest hasn't been paid for yet! But really, if you knew me....
> *Isaac.* Oh, I wasn't worried, monsieur Rabourdin. We all know what we know. I could only wish you owed me a hundred times that much.

Then some frantic stage-business, Rabourdin pretending that he's misplaced the key to the money-box, a lot of bustling about, fake attempts to recover the key, and finally:

> *Rabourdin.* You're not by any chance in a terrible hurry? Otherwise, you know, I could easily send it to you this afternoon....
> *Isaac.* I have time.

The money is produced, naturally; Isaac pockets it (not greedily, but rather carelessly, as a matter of course) and, perfectly willing to be jocose now that he has what he came for and what he knew all along he would get, he even loosens up enough to descend to moral small-talk: "Ah, yes, yes: sound accounts make good friends"; and then, after fishing a few trinkets out of his pocket which he wouldn't mind selling, he leaves — *je suis content*.

Even more direct than this (to cite one last example) is the walk-on Jew — neither Isaac nor Moses but unnamed — who is hurried through Kotzebue's frightfully popular, mercifully forgotten bourgeois drama *Der Opfertod*, a play of the 1790s. Desperate Christian debtor (obsessive gambler) versus Jewish money-lender. The scene (I 11) is London, and the conversation might have been written expressly to be included in a primer for a class in Elementary German. It will lose nothing in bilingual transcription; I cite the opening snatches:

Jew. Guten Tag, Sir.	Good day, Sir.
Maxwell. Den gebe mir Gott!	God give it to me!
Jew. Sie sind mir fuenfzig Pfund schuldig.	You owe me fifty pounds.
Maxwell. Allerdings.	So I do.
Jew. Koennen Sie bezahlen?	Can you pay?
Maxwell. Nein.	No.
Jew. Das ist schlimm.	That's bad.
Maxwell (zuckt die Achseln)	(shrugs his shoulders)
Jew. Ich habe Ihren Wechsel.	I have your note.
Maxwell. Ich weiss es.	I'm aware of it.
Jew. Und wissen auch, was ich thun kann?	And are also aware of what I can do?
Maxwell. Mich ins Gefaengnis fuehren.	Send me to jail.
Jew. Ich thaete es aber ungern.	I shouldn't care to do it, though.

In fairness to Kotzebue, it should be added that the Jew here turns out to be pliable, not adamant, and tears up the note at the end of the scene — the play reflects the philo-Semitic attitude generally traced to *Nathan the Wise* but already in fact apparent in some of the earlier *Sturm-und-Drang* plays of the 'seventies. (In one of the more intersting of these, a play entitled *Die Reue nach der Tat* by one of the minor *Sturm-und-Drang* writers, Goethe's friend Heinrich Leopold Wagner, Jew-baiting is exposed as so unambiguously revolting that when the play was republished in 1939, the editor, obviously embarrassed by Wagner's unorthodoxy but unwilling to drop the scene, endeavoured to explain it away in the sort of abstruse gobbledygook for which dictatorships provide). Kotzebue himself, for that matter, had already written a benevolent Jew into his earlier *Kind der Liebe*, the play which young Fanny Price found so shaming at Mansfield Park — though the version in which she performed omitted the Jew-scene. The thing to notice in all these dramas, however, is that one of the stock-traits of the good Jew requires him to come on just like Shylock, whom everybody anyhow takes him to be; all these plays are going to hinge on the discovery of a popular delusion, the explosion of a vulgar error. In this respect, Cum--berland's *The Jew* runs absolutely true to type. Behind every Sheva lurks the spectre of Shylock.

In *The Merchant of Venice*, then, after the Rialto salutatories, everybody knows where he stands and what to expect. The problem is really a very simple one, epitomized, as I suggested, in the ambiguity of *goodness* which is sounded as an introductory motif. The conflict between Antonio and Shylock is the conflict, essentially, between the ethics of generosity and the ethics of avarice; between prodigality in the widest sense and "sufficiency"; between those who love their neighbours and place their faith in the possibility of decent human relationships and those who are ruled by the old excuse that it's a dog-eat-dog world and who pay for their conviction by turning into peevish and embittered old gaffers; between the judicial "spiritualists," whose attitude toward justice is, not lax, but relaxed, tempered by a respect for the circumstantial and conditional, and the literalists, whose minds have been perverted by their insistence on unconditional obedience to the letter of the law. The whole burden of Portia's famous piece of oratory, after all, is that justice isn't in itself enough, "that in the course of justice none of us / Should see salvation." Allowing for this qualification and that, I do not see how the play can be taken in any other way. In answer to the obvious objection that Portia herself, in her definition of the pound of flesh, is being more narrowly legalistic than anybody, I can only suggest that these technical quibbles were more enjoyable to Shakespeare's audience than they are to us; one finds them — a slightly silly convention — in any number of Elizabethan and Jacobean comedies.

As a usurer, Shylock could anyhow be trusted to arouse the scorn of Shakespeare's audience. The money-lender's special aptitude for playing the comic villain has never perhaps been more astutely formulated than in Bentham's *Defense of Usury:*

> Those who have the resolution to sacrifice the present to the future, are natural objects of envy to those who have sacrificed the future to the present. The children who have eaten their cake, are the natural enemies of the children who have theirs.... Now I question whether, among all the instances in which a borrower and a lender have been brought together upon the stage, from the days of Thespis to the present, there ever was one, in which the former was not recommended to favour in some shape or other — either to admiration, or to love, or to pity, or to all three; — and the other, the man of thrift, consigned to infamy.

To this may be added an historical footnote or two. Even though money-lending had been legalized in England in 1571 and was openly practiced by Christians, at bottom usury continued to be looked on as a peculiarly

Jewish monopoly. (As a matter of fact, whereas stage-usurers weren't necessarily Jews, conversely, stage-Jews were almost prescriptively extortionists). As one of the historians has noted (E. C. Pettet, in *Essays and Studies*, 1945), for plays which dealt with the problem of usury, "a Jew had two particular points of significance: in the first place, Jews were certainly prominent in the business abroad, and in the second, it is possible that Shylock symbolizes the feeling, shared by Shakespeare, that usury is something alien to the national and traditional way of life." Usury had been proscribed as both economically unsound and religiously damnable by one patristic writer after another: Lactantius had labeled the practice outright robbery; Ambrose called it murder; Jerome saw no distinction "betwixt usury, fraud, and violent robbing, as who should say, he that is a usurer is a deceitful false man, an errant thief and an extreme extortioner"; Benevenuto a Imola, writing in the fourteenth century, declared that "he who practiceth usury goeth to hell," and by then Dante (in Canto XIV) had already put the practitioners there. Moreover, the economic situation in the latter part of the sixteenth century encouraged and reinforced the religiously based prejudice against money-lending. The popular nobility were constantly and deeply in debt — some, like the Earl of Leicester, by as much as 60,000 pounds, and, as Pettet reminds us, "Shakespeare's own patron, the Earl of Southampton, who, at one time, had surrendered his estates to creditors . . . 'scarce knows what course to take to live.'" In the eyes of the conservative majority, the usurer was therefore regarded as a disagreeable and dangerous parvenu, a threat to the continuance of the old order. In any contest between the tight-fisted money-lender and the irresponsibly lavish nobility, the money-lender was bound to get the worst of it by the playwright.

These things need to be borne somewhat in mind if one is to see the "Shylock problem" in perspective and if one is to make anything of the political climate in which Shakespeare wrote *The Merchant of Venice*. Translated very crudely into modern terms (and inverting the politics), you can take a — crudely — comparable figure — say, an obsessed fundamentalist smalltown Southern bigot, typical of a whole class of obsessed fundamentalist smalltown Southern bigots, whose hatred of Negroes is instinctive, inherited, and a function of his social and economic insecurity, and whose daughter, bored to death by his fundamentalist twaddle and herself relatively color-blind, runs off with a Negro — and you have something like an updated tabloid version of Shylock. No reason why this couldn't be played for laughs, provided the bigot is sufficiently rigid in his response to the situation. The chief difference lies in the choice of political norms — in Shakespeare's case conservative rather than innovative. Though Antonio, from the commercial viewpoint, is committed to the ambitions of the new class of burghers, in his ethical and political context he represents the older genteel-liberal traditions: for example, he takes it for granted that he should freely share his wealth with a friend whom he knows perfectly well to be the worst spendthrift, and that he should persistently disparage Bassanio's conscientious reminders of the risk involved in signing the bond. Within this framework, Bassanio himself, whose lavishness has always provided Shylock's apologists with the desired pretext to whitewash their man, falls easily enough into the role of the morally acceptable protagonist: a little wild perhaps, but also completely charming and courteous: Portia's preference for him, long before he has to go off on his ritual quest, is a measure of his character. For Shakespeare, reflecting the post-medieval nostalgia for the open-handed ways of the old gentry, Bassanio's expensive party-going argues on the whole a fundamentally honest heart and a virtuous disposition, and Antonio's willingness to underwrite his carnivals argues a positively Christian forbearance. The play keeps coming round to the point that between the miser and the prodigal the choice is a foregone conclusion.

VI

When at the beginning of the table-turning courtroom scene, the Duke warns Antonio that he had better be prepared to answer

> A stony adversary, an inhuman wretch,
> Uncapable of pity, void and empty
> From any dram of mercy,

he thus not only expresses a sentiment which is shared by all the other characters but delivers in effect a judicial opinion which, since it comes from the magisterial fount of order himself, may be taken safely at face value. Besides, the Duke knows his man, has met Shylock before, or at least heard from him; the old Jew, the insufferable old enemy alien, has been peppering him with one petition after another. Shylock's own attitude toward the governing bodies of Venice is really in many ways the attitude of the old refugee the world over: deferential to authority, rather paranoid because he is both old and alien, at once submissive and entirely correct in his posture before his tribunes.

> *Portia.* Is your name Shylock?
> *Shylock.*   Shylock is my name.

It's only when Portia affronts him with extra-legal arguments — to him no arguments at all — that his composure gives way to irritation and finally to fury: evidently these people don't speak his language.

For Shylock (to descend to comparisons) is of course much more narrowly the *old* Jew than someone like Barabas — one isn't surprised that Charles Macklin could still tackle the role when he was close to ninety and do a very creditable job at it: the poor absurd embittered persecuted old man, who smells conspiracies round every corner, who is forever bedevilled by the habits of these crazy young Venetian swells — he'll not be made a soft and dull-eyed fool by *them*; he is also much more narrowly than Barabas the ghetto Jew, who could never acclimate himself to the customs of the country, even if he were accepted by these impossible wastrels. "Ein alter Mann ist stets ein Koenig Lear!" Goethe tells us; he might equally well have said: "Ein alter Mann ist stets ein Jud Shylock." Barabas by comparison seems to be in the prime of his physical powers; he has nothing of the nasty old man about him; if he is in fact older than his Spanish and Ottoman playmates, it is more than we know. But in a play like *The Merchant*, in which the Jew is presented much more nearly in his "low mimetic" role than his Marlovian double, and in which the contrast between rioting youth and crabbed age is always before us, Shylock's presence as the single senescent character in the comedy (apart from old Gobbo, whom we can do without, and the Duke, who is purely figurehead) substantiates his comic function, helps to explain his dogged and helpless hatreds.

The generic difference between Marlowe's "tragedy" and Shakespeare's romantic comedy accounts, too, for the entirely different social, or extra-social, orbits in which the two Jews make themselves at home. Shylock is very much more the private person than Barabas; he is humanized, even when he is being most unpleasant and most grimly isolated, by one's sense of a domestic and congregational world through which he moves. The old man's mind ruminates on such familiar household stuff as his food, his dieting, his clowning servant — he is rather fond of the fellow, simply can't afford to keep such expensive gluttons — his fear of burglars, his walks to synagogue. Barabas, performing colossally *in coram publico*, is virtually his opposite in this: *his* mind teems with international conspiracies, affairs of state, military conquests, backstairs intrigues; the man has been in collusion with Hapsburgs and Medicis:

> Why, is not this
> A kingly kind of trade, to purchase towns
> By treachery and sell 'em by deceit?

Or:

> Now, whilst you give assault unto the walls,
> I'll lead five hundred soldiers through the vault
> And rise with them i' th' middle of the town,
> Open the gates for you to enter in,
> And by this means the city is your own.

Merely try to imagine Shylock storming the Venetian city-gates or being offered, if only as a joke, the governorship of Devil's Island: the prospect bogs the mind. Again, where Shylock maintains his religious ties with his Tubals and his Chuses — this has been said — Barabas treats his Three Jews to the same contemptuous epithets to which he treats Lodowick or the friars: base slaves, gentle maggot, religious caterpillars. And though he talks about the synagogue every so often and indulges in the customary sneers against the swine-eating Christians, one is not to suppose that he actively practices the false religion, he who is the god of his own idolatry.

Again their different stations and perspectives are reflected in such things as their attitudes toward property. As between the two, Shylock conforms much more narrowly to the role of the conventional miser, partly because Barabas has so many other fish to fry — wars to make, nunneries to poison, traps to spring — partly because Shylock's function in the comedy requires him to be exactly the humourless tightwad he is. The man is such a Scrooge! What a curmudgeon and killjoy! No wonder Jessica can't bear to stay another day in this dreary atmosphere of fastings and locked doors. "Our house is hell" — will be more intolerable than ever now that the clown has found himself a more congenial employer. Shylock's affinity to the Puritan usurers of his day has been noticed in print a number of times: how he detests with a Puritan's narrow mistrust and an old man's loathing — "gravity's revolt 'gainst wantonness" — the prospect of that brawling and parading in the streets.

> What, are there masques? Hear you me, Jessica,
> Lock up my doors, and when you hear the drum
> And the vile squealing of the wry-neck'd fife,
> Clamber not you up to the casements then
> Nor thrust your head into the public street
> To gaze on Christian fools with varnish'd faces:
> But stop my house's ears, I mean my casements,
> Let not the sound of shallow fopp'ry enter
> My sober house.

Sobriety is the last thing Barabas has any use for:

> I have bought a house
> As great and fair as is the governor's;
> And there, in spite of Malta, will I dwell,
> Having Ferneze's hand, whose heart I'll have —

and the difference is again spelled out in the testimonials of the two hirelings, Lancelot and Ithamore. Where Lancelot's impatience with Shylock's penny-pinching is supported by the actualities of the household, Ithamore's ludicrous lies about Barabas, "'Tis a strange thing of that Jew; he lives upon pickled grasshoppers and sauced mushrooms," reflects the superstitious, fictive view of the Jew and rather appals Barabas: "What a slave's this! The governor feeds not as I do." Where Shylock tends to look on money-making as virtually an end in itself (his horizons are not large), Barabas' attitude toward wealth is more relaxed and pragmatic: it buys him his lordly manor house, his connections, his power. Shylock doesn't care a straw for power; he shouldn't know what to do with it. He wants justice, according to his lights. Barabas doesn't care a straw for justice. He is much too mundane to know that he isn't going to get it anyway, and too superb to dispense it. He enjoys sacking a city or two, though.

For the later history of the stage-Jew, Shylock's penny-pinching was to set a much more useful example than Barabas's expansive greed. Not simply because Marlowe was far less well-known outside England than Shakespeare, but because the eighteenth-century comic writers found a more intelligible type in Shylock, one who more nearly approximated both the acknowledged stock-miser and their notion of the Jew *chez soi*, whereas Barabas would have been difficult to generalize, even if they had understood him. Barabas simply led you straight back to Marlowe; Shylock led you to other Jews. Thus even a decent Hebrew like Cumberland's Sheva, handing out cash to the thousand neediest, subscribes to Shylock's principle that Avarice Begins at Home, starves his servant, promotes the sanitary uses of cold water lest his guests might get the unhealthy idea of thirsting for wine. The money-lender in Voltaire's *La femme qui a raison*, an amiable enough old rogue — no longer quite Shylock, not yet quite Sheva, certainly not Nathan — shares Shylock's horror of anything that smacks of noise and revelry, wants his "noce frugale":

> Mais surtout plus de bal; je ne prétends plus voir
> Changer la nuit en jour, et le matin en soir;

the examples could be multiplied *ad infinitum*.

A Jew who is the heroic villain of the play, finally, may be expected to speak an entirely different language from one who is depressed into the role of comic foil. One tends to remember all of Barabas's great speeches as soliloquies when, as a matter of fact, almost all of them (though not quite all) are either debate or aside — just as one tends to think of Shylock's speeches as petulant arguments or sneaky asides, when in fact they are often rather tortured monologues. The structure of *The Jew of Malta* allows Barabas to engage in the same stylized, boastful, ultimately theatrical magniloquence with which the other grandees express themselves; the structure of *The Merchant of Venice* requires Shylock to articulate his grievances in language which makes the most of the dramatic opposition between Gentile and Jew. Barabas swears by the plagues of Egypt and the curse of heaven, by eternal night, by clouds of darkness and the Primus Motor; invokes fiery pillars and dismal shades; indulges in the resonant names of his far-flung brother-merchants: "Kirriah Jairim, the great Jew of Greece, / Obed in Bairseth, Nones in Portugal, / Myself in Malta." He reaches out easily to classical allusions and historical analogies:

> As fatal be it to her as the draught
> Of which great Alexander drunk and died,
> And with her let it work like Borgia's wine,
> Whereof his sire, the Pope, was poisonèd.
> In few, the blood of Hydra, Lerna's bane,
> The juice of Hebon, and Cocytus' breath,
> And all the poisons of the Stygian pool
> Break from the fiery kingdom, and in this
> Vomit your venom, and envenom her
> That like a fiend hath left her father thus.

(Marlowe doesn't quite let him get away with it, undercuts it with Ithamore's ironic commentary: "What a blessing has he given't? Was ever pot of rice porridge so sauced?") In *The Merchant of Venice* all the lovely classical allusions are sounded in Belmont — Portia's girlishly-wise talk about young Alcibiades and Hercules and the Dardanian wives; the swift rush of Homeric narratives in the amorous duet between Lorenzo and Jessica in Portia's garden; and Shylock himself tends to take his conceits from the Old Testament whenever he doesn't coin his own preposterous and indecorous similes.

Barabas's syntax is the syntax of dignity and self-control:

> Well, then, my lord, say, are you satisfied?
> You have my goods, my money, and my wealth,
> My ships, my store, and all that I enjoyed.

> And, having all, you can request no more,
> Unless your unrelenting flinty hearts
> Suppress all pity in your stony breasts,
> And now shall move you to bereave my life.

One might be tempted to discover a similar kind of nobility in Shylock: in the famous lecture to Antonio, for example, full of reproach and righteousness, beginning, "Signior Antonio, many a time and oft / In the Rialto you have rated me / About my moneys and my usances," and ending

> moneys is your suit.
> What should I say to you? Should I not say
> 'Hath a dog money? Is it possible
> A cur can lend three thousand ducats?' or
> Shall I bend low, and in a bondman's key
> With bated breath, and whis'pring humbleness
> Say this:
> 'Fair sir, you spet on me on Wednesday last,
> You spurn'd me such a day — another time
> You call'd me dog: and for these courtesies
> I'll lend you thus much moneys?'

This may be eloquence of a kind. But isn't it also a nasty sort of eloquence? There is something crooked, petulant, taunting in these imagined retorts to Antonio: the note that finally won't go away is the note of whining, the bondman's key; and to an audience already stirred up to distrust the Jew, the speech is apt to communicate itself as something less than noble. And in the most famous conversation of all — "Hath not a Jew eyes?" — which is always (perversely) excerpted as a soliloquy when Shylock in fact springs it on Salerio in reply to a leading question, it's been noted often enough how easily these quick, excited, rhetorical questions, with their funny lilt, lend themselves to comic recitation and comic gesture. For that matter, one's willingness to take the speech straight is always being undercut by Shylock's characteristically twisted parrallels: "If you prick us, do we not bleed? if you tickle us, do we not laugh? if you poison us, do we not die?" Is this really an affirmation of the Jew's humanity? Isn't it rather — this bleeding and tickling and dying in one and the same breath — merely another instance of Shylock's grotesque inability to brush the cobwebs out of his mind?

In a play in which the element of music turns into the paramount symbol of concord, Shylock's very syntax is purposefully discordant, ugly; the man's aversion to music, to harmony, to "the vile squealing of the wry-neck'd fife" betrays itself in his violent, frantic, broken onslaught on language, disconnected and disconcerting in its mumbo-jumbo; the others can only laugh and marvel at it:

> I never heard a passion so confus'd,
> So strange, outrageous, and so variable
> As the dog Jew did utter in the streets, —
> 'My daughter! O my ducats! O my daughter!
> Fled with a Christian! O my Christian ducats!
> Justice, the law, my ducats, and my daughter!
> A sealéd bag, two sealéd bags of ducats,
> Of double ducats, stol'n from me by my daughter!'

Or the concatenation of discrete detail, the total breakdown of rhythm in the wake of Jessica's flight — I follow Van Doren's legitimate extracts from III 1:

> Why, there, there, there, there! A diamond gone, cost me two thousand ducats in Frankfort! A curse never fell upon our nation till now. I never felt it till now. Two thousand ducats in that; and other precious, precious jewels. I would my daughter were dead at my foot, and the jewels in her ear! Would she were hears'd at my foot, and the ducats in her coffin! . . . I thank God, I thank God. Is't true? is't true? . . . I thank thee, good Tubal; good news, good news! Ha, ha! . . . Thou stick'st a dagger in me. I shall never see my gold again. Fourscore ducats at a sitting! Fourscore ducats! I am very glad of it. I'll plague him; I'll torture him. I am glad of it. . . . Nay, that's true, that's very true. Go, Tubal, fee me an officer; bespeak him a fortnight before. . . . Go, go, Tubal, and meet me at our synagogue; go, good Tubal; at our synagogue, Tubal.

A person who betrays his spiritual disconcertedness in such syncopated sounds — "Ho, no, no, no, no!" "Why, there, there, there, there!" "Out upon her! Thou torturest me, Tubal!" — and who succumbs to rhythms "so confus'd, so strange, outrageous, and so variable" would be stifled by the pure music-filled air of Belmont. For language, too, is the mirror of the soul; and in a play in which music surrounds and penetrates the Christian lovers, the simple moral — "Da wo man singt, da lass Dich ruhig nieder / Boese Menschen haben keine Lieder" — is spelled out, very close to the end, in a pretty recital by Shylock's brand-new son-in-law, the robber of his Christian ducats and the perverter of his daughter:

> The man that hath no music in himself,
> Nor is not moved with concord of sweet sounds,
> Is fit for treasons, stratagems, and spoils,
> The motions of his spirit are dull as night,
> And his affections dark as Erebus:
> Let no such man be trusted: — mark the music.

And a little earlier, in his duet with Jessica:

> In such a night
> Did Jessica steal from the wealthy Jew,
> And with an unthrift love did run from Venice,
> As far as Belmont.

"An unthrift love," " a spendthrift lover." To the old Jew-miser the coupling of such terms provides the final outrage; and to try to seduce him into acquiescence were love's labour's lost. People like that, says Shakespeare, have to be dragged to the baptismal font.

VII

In trying to pinpoint the elements which Shylock shares with Barabas, one is sooner or later bound to be struck by their patently external character. The qualities they share are the fixed components of an age-old legend, a religious fiction (or an unending historical nightmare, though they would hardly have thought of it that way); whatever these two plays have in common are the stuff of tradition, of mythology — the "given." Faust always sells his soul to the devil; the wolf always eats Red Riding Hood's grandmother; the Jew always feeds on the Christians. So we have our routine motions, our basic businesses. To expect anything like a realistic transcription of the Jews from people who have never seen one, who know of them only by hearsay and disquieting rumors, and to judge these plays by the criteria of naturalism — really, were it not to consider too curiously to consider so? What other "evidence" have these writers to go on? The Authority of Scripture; the polemics of the Church Militant; perhaps also the superstitious belief which clings to us all that there is something frightful about people to whom frightful things keep happening: one's touchy suspicion of the accident-prone person. But hardly the evidence of their senses. When Charles Macklin, some eighty-five years after the readmission of the Jews, revived Shylock at Drury Lane in 1741, inducing insomnia in King George II and frightening his subjects out of their living wits (for who in that audience could forget for a second that Macklin himself had killed a fellow-actor in a quarrel over a wig a few years back, had been tried for murder, and was rumored in private life to be the devil?), the great actor, in preparing for his role, "made daily visits to the center of business, the 'Change and the adjacent Coffee-houses, that by a frequent intercourse and conversation with the 'unforeskinned race' he might habituate himself to their air and deportment." But the generations of Edward Alleyn hardly enjoyed Macklin's research facilities — to say nothing of his unique prestige. Whether these enriched his performance is another question.

Beyond these operatives, a few conventions of the stage. As lineal descendant of the Devil, the Jew of Shylock's vintage inevitably moves in an atmosphere of laughter — but of apprehensive laughter: tentative, wary, inhibited, checked by one's instinct for watchful waiting and hedging one's bets. (Only a later playwright like Granville, who in a way anticipates the conception of the "dirty little Jew" favored by mindless Victorian cheapjacks like Tom Taylor and Dion Boucicault, disinfects the danger and removes the inhibitions by downgrading Shylock to a figure of sordid contempt, performing his ugly little monkey-business in an atmosphere of squalid farce.) You cannot quite call him a stock-figure, comprehended in this one trait or that — pure miser, pure butcher; the type is just flexible enough to permit of mutations, changes in posture, adjustments in perspective, and to generate, here and there, a small shock of surprise. Monomaniacs like Shylock are not simply types; in certain ways Shylock's single-minded and indestructible avarice has much more of old Grandet's ruling passion in it than of Harpagon's blandly innocuous clowning.

If it is true that the stage-Jew transcends the simplistic character of the stock type, it is equally plain that the dramatic sphere which defines him and his bearings remains essentially the sphere of *popular* drama. Rooted as he is in the popular plays of the Middle Ages, the Jew-figure persistently flourishes in dramas (and novels) which thrive on elements that magnetize the crowds: on superficially complex plots; spectacular adventures; extremes of innocence and depravity; intoxicating emotions; a densely cluttered cast of characters ranging from Duke to thief, Emperor to clown; language which oscillates feverishly between outrageous bombast and banal *niaiserie*; whirlwind changes in mise-en-scène, from the moonlit terraces to the stews and ghettos. The classic theatre, with its handful of exemplary personnages, its few austere motifs and situations, its fastidious avoidance of physical and verbal frenzy — a theatre such as this, which places the highest premium on self-control and elevated norms of seemliness, has no use for the Jew, or for eccentric or distorted figures of any kind: Jews, blackamoors, hunchbacks, stammerers, drunkards and prestidigitators — why, their intrusion into this hermetic society would at once disrupt the severity of its sentiments and the symmetry of appearances: the flies on the marble floors, the wart on Cleopatra's nose. The history of the stage-Jew is therefore essentially bound up with the history of the popular stage: with medieval church plays, the Elizabethan theatre, *Sturm und Drang*, sentimental comedy, Romantic and Victorian melodrama, Biedermeier play. (Later on, in the kind of "cross-section" drama — almost intrinsically second-rate — which depends for its choreography on the inclusion of multiple representative social or professional types, the Jew may appear simply as one more available specimen, though his presence is often little more than arbitrary: in Tolstoy's satire on quack science, *The Fruits of Enlightenment*, for example, in which Tolstoy opposes the simple superstitions of the peasantry to the stupid pretensions of the upper classes to spiritualistic hocus-pocus, the excitable Jewish medium in the crowd is presented as merely another minor exemplar of fake culture, along with The Professor, The Physician, and so on.) It's scarcely a coincidence that the one great Jew-play of the eighteenth century which falls outside the strictly popular categories, Lessing's *Nathan the Wise*, should have remained sufficiently *sui generis* for almost two hundred years to discourage imitators; and, great as the play remains after many readings, hardly anybody nowadays would claim much liveliness or sharp individuation for its hero: the play is essentially polemic, though polemic on the loftiest scale. Where the Jew does appear among the neo-classic writers — in Dryden's *Love Triumphant*, say, or later on in Voltaire's *La femme qui a raison* — the playwright makes sure that he leaves his august principles at home and writes farce or situation comedy. In Dryden's so-styled "tragicomedy," for example, Sancho, the apostate Jew who figures in the comedic subplot (where Jews are generally told to make themselves at home) simply talks in the coarse undifferentiated language of Restoration comedy, without regard to race, creed, or color: "Pr'ythee, sweet devil, do not ogle me, nor squeeze my palm so feelingly; thou dear infernal, do not;" "take back your trumpery, I mean your daughter; or I'll send for the scavenger with a dungcart." (On merely esthetic grounds one may prefer this to the heroic twaddle which Dryden foists on the "tragic" plotters upstairs: "What words are these? I feel my vital heart / Forsake my limbs, my curdled blood retreat!" and the like.) The degree to which Dryden's Jew has been disarmed in the century since the palmy days of Barabas (*Love Triumphant* was first acted in 1693) may be gauged by stage-direction:

"Enter Sancho, picking his teeth."

Where the knife has been whittled down to a toothpick, the gentile spectator no longer has anything to fear, and the laughter, coarse and unrestrained, may explode in box, pit, and gallery, free from anxiety.

Finally, once you have gotten past the theological sanctions and the historical sources, and past the more durable theatrical conventions, you come up against an occasional critical manifesto, a professorial word-to-the-wise. The good Rymer, for example, didn't think Othello quite the proper article for tragedy, because Othello is black and the tragic hero, says Rymer, ought always to be white; and as late as 1873, the younger Dumas, in the Preface to *La femme de Claude*, written as a showpiece for the greatest Jewish actress of modern times, maintained in all seriousness that on the stage the Jew must axiomatically be ludicrous — and, as Landa reminds us, similar opinions were defended with obstinacy by Scribe and Scarcey. It may be difficult to find stimulating excuses for Dumas & Company, but one's sense of the proprieties revolts against even trying to find the same excuses for Marlowe and Shakespeare. For the purposes of making a play, these writers could live with certain elementary assumptions about the Jews, but I doubt that they worried about these things very much. This needs to be said, because every so often one hears the argument that both Marlowe and Shakespeare must have been keenly alive to the oppression of the Jews and sufficiently perturbed to bring this out into the open; why else should they have gone out of their way to allow Barabas and Shylock to articulate their grievances so explicitly and so eloquently? Without for the moment making too much of the eloquence (which rather begs the question), surely the simplest answer is that every great writer is as it were trained to a sense of equity; a sense, also, that things are not simple, and that the blood-thirstiest Hottentot deserves to have the grounds of his thirst looked into if he is to be taken at all seriously to begin with; a consciousness, finally, that not everything is capable of being explained, that there remains, when all is said and done, an element of the submerged, the irrational and gratuitous: Shylock's "I'll not answer that! / But say it is my humour, — is't answered?" Sometimes, in listening to critics who try to whitewash Shakespeare by foisting on him public-spirited opinions about the Jews and prophylactic intentions toward them — the Playwright as Thinker — I keep hearing in the background one of those inane scraps of conversation between Peter Cooke and Dudley Moore — they happen to be talking about Queen Victoria's assumptions of the royal prerogative:

> *Cooke.* Of course, Queen Victoria used the royal prerogative a great deal, didn't she?
> *Moore.* I think some people would say she *over*used it.
> *Cooke.* Would they?
> *Moore.* They would, yes!
> *Cooke.* I think others would say she *under*used it.
> *Moore.* I think most people would say nothing at all. Hm. Yes — I think I'm one of those.

Admitting the lameness of the analogy (strictly Shandean association), I think Shakespeare was one of those. Very likely (but who is to say?) he found in his Jew a grateful antagonist to his sporty, fun-loving, extravagant crew of rioters and lovers; the literary sources he had ready at hand; since his innate dignity and his instinct for dramatic finesse kept him from turning Shylock loose as merely another swine like Gernutus, he invested him with his moral fervor, his motives, and his cue for wrath; tact and imagination did the rest — are you answered yet?

Even murkier, in its failure to distinguish between the extrinsic and the intrinsic, is the obverse argument — that Shylock's Jewishness is dramatically irrelevant and that Shylock is no more essentially the Jew than Iago is essentially the Italian, or Macbeth the Scotsman, or Claudius the Dane; pigstickers all. It seems to me that all it takes to defuse that particular fog-bomb is to respect the text; and if you do that no amount of special pleading can obscure the fact that Shakespeare wrote *Jew* into Shylock's every line and gesture, and that Shylock's Jewishness is the source of all his hatreds and his sufferings, his clean-cut crimes, and his questionable reward. The national definitions of Macbeth and Claudius are flimsy by comparison, largely the accidental yield of Shakespeare's historical source materials: by altering a few lines here and there, the writer could have shifted the setting without violence. How *The Merchant of Venice* could survive as the play it is if the Jew were yanked out of it and a non-Jew put in his place is not clear to me. The phrase "because I am a Jew!" runs through the play — defensive, accusatory, petulant, self-pitying — like a refrain. "Because he is a Jew" the Christians behave as they do; they base all their expectations on his Jewishness and predicate all their businesses on it, and they damn him for a Jew with monotonous regularity. Naturally it's idle to blame Shakespeare for the public misuse of Shylock's name by later generations; but if *Shylock* has passed into the vocabulary as a damning epithet for *Jew*, then this is something which (despite Shakespeare) is deeply latent in the play, and there is no point in blinking the fact. (The distinction may be supersubtle, but when Sir Oliver Surface in Sheridan's *School for Scandal* delivers himself of the lines, "Odds life, do you take me for Shylock in the play, that you would raise money of me on your own flesh and blood?" one feels that Sheridan is still close enough to Shakespeare to appreciate the dramatic artifice involved in the portrayal, without generalizing this beyond its dramatic application; in later writers the phrase "in the play" will be automatically dropped.) On the other hand, I shouldn't think that in calling his step-father a murderous damned incestuous Dane, Hamlet expresses sentiments which are of interest to the nation; if the Italians are worried about Iago, I have yet to hear about it; and the last time I asked young Ian MacGregor III (Cornell, Class of '70) what he thought of Lady Macbeth's Scottish features, he rolled his eyes for all the world like Owen Glendower and very politely asked me whether I had been reading *The Merchant of Venice*, by any chance.

So there we are.

VIII

A figure like Shylock not only foreshadows later stage-Jews; in a sense he recapitulates them all. Whatever you take him to be — literary stereotype; vestigial morality figure, the embodiment of an abstract vice; Elizabethan bogeyman; symbol of religious persecution; comic figure in a piece of artifice (it's just a *movie*, dear, don't cry, it's just a *movie*) — Shakespeare's man, though he may not have gotten his pound of flesh, has at least gotten under everybody's skin. Until the end of the nineteenth century, the playwrights were to find him virtually intractable. During the seventeenth century, which reveals itself increasingly as a blank to the historian of the stage-Jew in England, you get a handful of crude adaptations of Shakespeare's play — trashy, of interest perhaps to the anthropologist or historian of manners. For the sentimentalists of Cumberland's and Dibdin's generation who emerged at the end of the eighteenth century, the point was to turn Shylock as nearly as possible upside down; but naturally a man doesn't disappear by being stood on his head: he merely reveals his oddity. The trouble with simple antitypes like Sheva and Dibdin's small creatures is that they exist only by virtue of the type which they've been commissioned to liquidate, and so the point of reference remains the same. The intentions of people like Cumberland and Dibdin and Mrs Inchbald, and Kotzebue and Iffland in Germany, may have been perfectly laudable, but simple souls and bad writers that they were, the results were not especially encouraging. (Cumberland's philo-Semitism, for that matter, rested on a fairly cynical and transparent profit-motive: he had produced an unexpected hit by presenting a virtuous West Indian and Irishman — traditional objects of scorn — in one of his comedies, then presented a virtuous Scotsman, and when he consulted his Muse whom to rescue next for box-office purposes, lo, the Muse answered: The Jews. The Jews it was. Rather the same story with Dibdin: one of the officials of Drury Lane having "lamented that he could not get the character of a comic Jew to perform in town" and put in a requisition for "one [Jew] quite as benevolent, but more farcical, than Mr. Cumberland's Sheva," Dibdin went to work and delivered the article in breathtakingly short time.)

The sentimentalists perhaps created gratuitous difficulties for themselves in trying to talk Shylock out of the public mind by explicit argument and sententiousness. Instead of creating dramatically compelling figures, they blurred their anti-Shylocks by intellectualizing the issues, and their intellects were not precisely razor-sharp. In trying to prove that Jews did have affections, organs, and dimensions, they succeeded in proving very nearly the opposite by presenting, not a Man, but a formula-on-legs. After a while, the dramatic situation itself, to say nothing of the characters, lost whatever force it might have had by monotonous repetition: elderly widowed Jewish money-lender, usually of foreign origin but domiciled in England, who speaks ludicrous stage-gibberish, is axiomatically presumed by the Christians in the play to be the old Shylock writ small ("Here comes old Sheva, the rich Jew, the merest muckworm in the city of London"), until the crisis on which the play hinges reveals him to be a paragon of generosity, samaritan self-sacrifice — the seven deadly virtues rolled into a cotton-ball. In the final scene of Cumberland's *The Jew*, Sheva is solemnly led onstage by the Bassanio of the ensemble and presented to his half-dozen beneficiaries as "the widow's friend, the orphan's father, the poor man's protector, the universal philanthropist"; but before this purification rite can have any meaning, Sheva has to be mistaken (with his own consent and encouragement) for "a blood-sucker, an extortioner, a Shylock, an uncharitable dog, a muckworm, a baboon, an ass, a fool, a jack-a-dandy, an imp of Beelzebub" — Sheva himself rattles off the insults with some of Shylock's pleasant sense of his antagonists, not because they provide him with an incentive to revenge but because they place his generosity on the highest possible scale and show up the perverse measure of his goodness. (Of course this, too, is a form of revenge: avenging yourself on your former enemy by showering him with financial aid: you not only exact gratitude that way but show up his misconceptions in the most glaring light. Translated into politics, this sometimes creates areas of friction where there were none before.) The motives for the Jew's conduct are apt to be disclosed, as explicitly as possible, in pat announcements, embarrassing in their bad taste — commercials, really:

> *The Jew and the Doctor.* Ma dear, I always minds de main chance. The panker on whom I draw for payment, is Providence; he placed you in ma hands as a pledge in his favour. . . . If ever you see a helpless creature vat needs your assistance, give if for ma sake, etc etc.

The School for Prejudice. If I have any goodness apout me, I didn't learn it out of de Jews, noder out of de Christians — it was part of the shtock in trade given me from a better world.

The Jew. I do not bury [my moneys] in a synagogue, or any other pile; I do not waste it upon vanity, or public works; I leave it to a charitable heir, and build my hospital in the human heart.

The Jew as Christian, the Jew as Florence Nightingale; indeed this paradox, too, is worked for all it's worth by the playwright: "I'll you call you Christian, then; and this proud merchant Jew"; to which the only respectable answer is Sheva's ironic retort: "I shall not thank you for that compliment."

To be fair to them, the sentimentalists laboured under extraordinary handicaps in trying to deal honestly with the underdeveloped tribes in their midst. In a way, the whole sentimental tradition worked against anything like a fair picture of minority races, whom it was so much easier to patronize and gape at than to treat as equals. Moreover, a generation of writers who believe in the primacy of the emotions, unspoilt by the civilized and schooled intellect, are apt to search out their exemplary types of virtue among animals, children, and primitives, often without a sense of discriminating among these. Ideally the sentimentalist wants his characters raw and rustic — one remembers Rousseau's recipe for the good life: a charming woman, a faithful friend, a little boat, and a cow. The sentimental depiction of the Jews thus raised problems which the portrayal of outlandish primitives — Africans, say, or Cherokees — didn't raise. These were nobly savage or tamely savage; they were kind and dumb because in their peacefully anarchic state of nature they retained their natural innocence, simplicity, simple-mindedness. But the Jews, unlike the Hottentots and the Jamaican Negroes and the American Indians, were traditionally associated with large metropolitan nerve-centers, and therefore neither fine and solitary enough to keep a fever-chart of their sensibilities nor savage enough to assimilate to the trees and the rocks and the beasts in the field. They were very much part of the fair; these tents of Israel, pitched in Pettycoat Lane, were occupied by people whose profession called for the constant exercise of mental skill, mathematical aptitude, a talent — precisely — for calculation. As a result, Cumberland and Smollett and Dibdin were forever forced to blink at the paradox of intelligent kindness, cerebral benevolence: virtuous misers. They had somehow to explain away not merely the case-history of Judas but the whole spectacle of a sentimental usurer. "Money-lenders with hearts!" says a character in Dibdin's *The Jew and the Doctor.* "Come, I like that!" "Is it for a

Jew Cloaths Man to have a *soul?*" asks somebody in a foolish play entitled *Mordechai's Beard.* The question obviously begs for a rhetorical answer; it'll be a long one; so all one gets for one's pains is talk.

To trace the development of the stage-Jew with any degree of exhaustiveness past Shylock is not, in the jargon of my profession, "within the scope of this paper"; besides, the bibliographer himself has sketched the history of the subject for us. If one were to look for any single term to describe the contemporary stage-Jew from the Middle Ages down to the end of the nineteenth century, the term *parasite* will perhaps do as well as any: whatever else defines Shylock, the two traits which cling to him and which trail after him are his cannibalism and his usury: parasite either way. After the readmission of the Jews to England in 1655, a certain domestication of the tribe inevitably set in, on the stage as elsewhere, though it is idle to pretend that literature functions as a direct index to social change. Secularized and inoculated, Shylock the parasite persists, in one guise or another, throughout the nineteenth century: in Grabbe's obscene fairy-play *Cinderella,* in Hebbel's *The Diamond,* Gustav Freytag's *Journalists,* Tom Taylor's *Ticket-of-Leave Man,* and (saddest of all) in the very young Chekhov. Shylock's blade, dulled by the centuries, still flashes occasionally; the old phrase "Here shal be Cannibals" from the forgotten play by Day, Rowley, and Wilkins, is still sounded here and there; and if the Jew no longer wields the knife himself, he'll sell it to you at a bargain and let you do your own killing. Here is Shylock, 1836. Buechner's *Woyzeck.* Scene 18. Pawnshop: Woyzeck and Jew:

> *Woyzeck.* The little pistol is too much.
> *Jew.* Buy it or don't buy it, suit yourself.
> *Woyzeck.* How much is the knife?
> *Jew.* It's a sharp one. Going to cut your throat with it? Well: how about it? I'll give it to you as cheap as another. You can have your death cheap, but not for nothing. How about it? You can have your death at a bargain.
> *Woyzeck.* That'll cut more than bread.
> *Jew.* Two pennies.
> *Woyzeck.* There. (Goes).
> *Jew.* "There!" As if it was nothing! It's money, ain't it? The dog!

Fifty years later, in Chekhov's *Platonov,* the Jewish owner of a restaurant chain (sixty-three pubs), Vengerovich Sr., instructs a young horse-thief to cripple the title-figure of the play, a decadent, self-destructive Don Juan schoolteacher who has been giving the Jew a bad time: "I mean cripple, not kill. Cripple him; that is, give him such a beating that he'll remember it all his life.... Break some bones, or disfigure his face." And later on, with a perhaps unintended echo from Shylock: "When you're beating him, don't forget to say, 'This is from the grateful publican.'" But even at that precocious age — he wrote the play as a student, in his very early twenties — Chekhov is much too clear-eyed and clinical a writer to be fairly paired off with those mouldy Victorian puppeteers, with their tabloid versions of cheats and cutthroats: Vengerovich, no more the simple butcher than Shylock, resents being insulted by this mealy-mouthed fainéant Romeo as Shylock resents being insulted by these noisy spendthrifts. In his more leisurely moments, Chekhov's man moves with a certain aplomb among the Russian landowning classes, on whom he preys all the more easily because they themselves are too far gone in sloth to keep their estates intact; while the Jew's son, Isaac Abramovich to Abram Abramovich, already (these are the eighteen-eighties) indulges in the melancholia, the neurotically defensive arrogance, the self-tormented irony associated with the new generation.

By and large, though, as the fleshly theme sounded increasingly thin and out of tune with the times, the music of the three thousand ducats, the dreams of money-bags tonight, Shylock as Economic Man, as entrepreneur, went on and on and on. Roughly the first half of the nineteenth century devoted itself to the Jew who is little and dirty both: the pedlar, the fence, the old clothes' man, the picker up of filthy trifles. In a nasty review of Disraeli's *Tancred*, James Russell Lowell tried to impose some sense of history on things to account for the Jew's magpie instincts, as he saw them:

> That the idolators of ceremony and tradition should become the venders of old clothes, that the descendants of those who, within earshot of the thunders of Sinai, could kneel before the golden calf, should be the money-changers of Europe, has in it something of syllogistic completeness. The work by which the elder D'Israeli will be remembered is the old curiosity shop of literature. The son, with his trumpery of the past, is clearly a vender of the same wares, and an offshoot from the same stock.

By the time Lowell wrote this — the review appeared in 1847 — the contemporary stage-Jew, for the first time since the Renaissance, was again beginning to rise in social and economic status (though hardly in social esteem) and, putting on a clean shirt, went off to dine with the de Nucingens — also rich and Jewish. The Jew-muckworm of sentimental comedy and Romantic melodrama, by a series of successful deals (like fixing the World Series) is getting on in the world; the history of the nineteenth and early twentieth-century stage-Jew, with a squint at the actualities of the New Rialto, is largely the history of the Jew's rise from rags to riches, pedlar to tycoon: back to Barabas. His morals haven't necessarily improved in the process, and his manners only so much. The type that begins to emerge from about mid-century past 1914 is the social parasite, the unctuous social climber — successfully or unsuccessfully, but almost always disreputably, the would-be assimilationist, whom it would be so much less painful to assimilate if his nose were shorter, his skin less tawny, his conversation less vulgar, his cufflinks less shiny. The type is to be found in the plays of Pinero and Somerset Maugham, and those of lesser men.

By the end of the nineteenth century and at the outset of the twentieth, the Jew's problematic social status generally, divorced from the cash-nexus, is beginning to engage the playwright's solicitude in dozens of comedies *de thèse:* Nordau's *Dr. Kohn,* Schnitzler's *Professor Berhardi,* Henri Nathansen's *Within the Walls.* What interests these writers are the Jew's attitude toward his own religion in an increasingly secular and pluralistic society, toward intermarriage, toward social anti-Semitism. *La belle juive,* in the meantime, remains about as boringly *belle juive* as ever; but these things, like all others, depend finally on the playwright's ability to disengage himself from the stereotype and affirm his freedom; and if the playwright is only great enough, as Grillparzer and Hauptmann are, the *belle juive* will naturally be drawn into the sphere of his integrity. In Grillparzer's splendid *Jewess of Toledo,* for example, a late version of the quasi-historical legend already picked up by the earlier Spanish playwrights — by Lope de Vega, Mira de Amescua, García Huerta — the Jewess Rachel who charms King Alphonso to bed emerges as a rather gorgeous, sophisticated combination of go-getting, promiscuity, and lofty bitchiness; and the neurotic Jewess in Hauptmann's *Gabriel Schilling's Flight,* though the play is hardly vintage Hauptmann, has a lot more in common with Hedda Gabler than with Ivanhoe's heroic sweetheart.

Edward Coleman, our patient bibliographer, died in September 1939, two days after Hitler's invasion of Poland. He escaped by a few years the two nightmares of the times: the genocide of the Jews and the explosion of the A-bomb. The Nazi persecution of the Jews had already occupied a few of the playwrights before the war: Brecht in the dramatic sketches collected under the title *Furcht und Elend des Dritten Reiches;* the Danish playwright-priest Kaj Munk (he was shot of course); and the subject was to occupy others during and after the war: Werfel, Sartre, Hochhuth. Where millions perish, the individual turns into a non-person, disappears on these dunghills of death. So you fix the event in a place-name instead and talk about Auschwitz and Hiroshima. In the theatre, where Thingism doesn't work, where you need minimally A and B, or Mr Zero-sub-One and Mr Zero-sub-Two, the focus begins to shift: the stage-Jew is no longer assimilated to a prelogical tradition (that's been exploded, at last), is no longer a person meaningfully defined by his social and professional commitments — husband, doctor, rabbi, playboy, kidnapper; what defines him is the external event, the common catastrophe. How will he escape? How will he go to his death? How long can he hold out? Is he going to scream now? No, he won't escape. Yes, of course, he is going to scream. The crisis turns more than ever into a test of "character," if you like, but the dramatic motive is implicit in the general havoc, not individually determined. Here are the camps. Will his murderers feel guilty? Will *he* feel guilty for being murdered?

Our text for today is *The Investigation*. A boy of nine is loaded into a truck. 7th Witness, *loquitur:*

> I heard
> a guard talking through the barbed wire
> to a nine-year-old boy
> You know a lot for a boy your age
> he said
> The boy answered
> I know that I know a lot
> and I also know
> I'm not going to learn any more
> He was loaded into a truck
> with a group
> of about 90 children
> When the children started
> screaming and struggling
> the boy yelled
> Get in here
> Get in the truck
> Stop your crying
> You saw the way
> your parents and grandparents
> went
> Climb in
> then you'll get to see them again
> And as they were being driven off
> I heard
> him shout back to the guard
> You won't be forgiven
> anything

One thinks of Chaucer's "litel clergeon, seven yeer of age," who had his throat cut by the Jews; of the Croxton Play; and of — Oh, the Chimneys. — How these old griefs return.

Note

Anyone familiar with the literature will recognize my debt, even where this has not been indicated in the text, to the book-length studies by J. L. Cardozo, M. J. Landa, H. Sinsheimer, Bernard D. Grebanier, and Toby B. Lelyveld. On *The Merchant of Venice*, the literature is so large that one has to pick and choose: the essays I have read with particular pleasure are those by Mark Van Doren, Harley Granville-Barker, E. E. Stoll, E. M. W. Tillyard, Frank Kermode, W. H. Auden, C. L. Barber, and Cecil Roth. In my comments on usury, I have lifted two or three paragraphs from an earlier study of mine, *From Shylock to Svengali* (Stanford 1960); these are reprinted by permission of the Stanford University Press. For Marlowe and Shakespeare the texts I have used, as both reliable and very generally available, are Irving Ribner's one-volume edition of Marlowe's Complete Plays published by the Odyssey Press (N Y 1963) and J. R. Brown's edition of *The Merchant of Venice*, vol 23 in the New Arden Shakespeare (Cambridge, Mass 1955); and also the extracts of *The Merchant* from Mark Van Doren's *Shakespeare* (N Y 1939). The quotations from Nashe's *Unfortunate Traveller* are based on the text of Ronald B. McKerrow and F. P. Wilson (Oxford 1958) but I have modernized the spelling throughout. The Croxton Play has been included in Joseph Quincy Adams's *Chief Pre-Shakespearean Dramas* (Boston 1924). The quoted matter from Chekhov's *Platonov*, as translated by David Magarshack (N Y ©1964), is reprinted by permission of Hill and Wang; and I am grateful to Atheneum for permission to reprint the excerpt from Peter Weiss's *The Investigation*, "Song of the Camp" I, English version by Jon Swan and Ulu Grosbard (N Y ©1966). A brief tribute to Edward Coleman by Abraham Berger appears in the *Bulletin of The New York Public Library* LXIII (August 1959).

PREFACE

"If your playwrighters want a butt, or a buffoon, or a knave to make sport of, out comes a Jew to be baited and buffeted through five long acts for amusement of all good Christians."

Richard Cumberland, The Jew (1794) Act 1, Sc. 1.

THE list of works dealing with the Jew in English Drama, which is presented here, is offered as a continuation of the one published by the Library in 1931 under the title *The Bible in English Drama*. To the compilation of both lists the late Mr. Edward D. Coleman (1891–1939) devoted much of his leisure time and effort. To the faithful performance of this task, which he regarded as a labor of love, he gave many years of scholarly and enthusiastic attention. From his student days at Harvard University until the end of his life, he was fond of English literature and he evinced a keen interest in the Jew as a character in it. This fondness not only was expressed in omnivorous reading but also led him to collect with an almost contagious enthusiasm the literature to which he had been devoting so much of his interest and attention. Cultivating that hobby for over a quarter of a century enabled him to bring together what appears to be an unrivalled collection of books and related materials, representing a veritable laboratory for the student of the subject — the Jew in literature — which he himself had mastered so well. Virtually the entire literature recorded in his lists forms an integral part of his personal library. It is hoped that his collection of books will, before long, find a permanent place in a great reference library. Works of fiction — dramas, novels, short stories and poetry — containing Jewish characters and critical literature dealing with such writings, in the English language, both originals and translations, are most adequately represented in the Coleman Collection.

The untimely death of Mr. Coleman which occurred on September 3, 1939, deprived this publication of the benefit of the author's careful proofreading and of such improvements as he no doubt would have introduced in it while it was in process of publication. Mr. Daniel C. Haskell, the Bibliographer of The New York Public Library gave the manuscript the revision it required and saw it through the press. What Mr. Coleman said of Mr. Haskell's share in his earlier work (*The Bible in English Drama*, New York, 1931, p. 13) is certainly true of the present publication: he "has fashioned this material into the form in which it here appears, and is also responsible for the indices."

JOSHUA BLOCH

INTRODUCTION

BETWEEN 1584, the publication date of *The Three Ladies of London,* the first definitely secular play in which one of the characters is a Jew, and the year 1820, eighty plays of Jewish interest were published in the English language and most of them were staged. Between 1584 and the closing of the theatres, in 1648, plays were produced in fifteen different years; during the Restoration period, 1660–1700, only in five years; during the eighteenth century, in fifty years; during 1801–1837, in twenty years; during the Victorian period, 1838–1895, nearly every year; and from 1896 to the present, once or more every year. Such is the quantitative measure of the interest of English and American dramatists in plays with Jewish characters.

No living models for the Jew were easily available to English dramatists during the sixteenth and the greater part of the seventeenth century, because there were no Jews in England, at least none recognizable as such, during the period of the rise and early progress of the modern drama in that country. Jews were expelled from England in 1290 and their return was not permitted until 1656. The only English models existed in the ballads, miracle plays and romances of mediaeval times — nay, in the entire body of English literature, in which the seeds of anti-Jewish thought had been scattered far and wide.[1] If it be true that plays at their best are a reflection or a *re*-presentation of life, we must, therefore, deny high merit to the drama in England before Cromwell's time as far as the Jews were concerned, because there were no Jews there, during the greater part of that period, whose lives might conceivably have served for *re*-presentation. To be sure, there was at least one playwright during that time whose genius was not touched by any such limitation. But are we to believe the same of the rest?

A proper perspective, for our purposes, of the Jewish position in England may be had from the following events, chronologically set down. In 1594, Doctor Rodrigo Lopez, a Jewish convert, was hanged and quartered in the Tower on the charge of having plotted to poison Queen Elizabeth. He had become involved in English court intrigues and incurred the enmity of Elizabeth's friend, the powerful Earl of Essex.[2] By most historians his execution is considered a case

---

[1] See Edward D. Coleman, *The Bible in English drama;* an annotated list of plays, New York, 1931 (repr.: New York Public Library *Bulletin,* v. 34–35), p. 6–8; and H. Michelson, *The Jew in early English literature,* Amsterdam, 1926.

[2] See Sir Sidney Lee, "Elizabethan England and the Jews," in New Shakspere Society, *Transactions,* series 1 (1887–1892), no. 12, p. 143–166, and his "The original of Shylock" in *Gentleman's magazine,* 1880, v. 246, p. 185–200.

of judicial murder. The Lopez incident greatly exercised the contemporary dramatists and was much exploited by them.[3]

Five years later came Shakespeare's *The Merchant of Venice*. Though this drama is not treated bibliographically in the present list, beyond its mere inclusion under one entry, its influence is all-pervading. It must always have occurred to any author who meant to include a Jew in a play's cast of characters that an incomparable predecessor had already created Shylock. Let it be further remembered that the only interpretation of Shylock known to the stage (and consequently to the general public) till almost the middle of the nineteenth century was that of a bloodthirsty villain. The conception of a Shylock wronged and more sinned against than sinning is entirely modern and was first so portrayed by Sir Henry Irving.[4]

In 1656 London Maranos (secret Jews conforming outwardly to Christianity) first openly professed Judaism. During 1658–1660 attempts were made to bring about their re-expulsion. Further proceedings against them under the Conventicle Act were tried in 1673 but stopped by the King. In 1753 the Jew Bill was passed in their favor but promptly repealed. Their rights remained circumscribed for many, many years. Toleration and equality came about grudgingly and gradually. It took twenty years, 1836–1856, for the Jewish Emancipation Bill to become enacted. Complete political freedom did not come till 1858 and the University Tests were not abolished till 1871.[5]

---

[3] The references to Lopez are to be found in Marlowe's *Doctor Faustus*, Middleton's *Game at chesse*, Dekker's *The whore of Babylon*, Fletcher's *Women pleased, Hispanus*, a Latin play acted at Cambridge, March, 1596/7, and in *England's joy*, a spectacle (1602), besides allusions to and mentions of him in contemporary poetry.

[4] This more lenient interpretation given to Shylock owes not a little to later Shakespearean and historical research into all aspects of the bond episode. In the *Connoisseur*, London, May 16, 1754, p. 122–129, it was first suggested (? by Thomas Percy) that the bond story may have become known to Shakespeare with the contracting parties reversed as to race or religion. Gregorio Leti's *Life of Pope Sixtus V*, translated from the Italian by Rev. Farnsworth, is cited. The story is there told how Secchi, a Venetian Christian merchant, placed a wager with the Jew Samson Cenedo on the veracity of a current report that Drake had seized St. Domingo. The price of the wager was a pound of flesh. The Jew lost the wager. When the forfeiture fell due the Pope was called in as arbiter. Shocked by the inhumanity of the Christian merchant who demanded his pound of flesh, the Pope defeated Secchi's purpose by deciding in his favor in the same manner in which Portia decided in favor of Shylock in order to thwart him later. [Cf. Charles Reznikoff, "Note on *The Merchant of Venice*," in *The Menorah Journal*, New York, 1940, v. 28, p. 276–278 — J. Bl.]
See also Heinrich Graetz, *Shylock in der Sage, im Drama und in der Geschichte*, Krotoschin, 1880.

[5] The eminent mathematician James J. Sylvester who taught at the University of Virginia and Johns Hopkins University (see a sketch of him in the *Dictionary of American biography*) completed his studies at Cambridge in 1837, but did not get his degree till 1872, when the Test Act no longer intervened.

All writers on the subject of the present list have emphasized the unfavorable delineation of the Jew in English drama from earliest days till almost our own time. They have pointed out that in the drama before 1700 the Jew is a dark villain to be hated and avoided, and after 1700 a lesser villain and a caricature to be hissed and laughed at. Audiences before 1700, ready to believe all manner of atrocities on the part of a mysterious people upon whom they never or very seldom set their eyes, accepted all Jewish stage monstrosities as genuine and quite natural.[6] It takes much time to change a type which becomes established as the personification of wickedness. Since the dramatists had to have their villains, and since it is difficult to find villains in one's own group or sect it was much easier to choose them from among the Jews during the eighteenth century and long thereafter. In being so treated the Jews shared the fate of other English minorities and other unpopular and dissenting groups, such as the Puritans, the Quakers or the Plymouth Brethren, with the one important difference that in the case of the latter groups the practice was comparatively short-lived. In the case of the Jews it was persistent and continuous. One is justified in concluding that, as regards the Jews, the English stage did not hold up a mirror to nature and that the resulting types bear no truthful relation — political, social or cultural — to existing conditions and persons.

Our list, if it were arranged chronologically by successive years, would be headed by the *Croxton play of the Sacrament,* based on the mediaeval legend of the miracle of the desecration of the Host. This dramatic fragment was written in the second half of the fifteenth century, probably not long after 1461, the date given in its colophon as that of its alleged occurrence. The story was very popular in the middle ages. The earliest fifteenth-century version of a similar play was Italian, based on a Paris legend of 1290. In our English piece five Jews are named, a main villain and four conspirators. It differs from its continental models in its *dénouement,* in that the Jew and his accomplices are converted by the miracle and allowed to be baptized, instead of being burned in punishment.[7] In English literature the story is best known, in another form, in the beautiful ballad of Hugh of Lincoln. Usually styled a miracle play and in its latest edition printed as one of the *Non-Cycle Mystery Plays* by the Early English Text Society, the *Croxton Play* is nonetheless a secular one. Its dramatis personae are not biblical nor apocryphal and its central theme is distinctly historical.

[6] Prof. L. Wann, in preparing his *The Oriental in Elizabethan drama,* examined forty-seven Elizabethan plays and found six of Jewish interest. In *Modern philology,* 1915, v. 12, p. 441–442, he states: "The Jew, whom I have not considered an Oriental, appears in six plays and in every one he is *the* villain or *one* of them. He is a grasping miser or a treacherous tool, and no sympathy is ever shown for him."

[7] The miracles were held to prove the doctrine of Real Presence. A less spiritual result, on the continent, was the excuse for murder of wealthy Jews and the confiscation of their property.

The next play, *The Three Ladies of London,* by R. W. (? Robert Wilson, c. 1572–1600), surprises us by the presence in it of a decent and honorable Jew. J. P. Collier was the first one to point out its philo-Semitic nature.[8] Gerontus the Jew is represented in a very favorable light while his antagonist, the Christian merchant Mercatore, endeavors to defeat him by fraud, perjury and readiness to apostatize. Gerontus consents to lose all his money rather than allow it to be said of him that he had compelled the Christian to abandon his religion. The Jew's conduct is commended by the judge in a left-handed compliment: "Jews seek to excel in Christianity, and Christians in Jewishness." *The Three Ladies of London* proved a solitary relapse or a leader which had no followers. Ten years later, 1594, brought forth the wholesale and demoniac murderer Barabas in Marlowe's *The Jew of Malta,* and Abraham the poisoner in Robert Greene's *Selimus.* Shylock, made human and understandable by one who knew how, was followed by others not so human and not so understandable. They are listed here, with several exceptions, in chronological order: in 1601, Mammon the usurer in the anonymous *Jack Drum's Entertainment;* in 1607, Zariph, a travesty on Shylock in John Day's *The Travels of Three English Brothers;* in 1612, Benwash, a usurer, slavedealer and bawd in Robert Daborne's *A Christian Turn'd Turk;* in 1619, Zabulon, a slave panderer in Fletcher's *The Custom of the Country;* in 1623, Francisco disguised as a Jewish doctor poisoner in Massinger's *The Duke of Milan;* the same year, Romelio in another Jewish disguise to perform a nefarious operation in John Webster's *The Devil's Law Case;* in 1631, two Jewish monstrosities brought over from America in Killigrew's *Thomasso the Wanderer* (plagiarously repeated by Mrs. Aphra Behn in her *The Second Part of The Rover,* 1681); the same year, Hamon, a foul murderer in Thomas Goffe's *The Raging Turk;* and in 1694, Sancho, conceited coxcomb and apostate Jew in Dryden's *Love Triumphant.* There is little virtue in the composition of all of them and their roguery is of degree only. The woodenness of the result as evinced by these Jewish creations of our post-Shakespeareans is not improperly the measure of their difference from their great predecessor, who alone had the genius to make credible human beings do incredible things.

In 1697 the number of Jews on the London stock-exchange was limited to twelve, proof positive that many more applied for the privilege. Bearing in mind the topicalness of the drama it is not surprising that the furor caused by this legislative incident prompted the emergence, soon thereafter, of a Jewish stock-jobber on the London stage. Such a figure appeared at the very beginning of the eighteenth century in George Granville's (Lord Lansdowne) *The Jew of*

---

[8] In *Athenæum,* London, 1850, p. 475–476. See also Adolphus W. Ward, *A history of English dramatic literature to the death of Queen Anne,* London, 1899, v. 1, p. 141.

Venice, May, 1701. Dogget, who impersonated Sancho in Dryden's *Love Triumphant*, played the part of Shylock who was conceived as a purely comical character.[9] ("To day we punish a Stock-jobbing Jew. A piece of justice, terrible and strange; Which, if pursu'd, would make a thin Exchange:" reads part of the Prologue, spoken by Shakespeare and written by Bevill Higgons.) All the Shakespearean motivation was removed and, instead, a mere travesty of *The Merchant of Venice* was evolved. Throughout the eighteenth century, ushered in so inauspiciously, the Portuguese Jews then dominant and overwhelmingly more numerous than their German co-religionists, were extending their influence as merchant princes, physicians, scholars, Maecenases and members of learned societies. One of them, Moses Mendez, d. 1758, achieved contemporary fame as a poet and dramatist. It became, therefore, no longer possible to portray the Jew in the Elizabethan fashion. He ceased to be murderous and cruel. Instead he became the profligate in Cibber, Fielding and O'Keefe; the ridiculous fool in Knipe, Macklin and Sheridan; the would-be social climber in Foote; the hardhearted master in Morton, and generally detestable and to be avoided in the rest of them. The entire story is told in full in H. R. S. van der Veen's book.[10]

Veen, p. 261, lists five printed plays with Jewish characters between 1701 and 1749, and seventeen such between 1759 and 1798. He states that there are no new stage Jews between 1701 and 1733 and he considers *The Harlot's Progress* of 1733 as the first real play of Jewish interest in that century, p. 104. He ascribes the greater attention paid to Jewish characters in the second half of the century to the unfortunate Jew Bill of 1753, which focused unfavorable attention on the Jews and consequently inclined playwrights to burden them with ignoble rôles.[11] It is quite true that the abortive Jew Bill set back Jewish emancipation in England

---

[9] See J. H. Wilson, "Granville's 'stock-jobbing Jew,'" in *Philological quarterly*, 1934, v. 13, p. 1–15. Prof. Wilson quotes a 1700 dictionary definition of *stock-jobbing* as "a sharp, cunning, cheating Trade of Buying and Selling Shares of Stock."

Later actors made the part "a vehicle of most disgraceful buffoonery." See John Bernard, *Retrospections of the stage*, London, 1830. It was not till February 14, 1741, that Granville's conception of Shylock was abandoned forever on the English stage. On that night Macklin gave his version of a tragic Shylock, malevolent and furious, — a characterization which allegedly drew from Pope the epigram, "This is the Jew that Shakespeare drew." Shylock as conceived by Macklin held the stage for over a hundred years.

[10] *Jewish characters in eighteenth-century English fiction and drama*, Groningen, 1935. 308 p.

[11] The echo of the Jew Bill was heard in drama as late as 1769, in Garrick's *The Jubilee* (Drury Lane, Oct. 14, 1769). The speakers are two Stratford girls:

> NANCY: ...I swear I know no more about the Jubillo as you call him, than I do about the Pope of Rome...
>
> SUKEY: ...had you lived in Burmingham or Coventry, or any other polite Cities as I have done, you would have known better than to talk so, of Shakespeare and the Jew-bill.

for a long time. However, whether this contributed also to lower them in the estimation of the dramatists to the extent believed by Veen is open to question. Firstly, Veen errs in placing the number of Jewish plays in the first half of the century at five. At least four more plays, all printed and staged during that period, are apparently unknown to him.[12] The proportion becomes nine to seventeen against his five to seventeen — a not inconsiderable difference when so few are involved. What is more important is the fact that in the latter half of the century not *more,* as Veen himself admits, but *incomparably many more* plays were written than in the first half. A comparison of the hand-lists given by Allardyce Nicoll in his *A History of the Early Eighteenth-Century Drama, 1700–1750,* and in his 1750–1800 volume will prove this quite conclusively. Besides, the suggestion is here ventured that the greater number of derogatory Jewish types in the second half may not improperly be explained by what E. N. Adler describes in the chapter entitled "The Seamy Side" in his history of London Jewry.[13] Adler in this chapter refers to Peter Colquhoun's *Treatise on the Police of the Metropolis,* in which Jewish criminality in the London of the late eighteenth century is recorded. Joshua Van Oven contraverted Colquhoun but he admitted more than was pleasant. Veen's theory, therefore, as to the cause of the greater prevalence of unfavorable Jewish types during 1759–1800 is open to serious challenge.

In the slow movement of justice and fair dealing to the Jew in English dramatic literature and his emancipation from the contumely to which he seemed shackled Richard Cumberland holds first place. In an age when the Rights of Man were talked about and the slogans of the French Revolution were heard loud in the land not even English insularity could hold out. *Nathan the Wise,* itself the cause and effect of the humanitarian liberalism of the late eighteenth century, enunciated a new doctrine and introduced a new type of Jew in drama. It was high time for some one in England to perform the *amende honorable.* The Terence of England rose to the occasion. There was something in him which fitted him for the task. In his early youth he had prowled about in the London Jewish quarters. In epic verse he had sung the ancient glories of Israel and in journalism he championed the imaginary Abraham Abrahams. In two earlier plays he had vindicated the characters of the Scotch and the Irish on the boards of Drury Lane. At last, at the same theatre, on May 8, 1794, he brought forth his *The Jew,*

---

[12] Aaron Hill, *The walking statue* (Drury Lane, Jan., 1709/10); Thomas Baker, *An act at Oxford* (produced in a revised version as *Hampstead-Heath,* Drury Lane, Oct., 1705); Charles Knipe, *A city ramble* (Lincoln's Inn Fields, June, 1715); and Thomas Southerne, *Money the mistress* (Lincoln's Inn Fields, Feb., 1725). The number of such Jewish plays of the second half unrecorded by Veen, and formerly by Landa, is ten.

[13] E. N. Adler, *London,* Philadelphia, 1930, p. 150–160.

in which Jack Bannister played Sheva, outwardly a stock Jew of dramatic convention, but with a heart of gold. It was an instantaneous stage success and no less than seven editions were printed before 1800, besides the usual pirated editions. It was reprinted in 1824, 1829 and 1834 and, in the first year of its appearance, translated into French and German. It had a considerable vogue on the continent. It was seen in Boston on December 19, 24, and 29, 1794, and revived again and again there and in other cities during 1795–1796.[14] Everywhere it was hailed. Our own William Dunlap wrote: "The idea of vindicating the Jews is a very happy one. . . The serious part of the comedy is certainly deserving of praise." In England some of the reviewers denied merit to the plot but all joined in a chorus of praise for its purpose.[15] Henceforth, though the age of darkness for the Jew on the stage was by no means over, favorable Jewish types ceased to be rarities and the fashion for Jewish heroes became established. Cumberland returned to a Jewish theme three years before his death.[16] In 1808 his *The Jew of Mogadore,* the scene of which is laid in Africa (Drury Lane, May 3, 1808), was presented. Dowton played Nadab, another and even more admirable Sheva. It did not please the theatregoers; moreover, a good Jew was no longer a novelty.

The popularity and persistence of the so-called Jewish dialect, accompanied by prescribed gestures and occasionally by suitable habiliment, beginning in the eighteenth century and continued to our own times, has always plagued sensitive Jewish auditors. Dramatists, managers and actors refused to give it up, for the good reason that it always presumably "raised a laugh." Certain actors excelled in it, notably Baddeley, Wewitzer, Quick, Dowton, and Fawcett. Landa, in the chapter "Gibberish" in his *The Jew in Drama,* ascribes its invention to John O'Keefe in his play *The Young Quaker* (July 26, 1783). He calls O'Keefe "master of gibberish. He set a new fashion, planted a fungous growth which spread with devastating rapidity."[17] This is not quite correct.[18] Charles Knipe used it in 1715 in his *A City Ramble* (not mentioned by Landa) for Mordecai's

[14] For a detailed stage history of *The Jew* in America, see E. D. Coleman, "Plays of Jewish interest on the American stage, 1752–1821," in *Publications* of the American Jewish Historical Society, No. 33, p. 182–184. See ibid., p. 171–198 for a study of the subject given in the title.

[15] "The design is...deserving of every encomium," *British critic,* London, v. 6, p. 11–14. "Nothing has contributed more, in later times, to diffuse and establish this disgraceful prejudice against a set of unhappy wanderers, than the manner in which they have been represented on the stage," *Monthly review,* London, series 2, v. 16, p. 153. All other reviewers wrote in a similar vein.

[16] All writers on the present *The Jew* have recorded Cumberland's early lapse in presenting a conventional, disagreeable Jewish character in Ephraim in his *The fashionable lover,* 1772. None has mentioned that a similar, unfavorable type was included by him in the person of Issachar, a moneylender, in his *The note of hand; or, Trip to Newmarket* (Drury Lane, Feb. 9, 1774).

[17] supra, p. 120.

[18] Earlier, in this chapter, Landa qualified his assertion by saying that Cumberland "nibbled at the dialect" in his *The fashionable lover* in 1772.

lines, with more terrifying results than O'Keefe produced in the mouth of Shadrach Boaz. The same dialect, although not as pronounced, is used in the ballad opera *The Jew Decoy'd* and in Theophilus Cibber's *The Harlot's Progress* (both 1733). Miles P. Andrews did the same with Ephraim Labradore in his *Dissipation* (March 10, 1781) (another play unknown to Landa). Others, antedating Landa's given date, 1783, can be cited. Besides, the late R. Compton Rhodes disputes Landa's statement that Sheridan provided correct English for Isaac Mendoza in *The Duenna* and for Moses in *The School for Scandal*. "Actually," says Rhodes "they always spoke what was called 'the Jewish cant' though, in point of fact, it was more closely allied to the broken English of a Dutch man ... The dramatic authors rarely indicated the dialect they intended; that part they looked upon as the business of Jewish impersonators, like Baddeley..."[19]

In the printed copies of certain plays, speeches by Jewish characters are not given in dialect, but they are always so spoken. Rhodes illustrates this by some of the lines spoken by Hardy who is disguised as "cunning little Isaac Mendoza" in Mrs. Cowley's *The Belle's Stratagem* (Feb. 22, 1780). A reviewer of the production of Cumberland's *The Jew of Mogadore* (1808) writes: "The mongrel dialect used by Dowton [who played the part of Nadab, 'the benevolent Jew'], sometimes Duke's Place gibberish was very bad. Mr. Wewitzer is the only actor in London who has the Jewish dialect in any perfection."[20] On April 16, 1807, Sherenbeck, a Rochester actor, played Shylock with new readings or, rather, with new tones of readings. He delivered all his speeches in the Jewish dialect.[21] He played the same rôle, again in the Jewish dialect, at Covent Garden, London, on July 9, 1817, for the benefit of Mrs. Faucit.[22] Some historians of Yiddish literature, with more zeal for their language than facts for the case, have promised to prove that the "Jewish dialect" used at that time on the London stage was actual Yiddish. There is not a shred of evidence to support this belief.

Social chroniclers testify that Jews were assiduous theatregoers in early days as they are now. The question not unnaturally arises: How did they react to the continuous denigration? There is no indication of any mass-protest on their part till December 18, 1802. On that evening T. J. Dibdin's *Family Quarrels* was first seen at the Covent Garden. In it Fawcett (who had already sustained the "kindly" Jewish parts of Abednego and Ephraim respectively in Dibdin's *The Jew and the Doctor,* Nov. 23, 1798, and in his *The School for Prejudice,* Jan. 3, 1801) acted the rôle of Proteus in disguise as a Jew, who comes to rescue the girl. At the end of the second act Proteus offers the contents of his box [called the *Jew's*

---

[19] *Review of English studies,* 1929, v. 5, p. 138–139.
[20] *Monthly mirror,* 1808, new series, v. 3, p. 394–398.
[21] ibid., 1807, new series, v. 1, p. 293.
[22] *Era almanack,* 1881, p. 70.

box] to Argus who replies that "he never bought anything of such people."[23] A great disturbance arose, at this remark. The Jews, forming a considerable part of the audience, evidently resented it as a reflection upon all of them. The act, however, proceeded amid a general uproar.[24] Fawcett appeared on the stage during the intermission and explained that no insult was intended.[25] This apology allayed the storm, but broke out again on another allusion. Fawcett's "Jew song" in the third act — "First, dere vash Miss Levi, pretty Miss Levi — oh, vat a Miss Levi vas she!" was encored by the majority of the audience, but the opposition continued. The noise rendered it inaudible to any part of the house. In retrospect of 135 years, one can now judge this demonstration unfortunate in that the choice fell upon a play comparatively inoffensive.

Sufferance was no longer the badge of the Jew in December, 1802. Dan Mendoza, the "star of Israel" had been the pugilistic champion of England from 1792 to 1795, sheriff's officer in the county of Middlesex and a foe, feared if not respected, of those who would traduce the Jewish name. No less a star was Elias Samuel (better known as Dutch Sam, 1775–1816). In his heyday then, he was the hardest hitter the prize ring had ever seen and enriched his art by the introduction of the "upper-cut." With two such potential supporters, the pugnacious Jewish theatregoers were emboldened to protest. No wonder the Dramatic Guardian upbraided them as follows:[26] "They now grow arrogant and presuming, appearing to claim as a right what we [Cumberland in the portrayal of Sheva] have liberally conceded them as an indulgence. . . If the tribe proceed to further outrage, the Dramatic Guardian has much more and serious arguments in reserve." Dibdin himself made a dignified defence in a preface to the printed play, which Landa reprints in his volume, p. 145 (but which does not appear in the edition known to us).

[23] This line does not occur in the printed play (London: Longman, 1805) in the Library's possession, which is also the only separate edition listed in the British Museum Catalogue. Another edition of *Family quarrels* is included, according to the British Museum Catalogue, in Cumberland's British Theatre, v. 32, which perhaps does contain the missing line quoted above. However, the Library's set of Cumberland's British Theatre, in 42 volumes, does not contain the play at all. This is told here in detail to illustrate the bibliographical difficulties one constantly comes across among the English printed plays of the eighteenth and early nineteenth centuries. The genuine author's text is always in question, due to lack of protection in the existing copyright laws and the consequent prevalence of unauthorized and pirated editions. R. S. Rhodes discusses some of these problems in his "Some aspects of Sheridan bibliography" in *The Library*, London, Dec., 1928.
Argus's missing objectionable line is in our 1805 edition, probably the one reading, "I can't see what business you have here" or "Go along, I say." The compiler owns a copy of *Songs, duets, Chorusses, &c. in the new comic opera called Family quarrels* (London: Barker and Son, 1803), in which one can again observe variations as compared with the song texts given in the 1805 edition.
[24] See *European magazine*, 1802, v. 42, p. 457; and *Universal magazine*, 1802, v. 111, p. 455–456.
[25] He addressed them: "Ladies and gentlemen, I appear to you in behalf of the author who on no occasion has given offence to that part of the audience which, I fear, are now offended. I wish you would recollect the other pieces which he has written...in none of which is there a single passage that is not rather complimentary than otherwise. And, ladies and gentlemen, if you suffer this piece to proceed, I pledge myself and its success upon the truth of what I say. (Loud applause.)"
[26] The dramatic critic in *The monthly mirror*, 1802, v. 14, p. 404–405.

No record of similar demonstrations of displeasure is known. In later years Jewish audiences protested by their absence. An instance of it is told by the dramatist Charles Bucke in the prefaces to his play *The Italians,* London, 1820. It appears that Bucke had been promised that his piece would be staged by the Drury Lane Theatre. Instead, Penley's version of Marlowe's *The Jew of Malta* was substituted on April 24, 1818, to star Edmund Kean as Barabas. Bucke writes: "Previous to its [*Jew of Malta*] appearance, I was requested to write the Prologue. This I thought proper to decline: first, because I felt a reluctance to be in any way assisting in the revival of a Tragedy so barbarous, and so entirely unfitted for the present age, as *The Jew of Malta*: but, principally, because I felt ashamed, in being accessory to the cruelty of offering such an undeserved, as well as an unprovoked, insult to the great body of Jews: — all of whom took so much offence at the presentation — particularly as it occurred during the week of Passover — that, for the whole of the remaining season, it was more difficult to recognize a Jew in the house, than even a Woman of Fashion."[27] Henceforth the Jewish periodical press assumed the task of crying out whenever a particularly disagreeable type made his appearance. In our own century and country the Jewish Anti-Defamation League was organized for the purpose. If it is apparent that a play gives an untrue or unfair portrayal the League endeavors to prevent its production or to secure the elimination of objectionable matter.

The readiness of a theatre audience to laugh is unconquerable. An everyday psychologist pointed out that even a group of *highbrows* seated on a platform, would break into laughter to see a pompous individual, fashionably dressed, slip and fall headlong on the waxed floor, as he struts in full consciousness of his importance to his place. Our vaudeville dramatists know this and one can't blame them for capitalizing it. In our list are many plays of this vaudeville variety, far too many for the compiler's taste. They can be recognized in most cases by their titles and they are mostly the creations of hired hacks attached to the offices of certain dramatic publishers who specialize in this variety. In our third section these authors can be identified by the multitudinous titles to their credit. In the descriptions of these pieces in the publishers' catalogues they are invariably "mirth-provoking," "sure-fire hits," or "packed with pathos, action and comedy." The popular demand for them is apparently insatiable; otherwise, they would not have been printed continuously over so long a period. That they are funny even the most fastidious must admit and not much damage would have been done if they had been confined to "mirth-provoking" only.

Formerly the stage Irishman paraded with green whiskers and a corrugated brogue until the Irish, without benefit of an anti-defamation league, arose en

---

[27] *Monthly magazine,* London, 1822, v. 53, p. 59.

masse and smote him hip and thigh with effective weapons. The stage Jew, with hooked nose, flapping hands, sing-song English and Yiddish expletives, survived much longer. (*Abie's Irish rose,* by some considered an authentic Manhattan folk-tale, which enjoyed an unprecedented run of five years on the Broadway boards and the *Potash and Perlmutter* series of plays in 1913–1917, are essentially of this type, forming its crown and glory.) The stage Irishman, moreover, while funny, was at the same time winsome, chivalrous and lovable. Not so was the stage Jew. The latter, when he was not merely comical, was drawn as repulsive and contemptible, with no pride of ancestry, ready to sacrifice everything for love of money, sycophantic and craven, the beneficiary and inciter of crimes which he dared not commit. This is a fair description of most of them. It was a rare exception to represent one of them as decent and unselfish. There was always great difference of opinion in Jewish circles whether to fight this devil with irony or with fire. Certain it is that these vaudeville types of the Joe Welch brand did incalculable harm to the Jewish name throughout this country. Of late some of the publishers of this category of literature have called a halt. One of the best-known of them stated in 1933: "We are not proud of them. Such material, I think, had best be left unsung in their present obscure places... For ourselves, we're breaking away from introducing characters that are out and out caricatures. That sort of stage humor... is definitely out."

The larger part of the nineteenth century, for the purposes of this brief survey, can be dismissed with but a few words. It is so dismissed in general histories of the drama as well. It was the age of blood-and-thunder melodrama. Dibdin's imitations of Cumberland's *The Jew* (1798, 1800), H. M. Milner's *The Jew of Lubeck* (1819), the dozen or more dramatizations of Scott's *Ivanhoe* (1820 on), Charles Reade's *It's Never Too Late to Mend* and his *Gold* (1853, 1865), the versions of Scribe's *The Jewess* (1835 on), and the English adaptations of Mosenthal's *Deborah* (1862 on) are some of the sympathy-evoking plays of Jewish content. The majority of the others during that century are of the opposite kind, where the Jew is the conventionalized stage type, not as detestable as in the earlier centuries but still more than unpleasant. In modern times — the period begun in the nineties by Pinero and Jones and continued by Shaw, Barrie and Galsworthy — while the Jew is still introduced occasionally as the villain, the comic or, less often, as an exalted character — as a rule he is not distinguished, because of race, from the other characters. This is due to the fact that in modern times he is an integral part of society and is so considered. Any play which depicts social life and conditions occasionally includes a Jewish character without necessarily causing him to stand out as a Jew. Moreover, inasmuch as Jews predominate or are largely represented in certain businesses and occupations, it is usual and perhaps inevitable that a Jewish name should be given to a character representing such business or occupation, e.g., an art dealer in Arnold Bennett's *The Great Adventure;* an impresario in Margaret Kennedy's *The Constant Nymph;* a jeweler in S. N. Behrman's *Serena Blandish;* a physician in Franz V. Werfel's *Juarez and Maximilian;* a professional gambler in F. S. K. Fitzgerald's *The Great Gatsby;* or a movie magnate in G. S. Kaufman's *Merton of the Movies.*

* * *

The present list is the result of the compiler's attempt to offer a complete and annotated list of printed plays, including translations from other languages, of Jewish interest, based on material available at The New York Public Library and in the compiler's own collection. Whenever a copy of a desired play was not available at either of these two sources, the Library of Congress or the Harvard College Library was made use of. A very limited number of entries from other libraries was also included, for the sake of completeness. All entries bear the classmark of The New York Public Library or the name of the library from which they were taken. Those not so marked are from the compiler's collection. The term "dramatic composition" was used in its most comprehensive sense. Any errors of judgment will be found in the direction of too great inclusiveness, rather than that of rejections. The test for the inclusion of any work was the existence of speeches in character, provided it had an inherent dramatic element, or was primarily intended for the stage or public entertainment. Mere dialogues which postulate no mimic accompaniment were excluded, but monologues designed for stage or public presentation were included. The object being to dig out the less known and the less formally dramatic pieces, to illustrate the ramifications of Jewish interest throughout the entire range of English dramatic literature, this list is designed to offer a place for every possible work which can lay claim to any of the criteria of a drama. A certain number of exceptional cases were decided on their own merits.

A play is here considered of Jewish interest whenever one or more of its characters is designated in the dramatis personae as a Jew; whenever the text clearly indicates any of the characters to be taken as such; or whenever the author has bestowed upon the character an unmistakably Jewish name. Plays in which a Jewish historical figure is represented, and plays translated from Hebrew or Yiddish, of whatever kind, are also deemed of interest for this list. "Mention plays," i. e., those which are of Jewish interest because of some remarks about Jews or things Jewish, but in which there is no Jewish character, have not been included. The number of such plays is large, immeasurably more than the approximate dozen and a half, which Landa listed and quoted from.[28] Those to be found

[28] M. J. Landa, supra, p. 86–127, passim.

in the English drama of the sixteenth and seventeenth centuries, prior to the Re-settlement of the Jews in England and soon thereafter, are of especial importance, and the compiler hopes for an early opportunity to publish, with bibliographical annotations, those "mention plays" that originated before 1800. It was thought best to omit Shakespeare's *The Merchant of Venice* from this list. The traceable editions are so numerous, the commentative literature so great and the periodical reviews occasioned by its long and glorious stage history are so vast that it would have overshadowed the rest of our work. The compiler hopes to return to it at a later date.

A few early plays the texts of which have been lost have been admitted here. The authority for the information and such other facts as are known are stated. Opera librettos have been excluded as not belonging here. Pageants where the text is in dialogue, spoken by actors and not recited by a reader to the accompanying action of the performers, have been included. Foreign translated plays, and foreign plays unpublished in translation which were produced in English on the English or American stage are likewise included. Non-printed plays based on a pre-existing published novel, those which served as the basis for a subsequently-published novel or story, plays which exist only in extensive and detailed prose synopses, those the text of which is available only in substantial and numerous extracts with a running commentary (such as are given in Burns Mantle's series *The Best Plays*), and those not printed but the texts of which exist in manuscript at a public library where the compiler was able to examine them, were all considered for our purpose as printed plays and, therefore, included.

Our list has been arbitrarily arranged in three divisions — from earliest times to 1837, 1838–1914, and 1915 to date. Illumination of the Jewish interest of a play, particularly of those the titles of which do not indicate a Jewish connection, has been brought out by short excerpts from the preface, by published periodical reviews, or by the cited interpretation given to the character at the stage production. Each main entry, in the case of plays that have been staged, was supplemented by notes giving, whenever possible, the time and scene of the play, the name and nature of the Jewish character, when and where first produced, and the name of the actor who played the Jewish rôle. In the case of translated plays only English reviews were included. Of dramas originally written in English, reviews in all languages were admitted.

The kinds of play one comes across in our list are as diverse and manifold as those in any representative list compilable from the body of English dramatic literature. All classes and kinds are represented. Since no subject classification is given in the list it is not improper to indicate here some of the classes. The greater part comes within two broad divisions — plays in which the Jewish character (or characters) is incidental and replaceable and those in which he is essential, though he be one of many (e.g. De Levis in Galsworthy's *Loyalties*). Those of the first category are found among all classes of drama, whether in comedy or tragedy; those of the second category are usually those in which the Jew is the problem in questions of racial relations. The remaining kinds of play can be listed under the following headings as to their Jewish interest: Plays containing historical personages, such as Heine, Disraeli (in Laurence Housman's series of plays about Queen Victoria, and by other authors), the American Rebecca Franks, the patriot Haym Salomon, or certain of the characters connected with Columbus's first voyage to America; Zionist plays, the *milieu* of which is usually the Jewish effort in modern Palestine. (Many of these are issued by Zionist organizations, such as the Hadassah, and affiliated bodies, and are propagandic); miscellaneous plays by Jewish authors based largely on themes from Jewish history or current Jewish problems in this country;[29] plays dealing with the persecution of non-Aryans in Nazi Germany; humorous skits of minor Jewish interest or Jewish monologues; translations from the Yiddish and Hebrew, the locale mostly the old country or the so-called ghetto of New York.

The subject of this list has been treated in more or less complete studies by a number of students, at first — significantly enough — by three American rabbis, David Philipson, Harry Levi and Edward N. Calisch. During the last decade there have appeared volumes by Myer J. Landa (most comprehensive of all), H. Michelson on the period before the Resettlement, J. L. Cardozo on the Elizabethan period, and H. R. S. van der Veen on the eighteenth century. Nor should the names of T. F. Dillon Croker, Sir Sidney Lee and Charles Mabon be omitted in this connection. The works of each of them can justly be regarded as pioneer in part or in whole, and each has extended our bibliographical knowledge of the subject by the discovery of new plays and the elucidation of them. The present list adds many not mentioned by any of them. Information as to any omissions will be gratefully acknowledged.

The compiler is happy to have the opportunity here to express his gratefulness to his friends, Dr. Joshua Bloch, Chief of the Jewish Division of The New York Public Library, and Professor Harry A. Wolfson of Harvard University, for the advice and encouragement given him during the long preparation of this list. Mr. Frank A. Peterson was of great assistance during the early period of the work. Many friends, who must remain anonymous, have aided him in many ways. To all of them and, last but not least, to Mr. Daniel C. Haskell, Bibliographer of the Library, the compiler renders his most earnest thanks.

---

[29] Of a somewhat similar kind are the "Jewish Festival plays," q.v. in *The Bible in English drama*, supra, p. 154–166.

THE JEW IN ENGLISH DRAMA

ORDER OF ARRANGEMENT

BIBLIOGRAPHY
GENERAL WORKS
COLLECTIONS

INDIVIDUAL PLAYS
EARLIEST TIMES TO 1837
1838–1914
1915–1938

BIBLIOGRAPHY

ACKLAM, F. ELVA. Drama. (In her: Jewish life in modern literature; a bibliography. Madison, Wis., 1930. 4°. f. 19–25.)
Diss.: Library School of the University of Wisconsin.
A brief characterization is given of each title.

BAKER, WALTER H., AND COMPANY. Plays for Jewish groups. [Boston, 1932.] 4 l. 12°.
Caption-title.

—— —— [Boston, 1934.] 6 l. 12°.
Caption-title.

BLOCH PUBLISHING COMPANY. ...List of English plays, Biblical...adult plays, miscellaneous ... New York, 1938. 13 p. 12°.
Cover-title.
Similar lists have been issued by this firm in the past.

CALISCH, EDWARD NATHANIEL. A list of non-Jewish [and Jewish] authors who have written on or about the Jews. (In his: The Jew in English literature. Richmond [cop. 1909]. 12°. p. 199–265.) *PAO

CLARK, BARRETT HARPER. The Yiddish drama. (In his: A study of modern drama. New York and London, 1925. 8°. p. 411–420.) *R–NAF
Many works of several authors, appearing in our list, are recorded.

COLEMAN, EDWARD DAVIDSON. The Bible in English drama; an annotated list of plays including translations from other languages... New York: The New York Public Library, 1931. iv, 212 p. 4°. NCOD or *P–* PZB
Repr.: New York Public Library. Bulletin, Oct.–Dec., 1930, Jan. – March, 1931, *HND.
Classified with indexes of authors, plays, special topics and English translations of foreign plays.
See especially lists of quasi-Biblical plays, p. 151–166.
Reviewed by S. B. Liljegren in *Anglia Beiblatt*, Halle, 1933, Bd. 44, p. 238–239, *RNA;* by Zoltán Haraszti in Boston Public Library, *More books*, Boston, 1931, v. 6, p. 295, *GW;* by W. P. Schirmer in *Deutsche Literaturzeitung*, Leipzig, 1932, Jahrg. 53, col. 682–684, *NAA;* by Hugh Harris in *Jewish chronicle*, London, Oct. 9, 1931, p. 13, *PBE;* by Peter Wiernik in *Jewish morning journal*, New York, March 6, 1932, *PBB;* in *Jewish quarterly review*, Philadelphia, 1932, new series, v. 22, p. 436–437, *PBE;* in *Journal of religion*, Chicago, 1932, v. 12, p. 155, *ZAA;* by C. J. Graves in *Journal of theological studies*, Oxford, 1933, v. 34, p. 109, *PGH;* by S. Shunami in *Kirjath Sepher*, Jerusalem, 1932–33, Jahrg. 9, p. 39–40, *PAA;* and by Hans Hecht in *Theologische Literaturzeitung*, Leipzig, 1932, Jahrg. 57, col. 112.

DOBSEVAGE, I. GEORGE. Drama [and juvenile plays]. (In: American Jewish year book 5684. Philadelphia, 1923. 8°. v. 25, p. 213–214, 232–237.) *PXX
Part of his: A classified list of standard books in English on Jewish subjects.

FRIEDMAN, HELEN MARIE. Yiddish drama. (In her: Suggestive outline for the study of English translations of Yiddish fiction, drama, poetry, etc. Cleveland, 1931. 4°. f. [10–14.])

GOLDBERG, ISAAC. David Pinski. (In his: The drama of transition. Cincinnati [cop. 1922]. 8°. p. 379–403.) NAF

—— Perez Hirschbein. (In his: The drama of transition. Cincinnati [cop. 1922]. 8°. p. 404–420.) NAF

GOLDSTEIN, FANNY. Drama. (In: Boston Public Library. Brief reading lists. Boston, 1931–38. 8°. no. 44, May, 1931, p. 34–36; no. 44, April, 1934, p. 36–44; no. 44, May, 1936, p. 10–12; no. 45, April, 1937, p. 9; no. 46, May, 1938, p. 14–15.) *HND
These lists, representing the holdings of the Boston Public Library, bear the title Judaica, or Recent Judaica.
Each play is briefly described.

JEWISH WELFARE BOARD. English plays of Jewish interest translated from the Yiddish (suitable for intermediate and senior groups). New York: Jewish Welfare Board, 1933. 6 l. f°.
Typewritten.

—— English plays of Jewish interest in two or more acts, suitable for intermediate and senior groups. New York: Jewish Welfare Board [1933]. 7 l. 4°.
Caption-title.
Typewritten.
A revised list, 7 l., with added entries, was issued in 1937.

—— List of plays of Jewish interest for juniors and intermediates. New York: Jewish Welfare Board [1937]. 5 l. 4°.
Caption-title.
Reproduced from a typewritten copy.

—— Selected list of English plays of Jewish interest in one act (for seniors. Exclusive of holiday plays). New York: Jewish Welfare Board, 1933. 4 l. f°.
Caption-title.
Typewritten.
A list, 6 l., had been issued in 1929, and a revised issue, 5 l., was issued in 1937.

[1]

Bibliography, continued

LANDA, MYER JACK. Index of plays. (In his: The Jew in drama. London, 1926. 8°. p. 315–320.) * PZB

LEVINGER, ELMA C. (EHRLICH). List of plays suitable for Jewish groups. (Drama. Mt. Morris, Ill., 1928. 4°. v. 18, p. 153–154.) NAFA

—— A selective play-list for a Jewish dramatic group. (Youth leader. Cincinnati, 1937. 4°. v. 5, May, p. 19–27.) * PBD

MELS, EDGAR. The Jew in modern drama. (In: Jewish encyclopedia. New York, 1903. 4°. v. 4, p. 651–653.) * R–* PBZ

—— The Jews as portrayed in stage fiction. (Reform advocate. Chicago, 1908. 4°. v. 35, p. 218–221, 252–255.) * PBD
Printed also in *Jewish tribune*, Portland, Ore., 1908, v. 11, June 19, p. 12–13, * *PBD.*
Repr.: Illustrated Sunday magazine.

THE NEW YORK PUBLIC LIBRARY. List of dramas in The New York Public Library relating to the Jews, and of dramas in Hebrew, Judeo-Spanish, and Judeo-German; together with essays on the Jewish stage. Prepared by Mr. A. S. Freidus. [New York, 1907.] 34 p. 4°. * PAQ
Repr.: New York Public Library Bulletin, v. 11, p. 18–51, * *HND.*

STOKES, HENRY PAINE. The Jew in English literature. (In his: A short history of the Jews in England. London, 1921. 12°. p. 59–63, 108–114.) * PXQ

UNION OF AMERICAN HEBREW CONGREGATIONS. — DEPARTMENT OF SYNAGOGUE AND SCHOOL EXTENSION. Plays. (In its: Book catalog, 1937–1938. Cincinnati [1938]. 12°. p. 46–48.)

UNITED STATES. — WORKS PROGRESS ADMINISTRATION: FEDERAL THEATRE PROJECT, NEW YORK. ...Anglo-Jewish plays in English and Yiddish. New York: National Service Bureau, Federal Theatre Project, 1938. 4 l., 25, 25 f., 2 l. 4°. (National Service Bureau publication no. 20–S.) MWED
Mimeographed.
Text in English and Yiddish.
Compiled by "Jewish research workers."
Foreword: by Benson Inge.
Contents: Comedy. Comedy-drama. Drama. Fantasy. Twenty-five plays are listed, with synopsis and essential information for each.

—— ...Anti-war plays, foreign, and Anglo-Jewish lists. New York: National Service Bureau, Federal Theatre Project, 1937. 2 l., 2–54 f. 4°. (National Service Bureau publication no. 28.) MWED
Mimeographed.
Compiled by the Anglo-Jewish Play Department.
The Anglo-Jewish list occupies f. 45–54.

—— ...Jewish non-royalty plays and pageants, holiday — historical — general. New York: National Play Bureau, Federal Theatre Project, 1937. 3 l., 84 f. 4°. (Play Bureau publication. no. 8.) MWED
Mimeographed.
Compiled by Harold W. Rosenthal and Samuel J. Kreiter.
"A preface concerning the first Jewish play list:" by Benson Inge, f. [3].
Eighty-four plays are recorded. A brief description, a synopsis, and other information designed to aid amateur groups in a practical manner, are given about each play. The majority is Biblical, but there are a good many general Jewish plays.

GENERAL WORKS

ABRAHAMS, ISRAEL. Jews and the theatre. (Jewish chronicle. London, 1891. f°. Nov. 13, 1891, supplement, p. 21–23.) * PBE
A German translation by L. Cohen appeared in *Juedisches Litteratur-Blatt*, Magdeburg, 1892, Jahrg. 21, p. 14–15, 30–31, 34–35, 39, 42–43, * *PBC.*
Deals largely with the attitude towards the theatre in Rabbinic literature, and performances of Purim and other Biblical plays by Jewish amateur actors. Contains also remarks on the treatment of Jews as characters in several English dramas.

—— The Jews and the theatre. (In his: Jewish life in the middle ages. Philadelphia, 1896. 8°. p. 256–259.) * PYA
Cf. also new edition, London, 1932, p. 278–281, * *PYA.*
The stage Jew... The Jews in the Elizabethan drama. Generosity to the Jewess on the stage. Shakespeare, Marlowe, and Lessing.

ADLER, ELKAN NATHAN. Modern London Jews in drama. (In his: London. Philadelphia, 1930. 12°. p. 183–186.) * PXQ
Jewish communities series.

ANGLO-JEWISH plays. (Jewish chronicle. London, 1932. f°. Nov. 11, 1932, p. 8–9.) * PBD

BELDEN, MARY MEGIE. ...The dramatic works of Samuel Foote. New Haven: Yale University Press; London: H. Milford, Oxford University Press, 1929. viii, 224 p. 8°. (Yale studies in English. [no.] 80.) NCC (Foote)
Bibliography: p. 196–206.

BIBEN, AUGUSTA C. The Jew in English literature. (Jewish ledger. New Orleans, 1928. f°. v. 67, June 15, 1928, p. 3, 18.) * PBD

BIENENSTOK, MONTEFIORE. The Hebrew comedian. (Reform advocate. Chicago, 1912. f°. v. 44, p. 107–108.) * PBD
Reprinted in *American citizen*, New York, 1912, v. 1, p. 314–317, * *PBD.*

BOURCHIER, ARTHUR. The Jew in drama. (Contemporary review. London, 1915. 8°. v. 107, p. 376–384.) * DA

CAINE, SIR HALL. The Jew in literature. (Literary world. London, 1892. 4°. v. 45, p. 482–484.) * DA

CALISCH, EDWARD NATHANIEL. The Jew in English literature, as author and as subject. Richmond, Va.: The Bell Book and Stationery Co. [cop. 1909.] 277 p. 8°. * PAO
Reviewed by J. in *American Hebrew*, New York, 1909, v. 85, p. 149, * *PBD;* by B. in *Jewish comment*, Baltimore, v. 29, p. 202–203, * *PBD; Jewish outlook,*

General Works, continued

Denver, Colo., v. 6, June 4, 1909, p. 1, * *PBD;* and (reprinted from *London Daily Telegraph*) in *Jewish record,* Richmond, Va., v. 1, Sept. 26, 1909, p. 3, * *PBD.*

CARB, DAVID. The racial theatre. (American Hebrew. New York, 1926. 4°. v. 119, p. 259.)
* PBD

CARDOZO, JACOB LOPES. The contemporary Jew in the Elizabethan drama. Amsterdam: H. J. Paris, 1925. xii, 335 p. 8°. * PZB
"A select bibliography": p. 331–335.
"Were there as a matter of fact any recognizable Jews commonly known to be living in London between the accession of Queen Elizabeth and the closure of the theatres by the Puritans in 1640?" Cardozo, judging from the dramatic literature of that period, answers this question in the negative. Sidney Lee and Lucien Wolf are the writers whom this author aims to refute.
Reviewed by E. R. Adair in *English studies,* Amsterdam, 1926, v. 8, p. 122–124, *RNA;* by Sarah Adler in *Jewish quarterly review,* Philadelphia, new series, v. 19, p. 321–325, * *PBE;* by B. A. P. van Dam in *Museum,* Leiden, 1927, jaarg. 34, col. 97–99; *New Judaea,* London, v. 2, p. 532, * *PZX;* and in *Times literary supplement,* London, v. 25, p. 76, † *NAA.*

CARO, JOSEF. Bernard Shaw. (In: Festschrift zum 75jährigen Bestehen der Realschule mit Lyzeum der isr. Religionsgesellschaft Frankfurt am Main. Frankfurt a. M., 1928. 4°. p. 68–78.) * PBN
On the Jewish interest in certain of Shaw's plays.

CHANG, Y. Z. The Jew in the drama of the English renaissance. 1930. 62 f.
Ms. thesis. Unpublished.
Johns Hopkins University Library.
Title from S. A. Tannenbaum, *Christopher Marlowe; a concise bibliography,* item 559.

COLEMAN, EDWARD DAVIDSON. Plays of Jewish interest on the American stage, 1752–1821. (American Jewish Historical Society. Publications. [Baltimore,] 1934. 8°. no. 33, p. 171–198.)
* PXX

COLLINS, CHARLES WILLIAM. The drama of the Jew. illus. (Theatre magazine. New York, 1909. f°. v. 9, p. 58–62.) † NBLA

CORBIN, JOHN. Drama and the Jew. (Scribner's magazine. New York, 1933. 4°. v. 93, p. 295–300.) * DA
Subtitle reads: "Beginning with the vital spirit of the Yiddish theatre in the Bowery, the Jew has come to dominate the dramatic art of Broadway. Corrosive, vitriolic, animated by the spirit of a separate minority, the intellectual theatre has now given itself over to the drama of acid intelligence. Is this a reason for the present state of the theatre in America?" Mr. Corbin illustrates his thesis by a number of plays which are recorded in this list.
Cf. Gilbert Seldes in *New York Evening Journal,* April 27, 1933, p. 30, * *A.*

―― The Jew as a dramatic problem. (B'nai B'rith news. Chicago, 1919. f°. v. 11, March, 1919, p. 12.) * PYP
Repr.: New York Times, Jan. 4, 1919, section 4, p. 2, * *A.*

―― The new plays. (Saturday evening post. Philadelphia, 1909. f°. v. 182, Nov. 6, 1909, p. 18–19.) * DA
On the season's Jewish plays.
Cf. "The Jew in drama" in *Jewish comment,* Baltimore, 1909, v. 30, p. 86, * *PBD.*

COSULICH, GILBERT. Three Jewish fathers [Barabas, Shylock, Isaac of York]. (English journal. Chicago, 1914. 8°. v. 3, p. 558–561.)
RNA

CRABOS, GILBERT PIERRE. Le sémitisme au théâtre. (Revue critique des idées et des livres. Paris, 1908. 12°. année 2, tome 1, p. 28–49, 97–115.) * DM

CROKER, THOMAS FRANCIS DILLON. The stage Israelite. (Era almanack, 1881. [London, 1881.] 8°. p. 70–72.) NCOA

DEJOB, CHARLES. Le Juif dans le comédie au XVIIIe siècle. (Revue des études juives. Paris, 1899. 8°. v. 39, p. 119–128.) * PBF

THE DRAMA and the Jews. (Jewish chronicle. London, 1879. f°. Nov. 7, 1879, p. 4–5.) * PBE

DREYFUS, ABRAHAM. Le Juif au théâtre. Paris: Quantin, 1886. 36 p. 4°. * PZB
Repr.: Revue des études juives, Actes et conférences, 1886–1889, p. xlix–lxxi, * *PBF.*
Address delivered before the Société des études juives, March 1, 1886.

DURNING-LAWRENCE, SIR EDWIN. The Jew in drama. London, 1914. 2 p. 4°.
Repr.: Referee, London.

EATON, WALTER PRICHARD. Drama: a bond of fellowship. (In: Isaac Landman, editor, Christian and Jew; a symposium for better understanding. New York, 1929. 8°. p. 201–212.)
* PZA

ECKHARDT, EDUARD. Die Juden: äussere Merkmale. Charaktereigenschaften. Die Juden in den einzelnen Dramen. (In his: Die Dialekt- und Ausländertypen des älteren englischen Dramas. Louvain, 1911. 4°. Teil II, Die Ausländertypen, p. 144–162.) NCO (Materialien)
Materialien zur Kunde des älteren englischen Dramas. Bd. 32.

FINK, M. R. The dramas of Jacob Gordin. (Play-book. Madison, Wis., 1913. 8°. v. 1, Nov., 1913, p. 5–15.) NAFA
Reprinted, under the title, "Gordin's plays; American aspect," in *American Hebrew,* New York, 1915, v. 97, p. 280–281, * *PBD.*
Many of Gordin's plays recorded in our list are discussed here.

FRANK, FLORENCE KIPER. The Jew as Jewish artist. (Poetry. Chicago, 1923. 12°. v. 22, p. 209–212.) * DA
"The Jew in modern American poetry has nothing to say as Jew."

GABRIEL, GILBERT WOLF. Are we like that? The Jew as a theatrical commodity. (Jewish chronicle. Newark, N. J., 1933. f°. v. 25, May 12, 1933, p. 5.)
Reprinted in *Scribe,* Portland, Ore., v. 28, Aug. 25, 1933, p. 3, 7, * *PBD.*
A dozen plays are discussed to prove the point implied in the title.

―― The Jew in falseface; a number of character studies for the current stage. (New Palestine. New York, 1929. 4°. v. 16, p. 279–280.)
* PXL

General Works, continued

GALL, ELLEN M., AND L. H. CARTER. [Jewish make-up for the stage.] illus. (In their: Modern make-up. San Francisco [cop. 1928]. 12°. p. 79–82, 123.) MWET

GOITEIN, EDWARD DAVID. The stage Jew of the XVI century. (Jewish chronicle. London, 1923. f°. July, 1923, supplement 31, p. vii.) *PBE

GOLDBERG, ISAAC. The dramatic art of David Pinski, greatest of Yiddish dramatists and one of the most significant of living playwrights. (Stratford journal. Boston, 1917. 8°. v. 1, June, 1917, p. 3–13.) *DA
Contains, at end, a chronological list of Pinski's plays, 1899–1916.

—— The Yiddish theatre; a literature created by the wandering Jew. illus. (Theatre Guild magazine. New York, 1930. 4°. v. 7, April, 1930, p. 26–33, 56–57.) NBLA
A number of plays in this list are discussed.

GOLDBERG, SARAH. David Pinski; dramatist of depth and vision. illus., port. (B'nai B'rith magazine. Chicago, 1927. 4°. v. 41, p. 263–265, 269.) *PYP

GOODMAN, HENRY. Perez the playwright. (East and West. New York, 1916. 4°. v. 1, p. 345–346.) *PBD

HARRISON, CHARLES. [Jewish make-up for the stage.] illus. (In his: Theatricals and tableaux vivants for amateurs. London, n.d. 8°. p. 41–43.) MZB

HAWKINS, FREDERICK. Shylock and other stage Jews. (Theatre. London, 1879. 8°. series 2, v. 3, p. 191–198.) NCOA
Reprinted in *American Hebrew*, New York, 1879, v. 1, p. 9–10, 20–21, *PBD.

HEARN, LAFCADIO. The Jew upon the stage. (In his: Occidental gleanings... collected by Albert Mordell. New York, 1925. 8°. v. 2, p. 184–189.) NBQ
Repr.: Times-Democrat, New Orleans, April 18, 1886.
Reprinted in *American Hebrew*, New York, 1925, v. 118, p. 58, *PBD.

HYAMSON, ALBERT MONTEFIORE. The Jew in English drama. (In his: A history of the Jews in England. London, 1908. 8°. p. 134–135.)
In the 1928 edition, p. 115–116, *PXQ. *PXQ

THE JEW in caricature [on the stage]. (Jewish comment. Baltimore, 1906. f°. v. 23, April 27, 1906, p. 6.) *PBD

THE JEW in drama. (Jewish outlook. Denver, 1909. f°. v. 6, Oct. 22, 1909, p. 1; v. 7, Oct. 29, p. 1.) *PBD

THE JEW on the English stage. (Jewish comment. Baltimore, 1905. f°. v. 21, Sept. 22, 1905, p. 3.) *PBD
On the Jewish rôles acted by Sir Herbert Beerbohm Tree, 1853–1917.

THE JEW on the stage. (Reformer and Jewish times. New York, 1878. f°. v. 10, April 5, 1878, p. 4; April 12, p. 4.) *PBD

JEWS in fiction and drama. (Notes and queries. London, 1909. 8°. series 10, v. 11, p. 169, 254–255, 316, 394, 458; v. 12, p. 118.) *DA

KANE, JOSEPH NATHAN. The Jew on the modern English stage. (American Hebrew. New York, 1919. f°. v. 106, p. 72, 101.) *PBD

KOEPPEL, EMIL. Konfessionelle Strömungen in der dramatischen Dichtung des Zeitalters der beiden ersten Stuart-Könige. (Deutsche Shakespeare Gesellschaft. Jahrbuch. Berlin, 1904. 8°. Jahrg. 40, p. xvi–xxix.) *NCK
Festvortrag delivered before the Deutsche Shakespeare Gesellschaft, April 23, 1904.

KOHLER, MAX JAMES. The Jew in pre-Shakespearean literature. (Jewish exponent. Philadelphia, 1902. f°. v. 35, July 11, 1902, p. 1–2.) †*PBD
Read before the Jewish Chautauqua Summer Assembly, July 7, 1902.

KORNFELD, MURIEL G. Drama and the Jew. (Hebrew standard. New York, 1920. f°. v. 76, Nov. 5, 1920, p. 4–6.)

KROHN, MRS. HARRY N. The Jew in present day drama. (Jewish outlook. Denver, 1910. f°. v. 7, Feb. 18, 1910, p. 1; Feb. 25, p. 1–2.) †*PBD

LANDA, MYER JACK. Do Jews lisp? (Jewish chronicle. London, Dec., 1924. f°. supplement 48, p. vii.) *PBE
Apropos the lisping of the stage Jew.

—— The Jew and the [English] drama. (Jewish chronicle. London, 1920. f°. Aug. 27, 1920, p. 21.) *PBE
Abstract of a lecture delivered at the Oxford Summer School.

—— The Jew in drama. London: P. S. King & Son, Ltd., 1926. 340 p., front. (port.) 8°. *PZB
Reviewed by Elma C. E. Levinger in *B'nai B'rith magazine*, Cincinnati, v. 41, p. 457, *PYP; by David Philipson in *Jewish center*, New York, v. 5, Sept., 1927, p. 20–22, *PYR; in *Jewish tribune*, New York, Feb. 5, 1926, p. 23 (reprinted from *Stage*, London), *PBD; *Mask*, Florence, Italy, v. 12, p. 124–125, NAFA; *Nation*, London, v. 38, p. 719, *DA; by L. S. in *New Palestine*, New York, v. 10, p. 617, *PXL; by Rosamond Gilder in *Theatre arts monthly*, New York, v. 11, p. 879–880, NBLA; *Times literary supplement*, London, v. 25, p. 76, †NAA; and by J. Lifshitz in Yiddish Scientific Institute, *Archiv far der geschichte fun Yidishen teater un drama*, Vilna, 1930, p. 486–488, *PTQ.
Reviewed also by J. L. Cardozo in *English studies*, Amsterdam, 1927, v. 9, p. 17–19, RNA.
An interview with Mr. Landa, who states the difficulties he encountered and the aim he set himself while writing the book is printed, with his portrait, in the *Jewish chronicle*, London, Nov. 13, 1925, p. 18–19, *PBE.

—— The name "Moss." (Jewish chronicle. London, 1928. f°. Sept. 28, 1928, p. 12.) *PBE

LANDMAN, ISAAC. Jews and present-day dramatic art. (Jewish exponent. Philadelphia, 1908. f°. v. 48, Nov. 20, 1908, p. 1.) *PBD
I. Zangwill, H. Bernstein, C. Klein.

General Works, continued

LANDSTONE, CHARLES. The future of Anglo-Jewish drama. (Jewish chronicle. London, June, 1928. f°. supplement 90, p. i–ii.) *PBE
On the themes that constitute proper material for English-Jewish plays.

LEDERER, MORITZ. Der Jude im Drama. (In his: Aus jüdischer Sphäre. Brünn [1909]. 12°. p. 21–32.) *PBS

LEE, SIR SIDNEY LAZARUS. Elizabethan England and the Jews. (New Shakspere Society. Transactions. London, 1888. 8°. 1887/92, part 2, p. 143–166.) *NCK
Also listed as series 1, 1887/92, no. 12.
In this pioneer paper, read before the Society, Sir Sidney points out that Jews figured as characters "at all stages of the development of the Elizabethan drama" and argues therefrom the physical presence of Jews in England during the corresponding period.
A synopsis of a lecture, bearing the same title, delivered by the author, Jan. 22, 1888, before the Jews' College Literary and Art Society of London, and setting forth similar conclusions, is printed in *Jewish chronicle,* London, Jan. 27, 1888, p. 12, * *PBE*. The ensuing discussion, in which A. Löwy, I. Abrahams and M. Gaster participated, is also given. See Cardozo, above.

LEISER, JOSEPH. The development of the Jew in the drama. (Review. Philadelphia, 1914. 12°. v. 9, May, 1914, p. 11–21.)

LEVI, HARRY. Jewish characters in fiction. English literature. Philadelphia: Jewish Chautauqua Society [1903]. 140 p. 12°. (Jewish Chautauqua Society. The Chautauqua system of education. Course book.) * PZB

—— 2d ed. — rev. and enl. Philadelphia, Pa.: The Jewish Chautauqua Society, 1911. 173 p. 12°. (The Chautauqua system of Jewish education.) * PZB
"Supplementary bibliography of English fiction in which Jewish characters appear": p. 170–173.

LEVINGER, ELMA C. (EHRLICH). Why no Jewish plays? (Jewish advocate. Boston, 1931. f°. v. 59, March 27, 1931, p. 6.) * PBD

LYON, MABEL. Some recent plays of Jewish interest. (Jewish exponent. Philadelphia, 1913. f°. v. 58, Oct. 17, 1913. p. 1–2.) †* PBD

MABON, C. B. The Jew in English poetry and drama. (Jewish quarterly review. London, 1899. 8°. v. 11, p. 411–430.) * PBE
Reprinted in *Jewish exponent,* Philadelphia, v. 29, June 16, 1899, p. 1–2; June 23, p. 9; June 30, p. 6–7, * *PBD*.

MADISON, CHARLES A. David Pinski, the dramatist. (Poet lore. Boston, 1924. 8°. v. 35, p. 562–568.) * DA

—— The Yiddish theatre. (Poet lore. Boston, 1921. 8°. v. 32, p. 497–519.) * DA

MEDOFF, JOSEPH. The Jew in the world's drama. (B'nai B'rith news. Chicago, 1922. f°. v. 14, June, 1922, p. 4.) * PYP

MERSAND, JOSEPH. Jewish dramatists and the American drama. illus. (Opinion. New York, 1937. 4°. v. 7, Oct., 1937, p. 8–11.) * PBD

MEW, JAMES. Yiddish literature and drama. (Contemporary review. London, 1907. 8°. v. 91, p. 260–269.) * DA

MEYER, WILHELM. Der Wandel des jüdischen Typus in der englischen Literatur... Marburg a. L.: Robert Noske, 1912. xi, 88 p., 2 l. 8°.
Bibliography: p. ix–xi. * PZB p.v.1

MICHELSON, H. The Jew in early English literature. Amsterdam: H. J. Paris, 1926. viii, 175 p. 8°. * PZB
Bibliography: p. 174–175.
Reviewed by Sarah Adler in *Jewish quarterly review,* Philadelphia, new series, v. 19, p. 321–325, * *PBE*; and in *Times literary supplement,* London, 1926, v. 25, p. 822, † *NAA*.

PFITZNER, KÄTHE. ...Die Ausländertypen im englischen Drama der Restorationszeit... Breslau, 1931. 99(1) p. 8°. NAFH p.v.88
"Literaturverzeichnis:" p. 97–99.
See "Die Juden," p. 71–72.

PFLAUM, HEINZ. Les scènes de Juifs dans la littérature dramatique du moyen-âge. (Revue des études juives. Paris, 1930. 8°. tome 89, p. 111–134.) * PBF

PHILIPSON, DAVID. The Jew in English fiction ... Cincinnati: R. Clarke & Co., 1889. 4 p.l., 5–156 p. 12°. * PZB

—— —— New ed., rev. and enl. Cincinnati: The Robert Clarke Company, 1911. 4 p.l., 5–207 p. 8°.

—— —— New York: Bloch Pub. Co., 1918. 2 p.l., 220 p. 4. ed. enl. 12°. * PZB
Contents: Introductory. Marlowe's "Jew of Malta." Shakespeare's "Merchant of Venice." Cumberland's "The Jew." Scott's "Ivanhoe." Dickens's "Oliver Twist" and "Our mutual friend." Disraeli's "Coningsby and Tancred." George Eliot's "Daniel Deronda." Zangwill's "Children of the ghetto" and others.

PHILLIPS, P. D. The Jew in English literature. Read before the Melbourne Jewish Literary Society, 18th June, 1888. Melbourne, 1888. 16 p. 8°.

PLAYS that offend. (Jewish exponent. Philadelphia, 1911. f°. v. 54, Dec. 8, 1911, p. 4.) * PBD
On the misrepresentation of the Jews on the stage.

REINICKE, WALTER. Der Wucherer im älteren englischen Drama... Halle a. S.: C. A. Kaemmerer & Co., 1907. 78 p., 1 l. 8°.

RODENBERG, JULIUS. The Jews in England. (In his: England, literary and social, from a German point of view. London, 1875. 8°. p. 275–339.)
Barabas, Shylock, Sheva.

ROGOFF, HILLEL. אידישע פיעסען אויף דער ענגלישער ביהנע. (צוקונפט). New York, 1914. 4°. v. 19, p. 207–212.) * PBB

SABATZKY, KURT. ...Der Jude in der dramatischen Gestaltung. Königsberg i. Pr.: Hartung [1930]. 67 p. 16°. * PBM p.v.166

SELDES, GILBERT. Jewish plays and Jew-plays in New York. (Menorah journal. New York, 1922. 8°. v. 8, p. 236–240.) * PBD

General Works, continued

SHILLMAN, BERNARD. Legends of the Jew in English literature. (Jewish chronicle. London, Jan., 1923. f°. supplement 25, p. vi–viii.) * PBE
Reprinted in *Reflex*, Chicago, v. 4, Feb., 1929, p. 17–24, * *PBD.*

SHOSTAC, PERCY B. The modern Yiddish stage. (Menorah journal. New York, 1916. 8°. v. 2, p. 173–182.) * PBD
In this section, part of a larger paper, many of the plays of this list are discussed.

SIMON, ABRAM. Prejudice and literature. (In: Bruno Lasker, editor, Jewish experiences in America. New York [cop. 1930]. 12°. p. 125–130.) * PXY

STAGE caricatures of Jews. (American Israelite. Cincinnati, 1901. f°. v. 47, April 4, 1901, p. 1.)
Repr.: Indianapolis News. * PBD

THE STAGE Jew. (Jewish comment. Baltimore, 1913. f°. v. 41, p. 66.) * PBD

STAGE Jew. (Memphis Morning News. Memphis, Tenn., Nov. 1, 1903, p. 4.)

THE STAGE Jew. (Saturday review. London, 1886. 4°. v. 62, p. 451–452.) * DA
Deals largely with the presentation of the Jews on the French stage.

STAGE Jew. (Jewish American. Detroit, 1908. f°. v. 15, March 13, 1908, p. 1, 3, 4.) * PBD
Repr.: Detroit news tribune.

STOECKER, WILHELM. Pinero's Dramen; Studien über Motive, Charaktere und Technik... Marburg a. L., 1911. vi, 78 p., 1 l. 8°.
"Verzeichnis der benutzten Literatur:" p. 1–3.
Reprinted from *Anglia*, Halle a. S., 1911, Bd. 35, p. 1–79, *RNA.*
The Cabinet minister, p. 25–26; Trelawney of the "Wells," p. 51–54; Iris, p. 57–59; Letty, p. 59–62.

STONEX, ARTHUR BIVINS. The usurer in Elizabethan drama. (Modern Language Association of America. Publications. Baltimore, 1916. 8°. v. 31, p. 190–210.) RAA
Reprinted as a separate, 1916, NCC *p.v.20.*

SYMPOSIUM on "The Jew in literature and on the stage." (Jewish exponent. Philadelphia, 1913. f°. v. 58, Dec. 5, 1913, p. 8.) * PBD
Abstract of addresses by S. T. Witz on "The Jew on the dramatic stage" and by H. S. Platowsky on "The Jew on the comedy stage."

LE THÉÂTRE juif dans le monde. Paris: Nouvelle revue juive [1930]. 144 p. 4°. * PTQ
Cover-title.

THREE Jews in drama. ports. (Jewish comment. Baltimore, 1902. f°. v. 14, Feb. 28, 1902, p. 2–3.)
* PBD
The characters of Shylock, Nathan the Wise, and Eleazar.

VEEN, HARM REIJNDERD SIENTJO VAN DER. Jewish characters in eighteenth century English fiction and drama. Groningen, Batavia: J. B. Wolters' uitgevers-maatschappij n. v., 1935. 308 p., folded front. 8°. * PZB
"Bibliography": p. 291–294.
Reviewed in *Archiv für das Studium der neueren Sprachen*, Braunschweig, 1935, Bd. 168, p. 293, *RAA*; and by Abraham Mordell in *Jewish quarterly review*, Philadelphia, 1937, new series, v. 28, p. 69–72, * *PBE.*

WANN, LOUIS. The Oriental in Elizabethan drama. (Modern philology. Chicago, 1915. 4°. v. 12, p. 423–447.) NAA
Forty-seven plays, 1579–1642, are studied. "The Jew, whom I have not considered an Oriental, appears in six plays, and in every one he is *the* villain or *one* of them."

WATCHMAN, PSEUD. The stage, the Jew, and the Jewish Drama League. (Jewish chronicle. London, 1932. f°. May 20, 1932, p. 9–10.) * PBE
On the functions and the achievement of the Jewish Drama League, London.

WERNE, ISAAC. תיהודי בגיא החזיון. מאת יצחק ווירניקובסקי. (הלאם). New York, 1903–04. 4°. v. 3, p. 125–126, 133, 137, 149–150, 157–158, 167–168, 171–172, 181–182.) * PBA

WHY is the Jewish question avoided? Great dramatic material unused. Jewish actors, playwrights and public. (Jewish chronicle. London, 1936. f°. Sept. 11, 1936, p. xix–xx.) * PBE

WOLLMAN, MAURICE. The Jews in G. B. Shaw's plays. (Jewish chronicle. London, Jan., 1926. f°. supplement 61, p. vii–viii.) * PBE

ZANGWILL, ISRAEL. The Jew in drama and in life...from Shakespeare to Beilis. (New York American. March 29, 1914, part 2, p. 4.) * A
Reprinted in *American Hebrew*, New York, 1914, v. 94, p. 645, * *PBD.*
On "the treatment accorded the Jews on the stage and how even great dramatists have failed to picture him with truth and understanding."

—— Shylock and other stage Jews. (In his: The voice of Jerusalem. London, 1920. 8°. p. 228–243.) * PBT
Also in the New York edition, 1921, p. 238–253.

COLLECTIONS

BLOCK, ETTA, TRANSLATOR. One-act plays from the Yiddish; authorised translations by Etta Block. Cincinnati: Stewart Kidd Company [cop. 1923]. 5 p.l., 3–165 p. 8°. * PTP
Contents: Champagne, by I. L. Perez. Mother and son, by J. Halpern. The stranger, by P. Hirschbein. The snowstorm, by P. Hirschbein. When the dew falleth, by P. Hirschbein. The eternal song, by M. Arnstein.
Reviewed in *New York Times book review*, v. 29, Feb. 17, 1924, p. 5, † *NAA*; and in *Theatre arts magazine*, 1924, v. 8, p. 350, 352, *NBLA.*

—— One-act plays from the Yiddish. Second series. By Isaac Loeb Peretz, Perez Hirschbein, Abraham Raisen, F. Bimko; authorized translation by Etta Block. New York: Bloch Publishing Company, 1929. xi, 123 p. 12°. * PTP
Contents: Prologue, by M. Nadir. Bebele, by P. Hirschbein. Lone worlds! by P. Hirschbein. After the funeral, by I. L. Peretz. Brothers, by A. Raisen. "Liars!" by Shalom Alechem. Of an early morning, by I. L. Peretz. The sisters, by I. L. Peretz.
Reviewed by Elma C. E. Levinger in *B'nai B'rith magazine*, Cincinnati, 1930, v. 44, p. 238–239, * *PYP*;

Collections, continued
by Harold Silver in *Jewish social service quarterly,* New York, 1930, v. 6, p. 185–186, * *PYS;* and in *Young Judaean,* New York, v. 20, April, 1930, p. 18, * *PBD.*

BRODY, ALTER. Lamentations; four folk-plays of the American Jew... with a frontispiece by Hugo Gellert. New York: Coward-McCann, Inc., 1928. 4 p.l., 3–89 p., front. 8°.   NBM
Contents: Lowing in the night. Recess for memorials. Rapunzel. A house of mourning.
Reviewed in *Boston Transcript,* Dec. 26, 1928, section 3, p. 4, * *A; Jewish quarterly review,* Philadelphia, 1929, new series, v. 20, p. 108, * *PBE;* by E. Seaver in *New republic,* New York, 1929, v. 58, p. 340, * *DA;* by A. B. in *United Synagogue recorder,* Newark, N. J., v. 9, Jan., 1929, p. 3; and by H. Salpeter in *World,* New York, Nov. 4, 1928, * *A.*

GOLDBERG, ISAAC, EDITOR AND TRANSLATOR. Six plays of the Yiddish theatre, by David Pinski — Sholom Ash — Perez Hirschbein — Solomon J. Rabinowitsch, tr. and ed. by Isaac Goldberg, PH.D. Boston: J. W. Luce and Company [cop. 1916]. vii p., 1 l., 210 p. 12°.   * PTP
Contents: D. Pinski: Abigail, Forgotten souls. S. J. Rabinowitsch: She must marry a doctor. S. Ash: Winter, The sinner. P. Hirschbein: In the dark.
Reviewed by B. K. in *Boston Evening Transcript,* Dec. 13, 1916, part 3, p. 6, * *A.*

—— Six plays of the Yiddish theatre, second series, by David Pinski, Perez Hirschbein, Z. Levin [and] Leon Kobrin, tr. and ed. by Isaac Goldberg, PH.D. Boston: John W. Luce and Company [cop. 1918]. 3 p.l., 197 p. 12°.   * PTP
Contents: Pinski, D., Little heroes, The stranger. Hirschbein, P., On the threshold. Levin, Z., Poetry and prose. Kobrin, L., The black sheep, The secret of life.
Reviewed by Elias Lieberman in *American Hebrew,* New York, 1919, v. 104, p. 210–211, 215, * *PBD;* and by Babette Deutsch in *Bookman,* New York, v. 49, p. 711–712, * *DA.*

HOUSMAN, LAURENCE. Angels & ministers; three plays of Victorian shade & character... London: Jonathan Cape [1921]. 2 p.l., 9–85(1) p., 1 l. 8°.   NCR
Partial contents: The Queen: God bless her! His favourite flower.

—— Angels & ministers; four plays of Victorian shade & character... New York: Harcourt, Brace and Company, 1922. 150 p. 8°. NCR
Reviewed by F. L. Birch in *New statesman,* London, v. 20, p. 360, * *DA;* and O. W. Firkins in *Yale review,* New Haven, new series, v. 12, p. 195, * *DA.*

KOHUT, GEORGE ALEXANDER, EDITOR. A Hebrew anthology; a collection of poems and dramas inspired by the Old Testament and post Biblical tradition gathered from writings of English poets, from the Elizabethan period and earlier to the present day. Edited by George Alexander Kohut; with an introduction by Hudson Maxim ... Cincinnati: S. Bacharach, 1913. 2 v. 8°.
Paged continuously.   * PSO
Contents: v. 1. Lyrical, narrative and devotional poems. v. 2. Selections from the drama.
Partial contents of v. 2: Nathan the Wise, G. E. Lessing. Torquemada, Victor Hugo [extract]. The Spanish gypsy, George Eliot (selections from book ii). The Merchant of Venice, Shakespeare [extract].
For reviews of this work see E. D. Coleman, *The Bible in English drama,* New York, 1931, p. 17–18, *NCOD,* or * *RB–NCOD.*

KRAFT, IRMA. The power of Purim, and other plays; a series of one act plays designed for Jewish religious schools. Philadelphia: The Jewish Publication Society of America, 1915. 189(1) p. illus. 12°.   * PSQ
Contents: The power of Purim (Purim). A Maccabean cure (Hanukkah). To save his country (Pesah). Ambition in Whitechapel (Shabuot). Because he loved David so (closing of school).

NEEDOFF, SYDNEY, EDITOR. Five one-act plays of Jewish interest, edited by Sydney Needoff... Published under the auspices of the Federation of Northern Jewish Literary Societies, Gt. Britain. [Manchester, Eng.: Feltone Beck, Ltd., 1937.] 80 p. 8°.
Contents: Preface, Neville J. Laski. Introduction, F. E. Doran. And it came to pass, E. Levy. The miracle of Lodz, Alan Peters. Esther, S. F. Bock. The dictator, C. Drapkin. I believe, E. Levy.

PINSKI, DAVID. ...Ten plays, translated from the Yiddish by Isaac Goldberg. New York: B. W. Huebsch, 1920. 5 p.l., 3–209 p. 12°. * PTP
"The original translation of 'A dollar' was made by Mr. Joseph Michael and of 'Diplomacy' by Mr. Harry Birnbaum. These have been revised by Dr. Isaac Goldberg."
Contents: The phonograph. The god of the newly rich wool merchant. A dollar. The cripples. The inventor and the king's daughter. Diplomacy. Little heroes. The beautiful nun. Poland, 1919. The stranger.
Reviewed by K. M. in *Freeman,* New York, 1920, v. 1, p. 548–549, * *DA;* and in *Review,* 1920, v. 3, p. 133, * *DA.*

—— Three plays, by David Pinski, authorized translation from the Yiddish, by Isaac Goldberg. New York: B. W. Huebsch, 1918. viii p., 2 l., 3–234 p. 12°.   * PTP
Contents: Isaac Sheftel. The last Jew. The dumb Messiah.
Reviewed by D. L. M. in *Boston Evening Transcript,* Boston, July 31, 1918, part 2, p. 7, col. 4, * *A;* by M. C. D. in *Nation,* New York, v. 107, p. 210, * *DA;* and by L. R. in *New republic,* New York, v. 16, p. 26, 29, * *DA.*

REZNIKOFF, CHARLES. Nine plays. New York: C. Reznikoff [cop. 1927]. 3 p.l., 113 p., 1 l. 8°.   NBM
Partial contents: Uriel Acosta. The black death. Rashi.

RUBINSTEIN, HAROLD FREDERICK. Israel set free; five one-act plays... London: Jonathan Cape [1936]. 186 p. 8°. (New play series. no. 7.)   NCR
Contents: Preface. The deacon and the Jewess. Whitehall, 1656. Jew Dyte. They went forth. To the poets of Australia.
Reviewed in *Jewish chronicle,* London, June 5, 1936, p. 23, * *PBE.*

TAYLOR, RICA BROMLEY. Four Jewish sketches ... London: S. French, Ltd.; New York: S. French, cop. 1927. 64 p. 12°. (French's acting edition. no. 704.)
Contents: Benny proposes. The boomerang. Damages — two hundred. Paul robs Peter.

Collections, continued

WHITE, BESSIE (FELSTINER), TRANSLATOR. Nine one-act plays from the Yiddish, translated by Bessie F. White. Boston: J. W. Luce and Company [1932]. 4 p.l., (1)4–235 p. 12°. * PTP
  Contents: The golem, by H. Leivick (first two scenes from the poetic drama). Captain Dreyfus, by Jacob Gordin. The doctor's first operation, by Z. Levin. After midnight, by Samuel Daixel. The sewing of the wedding gown, by I. L. Peretz. Landsleit, by I. D. Berkowitz. Colleagues, by Z. Libin. Sorrows, by David Pinski. Gymnazie, by Sholom Aleichem.
  Reviewed by Rose W. Golub in *Jewish education,* Chicago, 1932, v. 4, p. 191, * PYW.

ZIMMERMAN, HARRY, COMPILER. Plays of Jewish life; compiled by Harry Zimmerman. [London: The New Arts Pub. Guild, 1931.] 106 p. 12°. NCO
  Half-title.
  Contents: Gordon, S., The resting place. Landa, G., and M. J. Landa, For all eternity. Jacobs, B., The man with the puckel. Gorsky, J. A., Kislev. Zimmerman, H., David's Barmitzvah.
  Reviewed by Hugh Harris in *Jewish chronicle,* London, Nov. 13, 1931, p. 21, * PBD; and in *Jewish quarterly review,* Philadelphia, 1932, new series, v. 23, p. 101, * PBE.

INDIVIDUAL PLAYS
EARLIEST TIMES TO 1837

ALLINGHAM, JOHN TILL. Transformation; or, Love and law. [By J. T. Allingham.] A musical farce in two acts. As performed at the theatres, London, Philadelphia and Baltimore. First edition from the original manuscript. Baltimore: J. Robinson, 1814. 30 p. 24°. NCO p.v.299, no.12
  Produced by the Drury Lane Company at the Lyceum Theatre, London, Nov. 30, 1810, with Matthews as Cameleon in a Jewish disguise and Wewitzer as Malachi, "the genuine Jew." The meeting of the two in act II is the occasion for much of the humor of the play. Both speak their lines in dialect. Genest, VIII:211, states: "This musical farce is attributed to Allingham, and is not printed." Reviewed in *European magazine,* London, 1810, v. 58, p. 454, * DA.
  Produced at the Park Theatre, New York, Dec. 30, 1816, with J. Darley as Malachi and Thos. Hilson as Cameleon.

AMHERST, J. H. ...Napoleon Buonaparte's invasion of Russia; or, The conflagration of Moscow; a grand military and equestrian spectacle in three acts... London: Duncombe [1825?]. 2 p.l., (1)6–48 p., 1 folded col'd plate. 12°.
  At head of title: Duncombe's edition. NCR
  Also issued in v. 13 of Lacy's acting edition of plays, *NCO (Lacy),* and as no. 194 of French's acting edition.
  First acted at Astley's Royal Amphitheatre, London, April 4, 1825, with J. Amherst as Benjamin, "an aged Muscovite Jew," 100 years old, who offers the governor of Moscow 200,000 rubles to help "drive out the invader of my country" from the city where, he says, he had lived his entire life. Benjamin further promises the governor the financial help of his co-religionists.
  Reviewed in *The Times,* London, April 5, 1825, p. 2, col. 4, * A.

────── ...Will Watch; or, The black phantom: a melo-drama, in two acts... As now performed at the London theatres. Embellished with a fine engraving, by Mr. Findlay... London: J. Duncombe [18—?]. 28 p., front. 16°. NCOF
  At head of title: Duncombe's edition.
  Prompter's copy, interleaved ms. notes.
  In the Library of Congress copy the engraver's name is given as Jones.
  Announced for production at the Coburg Theatre, London, on Feb. 8, 1830.
  Villiers adapted Levi Lyons, peddler and leader of a band of smugglers.
  Produced under the title *Will Watch, the bold smuggler,* at the Chatham Theatre, New York, May 9, 1831, with Judah as Levi Lyons. This Judah is the notable dramatist and author, Samuel Benjamin Herbert (or Helbert) Judah, 1799–1876, an account of whose life is given by C. P. Daly in his *The Settlement of the Jews in North America,* New York, 1893, p. 139–145, * PXY. See also *Dictionary of American biography,* v. 10, p. 228–229. Odell, III:530, quotes a contemporary account that Judah "made a hit" in his part as Lyons.

ANDREWS, MILES PETER. Dissipation. A comedy, in five acts; as it is performed at the Theatre-Royal, in Drury-Lane. London: T. Becket, 1781. vi p., 1 l., 80 p. 8°. NCO p.v.108
  Based in part on Garrick's *Bon ton.*
  Reviewed in *Critical review,* London, 1781, v. 51, p. 318, *NAA.*
  Produced at the Drury Lane, London, March 10, 1781, with Baddeley as Ephraim Labradore, a dissolute money-lender and Miss Kirby as "the Jew's daughter." The daughter figures in a sub-plot exactly as does Jessica in *The Merchant of Venice,* with the French valet, Coquin, in the rôle of a Lorenzo. Reviewed in *London chronicle,* London, 1781, v. 49, p. 245, * A; *London magazine,* London, 1781, v. 50, p. 134–135, * DA; and in *Universal magazine,* London, v. 68, p. 136–137, * DA.

ARNOLD, SAMUEL JAMES. See sub-entry under MAID AND MAGPIE.

AYMAR, BENJAMIN, AND J. R. BLAKE. *See* sub-entry under SCOTT, SIR WALTER.

BAILLIE, JOANNA. The siege; a comedy in five acts... <from the first London edition of 1812.> New York: Published by the Longworths, at the Dramatic Repository, Shakspeare-Gallery, 1812. 67 p. 16°. NCO p.v.259
  Reprinted in her *Complete poetical works,* Philadelphia, 1832, p. 384–406, *NCR.*
  The scene is "a castle on the French confines of Germany." Baron Baurchel in one of his stage disguises assumes the part of an Armenian Jew, and speaks in dialect.

BAKER, THOMAS. An act at Oxford; a comedy by the author of The yeoman o' Kent [Thomas Baker]... London: Bernard Lintott, 1704. 8 p.l., 60 p. 8°. NCO p.v.309
  "Afterwards altered and brought out under the title of Hampstead Heath." — *Biographia dramatica.*

────── Hampstead Heath; a comedy. As it was acted at the Theatre Royal in Drury Lane. By the author of The yeoman of Kent [Thomas Baker]. London: Bernard Lintott, 1706. 2 p.l., 51(1) p., 1 l. 8°.
  Copy: Harvard College Library.
  Contains a Prologue and an Epilogue, which were not printed in *An Act at Oxford.* The last line of the Prologue is: *Let Hampstead Heath excuse Oxford Act.* It was produced at Drury Lane, Oct. 30, 1705. The Epilogue was spoken by Pinkethman.

BARBER, JAMES. *See* sub-entry under MAID AND MAGPIE.

THE JEW IN ENGLISH DRAMA 9

Individual Plays—Earliest Times to 1837, cont'd

BARNETT, CHARLES ZACHARY. The rise of the Rotheschildes; or, The honest Jew of Frankfort. A drama in two acts, founded upon facts ... As performed at the Garrick Theatre... London: J. Pattie [1839–40]. 2 p.l., (1)8–46 p., front. 24°. (Pattie's modern stage. no. 66.)
    NCO p.v.315
A lurid melodrama, with no basis in history, centred around the Rothschild family in Frankfurt a. M. The landgrave of Hesse Cassel, Anselmo Rothschild (J. R. Williams), Dieter, a Jewish priest (?) (Gannon), his daughter Esther (Mrs. Pope), and the villain Zodiah, an apostate Jew (Green) are the main characters. It was produced at the St. James' Theatre, London, Feb. 15, 1836.

BARRETT, EATON STANNARD. The school for profligacy; or, The land we live in. (In his: The rising sun. By Cervantes Hogg [pseud.]. London, 1809. 16°. v. 1, p. 97–136.) NCW
First edition, 1807.
Chapters 11–14 of this romance are in the form of a play, in eight scenes, in which one of the characters is named Moses, a regulation moneylender.

BATES, WILLIAM. Gil Blas: or, The fool of fortune. A new pantomimic entertainment in two parts, as performing at the Royalty Theatre, Well-street, Goodman's-Fields. The pantomimes, songs, duets, trios, &c. by Mr. Bates. The overture and music by Mr. Reeves... London: J. Skirven for W. Bates [1788?]. 1 p.l., 32 p. 8°.   NCO p.v.186
Without the music.
In act I, sc. 5, "a Jew with a box trinkets" is brought in as prisoner of the banditti. The others captured, for whom no sympathy is intended, are a miser, a young beau, a dancing master and a lawyer. Act II, sc. 2, is a tavern in Valladolid, Spain. At a gaming table a Jew wins Gil Blas' money as well as his outer garments, down to his waistcoat.

BEACONSFIELD, BENJAMIN DISRAELI, 1ST EARL OF. The wondrous tale of Alroy. The rise of Iskander... Philadelphia: Carey, Lea and Blanchard, 1833. 2 v. 8°.   NCW
Dramatized into a "romantic play" by John Templeton, in 1873. See United States.—Copyright Office, *Dramatic compositions copyrighted in the United States, 1870–1916*, no. 1003.

BEAZLEY, SAMUEL. *See* sub-entry under SCOTT, SIR WALTER.

BEHN, MRS. APHRA (AMIS). The second part of The rover [in five acts]. As it is acted by the Servants of His Royal Highness. Written by A. Behn. London: Printed for Jacob Tonson ...1681. 4 p.l., 85(1) p., 1 l. 4°.   *KC 1681
Reprinted in her *Plays, histories and novels*, London, 1871, v. 1, p. 93–185, *NCP*; and in her *Works*, ed. by Montague Summers, London, 1915, v. 1, p. 109–213, *NCF*. The Jewish part of it is taken almost verbatim from Killigrew's *Thomasso; or, The Wanderer* (see under Killigrew). It was produced at the Dorset Gardens, London, in 1681, with Freeman as the Jewish guardian, but, unlike the first part, it was not successful. W. C. Hazlitt, in his *Manual*, p. 198, says: "[The Rover] contains much business, bustle, and intrigue, supported with an infinite deal of sprightliness."

Pfitzner, Käthe. Die Juden; äussere Merkmale. Charakterzüge. (In her: Die Ausländertypen im englischen Drama der Restorationszeit. Breslau, 1931. 8°. p. 71–72.) NAFH p.v.88
The author apparently found only this one play by Mrs. Behn to illustrate her thesis as regards the Jews as a foreign type.

BEN-ZION, BENEDIX. *See* sub-entry under SCOTT, SIR WALTER.

BOUILLY, JEAN NICOLAS. Une folie. A comick opera, in two acts. Being a translation from the original [by J. N. Bouilly] of Love laughs at locksmiths. A piece performed at the Theatre Royal, Hay-Market, with universal applause. London: Lackington, Allen, and Co. [etc.], 1804. 56 p. 2. ed. 8°.
Running title: A wild goose chace; or, The model. Probably translated by James Wild. *cf.* Baker, Biog. dram.; Biog. dict. living authors.

Colman, George, 1762–1836. Love laughs at locksmiths; a farce, in two acts. By George Colman, the younger. London: Printed by D. Deans, for J. Cawthorn [etc.], 1808. 52 p. 8°.
Without the music.   NCO p.v.148

——— Love laughs at locksmiths; a comic opera, in two acts. By George Colman, the younger. As performed at the Hay-Market and New-York theatres, from the prompt book. (second American from the first London edition of 1806.) New York: Published by D. Longworth, at the Dramatic Repository, Shakspeare-Gallery, 1808. 47 p. 24°.   *KL
Two undated casts are given for Boston and New York, with Darley in both as Capt. Beldare.

——— Love laughs at locksmiths, a farce; by George Colman, Esq. With prefatory remarks ...faithfully marked with the stage business, and stage directions, as it is performed at the Theatres Royal. By W. Oxberry, comedian. London: Pub. for the Proprietors, by W. Simpkin, and R. Marshall [etc.], 1822. 1 p.l., iii[1] p., 1 l., 38 p. front. (port.), diagr. 12°. (Oxberry, William. The new English drama. London, 1822. v. 13 [no. 4].)   NCO (Oxberry)
At head of title: Oxberry's edition.
Remarks, by P. P.: p. i–iii.

——— ——— A second copy. Prompter's copy. Interleaved ms. notes.   NCOF

——— Love laughs at locksmiths. [New York, 1824.] 47 p. 24°.   NCI p.v.27
Caption-title.
Also issued in Cumberland's British theatre, v. 37, [no. 10], *NCO (Cumberland)*, and in Lacy's acting edition of plays, v. 94, pt. 9. [no. 1401], *NCO (Lacy)*.
Produced at the Haymarket, London, July 25, 1803, with Elliston as Capt. Beldare, disguised as Levi Kaiserman, "a Jew picture-dealer, from Germany." Announced, when staged, as written by Arthur Griffinhoof. The author, who adapted it from Bouilly's *Une Folie*, wished to be considered as "one of his lighter labours on which he does not choose to risk his literary fame."
Reviewed in *European magazine*, London, 1803, v. 44, p. 131–132, **DA*; and in *Monthly mirror*, London, v. 16, p. 58–59, **DA*.
Produced at the Park Theatre, New York, May 23, 1804, with Fennell as Beldare.
Nicoll, *Early nineteenth century*, p. 486, records an anonymous burletta of the same name as having been produced at the Regency Theatre, London, in November, 1811.

BROME, RICHARD. The Jewish gentleman. Entered on the books of the Stationers' Company, August 4, 1640, but not printed.

Individual Plays—Earliest Times to 1837, cont'd

BROUGH, ROBERT BARNABAS, AND W. BROUGH. See sub-entry under SCOTT, SIR WALTER.

BROWN, MURIEL. See sub-entry under SCOTT, SIR WALTER.

BUCKSTONE, JOHN BALDWIN. Luke the labourer; or, The lost son. A domestic melodrame in two acts. As performed at the Adelphi Theatre, Strand... London: Printed for William Kenneth, 1828. 63 p. 2. ed. 12°. NCO p.v.154
Dedication to Daniel Terry.

—— —— Philadelphia: Weikel and Bunn; New York: W. Whale, 1829. 62 p. 16°.

—— —— Printed from the acting copy. To which are added, cast of the characters...and the whole of the stage business, as now performed in the Theatres Royal, London... Baltimore: J. Robinson, 1838. 50 p. 12°.
Copy: Library of Congress.

—— —— Printed from the acting copy, with remarks, biographical and critical, by D.-G.... As performed at the metropolitan minor theatres... London: J. Cumberland, n.d. 47 p. incl. front. 16°. (Cumberland's minor theatre. v. 2 [no. 3].) NCO (Cumberland)
Remarks by George Daniel, editor of the series.

—— —— Prompter's copy; interleaved ms. notes. NCOF

—— —— With the stage business, cast of characters, relative positions, etc. New York: Samuel French [1846?]. 45 p. 12°. (Minor drama. no. 13.) NCOF
Prompter's copy, interleaved ms. notes.

—— —— Another prompter's copy. NCOF p.v.10
Also issued in Dicks standard plays, no. 830 (copy: Coleman); in Lacy's acting edition of plays, v. 69, *NCO (Lacy)*; and in Turner's dramatic library of acting plays, new series [no. 77] (copy: Library of Congress).
First produced at the Adelphi Theatre, London, Oct. 7, 1826. One of the characters is Aaron Mordica, "a Jew pedlar." He is listed as one of the *dramatis personae* only in the Dicks edition. In the other editions, which differ textually from the Dicks edition, he does not appear.
Produced at the Park Theatre, New York, Feb. 17, 1827. Reviewed in *New York mirror*, 1827, v. 4, p. 247, * *DA*.

BUNG-YOUR-EYE, SOLOMON, PSEUD. The informers outwitted; a tragi-comical farce... [in two acts, and in prose.] Written originally in Hebrew, and translated by S. B. London, 1738. 8°.
Copy: Library of Congress, entered under title. Baker states "never acted."

BUNN, ALFRED. See sub-entry under SCOTT, SIR WALTER.

BURROUGHS, WATKINS. See sub-entry under SCRIBE, AUGUSTIN EUGÈNE.

BYRON, HENRY JAMES. See sub-entries under MAID AND MAGPIE; SCOTT, SIR WALTER.

THE CALIPH's buffoon. (In: Oliver's complete collection of comic songs. Edinburgh: Oliver & Boyd [1825]. 3. ed. 24°. p. 35–38.)
NDF (Oliver's)
A comic song. The speakers are in character. One of them is a Jew, who speaks in dialect, as do the others.

CAMPBELL, ANDREW LEONARD VOULLAIRE. The forest oracle; or, The bridge of Tresino. An operatic drama in three acts, by M. Campbell, Esq. The music by Mr. Nicholson... With remarks biographical and critical, by D.-G. [i.e. Geo. Daniel]... As now performed at Sadler's Wells Theatre... London: John Cumberland [1825–55?]. 48 p. incl. front. 24°.
NCO p.v.455
Aaron, a Polish Jew, "a very good sort of a man, as times go, but quite attentive to the main chance." Landa believes that Campbell was the first English playwright who reveals acquaintance with the Yiddish language. He further states, erroneously, that Aaron is the first Polish Jew on the English stage (see *Zorinski* by Thomas Morton, 1795). Scene: The Alps. First produced at Sadler's Wells, Nov. 9, 1829. Villiers as Aaron: speaks the usual dialect.
Reviewed in *The Times*, London, Nov. 10, 1829, p. 2, col. 6, * *A*.

—— —— By A. L. V. Campbell... As now performed at the metropolitan minor theatres ... London: J. Cumberland [18—?].
The publisher's address varies from the one preceding.

CARNARVON, HENRY JOHN GEORGE HERBERT, 3RD EARL. Don Pedro, king of Castile. A tragedy. By Lord Porchester... London: H. Colburn, 1828. 1 p.l., (i) vi–vii p., 1 l., 99 p. 8°.
NCO p.v.237
Reviewed in *London magazine*, London, 1828, series 3, v. 1, p. 148–150, * *DA*.
Produced at the Drury-Lane, London, March 10, 1828. Wallack as Raban the Jew "one of Shylock's class, seeking revenge for accumulated wrongs." The action of the play is laid during the reign of Peter the Cruel, 1350–1386, and the rôle assigned to Raban is based partly on historical facts.
Reviewed in *Examiner*, London, 1828, p. 178–179, * *DA*; *Literary gazette*, London, 1828, p. 172–173, * *DA*; *New monthly magazine*, London, v. 24, p. 151–152, * *DA*; and in *The Times*, London, March 11, 1828, p. 3, col. 4, * *A*. Most of the reviewers condemned it.

CHANTILLY... London: Edward Bull, 1832. 3 v. 8°.
Copy: Harvard College Library.
Divided into three tales: D'Esprignac, The Page, and Ash Wednesday.
The Jewish interest is in the second tale, The Page, where Ben Israel and his son, El Adhel, figure.
"The author was probably a woman."
A synopsis is given in *Athenæum*, London, 1832, v. 5, p. 121–122, * *DA*. Reviewed in *Gentleman's magazine*, London, 1832, new series, v. 102, p. 437, * *DA*; and in *Literary gazette*, London, 1832, p. 114, * *DA*.
Deals with the period of Charlemagne, when the knights were fighting the Saracens. This tale was dramatized by Henry M. Milner into *The Moorish page; or, The days of chivalry*, and was produced in Liverpool, Feb. 6, 1838, with Burton as Ben Israel.

CHARLEMAGNE, ARMAND. The uncle's will, who wins?; or, The widow's choice. A farce in two acts, freely translated from the French of Mr. Charlemagne, by Peter Berard.. London: Printed for the author, by A. Macpherson, 1808. 3 p.l., (1)6–30 p. 8°. NCO p.v.154
Never acted.
The author, in his *Preface*, apologizes for his effort, since "*the Uncle's will* is at present before the public

Individual Plays—Earliest Times to 1837, cont'd

from a much more competent Pen." The reference here is to J. T. Allingham's *Who wins?; or, The Widow's choice*, produced at Covent Garden, London, Feb. 25, 1808, and printed as *The Widow; or, Who wins?* (in Cumberland's British theatre, v. 32, *NCO*). The plot of our present farce is very much like that of Allingham's.
Moses Balthasar, "a Jew usurer." He comes to collect a note from the poet De Valencourt, and is called by his debtor *hard-hearted villain, inexorable usurer, damned Hebrew, one of the infernal, cursed race of usurers*, etc. He is made to speak in dialect.

CIBBER, THEOPHILUS. *See* sub-entry under HOGARTH, WILLIAM.

CLEMPERT, JOHN. *See* sub-entry under SCRIBE, AUGUSTIN EUGÈNE.

COBB, JAMES. A house to be sold, a musical piece, in two acts. As performed at the Theatre-Royal, Drury-Lane... The music composed and selected by Michael Kelly. London: Printed for G. and J. Robinson, by J. Crowder and E. Hemsted, 1802. 2 p.l., 56 p. 2. ed. 8°.
NCO p.v.170
Adapted from Alexandre Duval's *Maison à vendre*. Without the music.

—— —— As performed at the New-York Theatre. New-York: Printed and published by D. Longworth, at the Shakspeare-Gallery. 1803. 48 p. 16°.
Without music.
Reviewed in *European magazine*, London, 1802, v. 42, p. 378–379, * *DA*. "The Jew, by Wewitzer, must be noticed as a chaste, natural, and truly comic performance."
"An alteration from a successful French drama, in one act, entitled, 'Maison à vendre,'" which M. Kelly brought from Paris from the Théâtre Feydeau. Produced at the Drury Lane, Nov. 17, 1802. Wewitzer as Melchizedek, a Jew, who is fooled in a commercial bargain, while buying a house from one who did not own it. Speaks in dialect. Bannister as Kelson played the counter role.
It was staged as an afterpiece at the Park Theatre, New York, with John Hogg as Meshoc, May 25, 1803 and revived, Jan. 13, 1804.
Nicoll, p. 252, lists *A house to be sold*, by John Baylis, [London] 1804, as another printed adaptation of *La Maison à vendre*.

COLE, JOHN WILLIAM. *See* sub-entry under SCOTT, SIR WALTER.

COLMAN, GEORGE, 1732–1794. Man and wife; or, The Shakespeare jubilee. A comedy, of three acts, as it is performed at the Theatre Royal in Covent Garden... London: T. Becket and Co. [etc.], 1770. 3 p.l., v(i), 64 p. 8°.
NCO p.v.102
Taken in part from Destouches' *La Fausse Agnès*. A second edition was printed the same year, NCO p.v.618.
The second act ends with a Pageant "exhibiting the characters of Shakespeare." In the division called "the Comic Muse," Shylock "with Knife, Scales, and Bond" brings up the rear of the procession.
Produced at the Covent Garden, London, Oct. 7, 1769, and revived there Dec. 20, 1777. See Genest, v. 5, p. 278–279. The pageant was introduced in this piece with a view to forestall the pageant in the *Jubilee* of Garrick, which was then in preparation at the Drury Lane. "But this Pageant was very inferior to the other."
"In the Larpent collection [now at the Henry E. Huntington Library] is *Ye jubilee of Covent Garden Theatre*, dated 1769 (9 S) and also the present *Man and wife*, dated Oct. 3, 1769." — Nicoll, p. 246.

COLMAN, GEORGE, 1762–1836. *See* sub-entry under BOUILLY, JEAN NICOLAS.

COMOEDIA genandt Dass wohl gesprochene Uhrtheil eynes weiblichen Studenten; oder, Der Jud von Venedig. (In: Johannes Meissner. Die englischen Comoedianten zur Zeit Shakespeares in Oesterreich. Wien, 1884. 8°. p. 131–189.)
* NDD p.v.5
In five acts of four, five, seven, nine and eight scenes respectively.
The Jewish character is called Jud Barrabas, hernach Joseph, and the scene is Cyprus.
It was produced by an English strolling company in Gräz, 1608; at Halle, Germany, in 1611, and as late as 1674 in Dresden. Whether this is a "mixture" of Shakespeare's *The Merchant of Venice* and Marlowe's *The Jew of Malta*, or possibly the source of Shakespeare's comedy, or the substance of Dekker's lost *The Jew of Venice*, is discussed ibid., p. 103–112, 127–130; and by J. Bolte in Deutsche Shakespeare Gesellschaft, *Jahrbuch*, Weimar, 1887, Jahrg. 22, p. 189–201, * *NCK*. Bolte inclines to the belief that it is a revamped form of Shakespeare's play.
A synopsis and translation of parts from acts IV and V are given by H. H. Furness, in the Variorum edition of *The Merchant of Venice*, Philadelphia, 1888, p. 324–331, * *NCM*.

COOPER, FREDERICK FOX. Hercules, king of clubs! A farce in one act... Printed from the acting copy, with remarks, biographical and critical, by D. G. [i.e. Geo. Daniel]... As performed at the metropolitan minor theatres... London: John Cumberland [183–?]. 23 p. incl. front. 24°. (Cumberland's minor theatre. v. 13 [no. 7].)
NCO (Cumberland)
Also issued in Lacy's acting edition of plays, v. 89, [no. 1334,] *NCO* (Lacy).
Produced at the Strand Theatre, London, July 28, 1836. Fox Cooper played Capt. Darling in disguise of Isaacs, an antique dealer, and spoke his lines in dialect. Reviewed in *Literary gazette*, London, 1836, p. 460, * *DA*.
Odell, IV:286, mentions a performance at the Park Theatre, New York, May 7, 1839, and again, IV:362, at the Park Theatre, June 15, 1840, with A. Andrews as Captain Darling.

—— *See also* sub-entry under SCOTT, SIR WALTER.

COWIE, R. *See* sub-entry under SCOTT, SIR WALTER.

COWLEY, MRS. HANNAH (PARKHOUSE). The belle's stratagem, a comedy, as acted at the Theatre-Royal in Covent-Garden. By Mrs. Cowley. London: T. Cadell, 1782. 2 p.l., 84 p. 8°.
NCO p.v.108
This is the first authorized edition; dedicated to the Queen. It was preceded in 1781 by an unauthorized edition, published by T. Bathe, Dublin. Cf. *Review of English studies*, London, 1929, v. 5, p. 131, *RNA*.
Reviewed in *Critical review*, London, 1782, v. 53, p. 314, *NAA; European magazine*, London, v. 1, p. 292, * *DA*; and in *Monthly review*, London, v. 66, p. 287–292, *NAA*.

—— The belle's stratagem, a comedy. By Mrs. Cowley. With alterations and amendments. As performed at the New Theatre, in Boston. Printed at the Apollo Press, in Boston, for David West, No. 36, Marlboro' Street, and John West, No. 75, Cornhill. 1794. 73 p. 12°.
Copy: Library of Congress.

—— —— Printed at the Apollo Press, in Boston, for John West, no. 75, Cornhill. 1794. 73 p. 12°.
Copy: Harvard College Library.

Individual Plays—Earliest Times to 1837, cont'd

COWLEY, MRS. HANNAH (PARKHOUSE). The belle's stratagem; a comedy in five acts... As acted at the Theatres Royal, Drury Lane and Covent Garden... With remarks by Mrs. Inchbald. London: Longman, Hurst, Rees and Orme [1806?]. 86 p., front. 16°. NCO p.v.543
With corrections and additions in ms.

—— —— As acted at the Theatre Royal, in Covent Garden... London: Longman, Hurst, Rees and Orme, 1806. 2 p.l., 84 p. new ed. 8°.

—— The belle's stratagem; a comedy, in five acts. By Mrs. Cowley. As performed at the Theatre Royal, Covent Garden, and at the Boston Theatre. Boston: Published by John West & Co. 75, Cornhill. 1810. E. G. House, Printer. 83(1) p. 12°.
Copy: Library of Congress.

—— The belle's stratagem. A comedy. By Mrs. Cowley. Correctly given, from copies used in the theatres, by Thomas Dibdin... London: Printed at the Chiswick Press for Whittingham and Arliss, 1815. 75(1) p. illus. 24°. (T. J. Dibdin, London theatre. v. 1 [no. 6].)
Copy: Library of Congress.

—— ...The belle's stratagem; a comedy... With prefatory remarks... As it is performed at the Theatres Royal. By W. Oxberry, comedian. London: Published for the proprietors by W. Simpkin and R. Marshall [etc.], 1819. 1 p.l., ii p., 3 l., 72 p., front. (port.) 12°. (William Oxberry. The new English drama. v. 6 [no. 4].) NCO (Oxberry)
At head of title: Oxberry's edition.
"Prefatory remarks," by W. H. i.e. William Hazlitt.

—— The belle's stratagem; a comedy, in five acts... [London, 182–?] 20 p. 8°. NCO p.v.454
Caption-title.
Excerpt.

—— ...The belle's stratagem; a comedy. By Mrs. Cowley. With prefatory remarks. The only edition existing, which is faithfully marked with the stage business, and stage directions. As it is performed at the Theatres Royal. By W. Oxberry, comedian. Boston: Wells and Lilly; New York: A. T. Goodrich & Co., 1822. 109 p. 24°. NCO p.v.430
At head of title: Oxberry's edition.
No American casts are given.

—— ...The belle's stratagem, a comedy; in five acts. By Mrs. Cowley. Printed under the authority of the managers, from the prompt book. With notes, critical and explanatory. Also an authentic description of the costume, and the general stage business. As performed at the Theatres Royal, London... London: Printed and pub. by T. Dolby, 1823. iv p., 1 l., (1) 8–74 p., 1 l., front. 12°. (Cumberland's British theatre. v. 2 [no. 4].) NCO (Cumberland)
"Remarks," p. iii, iv.

—— —— London: John Cumberland [182–?]. 70 p. incl. front. 16°. (Cumberland's British theatre. no. 11.) NCO p.v.533
"Remarks," by Geo. Daniel, p. 5, 6.

—— —— 3 p.l., (1) 10–70 p., 1 l. 24°. NCO p.v.2
"Critical remarks — 1825," 2nd p.l.

—— The belle's stratagem; a comedy in five acts... New York, Philadelphia, Boston: Charles Wiley [etc.], 1825. 88 p. 24°.
Illustrated title-page. NCO p.v.721

—— The belle's stratagem. Condensed from Mrs. Cowley's comedy and arranged in three acts, by Augustin Daly. As first produced at the Daly's Theatre, New York, April, 1892. Printed from the prompt book of Daly's Theatre. [New York,] 1892. 41 p. 4°. † NAC p.v.121

—— —— As first produced at Daly's Theatre, New York, January 3, 1893. [New York:] Printed from the prompt book of Daly's Theatre, 1893. 57 p. 8°. 8–† NCOF
Added t. p.: Two old comedies, The Belle's stratagem and The Wonder...
"Representative old comedies. The Wonder and The Belle's stratagem. A preface," by William Winter.
Text inlaid, and 1 playbill, printed on satin, and newspaper clippings mounted, on folio size sheets.
With autograph of Miss Ada Rehan.
With this is bound: S. Centlivre, The Wonder. [New York,] 1893. 8°.

—— The belle's stratagem; a comedy in five acts... With remarks biographical and critical, by D.-G. [i.e. Geo. Daniel]... As performed at the Theatres Royal... London: G. H. Davidson [1849–55]. 70 p., 1 l., incl. front. 16° (Davidson's shilling volume of Cumberland's plays. v. 1 [no. 4].) NCO (Davidson)

—— —— Prompter's copy; interleaved ms. notes; front. missing. NCOF

—— The belle's stratagem; a comedy in five acts... Correctly marked and arranged by Mr. J. B. Wright. New York: S. French [1850–76]. 52 p. 12°. (French's standard drama. The acting edition. no. 281.) *C p.v.1705
Twenty casts of characters of American productions, during 1827–1856, are given on p. 2–3.

—— —— Prompter's copy; ms. notes. NCOF

—— —— With variant publisher's address on t.-p. Prompter's copy; interleaved ms. notes. NCOF

—— The belle's stratagem; a comedy, in five acts... The whole of the stage business, correctly marked and arranged by Mr. J. B. Wright... Boston: W. V. Spencer [186–?]. 52 p. 12°. (Spencer's Boston theatre. [v. 12], no. 95.) NCO p.v.574

—— —— Second-fifth copies; prompter's copies, with interleaved ms. notes. NCOF

—— —— Sixth copy; prompter's copy, not interleaved. NCOF

THE JEW IN ENGLISH DRAMA 13

Individual Plays—Earliest Times to 1837, cont'd

COWLEY, MRS. HANNAH (PARKHOUSE). The belle's stratagem; a comedy in three acts... London: T. H. Lacy [1866–73]. 65 p., 1 plate. illus. 12°. (Lacy's acting edition of plays. v. 72.) NCO (Lacy)

—— —— Prompter's copy; interleaved ms. notes. NCOF p.v.8
"This edition...is the first acting one ever printed containing Mrs. Cowley's text," p. 3. See R. C. Rhodes in *Review of English studies*, v. 5, p. 132–133, *RNA*, who states that the Lacy edition may be described as the author's draft, and the earlier editions as the acting copy. Lacy omitted the insulting words addressed by a masquerader to Isaac Mendoza in the person of Hardy, in act II, scene 5 — the masquerade scene (act IV, scene 1, of the earlier editions). Augustin Daly followed suit in his printed acting version of 1892.

—— ...The belle's stratagem; a comedy in five acts... London: J. Dicks [1883–92]. 23 p. illus. new and complete edition. 12°. (Dicks' standard plays. no. 58.) NCO p.v.358
Cover-title.

—— The belle's stratagem; a comedy in five acts. (British drama. London, 1824. 8°. v. 1, p. 532–553.) NCO (British)
Caption-title.
Other editions published at Philadelphia, 1835 and 1838, *NCO*.
Also published in *English comedy*, London, 1810, v. 5, p. 1–79, *NCO (English)*, *The London stage*, London [1824–27], v. 2, [no. 1], *NCO (London)*, and *Select London stage*, London [1830?], [no. 10], *NCO (Select)*.
A selection from act II, scene 1, is given in *Universal magazine*, London, 1782, v. 71, p. 20–24, * *DA*.
It was produced at the Covent Garden, Feb. 22, 1780. Hardy, father of the belle, acted by Quick, who had played the part of Isaac Mendoza in Sheridan's *The Duenna*, disguises himself as Mendoza at a masquerade ball and is addressed insultingly by another masquerader. Landa, p. 122, states that the remarks refer to Samson Gideon, 1699–1762, eminent English financier.
Reviewed in *London chronicle*, London, 1780, v. 47, p. 189–190, * *A*; *London magazine*, London, v. 49, p. 55–56, * *DA*; and in *Universal magazine*, London, v. 66, p. 119–120, * *DA*.
It was first produced at Kingston, Jamaica, Dec. 8, 1781, with Morris as Hardy. The American Company, which produced it in Jamaica, first presented it in New York, under Hallam and Henry, June 17, 1786, and kept it on the boards for many seasons. Baltimore saw it, Sept. 24, 1790.

Rhodes, Raymond Crompton. Belle's stratagem [a contribution to its bibliography]. (Review of English studies. London, 1929. 8°. v. 5, p. 129–142.) RNA

CRAWFORD, ALICE. See entry under SCOTT, SIR WALTER.

CROSS, JAMES C. The false friend; or, Assassin of the rocks. A new melo dramatic ballet of action [in nine scenes]. Performed for the first time, September 7, 1806. (In his: Dramatic works. 2. ed. London, 1812. 12°. v. 2, p. 33–71.) NCO p.v.194
On the t.-p.: "The incidental dances by Mr. Bolgna, Jun. The music by Messrs. Russel and Corri, Jun. The machinery by Mr. Cabanall, Jun., and the scenery by Mr. Marchbanks."
Published in *Circusiana*, 1809. According to A. Nicoll it was produced at the Circus Theatre, London, Aug. 25, 1806. The Jewish character is one Zaluch, described as "a friendly" and benevolent Jew.

CROWNE, JOHN. Caligula. A tragedy, as it is acted at the Theatre Royal, by His Majesty's servants. Written by Mr. Crowne. London: Printed by J. Orme, for R. Wellington, at the Lute in St. Paul's Church-Yard, and sold by Percivil Gilborne [etc.], 1698. 6 p.l., 52 p. 8°. Reserve
Also printed in his *Dramatic works*, Edinburgh, 1874, v. 4, p. 337–426 (issued as one of the volumes of the series Dramatists of the Restoration, ed. by J. Maidment and W. H. Logan), *NCO (Dramatists)*.
For a detailed bibliographical description of the first edition see *Harvard Library notes*, Cambridge, 1920, no. 2, p. 47, * *HA*.
Philo appears as a messenger to Caligula, on behalf of the Alexandrian Jews. Philo's daughter Salome, in a minor sub-plot, is represented in love with a Roman. The mission of Philo in 40 A.D. is historical; the story of Salome in this play is fictitious. The chief source of Crowne's material, as to Caligula, is Suetonius' life of Caligula; as to Philo, the writings of Philo himself.
For a historical discussion of the play see A. F. White, *John Crowne; his life and dramatic works*, Cleveland, 1922, p. 171–176, *NCC (Crowne)*.
Mr. Winship calls the author the first Harvard man who succeeded in making a living by practising a recognized form of literature, Crowne having attended Harvard College while his father resided in Boston during the Protectorate.
It was acted at the Drury Lane Theatre, about the middle of March, 1698, with Mr. Disney as Philo and Mrs. Cross as Salome.

CUMBERLAND, RICHARD. The fashionable lover; a comedy. As it is acted at the Theatre-Royal, in Drury-Lane. London: W. Griffin, 1772. x p., 1 l., 63 p. 8°. NCO p.v.14

—— —— London: W. Griffin, 1772. x p., 1 l., 63 p. new ed. 8°.

—— —— Dublin: A. Leathley [etc.], 1772. 4 p.l., 64 p. 16°.

—— —— London: B. Law [etc.], 1781. x p., 1 l., 63 p. new ed. 8°.

—— —— Philadelphia: Printed for William Woodhouse, 1773. 72 p. 12°.
Copy: Library of Congress.

—— —— Adapted for theatrical representation ... London: J. Bell, 1793. 1 p.l., vii(i), (1) 10–102 p., front. 16°. NCP p.v.1

—— —— Correctly given, from copies used in the theatres, by Thomas Dibdin... London: Printed at the Chiswick Press for Whittingham and Arliss, 1814. 68 p. illus. 24°. (Dibdin, T. J. London theatre. v. 4 [no. 8].)
Also published in *Bell's British theatre*, v. 18, *NCO (Bell)*, *The London stage*, v. 2, *NCO (London)*, *Select London stage*, [no. 17], *NCO (Select)*, *Sharpe's British theatre*, v. 8, *NCO (Sharpe's)*, and, with an introduction, in Montrose J. Moses, *British plays from the Restoration to 1820*, Boston, 1929, v. 2, p. 705–744, *NCO (Moses)*.
Reviewed in *Critical review*, London, 1772, v. 33, p. 85, *NAA*; *Gentleman's magazine*, v. 42, p. 80–81, * *DA*; *Monthly review*, v. 46, p. 167–168, *NAA*; and (with numerous extracts from the text) in *Universal magazine*, v. 50, p. 42–47, * *DA*. See also William Mudford, *A critical examination of the writings of Richard Cumberland*, London, 1812, v. 1, p. 284–300, *AN*.
The design of the piece was a compliment to the Scotch, in the person of Colin Macleod, at the expense of the English. The Jewish character is Napthali (a Jew broker), a little ugly fellow with a broken accent. "He is not a very bad case, but just an average case of an average incidental figure." Cumberland afterwards regretted him and made the amende honorable in his *The Jew*, 1794. First produced at the Drury

Individual Plays—Earliest Times to 1837, cont'd

CUMBERLAND, RICHARD, *continued*

Lane, London, Jan. 20, 1772, with Waldron as Napthali. Reviewed in *London chronicle*, London, 1772, v. 31, p. 73, * *A; London magazine*, London, 1772, v. 41, p. 70–73, * *DA;* and in *Town and country magazine*, v. 4, p. 41–44, * *DA.*

Seilhammer, judging from an announcement of this play, dated May 7, 1772, Williamsburg, Va., says that it was probably produced there, on that date, for the first time in America, by the American Company. It was seen in Philadelphia, at the Southwark Theatre, during the season of 1772–73, with Mr. Wall as Napthali, Nov. 30, 1772, and March 8, 1773. It was played at Charleston, S. C., March 7, 1774, and was staged in New York, June 2, 1781, by the British garrison.

—— The Jew, a comedy. Performed at the Theatre-Royal, Drury-Lane... London: C. Dilly, 1794. 2 p.l., 75(1) p. 8°. NCO p.v.115

—— —— The 2d ed. London: C. Dilly, 1794. 2 p.l., 75(1) p. 8°.

—— —— London: Printed for the booksellers, 1794. 48 p. 12°.
A pirated (?) edition. Without prologue and epilogue.

—— —— London: C. Dilly, 1795. 2 p.l., 75(1) p. 3. ed. 8°.

—— —— London: C. Dilly, 1795. 2 p.l., 75(1) p. 4. ed. 8°.

—— The Jew: or, Benevolent Hebrew. A comedy. As performed, with universal applause, at the theatre in Boston... Boston: Printed for, and sold by John West, 1795. 48 p. 12°. * KD
No. 100 in the Rosenbach bibliography.

—— The Jew. A comedy. Performed in London, and by the Old American Company in New-York, with universal applause... New-York: Printed and sold by Samuel Campbell, 1795. 54 p., 1 l. 12°. * KD 1795
No. 102 in the Rosenbach bibliography.

—— The Jew: or, Benevolent Hebrew. A comedy. As performed with universal applause, at the New Theatre, in Philadelphia... Philadelphia: Printed for Henry & Patrick Rice, and James Rice & Co., Baltimore. 1795. 48 p. 12°.
Without the prologue and epilogue. * KD 1795
No. 101 in the Rosenbach bibliography.
Imperfect; p. 47–48 wanting, supplied by photostatic reproduction.

—— The Jew; a comedy. Performed at Theatre Royal, Drury Lane... London: C. Dilly, 1797. 2 p.l., 64 p., 1 l. 6. ed. 8°. NCOF
Prompt book.

—— —— London: J. Mawman, 1801. 2 p.l., 64 p., 1 l. 7. ed. 8°.

—— —— As performed at the Philadelphia Theatre. Philadelphia: T. H. Palmer, 1823. 67(1) p. 16°.
Copy: Library of Congress.

—— —— New York, London: Samuel French [1910–24]. 47(1) p. 12°.
Also published in *Cumberland's British theatre*, v. 38, *NCO (Cumberland),* also a prompter's copy, with interleaved ms. notes, *NCOF;* in Mrs. Elizabeth Inchbald, *The British theatre,* v. 18, *NCO (Inchbald); Lacy's acting edition of plays,* v. 84, *NCO (Lacy);* and *The London stage,* v. 1, *NCO (London).* With varying frontispieces.

Printed, as abridged by Ernestine P. Franklin, in Louis I. Newman, *Richard Cumberland,* New York, 1919, p. 61–124, * *PSQ (Newman)* (reprinted from the English page of the *Jewish Daily News,* New York, July 15 – Aug. 2, 1919, * *PBA).* This version, with the dialect omitted, was produced in New York, June (or July) 15, 1919.

An extract from act III, scene 2, is printed in Allardyce Nicoll, editor, *Readings from British drama,* New York [1928], p. 245–247, * *R–NCO.*

Reviewed in *Analytical review,* London, 1794, v. 20, p. 436–439, *NAA; British critic,* London, v. 6, p. 11–14, * *DA; Critical review,* London, series 2, v. 14, p. 191–196, *NAA;* and in *Monthly review,* London, series 2, v. 16, p. 153–156, *NAA.* Cumberland "thinking that it is high time that something should be done for a persecuted race" gives his reasons for writing this play in his *Memoirs,* London, 1807, v. 2, p. 202–203, 279–280, *AN.* William Mudford gives an appraisal of the play in his *Critical examination of the writings of Richard Cumberland,* London, 1812, v. 2, p. 547–553, *AN.* John Adolphus evaluates the character of Sheva, acted by Jack Bannister, in his *Memoirs of John Bannister,* London, 1839, v. 1, p. 338–342, *MWES (Bannister).*

This drama, produced at the Drury Lane, May 9, 1794, is the first full-length pro-Jewish play in English literature. The prologue avowed the liberal design of the author, "to cut down the creeper Prejudice from the British oak" and to take the part of a victim who never yet had known the comfort of one applauding scene. In *The Jew* Cumberland set out to do for the Jews what he professed to do for the Scotch in his *Fashionable lover* and for the Irish in his *The West Indian.* It held the English and American stage for nearly a hundred years, having been produced professionally in New York as late as Oct. 28, 1859. The hero is Sheva an "honest" and benevolent Jew acted by Jack Bannister. Suett played the part of Jabal, Sheva's attendant. The reviewers, while disagreeing as to the merits of the play, joined in lauding the motives which prompted Cumberland to write it.

Reviewed in *European magazine,* London, 1794, v. 25, p. 386–387, * *DA; Lady's magazine,* London, v. 25, p. 255–256, * *DA; London chronicle,* London, v. 75, p. 442, * *A;* and in *Universal magazine,* London, v. 94, p. 372, * *DA.*

It was revived by M. J. Landa, for the benefit of a War charity, at the Strand Theatre, London, May 8, 1917, with S. Teitelbaum as Sheva. For reviews see *Era,* London, v. 80, May 9, 1917, p. 8, † *NAFA;* and *Jewish chronicle,* London, May 11, 1917, p. 18, * *PBE.*

It was first seen in Boston, Dec. 19, 1794, with Hipworth as Sheva and Villiers as Jabal, and revived there, Dec. 24, 29, 1794, and Jan. 2, 21, Feb. 16, May 13, 1795; again at the Boston Theatre under Col. John S. Tyler, Feb. 15 and March 14, 1796; during the season of 1796–97, under Williamson, Feb. 17, 1797, with Williamson as Sheva; and at the Boston Haymarket, under Chas. S. Powell, Jan. 9, 1797. Wignell and Reinagle staged it in Philadelphia, Feb. 11, 1795, with Wignell as Sheva and Harwood as Jabal, and revived it during the season of 1795–96, Aug. 1, Sept. 19, Nov. 4, Dec. 30, and April 2. In New York, Hallam and Hodgkinson brought it out Feb. 25, 1795, and repeated it March 4 and 23. Hodgkinson played Sheva; Hallam, Jabal. During the season of 1796–97, the old American Company again produced it, March 21, and another rival company, at the Greenwich Theatre, Sept. 30, with John Bernard as Sheva. Solee's Charleston Company brought it to Charleston, S. C., Nov. 24, 1795, with Mr. Jones as Jabal. Joseph B. Harper's Rhode Island Company played it at Providence, June 13, 1796, with Mr. Williamson as Sheva. Hallam, Hodgkinson, & Dunlap brought it to Hartford, Conn., Aug. 1, 1796. It continued to be revived throughout the nineteenth century. Odell mentions *Der Jude* acted on May 10, 1858, at Mitchell's Hotel, Union Hill; again "neu bearbeitet von Carl Seydelmann" at Lindenmüller's Odeon, 49 Bowery, Oct. 1 and 4, 1858, with Eduard Wissig as Shewa; and at Eustachi's New-Yorker Volks-Theater, Fourth Street, Oct. 28, 1859, with Volkland as Shewa, "der edle Jude."

Individual Plays—Earliest Times to 1837, cont'd

CUMBERLAND, RICHARD. Der Jude; ein Schauspiel in fuenf Aufzuegen...aus dem Englischen uebersetzt von Brockmann, für das k. k. National - Hoftheater. Wien: J. B. Wallishauser, 1795. 94 p. 12°.

—— Der Jude; Schauspiel in fünf Aufzügen, nach Richard Cumberlands englischem Originale. [Translated by Dengel.] Königsberg: Friedrich Nicolovius, 1798. 148 p. 16°.
Reviewed in *Neue allgemeine deutsche Bibliothek*, Kiel, 1799, Bd. 44, p. 316–317, NAA.

—— Der Jude; Schauspiel in fünf Aufzügen ... Aus dem Englischen übersetzt von Brockmann. Nach dem Aufführungs-Exemplare des k. k. Hofburgtheaters. Wien: J. B. Wallishausser, 1838. 68 p. 2. Aufl. 12°. * PSQ

—— Der Jude; ein Schauspiel in fünf Aufzügen. Von Richard Cumberland, aus dem Englischen. Leipzig: Philipp Reclam, jun., n.d. 64 p. 16°. (Universal Bibliothek. Nr. 142.) * PSQ

—— Der Jude; Schauspiel in fünf Akten... Stuttgart: Hoffmann'sche Verlagsbuchhandlung, n.d. 52 p. 12°.
Text in double columns.
Copy: Library of the Jewish Theological Seminary of America.

איש יהודי. מחזה שעשועים בחמש מערכות...
הסופר... ריצארד קומבערלאנד. העתק לעברית על
ידי יוסף בריל... ווילנא: דפוס יהודה ליב
ליפמאן מ״ץ, תרל״ח.
Wilna: L. Matz, 1878. 84 p. 16°. * PSN

—— Одинъ изъ нашихъ или рѣдкій еврей... Переводъ М. Я. Хашкеса. Вильна: тип. Яловцера и Вайнштейна, 1875. 95 p. 12°. * PBM p.v.158

—— Der Jud Menachem; oder, Die bescheidene Tugend. Komödie in 5 Akten. Übergesetzt vinem Englischen vin Benedix Ben-Zion. Odessa, 1882. 36 l. sq. 8°.
Judeo-German ms.
Title from A. S. Freidus' *List of dramas in The New York Public Library relating to the Jews*, item 260.

—— Zid; aneb. Dědicové Bělohorští. By E. Peškové. Prague, 1880.
Title from Allardyce Nicoll, *Late eighteenth century drama*, p. 128.

Auch ein Schreiben über das Schauspiel Der Jude, nicht an den Direktor Iffland. Berlin: J. F. Unger, 1798. 18 p. 16°.
Signed: Ihr unbekannter Freund.

Benevolent Jew; or, Sheva's creed. (Jewish Historical Society of England. Transactions. London, 1915. 4°. v. 7, p. 177–179.) * PXQ
A broad-sheet ballad, current in 1794. Original size, 10 x 3½ in.

Bril, Joseph. קטיגור וסניגור.
(חיום). St. Petersburg, 1887. f°. v. 2, no. 172, p. 2–3.) †* PBA
Signed: J. B.

Bump, Charles R. Cumberland's drama of "The Jew." (American Hebrew. New York, 1891. 4°. v. 46, p. 43–44.) * PBD

Carlos, pseud. Observations and strictures on the characters of Shylock and Sheva. (Monthly visitor. London, 1797. 16°. v. 1, p. 49–55.) * DA
The author posits the question: "Which is most consistent with the character of an Israelite, Shakespeare's Shylock or Cumberland's Sheva?" Although he lauds Cumberland for his attempt at "dissipating the mists of prejudice," he holds that Shakespeare is the truer copier of nature.

Cumberland, Richard. The generous Jew. For six males. [In four scenes.] (In: Beadle's dime dialogue. New York [cop. 1867]. 12°. no. 6, p. 43–60.)
An adaptation of part of the author's *The Jew*.

Fehler, Kurt. The Jew. [Analyse. Quellen. Kritik.] (In his: Richard Cumberlands Leben und dramatische Werke. Erlangen, 1911. 8°. p. 66–76, 111–112.) NCO p.v.381

Iffland, August Wilhelm. Antwort des Direktor Iffland auf das Schreiben an ihn über das Schauspiel Der Jude und dessen Vorstellung auf dem hiesigen Theater. Berlin: J. F. Unger, 1798. 20 p. 16°.
Reviewed in *Neue allgemeine deutsche Bibliothek*, Kiel, 1799, Bd. 44, p. 317–318, NAA.

Laujon, Pierre. Le Juif bienfaisant; ou, Les rapprochemens difficiles. Comédie en cinq actes et en prose, imitée de l'anglais [de R. Cumberland]. (In his: Oeuvres choisies. Paris, 1811. 8°. tome 3, p. 151–293.)
Copy: Harvard College Library.
"Représentée à Rouen, en juin 1806."
In a note, p. 288, the author states that the plot of the play was communicated to him by his son, who, as a cadet in the French navy, had first seen it in Philadelphia, at the opening of a theatre there. The basis of it is Cumberland's *The Jew*. Sheva is described, instead of a stock broker, as "Juif français, peintre et commerçant en tableaux." Another character is le petit Isaac, "jeune Juif allemand." A review of the French text is given in *Monthly review*, London, 1812, series 2, v. 68, p. 490–491, NAA.

Levi, Harry. "The Jew." (In his: Jewish characters in fiction; English literature. Philadelphia [cop. 1903]. 12°. p. 37–41.) * PZB
Revised and enlarged in a second edition, 1911, p. 36–43, * PZB.

Newman, Louis Israel. Richard Cumberland, critic and friend of the Jews. New York: Bloch Pub. Co., 1919. 2 p.l., vii–xv, 124 p. 24°. * PSQ
Reprinted from the English page of the *Jewish Daily News*, New York, June 26 – July 14, 1919, * PBA.
Suggestion is here made of Abraham Goldsmid (1756?–1810) as the possible prototype of Sheva. Landa, p. 138, suggests Baron Ephraim Lopez Pereira d'Aguilar (1739–1802) or Joshua Manasseh in Tobias Smollett's *The Adventures of Ferdinand, Count Fathom*, (1753) as the original. Cf. also John Adolphus, *Memoirs of John Bannister, comedian*, London, 1839, v. 1, p. 338–342, MWES (Bannister).

Individual Plays—Earliest Times to 1837, cont'd

CUMBERLAND, RICHARD, *continued*

Philipson, David. Cumberland's "The Jew." (In his: The Jew in English fiction. Cincinnati, 1889. 12°. p. 54–69.) * PZB
Other editions published at Cincinnati, 1903, and 1911 and at New York, 1918.

Zangwill, Louis. Richard Cumberland centenary memorial paper. Read before the Jewish Historical Society of England, on July 10, 1911. port. (Jewish Historical Society of England. Transactions. London, 1915. 4°. v. 7, p. 147–179.) * PXQ

CUMBERLAND, RICHARD. The Jew of Mogadore, a comic opera, in three acts... London: S. Tipper, 1808. 2 p.l., 76 p. 8°. NCO p.v.174
Without the music (by Kelly).

—— The | Jew of Mogadore, | A comic opera, | in three acts. | By Richard Cumberland, Esq. | Sit mihi musa lyrae solers, et cantor Apollo! <published in London, 1808> | New-York: | Published by David Longworth, | at the Dramatic Repository, | Shakpeare [sic]-gallery. | 1808. 56 p. 16°. NCO p.v.528
Reviewed in *British critic*, London, 1809, v. 34, p. 407–408, * DA.
First produced at the Drury Lane, London, May 3, 1808, with Dowton as Nadab, a "benevolent" Jew, and Penley as Palti, a "knavish" Jew. Reviewed in *Edinburgh annual register*, Edinburgh, 1808, v. 1, part 2, p. 275–276, *BAA*; *European magazine*, London, v. 53, p. 381–382, * *DA*; *Examiner*, London, 1808, p. 299–300, * *DA*; and in *Monthly mirror*, London, new series, v. 3, p. 394–398, * *DA*. The last reviewer comments on the Jewish dialect essayed by the Jewish characters.

Mogadoriensis, pseud. [A letter to the editor.] (Gentleman's magazine. London, 1809. 8°. v. 106, p. 910–911.) * DA
The writer takes exception to the portrayal of a Jew as ransoming Christian captives. "A Nadab in Barbary would be a rara avis" asserts this correspondent.

Zangwill, Louis. Richard Cumberland centenary memorial paper... port. (Jewish Historical Society of England. Transactions. London, 1915. 4°. v. 7, p. 147–179.) * PXQ

CUMBERLAND, RICHARD. The note of hand; or, A trip to Newmarket... London: T. Becket, 1774. 3 p.l., 48 p. 8°. NCO p.v.142
Title in vignette.
In two acts.
The Epilogue is also printed in *Universal magazine*, London, 1774, v. 54, p. 97–98, * DA.
Reviewed in *Critical review*, London, 1774, v. 37, p. 158, *NAA*.
A farce about gambling and gamblers. In act II, sc. 3, Revell promises to help Rivers thus: "I'll lend thee Issachar; I'll promote thee to [bring you to the attention of] my Jew, the ablest financier of Christendom... Issachar will raise money as a witch does wind." In act I, sc. 2, Revell meets Issachar at the Newmarket races. The following colloquy ensues: Revell: Which way look your bargains in the Alley; is war or peace your game? Issachar: War, war; loss of credit; fall of stocks; heavy, heavy is the word with me; debt upon debt; long arrears and short payments; other people's loss is my gain — so lies my account.
Produced at the Drury Lane, London, Feb. 9, 1774. Reviewed in *London magazine*, 1774, v. 43, p. 59, * DA.
The Jewish interest of this farce has not been pointed out by any of the many writers on Cumberland and the Jews.

DABORNE, ROBERT. A Christian turn'd Turke: Or, The Tragicall Liues and Deaths of the two Famous Pyrates, Ward and Dansiker. As it hath beene publickly Acted. VVritten by Robert Daborn, Gentleman. *Nemo sapiens, Miser est*. [*Printer's mark*] London: Printed by for William Barrenger, and are to be sold at the great North-doore of Pauls. 1612. [70] p. 4°.
Copy: Library of Congress.
Reprinted by A. E. H. Swaen in *Anglia*, Halle, 1898, Bd. 20, p. 188–256, *RNA*. See his analysis of the play, ibid., p. 174–187.
The dramatis personae are divided as ten Christians, three Turks and three Jews (Benwash, Rabshake and Ruben).

Cardozo, Jacob Lopes. A Christian turn'd Turk (1612). (In his: The contemporary Jew in the Elizabethan drama. Amsterdam, 1925. 8°. p. 156–168.) * PZB

DAY, JOHN. The Travailes Of The three English Brothers.

Sir Thomas ⎫
Sir Anthony ⎬ Shirley
Mr Robert ⎭

As it is now play'd by her Maiesties Seruants. [*Ornament*] Printed at London for Iohn Wright, and are to bee sold at his shoppe neere Christ-Church gate. 1607. [64] p. 4°.
Copy: Library of Congress.
Manuscript note on t.-p.: First edition.
The "Kemble-Devonshire copy," with marginal note on first page: Collated & perfect. I: P: K. 1798. cf. Anderson sale catalogue.
Imperfect? According to the reprint in *Works of John Day*, ed. by A. H. Bullen, Chiswick Press, 1881, and descriptions in Greg's *List of Eng. plays*, *Cambridge hist. of Eng. lit.*, and the *Dict. nat. biog.*, this copy lacks a dedicatory epistle, "To honours fauourites, and the intire friends to the familie of the Sherleys, health," signed: Iohn Day. William Rowley. George Wilkins.

—— —— (In: John Day, Works. With an introduction and notes by A. H. Bullen. London, 1881. 8°. [part 5.])
Copy: Harvard College Library.
Historical and critical notes by the editor are given on p. i–viii of part 5, and p. 19–20 of the general Introduction.
See also John Fry, *Bibliographical memoranda*, Bristol, 1816, p. 345–350, *NCB*.
The *Travels* was entered on the Stationers' Register, June 29, 1607, and was printed the same year. The address "to the familie of the Sherleys" is signed by John Day, William Rowley and George Wilkins. The source of the play is Anthony Nixon's tract *The Three English brothers* (Stat. Reg. June 8, 1607) published in 1607, so that *The Travels* must have been composed within about three weeks. See article "Day and Wilkins as collaborators" in *Notes and queries* for June 12, 1926, p. 417–421, 436–438, * R–* DA. Golding tabulates his own results and those of four other scholars, with regards to the respective shares of the three authors in each scene of the play.
See J. L. Cardozo, *The Contemporary Jew in the Elizabethan drama*, Amsterdam, 1925, p. 141–156, * PZB.

DELAVIGNE, JEAN FRANÇOIS CASIMIR. The monastery of St. Just; a play in three acts. Adapted from the French of Casimir Delavigne...by John Oxenford... London: T. H. Lacy [186–?]. 53 p. nar. 12°. (Lacy's acting edition of plays. v. 63.) NCO (Lacy's)
The passion of Don Juan for a supposedly Jewish

THE JEW IN ENGLISH DRAMA 17

Individual Plays—Earliest Times to 1837, cont'd
girl is the foundation of the play. Its plot is patently copied from Scribe's *La Juive*. In the original French, as *Don Juan d'Autriche*, it was produced at the Théâtre Français, Paris, Oct. 17, 1835, with Mme. Volnys as Florinde de Sandoval.
   In an English translation, *Don Juan of Austria*, it was produced at the Covent Garden, London, April 23, 1836, with Helen Faucis in the principal part. Reviewed in *Athenæum*, London, 1836, v. 9, p. 291–292, * *DA*; and in *Literary gazette*, London, 1836, p. 267–268, * *DA*.
   The present Oxenford version, under its original title, was given a happy ending and was so produced at the Princess Theatre, London, June 27, 1864, with Stella Colas as Florinde. Reviewed in *Athenæum*, London, 1864, v. 44, p. 25, * *DA*; and in *Era*, London, v. 26, July 3, 1864, p. 10–11, † *NAFA*.

DIBDIN, THOMAS JOHN. Family quarrels, a comic opera, in three acts: as performed at the Theatre-Royal, Covent-Garden. Written by Thomas Dibdin... London: Longman, Hurst, Rees, and Orme, 1805. 2 p.l., 74 p. 8°.
NCO p.v.172
   Without the music (by Moorehouse, Braham and Reeve).

—— Songs, duets, chorusses, &. in the new comic opera, called Family quarrels... The music entirely new, and composed by Messrs. Reeve, Moorehead, Davy and Braham. The overture by Mr. Reeve. London: Barker and Son, 1803. 27 p. 8°.
   The song, First dere vath Miss Devy, from act II, as sung by Proteus, is ascribed to Reeve.
   First produced at the Covent Garden, London, Dec. 18, 1802. Fawcett played Proteus and in one of his disguises as a Jewish peddler sang a song which offended greatly the Jewish part of the audience and caused a great disturbance. Reviewed in *European magazine*, London, 1802, v. 42, p. 456–457, * *DA*; *Monthly mirror*, London, 1803, v. 15, p. 54–56, * *DA*; and in *Universal magazine*, London, 1802, v. 111, p. 455–456, * *DA*.

—— Humphrey Clinker; a farce, in two acts [from the novel by T. Smollett]... With remarks biographical and critical, by D.-G. [i.e. George Daniel]... As now performed at the metropolitan minor theatres... London: John Cumberland [1828?]. 36 p. front. 24°. (Cumberland's minor theatre. v. 4.) NCO (Cumberland)
   First produced at Sadler's Wells Theatre, London, March 17, 1828. Mordecai, a Jew, played by Mr. Mortrum. His clothes are borrowed for a Jewish disguise.
   First produced in New York, at the Park Theatre, June 7, 1838.

—— The Jew and the doctor, a farce in two acts, written by M. [*sic*] Dibdin, Jun. As performed at the Theatres-Royal, London and Dublin, with universal applause. Dublin: T. Burnside, 1799. 2 p.l., 26 p. 12°.

—— —— As performed at the Theatre-Royal, Covent-Garden. By Thomas Dibdin. London: Printed by A. Strahan, for T. N. Longman and O. Rees, 1800. 3 p.l., 32 p. 8°. NCO p.v.147

—— —— As performed at the Boston Theatre and Theatre-Royal, Covent-Garden. By Thomas Dibdin. New York: Published by D. Longworth, at the Dramatic Repository, Shakspeare-Gallery, 1807. 36 p. 24°.
NCO p.v.436
   No. 137 in the Rosenbach bibliography.
   A Boston cast is given, with Bernard as Abednego.

—— —— As performed at the Philadelphia Theatre. By Thomas Dibdin. Philadelphia: Published by Thomas H. Palmer, 1823. 36 p. 24°.
   No. 236 in the Rosenbach bibliography.
   Also published in *Cumberland's British theatre*, v. 34, NCO (Cumberland), and in Mrs. Elizabeth Inchbald, *A Collection of farces and afterpieces*, London, 1809, v. 2, p. 47–78, NCO (Inchbald).
   Reviewed in *Critical review*, London, 1800, series 2, v. 30, p. 227–229, *NAA*; *Monthly mirror*, London, v. 9, p. 292, * *DA*; *Monthly review*, London, series 2, v. 33, p. 106–107, *NAA*; and in *New London review*, London, v. 3, p. 283, * *DA*.
   The benevolence of a Jew (Abednego) toward a foundling who turns out afterwards to be the lost and long regretted daughter of the doctor is the groundwork of the piece. It was produced at the Covent Garden, London, Nov. 23, 1798, with Fawcett as Abednego, who is modelled after Sheva in Cumberland's *The Jew*. In a note to the printed play, Dibdin denied the charge of copying. Reviewed in *European magazine*, London, 1798, v. 34, p. 400, * *DA*; *London chronicle*, London, v. 84, p. 502, * *A*; *Monthly mirror*, London, v. 6, p. 366–367, * *DA*; *Monthly visitor*, London, v. 5, p. 393–394, * *DA*; and in *Universal magazine*, London, v. 103, p. 362, * *DA*.
   The first New York production was at the New Park Theatre, Feb. 19, 1808, with John Bernard as Abednego. It was revived at the Lyceum Theatre, Warren St. and Broadway, Feb. 11, 1809. In Boston it was seen at the Boston Theatre, Feb. 23, 1807.

—— The school for prejudice: a comedy, in five acts. Performed at the Theatre-Royal, Covent-Garden... London: Printed by A. Strahan, for T. N. Longman and O. Rees, 1801. 84 p., 1 l. 8°.
   Also printed in Mrs. Elizabeth Inchbald, *Modern theatre*, v. 4, p. 331–411, NCO (Inchbald).
   Originally produced in three acts, under the title of *Liberal opinions*, at the Covent Garden, May 12, 1800. Reviewed in *European magazine*, London, 1800, v. 37, p. 387–388, * *DA*; and in *Monthly mirror*, London, v. 9, p. 366, * *DA*. Under its printed title it was re-acted at the same theatre on Jan. 3, 1801. Reviewed in *European magazine*, London, 1801, v. 39, p. 41–42, * *DA*, where the prologue and epilogue are also given; and in *Monthly mirror*, London, v. 11, p. 126, * *DA*. Fawcett played the Jewish part — that of Ephraim, a "good and honest Jew" — both times.
   With the sub-title, *The Jew and the Yorkshireman*, it was produced at the Drury Lane on June 28, 1814. "Renamed *The Lawyer, the Jew and the Yorkshireman*, a three-act burletta, *The School for prejudice*, was revived at Sadler's Wells on Aug. 22, 1825. Mr. Vining played Abednego," Landa, p. 145–146. Abednego, however, is not the Jewish character in this play, but in another one by Dibdin.
   Under the title of *Liberal opinions*, it was produced at Philadelphia, Jan. 1, 1801 and Jan. 21, 1801, and by Dunlap, at the Park Theatre, New York, with Jefferson as Ephraim, Jan. 21 and 28, 1803. Under its title *The school for prejudice*, it was staged in Philadelphia, Nov. 11, 1801. There is no record of a New York production under its printed title. The two Philadelphia versions, staged Jan. 1, and Nov. 11, 1801, were reviewed in *The Portfolio*, Philadelphia, v. 1, p. 11, 36, 365, * *DA*.

—— *See also* sub-entry under SCOTT, SIR WALTER.

Individual Plays—Earliest Times to 1837, cont'd

DODSLEY, ROBERT. Rex et pontifex, being an attempt to introduce upon the stage a new species of pantomime. London: Printed for M. Cooper, 1745. 15 p. 8°.
Copy: Harvard College Library.
Reprinted in his *Trifles*, London, 1745, v. 1, p. 151-159, *NCF*.
"This piece was intended for the stage; but other avocations preventing the author from taking upon himself the trouble of bringing it on, if either of the Managers think it for their purpose, they are very welcome to it." — *Advertisement*, p. ii.
A kind of morality play. Dodsley endeavored to have it staged, but could find no producer. The curtain rises upon a temple, where "a cabal of Egyptian priests, Jewis Rabbins, Mahometan Muftis, a Pope, a cardinal, Jesuit, and Capuchin...are earnestly employed in dressing up the figure of Imposture." The remaining characters are abstractions, such as Liberty, Persecution, Corruption, etc.

DRYDEN, JOHN. Love triumphant; or, Nature will prevail. A tragi-comedy. As it is acted at the Theatre Royal, by Their Majesties servants. [*Two lines from Virgil*] Written by Mr. Dryden. London: Printed for Jacob Tonson, at the Judges Head near the Inner-Temple-Gate in Fleet-street. 1694. 6 p.l., 82 p., 1 l. 8°.
Copy: Library of Congress (imperfect: half-title wanting).

—— —— (In his: Works. With notes by Walter Scott. London, 1808. 8°. v. 8, p. 331-435.) NCF
A second edition, Edinburgh, 1821, *NCF*.
Also printed in Dryden's *Dramatic works*, edited by Montague Summers, London, 1932, v. 6, p. 399-476, explanatory notes, p. 577-589, * *KP (Nonesuch)*.
Gildon in his continuation of Langbaine says: "I take this play to be founded on the story of the *King and no King* of Fletcher." One of the characters, in a comic underplot, is Sancho, a conceited coxcomb and apostate Jew, son of a usurer. He is favored by the father of his mistress for his wealth only. Scott remarks that he "has some resemblance in manners and genealogy to a much more pleasant character, that of Isaac in the 'Duenna.'" This play, the last Dryden ever wrote, was produced at the Theatre Royal, London, in January, 1694, with Dogget in the part of Sancho, but did not keep the stage. See Genest, II:51-54. Scott's judgment was that "it affords little pleasure when perused."

EDGAR, RICHARD HORATIO. *See* sub-entry under SCOTT, SIR WALTER.

ELLISON, JAMES. The American captive, or Siege of Tripoli. A drama in five acts. Written by Mr. James Ellison. Boston: Printed by Joshua Belcher, 1812. 54 p. 24°.
Copy: Harvard College Library.
Produced at the Boston Theatre, Boston, in 1812. It is based on Susanna H. Rowson's *Slaves in Algiers*, and the Jewish character Abdomelick is modelled after that of Ben Hassan. See E. D. Coleman, "Plays of Jewish interest on the American stage, 1752–1821," in American Jewish Historical Society, *Publications*, no. 33, 1934, p. 192–194, * *PXX*.

L'ÉMIGRÉ à Londres; drame en cinq actes [in prose] par un émigré. Londres: J. Barker [1795]. 117(1) p., 1 l. 8°. NKO
Additional t.-p. in English.
Text in French and English on opposite pages.
Our character is un Juif who comes to buy jewels from the émigré count. He speaks of himself thus: "With us Jews, a mother and children are commodities whereon we do not set any value."
According to Genest, never acted.

ESTABROOK, H. D. *See* sub-entry under SCOTT, SIR WALTER.

FENWICK, JOHN. The Indian: a farce. As it was performed at Drury-Lane Theatre... London: West and Hughes [1800]. 2 p.l., 49(1) p. 8°. NCO p.v.147
Prologue "written by Dr. Houlton."
"The subject...is taken from a French comedy, in three acts, called Arlequin sauvage [by L. F. Delisle de la Drévetière] formerly acted ..at Paris." — *From the Advertisement*. Produced, Oct. 6, 1800, with Grimaldi as a "Jew pedlar."
Reviewed in *European magazine*, London, 1800, v. 38, p. 287–288, * *DA*; and in *Monthly mirror*, London, v. 10, p. 252, * *DA*.

FIELDING, HENRY. Miss Lucy in town; a sequel to The virgin unmasqued. A farce with songs. As it is acted... by his majesty's servants. London: A. Millar, 1742. 2 p.l., 44 p. 12°.
 * C p.v.1357
Reprinted in his *Works*, London, 1783, v. 4, p. 257–286, *NCF*; *Works*, London, 1806, v. 3, p. 427–459, *NCF*; *Works*, ed. T. Roscoe, London, 1840, p. 1070–1077, *NCV* (another ed., London, 1851, *NCF*); *Works*, ed. J. P. Browne, London, 1871, v. 3, p. 449–482, *NCF*; and in his *Works*, ed. L. Stephen, London, 1882, v. 10, p. 299–329, *NCF*.
It was produced at the Drury Lane, London, May 4, 1742, with Macklin as Zorobabel.
Zorobabel in this farce is modelled after the Jew in Hogarth's *The Harlot's progress*. For a full discussion of this farce see H. R. S. Van der Veen, *Jewish characters in eighteenth century English fiction and drama*, Groningen, 1935, p. 109–121, * *PZB*.
As a pantomime or ballad-farce, it was produced, under the title *The Country mad-cap in London*, at the Covent Garden, London, Dec. 12, 1770. See *Town and country magazine*, London, 1770, v. 2, part 2, p. 658–659, * *DA*.

FINDLAY, MAUD I. *See* sub-entry under SCOTT, SIR WALTER.

FITZBALL, EDWARD. *See* sub-entry under MAID AND MAGPIE.

FLETCHER, JOHN, AND PHILIP MASSINGER. The custom of the country. Written by Mr. Francis Beaumont and Mr. John Fletcher. London: Printed for J. T. and sold by J. Brown, 1717. 67(1) p. 4°.
Copy: Library of Congress.
"By Fletcher and Massinger, founded on the *Persiles y Sigismunda* of Cervantes." — *Cambridge history of English literature*.
Also printed in Beaumont and Fletcher, *Works*, London, 1711, v. 1, p. 307–394, *NCP*; *Works*, ed. by L. Theobald and others, London, 1750, v. 2, p. 1–95, *NCP*; *Works*, ed. by George Darley, London, 1840 (another ed., 1859), v. 1, p. 105–132, *NCP*; *Works*, ed. by Alexander Dyce, London, 1844, v. 4, p. 385–496, *NCP*; *Works*, ed. by A. Dyce, Boston, 1854, v. 1, p. 720–755; ed. by R. W. Bond in their *Works, Variorum edition*, ed. by A. H. Bullen, London, 1904, v. 1, p. 475–589, *NCP*; and in *Works*, ed. by Arnold Glover, Cambridge, 1905, v. 1, p. 302–388, *NCP*.
Also in *Dramatic works of Ben Jonson, Beaumont and Fletcher*, London, 1811, v. 2, p. 145–183 (notes by George Colman), *NCP*.
As to Massinger's part in this play see Robert Boyle in New Shakspere Society, *Transactions*, series 1, no. 10 (1880/6, part 3), p. 602–603, * *NCK*. For a discussion of the Jewish interest of the play see J. L. Cardozo, *The Contemporary Jew in Elizabethan drama*, Amsterdam, 1925, p. 168–178, * *PZB*.

The Stallion. (In: Wits; or, Sport upon sport, edited by J. J. Elson. Ithaca, N. Y., 1932. 8°. p. 104–110, 375.) NCO
A droll based on *The Custom of the country*, act III, scene 3, and act IV, scene 5.

Individual Plays—Earliest Times to 1837, cont'd

C., J. A note on Cervantes and Beaumont and Fletcher. (Fraser's magazine. London, 1875. 8°. new series, v. 11, p. 592–597.)   *DA
The writer argues that Fletcher alone wrote this play. "Fletcher has in a great measure copied word for word" from an English translation, by one M. L., London, 1619, of Cervantes' *Los Trabajas de Persiles y Sigismunda*. Beaumont had no hand in it, since he died in 1615, before the Persiles was first published in Spain.

FOOTE, SAMUEL. The cozeners; a comedy of three acts. As it was performed at the Theatre Royal in the Hay-Market. London: John Wheble, 1778. 2 p.l., 79 p. 8°.

—— —— Published by Mr. Colman. London: Printed by T. Sherlock for T. Cadell, 1778. vi p., 1 l., 94 p. 8°.   NCO p.v.106

—— The cozeners; a comedy, in three acts. By Samuel Foote, Esq. <first published in London, 1778.> New-York: Published by D. Longworth, At the Dramatic Repository, Shakspeare-Gallery. Oct. — 1813. 64 p. 16°.
   NCO p.v.254
Appended (p. 62–64): Circumstantial evidence.
Reviewed in *Critical review*, London, 1778, v. 45, p. 155–156, *NAA*.
Reprinted in his *Dramatic works*, Dublin, 1778, v. 2, p. 225–278, *NCP; Dramatic works*, London, 1797, v. 2, p. 151–211, *NCP*; as a separate, 1795, 77 p., in his *Dramatic works*, London, 1809, v. 2 [no. 4], *NCP*; as a separate, 1813, 64 p., in his *Works*, New York, 1814, v. 3 [no. 1], *NCP*; and in his *Works*, ed. by John Bee, London, 1830, v. 3, p. 301–377.
A satire against the corruption and venality of the age. Flaw and Mrs. Fleece'em are the cozeners. Moses Manasses, having made several unsuccessful attempts to gain membership into some fashionable club, solicits Mrs. Fleece'em to get him admitted "into de Boodles, de Almacks, or von of de clubs." This is the first instance in English dramatic literature of a Jew with an ambition such as this. The part was played by Burton, according to the printed edition of Colman. The Wheble edition ascribes this part to Baddeley, while the reviewer of *Universal magazine* names a third one, Palmer. It was produced at the Haymarket Theatre, July 15, 1774; with Burton as Moses. See Genest, v:430–433.
Reviewed in *London chronicle*, London, 1774, v. 35, p. 55–56, * *A; London magazine*, London, v. 43, p. 309–310, * *DA*; and in *Universal magazine*, London, v. 55, p. 35, * *DA*. A detailed synopsis of the plot, with extracts from the dialogue, is given in *Hibernian magazine*, Dublin, 1774, v. 4, p. 451–456, * *DA*.

—— The devil upon two sticks; a comedy, in three acts. As it is performed at the Theatre-Royal in the Haymarket. Written by the late Samuel Foote, Esq., and now published by Mr. Colman. London: Printed by T. Sherlock, for T. Cadell, 1778. 1 p.l., [v]–vi p., 1 l., 69 p. 8°.
   NCO p.v.106

—— The devil upon two sticks: a comedy, in three acts. By Samuel Foote, Esq. <first published in London, 1778.> New-York: Published by D. Longworth, At the Dramatic Repository, Shakspeare-Gallery. Nov. — 1813. 47 p. 16°.
Copy: Library of Congress.
Reprinted, as a separate, 1778, 48 p., in his *Dramatic works*, Dublin, 1762–78, v. 2, *NCP; Dramatic works*, Dublin, 1778, v. 3, p. 275–324, *NCP; Dramatic works*, London, 1797, v. 2, p. 302–347, *NCP*; as a separate, 1795, 58 p., in his *Dramatic works*, London, 1809, v. 2 [no. 7], *NCP*; as a separate, 1813, 47 p., in his *Works*, New York, 1814, v. 3 [no. 3], *NCP*; and in his *Works*, ed. by John Bee, London, 1830, v. 3, p. 1–57.
Also printed in *British drama*, London, 1804, v. 3, p. 477–493, *NCO (British)*, and in *Modern British drama*, London, 1811, v. 5, p. 377–393, *NCO (Modern)*.
Reviewed in *Critical review*, London, 1778, v. 45, p. 314–315, *NAA*; and in *Monthly review*, London, v. 58, p. 240–241, *NAA*.
"A play opening like melodrama, passing into magic and ending in a scientific debate among doctors at the physicians' college. All are about to demand their rights of Parliament...the Jew won't go on the Sabbath." Produced at the Haymarket, London, May 31, 1768, with Pierce as Habakkuk. See Genest, v: 212–214.
Reviewed in *London chronicle*, London, 1768, v. 23, p. 525, * *A; London magazine*, London, 1768, v. 37, p. 317–319, * *DA*; and in *Universal museum*, London, June, 1768, p. 275–276, * *KSD*.
Dr. Last's examination before the College of Physicians, an interlude from this play, was, according to Genest, vi:454, staged at the Haymarket Theatre, London, Aug. 21, 1787. In this country it was given by the Kenna family troupe, playing as the New American Company, at Annapolis, Feb. 17, 1790.

—— The nabob; a comedy, in three acts. As it is performed at the Theatre-Royal in the Haymarket. Written by the late Samuel Foote, Esq. and now published by Mr. Colman. London: Printed by T. Sherlock, for T. Cadell, 1778. vi p., 1 l., 71 p. 8°.   NCO p.v.107

—— The nabob: a comedy, in three acts. By Samuel Foote, Esq. <first published in London, 1778.> New-York: Published by D. Longworth, At the Dramatic Repository, Shakspeare-Gallery. Dec. — 1813. 47 p. 16°.
Copy: Library of Congress.
Reprinted, as a separate, 1778, 55 p., in his *Dramatic works*, Dublin, 1762–78, v. 2, *NCP; Dramatic works*, Dublin, 1778, v. 3, p. 141–193, *NCP*; as a separate, 1778, 1 p.l., v–vi p., 1 l., 71 p., in his *Dramatic works*, London, 1778, v. 4 [no. 3], *NCP; Dramatic works*, London, 1797, v. 2, p. 256–301, *NCP*; as a separate, 1795, 59 p., in his *Dramatic works*, London, 1809, v. 2 [no. 6], *NCP*; as a separate, 1813, 47 p., in his *Works*, New York, 1814, v. 3 [no. 4], *NCP*; and in his *Works*, ed. by John Bee, London, 1830, v. 3, p. 179–237.
Reviewed in *Critical review*, London, 1778, v. 45, p. 315, *NAA*; and in *Monthly review*, London, v. 58, p. 241, *NAA*.
In this play the East India Company was the object of Foote's ridicule and castigation. Produced at the Haymarket Theatre, London, June 29, 1772, with Jacobs and Castle as Moses Mendoza and Nathaniel Bensaddi, the nabob's agents in the City. Both speak their parts in dialect.
Reviewed in *London chronicle*, London, 1772, v. 32, p. 1–2, * *A; London magazine*, London, 1772, v. 41, p. 307–310, * *DA; Town and country magazine*, London, v. 4, p. 373–375, * *DA*; and in *Universal magazine*, London, v. 50, p. 363–364, * *DA*.

FRANKLIN, ANDREW. The wandering Jew: or, Love's masquerade. A comedy, in two acts. As performed by Their Majesty's servants at the Theatre-Royal, Drury-Lane... London: Printed and pub. by G. Cawthorn, 1797. 55 p. 8°.
   NCO p.v.147
A second and a third edition were also printed the same year.
Reviewed in *Monthly review*, London, 1797, series 2, v. 24, p. 465, *NAA*; and in *Monthly visitor*, London, 1797, v. 2, p. 383–384, * *DA*.
The first English play with the Wandering Jew theme. Produced at the Drury Lane, London, May 15, 1797. J. Bannister played the part of Major Atall and assumed the disguise of the Wandering Jew to elude the vigilance of Lydia's guardian. R. Palmer, as Capt. Marall, acted the part of the Jew's attendant.
Reviewed in *Monthly mirror*, London, 1797, v. 3, p. 309–310, * *DA*; and in *Monthly visitor*, London, 1797, v. 1, p. 451–452, * *DA*.
Produced at the New Park Theatre, New York, May 2, 1798, with John Martin in the rôle of Major Atall.

Individual Plays—Earliest Times to 1837, cont'd

GALLATIN, ALBERTA. *See* sub-entry under SCOTT, SIR WALTER.

GARRICK, DAVID. The jubilee [in two parts]. facsims. (In his: Three plays, ed. Elizabeth P. Stein. New York, 1926. 8°. p. 55–111.) NCP
To accompany the Shakespeare Jubilee pageant at Drury Lane in 1769, based on the Stratford Jubilee of the same year.
Copy: Library of Congress.
The *Jubilee* was written primarily as a pageant of Shakespeare's characters and was scheduled for presentation at Stratford in Sept., 1769. The pageant was abandoned on account of the bad weather. Besides, the townspeople were hostile to the "invasion" by the London actors. It was, therefore, put on at London, at the Drury Lane, Sept. 14, 1769, and repeated yearly for many years afterwards. See *Introduction*, ibid., p. 59–64, and *Notes*, p. 105–111; also Genest, v. 252–254, 256–257. In the procession of the comedies, *The Merchant of Venice* is the third, and Shylock marches "with a knife, and bond & scales."

—— Songs, chorusses, &c., which are introduced in the new entertainment of the Jubilee, at the Theatre Royal, in Drury-Lane. London: T. Becket and P. A. De Hondt, 1770. 1 p.l., 18 p. 12°.
Without the music (by Dibdin).

—— Garrick's vagary; or, England run mad... [Six dramatic scenes in prose.] With particulars of the Stratford Jubilee. London, 1769. 8°.
Title from the British Museum catalogue.

GHERARDI DEL TESTA, TOMMASSO, CONTE. *See* sub-entry under MAID AND MAGPIE.

GOFFE, THOMAS. The Raging Tvrke, Or, Baiazet The Second. A Tragedie vvritten by Thomas Goffe, Master of Arts, and Student of Christ-Church in Oxford, and Acted by the Students of the same house. [*Two lines in Latin. Ornament*] London: Printed by Avgvst. Mathevves, for Richard Meighen. 1631. [104] p. 8°.
Dedication signed: Rich. Meighen.

—— —— London: Printed for G. Bedell and T. Collins, 1656. 113 p. 2. ed. 12°. (In his: Three excellent tragedies. London, 1656.)
Includes the dedication to The raging Turk, signed Richard Meighen, first printed in the original edition.
No female characters in this play. Goffe was a professed enemy of the female sex.

GRANVILLE, GEORGE. *See* LANSDOWNE, GEORGE GRANVILLE, BARON.

GREENE, ROBERT. Selimus. 1594. (In: The life and complete works...of Robert Greene. Edited by Alexander B. Grosart. London, 1881–86. 8°. v. 14, p. 189–291.) NCF
Huth library.
Original title: The first part of the tragicall raigne of Selimus, sometime Emperour of the Turkes, and grandfather to him that now raigneth. Wherein is showne how hee most unnaturally raised warres against his owne father Baiazet, and prevailing therein, in the end caused him to be poysoned. Also with the murthering of his two brethre, Corcut, and Acomat. As it was played by the Queenes Maiesties Players. London: Printed by Thomas Creed, dwelling in Thames Streete at the signe of the Kathren whelle, neare the olde Swanne. 1594.
First published 1594. Reprinted with a new title page, London, 1638, with addition on it, "Written by T. G.," which led Langbaine to ascribe it erroneously to Thomas Goffe. Variously attributed to Marlowe, Peele, Greene and Lodge, and R. Greene alone. Dr. A. B. Grosart claimed this play for Robert Greene and so included it in the Huth Library edition of Greene's works, v. 14. Cf. ibid., the editor's observations, v. 1, p. lxxi–lxxvii. Dr. Grosart's theory is challenged by A. W. Ward. The play was presented at the Theatre by the Queen's Company sometime between 1588 and 1592. Abraham, "a cunning Jew professing physicke" administers poison to Bajazet and Aga, at the instigation of Selimus, and dies by the same means.
Selections from act I, scene 2, are given in W. H. Williams, *Specimens of the Elizabethan drama from Lyly to Shirley*, Oxford, 1905, p. 50–55, NCO.

—— The tragical reign of Selimus, sometime emperor of the Turks; a play reclaimed for Robert Greene...ed. with a preface, notes and glossary by Alexander B. Grosart... London: J. M. Dent and Co., 1898. xxii p., 1 l., 106 p., 1 l. front. 24°. (The Temple dramatists.) NCP

—— The tragical reign of Selimus, 1594... [London: Printed for the Malone Society by Charles Whittingham & Co. at the Chiswick Press, 1909.] viii, [75] p., 4 facsims. 8°. (The Malone Society reprints, 1908.) NCO (Malone)
"Prepared by W. Bang and checked by the general editor, W. W. Greg."

—— The tragical reign of Selimus, sometime emperor of the Turks. Edited with an introduction and notes by A. F. Hopkinson. For private circulation. London: M. E. Sims & Co., 1916. 2 p.l., xxxiv p., 4 l., (1) 4–155 p. 12°.

Blass, Jakob Leonhard. Die Entwickelung der Figur des gedungenen Mörders im älteren englischen Drama bis Shakespeare... Mainz: Philipp von Zabern, 1913. 77 p., 1 l. 8°.
See p. 23–25.

Brion, Marcel. Robert Greene. (Correspondant. Paris, 1930. 8°. nouv. série, tome 282, p. 734–745.) *DM

Buland, Mable. [Its time element.] (In her: The presentation of time in the Elizabethan drama. New York, 1912. 8°. p. 254–257.) NCOD

Daniel, P. A. Locrine and Selimus. (The Athenæum. London, 1898. 4°. v. 111, p. 512.) *DA

Ehrke, Karl. Selimus. (In his: Robert Greene's Dramen. Greifswald, 1904. 8°. p. 12–13.)
NCE p.v.91
"Der ästhetische Wert des Stückes ist ein sehr geringer."

Fox, Arthur W. Tragedy as it was written. Manchester: Sherratt & Hughes, 1899. 1 p.l., 283–291 p. 8°. AGH p.v.12
Repr.: Manchester quarterly, July, 1899, v. 18, p. 283–291, *DA.

Gilbert, Hugo. Robert Greene's Selimus. Eine litteratur-historische Untersuchung. Kiel: H. Fiencke, 1899. 2 p.l., 74 p., 2 l. 8°.
Reviewed by Robert Boyle in *Englische Studien*, Leipzig, 1901, Bd. 29, p. 434–436, RNA.

Ross, Crystal Ray. The Machiavellian man in Elizabethan drama... [New York, 1921.] 135, iv f. 4°.
Typewritten copy. Master's thesis. Columbia University. M.A. theses. 1921. v. 24.

THE JEW IN ENGLISH DRAMA 21

Individual Plays—Earliest Times to 1837, cont'd

GUNNISON, BINNEY. *See* sub-entry under SCOTT, SIR WALTER.

HAINES, JOHN THOMAS. *See* sub-entry under HOGARTH, WILLIAM.

HALLIDAY, ANDREW. *See* sub-entry under SCOTT, SIR WALTER.

HARRISON, THOMAS. Belteshazzar; or, The heroic Jew. A dramatic poem. London, 1727. 82 p. 8°.
Title from Halkett and Laing.
Copy: Bodleian Library.

HAYMAN, PHILIP, AND E. SOLOMON. *See* sub-entry under SCOTT, SIR WALTER.

HILL, AARON. The walking statue; or, The devil in the wine cellar. A comedy, as it is acted at the Theatre Royal in Drury-Lane. [Dublin:] Printed in the year 1709. 24 p. 12°.
NCI p.v.5

—— —— [Dublin:] Printed in the year 1709. 1 p.l., 22 p. 12°. NCO p.v.632

—— —— As it is acted at the theatres with great applause... Dublin: H. Saunders, 1762. 22 p. 12°. NCO p.v.650
In one act of five scenes.
Reprinted in his *Dramatic works*, London, 1760, v. 1, p. 53–70, NCP.
Sprightly, in order to gain admittance into his sweetheart's home, arranges a Jewish disguise for his man Toby, who manages to bring into the lady's house a statue from a Mr. Chissel, which had been ordered by the girl's father. Toby, when asked to identify himself, replies "I am by profession a statuary, by country a Portuguese, but brought up in England; by quality a journeyman, and by religion a Jew."
First produced at the Drury Lane, Jan., 1709/10.

HOGAN, ALFREDO POSSOLO. *See* sub-entry under SCOTT, SIR WALTER.

HOGARTH, WILLIAM. The Harlot's progress.

Cibber, Theophilus. The harlot's progress; or, The ridotto al' fresco. A grotesque pantomime entertainment. As it is performed by His Majesty's company of comedians at the Theatre-Royal in Drury-Lane. Composed by Mr. Theophilus Cibber, comedian. The songs made (to old ballad tunes) by a friend. [London:] Printed for the benefit of Richard Cross the prompter, and sold at the Theatre, 1733. 12 p. 8°.
Copy: Boston Public Library.
"This entertainment is dedicated to the ingenious Mr. Hogarth (on whose celebrated designs it is plan'd)." — *p. [iii].* Dated March 31, 1733.
This is a synopsis in dramatic form of the action represented in the plates, and includes six "airs."
Produced at the Drury Lane, London, March 31, 1733, with Stoppelaer as Beau Mordecai.

Haines, John Thomas. The life of a woman, or, The curate's daughter: a pictorial drama of interest, founded on Hogarth's "Harlot's progress"... As performing at the Royal Surrey Theatre, correctly printed from the prompt copy... London: J. Pattie [1840]. xi, (1)12–56 p. 12°. (Pattie's Universal stage. no. 12.)
In three acts.
Also included in *Universal stage*, London, 1840, v. 2, no. 3 (copy in Library of Congress).
Produced at the Royal Surrey Theatre, London, April 20, 1840, with W. Smith as Malachi Benledi, a rich Jew, according to the original bill, reprinted in the play. It is there styled a village tragedy. "To point a moral e'en from basest shame... To win wild youth is here the Drama's aim." According to the reviewer in *The Times*, London, April 21, 1840, p. 5, col. 3, * A, the Jewish part was sustained by H. Vining.

The Jew decoy'd; or, The progress of a harlot. A new ballad opera of three acts. The airs set to old ballad tunes... London: E. Rayner [etc.], 1733. 53 (i.e. 55) p. folded front. 8°.
In prose and verse.
Suggested by Hogarth's famous paintings "Progress of a harlot."
Perhaps based on Breval's *Harlot's progress*.
Caption-title: The progress of a harlot. Frontispiece after Hogarth.
Without the music.
Errors in paging: p. 53–55 numbered 51–53.

—— London: Printed by W. Rayner, 1735. 48 p. 8°.
Copy: Library of the Jewish Theological Seminary of America.
The time-teller in the opening of the first act says, "From the keen satyr in sly Hogarth's prints, We own we took for most that follows — hints." In the list of the dramatis personae, the Jew is named Ben Israel. The harlot Moll speaks of him as "old Manasseh Ben Israel." He is described as carrying a stiletto, and he hints that he hails from Portugal. He is disposed of at the end of the first act, where Moll and her accomplice attack him and rob him. He is one of the first Jewish characters in English drama to speak his lines in dialect. Here are two specimens of what was later much copied and made a great deal worse: "No passion, Molly, no passion; I come a from Richmond dis morning by six o'clock, I want my breakfast very much; let us drink a de tea, and be friends..." Again, in act I, scene 6, "Den you shall sing me song, come 'tis past eleven; sing a de song and I will drink one dish of tea, and so to Shange." It was never produced.

HOLBERG, LUDVIG, BARON. Captain Bombastes Thunderton (Diederich Menschenskræk). A comedy in three acts. [Translated from the Danish by H. W. L. Hime.] (In his: Three comedies. London, 1912. 12°. p. 73–115.) NIY
The scene is Venice, about 1718. The villain is the Jew Ephraim, the custodian of a captured Christian girl. First performed in Copenhagen in 1724.

—— Ulysses von Ithacia. [Selections translated by William M. Payne.] (In: Library of the world's best literature. New York [cop. 1897]. 8°. v. 13 or 18, p. 7417–7420.) NAC
The full title translated is *Ulysses of Ithaca; or, A German comedy*, in five acts and a prologue. It is made up of a jumble of incidents connected with the Trojan war. Two Jews are among the dramatis personae. It was first produced June 1, 1724.
Holberg, although a known liberal and sympathetic to the Jews in his *Jewish history from creation to the present day*, Copenhagen, 1747, was uniformly unfriendly in regard to the Jewish characters which he introduced into his plays.
The following three comedies by him also contain minor Jewish characters: Den ellevete Juni (The eleventh of June) in five acts, produced June 11, 1723; Det Arabiske Pulver (The Arabian powder), a comedy in one act, produced Jan. 1, 1724; and Een Danske Komedies ligbegæ ngelse (A funeral of Danish comedy), a one-act afterpiece, produced Feb. 25, 1727.

Individual Plays—Earliest Times to 1837, cont'd

HOLCROFT, THOMAS. Hear both sides: a comedy, in five acts. As it is performed at the Theatre Royal, Drury-Lane... London: R. Phillips, 1803. 4 p.l., (1)6–90 p., 1 l. 2. ed. 8°.
NCO p.v.122
The compiler of the list has the first, third and fourth editions.

—— —— Philadelphia, Baltimore: J. Conrad & Co. [etc., etc.], 1803. 91(1) p., 1 l. 16°.
NCO p.v.249
For bibliographical details of the published editions see Elbridge Colby, *A Bibliography of Thomas Holcroft*, New York, 1922, p. 84, *NCE p.v. 37* or * *HND (N.Y.P.L.) p.v.3*.
In the prologue spoken by Bannister, the Transit of the play, occur the following lines: "We dread newspapers, magazines, reviews: We dread the Christians; nay, we dread the Jews." Epilogue spoken by Mrs. Jordan, Eliza in the play. The moral of the play is implied in its title. It was condemned by the critics and the author defended it in the printed preface to the play. Genest pronounces the play to be good as regards plot and language, but deficient in comic force.
First produced at the Drury Lane, London, Jan. 29, 1803. Wewitzer played the part of a bailiff and spoke his lines in dialect. A synopsis of the play and its prologue are printed in *European magazine*, London, 1803, v. 43, p. 143–144, 146–147, * *DA*.

—— The vindictive man: a comedy, in five acts, as it was performed at the Theatre Royal, Drury Lane... London: H. D. Symonds, 1806. vii(i), 84 p. 8°.
Library also has 2. ed., 1807, NCO p.v.125.
For bibliographical details of the published editions see Elbridge Colby, *A Bibliography of Thomas Holcroft*, New York, 1922, p. 86, *NCE p.v.37* or * *HND (N.Y.P.L.) p.v.3*.
In the preface to the published play the author says "*L'Heritage, conte morale et dramatique*, par M. Bret, furnished much of the character and story." Produced at the Drury Lane, Nov. 20, 1806. Reviewed in *European magazine*, London, 1806, v. 50, p. 396–398, * *DA*; and in *Monthly mirror*, London, v. 22, p. 347–348, * *DA*. Wewitzer as Abrahams acted as a Jewish dealer. In some contemporary reviews he is called Isaacs. He appears in act 3, scene 4, and throughout act 4, and speaks the usual dialect. "The part of the Jew was remarkably well supported by Wewitzer." It was played but twice, and damned. See the author's *Memoirs*, London, 1816, v. 3, p. 176–177, and Charles Lamb's *On the custom of hissing in the theatres*.

HOLFORD, MRS. MARGARET (WRENCH). Neither's the man; a comedy, in five acts: as performed at the Theatre-Royal, Chester... Chester: W. Minshull [etc., etc., 1799?]. 82 p. 8°.
A young and beautiful heiress decides that neither the effeminate lord nor the usurious Jew, both of whom are urged upon her, with equal favor, by her guardian, is the man for her. She chooses the poor suitor, who turns out to be a wealthy nobleman. The play was produced at Chester, and apparently never reached the London stage. Obviously modelled after Macklin's *Love a la mode*, including the naming of the Jewish character, Mordecai, who, in the dramatis personae, is listed as having been acted by Mr. Saunders. It was licensed on Oct. 31, 1798.
Reviewed in *Analytical review*, London, 1799, v. 29, p. 147, *NAA*; *British critic*, London, v. 14, p. 428–429, * *DA*; *Critical review*, London, series 2, v. 27, p. 236–237, *NAA*; *Monthly mirror*, London, v. 7, p. 293, * *DA*; and *New London review*, London, v. 1, p. 619, * *DA*. The last reviewer says: "The characters, humour, and incidents of the play are chiefly borrowed from other plays."

HOOK, THEODORE EDWARD. The invisible girl; a piece in one act, as performed at the Theatre Royal, Drury Lane... London: C. and R. Baldwin, 1806. vi p., 1 l., (1)10–38 p. 8°.
NCO p.v.148

—— The invisible girl; a comic piece, in one act... Printed from the acting copy, with remarks biographical and critical, by D.-G. [i.e. Geo. Daniel]... As performed at the Theatres Royal... London: John Cumberland [1840?]. 22 p. incl. front. 24°. (Cumberland's British theatre. v. 40 [no. 8].)
NCO (Cumberland)
"Neither translation, nor adaptation. It is the hint ...that is borrowed from *Le Babillard*, by C. Maurice." cf. Remarks by George Daniel, editor of the series.

—— —— London: Davidson, n. d. 22 p. incl. front. 16°. (Cumberland's British theatre. no. 322.)
Reissue of Cumberland's earlier edition.
Reviewed in *British critic*, London, 1807, v. 28, p. 198, * *DA*; and in *Monthly review*, London, series 2, v. 51, p. 212–213, *NAA*.
Produced at the Drury Lane Theatre, April 28, 1806. Mr. Webb as Moses Melchisedeck, and Bannister as Capt. All-clack, who impersonates him in dress and dialect speech. "The title has little or no reference to the play." — *Genest*. Reviewed in *European magazine*, London, 1806, v. 49, p. 371, * *DA*.
Produced at the Park Theatre, New York, Jan. 26, 1807.

HUGO, VICTOR MARIE, COMTE. Cromwell. (In his: Dramas. Boston and New York [18—?]. 12°. v. 3, p. vii–xi, 1–448.) NKP
Included also in his *Works* (International limited edition), Boston [191–?], v. 13, *NKF*, and in his *Dramatic works*, New York [1909], v. 3, p. 1–419, *NKF*.
In five acts, respectively named The conspirators, The spies, The fools, The sentinel, The workmen.
Manasseh ben Israel, who figures a great deal in this drama, is represented as actuated by mean and petty motives.

Phillips, Frederick. Cromwell; a tragedy based on Hugo's play of the same name, was produced at the Surrey Theatre, London, during the week beginning Feb. 14, 1859.
Reviewed in *Athenæum*, London, 1859, v. 33, p. 292, * *DA*; and in *Era*, London, v. 21, Feb. 20, 1859, p. 11, † *NAFA*. Whether the character of Manasseh ben Israel was retained and, if so, whether portrayed in the Hugo fashion, is not certain.

Kohut, George Alexander. Victor Hugo and the Jews; a discordant note on the occasion of his centenary, February, 1902. New York: Cameron & Co., 1902. 2 parts in 1 v. 12°.
NKD p.v.5
Repr.: American Hebrew, v. 70, p. 516–518, 601–602, * *PBD*.
Hugo's anti-Jewish allusion in his drama, *Les Burgraves*, 1843, is pointed out, but no mention is made of his *Cromwell* nor his other dramas of Jewish interest.

HUGO, VICTOR MARIE, COMTE. Mary Tudor. (In his: Dramas. Boston and New York [18—?]. 12°. v. 1, p. 1–122.) NKP
Included also in his *Works* (International limited edition), Boston [191–?], v. 12, *NKF*, and in his *Dramatic works* (translated by George Burnham Ives), New York [1909], v. 3, p. 421–524, *NKF*.
In four acts, designated respectively first, second, third day, part one, and third day, part two. Produced at the Théâtre Porte-Saint-Simon, Paris, Nov. 6, 1833, and first published Berlin, 1834.

Individual Plays—Earliest Times to 1837, cont'd

HUGO, VICTOR MARIE, COMTE. Mary Tudor, queen of England. A drama in four acts. Translated from the French... Boston, 1835. 4 pamphlets. f°. † NCOF
Manuscript. Prompter's copy.
The name Eliza P. Asbury appears on the cover.
The names of an acting cast are illegibly given, but the compiler has not been able to identify the production as to place and date.
The scene is London, in 1553. Among the characters is a Jew, who describes himself as a moneylender and silversmith from Brussels — in possession of important state documents.

IFFLAND, AUGUST WILHELM. Crime from ambition: a play, in five acts. Translated from the German of Wilhelm Augustus Iffland, by Maria Geisweiler... London: Printed for C. Geisweiler [etc.] by G. Sidney, 1800. 3 p.l., 5–131 p. 8°.
Copy: Library of Congress.
Reviewed by Za. in *Neue allgemeine deutsche Bibliothek*, Anhang zu Band 29–68, Abtheil. 2, Berlin, 1803, p. 842, *NAA*.
Iffland, at the age of eighteen, on March 15, 1777, played professionally the part of the Jew in Johann Jacob Engel's *Der Diamant*. The original German was first published in 1784 and, under its title of *Verbrechen aus Ehrsucht*, was staged at the k. k. National-Hoftheater, Vienna, 1784.
There is no record of an English production.

THE ISRAELITES; or, The pampered nabob [in two acts]. (In: H. R. S. van der Veen, Jewish characters in eighteenth century English fiction and drama. Groningen, 1935. 8°. p. 270–290.)
* PZB
Printed from Larpent MS. 39 M, in the Henry E. Huntington Library.
Produced at the Covent Garden, London, April 1, 1785, with Wewitzer as Mr. Israel and Bonner as his profligate son, Enoch. The *European magazine*, London, 1785, v. 7, p. 284–285, * *DA*, in its review of the piece, states: "written by the late Dr. Smollett. It contained many strokes of humour peculiar to the author... it was very ill attended, and but indifferently received." Veen, *supra*, p. 198–209, concludes that it is not by Smollett, but by "a dramatist who was influenced by Joshua Manasseh in [Smollett's novel] *Count Fathom*." The delineation of Mr. Israel is favorable to the Jew, nine years ahead of Cumberland's *The Jew*. No dialect is used in his speech and Veen calls it "the first feeble attempt in English drama to depict the Jew as a serious character." See also *Town and country magazine*, London, 1785, v. 17, p. 183, * *DA*.

JACK DRUM'S ENTERTAINMENT. Iacke Drums Enter- | tainment: | Or | The Comedie | Of Pasquill *and* Katherine. | *As it hath bene sundry times plaide by the* | *Children of Powles*. | [*Printer's device*] | At London | Printed for Richard Oliue, dwelling in Long | Lane. 1601. [70] p. 4°.
Ascribed to John Marston.
Copy: Library of Congress.

—— ... Jack Drum's entertainment. 1601. [London?] Issued for subscribers by the editor of the Tudor facsimile texts, 1912. 3 p.l., facsim.: 1 l., [68] p. 4°. (The Tudor facsimile texts...)
"This facsimile is from a copy of the earliest known edition of 1601."
Copy: Library of Congress.

—— —— At London, Printed for Richard Oliue, dwelling in Long Lane. 1601. [Amersham, Eng.: Issued for subscribers by John S. Farmer, 1913.] 1 p.l., [68] p. 8°. (Old English drama. Students' facsimile edition.) NCP
Also printed, with introduction and notes, in Richard Simpson, editor, *The School of Shakspere*, London, 1878, v. 2, p. 125–208, * *NDD* (Simpson).

Jones, Fred L. Echoes of Shakspere in later Elizabethan drama. (Modern Language Association of America. Publications. Menasha, Wis., 1930. 8°. v. 45, p. 791–798.) RAA
Parallels are drawn between the language and manners of Mamon in *Jack Drum's entertainment* and Shylock in *The Merchant of Venice*.

JACKSON, JOHN P. *See* sub-entry under SCOTT, SIR WALTER.

JEPHSON, ROBERT. Julia; or, The Italian lover. A tragedy, as it is acted at the Theatre-Royal in Drury-Lane... London: C. Dilly, 1787. 4 p.l., 89 p., 1 l. 8°. NCO p.v.208
Prologue, by Edmund Malone. Epilogue, by John Courtenay.
A tragedy of passion. Manoa, an artist jeweller, who had been unjustly driven out of Genoa, is rescued at sea by a nobleman, brought back to the city, treated kindly by his rescuers, and helps to unravel the mystery developed in the plot. Produced at the Drury Lane, London, April 14, 1787, with J. Aikin as Manoa. Reviewed in *European magazine*, London, 1787, v. 11, p. 289–290, * *DA*; and in *New lady's magazine*, London, 1787, v. 2, p. 222–223, * *DA*. See also Genest, VI:433–434.

JERROLD, DOUGLAS WILLIAM. The painter of Ghent; a play in one act... As performed at the Strand Theatre. London: John Duncombe and Co. [preface 1836.] 23 p. front. 24°.

—— —— Clyde, Ohio: A. D. Ames [187–?]. 12 p. 12°. (Ames' series of standard and minor drama. no. 29.)

—— —— Clyde, Ohio: Ames Publishing Co. [189–?] 15 p. 12°.
Also published in *Lacy's acting edition of plays*, v. 92, *NCO (Lacy)*.
Reviewed in *Monthly repository*, London, 1836, new series, v. 10, p. 377–379, *ZXDA*.
A curious tragedy in which one of the characters is old Ichabod, a Jewish picture dealer, played by Mitchell. It is called a burletta of serious interest, but lacks a sustained plot. Produced at the Strand Theatre, London, April 25, 1836. Reviewed in *Literary gazette*, London, 1836, p. 283–284, * *DA*; and *The Times*, London, April 26, 1836, p. 6, col. 4, * *A*. It was revived at Edinburgh in Aug., 1837. Cf. review in *Dramatic spectator*, Edinburgh, 1837, no. 6, p. 48, *NCOA*, in which the opinion is expressed "it will never do. It is hopelessly dull — all talkee, talkee, without action."
It was produced at Burton's Theatre, New York, June 19, 1855, with Humphrey Bland as Ichabod.

THE JERUSALEM infirmary; or, A journey to the valley of Jehosaphat. A farce. [*Design*] Venice: Printed in the year MDCCXLIX. 16 p. 8°.
"To be acted next *Southwark* Fair."
"Dramatis Personae, as in the Print to which the Reader is referr'd."
Copy, probably unique: Henry E. Huntington Library.
Photostated copy: Collection of the compiler.
"It is a piece of the most unintelligible, and at the same time abusive, jargon ever seen and is written with a view to expose and calumniate a number of private personal characters among the Jews... Never was, nor ever is, intended to be acted." — Baker's *Biographia dramatica*.
Venice, in the imprint, is not Venice but, probably, London.

Individual Plays—Earliest Times to 1837, cont'd

THE JERUSALEM infirmary..., *continued*

The plot, in one act, is based on the print mentioned above (not vice versa). The print is described in British Museum, *Catalogue of prints and drawings, Division 1, Political and personal satires*, v. 3, part 1, p. 791–793 (no. 3106), MDE. It is reproduced by Alfred Rubens, in his *Anglo-Jewish portraits*, London, 1935, facing p. 124, * PWW. Rubens, ibid., p. 119–123, gives a historical sketch of the circumstances which in 1749 evoked this pasquil and identifies the prototypes of all the dramatis personae.
On the basis of Rubens, here cited, H.R.S. van der Veen reconstructed fairly accurately the plot and dialogue of the play in his *Jewish characters in eighteenth century English fiction and drama*, Groningen, 1935, p. 123–132, * PZB.
None of those who wrote about this lampoon, with the possible exception of Baker in his *Biographia dramatica*, ever saw the text of it.

THE JEW; a play, the subject of which was "the greedinesse of worldly chusers and the bloody mindes of usurers," is mentioned in Stephen Gosson's *School of abuse*, 1579, as having been "showne at the Bull."
See Edward Scott, "Shakespeareana," in *Athenæum*, London, 1881, v. 78, p. 14, * DA.

Biesecker, C. E. A comparison of *The Jew* and the *Merchant of Venice*. 1927.
Ms. thesis, unpublished, Ohio State University Library.
Title from S. A. Tannenbaum, *Christopher Marlowe, a concise bibliography*, item 436.

Small, Samuel Asa. 'The Jew.' (Modern language review. London, 1931. 8°. v. 26, p. 281–287.) NAA
An analysis of the probable incidents which formed its plot.

THE JEW decoy'd. *See* sub-entry under HOGARTH, WILLIAM.

JOHNSON, PHILIP, AND HOWARD AGG. *See* subentry under SHERIDAN, RICHARD BRINSLEY BUTLER.

JONATHAS THE JEW *(Miracle-play)*. [The conversion of Jonathas the Jew by the miracle of the blessed sacrament, reproduced in facsimile from ms. F. 4. 20 in the Library of Trinity College, Dublin.] 1 p.l., facsim.: 37 mounted l. f°. ([The Modern Language Association of America. Collection of photographic facsimiles. no. 7. 1923.]) † NACM (Modern)
The original, a paper ms., 21 x 15cm. is included in a quarto volume of 8 miscellaneous 16th–17th century mss. listed as no. 652 in the *Catalogue of manuscripts in the Library of Trinity College, Dublin*, comp. by T. K. Abbott (Dublin [etc.], 1900).

—— <The play of the sacrament.> (In: Non-cycle mystery plays, together with the Croxton play of the sacrament, re-edited by Osborn Waterhouse. London, 1909. 8°. p. 54–87.) NCE (Early)
Early English Text Society. Extra series. no. 104. In 927 lines.
Editorial introduction, p. liv–lxiv.
On the basis of this edition, collated with the earlier editions, it is reprinted in J. Q. Adams, editor, *Chief pre-Shakespearean dramas*, Boston [1924], p. 243–262, * R–NCO.

—— The play of the sacrament [Croxton]. A Middle-English drama, edited from a manuscript in the Library of Trinity College, Dublin, with a preface and glossary by W[hitley] S[tokes]. Berlin: Published for the Philological Society, 1862. 54 p. 8°. NAFM (Play)
Text of the play, in 1005 lines, p. 7–44.
The colophon reads: Thus endyth the play of the blyssyd sacrament whyche myracle was don in the forest of Aragon   In the famous Cite Eraclea the yere of ow^r lord God .M^1 cccc.lxi. to whom be honow^r amen
Reprinted from Philological Society, London, *Transactions*, Berlin, 1860–61, Appendices, p. 101–152, RAA, where it appeared for the first time.
Textual emendations for this edition are given by F. Holthausen in *Englische Studien*, Leipzig, 1892, Bd. 16, p. 150–151, RNA; and in *Anglia*, Halle a. S., 1893, Bd. 15, p. 198–203, RNA.
On the basis of Stokes' text, collated with the ms., J. M. Manly reprinted it in his *Specimens of the pre-Shaksperean drama*, Boston, 1897, v. 1, p. 239–276.

Barns, Florence Elberta. The background and sources of the Croxton play of the sacrament. [Abstract of thesis.] (University of Chicago. Abstracts of theses. Humanistic series. Chicago [cop. 1928]. 8°. v. 5, p. 443–446.) STG (Chicago)

The Play of the sacrament [with extracts]. (Saturday review. London, 1862. f°. v. 13, p. 159–161.) * DA
The writer calls it the oldest existing secular drama.
Deals with the miracle or legend of the desecration of the Host by Jews (five are named: Jonathan, Jason, Jasdon, Masphat and Malchus). "The handwriting [of the ms.] is of the latter half of the fifteenth century; and the scribe (the initials of whose name are R. C.) probably finished his work soon after the year 1461—the date given at the end of the play as that of the occurrence on which it is founded." — *From the Introduction.*

KELSALL, CHARLES. The first sitting of the committee on the proposed monument to Shakspeare. Carefully taken in short-hand by Zachary Craft [pseud.]... Cheltenham: Printed for G. A. Williams, 1823. 88 p., 2 l. 16°. * NCLF
Melchisedech Levi, residing at no. 239 Old Jewry, at a meeting arranged to raise funds for a Shakespeare monument, "will shuscribe noothing" for the creator of "King Sheelock." See p. 64–65.

KENNEY, JAMES. Ella Rosenberg: a melodrama. In two acts. As it is performed at the Theatre Royal, Drury Lane... London: Longman, Hurst, Rees, and Orme, 1807. 2 p.l., 41 p., front. (port.) 8°. NCO p.v.76

—— —— Prompter's copy; ms. notes. Lacks plate. NCOF

—— ...Ella Rosenberg, a grand melodrama, in two acts. Written by Mr. Kenny. As it is performed at the Theatre Royal, Drury Lane. London: J. Scales [1807?]. 26 p. incl. col'd front. 12°.
At head of title: Scales's edition.
Copy: Library of Congress.

Individual Plays—Earliest Times to 1837, cont'd

KENNEY, JAMES. Ella Rosenberg; a melodrama, in two acts. As it is performed at the Theatre-Royal, Drury Lane... New York: Published by David Longworth, at the Dramatic Repository, Shakspeare-Gallery, 1808. 35 p. 24°. NCO p.v.446
No American cast is given.

—— —— Boston: West & Richardson [18—?]. 35 p. 24°. NCO p.v.407

—— —— Prompter's copy; interleaved ms. notes. NCOF

—— —— The whole of the stage business, correctly marked and arranged by J. B. Wright ... Boston: W. V. Spencer [1856?]. 26 p. 12°. (Spencer's Boston theatre. [v. 14,] no. 112.) NCOF
Prompter's copy; interleaved ms. notes.
Two English, and eight American, casts are given. Also published in Mrs. Elizabeth Inchbald, *A Collection of farces and other afterpieces*, London, 1809, v. 1, p. 187–223, *NCO (Inchbald), Cumberland's British theatre*, v. 27, *NCO (Cumberland)*, and *French's standard drama, the acting edition*, no. 289. Reviewed in *Annual review*, London, 1808, v. 7, p. 571, *NAA*.
First produced at the Drury Lane, London, Nov. 19, 1807. De Camp as Col. Mountfort, in disguise as a Jewish messenger (act I, scene 1) from "Isaac, the picture merchant," comes to Ella with a commission for a painting. Speaks the usual dialect. Reviewed in *European magazine*, London, v. 52, p. 392–393, * *DA*; *Monthly mirror*, London, new series, v. 2, p. 351–352, * *DA*; and in *The Times*, London, Nov. 20, 1807, p. 3, col. 1, * *A*.
Produced at the Park Theatre, New York, June 15, 1808, with Robertson as Col. Mountfort. In Philadelphia it was seen at the Chestnut Street Theatre, Nov. 27 and Dec. 4, 1809. An abstract and a review are given in *Mirror of taste*, Philadelphia, 1810, v. 1, p. 69–71, 74–76, *MWA*.

KENRICK, WILLIAM. The duellist; a comedy. As it is acted at the Theatre Royal; in Covent Garden. Written by W. Kenrick, LL.D. London: T. Evans [1773]. 6 p.l., 80 p., 1 l. 8°.
* KL (Bickerstaffe)
Bound with: I. Bickerstaffe, Doctor Last in his chariot. London, 1773.

—— —— The 2d ed. London: T. Evans, 1773. 2 p.l., x p., 1 l., 80 p., 1 l. 8°.
Copy: Library of Congress.
Reviewed in *Gentleman's magazine*, London, 1773, v. 43, p. 610–611, * *DA*; and in *Monthly review*, London, v. 49, p. 396, *NAA*.
Based in part on Fielding's novel *Amelia*. "This hapless comedy insulted taste continuously; the incidents were few and detached from each other." It intended to ridicule and discourage the prevalent custom of duelling. Act III, scene 3, represents a levee with "Jew brokers and others." It was produced at the Covent Garden, London, Nov. 20, 1773. Genest says that it was "acted but once." Thompson and Holtom played the part of the brokers. Reviewed in *London chronicle*, London, 1773, v. 34, p. 501, * *A*; and in *London magazine*, London, 1773, v. 42, p. 524–526, * *DA*.

KILLIGREW, THOMAS. Thomaso; or, The wanderer. A comedy. The scene Madrid. Written in Madrid... In two parts. London: Printed by J. M. for Henry Herringman, 1663. (In his: Comedies and tragedies. London, 1664. 4°. p. 311–382.)
Copy: Harvard College Library.
The scene is Madrid. There are introduced two Jewish female monstrosities, a dwarf and her sister, an overgrown giantess, accompanied by a guardian of their faith. "Two sisters came from Mexico: Jews, 'tis thought of vast Fortunes, no wonder [with] a Guardian of the same Tribe, though the Rogue eats Bacon; their Father and Families were both drown'd coming from the Indies; they are worth a million of Crowns." — Act IV, sc. 2, first part. They are both married off to Edwardo and Ferdinando, two adventurers.
For possible sources of the play, a synopsis and criticism, see Alfred Harbage, *Thomas Killigrew, cavalier dramatist*, Philadelphia, 1930, p. 218–231, *AN*.
Cf. Aphra Behn's *The Second part of The Rover*.

KNIPE, CHARLES. A city ramble: or, The humours of the compter. As it is acted at the theatre in Lincoln's-Inn-Fields... London: E. Curll [etc.], 1715. 3 p.l., 57 p., front. 12°.
A scurrilous play, aimed chiefly against the Quakers. Scene is laid in a night court, crowded with types of London night life. Among them is a country justice, a Presbyterian parson, a Quaker, and one Mordecai, styled a French Jew, on charge of drunkenness. "This farce has not even the shadow of a plot, but the dialogue is written with a tolerable degree of low humour." It was produced at Lincoln's Inn Fields, June 2, 1715, with Knap as Mordecai. It was reprinted in 1736 and revived at the Covent Garden, March 27 or 28, 1736.
Nicoll records *The Humours of the compter*, London, 1717, 12°, produced in November of that year, as being most likely Knipe's piece.

KOTZEBUE, AUGUST FRIEDRICH FERDINAND VON. Family distress; or, Self immolation. A play, in three acts, by Augustus von Kotzbue. As it is now performing *verbatim* from this translation with universal applause, at the Theatre Royal, in the Hay Market. Faithfully translated from the German by Henry Neuman, Esq. [London:] Printed for R. Phillips, sold by H. D. Symonds [etc.], 1799. vii(i), 49 p. 8°. NCO p.v.71

—— Self immolation; or, The sacrifice of love. A play, in three acts: by Augustus von Kotzebue. Faithfully translated from the German by Henry Neuman, Esq. London: Printed for R. Phillips, sold by H. D. Symonds [etc.], 1799. vii(i), 49 p. 8°.
Reviewed in *Monthly mirror*, London, 1799, v. 8, p. 33, * *DA*.

—— Boston: Printed for W. P. and L. Blake, at the Boston book-store, Cornhill. 1799. 57 p. 12°.
Copy: Library of Congress.

—— Self immolation: or, The sacrifice of love. A play in three acts. Translated from the German of Kotzebue. New-York: Printed for Charles Smith and S. Stephens. 1800. 54 p. 8°.
Translated by Henry Neuman. * KD
Also printed in his *A Selection of the best plays*, London, 1800.
Produced at the Haymarket Theatre, London, June 15, 1799, with Waldron as the Jew, whom Kotzebue again represents as kind hearted when most of the Christian characters are not. Reviewed in *European magazine*, London, 1799, v. 35, p. 404–405, * *DA*.
Under the title of *Self immolation* it was produced by Dunlap in New York, Nov. 29, 1799, with Jefferson as the Jew. Neither Seilhammer nor Brede record a production of it outside of New York.

Individual Plays—Earliest Times to 1837, cont'd

KOTZEBUE, AUGUST FRIEDRICH FERDINAND VON. Lovers' vows; or, The child of love. A play, in five acts. Translated from the German of Augustus von Kotzebue: with a brief biography of the author, by Stephen Porter... London: Printed for J. Parsons, and sold by J. Hatchard [etc.], 1798. 2 p.l., vii(i), 111 p. 8°.
Copy: Library of Congress.

—— Lovers' vows; a play in five acts. Performing at the Theatre Royal, Covent-Garden. From the German of Kotzebue, by Mrs. Inchbald... London: G. G. and J. Robinson, 1798. 1 p.l., iv p., 1 l., 90 p., 1 l. 5. ed. 12°.   NCO p.v.70

—— The natural son; a play, in five acts, by Augustus von Kotzebue... Being the original of Lovers' vows, now performing, with universal applause, at the Theatre Royal, Covent Garden. Translated from the German by Anne Plumptre... who has prefixed a preface, explaining the alterations in the representation; and has also annexed a life of Kotzebue. London: Printed for R. Phillips: sold by H. D. Symonds [etc.], 1798. 1 p.l., vii(i), 83 p. 8°.

—— —— Dublin: H. Fitzpatrick, 1798. xi(i), (1)14–108 p. 12°.
"The translation here given is from the genuine Leipsick edition, published...in 1791." p. xi.
This translation is also printed in his *A Selection of the best plays*, London, 1800.

—— Lovers' vows; or, The natural son. A drama, in five acts. Translated from the German...by Benjamin Thompson, Esq. London: Printed by T. Maiden for Vernor and Hood, 1800. 2 p.l., 99 p., front. 8°. (In: Benjamin Thompson, translator, The German theatre. 1801. v. 2 [no. 1].)
Also printed in the 1806 edition.
Reprinted in Alfred Bates, editor, *The Drama*, London, 1904, v. 21, p. 143–220, NAF.
This translation reviewed in *European magazine*, London, 1800, v. 37, p. 302, *DA*.

—— —— Baltimore: Printed for Thomas, Andrews & Butler, by John W. Butler, corner Gay & Water Streets, 1802. 66 p. 12°.
NGB p.v.172

—— Lovers' vows... from the German... by Mrs. Inchbald. London: Longman, Hurst, Rees, and Orme, 1805. vi p., 1 l., 66 p., 1 l. 5. ed. 12°.   NAC p.v.217

—— Lovers' vows: a play, in five acts, altered from the German of Kotzebue, by Mrs. Inchbald... Printed from the acting copy, with remarks, biographical and critical [by D.—G.] ... As now performed at the Theatres Royal... London: J. Cumberland, n.d. 58 p. incl. front. 16°. (Cumberland's British theatre. v. 17 [no. 7].)   NCO (Cumberland)
This translation is also printed in *The London stage*, v. 3, NCO (London), in *Select London stage*, [no. 41], NCO (Select) and in Mrs. Elizabeth Inchbald, *The British theatre*, v. 23, NCO (Inchbald).

—— Lovers vows; a play, in five acts. From the German of Rotzebue [!]. By William Dunlap. As performed at the New-York Theatre. New-York: Published by David Longworth, At the Dramatic Repository Shakspeare-Gallery. Feb.—1814. 74 p. 24°.   *KL
An adaptation of *The natural son*, Anne Plumptre's translation of Kotzebue's *Das Kind der Liebe*.

—— Lovers' vows; a play, in five acts. Altered from the translations of Mrs. Inchbald and Benjamin Thompson; by J. H. Payne. Baltimore: Printed by G. Dobbin and Murphy, 1809. vii(i), (1)10–90 p. 16°.   *KL
Produced for the first time, at the Liebhabertheater, Reval, February 10, 1790.
"A Jew as a kindly passer-by, who gives a coin to a destitute woman. The heart and the creed have no concern with each other." — Act I.
The Inchbald translation was produced at the Covent Garden, London, Oct. 11, 1798. Reviewed in *European magazine*, London, 1798, v. 34, p. 255–258, *DA*, where are given the Prologue, written by John Taylor and spoken by Murray, and the Epilogue, written by Thomas Palmer, and spoken by Munden. These are not included in all the printed editions listed here.
The Inchbald version was staged in Philadelphia, May 24, 1799. Dunlap's version was produced at the Park Theatre, New York, March 11, 1799, with Miller as the Jew.

Dodds, Madeleine Hope. 'Lovers' vows.' (Library. London, 1917. 8°. series 3, v. 8, p. 1–23.)
*HA

Reitzel, William. Mansfield Park and Lovers' vows. (Review of English studies. London, 1933. 8°. v. 9, p. 451–456.)   RNA
What it was in the play which made it so shocking to the political and social views of that time.

KRASIŃSKI, ZYGMUNT, HRABIA. The undivine comedy. (In his: The undivine comedy and other poems. Translated by Martha Walker Cook. Philadelphia, 1875. 12°. p. 173–274.)
**QPH
First published anonymously in Paris, 1835, under its Polish title *Nie-boska komedyja*.
"Translation collated from the version in German by R. Bartonicki, Leipsic, 1841; from the version in French in the Revue des deux mondes, Oct. 1, 1846; and from that published by Ladislas Mickiewicz, in Paris, 1869; 'Œuvres complètes du Poëte Anonyme.'"
Pages 41–52 are an analysis of the play by the translator, extracted from *Les Slaves*, a course of lectures delivered before the Collège de France (1842–43), by Adam Mickiewicz.
A leading character, called Neophyte, chief of a band of Jews newly baptized, is introduced. The Neophytes are first discovered studying the Talmud, singing in chorus a song of praise to Jehovah, and heaping curses upon the Christian nobles. The translator in the *Revue des deux mondes* notes that "it is the Frankists, and not the genuine Hebrews, whom our author here depicts."
A critical synopsis, with numerous translated extracts, is given by Monica M. Gardner, who regards this play as the portrayal of an imaginary conflict between Aristocracy and Democracy, in her *The Anonymous poet of Poland; Zygmunt Krasinski*, Cambridge, 1919, p. 92–134, *QPH*.
Six selections in this translation are given in *Library of the world's best literature*, v. 15 or 22, p. 8737–8745, NAC.

—— The un-divine comedy, by Zygmunt Krasiński, translated by Harriette E. Kennedy, B.A., and Zofia Umińska; preface by G. K. Chesterton, introduction by Arthur Górski.

Individual Plays—Earliest Times to 1837, cont'd

London: G. G. Harrap & Co., Ltd.: Warsaw: Książnica polska [1924]. xvii p., 1 l., 111(1) p. 8°.   *QPK
Printed in Poland.
The Neophytes are, in this translation, called "The baptized Jews." G. K. Chesterton, in his Preface, p. ix, remarks: "It is notable that it is especially a conspiracy of Jews who do not call themselves Jews ... The whole story of the popular revolt begins in a sort of secret Sanhedrim; in which these Jews plot the destruction of our society almost in the exact terms which have since been attributed to the Elders of Zion... Krasinski must have perceived this element of Bolshevism, either because it was quite obvious even then in eastern Europe, or because he was a man of extraordinary penetration and prevision."
Orval; or, The Fool of time, London, 1869, by the first earl of Lytton, is based on this play, but differs considerably from the Polish original. The characters of Jewish interest are omitted.

LACY, MICHAEL ROPHINO. *See* sub-entry under SCOTT, SIR WALTER.

LACY, THOMAS HAILES. *See* sub-entry under SCRIBE, AUGUSTIN EUGÈNE.

LANSDOWNE, GEORGE GRANVILLE, BARON. The Jew of Venice. A comedy. As it is acted at the theatre in Little-Lincolns-Inn-Fields, by His Majesty's servants. London: Printed for Ber. Lintott, 1701. 4 p.l., 46 p., 1 l. 4°.   *KC

──── ──── London: Printed for Bernard Lintot [etc.], 1732. 4 p.l., [174]–175, 175–226 p., 1 l. front. 12°.
Copy: Harvard College Library.
Reprinted in his *Three plays,* London, 1713, p. 171–239; and in his *Genuine works in verse and prose,* London, 1732, v. 2, p. 129–221, and London, 1736, v. 3, p. 107–177.
Jaggard, *Shakespeare bibliography,* p. 394, lists seven other editions, between 1711 and 1736.
An adaptation of Shakespeare's *Merchant of Venice,* in a prologue (by Bevill Higgons), five acts and an epilogue. A Masque of Peleus and Thetis is introduced, between acts II and III, during the performance of which Shylock, supping at a separate table, drinks a toast to his lady-love Money. Baker's *Biographia Dramatica* regards this interlude as "a happy thought." Prof. A. W. Ward calls it "a hash, prepared and announced in a spirit of convinced superiority." The prologue announces that "the first rude sketches Shakespear's pencil drew, but all the Shining Masterstroaks are new." Shylock, played by Dogget, is a comic character ("Today we punish a stock-jobbing Jew") and this conception ruled the stage till Macklin's memorable version of Shylock in 1741. Mrs. Bracegirdle played Portia, and Mrs. Porter, Jessica. The profits of the play were given to Dryden's family.

Handasyde, Elizabeth. 'The Jew of Venice.' (In her: Granville the polite. Oxford, 1933. 8°. p. 54–71.)   AN (Lansdowne)

Spencer, Hazelton. Granville's *The Jew of Venice.* (In his: Shakespeare improved. Cambridge, 1927. 8°. p. 338–344.)   *R-*NDB

Wilson, J. Harold. Granville's "stock-jobbing Jew." (Philological quarterly. Iowa City, Iowa, 1934. 8°. v. 13, p. 1–15.)   NAA

Wood, Frederick T. The Merchant of Venice in the eighteenth century. (English studies. Amsterdam, 1933. 8°. v. 15, p. 209–218.) RNA

LAURENT, MADAME, AND W. H. OXBERRY. ...The Truand chief! Or, The provost of Paris! A melo drama in three acts... The only edition correctly marked, by permission, from the prompter's book... London: J. Duncombe & Co. [1839.] 32 p. incl. front. 24°.   NCO p.v.744
At head of title: Duncombe's edition.
A melodrama about a Jewish chief of brigands and his sister wronged by the "provost of Paris." Produced at the Victoria Theatre, London, Oct. 9, 1837, with Denvil as Zarac, the chief, and Mrs. Hooper as Zabina. In the cast were also Emanuel, their father, and a sister, Sarah.

LEE, NELSON. *See* sub-entry under MAID AND MAGPIE.

LENZ, JOHANN REINHOLD. *See* sub-entry under SCOTT, SIR WALTER.

LEO, MRS. Salomme and Eleazer; an Oriental dramatic poem [in three acts]. The event supposed to have happened in the time of the primitive Christians; the scene in Palestine on the banks of the Jordan, by a lady of Chester [Mrs. Leo]. Chester: J. Monk, 1785. 2 p.l., iii(i), 24 [correctly 28] p. 4°.

LEROY-DENIS, JEANNE. *See also* sub-entry under SCOTT, SIR WALTER.

LESSING, GOTTHOLD EPHRAIM. The Jews; a comedy in one act. (In his: Dramatic works, ed. by Ernest Bell. London, 1878. 8°. p. 185–217.)
Written in Berlin in 1749. It first appeared in his *Schriften,* Teil 4, Berlin: C. F. Voss, 1754; and was issued separately for the first time as publication no. 10, by the Soncino-Gesellschaft der Freunde des jüdischen Buches, Berlin, 1929, *NGC.*
An early English synopsis of it, which translates the title as "Mock-Jews," is given in *Monthly magazine,* London, 1806, v. 21, p. 401, * *DA.*
Also printed in the edition of 1909, [v. 2,] Comedies, p. 185–217, NGC.

Abrahams, Israel. Lessing's first Jewish play. (In his: By-paths in Hebraic bookland. Philadelphia, 1920. 8°. p. 166–170.)   *PAT

Kies, Paul Philemon. Lessing's relation to early English sentimental comedy. (Modern Language Association of America. Publications. Menasha, Wis., 1932. 8°. v. 47, p. 807–826.)   RAA
"In the present article I hope to show that Lessing's Der Freigeist (1749) and Die Juden (1749) were influenced by early English sentimental comedy."

──── The sources of Lessing's *Die Juden.* (Philological quarterly. Iowa City, 1927. 8°. v. 6, p. 406–410.)   NAA
"*The relapse* [by Vanbrugh] and *The Beaux stratagem* [by Farquhar] are the chief sources of *Die Juden.*"

Mersand, Joseph. Lessing and the Jews. (Jewish outlook. New York, 1937. f°. v. 2, Dec., 1937, p. 5–9.)

Zinnecker, W. D. Lessing the dramatist. (German quarterly. Lancaster, 1929. 8°. v. 2, p. 48–53.)   RLA
A radio address broadcasted Jan. 27, 1929, by the Permanent Commission for Better Understanding between Jews and Christians in America.

Individual Plays—Earliest Times to 1837, cont'd

LESSING, GOTTHOLD EPHRAIM. Nathan the Wise. A philosophical drama. From the German of G. E. Lessing... Translated into English by R. E. Raspe. London: Printed for J. Fielding, 1781. 2 p.l., 103 p. 8°.
In five acts.
"Rudolf Eric Raspe, the original of the character whom Scott so mercilessly caricatures as Dousterswivel in his novel 'The Antiquary,' was not only the author of 'Baron Münchausen,' but was also the first translator into English of Lessing's 'Nathan der Weise' (London, 1781)."— Israel Abrahams, *Bypaths in Hebraic bookland*, p. 194.
Raspe has prefixed a Preface to his play — referring to the injustice meted out to the Jewish race, and the influence which Shakespeare's character of Shylock had in England. He adds that the purpose of the translation was not for representation but to serve as an antidote against the rancor of religious bigotry, with which the Jews were treated. It is extremely rare, and unknown to Genest.
Reviewed in *Critical review*, London, 1781, v. 52, p. 236, *NAA*. ("A heap of unintelligible jargon very badly translated"); *European magazine*, London, v. 1, p. 56–57, * *DA*; and in *Monthly review*, London, v. 66, p. 307–308, *NAA*.

—— Nathan the Wise; a dramatic poem. Written originally in German... Norwich [Eng.]: Printed by Stevenson and Matchett in 1791 and published in 1805 by R. Philips, London. 4 p.l., (1)6–293 p. 12°.   NCO p.v.81
The translation by Wm. Taylor.
"The translation... was undertaken in March, 1790, when questions of toleration were much afloat."— *Translator*.
The compiler has a large-paper copy, interleaved.

—— Nathan the Wise; a dramatic poem in five acts...translated by W. Taylor. (In his: Nathan the Wise...Emilia Galotti. Leipzig, 1868. 12°. p. 1–176.)
Collection of German authors. v. 9.

—— Nathan the Wise; a dramatic poem in five acts. Translated by William Taylor of Norwich, from the German of Lessing. Boston [etc.]: Educational Publishing Company, n.d. 192 p. 16°.
Introduction by H. M., p. 5–10.
Copy: Library of the Jewish Theological Seminary of America.
This Taylor translation was reviewed in *Annual review*, London, 1805, v. 4, p. 634–639, *NAA*; *British critic*, London, v. 27, p. 549–550, * *DA*; by F. Jeffrey in *Edinburgh review*, Edinburgh, v. 8, p. 148–154, * *DA*; *Monthly review*, London, series 2, v. 49, p. 243–248, *NAA*; and in *Retrospective review*, London, v. 10, p. 265–285, * *DA*.

—— Nathan the Wise; a dramatic poem, in five acts... Translated from the German, with a biography of Lessing, and a critical survey of his position, writings, etc., by Adolphus Reich. London: A. W. Bennett, 1860. xxxv(i), 219(1) p. 12°.

—— Nathan the Wise; a dramatic poem.. translated by Ellen Frothingham, preceded by a brief account of the poet and his works and followed by Kuno Fischer's essay on the poem. New York: H. Holt and Company [cop. 1867]. xxiii, 259 p. 12°.   NGC

—— —— 2d ed., rev. New York: Leypoldt & Holt, 1868. xxiii, 259 p. 12°. ([Library of foreign poetry. III.])

—— —— 3d ed., rev. New York: H. Holt and Company, 1873. xxiii, 259 p. 12°. ([Library of foreign poetry. III.])
Copy: Library of Congress.
Reprinted in G. A. Kohut, *A Hebrew anthology*, Cincinnati, 1913, v. 2, p. 1237–1329, * *PSO*.
Reviewed in *The Athenæum*, London, 1868, v. 52, p. 250–251, * *DA*; *Atlantic monthly*, Boston, v. 21, p. 250–252, * *DA*; and in *North American review*, New York, v. 106, p. 704–712, * *DA*.

—— Nathan the Wise, a dramatic poem... From the German. With an introduction on Lessing and the "Nathan": its antecedents, character and influence. [By R. Willis, M.D.] London: N. Trübner and Co., 1868. 1 p.l., xxxviii p., 1 l., 214 p. 12°.
The translator's name is given on the t.-p., in ms., where it usually appears in print.

—— Nathan, the Wise. A dramatic poem of five acts, by Lessing. Translated into English prose by Dr. Isidor Kalisch. New York: Waldheimer & Zenn, 1869. 2 p.l., ix p., 1 l., (1)6–212 p., 1 l. 12°.   8–NGC

—— Nathan the Wise; a drama, in five acts, by E. Lessing. Abridged and translated from the German by E. S. H. London: Henry Sotheran and Co., 1874. 3 p.l., (1)4–128 p. 4°.

—— Nathan the Wise, a dramatic poem by Lessing, translated into English blank verse by Andrew Wood... London and Edinburgh: William P. Nimmo, 1877. xxiv, 212 p. 12°.
Reviewed in *Contemporary review*, London, 1878, v. 31, p. 896–897, * *DA*; and in *Spectator*, London, v. 51, p. 1162, * *DA*.

—— Nathan the Wise; a dramatic poem in five acts. (Translated by R. Dillon Boylan.) (In his: Dramatic works. Edited by Ernest Bell. London, 1878. 8°. [v. 1.] Tragedies. p. 227–382.)

—— ...Lessing's Nathan the Wise. Translated from the German [by R. D. Boylan]. New York: Hinds, Noble & Eldredge [191–?]. 156 p. 16°.
At head of title: Handy literal translations.
In this translation, and an adaptation of it by M. J. Landa, it was produced by the Jewish Drama League at the Strand Theatre, London, May 2, 1925, with Wilfrid Walter as Nathan and Ann Trevor as Recha. Reviewed in *Era*, London, v. 88, May 9, 1925, p. 8, † *NAFA*; by M. M. in *Jewish chronicle*, London, May 8, 1925, p. 34, * *PBE*; *Jewish guardian*, London, v. 6, May 8, 1925, p. 5, * *PBE*; and in *The Times*, London, May 4, 1925, p. 10, * *A*. "It is remarkable that it [Nathan the Wise] should still, 150 years after it was brought out, retain so firm a grip of the imagination." — *Times reviewer*.

—— Lessing's Nathan the Wise. Translated into English verse by E. K. Corbett. With an introduction and notes... London: Kegan Paul, Trench & Co., 1883. lvi p., 1 l., 185 p. 12°.   NGC

—— Nathan the Wise; a dramatic poem in five acts... Translated by William Jacks. Introduction by Archdeacon Farrar, etchings by William Strang. Glasgow: Published for the translator by James Maclehouse and Sons, 1894. xxxiv p., 1 l., 252 p., front., 7 pl. 12°.

Individual Plays—Earliest Times to 1837, cont'd

LESSING, GOTTHOLD EPHRAIM. Nathan the Wise. A dramatic poem in five acts... Translated from the German of G. E. Lessing. New Orleans: J. P. Hopkins, printer, 1894. 181 p. 8°.
Copyrighted by L. C. K. Mannering.
Copy: Library of Congress.

—— Lessing's Nathan the Wise. Translated, with an introduction and notes, by Major-General Patrick Maxwell. London: Walter Scott, Ltd. [1895.] xxii p., 2 l., (1)4–264 p. 12°. (Scott library. [v. 99.])

—— Nathan the Wise, a dramatic poem, by Gotthold Ephraim Lessing... translated from the German by Patrick Maxwell, ed., with an introduction, comprising a biographical sketch of the author, a critical analysis of the poem, and an account of the relations between Lessing and Moses Mendelssohn, by George Alexander Kohut. New York: Bloch Publishing Company, 1917. 388 p. front., plates, ports., facsims. 12°.   8–NGC
Reviewed by Isidor Singer in *American Hebrew*, New York, 1917, v. 101, p. 215, * *PBD*; by D. de Sola Pool in *American Jewish chronicle*, New York, 1917, v. 3, p. 178, 182, * *PBD*; by J. B. in *Hebrew standard*, New York, v. 69, June 22, 1917, p. 11, * *PBD*; by C. D. Matt in *Jewish exponent*, Philadelphia, v. 68, Nov. 22, 1918, p. 1, * *PBD*; in *Zionist review*, London, 1917, v. 1, p. 79, * *PZX*; *Evening Post*, New York, June 6, 1917, p. 10, col. 5–6, * *A*; and in *New York Tribune*, May 26, 1917, p. 9, col. 3–4, * *A*.

—— Nathan the Wise; a dramatic poem, in five acts [translated by W. A. Steel]. (In his: Laocoön, Nathan the Wise & Minna von Barnhelm. London [etc., 1930]. 12°. p. 111–220.)
Everyman's library. Poetry and the drama. no. 843.
Nathan's narration of the story of the three rings is reprinted by T. W. H. Rolleston in his *Sea spray: verses and translations*, Dublin, 1909, p. 54–64, *NCM;* and (with illus.) in *Young Judaean*, New York, v. 13, p. 112–115, * *PBD*. More selections are given in Julian Hawthorne, editor, *Masterpieces and the history of literature*, New York, 1906, v. 8, p. 27–39, *NAB;* and in *Library of the world's best literature*, v. 15 or 23, p. 9011–9017, *NAC*.
A discussion as to Lessing's source of the story of the three rings is printed in *Jewish chronicle*, London, Dec. 27, 1878, p. 3; Jan. 3, 1879, p. 6 and Jan. 10, 1879, p. 6; Jan. 23, 1891, p. 9, and Jan. 30, 1891, p. 8, * *PBE*. Hermann Gollancz holds that Lessing derived it from *Schebet Jehudah* by Solomon Ibn-Verga, end of the 15th century. W. Heinemann quotes Lessing's statement that he found it in Boccaccio.
Produced for the first time in English at St. Mark's Hall of St. Mark's Episcopal Church, New York (Wm. N. Guthrie, rector), May 27, 1912, with Howard Kyle as Nathan and Ethel H. Gray as Recha. Repeated by the same group at the Hotel Astor (privately) on Friday afternoon, Oct. 25, 1912. See *New York dramatic mirror*, New York, v. 67, June 19, 1912, p. 3; v. 68, July 3, 1912, p. 12, and Oct. 30, 1912, p. 7, * *T–* *DA*. See also illustration in *Theatre magazine*, New York, v. 16, p. 192, † *NBLA*.

—— The three rings. For two males. (In: Beadle's dime dialogues. New York [cop. 1867]. 12°. no. 6, p. 93–96.)
An adaptation of act III, scene 7. The speakers are an Inquisitor and Nathan, instead of Saladin and Nathan.

Bradfield, Thomas. Lessing's story of the three rings. (Westminster review. London, 1895. 8°. v. 144, p. 666–669.)   * DA

Buchheim, Karl Adolf. Introduction [to Nathan the Wise]. (In: G. E. Lessing, Nathan der Weise, ed. by C. A. Buchheim. Oxford, 1888. 16°. p. xi–lvi.)   8–NGC
Library also has another edition, 1893, *8–NGC*.
Contents: History of the composition. The tendency of the drama. The parable of the three rings. Time and place of the action. Analysis of the characters. The language of the drama. A dramatic poem and a stage-play. On the motto [Introite, nam et hic Dii sunt].

Calkins, Raymond. "Nathan der Weise"; poem or play? (Modern language notes. Baltimore, 1893. 4°. v. 8, col. 193–205.)   RAA

Carruth, William Herbert. Lessing's treatment of the story of the ring and its teaching. (Modern Language Association of America. Publications. Baltimore, 1901. 8°. v. 16, p. 107–116.)   RAA

Cohen, Rose. Nathan the Wise. An essay read before B'rith Sholom Congregation of Louisville, Ky. (Jewish review and observer. Cleveland, 1903. f°. v. 27, Feb. 20, 1903, p. 1, 4.)
Repr.: Jewish spectator.   * PBD

Davis, W. W. Lessing's unfairness in "Nathan the Wise." (Methodist review. New York, 1894. 8°. v. 76, p. 746–757.)   * DA
Maintains that Lessing presented Christianity unfairly, since he let the Christian be most biased by his prejudice, and placed Christianity on a level not higher than the other religions.

Deering, Robert Waller. Lessing's "Nathan the Wise" [a critical study]. (Chautauquan. Cleveland, 1902. 8°. v. 34, p. 519–528.)   * DA

Diekhoff, Tobias J. C. Introduction [to Nathan the Wise]. (In: G. E. Lessing, Nathan der Weise, ed. by T. J. C. Diekhoff. New York [etc., cop. 1902]. 8°. p. 7–73.)   8–NGC
Nathan as a religious polemic. Nathan as a work of art. The sources of Nathan. Historical foundation.

Forster, Joseph. Lessing. (London society. London, 1890. 8°. v. 58, p. 577–588.)   * DA
See comment in *Jewish chronicle*, London, Jan. 21, 1891, p. 9, * *PBE*.

Friedlander, Gerald. A Jew in post-Shakespearian drama. (In his: Shakespeare and the Jew. London, New York, 1921. 16°. p. 67–79.)   * NCVF (Merchant)

Grossman, Rudolph. Shylock and Nathan the Wise. (Menorah. New York, 1894. 8°. v. 16, p. 168–180.)   * PBD
Reprinted in *New era*, Boston, v. 2, Dec., 1902, p. 33–40, * *PBD*.

Gruener, Gustav. The genesis of the characters in Lessing's 'Nathan der Weise.' (Modern Language Association of America. Publications. Baltimore, 1892. 8°. v. 7, no. 2, p. 75–88.)   RAA

Individual Plays—Earliest Times to 1837, cont'd

LESSING, GOTTHOLD EPHRAIM, *continued*

Grusd, Edward E. Lessing; friend of the Jews. illus. (B'nai B'rith magazine. Chicago, 1929. 4°. v. 43, p. 137.) * PYP

Gubalke, vicar. Must Lessing's 'Nathan' be a Jew? (American Hebrew. New York, 1892. 4°. v. 51, p. 789–790.) * PBD
Translated from the German in the *Berlin Zeitgeist*, by M. Blanzger.

Hase, Karl August von. Hans Sachs and Lessing's "Nathan." (In his: Miracle plays and sacred drama. London, 1880. 8°. p. 141–176, 260–266.)

Hellstern, Sadie. Teachings of "Nathan the Wise." (Jewish record. Richmond, Va., 1909. f°. v. 1, Dec. 26, 1909, p. 8–9.) * PBD

Herford, Charles Harold. Lessing['s Nathan the Wise]. (John Rylands Library. Bulletin. Manchester, 1923. 8°. v. 7, p. 225–232.)
* GX (Manchester)

Iliowizi, Henry. Shylock and Nathan. (Jewish exponent. Philadelphia, 1889. f°. v. 5, April 12, 1889, p. 1.) * PBD

Kohut, Adolph. Lessing and "Nathan the Wise." Adapted from the German, by George D. M. Peixotto. (Menorah. New York, 1887. 8°. v. 2, Feb., 1887, p. 49–57.) * PBD

Kopald, Louis J. The friendship of Lessing and Mendelssohn in relation to the good-will movement between Christian and Jew. (Central Conference of American Rabbis. Yearbook. Detroit, 1929. 8°. v. 39, p. 370–387.) * PXY
Treats of the historical background out of which Nathan the Wise arose. See also "Discussion," ibid., p. 387–401.

Krauskopf, Joseph. Nathan the Wise, the historic Jew. A Sunday lecture before the Reform Congregation Keneseth Israel, Nov. 15, 1891. Philadelphia: S. W. Goodman, 1891. 1 p.l., 14 p. 8°. (In his: Sunday lectures. series 5 [no. 4].) * PLM
Reprinted in *Our pulpit*, v. 5, no. 4.

Landa, Myer Jack. Nathan the neglected. (Jewish chronicle. London, June, 1923. f°. Supplement no. 30, p. vi–viii.) * PBE
Neglected by English stage producers.

Leiser, Joseph. The genesis of religious tolerance. (American Israelite. Cincinnati, 1917. f°. v. 63, June 14, 1917, p. 1.) * PBD

Marcus, Michael. Lessing's Nathan der Weise. (Jewish chronicle. London, Dec., 1928. f°. Supplement no. 96, p. v–vi.)

Mayer, Eli. Shakespeare, Lessing and the Jew. (Jewish exponent. Philadelphia, 1905. f°. v. 40, April 14, 1905, p. 8; v. 41, April 21, 1905, p. 8.)
* PBD
Reprinted in *Jewish American*, Detroit, v. 10, April 28, 1905, p. 1–3, May 5, 1905, p. 1–3, * PBD.

Pavey, Charles C. The stories of "the three rings." (Kit-kat. Columbus, Ohio, 1919. 12°. v. 8, p. 170–184.)

Price, Samuel. Lessing, the Christian liberal ... author of "Nathan" and "Die Juden." (American citizen. New York, 1913. 4°. v. 2, p. 275–276, 289.)

Primer, Sylvester. Lessing's religious development with special reference to his Nathan the Wise. (Modern Language Association of America. Publications. Baltimore, 1893. 8°. v. 8, p. 335–379.) RAA

Silverman, Joseph. Nathan the Wise. (American Hebrew. New York, 1917. f°. v. 102, p. 88, 102.) * PBD

Wagener, Edward A. The Jew of Lessing and of Shakespeare. (Jewish outlook. Denver, 1904. 4°. v. 1, March 4, 1904, p. 1–2.) * PBD
Reprinted in *Jewish American*, Detroit, v. 8, May 20, 1904, p. 1–2, * PBD.

Weinman, Nettie C. Companionship of Mendelssohn and Lessing. (Sabbath visitor. Cincinnati, 1899. 8°. v. 18, p. 606–608.) * PBD

Zangwill, Israel. Two unjewish Jewish plays. (New century review. London, 1900. 8°. v. 8, p. 480–482.) * DA
Reprinted in *American Hebrew*, New York, 1900, v. 68, p. 73–74, * PBD.
This paper was occasioned by the production of Nathan in German at the Comedy Theatre, London, Nov., 1900, with Max Behrend in the title rôle.

Zinnecker, W. D. Lessing the dramatist. (German quarterly. Lancaster, Pa., 1929. 8°. v. 2, p. 48–53.) RLA
A radio address broadcasted Jan. 27, 1929, by the Permanent Commission for Better Understanding between Jews and Christians in America.
Critiques of the play are given, by Alexander H. Japp in his *German life and literature in a series of biographical studies*, London [1880], p. 55–58, 69–70, 79–81, *NFC*; by T. W. H. Rolleston in his *Life of Gotthold Ephraim Lessing*, London, 1889, p. 179–189, * PSQ (*Lessing*); and by James Sime in his *Lessing*, London, 1877, v. 2, p. 232–260, AN (*Lessing*). See also *Edinburgh review*, London, v. 82, p. 464–466, * DA; and an abstract of a lecture by Charles I. Hoffman before the Mikveh Israel Association in *Jewish exponent*, Philadelphia, v. 44, March 15, 1907, p. 2, * PBD. The centenary of its first production at Berlin on April 14, 1783, was the occasion for an article in *Jewish chronicle*, London, May 4, 1883, p. 4, * PBE.

LINDSEY, THEOPHILUS. The Polish partition, illustrated; in seven dramatick dialogues, or, Conversation pieces, between remarkable personages, published from the mouths and actions of the interlocutors. By Gotlieb Pansmouzer [pseud. of Theophilus Lindsey] the baron's nephew... London: Printed for P. Elmsly [1773]. 2 p.l., 89 p. 8°.
Among the interlocutors are the rulers of Europe who shared in the partition of Poland, and Ephraim, baron of Joppa, who is commissioned by the King of Prussia to melt down the coin and distribute it in Poland. The prototype of Ephraim is Veitel-Heine Ephraim, mintmaster (Münzjude) under Frederick William I and Frederick the Great, and partner in business to the notable Daniel Itzig. Ephraim died in 1775. See *Jewish encyclopedia*, v, 192–193. Ephraim is announced towards the end of the first dialogue, "an admirable hand towards circumcising difficulties and ducats; one who can make a dollar appear double when it is paid, and single when it is received." The universal condemnation of the partition of Poland

Individual Plays—Earliest Times to 1837, cont'd
probably accounts for the translation of this piece into almost all the European languages.
Reviewed in *Critical review*, London, 1774, v. 37, p. 236, *NAA*; *Gentleman's magazine*, London, 1774, v. 44, p. 269–270, * *DA*, and in *Monthly review*, London, v. 50, p. 233, *NAA*.

—— Divisione della Polonia. In sette dialoghi a guisa di dramma. Conversazione tra potenze distinte, in cui si fanno parlare gli interlocutori secondo i loro principi, e la loro condotta. Opera di G. Pansmouser [pseud.]. Tradotta dall' inglese. All'Haja, 1775. 94 p., 1 l. nar. 8°.

—— Die Theilung von Pohlen, in sieben Gesprächen, oder Unterredung zwischen hohen Personnen, worinn sich dieselben ihren Grundsaetzen und Vertragen gemäss ausdrücken .. Aus dem Englischen übersetzt, von Miladi * * * Herzogin von * * * ... Hanau, 1775. 80 p. 12°.

—— Le partage de la Pologne, en sept dialogues en form de drame, ou Conversation entre des personnages distingués... Traduit de l'anglois, par Miladi * * * duchesse de * * * ... Londres: P. Elmsy [177–?]. 64 p. nar. 8°.

—— De verdeeling van Polen, in 7 samenspraken, tusschen hooge standspersonen, tooneelswijze voorgedragen... Uit het Engelsch vertaeld, door eene Kleefsche Mevrouw. Keulen: J. Kreitzer, 1775. 2 p.l., 112 p. 8°. GME p.v.2
For full record of this work see K. J. T. Estreicher, *Bibliografia polska*, tom 21, p. 288–290, * *QP*.

LUCAS, WILLIAM JAMES. Traitor's gate; or, The tower of London in 1553. An historical drama in three acts... London: T. H. Lacy [18—?]. 37 p. nar. 12°. (Lacy's acting edition of plays. [no. 1418.] v. 95.) NCO (Lacy)
Produced at the Royal Pavillion Theatre, London, March 31, 1834, with Farrell as Barnabas, "a Flemish usurer." Revived at the Victoria Theatre, London, in 1835, with Moss as Barnabas.

LUZZATTO, MOSES HAYYIM. Moses Haym Luzzatto's Lah-y' shaw-riem tehilaw ("Praise for righteousness") translated from the Hebrew by Rabbi Herbert S. Goldstein and Rebecca Fischel, March 7, 1915. New York: Bloch Publishing Company, 1915. 55 p. 16°. * PSH
An allegorical play, first published at Amsterdam, 1743.
The dialogue between Uprightness and Search, in act II, scene 1, translated by Israel Abrahams, is printed in *Jewish chronicle*, London, Sept. 2, 1892, p. 10, * *PBE*, and reprinted in *American Hebrew*, New York, 1892, v. 51, p. 665–666, * *PBD*. The dialogue between Understanding and Uprightness, act II, scene 1, is printed in B. Halper, *Post-Biblical Hebrew literature*, Philadelphia, 1921 [v. 2], English translation, p. 243–246, * *PAT*.

Abrahams, Israel. Guarini and Luzzatto. (In his: By-paths in Hebraic bookland. Philadelphia, 1920. 12°. p. 122–128.) * PAT
"Luzzatto derived his whole dramatic inspiration from Guarini [author of *Il Pastor fido*]".

Ginzburg, Simon. Dramas and lyrical poems. (In his: The life and works of Moses Hayyim Luzzatto. Philadelphia, 1931. 8°. p. 96–117.)
* PWZ (Luzzatto)

Marcus, Joseph. Luzzatto's Sefer ha-Mahzot. (*Jewish quarterly review*. Philadelphia, 1929. 8°. new series, v. 19, p. 501–504.) * PBE

LUZZATTO, MOSES HAYYIM. [Migdol Oz; or, Tummat Yesharim (The tower of strength; or, Innocence of the just) an allegorical drama in four acts, abstracted with numerous extracts, under title of] Specimens of the modern Jewish drama from the Hebrew of Moses ben Jacob Luzzatto. (*Monthly magazine*. London, 1841. 8°. series 3, v. 6, p. 127–137.) * DA
Written in 1727. First printed in Leipzig, 1837.
Reprinted, with some changes in the first few paragraphs, in *Albion*, New York, Sept. 23, 1843, new series, v. 2, p. 461–462, * *A*.

MACFARREN, GEORGE. Malvina: an opera, in three acts... The music by Mr. T. Cooke. Printed from the acting copy, with remarks, biographical and critical, by D.—G.... As performed at the Theatres Royal... London: J. Cumberland, n.d. 52 p. incl. front. 16°. (Cumberland's British theatre. v. 36 [no. 8].)
NCO (Cumberland)
Remarks by George Daniel, editor of the series.
Without the music.
Embellished with an engraving by Mr. Armstrong after a drawing by Mr. R. Cruikshank.
Produced at the Drury Lane, London, Jan. 28, 1826.
Listed wrongly in E. N. Calisch, *The Jew in English literature* [1909], p. 217. This ballad-opera is of no Jewish interest. There is a peddler in it, but he is a Caledonian, Shilric by name, a "jolly pedlar-man who sang of lasses and o'er the hills did wander."

MACKLIN, CHARLES. Love a-la-mode, a comedy of two acts, as it is performed at the Theatre Royal in Covent Garden. By Mr. Macklin... London, 1782. 1 p.l., 10, 13–24 p. 12°.
No. 11–12 omitted in paging, text continuous.
Copy: Library of Congress.

—— Love a la mode; a farce... As performed at the Theatres-Royal, Drury Lane and Covent-Garden. London: John Bell, 1793. 42 p. 12°.
NCO p.v.147

—— —— London: Printed by J. Bell, 1793. 2 p.l., 32 p. obl. 4°. † NCP
Bound with his: The man of the world. London, 1793.

—— —— London: J. Cawthorn, 1806. ix p., 1 l., (1)14–64 p. port. 24°. (Cawthorn's minor British theatre. no. 24.) NCO p.v.347

—— —— Prompter's copy; interleaved ms. notes. front. (port.) missing. NCOF

—— —— Love a-la-mode, a comedy. As it is performed at the Theatre Royal, Covent Garden ... London, 1810. 24 p. 24°. NCP p.v.1

—— —— Love à la mode: an afterpiece, in two acts... London: Printed by D. S. Maurice [1819?]. 42 p. front. 24°. ([Cabinet theatre. v. 7, no. 6.])
Copy: Library of Congress.

—— —— Love a-la-mode; a comedy. In two acts ... As performed at the Philadelphia Theatre. Philadelphia: Published by Thomas H. Palmer, 1823. 38 p., 1 l. 24°. NCP (Home)
An unidentified cast is given, with Francis as Mordecai.
Bound with: John Home. Douglas, a tragedy.

Individual Plays—Earliest Times to 1837, cont'd

MACKLIN, CHARLES. Love a la mode. An afterpiece, in two acts... Correctly given, as performed at the Theatres Royal. With remarks. New-York: Published by C. Wiley, no. 3, Wall-Street, 1824. 42 p. 32°. NCO p.v.426
Illustrated title page.
An unidentified cast is given, with Simmons as Mordecai.

—— ...Love a la mode, a farce... With prefatory remarks... Faithfully marked with the stage business and stage directions, as it is performed at the Theatres Royal. By W. Oxberry, comedian. London: Pub. for the proprietors, by W. Simpkin and R. Marshall [etc.], 1825. 1 p.l., vii(i) p., 1 l., 30 p. 12°. (Oxberry's New English drama. no. 115.) NCO p.v.632

—— —— Edinburgh: Stirling & Kenney, 1829. 36 p. front. 24°. NCE p.v.44

—— —— Edinburgh: Oliver & Boyd [18—?]. 36 p. 24°. NCO p.v.331

—— —— London: J. Dicks, n.d. 179–192 p. illus. new ed. 12°. (Dicks' standard plays. no. 123.)
Cover-title.

—— Love à la mode; an afterpiece... Correctly given, as performed at the Theatres Royal. With remarks... London: T. Hughes [18—?]. 42 p., 1 pl. 24°. (English theatre. no. 30.) NCO p.v.348
Also published in *British drama*, London, 1826, v. 2, p. 1163–1173, *NCO (British)*, *British drama*, Philadelphia, 1838, v. 2, p. 355–365, *NCO (British)*, Mrs. Elizabeth Inchbald, *A Collection of farces and other afterpieces*, London, 1809, v. 1, p. 299–337, *NCO (Inchbald)*, W. Jones, *British theatre*, Dublin, 1793, v. 6, p. 163–202, *NCO (Jones)*, *The London stage*, v. 3, *NCO (London)*, *Modern British drama*, London, 1811, v. 5, p. 492–505, *NCO (Modern)*, and in *Select London stage* [no. 56], *NCO (Select)*.
Produced at the Drury Lane, Dec. 12, 1759. Blakes as Beau Mordecai, an Italian Jew, suitor to the hand of the wealthy heiress. Reviewed in *Grand magazine of universal intelligence*, London, 1760, v. 3, p. 132–133, *Reserve*. ("The characters in themselves (excepting the Jew, which is really made no character at all) are not ill-drawn."
It was produced in America, at the John Street Theatre, New York, May 13, 1768, with Owen Morris as Mordecai; at Philadelphia, Southwark Theatre, Nov. 4, 1768; at Charleston, S. C., Jan. 19, 1774. During the season of 1779–1780 it was staged by the "Clinton Thespians" at the Theatre Royal. Denis Ryan produced it in a post-season performance at the John Street Theatre, New York, Aug. 20, 1783. It held the stage for many years. An Albany, N. Y., production is recorded, Jan. 20, 1786, and another in Annapolis, Nov. 16, 1786.

Matthews, W. The piracies of Macklin's Love à-la-mode. (Review of English studies. London, 1934. 8°. v. 10, p. 311–318.) RNA
The first act, as pirated by Tate Wilkinson, and published first in *Court miscellany*, London, 1766, v. 2, p. 217 et seq., is reprinted with critical notes.

Newbery, Francis. Epilogue to Love a-la-mode. (In his: Donum amicis. London, 1815. 8°. p. 17–21.)
Recited during a production on Jan. 2, 1794, at Heathfield Park, by Miss N. in the character of Charlotte. Beau Mordecai is one of the characters singled out for ridicule.

A *Scotsman's* remarks on the farce of Love a la mode, scene by scene. As it is acted at the Theatre Royal in Drury Lane. London: J. Burd, 1760. 1 p.l., 38 p. 12°.
"That [treatment] given of the Jew beau Mordecai, as well as the treatment of him throughout, is idly and grossly insulting a body of people, since the Jew-act has not taken place, and who ought to meet with better treatment from a man who owed his getting any footing on the stage to the supposition of his having well represented one of their community." — *p. 8.*

MACLARIN, ARCHIBALD. Britons to arms! or, The consul in England. A musical drama [in two acts]. London: For the author by A. Macpherson, 1803. 24 p. 12°. NCO p.v.335
This piece deals farcically with Napoleon's threatened invasion of England. There is no record of its being produced.
In act II, sc. 3, is introduced a Mr. Reuben. There follows the ensuing conversation:
Thomas: Reuben, wou'd not you fight them?
Reuben: Fight them! — there's a pretty question... By all the ancient hero's of my race, if Bonaparte himself was to come, I wou'd let him see that I am a Jew and a Briton, ready to fight and die in defence of my king and country, and my property.
Thomas: Mr. Reuben, give me your hand — I hear that your people in London have shew'd a spirit of patriotism —
Reuben: Not inferior to any of their neighbours, I hope.
He then proceeds to sing a song with the refrain
Whether Gentile or Jew, may we ever prove true
To the king and the country we live in.
A rather rare instance in dramatic literature of extolling Jewish patriotism. Maclarin, a Scotchman, fought with the British during the American Revolution and later in the Napoleonic wars. See an account of him in the *Dictionary of national biography*.

—— The ways of London; or, Honesty the best policy. A dramatic piece with songs. In two acts... London: For the author by A. Macpherson, 1812. 24 p. 12°. NCO p.v.335
Act I, sc. 3, is the meeting time of Breaklock, Snatchpurse, and several other rogues. Breaklock disguised with a long beard, to look "as true a Jew as ever opened a bag in Petticoat-lane." He is addressed as Moses and asked to sing. He obliges with a ditty on the virtues of British ale. At the conclusion of the song:
Landlord: That's a scurvy reflexion! You Jews are —
Breaklock: Every thing but good. If there's a bad shoe, bad gold, bad monies, bad any thing, the poor Jew get all the blame, though the Christian get often the profit.
An observation of this sort in favor of the Jews is rather unusual. Maclarin seemed to have been favorably disposed to the Jews.

MAID AND MAGPIE. [1815.]

Arnold, Samuel James. The maid and the magpye; or, Which is the thief? A musical entertainment, in two acts. Freely translated, with alterations, from the French... First performed at the Theatre-Royal, Lyceum, on Monday, August 21, 1815. The musick composed and selected by Mr. H. Smart. London: John Miller, 1815. 2 p.l., 52 p. 8°.
This is the first of many English adaptations, listed below, of *La Pie voleuse; ou La servante de Palaiseau* by L. C. Caigniez and T. M. T. Baudouin, which was first produced at the Théâtre de la Porte-Saint-Simon, Paris, April 29, 1815, with M. Vissot as Isaac, "Juif, marchand, forain." It was called "mélodrame historique" because of the alleged fact on which it is based. The plot turns upon a spoon stolen by a magpie. A female domestic is blamed for the theft but she

Individual Plays—Earliest Times to 1837, cont'd

is exonerated largely through the efforts of a Jewish peddler, variously named in the many versions. The date of production is not Aug. 21st, as given on the t.-p., but Aug. 28th. W. Oxberry played Isaac, the peddler. Reviewed in *European magazine*, London, 1815, v. 68, p. 251, * *DA;* and in *The Times*, London, Aug. 30, 1815, p. 3, col. 5, * *A.*

Barber, James. Which is the thief? a burletta, a new version of *The Maid and the magpie*, was produced at the Princess Theatre, London, March 9, 1843.
See Nicoll, p. 249.

Byron, Henry James. The maid and the magpie; or, The fatal spoon! A burlesque burletta, founded on the opera of "La gazza ladra"... London: T. H. Lacy [185–?]. 36 p. 12°. (Lacy's acting edition of plays. v. 37 [no. 552].)
  NCO (Lacy)
Running title: Maid and the magpie travesty.
First performed at the Strand, London, Oct. 11, 1858. In this version, The Jew is Isaac "old clothesman and general merchant — Ladies' and gentlemen's cast-off wardrobes purchased," acted by J. Clarke. Reviewed in *Era*, London, Oct. 17, 1858, p. 11, † *NAFA;* and in *The Times*, London, Oct. 14, 1858, p. 8, col. 6, * *A.*

Fitzball, Edward. Ninetta; or, The maid of Palaiseau. An opera in three acts, translated and altered from the French and Italian... The music from Rossini's opera "La gazza ladra." First performed at the Theatre Royal, Covent Garden, on Thursday, 4th of February, 1830. London: J. Ebers [1830]. 47 p. 8°. NCO p.v.191
Text by Fitzball. The music by Henry R. Bishop. Without the music.
"The present version is another translation... with alterations and additions from the Italian opera, 'La gazza ladra' [first staged in Milan, 1817]". — *From the Advertisement to the printed play.* The peddler is here called Shadrach; the part was acted by J. Russell. Reviewed in *Athenæum*, London, 1830, v. 3, p. 77–78, * *DA; Belle assemblée*, London, v. 11, p. 130, * *DA;* and in *The Times*, London, Feb. 5, 1830, p. 4, col. 1, * *A.*
Another version of *La gazza ladra* by Fitzball, under the sub-title *The maid of Palaiseau*, was produced at the Drury Lane, London, Oct. 13, 1838.

Gherardi del Testa, Tommasso, conte. La gazza ladra... A semi-serio opera in two acts ... The music by G. Rossini; the translation by Mr. W. J. Walter. London: J. Ebers [1821]. 109 p. 8°.
Text in Italian and English.
Title from British Museum catalogue.
See W. D. Adams, *A book of burlesque*, London, 1891, p. 180–182.

Lee, Nelson. The maid and the magpie; a melodrama was produced at the Grecian Theatre, London, in 1844.
Title from Nicoll, p. 332.

...*The Magpie*; or, The maid of Palaiseau. A melo-drame. With prefatory remarks... By W. Oxberry, comedian. London: W. Simpkin and R. Marshall, 1820. 1 p.l., ii p., 1 l., 36 p. front. (port.) 12°. (W. Oxberry, ed., New English drama. v. 11 [no. 1].)   NCO (Oxberry)
At head of title: Oxberry's edition.
This version was attributed by Oulton, and later by Genest, to T. J. Dibdin, but was disclaimed by him. See his *Reminiscences*, v. 2, p. 55, 67. Produced at the Drury Lane, London, Sept. 12, 1815, with W. Oxberry again as Isaac, the peddler. Reviewed in *European magazine*, London, 1815, v. 68, p. 252, * *DA;* and in *New monthly magazine and universal register*, London, v. 4, p. 247–249, * *DA.*

...*The Maid and the magpie;* a drama, in three acts, and written expressly for, and adapted only to Skelt's characters and scenes in the same. London: B. Skelt [1854?]. [3]–18 p. front. 16°. (Skelt's juvenile drama.)
t.-p. and front. missing.   NCR p.v.8

...*The Maid and the magpie;* a drama in three acts. Written expressly for, and adapted only to, Webb's characters and scenes in the same. London: W. Webb [18—?]. 18 p. 16°. (Webb's juvenile drama.)   NAC p.v.319

The Maid and the magpie; or, Which is the thief? A pathetic tale founded upon the well-known fact of an interesting female, who was condemned to death upon the strong circumstantial evidence of stealing various articles of plate, which were afterwards found to have been stolen by a magpie. London: Thomas Marden [1815]. 28 p. incl. col'd front. 12°.

The Maid and the magpie; a drama, in three acts. Adapted only for Pollock's characters and scenes. London: B. Pollock [185–?]. 16 p. 12°. (Pollock's juvenile drama.)
Isaac, a "travelling Jew."
Accompanied by 13 colored plates of scenes, entitled Pollock's Characters and scenes in The Maid and the magpie, obl. 12°.

Payne, John Howard. Trial without jury; or, The magpie and the maid. Not printed and never produced.
The ms. of this play is in the Theatre Collection of the Harvard College Library. Payne, comparatively unknown in London in 1815, was turned down with his Magpie version. He, too, introduced a Jewish character and named him Isaac. See Lillian A. Hall, in *Harvard Library notes*, Cambridge, Mass., 1935, no. 26, p. 89, * *HA.*
It is announced for publication by the University of Pennsylvania Press, in a series of *Manuscript American plays*, under the general editorship of B. H. Clark.
The Maid and the magpie; or, *Harlequin and the magic spoon*, by C. Stanfield James, is listed in Allardyce Nicoll, *A History of early nineteenth century drama*, 2:320, as having been produced at the Queen's Theatre, London, Dec. 23, 1848. The same authority, 2:417, cites a burlesque entitled *Another maid and another magpie* as having been presented at the Olympic Theatre, London, Nov. 3, 1815.

Pocock, Isaac. The magpie, or the maid? a melo drame, in three acts. Translated and altered from the French by I. Pocock. First performed at the Theatre-Royal, Covent-Garden, on Friday, September 15, 1815. The music composed by Mr. Bishop. London: John Miller, 1815. 1 p.l., 52 p. col'd front. 8°. NCO p.v.192

—— —— London: John Miller, 1816. 56 p. front. 2. ed. 8°.   NCR

—— —— From the first London edition of 1816. New York: D. Longworth, 1816. 46 p. 16°.   NCR p.v.11

—— —— Baltimore: J. Robinson, 1831. 48 p. 16°.   NCO p.v.299
Also printed in *Lacy's acting edition of plays*, v. 87, NCO (Lacy), and in *Cumberland's British theatre*, v. 28, NCO (Cumberland).
The text in the Cumberland and Lacy editions differs slightly from that in the earlier editions in 1815, 1816 and 1831. Produced at the Covent Garden, Sept. 15, 1815. The peddler is here called Benjamin, and was acted by Farley. Reviewed in *European magazine*, London, 1815, v. 68, p. 253, * *DA;* and in *New monthly magazine and universal register*, London, v. 4, p. 247–249, * *DA.*

Individual Plays—Earliest Times to 1837, cont'd

MAJOR, S. A gallant Jew; a dramatic sketch.
Title from E. N. Calisch, *The Jew in English literature*, p. 252.

MARLOWE, CHRISTOPHER. The Famous Tragedy of the Rich Ievv of Malta. As it was playd before the King and Qveene, in his Majesties Theatre at White-Hall, by her Majesties Servants at the Cock-pit. Written by Christopher Marlo. [*Printer's mark*] London: Printed by I. B. for Nicholas Vavasour, and are to be sold at his Shop in the Inner-Temple, neere the Church. 1633. [74] p. 4°.
Dedication signed by the editor: Tho. Heyvvood.
Copy: Harvard College Library.
"Although 'The Jew of Malta' was written between 1588 and 1592, there is no earlier edition of the play than the quarto of 1633. This was furnished with a brace of Prologues and Epilogues by Thomas Heywood, the dramatist... The source of the story is unknown; Mr. [J. A.] Symonds, arguing chiefly from its unrelieved cruelty, thinks it may be taken from some Spanish novel." It was entered at Stationers' Hall for publication, May 17, 1594.
Performed by Lord Strange's men at the Rose, Feb. 26, 1591/2 and thence (also by other companies) 35 more times till June 21 (23), 1595/6. See Philip Henslowe, *Diary*, ed. W. W. Greg, London, 1908, v. 2, p. 151, 389, *NCOM*. As to its relation to other early plays of Jewish interest, see ibid., under French doctor, p. 170–171.

—— The famous historical tragedy of the Rich Jew of Malta, as it was acted before the King and Queen in His Majesty's Theatre, at Whitehall, by Her Majesty's servants at the Cockpit. Imitated from the works of Machiavelli, by Christopher Marlo. London: Re-printed by Reynell and Son, and sold by Richardson, 1810. x p., 1 l., 77 p. 8°.
Edited by W. Shone.
Reviewed in *Monthly review*, London, 1812, new series, v. 67, p. 434–435, *NAA*.
A review of the play in an unidentifiable edition is given in *European magazine*, London, 1821, v. 79, p. 310–311, * *DA*.

—— Marlowe's celebrated tragedy of the Jew of Malta. In five acts, with considerable alterations and additions, by S. Penley, comedian. As performing with unanimous approbation at the Theatre Royal, Drury Lane. London: Richard White, 1818. 2 p.l., ii, (1)10–96 p. 8°.
Staged at the Drury Lane, London, April 24, 1818, with Edmund Kean as Barabas, Wewitzer as one of the three Jews, Mrs. Bartley as Abigail, and Harley as Ithamore. Reviewed in *Blackwood's magazine*, London, 1818, v. 3, p. 208–210, * *DA*; *European magazine*, London, 1818, v. 73, p. 429–430, * *DA*; *Literary gazette*, London, 1818, p. 285–286, * *DA*; *New monthly magazine and universal register*, London, 1818, v. 9, p. 444–445, * *DA*; and in *The Times*, London, April 25, 1818, p. 2, col. 1, * *A*. See also F. W. Hawkins, *The Life of Edmund Kean*, London, 1869, v. 2, p. 39–44, *MWES* (Kean).
The changes made by Penley are pointed out and discussed by C. F. Tucker Brooke in Connecticut Academy of Arts and Sciences, *Transactions*, New Haven, 1922, v. 25, p. 398–403, * *EA*.
One of the reviewers wrote "He [Kean] was as violent, raving, and fiendish as the heart of the spectator could desire, save when he sung a song to the harp which, mirabile dictu, has been composed by Mr. Nathan, a Jew, for the play." The Nathan referred to is Isaac Nathan, 1792–1864, English musician and composer, who set Byron's Hebrew melodies to music. The first of the four stanzas of this song reads:

Scarcely had the purple gleam of day
Glanc'd lightly on the glowing sea
When forc'd by fortune's shafts away
My native land, I quitted thee.

The following apology for the revival of the play occurs in the Prologue, spoken by Mr. Barnard (the Selim Calymath of the play):

Nor have we vainly sought from ev'ry page
T' expel that prejudice which mark'd the age
When persecution darken'd all our isle
And veil'd in terror true religion's smile
Then far from us long be th' invidious aim
To cast opprobrium o'er the Hebrew name.

In Penley's version it was first produced in America, at the Anthony Street Theatre, New York, March 26, 1821, with Kean as Barabas and Miss Johnson as Abigail.

—— The Iew of Malta. Herausgegeben von Albrecht Wagner. Heilbronn: Gebr. Henninger, 1889. xiv, 111 p. 12°. (Englische Sprach- und Literaturdenkmale des 16., 17. und 18. Jahrhunderts. Bd. 8.)
Forms Bd. 3 of Marlowe's Werke, ed. by H. Breymann and A. Wagner.
Reviewed by Leon Kellner in *Englische Studien*, Leipzig, 1890, Bd. 14, p. 139–141, *RNA*.

—— ...The Jew of Malta. (Condensed.) With introduction and explanatory notes. By J. Scott Clark... New York: E. Maynard & Co., 1892. 55 p. 16°. (English classic series. no. 101.)
NCO p.v.305

—— The Jew of Malta; a tragedy in five acts, by Christopher Marlowe, M. A. Adapted acting version of the Williams College English Department, with a preface by Solomon Bulkley Griffin... and an introduction by Lewis Perry... Williamstown, Mass., 1909. 3 p.l., xi–xix, 83 p., 1 l. incl. mounted front., mounted illus. (incl. ports.) 8°.
Copy: Library of Congress.
Produced in 1909 by the students of Williams College, with Graves as Barabas and Mr. Arnold as Abigail. The text was considerably cut in order to play down to the usual acting time. "The attitude of mind which an Elizabethan audience had toward a Jew is not ours, but the thrilling moments which came in the performance at Williamstown...were as real and as effective as...in 1590." The sustained interest of the spectators lasted not only during the first two acts, which critics say is usually the case, but "was a steadily rising one from first to last."
The English Dramatic Association of Princeton College staged it at Princeton, N. J., with T. Q. Beesley as Barabas, April 17, 1912, and subsequently at the Princeton Club of New York. See *New York dramatic mirror*, New York, v. 67, April 24, 1912, p. 4, * *T–* *DA*.

—— The famous tragedy of the rich Jew of Malta... Newly imprinted with engravings by Eric Ravilious. London: For the Golden Hour Press, 1933. 3 p.l., 86 p., 1 l., 4 pl. incl. front. 4°.
"Of this volume 250 copies have been printed."
The Phoenix Society revived it at Daly's Theatre, London, Nov. 5, 1922, with Balliol Holloway as Barabas, Isabel Jeans as Abigail, and Ernest Thesiger as Ithamore. Reviewed in *Blackwood's magazine*, Edinburgh, 1922, v. 212, p. 833–834, * *DA*; *Curtain*, London, v. 1, p. 141, *NAFA*; *Era*, London, v. 86, Nov. 9, 1922, p. 13, † *NAFA*; by W. J. Turner in *London mercury*, London, v. 7, p. 199–201, * *DA*; by Francis Birrell in *New statesman*, London, 1922, v. 20, p. 175, * *DA*; *Spectator*, London, v. 129, p. 695–696, * *DA*; and in *Truth*, London, v. 92, p. 823, * *DA*.
Reprinted in his *Works* edited by George Robinson, which edition A. Dyce characterizes as "abounding with the grossest errors"), London, 1826, v. 1, p. 183–284, *NCP*; *Works*, edited by A. Dyce, London, 1850, v. 1, p. 227–349, *NCP* (a new and revised edition, London and New York, 1876, p. 139–178); *Works*, edited by A. H. Bullen, London, 1885, v. 2, p. 1–113, *NCP*; *Christopher Marlowe*, edited by Havelock Ellis (Mermaid series), London [1887], p. 229–320,

Individual Plays—Earliest Times to 1837, cont'd

NCP (another edition, 1893, *NCP*); *Christopher Marlowe*, with introduction by Wm. L. Phelps, New York [etc., 1912], p. 231–312; *Doctor Faustus, Edward the Second, The Jew of Malta*, Leipzig, 1917, p. 191–296 (Collection of British authors, v. 4517); *Plays*, edited by Edward Thomas, London [1929], p. 159–224 (Everyman's library, no. 383); *Works*, edited by C. F. Tucker Brooke, Oxford [1929], p. 230–306, * *R-NCP;* and in his *Works and life*, New York, 1931, v. 3, edited by H. S. Bennett, p. 1–166, *NCF* (another edition, London [1931]).
The last-mentioned edition by Bennett is reviewed by H. S. V. Jones in *Journal of English and Germanic philology*, Urbana, Ill., 1933, v. 32, p. 101–103, *RKA;* by Sir Edmund K. Chambers in *Modern language review*, Cambridge, 1932, v. 27, p. 77–79, *NAA;* by Ethel Seaton in *Review of English studies*, London, 1933, v. 9, p. 328–330, *RNA;* and in *The Times literary supplement*, London, 1931, v. 30, p. 323, † *NAA*.
Reprinted in Robert Dodsley, *A Select collection of old plays*, London, 1780, v. 8, p. 299–394, *NCO;* ibid., London, 1825–27, v. 8, p. 241–327, *NCO; Ancient British drama*, edited by W. Scott, London, 1810, v. 1, p. 250–279, *NCO;* W. R. Thayer, *Best Elizabethan plays*, Boston [1890], p. 21–112, * *R-NCO;* William A. Neilson, *The Chief Elizabethan dramatists excluding Shakespeare*, Boston and New York [1911], p. 96–121; Charles F. T. Brooke and N. B. Paradise, *English drama, 1580–1642*, Boston [1933], p. 193–224; Hazelton Spencer, *Elizabethan plays*, Boston, 1933, p. 65–100; and in E. W. Parks and R. C. Beatty, editors, *The English drama; an anthology, 900–1642*, New York [1935], p. 420–479.
Extracts are also given from act I, scene 1, in Charles Lamb, *Specimens of English dramatic poets*, London, 1808, p. 29–31, * *KL;* ibid., edited by I. Gollancz, London, 1893, v. 1, p. 44–46, 293 (Temple library); in C. Marlowe, *Dramatic works, selected*, edited by P. E. Pinkerton, New York, 1885, p. 35–45, *NCP* (another edition, New York, 1889); from act II, scene 1, by William H. Williams in his *Specimens of the Elizabethan drama*, Oxford, 1905, p. 32–34, *NCO;* by A. R. Headland and H. A. Treble, compilers, in their *A Dramatic reader*, Oxford, 1921, book 3, p. 15–24; from act I, scene 1, and act II, scene 1, in C. Marlowe, *Scenes from Marlowe's plays*, chosen by A. T. Quiller-Couch, Oxford, n. d., p. 22–28 (Select English classics); in C. Marlowe, *Passages from the works of Marlowe*, edited by J. LeG. Brereton, Sydney, n. d., p. 38–49, 135–148 (Kealy and Philip's Australian tutorial series); and in *Library of the world's best literature*, v. 17 or v. 24, p. 9727–9728, *NAC*.
Conjectural readings, emendations and notes are given by Chris. Brennan in *Anglia: Beiblatt*, Halle a.S., 1905, Bd. 16, p. 208, *RNA;* by J. LeG. Brereton, ibid., p. 205, *RNA;* by Brereton also in *Modern language review*, Cambridge, 1911, v. 6, p. 95, *NAA;* by F. C. Danchin in *Revue anglo-américaine*, Paris, 1933, année 10, p. 330, * *DM;* by Kenneth Deighton in his *The Old dramatists; conjectural readings*, Westminster, 1896, p. 120–122; by Karl Elze in his *Notes on Elizabethan dramatists*, Halle, 1889, p. 2–3, 12, 110, *NCOD;* by F. Holthausen in *Englische Studien*, Leipzig, 1909, Bd. 40, p. 395–401, *RNA;* by Baldwin Maxwell in *Modern language notes*, Baltimore, 1931, v. 46, p. 552–553, *RAA;* by Hazelton Spencer in *Philological quarterly*, Iowa City, 1932, v. 11, p. 222–223, *NAA;* and by Wilhelm Wagner in Deutsche Shakespeare Gesellschaft, *Jahrbuch*, Weimar, 1876, Jahrg. 11, p. 70–77, * *NCK*.

—— La fameuse tragédie du riche Juif de Malte. (In his: Théâtre. Trad. de F. Rabbe, avec une préface par Jean Richepin. Paris, 1889. 12°. v. 2, p. 83–174.)

—— Le Juif de Malte. (In: Les Contemporains de Shakespeare: Ben Jonson, Marlowe, Dekker, Middleton; Volpone; ou, le Renard, le Juif de Malte, le Mardi-gras du cordonnier, le Moyen d'attraper un vieillard. Traduction de Georges Duval. Paris [1920]. 8°. p. 122–199.) (Les Meilleurs auteurs classiques français et étrangers.)

—— Der Jude von Malta. (In: Alt-englische Schaubuehne; uebersetzt und herausgegeben von Eduard von Buelow. 1. Theil. Berlin, 1831. 12°. p. 283–426.)
Parts of acts I and II are translated in F. M. Bodenstedt, editor, *Shakespeare's Zeitgenossen und ihre Werke*, Berlin, 1860, Bd. 3, p. 319–350, *NCO;* and in Adolf F. von Schack, *Die Englischen Dramatiker vor, neben und nach Shakespeare*, Stuttgart, 1893, p. 84–87, *NCO*.

—— ...Мальтійскій жидъ. Трагедія въ пяти дѣйствіяхъ... Переводъ Мих. Шелгунова. St. Petersburg: S. Dobrodeyev, 1882. vii, 1, 132 p. illus. 8°. (Библіотека избранныхъ произведеній.)

—— [Extracts, translated into Russian, by N. I. Storozhenko.] (In: N. I. Storozhenko, Предшественники Шекспира... Лилли и Марло. St. Petersburg, 1872. 8°. p. 242–261.) *QDK

Akers, D. A project in stage design for Jew of Malta, 1933.
Ms. thesis, unpublished, State University of Iowa Library, Iowa City, Iowa.
Title from S. A. Tannenbaum, *Additions to Christopher Marlowe; a concise bibliography*, 1937, item 380c.

Beljame, A. Les premières oeuvres dramatiques de Shakespeare. (Revue des cours et conférences. Paris, 1898. 8°. série 2, année 6, p. 743–752.)
Copy: Columbia University Library.

Benson, Nelson P. A study in character delineation. Shylock in The Merchant of Venice, and Barabas in The Jew of Malta. (Pennsylvania Central State Normal School, Lock Haven. The normal bulletin. Lock Haven, 1912. 8°. v. 13, no. 1, p. 22–25.) SSGC

Booth, William Stone. [Francis Bacon and The Jew of Malta.] (In his: Some acrostic signatures of Francis Bacon. Boston and New York, 1909. 4°. p. 211–222.) *NCZB

Boyer, Clarence Valentine. Marlowe and the Machiavellian villain-hero. (In his: The villain as hero in Elizabethan tragedy. London [1914]. 8°. p. 40–59.) NCOD

Brooke, Charles Frederick Tucker. Marlowe's versification and style. (University of North Carolina. Philological Club. Studies in philology. Chapel Hill, N. C., 1922. 8°. v. 19, p. 186–205.) RNA (North Carolina)

—— The prototype of Marlowe's Jew of Malta. (Times literary supplement. London, 1922. f°. v. 21, p. 380.) *A
Bound with: *The Times*, London, June 8, 1922.
The suggestion is here made that David Passi, fl. 1585–1591, about whose adventurous career Marlowe may have learned from English government circles, served as the prototype. Passi's career, rather than that of Joseph ha-Nasi, as suggested by Kellner (see Kellner, infra), corresponds more nearly to the various

Individual Plays—Earliest Times to 1837, cont'd
MARLOWE, CHRISTOPHER, *continued*
plots in which Barabas figures. "Marlowe was fond of introducing the immediate present and current talk into his dramas." As to the career of Passi, see Lucien Wolf, "Jews in Elizabethan England," in Jewish Historical Society of England, Transactions, v. 11, p. 1–91, * PXQ.

Broughton, James. The Jew of Malta, 1633. (Gentleman's magazine. London, 1830. 8°. v. 147, p. 593–594.) *DA

Buland, Mable. [Time element in the Jew of Malta.] (In her: The presentation of time in the Elizabethan drama. New York, 1912. 8°. p. 272–275.) NCOD

Chiarini, Giuseppe. Il giudeo nell' antico teatro inglese: Barabbo e Shylock. (Nuova antologia. Roma, 1892. 8°. v. 124 [serie 3, v. 40], p. 62–88.) NNA
Reprinted in his *Studi shakespeariani*, Livorno, 1896, p. 183–222, * NCV.

Clark, Arthur Melville. The Jew of Malta. (In his: Thomas Heywood; playwright and miscellanist. Oxford, 1931. 8°. p. 287–294.) AN (Heywood)
As to Heywood's share in this play of Marlowe, Mr. Clark concludes, "There ought to be no doubt, in the face of both the stylistic and the structural evidence, that the chief blame for the corruption of the play must attach to its editor [T. Heywood]."
Reviewed in *Times literary supplement*, London, 1931, v. 30, p. 589–590, † NAA.

Courtney, William Leonard. [Imitations of passages from Marlowe's play in Shakespeare's *Merchant of Venice*.] (Fortnightly review. London, 1905. 8°. v. 84, p. 685–686.) *DA

D., W. Marlow's Jew of Malta. (Athenæum. London, 1829. f°. v. 2, p. 725–26, 743–44.) *DA

Davidson, Israel. Shylock and Barabas; a study in character. [Sewanee? 1901?] 14 p. 8°.
Cover-title. * NCVB p.v.1
Bibliographical footnotes.
Repr.: Sewanee review, v. 9, p. 337–348.

——— היהודי בספרות האנגלית.
(נר המערבי) New York, 1895. 8°. v. 1, no. 6, p. 38–40; no. 7, p. 7–15.) * PBA
Reprinted as a separate, New York: A. H. Rosenberg, 1895, 15 p., * PZB.

Enelow, Hyman Gerson. "The Jew of Malta." (In his: Selected works. [Kingsport, Tenn.,] 1935. 8°. v. 2, p. 197–208.) * PBT

Fischer, Rudolf. [Marlowe's Jew of Malta.] (In his: Zur Kunstentwicklung der englischen Tragödie. Strassburg, 1893. 8°. p. 136–145.) NCOD
Gruppirung der Handlungselemente. Wirkungsvolle Gliederung des Dramas. Ungleichmässige Ausarbeitung. Auflösung der Figurengruppen.

Fitz-Hugh, Alexander. The Jew of Malta and the Jew of Venice. (University of Virginia magazine. Charlottesville, Va., 1895. 4°. new series, v. 38, p. 288–294.) STG (Virginia)

Frazer, Helen. A glimpse of the seventeenth century Jew in the drama. (Mount Holyoke. South Hadley, Mass., 1903. 8°. v. 12, p. 363–365.) STG

Hastings, E. E. Comparative study of *The Jew of Malta* and *The Merchant of Venice*. 1913. 12 p.
Ms. thesis, unpublished; Ohio University Library, Athens, Ohio.
Title from S. A. Tannenbaum, *Christopher Marlowe; a concise bibliography*, item 804.

K., E. E. Barrabas and Shylock compared. (Franklin and Marshall College. College student. Lancaster, Pa., 1898. 8°. v. 18, p. 252–255.) STG

Kellner, Leon. Die Quelle von Marlowe's "Jew of Malta." (Englische Studien. Heilbronn, 1887. 8°. Bd. 10, p. 80–111.) RNA
Argues that João Miguez, or Jean Miques, or Johannes Michesius, later known as Joseph ha-Nasi, Duke of Naxos under Selim II, 1566–1579, suggested Barabas to Marlowe. See Moritz A. Levy, *Don Joseph Nasi*, Breslau, 1859, * PWZ.

Klein, Julius Leopold. The Jew of Malta. (In his: Geschichte des Drama's. Leipzig, 1876. 8°. Bd. 13, p. 667–708.) NAF

Kraemer, Georg. [Characterization of Barabas in The Jew of Malta.] (In his: Unmittelbare Selbstcharakterisierung und Charakterisierung durch Mithandelnde im englischen Drama der Renaissencezeit. Breslau, 1930. 8°. p. 35–40, 44–45.) NAFH p.v.88

Landa, Myer Jack. Marlowe's Jew. (Jewish chronicle. London, Oct., 1922. f°. supplement 22, p. vii–viii.) * PBE
On the occasion of the Phoenix production in 1922.

——— Marlowe's "Jew of Malta." (In his: The Jew in drama. London, 1926. 8°. p. 56–69.) * PZB

Levi, Harry. "The Jew of Malta." (In his: Jewish characters in fiction. English literature. Philadelphia [cop. 1903]. 12°. p. 13–20.) * PZB
Revised and enlarged in a second edition, 1911, p. 10–19, * PZB.

M., H. Jew of Malta — Marlow. (Blackwood's magazine. Edinburgh, 1817. 8°. v. 2, p. 260–266.) *DA
Analytical essays on the early English dramatists, no. 3.

Meyer, Edward Stockton. [Machiavelli and the Jew of Malta.] (In his: Machiavelli and the Elizabethan drama. Weimar, 1897. 8°. p. 30–56.) NABM (Literaturhistorische)
Literaturhistorische Forschungen. Heft 1.

Michelson, H. Marlowe's Jew of Malta. (In his: The Jew in early English literature. Amsterdam, 1926. 8°. p. 70–82.) * PZB

Mory, E. Marlowes Jude von Malta und Shakespeares Kaufmann von Venedig... Basel: Schweighauserische Buchdruckerei, 1897. cover-title, 27 p. 4°.

Individual Plays—Earliest Times to 1837, cont'd

MARLOWE, CHRISTOPHER, *continued*

O'Brien, J. F. A character study of Barabas. 1923.
   Ms. thesis, unpublished; Catholic University of America Library.
   Title from S. A. Tannenbaum, *Christopher Marlowe; a concise bibliography*, item 1048.

O'Hara, Julie Caroline. Christopher Marlowe's Jew of Malta. (Jewish comment. Baltimore, 1905. f°. v. 21, Sept. 8, 1905, p. 7–8.)   *PBD

Passmann, Hanns. Der Typus der Kurtisane im elisabethanischen Drama... Borna-Leipzig: R. Noske, 1926. vii, 75 p., 1 l. 8°.
   "Literaturverzeichnis," p. v–vii.
   See p. 4–5.

Philipson, David. [Abstract of] a lecture. (Jewish exponent. Philadelphia, 1887. f°. v. 2, no. 8, p. 13.)   *PBD

—— Marlowe's Jew of Malta. (In his: The Jew in English fiction. Cincinnati, 1889. 12°. p. 19–33.)   *PZB
   The Library also has the editions of 1903 and 1918, *PZB.

Pietzker, Annemarie. Der Kaufmann in der elisabethanischen Literatur... Quakenbrück i. Hann.: C. Trute, 1931. vi, 76 p., 1 l. 8°.
   Dissertation: Freiburg i. Br.
   See p. 13.

Poel, William. Shakespeare's Jew and Marlowe's Christians. (Westminster review. London, 1909. 8°. v. 171, p. 54–64.)   *DA

Ross, Crystal Ray. The Machiavellian man in Elizabethan drama... [New York, 1921.] 135, 4 f. 4°.
   Typewritten copy.
   Master's thesis.
   Columbia University. M.A. Theses. 1921. v. 24.
   See f. 17–23.

Schau, Kurt. Sprache und Grammatik der Dramen Marlowes... Halle a. S.: Heinrich John, 1901. 102 p., 1 l. 8°.
   Dissertation: Leipzig.

Schick, J. Christopher Marlowe: seine Persönlichkeit und sein Schaffen. (Deutsche Shakespeare Gesellschaft. Jahrbuch. Leipzig, 1928. 8°. Jahrg. 64, p. 159–179.)   *NCK
   Der Jude von Malta, p. 175.

Schipper, Jacobus. De versu Marlovii... Bonnae: Typis Caroli Georgi [1867]. 2 p.l., 43 p., 1 l. 12°.
   Dissertation: Bonn.
   Bibliographical footnotes.

Schneider, Rudolf Konrad. ...Der Mönch in der englischen Dichtung bis auf Lewis's 'Monk' 1795... Leipzig: Mayer & Müller, 1928. ix, 204 p. 8°. (Palaestra 155...) NCI p.v.433
   See p. 89.

Seaton, Ethel. Fresh sources for Marlowe. (Review of English studies. London, 1929. 8°. v. 5, p. 385–401.)   RNA
   See *Juan Miques*, p. 390–393.
   Philippus Lonicerus, who cited references to Juan Miques, alias Joseph ha-Nasi, was Marlowe's probable source for his prototype of Barabas. See Kellner, *supra*.

Spencer, Hazelton. Marlowe's rice "with a powder" [in act III, scene 4]. (Modern language notes. Baltimore, 1932. 4°. v. 47, p. 35.)   RAA

Stockley, William Frederick Paul. The Jews of Marlowe and Shakespeare. (Queen's quarterly. Kingston, Ont., 1918. 4°. v. 26, p. 159–180.)   *DA
   Reprinted in *Irish ecclesiastical record*, Dublin, 1934, series 5, v. 44, p. 67–88, ZLPS.
   "Shakespeare's Jew is *much* less a call to anti-Semitism than had been Barabas, if any such call there be, in Shylock."

Swan, Arthur. "The Jew that Marlowe drew." (Sewanee review. New York, 1911. 8°. v. 19, p. 483–497.)   *DA

Symonds, John Addington. [Transfigured avarice.] (In his: Shakespere's predecessors in the English drama. London, 1900. 12°. p. 493–497.)   NCOD

Tarnawski, Władysław. [A critique.] (In his: Krzysztof Marlowe; jego życie, dzieła i znaczenie... Warsaw, 1922. 8°. p. 99–123.)   *QP

Thimme, Margarete. Marlowes "Jew of Malta"; Stil- und Echtheitsfragen. Halle a. S.: Max Niemeyer, 1921. xi, 48 p. 8°. (Studien zur englischen Philologie. Heft 61.)   NCO p.v.476
   Reviewed in *Zeitschrift für französischen und englischen Unterricht*, Berlin, 1922, Bd. 21, p. 226–227, NAA.

Uvarov, S. [A critical study, in his Марло, одинъ изъ предшественниковъ Шекспира.] (Русское слово. St. Petersburg, 1859. 8°. no. 2, Feb., 1859, p. 38–53.)   *QCA

Ward, Adolphus William. [Marlowe's Jew of Malta and its resemblance to Shakespeare's Merchant of Venice.] (In his: A history of English dramatic literature. London, 1899. 8°. v. 1, p. 337–347.)   *R – NCOD
   From the resembling passages of the two plays, Prof. Ward concludes that Marlowe's play was in Shakespeare's mind when he wrote his *Merchant of Venice*.

Wynne, Arnold. [The Jew of Malta.] (In his: The growth of English drama. Oxford, 1914. 12°. p. 242–248.)   NCOD

THE MASQUE of flowers. (In: Herbert A. Evans, editor, English masques. London, 1897. 12°. p. 100–113.)   NCO
   This anonymous masque, the foreword to which is signed by J. G., W. D., and T. B., was presented in Whitehall by the Gentlemen of Gray's Inn, Dec. 26, 1613, at the marriage of the Earl of Somerset to the daughter of the Earl of Suffolk. "To this masque belongs the unique distinction of a modern revival; it was performed at Gray's Inn on July 7, 1887, the year of the Queen's Jubilee."
   In the Dance, in the middle of the Masque, eight couples take part; four enter on the side of Silenus and four on the side of Kawasha, the god of tobacco. One of the couples on Kawasha's side is designated "mountebank and Jewess of Portugal." The Dance is repeated at the end; the masquers pay homage to the royal family and are invited to the banquet.

Individual Plays—Earliest Times to 1837, cont'd

MASSINGER, PHILIP. The Dvke Of Millaine. A Tragædie. As it hath beene often acted by his Maiesties seruants, at the blacke Friers. Written by Philip Massinger Gent. [*Ornament*] London, Printed by B. A. for Edward Blackmore, and are to be sold at his shop at the great South doore of Pauls. 1623. [93] p. 4°.
Copy: Library of Congress.
The background of the story is taken from Guiciardini's narrative of the historical conflict between Ludovico Sforza and Emperor Charles v. Langbaine gives Josephus' account (*De antiquitatibus Judaicis*, book 15) of Herod's love for Mariamne as the true source of the plot. It is said on the title-page to have "been acted by his Majesty's Servants at the Black Friars." In this play there is another early instance of a Christian disguised as a Jew for a nefarious purpose. Francisco, in act v, scene 2, is disguised as a Jewish doctor to avenge his sister Eugenia. He is introduced as "a Jew by birth and a physician by his profession."

—— The duke of Millaine; a tragedy. London: Printed by I. Raworth for E. Blackmore, 1638. 80 p. sm. 4°.
Copy: Harvard College Library.

—— The Duke of Milan; a tragedy, in five acts. Written by Philip Massinger, Gent., and now performed at the Theatre-Royal Drury Lane. London: Printed for W. Lowndes, 1816. 2 p.l., (1) 4–62 p. 8°.

—— —— Revived at the Theatre-Royal, Drury-Lane, with alterations and additions, on Saturday, March 9, 1816. London: Printed for J. Miller by B. M'Millan, 1816. 2 p.l., (1) 4–67 p. 8°. NCO p.v.223
The 1816 editions are alterations by an anonymous author or authors. Produced at the Drury Lane, London, March 9, 1816, with Edmund Kean as the Duke Sforza, and Rae as Francisco. Reviewed in *European magazine*, London, 1816, v. 69, p. 243–244, *DA*; by William Hazlitt, in his *A View of the English stage*, London, 1818, p. 251–255, *NCOM*; and in *The Times*, London, March 11, 1816, p. 2, col. 5–p. 3, *A*. The Henry E. Huntington Library possesses an *Address to the revived play of The Duke of Milan*, spoken at that theatre that evening. See its *Catalogue of the Larpent plays*, compiled by Dougald MacMillan, 1939, no. 1914, **RS–NCO*. See also detailed account in Genest, v. 8, p. 527–531. One of the alterations was staged at Bath, England, with Bengough as Francisco, July 5, 1816.
An altered version, attributed to Richard Cumberland, was produced at the Covent Garden, London, Nov. 10, 1779, with Aikin as Francisco. Cf. Genest, v. 6, p. 141–142.
A *Prologue* ("This night, we set to view a Guiltless Wife") and *Epilogue* ("When Senators attend St. Stephen's call"), spoken at this production, are owned by the Huntington Library. See its *Catalogue of Larpent plays*, no. 495.

—— An edition of Philip Massinger's Duke of Milan... by Thomas Whitfield Baldwin... Lancaster, Pa.: Press of the New Era Printing Company, 1918. ix, 197 p. 8°. NCP
Printed in his *Plays*, edited by W. Gifford, London, 1805 (2. ed., 1813), v. 1, p. 231–343, *NCP*; 3. ed., London, 1840 (another ed., 1853), p. 61–89, *NCP*; in his *Plays adapted for family reading and the use of young persons by the omission of objectionable passages*, New York, 1831, v. 2, p. 1–96 (Harper's family library, no. 89), *NCP*; in Massinger and Ford, *Dramatic works*, edited by Hartley Coleridge, London, 1840 (other editions, 1848, 1859, 1869), p. 49–73, *NCP*; in his *Plays*, edited by F. Cunningham from the text of Gifford, London, 1870 (another ed., 1871), p. 65–98, *NCP*; and in *Philip Massinger*, edited by Arthur Symons (Mermaid series), London, 1887 (another ed., 1893), v. 1, p. 1–101, *NCP*.
Also printed in T. J. Dibdin, *London theatre*, London, 1815, v. 4; in *The London stage*, London [1824–27], v. 2, *NCO (London)*, and in J. S. Keltie, editor, *Works of the British dramatists*, Edinburgh, 1870, p. 411–434, *NCO*.
An extract from Act i, scene 3, is printed in Allardyce Nicoll, editor, *Readings from British drama*, New York [1928], p. 147–149, * R–NCO.

D., O. [A passage in act III, scene 1.] (Notes and queries. London, 1861. 8°. series 2, v. 11, p. 261–262.) *R–*DA
"To set these chuffs, that every day may spend."

Dunstan, Arthur Cyril. E. C.'s drama and "The duke of Milan." (In his: Examination of two English dramas: "The Tragedy of Mariam" by Elizabeth Carew; and "The True tragedy of Herod and Antipater: with the death of faire Marriam," by Gervase Markham and William Sampson. Königsberg i. Pr., 1908. 8°. p. 39–40.)
NCO p.v.308

Gerhardt, Erich. Massinger's "The duke of Milan" und seine Quellen... Halle a. S.: C. A. Kaemmerer & Co., 1905. 48 p. 8°.

Grack, Walter. Studien über die dramatische Behandlung der Geschichte von Herodes und Mariamne in der englischen und deutschen Litteratur. (Massinger, Fenton, Hebbel, Stephen Phillips.) Königsberg i. Pr.: H. Jaeger, 1901. 135 p., 2 l. 8°. NCO p.v.317
Litterat: p. 133–135.
"The Duke of Milan," p. 19–42.

Greg, Walter Wilson. Massinger's autograph corrections in 'The Duke of Milan,' 1623. (Library. London, 1923. 8°. series 4, v. 4, p. 207–218.) *HA
See also series 4, v. 5, p. 72.

Macauley, Elizabeth Wright. The duke of Milan. illus. (In her: Tales of the drama. Exeter, N. H., 1833. 12°. p. 9–30.) NCT
Another edition, Boston, 1834, *NCW*.

Mills, J. W. The repulsiveness of *The duke of Milan*. (Academy. London, 1891. 4°. v. 40, p. 566–567.) *DA
Abstract of a paper read before the Clifton Shakespeare Society. Abstracts are also given of *The key note of 'The duke of Milan,'* and *Womenfolk in 'The duke of Milan,'* by Walter Strachan and Florence Herapath, respectively.

Silbermann, Abraham Moritz. Untersuchungen über die Quellen des Dramas "The true Tragedy of Herod and Antipater with the death of faire Marriam" by Gervase Markham and William Sampson (1622). Wittenberg: Herrosé & Ziemsen [1930]. 86 p., 1 l. 8°.
The author concludes that Massinger's *Duke of Milan* is taken not from Josephus but from Markham and Sampson's play. See especially p. 64–80.
Reviewed by T. W. Baldwin in *Journal of English and Germanic philology*, Urbana, Ill., 1929, v. 28, p. 439–440, *RKA*.

Tomlinson, Warren E. "The Duke of Milan" von Philip Massinger. (In his: Der Herodes-Charakter im englischen Drama. Leipzig, 1934. 8°. p. 109–110.) NCOD

MELVILLE, WALTER. *See* sub-entry under SCOTT, SIR WALTER.

Individual Plays—Earliest Times to 1837, cont'd

MIDDLETON, THOMAS. The triumphs of honour and industry. (In his: Works, ed. by A. Dyce. London, 1840. 12°. v. 5, p. 605–620.) NCP

Reprinted in A. H. Bullen's edition of Middleton's works, London, 1886, v. 7, p. 291–307. In Dyce's edition, on p. 607, is given a copy of the t.-p. of the original 1617 quarto.

This is a pageant or masque which was given on Oct. 29, 1617, at the induction of George Bowles as mayor of London. Middleton describes one of the episodes as the pageant of several nations. Representatives of ten nationalities are enumerated, among them a Jew, who speak lines appropriate for the occasion.

MILLINGEN, JOHN GIDEON. The miser's daughter; a drama in two acts... London: John Miller, 1835. v(i), 25 p. 8°. (Modern acting drama. new series, no. 5.)

Copy: Harvard College Library.
Produced at the Drury Lane, London, Feb. 24, 1835. Farren played Isaac Ivy the miser, and Ellen Tree, his daughter Ann Ivy. It lasted only two nights. Reviewed in Literary gazette, London, 1835, p. 185, col. 2, * DA.

As to its Jewish interest, see Landa, p. 154–155. Odell, IV:289, 631, and Ireland, II:272, 394, record New York productions of *Miser's daughter*. These, however, are meant for either E. Stirling's piece of that name or another unidentifiable one.

MILNER, HENRY M. The Jew of Lubeck; or, The heart of a father. A serious drama in two acts... First performed at the Theatre Royal, Drury-Lane, on Wednesday, May 12, 1819. The music composed by Mr. T. Cooke. London: J. Lowndes, 1819. 4 p.l., 27 p. 2. ed. 8°. NCO p.v.86

The Jew is not a Jew, but an Austrian nobleman, who, denounced as a traitor, escapes to Lubeck and there hides by living as a Jew. In the preface the author states, "I believe I ought to apologize to that body of people, to whose restoration to their former splendor and a yet more blessed theocracy I devoutly look, for giving to my production a title, which should excite their curiosity, and occasion an ultimate disappointment."

Licenser's ms. shows "numerous deletions...one scene and long passage in ms. not printed; numerous minor differences." See *Catalogue of Larpent plays*, no. 2082. The date of production is given, ibid., May 11.

Rae played the Jew; Oxberry, Van Fursten, his principal servant; and Mrs. West, Rosa, his daughter. It was acted six times. Genest and the reviewers give May 11, 1819, as the date of the first production. Reviewed in *European magazine*, London, 1819, v. 75, p. 448–449, * *DA*; *Examiner*, London, 1819, p. 317, * *DA*; and in *Literary gazette*, London, 1819, p. 318, * *DA*.

It was produced at the Park Theatre, New York, Oct. 8, 1819, with R. C. Maywood as *The Jew*, and was given at the Chestnut Street Theatre, Philadelphia, March 13, 1820, with Hughes in the title-rôle.

MONCRIEFF, WILLIAM THOMAS. The heart of London; or, The sharper's progress. A drama in three acts; first performed at the Adelphi Theatre, Monday, February, 1830. [London: H. Robertson, 1839.] viii, 80 p. 8°.

The first one of the so-called Jack Sheppard plays See under Ainsworth, in the following section. "The object of the [play]...is to hold out a strong moral lesson to the rising generation by exhibiting, in the most appalling colours, the ruinous dangers attendant on the slightest deviation from the paths of rectitude."

Also printed in his *Selection from the dramatic works of W. T. Moncrieff*, London, 1851, v. 1 [no. 6]. Also issued as no. 430 of Dicks' standard plays, NCO p.v.666.

"The heart of London" is the nickname for the Newgate prison in London. The three acts are dated 1796, 1798, and 1802 respectively. In act 2 Aby Houndsditch (so named after the quondam Jewish quarter of London), played by Mr. Barnett, appears as one of the prisoners of Newgate and is addressed by the jail jester in part thus: "Of the Rag Fair fencibles...what would you say to a parcel of swag in the shape of a few chests of plate—do you think you couldn't make white soup and brown gravy of them?" Aby is the later Abraham Mendes in the Jack Sheppard plays.

Produced at the Adelphi Theatre, London, Feb. 15, 1830. Aby Houndsditch is the Jewish character. Reviewed in *The Times*, London, Feb. 16, 1830, p. 3, col. 5, * *A*.

—— Rochester; or, King Charles the Second's merry days: a burletta, in three acts. As performed at the Olympic New Theatre... London: J. Lowndes, 1819. 2 p.l., 63 p. 8°.
NCO p.v.780

Licenser's ms. shows "extensive differences" from printed text. See *Catalogue of Larpent plays*, no. 2056.

The Library has three prompter's copies with interleaved ms. notes, *NCOF*.

Reprinted in *Modern English dramas*, London, 1820, v. 2 [no. 2].

—— Rochester; or, King Charles the Second's merry days. A musical comedy in three acts. As performed at the Olympic, Adelphi and other theatres... London: W. T. Moncrieff [pref. 1823]. 2 p.l., viii, (1)6–75 p. 8°.

—— —— London: W. T. Moncrieff, 1825. new ed. 8°. NCOF

Prompter's copy with interleaved ms. notes.
In the Advertisement, p. iii, the author states that this drama was written "to give Elliston an opportunity of displaying his extraordinary talents in the character of Rochester."

—— —— Printed from the acting copy, with remarks... London: T. Richardson [pref. 1828]. vi, 7–64 p. incl. front. 24°. NCO p.v.443

Also issued as no. 93 of Cumberland's minor theatre, *NCO p.v.407*. Of this edition the Library also has two prompter's copies with interleaved ms. notes in *NCOF*. Also appeared in v. 83 of Lacy's acting edition of plays, *NCO (Lacy)*.

First performed at the Olympic Theatre, London, Nov. 16, 1818, and styled then "a comic historical burletta." The plot is founded on an anecdote related in a letter by the celebrated St. Evremond to the Duchess of Mazarine. Rochester and Buckingham, two of the dramatis personae, disguise themselves as Jewish old-clothes men. Each considers the other a fake and each demands of the other that he speak Hebrew to prove his Jewishness. Elliston played Rochester and Pearman, Buckingham.

First produced in this country, at the Park Theatre, New York, March 23, 1820.

—— Van Diemen's Land; an operatic drama, in three acts... Printed from the acting copy, with remarks biographical and critical, by D.-G. [i.e. Geo. Daniel]... As performed at the metropolitan minor theatres... London: John Cumberland [18–?]. 76 p. incl. front. 24°. (Cumberland's minor theatre. v. 10.)
NCO (Cumberland)

First produced on Feb. 11, 1830, with Yardley as Ikey Solomons "(from the East)." Landa states that he saw a British Museum playbill of the first production where the Jewish character is named Barney Fence. The change to Solomons was occasioned by the trial and conviction of a notorious Solomons, who was sentenced to Van Diemen's Land (a penal colony). Cf. Landa, p. 161–162. The production took place at the Surrey Theatre, London. Reviewed in *The Times*, London, Feb. 12, 1830, p. 3, col. 4, * *A*.

Odell, IV:250, mentions a performance at the Olympic Theatre, New York, Dec. 20, 1837, but it is doubtful whether this is the play referred to.

Individual Plays—Earliest Times to 1837, cont'd

MONCRIEFF, WILLIAM THOMAS. *See also* sub-entries under SCOTT, SIR WALTER; SCRIBE, AUGUSTIN EUGÈNE.

MORTON, THOMAS. Zorinski: a play, in three acts, as performed at the Theatre Royal, Hay-Market... London: Printed by G. Woodfall, for T. N. Longman, 1795. 2 p.l., 73 p. 8°.
Without the music (by Arnold). NCO p.v.166
The ms. submitted to the Licenser bore the title *Casimir the Great*. It has "a few corrections in another hand...a few differences" from the printed text. See *Catalogue of Larpent plays*, no. 1081.

—— —— As it is performed at the Theatre-Royal, Crow-Street, with universal applause... Dublin: Printed by H. Fitzpatrick for G. Kingsley, 1796. 59 p. 12°.
A cast gives Meadows as Amalekite.

—— —— As performed at the Theatre Royal, Hay-Market... A new edition. London: Printed by A. Strahan, for T. N. Longman and O. Rees, 1800. 72 p. 8°. NCO (Morton) p.v.1
Also printed in Mrs. E. Inchbald, *Modern theatre*, London, 1811, v. 3, p. 85–139, NCO (Inchbald).
A compound of serious, almost tragic drama, mixed with scenes of comedy. An Irishman and a Jew, who is named Amalekite Grabowski, in the environs of Cracow, provided the farcical elements. The plot was founded historically on events in the life of King Stanislaus of Poland (Casimir in the play). Produced at the Haymarket, June 20, 1795, and played twenty times. Suett played Amalekite.
First produced at the Haymarket Theatre, Boston, May 15, 1797, and repeated there, June 5 and 14, with Mr. Hughes as Amalekite. It was seen in New York, March 23, 1798, but the character of Amalekite is not given in any available cast.
An anonymous *Zorinski; or, The Salt mine of Cracow* was produced at Sadler's Wells Theatre, London, Jan. 8, 1841. See Nicoll, p. 548.

Truth, pseud. Mr. Morton's *Zorinski* and Brooke's *Gustavus Vasa* compared; also a critique on Zorinski...by Mr. Morton and his friends in a weak and wild attempt to confute Truth. With alterations and additions by Truth. London: Printed for the author, 1795. 50 p. 8°. NAC p.v.337
The author, in analyzing the possible or obvious models for the dramatis personae of Morton's *Zorinski*, characterizes Amalekite thus — "the soul of Yuseph ben Mustapha in [James Cobb's] *The Siege of Belgrade*, transmigrated into the body of a Jew." — p. 28.

MOSER, JOSEPH. The bubbles; or, The matrimonial office. A comedy in three acts. (European magazine. London, 1808. 8°. v. 53, p. 9–15, 89–97, 169–178.) *DA
Unknown to Nicoll. The scene is London. The Jewish characters are Daniel (speaks in dialect), his clerk Jonas and his daughter Abienda.
For a memoir of the author see *European magazine*, London, 1803, v. 44, p. 83–85, *DA.

MURPHY, ARTHUR. The temple of Laverna [in one scene]. (In his: Works. London, 1786. 8°. v. 5, p. 149–158.) NCP
Reprinted from *Gray's Inn journal*, of Feb. 17, 1752, which Murphy edited, 1752–1754. He describes the scene as "taken from the life and is the opening of a farce intended to be worked up, for the winter season, into two acts."
"The curtain draws and discovers a group of circumcised exotic figures, all having selfishness, and a thorough contempt of what ideal moralists call benevolence, strongly depicted in their countenances." They are here named Moses Aaron, Judas, and Caiaphas. The last one, though about to become Christian, is still considered by the group as one of the faith.

Their talk concerns money and Exchange affairs. All the aversion which Murphy, in much of his writings, showed towards the Jews is concentrated in this skit.

MURRAY, WILLIAM HENRY WOOD. *See* sub-entry under SCOTT, SIR WALTER.

NORRIS, CHARLES GILMAN. See sub-entry under SCOTT, SIR WALTER.

O'KEEFFE, JOHN. The little hunch-back; or, A frolic in Bagdad. A farce. In two acts. As it is performed at the Theatre Royal, Covent-Garden, with universal applause... London: J. Debrett, 1789. 2 p.l., 35 p. 8°. NCO p.v.146
Also printed in his *Dramatic works*, London, 1798, v. 2, p. 281–334, NCP.
Licenser's ms. bears "some erasures and corrections ...several differences, with printed text longer than the ms." See *Catalogue of the Larpent plays*, no. 824. No. 2158, ibid., records an alteration of this farce by, probably, Samuel J. Arnold, who applied for the license and produced it at the English Opera House, London, July 8, 1820. An attempt to find periodical reviews of its reception was not successful.
Reviewed by C. C. in *Analytical review*, London, 1790, v. 6, p. 329–330, NAA.
Zebede, the purveyor, and his nephew Absalom, the barber, are the two Jewish characters. One of the earliest modern intermarriage plays.
"Jew, Christian, and Mahomedan are alike unpleasant." — *Landa, p. 122.*
First produced at Covent-Garden, April 14, 1789. The story is almost literally taken from the *Arabian Nights entertainment*, as far as relates to the hunchback.
No two casts agree as to the actors who played Zebede and Absalom. The *European magazine* gives Wewitzer and Milburn; *Town and country magazine*, Wewitzer and Macready; the printed London edition of 1789, Reeve and Macready; and the edition of 1798, Wilson and Macready. Absalom variously appears in the different casts as the Jew's man, a barber, or under his own name. Reviewed in *European magazine*, London, 1789, v. 15, p. 327–328, *DA; *London chronicle*, London, v. 65, p. 363, *A; and in *Town and country magazine*, London, v. 21, p. 181–182, *DA.
Presented for the first time in America at the Southwark Theatre, Philadelphia, May 27, 1791, by the American Company, with Mr. Martin as Absalom. In New York it was produced at the John Street Theatre, by the same company, Dec. 14, 1791, and by the Alexander Placide troupe, at the same theatre, April 13, 1792.

—— —— The London hermit; or, Rambles in Dorsetshire, a comedy, in three acts, as performed with universal applause at the Theatre Royal, Haymarket... London: J. Debrett, 1793. 3 p.l., 103 p. 8°.
Copy: Library of Congress.
Licenser's ms. has "prologue and epilogue [no epilogue in the printed text]...numerous differences." See *Catalogue of Larpent plays*, no. 988.

—— —— Second edition. London: Printed for J. Debrett, 1793. 4 p.l., 103 p. 8°.

—— —— Third edition. London: Printed for J. Debrett, 1793. 4 p.l., 103 p. 8°. *C p.v.306

—— —— Fourth edition. London: Printed for J. Debrett, 1793. 4 p.l., 103 p. 12°.

—— —— London: J. Barker, 1798. 3 p.l., 103 p. 5. ed. 8°. NCO p.v.119
The Library also has a prompter's copy, with ms. notes, of this ed., NCOF.
Also printed in his *Dramatic works*, London, 1798, v. 3, p. 209–290, NCP.
Reviewed in *Analytical review*, London, 1793, v. 17, p. 151–152, NAA; and in *English review*, London, 1793, v. 22, p. 306–307, *DA.
Produced at the Haymarket Theatre, London, June 29, 1793. Wewitzer as Barebones, described in the play

Individual Plays—Earliest Times to 1837, cont'd

as a "Methodist preacher, informer, pedlar, money-lender, old-cloaths man." He is made to speak in Jewish dialect — "Vhen I vas a coal-heaver, my face vas a black angel, but my inward man vas as vhite as a vhite vall that is vhite." — Act 2. Reviewed in *European magazine,* London, 1793, v. 24, p. 65–66, * *DA; London chronicle,* London, v. 74, p. 3, * *A;* and in *Universal magazine,* London, v. 93, p. 69–70, * *DA.*
Produced at the Park Theatre, New York, April 30, 1798, with John Martin as Barebones.

—— The comic opera of Peeping Tom of Coventry. In two acts. As performed at the Theatre-Royal, Smoke-Alley. [Dublin,] 1792. 39 p. 16°. NCO p.v.415
Without the music by S. Arnold.
The Examiner's ms. shows "conspicuous differences throughout." See *Catalogue of Larpent plays,* no. 662.

—— Peeping Tom of Coventry; a musical farce in two acts... Printed from the acting copy, with remarks, biographical and critical, by D. G. [i.e. Geo. Daniel]... As now performed at the Theatres Royal, London... London: J. Cumberland [1833?]. 36 p. incl. front. 12°. (Cumberland's British theatre. v. 31 [no. 9].) NCO
Three editions were printed in Dublin, all pirated, in 1784, 1786, and 1787. "Acted at the Haymarket [London, Sept. 6, 1784] with great success." — Baker, *Biographia dramatica.* Bannister played Harold. See Genest, VI:320–322. It was revived at the Covent Garden, April 20, 1789, and at the Drury Lane, Oct. 29, 1795.
In this comic opera George Colman, who was manager of the Haymarket in 1792, embodied a ballad called *The Little farthing rushlight,* the hero of which was Sir Solomon Simons, a knighted Jew. Bannister, noted for his Jewish parts, sang it in the Haymarket production of Aug. 22, 1792. See John Adolphus, *Memoirs of John Bannister, comedian,* London, 1839, v. 1, p. 277, *MWES* (Bannister).

—— The young Quaker; a comedy. As it is performed at the Theatre Royal in Smock-alley, with great applause. Dublin: Printed by P. Wogan, 1784. 56 p. 16°.
Copy: Library of Congress.
The Examiner's ms. shows "a few passages marked for omission; prologue and epilogue [by George Colman, manager of the Haymarket, who applied for the license]... differs greatly in content, order of scenes, and phraseology." See *Catalogue of Larpent plays,* no. 627.

—— —— Dublin: Printed for the booksellers, 1784. 36 p. 16°.
A pirated edition.
In the cast given, Mr. Cornellys played Shadrach Boaz.

—— —— n. p.: Printed for the book-sellers, 1788. 62 p. 16°.
Copy: Library of Congress.

—— The young Quaker, a comedy; as performed at the Theatre-Royal, Smoke-alley, and by the Old American Company. Philadelphia: Printed by Thomas Bradford, No. 8 South Front-street. 1794. 62 p., 1 l. 16°. * KD 1794
Evans 27448.

—— The fair American; or, The young Quaker... In five acts... Philadelphia: Published by Thomas H. Palmer, 1823. 63 p. 16°. NCO p.v.253
The Library also has a prompter's copy, with interleaved ms. notes, *NCOF.*

—— The young Quaker; a comedy, in five acts... Printed from the acting copy, with remarks biographical and critical, by D.-G. [i.e. Geo. Daniel]... As performed at the Theatres Royal, London... London: G. H. Davidson [18—?]. 59 p. incl. front. 24°. NCP
Bound in his: Dramatic works. London, 1798. v. 2 (copy 2).
Also issued in v. 37 of Cumberland's British theatre, *NCO (Cumberland).*
First produced at the Haymarket Theatre, London, July 26, 1783. Wewitzer played Shadrach Boaz, "the most repugnant stage Jew of the century, without a redeeming feature... a comic cowardly villain who epitomized what had gone before, standardized it afresh, and fashioned an 'improved type' for subsequent dramatists to copy slavishly." See Landa, p. 121. Reviewed in *European magazine,* London, 1783, v. 4, p. 148–149, * *DA; London chronicle,* London, v. 54, p. 99, * *DA; Town and country magazine,* London, v. 15, p. 403–404, * *DA;* and in *Universal magazine,* London, v. 73, p. 75–76, * *DA.*
Revived at the Theatre Royal, Haymarket, 1824, with Mr. Williams as Shadrach, and in 1827, with Mr. Wilkinson as Shadrach.
It was first produced in America by the Old American Company, in New York, May 12, 1794, with Mr. Hammond as Shadrach, and repeated there, June 9. In Philadelphia, where the play was given the additional sub-title The fair Philadelphian, it was staged at the Southwark Theatre, Sept. 26, 1794, and was repeated many times during that season, with Mr. Hammond or John Martin in the role of Shadrach. In Boston, it was seen Feb. 13 and 18, 1795. On Feb. 16, 1796, it was produced by Sollee's Charleston Company at Charleston, S. C., with Mr. Miller as Shadrach.
As *The fair American* it was seen at Alexandria, Va., Nov. 26, 1817, May 4 and Sept. 21, 1818; at Washington, D. C., July 16, 1818 and Sept. 13, 1821.

Colman, George, the elder. Prologue [and] epilogue [to the play]. (*European magazine,* London, 1783. 8°. v. 4, p. 149–150.) * DA
Printed also in *London chronicle,* London, 1783, v. 54, p. 159, * *A.*
Neither the prologue nor the epilogue appears in any of the published editions of the play.

PACE, WILLIAM. Lydia; or, Conversion; a sacred drama; inscribed to the Jews, by a clergyman of the Church of England [William Pace] ... London: J. G. and F. Rivington [etc.], 1835. vii(i), 75(1) p. 8°.
Plot laid at Antioch in the first century A. D. In the preface the author declares the purpose of the play to help promote conversion of the Jews to Christianity.

PALMER, WILLIAM. *See* sub-entry under SCOTT, SIR WALTER.

PASQUIN, P. P. Jewish conversion; a Christianical farce, got up with great effect under the direction of a society for making bad Jews worse Christians. Dedicated to His Royal Highness, the Duke of Kent, with whose approbation it has been recently played... London: J. Wooler, 1814. 8 p. 8°.
Copy: Library of Jewish Theological Seminary of America.
A poem with a title page suggesting a play. The author's name is probably pseudonymous. The piece is a satire on the London Society for the Conversion of the Jews and reflects the Jewish attitude towards organized Christian efforts to convert the Jews. The Duke of Kent, here referred to, was Edward, 4th son of King George III, Duke of Kent and Duke of Brunswick-Lüneberg, 1767–1820, father of Queen Victoria. The chief object of ridicule is Joseph Samuel Christian Frederick Frey, 1771–1850, born Joseph Samuel Levi, a Jewish convert and missionary to the Jews in England and the United States. He is here called Josh Shimel Christin Ferdick Vray. Cf. L. M. Friedman, *The American Society for Meliorating the Condition of the Jews and Joseph C. S. Frey, its missionary; a study in American Jewish history,* Boston, 1925, 1 p.l., 21 p. * *PG p.v.1.*

Individual Plays—Earliest Times to 1837, cont'd

PAYNE, JOHN HOWARD. See sub-entry under MAID AND MAGPIE.

PEAKE, RICHARD BRINSLEY. The bottle imp; a melo-dramatic romance, in two acts. Produced at the Theatre Royal, English Opera House, July, 1828... The overture and music composed by G[eorge] H. B. Rodwell... London: Chapman & Hall [1837-49]. 29(1) p., front. 12°.
Prompter's copy; interleaved ms. notes.   NCOF
Also issued in B. N. Webster, editor, *Acting national drama*, v. 2, with different imprint.
The exact date of production is July 7, 1828.
Reviewed in *Examiner*, London, 1828, p. 452-453, * *DA*; *Literary gazette*, London, 1828, p. 445, * *DA*; and in *New monthly magazine*, London, v. 24, p. 342-343, * *DA*. Genest gives Oct. 17, 1828, as the date of the first production, at the Covent-Garden, London, with Turnour as Shadrack.
"First announced here [Park Theatre, New York] on November 25th [1828], although Ireland places the première on February 14th, wrongfully." — Odell, 3:385.

PELLICO, SILVIO. Esther of Engaddi; a tragedy. From the Italian of S. Pellico. London: Whittaker, Treacher & Co.; Liverpool: W. Grapel [1836]. vii(i), 84 p. 8°.   NCO p.v.243
In five acts.
Scene: the Valley of Engaddi. Time: the second century of the Christian era.
The translator is Dr. James Vose. See Manchester Literary Club, *Papers*, v. 6, p. 216, *NAA*.

PHILLIPS, FREDERICK. See sub-entry under HUGO, VICTOR MARIE, COMTE.

PLANCHÉ, JAMES ROBINSON. See sub-entry under SCRIBE, AUGUSTIN EUGÈNE.

PLOWMAN, THOMAS FORDER. See sub-entry under SCOTT, SIR WALTER.

POCOCK, ISAAC. See sub-entry under MAID AND MAGPIE.

REDE, WILLIAM LEMAN. The skeleton witness; or, The murder of the Mount. A drama in three acts [and in prose and verse]. London: J. Miller, 1835. 43 p. 12°.
Title from British Museum catalogue.

——...The skeleton witness; or, The murder at the Mound. A domestic drama in three acts... As performed at the principal English and American theatres. New York: Samuel French [185-?]. 44 p. 12°. (French's standard drama. The acting edition. no. 197.)
As *The Skeleton witness; or, The king's evidence*, it was produced at the Surrey Theatre, London, April 27, 1835.
A murder mystery story in which one Simon Levi, money lender and pawnbroker, is involved. The theme of Rede's melodrama harks back to certain criminal offences in which certain Jews of the 1740-1770 period were implicated. See E. N. Adler, "The seamy side," in his *London*, Philadelphia, 1930, p. 151, * *PXQ*.
It enjoyed great popularity in this country. It was first seen at the Park Theatre, New York, July 31, 1835, with Henry Lewis as Simon Levi. Odell states: "Lewis made a hit in a Jewish part." The printed text gives casts for a Louisville, Ky., presentation in 1838; Walnut Street Theatre, Philadelphia, in 1837; and Bowery Theatre, New York, in 1857.
The Murder of the Mount; or, Whitechapel in 1740 (anon.), dealing with the same story, was produced at the Royal Pavillion, London, Oct. 20, 1834. See Nicoll, p. 498.

ROWSON, SUSANNA HASWELL. Slaves in Algiers; or, A struggle for freedom. A play interspersed with songs, in three acts... As performed at the new theatres in Philadelphia and Baltimore. Philadelphia: Printed for the author by Wrigley and Berriman, 1794. 2 p.l., ii p., 1 l., (1)6-72 p., 1 l. 16°.   NBL p.v.121
This play, by the author of *Charlotte Temple*, first produced at the New Theatre, Philadelphia, June 30, 1794, to the music composed by Reinagle, deals with the American difficulties with the Mediterranean pirates, and is the first American play containing Jewish characters. Francis acted Ben Hassan and Mrs. Marshall, Fetnah, his estranged daughter. For a synopsis of the play and its early American stagings, see E. D. Coleman, "Plays of Jewish interest on the American stage, 1752-1821," in American Jewish Historical Society, *Publications*, Baltimore, 1934, no. 33, p. 180-182, *IAA*.
See also R. W. G. Vail, "Susanna Haswell Rowson; a bibliographical study," in American Antiquarian Society, *Proceedings*, 1932, new series, v. 42, p. 47-90, 144, *IAA*.
It was never produced in England.

SCOTT, SIR WALTER. Ivanhoe; a romance...
The first dramatization to be produced in America was seen at the Anthony Street Theatre, New York, June 19, 1820, with R. C. Maywood as Isaac and Mrs. Barnes as Rebecca. No contemporary review of it has been found. Odell questions whether it was of American authorship. It may have been the version of Dibdin, Moncrieff, Soane, or any of the five other versions which had already appeared in England.

Aymar, Benjamin, and J. R. Blake. Ivanhoe, a modification of H. J. Byron's *Ivanhoe*, was produced by the Columbia University Dramatic Club, "The Strollers," at the Irving Place Theatre, New York, May 8, 1893.
Giles A. Faintor played Isaac; Melvin H. Dalberg, Rebecca.
Reviewed in *New York Times*, May 9, 1893, p. 5, col. 3, * *A*; and in *New York Herald*, May 9, 1893, p. 8, col. 5, * *A*.

Beazley, Samuel. Ivanhoe; or, The knight templar: adapted from the novel of that name. First performed the 2nd of March, 1820, at the Theatre Royal, Covent Garden. The music selected by Dr. Kitchener, the stage management and the whole piece produced under the direction of Mr. Farley. London: Printed by W. Smith, sold by Simpkin and Marshall [etc.], 1820. 72 p. 8°.
Copy: Library of Congress.
The Examiner's ms. has "two short deletions... extensive differences, chiefly long passages in ms. not in printed text; minor differences throughout." See *Catalogue of Larpent plays*, no. 2140.
Attributed to Samuel Beazley. *cf.* Theatrical inquisitor, v. 16, p. 125-127, 136, 225; Eitner, v. 5, p. 377.
This version, ascribed by the Library of Congress to Beazley, is recorded anonymously in the British Museum and Harvard College Library catalogues.
Produced at the Covent Garden, London, March 2, 1820, with Farren as Isaac and Miss Foote as Rebecca. This version, described as a magnificent spectacle, commencing after the tournament and concluding with the burning of Front de Boeuf's castle, followed the plot of the novel more closely than the other versions. More of the episodes were included. Ivanhoe (Charles Kemble) is represented in love with Rebecca.
Reviewed in *European magazine*, London, 1820, v. 77, p. 258, * *DA*; *Literary gazette*, London, 1820, p. 157, * *DA*; *London magazine*, London, 1820, v. 1, p. 437-440, * *DA*; *Monthly magazine*, London, v. 49, p. 266, * *DA*; *New monthly magazine and universal register*, London, v. 13, p. 474-475, * *DA*; and in *The Times*, London, March 3, 1820, p. 3, col. 5, * *A*.
For colored plates and stage designs, as well as other illustrations, see *MWEZ* n.c.773, p. 20, 21, 34, 35 and *MWEZ* n.c.1308, p. 20.

Individual Plays—Earliest Times to 1837, cont'd

SCOTT, SIR WALTER, *continued*

Brough, Robert Barnabas, and W. Brough. The last edition of Ivanhoe, with all the latest improvements. An extravaganza in two acts, by the Brothers Brough... As first performed at the Theatre Royal, Haymarket [April 1, 1850]... London: National Acting Drama Office [185–?]. 43 p., 1 pl. 12°.

Isaac of York, principal partner in the eminent firm of "Isaacs & Son," cheap tailors, armourers, &c., Houndsditch, York — a picture in Mosaic, by Mr. Keeley. Rebecca the maid of Judah par excellence. The artist is Miss P. Horton. Reviewed in *The Times*, London, April 2, 1850, p. 5, col. 2, * A.

Brown, Muriel. Ivanhoe; a play in four acts, dramatized from the novel of Sir Walter Scott... Edited by Claude Merton Wise... Art work by Don Ament... Evanston, Ill.: Row, Peterson & Company [cop. 1930]. 5 p.l., 106 p. col'd illus., diagrs. 12°.

On cover: The gateway series of tested plays. "First produced, Nov. 23, 1929, at the Kenneth Sawyer Goodman Memorial Theatre, Chicago, Illinois," with Estherle Andrews as Rebecca and Peter Martin as Isaac.

Bunn, Alfred. Ivanhoe; or, The Jew of York. A new grand chivalric play, in three acts. Compiled by A. Bunn, Esq., and now performing with the greatest success at the new Theatre Royal, Birmingham. Birmingham: Beilby and Knotts [etc.], 1820. 3 p.l., (1)4–76 p. 8°.
NCO p.v.93

"The play... was compiled... from the... novel of that name, and from contemporary plays on the subject." — *Preface*.

A play, similarly entitled, is recorded by Nicoll as having been staged at the Coburg Theatre, London, Jan. 24, 1820. It is probably not the version arranged later by Bunn.

Byron, Henry James. Ivanhoe, in accordance with the spirit of the times; an extravaganza [in six scenes]... London: T. H. Lacy [186–?]. 48, 13–16 p. 12°. (Lacy's acting edition of plays. v. 59.) NCO (Lacy)
p. 11–12, omitted.

—— —— London, New York: S. French [1863–75]. 2 p.l., (1)8–48 p. 12°. NCO p.v.267

Produced at the Strand Theatre, London, Dec. 26, 1862. Mr. J. Clark as Isaac of York is represented as a speculating army clothier, bill discounter and general outfitter. Mr. James Rogers as Rebecca has formed a clandestine attachment to Ivanhoe. Reviewed in *Era*, London, Dec. 28, 1862, p. 13, † *NAFA;* and in *The Times*, London, Dec. 27, 1862, p. 3, col. 5–6, * A. "The rage of the Jew... is something wonderful to witness. From cursing it passes to shrieking and finally culminates in a song and a jig."

This travesty served as a basis for another one, played by the Cambridge Amateur Dramatic Company in 1891, under the title of *Ivanhoe à la carte,* in allusion to Mr. D'Oyly Carte's production of Sir Arthur Sullivan's *Ivanhoe.* See below under Stone, Dalton.

The Pi Eta Society of Harvard College presented it at Beethoven Hall, New York, April 24, 1876. See Theatre Collection, Programme folder "Chums."

Cole, John William. Ivanhoe; or, The Jewess. Founded on the celebrated romance of Ivanhoe by the author of Waverley. Edinburgh: John Anderson, 1825. 3 p.l., 79 p. 16°.

In five acts.
Dedication, p. iii, signed by John William Calcraft [pseud.].
Copy: Harvard College Library.

Cooper, Frederick Fox. Ivanhoe. (A historical drama in three acts. Dramatized from Sir W. Scott's novel.) [1885.] 16 p. 12°. (Dicks' standard plays. no. 385.)

Title from British Museum catalogue.
H. A. White states that it was produced at Astley's Theatre, London, Easter Monday, 1869. This is in error, since the play at Astley's on that evening, March 28, was Boucicault's London assurance.

Cowie, R. Ivanhoe. Produced at the Royal Theatre, Dundee, Feb. 15, 1875.

Crawford, Alice. Rebecca and Rowena; or, The triumph of Israel. A tragic burlesque in five acts — for amateur parlor representation — based on Thackeray's sequel to Ivanhoe. New York: G. B. Vaux, 1883. 28 p. 16°. NBL p.v.12

—— —— New York: Roorbach & Co. [cop. 1883.] 28 p. 12°. (The acting drama. no. 185.)
NBL p.v.9

Rowena "dies." Rebecca turns Christian and marries Ivanhoe.
Produced at the Columbia Institute, New York, for the benefit of the New York Canoe Club, April 16, 1883, with Miss Seavey as Rebecca. The play was printed anonymously, and is so given in the Library's catalogue, but the programme in the Theatre Collection discloses the authorship.

Dibdin, Thomas John. Ivanhoe; or, The Jew's daughter. A melo dramatic romance, in three acts. First performed at the Surrey Theatre, on Thursday, January 20, 1820. London: Roach and Co., 1820. viii, (1)10–71 p. 8°.

Prologue, spoken by Miss Copeland, p. vii–viii.
Also published in Cumberland's Minor theatre, v. 2, *NCO (Cumberland);* French's standard drama, the acting edition, no. 319; Lacy's acting edition of plays, v. 92, *NCO (Lacy);* and Spencer's Boston theatre, no. 196, *NCR p.v.4.*

It follows the course of the romance closely and includes all the important characters. Produced at the Surrey Theatre, London, Jan. 20, 1820, with Huntley as Isaac and Miss Taylor as Rebecca. Reviewed in *European magazine*, London, 1820, v. 77, p. 62–63, * *DA;* and in *New monthly magazine and universal register*, London, v. 13, p. 475–476, * *DA.*

This play was produced at the Coburg Theatre, London, Feb. 15, 1830, as *Ivanhoe; or, The Knights Templars; or, Isaac the Jew of York.* See Nicoll, p. 292.

A version, definitely ascribed to Dibdin, was produced at the Howard Athenaeum, Boston, 1853, with W. R. Goodall as Isaac and Mrs. A. Knight as Rebecca, and at the Broadway Theatre, New York, in 1859, with E. Eddy as Isaac and Mme. Ponisi as Rebecca.

Edgar, Richard Horatio. Ivanhoe; or, The maid of York, based on Scott's novel, was produced at the Royal Amphitheatre, Liverpool, Nov. 27, 1871.

J. Lunt was Isaac and Miss Marriott, Rebecca. Reviewed in *Era*, London, v. 34, Dec. 3, 1871, p. 6, col. 6, † *NAFA.*

Estabrook, H. D. The joust; or, Tournament. An operetta in two acts... Libretto by H. D. Estabrook. Chicago: W. P. Dunn & Co., 1883. 32 p. 8°.

Words only.
See United States. — Copyright Office, *Dramatic compositions copyrighted in the United States, 1870 to 1916,* item 23075.

Findlay, Maud I. Scott's Ivanhoe dramatised for school use. London, New York [etc.]: H. Milford, Oxford University Press [1917]. iv, 5–36 p. 12°. NCO p.v.417

In eight scenes.
Also issued in 1922.

Individual Plays—Earliest Times to 1837, cont'd

SCOTT, SIR WALTER, *continued*

Gallatin, Alberta. A dramatization of Sir Walter Scott's novel "Ivanhoe"... n. p. [1907?] 4 1. 12°. Theatre Collection "Ivanhoe" folder
In four acts.
A scenario.

Gunnison, Binney. The baron and the Jew. Adapted from the novel, "Ivanhoe," by Sir Walter Scott. (In his: New dialogues and plays. New York, 1900. 8°. Intermediate dialogues, p. 135–138.) NACG–NDP

Halliday, Andrew. Rebecca, an adaptation in four acts of Scott's Ivanhoe, was produced at the Drury Lane, London, Sept. 23, 1871.
Samuel Phelps played Isaac and Miss Lilian A. Neilson, Rebecca. The rôle of Rebecca was made most prominent, in order to feature Miss Neilson. "Of the Jew [Isaac] even Mr. Phelps can make no more than a trembling old man." — *The Times* reviewer. Reviewed in *Era*, London, Oct. 1, 1871, p. 13, † *NAFA*; *Graphic*, London, v. 4, p. 323, * *DA*; *Illustrated London news*, London, v. 59, p. 315, * *DA*; *The Times*, London, Sept. 26, 1871, p. 4, col. 2, * *A*; and in *Vanity fair*, London, v. 6, p. 115–116, * *DA*.

Hayman, Philip, and E. Solomon. All my eyevanhoe, a two-act burlesque, was produced at the Trafalgar Theatre, London, Oct. 31, 1894.
James Stevenson acted Mithter Ithaacth of York; Phyllis Broughton, Rebecca Hothouse Peach. The music was by John Crook, Howard Talbot, Philip Hayman and Edward Solomon. Reviewed in *Theatre*, London, 1894, new series, v. 24, p. 318, *NCOA*; *The Times*, London, Nov. 1, 1894, p. 3, col. 6, * *A*; and by William Archer in his *Theatrical 'World' of 1894*, London, 1895, p. 298–300, *NCOA (Archer)*.

Ivanhoe; or, The Jew of York: a drama, in three acts. [Adapted from Sir W. Scott's romance.] London [1822]. 12°. (Hodgson's Juvenile drama.)
Title from British Museum catalogue.

Ivanhoe; or, The Saxon chief, an adaptation from Scott, is recorded by Nicoll as having been staged at the Adelphi Theatre, London, Feb. 14, 1820.
The Licenser's ms. terms it a "melodramatic burletta, 3 acts...some deletions" made by the Examiner, to be observed during the performance. Application was made Jan. 1, 1820. See *Catalogue of Larpent plays*, nos. 2141 and 2135.

Jackson, John P. The Templar and the Jewess. [ca. 1833.] 8°.
A version of Wohlbrueck and Marschner.
Title from Nicoll, p. 320.

Lacy, Michael Rophino. The maid of Judah: or, The Knights Templars: a serious opera, in three acts, (dramatised from Sir Walter Scott's Ivanhoe,) by M. Rophino Lacy... The music composed by Rossini. Printed from the acting copy, with remarks biographical and critical, by D.—G. ... As performed at the Theatres Royal... London: J. Cumberland, n. d. 63 p. incl. front. 16°. (Cumberland's British theatre. v. 25 [no. 5].) NCO (Cumberland)
Remarks by George Daniel, editor of the series.
Without the music.
Library also has a prompter's copy, with interleaved ms. notes, *NCOF*.

—— —— London: Davidson [ca. 1849–55]. NCOF
Library also has another prompter's copy, with interleaved ms. notes, *NCOF*.
p. 61–63 missing in both and supplied partly in ms. One of these is the volume about which H. A. White states: "The New York Public Library has an independent text that shows some changes." H. A. White, in his *Sir Walter Scott's novels on the stage*, p. 113, calls it "a bad translation and adaptation" of the French opera *Ivanhoé* by Émile Deschamps and Gabriele Gustave de Wailly.
Scene passes in England after the third Crusade, 1194. First produced at the Covent Garden, London, March 7, 1829, with Egerton as Isaac and Miss Paton as Rebecca. The whole interest of the piece is made to devolve upon the character of Rebecca. Reviewed in *Literary gazette*, London, 1829, p. 180, * *DA*; and in *The Times*, London, March 9, 1829, p. 5, col. 2, * *A*.

Melville, Walter. Ivanhoe, drama in four acts, was produced by Walter Melville, at the Lyceum Theatre, London, May 22, 1913.
Hubert Carter as Isaac of York and Miss Tittell-Brune as Rebecca. Reviewed in *Era*, London, v. 76, May 24, 1913, p. 13, † *NAFA*.

Moncrieff, William Thomas. Ivanhoe! or, The Jewess. A chivalric play, in three acts, founded on the popular romance of "Ivanhoe"... London: Printed for John Lowndes, 1820. 2 p.l., 80 p. 8°.
"I have a strong suspicion my drama will prove the best that may appear on the subject, from the circumstance of its containing less original matter than any other." — p.l. 2.
"Seems never to have been produced," White, p. 111; but Nicoll, p. 348, gives Coburg Theatre, London, Jan. 24, 1820.

Murray, William Henry Wood. Ivanhoe; a historical drama, founded on the celebrated romance of the same name, by the author of "Waverley," &c., &c., performed at the Theatre-Royal, Edinburgh... Edinburgh: Printed for J. L. Huie, and sold by Oliver & Boyd [etc.], 1823. 76 p. front. 12°. (In: The Waverley dramas, from the novels... London, 1845. [no. 8.])
Half-title: Dramas from the novels, tales, &c. of the author of "Waverley." no. VII.
Adapted by Murray in three acts from Beazley's *Ivanhoe; or, The knight templar*, from *Rebecca*; or, *The Jew's daughter* (probably Dibdin's version) and Calcraft's (Cole, J. W., in this list) *Ivanhoe*. cf. J. C. Dibdin's *Annals of the Edinburgh stage*, p. 307.
Without the music (arranged from Bishop by Dewar).
Halkett and Laing, following the British Museum catalogue, ascribes this play to Daniel Terry. The Library of Congress and the Harvard College Library ascribe it to Murray.
Produced at the Edinburgh Royal Theatre, Nov. 24, 1823, with Mason as Isaac and Mrs. H. Siddons as Rebecca. It ran seventeen evenings, Nov. 24 – Dec. 13, 1823. Reviewed daily while it was being performed, in *Edinburgh dramatic review*, Edinburgh, 1823, v. 6, p. 84–146, 152–154, *NCOA*.

Norris, Charles Gilman. Ivanhoe; a grove play ...music by Harry I. Wiel. San Francisco: Bohemian Club, 1936. 107 p. 8°. NBM
Without music.
This, the 35th Grove play of the Club, was produced by the Club, Aug. 1, 1936, with H. H. Chalmers as Isaac and Templeton Crocker as Rebecca. The plot of the original *Ivanhoe* is closely followed.

Palmer, William. Ivanhoe; a dramatic version of Sir Walter Scott's novel, was produced at the Queen's Theatre, Manchester, Sept. 10, 1906.
Title from *"The Stage" cyclopaedia*.

Individual Plays—Earliest Times to 1837, cont'd
SCOTT, SIR WALTER, continued

Plowman, Thomas Forder. Isaac abroad; or, Ivanhoe settled and Rebecca righted. A second travesty. Produced at the Theatre Royal, Oxford, Jan. 15, 1878.

—— Isaac of York; or, Saxons and Normans at home, "a burlesque-extravaganza" in three scenes, was produced at the Court Theatre, London, Nov. 29, 1871.
This was a parody of Halliday's *Rebecca*. Mr. Righton played Isaac and Miss M. Oliver, Rebecca. Reviewed in *Era*, London, v. 34, Dec. 3, 1871, p. 11, † *NAFA*.
Two extracts from the script are given by W. D. Adams in his *A Book of burlesques*, London, 1891, p. 196–198.

Scott, Sir Walter. Scene from "Ivanhoe." (In: Humorous monologues and dramatic scenes, by Belle Marshall Locke and others. Boston, cop. 1907. 12°. p. 40–42.) NBL p.v.77
Rebecca and Rowena speaking.

Simons, Sarah Emma, and C. I. Orr. Ivanhoe. [In three episodes.] (In their: Dramatization: selections from English classics adapted in dramatic form. Chicago, New York [cop. 1913]. 8°. first year, p. 24–46.)

Soane, George. The Hebrew; a drama in five acts. As performed at the Theatre Royal, Drury-Lane... London: John Lowndes, 1820. 64 p. 8°.
Prologue, by R. Barlow, contains the following: Our "Hebrew" of to-night attention claims. No longer scoff'd, in peaceful compact blend, Christian and Jew by turns each other's friend.
Produced at the Drury Lane, London, March 2, 1820, the same evening when Beazley's version was staged at the Covent Garden, with Edmund Kean as Isaac, Mrs. West as Rebecca, and Miss Carew as Miriam, Rebecca's attendant. One reviewer wrote as follows: "Isaac in his [author's] hands is not the Jew of York — nor any Jew at all — but a passionate and metaphysical old man in a strange gaberdine. There are...few of those admirable Hebraisms which in the novel carry back the mind to the old glories of the race of Judah... The Jew of Walter Scott would have been rich, indeed, in the hands of the performer [Edmund Kean] whose Shylock and whose Jew of Malta prove how finely he can depict the peculiarities of the race of Abraham."
Reviewed in *European magazine*, London, 1820, v. 77, p. 256–257, * *DA*; *Literary gazette*, London, 1820, p. 157, * *DA*; *London magazine*, London, 1820, v. 1, p. 437–440, * *DA*; *Monthly magazine*, London, v. 49, p. 266, * *DA*; *New monthly magazine and universal register*, London, v. 13, p. 473–474, * *DA*; and in *The Times*, London, March 3, 1820, p. 3, col. 5, * *A*. See also F. W. Hawkins, *The Life of Edmund Kean*, London, 1869, v. 2, p. 116–117, *MWES* (Kean).
It was licensed under the Lord Chamberlain on Feb. 9, 1820, under the title *The Pilgrim from Palestine*, a "tragicomedy." Ms. bears "some corrections and excisions...differs extensively" from the printed text, *The Hebrew*. See *Catalogue of Larpent plays*, no. 2143.
Produced at the Park Theatre, New York, Dec. 15, 1823, with Thomas Hilson as Isaac and Ellen Johnson as Rebecca. Noted briefly in *New York mirror*, 1823, v. 1, p. 165, * *DA*.

Stevens, Ernest. Ivanhoe; a drama, adapted from Sir Walter Scott's novel, was produced at the Grand Theatre, Glasgow, March 14, 1896.
Title from *"The Stage" cyclopaedia*.

Stevenson, Augusta. Ivanhoe. [In three acts.] illus. (In her: Children's classics in dramatic form. Book five. Boston [etc., cop. 1912]. 8°. p. 166–204.)

Stone, Dalton. Ivanhoe a la carte; a burlesque in imitation of H. J. Byron's *Ivanhoe according to the spirit of the times*.
Produced at Cambridge, England, July, 1891, with Bromley Davenport as "old clo" Isaac of York. Reviewed in *Theatre*, London, 1891, new series, v. 18, p. 93, *NCOA*.

Sturgis, Julian Russell. Ivanhoe, a romantic opera, adapted from Sir Walter Scott's novel. Words by J. Sturgis; music by Arthur Sullivan. London: Chappell & Co. [1891.] 36 p. 8°.
* MZ (Sullivan)
Produced at the Royal English Opera, London, Jan. 31, 1891. Margaret Macintyre and Miss Thudichum as Rebecca; Charles Copland as Isaac of York. Reviewed in *Jewish chronicle*, London, Feb. 6, 1891, p. 12, * *PBE*; and (with illus.) in *Pall mall budget*, London, 1891, v. 39, Feb. 5, 1891, p. 1, 8–10, * *DA*. Illustrations are also in *Illustrated London news*, London, v. 98, p. 132, 165, 168, 170, 385, * *DA*; *Graphic*, London, v. 43, p. 144–145, * *DA*; *Illustrated sporting and dramatic news*, London, v. 34, p. 678, 715, 768–769, * *DA*; and in *MWEZ* n.c.774, p. 40.

Hind, Lewis. A souvenir of "Ivanhoe"...with twenty-one illustrations from drawings by Maurice Greiffenhagen, Herbert Railton, John Jellicoe, and others. London: Published for the Royal English Opera, by J. S. Virtue & Co., Ltd. [1891.] 32 p. incl. front., illus. obl. 12°.
Theatre Collection "Ivanhoe (Sturgis and Sullivan)" folder.
Detailed synopsis of the story, with extracts from the text.

———

The following Ivanhoe plays are recorded as copyrighted, but no record of their production is available: by Hiram W. Hayes in 1899; by C. H. Curtis in 1901; by Paul D. Emmons in 1913; and by Elizabeth Hawxby in 1915; by James M. Martin in 1904, under the title *By wager of battle* ("a drama from the time of the Norman conquest of England*, A.D. 1175–1200"); and by Wm. H. Duncan, Jr., in 1908, under the title *The tournament; or, Ivanhoe and the black knight*. See United States. — Copyright Office, *Dramatic compositions copyrighted in the United States, 1870 to 1916*, items 22270–22273a, 5728 and 46631.

Ben-Zion, Benedix. A varumglücktes Auto-dafé oder Rebecca die 18 jährige Mechaschefoh. Drame in 5 Akten und zwölf Bilder. Die Maasse is arausgenumen vum Walter Scott's Roman "Ivanhoe" (Englisch) übersetzt, arrangirt und baarbet far der jüdischer Bühne. Odessa, 1882. 1 p.l., 88 p. sq. 8°.
Judeo-German ms.
Title from A. S. Freidus' *List of dramas in The New York Public Library, relating to the Jews*, item 210.

Lenz, Johann Reinhold. Das Gericht der Templar; Schauspiel in drei Aufsätze. Mainz, 1825. (In his: Schauspiele nach Walter Scott.)
Title from C. G. Kayser, *Vollständiges Bücher-Lexicon, 1750–1832*.

Leroy-Denis, Jeanne. ...Ivanhoé; grand drame historique en 5 actes, d'après le célèbre roman de Walter Scott. Niort: H. Boulord [1934?]. 159 p. 12°. (Collection mon théâtre.)
NKM p.v.748
"Cette pièce a été radiodiffusée par l'ensemble des stations du réseau d'État français, en septembre 1932, lors de la célébration du centenaire de Walter Scott."

Individual Plays—Earliest Times to 1837, cont'd
SCOTT, SIR WALTER, *continued*

Possolo Hogan, Alfredo. Ivanhoe; drama em cinco actos e nove quadros. Extrahido do romance de Sir Walter Scott Ivanhoe, ou a volta do Cruzado... Lisboa: Typ. da Rua de Bica de Duarte Bello, 1849. 111 p. 12°. NQM p.v.103

Wohlbrück, Wilhelm August. Der Templer und die Jüdin. Grosse romantische Oper in drei Aufzuegen, nach Walter Scott's Roman: "Ivanhoe." Frei bearbeitet... Leipzig: Carl Focke, 1829. 164 p. 16°.

—— Der Templer und die Jüdin; romantische Oper in drei Aufzügen, von Heinr. Aug. Marschner. Dichtung nach Walter Scott's "Ivanhoe," von W. A. Wohlbrück... Hrsg. von C. F. Wittmann. Leipzig: Philipp Reclam, jun., n. d. 109 p. plans. 24°. (Universal Bibliothek. Nr. 3553.)
First produced, to the music of Marschner, at the Hoftheater, Leipzig, Dec. 22, 1829.

—— Tempelherren og Jødinden; romantisk Opera, i fire Acter. Musiken af Heinrich Marschner. Oversat af Th. Overskou. Kjøbenhavn, 1834. 19 p. 8°. (Kongelige Theaters Repertoire. v. 3.) NAFH (Kongelige)
Caption-title.
A translation into Danish of the preceding entry.
Nicoll records *The Templar and the Jewess*, by Wohlbrück and Marschner as having been produced at the Drury Lane, London, May 26, 1841.

On the dramatic powers of the author of Waverley. (Blackwood's magazine. Edinburgh, 1826. 8°. v. 19, p. 152–160.) *DA
Particular references are made to the episodes in Ivanhoe which lend themselves to dramatization.

White, Henry Adelbert. [The dramatizations of Scott's Ivanhoe.] (In his: Sir Walter Scott's novels on the stage. New Haven: Yale University Press, 1927. 8°. p. 102–123, 237–238.) NCC (Scott)

Wilstach, Paul. Dramatisations of Scott. illus. (Bookman. New York, 1902. 8°. v. 15, p. 129–137, 280–282.) *DA

SCRIBE, AUGUSTIN EUGÈNE. La Juive. The Jewess. A grand opera in four acts. The music by Halévy. [Libretto. Italian and English text.] New York: C. Breusing, 1860. 2 p.l., (1) 4–23, 5 p. 8°. *MZ (Halévy)
The scene is Constance, 27th and 28th of January, 1417, during the session of the Council of Constance, when the emperor Sigismund visited the city.
First staged at the Paris Opéra, Feb. 23, 1835, and in England, at the Drury Lane, London, in French, July 29, 1846.

Burroughs, Watkins. The Jewess; a drama, was produced at Edinburgh, June 1, 1836.

Clempert, John. Jedorka (the Jewess); a dramatic sketch was produced at the Manchester Palace, Manchester, England, April 15, 1907.
Title from "The Stage" cyclopædia.

The Jewess; or, The cardinal's daughter, by an anonymous adapter, was produced, November 23, 1835, at the Pavillion Theatre, London, with Denvil as Eleazer. Reviewed in *Athenæum*, London, 1835, p. 892, *DA.

Lacy, Thomas Hailes. The Jewess; or, The Council of Constance. A romantic drama, in three acts, adapted from Scribe's "La Juive"... London: T. H. Lacy [1857–73]. v(i), 7–40 p. 12°. (Lacy's acting edition of plays. v. 33.) NCO (Lacy)

Moncrieff, William Thomas. ...The Jewess; or, The Council of Constance. A romantic drama, in three acts... The only edition correctly marked by permission, from the prompter's book... As performed at the London theatres... London: J. Duncombe & Co. [1835?] 54 p., incl. front. 16°. (Duncombe's acting edition of the British theatre. no. 149.) NCO p.v.304

—— ...The Jewess; or, The Council of Constance. An historical drama, in three acts. By W. T. Moncrieff... As performed at the London and New-York theatres... New-York: O. Phelan [ca. 1840]. 62 p. 16°.
Copy: Library of Congress.
Also issued in French's American drama, the acting edition, no. 37, NCR p.v.6.
First produced at the Victoria Theatre, London, Nov. 30, 1835, with Archer as Eleazer Mendizabel, and Mrs. Selby as Rachel.
Moncrieff's version was produced in this country at the Bowery Theatre, New York, March 7, 1836, with Jackson as Eleazer and Mrs. Flynn as Rachel. Besides this production and Planché's at the Park, on March 11, a third, an anonymous version, was staged at the Franklin Theatre, New York, March 15, 1836, with Wm. Sefton as Eleazer. See an extensive account in Odell IV: 80–81.

Planché, James Robinson. The Jewess, a grand operatic drama, in three acts, founded on M. Scribe's opera, "La juive," by J. R. Planché... First performed at the Theatre Royal, Drury-Lane, Monday, Nov. 16, 1835. London: Porter and Wright, 1835. vii(i), 48 p. 8°.
"Although I have adhered pretty closely...to the plot of Mons. Scribe's drama, the language, such as it is, is my own." — *Note at end, signed J. R. P.*
Planché, instead of allowing his Jewess to be cast into the boiling cauldron, causes her to be rescued at the last moment. He defends this alteration of the denouement in his *Recollections and reflections*, London, 1872, v. 1, p. 240–244, AN.
Vandenhoff played Eleazer and Ellen Tree, Rachel. Reviewed in *Athenæum*, London, 1835, v. 8, p. 876, *DA; in *Literary gazette*, London, 1835, v. 17, p. 748, *DA; in *New monthly magazine*, London, 1835, v. 45, p. 519–521, *DA; and in *The Times*, London, Nov. 17, 1835, p. 3, col. 3, *A.
First American production at the Park Theatre, New York, March 11, 1836, with Harrison as Eleazer and Mrs. Hilson as Rachel.
The staging of the earliest American version, by an unknown adapter, took place at the Franklin Theatre, New York, Feb. 29, 1836, with William Isherwood as Eleazer and Mrs. Blake as Rachel.

SESSA, KARL BOROMÄUS ALEXANDER. The ways of our tribe; a bluette in one act. Altered from the German farce of "Unser Fakehr [*sic*]"... London: John Lowndes [181–?]. 19 p. 8°.
Copy: Library of Jewish Theological Seminary of America. Israel Solomons Collection.
A viciously anti-Semitic play which was first produced at the Breslauer Theater, Feb. 11, 1813, under its original title *Die Judenschule*. On account of its inflammatory nature, it was for a time forbidden by

Individual Plays—Earliest Times to 1837, cont'd

Chancellor Hardenberg. It was seen in Danzig, Hamburg, Königsberg and reached Berlin in 1815, where it was staged under the printed title, *Unser Verkehr*. The main characters are a father and son, Abraham and Jacob Hirsch; the latter part was first acted in Breslau by Ludwig Deverient, and by Ferdinand A. A. Wurm in the provinces. Goethe refused to have it staged at Weimar, while he was manager of its Opera.

Against this farce appeared in 1815 *Edelmuth und Schlechtsinn; ein Seitenstück zu Unser Verkehr*, by L. T. H. W. Wichmann, and *Euer Verkehr*, by Julius von Voss, Berlin, 1816. Sessa himself wrote an afterpiece in continuation which he called *Jakobs Kriegsthaten und Hochzeit; Fastnachts-Posse in drei Akten*, Kanaan, 1816.

Gotthard Deutsch gives bibliographical data about the history of the controversy aroused by this farce in *Jewish chronicle*, London, Jan. 29, 1915, p. 21, * PBE. See Ludwig Geiger in *Allgemeine Zeitung des Judentums*, Berlin, 1903, Jahrg. 67, p. 78–81, * PBC; his *Geschichte der Juden in Berlin*, Bd. 2, p. 191–192, * PXS; and G. R. Philon, *Über die Juden auf Veranlassung der Posse Unser Verkehr; hierzu noch einige Anmerkungen*, Königsberg u. Leipzig, 1815 (copy in Library of the Jewish Theological Seminary, in a volume labelled *Schriften über Juden*).

On the t.-p. of the English translation is given the first part of Barabas' speech to Ithamore in act II, scene 3, of Marlowe's *Jew of Malta*, "As for myself, I walk abroad o' nights, and kill sick people groaning under walls," etc. In this spirit, the translator apparently conceived his work. No record is known to the compiler about a stage production of it in England. As to Voss's *Euer Verkehr* and his views on the Jews as expressed in his plays, see Johannes Hahn, *Julius von Voss*, Berlin, 1910, p. 48–54 (Palaestra, No. 94), NFF p.v.27.

SHAKESPEARE, WILLIAM. The Merchant of Venice. 1600.

The Library has numerous editions of the *Merchant of Venice* but they are so many and the literature of the subject so voluminous that it has seemed best to do nothing except to call attention to it.

SHELLEY, PERCY BYSSHE. Œdipus tyrannus; or, Swellfoot the tyrant. A tragedy, in two acts. Translated from the original Doric. (In his: The poetical works of Percy Bysshe Shelley. Edited by Mrs. Shelley. London: Edward Moxon, 1840. 8°. p. 181–190.) NCM

Printed also in all the collected editions of Shelley's works.

A political satire of the day — one of Shelley's least successful works. Written in Italy in 1820. For the circumstances which occasioned the writing of it, see *Note on Œdipus tyrannus*, by Mrs. Shelley, ibid., p. 191. Among the characters are Moses, a sow-gelder, Solomon, a porkman, and Zephaniah, a pig-butcher. They are summoned as Jews by the king, and ordered to slay the pigs.

—— Oedipus tyrannus; czyli, Opuchłolydziec król. (In: J. Kasprowicz, editor and translator, Arcydzieła europejskiej poezyi dramatycznej. Lwów, 1912. 8°. tom 1 [dział 4].) * QPK

White, Newman I. Shelley's Swell-foot the tyrant in relation to contemporary political satires. (Modern Language Association. Publications. Baltimore, 1921. 8°. v. 36, p. 332–346.) RAA

"The remaining unidentified characters — Solomon, Zephaniah and Moses — have no discoverable parallels in the satires of the day. Todhunter's suggestion that they may be, respectively, Rothschild [who in 1820 was coming into prominence], physical force, and the Malthusians is as good as any, but one may doubt whether these characters were intended to represent real persons." See John Todhunter, *A Study of Shelley*, London, 1880, p. 206–208, NCC (Shelley).

SHERIDAN, RICHARD BRINSLEY BUTLER. The duenna: a comic opera in three acts. As performed at the Theatre Royal, Covent Garden, with universal applause... London: Printed for T. N. Longman, 1794. 2 p.l., (1) 10–78 p. 12°. NCO p.v.165

Printed from a copy supplied by Thomas Harris, manager of Covent Garden, owner of the copyright.

This, according to Rhodes, is the genuine text, first edition, first issue. The Library also has a Dublin, 1794, edition, NCO p.v.784, which he calls first edition, second issue.

Reviewed in *Monthly review*, London, 1794, series 2, v. 14, p. 349, NAA.

—— The duenna; a comic opera in three acts ... With an introduction by Nigel Playfair. And illustrated with the design for costumes and scenery used in the production at the Lyric Theatre, Hammersmith [Oct. 23, 1924], and other drawings by George Sheringham. London: Constable and Co., Ltd. [1925.] xxvii(i), 105 p. front., 12 illus. 8°.

—— Songs, duets, trios, &c. in The duenna, or, The double elopement. As performed at the theatre-royal in Covent-Garden... London: Printed for J. Wilkie and T. Evans, 1776. 2 p.l., 20 p. 12. ed. 8°.

The London production was reviewed in *Lady's magazine*, London, 1775, v. 6, p. 605–608, * DA; with some of the songs reproduced in *London magazine*, London, 1775, v. 44, p. 610–612, * DA; on the occasion of its thirty-fifth successive performance, ibid., 1776, v. 45, p. 47–48, * DA; *Town and country magazine*, London, v. 7, p. 602–603, * DA; and in *Universal magazine*, London, 1775, v. 57, p. 262–263, * DA.

First produced in Jamaica, Nov. 27, 1779, and revived there, March 11, 1780, with T. Wignell as Isaac Mendoza. Under the title of Elopement, it was brought out at Charleston, at Harmony Hall, Oct. 10, 1786, with Mr. Goodwin as Mendoza. The American Company, with Wignell again as Mendoza, produced it in New York, June 1, 1787; in Philadelphia, July 7; and in Baltimore, Sept. 5, 1787.

The Library has also the following three editions: Edinburgh: Sterling & Kenney, 1828 (Huie's British drama, no. 10), NCO p.v.346; New York: John Douglas, 1848 (Modern standard drama, no. 54), NCO p.v.495; and New York: Douglas, 1848, NCO p.v.496.

The Harvard College Library has the following two editions not listed elsewhere in this list: New-York: David Longworth, 1808; and Boston: Wells and Lilly, 1822 (on cover: Oxberry's new English drama, no. 10).

Reprinted in *British drama*, London, 1826, v. 2, p. 1102–1119 (another edition, Philadelphia, 1838, v. 2, p. 294–311), NCO (British); *Cumberland's British theatre* (with Remarks) v. 2 [no. 2], NCO (Cumberland); *Davidson's shilling volume of Cumberland's plays*, v. 3, NCO (Davidson's); in John Dicks, *The British drama*, London, 1865, v. 4 [no. 26], p. 1055–1072, illus.; in Mrs. E. S. Inchbald, *British theatre*, London, 1808, v. 19 [no. 3], NCO (Inchbald); *The London stage*, London [1824–27], v. 1 [no. 5], NCO (London); *Select London stage*, London [1830?], NCO (Select); in William Oxberry, *The new English drama*, London, 1818, v. 2 [no. 2], NCO (Oxberry) and NCO p.v.409; in R. B. B. Sheridan, *Dramatic works*, London, 1798, 42 p.; and in all later editions of the author's collected works.

An extract, Isaac and the duenna, from act II, scene 2, is printed in Allardyce Nicoll, editor, *Readings from British drama*, New York [1928], p. 264–266, * R-NCO.

—— La duègne; opéra-comique en trois actes. (In his: Oeuvres complètes, trad. par Benjamin Laroche. Paris, 1841. 12°. p. 103–174.)

Levi, Harry. "The duenna." (In his: Jewish characters in fiction: English literature. Philadelphia [cop. 1903]. 12°. p. 30–36.) * PZB

Revised and enlarged in a second edition, 1911, p. 28–36, * PZB.

Individual Plays—Earliest Times to 1837, cont'd

SHERIDAN, RICHARD BRINSLEY BUTLER, *cont'd*

O'Keeffe, John. Cunning Isaac's escape. From The duenna. A comic-poetic bagatelle, by O'Keefe. (In: W. Oxberry, compiler, Actor's budget. Calcutta, 1824. 12°. p. 43–46.)
    NCO (Oxberry)

Rhodes, R. Crompton. Bibliography of The Duenna. (In: Richard B. B. Sheridan, The plays & poems, edited by R. C. Rhodes. Oxford, 1928. 8°. v. 1, p. 269–276.) 8-NCF
See also Appendices I and II, ibid., p. 248–268.

—— Sheridan; a study in theatrical bibliography. (London mercury. London, 1927. 8°. v. 15, p. 381–390.) *DA

Weiss, Kurt. Richard Brinsley Sheridan als Lustspieldichter... [Erfurt: O. Conrad,] 1888. 3 p.l., 110 p., 1 l. 8°. NCC p.v.19

Wollman, Maurice. Some notes on Sheridan, "The duenna," and Isaac Mendoza. (Jewish chronicle. London, June, 1927. f°. supplement 78, p. vii–viii.) *PBE

—— The governess; a comic opera, by R. B. Sheridan, Esq. Adapted for theatrical representation. As performed at the theatres-royal, Drury-Lane, Covent-Garden, and Smock-Alley. Regulated from the prompt-books, by permission of the managers... Dublin: W. Jones, 1793. 59 p. 16°. (Jones's British theatre. London, 1795. v. 6 [no. 4].) NCO (Jones)
The names of all the characters are here altered. Mendoza becomes Enoch Issachar. The dialogues are paraphrased, but the songs are given correctly. R. C. Rhodes says that this text is the acting version of Ryder's production at the Theatre-Royal, Crow Street, Dublin, on Jan. 31, 1777, which, in turn, was the same as The Duenna version used by Tate Wilkinson at York, Easter Monday, 1776.
On the relation of *The Duenna* and *The Governess*, 1777, see R. C. Rhodes in *Times literary supplement*, London, 1925, v. 24, p. 599, † *NAA*.

—— The school for scandal. A comedy... Dublin: Printed for J. Ewling [1778?]. vi, 93(1) p., 1 l. 8°. *KL
First edition? See Iolo A. Williams, *Seven* XVIIIth *century bibliographies*, London, 1924, p. 216–217, *NCB*.
Blank leaf wanting at end.
The Library has also the following separate editions: Dublin, 1781, 70 p., 1 l., *NCO p.v.58*; "Adapted for theatrical representation," Dublin: W. Jones, 1792, *NCO (Jones's British theatre, v. 5)*; Philadelphia [etc.], 1802 (Conrad & Co.'s edition of select plays), *KL*; New York: David Longworth, 1807, *NCO p.v.436*; Washington: Davis and Force, 1824, *NCO p.v.435*; edited by Epes Sargent, New York, 1845 (Modern standard drama, no. 7); New York: William Taylor & Co. [1846?], *NCO p.v.432*; New York: Berford & Co., 1847, *NCO p.v.394*; edited by John M. Kingdom, New York [1876] (De Witt's acting plays, no. 201), *NCO p.v.504*; Boston: W. H. Baker & Co., 1915 (Introduction by F. E. Chase), *NCO p.v.390*; and edited by R. Crompton Rhodes, the decorations by Thomas Lowinsky, Oxford, 1930, *KP (Shakespeare Head)* and, with an introduction by Carl Van Doren, Oxford, 1934, *KP (Limited)*.
The Library also has prompter's copies, *NCOF* and † *NCOF*.
The Harvard College Library has the following editions not listed elsewhere: "The fifth edition," Paris: T. Barrois, 1789; Boston: J. Belknap and T. Hall, 1792; Campe's edition, Nürnberg and New York [18—?]; "Carefully corrected from the prompt books ...by M. Lopez," Philadelphia: F. C. Wemyss [etc., 1827] (The acting American theatre, Lopez and Wemyss' edition); edited by Christopher T. Voigtmann, Coburg and Leipsic, 1839; Philadelphia, New York: Turner and Fisher, 1846 (Turner's dramatic library); with notes by O. J. Victor, New York [1860] (The dime drama); and edited by F. Fischer, Berlin, 1885 (Rauch's English readings, Heft 1).
The Library of Congress has the following editions: "as it is performed at the Theatre-Royal in Crow-street," Dublin, 1782; "from a manuscript copy in the possession of John Henry," New York: Hugh Gaine, 1786 (contains numerous slight variations in text from the authorized English editions); London: E. Powell, 1798; Dublin: Printed for the booksellers, 1800; illustrated by Frank M. Gregory, New York, 1892; New York and Boston: H. M. Caldwell Company [1900]; edited with a preface and notes by G. A. Aitken, London, 1911 (The Temple dramatists); and edited by Hanson H. Webster, Boston [cop. 1917] (The Riverside literature series).
In the compiler's collection are the following additional editions: London, 1797, included in the author's *Dramatic works*, London, 1798; edited by Karl F. C. Wagner, Helmstädt, 1834; Berlin: B. Behr's Library, 1837 (British theatre: a collection of the best dramatic pieces [no. 21]); edited by Carl Meissner, Göttingen, 1863; edited by Otto Dickmann, Leipzig, 1873; edited by Leo Türkheim, München, 1897 (Französisch-englische Klassiker Bibliothek, hrsg. von J. Bauer u. Th. Link); with illustrations by Lucius Rossi, London [1900?]; with notes by Ch. Clermont, Paris: Hachette [1908]; and edited by E. M. Jebb, Oxford: Clarendon Press, 1928.
The Library has the following translations: in Danish, in Kongelike theaters repertoire, Kjøbenhavn [1828–45?], v. 6, *NAFH*; in Dutch by C. van Bruggen, in *Groot-Nederland*, Amsterdam, 1923, deel 2, p. 420–447, 552–589, 652–672, *NHA*; in German by F. L. Schroeder, Wien, 1847, *NCP*; in Italian, in Biblioteca teatrale economica, cl. 2, v. 7, *NNO p.v.44*; and in Russian by Vyetrinski, in *Panteon literatury*, v. 5, no. 1–2, * *QCA*.
The Harvard College Library has the following translations: in French by Bunel Delille, London: Galabin, 1789; in French, translated and edited by A. Châteauneuf, Paris: Delaunay, 1834; in German, translated and edited by Christoph G. Voigtmann [Coburg and Leipsic: J. G. Riemann, 1839]; in Siamese by Sri Ayudha, pseud., Bangkok, n. d.; and in Greek comic iambics by Algernon E. F. Spencer (of act IV, scene 1), Oxford, 1909 (with English and Greek on opposite pages).
In the compiler's collection are the following translations: in French, in R. B. Sheridan, *Oeuvres complètes*, translated by Benjamin Laroche, Paris, 1841, p. 284–399; in French, translated with notes by A. Barbeau, Paris [1924] (Les cent chefs-d'œuvre étrangers [no. 52]); in German, Stuttgart: Freya, 1868 (Classische Theater-Bibliothek aller Nationen, Nr. 30); in German by Schroeder, Leipzig [1872] (Universal-Bibliothek [Nr.] 449); and translated by G. Humbert, Berlin: S. Fontane & Co., 1904.
Other existing French translations are in *Théâtre anglais*, 1784; by Famin in *Théâtre des variétés*, Paris, 1807; by Merville in *Les Chefs-d'œuvre des théâtres étrangers*, Paris, 1822; by Pinchot, Paris, 1852; by Guillemot, Paris, 1867; and by Cler, Paris, 1879.
Reprinted in the following collections: *British drama*, London, 1826, v. 2, p. 1600–1624 (another edition, Philadelphia, 1838, v. 2, p. 792–816), *NCO (British)*; Cumberland's *British theatre*, v. 14 [no. 4], with remarks by George Daniel, *NCO (Cumberland)* and *NCO p.v.455*; in John Dicks, *The British drama*, London, 1864, v. 2 [no. 7], p. 385–410; the same, new and complete edition, London [1873?] (Dicks' standard plays, no. 2), *NCO p.v.344* and *NCO p.v.301*; Lacy's *acting edition of plays*, v. 27, *NCO (Lacy)*; *London stage*, London [1824–27], v. 4 [no. 41], *NCO (London)*; and *New York drama*, New York [cop. 1876], v. 1, no. 10.
Reprinted also in *Harvard classics*, New York, [cop. 1909], v. 18, p. 103–196, *NAC*; J. S. P. Tatlock and R. G. Martin, editors, *Representative English plays*, New York, 1916, p. 671–714, *NCO (Tatlock)*; J. B. Matthews and P. R. Lieder, editors, *Chief British dramatists*, Boston [1924], p. 739–789, *NCO (Matthews)*; J. B. Hubbell and J. O. Beaty, compilers, *An Introduction to drama*, New York, 1927, p. 425–473, *NAFH (Hubbell)*; H. F. Rubinstein, editor, *Great English plays*, New York (another edition,

THE JEW IN ENGLISH DRAMA 49

Individual Plays—Earliest Times to 1837, cont'd

London) 1928, p. 972–1023, *NCO (Rubinstein)*; R. M. Smith, editor, *Types of social comedy*, New York, 1928, p. 351–456, *NCO (Smith)*; M. J. Moses, editor, *British plays from the Restoration to 1820*, Boston, 1929, p. 797–850, plates, ports., *NCO (Moses)*; G. R. Coffman, editor, *Five significant English plays*, New York, 1930, p. 225–323, *NCO (Coffman)*; D. MacMillan and H. M. Jones, editors, *Plays of the Restoration and eighteenth century*, New York [cop. 1931], p. 824–866, *NCO (MacMillan)*; and in B. H. Clark, editor, *World drama; an anthology*, New York, 1933, [v. 1], p. 615–660, *NAFH*; in *Twelve famous plays of the Restoration and eighteenth century*, New York, 1933, p. 873–952, *NCO (Twelve)*; F. and J. W. Tupper, editors, *Representative English dramas from Dryden to Sheridan*, New York, 1934, p. 645–681, *NCO (Tupper)*; and in R. B. Thomas, editor, *Plays and the theater*, Boston, 1937, p. 249–329, *NAFH*. Also printed in all editions of his works.

The first London production was reviewed in the *London chronicle*, 1777, v. 41, p. 444, * *A*; *Universal magazine*, London, 1777, v. 60, p. 251–253, * *DA*; and in *Westminster magazine*, London, 1777, v. 5, p. 258–259, * *DA*.

Sheridan, as manager of his theatre, knew the aptitudes of each actor for whom he was writing. In assigning the part of Moses to Baddeley, he but confirmed the reputation of the latter as an actor of Jewish rôles.

It was first produced in Jamaica, by the American Company, May 26, 1781, with Mr. Moralis as Moses. In the United States it was first seen in Baltimore, Feb. 3, 1784, in a production headed by Dennis Ryan, who played the Jewish part. In New York it was first staged professionally, Dec. 12, 1785. Other productions are too numerous to be given. Seilhammer records no less than fifty-five revivals between 1785 and 1797. Neither Seilhammer for Baltimore nor Odell for New York could locate a contemporary review of the first production.

A musical version of *The School for scandal* (book by John Kendrick Bangs and Roderic C. Penfield; music by A. Baldwin Sloane) was staged at the Casino Theatre, New York, Dec. 24, 1904, under the title *Lady Teazle*, with Lillian Russell in the title rôle and Edmund Lawrence as Moses. Reviewed in *New York dramatic mirror*, v. 53, Jan. 7, 1905, p. 14, * *T*–* *DA*.

Brereton, Austin. The school for scandal. illus. (In his: A short history of She stoops to conquer, The rival, and The school for scandal. London, 1900. 12°. p. 16–21.)

Cook, Sherwin Lawrence. Looking back at the "School for scandal." (Emerson quarterly. Boston, 1930. f°. v. 10, May, 1930, p. 1–6, 28.) † NANA

"Large part of this ...was published in the *Boston evening transcript*," in celebration of the sesquicentennial of the first performance.

Hartmann, Hermann. Sheridan's School for scandal; Beiträge zur Quellenfrage... Königsberg i. Pr.: Hartung, 1900. 46 p. 8°. (Königliche Oberrealschule auf der Burg. Ostern 1900. Progr. No. 23. Beilage.)
"Litteratur": p. 3–4.
Reviewed by O. Glöde in *Englische Studien*, Leipzig, 1902, Bd. 31, p. 132–133, *RNA*.

Hazlitt, William. The school for scandal. (In his: A view of the English stage. London, 1818. 8°. p. 164–167.) NCOM

Nettleton, George Henry. The first editions of The school for scandal. (Times literary supplement. London, 1934. f°. v. 33, p. 695.) † NAA

Rhodes, R. Crompton. The genuine and piratical texts; with a bibliography. (In: Richard B. B. Sheridan, The plays & poems, edited by R. C. Rhodes. Oxford, 1928. 8°. v. 2, p. 154–174.) 8–NCF

—— Sheridan; a study in theatrical bibliography. (London mercury. London, 1927. 8°. v. 15, p. 381–390.) * DA

—— Some aspects of Sheridan bibliography. (Library. London, 1928. 8°. series 4, v. 9, p. 233–261.) * HA

Sheridan, Richard Brinsley Butler. An ode to scandal... By the late Right Hon. R. B. Sheridan... London: Printed for W. Wright, 1819. 2 p.l.,(1)8–23 p. 3. ed. 8°. NCI p.v.50
"The comedy of the School for Scandal was founded on the above Ode," t.-p.

Weiss, Kurt. Richard Brinsley Sheridan als Lustspieldichter... [Erfurt: O. Conrad,] 1888. 3 p.l., 110 p., 1 l. 8°. NCC p.v.19

Johnson, Philip, and H. Agg. ...The new School for scandal; an impertinence in three acts... London: H. W. F. Deane & Sons; Boston, Mass.: The Baker International Play Bureau [cop. 1936]. 70 p., 1 l. 8°.
At head of title: The year book press series of plays.
Sheridan's play in a modern setting and in modern idiom. Most of the original characters, including Moses, are here. The part assigned to Moses is very much the same as in the 1774 play.

School for scandal. A comedy... The third edition... London: Printed. Philadelphia: Reprinted and sold by Thos. Bradford, 1779. iv p., 1 l., 46 p. 8°. * KD 1779
Attributed by Cushing to John Leacock.
An adaptation of Sheridan's play to the exigencies of English politics relating to the American Revolution. The part of Moses is assigned to Lord Boreas, the Lord North of history. Reference is made to the American Revolution by Lord Boreas who (p. 15) tells Sir Benjamin: "Perhaps General Washingball's servants are defeated."
Reviewed unfavorably in *Critical review*, London, 1779, v. 47, p. 73, *NAA*; *Gentleman's magazine*, London, 1779, v. 49, p. 92, * *DA*; and in *Monthly review*, London, 1779, v. 60, p. 64, *NAA*. See also comment in *Athenæum*, London, 1884, v. 84, p. 570, * *DA*.

The School for scandal; a comedy. ["A poetical satire on the India Bill and the Coalition."] In five acts. As it is performed by his Majesty's servants, &c. Never before printed. London: G. Lister, 1784. vi p., 1 l., 42 p. 8°.
Copy: Harvard College Library.
Reviewed in *Critical review*, London, 1784, v. 57, p. 394, *NAA*.

A School for scandal; or, Newspapers. A comedy [in five acts and in prose]. London: H. D. Symonds, 1792. 96 p. 8°.
Title from British Museum catalogue.
A satire on the conductors of newspapers.
D. E. Baker, in *Biographia dramatica*, states that it was "never acted."
Whether any or all of the characters, as named by Sheridan, were retained has not been ascertained.
The *Catalogue of the Larpent plays*, no. 470, records *The School for scandal scandalized*, a one-act interlude (the ms. in the hand of John Philip Kemble), produced by Tate Wilkinson at the Theatre Royal, York, March 27, 1779. Nicoll, p. 343, states that it was also produced at Covent Garden, London, March 18, 1780. No mention of it in the theatrical reviews of the period, nor official listing of it in Covent Garden's advertisements for March 18, 1780, or 1779, has been found.

Individual Plays—Earliest Times to 1837, cont'd

SHIEL. The passing of the bill; a new tragedy. Still in ms. (Athenæum. London, 1829. 4°. April 22, 1829, p. 249-250.) *DA
Résumé, with extracts, of a play, in five acts, centered around the subject of the Catholic Emancipation Bill in England. One of the characters, in the fourth act, is a Mr. Isaacson.

SIMONS, SARAH EMMA, AND C. I. ORR. *See* sub-entry under SCOTT, SIR WALTER.

SMITH, JONATHAN S. The siege of Algiers; or, The downfall of Hagdi-Ali-Bashaw. A political, historical, and sentimental tragi-comedy, in five acts. By Jonathan S. Smith, of Philadelphia... Philadelphia: Printed for the author, by J. Maxwell, 1823. 140 p., 1 l. 12°.
Copy: Library of Congress (imperfect; p. 5-6 wanting).
The theme of the play centers about the difficulties of the United States with the Barbary states in the early part of the last century. The European states are rebuked for their compromises with the piratical Algerians. John Bull is especially taken to task. The Jewish character, not unsympathetically drawn, is David Brokereye, "a Hebrew money changer of great note, decapitated by the Dey, through the intrigues of his prime minister [Muley Mahomet]." The author shows accurate knowledge of the condition of the Jews in north Africa during the period when the action of the play takes place. It is significant to note that Mordecai Manuel Noah, U. S. Consul to Tunis in 1813-16, who had much to do in protecting American merchants and sailors during his incumbency, was a journalist who had been writing under the pseudonym of Muley Molock. One of the dramatis personae is citizen Yankoo, "a native of Delphia in the west"; another is Commodore Intrepid "with a squadron of ships from the nation of the west," and the play ends with the famous statement of Pinckney, "Millions for defence, but not one cent for tribute." It was apparently never acted.

SMOLLETT, TOBIAS GEORGE. The adventures of Ferdinand, Count Fathom... London: Harrison and Co., 1782. v, 220 p., 3 pl. 8°. (The Novelist's magazine. v. 7.) NAC (Novelist's)
This novel is one of the earliest in English literature to introduce a Jewish character — Joshua Menasseh — in a sympathetic light. See M. J. Kohler, "Scott, Smollett and the Jews," in *American Hebrew*, New York, 1929. v. 125, p. 136, * PBD.
It was dramatized by T. J. Dibdin into a burletta named *Ferdinand, Count Fathom*, and produced at the Royal Circus, London, July 31, 1818.

SOANE, GEORGE. *See* sub-entry under SCOTT, SIR WALTER.

The SOUTH Briton: a comedy of five acts: as it is performed at the theatre in Smock-alley, with great applause. Written by a lady. London: J. Williams, 1774. 72 p. 8°. *KL
Reviewed in *Critical review*, London, 1774, v. 38, p. 237-238, *NAA*.
In the Dublin production, on Jan. 21, 1773, T. Jackson played the part of Issachar, the Jewish villain of the play, and Mrs. Barry that of Mrs. Issachar. In England, it was produced at the Covent Garden, London, April 12, 1774. Genest, v: 421-422, gives the name of Quick as the probable actor of the part of Issachar.

SOUTHERNE, THOMAS. Money the mistress; a play. (In his: Plays. London, 1774. 12°. v. 3, p. 173-243.) NCP
This play is Southerne's last and poorest. It lasted on the stage only a few evenings. The crisis of the plot turns upon the pawning of jewels, which takes place through Nathan, the Jew, a minor character. Genest does not state who acted the part of Nathan. There is the usual abusive reference in it to Jews. It was produced at Lincoln's Inn Fields, Feb. 19, 1726.

See Montague Summers, *The Restoration theatre*, London, 1934, p. 142, 143, * R-NCOM.
As to sources, synopsis and criticism, see John W. Dodds, *Thomas Southerne, dramatist*, New Haven, 1933, p. 194-203, *NCC (Southerne)*. See also Genest, III: 179-181.

SPINDLER, KARL. The Jew... [Translated from the German.] New York: Harper & Brothers, 1844. 173 p. 8°. (On cover: Library of select novels. no. 31.) NGL
In double columns.
This novel which appeared in 1827 is described by the author as a German *Sittengemälde* of the first half of the fifteenth century. It was dramatized by Bernhard Neustadt under the title *Ben David, der Knabenräuber; oder, Der Christ und der Jude*, and as such produced at the Stadt Theater, New York, April 11, 1856. See Odell, VI: 483.

STEVENS, ERNEST. *See* sub-entry under SCOTT, SIR WALTER.

STEVENSON, AUGUSTA. *See* sub-entry under SCOTT, SIR WALTER.

STONE, DALTON. *See* sub-entry under SCOTT, SIR WALTER.

STUART, CHARLES. The distress'd baronet; a farce, in two acts... London: Printed for J. Debrett, 1787. 1 p.l., (i) vi-viii, (1) 10-32 p. 8°. NCO p.v.145
The Library also has the 2. ed., published by Debrett the same year, *NCO p.v.342*.
Licenser's ms. shows "numerous and extensive differences." See *Catalogue of the Larpent plays*, no. 776. The production date is given here, wrongly, as May 11.
Reviewed in *Critical review*, London, 1787, v. 63, p. 473, *NAA*; and in *Monthly review*, London, v. 77, p. 245, *NAA*.
Produced at the Drury Lane, London, May 3, 1787. Burton as Aminadab Lebanon, who deals in bails and bankruptcies, comes with a friend to negotiate bankruptcy proceedings with Sir George Courteous, the distressed baronet. Bannister in the published prologue, hits the part off thus: "Vatch dat to do Bar'-netch in distress? I will relieve him — let him come to me, Dat ish if he has jewels, d'ye see." There is a usurious pawnbroker, Peter Pop, acted by Suett, in this comedy, who is allowed to be straight English. Reviewed in *European magazine*, London, 1787, v. 11, p. 301-302, * DA; *London chronicle*, London, v. 61, p. 428, * A; and in *New lady's magazine*, London, v. 2, p. 278, * DA.
Pinero used the name Lebanon for his Jewish character in his *The Cabinet minister*, 1890.

STURGIS, JULIAN RUSSELL. *See* sub-entry under SCOTT, SIR WALTER.

THE THREE LADIES OF LONDON. A right excellent and famous Comœdy called the three Ladies of London. Wherein is notablie declared and set foorth, how by the meanes of Lucar, Loue and Conscience is so corrupted, that the one is married to Dissimulation, the other fraught with all abhomination... Written by R. W. as it hath beene publiquely played. At London, Printed by Roger Warde, dwelling neere Holburne Conduit, at the signe of the Talbot. 1584. (In: J. Payne Collier, editor, Five old plays, illustrating the early progress of the English drama. Printed for the Roxburghe Club. London: W. Nicol, 1851. 4°. p. 157-244.)
9-* KP (Roxburghe)

—— —— [Amersham, Eng.: Issued for subscribers by John S. Farmer, 1913.] 1 p.l., [44] p. 8°. (Old English drama. Students' facsimile edition.)

Individual Plays—Earliest Times to 1837, cont'd

...The Three Ladies of London, by R. W. 1584. [London?] Issued for subscribers by the editor of the Tudor facsimile texts, 1911. 3 p.l., facsim.: 1 l., [44] p. 4°. (The Tudor facsimile texts.)   NCO (Tudor)
Ascribed to Robert Wilson, the elder. cf. Preface.
Also printed in Robert Dodsley, editor, *A Select collection of old English plays.* 4th edition by W. C. Hazlitt, London, 1874-76, v. 6, p. 245-370, NCO (Dodsley).
"Most of the dramatis personae are indisputably allegorical or representative, the embodiments of certain virtues and vices; but individuals are also employed, such as Gerontus, a Jew, and Mercadore, a merchant, besides a Judge who is called upon to determine a dispute between them. This portion of the piece may be said to belong to a more advanced period of our stage, and distinguishes it, as far as we are aware, from anything of the kind known anterior to the date when the production first came from the press. The name Gerontus, can hardly fail to bring to mind that of the hero of the old ballad of 'Gernutus, the Jew of Venice'; but there is a remarkable difference between the two persona; in the play before us Gerontus is represented in a very favourable light, as an upright Jew, only anxious to obtain his own property by fair means, while his antagonist, a Christian merchant, endeavors to defeat the claim by fraud, perjury and apostacy. So far the drama of 'The three Ladies of London' contradicts the position, founded mainly upon Marlowe's Barabas (in his Jew of Malta) and Shakespeare's Shylock, that our early dramatists eagerly availed themselves of popular prejudices against the conscientious adherents to the old dispensation." — From the introduction to *Five old Plays,* ed. J. P. Collier, p. x-xi.

Collier, John Payne. Jews in our early plays. (Athenæum. London, 1850. 4°. v. 23, p. 475-476.)   * DA

Fernow, Hans. The three lords and three ladies of London, by R(obert) W(ilson). London, 1590; ein Beitrag zur Geschichte des englischen Dramas. Hamburg: Th. G. Meissner, 1885. 29 p. sq. 4°. (Realgymnasium des Johanneums zu Hamburg. Ostern 1885. Programme No. 661.)
Contains critical discussion of the same author's *Three ladies of London.*

Friedlander, Gerald. A Jew in pre-Shakespearian drama. (In his: Shakespeare and the Jews. London, 1921. 16°. p. 29-38.)
                                                        * NCVF (Merchant)

Goitein, E. David. A stage Jew of the xvi. century. (Jewish chronicle. London, July, 1923. f°. Supplement 31, p. vii.)   * PBD

Gourvitch, I. Robert Wilson: "The elder" and "the younger." (Notes and queries. London, 1926. 8°. v. 150, p. 4-6.)   * R-* DA
There were two Robert Wilsons, the elder and the younger. The Robert Wilson, supposed author of this play, is by most authorities held to be Wilson senior. Which one of the Wilsons died in 1600, the date of our author's death?

Lee, Sir Sidney. Shylock and his predecessors. (Academy. London, 1887. 4°. v. 31, p. 344-345.)   * DA

Tilbury, William Harries. ...The German Jew; or, The forest of Remival. A drama in three acts... The only edition correctly marked, by permission from the prompter's book... As performed at the London theatres... London: J. Duncombe & Co. [1830-1852.] 48 p. incl. front. (port.) 24°.
At head of title: Duncombe's edition.
Produced at the Sadler's Wells Theatre, London, Aug. 16, 1830, with Villiers as Isaac Samuel, the kindly "German Jew." Allardyce Nicoll, in his *A History of the early eighteenth century drama,* lists the Sadler's Wells production of that evening as *The German Jew; or, The deserter from Orleans.* Landa, p. 154, thinks this melodrama is indebted to Lessing's one-act play *The Jews.*

Tobin, John. The faro table; or, The guardians. A comedy, now performing at the Theatre-Royal, Drury-Lane. By the late John Tobin... London: J. Murray, 1816. 4 p.l., 54 p., 1 l. 8°.
                                                       NCO p.v.129

—— —— New York: D. Longworth, 1817. 58 p. 16°.   NCO p.v.248
Prologue, written by E. Peacock, and epilogue.
In five acts.
Licenser's ms. has "two prologues and two epilogues [the printed text has but one of each]...some differences." See *Catalogue of Larpent plays,* no. 1495.
This piece was announced for presentation at the Drury Lane for Oct. 20, 1806, but was withdrawn by R. B. Sheridan, the then proprietor, on account of a supposed personal allusion to a lady of high rank. First produced under the name of Guardians, at the Drury Lane, London, Nov. 5, 1816. Dowton, as Barton, disguised as Levi, speaks in dialect. The plot chiefly turns upon a guardian's assumption of a Jewish character. "Probability would have been preserved and the interest of the piece considerably heightened if the Jew had been included in the dramatis personae." — Oulton, *A History of the theatres of London...from...1795 to 1817,* v. 1, p. 346-347. Reviewed in *European magazine,* London, 1816, v. 70, p. 453, * DA; and in *The Times,* London, Nov. 6, 1816, p. 2, col. 5-p. 3, * A.
Produced at the Park Theatre, New York, April 9, 1817. Reviewed in *American monthly magazine,* New York, 1817, v. 1, p. 52, * DA. "A patch-work but splendidly produced."

—— The fisherman; an opera in three acts. (In his: Memoirs... By Elizabeth O. Benger. London, 1820. 12°. p. 365-444.)
Copy: Harvard College Library.
Examiner's ms. is "dated by Larpent, (?), Oct. 17, 1817 <sic>; prologue and epilogue." The authorship of Tobin is questioned by D. MacMillan. See *Catalogue of Larpent plays,* no. 2118.
"The groundwork of the serious part is borrowed from the commencement of an episode in *Diable boiteux.* For the comic scenes the author appears to have been indebted solely to his own invention."
Produced under the title *The Fisherman's hut,* at the Drury Lane, October 20, 1819, with Dowton as Balthazar, a Jewish dealer, and Miss Carew as his daughter Leah. "The comic part is composed of the chaste loves of Leah, the handsome Jewess...and Nicolino, the fisherman, and the unholy intrigues of ...Balthazar to procure the favor of Martha, the sister of Nicolino." It was acted but three times. Reviewed in *European magazine,* London, 1819, v. 76, p. 351-352, * DA; and in *British stage and literary cabinet,* London, 1819, v. 4, p. 28-30 (with illus. of Dowton as Balthazar, facing p. 25). Dowton made his stage debut Oct. 10, 1796, in the part of Sheva in Cumberland's *The Jew.*

Venetian comedy, 1594. The text is lost. Recorded by Henslowe as having been first acted, by the Lord Admiral's men at the Rose, August 25 (27), 1594, and thence 11 more times till May 8, 1595.
See P. Henslowe, *Diary,* edited by W. W. Greg, London, 1904-08, v. 2, p. 167, NCOM. For its relation to T. Dekker's *Jew of Venice, Love of an English lady* (Portia?), Marlowe's *Jew of Malta,* and the *Comoedia genandt Das wohl gesprochene Uhrtheil eynes weiblichen Studenten; oder, Der Jud von Venedig* (published by Meissner in 1884), see ibid., v. 2, p. 170-171.

Individual Plays—Earliest Times to 1837, cont'd

WADE, THOMAS. The Jew of Aragon; or, The Hebrew queen. A tragedy in five acts [and in verse]... London: Smith, Elder & Co., 1830. xi, 82 p., 1 l. 12°.   NCO p.v.232
Reviewed in *Athenæum*, London, 1830, v. 3, p. 727, * *DA;* and with many extracts in *Monthly repository,* London, 1837, new series, v. 11, p. 153–157, *ZXDA.*
First produced at Covent Garden, London, Oct. 20, 1830. Fanny Kemble played Rachel the Jewess, in her first appearance on the English stage. Reviewed in *Court journal*, London, 1830, v. 2, p. 683, * *DA;* and in *Literary gazette,* London, 1830, p. 692–693, * *DA.*
The reviewer in *Literary gazette,* London, 1830, p. 716–717, * *DA,* prints the passages which the Licenser, George Colman the younger, caused to be expunged from the text as staged and which in the printed play are given in capitals.

Cohen, A. Some precursors of Anglo-Jewish emancipation. (Jewish chronicle. London, March, 1930. f°. supplement 111, p. v–vi.)
* PBE

Forman, H. Buxton. Thomas Wade: the poet and his surroundings. [A critical appreciation.] (In: Literary anecdotes of the nineteenth century. Edited by W. R. Nicoll and T. J. Wise. London, 1895. 8°. v. 1, p. 43–67.)   NCB
"In, the dedication of the Jew of Arragon, there is a passage on liberty of conscience and against the civil disabilities of the Jews, written in the very spirit of Shelley, and ending with a quotation from Shelley's 'Liberty.'"

Landa, Myer Jack. "The Jew of Arragon." (Jewish chronicle. London, March, 1921. f°. supplement 3, p. vi–vii.)   * PBE

WALLACE, EGLANTINE (MAXWELL), LADY. The ton; or, Follies of fashion. A comedy. As it is acted at the Theatre Royal, Covent Garden. By Lady Wallace. London: T. Hookham, 1788. 1 p.l., iv, ii p., 1 l., 99(1) p. 8°.   NCO p.v.112
The Licenser's ms. shows "numerous corrections and cancellations... slight differences" from the printed text. See *Catalogue of Larpent plays,* no. 801.
Reviewed in *Critical review,* London, 1788, v. 65, p. 404–405, *NAA;* with many extracts in *English review,* London, 1788, v. 11, p. 361–371, * *DA;* and in *Monthly review,* London, v. 78, p. 437–438, *NAA.*
The Jewish character is Ben Levy, acted by Quick, referred to as the Jew broker and introduced as "honest Levy, the Israelite without guile." He speaks broken English. One of the reviewers corrects the name to read Levi. First produced at the Covent Garden, London, April 8, 1788. Lady Wallace's play was hooted off the stage at its first presentation in Edinburgh, May 24, 1788, and was never repeated there. Reviewed in *London chronicle,* London, 1788, v. 63, p. 347, * *A;* and in *New lady's magazine,* London, v. 3, p. 260–261, * *DA.*

WEBSTER, JOHN. The Deuils Law-case. Or, When Women goe to Law, the Deuill is full of Businesse. A new Tragecomædy. The true and perfect Copie from the Originall. As it was aprooueedly well Acted by her Maiesties Seruants. Written by Iohn Webster. *Non quam diu, sed quam bene.* [Printer's device] London: Printed by A. M. for Iohn Grismand, and are to be sold at his Shop in Pauls Alley at the Signe of the Gunne. 1623. [87] p. 4°.
Copy: Library of Congress.
Printed in his *Works,* edited by A. Dyce, London, 1830, v. 2, p. 1–135, *NCP;* in his *Works,* edited by A. Dyce, London, 1859 (another ed., 1871), p. 103–145, *NCP;* and in his *Dramatic works,* edited by William Hazlitt, London, 1857, v. 3, p. 1–121, *NCP;* and, with introduction, commentary and textual notes, in his *Complete works,* edited by F. L. Lucas, London, 1927, v. 2, p. 211–372, *8–NCP.*
Written, Fleay thinks, in 1610. Acted by the Queen's servants. As to the dates of composition and publication and the sources of the play, see E. E. Stoll, *John Webster; the periods of his work,* Boston, 1905, p. 30–32, 153–160, *NCC (Webster).*
The first instance in English drama of a Christian disguising himself as a Jew. Romelio, when so disguised, soliloquizes, "Excellently, well habited! Why methinks I could play with mine own shadow now, and be a rare Italianated Jew."— Act. III, Sc. 2. See Landa, p. 90–91.

—— Des Teufels Rechtshandel. (In: F. M. Bodenstedt, editor, Shakespeare's Zeitgenossen und ihre Werke. Berlin, 1858. 12°. Bd. 1, p. 265–285.)   NCO (Bodenstedt)
Translation of parts of the drama.

Deighton, Kenneth. [Conjectural readings.] (In his: The old dramatists; conjectural readings. Westminster, 1896. 12°. p. 197–198.)

Sturge, L. J. Webster and the law: a parallel. (Deutsche Shakespeare Gesellschaft. Jahrbuch. Berlin-Schöneberg, 1906. 8°. Jahrg. 42, p. 148–157.)   * NCK
Webster's knowledge of the theory and practice of the law is evidenced particularly in the fourth act of the *Devil's law case.*

WILKS, THOMAS EGERTON. Rinaldo Rinaldini; or, The brigand and the blacksmith! A romantic drama, in two acts... As performed at the London theatres. London, New York: Samuel French [1876–86?]. 1 p.l., (1)6–36 p. 12°. (French's acting edition of plays. v. 117, [no. 1743].)   NCO (Lacy)
First produced at Sadler's Wells Theatre, Jan. 4. 1835. Campbell in the title rôle assumes the character of Moses, "a German Jew pedlar" in the first of his many disguises.
Nicoll, p. 410, gives Jan. 7, 1836, as the date of the first production.

WILSON, JOHN. Belphegor: or The marriage of the devil. A tragi-comedy. Lately acted at the Queen's Theatre in Dorset-Garden. By Mr. Wilson... Licens'd, October 13. 1690. London: Printed by J. Leake, and are to be sold by Randal Taylor, in Amen-Corner, near Stationers-Hall, 1691. 4 p.l., 63(1) p. 4°.
Copy: Library of Congress.
"Matchiavel (whether the original were his own, or Straporola's...) gave me the argument of the ensuing play." — "The author to the reader."
Another issue with a slightly different imprint, "Printed by J. L. for Luke Meredith," appeared the same year.
It was produced at the Duke's Theatre, Dorset Garden, about Oct., 1690.
Also printed in his *Dramatic works,* Edinburgh, 1874, p. 279–401, *NCO (Dramatists).*
Jews are introduced who act as bailiffs. There are also several allusions to Jews.

Hollstein, Ernst. Verhältnis von Ben Jonson's "The devil is an ass" und John Wilson's "Belphegor; or, The marriage of the devil" zu Machiavelli's Novelle vom Belfagor... Halle a. S.: C. A. Kaemmerer & Co., 1901. 52 p., 1 l. 8°.

WISDOM OF DOCTOR DODYPOLL. The Wisdome of Doctor Dodypoll. As it hath bene sundrie times Acted by the Children of Powles. [Printer's mark] London, Printed by Thomas Creede,

THE JEW IN ENGLISH DRAMA 53

Individual Plays—Earliest Times to 1837, cont'd
for Richard Oliue, dwelling in Long Lane. 1600. [60] p. 4°.
Sometimes ascribed to Peele.
Copy: Library of Congress.

—— [Amersham, Eng.: Issued for subscribers by John S. Farmer, 1913.] 1 p.l., [58] p. 8°. (Old English drama. Students' facsimile edition.) NCP

—— ...The wisdom of Doctor Dodypoll. 1600. [London:] Issued for subscribers by the editor of the Tudor facsimile texts, 1912. 3 p.l., facsim.: 1 l., [58] p. 4°. (The Tudor facsimile texts.)
Also printed in A. H. Bullen, editor, *A Collection of old English plays,* London, 1882-85, v. 3, p. 95-159, NCO (Bullen).
"In many respects reminds us of the Jew. In the first place the broken English spoken by the Doctor. In the second place his desire to marry the heroine (think of Jacuppus in *Machiavellus*). In the third place several traits which were at any rate thought to be Jewish. He has a servant called Zaccharee, which is a Jewish name. All this is not conclusive proof that a Jew was meant, but if no Jew was meant, most of the details were at any rate derived from the Jew of literature." — *Michelson, p. 87.*
A. W. Ward states that an allusion to this play is to be found in 1596.
Neither Landa nor Cardozo mentions this play.

WOHLBRÜCK, WILHELM AUGUST. *See* sub-entry under SCOTT, SIR WALTER.

INDIVIDUAL PLAYS — 1838-1914

ABEL, W. H. *See* sub-entry under DE LA RAMÉE, LOUISE.

ADAMS, OSCAR FAY. The merchant of Venice: act VI. (Cornhill booklet. Boston, 1903. 16°. v. 3, p. 57-66.) NBI
Note by William J. Rolfe, p. 57-58.
Reprinted in his *A Motley jest,* Boston, 1909, p. 49-62, * NCS.
Shylock, though publicly a Christian, secretly remains true to his old faith and nurses his passion for revenge.
"Written for an evening entertainment of the 'Old Cambridge Shakespeare Assn.'"
Reviewed in *The Nation,* New York, 1909, v. 88, p. 231, * DA.

ADAMS, MRS. SARAH FULLER (FLOWER). Vivia Perpetua; a dramatic poem in five acts... London: Charles Fox, 1841. 5 p.l., (1)4-200 p. 8°.
Copy: Harvard College Library.
Vivia Perpetua was a Christian martyr in Carthage, North Africa, in the year 203. Her feast day, that of Saints Felicitas and Perpetua, is on March seventh. In this poem, Barcas, a Jew, is represented as denouncing her to the Roman authorities. Reviewed in *Albion,* London, 1842, new series, v. 1, p. 321-322, * A; and in *Examiner,* London, 1841, p. 99-100, * DA.
A synopsis, with many extracts, is printed in *Eclectic review,* London, 1841, series 4, v. 10, p. 166-177, * DA.

ADDISON, THOMAS. *See* sub-entry under TILTON, DWIGHT, PSEUD. OF G. T. RICHARDSON AND W. D. QUINT.

AGUILAR, GRACE. The vale of cedars; or, The martyr. New York: D. Appleton & Company, 1850. 1 p.l., (i)vi-xii, (1)14-256 p., front. 12°. NCW
This romance about the Jews of Spain of the fifteenth century, written before 1835 and first published in 1850, was adapted into a drama of five acts by Sigmund Herzberg, under the title *Jewess of Spain.*
See United States. — Copyright Office, *Dramatic compositions copyrighted in the United States, 1870 to 1916,* item 22709.

AINSWORTH, WILLIAM HARRISON. Jack Sheppard; a romance... with illustrations by George Cruikshank... London: R. Bentley, 1839. 3 v. 30 pl. 8°. MEM C955ai

ALMAR, GEORGE. Jack Ketch; or, A leaf from Tyburn tree. Drama in three acts. London: J. Dicks [1841].
Produced at Sadler's Wells Theatre, London, Sept., 1841. Reviewed in *Punch,* London, 1841, v. 1, p. 131-132, * DX.

Buckstone, John Baldwin. Jack Shepherd; a drama, in four acts... As performed at the Theatre Royal, Adelphi... Illustrated with an etching by Pierce Egan, the younger... London: Webster and Co. [184–?] 1 p.l., 17-72 p. front. 12°. NCOF
Prompter's copy, with interleaved ms. notes.
Fourteen pages missing at beginning.

—— —— New York: W. Taylor & Co., 1854. 92 p. nar. 12°. NCOF
At head of title: Minor drama, ed. by F. C. Wemyss, no. 53.
Prompter's copy with ms. notes.

—— —— New York: Samuel French [187–?]. 3 p.l., (1)10-92 p. 12°. NCO p.v.512
At head of title: Minor drama, ed. by F. C. Wemyss, no. 53.
Also printed in Benjamin N. Webster, editor, *Acting national drama,* v. 7.
Produced at the Adelphi Theatre, London, Oct. 28, 1839, with Yates as Abraham Mendez. Reviewed in *Athenæum,* London, 1839, v. 12, p. 830, * DA; *Spectator,* London, 1839, v. 12, p. 1039, * DA; and in *The Times,* London, Oct. 29, 1839, p. 5, col. 3, * A.
Produced at the Bowery Theatre, New York, Nov., 1853, with Leffingwell as Abraham Mendez.

—— The stone jug; a new version of Jack Sheppard. Produced at the Adelphi Theatre, London, March 24, 1873.
The censor having banned all *Jack Sheppard* plays, the present version as well as most of the dramatis personae were renamed. Jack Sheppard became Robert Chance and Mendez was transformed into Moses Mordecai, "the Jew Janizary." This part was acted by C. J. Smith. Reviewed in *Athenæum,* London, 1873, p. 417, col. 2-3, * DA; and in *Era,* London, v. 35, March 30, 1873, p. 12, † *NAFA.* Landa, p. 168, gives the date of this production as March 29, 1873, and H. Cooper as the adapter.

Greenwood, Thomas. Jack Sheppard; or, The house-breaker of the last century. A romantic drama in five acts (Dramatised from Harrison Ainsworth's novel.)... Printed from the acting copy, with remarks, biographical and critical, by D.-G. [i.e. George Daniel.] As performed at the metropolitan minor theatres... London: John Cumberland [1828-40]. 68 p. incl. front. 24°. (Cumberland's minor drama. v. 15.)
An extract, act v, scenes 2, 3, and 4, is printed in Allardyce Nicoll, editor, *Readings from British drama,* New York [1928], p. 280-282, * R-NCO.
Produced at the Sadler's Wells Theatre, London, Oct. 28, 1839. Mr. Hance played Abraham Mendez. The scene is laid in London, from the year 1703 to 1724.

Individual Plays — 1838-1914, continued

AINSWORTH, WILLIAM HARRISON, *continued*

Haines, John Thomas. Jack Sheppard; a domestic drama, in three acts... As performed at the London theatres, correctly printed from the prompt book with...plots of the scenery, properties, calls, copy of original bill, incidents, etc. [London:] James Pattie, 1839. xx, 70 p. front. 12°. (Pattie's universal stage. no. 4.)
Copy: Library of Congress.
Produced as "a new and singularly graphic, melodramatic, and panoramic adaptation," Oct. 21, 1839, at the Surrey Theatre, London, with Morelli as Abraham Mendez, one of Jonathan Wild's Janizaries.
Ainsworth having witnessed the rehearsals gave his written sanction to the performance. George Cruikshank designed the scenery. See p. x.

The Life and death of Jack Sheppard. A drama, in four acts. Adapted from Harrison Ainsworth's popular romance. London: T. H. Lacy [185–?]. 63 p., 1 pl. nar. 12°. (Lacy's acting edition of plays. v. 23.)   NCO (Lacy)

Phillips, Jonas B. Jack Sheppard; or, The life of a rotter. Melodrama in three acts, founded on Ainsworth's novel. [New York, 1839.] 2, 40, 25, 24 f. f°.
Ms., in possession of the Theatre Collection of Harvard College Library.
"First performed at the Bowery Theatre, New York, December 30, 1839." See Odell, IV: 367.
Nab Mendez is the name of a Jew, one of the Janizaries of Jonathan Wild. He is made to speak in dialect.

Stephens, Henry Pottinger, and W. Yardley. Little Jack Sheppard; a three-act burlesque-operatic-melodrama. London: W. S. Johnson, 1886. 56 p. 8°.
The date on the cover is 1885.
Cf. W. D. Adams, *A Book of burlesques*, London, 1891, p. 209–210.
Produced at the Gaiety Theatre, London, Dec. 26, 1885, with F. Wood as Abraham Mendez. Reviewed by H. Saville Clarke in *Theatre*, London, 1886, series 4, v. 7, p. 44–46, *NCOA*.
Produced at the People's Theatre, New York, Sept. 4, 1886, with F. T. Ward as Mendez.
The Library has a playbill of a Jan. 10, 1887, production, at the Alcazar Theatre, San Francisco, with George Osbourne as Mendez. See *MWEZ n.c.708*, p. 44.

The following are some of the ascertainable Jack Sheppard plays produced in England:
Harlequin Jack Sheppard; or, The blossom of Tyburn Tree (anon.) at the Drury Lane, Dec. 26, 1839. (See Nicoll, p. 464.)
The Idle apprentice; or, The two roads of life (anon.). Produced at the City of London Theatre, June 5, 1865. Reviewed in *Era*, London, v. 27, June 11, 1865, p. 11, † *NAFA*.
Jack Sheppard, by Joseph Hatton. Produced at the Pavillion Theatre, London, in four acts, April 9, 1898. Reviewed in *Illustrated sporting and dramatic news*, London, 1898, v. 49, p. 244, * *DA*.
Jack Sheppard (a melodrama), by William H. W. Murray. Produced at Edinburgh, Feb. 17, 1840. (See Nicoll, p. 355.)
Jack Sheppard (a sketch), by R. A. Roberts. Produced at the Palladium, London, Sept. 3, 1923. (*Stage year book*, 1921-25, p. 171.)
Jack Sheppard (a new version; drama in four acts and fourteen scenes), by Matt Wilkinson. Produced at the Elephant and Castle Theatre, London, April 30, 1928, with Richard Burn as Abraham Mendez. Reviewed in *Era*, London, v. 91, May 2, 1928, p. 4, † *NAFA*.

Jack Sheppard; or, The progress of crime, by W. T. Moncrieff. Produced at the Victoria Theatre, London, Oct. 21, 1839. His *Jack Sheppard the housebreaker; or, London in 1724*, was staged at the Coburg Theatre, London, April 18, 1825 — long before the appearance of Ainsworth's novel.
Jonathan Wild (a drama), by C. Stanfield James. Produced at the Queen's Theatre, London, Sept. 25, 1848. (See Nicoll, p. 320.)
Jonathan Wild (a drama in five acts), by Henry Young. Produced at the Elephant and Castle Theatre, London, Nov. 27, 1886.
Jonathan Wild; or, The storm on the Thames (a drama in four acts), by Mrs. H. Young. Produced at the New East London Theatre, July 13, 1868. Reviewed in *Era*, London, v. 30, July 19, 1868, p. 11, † *NAFA*.
Old London, adapted by John Oxenford from A. P. Dennery and E. Bourget's French version of Jack Sheppard (called *Les chevaliers du Broniliard*). Produced at the Queen's Theatre, London, Feb. 5, 1873. Reviewed in *Athenæum*, London, 1873, v. 61, p. 190, * *DA*; and in *Era*, London, v. 35, Feb. 9, 1873, p. 11, † *NAFA*.
Old London bridge in the days of Jack Sheppard and Jonathan Wild, by Arthur Shirley and W. M. Tilson. Produced at the Marylebone Theatre, London, Aug. 29, 1892, and revived March 12, 1894, at the Standard Theatre, London.
The Two Jack Sheppards (a burletta. Anon.). Produced at the Olympic Theatre, London, April 26, 1841. (See Nicoll, p. 536.)

The first American *Jack Sheppard* play was produced at the Bowery Theatre, New York, Dec. 30, 1839. The ascertainable adaptations and versions since then are as follows:
Blueskin; or, Jack and his pals, by John F. Poole, at the New Bowery, New York, Nov. 8, 1862. (Brown, II: 198.)
The Felon's last dream; or, Jack Sheppard in France (anon.), at the Bowery Theatre, New York, Aug. 12, 1850.
Harlequin Jack Sheppard; or, All right, my covey (a comic pantomime), by Joseph C. Foster, at the New Bowery Theatre, New York, Dec. 8, 1862. (Brown, II: 199.)
He's Jack Sheppard (a farce), by J. R. Planché, at the Winter Garden, New York, May 8, 1863. Noted in *Albion*, New York, 1863, v. 41, p. 235.
Jack Sheppard, by Owen Davis, at the Academy Theatre, Chicago, Aug. 26, 1908.
Jack Sheppard (in four acts) by Olive Harper, at the Grand Street Theatre, New York, Nov. 16, 1908. Reviewed in *New York dramatic mirror*, v. 60, Nov. 28, 1908, p. 3, * *T-* *DA*.
Jack Sheppard and his dog (anon.), at the Bowery Theatre, New York, Dec. 5, 1863. (Brown, I: 138.)
Jack Sheppard on horseback (anon.), at the Stadt-Theater, New York, Aug. 2, 1864. (Odell, v: 7.)
Jerry Ledrew; or, The American Jack Sheppard, by John F. Poole, at the Bowery Theatre, New York, March 28, 1864. (Brown, II: 206–207 and Odell, VII: 572.)
Knights of the mist (anon.), at the Chatham Theatre, New York, Nov. 8, 1858, and (according to Odell, VII: 142) the same evening at the National Theatre, New York. With the sub-title or, *Jack Sheppard from his cradle to his grave*, it was produced at the New Bowery Theatre, New York, Nov. 29, 1862. (Brown, II: 199.)
Three blueskins (anon.), at the New Bowery Theatre, New York, April 7, 1865. (Odell, VII: 662.) Odell, ibid., also records an anonymous *Three Jack Sheppards* at the same theatre a few evenings later.
Jack Sheppard; or, Newgate routed (a burlesque in two acts) of which there is no record of production, is credited to Wm. G. Baker and J. C. Arnold. (United States. — Copyright Office, *Dramatic compositions copyrighted in the United States, 1870 to 1916*, item 22359.)
The following anonymous *Jack Sheppard* versions without place and date of production, are given by H. C. Newton, p. 67: *Boy burglar, London apprentice, Storm in the Thames, Thames Darrell*, and *Young housebreaker*.

Individual Plays — 1838-1914, continued

AINSWORTH, WILLIAM HARRISON, *continued*

Ellis, Stewart Marsh. Jack Sheppard: the youth; the book and the play. illus. (In his: William Harrison Ainsworth and his friends. London, 1911. 8°. v. 1, p. 352-382.)
AN (Ainsworth)

—— Jack Sheppard in literature and drama. (In: H. W. Bleackley, Jack Sheppard. Edinburgh and London [1933]. 8°. p. 64-126.)
SLN (Bleackley)

Newton, Henry Chance. All the Jack Sheppards; Jonathan Wild and Claude Duval. (In his: Crime and the drama; or, Dark deeds dramatized. London [1927]. 8°. p. 64-75.) NAF

Roberts, W. Jack Sheppard in literature. (National review. London, 1924. 8°. v. 83, p. 432-440.) *DA

ALLEN, HORACE. *See* sub-entry under ERCKMANN, ÉMILE, AND ALEXANDRE CHATRIAN.

ALMAR, GEORGE. *See* sub-entries under AINSWORTH, WILLIAM HARRISON; DICKENS, CHARLES.

AMONG the musicians. (Dialogues of the dead, no. 6.) (Once a week. London, Dec. 19, 1868. 8°. [series 3,] v. 2 [i.e. v. 19], p. 509-512.) *DA
Among the characters are Meyerbeer and Mendelssohn, in heaven.

ANDREYEV, LEONID NIKOLAYEVICH. Anathema, a tragedy in seven scenes, by Leonid Andreyev; authorized translation by Herman Bernstein. New York: The Macmillan Company, 1910. vi, 211 p. 12°. **QDK
Reviewed in *American Hebrew*, New York, 1910, v. 88, p. 40, *PBD; by Richard Burton in *The Dial*, Chicago, v. 49, p. 523, *DA; *The Nation*, New York, 1910, v. 91, p. 397-398, *DA; *The Nation*, London, v. 7, p. 180, *DA; *New York dramatic mirror*, 1910, v. 64, Nov. 9, p. 8, *T-*DA; and in *New York Times book review*, v. 16, p. 43 (Jan. 29, 1911), † NAA.
A synopsis from the original Russian edition is given in *American Hebrew*, New York, 1909, v. 84, p. 622-623, *PBD.
The motif is that of the Faust legend. Anathema is the spirit that doubts or Mephisto. Faust in this case is a poor, Job-like Jew, David Leizer. Originally produced at the Moscow Art Theatre, Moscow, with Kachalov as Anathema. It was produced in Yiddish at the Lipzin Theatre, New York, with Maurice Moschcovitch in the title-rôle and S. Tobias as David, Nov. 25, 1910. Reviewed in *New York dramatic mirror*, v. 64, Nov. 30, 1910, p. 7, *T-*DA.

—— —— New York: The Macmillan Company, 1923. 4 p.l., 3-211 p. 12°.
Reviewed by Harrison Goldberg in *Hebrew Union College monthly*, Cincinnati, 1924, v. 10, Feb., p. 15-17, *PBD; and by Isadore Lhevinne, in *Literary review of the New York Evening Post*, April 21, 1923, p. 622, *A.
A second dramatization was staged at the Yiddish Art Theatre, New York, with Maurice Schwartz as Anathema and Paul Muni as David, Feb. 9, 1923. Reviewed in *American Hebrew*, New York, v. 112, p. 565, 577 (with illus.), *PBD; and in *Theatre magazine*, New York, v. 37, April, 1923, p. 14, † NBLA. See also *Collection of newspaper clippings of dramatic criticism, 1922-1923*, vol. A-F, † NBL.

Thomson, Osmund Rhodes Howard. Andreyev's "Anathema" and the Faust legend. (North American review. New York, 1911. 8°. v. 194, p. 882-887.) *DA

ANDREYEV, LEONID NIKOLAYEVICH. To the stars (a drama in four acts) by Leonid Andreieff. Translated from the Russian by Dr. A. Goudiss. (Poet lore. Boston, 1907. 8°. v. 18, p. 417-467.) *DA

—— —— Translated by Maurice Magnus. London: C. W. Daniel, Ltd., 1921. 84 p. 12°. (Plays for a people's theatre. no. 10.)
First appeared in *Sbornik tovarishchestva "Znaniye,"* St. Petersburg, 1906, v. 10, p. 1-33, *QDA. A synopsis of the Russian text appeared in *American Hebrew*, New York, 1906, v. 78, p. 499, *PBD; and in *Current literature*, New York, v. 40, p. 312, *DA. For a critical analysis see Joshua Kunitz, *Russian literature and the Jew*, New York, 1929, p. 140-144, *PZB. The Jewish character is Joseph Abramovich Luntz, whose relatives had been massacred in Russia and who is, during the action of the play, a fellow refugee in the household of a Russian astronomer.

ANZENGRUBER, LUDWIG. The farmer forsworn [in three acts] translated by Adolf Busse. plates. (In: Kuno Francke and W. G. Howard, editors, The German classics. New York [cop. 1914]. 8°. v. 16, p. 112-188.) NFF (Francke)
Its German title is Der Meineidbauer.
Cf. The life of Ludwig Anzengruber, by the translator, p. 100-111.
A play of Austrian peasant life. Levy, a peddler, appears in it in a minor part.

ARCHER, THOMAS. The three red men; or, The brothers of Bluthaupt. A romantic drama in three acts... London: T. H. Lacy [186-?]. 50 p. 12°. (Lacy's acting edition of plays. v. 41.)
NCO (Lacy)
The New York Public Library has also a prompter's copy, interleaved with ms. notes, NCOF.
A version of Paul Jéval's *Les Trois hommes rouges*, Paris, 1847.
Produced at the City of London Theatre, May 1, 1848, with Grant as Baron de Geldberg, "otherwise Moses Geld and Araby the Jew." The legend as printed on the original play-bill reads thus: "Once upon a time there were three illegitimate brothers, who wandered about to protect a race, and so changed their features at will as to deceive a combination of powerful and artful enemies of the house of Bluthaupt, for its ruin and the destruction of the rightful heir. Their death was often sought, but their ingenuity frustrated every attempt; — their tomb remains to this day in Frankfort."
The time of the action is 1829.
Nicoll, p. 532, lists an anonymous play, *The Three red men*, as having been produced at the Coburg Theatre, London, May 8, 1848.

ARNSTEIN, MARK. The eternal song; a picture of labor life. (In: Etta Block, translator, One-act plays from the Yiddish. Cincinnati [cop. 1923]. 12°. p. 139-165.) *PTP
Reprinted in Constance M. Martin, editor, *Fifty one-act plays*, London, 1934, p. 751-768, NAFH.
"A picture of labor life, amid whose hardships and despairs love lingers and is born." Time: past, present, or future, in a large city. It first appeared in Polish in *Wschód*, Lwow, 1901, and first produced in that language at the Teater Rozmaitosci, Warsaw, Sept. 25, 1901. A Yiddish version was staged in Riga, Aug. 28, 1905. The original Yiddish was printed in *Teater-Bibliothek*, no. 3, Warsaw, 1907.

Individual Plays — 1838–1914, continued

ASCH, SHALOM. The God of vengeance [in three acts]. Translated by S. P. Rudens and H. Champvert. (East and West. New York, 1916. 4°. v. 1, p. 324–340.)   * PBD

—— The God of vengeance; drama in three acts, by Sholom Ash, authorized translation from the Yiddish, with introduction and notes by Isaac Goldberg, preface by Abraham Cahan ... Boston: The Stratford Co., 1918. xiv p., 1 l., 99 p. 12°.   * PTP
Reviewed in *Dramatist*, Easton, Pa., v. 14, p. 1156–1157, *NAFA;* by M. C. D. in *The Nation*, New York, v. 107, p. 210, * *DA;* and in *Stratford journal*, Boston, v. 4, p. 53, * *DA.*
A decadent play, the action of which is laid in a house of prostitution. The original was published in Wilna, 1907, and was reviewed by David Pinski, in *Zukunft*, New York, 1907, v. 12, p. 659–662, * *PBB.* First produced by Reinhardt at the Deutsches Theater, Berlin, March 19, 1907, and reviewed by Hermann Kienzl, in his *Die Bühne; ein Echo der Zeit (1905–1907)*, Berlin, 1907, p. 231–235, *MWEF (Berlin)*. Produced in Yiddish at the Thalia Theatre, New York, Oct. 13, 1907, with David Kessler as Shepshelovitz, keeper of the brothel. Reviewed in *American Hebrew*, New York, 1907, v. 81, p. 598, * *PBD;* and in *Modern view*, St. Louis, v. 16, Oct. 2, 1908, p. 6, * *PBD.*
An English version was staged at the Provincetown Theatre, New York, Dec. 19, 1922, with Rudolf Schildkraut in the main rôle. Reviewed in *Life*, New York, v. 81, March 8, 1923, p. 18, * *DA;* by Isaac Goldberg in *Talmud magazine*, Boston, v. 3, no. 2, p. 37–40, 46, * *PBD;* and in *Theatre magazine*, New York, v. 37, April, 1923, p. 20, 68, † *NBLA.* See also *Collection of newspaper clippings of dramatic criticism, 1922–1923*, vol. G–L, † *NBL.*

Apollo Theatre, New York. Opinions of Frank Crane and other prominent men and women. [New York: Marston Press, 1923.] 18 p. facsim., ports., illus. 8°.
On cover: "The God of vengeance," is the play immoral? — is it a great drama? Read what Frank Crane and others say.
"To the public," by Harry Weinberger, p. 1–2.

New York (state). — Courts: Supreme Court. ... The people of the state of New York, respondents, against Harry Weinberger, Rudolph Schildkraut ... [and others], defendant-appellants. Respondents' brief. [New York, 1924.] 74 p. 8°.   SEKD (American) n.c.13
Caption-title.
At head of title: Garrett Wallace... New York Supreme Court. Appellate Division — First Department.
Case of producer and actors of The God of vengeance, by Shalom Asch.
The final adjudication of the case, as given by the New York Court of Appeals, Jan. 21, 1925, is printed in *Northeastern reporter*, St. Paul, Minn., 1925, v. 146, p. 434–438.

ASCH, SHALOM. Night. [In one act.] Translated by Jacob Robbins. (East and West. New York, 1915. 4°. v. 1, p. 75–78.)   * PBD
Night in the market place. A prostitute, a thief, a beggar, a bastard, and a fool speak. The original appeared in *Zukunft*, New York, 1913, v. 18, p. 869–874, * *PBB.*
Reprinted in Frank Shay and P. Loving, editors, *Fifty contemporary one-act plays*, Cincinnati [cop. 1920], p. 537–544, *NAFH (Shay);* and in Constance M. Martin, editor, *Fifty one-act plays*, London, 1934, p. 769–781, *NAFH (Martin).*
Produced by the East-West Players at the Berkeley Theatre, New York, April 7, 1916, with Mark Hoffman as the drunkard and Gustav Blum as the thief.

—— Sabbatai Zevi; a tragedy in three acts and six scenes with a prologue and an epilogue, by Sholom Ash; authorized translation from the Russian version by Florence Whyte and George Rapall Noyes. Philadelphia: The Jewish Publication Society of America, 1930. 131 p., front. 12°.   * PTP
Reviewed by John Cournos in *B'nai B'rith magazine*, Cincinnati, 1930, v. 44, p. 335, * *PYP;* Jewish quarterly review, Philadelphia, 1931, new series, v. 21, p. 351, * *PBE;* and in *The Times literary supplement*, London, 1930, v. 29, p. 570, † *NAA.*
The original Yiddish appeared in *Literarische Monats-schriften*, no. 3, 1908, * *PBB*, and reviewed by Ben-Zion Hoffman in *Zukunft*, New York, 1908, v. 13, p. 517–519, * *PBB.* The action centers around Sabbethai Zebi, pseudo-Messiah, 1626–1676.

—— The sinner [a drama in one act]. Translated by Jacob Robbins. (East and West. New York, 1915. 4°. v. 1, p. 5–9.)   * PBD
See criticism by John Erskine, *ibid.*, p. 21–23, who points out that this is the only piece, among other translations from the Yiddish, which is entirely understandable by a non-Jew.
A second translation appeared in Isaac Goldberg, translator, *Six plays of the Yiddish theatre*, Boston [cop. 1916], p. 151–175, * *PTP.*
Reprinted in Leo W. Schwarz, editor, *A golden treasury of Jewish literature*, New York [cop. 1937], p. 528–536, * *PSY.*

—— Winter; a drama in one act. (In: Isaac Goldberg, translator, Six plays of the Yiddish theatre. Boston [cop. 1916]. 12°. p. 123–149.)   * PTP
The original, Um Winter, was published by the Verlag Progress, Warsaw, 1910.
Grim drama of a woman's self-sacrifice.
Presented by the Jewish Drama League at the Strand Theatre, London, May 22, 1927. Reviewed in *Jewish chronicle*, London, May 27, 1927, p. 34, * *PBE.*

—— With the current. [In one act.] Translated by Jacob Robins [*sic!*]. (East and West. New York, 1915. 4°. v. 1, p. 195–199.)   * PBD
This, first of Asch's plays, appeared in Hebrew under the title of Yatza we-hazar in *Hashiloah*, Krakau, 1904, Bd 13, p. 201–212, 304–312, * *PBA.* Originally it is in two parts; only the first is here translated. The scene is in a little town in the Russian Pale, in the seventies of the last century, and pictures the struggle of a young scholar between the old forms of Jewish life and the new currents of thought. It was first produced in Polish at the Municipal theatre of Cracow, Jan. 9, 1905.
Produced in English by the Neighborhood Playhouse, Grand Street, New York, April 22, 1916. In an English translation by Mrs. Bessie F. White, entitled *Down stream*, it was staged by the Little Theatre of Temple Israel, Boston, Dec. 10, 1930. See *Jewish advocate*, Boston, 1930, v. 58, Dec. 5, p. 1, 5, * *PBD.*

AUGIER, GUILLAUME VICTOR ÉMILE, AND JULES SANDEAU. Monsieur Poirier's son-in-law. <Le gendre de M. Poirier.> A comedy in four acts. (In: Émile Augier. Four plays, translated by B. H. Clark. New York, 1915. 8°. p. 71–140.)   NKP
Reprinted in B. H. Clark, editor, *World drama; an anthology*, New York, 1933 [v. 2], p. 346–378, *NAFH;* and, under the title *A son-in-law of M. Poirier*, in Brander Matthews, editor, *Chief European dramatists*, Boston [etc., cop. 1916], p. 411–446, *NAFH.*
For summaries and appreciations of the play see G. V. E. Augier, *Le gendre de M. Poirier*, ed. by Petilleau, London, 1896, p. v–xv, *NKM p.v.367*, and ed. by B. W. Wells, Boston [cop. 1896], p. iii–xii, *NKP.* See also the introductions in the editions of S. Symington, New York, 1899; of Edwin C. Roedder, New York [1903]; of Richmond L. Hawkins, New York [1921]; of Clifford S. Parker, Boston [1926];

THE JEW IN ENGLISH DRAMA 57

Individual Plays — 1838-1914, continued
and of L. P. Irvin and H. L. Cook, New York, 1930. Cf. also *Essential qualities of the work of Émile Augier*, n. p. [18—?], f. 11–13, NAC p.v.76.
Two extracts from Act II are printed in *Library of the world's best literature*, v. 2 or 3, p. 1006–1011, NAC.
W. N. Guthrie called it "Moliere's '*Bourgeois gentilhomme*' brought down to date." It was produced at the Théâtre Gymnase, Paris, April 8, 1854. Salomon is one of three creditors.
Odell, VII: 164–165 records an advertisement of a New York production in French scheduled for April 2, 1859. It was staged again at the French Theatre, New York, May 5, 1860. Under the title *My noble son-in-law*, it was produced at Wallack's Theatre, New York, April 7, 1863, with G. F. Browne as Salomons and C. T. Parsloe as Isaacs. Reviewed in *Spirit of the times*, New York, 1863, v. 8, p. 112, † *MVA*.

Greville, Lady Violet. Equals; a comedy in three acts, based on Le gendre de M. Poirier, was produced at the Criterion Theatre, London, March 31, 1894.
An almost literal version of the French. The characters are given English names and the scene is placed in London. Reviewed in *The Times*, London, April 2, 1894, p. 4, col. 2, * A.

Rose, Edward. Equals; a comedy in three acts. Freely adapted from "Gendre de M. Poirier"... London, New York: Samuel French [1883–86]. 34 p. nar. 12°. (French's acting edition of plays. v. 119 [no. 1783].) NCO (Lacy)
Produced at the Prince's Theatre, Manchester, June 28, 1883. Mr. Kenward as Isaacs, Sen., one of three money-lenders. The others are named McNab and Higson. Isaacs has a minor part, at end of the first act.

B., J. H. Patriots; a tragedy [in two acts]. (Jewish comment. Baltimore, 1909. f°. v. 29, p. 197.) * PBD
A comic sketch about the wrangling of delegates at a Zionist convention.

BAAR, HERMAN. Dialogue on cooking. (Sabbath visitor. Cincinnati, 1888. 8°. v. 18, p. 201–203.) * PBD

—— Dialogue on prizes. (Sabbath visitor. Cincinnati, 1888. 8°. v. 18, p. 346–347.) * PBD

—— Fashion; a dialogue. (Sabbath visitor. Cincinnati, 1887. 8°. v. 17, p. 405–407.) * PBD

—— Visitors; a dialogue. (Sabbath visitor. Cincinnati, 1887. 8°. v. 17, p. 357–358.) * PBD
These dialogues were spoken by the inmates of the Hebrew Orphan Asylum, New York, at public entertainments.

BAKER, GEORGE MELVILLE. Conjuration; a charade of four syllables, in operetta. [Boston: Geo. M. Baker & Co., cop. 1873.] 103–114 p. 12°. (Parlor opera. no. 4.)
Caption-title.
One of the characters in the charade is a Jew.

—— The peddler of Very Nice; a burlesque... Boston: Lee & Sheppard, W. V. Spencer, 1866. 16 p. 12°.
Reprinted in his *Amateur dramas for parlor theatricals*, Boston and New York [cop. 1866], Boston [cop. 1876], and Boston [cop. 1894], p. 201–214; and in his *Original entertainments and burlesques*, Boston [cop. 1898], and Boston, 1902, p. 79–92.
A burlesque on the trial scene in *The Merchant of Venice*. Shylock is represented as a pawnbroker; Antonio, the peddler of Very Nice; and Portia, a Very Nice bloomer.

BANKS, CHARLES EUGENE. An American woman; a drama in four acts. Chicago and New York: Dramatic Pub. Company, cop. 1905. 51 p. 12°. (Sergel's acting drama. no. 577.)
NBL p.v.4
First produced Jan. 11, 1905, at the Burtis Opera House, Davenport, Iowa. Bradlee Martin as Solomon Slupski, merchant. Speaks in dialect.

BARNETT, CHARLES ZACHARY. Dream of fate; or, Sarah the Jewess. A drama in two acts... London, New York: Samuel French [1876–86]. 36 p. 12°. (French's acting edition. [no. 1296.] v. 129.) NCO (Lacy)
Included in *Duncombe's Dramatic tales*, London [1840?], new series, no. 1.
The scene is laid in Frankfort and Paris. The first act opens during a Jewish celebration of the feast of Purim. The events of the play, a synopsis of which is given in Landa, p. 184, prove to be a dream. It was produced at Sadler's Wells Theatre, London, Aug. 20, 1838, with Cathcart as David Stolberg the rich Jew of Frankfort; Dry as Zodiah an apostate Jew; Mrs. R. Honner as Sarah the Jewess, and Miss Pincott as Rebecca, maid in the household of the Stolbergs.
Produced at the Franklin Theatre, New York, Dec. 19, 1838, with W. Jones as David Stolberg and Mrs. C. Thorne as Sarah.

—— The mariner's dream; or, The Jew of Plymouth. An original drama in three acts... As performed at the Pavillion Theatre... London: J. Pattie [1839–40?]. 2 p.l., ii, (1)8–49 p., front. (plate.) 24°. NCO p.v.315
Produced at the Royal Pavillion, Oct. 17, or Oct. 18, 1838, with J. R. Williams as Isaac Waldorf, the Jew. Scene: near Plymouth and on board H. M. S. *Enterprise*. The time: 1815.

—— See also sub-entry under DICKENS, CHARLES.

BARRETT, ALFRED WILSON. The Jew of Prague... London: F. V. White, Ltd., 1912. 311 p. 8°.
Dramatized by the author into a play of four acts and seven scenes. A violent romantic drama which, despite its melodramatic absurdities, was fairly well received. Produced at the Whitney Theatre, London, May 8, 1912. Reviewed in *Truth*, London, 1912, v. 71, p. 1244, * DA. See illustration in *Illustrated sporting and dramatic news*, London, v. 77, p. 409, * DA.

BARRETT, WILSON, AND R. S. HICHENS. The daughters of Babylon; a novel... Philadelphia: J. B. Lippincott Company, 1899. 324 p. incl. front. 12°. NCW
This novel by the two authors is based on Barrett's play of the same title, in four acts, which was produced at the Lyric Theatre, London, Feb. 6, 1897, with great success. *The Times* reviewer wrote: "Mr. W. B. does this time for the Synagogue what before [in his Sign of the cross] he attempted for the Church. He seeks to glorify Hebraism as he did early Christianity. The period is that of the Jewish captivity in Babylon — 500 or 400 B. C. The Israelites are depicted as still leading a pastoral life."
Production reviewed by A. B. Walkley in *Cosmopolis*, London, 1897, v. 6, p. 77–78, * DA; by G. B. Shaw in *Saturday review*, London, 1897, v. 83, p. 168–170, * DA; by William Archer in his *Theatrical world of 1897*, London, 1898, p. 23–30, NCOA; *Truth*, London, 1897, v. 41, p. 334–335, * DA; and in *The Times*, London, Feb. 8, 1897, p. 12, * A.

Souvenir of "The daughters of Babylon" by Wilson Barrett. Illustrated by W. & D. Downey. London: W. & D. Downey [1897]. 4°.
Title from British Museum catalogue.

Individual Plays — 1838–1914, continued

BASWITZ, CHARLES. Jakey Einstein; or, Life on the road. A comedy drama in four acts... Springfield, Ill.: State Journal Book and Job Printing Co., 1886. 50 p. 8°.
See United States. — Copyright Office, *Dramatic compositions copyrighted in the United States, 1870 to 1916*, item 22434.

BAUMAN, J. HOWARD. The country squire; a comedy drama in four acts... Clyde, Ohio: Ames Publishing Co., cop. 1906. 52 p. 12°. (Ames' series of standard and minor drama. no. 465.)
Solomon Isaac, "a Jew pedler."

BEACONSFIELD, BENJAMIN DISRAELI, 1ST EARL OF. Tancred; or, The new crusade. London: Henry Colburn, 1847. 3 v. 12°.

Nuttall, Edith (Smith), "Mrs. Harry Nuttall." Tancred, a play in a prologue and three acts, adapted by Edith Millbank [pseud.] from Disraeli's novel of the same name, was produced at the Kingsway Theatre, London, July 16, 1923.
A dramatization into a romantic melodrama of the novel which Disraeli himself considered his greatest. It reveals Disraeli's racial patriotism and his attitude towards a "wider Judaism" which he termed Christianity. The action takes place in Palestine whither Tancred has travelled in quest of spiritual peace. There he meets and marries Eve, Rose of Sharon. Tancred is Lord Beaconsfield himself. Sidonia, the prototype of whom was Baron Lionel Nathan de Rothschild, 1806–1879, was omitted in the dramatization. Charles Carson played Tancred, Lord Montacute; Henzie Raeburn, Eve. The critics condemned the play. Cf. Robert Arnot, editor, *The Earl of Beaconsfield, K. G., keys to the famous characters delineated in his historical romances*, New York [cop. 1904], p. 21, 42–43, *NCC (Beaconsfield).*
Reviewed in *Curtain*, London, 1923, v. 2, p. 89, *NAFA*; *Era*, London, v. 86, July 18, 1923, p. 5, † *NAFA*; *London mercury*, London, v. 8, p. 650, * *DA*; by L. W. in *Nation*, London, v. 33, p. 554, 556, * *DA*; and by Cheviot Hill in *Time and tide*, London, v. 4, p. 757–758, * *DA*.

Badt-Strauss, Bertha. Disraeli und Palästina. illus. (Menorah. Wien, 1927. 8°. Jahrg. 5, p. 640–643.) * PBC

BECKETT, DAN. *See* sub-entry under DICKENS, CHARLES.

BEDDOES, THOMAS LOVELL. The second brother; an unfinished drama. (In his: Poems; posthumous and collected. [Edited by Thos. F. Kelsall.] London, 1851. 12°. v. 1, p. 1–56.) NCM
Also printed in his *Poems*, edited by Ramsay Colles, London and New York [1914], p. 217–258, *NCR*; in his *Complete works*, edited by Sir Edmund Gosse, London [1928], p. 493–536, * *KP (Fanfrolico)*; and by F. L. Lucas, in his *Thomas Lovell Beddoes; an anthology*, Cambridge, 1932, p. 89–130, *NDH (Beddoes)*.
This drama in three acts and two short scenes of a fourth act was written sometime during 1823–1825. It derives its name from the return of the second brother Marcello, long thought dead, to claim the dukedom from his younger brother Orazio, who believes himself the rightful heir in the order of succession. The Jew Ezril is Marcello's servant, physician and confidant. The scene is Ferrara, Italy. Ezril appears again as the main character in *The Israelites amid Philistines* and in *Prison thoughts*, the third and the fifth fragments of Beddoes' *Dramatic scenes and fragments*.

Reviewed in *Athenæum*, London, 1851, v. 24, p. 989–990, * *DA*; *Examiner*, London, 1851, p. 612–613, * *DA*; and in *Sewanee review*, New York, v. 11, p. 318–320, * *DA*. For a bibliography of Beddoes see R. H. Snow, *Thomas Lovell Beddoes; eccentric & poet*, New York, 1928, p. 222–227, *NCC (Beddoes)*.
Detailed analyses and synopses are given by Alwin L. W. Feller in his *Thomas Lovell Beddoes; Untersuchungen über sein Leben und Dichtungen*, Marburg a. L., 1914, p. 59–64, *AN (Beddoes)*; and by Grete Moldauer in her *Thomas Lovell Beddoes*, Wien and Leipzig, 1924, p. 136–138 (Wiener Beiträge zur englischen Philologie, Bd. 52, *NCB, Wiener*).

BEEBE, M. N. The all America eleven; an entertainment for boys in one scene... Boston: Walter H. Baker & Co., 1909. 8 p. 12°. (Baker's edition of plays.)
One of the boys on the team is Jewish.

——— Wanted — a pitcher; a farce in one act. Boston: Walter H. Baker Company, cop. 1913. 23 p. 16°. (Baker's edition of plays.)
Isaac Steinberg, peddler, who comes with a pitcher, when a pitcher is needed.

BELL, KENNETH. Anti-clericalism in France. (Forum. New York, 1911. 8°. v. 45, p. 320–333.) *DA
A dialogue between an English country gentleman and his two guests, a deputy of the moderate Left in the French Chamber and a former deputy, member of the Right. The Dreyfus affair and the so-called Jewish question are discussed.

BENAVENTE Y MARTINEZ, JACINTO. Saturday night, a novel for the stage in five tableaux. Translated from the Spanish by John Garrett Underhill. (Poet lore. Boston, 1918. 8°. v. 29, no. 2, p. 127–193.) *DA
See the translator's "Benavente as a modern," ibid., p. 194–200.

——— ——— [Boston: R. G. Badger,] cop. 1918. (1)128–193 p. 4°. (Poet lore plays. series 2.)
A pageant of life upon the Riviera, which unfolds certain dominant moods in the life of the heroine Imperia. It was first produced at the Teatro Español, Madrid, March 17, 1903.

——— Saturday night; translated from the Spanish with a preface by John Garrett Underhill. Authorized ed. New York: C. Scribner's Sons, 1926. 5 p.l., 41–129 p., front. 12°.
The present edition, reprinted from his *Plays; third series*, New York, 1923, p. 39–129, *NPO*, was issued on the occasion of its first English presentation by Eva La Gallienne at the Civic Repertory Theatre, New York, Oct. 25, 1926. Egon Brecher played Mr. Jacob, proprietor of a music hall; Nancy Bevill, Zaida, an Algerian Jewish dancing girl. For reviews see *Collection of newspaper clippings of dramatic criticism, 1926–1927*, vol. R–S, † *NBL*.

——— ...The smile of Mona Lisa; a play in one act...translated from the Spanish by John Armstrong Herman. Boston: R. G. Badger [etc., cop. 1915]. 3 p.l., 5–12 p., 2 l., 15–34 p. 12°. (Contemporary dramatists series.) NPO

——— ——— Boston: Four Seas Company, 1919. 34 p. 12°.
Known in the original as *La Sonrisa de La Gioconda*. Among the characters are Leonardo Da Vinci, and the Jew Ismael, one of his patrons and admirers.

BENEDICT, GEORGE. The masterpiece; a Purim comedietta in two acts. (London Jewry sketches. vi.) (Jewish exponent. Philadelphia, 1901. f°. v. 32, March 1, 1901, p. 1–2.) †* PBD
A sketch of Jewish home life in a Whitechapel back street.

THE JEW IN ENGLISH DRAMA 59

Individual Plays — 1838–1914, continued

BENJAMIN, PSEUD. Between ourselves. [In one scene.] (Israel. London, 1900. 4°. v. 4, p. 1–2.)
Copy: Library of American Jewish Historical Society.
The speakers are the hon. officers of the United Synagogue, London.

BENNETT, ARNOLD. The great adventure; a play of fancy in four acts... London: Methuen & Co., Ltd. [1913.] 152 p. 16°.   NCR

—— —— London: Methuen & Co., Ltd. [1924.] 152 p. 7. ed. 12°.

—— —— New York: George H. Doran Company [cop. 1913]. 152 p. 12°.

—— The great adventure; a comedy in four acts. New York: George H. Doran Company [cop. 1913]. 145 p. 12°.
Reprinted in R. A. Cordell, editor, *Representative modern plays, British and American*, New York, 1929, p. 208–252, *NCO (Cordell)*; and in Virginia W. F. Church, editor, *Curtain!* New York and London, 1932, p. 25–115, *NCO (Church)*.
An extract from act I, scene 1 is printed in Allardyce Nicoll, editor, *Readings from British drama*, New York [1928], p. 417–421, * *R-NCO*; and in A. R. Headland and H. A. Treble, compilers, *A dramatic reader*, book III, Oxford, 1921, p. 129–133.
Dramatized from the author's novel. An eminent painter, Carve, causes his valet to be buried in Westminster Abbey as the supposedly dead Carve. Ebag, a Jewish picture dealer, discovers later his identity.
"Carve. Damned Jew!
"Ebag. (Smoothly) Damned — possibly. Jew — most decidedly. But in this particular instance I behaved just like a Christian. I paid a little less than I was asked, and sold for the highest I could get."
The play was first tried out at the Royalty Theatre, Glasgow, Sept. 18, 1911, and brought to London, at the Kingsway Theatre, March 25, 1913, with Clarence Derwent as Ebag. Reviewed in *Academy*, London, 1913, v. 84, p. 435–436, * *DA*; and by John Palmer in *Saturday review*, London, 1913, v. 115, p. 419–420, * *DA*. A revival, which ran 160 times, was seen at the Haymarket Theatre, London, June 5, 1924, with Lewin Mannering as Ebag. Reviewed by Horace Shipp in *English review*, London, 1924, v. 39, p. 140–141, * *DA*.
Produced at the Opera House, Providence, R. I., Oct. 6, 1913, and at the Booth Theatre, New York, Oct. 16, 1913, with Edgar Kent as Ebag. Reviewed by Channing Pollock in *Green book album*, Chicago, 1914, v. 11, p. 69–71, *NBLA*; and (with illus.) in *Theatre magazine*, 1913, v. 18, p. 142, 179, *NBLA*. Copious extracts from the text, with illus., are printed in *Hearst's magazine*, 1913, v. 24, p. 965–975, * *DA*.

BERGSTRØM, HJALMAR. Lynggaard & Co.; a drama in four acts. (In his: Karen Borneman, Lynggaard & Co. Translated with an introduction by Edwin Björkman. New York, 1923. 12°. p. 93–255.)   NIY
The basis of the play is the conflict between capital and labor. The action takes place at Copenhagen. George Heymann, played by James Hearne, is the Jewish manager of the Lynggaard firm, in love with the daughter of the head of the firm.
The head of the firm; adapted from the Danish Lynggaard & Co., by Leslie Faber, was produced at the Buxton Opera House, June 13, 1908, and at the Vaudeville Theatre, London, March 4, 1909. Reviewed in *Illustrated London news*, 1909, v. 134, p. 370, * *DA*; and by Max Beerbohm in *Saturday review*, London, 1909, v. 107, p. 367–368, * *DA*.

BERLYN, IVAN. See sub-entry under DICKENS, CHARLES.

BERNARD, WILLIAM BAYLE. The philosophers of Berlin; a comedy, in two acts. London [1886]. 14 p. 8°. (Dicks' standard plays. no. 779.)
Entry from British Museum catalogue.
Voltaire and Frederick the Great are the two central characters. It was produced at the Haymarket Theatre, London, May 18, 1841, with Strickland and Rees as "two Hebrew merchants deporting themselves as a couple of Jew clothesmen in a farce." Reviewed in *The Athenæum*, London, 1841, v. 14, p. 412, * *DA*; and in *The Spectator*, v. 14, p. 495, * *DA*.

BERNSTEIN, HENRY. Israël, pièce en trois actes. [Paris,] 1908. 32 p. illus. f°. (Illustration théâtrale. no. 102.)   NKM p.v.284
First produced at the Théâtre Réjane, Paris, Oct. 13, 1908, with Gautier as Thibault and Signoret as Justin Gottlieb. Reviewed in *The Nation*, New York, 1908, v. 87, p. 471, * *DA*.
A translated excerpt from act I, scene 6, is given in Edmond Fleg, *Jewish anthology*, translated by Maurice Samuel, New York [cop. 1925], p. 357–359, * *PS*.
A synopsis of the plot is given in *Modern view*, St. Louis, v. 18, Feb. 19, 1910, p. 7, * *PBD*; with copious extracts, in *Current opinion*, New York, v. 48, p. 193–199, * *DA*; and by Charles W. Collins, in *Theatre magazine*, New York, v. 9, p. 57–62, † *NBLA*.
A young aristocrat insults a dignified old Jewish banker wishing to involve him in a duel. The Jew applies to the youth's mother who in turn beseeches her son not to press the quarrel. In a gruelling cross-examination the boy follows up the motive of this strange request until at last he wrings from her the confession that he is the illegitimate son of this banker. Despite the latter's attempt to reconcile him to his fate the boy commits suicide. Produced at the Criterion Theatre, New York, Oct. 25, 1909, with Edwin Arden as Justin Gottlieb, and Graham Browne as his son Thibault. As staged in New York, the scene in the last act between Thibault and Father Silvian who urges him to enter upon a monastic life, is omitted, and Thibault, instead of destroying himself, marries and presumably lives happily ever afterwards.
The New York production was reviewed by Louis Lipsky in *American Hebrew*, New York, 1909, v. 85, p. 647, * *PBD*; *Dramatist*, Easton, Pa., v. 1, p. 16–17, *NAFA*; (with illus.) in *Everybody's magazine*, New York, v. 22, p. 126, 129–130, * *DA*; by Clayton Hamilton, in *Forum*, New York, v. 42, p. 571–575, * *DA*; *Hampton's magazine*, New York, v. 23, p. 535–540, * *DA*; *Jewish comment*, Baltimore, v. 30, p. 35, * *PBD*; by Harriet Quimby in *Leslie's weekly*, New York, v. 109, p. 462, * *DA*; by J. S. Metcalfe in *Life*, New York, v. 54, p. 629, * *DA*; *The Nation*, New York, v. 89, p. 414, * *DA*; *New York dramatic mirror*, New York, v. 62, Nov. 6, 1909, p. 5, * *DA*; and in *Theatre magazine*, New York, v. 10, p. 169, † *NBLA*.
See also correspondence between Joseph Jacobs, editor, and Charles Frohman, producer, relative to the advisability of staging so anti-Jewish a play, in *American Hebrew*, New York, v. 84, p. 340, * *PBD*. Cf. ibid., v. 85, p. 656–657, * *PBD*.

—— —— Israel; a drama. Translated and adapted by Sidney L. Isaacs for the Jewish Drama League, London. Produced at the Everyman Theatre, London, Oct. 10, 1927, with Herbert Lomas as Justin Gottlieb and Harcourt Williams as Thibault.
Reviewed by James E. Agate in his *Contemporary theatre*, 1926, London, 1927, p. 102–106, *NAFA*; by G. W. B. in *Era*, London, v. 91, Oct. 12, 1927, p. 5, † *NAFA*; and in *Jewish chronicle*, London, Oct. 14, 1927, p. 29, * *PBE*.

Allary, J. The dramas of Henry Bernstein and the worship of strength. (Fortnightly review. New York, 1920. 8°. v. 114, p. 301–307.) * *DA*

Crabos, Pierre Gilbert. Le Juif dans le théâtre de M. Bernstein; essai de critique psychologique. (Revue critique des idées et des livres. Paris, 1912. 8°. tome 16, p. 427–448.) * *DM*

Individual Plays — 1838–1914, continued
BERNSTEIN, HENRY, *continued*

Eaton, Walter Prichard. "Israel" and the happy ending. (In his: At the New Theatre and others. Boston [cop. 1910]. 12°. p. 116–124.)
MWED

Feraru, Leon. Henri Bernstein and "Israel." illus. (Maccabaean. New York, 1915. 4°. v. 26, p. 116–117.) * PBD

Norman, Hilda Laura. The sons of Turcaret. (In her: Swindlers and rogues in French drama. Chicago, 1928. 8°. p. 211–232.) NKL

BERNSTEIN, HENRY. Samson; pièce en quatre actes. [Paris,] 1908. 36 p. illus. f°. (Illustration théâtrale. no. 83.) NKM p.v.275
A synopsis of the play with copious translated extracts are given in *Current opinion*, New York, 1909, v. 46, p. 189–200, * DA.
Samson was first produced at the Théâtre Renaissance, Paris, Nov. 6, 1907, with Lucien Guitry as Jacques Brachart, self-made Jewish millionaire risen from a dock-laborer's position, who like the Biblical Samson destroys himself while achieving the ruin of his wife's lover.
Produced at the Criterion Theatre, New York, Oct. 19, 1908, with William Gillette as Maurice Brachard. Reviewed in *The Nation*, New York, 1908, v. 87, p. 392–393, * DA; and in *New York dramatic mirror*, New York, v. 60, Oct. 31, 1908, p. 3, * T–* DA; and in *Theatre magazine*, New York, v. 8, p. 314–315 (illus. on p. 234, 332–333), † NBLA.
Originally produced at the Grand Theatre, Swansea, Jan. 25, 1909, and brought to the Garrick Theatre, London, Feb. 3, 1909, with Bourchier as Brachard. Reviewed in *The Athenæum*, London, 1909, v. 133, p. 207, * DA; and in *Illustrated sporting and dramatic news*, London, v. 70, p. 932 (illus. on p. 952), * DA.

Allary, J. The dramas of Henry Bernstein and the worship of strength. (Fortnightly review. New York, 1920. 8°. v. 114, p. 301–307.) * DA

Crabos, Pierre Gilbert. Le Juif dans le théâtre de M. Bernstein; essai de critique psychologique. (Revue critique des idées et des livres. Paris, 1912. 8°. tome 16, p. 427–448.) * DM

Stephenson, Edgar. Henry Bernstein — France's new high-pressure playwright. (Theatre magazine. New York, 1909. 4°. v. 9, p. 155–158.) † NBLA

BIRD, CHARLES S. Peck vs. Peck; a mock trial in one act... New York: Samuel French, cop. 1911. 43 p. 12°. (French's international copyrighted...ed. of the works of the best authors. no. 166.)
Mr. Jacob Gobsky, one of the witnesses for the defendant.

BISSON, ALEXANDRE CHARLES AUGUSTE, AND P. GÉRARD. Disparu!!! Comédie en 3 actes. Paris: P. V. Stock, 1898. 180 p. 12°. NKM p.v.671
Produced at the Théâtre Gymnase, Paris, March 19, 1896.
All alive, oh! a farce in three acts, adapted, by Arthur Bourchier, from MM. Bisson and Gérard's Disparu!!!, was produced at the Strand Theatre, London, June 16, 1897.
William Archer suggests Ralph Lumley as the adapter. Coventry Davies acted Jacob Caratstein and Claude Agnew, Abrahams. Reviewed in *The Athenæum*, London, 1897, v. 109, p. 820, * DA; *The Theatre*, London, 1897, series 4, v. 30, p. 35, *NCOA*; by W. Archer in his *Theatrical 'world' of 1897*, London, 1898, p. 192, 402–403, *NCOA*; and in *The Times*, London, June 17, 1897, p. 9, col. 2, * A.

BITNEY, MAYME RIDDLE. Cohen's views on business. (In her: Monologues grave and gay. Chicago [cop. 1911]. 12°. p. 107–108.)
Cohen speaking. This one is among the gay ones.

BIXBY, FRANK L. The little boss; a comedy drama in four acts. Boston: W. H. Baker & Co., 1901. 44 p. 12°. (Baker's edition of plays.)
Copyrighted by Doré Davidson. NBL p.v.14
Mo Simons, "character heavy, Jew."
The action takes place in the Tennessee hills.

BLANEY, CHARLES E. The child slaves of New York. A novel. Founded upon the melodrama of the same name, by Charles E. Blaney and Howard Hall... New York: J. S. Ogilvie Publishing Company, 1904. 128 p. front., plates. 12°. (The Sunnyside series. no. 129.)
This melodrama, in four acts, was produced at Proctor's Fifty-eighth Street Theatre, New York, Sept. 7, 1903, with Frank Opperman as Abraham Levy. Reviewed in *New York clipper*, New York, 1903, v. 51, p. 680, * T–MVA; and in *New York dramatic mirror*, New York, v. 50, Sept. 19, 1903, p. 18–19, * T–* DA.

——— Old Isaacs from the Bowery; a novel founded upon the melodrama of the same title ... New York: J. S. Ogilvie Publishing Company, 1906. 115 p. port. 12°. NBO
Produced at the American Theatre, New York, May 14, 1906. Abraham Isaacs (Harry First) pawnbroker and "kindest of man" is ruined financially by his worthless step-daughter Rachel (Louise Mitchell) and her villainous non-Jewish husband. Virtue triumphs by the aid of his adopted Gentile daughter Sadie Paulding (Minnie Barrie) betrothed to his son Sam (Robert G. Vignold). There are thirty-two characters in this melodrama. Reviewed in *New York clipper*, New York, 1906, v. 54, p. 368, * T–† MVA; and in *New York dramatic mirror*, New York, v. 55, May 26, 1906, p. 3, * T–* DA.

BLUNT, WILFRID SCAWEN. The bride of the Nile; an extravaganza in three acts. (In his: Poetical works. London, 1914. 8°. v. 2, p. 355–398.) NCM
On the banks of the Nile, 7th century A. D. Benjamin, a Samaritan Jew, and his daughter, Joel, in revolt against Rome.
First acted privately, Aug. 23, 1893.

BOGGS, ROBERT. A stepdaughter of Israel... New York [etc.]: F. T. Neely Co. [cop. 1900.] 1 p.l., 281 p. 8°.
Adapted by the author into a drama of five acts, in 1903, under the title *Beneberak, the Spanish Jew*. See United States. — Copyright Office, *Dramatic compositions copyrighted in the United States, 1870 to 1916*, item 3495.

BOUCICAULT, DION. After dark; a drama of London life in 1868, in four acts. (Authorized adaptation of Messrs. Grangé and Dennery's "Les oiseaux de proie")... Chicago: Dramatic Publishing Company [18—?]. 37 p. 12°. (Sergel's acting drama. no. 364.)
"Derived from a melodrama [Les oiseaux de proie] by Mess. Dennery & Grange." It was first produced at the Royal Princess Theatre, London, Aug. 12, 1868, with Dominick Murray as Dicey Morris, a Jewish keeper of a gaming house. Reviewed in *Athenæum*, London, 1868, v. 52, p. 218–219, * DA; and in *Era*, London, v. 30, Aug. 16, 1868, p. 11, † NAFA.

Individual Plays — 1838–1914, continued

BOUCICAULT, DION. After dark; a tale of London life. Drama in three acts. London, 1868. 3 pamphlets. 8°. † NCOF
With the parts of the different characters, in 8 pamphlets. 12°; and a musical score. Ms.

—— —— Another copy, made in America. 3 pamphlets. 4°. NCOF
The two pamphlets bound together.
From the manuscripts in The New York Public Library, listed above, Mr. Cleon Throckmorton adapted a version which he called *After dark; or, Neither maid, wife, nor widow*, and which Christopher Morley produced at the Old Rialto Theatre, Hoboken, N. J., Dec. 10, 1928. John A. Regan played Dicey Morris. For reviews see *Collection of newspaper clippings of dramatic criticism, 1928–1929*, v. A–B, † *NBL*; and Mary H. Vorse in *Nation*, New York, v. 128, p. 54, * *DA*.
"After dark has been rehearsed to a pitch of absolute perfection and we are to have this great London sensation Monday next [Nov. 16, 1868, at Niblo's Garden, New York, where E. Coleman will play Dicey Morris]." See *Spirit of the times*, New York, 1868, v. 19, p. 208, † *MVA*. See also ibid., affidavit by Boucicault which was prompted by the unauthorized production of the play at the Bowery Theatre, New York, Nov. 2, 1868. Boucicault in his affidavit calls it *London by night*.
A notable revival was seen at the Princess Theatre, London, Nov. 9, 1891, with W. E. Shine as Morris. Reviewed in *Theatre*, London, 1891, new series, v. 18, p. 279–280, * *T–* *DA*.

Williams, Henry Llewellyn. After dark. Founded on the popular drama of D. Boucicault... by the author of the dramatic tales of Two orphans, etc. London [1880]. 7 p. 4°.
Title from British Museum catalogue.

BOUCICAULT, DION. Flying scud; or, Derby day [in three acts]... [Chicago, Ill., 191–?] 1, 35 f. 4°.
Reproduced from typewritten copy.
The text is probably pirated and abbreviated.

—— Flying scud [or, A four-legged fortune]. A drama in four acts. n. p. [191–?] 116 [i.e. 118] p. 8°. † NCR
Photostatic reproduction.
It is announced for publication by the University of Pennsylvania Press, in a series of *Manuscript American plays*, under the general editorship of B. H. Clark.
Produced at the opening of the Holborn Theatre, London, Oct. 6, 1866, with Vollaire as Mo Davis, "the Jew sharper," one of the satellites of the villain Capt. Goodge. Reviewed in *Era*, London, v. 28, Oct. 14, 1866, p. 14, † *NAFA*.
In this country it was first seen at the Wallack Theatre, New York, April 24, 1867, with Charles Fisher as Mo Davis. In later American productions, Davis was often billed as Old Moses, "a sporting Jew," and made into a comic character.

—— London assurance; a comedy, in five acts... London: J. Andrews, 1841. viii, 86 p. 8°.
Prompter's copy; ms. notes. NCOF

—— —— First American edition. Philadelphia, New York: Turner & Fisher [1841?]. 2 p.l., (1)10–76 p. 24°. NCR p.v.8
At head of title: Turner's dramatic library.
The Library has a prompter's copy, with interleaved ms. notes, 24°, mounted as 8°, *NCOF*.

—— —— [London: T. H. Lacy, 185–?] 72 p. nar. 12°. (Lacy's acting edition of plays. v. 34.) NCO (Lacy)

—— —— As performed at the Park Theatre. New York: S. French [1864?]. v, (1)8–71 p. 12°. (French's standard drama. no. 27.) NCO p.v.323
The Library also has a prompter's copy, with interleaved ms. notes, *NCOF*.

—— —— An entirely new acting ed. With full stage directions...notes, etc. Ed. by Alfred B. Sedgwick... New York: C. T. De Witt, cop. 1877. 54 p. diagrs. 8°. (De Witt's acting plays. no. 212.)

—— —— New American ed., correctly reprinted from the original authorized acting ed. ... New York: H. Roorbach, cop. 1889. 67 p. diagrs. 12°. (Roorbach's American edition of acting plays. no. 19.)

—— —— New York: Dick & Fitzgerald, cop. 1889. 67 p. 12°.
Synopsis of incidents, p. 3–6.

—— —— Acting version of the Yale University Dramatic Association (Incorporated) with an introduction by William Lyon Phelps... New Haven, Conn.: Pub. under the supervision of P. Roberts, 1910. xvii p., 2 l., 87 p. front., illus. (facsim.), ports. 8°. NCO p.v.381
Produced at the Waldorf-Astoria Hotel, New York, Jan. 3 and 4, 1910, with D. E. Chantler as Isaacs. Reviewed in *New York dramatic mirror*, New York, v. 63, Jan. 15, 1910, p. 5–6, * *T–* *DA*.

—— —— Boston: W. H. Baker & Co., 1911. 78 p. 12°. (The William Warren ed. of standard plays.)
"This version is based upon the text employed in the prompt-book of the Boston Museum and gives the stage business used in the performances of the play at that once famous house."
Reprinted in G. H. Lewes, editor, *Selections from the modern British dramatists*, Leipzig, 1867, v. 2, p. 257–322, *NCO*; *New York drama*, New York [cop. 1875], v. 1, no. 2, 22 p., *NCO p.v.310*; Alfred Bates, editor, *The Drama*, London, 1904, v. 22, p. 197–270, *NAF*; M. J. Moses, editor, *Representative British dramas, Victorian and modern*, Boston, 1918, p. 137–179, *NCO* (another ed., Boston, 1931, * *R–NCO*); and in J. B. Matthews and P. R. Lieder, editors, *Chief British dramatists*, Boston [1924], p. 843–880, *NCO*.
Solomon Isaacs, a writ server, appears in a small part at the end of the play. His name does not appear in the casts of character in any of the printed early editions; neither do the contemporary reviewers note the actor who played the part. First produced at the Covent Garden, March 4, 1841. Reviewed in *Examiner*, London, 1841, p. 149–150, * *DA*; *Literary gazette*, London, 1841, p. 157, * *DA*; *The Spectator*, London, v. 14, p. 228, * *DA*; and in *The Times*, London, March 5, 1841, p. 5, * *A*.
The American popularity of this play is evidenced by 69 references to it in Brown, and 116 in Odell, v. 4–7. The first American production was at the Park Theatre, New York, Oct. 11, 1841. See Odell, IV: 534–536 where it is reviewed at length and numerous contemporary notices are cited. On May 9, 1842 it was revived at both the Bowery and Chatham theatres.

Paul, Howard. The genesis of London assurance. (New York dramatic mirror. New York, 1905. f°. v. 53, April 29, 1905, p. 2.)
* T–* DA
See "How Boucicault wrote his comedy 'London assurance'" in Robinson Locke collection, v. Boucicault, † *NAFR*.

Individual Plays — 1838-1914, continued

BOUCICAULT, DION. The queen of spades; a drama in two acts. Adapted from "Le dame de pique," by Dion Boucicault. London: T. H. Lacy [185-?]. 30 p. nar. 12°. (Lacy's acting edition of plays. v. 24.) NCO (Lacy)
A melodrama the scene of which is in Russia and Bohemia. Produced at the Drury Lane, March 29, 1851, with Barrett as Kopeck, keeper of a gaming house. He is introduced as "the most conscientious of Jews, the most confiding of creditors." Reviewed in *Era,* London, v. 13, April 6, 1851, p. 11, † *NAFA;* and in *The Spectator,* London, 1851, v. 24, p. 325, * *DA.* The *Era* reviewer states: "Barrett threw into the part of the gambling banker a degree of pungency in which lay all the humour of the piece."

BRAND, OSWALD. *See* sub-entry under DICKENS, CHARLES.

BROOKFIELD, CHARLES HALLAM ELTON, AND W. YARDLEY. *See* sub-entry under DU MAURIER, GEORGE LOUIS PALMELLA BUSSON.

BROOKS, SHIRLEY. The creole; or, Love's fetters. An original drama, in three acts... London: Printed for the author by F. Ledger [pref. 1847]. v, [6]-48 p. 12°.

—— —— London: T. H. Lacy [18—?]. 42 p. 12°. (Lacy's acting edition of plays. v. 1.) NCO (Lacy's)

—— —— [London: J. Dicks,] n. d. 18 p. illus. 12°. (Dicks' standard plays. no. 1009.)
Cover-title.
The play proposes to illustrate the state of society on the island of Mauritius, in 1794, when it belonged to France. It was written within three days at the request of Mrs. Kelley who played the part of Bellona St. Mars, a vivandiere. Performed at the Lyceum Theatre, London, April 8, 1847, with Mr. Keeley as Bokes, a cockney Jewish money lender, represented as an alien without civic rights. Reviewed in *The Athenæum,* London, 1847, v. 20, p. 418, * *DA; Literary gazette,* London, 1847, p. 285, * *DA;* and in *The Times,* London, April 9, 1847, p. 4, col. 6, * *A.*
Produced at Thorne's St. Charles Theatre, New York, Aug. 5, 1853, with Brunton as Bokes. It was revived in New York, at Wallack's Theatre, Jan. 12, 1857, with Holland as Bokes, and ran only three nights.

BROUGH, ROBERT BARNABAS. The overland journey to Constantinople, as undertaken by Lord Bateman, with interesting particulars of the fair Sophia. An extravaganza in two acts ... London: T. H. Lacy [1854?]. 36 p. nar. 12°. (Lacy's acting edition of plays. v. 15.) NCO (Lacy)
On copy of original play-bill, p. 2, "Turks, Jews, and heretics." First produced at the Adelphi Theatre, London, April 17, 1854. Reviewed in *Era,* London, v. 16, April 23, 1854, p. 11, † *NAFA; Examiner,* London, 1854, p. 247, * *DA;* and in *The Times,* London, April 18, 1854, p. 7, col. 5, * *A.*

BROUGHAM, JOHN. ...Columbus el filibustero! A new and audaciously original, historico-plagiaristic, ante-national, pre-patriotic, and omni-local confusion of circumstances, running through two acts and four centuries... As performed at Burton's Theatre, December, 1857. New York: Samuel French [1850-76]. 24 p. 12°. (Minor drama. The acting edition. no. 145.) NBM p.v.1
Produced at Burton's New Theatre (Tripler Hall), New York, Dec. 30, 1857.
Alleyne played Luis de St. Angel, "a contented office-holder, pursuing the even tenor of his way." Santangel succeeded in 1476 his father of the same name as farmer of the royal taxes to the king of Spain. He took an important part in the discovery of America. It was Santangel who received Columbus' first detailed report of his voyage and discoveries.

—— ...The great tragic revival. A new and undoubtedly original contemporaneous dramatic absurdity, in one act and several tableaux... As performed at Burton's Theatre... New York: S. French, cop. 1858. 10 p. 12°. (The minor drama. The acting edition. no. 154.)
Copy: Harvard College Library.
Produced at Burton's Theatre, New York, April 17, 1858, with Burton as Cassius Marc Anthony Shylock Barown; Polly Marshall as Julietta Jessica Barown. Reviewed in *New York Tribune,* April 19, 1858, p. 7, col. 2, * *A.* "The fun consisted in dressing up every-day business and commonplace occurrences in the 'hifalutin' language of the stage and cheap romance tragedy heroes."

—— The lottery of life, a story of New York. An original local drama in five acts... London: S. French; New York: S. French & Son, cop. 1867. 41(1) p. 12°. (French's acting edition. no. 1566.)

—— —— Another edition. [1867-76.] NCO p.v.529

—— —— Another edition. [1876-86.] (Lacy's acting edition of plays. v. 105.) NCO
Designated on the programmes as "a dramatic satire," it was produced at Wallack's Theatre, New York, June 8, 1868. Charles Fisher played the "double-faced character" of Mordie Solomons and Mr. Allcraft. Full cast with detailed descriptions of the parts is given in *Stage,* New York, v. 5, July 9, 1868, p. 1. Reviewed in *Spirit of the times,* New York, 1868, v. 18, p. 308, † *MVA.*

—— Much ado about a merchant of Venice. From the original text — a long way. [New York, 1869.] 15 p. cover-illus. 8°.
Caption-title.
"Inductive analysis...touching the ancient and modern versions of the story:" p. 5-8.

—— —— New York: Samuel French [1868]. 24 p. nar. 12°. (French's minor drama. no. 308.) NCOF
Prompter's copy; interleaved ms. notes.
"Shylock. A shamefully ill-used, and persecuted old Hebrew gentleman — in fact, an Israelite of other days, whose character was darkened by his Christian contemporaries simply to conceal their own nefarious transactions; victimized as he was by sundry unjustifiable confidence operations."
"Jessica. The Jew's undutiful daughter, who makes a jubilee of her sire's sorrow."
"Tubal. A Christianized Hebrew serf — in fact, a converted bond-man."
Produced at Brougham's Theatre, New York, March 8, 1869, with Brougham as Shylock. Consists largely of hits on Wall Street individuals and operations of that time. Reviewed in *Evening Post,* New York, March 9, 1869, p. 4, col. 3, * *A;* and in *New York Daily Tribune,* March 9, 1869, p. 8, col. 1, * *A.* "Scarcely a line that was spoken last night that did not glitter." It was preceded on the opening night by a comedietta called *Perfection.*

BUCHANAN, ROBERT WILLIAMS, AND F. HORNER. *See* sub-entry under DAUDET, ALPHONSE.

THE JEW IN ENGLISH DRAMA　　　63

Individual Plays — 1838–1914, continued

BUCKINGHAM, LEICESTER SILK. Belphegor; a new and original, acrobatic, dramatic, epigrammatic, and decidedly un-aristocratic burlesque... London: T. H. Lacy [1856?]. 45 p. 12°.
In one act of five scenes, and in verse.
Founded on the play adapted from the French of E. Phillippe and M. Fournier by T. H. Higgie.
Copy: Harvard College Library.
Chevalier de Rolac of the Higgie text is here transformed into a Jewish agent named Ikey, who tempts the heroine away from her home, under the pretense of a large salary at a theatre. Produced at the Strand Theatre, London, Sept. 29, 1856, with J. Clarke as Rolac. He is supposed to possess a ticket-of-leave, but really is absent without leave. Reviewed in *The Athenæum*, London, v. 29, part 2, p. 1250, col. 2, * *DA*; and in *Era*, London, Oct. 5, 1856, p. 11, † *NAFA*.

BUCKSTONE, JOHN BALDWIN. See sub-entry under AINSWORTH, WILLIAM HARRISON.

BUECHNER, GEORG. Wozzeck; a fragment [in twenty-seven scenes and variants to four scenes]. (In his: Plays. Translated by G. Dunlop. London [1927]. 12°. p. 219–274.)　　NGE
"The ms. of this play...published for the first time by K. E. Franzos, in 1879."
Jew, a peddler.

Kupsch, Walther. Wozzeck. Ein Beitrag zum Schaffen Georg Büchners (1813–1837). Berlin: Emil Ebering, 1920. 115 p., 2 l. 8°. (Germanische Studien. Heft 4.)
　　NFCA (Germanische)

BULWER-LYTTON, EDWARD GEORGE EARLE LYTTON, 1ST BARON LYTTON. Leila; or, The siege of Granada. By the author of "Pelham"... New York: Harper & Brothers, 1838. viii, (1) 10–180 p. 12°.　　NCW
Privately published in 1835. No copy of this edition could be located. The date given here, 1838, is that of the first trade edition. *Leila* is a romance dealing with the reconquest of Spain from the Moors. The interest centers in Almamen, "the unavowed Jew and master of magic," and his daughter Leila. For an abstract of the plot, see E. G. Bell, *Introduction to the prose romances, plays and comedies of Edward Bulwer, Lord Lytton*, Chicago, 1914, p. 120–122, *NCC (Bulwer)*.
Dramatized and produced at the Sadler's Wells Theatre, London, Oct. 22, 1838. Reviewed in *Literary gazette*, London, 1838, p. 685, * *DA*; and in *Spectator*, London, v. 11, p. 1182, * *DA*.
As "a spectacular, Oriental romance," it was produced at the National Theatre, New York, April 30, 1838, with Henry Wallack as Almamen.

L'Ebreo; melodramma tragico in un prologo e tre atti [in verse. Founded on Bulwer's "Leila; or, The siege of Granada"]. Milano [1855?]. 35 p. 12°.
Title from British Museum catalogue.

Wallace, William Ross. Leila; or, The siege of Grenada: a melo-drama, in three acts from E. L. Bulwer's novel of that title. Lexington [Ky.]: J. C. Noble, 1838. 45 p., 1 l. 16°.
Copy: Library of Congress.
p. [1], t.-p.; p. [2], copy-right; p. [3], advertisement by the author; p. [4], dedication; p. [5], publisher's advertisement; p. [6], original cast; p. [7]–45, text; last leaf, recto, prologue <spoken by Mrs. Dyke>; last leaf, verso, costume.
In the Advertisement, p. 3, the author "hopes to be forgiven" for the rhythm of some of his lines and acknowledges his indebtedness to "a gentleman of this city" and to a certain Joe Davies. The Dedication, p. 4, is to David Ingersoll, "the splendid and distinguished actor," who had the part of Almamen, "Jew and enchanter," and to Mrs. R. Dyke, "the accomplished actress," who acted Leila, daughter of Almamen.
The publisher's Advertisement, p. 5, is a pre-publication review, by W. B., of the play, reprinted from the *Lexington Intelligencer*. The dramatist is described as a "young writer, now in this city, highly talented, and extensively 'known to fame' as a poet of rare genius."
R. L. Rusk, in his *The Literature of the middle western border*, New York, 1925, v. 1, p. 425–426, *NBB*, states that "there is no evidence that it went beyond two performances," in Lexington, Ky., on or about May 9 and 16, 1838, and in St. Louis, Mo., on or about July 9, 1838. For contemporary notices see the references cited ibid. The spectacular quality of the action and setting of the play, the popularity of the novel which had just then reached the Ohio Valley, and the dramatist's fame as a Western poet encouraged the producers to stage *Leila*, but did not help to make it successful.

BURNAND, FRANCIS COWLEY. See sub-entries under ERCKMANN, ÉMILE, AND ALEXANDRE CHATRIAN; PRAED, ROSA CAROLINE (MURRAY-PRIOR), "MRS. CAMPBELL PRAED."

BURTON, HENRY BINDON. The battle of the lords; a political drama [in two acts]... Dublin: Hodges, Figgis & Co., Ltd., 1910. 70 p. 12°.
　　NCR
Deals with the Irish Home Rule question. The characters are the Liberal and Unionist Lords. The time is at the death of Edward VII and the accession of George V, under the premiership of Asquith. Neil Primrose, son of the Earl of Rosebery and Hannah Rothschild, killed in action in 1917 during the Palestine campaign, is one of the characters and is listed as one of the members of the Primrose League.

BUSH, THOMAS. Santiago; a drama in five acts ... Toronto [:Rollo & Adam, 1866]. 55 p., 1 l. 8°.　　* C p.v.613
An anti-Catholic play. The action is laid in Santiago, Chile. Sheeram, a Jew, speaking in dialect, is one of the many villains.

BUTLER, ARTHUR GRAY. Harold. (In his: Harold; a drama in four acts, and other poems. London and Oxford, 1892. 12°. p. 1–143.)

—— Harold; a drama in four acts... London: Henry Frowde, 1906. 4 p.l., 118 p. 2. ed. 12°.
　　NCR
Based on *Harold, last of the Saxon kings*, a novel by Lord Bulwer-Lytton. The scene is laid during the time of Edward the Confessor, and his successor Harold. Simon, a Jew, appears in the cast of characters.

BUTLER, RICHARD WILLIAM, AND H. C. NEWTON. See sub-entry under DUMAS, ALEXANDRE, THE ELDER.

CAINE, SIR HALL. The Christian; a drama in four acts... London: Collier and Co., 1907. x, 178 p. 12°.
Copy: Harvard College Library.
Based thinly on the author's novel of the same name. The scene is London and it deals with "the problem of the fallen woman."
A copyright performance took place on Aug. 7, 1897. It was brought to London, to the Duke of York's Theatre, Oct. 16, 1899. See reviews in *The Athenæum*, London, 1899, v. 114, p. 564, * *DA; Graphic*, London, 1899, v. 60, p. 570 (full-page illus. on p. 571), * *DA*; and in *The Times*, London, Oct. 17, 1899, * *A*. This early version was also seen in New York, at the Knickerbocker Theatre, Oct. 10, 1898, with Edgar

Individual Plays — 1838-1914, continued

CAINE, SIR HALL, *continued*
Norton as the theatrical manager. Reviewed in *New York dramatic mirror*, v. 40, Oct. 15, 1898, p. 16, * T-* DA.
As printed in the present text it was revived at the Lyceum Theatre, London, Aug. 31, 1907, with Thomas Barry as Rosenberg, the manager who, in the text, is described "middle-aged, Semitic features, many diamonds." Reviewed (with illus.) in *Graphic*, London, 1907, v. 76, p. 318, * DA; and in *Illustrated London news*, 1907, v. 131, p. 330, * DA.

FITZSIMONS, SIMON. "The Christian" and the critics. (Catholic world. New York, 1898. 8°. v. 68, p. 341–347.) *DA

CALLAHAN, C. E. *See* sub-entry under DICKENS, CHARLES.

CALMUS, P. H. The Jew of Zemplin; a drama in five acts... Hawkinsville, Ga.: J. R. Beverly, 1886. 31 p. 8°.
Copy: Library of Congress.
The scene is laid in Hungary.

CAMPBELL, BARTLEY T. "Siberia"; a picturesque romantic drama of Russian life in six acts, by Bartley Campbell. [New York?] H. C. Kennedy, cop. 1911. [95] f. 8° bound as obl. 4°.
Various paging. † NCOF
Photostatic reproduction on 52 leaves.

—— Siberia [a drama in six acts]. 47 l. diagrams. 4°.
Typewritten.
Deals with the persecution of the Jews in Russia, under the old regime. The second act portrays a massacre in a Russo-Jewish town; the last, departure of the refugees for America. Scene: Siberia and Odessa.
It is announced for publication by the University of Pennsylvania Press, in a series of *Manuscript American plays*, under the general editorship of B. H. Clark.
First produced at the California Theatre, San Francisco, Nov. 28, 1882. Noted in *New York dramatic mirror*, v. 8, Dec. 16, 1882, p. 4, * T-* DA. The New York première was at Haverly's Theatre, Feb. 26, 1883, with Georgia Cayvan as Sara and Blanche Mortimer as Maria, daughters of David Janoski. Reviewed in *New York dramatic mirror*, v. 9, March 3, 1883, p. 2, * T-* DA. In New York it ran five weeks.
Brown lists seventeen revivals in New York alone between 1884 and 1900. The Kishineff massacre of April 19-21, 1903, and the consequent American sympathy and protest demonstrations caused the revival of this melodrama with the interpolation of scenes supposedly portraying scenes from the massacre. It was so first staged at McVicker's Theatre, Chicago, Oct. 9, 1904, with Frank Russell as Janoski, the Jew in the play whose home is pillaged, and was brought to New York, at the Academy of Music, Jan. 2, 1905. See review in *New York dramatic mirror*, v. 53, Jan. 14, 1905, p. 17, * T-* DA. An announcement of an intended revival by Robert Campbell, son of the author, is printed ibid., v. 71, April 15, 1914, p. 13, but whether it was actually staged again is uncertain. See folder *Siberia* in the Library's Theatre collection.
In England it was produced for the first time at the Princess Theatre, London, Dec. 14, 1887, with Grace Hawthorne and Mary Rorke as David's daughters. Reviewed in *Illustrated sporting and dramatic news*, London, 1887, v. 28, p. 404, * DA; by Cecil Howard in *Theatre*, London, 1888, series 4, v. 11, p. 45–46, *NCOA*; and in *The Times*, London, Dec. 15, 1887, p. 9, col. 5, * A. It was revived at the Olympia Theatre, Liverpool, May 5, 1913.

GELLER, JAMES JACOB. Siberia. (In his: Grandfather's follies. New York [cop. 1934]. 8°. p. 103–105.) MWED

KENNEDY, H. C. Siberia; a picturesque play. In six acts. Revised by H. C. Kennedy. 129 p. 4°.
Typewritten.
cop. March 9, 1911.
Title from United States. — Library of Congress, *Dramatic compositions copyrighted in the United States, 1870 to 1916*, item no. 42228.
A version of Campbell's play.

CARB, DAVID. The voice of the people; a play in three acts. Boston: The Four Seas Company, 1912. 3 p.l., 129 p. 12°. NBM
A play dealing with the fortunes of a political boss and his ward heelers. David, "a young Polish Jew," his fiancée Becky, and Jacobs (the last one not mentioned in the cast) are the Jewish characters.

CARDOT, LOUIS. *See* sub-entry under ERCKMANN, ÉMILE, AND ALEXANDRE CHATRIAN.

CARPENTER, EDWARD C. The tongues of men; a comedy in three acts... New York, London: S. French [cop. 1913]. 102 p. 12°. (French's standard library edition.) NBL p.v.161
The wagging tongues of men. Treats of one angle of the relation of church and stage. The plot involves a prima donna and a clergyman. Produced at the Harris Theatre, New York, Nov. 10, 1913. Sheridan Block as Herman Geist, manager of the Metropolitan Opera Company, "a cultivated Hebrew of fifty — well dressed, but not loudly, with a suspicion of accent in his voice." The action takes place in London. Reviewed in *New York dramatic mirror*, New York, v. 70, Nov. 12, 1913, p. 6, * DA; in *Theatre magazine*, New York, v. 18, Dec., 1913, p. xvi, † *NBLA*.

CARR, JOSEPH WILLIAM COMYNS. *See* sub-entry under DICKENS, CHARLES.

CATTELL, WILLIAM F. A receipt for 10,000 dollars; a comedy drama in four acts and four scenes... Clyde, Ohio: Ames Publishing Co., 1904. 39 p. 12°.
On cover: Ames' series of standard and minor drama. no. 445.
"Ikey Cohen, character comedy."

CHASE, FRANK EUGENE. The great umbrella case; a mock trial [in one act]. Boston: W. H. Baker Co. [cop. 1883.] 36 p. new ed. 12°. (Baker's novelty plays.) NBL p.v.5
Originally published in the *Amateur theatrical journal*, 1881. "For the plot and some of the incidents of the piece, the author is indebted to a sketch bearing the same title by Mr. W. L. Balch." — *p. 2*.
Godonli Nozouski, a rejected juror, "a Bulgarian or Oirish Jew."

—— In the trenches; a drama of the Cuban war, in three acts. By Abel Seaman [pseud.] ... Boston: W. H. Baker & Co., 1898. 37 p. 12°. (Baker's edition of plays.)
Patrick Green, an Irishman, and Moses Bullheimer constitute the firm of Bullheimer and Green, "army contractors and general speculators."

—— A ready-made suit; a mock trial [in one act]. Boston: W. H. Baker Company, cop. 1913. 41 p. 16°. (Baker's edition of plays.)
Isaac Gutentag and Levi Cohen as defendants, witnesses for the prosecution, and jurors.

Individual Plays — 1838–1914, continued

CHEKHOV, ANTON PAVLOVICH. Ivanoff [a play in four acts]. (In his: Plays. Translated by Marian Fell. New York, 1912. 12°. p. 73–153.) ** QDK
Written in 1887 and printed at St. Petersburg, 1889. Reprinted in his *Three sisters and other plays*, London, 1923, p. 97–191, ** *QDK;* and in *The Moscow Art Theatre series of Russian plays*, second series, New York [cop. 1923], ** *QDK.*
The Moscow Art Theatre produced it in Russian at the Jolson Theatre, New York, Nov. 26, 1923, with Olga Knipper-Chekhova as Anna. For reviews see *Collection of newspaper clippings of dramatic criticism, 1923–1924,* vol. M (Moscow), † *NBL.*
Produced in the translation of Marian Fell by the Incorporated Stage Society, at the Duke of York's Theatre, London, Dec. 6, 1925, with Miss Jeanne de Casalis, as Anna Ivanoff, née Sarah Abramson, wife of Nicholas, one of Russia's "useless people," who had been warned not to marry a Jewess. Reviewed by Desmond MacCarthy in *New statesman*, London, 1925, v. 26, p. 301, * *DA;* by N. G. Royde-Smith in *Outlook,* London, v. 56, p. 405, * *DA;* and by Ivor Brown in *Saturday review,* London, v. 140, p. 698–699, * *DA.*

CHELTNAM, CHARLES SMITH. The ticket-of-leave man's wife; or, Six years after. A new and original drama, in three acts; being a continuation of Tom Taylor's drama of "Ticket-of-leave man." London: T. H. Lacy [pref. 1866]. 72 p. nar. 12°. (Lacy's acting edition of plays. v. 69.) NCO (Lacy)
Also issued as no. 1032 of French's acting edition of plays.
"The happy idea of continuing the interesting story embodied in Mr. Tom Taylor's renowned 'Ticket-of-leave man' originated with Mr. Sefton Parry... At his suggestion and in consultation with him, the present Drama was constructed and written." The action of the drama is supposed to take place six years after that of *The Ticket-of-leave man.*
Produced at the New Theatre, Greenwich, April 2, 1866, with Edwin Shepherd as Melter Moss. Reviewed in *Era,* London, v. 28, April 8, 1866, p. 11–12, † *NAFA.* "Moss is the prime mover of the machinery... Too much importance has been given by the author to this character."

——— *See also* sub-entry under MOSENTHAL, SALOMON HERMANN, RITTER VON.

CHERBULIEZ, VICTOR. Samuel Brohl and Company. Translated from the French [by Auber Forestier, pseud. of A. A. W. Moore]. New York: D. Appleton and Company, 1877. 1 p.l., 271 p. 12°. (Collection of foreign authors. no. 1.) NKV
Adapted into a drama of four acts by Junius Brutus Booth, in 1896. See United States. — Copyright Office, *Dramatic compositions copyrighted in the United States, 1870 to 1916,* item 40675.

CHIRIKOV, YEVGENI NIKOLAYEVICH. The Jews; a drama in four acts. Translated from the Russian by M. S. Mandell, and revised by the editors of the Maccabaean. (Maccabaean. New York, 1905–06. 4°. v. 9, p. 175–183, 228–236, 285–292; v. 10, p. 23–27.) * PBD

——— ...The chosen people; a drama in four acts. By Eugen Tchirikow. Translated from the Russian for the Maccabaean. [New York:] Maccabaean Pub. Co. [1906.] 33 p. 4°. * PSQ
At head of title: Zionist publications.
Repr.: Maccabaean.

——— ...The chosen people; a dramatic portrayal of Jewish life in Russia, in three acts, by Eugene Tchirikoff... [New York: The International Press, 1905.] 15(1) p. illus. 8°.
At head of title: Synopsis. * Q p.v.33
A play of the pogroms in Russia. The action takes place in one of the cities of the Pale, in the southwestern district of Russia, during 1903–1904. Three problems are presented: parents and children, racial intermarriage, and Zionism or Socialism as the solution for the Jewish difficulties of that period. Nachman is the Zionist, and Isserson, the revolutionary Socialist. Leah, sister of Nachman, and daughter of old Leiser, is at one time in love with a Russian Christian student.
Produced in Russian by the St. Petersburg Dramatic Company at the Herald Square Theatre, New York, March 23, 1905, with Paul Orlenoff as Nachman and Alla Nazimova as Leah. Reviewed by Philip Davis in *Jewish advocate,* Boston, Dec. 1, 1905, p. 6 and Dec. 8, p. 6, * *PBD;* by I. L. Bril in *Jewish comment,* Baltimore, v. 20, March 24, 1905, p. 1–2, * *PBD;* and in *New era,* New York, 1905, v. 6, p. 537–539, * *PBD.*
Produced in Yiddish at the People's Theatre, New York, Nov. 23, 1905 with B. Thomashevsky as Nachman. Reviewed by A. D. DeCastro in *Jewish exponent,* Philadelphia, v. 42, Dec. 8, 1905, p. 10, * *PBD.*
Translated anew by Leon Kobrin, it was again staged in Yiddish under the title Jews in Russia, at the Peoples' Theatre, New York, Jan. 11, 1910, with Gustav Schacht as Nachman and Mrs. Shapiro as Leah. Reviewed by Louis Lipsky in *American Hebrew,* New York, 1910, v. 86, p. 259, 289, * *PBD;* and in *New York dramatic mirror,* New York, v. 63, Jan. 22, 1910, p. 6, * *DA.* It was revived in Russian at the Garrick Theatre, New York, March 21, 1912, with Orlenoff as the original Nachman, and Lina Koroleva as Leah. Reviewed on that occasion in *New York dramatic mirror,* New York, v. 67, March 27, 1912, p. 6, * *DA.*

Eisenbett, I. G. "Евреи" въ драмѣ г. Чирикова... (Еврейская жизнь. С.-Петербургъ, July, 1904. 8°. p. 137–160.) * PBI

Kunitz, Joshua. [Chirikov's Jewish play.] (In his: Russian literature and the Jew. New York, 1929. 8°. p. 156–161.) * PZB
"The play is the nearest approach a Russian author has made to an adequate study of the intellectual and spiritual conflicts and problems within the Pale... Iserson is the first, and up to 1912 the only, revolutionary class-conscious Jewish worker in Russian literature."

CLARK, WILLIAM M. A queer fit. (In his: Model dialogues. Philadelphia, 1906. 12°. p. 97–101.)

——— (In his: Model dialogues. Philadelphia, 1913. 12°. p. 97–101.) NACG-MD
In two scenes.
Mr. Isaacs, "Jew clothier."

COLLINGHAM, GEORGE. *See* sub-entry under DICKENS, CHARLES.

CONQUEST, GEORGE AUGUSTUS. *See* sub-entry under MOSENTHAL, SALOMON HERMANN, RITTER VON.

CORALNIK, ABRAHAM. Red snow; one-act play of Russo-Jewish life. Authorized translation by Oscar Leonard. (Reform advocate. Chicago, 1909. 4°. v. 36, p. 747–752.) * PBD
Originally appeared, in seven scenes, in *Die Welt,* Köln, 1907, Jahrg. 11, No. 23, p. 18–21, * *PBC.*

Individual Plays — 1838-1914, continued

CORBIN, JOHN. Husband; a comedy in three acts. (In his: Husband and The forbidden guests; two plays. Boston and New York, 1910. 12°. p. 1–233.) NBM
See Wife, a preface, p. v–xxxiii.
Rebecca Levine, LL.B., "lithe, feline," head of the Legal Aid Society, social worker and advocate of free love. Reviewed in *Independent*, New York, 1910, v. 69, p. 988, * *DA*; and in *The Nation*, New York, v. 91, p. 450–451, * *DA*.

CORELLI, MARIE. "Temporal power"; a study in supremacy... New York: Dodd, Mead and Company, 1902. 3 p.l., 559 p. 12°. NCW
David Jost, sole proprietor of the most influential newspaper in the kingdom, exerts political influence which he uses for his own selfish ends. The character is incidental to the general plot. It was dramatized by the author and produced as a play, in five acts, at Morecambe, Lancashire, England, August 23, 1902.

COURTNEY, JOHN. The soldier's progress; or, The horrors of war, a pictorial drama in four acts, illustrative of the celebrated series of plates issued under the patronage of the Peace Society... London: T. H. Lacy [1857–73]. 53 p. 12°. (Lacy's acting edition of plays. v. 1.) NCO (Lacy)

———— Prompter's copy, with interleaved ms. notes. NCOF
Also issued as no. 3 of French's acting edition, NCO p.v.758.
Produced at the National Theatre, New York, May 18, 1853.
First performed at the Victoria Theatre, London, Nov. 5, 1849. Mr. Franklin as Levi Solomons, "a poor old Jew clothes-man, with the pity for the unfortunate, generosity for the unfriended, and possessing a heart of which many a Christian might be proud of." Speaks in dialect.

———— *See also* sub-entry under MOSENTHAL, SALOMON HERMANN, RITTER VON.

COYNE, JOSEPH STIRLING. This house to be sold (the property of the late William Shakespeare). Inquire within. A musical extravaganza in one act... As performed at the Theatre Royal, Adelphi... London: Webster and Co. [1847.] 16 p., front. (plate.) 12°. (Webster's acting national drama. [v. 14,] no. 144.)
A cockney gentleman deciding to begin business in the house of the bard, hangs out a sign "Chopkins, late Shakespeare." He falls asleep and in his dream he sees the characters in Shakespeare's plays perform before him. This piece was produced at the Adelphi Theatre, London, Sept. 9, 1847, with C. J. Smith as Shylock. Reviewed in *Literary gazette*, London, 1847, p. 662, * *DA*.

———— *See also* sub-entries under DICKENS, CHARLES; SEJOUR, VICTOR.

CRAVEN, HENRY THORNTON. Philomel; a romantic drama in three acts... New York: R. M. De Witt [1870?]. 41 p. 12°. (De Witt's acting plays. no. 293.) NCO p.v.301
"The serious part is chiefly derived from Louis Ulbach's novel entitled in English form *Which wins — love or money?*"
A melodrama. Produced at the Globe Theatre, London, Feb. 10, 1870, with J. Clarke as Judah Lazarus, "a money lender from London," but not of the conventional type. Of Clarke in the rôle it was written: "It would be almost impossible for the character to be better played. Judah Lazarus is emphatically one of Mr. Clarke's greatest triumphs, and this character alone will make the play a great success." In his mouth the author placed many corrupted Hebrew words, which were at that time considered part of the current English slang. Reviewed in *The Athenæum*, London, 1870, v. 55, p. 270, * *DA*; *Era*, London, v. 32, Feb. 13, 1870, p. 10, † *NAFA*; and in *Illustrated London news*, 1870, v. 56, p. 207, * *DA*.

CUMBERLAND, STUART C. ...The rabbi's spell ... New York: J. W. Lovell Company [1889]. cover-title, 81 p. 12°. (Lovell's library. no. 1338.) * PST
First published in 1885. See review in *Jewish chronicle*, London, 1885, Dec. 4, p. 13, * *PBD*. This romance is modelled after Annette E. von Droste-Hülshoff's *Die Judenbuche; ein Sittengemälde aus dem gebirgichten Westfalen*.
Dramatized by M. H. Billings, in 1915, under the title *The rabbi's spell; a romance of Russian Poland*, in four acts and seven scenes.
See United States. — Copyright Office, *Dramatic compositions copyrighted in the United States, 1870 to 1916*, item 38262a.

DALRYMPLE, C. LEONA, "MRS. C. ACTON WILSON." A white shawl; a farce comedy in two acts... New York: Dick & Fitzgerald [1905]. 25 p. 16°. NBL p.v.1, no.2
There is also an edition cop. by Fitzgerald Pub. Corp., 1905.
Dr. Adolphus Katz, in the rôle of a wooer.

DALY, AUGUSTIN. The last word; a comedy, in four acts (from the German of Franz von Schoenthan)... As originally produced at Daly's Theatre, New York, Oct. 28, 1890. [New York:] Privately printed for A. Daly, 1891. 3 p.l., (1)6–71 p. 8°. NCOF
Prompter's copy; interleaved ms. notes.
Contains "Dramatis personae and original cast."
Playbill inserted.
Frederic Bond played the part of Moses Mossop, "an overdressed and presuming person of evident Hebrew extraction; slow, oily, foreign accent," who is employed in a confidential capacity by the President of the United States. The words "of evident Hebrew extraction" are deleted by the prompter in the Library's copy. Reviewed in *Town topics*, New York, v. 24, Oct. 30, 1890, p. 10, * *DA*. For further reviews of this and later productions see *Daly's Theatre scrapbooks, 1890–1891*, v. 25, p. 44–57, † *NBL*.
Produced for the first time in England, at the Lyceum Theatre, London, Sept. 19, 1891, with Charles Leclercq as Moses Mossop. Reviewed in *Theatre*, London, 1891, new series, v. 18, p. 185–186, * *T*–* *DA*.

———— *See also* sub-entry under MOSENTHAL, SALOMON HERMANN, RITTER VON.

DAUDET, ALPHONSE. La lutte pour la vie; pièce en 5 actes, 6 tableaux... Paris: C. Lévy, 1890. xii, 152 p. 8°.
Produced at the Gymnase-Dramatique, Paris, Oct. 30, 1889.
Published in *Lettres et les arts*, Paris, 1889, année 4, tome 4, partie 2, p. 121–204, *NKA*.

———— The battle of love (La lutte) ... A realistic novel... Translated by Henry Llewellyn Williams... Chicago: Donohue, Henneberry & Co., 1892. 1 p.l., 7–278 p. front., plates. 8°. (Optimus series. 19.)
Reviewed by F. M. in *Reform advocate*, Chicago, 1892, v. 3, p. 394, * *PBD*.

Individual Plays — 1838–1914, continued

DAUDET, ALPHONSE, *continued*

Buchanan, Robert Williams, *and* F. Horner. The struggle for life, a drama in four acts, adapted from A. Daudet, was produced at the Avenue Theatre, London, Sept. 25, 1890.
One of the principal characters is Esther de Séléney, daughter of la Maréchalle, acted by Alma Stanley. She is referred to as the Jewess throughout the play. Reviewed in *Athenæum*, London, 1890, v. 96, p. 457–458, * *DA; Jewish chronicle*, London, Oct. 3, 1890, p. 6, * *PBD; Queen*, London, v. 88, p. 500, * *DA; Saturday review*, London, v. 70, p. 372–373, * *DA;* and in *Theatre*, London, series 4, v. 16, p. 232–234, *NCOA.* No record of an American production has been found. The play called *Struggle for life* which was staged at the Standard Theatre, New York, Sept. 7, 1891, and reviewed in *New York dramatic mirror*, v. 26, Sept. 12, 1891, p. 2, * *T-* *DA,* is not to be confused with the original of Daudet's, similarly entitled.

DAVENTRY, G. *See* sub-entry under DE LA RAMÉE, LOUISE.

DAVIS, ALLAN. Gloomy Fanny; a comedy in four acts... [New York,] cop. 1913. 28, 43, 31, 20 f. 4°. NBL p.v.212
Typewritten.
Based on a story similarly entitled, by Morley Roberts, which appeared in *Saturday evening post*, v. 183, May 13 and 20, 1911. The action is laid in London. Joseph Levison and his wife Jennie are the Jewish characters.

—— The iron door; an American play, in a prologue and three acts... n. p., cop. 1912. 26, 40, 21, 21 f. 4°. NBL p.v.213
Typewritten.
A play of American politics. The action takes place in an industrial city of the Middle West. Magistrate Louie Rosenberg is thus described "short...sports a pincenez. His manner is at once shrewd, bristling, and conciliatory."

—— The promised land; a drama in four acts ... [Cambridge:] The Harvard Dramatic Club, 1908. 16, 20, 17, 14 f. 4°. NBL p.v.213
Typewritten.

—— —— [Cambridge:] The Harvard Dramatic Club, 1908. 6 p.l., (1)12–69 p. 8°. NBL p.v.13
The characters of this play, which was produced by the Harvard Dramatic Club, at Brattle Hall, Cambridge, Mass., Dec. 15, 1908, are, in a thin disguise, the leaders and opponents of the Zionist movement in the late nineties of the last century. The events take place in eastern Germany. Theodor Herzl, Menahem Ussishkin, the Rothschilds and Jacob H. Schiff can easily be identified. It is probably the first serious drama of Jewish interest to be presented by a non-Jewish amateur organization.
Reviewed in *American Hebrew*, New York, 1909, v. 84, p. 167–168, * *PBD;* and by James C. Savery (with illus.) in *Burr McIntosh monthly*, New York, 1909, v. 18, no. 71, 3 p., † *MFA.*

DAVIS, PAUL P. An amateur triumph; a comedietta in one act... Philadelphia: The Penn Publishing Company, 1915. 11 p. 12°. NBL p.v.49
Mr. Sydenham, a journalist, in disguise of Mr. Bernstein, theatrical promoter, in order to dissuade his wife from a stage career.

DAVIS, RICHARD HARDING. Peace manoeuvres; a play in one act. New York: S. French [etc.], cop. 1914. 18 p. 12°. (French's international

copyrighted...edition of the works of the best authors. no. 278.) NBL p.v.116
Reprinted in *One act plays for stage and study*, New York, 1924 [series 1], p. 160–173, *NCO (One).*
Ikey Schwab, one of two gunmen, "small, rat-like, Hebrew, cynical, doubting, carries a constant 'grouch.' "

DE LA RAMÉE, LOUISE. Under two flags; a novel, by "Ouida" [pseud.]. Philadelphia: J. B. Lippincott & Co., 1867. iv, 5–652 p. 12°. NCW
The first British edition, in 3 v., has sub-title: a story of household and the desert.
"Ouida's best novel." In this romance the characters are all idealizations of either good or bad. Baroni, the Jewish character, is placed in the latter category. The scene is England and Algiers.

Abel, W. H. Under two flags; a dramatized version by W. H. Abel was produced at the Norwich Theatre Royal, Nov. 14, 1870.
Reviewed in *Era*, London, Nov. 20, 1870, p. 12, † *NAFA.*

Daventry, G. Under two flags; a dramatized version by G. Daventry, was produced at the Dundee Theatre Royal, Sept. 15, 1882, and at the Pavillion Theatre, London, Aug. 11, 1884.

Elsner, E. Under two flags, a dramatized version by E. Elsner, was produced at the Cork Opera House, March 3, 1902.

Mayo, Margaret. Under two flags, a dramatized version in five acts, was produced at the West End Theatre, New York, June 6, 1904.
Otto F. Hoffman played the rôle of Baroni, "a cringing enough Jew money-lender." Reviewed in *New York dramatic mirror*, v. 51, June 18, 1904, p. 15, * *T-* *DA.*

Mitchell, A. ...Under two flags; a romantic play, in four acts. Dramatized from Ouida's famous novel... Chicago: Dramatic Publishing Company, cop. 1893. 31 p. 12°. (Sergel's acting drama. no. 396.) NBL p.v.116

Potter, Paul Meredith. Under two flags; a dramatized version in five acts was produced at the Garden Theatre, New York, Feb. 5, 1901.
It ran 133 consecutive evenings. Albert Bruning played Baroni, keeper of a curiosity shop at Rouen, and Grace Elliston his daughter, Rehee Baroni. Reviewed in *New York dramatic mirror*, New York, v. 45, Feb. 16, 1901, p. 16, * *T-* *DA.*

Under two flags; a dramatization by an unknown author was produced at the Royal Theatre, Stratford, July 26, 1909.

Watkins, Harry. Under two flags; or, Trodden down. Produced at the Olympic Theatre, New York, July 3, 1873.

DE MILLE, HENRY CHURCHILL, AND DAVID BELASCO. "Men and women"; a drama of our times in four acts. [New York, 1890.] 4 parts in 1 v. 4°. † NCOF
Typewritten.
Prompt-book.

—— —— n. p., n. d. 44, 31, 31, 19 p. 4°. † NCOF
Photostatic reproduction, in 66 leaves, of typewritten copy.
It is announced for publication by the University of Pennsylvania Press in the series *Manuscript American plays*, under the editorship of Barrett H. Clark.
An American Wall Street drama. Its principal charac-

Individual Plays — 1838-1914, continued
DE MILLE, H. C., & DAVID BELASCO, *continued*

ters are bank directors and their employees. It was first produced at Proctor's 23rd Street Theatre, New York, Oct. 21, 1890, with Frederick de Belleville as Israel Cohen, the Jewish president of the Jefferson National Bank, a man of integrity, broad-mindedness and kindness. Reviewed in *New York dramatic mirror*, v. 24, Nov. 1, 1890, p. 6, * *T-* DA*. The reviewer here states that the character of Israel Cohen was drawn merely to please the Jewish playgoers.

It was revived at the New Park Theatre, Brooklyn, N. Y., Nov. 9, 1891, and again by the William Morris Stock Co., at the Lincoln Square Theatre, New York, April 8, 1907, with Austin Webb as Israel Cohen. Reviewed in *New York dramatic mirror*, v. 57, April 20, 1907, p. 3, 13, * *T-* DA*.

Under the title *Man and woman*, and with the fourth act rewritten by Malcolm Watson, it was seen in London, at the Opera Comique, March 25, 1893, with Arthur Elwood in the rôle of the Jewish bank president. Reviewed unfavorably by William Archer in his *Theatrical 'World' of 1893*, London, 1894, p. 88–90, *NCOA; Theatre*, London, 1893, series 4, v. 21, p. 282–283, *NCOA;* and in *The Times*, London, March 27, 1893, p. 8, * *A*.

B., C. The advancement of the stage Jew. (Jewish exponent. Philadelphia, 1890. f°. v. 8, Oct. 31, 1890, p. 8.) * PBD
Repr.: Sunday mercury, Philadelphia.

DENISON, THOMAS STEWART. A dude in a cyclone; a farce [in one act]. Chicago: T. S. Denison & Co. [cop. 1895.] 12 p. 12°. (Amateur series.)
Solomon Isaacstein, insurance agent and "bromoter." He tries to ply his trade while a cyclone rages.
Reprinted in his *Lively plays for live people*, Chicago [1895].

DE NOIE, VERA, AND A. D. HALL. The Dreyfus affair. [New York, 1898.] 16 p., 6 ports. 8°.
DLX p.v.13
Outline of the melodrama *Devil's Island*, in four acts, which was produced at the Fourteenth Street Theatre, New York, Aug. 29, 1898, with William Harcourt as Capt. De la Tour (Dreyfus), and Ralph Delmar as Prince Orloff (Esterhazy). Reviewed in *Jewish exponent*, Philadelphia, v. 27, Sept. 9, 1898, p. 5, * *PBD;* and in *New York dramatic mirror*, v. 40, Sept. 3, 1898, p. 14, * *T-* DA*.
Two productions entitled *Devil's Island*, dealing with the same theme, were staged at the Harlem Opera House, New York, Sept. 26, 1899, and at the Third Avenue Theatre, Feb. 26, 1900. See Brown, III:556, 234.

DEUTSCH, GOTTHARD. Israel Bruna; an historical tragedy in five acts. Boston: R. G. Badger, 1908. 95 p. 8°. * PSQ
The central character is Israel ben Hayyim of Brünn who, after the expulsion of the Jews from that city in 1454, settled at Ratisbon. The action takes place at about that time and around this rabbi the author has designed the plot, which deals with the blood accusation libel and the local Inquisition.
Reviewed in *Modern view*, St. Louis, v. 18, Oct. 1, 1909, p. 7, * *PBD*.

DE VERE, AUBREY. Alexander the Great. A dramatic poem. London: H. S. King & Co. [1874.] xxiv, 231 p. 16°. NCR
Act II, scene 7, relates to the visit of Alexander to Jerusalem; Alexander and the Jewish high-priest are the speakers.
Reviewed in *Dublin review*, London, 1874, new series, v. 23, p. 412–440, * *DA*.

DEXTER, WALTER, AND F. T. HARRY. *See* subentry under DICKENS, CHARLES.

DICKENS, CHARLES. Oliver Twist; or, The parish boy's progress. By "Boz." [Illustrated by G. Cruikshank.] London: R. Bentley, 1838. 3 v. 24 pl. 8°. MEM C 955 dic

Almar, George. Oliver Twist; a serio-comic burletta, in three acts... As correctly printed from the prompter's copy... London: Chapman & Hall [1843?]. 60 p. front. 12°. NCR
The Library also has a prompter's copy, [3]–42 p., with interleaved ms. notes and additional ms. leaves to replace missing text, *NCOF*.
Also issued in Dicks' standard plays, no. 293; in French's standard drama, no. 228; in Ludwig Hilsenberg, The modern English comic theatre, series 1 (text in English, notes in German); and in Benjamin N. Webster, editor, The acting national drama, v. 6.
Produced at the Surrey Theatre, London, Nov. 19, 1838, with Heslop as Fagin. Reviewed in *Athenæum*, London, 1838, v. 11, p. 844, * *DA; Literary gazette*, London, 1838, p. 748, * *DA;* and in *The Times*, London, Nov. 21, 1838, p. 5, col. 2, * *A*.
A new adaptation, credited in Ireland, II:701, to Joseph Jefferson, was produced at the Winter Garden, New York, Feb. 2, 1860, with J. Wallack, Jr. as Fagin. Wallack revived it at the Grand Opera House, New York, Feb. 12, 1876. See *New York Tribune*, Feb. 14, 1876, p. 5, col. 1, * *A*.

Barnett, Charles Zachary. Oliver Twist; or, The parish boy's progress. A drama in three acts. Adapted from the celebrated novel by Mr. Charles Dickens. London: T. H. Lacy [1857–73]. 48 p. nar. 12°. (Lacy's acting edition of plays. v. 33.) NCO (Lacy)
Also issued as no. 494 of French's acting edition.
According to Fitz-Gerald, p. 99, this Barnett version was produced at the Pavillion Theatre, London, May 21, 1838. The cast given here is the one which acted in Almar's version at the Surrey, Nov. 19, 1838. The text, however, is not Almar's.

Beckett, Dan. The thief maker; a protean sketch. Adapted by D. Beckett from Dickens' Oliver Twist. Produced at the Rehearsal, London, Nov. 27, 1910.

Berlyn, Ivan. Fagin, an episode. Produced at the Empress Theatre, Brixton, Oct. 28, 1907.
Noted in Fitz-Gerald, p. 114–115.

Brand, Oswald. Oliver Twist, in four acts. Produced at the Grand Theatre, Islington, March 30, 1903, with Ivan Berlyn as Fagin.
Noted in Fitz-Gerald, p. 113–114.

Callahan, C. E. Oliver Twist; a new dramatization. Produced at the American Theatre, New York, March 2, 1904, with Paul Scott as Fagin.

Carr, Joseph William Comyns. Oliver Twist; a new version. Produced at His Majesty's Theatre, London, July 10, 1905, with Herbert Beerbohm Tree as Fagin.
Reviewed in *Academy*, London, 1905, v. 69, p. 738, * *DA; Queen*, London, v. 118, p. 480, * *DA;* (with illus.) in *Rapid review*, London, v. 4, p. 343, * *DA;*

THE JEW IN ENGLISH DRAMA

Individual Plays — 1838–1914, continued

DICKENS, CHARLES, *continued*

by William T. Stead in *Review of reviews*, London, v. 32, p. 603–605, "The Jewishness of the villain was accidental... Of anti-Semitism at His Majesty's there was no trace." * *DA;* in *The Times*, London, July 11, 1905, p. 5, col. 5–6, * *A; Truth*, London, v. 58, p. 152–153, * *DA;* and by William Winter in *World*, London, 1905, p. 121–122, * *DA.* A revival of it by Tree was seen at London, June 11, 1912, which was reviewed in *Academy*, London, v. 82, p. 760–761, * *DA.* Another revival took place on April 19, 1915. Reviewed in *Athenæum*, London, v. 145, p. 390, * *DA; Era*, London, v. 78, April 21, 1915, p. 11, † *NAFA;* and in *The Times*, London, April 20, 1915, p. 12, col. 6, * *A.*
Also produced at the Fifth Avenue Theatre, New York, Nov. 13, 1905, with J. E. Dodson as Fagin. Reviewed in *New York dramatic mirror*, New York, v. 54, Nov. 25, 1905, p. 16, * *T–* DA;* and (with illus.) in *Theatre magazine*, v. 5, Dec., 1905, p. 291, xvi–xvii, † *NBLA.* A revival, with Nat C. Goodwin as Fagin, took place at the New Amsterdam Theatre, Feb. 26, 1912. Reviewed by Louis Lipsky in *American Hebrew*, New York, v. 90, p. 531, * *PBD; New York dramatic mirror*, New York, v. 67, Feb. 28, 1912, p. 6–7 (illus. in March 6, p. 8 and April 10, p. 2), * *T–* DA;* and in *Theatre magazine*, New York, v. 15, April, 1912, p. xvi–xvii (illus. on p. 127, 167), † *NBLA.*
For certain details connected with the first staging of Carr's dramatization by Tree, see Alice V. Carr, *Reminiscences*, London [1926], p. 226–228, *AN.*

His Majesty's Theatre, London. "Oliver Twist" portfolio, 1905. [London: Carl Hentschell, Ltd., 1905.] 10½ × 8½ in.
A souvenir portfolio issued on the occasion of the production of Carr's play. Consists of a programme; A night with Fagin, by James Douglas, reprinted from the Morning leader of Nov. 20, 1905, 2 1.; facsim. page from the original ms.; and 6 ports. of characters in the play, 2 of which are in color.

Collingham, George. Oliver Twist, an American adaptation, was produced at the Olympic Theatre, London, Dec. 21, 1891, with Henry De Solla as Fagin. Reviewed in *Theatre*, London, 1892, series 4, v. 19, p. 118, *NCOA;* and in *The Times*, London, Dec. 22, 1891, p. 4, col. 6, * *A.*

Coyne, Joseph Stirling. Oliver Twist; based on Charles Dickens' novel. Produced at the Adelphi Theatre, London, Feb. 25, 1839 with Yates as Fagin.
Nicoll, p. 396, ascribes the production of this date to Edward Stirling.
Reviewed in *Athenæum*, London, 1839, v. 12, p. 174, * *DA; Literary gazette*, London, 1839, p. 141, * *DA; Spectator*, London, v. 12, p. 205–206, * *DA;* and in *The Times*, London, Feb. 26, 1839, p. 5, col. 3, * *A.*

Dexter, Walter, and F. T. Harry. Oliver Twist, a new version in five acts, was produced at the Broadway Theatre, New Cross, Dec. 13, 1909, with Bransby Williams as Fagin.
Noted in Fitz-Gerald, p. 115. It was revived at the King's Theatre, Hammersmith, Sept. 4, 1922, and reviewed in *Era*, London, v. 86, Sept. 6, 1922, p. 5, † *NAFA.* "His [Williams'] Fagin of the play is the Fagin of our dreams." For illus. see *Illustrated sporting and dramatic news*, London, v. 98, p. 123, * *DA.* All reviewers commended this version highly.

Doughty, G. Henry. Oliver Twist, a new version in four acts, was given at the Lyceum Theatre, Sheffield, May 12, 1913.
Information from *Stage cyclopedia*, 1914, p. 199.

Ford, Alexander Hume. Oliver Twist; a new version. Produced Jan. 10, 1903 at the Carnegie Lyceum, New York, with Lemuel B. C. Josephs as Fagin.
Reviewed in *New York dramatic mirror*, New York, v. 49, Jan. 17, 1903, p. 16, * *T–* DA.*

Greenwood, Thomas. "Boz's" Oliver Twist; or, The parish boy's progress was produced at the Sadler's Wells Theatre, London, Dec. 3, 1838, with Robert Honner as Fagin.
Reviewed in *Spectator*, London, v. 11, p. 1183, * *DA.*

Johnstone, J. B. Oliver Twist, a new adaptation, was staged at the Surrey Theatre, London, May 18, 1868, with John Vollaire as Fagin.
Reviewed in *Era*, London, v. 30, May 24, 1868, p. 11, † *NAFA.*

Mordaunt, John. Oliver Twist, a new version, was produced at Marylebone Theatre, London, June 9, 1856, and revived at the Alexander Theatre, Camden Town, London, April 10, 1869.

Murray, William Henry Wood. Oliver Twist. Produced at the Theatre Royal, Edinburgh, March 23, 1840, with Skerrett as Fagin.
Noted in Fitz-Gerald, p. 107, and in Nicoll, v. 2, p. 355.

Oliver Twist, starring Dickie Moore with William Boyd and Irving Pichel. A monogram picture based on the famous story by Charles Dickens... New York: Engel-Van Wiseman, Inc. [cop. 1935.] 2 p.l., 9–154 p., 1 l. ports., illus. 24°. (Five star library. no. 11.)
Irving Pichel played the part of Fagin.

Oxenford, John. Oliver Twist; a new version, was produced at the New Queen's Theatre, London, April 11, 1868, with J. Ryder as Fagin.
Reviewed in *Athenæum*, London, 1868, v. 51, p. 567, * *DA; Era*, London, v. 30, April 19, 1868, p. 14, † *NAFA;* and in *Queen*, London, v. 43, p. 335, * *DA.*

Pertwee, Guy, editor. Oliver Twist in Fagin's den. illus. (In his: Scenes from Dickens, for drawing-room and parlor delivery. London, New York [1911]. 12°. p. 177–206.)

Pink, Wal. Oliver twisted; or, Dickens up a tree. Music by J. S. Baker. Produced at the Pavillion Theatre, London, Nov. 13, 1905.
Noted in Fitz-Gerald, p. 116.

Pollock's characters & scenes in Oliver Twist [a toy theatre play]. With book to the above. London: B. Pollock, n. d. 23 col'd sheets, 7 x 9 in., comprising six plates in character, 1 set piece, 3 wings and 13 scenes.

Ravold, John. Oliver Twist; a play in three acts, from the book of Charles Dickens... New York: S. French, cop. 1936. 94 p., 1 l. 16°.

Robinson, Marvin G. Oliver Twist; a dramatization in six episodes, by Marvin G. Robinson. Boston, Mass., Los Angeles, Calif. [W. H. Baker Company, cop. 1936.] 31 p. 12°. (Junior high series.)
"Arranged expressly for boys and girls of the junior and senior high school ages."
Produced at the Theodore Roosevelt Junior High School, Amsterdam, N. Y., March 23, 1934.

Individual Plays — 1838–1914, continued

DICKENS, CHARLES, *continued*

Roby, Bernard Soane. Bill Sykes; a dramatic episode in one act, adapted by B. Soane-Roby, from Dickens' Oliver Twist. Produced at the Palace Pier, Brighton, Oct. 4, 1909, with the author as Fagin.

Rosener, George M. Under London; a dramatization of Oliver Twist, in one act... New York: Wetzel, Rosener & James, 1912. 14 p. 24°.
See United States. — Copyright Office, *Dramatic compositions copyrighted in the United States, 1870 to 1916,* item 48118.

Searle, Cyril. Nancy Sikes, a dramatic version of Dickens' Oliver Twist, in five acts was produced at the Olympic Theatre, London, July 9, 1878, with G. W. Anson as Fagin.
Reviewed in *Athenæum,* London, 1878, v. 72, p. 60, * *DA; Theatre,* London, 1878, series 2, v. 1, p. 66–67, *NCOA;* and in *The Times,* London, July 11, 1878, p. 8, col. 2, * *A.* "Mr. Anson played the Jew — closely after Cruickshank's famous portrait."

Skeen, W. H. ...Oliver Twist. Adapted by W. H. Skeen. London: Samuel French, Ltd. [1926?] 16 p. 12°. (French's scenes from Dickens.)
At head of title: Scenes from Dickens.
Contents: The thieves' kitchen (in two scenes). The condemned cell (in one scene).
Fagin is the principal character in both adaptations.

Stirling, Edward. Oliver Twist, a new version, was produced at the City of London Theatre, London, Dec. 3, 1838, with Campbell as Fagin.

Suter, Henry Charles. An episode from Dickens' "Oliver Twist." Fagin's last night alive [in one scene]. (In his: Dramatic episodes from Dickens. London [1930]. 12°. p. 43–50.)
NCR (Dickens)

Vance, Daisy Melville. A lamb among wolves. From "Oliver Twist" [in two scenes]. (In her: Short plays from Dickens. New York [etc.], cop. 1935. 12°. p. 41–55.) NBL p.v.360

—— Vengeance. From "Oliver Twist" [in one scene]. (In her: Short plays from Dickens. New York [etc.], cop. 1935. 12°. p. 89–99.)
NBL p.v.360
The scene in both above dramatizations is Fagin's den, London, 1838.

Wallace, Sarah Agnes. Scenes from "Oliver Twist." (Education. Boston, 1930. 8°. v. 50, p. 499–506.) SSA
In five scenes. Scene IV is Fagin's den, with Fagin as one of the characters.

Whyte, H., and R. Balmain. Oliver Twist; a new version produced at the King's Theatre, Walthamstow, Essex, Oct. 2, 1905.
Noted in Fitz-Gerald, p. 114.

The following anonymous versions were staged in London:
At the St. James' Theatre, March 27, 1838. Reviewed in *Literary gazette,* London, 1838, p. 203, * *DA.*
"It was acted, we regret to say, with great ability, for a thing more unfit for any stage...we never saw"; and in *Spectator,* London, v. 11, p. 300, * *DA.*
At the Elephant and Castle Theatre, April 13, 1903, with Trant Fischer as Fagin.
Two "new" versions were advertised in the London *Times* for the evening of April 10, 1869, one to be produced at the New National and the other at the Standard Theatre.
The first American *Oliver Twist* play (according to Odell, IV: 308) was produced at the Franklin Theatre, New York, Jan. 7, 1839, with C. R. Thorne as Fagin. Another production, with Chippindale as Fagin, was seen at the Park Theatre, New York, Feb. 7, 1839. Other New York productions were: July 29, 1844, with Davenport as Fagin, at the Bowery Theatre; and Dec. 27, 1851, with Russell as Fagin, at Burton's Theatre. It is impossible to determine the authorship of any of the above New York adaptations.
The following additional dramatizations are recorded: by Abram Van Deventer (drama in five acts), 1905; by Beaumont Claxton [pseud. of Thomas C. Taylor], 1912; by William Francis Burke, 1912; and by J. H. Hoffman, under the title *Fagin's pupil,* 1909. See United States. — Copyright Office, *Dramatic compositions copyrighted in the United States, 1870 to 1916,* items 33712, 33713, 33714, and 13354.
A novelization by Norman Bruce of an Oliver Twist scenario, in which Jackie Coogan was featured, is printed, with illus., in *Motion picture magazine,* Jamaica, N. Y., v. 24, Sept., 1922, p. 66–70, 112–113, 120–121, † *MFL.*

Fitz-Gerald, Shafto Justin Adair. "Oliver Twist." (In his: Dickens and the drama. London, 1910. 8°. p. 97–116.) MWEM (Dickens)
A survey of the English productions, 1838–1909.

Landa, Myer Jack. The original of Fagin. (In his: The Jew in drama. London, 1926. 8°. p. 159–168.) * PZB

DINGMAN, MRS. W. B. Our own beloved America; an exceptionally unique patriotic exercise... Lebanon, Ohio: March Brothers [cop. 1914]. 10 p. 12°.
Cosmopolitan character of Americans by introducing loyal contributions of various nationalities. One of the speakers is designated "Hebrew."

DON ADRIAN; or, The harp of Judah; a dramatic poem in ten acts, or two parts. (Jewish chronicle. London, 1849. f°. v. 6, p. 31, 46, 62, 69, 77.) * PBE
Résumé and extracts are given from the manuscript. The editor states that it is founded upon historical events of the 15th century, in Spain. It was put out as an effort "to advocate the claim of the 'Children of Israel' to equal rights." Calisch, p. 213, lists it as published 1849, but gives no other information except that it is pro-Jewish. The compiler has not been able to find a full bibliographical description of it.

DONNAY, MAURICE CHARLES. ...Le retour de Jérusalem; comédie en quatre actes... Paris: Librairie Charpentier & Fasquelle, 1904. 2 p.l., xlii p., 1 l., 285 p. 12°. * PSQ
The author attempted the problem: Is real intimacy, intellectual and physical, possible between members of two races? A triangle with a Jewess as one of the angles.
Produced for the first time at the Théâtre du Gymnase, Paris, Dec. 3, 1903, with M. Duményas Michel Aubier, and, in French, at the Coronet Theatre, London, June 18, 1906. Reviewed in *Graphic,* London, 1906, v. 73, p. 827, * *DA.*

Individual Plays — 1838–1914, continued
DONNAY, MAURICE CHARLES, *continued*

Johnson, Owen. Return from Jerusalem, an English adaptation, was produced at the Hudson Theatre, New York, Jan. 10, 1912.
Arnold Daly played Michael Aubier; Mme. Simone, Henriette de Chouze; and Selene Johnson, Suzanne Aubier. Reviewed by Louis Lipsky in *American Hebrew*, New York, 1912, v. 90, p. 414, and by Rachel Ellison, ibid., p. 468, * *PBD;* by Channing Pollock in *Green book album,* Chicago, 1912, v. 7, p. 565, and by G. J. Nathan, ibid., p. 763–764, *NAFA; Jewish exponent,* Philadelphia, v. 54, Jan. 19, 1912, p. 8, * *PBD; Nation,* New York, v. 94, p. 67–68, * *DA; New York dramatic mirror,* New York, v. 67, Jan. 17, 1912, p. 6–7, * *T–* DA;* and in *Theatre magazine,* New York, v. 15, *p. 39–40,* † *NBLA.*

DORÉE, NADAGE. Gilta; or, The Czar and the cantatrice. A novel... New York: Hurst & Company [cop. 1897]. 234 p. incl. front. (port.) 12°.
A second ed., called *Gelta; or, The Czar and the songstress* appeared in 1900. Reviewed in *Book world,* New York, 1900, v. 5, p. 298–299, * *DA.*
Under its 1900 title it was dramatized that year into a drama of four acts and five scenes. *See* United States. — Copyright Office, *Dramatic compositions copyrighted in the United States, 1870 to 1916,* item 16021.

DOROSHEVICH, VLASI MIKHAILOVICH. A dream of a Russian subject [in one act]. Translated from the Russian by Marie G. Sabsovich. (Jewish comment. Baltimore, 1907. 4°. v. 25, p. 101–103, 113.) * *PBD*
On the precariousness of Russian representative government in 1907. Paul Alexandrovich Krushevan, 1860–1909, notorious anti-Semite, editor of the *Kishineff Bessarabetz,* and member of the Russian Douma in 1907 is the central character.

DOUGHTY, G. HENRY. *See* sub-entry under DICKENS, CHARLES.

DOWNING, HENRY FRANCIS. The shuttlecock; or, Israel in Russia, an original drama in four acts. London: F. Griffiths [cop. 1913]. 96 p. 12°. NBL p.v.32
Place: St. Petersburg. Time: 1900.

DRAMA LEAGUE OF AMERICA. ...Shakespeare festival in honor of the poet's birthday, April 23, 1912, Lincoln Park, Chicago. Chicago: R. F. Seymour Co. [cop. 1912.] 37 p. illus. 8°.
Engraved t.-p. * NCV p.v.7
At the head of title: Drama League of America.
The Merchant of Venice, with Shylock as one in the procession, constitutes the second group.

DROVIN, GEORGE ALBERT. In Hades; a farce, in one act. Philadelphia: Penn Pub. Co., 1911. 25 p. 12°.
Historic and fictional characters. Among them is Shylock as a pawnbroker. Lady Macbeth attempts to murder him for his money.

DUMAS, ALEXANDRE, THE ELDER. Monte-Cristo ... (In his: Théâtre complet. Paris, 1874. 12°. tome 2.) NKP
Dramatized by the author from his novel, published in 1845, into a drama in two parts, of five acts each. It was first staged at the Théâtre-Historique, Paris, Feb. 3 and 4, 1848, with M. Dupuis as Noirtier, in one of his disguises as a Jewish peddler.

Butler, Richard William, and H. C. Newton. Monte Christo, Jr.; a burlesque melodrama, in three acts. By Henry Richard, pseud. Produced at the Gaiety Theatre, London, Dec. 23, 1886, with Fred Leslie as Noirtier.
That Richard Henry is the pseudonym of two collaborators, Richard W. Butler and Henry C. Newton, is disclosed by H. C. Newton in his *Cues and curtain calls,* London [1927], p. 86, *AN.*
Reviewed by A. B. in *Theatre,* London, 1887, series 4, v. 9, p. 47–48, *NCOA.*
Fred Leslie brought this popular burlesque to New York, at the Standard Theatre, Nov. 15, 1888. See review in *New York dramatic mirror,* v. 20, Nov. 24, 1888, p. 2, * *T–* DA.*

Webster, Benjamin Nottingham. Monte Cristo; in a prologue and four acts, dramatized from Dumas' novel. Produced at the Adelphi Theatre, London, Oct. 17, 1868, with the author as Noirtier.
Reviewed in *Era,* London, v. 31, Oct. 25, 1868, p. 14, † *NAFA;* and in *The Times,* London, Oct. 19, 1868, p. 10, col. 4, * *A.*
This, the first English version, was revived as a "romantic drama" at the Avenue Theatre, London, Feb. 7, 1891, with Lee as Noirtier. Reviewed in *Jewish chronicle,* London, Feb. 13, 1891, p. 6, * *PBD;* and in *Theatre,* London, 1891, series 4, v. 17, p. 145–147, *NCOA.*
The third act of the Webster adaptation was presented at the Academy of Music, New York, Nov. 1, 1877, with F. B. Warde as Noirtier. On Dec. 17, 1877 the full play, with Warde again, was produced at the Broadway Theatre, New York. An anonymous version in which Chas. Wheatleigh played Noirtier was staged at the Grand Opera House, New York, April 28, 1873. Reviewed in *Spirit of the times,* New York, 1873, v. 28, p. 192, † *MVA.*

DU MAURIER, GEORGE LOUIS PALMELLA BUSSON. Trilby... London: Osgood, McIlvaine & Co., 1894. 3 v. 12°. NCW

Brookfield, Charles Hallam Elton, and W. Yardley. Model Trilby; or, A day or two after Du Maurier. A one-act sketch burlesquing the Potter play Trilby.
First produced at the Opera Comique, London, Nov. 16, 1895, with Robb Howard as Svengali. Reviewed (with illus.) in *Sketch,* London, 1895, v. 12, p. 172–173, 451, * *DA; Vanity fair,* London, v. 54, p. 365, * *DA;* and by William Archer in his *Theatrical 'World' of 1895,* London, 1896, p. 351–352, *NCOA (Archer);* and *The Times,* London, Nov. 18, 1895, p. 3, col. 5, * *A.*

Hearn, James, and Paul Rubens. A Trilby triflet was staged by the Oxford University Dramatic Society at Oxford, Dec., 1895, with Paul Rubens as Svengali.
See review and illus. in *Sketch,* London, 1895, v. 12, p. 448, * *DA.*

Herbert, Joseph N. Thrilby; a travesty. Produced at the Garrick Theatre, New York, June 3, 1895, with Alexander Clark as Spaghetti.
Brown, II:646, records Thrilby, another burlesque, at the Grand Opera House, New York, Feb. 3, 1896. Whether it is different from the Herbert version is not certain.

Muskerry, William. "Thrillby"; a shocker, in one scene and several spasms... With special songs composed by F. Osmond Carr. London, New York: Samuel French [1896–1910?]. 16 p., 1 pl. nar. 12°. (French's acting edition of plays. v. 140.) NCO (Lacy)
Without the music.
Produced at the Theatre Royal, Richmond, England, May 11, 1896. Lee Trevor as Svengali.

Individual Plays — 1838–1914, continued

DU MAURIER, GEORGE L. P. B., *continued*

Potter, Paul Meredith. Trilby, a play in four acts dramatized from George Du Maurier's novel, was first produced at the Boston Museum, Boston, March 4, 1895 and brought to the Garden Theatre, New York, April 15, 1895, with Wilton Lackaye as Svengali.

Trilby O'Ferrall becomes a great prima donna under the hypnotic influence of Svengali, but is finally rescued by her three artist friends, Taffy, the Laird, and Little Billee. Svengali, "the weird, lank, Hebrew hypnotist, with his music, his mysticism, his livid face and masterful deviltry" is the character which in the present adaptation becomes the pivot of the action. E. F. Walbridge in his *Do novelists use real people?* states that Felix Moscheles, 1833–1917, son of a famous pianist and author of *In Bohemia with Du Maurier* has been suggested as the original of Svengali.

Reviewed by W. B. H. (with illus.) in *Harper's weekly*, New York, 1895, v. 39, p. 320, 326, * *DA*; *New York clipper*, New York, v. 43, p. 102, * *T–* † *MVA*; *New York dramatic mirror*, New York, v. 33, April 20, 1895, p. 3, * *DA*; *Spirit of the times*, New York, v. 129, p. 480, † *MVA*; *Town topics*, New York, v. 33, April 18, 1895, p. 15–16, * *DA*; and *Vanity*, New York, v. 1, p. 169–170, * *DA*. See also "Trilby on the stage," in *Trilbyana*, New York, 1895, p. 8–10, *NCT* p.v.75.

It was revived, with Wilton Lackaye in his original rôle, at the Shubert Theatre, New York, April 3, 1915. See review by M. Morgan in *Theatre magazine*, New York, 1915, v. 21, p. 242–243, 274 (with illus.), † *NBLA*. Mr. Lackaye was again Svengali in a revival by the Cooperative Players at the National Theatre, New York, Dec. 23, 1921. Sir Herbert Tree as Svengali revived it in London at the Finsbury Park Theatre, July 5, 1915.

After a trial performance at the Theatre Royal, Manchester, Sept. 7, 1895, it was brought to the Haymarket Theatre, London, Oct. 30, 1895, with Herbert Beerbohm Tree as Svengali. Reviewed (with illus.) in *Queen*, London, 1895, v. 98, p. 886–887, * *DA*; *Sketch*, London, 1895, v. 12, p. 64 and (with illus.) in Dec. 25, Supplement, p. 1–8, * *DA*; *Speaker*, London, v. 12, p. 469–470, * *DA*; *The Times*, London, Oct. 31, 1895, p. 6, col. 3, * *A*; *Truth*, London, v. 38, p. 1136–1137, * *DA*; *Vanity fair*, London, v. 54, p. 324, * *DA*; and by William Archer in his *Theatrical 'World' of 1895*, London, 1896, p. 328–335, *NCOA*.

The compiler of this list has in his collection a folio-size scrapbook of provincial newspaper clippings, relating to Mr. Abud's Trilby companies, which toured England, outside of London, March to June, 1896.

Fletcher, Beaumont. Trilby as a play. illus. (Godey's magazine. New York, 1895. 8°. v. 130, p. 570–578.) * *DA*

Geller, James Jacob. "Trilby." (In his: Grandfather's follies. New York [cop. 1934]. 8°. p. 166–170.) MWED

Tree, Sir Herbert Beerbohm. A souvenir of "Trilby" by Paul M. Potter (founded on George Du Maurier's novel)... [London: John Walker & Co., 1895.] 8 ports. 4°. † NCOD

No text. Photographs of eight players in character, with two of Tree as Svengali.

DUMONT, FRANK. The depot lunch counter; a farce in one act. Philadelphia: Penn Pub. Co., 1916. 23 p. diagr. 12°. NBL p.v.44, no.1
Another edition was published in 1925.
A farce described as "a rollicking absurdity." Moses Slavinsky, a peddler.

—— The district convention; a burlesque in one act... Philadelphia: Penn Pub. Co., 1915. 13 p. 12°. NBL p.v.44, no.6
Another edition published in 1923.
An "uproarious" political nominating convention. Yipsil Rosinski, the Hebrew candidate.

—— The girl from "L Triangle" ranch; a drama in three acts... Philadelphia: Penn Pub. Co., 1915. 53 p. diagrs. 12°. NBL p.v.44, no.11
Another edition published in 1923.
Solomon Doanahue, "a wandering Hebrew, in search of 'Mazuma,'" among Western folks.

—— A gunner in the navy; a melodrama in three acts... Philadelphia: Penn Pub. Co., 1913. 46 p. diagrs. 12°. NBL p.v.44, no.5
Ikey Moritzski, "a Hebrew Jack of all trades."

—— Mock trial of the great kidnapping and breach of promise case; or, Balm for a wounded heart... New York [etc.]: M. Witmark & Sons [1905]. 24 p. 12°.
On cover: The Witmark stage publications.
Levi Hockheimer, "comic Hebrew peddler's make-up," one of the twelve jurors.

—— The night riders; a melodrama in three acts... Philadelphia: Penn Pub. Co., 1916. 62 p. diagrs. 12°. NBL p.v.46, no.15
Another edition published in 1919.
Ikey Bloomingall, "a Hebrew traveler" in a Ku Klux country.

—— The old New Hampshire home; a melodrama in three acts... Philadelphia: Penn Pub. Co., 1916 [cop. 1908]. 56 p. diagr. 12°.
Another edition published in 1925. NBL p.v.46
Moses Gazinski, a Hebrew glazier.

—— Sky-lark; or, The merchant of Ven-is it; burlesque on "Shylock; or, The merchant of Venice." New York [etc.]: M. Witmark & Sons, cop. 1905. 13 p. 12°. (The Witmark stage publications.)
p. 5 skipped in numbering.

ELIOT, GEORGE, PSEUD. OF MARY ANN (EVANS) LEWES CROSS. Daniel Deronda... Edinburgh and London: William Blackwood and Sons, 1876. 4 v. 8°.

Deronda and his mother; a scene from "Daniel Deronda." (Werner's magazine. New York, 1900. 8°. v. 24, p. 632–634.) MWA
A dramatization of that portion of the novel where Daniel Deronda meets his mother, the princess, at Genoa.

James, Henry, Jr. Daniel Deronda: a conversation. (Atlantic monthly. Boston, 1876. 8°. v. 38, p. 684–694.) * DA
A review in the form of a conversation among Theodora, Constantius and Pulcheria.

Ryan, James. Daniel Deronda, an adaptation of George Eliot's novel, was produced at the Baldwin Theatre, San Francisco, on Sunday, May 25, 1879, with James O'Neill, in the title-rôle.

It was announced for production as a benefit for Charles Goodwin, treasurer of the theatre on May 24, 1879, in the *Argonaut* and in the *San Francisco news letter*. Lewis Morrison played Mordecai; Kate Corcoran, Mirah; J. A. Herne, Herr Klesmer; Olive West, Gwendolyn Harleth; and Kate Denin, princess Halm-Eberstein, Deronda's mother. Reviewed on May 26, 1879, in the *San Francisco Call*, *San Francisco Examiner*, and the *Daily Alta California*; *New York dramatic mirror*, New York, June 7, 1879, p. 2, * *T–* * *DA*; and in *Spirit of the times*, New York, v. 97, p. 437, † *MVA*. See also *Jewish chronicle*, London, June 27, 1879, * *PBE*, quoting the contemporary *Hebrew* of San Francisco.

Individual Plays—1838–1914, continued

ELIOT, GEORGE, PSEUD., ETC., *continued*

Tobias, Mrs. Lily, and L. Lewisohn. Daniel Deronda, in three acts and a prologue, was produced by Jewish Drama League at the Q Theatre, London, Feb. 14, 1927.
Ernest Milton played the title rôle; Beatrice Lewisohn, Mirah; Victor Lewisohn, Mordecai; Sydney Benson, Ezra Cohn; and Nancy Price, Deronda's mother. Reviewed in *Jewish chronicle*, London, Feb. 18, 1927, p. 32, * PBE; *Jewish guardian*, London, Jan. 21, 1927, p. 8 and Feb. 18, p. 13, * PBE; and with extracts from the dramatized text in *New Judaea*, London, 1927, v. 3, p. 224–225, * PZX.
The following dramatizations of *Daniel Deronda* are recorded: by Wisner Gillette Scott (a play in five acts) in 1878; by Martha Morton in 1883; by Mrs. J. H. Selz in 1907; and by Jonah Spivack (a drama in four acts) in 1913. See United States. — Copyright Office, *Dramatic compositions copyrighted in the United States, 1870 to 1916*, items 9802–9805.

ELIOT, GEORGE, PSEUD. OF MARY ANN (EVANS) LEWES CROSS. The Spanish gypsy; a poem... Edinburgh and London: William Blackwood and Sons, 1868. 3 p.l., 358 p. 8°.

—— —— Boston: Ticknor and Fields, 1868. 2 p.l., 287 p. 12°. NCM
"Author's edition, from advance sheets."

—— —— New York: F. A. Stokes Company [1881?]. 1 p.l., 271 p. front. (plate.) 16°. NCM

—— —— New York: White, Stokes, and Allen, 1886. 3 p.l., (1)6–271 p. 16°. NCM

—— —— New illustrated ed. New York: Frederick A. Stokes Company [cop. 1893]. 1 p.l., 271 p., front., 11 pl. 12°. ([Wild rose series.])

—— —— (In her: Theophrastus Such; Jubal, and other poems; and The Spanish gypsy. Chicago [etc.], 1888. 12°. p. 289–504.) NDH

—— —— Condensed and arranged for reading with special adaptability for a woman, with directions for interpretation by Lily Hoffner Wood Morse... New York: E. S. Werner and Company, cop. 1906. iii p., 1 l., 82 p. 12°. NCR
Selections are given in M. L. Cobb, *Poetical dramas for home and school*, Boston, 1873, p. 33–87, *MZB*; and from book II in G. A. Kohut, editor, *A Hebrew anthology*, Cincinnati, 1913, v. 2, p. 1351–1361, * PSO.
A dramatic poem originally written in 1864–65 and later rewritten and amplified. The scene is the town of Bedmár, Andalusia, Spain, in the desert near by, and the Mediterranean coast. The time is about 1487. One of the characters is Salomo Sephardo, a Jewish sage, the astrologer of Abderahmen's tower, whose aid and counsel Duke Silva seeks after Fedalma's departure. See Books 2 and 4 of the Poem.
Reviewed in *Athenæum*, London, 1868, v. 51, p. 855–856, * DA; *Atlantic monthly*, Boston, v. 22, p. 380–384, * DA; *Blackwood's magazine*, New York, v. 103, p. 760–771, * DA; *British quarterly review*, London, v. 48, p. 503–534, * DA; by Parsons in *Dartmouth*, Hanover, N. H., v. 2, p. 386–392, STG; *Edinburgh review*, London, v. 128, p. 523–538, * DA; *Independent*, New York, v. 20, July 30, 1868, p. 6, col. 4–5, * DA; *London quarterly review*, London, v. 31, p. 160–188, * DA; by J. M. in *Macmillan's magazine*, London, v. 18, p. 281–287, * DA; *Nation*, New York, v. 7, p. 12–14, * DA; by Henry James, Jr., in *North American review*, Boston, v. 107, p. 620–635; * DA; *St. James' magazine*, London, new series, v. 1 [v. 22], p. 478–486, * DA; and in *Saint Pauls*, London, v. 2, p. 583–592, * DA. See also Leslie Stephen, *George Eliot*, New York, 1902, p. 158–171, AN.

Williams, Thomas John. A silent protector; a comedietta in one act... London: S. French; New York: S. French & Son [18—?]. 24 p. 12°. (Lacy's acting edition of plays. v. 80.)
NCO (Lacy)
First produced at the Prince of Wales' Theatre, London, March 7, 1868, with Montgomery as Nat Nobbler, a Hebrew sheriff.

Étienne, Louis. Un retour du réalisme à la poésie. (Revue des deux mondes. Paris, 1870. 8°. période 2, tome 90, p. 429–446.) * DM

Rands, William Brighty. George Eliot as a poet. (Contemporary review. London, 1868. 8°. v. 8, p. 387–396.) * DA
Signed: Matthew Browne [pseud.].
Reprinted in George Eliot, *Poems*, New York, 1900, p. 1–12, NCM.

ELSNER, E. See sub-entry under DE LA RAMÉE, LOUISE.

EMORY, S. See sub-entry under ERCKMANN, ÉMILE, AND ALEXANDRE CHATRIAN.

ERCKMANN, ÉMILE, AND ALEXANDRE CHATRIAN. Friend Fritz; a tale of the banks of the Lauter. Translated from the French... New York: Scribner, Armstrong & Company, 1877. 2 p.l., 401 p. 12°. NKV
Friend Fritz occupies p. 1–289.
This is the story of an old bachelor who marries a little country maiden, in an Alsatian village. In the original French it exists as a novel and in a printed dramatization by Émile Perrin. It was first produced at the Comédie Française, Paris, Dec. 4, 1876, with M. Got as Rabbi Sichel. For comment on its pro-Jewish interest see *Jewish chronicle*, London, June 1, 1877, p. 5, * PBE.
In a dramatization by Stanislaus Stange, it was first staged at Herrmann's Theatre, New York, Jan. 26, 1893. In a German version by Demetrius Schrutz, it was seen at the Irving Place Theatre, New York, Feb. 27, 1905, with Ferdinand Bonn as David Sichel. See *New York dramatic mirror*, v. 53, March 11, 1905, p. 16, * T–* DA. It was also presented by the Cambridge Latin School Club of Radcliffe College, Cambridge, Mass., April 1, 1911. See ibid., v. 65, April 12, 1911, p. 8, col. 4.

...Le juif polonais, par Erckmann-Chatrian, known on the English and American stage as "The bells"; ed. with introduction, notes and vocabulary by Edward Manley... Boston: D. C. Heath & Co., 1903. xiii, 108 p. 16°. (Heath's modern language series.) NKV
First performed at the Cluny Théâtre, Paris, June 15, 1869.

—— The bells; or, The Polish Jew. A romantic, moral drama. In three acts. Translated from the French of Messrs. Erckmann and Chatrain [!]. By Henry L. Williams, jr... New York: R. M. De Witt, 1872. 33 p. 12°. (De Witt's acting plays. no. 141.)

—— The Polish Jew [a dramatic study in three parts] by Erckmann-Chatrian. Translated from the French by Caroline A. Merighi. New York: George Munro's Sons, cop. 1884. 1 p.l., (1)6–49 p. 12°.
The Library has an 1885 edition (on cover: Seaside library. Pocket ed. no. 329), 8–* ITGB (U.S.: 1885).
The first American version was styled *The Polish Jew; or, The bells*, and was seen at the Bowery Theatre, New York, Aug. 19, 1872, with J. B. Studley as Mathias. It followed closely the translation of H. L. Williams. Brown, III: 21, records *The Polish Jew* on April 22, 1878, at the New Fifth Avenue Theatre, New York.

Individual Plays — 1838-1914, continued
ERCKMANN, É., & A. CHATRIAN, *continued*

Allen, Horace. Bells of the sleigh; a drama in a prologue and three acts. Adapted by Horace Allen. Produced at the Leigh (Lancashire) Theatre, Dec. 26, 1891.

Bells bell-esqued and the Polish Jew polished off; or, Mathias, the muffin, the mystery, the maiden, and the master. Produced at the Theatre-Royal, Norwich, March 13, 1883.

Burnand, Francis Cowley. Paul Zegers; or, The dream of retribution, a drama in three acts, founded on *Le Juif polonais*. Produced at the Royal Alfred Theatre, London, Nov. 13, 1871.
Reviewed in *Graphic*, London, 1871, v. 4, p. 494, * *DA*.
The scene of the play is changed from Alsace to Cornwall. The Jewish peddler is converted into a Dutch captain. In the French original the action of the play begins after the murder; in the present version the murder takes place on the stage.

Cardot, Louis. The bells, a new version, in which Thos. E. Shea played Mathias and J. I. Southard was named Joseph Cavenski (the Polish Jew) was seen in New York, on May 10, 1897.

Emery, S. The Polish Jew, a drama. Produced at the Theatre-Royal, Bradford, March 18, 1872.

Hazlewood, Colin Henry. The bells in the storm. Produced at the Sadler's Wells Theatre, London, Feb. 14, 1874, with Jackson in the part of the Jew.
Reviewed in *Era*, London, v. 36, Feb. 22, 1874, p. 11, † *NAFA*.

Hoggan-Armadale, E. Sleigh bells, a sketch. Produced at the Empire Theatre, Camberwell, Jan. 6, 1908.

Lewis, Leopold David. The bells, a drama in three acts. (Adapted from "The Polish Jew," a dramatic study, by MM. Erckmann-Chatrian.) By Leopold Lewis. London, New York: Samuel French [188–?]. 30 p. 8°.   NKM p.v.327
The Library also has a prompter's copy, with interleaved ms. notes, *NCOF*.

—— —— Philadelphia: Penn Pub. Co., 1918. 39 p. 12°.

—— The bells; drama in three acts, by Leopold Lewis; adapted for performance by male characters, and supplied with full directions for stage management, diagrams, etc., by C. J. Birbeck... New York: J. F. Wagner [1904]. 46 p. diagrs. 12°. ([Classical dramas arranged for performance by male characters only. no. 3.])
"Adapted from Sir Henry Irving's version."
In this version the "Polish Jew" appears as one of the characters.
First produced at the Lyceum Theatre, London, Nov. 25, 1871, and performed for 151 consecutive nights. Scene: Alsace. Period: Dec. 24–26, 1833. Reviewed in *Athenæum*, London, 1871, v. 58, p. 728–729, * *DA*; *Era*, London, v. 33, Dec. 3, 1871, p. 13, † *NAFA*; *Graphic*, London, v. 4, p. 542, * *DA*; *Illustrated London news*, London, v. 59, p. 526–527, * *DA*; and in *The Times*, London, Nov. 28, 1871, p. 4, col. 6, * *A*. See also Clement W. Scott, *From "The bells" to "King Arthur,"* London, 1896 (another ed., 1897), p. 1–7, *NCOD*. A discussion of the rôle of Mathias as conceived by M. Coquelin and Henry Irving is given in *Saturday review*, London, 1887, v. 64, p. 657–658, * *DA*.

Robinson, W. Bevan. Bells across the snow, romantic drama in four acts, by W. Bevan Robinson. Produced at the Greenwich Theatre, Greenwich, Eng., Jan. 2, 1905.

Rosenfeld, Sidney. Those bells, a version to the music by G. A. Kerker, was staged at the Bijou Opera House, New York, in 1884, with Nat Goodwin impersonating Henry Irving's rôle of Mathias and H. E. Brew as Solomon Lescynski.

Rowe, George Fawcett. The sleigh bells, a drama. Produced at the Prince of Wales' Theatre, Liverpool, March 11, 1872, with Joseph Eldred as Mathias and Richards as the Jew.
Reviewed in *Era*, London, v. 34, March 17, 1872, p. 6, col. 2, † *NAFA*.

Russell, Livingston. The death dream, dramatic monologue for a man. Arranged from the play of "The bells." New York: E. S. Werner & Company, cop. 1907. 14 p., 5 ports. 12°.

Ware, J. Redding. The Polish Jew, a new version. Produced at the Grecian Theatre, London, March 4, 1872.
Reviewed in *Era*, London, v. 34, March 10, 1872, p. 11, † *NAFA*.

Hawkins, Frederick. The first production of The bells. (Theatre. London, 1896. 8°. new series, v. 28, p. 304–307.)   * T–* DA

ESMOND, HENRY VERNON. When we were twenty-one; comedy in four acts... New York, London: S. French, cop. 1903. 80 p. 12°. (French's standard library edition.)   NCR
First produced at the Chestnut Street Opera House, Philadelphia, March 12, 1900, with Thomas O'Berle as David Hirsch. It was brought to New York, at the Knickerbocker Theatre, March 28, 1900.
Performed at the Comedy Theatre, London, Sept. 2, 1901. Mr. Bassett Roe as David Hirsch. Reviewed in *Graphic*, London, 1901, v. 64, p. 315, * *DA*; *Sketch*, London, v. 35, p. 288, 329 (illus. on p. 273), * *DA*; by P. C. in *Speaker*, London, new series, v. 4, p. 643–644, * *DA*; *The Times*, London, Sept. 3, 1901, p. 7, col. 6, * *A*; and in *Truth*, London, v. 50, p. 662–663, * *DA*. For more illustrations see *Illustrated sporting and dramatic news*, London, v. 56, p. 435, * *DA*.

FAGAN, JAMES BERNARD. *See* sub-entry under HICHENS, ROBERT SMYTHE.

FALCONER, EDMUND, PSEUD. OF EDMUND O'ROURKE. Chrystabelle; or, The rose without a thorn. An extravaganza [in six scenes]... London: T. H. Lacy [186–?]. 36 p. nar. 12°. (Lacy's acting edition of plays. v. 49.)
NCO (Lacy)
Produced at the Lyceum Theatre, London, Dec. 26, 1860, with Clara Danvil as Pippo, a page. Reviewed in *Era*, London, v. 23, Dec. 30, 1860, p. 11, † *NAFA*. In scene 4, enter Pippo as a "Jewboy" old clo' seller. The *Era* reviewer states: "The best piece of acting was certainly the performance of Pippo...who got the only encore in a familiar parody," about spendthrifts casting away their old clothing before being certain of new.

Individual Plays — 1838-1914, continued

THE FALL of Haman; a tragedy appropriate for school theatricals... Leeds: R. Jackson, 1874. 16 p. 16°. NCO p.v.636
A three-act play in verse dealing with Dr. Henry Hayman's term as head master (1869-1874) at Rugby, and his resignation (1874).
Haman, "Head of Rokeby," is Dr. Henry Hayman, 1823-1904; Temenus, his predecessor, is Frederick Temple, 1821-1902, later archbishop of Canterbury. Disraeli, "Vizier to the Queen," is represented as commissioning Dr. Hayman, upon his resignation, with the rectorship at Addingham, Lancashire. Cf. Henry Hayman, "My time at Rugby (1869-1874)," in *Bibliotheca sacra*, Oberlin, Ohio, 1899-1900, v. 56, p. 505-531; v. 57, p. 95-118, * DA.

FERBER, EDNA. Roast beef medium served hot by Emma McChesney. (American magazine. New York, 1911. 8°. v. 73, p. 157-164.) * DA

Hobart, George Vere, and Edna Ferber. Our Mrs. McChesney; a comedy in three acts, based on the McChesney stories by Edna Ferber, was produced at the Lyceum Theatre, New York, Oct. 19, 1915, with Thomas Reynolds as Joe Greenebaum and Jack Kingsberry as Mr. Perlman.
Reviewed in *Billboard*, Cincinnati, v. 27, Oct. 30, 1915, p. 4, † *MZA*; by Montrose J. Moses in *Book news monthly*, Philadelphia, v. 34, p. 179-180, * DA; (with illus.) in *Harper's weekly*, New York, v. 61, p. 440, * DA; *Nation*, New York, v. 101, p. 527-528, * DA; by William E. Merrill (with illus.) in *National magazine*, Boston, v. 43, p. 244-247, * DA; *New York dramatic mirror*, New York, v. 74, Oct. 19, 1915, p. 8, * DA; and in *New York clipper*, New York, v. 63, Oct. 30, 1915, p. 28, * T-† *MVA*. For illustrations see *Theatre magazine*, New York, v. 22, p. 307, † *NBLA*.
See also Ethel Barrymore, "Why I want to play Emma McChesney," in *American magazine*, New York, v. 80, Nov., 1915, p. 40-42, 96-97, * DA.

FIELD, MICHAEL, PSEUD. OF KATHERINE H. BRADLEY AND EDITH E. COOPER. A messiah. [In three acts.] (In their: The accuser, Tristram de Léonois, A messiah. London, 1911. 8°. p. 151-235.)
The first and the only play in English of high literary merit on the subject of the pseudo-Messiah, Sabbethai Zebi, 1626-1676.

FITCH, CLYDE. Beau Brummel; a play in four acts, written for Richard Mansfield by Clyde Fitch. New York: J. Lane Company, 1908. 142 p. front. (port.), plates. 8°. NBM
Reprinted in his *Plays*, edited with an introduction by M. J. Moses and Virginia Gerson, Boston, 1915, v. 1, p. 1-208, *NBM*; and, with an introduction, in Helen L. Cohen, editor, *Longer plays by modern authors (American)*, New York [cop. 1922], p. 1-84, *NBL (Cohen)*.
First produced at the Madison Square Theatre, New York, May 19, 1890, with Richard Mansfield as the Beau and W. H. Crompton as Abrahams, one of his creditors. Reviewed in *New York dramatic mirror*, v. 23, May 24, 1890, p. 4, * T-* DA. See also *Evening Post*, New York, May 20, 1890, p. 7, col. 1, * A; and *New-York Daily Tribune*, May 20, 1890, p. 6, col. 5, * A.

—— The woman in the case; a play in four acts. Boston: Little, Brown, and Company, 1915. 195 p. 12°.
Published also, with same pagination, in v. 4 of the author's *Plays*... Memorial ed., Boston, 1915, *NBM*. First produced at the Herald Square Theatre, New York, Jan. 31, 1905, with Samuel Edwards as Louis Klauffsky. Reviewed in *New York dramatic mirror*, New York, v. 53, Feb. 11, 1905, p. 16, * T-* DA; and in *Theatre magazine*, New York, v. 5, p. 54-55 (illus., ibid., p. 54, 115), † *NBLA*.
Produced at the Garrick Theatre, London, June 2, 1909, with E. Dagnall as Klauffsky. Ran there 226 times. Reviewed in *The Athenæum*, London, 1909, v. 133, p. 711, * DA; and in *The Times*, London, June 3, 1909, p. 12, col. 4, * A. Illustration of the stage production is given in *Illustrated sporting and dramatic news*, London, v. 71, p. 588, * DA.

FITZBALL, EDWARD. ...Azael, the prodigal. Grand operatic spectacle. In three acts... As performed at the London theatres... London: J. Duncombe [185-?]. 26 p., front. 24°. NCOF
At head of title: Duncombe's edition.
Front. missing.
Without the music, by Auber.
Prompter's copy, with signature of E. F. Taylor.
The Library also has a second prompter's copy (p. 25-26 missing), interleaved with ms. notes, and with the signature of Mrs. F. B. Conway, *NCOF*.

—— Azael the prodigal. A grand, romantic spectacle, in three acts... London: T. H. Lacy [186-?]. 28 p., 1 pl. nar. 12°. (Lacy's acting edition of plays. [no. 827.] v. 56.) NCO (Lacy)
The motif of the plot is the parable of the prodigal son. Founded on Auber's popular opera *L'Enfant prodigue*. The scene is laid in the desert home of the father and at Memphis, Egypt, whereto the son wanders away. First performed at the Drury Lane, London, Feb. 19, 1851, with Vandenhoff as Reuben, the father, chief of a tribe of Israelites, Miss F. Vining as Jephtele, the prodigal's betrothed, and Anderson in the title rôle. Reviewed in *The Athenæum*, London, 1851, v. 24, p. 225-226, * DA; *Era*, London, v. 13, Feb. 23, 1851, p. 10, † *NAFA*; *Figaro*, London, 1851, p. 118, * DA; *Queen*, London, v. 9, p. 108, * DA; *Spectator*, London, v. 24, p. 178, * DA; and in *The Times*, London, Feb. 20, 1851, p. 5, col. 5, * A. A burlesque version, with London instead of Memphis as the scene of dissipation, was produced at the Olympic Theatre, London, Oct., 1851. See *Examiner*, London, 1851, p. 693, col. 3, * DA.

FLATTERY, MAURICE DOUGLAS. The conspirators; a drama in four acts. (In his: Three plays. Boston [cop. 1921]. 12°. p. 79-147.) NBM
This was alleged to be a play of Boston life. Produced at the Park Theatre, Boston, under title of *Faith Mather*, Sept. 4, 1905, with Russell Bassett as Joe Leavitt, formerly Joe Levi, a renegade and a forger. Reviewed in *New York dramatic mirror*, New York, v. 54, Sept. 16, 1905, p. 12, col. 3, * A. It never reached the New York stage.

FLECKER, JAMES ELROY. The golden journey to Samarkand... London: M. Secker [1915]. xi, 65(1) p. 8°. NCM
"First published July, 1913."
"The golden journey to Samarkand": p. 3-9.
A dramatic poem in a prologue and an epilogue. At the gate of the Sun, Bagdad, in olden time. Among the speakers are "the principal Jews."
Reprinted in his *Collected poems*, London [1921], p. 144-150, *NCM*; and, without the prologue, in W. S. Braithwaite, editor, *The Book of modern British verse*, Boston [cop. 1919], p. 101-104, *NCI*.

FORBES, JAMES. The show shop; a farcical satire in four acts... New York: Samuel French, cop. 1920. 3 p.l., 93-197 p. 12°. (French's standard library edition.)
Reprinted from his *The Famous Mrs. Fair and other plays*, New York [cop. 1920], p. 89-197.
Concerns the theatrical profession and deals with a play within a play. Produced at the Hudson Theatre, New York, Dec. 31, 1914, with George Sidney as Max Rosenbaum, theatre manager, and George Colt as Goldman. Reviewed in *New York dramatic mirror*, v. 73, Jan. 6, 1915, p. 8-9, * T-* DA; and (with illus.) in *Theatre magazine*, New York, 1915, v. 21, p. 57-58, † *NBLA*.
Produced at the Globe Theatre, London, April 18, 1916, with Edmund Gwenn as Rosenbaum.

Individual Plays — 1838-1914, continued

FORD, ALEXANDER HUME. *See* sub-entry under DICKENS, CHARLES.

FRAENKEL, J. Esther Guiladi; an episode of Jewish persecution in the eighteenth century. A story in dramatic form [in three acts]. (Translated from the French.) London: John Kensit, 1892. 96 p. 12°.
Scene: Lithuania, 1741 A. D. Its theme, the libel of blood accusation.
Reviewed in *Jewish chronicle*. London, Aug. 19, 1892, p. 6, * *PBE*. "Throughout the narrative we catch glimpses of the cloven hoof of the conversionist... It is a clumsy tissue of inartistic coincidences on the level of probability of a comic opera."

FRANK, ETHEL. Gossip; a one-act play. (Ark. Cincinnati, 1912. f°. v. 2, p. 868.) *PBD

FRANKAU, MRS. JULIA (DAVIS). The heart of a child; being passages from the early life of Sally Snape, Lady Kidderminster, by Frank Danby [pseud.]... New York: The Macmillan Company, 1908. 3 p.l., 388 p. 12°. NCW
A dramatization in four acts of this novel was produced by the Premier Stock Co., at the Baker Theatre, Rochester, N. Y., April 28, 1913, with Robert Graceland as Joe Aarons, the overbearing theatrical manager who pays odious attention to Sally. See *New York dramatic mirror*, v. 66, May 7, 1913, p. 12, * *T-* DA*.
In England it was produced at the Royal Theatre, Huddersfield, Sept. 6, 1920, and at the Kingsway Theatre, London, March 26, 1921. The character of Aarons, played by Will West, is here called Sir Thomas Peters. Reviewed in *Era*, London, v. 84, March 30, 1921, p. 5, † *NAFA*.

FRASER, FREDERICK JOHN. ...A burlesque extravaganza...entitled "The merry Merchant of Venice." A peep at Shakespeare through the Venetians. Allahabad [1895]. 8°.
At head of title: Railway Theatre, Allahabad.
Copy: British Museum.
"Shylock: In the pawnbroking and old clo' line, the uncle of the indigent."
"Jessica: Miss Shylock, who, not receiving enough to dress on from dear pa, runs an ice-cream cart on her own account."
See Otto Burmeister, *Nachdichtungen und Bühneneinrichtungen von Shakespeare's Merchant of Venice*, Rostock, 1902, p. 99-108, *NDD p.v.3*.

FREYTAG, GUSTAV. The journalists; comedy in four acts. Translated by Roy Temple House. (Drama. Chicago, 1913. 12°. no. 9, p. 30-140.) NAFA
See also Martin Schütze, "Gustav Freytag," ibid., p. 3-28.

—— ...Die Journalisten...literally translated by Vivian Elsie Lyon. New York: Translation Pub. Company, Inc. [cop. 1916.] 159 p. 16°.
At head of title: The students' literal translations.
Another translation by Ernest F. Henderson is given in Kuno Francke, editor, *The German classics*, New York [cop. 1914], v. 12, p. 10-108, illus., *NFF*.
German critics rank this comedy as the most outstanding one of the last century, and it still holds the German stage. It was produced at Breslau, Dec. 8, 1852, and printed in 1854. The plot deals with politics and with the rivalry of two newspapers during an election. Among the characters is the farcical Schmock, general utility man of the *Coriolanus* office, who is made to speak his lines in dialect. The hero is Konrad Bolz, clever man of the world. Cf. introduction in *Die Journalisten*, edited by W. D. Toy, Boston, 1908, p. ii-ix, *NGE*.
This comedy was produced in German at the Bowery Theatre, New York, April 4, 1888, with Herr Possart as Schmock.
See "Gustav Freitag on anti-Semitism," in *American Hebrew*, New York, 1894, v. 54, p. 397-398, * *PBD*.

FRIEL, THORNTON. The case against Casey; a burlesque breach of promise trial, in one scene. Chicago: T. S. Denison & Co. [cop. 1905.] 24 p. 12°. (Denison's specialties.)
Izzy Marks, second-hand clothing store proprietor, one of the witnesses.

FRISCHMANN, DAVID. "For Messiah, King." Translated by Jessie E. Sampter. [Adaptation and dramatization by Rose G. Schnitzer.] (In: Jewish Education Committee, Chicago, Portfolio for the observance of peace day. Chicago [1929?]. 6 f. 4°.) *PKB
Mimeographed.
The Hebrew poem "Messiah," first appeared in השלח, v. 1, p. 263-267, * *PBA*.

GERSONI. A dignified and honorable interview [between A. Kraus, president of I. O. B. B. and M. Witte's secretary]. (Jewish comment. Baltimore, 1905. f°. v. 21, Aug. 11, 1905, p. 7.)
*PBD
A satiric sketch about the efforts to intervene on behalf of the Jews with M. Witte, peace negotiator with the Japanese in Portsmouth, in 1905.

GILBERT, SIR WILLIAM SCHWENCK. Creatures of impulse; a musical fairy tale, in one act... Music composed by Alberto Randegger. London: T. H. Lacy [187-?]. 20 p. nar. 12°. (Lacy's acting edition of plays. v. 91.) NCO (Lacy)
Also issued as no. 1364 of French's acting edition.
Reprinted in his *Original plays; fourth series*, London, 1911, p. 309-327, *NCR*; and in Frank Shay, editor, *Plays for strolling mummers*, New York, 1926, p. 149-174, *NAFH* (Shay).
Reviewed in *The Athenæum*, London, April 22, 1871, p. 507, * *DA*.
Founded on the author's own *Story about a strange old lady* and first performed at the Court Theatre, London, April 15, 1871. E. E. Righton as Boomblehardt, the miser. Although the printed text does not identify the miser as a Jew, the part was acted as such.

—— An old score, an original comedy-drama. In three acts... London: T. H. Lacy [187-?]. 42 p. nar. 12°. (Lacy's acting edition of plays. v. 85.) NCO (Lacy)
Also issued as no. 1610 of French's acting edition, *NCO p.v.263*.
Announced for production at the Gaiety Theatre, London, on July 19th, but not staged there till July 26, 1869. Mr. Joseph Eldred played Manasseh, a Jewish bill discounter. Reviewed in *The Athenæum*, London, 1869, v. 54, p. 154-155, * *DA*; and in *Era*, London, v. 31, Aug. 1, 1869, p. 11, † *NAFA*.

GLADSTONE and the House of Lords; a lyrical serio-comic drama. In one act. To be performed in the House of Lords during the session of 1872... London: E. Stanford, 1872. 23 p. 16°.
NCO p.v.683
In 1872 Gladstone was premier and Beaconsfield (Dizzy in this piece) leader of the opposition. At one place Gladstone addresses him:
"Swear by thine Old Jewry
I abhor ye, I abjure ye—
In thy last state,
Base apostate."

Individual Plays — 1838-1914, continued

GLASCOCK, WILLIAM NUGENT. Land sharks and sea gulls. By Captain Glascock... Philadelphia: Lea & Blanchard, 1838. 2 v. 12°. NCW
Contents: v. 1. Wife-hunting. The widow. v. 2. The man-of-war.
Dramatized under the title *Elizabeth Lazarus*, by J. T. Haines, and produced at the Surrey Theatre, London, Jan. 17, 1842. Reviewed in *The Times*, London, Jan. 18, 1842, p. 3, col. 2, * *A*. "Bet Lazarus, the heroine, a Jewess...of doubtful moral principles, but means well."

GLASS, MONTAGUE MARSDEN. Object: matrimony... Garden City, N. Y.: Doubleday, Page & Company, 1912. 3 p.l., 3–74 p., 1 l. front. obl. 16°.
Repr.: Saturday evening post, Dec. 11, 1909.
Dramatized by the author jointly with Jules E. Goodman into a comedy of three acts and produced at the Cohan and Harris Theatre, New York, Oct. 25, 1916. The Sachs and the Lesengelt families plan to arrange a marriage that will buttress a shaky business. Irving Cummings played Milton Sachs and Jean Temple, Birdie Lesengelt. Reviewed in *New York dramatic mirror*, v. 76, Nov. 4, 1916, p. 7, * *T-* *DA;* and by Arthur Hornblow in *Theatre magazine*, v. 24, p. 392, † *NBLA*. The plot is given by S. W. in *Nation*, New York, 1916, v. 103, p. 427, * *DA*. The cast which played it in New York tried it out in Washington, D. C., at the Belasco Theatre, Sept. 25, 1916.

—— Potash and Perlmutter; a play in three acts... New York, N. Y., Los Angeles, Calif.: S. French, Inc.; London: S. French, Ltd. [etc.], cop. 1935. 114 p., 2 l. plates, diagrs. 12°. (French's standard library edition.)
NBL p.v.361
Produced at Apollo Theatre, Atlantic City, N. J., Aug. 4, 1913, and at the George M. Cohan Theatre, New York, Aug. 16, 1913. Barney Bernard and Alexander Carr played the title rôles; Elita Proctor Otis, Mrs. Potash; Marguerite Anderson, the daughter Irma; and Leo Donnelly, Rabiner. Reviewed in *American Hebrew*, New York, 1913, v. 93, p. 457, * *PBD; Dramatist*, Easton, Pa., v. 5, p. 479–480, *NAFA; New York clipper*, v. 61, Aug. 23, 1913, p. 7, † *MVA; New York dramatic mirror*, v. 70, Aug. 13, 1913, p. 7 and Aug. 20, p. 6, * *DA;* (with illus.) in *Theatre magazine*, New York, v. 18, Oct., 1913, p. 115, ix–x, 133, † *NBLA;* and in *Town topics*, New York, v. 70, Aug. 21, 1913, p. 14, * *DA*. A synopsis, illustrations, and numerous extracts from the text are given in *Current opinion*, New York, v. 57, p. 172–176, * *DA;* and in *Hearst's magazine*, New York, 1914, v. 25, p. 845–855, * *DA*.
It was revived at the Park Theatre, New York, April 5, 1935, with Arthur S. Ross and Robert Leonard in the title rôles. For reviews see *Collection of newspaper clippings of dramatic criticism, 1934–35*, v. P, † *NBL*.
Produced in England, at the Theatre Royal, Plymouth, April 8, 1914, and at the Queen's Theatre, London, April 14, 1914, with Augustus Yorke, Robert Leonard, Mathilde Cottrelly, Elise Martin and Ezra Matthews in the parts named under the New York production. Reviewed in *Academy*, London, v. 86, p. 599, * *DA; Era*, London, v. 77, April 15, 1914, p. 12, and April 22, p. 15, † *NAFA;* (with illus.) in *Graphic*, London, v. 89, p. 724, 763, * *DA;* by J. W. (with illus.) in *Illustrated sporting and dramatic news*, London, v. 81, p. 313, 324, * *DA; Queen*, London, v. 135, p. 793, * *DA; The Times*, London, April 15, 1914, p. 11, * *A;* and in *Truth*, London, v. 75, p. 1000–1001, * *DA*. Illustrations are given in *Play pictorial*, London, v. 24, no. 147, p. 101–120, † *NCOA*.

GLASS, MONTAGUE MARSDEN, AND J. E. GOODMAN. Business before pleasure, comedy in three acts. Produced at the Apollo Theatre, Atlantic City, N. J., Aug. 6, 1917 and at the Eltinge Theatre, New York, Aug. 15, 1917.
The two partners are now in the "fillum" business. Alexander Carr played Perlmutter and Lottie Kendall, his wife Ruth. Reviewed in *Billboard*, New York, v. 29, Aug. 18, 1917, p. 78, † *MZA; New York clipper*, New York, v. 65, Aug. 22, 1917, p. 10, * *T-*† *MVA; New York dramatic mirror*, New York, v. 77, Aug. 25, 1917, p. 7, * *DA;* by Arthur Hornblow in *Theatre magazine*, New York, v. 26, p. 136 (illus., p. 221), † *NBLA;* and in *Town topics*, New York, v. 78, Aug. 23, 1917, p. 15, * *DA*.
Produced at the Savoy Theatre, London, April 21, 1919, with Vera Gordon and Ruth Gates in the respective parts of Mrs. Potash and Mrs. Perlmutter. Reviewed in *Era*, London, v. 82, April 23, 1919, p. 13, † *NAFA; Illustrated London news*, v. 154, p. 646, * *DA; Queen*, London, v. 145, p. 477, * *DA; The Times*, London, April 22, 1919, p. 7, * *A;* and in *Truth*, London, v. 85, p. 704, 706, * *DA*. Illustrations are given in *Illustrated sporting and dramatic news*, London, v. 91, p. 566, 569, 604, * *DA*. It ran in London 207 times.

—— His Honor Abe Potash, a comedy in three acts. Produced at the Bijou Theatre, New York, Oct. 14, 1919.
Abe, urged on by his daughter Irma, a college graduate by this time (played by Lucille English), enters politics, becomes the mayor of the town and gives an honest administration. Perlmutter is omitted in this comedy. Reviewed in *New York dramatic mirror*, 1919, v. 80, p. 1653, * *DA;* and in *Variety*, New York, v. 56, Oct. 17, 1919, p. 16, † *NAFA*. More reviews of New York dailies are in *Collection of newspaper clippings of dramatic criticism, 1919–1920*, v. F-K, † *NBL*. It was never staged in England.

—— Partners again; a comedy. Produced at the Selwyn Theatre, New York, May 1, 1922.
The two genial partners are this time in the automobile business. Jennie Moscovitz acted Mrs. Rosie Potash. Reviewed in *Billboard*, New York, v. 34, May 20, 1922, p. 19, † *MZA;* by Samuel O. Kuhn in *Jewish forum*, New York, v. 5, p. 394, * *PBD; New York clipper*, New York, v. 70, May 10, 1922, p. 20, * *T-*† *MVA;* and by Arthur Hornblow in *Theatre magazine*, New York, v. 36, p. 29–30, † *NBLA*. More reviews are in *Collection of newspaper clippings of dramatic criticism, 1921–1922*, v. M–R, † *NBL*.
A scrapbook of material about the play covering its production throughout the country can be seen in †† *NBL n.c.6*.
Produced at the Garrick Theatre, London, Feb. 28, 1928, with Lize Silbert as Mrs. Potash and Marie Ault as Tillie Friedman. Reviewed by Ashley Dukes in *Illustrated sporting and dramatic news*, London, v. 98, p. 49 (illus. in v. 99, p. 54), * *DA;* (with illus.) in *Sketch*, London, v. 121, p. 572, * *DA; The Times*, London, March 1, 1923, p. 10, * *A;* and in *Truth*, London, v. 93, p. 428, * *DA*. More illustrations are given in *Play pictorial*, London, v. 42, p. 109–128, † *NCOA*. Numerous extracts from the text of the play are printed in *Hearst's international*, New York, v. 42, Oct., 1922, p. 85–87, 119–121, * *DA*.

—— Potash and Perlmutter, detectives; a comedy in three acts. Produced at the Ritz Theatre, New York, Aug. 31, 1926.
Abe and Mawruss are reunited and go sleuthing. Ludwig Satz succeeded Barney Bernard as Abe Potash. Reviewed in *Billboard*, New York, v. 38, Sept. 11, 1926, p. 11, † *MZA*. See also *Collection of newspaper clippings of dramatic criticism, 1926–1927*, v. N–Q, † *NBL*.
In England it was shown as a pre-view at the Theatre Royal, Plymouth, Dec. 12, 1927, with Mildred Franklin as Mrs. Potash, but it never reached the London boards. Reviewed in *Era*, London, v. 91, Dec. 14, 1927, p. 6, † *NAFA*.

Individual Plays — 1838–1914, continued

GLASS, MONTAGUE MARSDEN, AND R. C. MEGRUE. Abe and Mawruss, a comedy in three acts. Produced at the Lyric Theatre, New York, Oct. 21, 1915.
Barney Bernard and Julius Tannen in the title rôles; Mathilde Cottrelly as Rosie; Claiborne Foster as Irma and Leo Donnelly as Rabiner. Reviewed in *Billboard,* New York, v. 27, Oct. 30, 1915, p. 15, † *MZA;* *New York clipper,* v. 63, Oct. 30, 1915, p. 26, † *MVA;* *New York dramatic mirror,* v. 74, Oct. 30, 1915, p. 9 (illus. in Nov. 5, p. 2, and Nov. 20, p. 2), * *DA;* (with illus.) in *Theatre magazine,* New York, v. 22, p. 299, 320, † *NBLA;* and in *Town topics,* New York, v. 74, Oct. 28, 1915, p. 16, * *DA.* In London it was staged later under the title of *Potash and Perlmutter in society.*

—— Potash and Perlmutter in society (earlier staged in New York as Abe and Mawruss), a comedy in three acts, was produced at the Queen's Theatre, Manchester, Eng., Sept. 4, 1916, and at the Queen's Theatre, London, Sept. 12, 1916.
Millie Hylton played Rosie (the original of this rôle in London, Mme. Cottrelly, having gone to the United States, to act this part with great applause); Peter Wiser played Rabiner. Reviewed in *Era,* London, v. 80, Sept. 6, 1916, p. 8, and Sept. 20, p. 1, † *NAFA;* *Illustrated London news,* London, v. 149, p. 372, * *DA;* (with illus.) in *Illustrated sporting and dramatic news,* London, v. 86, p. 97, 126–127, * *DA;* *Queen,* London, v. 140, p. 420, * *DA;* and in *The Times,* London, Sept. 13, 1916, p. 11, * *A.* Further illustrations can be seen in *Play pictorial,* London, v. 29, p. 65–80, † *NCOA.*

CARR, ALEXANDER, and B. BERNARD. The humor of the Jewish characters. (Theatre magazine. New York, 1914. 4°. v. 19, p. 136, 138, 144.)
† NBLA
An explanation by the two chief actors in the Potash and Perlmutter series of plays as to what they conceived to be the proper interpretation of their rôles.

The Truth about Potash and Perlmutter and their founder. port. (American hatter. New York, 1910. f°. v. 39, p. 55–56, 68.) 3–† VLW

GORDIN, JACOB. Captain Dreyfus; a drama. (In: Bessie F. White, translator, Nine one-act plays from the Yiddish. Boston [cop. 1932]. 12°. p. 37–57.) * PTP (White)
Isaac Goido states that it was produced on the Yiddish stage, in 1898, when the Dreyfus affair was the subject of great interest. It is included in the author's *Ein acters,* New York, 1917, p. 161–179, * PTP.

—— Gott, Mensch und der Teufel (God, man and the devil). A drama in 4 acts. [New York: Lipschitz Press, 1903.] 14 p., 1 l. incl. front. (port.) 8°. * PTP
Caption-title.
On cover: Souvenir programme. Grand benefit performance of J. Gordin's play...for the East Side Janitors' Society, Thalia Theatre, May 19th.
Consists of a translation of the Prologue and detailed synopsis of the four acts of the play.
A drama on the Faust theme, by some considered as Gordin's greatest play. Originally produced at the Thalia Theatre, New York, Sept. 21, 1900, with David Kessler as Hirshele Dubrovner and M. Moschkowitz as Uriel Masik (the Satan). Cf. I. Goldberg, *The Drama of transition,* Cincinnati [cop. 1922], p. 360–361, *NAF;* and H. Hapgood, *The Spirit of the ghetto,* New York, 1909, p. 140–149, 167–176, * *PXY.*
In a revised and modernized form by Maurice Schwartz who played the rôle of Satan, it was produced at the Yiddish Art Theatre, New York, Dec. 23, 1928. For reviews see *Collection of newspaper clippings of dramatic criticism, 1928–1929,* v. E–G, † *NBL;* and Robert Littell in *Theatre arts monthly,* New York, 1929, v. 13, p. 172–173, *NBLA.*

—— A new prologue in heaven. Translated by Louis Lipsky. (American Hebrew. New York, 1903. f°. v. 73, p. 243–244.) * PBD
Reprinted in *Menorah magazine,* New York, 1903, v. 35, p. 59–63, * *PBD.*
From Gordin's Yiddish Faust tragedy, *God, man and devil.*

—— The Jewish King Lear; a drama in four acts. Synopsis. (In: B'nai B'rith, Independent Order. George Jessel Lodge, No. 566. A special performance of Jacob Gordin's The Jewish King Lear. New York, 1905. 8°. p. 7–13.)
* PYP (B'nai B'rith)
The motif is that of Shakespeare's King Lear, with original material supplied from Jewish life. This drama, the second written by Gordin in this country, was first produced in the original Yiddish at the Union Theatre, New York, Oct.–Nov., 1892. The performance listed above was given at the Grand Theatre, Dec. 19, 1905.

—— Souvenir programme. Grand benefit performance of Jacob Gordin's play, The Jewish King Lear, by Jacob P. Adler and his company. Given under the auspices of the Emanu-El Brotherhood at Grand Theatre, 255–7 Grand St., Monday, April 11th, 1904, 8.15 p. m. [New York,] 1904. 3 l. ports. 8°. * PBM p.v.150
Cover-title.
Synopsis.

—— The Kreutzer sonata; a play in four acts. Adapted from the Yiddish of Jacob Gordin by Langdon Mitchell. New York: H. G. Fiske, 1907. 78 p. 12°. NBL p.v.169
Only the title points to Tolstoi's theme; the material and characters are taken from Jewish life in Russia and America. First produced in the original Yiddish at the Thalia Theatre, New York, June, 1902, with Bertha Kalich, for whom it was specially written, in the rôle of Hattie, and David Kessler as her father, Raphael Friedlander. Reviewed by Louis Lipsky in *American Hebrew,* New York, 1902, v. 70, p. 336–338, and again on p. 572, * *PBD.*
A synopsis for an English staging appears in *Theatre magazine,* New York, 1904, v. 4, p. 218, † *NBLA.* Translated by Samuel Shipman and adapted for the English stage by Lena R. Smith and Mrs. Vance Thompson, it became the first Yiddish play to be presented on the American stage. Wagenhals and Kemper staged it at the Court Theatre, Wheeling, W. Va., Nov. 21, 1904; at McVicker's Theatre, Chicago, Dec. 4, 1904; and brought it to New York, at the Manhattan Theatre, Aug. 13, 1906, with George Sumner as Friedlander, Blanche Walsh as Hattie and Helen Ware as her sister Celia. Reviewed (with illus.) in *Current literature,* New York, 1906, v. 41, p. 420–421, * *DA;* *New York dramatic mirror,* New York, v. 56, Aug. 25, 1906, p. 8, * *T–*DA;* and in *Theatre magazine,* v. 6, Sept., 1906, p. xv, † *NBLA.* See also Robinson Locke Collection, Blanche Walsh, v. 3, † *NAFR.*
Leopold Spachner and David Kessler obtained an injunction to restrain the Blanche Walsh production, which was argued before Supreme Court, Special term, Justice Giegerich, Aug. 17, 1906. See *New York dramatic mirror,* v. 56, Aug. 25, 1906, p. 14, * *T–*DA.* The present English translation and adaptation was thereupon staged by H. G. Fiske, first at Pittsburgh, Pa., Sept. 3, 1906, and at the Lyric Theatre, New York, Sept. 10, 1906, with Bertha Kalich as Miriam (originally Hattie). Reviewed in *New York dramatic mirror,* v. 56, Sept. 22, 1906, p. 3, * *T–*DA.* A revival of Mitchell's version was seen at the Frazee Theatre, New York, May 24, 1924, with Bertha Kalich, Edwin Maxwell and Clelia Benjamin in the leading parts. For reviews see *Collection of newspaper clippings of dramatic criticism, 1923–1924,* vol. I–L, † *NBL.*

Individual Plays — 1838–1914, continued

GORDON, SAMUEL. Daughters of Shem; a study in sisters. (In his: Daughters of Shem and other stories. London, 1898. nar. 8°. p. 1–78.)
*PST
An intermarriage-problem short story. Dramatized by the author and Carmel Goldsmid into a one-act play. It was first produced by the Pioneers at the Royalty Theatre, London, May 20, 1906. Reviewed then in *Jewish comment*, Baltimore, v. 23, June 8, 1906, p. 13, * *PBD; Jewish chronicle*, London, May 25, 1906, p. 34–35, * *PBD*. It was revived at the All-Jewish Matineé, London Pavillion, June 15, 1916, with S. Teitelbaum as Anshel, the father.

GOULD, ERNEST MOORE. On the sight-seeing car; a comedy sketch in one act. Philadelphia: Penn Pub. Co., 1915. 18 p. 12°.   NBL p.v.43, no.9
A Jew, who tries to pay his fare with a trolley transfer ticket, is one of the passengers.

GREENWOOD, THOMAS. See sub-entries under AINSWORTH, WILLIAM HARRISON; DICKENS, CHARLES.

GREVILLE, LADY VIOLET. See sub-entry under AUGIER, GUILLAUME VICTOR ÉMILE, AND JULES SANDEAU.

GRILLPARZER, FRANZ. The Jewess of Toledo; an historical tragedy in five acts. Translated by George Henry Danton and Annina Perian Danton. (In: Kuno Francke and W. G. Howard, editors, The German classics. New York [cop. 1914]. 8°. v. 6, p. 337–408.)
NFF (Francke)
Numerous translated extracts, with a running synopsis of the play, are given by Gustav Pollak in his *Grillparzer and the Austrian drama*, New York, 1907, p. 361–378, *NFD (Grillparzer)*.
A drama of passion in classical dignity of form, begun in 1824, finished after 1855, and published in Strassburg, 1873. Based on or adapted from Lope de Vega's *Las paces de los reyes y Judia de Toledo*, the main plot of which has been variously utilized in fiction and drama. It depicts the love of King Alfonso VIII of Castile (1166–1214) for Rachel (Fermosa) of Toledo. Some historians hold that the grandees of Spain, attributing their defeat by the Almohades at the battle of Alarcos to the king's love affair with Rachel, murdered her and her relatives, who originally had dissuaded her from the royal infatuation. The play follows this unauthenticated version.
Grillparzer's possible sources are given and discussed by Ludwig Geiger in *Allgemeine Zeitung des Judenthums*, Berlin, 1900, Jahrg. 64, p. 22–23, 32–33, 45–47, * *PBC*; by E. Lambert in *Revue de littérature comparée*, Paris, 1922, année 2, p. 238–279, *NAA*; also in Grillparzer-Gesellschaft, *Jahrbuch*, Wien, 1910, Jahrg. 19, p. 61–84, *NFD*; and by W. von Wurzbach, ibid., Jahrg. 9, p. 86–127, *NFD*. See also S. Lublinski, *Jüdische Charaktere bei Grillparzer, Hebbel und Otto Ludwig*, Berlin, 1899, p. 97–120, * *PZB*.
It was produced in German at the Amberg Theatre, New York, Dec. 26, 1891.

Burgess, Amy V. An analysis of the female characters of Grillparzer's dramas. Rahel and Esther. (University College of Wales. Aberystwyth studies. Aberystwyth, 1912. 8°. v. 1, p. 104–107.)   STK (Wales)

Lasher-Schlitt, Mrs. Dorothy. Grillparzer's attitude toward the Jews... New York [etc.]: G. E. Stechert & Co., 1936. xii, 128 p. 8°. * PZB
Bibliography: p. 123–128.
"How Grillparzer felt about the Jews is important only in so far as it gives the world an insight into his personality and *Weltanschauung* and...a more correct interpretation to his drama *Die Jüdin von Toledo*."

GROSSMAN, SAMUEL S. "The jewels of God." [A play in one act.] (The Ark. Cincinnati, 1914. 8°. v. 4, p. 619–620.)   * PBD
The characters are Rabbi Meir, fl. 2nd century, and his wife Beruriah. Based upon a legend which teaches resignation in affliction.

—— The trusted jewels. [In one act. New York: Young Judaea.] 2 l. 4°. (In his: [Holiday and other plays for Jewish children.])
Typewritten.   NASH
Based upon a Talmudic legend, touching the piety and bravery of Beruriah, wife of the Tanna Meir.

GRUNDY, SYDNEY. "A bunch of violets"; a play in four acts... New York, London: S. French, cop. 1901. 57 p. nar. 12°. (French's acting edition of plays. v. 148.)   NCO (Lacy)
Also published as no. 47 of French's international copyrighted...edition of the works of the best authors.
Produced at the Haymarket Theatre, London, April 25, 1894, with G. W. Anson as Jacob Schwartz, a grafting labor leader. He is not an Englishman, but describes himself as "an elder of the Anabaptists." Reviewed by W. M. Thomas in *Graphic*, London, 1894, v. 49, p. 523, * *DA; Theatre*, London, 1894, new series, v. 23, p. 324–326, * *T-* DA*; and by William Archer in his *Theatrical 'world' of 1894*, London, 1895, p. 118–127, *NCOA*.
The first American production took place at Abbey's Theatre, New York, Jan. 30, 1895, with Charles Allan as Schwartz. Reviewed in *New York dramatic mirror*, v. 33, Feb. 9, 1895, p. 6, * *T-* DA*.

—— An old Jew. An original comedy in five acts. New York: American & Foreign Dramatists, 1894. 130 p. 12°.   NCO p.v.660
Place: London. Time: Present.
Julius Sterne is the Jewish character.
Deals with the theme of corrupt journalism. The preface, p. 3–19, is a defense of the play against its critics, by the author.
Originally produced at the Garrick Theatre, London, Jan. 6, 1894, with John Hare as Sterne. Reviewed in *Academy*, London, 1894, v. 45, p. 41, * *DA*; by William Archer in his *Theatrical 'world' of 1894*, London, 1895, p. 9–21, *NCOA*; by W. M. Thomas in *Graphic*, London, v. 49, p. 46, * *DA*; by Israel Zangwill in *Jewish chronicle*, London, Jan. 12, 1894, p. 7, * *PBD*; by G., ibid., p. 7–8, * *PBD; Sketch*, London, v. 4, p. 628, * *DA*; by A. B. W., in the form of an imaginary correspondence from William Archer to Clement Scott, from Clement Scott to A. W. Pinero, from Joseph Knight to Justin H. M'Carthy, and from Sir Augustus Harris to Malcolm Salaman, in *Speaker*, London, v. 9, p. 43–44, * *DA; Theatre*, London, series 4, v. 23, p. 109–112, *NCOA*; *The Times*, London, Jan. 8, 1894, p. 12, col. 2, * *A*; and in *Truth*, London, v. 35, p. 76–77, * *DA*. This last reviewer thinks there is no such Jew as the one portrayed in the person of Julius Sterne.

—— ...A son of Israel; an original play, in four acts... London: Printed by J. Miles & Co., 1896. 52 p. diagr. 8°.
At head of title: Printed — as manuscript — for private circulation only.
This is the same as the preceding play, under another title.

W., W. R. "An old Jew." [In five acts.] (Theatre magazine. London, 1894. 8°. new series, v. 23, p. 95–103.)   NCOA
Condensed dramas. no. 7.
A satire on Grundy's play.

—— See also sub-entry under MIRBEAU, OCTAVE.

Individual Plays — 1838–1914, continued

GUEST, CARMEL HADEN (GOLDSMID). 'The proselyte'; a comedy in one act... With a foreword by Harry Zimmerman. London: The New Arts Publishing Guild, 1934. 16 p. 8°.
Glossary on inside back cover.   NAFH p.v.141
As "a comedietta" it was staged at Portman Rooms, London, May 13, 1912, with Michael Sherbrooke as father Isaacs and J. Henry as his son Solly.
In its present form it was staged by the Habima Players in the Jewish Drama League's annual competition, at the Grafton Theatre, London, Jan. 22, 1933, with D. Abrahams and A. Blitz in the rôles of father and son.
Reviewed in *Jewish chronicle*, London, Jan. 27, 1933, p. 29, * PBE.

GUNNISON, BINNEY. The suffering of Nehushta [in three parts]. Adapted from "Zoroaster," by F. Marion Crawford. (In his: New dialogues and plays. New York, 1905. 12°. p. 129–138.)
MZB
Nehushta, a Hebrew maiden, second wife of Darius, king of Persia.

GUTZKOW, KARL FERDINAND. Uriel Acosta, a tragedy in five acts... Translated from the German by M. M. New York: M. Ellinger & Co., 1860. 2 p.l., (1)8–104 p. 12°. NGB p.v.202
Translation in blank verse.

—— Gutzkow's Uriel Acosta. Tragedy in five acts. Translated by W. J. Tuska. New York: G. Van der Potendyk & W. Cahn, printers, 1867. 86 p. 12°.
Prose translation.

—— Uriel Acosta, in three acts. From the German of Gutzkow by Henry Spicer... London: Kegan Paul, Trench & Co., 1885. viii p., 1 l., 87 p. 8°.

—— Uriel Acosta. By Karl Gützkow. (Poet lore. Boston, 1895. 8°. v. 7, p. 6–18, 83–96, 140–149, 198–203, 263–270, 333–349.)   * DA
"Translated by Richard Hovey and François Stewart Jones."
A historical play, first produced at the Hoftheater in Dresden, Dec. 13, 1848, and based on the author's short story *Der Sadducäer von Amsterdam.*
Adolph Sonnenthal played Uriel at the Thalia Theater, New York, March 9. 1885, with Julie Schomberg as Judith. See *New York dramatic mirror*, v. 13, March 14, 1885, p. 2, * T–* DA. The Library has a playbill of an 1888 German production at the Academy of Music, New York, with Moritz Moritz as Acosta and Lili Petri as young Baruch Spinoza. In London it was given in German at the Great Queen Street Theatre, Nov. 21, 1905, with Herr Waldeck in the title rôle. Reviewed in *The Athenæum*, London, 1905, v. 126, p. 734, * DA; and in *Jewish chronicle*, London, Dec. 8, 1905, p. 23, * PDE.
Brown and Odell record the first American production at the Deutsches National Theater, New York, in German, on Dec. 28, 1852.
Jacob Adler in the title rôle produced it in Yiddish at the West End Theatre, New York, June 26, 1906. See review in *New York dramatic mirror*, v. 76, July 7, 1906, p. 2, * T–* DA.
In a prose version by Bertram Jacobs, it was staged for the first time in the English language, by the Jewish Drama League, at the Garrick Theatre, London, Dec. 11, 1927, with Paul Cavanagh in the title rôle and Phyllis Kohnstam as Judith. Reviewed by S. N. in *Jewish chronicle*, London, Dec. 16, 1927, p. 40, * PBE; and in *Jewish guardian*, London, Dec. 16, 1927, v. 9, p. 13, * PBE.
See I. Abrahams in his *By-paths in Hebraic bookland*, Philadelphia, 1920, p. 240–246, * PAT; Albert Bloch in *Revue d'art dramatique*, Paris, 1898, nouv. série, tome 4, p. 180–186, *NAFA*; Moritz Ellinger in *Menorah magazine*, New York, 1902, v. 33, p. 320–324, * PBD; A. J. Leventhal in *Jewish chronicle*, London, 1927, supplement no. 74, p. v, * PBE (re-printed in *Jewish exponent*, Philadelphia, v. 80, March 25, 1927, p. 12, * PBD); Raphael Löwenfeld in *Allgemeine Zeitung des Judenthums*, Berlin, 1890, Jahrg. 54, p. 280–282, 292–294, * PBC; and J. Perles in *Monatsschrift für Geschichte und Wissenschaft des Judenthums*, Krotoschin, 1877, Jahrg. 26, p. 193–213, * PBC. For further historical and literary comments, see K. F. Gutzkow, *Uriel Acosta*, edited by S. W. Cutting and A. V. von Noé, New York, 1910, p. v–xiii, 103–105.

HAGEMAN, MAURICE. Hector; a farce in one act... Chicago: Dramatic Pub. Company [cop. 1897]. 23 p. 12°. (Sergel's acting drama. no. 488.)   NBL p.v.19
Einstein, pawnbroker. Described as wearing flashy clothes and speaking in "Hebrew" dialect.

HAINES, JOHN THOMAS. Ruth; or, The lass that loves a sailor. A nautical and domestic drama in three acts... London: T. H. Lacy [18—?]. 49 p. 12°. (Lacy's acting edition of plays. v. 44.)   NCO (Lacy)
First produced at the Victoria Theatre, London, Jan. 23, 1843, with Mr. Morelli as Jabez Grimani, "a Jew and receiver of unlawful treasures," and Miss Martin as Leah Grimani, "the Jew's daughter, but no Jewess."
Odell, VII:490, records a performance at Fox's Old Bowery Theatre, New York, Dec. 3, 1862.

—— *See also* sub-entry under AINSWORTH, WILLIAM HARRISON.

HALLIDAY, ANDREW. The great city; a novel [founded upon the play of the same name]. London, 1867. 8°.
Copy: British Museum.
The novelization by the author is based on his play in four acts, which was produced at the Drury Lane, London, April 22, 1867. F. Villiers played Mendez, the Jew, and Mrs. Warlow, aunt Judith, his sister. Mendez is the landlord of a "crib." The villain Blount escapes with his daughter, and the Jew revenges himself accordingly. Mendez was not conceived in the best light, judging from the *Era* reviewer who states: "The sentiments he [Mendez] is enforced to utter are likely to keep alive popular prejudices which should long since have been consigned to oblivion." Reviewed in *The Athenæum*, London, 1867, v. 49, p. 558, * DA; *Era*, London, v. 29, April 28, 1867, p. 10, † *NAFA*; and in *The Times*, London, April 23, 1867, p. 12, col. 1–2, * A.

HALPERN, JONATHAN. Mother and son. (In: Etta Block, translator, One-act plays from the Yiddish. Cincinnati [cop. 1923]. 8°. p. 17–47.)
Place: in a small Polish village.   * PTP (Block)
"It presents the results of a tyrannical religious rule in a family; the revolt of the son; the anguish of a divided loyalty in the mother's heart."

HANCOCK, C. W. ...Down on the farm; a Yankee rural comedy in three acts... New York [etc.]: Samuel French, cop. 1906. 3 p.l., 3–87 p. diagrs. 12°. (French's American acting edition. no. 7.)   NBL p.v.139
Acts 1 and 3, "down on the farm"; Act 2, the Bowery, New York city.
Solomon Levi, a clothing dealer.

HANNAN, CHARLES. A cigarette maker's romance; a play in three acts. (As commanded to Sandringham)... Founded...upon Marion Crawford's novel of the same name. London, New York: Samuel French [1910–24?]. 1 p.l., 79 p. nar. 12°. (French's acting edition of plays. v. 160.)   NCO (Lacy)
First produced at the Court Theatre, London, Feb. 11, 1901. Mrs. B. M. de Solla as Akulina, a German-Jewess, "a bully and a miser." She is the mistress of the cigarette factory. The action of the play takes place in Munich, about the year 1850. Reviewed in *The Times*, London, Feb. 12, 1901, p. 6, col. 6, * A.

Individual Plays — 1838–1914, continued

HARDING, THOMAS WALTER. Nina Balatka; a play in five acts. (In his: Oliver...and Nina Balatka; or, A maiden of Prague. Cambridge, 1926. 12°. p. 59–150.) NCR
"Founded on an anonymous tale with the same name, which came out in 'Blackwood's magazine' in the year 1866," p. 59. The tale, here called anonymous, is by Anthony Trollope, and was republished in book form by Wm. Blackwood & Sons, Edinburgh and London, Feb. 1, 1867. The scene of the story is laid in Prague, about 1850, and the hero is a Jew, Anton Trendellsohn, around whose marriage to the Christian heroine, Nina Balatka, the plot revolves.

HARRIS, AUGUSTUS GLOSSOP. The avalanche; or, The trials of the heart. A romantic drama in three acts... London: T. H. Lacy [185–?]. 2 p.l., 9–50 p. nar. 12°. (Lacy's acting edition of plays. v. 16.) NCO (Lacy)
Also issued as French's acting edition, no. 237.
The period is during Napoleon's second Italian campaign. The scene is Switzerland. The plot originates from the presumed fatal result to a mountain guide by the sudden descent of an avalanche. First performed at the Surrey Theatre, London, Oct. 3, 1854, with Vollaire as Flashenhausen, "a German Jew," who is made to speak in dialect. Reviewed in *Era*, London, v. 17, Oct. 15, 1854, p. 11, † *NAFA*.
Produced at the Bowery Theatre, New York, March 26, 1855. Brown, 1:140, records a production at the same theatre, Oct. 2, 1866.

HARRIS, GEORGE. Two bad boys; a musical and farcical comedy in four acts... Clyde, Ohio: Ames Publishing Co., cop. 1884. 25 p. 12°. (Ames' series of standard and minor drama. no. 262.)
Solomon Isaacs, "proprietor of a little grocery store on the corner."

HATTON, JOSEPH. By order of the czar; the tragic story of Anna Klosstock, queen of the ghetto... London: Hutchinson and Co., 1891. ix(i), 397 p. 7. ed. 12°. NCW

—— By order of the czar; a drama in five acts. London: Hutchinson and Co., 1904. 172 p. 12°.
Dramatized from the author's novel of the same name.
Scene: Russia and Siberia. Period: 1881–87.
Deals with "the tyrannous acts of certain of His Imperial Majesty's governors of provinces and prisons."
The Jewish characters are Rabbi Losinski, a young learned Jew, betrothed to Anna Klosstock, afterwards the Countess Stravinsky, and Andrea Ferrari, known as Ferrari the Jew.

Hewson, J. James. Under the canopy; a Russo-Jewish drama in four acts, founded on an episode in Joseph Hatton's novel "By order of the czar," was produced at the Pavillion Theatre, London, Nov. 2, 1903.
Reviewed in *Jewish chronicle*, London, Nov. 6, 1903, p. 29, * *PBE*.

HAUENSTEIN, CONRAD. David Cohn, der New Yorker Heiratsvermittler; Original-Posse mit Gesang und Tanz in drei Aufzügen und fünf Bildern. New York [1896]. 65 p. 12°.
See United States. — Copyright Office, *Dramatic compositions copyrighted in the United States, 1870 to 1916*, item 10049.

—— Samuel Wolf; New Yorker Original-Posse. Mit Gesang und Tanz in vier Aufzügen und fünf Bildern. New York: Selbstverlag [cop. 1896]. 68 p. 12°.
Words only.
See United States. — Copyright Office, *Dramatic compositions copyrighted in the United States, 1870 to 1916*, item 40676.

HAUPTMANN, GERHART. The conflagration. (In his: Dramatic works. New York, 1912. 12°. v. 1, p. 511–649.) NGE
In four acts.
German title: Der rote Hahn.
Translated by Ludwig Lewisohn.
Dr. Boxer, "physician of Jewish birth."
For a synopsis see Paul H. Graumann in *Poet lore*, Boston, 1910, v. 21, p. 290–291, * *DA*. See also Otto Heller, *Studies in modern German literature*, New York [cop. 1905], p. 215–218, *NFCD*.

—— Florian Geyer, a tragedy of the Peasants' war [in five acts]. Translated by Bayard Quincy Morgan. (In his: Dramatic works. New York [cop. 1929]. 12°. v. 9, p. 1–262.) NGE
Also published in London [cop. 1929].
Joey, an old Jewish money lender, on the side of the peasants against the feudal lords, not unsympathetically presented.
See Otto Heller, *Studies in modern German literature*, New York [cop. 1905], p. 175–179, *NFCD*.

—— Gabriel Schilling's flight [in five acts]. (In his: Dramatic works. Edited by Ludwig Lewisohn. New York, 1915. 12°. v. 6, p. 281–419.) NGE
The translation is by the editor.
Also published in London [cop. 1915].
Hannah Elias is undoubtedly meant to be an East European Jewess. She dislikes the Germans. However, she might as well have been represented as any other foreigner, with an aversion to the native Germans.
In the original German it was staged at the Irving Place Theatre, New York, Feb. 18, 1913, with Mathilda Brandt as Hannah. See *New York dramatic mirror*, v. 69, Feb. 26, 1913, p. 7, * *T–* *DA*.

HAY, FREDERICK, AND W. CHAPMAN. The deep red rover; an o'piratic burlesque in three scenes... London, New York: Samuel French [1869–76?]. 28 p. 12°. (French's acting edition of plays. v. 111.) NCO (Lacy)
One of the mariners, named Ikey Homespun, a tailor by trade, sings the praises of his wares, and is referred to by the others as "this Jew."

HAZLEWOOD, COLIN HENRY. Capitola; or, The masked mother and the hidden hand... London: T. H. Lacy [18—?]. 35 p. 12°. (Lacy's acting edition of plays. v. 70.) NCO (Lacy)
Melodrama, in three acts.
In act II, sc. 2, Black Donald uses a Jewish disguise of a peddler's pack and gaberdine to gain admittance to the heroine and seize her. Produced at the City of London Theatre in 1860.

—— The stolen Jewess; or, Two children of Israel. An original romantic drama in three acts... London, New York: Samuel French [1872–76]. 36 p. nar. 12°. (French's acting edition of plays. [no. 1575.] v. 105.) NCO (Lacy)
A melodrama, the action of which is placed in Italy and Spain during 1807–1825. First produced at the Britannia Theatre, London, April 1, 1872, with Miss L. Macdonald as Izolina, a girl who educated as a Christian discovers that she is the daughter of Jewish parents, Balthazar played by J. Reynolds and Miriam, played by Miss J. Coveney. The usual cliche is here reversed. The Jewish heroine is more often discovered to be a Christian girl brought up by a Jew. See also Landa, p. 194–195. Reviewed in *Era*, London, v. 34, April 7, 1872, p. 14, † *NAFA*.

—— *See also* sub-entries under ERCKMANN, ÉMILE, AND ALEXANDRE CHATRIAN; READE, CHARLES.

Individual Plays — 1838–1914, continued

HEARN, JAMES, AND PAUL RUBENS. See sub-entry under DU MAURIER, GEORGE LOUIS PALMELLA BUSSON.

HEBBEL, CHRISTIAN FRIEDRICH. Der Diamant; eine Komödie in fünf Acten... Hamburg: Hoffmann und Campe, 1847. 1 p.l., iv p., 2 l., (1) 12–178 p. 12°.   NGE
First produced at Kremsier, 1852.
A detailed synopsis is given and the Jewish interest pointed out in Edna Purdie, *Friedrich Hebbel; a study of his life and work*, London, 1932, p. 88–91, NFD (Hebbel).

HEERMANS, FORBES. ...Down the black cañon; or, The silent witness. A drama of the Rocky Mountains in four acts... Chicago: Dramatic Pub. Company, cop. 1890. 40 p. 12°. (Sergel's acting drama. no. 357.)   NBL p.v.2, no.9
A melodrama of the Vigilante period, in a mining region in Colorado. Solomon Goldstein, sheriff of San Juan county.
In the Theatre Collection is a programme recording a production of it at Social Hall, St. George, Utah, Sept. 14, 1895, with Wm. A. Nelson as the sheriff.

HEIJERMANS, HERMAN. Ahasverus [in one act]. Translated from the Dutch by Caroline Heijermans-Houwink and Dr. J. J. Houwink. (Drama. Mount Morris, Ill., 1929. 4°. v. 19, p. 145–147.)   NAFA
Portrait on p. 135.

—— Ahasverus; a play in one act... Boston: Walter H. Baker Company [cop. 1934]. 18 p. 16°. (Baker's all star series.)

—— The wandering Jew; a powerful play of Jewish life in Russia. Translated by Gerson Rubinovitz. (Jewish comment. Baltimore, 1908. 4°. v. 26, p. 289–291, 305–307.)   * PBD
Ahasverus and *The Wandering Jew* are the same play. It is a dramatization of an incident dealing with the expulsion of a Jewish family from the interior of Russia in the nineties of the last century. First published pseudonymously in 1893 by Ivan Jelakowitsch, In continental translations it is known as *A Russian sabbath eve*. In 1894, it was produced at the Théâtre Libre, Paris.

Freed, Clarence I. A knock at the door; adapted from [Ahasverus] a play by Herman Heijermans. (American Hebrew. New York, 1922. f°. v. 110, p. 578, 616–617, 620–621.)   * PBD
This version was produced in English, by the Y. M. H. A. Players of New York, March 31, 1918; H. Eckstein as Mendel Rubinoff, the old father.

HEIJERMANS, HERMAN. The ghetto; a drama, in four acts. Freely adapted from the Dutch... by Chester Bailey Fernald. London: William Heinemann, 1899. 4 p.l., 144 p. 12°.   NHM
One of the earliest serious problem plays about intermarriage, the action of which is placed in the Jewish quarter of Amsterdam, 1817. Titheradge played the old Orthodox blind father Sachel; Kyrle Bellew, the son Rafael determined upon marrying the Christian domestic in his father's house; Constance Collier, Esther sister of Rafael; and Beveridge, rabbi Haezer of the community. Produced at the Comedy Theatre, London, Sept. 9, 1899. Reviewed (with illus.) in *Illustrated sporting and dramatic news*, London, 1899, v. 52, p. 88–89, * DA; by Max Beerbohm in *Saturday review*, London, v. 88, p. 356–357, * DA; *The Times*, London, Sept. 11, 1899, p. 6, col. 4, * A; *To-day*, London, v. 24, p. 212, * DA; and in *Truth*, London, v. 46, p. 636, * DA. The last reviewer stated: "This play is a triumph of ennui. Tedium dwells in every part of it." A synopsis is given by C. F. Fernald, translator, in *Jewish chronicle*, London, Sept. 1, 1899, p. 19, * PBE, which is reprinted in *Jewish comment*, Baltimore, v. 9, Sept. 15, 1899, p. 1–2, * PBD. See also letter by G. J. Webber, in *Jewish chronicle*, London, Feb. 17, 1928, p. 30, * PBE.
Produced at the Broadway Theatre, New York, Sept. 15, 1899, with Sidney Herbert as Sachel, Joseph Hawarth as Rafael, Mrs. McKee Rankin as Esther, Miss Bijou Fernandez as Rebecca, the girl who had been chosen for Rafael by his father, and George Heath as rabbi Haezer. Reviewed in *American Hebrew*, New York, 1899, v. 65, p. 609–610, * PBD; by J. S. Metcalfe in *Life*, New York, v. 34, p. 252–253, * DA; and in *New York dramatic mirror*, New York, v. 42, Sept. 23, 1899, p. 16, * DA. For illus. see *Illustrated sporting and dramatic news*, London, v. 52, p. 683, * DA. See also A. J. Barnouw in *Theatre arts monthly*, New York, 1925, v. 9, p. 109–112, NBLA.

HEILPERIN, FALK. Parents [in one act]. (Reflex. New York, 1928. 8°. v. 3, Dec., 1928, p. 56–62.)   * PBD
A scene of home life.
This is a translation from the Yiddish which appeared in his *Erzehlungen*, Wilna, 1911, p. 153–167, * PTP.

HELPS, SIR ARTHUR. Oulita, the serf; a tragedy. London: John W. Parker, 1858. 3 p.l., (1) 4–190 p. 12°.   NCR

—— London: Strahan & Co., 1873. 3 p.l., 207 p. 2. ed. 24°.
"A slight Jewish element is introduced in Sir Arthur Helps' tragedy, *Oulita*, the scene of which is laid in Russia." — *Mabon, p. 428.*

HENRY, MRS. RE (HENRY). Past, present, and future. (Jewish chronicle. London, 1889. f°. June 28, 1889, p. 12.)   * PBE
Spoken by three pupils of the Stepney Jewish School, June 20, 1889, at the annual graduation ceremonies.

HERBACH, JOSEPH. The rehearsal; a drama in one act. Philadelphia: J. H. Greenstone, 1911. 1 p.l., v, 7–62 p., front. 12°.
Deals with the subject of intermarriage and propounds definite advice.

HERBERT, JOSEPH N. See sub-entry under DU MAURIER, GEORGE LOUIS PALMELLA BUSSON.

HERON, MATILDA. See sub-entry under SEJOUR, VICTOR.

HERZL, THEODOR. ...Das neue Ghetto. Schauspiel in 4 Acten. Wien: Verlag der "Welt," 1903. 2 p.l., 100 p. [2. ed.] 8°.   * PSQ
Reviewed in *Jewish chronicle*, London, Jan. 7, 1898, p. 11, * PBE.
This Zionist play was written by the founder of the Zionist movement in 1894, and produced at the Carl-Theater, Vienna, Jan. 5, 1898. The action takes place in Vienna in 1893, and part of the plot is said to be based on a true incident. It appeared first, with illustrations, in *Die Welt*, Wien, Jahrg. 2, March 4, 1898, p. 13–16, and subsequent issues. Its appeal in a later production of it in England is greatly discounted by the absence of the European continental brand of anti-Semitism in Anglo-Saxon countries.

Landa, Myer Jack. New ghetto, an English adaptation by M. J. Landa, was produced by the Jewish Drama League at the Pavillion Theatre, London, June 23, 1919.
Reviewed in *Illustrated London news*, London, 1919, v. 155, p. 30, * DA; and in *Jewish chronicle*, London, June 27, 1919, p. 27, * PBE (reprinted in *Jewish exponent*, Philadelphia, v. 69, July 18, 1919, p. 2, * PBD).

HEWSON, J. JAMES. See sub-entry under HATTON, JOSEPH.

Individual Plays — 1838-1914, continued

HEYDEMANN, LILLIAN P. The American idea; a sketch in one act. By Lily Carthew [pseud.]. Boston: W. H. Baker Co., 1918. 14 p. 16°. (Baker's acting plays.)
Mignon Goldman turns down Solly Rosenbaum, her would-be suitor, and chooses John Kelly, formerly Yankele Opechinsky. "That's the American idea." Produced at the Peabody Playhouse, May 7, 1918.

HICHENS, ROBERT SMYTHE. Bella donna, a novel... Philadelphia: J. B. Lippincott Company, 1909. 537 p. 8°. NCW

Fagan, James Bernard. Bella donna; a play in five acts, dramatized from the novel of Robert Hichens by J. B. Fagan, was first produced at the St. James' Theatre, London, Dec. 9, 1911, with Sir George Alexander as Meyer Isaacson, a famous physician.
Reviewed in *Academy*, London, 1911, v. 81, p. 798-799, * *DA*; by E. B. McCormick in *English illustrated magazine*, London, new series, v. 46, p. 414-415, * *DA*; by S. O. in *English review*, London, v. 10, p. 354-356, * *DA*; (with illus.) in *Graphic*, London, v. 84, p. 948, * *DA*; by John Palmer in *Saturday review*, London, v. 112, p. 760-761, * *DA*; and in *The Times*, London, Dec. 11, 1911, p. 6, col. 1, * *A. The Times* reviewer says, "Why is the physician made a Jew? Nothing comes of it save the passing remark that when in the East he feels quite at home." Illustrations are to be seen in *Illustrated sporting and dramatic news*, London, v. 77, p. 468, * *DA*; and in *Play pictorial*, London, v. 20, no. 119, p. i-x, 25-44, † *NCOA*.
Produced at the Empire Theatre, New York, Nov. 11, 1912, with Charles Bryant as Meyer Isaacson. Reviewed (with illus.) by Arthur Ruhl in *Collier's*, New York, v. 50, Dec. 7, 1912, p. 24, 26, * *DA*; *Dramatist*, Easton, Pa., v. 4, p. 324-325, *NAFA*; *New York dramatic mirror*, v. 68, Nov. 20, 1912, p. 6, * *T-* *DA*; and in *Theatre magazine*, New York, v. 16, Dec., 1912, p. xx, † *NBLA*. Illustrations are given in *Harper's weekly*, New York, v. 56, Nov. 23, 1912, p. 18, * *DA*.

Blathwayt, Raymond. Bella donna; the authors, the play and the players. [London: St. James's Theatre.] 15 p. 8°.

—— *See also* sub-entry for Hichens under MIRBEAU, OCTAVE.

HILAND, FRANK E. Who caught the count; a farce in one act... Boston: Walter H. Baker & Co., 1899. 13 p. 12°. (Baker's edition of plays.)
Solomon Rosebaum, "a Jewish peddler."

HILL, ROLAND. Christopher Columbus; an historic drama in four acts. London: S. Low, Marston & Company, Ld., 1913. 2 p.l., (1) 4-55 p., 2 pl. (incl. front.) 8°. NCR
Luis de St. Angel and Roderigo Sanchez, the latter a Marano Jew who accompanied Columbus on his first voyage, are among the characters. See below Raymond, G. L., *Columbus the discoverer*.

HIRSCHBEIN, PEREZ. Elijah the prophet. [A comedy in one act.] Translated by Elias Lieberman. (East and West. New York, 1915. 4°. v. 1, p. 261-266.) * PBD
Elijah in the rôle of a stranger and guest at a Sabbath meal in the home of a poor country Jew.

—— The haunted inn; a drama in four acts, by Peretz Hirshbein, authorized translation from the Yiddish by Isaac Goldberg. Boston: J. W. Luce & Company [cop. 1921]. 1 p.l., v-ix, 163 p. 12°. * PTP
A folk play of the Russian Jewish Pale. Written in 1911, it was first printed in Wilna, 1914, and in the author's *Gesammelte Dramen*, New York, 1916. It was first staged at Liporski's Wilna Yiddish Theatre, with Rudolph Zaslavski as Itzig.

Wolheim, Louis, and I. Goldberg. The idle inn; a folk tale in three acts. Adapted for the English stage and produced at the Plymouth Theatre, New York, Dec. 20, 1921.
Ben-Ami, in his first appearance on the English stage, played Itsik; Wolheim, Bendet; and Eva MacDonald, the latter's daughter Meta. These are the main characters. It found no favor on Broadway. Reviewed in *American Hebrew*, New York, 1922, v. 110, p. 228, * *PBD*; by Ernest Boyd, in *Freeman*, New York, v. 4, p. 446-447, * *DA*; and by Arthur Hornblow in *Theatre magazine*, New York, v. 35, p. 165, † *NBLA*. See also *Collection of newspaper clippings of dramatic criticism, 1921-1922*, vol. E-L, † *NBL*.

HIRSCHBEIN, PEREZ. In the dark. Translated by Jacob Robbins. (East and West. New York, 1915. 4°. v. 1, p. 131-135.) * PBD

—— In the dark; a dramatic study in one act. (In: Isaac Goldberg, translator, Six plays of the Yiddish theatre. Boston [1916]. 12°. p. 179-210.) * PTP
Reprinted in Leo W. Schwarz, editor, *A golden treasury of Jewish literature*, New York [cop. 1937], p. 504-513, * *PSY*.
A scene from the life of the Jewish poor. "Poverty, abject, brutalizing, vivid to the point of revulsion, yet haunting in its quality."

—— Lone worlds! (In: Etta Block, translator, One-act plays from the Yiddish; second series. New York, 1929. 12°. p. 27-44.) * PTP
"The tragedy of persecution and fear and their effect on the human mind."

HIRSCHFELD, GEORG. The mothers, translated and with an introduction by Ludwig Lewisohn. Garden City, New York: Doubleday, Page & Company, 1916. xix, 122 p., 1 l. 12°. (The Drama League series of plays. v. 18.) NGE
Mrs. Printz, "Skalitzer Street, Berlin," is made to speak her lines in dialect German. This is also made evident in the translation.

HOBART, GEORGE VERE, AND EDNA FERBER. See sub-entry under FERBER, EDNA.

HODGES, HORACE, AND T. W. PERCYVAL. Grumpy; a play in four acts. New York: S. French; London: S. French, Ltd., cop. 1921. 1 p.l., 5-90 p., 1 l. illus. (plans). 12°. (French's standard library ed.) NCO p.v.481
Also issued as no. 2601 of French's acting edition. Produced at the Theatre Royal, Glasgow, Sept. 19, 1913, and at the New Theatre, London, May 13, 1914. Reviewed in *Era*, London, v. 77, May 20, 1914, p. 12, † *NAFA*; and in *Illustrated sporting and dramatic news*, London, 1914, v. 81, p. 487, * *DA*.
Produced at Wallack's Theatre, New York, Nov. 24, 1913, with Lenox Pawle as Isaac Wolfe, a small but well characterized rôle. Reviewed in *New York dramatic mirror*, v. 70, Nov. 26, 1913, p. 10, * *T-* *DA*; and in *Theatre*, New York, 1914, v. 19, p. 48, † *NBLA*.

HOGGAN-ARMADALE, E. *See* sub-entry under ERCKMANN, ÉMILE, AND ALEXANDRE CHATRIAN.

Individual Plays — 1838-1914, continued

HORNE, RICHARD HENRY. Laura Dibalzo; or, The patriot martyrs. A tragedy [in five acts] ... London: Newman & Co., 1880. vii(i), 98 p. 12°. NCR
Michael Skurdenka, a Polish Jew, martyr for Italian political freedom.
Reviewed in *The Athenæum*, London, 1880, v. 75, p. 450, * *DA*.

HORNIMAN, ROY. *See* sub-entry under LOCKE, WILLIAM JOHN.

HOWE, JULIA (WARD). The world's own... Boston: Ticknor and Fields, 1857. 141 p. 12°. NBM
Reprinted as *Leonora; or, The world's own*, in A. H. Quinn, editor, *Representative American plays*, New York, 1917, p. 385–427, * *R–NBL*.
The story is laid in northern Italy, in the early part of the eighteenth century. Jacob, a Jew, is involved with a gipsy in a kidnapping plot. "The Jew and the gipsy are alike unnecessary to the plot" and it is difficult to see any reason why the play was named as printed.
As *Leonora*, it was produced at Wallack's Theatre, New York, March 16, 1857. It ran for several weeks and was later seen in Boston. Reviewed in *Spirit of the times*, New York, 1857, new series, v. 2, p. 48, and again, ibid., p. 64, † *MVA*. See also Laura E. Richards and Maud H. Elliott, in their *Julia Ward Howe, 1819–1910*, Boston and New York, 1925, p. 70–71, *AN;* and A. H. Quinn, *A History of the American drama from the beginning to the Civil War*, New York, 1923, p. 365, * *R–NBL*.

HUBBARD, ELBERT. ...Ferdinand Lassalle & Helene von Donniges [in six acts]. East Aurora, N. Y.: The Roycrafters, 1906. 2 p.l., 97–131 p. 12°. (Little journeys to the homes of great lovers. Little journeys, Oct., 1906. v. 19, no. 4.) 8–AB

—— (In his: Little journeys to the homes of great lovers. Book two. Miriam edition. East Aurora, 1913. sq. 8°. p. 121–161.)
* KP (Roycroft)
Deals with the love affair of Lassalle and Helena von Rakowitza, 1862–1864. Among the characters, besides Lassalle, 1825–1864, is Karl Marx, 1818–1883. The Jewish origin of both is referred to throughout.

HUGHES, RUPERT. Excuse me; a farce-comedy in three acts... New York, N. Y., Los Angeles, Calif.: S. French, Inc.; London: S. French, Ltd. [etc.], cop. 1934. 132 p. plates, diagrs. 12°. (French's standard library edition.) NBL p.v.327
Characterized on the programme as "a Pullman carnival in three sections." Produced at the Gaiety Theatre, New York, Feb. 13, 1911, with Frank Manning as Max Baumann, "a flashy and impertinent Jewish individual." Reviewed in *New York dramatic mirror*, v. 65, Feb. 15, 1911, p. 7, * *T–* *DA;* and in *Theatre*, New York, v. 13, March, 1911, p. x, *NBLA*.

HUGO, VICTOR MARIE, COMTE. Torquemada. Part II. (In his: Dramas. Boston and New York [18—?]. 12°. v. 1, p. 351–424.) NKP
Included also in his *Works* (International limited edition), Boston [191–?], v. 12, *NKF;* and in his *Dramas*, published by P. F. Collier [188–?], p. 211–294 (translated by F. L. Slous and Mrs. Newton Crosland).
In three acts.
The original French edition was reviewed in *The Athenæum*, London, 1882, v. 79, p. 723–725, * *DA;* by Isidore Loeb in *Revue des études juives*, Paris,

1881, v. 4, p. 304–306, * *PBF;* and by Goetzel Selikovitsch in תמגיד, Lyck, 1882, v. 26, p. 202, * *PBA*.
Extracts from act II are given in G. A. Kohut, *A Hebrew anthology*, Cincinnati, 1913, v. 2, p. 1331–1349, * *PSO*.

—— Torquemada. A drama... Expounded and portions translated by Leo Haefeli. (Western galaxy. Salt Lake City, 1888. 8°. v. 1, p. 418–421.) ZZMA
Bound in: Tullidge's quarterly magazine, v. 3, 1884–85.
The translation was to be continued, but the periodical ceased publication with the following number, June, 1888.
Moses ben Habib, grand rabbi, at the head of a delegation of Jews, and Torquemada, Grand Inquisitor, in their pleas against, and for, the expulsion of the Jews from Spain, just before the year 1492. Moses b. Shem-Tob Ibn Habib, Hebrew poet and philosopher, flourished in the 15th–16th century (see *Jewish encyclopedia*, VI:125–126), but he had nothing to do with the events preceding the expulsion from Spain.

A HUNDRED years hence. (Princeton tiger. Princeton, N. J., 1913. 4°. v. 23, Jan., 1913, p. 10–11.) STG
Zabo Cohen, Polish Negro, keeper of the Royal Seals, and Neuralgia Cohen, his femme.
"A take-off on the Triangle show" of 1912.

HURD, ST. CLAIR. Counsel for the plaintiff; a comedy in two acts... Boston: Walter H. Baker & Co. [cop. 1891.] 27 p. 12°. (Baker's edition of plays.)
Mr. Solomon Nathan, "Hebrew banker."

HURWITZ, ISRAEL. The thief [in one act]. Adapted from the Yiddish of Z. Libin [pseud.]. (Jewish comment. Baltimore; 1911. f°. v. 36, Oct. 13, 1911, p. 16–17.) * PBD
The tribulations besetting the leadership of the trade-union movement among Jewish immigrant workers.

IMAGINARY conversation. (Punch. London, 1859. 4°. v. 37, p. 213.) * DX
Reprinted in *Albion*, New York, 1859, v. 37, p. 593, * *A*.
Mr. Gladstone and Mr. Disraeli in conversation in Hyde Park.

INVESTIGATE; an acting charade, in five scenes. (Jewish exponent. Philadelphia, 1906. f°. v. 42, April 13, 1906, p. 5.) †* PBD
One scene for each syllable of the word, and one for the whole word, — inn-vest-i-gate. Scene II has a Jewish (?) tailor in it.

JAKEY and old Jacob. (In: Werner's readings and recitations. New York, 1891. 12°. no. 27, p. 140–143.) NACG – W. R.
Boy, misunderstanding his Sunday School teacher's story of the patriarch Jacob's matrimonial experiences and his telling it to his mother, causes commotion at home, until the teacher comes and explains all.

JAY, HARRIET. ...Złoty wiek rycerstwa; komedya w trzech aktach przez C. Marlowe'a [pseud.]. Przekład z angielskiego. Lwow: B. Poloniecki [19—?]. 89 p. 12°. (Teatr dla wszystkich. nr. 20.) * QPK p.v.45
A country house gathering of today is shown transformed into a similar party of the ancestors in 1196. In the middle act the Jew and his daughter become Isaac and Rebecca of York. In the original English, which was very successful on the boards in England and the United States, the play was known as *When knights were bold*, but was never printed. The same forces were at work then as agitate the world to-day.

Individual Plays — 1838-1914, continued

It was first staged at the Royal Theatre, Nottingham, Eng., Sept. 17, 1906, and at Wyndham's Theatre, London, Jan. 29, 1907, with Arthur Grenville as Isaac Isaacson and Daisy Cordell as his daughter, Sarah. Reviewed in *Graphic*, London, 1907, v. 75, p. 175, * *DA;* (with illus.) in *Illustrated sporting and dramatic news*, London, 1907, v. 66, p. 1035, * *DA; The Queen*, London, 1907, v. 121, p. 259, * *DA;* (with illus.) in *Sphere*, London, 1907, v. 28, p. 120, 171, * *DA;* and in *Truth*, London, 1907, v. 61, p. 323–324, * *DA*. A synopsis of the text, with numerous illustrations, is given in *Play pictorial*, London, 1907, v. 9, p. 253–280, † *NCO*.
It was first seen in this country at the Criterion Theatre, New York, Aug. 20, 1907. George Irving and Margaret Gordon played the Jewish parts. Reviewed in *New York dramatic mirror*, v. 58, Aug. 31, 1907, p. 3, * *T–* DA;* and in *Theatre magazine*, New York, v. 7, Oct., 1907, p. xvii, † *NBLA*.

JEROME, JEROME KLAPKA. The passing of the third floor back; an idle fancy. [London, 1908?] [104] f. 8°.
Various paginations.
Reproduced from typewritten copy.
Ian Forbes-Robertson's copy, typed red and black, with his signature on t.-p. Many ms. notes and corrections, additions and excisions in the text. Inserted are lists of "props," sheet of music of Song in act III, programme of Sept. 1, 1908 production, and other notes.

—— The passing of the third floor back; an idle fancy in a prologue, a play and an epilogue ... London: Hurst & Blackett, Ltd., 1910. 212 p. front., plates. 12°. NCR

—— —— New York: Dodd, Mead and Company, 1921. 197 p. 8°.

—— —— New York: Samuel French [cop. 1921]. 197 p. 12°. (French's standard library edition.)
A synopsis in prose, suitable for a dramatic reading, is included in *Werner's readings and recitations*, New York, 1915, no. 56, p. 30–39.
The play, taken from the author's short story of the same name, is a morality. It turns upon a series of conversions. The conversion is effected by an appeal to the better-self of a group of boarders in a Bloomsbury flat, third floor back. It is written for the simple, the sentimental, and the optimistic. Critics usually compared it with C. R. Kennedy's *The Servant in the house*. The Jewish character is a rogue in the *Prologue*; in the *Play* he is Mr. Jake Samuels of the City, and in the *Epilogue* he is a Jew and proud of being so.
First shown at the Opera House, Harrogate, England, Aug. 13, 1908, and brought to the St. James' Theatre, London, Sept. 1, 1908, with Edward Sass as Jake Samuels. Reviewed in *Illustrated sporting and dramatic news*, London, 1907, v. 70, p. 5 (illus. on p. 1, 15), * *DA;* and in *The Queen*, London, v. 124, p. 487–488, * *DA*.
Produced at Maxine Elliott's Theatre, New York, Oct. 4, 1909, with A. G. Poulton as Jake Samuels. Reviewed in *American Hebrew*, New York, v. 85, p. 610, * *PBD;* (with illus.) in *American magazine*, New York, v. 69, p. 412–414, * *DA;* by George Jean Nathan (with illus.) in *Burr McIntosh monthly*, New York, v. 22, p. 54–56, † *MFA;* in *Collier's weekly*, New York, v. 44, Oct. 30, 1909, p. 24, * *DA; Everybody's magazine*, New York, v. 22, p. 121–127, * *DA;* by Clayton Hamilton in *Forum*, New York, v. 42, p. 440–441, * *DA;* by Channing Pollock in *Green book album*, Chicago, v. 2, p. 1265–1267, *NAFA;* (with illus.) in *Hampton's magazine*, New York, v. 23, p. 819–820, * *DA;* by William Winter (with illus.) in *Harper's weekly*, New York, v. 54, April 16, 1910, p. 24, 30, * *DA;* (with illus.) in *Independent*, New York, v. 67, p. 1121–1123, * *DA;* by Harriet Quimby in *Leslie's weekly*, New York, v. 109, p. 390, * *DA;* by J. S. Metcalfe in *Life*, New York, v. 54, p. 516–517, * *DA; Literary digest*, New York, v. 39, p. 629,
* *DA; The Nation*, New York, v. 89, p. 335, * *DA; New York dramatic mirror*, v. 62, Oct. 16, 1909, p. 5, * *DA;* by Adolph Klauber in *Pearson's magazine*, New York, v. 22, p. 797–800, * *DA;* (with illus.) in *Theatre magazine*, New York, v. 10, p. 133–134, † *NBLA;* and by Henry Frank in *Twentieth century magazine*, Boston, v. 4, p. 30–32, * *DA*. More illustrations can be seen in *Harper's weekly*, New York, v. 53, Oct. 30, 1909, p. 24, * *DA; Metropolitan magazine*, New York, v. 31, p. 682–683, * *DA;* and in *Play pictorial*, London, v. 12, no. 73, p. 81–104, † *NCO*.

—— Der Fremde. (The passing of the third floor back.) Eine Legende von heute in einem Prolog, einem Spiel und einem Epilog... Deutsch von Wilhelm Wolters... Leipzig: Philipp Reclam, Jun., n.d. 96 p. 24°. (Universal Bibliothek. No. 5392.)

—— ...Le locataire du troisième sur la cour (une rêverie). Pièce en trois actes, traduite et adaptée par Mme Andrée Méry... [Paris: L'Illustration,] cop. 1933. 26 p., 1 l. f°. (La Petite illustration...no. 637, 12 août 1933. Théâtre [nouv. sér.] no. 330.) † NKM
In this French translation it was produced at the Théâtre de la Comédie, Geneva, in April, 1928, and at the Théâtre des Arts, Paris, May 9, 1933, with Jean Hort as Samuels.

Odgers, J. C. Some expressions of opinions and a sermon on "The passing of the third floor back." n. p. [1910.] 8 p. 8°. NCO p.v.339
Title from cover.

JERROLD, DOUGLAS WILLIAM. The prisoners of war; a comedy, in two acts... London: T. H. Lacy [185–?]. 49 p., 1 pl. nar. 12°. (Lacy's acting edition of plays. v. 27.) NCO (Lacy)
Printed also in G. H. Lewes, editor, *Selections from the modern British dramatists*, Leipzig, 1867, v. 2, p. 83–126, *NCO (Lewes)*.
The action takes place in 1805, during the Napoleonic wars with England. It was first produced at the Drury Lane, London, Feb. 8, 1842. M. Barnett played the part of Boaz, a Jewish money lender to the English prisoners of war at Verdun. He is made to speak in dialect. See Landa, p. 156–157. Reviewed in *The Athenæum*, London, 1842, v. 15, p. 159, * *DA; Literary gazette*, London, 1842, p. 116, * *DA;* and in *The Times*, London, Feb. 9, 1842, p. 6, col. 6, * *A*.
Both Brown and Odell record a production of this play at the Park Theatre, New York, April 18, 1842, but Odell calls it *Prisoner at war*. It was again staged at the Broadway Theatre, New York, Oct. 16, 1847, with George Chapman as Boas.

JESSOP, GEORGE HENRY. Samuel of Posen [a comedy-drama in four acts. Chicago, 188–?]. 1, 45 f. 4°.
Typewritten.
The first New York production as *Samuel of Posen; or, The commercial drummer*, took place at Haverly's Fourteenth Street Theatre, May 16, 1881, with M. B. Curtis in the title rôle and R. O. Charles as uncle Goldstein, the pawnbroker. For miscellaneous information about the play and its principals see *MWEZ n.c.676*, p. 52–55.
In England it was seen for one afternoon, at the Gaiety Theatre, London, July 4, 1895, with Mary Jocelyn as Rebecca. Reviewed in *The Athenæum*, London, 1895, v. 106, p. 76, * *DA;* by A. B. (with illus.) in *Sketch*, London, 1895, v. 10, p. 564–565, * *DA;* and in *Theatre*, London, 1895, new series, v. 26, p. 110–111, * *T–* DA*. In the Library's Theatre Collection are 11 clippings in folder *Samuel of Posen*. See also comment in J. K. Hosmer, *The Jews; ancient, mediaeval and modern*, New York, 1908, p. 368, * *PXE*.
The success of this play was so great that it was seen in many revivals under different titles. M. B. Curtis and E. Marble changed it to *Spot cash; or,*

Individual Plays — 1838-1914, continued

JESSOP, GEORGE HENRY, continued

Samuel of Posen on the road. As such it was first staged in Chicago, at McVicker's Theatre, in the early part of Sept., 1884. See *New York dramatic mirror,* v. 12, Sept. 13, 1884, p. 4, col. 3, * *T-* *DA*. It was brought to New York at the Fifth Avenue Theatre, Feb. 16, 1885, with M. B. Curtis again as "the one, only, same Samuel of Posen," and Josie Wilmere as his daughter, Rebecca. William J. Shaw renamed it *Caught in a corner,* and produced it at the Fourteenth Street Theatre, New York, Nov. 1, 1886, where Curtis "took the audience by storm in his Jew garb...and moved the risibilities of the audience at will." See *New York dramatic mirror,* v. 16, Nov. 6, 1886, p. 2, * *T-* *DA*. The playing troupe barnstormed with it throughout the country, and on Oct. 10, 1887, brought it to the Alcazar Theatre, San Francisco. See *MWEZ n.c.708,* p. 63. A synopsis of the play is given in *American theatre,* period 1880, v. 1, p. 399–402, † *NBL*.

Between 1881 and 1887, when its popularity began to wane, it was adapted and burlesqued many times, under the following titles: *Our Hebrew friends,* by G. H. Jessop; *The Drummer, The Drummer from Posen, Der Innocent Drummer; Isidore, Samuel of Posen's brother; Samuel Posen as the drummer on the road,* by M. B. Curtis or M. B. Curtis and Edward Marble; *Samuel of Pilsen,* by ·Lester Franklin; and as *The Greenhorn from Breslau,* by Herbert H. Winslow. "The voice of the people declares it a portrait faithful to the life." — *Hosmer, p. 368.*

JOHNSON, OWEN. See sub-entry under DONNAY, MAURICE CHARLES.

JOHNSTONE, J. B. See sub-entry under DICKENS, CHARLES.

JONES, GEORGE. Tecumseh and the prophet of the West, an original historical Israel-Indian tragedy, in five acts; (with historical notes; original letters, &c). (In his: Tecumseh and the prophet of the West... Life and history of General Harrison [etc.]. London [1844]. 8°. p. 1–113, prefaced by 20 p. of introductory matter.)   NDH
The Library has a second copy in *HBC.*
Scene: Indiana and the Canadian border. The dramatis personae are divided into two classes: Anglo-Americans and Israel-Indians, the author being a proponent of the theory that the aborigines of the Western Hemisphere are descended from the ten lost tribes of Israel. See his *The History of ancient America — the identity of the aborigines with the people of Tyrus and Israel,* London, 1843, *HBC.*

JONES, HENRY ARTHUR. Judah; an original play in three acts. New York and London: Macmillan and Co., 1894. xxiii, 104 p. 12°.   NCR
Preface, signed: Joseph Knight, p. vii–xxiii.

—— —— (The second edition)... New York, London: Samuel French, cop. 1894. 117 p. 8°.   NCO p.v.637
On cover: The plays of Henry Arthur Jones.
Reprinted, with a critical introduction by Clayton Hamilton, in his *Representative plays,* Boston, 1925, v. 1, p. xliv-xlvi, 197–278, *NCR*; and in H. F. Rubinstein, editor, *Great English plays,* New York, 1928 (another edition, London, 1928), p. 1061–1101, *NCO (Rubinstein).*
Judah Llewellyn, a minister, son of a Welsh father and Jewish mother, the product thus of Celt and Jew. The action is laid in Wales at the present time. First produced at the Shaftesbury Theatre, London, May 21, 1890, with Willard as the Reverend Judah. Reviewed by Frederick Wedmore in *Academy,* London, 1890, v. 37, p. 396–397, * *DA; The Athenæum,* London, v. 95, p. 683, * *DA; Illustrated sporting and dramatic news,* London, v. 33, p. 358, * *DA;* and in *Saturday review,* London, v. 69, p. 640, * *DA*. A revival was staged at the Avenue Theatre, London, Jan. 30, 1892, with E. H. Vanderfelt as Judah, which was reviewed in *Theatre,* London, 1892, series 4, v. 19, p. 152–153, *NCOA.*
Produced, for the first time in America, at Palmer's Theatre, New York, Dec. 29, 1890, with E. S. Willard as Judah. The last performance was on Feb. 3, 1891. Reviewed in *New York dramatic mirror,* v. 25, Jan. 3, 1891, p. 2, * *T-* *DA.*
The author's ms. of the play was, in 1930, bequeathed to Columbia University, New York.

Winter, William. Edward S. Willard in The Middleman and Judah. (In his: Shadows of the stage. New York, 1893. 16°. p. 322–338.)   NADB

JOSEPH and his brethren. The Hebrew son; or, The child of Babylon. In three acts. [New York, 1860.] 3 pamphlets. f°.   † NCOF
Prompter's ms. copy, with the parts of the different characters on loose sheets. On the t.-p. appears the name of E. F. Taylor, where ordinarily the author's name is given. Brown gives the name of one E. A. Taylor as the stage manager of Barnum's Museum, New York, in the sixties of the last century. Since this play was produced at that theatre on Sept. 10, 1860, the two initials are probably those of the same person.
This piece is described as "a moral and religious spectacle highly adapted to the needs of the famous [Barnum's] 'lecture' room." Some of the characters are Imrod, king of Babylon; Izaack, an old Jewish mountaineer of Arrarat; Joseph, his son; and his seven brothers. The scene takes place in Babylon (?). See Odell, VII:336.

KAAPLANDER, M. H. ...The convert; a play in four acts. Wilmington, Del.: The author, 1913. 55 p., 1 l. front. (port.) 8°.
"This playlet belongs to the class of dramas whose object it is to instruct rather than to amuse. Each of the four acts aims to teach a lesson of its own, though all four aim at a unity." — *Preface.* The author, a rabbi, sets forth three evils in the first three acts; indifference towards the synagogue, narrow views regarding the instruction of Hebrew, and the card-playing habit which, he says, has become entirely too prominent in Jewish life in America.

KAMPF, LEOPOLD. ...On the eve; drama in three acts... New York: International Library Publishing Co., 1907. 2 p.l., 7–100 p., 3 l. 12°.   NGB p.v.169
At head of title: International library.
Port. of author on cover.

—— —— New York: Wilshire Book Co., 1907. 106 p. 16°.   NGB p.v.90
The theme deals with the Russian revolutionary movement during the first decade of the twentieth century. Tantal is the Jewish member in the revolutionary group. The action of the play takes place in a large Russian town.
Reviewed in *New York dramatic mirror,* v. 57, March 16, 1907, p. 16, * *T-* *DA.*
Adapted for the stage by Martha Morton, and produced at the Hudson Theatre, New York, Oct. 4, 1909, with J. Adelman as Tantul Vlasdor. Reviewed by Clayton Hamilton in *Forum,* New York, 1909, v. 42, p. 439–440, * *DA;* by Channing Pollock in *Green book album,* Chicago, 1909, v. 2, p. 1270, *NAFA*; (with illus.) in *Hampton's magazine,* New York, 1909, v. 23, p. 818–820, * *DA; New York dramatic mirror,* v. 62, Oct. 16, 1909, p. 5, * *T-* *DA;* and (with illus.) in *Theatre magazine,* New York, v. 10, Nov., 1909, p. xii, 135, *NBLA.*
Produced at the Gaiety Theatre, Manchester, Eng., Feb. 7, 1910, with Stanley Drewitt as Tantal.

Individual Plays — 1838-1914, continued

KAUFFMAN, REGINALD WRIGHT. The house of bondage. New York: Moffat, Yard and Company, 1910. 5 p.l., 466 p. 12°.

TOTTEN, JOSEPH BYRON. The house of bondage, a play in four acts, founded on a novel of the same name by R. W. Kauffman, was produced at the Cecil Spooner Theatre, New York, Dec. 8, 1913.
A white slave drama. Agnes Kelly played the rôle of Carrie Berkowicz, one of the inmates of the house of prostitution. Reviewed in *New York dramatic mirror,* v. 70, Dec. 17, 1913, p. 6, * *T-* DA*. For staging this unexpurgated version of the novel the producers and the principals of the cast were arrested by the police. After the court proceedings, the play was somewhat modified and was so seen on Broadway, New York, at the Longacre Theatre, Jan. 19, 1914, with Garia Marvelac in the part of Carrie. Reviewed in *New York dramatic mirror,* New York, v. 71, Jan. 21, 1914, p. 7, * *T-* DA*.

KELLEY, JESSIE A. The pedlers' parade; an entertainment in one act... Boston: Walter H. Baker Company [cop. 1903]. 26 p. music. 12°. (Baker's novelty plays.)
Salesmen of various nationalities are introduced through the medium of songs and recitations. The Jew is one of them; he sells suspenders and collar buttons.

KENNEDY, H. C. *See* sub-entry under CAMPBELL, BARTLEY T.

KITCHEL, MARY EVA. A literary reception [in one scene]. (Normal instructor. Dansville, N. Y., 1913. f°. v. 22, April, 1913, p. 34.) † SSA
The characters are from literature; among them Shylock and the Wandering Jew.

KLEIN, CHARLES. Maggie Pepper. New York: The H. K. Fly Company [cop. 1911]. 317 p. front., plates. 12°.
Copy: Library of Congress.

—— —— New York: S. French [etc.], cop. 1916. 106 p. illus. (plans.) 8°. (French's standard library edition.) NBM
Produced at the Harris Theatre, New York, Aug. 31, 1911. The part of Jake Rothschild, played by Lee Kohlmar, although intended to assist the plot, is merely that of a Jewish comedian. Reviewed in *Green book album,* Chicago, 1911, v. 5, p. 998, *NAFA*; and (with illus.) in *New York dramatic mirror,* v. 66, Sept. 6, 1911, p. 10, and Oct. 11, p. 4, * *T-* DA*.
On April 10, 1922, at the Vanderbilt Theatre, New York, it was turned by Oliver Morosco and George V. Hobart into a two-act musical comedy, entitled *Letty Pepper,* with Paul Burns as Abe Greenbaum. See *Collection of newspaper clippings of dramatic criticism, 1921-1922,* vol. E-L, † *NBL*.

—— The third degree, a narrative of metropolitan life, by Charles Klein and Arthur Hornblow... Illustrations by Clarence Rowe. New York: G. W. Dillingham Company [cop. 1909]. 356 p., front., 5 pl. 8°.
Copy: Library of Congress.

—— The third degree; a play in four acts... New York: Samuel French [cop. 1908]. 117 p. diagrs. 12°. (French's standard library edition.) NBL p.v.131
The third degree as practised by the American police. Produced at the Hudson Theatre, New York, Feb. 1, 1909, with George Barnum as Dr. Bernstein, the police physician. Reviewed in *New York dramatic mirror,* New York, v. 61, Feb. 13, 1909, p. 3, * *DA*. A synopsis of the play, with extracts from the text, is given in *Theatre magazine,* New York, v. 9, March, 1909, p. 96–99, † *NBLA*.
Under the title *Find the woman,* it was staged at the Garrick Theatre, London, June 17, 1912, with Kenyon Musgrave as Dr. Bernstein.

KLEIN, JOE. ... Hard luck Cohen; an up-to-date Hebrew monolog... New York [etc.]: M. Witmark & Sons, cop. 1907. 6 l. 12°.
At head of title: The Witmark edition of up-to-date monologs, etc.
On cover: The Witmark stage publications.

KNOBLOCK, EDWARD. "The faun"... Audacious pean of paganism. illus. (Current literature. New York, 1911. 4°. v. 50, p. 302–310.) *DA
A synopsis with copious extracts from the text of the play.
"*The Faun* comes to preach pantheism and natural laws." It was first produced at Daly Theatre, New York, Jan. 16, 1911, with Lionel Belmore in the rôle of a conventional Jewish money lender, ambitious to enter English high society. Reviewed in *New York dramatic mirror,* v. 65, Jan. 18, 1911, p. 10, * *T-* DA*; and in *Theatre magazine,* New York, v. 13, March, 1911, p. 74, vii, † *NBLA*.
Produced at the Prince of Wales's Theatre, London, June 10, 1913, with Charles Glenney as Maurice Morris. Reviewed in *Academy,* London, 1913, v. 84, p. 759–760, * *DA*; (with illus.) in *Graphic,* London, v. 87, p. 1016, * *DA*; (with illus.) in *Illustrated London news,* London, v. 142, p. 938, * *DA*; by John Palmer in *Saturday review,* London, v. 115, p. 738–739, * *DA*; and in *The Times,* London, June 11, 1913, p. 10, * *A*, where Morris is characterized as "a rather crude caricature of a Jew money-lender."

KNOWLES, JAMES SHERIDAN. The maid of Mariendorpt; a play in five acts... London: Edward Moxon, 1838. 4 p.l., 111(1) p. 8°. NCOF
Prompter's copy, with interleaved ms. notes.
Reviewed in *Court magazine,* London, 1838, part 2, p. 520–522, * *DA*.

—— —— Correctly printed from the most approved copy... As now performed at the principal theatres. Philadelphia, New York: Turner & Fisher [1838?]. 72 p. 24°. NCOF
At head of title: Turner's dramatic library.
Prompter's copy, with interleaved ms. notes.

—— —— Boston: James Fisher; Philadelphia, New York: Turner & Fisher. 24° bd. as 8°. NCOF
Prompter's copy, with interleaved ms. notes.
Also issued as Turner's dramatic library of plays, new series, v. 7, no. 47.

—— —— Correctly printed from the acting copy... As performed at the Theatre Royal, Haymarket, London. Baltimore: Jos. Robinson [1838?]. 60 p. 24°. NCO p.v.296
At head of title: Robinson's edition.
Library also has a prompter's copy with interleaved ms. notes, t.-p. missing, *NCOF*.
Reprinted in his *Dramatic works,* London, 1843, v. 3, p. 1–75, * *KZ* (31372–31403); London and New York, 1856 (other editions, 1859 and 1864), v. 2, p. 113–168, *NCR*.
There is a very "noble" Jew (Joseph) with all the cardinal virtues concerned in the plot and his Jewish steward by the name of Ahab. *The Times* reviewer called the part of Joseph "not striking, being but another version of Cumberland's Sheva." It is based on Anna M. Porter's novel *Village of Mariendorpt,* and the time is during the Thirty Years' war, in Germany. Produced at the Haymarket Theatre, London, Oct. 9, 1838, with Webster as Joseph and Gough as Ahab.

Individual Plays — 1838-1914, continued

KNOWLES, JAMES SHERIDAN, *continued*
Reviewed in *The Athenæum*, London, 1838, v. 11, p. 747-748, * *DA; Examiner*, London, 1838, p. 646, * *DA; Literary gazette*, London, 1838, p. 653, * *DA; New Yorker*, New York, v. 6, p. 200, * *DA* (reprinted from *Monthly chronicle*); *Spectator*, London, 1838, v. 11, p. 968-969, * *DA;* and in *The Times*, London, Oct. 10, 1838, p. 5, col. 2, * *A.* Cf. Landa, p. 179-181.
The first American performance was seen at the Park Theatre, New York, Dec. 28, 1838, with Richings as Joseph. Ireland says that it "was but moderately successful."

KRAFT, IRMA. Borderlands; an Alsatian love drama in one act and a series of tableaux. (Review. Philadelphia, 1914. 12°. v. 10, Nov., 1914, p. 7-37.)
Copy: Library of Jewish Theological Seminary of America.
Sept. 29, 1872, at Metz, Alsace-Lorraine. How German and French patriotism interfered between a German Jewish girl and her French fiancé, and how German harshness and Biblical love precedents enabled the French youth to win out. This prize playlet was announced for production by the Adath Jeshurun Assembly, at Mercantile Hall, Philadelphia, Feb. 1, 1915.

KREMER, THEODOR. *See* sub-entry under WHITE, GRACE (MILLER).

LANDA, MYER JACK. *See* sub-entry under HERZL, THEODOR.

LANGDON, WILLIAM CHAUNCY. The chapel masque of Christmas... Grace Chapel, New York City. [New York: Clover Press,] 1913. 16 p. 8°. NBL p.v.63
Grace Chapel is situated at Fourth Avenue and 10th Street, New York City. Towards the end of the masque, a Jew from the Chapel neighborhood enters and a conversation develops between him and the Chapel.

THE LARKS, PSEUD. The Shakespeare watercure, suggested and adapted from Place aux dames, and pirated from many authors living and dead, by The Larks [revised by Alice Crawford]. New York: Roorbach & Company, 1883. 40 p. 12°. ([The acting drama. no. 186.])

—— The Shakespeare water-cure; a burlesque comedy, in three acts... New York: H. Roorbach [cop. 1897]. 42 p. 12°. * NDD p.v.1, no.11
Another edition was published by the Fitzgerald Pub. Corp., cop. 1897.
Among the characters is Shylock, "crafty and greedy." "Shylock, wishing to possess Portia's gold, bribes Lady Macbeth to incite her husband to the murder of Bassanio, so that he may marry the fair heiress." — *From the Argument to the play.*

LA TOUCHE, HUGH N. D., AND O. SAVINI. The eagle; a comedy in four acts... Morland, Amersham: [T. Hutton,] 1914. 64 p. 8°.
NCO p.v.298
Samuel Swakan, a dunning creditor, is taken away by aeroplane to Mars. He is left there by Golpin, the aviator, but somehow manages to return.

LAVEDAN, HENRI LÉON ÉMILE. The Prince d'Aurec; a comedy in three acts. Translated by Barrett H. Clark. (In: Three modern plays from the French. New York, 1914. 12°. p. 51-129.) NKM
Baron de Horn, the Jew in the play, is treated "conventionally, as animated by ordinary human sentiments. Being, however, a millionaire, with a desire to break into high society, he squanders vast sums without overcoming the prejudice of exclusiveness." — Landa, p. 267.
It was first produced at the Théâtre de Vaudeville, Paris, June 1, 1892.

Norman, Hilda Laura. The sons of Turcaret. (In her: Swindlers and rogues in French drama. Chicago, 1928. 8°. p. 211-232.) NKL

LAZARUS, EMMA. The dance to death; a historical tragedy in five acts. (In her: Songs of a Semite. New York, 1882. 8°. p. 1-48.) * PSP
Repr.: *American Hebrew*, New York, 1882, v. 11, p. 83-84, 108-109, 120-121, 132-133, 144-145, 156-157; v. 12, p. 8, 20-21, * *PBD.*
Reprinted in her *Poems*, Boston, 1895, v. 2, p. 69-173, *NBI.*
"This is considered her finest work. The background is historical and the plot and incident have been taken from 'Der Tanz der Tode', a night-piece of the fourteenth century." The scene is laid in Nordhausen, Germany, May 4, 5, and 6, 1349. It is dedicated "in profound veneration and respect to the memory of George Eliot... who did most among the artists of our day towards elevating and ennobling the spirit of Jewish nationality."

Cohen, Rachel. Emma Lazarus [an appreciation]. (Jewish chronicle. London, June, 1927. f°. supplement no. 78, p. i-iii.) * PBE
Reprinted in *Reform advocate*, Chicago, 1927, v. 74, p. 184-189, * *PBD.*

Levi, Harry. "The dance to death," Emma Lazarus. (In his: Jewish characters in fiction. English literature. Philadelphia [cop. 1903]. 12°. p. 90-96.) * PZB
Revised and enlarged in a second edition, 1911, p. 99-108, * *PZB.*

LEAVITT, EZEKIEL. Ghetto silhouettes; a comedy in one act. (Jewish voice. St. Louis, 1908. f°. v. 44, Jan. 31, 1908, p. 6.) * PBD
A take-off on some of the contemporary contributors to the *Jewish Daily News*, the oldest Yiddish daily in America. Goetzel Selikovitch (1863-1926) is Getzel Ludlow-jail-sky; Hillel Malachovsky is Hilke Lemechovsky; Ezekiel Sarasohn is Chaim Sonsora; Morris Rosenfeld (1862-1923) is Moe Rose; and Moses Seiffert (1854-1922) is Max Zeif.

—— The "pleasures" of the Czar; a tragicomedy in one act. (Hebrew standard. New York, 1907. f°. v. 50, Feb. 8, 1907, p. 1-2.)
* PBD
Reprinted in his *The "Pleasures" of the Czar, etc.,* Washington, D. C. [1910], p. 10-17, * *PSY p.v.1.*
Nachman Heller translated it in a shortened form, from a Yiddish version by the author, in *Jewish American,* Detroit, v. 13, Jan. 25, 1907, p. 5, 8, * *PBD.*
"The Czar [late Nicholas II] is in misery. He wants happiness from 'pogroms.'"

—— "Professor" Getzel; a comedy in two acts. (In his: The "pleasures" of the Czar... Washington [1910]. 12°. p. 18-29.) * PSY p.v.1
An amplification of his *Ghetto silhouettes.* Gedaliah Bublick figures as Bub; Alexander Harkavy as Alex Rakovy; Jacob Fishman as Fish; I. J. Zevin, 1872-1926, as Tash; and Leon Kamaiky as Kom.

—— Stomachs and hearts; a comedy in one act. (Hebrew standard. New York, 1907. f°. v. 50, March 1, 1907, p. 9.) * PBD
Reprinted, under the title *Hearts and stomachs,* in his *The "Pleasures" of the Czar, etc.,* Washington, D. C. [1910], p. 30-33, * *PSY p.v.1.*

LECKIE, MRS. The Hebrew boy; a dramatic poem. Edinburgh, 1842. 8°.
Copy: British Museum.

Individual Plays — 1838-1914, continued

LEONARD, OSCAR. *See* sub-entry under ROMAN, RONETTI.

LEVEY, SIVORI. ...Mahmud, the Sultan, adapted by Sivori Levey from Shelley's "Hellas." Roehampton [London]: Fountain Pub. Co. [1919?] 11 p. 8°. (The Pilgrimage plays. no. 5.)
In one act. NCO p.v.460
"Mahmud, the Sultan, depressed at the news from all sides of defeat and disaster, summons a Jewish interpreter of dreams [Ahasuerus in the play] to reveal the future." From the Argument, p. 3. The play was presented in 1910 at the Royalty Theatre.

LEVIN, LOUIS HIRAM. Breadth and culture. [In one scene.] By Amiel [pseud.]. (Jewish comment. Baltimore, 1908. f°. v. 28, p. 119-120.)
About mixed marriages. *PBD

—— Clean. [In one scene.] By Amiel [pseud.]. (Jewish comment. Baltimore, 1909. f°. v. 28, p. 247-248.) *PBD
About the ritually-permitted meat question.

—— Desertion. [In two scenes.] By Amiel [pseud.]. (Jewish comment. Baltimore, 1909. f°. v. 28, p. 231-232.) *PBD
Children who desert their parents, in order to lead what they call their own lives.

—— Jewish missionaries. [In one scene.] By Amiel [pseud.]. (Jewish comment. Baltimore, 1908. f°. v. 28, p. 135-136.) *PBD
Reform rabbis and their vagaries.

—— The melting pot. [In one scene.] By Amiel [pseud.]. (Jewish comment. Baltimore, 1908. f°. v. 28, p. 103-104.) *PBD
Three "Bohemian" artists and America.

—— Not needed. [In one scene.] By Amiel [pseud.]. (Jewish comment. Baltimore, 1909. f°. v. 28, p. 215-216.) *PBD
A broker and a clothier at the club decide upon what is not needed.

—— The only language. [In one scene.] By Amiel [pseud.]. (Jewish comment. Baltimore, 1908. f°. v. 28, p. 199-200.) *PBD
Is it to be Hebrew or Yiddish?

—— Saving Judaism. [In one scene.] By Amiel [pseud.]. (Jewish comment. Baltimore, 1908. f°. v. 28, p. 151-152.) *PBD
The bewildered Orthodox rabbi and his American environment.

—— The two reforms. [In one scene.] By Amiel [pseud.]. (Jewish comment. Baltimore, 1908. f°. v. 28, p. 171-172.) *PBD
These sketches deal satirically with phases of Jewish life in this country.

LEVINGER, ELMA C. (EHRLICH). "False jewels" (an Arabian story retold in one scene). Jewish child. New York, 1914. f°. v. 2, May 8, 1914, p. 2-4.) *PBD

—— God's fool; a play in one act. (Review. Philadelphia, 1914. 12°. v. 10, Dec., 1914, p. 39-40.)
Copy: Library of the Jewish Theological Seminary of America.
"God has been making fools of us all these years, and still we trust Him."

—— The sad jester; a story for discontented folks [in one scene]. By E. C. Ehrlich. Music by Jennie Perlstein. music. (Ark. Cincinnati, 1913. f°. v. 3, p. 583-588.) *PBD

LEWIS, LEOPOLD DAVID. *See* sub-entry under ERCKMANN, ÉMILE, AND ALEXANDRE CHATRIAN.

THE LIFE and death of Jack Sheppard. *See* sub-entry under AINSWORTH, WILLIAM HARRISON.

LINDAU, PAUL. ...Maria and Magdalena. A play, in four acts. Adapted for the American stage from the German original of Paul Lindau, by L. J. Hollenius... New York: R. M. De Witt [1874]. 44 p. 12°. (De Witt's acting plays. no. 154.) NGB p.v.209
One of the characters is a Balthasar Schelmann, owner and editor of the Prompter's Box, who succeeds in extorting money from the actress Maria. He is described as "over-dressed; expensive jewelry...gray hair, hooked nose."

LIPSKY, LOUIS. In the forest; a drama in one act. illus. (American Hebrew. New York, 1908. 4°. v. 84, p. 3-7.) *PBD
Reprinted in *Maccabaean*, New York, 1908, v. 15, p. 193-199, *PBD; American Hebrew, New York, v. 121, p. 128, 130, *PBD; and in his *Selected works*, New York, 1927, v. 3, p. 237-247, *PBT.
A symbolic playlet of old world Jewish life. The characters are a father, mother, son, grandmother, and a stranger.

—— The shofar; a symbolic drama in one act. [New York: Young Judaea,] cop. 1907. 5 l. 4°.
Caption-title.
Mimeographed.
First appeared in *American Hebrew*, New York, 1907, v. 80, p. 685-687, *PBD. Reprinted in *Maccabaean*, New York, v. 12, p. 221-226, *PBD; and in his *Selected works*, New York, 1927, v. 3, p. 227-236, *PBT.
The scene is the interior of a Jewish household in western Russia, in the early years of the century. Deals with the mystic call of the Holy Land through all the ages.

LOCKE, WILLIAM JOHN. Idols... New York & London: John Lane, 1904. 3 p.l., 365 p., 1 l. 3. ed. 8°. (Canvasback library of popular fiction. v. 20.)
First published 1898.

Horniman, Roy. Idols, a drama in four acts, adapted from the novel of that name by W. J. Locke, was produced at the Theatre Royal, Birmingham, Aug. 24, 1908, and at the Garrick Theatre, London, Sept. 2, 1908.
A struggle arising out of antipathy between Jew and Gentile is given here a slight anti-Semitic tinge. The antagonists are Jacob Hart (Alfred Brydone) and the Gentile husband of his daughter Minna (Edyth Latimer). The third Jewish character is Anna Josephs (Mrs. Harry Cane), elderly sister of Hart.
Produced at New Haven, Conn., Oct. 18, 1909, and at the Bijou Theatre, New York, Nov. 1, 1909, with Sheldon Lewis as the father, Leonore Harris as his daughter, and Blanche Weaver as Anna Josephs. Reviewed in *American Hebrew*, New York, 1909, v. 86, p. 16, *PBD; *New York dramatic mirror*, v. 62, Nov. 13, 1909, p. 7, *T-*DA; and in *Nation*, New York, v. 89, p. 442, *DA.

LOEB, OSCAR. Up to the minute. [In one scene.] (Jewish comment. Baltimore, 1910. 4°. v. 31, p. 242-243.) *PBD
Moe Wasserman and James Leveries (originally Levy) discuss their reform rabbi, Dr. Hamilton.

Individual Plays — 1838-1914, continued

LONDON, WALTER. Hebrew monologues. [A monologue.] (Madison's budget. New York, 1903. 4°. no. 9, p. 29-31.) † NBW

LORD, ALICE E. A vision's quest; a drama in five acts, representing the hopes and ambitions, the love, marriage, pleadings, discouragements, and achievements of Christopher Columbus, discoverer of America... Baltimore: Cushing & Company, 1899. 3 p.l., (1)6-123 p., 1 pl. 12°. NBM

Luis de Santangel, a professing Jew as late as July, 1491, farmer of the royal taxes and counsellor to King Ferdinand, and Juan de Cabrera, a Marrano Jew, are among the characters. It was Santangel who lent 17,000 ducats to the Columbus expedition and received Columbus's first detailed report of the voyage and discoveries. Ferdinand thought so highly of him that he granted him, his children and grandchildren, royal exemption from liability to the possible charge of apostasy, the officers of the Inquisition being strictly forbidden to molest them on account of their religious beliefs.

LORD, WILLIAM WILBERFORCE. André; a tragedy in five acts. New York: C. Scribner, 1856. 138 p. 12°.
In verse.

—— —— Tarrytown, N. Y.: Reprinted W. Abbatt, 1932. 3 p.l., (1)8-74 p. 4°. (The Magazine of history, with notes and queries. Extra number. no. 179 [v. 45, no. 3].) IAG

Major David S. Franks is one of the main characters. See A. S. W. Rosenbach, "Documents relative to Major David S. Franks while aid-de-camp to General Arnold," in *American Jewish Historical Society, Publications*, Baltimore, 1897, no. 5, p. 157-189, * PXX. See also M. J. Kohler, ibid., no. 4, p. 84-87, and H. P. Johnston, "Colonel Varick and Arnold's treason" in *Magazine of American history*, New York, 1882, v. 8, p. 717-733, IAA.

LOUNSBERY, GRACE C. See sub-entry under WILDE, OSCAR.

LOYSON, PAUL HYACINTHE. The apostle; a modern tragedy in three acts, with an introduction by Professor George Pierce Baker. Garden City, N. Y.: Doubleday, Page & Company, 1916. xix p., 2 l., 3-120 p., 1 l. 12°. (The Drama League series of plays. v. 15.) NKP
Translated by Barrett H. Clark.
A play by the son of Père Hyacinthe about free thought and religious education. "He who foregoes religion unthinkingly...because he has never known it is likely to mistake his inheritance for license." Meyerheim, "well-known banker," is one of the characters. This drama had its first representation on May 3, 1911, at the Odéon, Paris.
Reviewed in *American review of reviews*, New York, 1916, v. 53, p. 763, * DA; by H. E. Woodbridge in *Dial*, Chicago, 1917, v. 62, p. 68-69, * DA; and in *Drama*, Chicago, 1916, v. 6, p. 469-470, NAFA.
Produced at His Majesty's Theatre, Carlisle, England, Sept. 11, 1913, with Basil Holmes as Meyerheim.

LYONS, MABEL. Chanuka in camp. [In two scenes.] (Helpful thoughts. New York, 1900. 8°. v. 6, p. 134-136.) * PBD
Celebration of Hanukkah in camp, during the Cuban campaign of the Spanish-American war.

MCINTYRE, JOHN T. The Bowery night school; a vaudeville sketch [in one act]. Philadelphia: Penn Pub. Co., 1916. 20 p. 12°. NBL p.v.48
Another edition published in 1923.
A teacher with his pupils of different nationalities. Among them is Issy Letzosky.

MADISON, JAMES. General Breakdown, U. S. A. A new Hebrew monologue. (Madison's budget. New York, 1913. 4°. no. 15, p. 20-21.) † NBW

—— Getting his goat. An act for two Hebrew comedians. (Madison's budget. New York, 1913. 4°. no. 15, p. 39-40.) † NBW

—— Ghetto get-backs between Cohen and Levi. (Madison's budget. New York, 1903. 4°. no. 9, p. 35.) † NBW

—— He would be a cop. An original act for two comedians. (Madison's budget. New York, 1913. 4°. no. 15, p. 32-34.) † NBW
Straight and Hebrew.

—— I'm your friend. A talking act for straight and Hebrew comedian. (Madison's budget. New York, 1913. 4°. no. 15, p. 34-36.) † NBW

—— More tribulations of Cohen & Levi. (Madison's budget. New York, 1903. 4°. no. 9, p. 34.) † NBW

—— Two Hebrew sports; none other than our friends Cohen & Levi. (Madison's budget. New York, 1903. 4°. no. 9, p. 32-33.) † NBW

MALBIM, MEIR LOEB. [Extract from the first act of Mashel uMelitzah, Fable and moral, a Hebrew allegorical play; translated by Israel Abrahams from text which originally appeared in the Hebrew periodical Lebanon, Paris, 1867.] (Jewish chronicle. London, 1892. f°. Sept. 23, 1892, p. 14.) †* PBE

MALONE, WALTER. Inez: a tragedy [in five acts]. (In his: Claribel and other poems. Louisville, Ky., 1882. 12°. p. 7-82.) NBI
Scene: Catalonia, northern Spain. Jacob, a Jew, follower of the reigning Duke Don Roderick of Censola, is the villain of the play. He is represented as a poisoner.

MANNERS, JOHN HARTLEY. The house next door; a comedy in three acts, by J. Hartley Manners, suggested by "Die von Hochsattel," by Lee Walther Stein and Ludwig Heller. Boston: W. H. Baker & Co. [cop. 1912.] vi p., 1 l., 157 p. 12°. NCR
Reviewed in *Dramatist*, Easton, Pa., 1912, v. 3, p. 261-262, NAFA.
A synopsis, copious extracts from the text, and illustrations are given in *Current literature*, New York, v. 49, p. 539-547, * DA. A novelization of the play, by Joseph O'Brien, is printed in *Green book album*, Chicago, v. 2, p. 673-711, NAFA; and by Lucy F. Pierce in *Hearst's magazine*, Chicago, v. 17, p. 1176-1185, * DA.
Cecil, the son of a poor and peppery baronet, Sir John Cotswold, loves Esther, the daughter of Sir Isaac Jacobson, his Jewish next-door neighbor, a man of wealth; but for reasons of racial prejudice, the parents' consent is withheld. In the end Sir John, overcome by the Jew's generosity and nobility of character, swallows his pride and, hat in hand, visits "the house next door" to ask forgiveness. Produced at the Gaiety Theatre, New York, April 12, 1909, with Thomas Findlay as Sir Isaac Jacobson, M. P., Regan Hughston as his son Adrian, and Fania Marinof as his daughter Esther. Reviewed by Louis Lipsky in *American Hebrew*, New York, 1909, v. 84, p. 634 (see also B. G. R., ibid., p. 29, and Jacob G. Asher, ibid., p. 30), * PBD; *New York dramatic mirror*, v. 61, April 24, 1909, p. 3, * T-* DA; and (with illus.) in *Theatre magazine*, New York, v. 9, May, 1909, p. viii-ix, 167, † NBLA.
In the original German, *Die von Hochsattel* was given at the Great Queen Street Theatre, London April 17, 1907.

Individual Plays — 1838–1914, continued

MANNERS, JOHN HARTLEY, *continued*

Calisch, Edward Nathaniel. "The house next door." [A sermon.] (Jewish record. Richmond, Va., 1910. f°. v. 2, March 18, 1910, p. 1–3.)
* PBD
Cf. Albert M. Gunst, "The Views of a layman," ibid., p. 4–5.

MAPU, ABRAHAM. The shepherd prince... A scenario in thirteen episodes with an epilogue, adapted for the screen from the historical romance of the same title. Scenario by B. A. M. Schapiro and A. Armband. New York: B. A. M. Schapiro, cop. 1923. 166 p. 8°. NAFH p.v.17
Cover-title.

THE MARCH on London; a masque [in three scenes]. (Vanity fair. London, 1884. f°. v. 32, p. 265–266.) * DA
Among the characters is "The Caucusite, a salaried Hebrew, retained by the dissenting Christians of Paradise Row."

MARKS, MILTON, AND OTHERS. God is one; an historical pageant of Israel's loyalty [in ten scenes], by Milton Marks, Henry Hart, Martin A. Meyer. New York: Bloch Publishing Company, 1914. 30 p. 12°.
Covers the range of Jewish history from the time of Pharaoh to modern America. Scene 7, in sunny Spain; scenes 9 and 10, America, the land of the free.

MARTEL DE JANVILLE, SIBYLLE GABRIELLE MARIE ANTOINETTE DE RIQUETTI DE MIRABEAU, COMTESSE DE. ...Le Friquet. Paris: E. Flammarion [1901]. 3 p.l., 312 p. 12°. NKV
At head of title: Gyp, author's pseud.
In an English translation of its adaptation by Pierre F. S. Berton, it was produced at the Savoy Theatre, New York, Jan. 31, 1905, with Frank Losee as Jacobson, proprietor of an American circus in a small French town. Jacobson is described "ainsi que [te] l'indiquent son visage et son nom, un abominable youpin." Reviewed in *New York dramatic mirror*, v. 53, Feb. 11, 1905, p. 16, * T-* DA; and (with illus.) in *Theatre magazine*, New York, 1905, v. 5, p. 56–57, † NBLA.

MARY AGNES, SISTER. At the court of Isabella; an historical drama [in three acts]. By S. M. A. Winnipeg, Man.: St. Mary's Academy, cop. 1914. 51 p. 12°.
A play about the discovery of America. Luis de Santangel, receiver of revenues for the Spanish court, is one of the characters.

MATHEWS, CHARLES JAMES. Patter versus Clatter; a farce in one act... London: Samuel French; New York: Samuel French & Son [1876–86?]. 22 p. 12°. (Lacy's acting edition of plays. v. 118.) NCO (Lacy)
Capt. Patter assumes the disguise of Mynheer Pierre Pytter, "a German Jew," to whom his rival, Capt. Clatter is financially indebted, and speaks his line in so-called German-Jewish dialect. This is a personation playlet, where one actor plays all the parts — in the present case it was C. J. Mathews (the author) who acted so, in seven different rôles. It was first produced at the Olympic Theatre, London, May 21, 1838. Reviewed in *The Times*, London, May 22, 1838, p. 6, col. 6, * A.

For portraits of the parts assumed by Mathews in this personation, see his *The life of Charles James Mathews, chiefly autobiographical*, edited by Charles Dickens, London, 1879, v. 2, facing p. 162, AN; and G. C. D. Odell, *Annals of the New York stage*, v. 4, facing p. 272, * R–MWED (New York).
Mathews came to America in the summer of 1838, and appeared in this piece at the Park Theatre, New York, Sept. 24, 1838. See *Knickerbocker*, New York, 1838, v. 12, p. 379–381, * DA. He revived it at the Fifth Avenue Theatre, New York, April 10, 1871.

MAUGHAM, WILLIAM SOMERSET. Lady Frederick; a comedy in three acts. London: W. Heinemann, 1912. viii, 163 p. 12°.
On cover: The plays of W. S. Maugham.

—— —— London: W. Heinemann [1914]. vii(i), 163 p. 16°. NCR
Reprinted in his *Plays*, London [1931], v. 1, p. 1–89, NCR.
Captain Montgomerie, second-generation usurer, and blackmailer besides. His father was Aaron Levitzki, an immigrant. "My father married an English woman, and I have all the English virtues." — Act II. First produced at the Court Theatre, London, Oct. 26, 1907, with A. Holmes-Gore as Captain Montgomerie. Reviewed in *Queen*, London, 1907, v. 122, p. 841, * DA; and in *The Times*, London, Oct. 28, 1907, p. 12, col. 2–3, * A.
Produced at Poughkeepsie, N. Y., Sept. 15, 1908 and at the Hudson Theatre, New York, Nov. 9, 1908, with Orlando Daly as Capt. Montgomerie. Reviewed in *New York dramatic mirror*, v. 60, Nov. 21, 1908, p. 2, * T-* DA.
A novelization of the play by Fred Jackson is printed in *Green book album*, Chicago, 1909, v. 1, p. 929–964, NAFA.
As to the evolution of the name Moses Moses into Montmorency, see verses by I. Zangwill entitled *What's in a name*, in a paper by Frank Jaffe, "Zangwill; some reminiscences," in *Jewish chronicle*, London, 1931, July supplement, p. v–vi, * PBE.

—— —— Smith; a comedy in four acts. Chicago: The Dramatic Publishing Company [1909]. vii(i), 200 p. 12°.
"Printed by Ballantyne & Company, Ltd., London, England."

—— —— London: W. Heinemann, 1913. vii(i), 200 p. 12°. NCR

—— —— London: W. Heinemann [1914]. vii(i), 200 p. 12°.
Reprinted in his *Plays*, London [1931], v. 2, p. 111–212, NCR.
A comedy of manners about a worthless, bridgeplaying set of social butterflies, one of whom is Mrs. Otto Rosenberg. She is represented as married to a German Jew, and after the death of her baby, presumably caused by her neglect, she gives up her cronies and returns to her home-loving husband. First produced at the Comedy Theatre, London, Sept. 30, 1909, with Lydia Bilbrooke as Cynthia, wife of Otto. Reviewed in *The Athenæum*, London, 1909, v. 134, p. 435–436, * DA; *Country life*, London, v. 26, p. 505–506, † MVA; by William Archer in *The Nation*, London, v. 6, p. 48–49, * DA; and in *Truth*, London, v. 66, p. 805–806, * DA. Illustrations are given in *Illustrated sporting and dramatic news*, London, v. 72, p. 331, 353, * DA.
Produced at the Empire Theatre, New York, Sept. 5, 1910, with Jane Laurel as Mrs. Otto Rosenberg. Reviewed in *New York dramatic mirror*, v. 64, Sept. 14, 1910, p. 11, * T-* DA; and (with illus.) in *Theatre magazine*, New York, v. 12, p. 98–99, 107, † NBLA.
A novelization by Lucy F. Pierce is printed (with illus.) in *Hearst's magazine*, New York, 1911, v. 20, p. 184–193, * DA. Another novelization was made by David Gray and published by Duffield & Company, New York, 1911.

Individual Plays — 1838-1914, continued

MAYHEW, HENRY, AND A. S. MAYHEW. Jubilee. A charade in three acts. illus. (In their: Acting charades. London [1850]. sq. 16°. p. 135–140.)
MZB
Reprinted in *Godey's lady book and magazine*, Philadelphia, 1865, v. 70, p. 430–432, * DA.
Act I: Ju- (Jew) is the trial scene of the Merchant of Venice. Among the actors are Shylock and Portia.

—— Passport. A charade in three acts. illus. (In their: Acting charades. London [1850]. sq. 16°. p. 24–28.) MZB
Reprinted in *Godey's lady's book and magazine*, Philadelphia, 1855, v. 50, p. 506–508, * DA.
Act II (-port) has Jews among the dramatis personae.

—— Watchman. A charade in three acts. illus. (In their: Acting charades. London [1850]. sq. 16°. p. 124–128.) MZB
Act I (Watch-). The characters are a sailor and a Jew.

MAYO, MARGARET. Polly at the circus; a comedy-drama in three acts...prepared by Nathaniel Edward Reeid [!]... New York: Longmans, Green and Co., 1933. 4 p.l., 3–98 p. 12°. (Longmans' play series.) NBL p.v.315
"The players' book."
Produced at the Liberty Theatre, New York, Dec. 23, 1907, with Mabel Taliafero in the title rôle. Reviewed in *New York dramatic mirror*, v. 59, Jan. 4, 1908, p. 2, * T-* DA; and in *Theatre magazine*, New York, v. 8, Feb., 1908, p. xi, † NBLA.
One of the circus performers, as given in the cast in the printed text, is a "Jew tramp," acted by Israel Fein. He has no speaking part.

—— *See also* sub-entry under DE LA RAMÉE, LOUISE.

MERCET, S. *See* sub-entry under WILDE, OSCAR.

MEYER, FELIX. Dialogue of the dead. (Australian Hebrew. Sidney, 1896. f°. v. 2, p. 71–72.)
* PBE
The characters are Haman, Torquemada, and Pfefferkorn, on the shores of the Styx. Translated from the French in *L'Univers israélite*, v. 51, partie 2, p. 173–176, * PBF.

MIDDLETON, JESSIE ADELAIDE. Red Sefchen, an incident in the life of Heinrich Heine [in one act]. [Boston, 1907.] 2 p.l., 23 p. 12°. NCM
Bound with her: Love songs and lyrics, Boston, 1907.
Red Sefchen is Josepha, the executioner's red-headed granddaughter, Heine's first love, whose charms he described in his *Memoiren*.

MILLER, MARION MILLS. *See* sub-entry under WILDE, OSCAR.

MILLER, WM. L. Life of Columbus; a dramatization [in 1 act]. (McEvoy magazine. Brooklyn, N.Y., 1913. 8°. v. 5, p. 345–352.) SSA
Luis de Santangel is one of the characters.

MILLS, SAMUEL ALFRED. Judith; or, The wife of Manasseh. A fictional drama. New York: Hamilton Printing Co. [1902.] 112 p. 8°.
See United States. — Copyright Office, *Dramatic compositions copyrighted in the United States, 1870 to 1916*, item 23179.

MINER, CARL S., AND OTHERS. Merchant of Venice by William Shakespeare. [In five acts.] Slightly revised and modernised by Carl S. Miner, James H. Emery, Robert A. Moore, Harry J. Spencer. [Cedar Rapids, Iowa: Record Printing Co., 1896?] 28 p. 5. ed. 12°.
The incidents of Shakespeare's play made to suit the contingencies of a high school football team, in a burlesque manner. Produced by the class of 1896 of the Cedar Rapids, Iowa, High School, May 5, 1896.

—— —— Chicago: Dramatic Pub. Company, 1908. 66 p. 12°. (Sergel's acting drama. no. 593.)

MIRBEAU, OCTAVE. Les affaires sont les affaires; comédie en trois actes. Paris: E. Fasquelle, 1903. 3 p.l., 288 p. 12°. NKP
First produced at the Comédie Française, Paris, April 20, 1903, with M. de Feraudy as Isidore Lechat, and revived in French at the Fulton Theatre, New York, by M. de Feraudy, March 10, 1924. See *Collection of newspaper clippings of dramatic criticism, 1923–1924*, vol. E–H, † NBL. A synopsis of the play was given in *Theatre magazine*, New York, 1903, v. 3, p. 190–191, † NBLA.

Grundy, Sydney. Business is business, a new English version. Produced at His Majesty's Theatre, London, May 13, 1905, with Beerbohm Tree as Izard (Isidore Lechat of the original French).
Reviewed in *Academy*, London, 1905, v. 68, p. 545–546, * DA; *Graphic*, London, v. 71, p. 583, * DA; (with illus.) in *Queen*, London, v. 117, p. 775, * DA; *Review of reviews*, London, v. 32, p. 29–31, * DA; *Sketch*, London, v. 50, p. 174 (illus. on p. 131), * DA; by Reginald Farrer in *Speaker*, London, new series, v. 12, p. 185–186, * DA; and in *Sphere*, London, v. 21, p. 186 (illus. on p. 167), * DA. Additional illustrations are in *Illustrated sporting and dramatic news*, London, v. 63, p. 486, * DA.
The *Academy* reviewer thought it wise on the part of Grundy to have represented Izard as a Jew. Mrs. E. H. Brooke played Mme. Izard; Viola Tree, the daughter Inez; and George Trollope, the son Cyril.

Hichens, Robert Smythe. Business is business, adapted from M. Mirbeau's *Les affaires sont les affaires*, was produced at the Criterion Theatre, New York, Sept. 19, 1904, with William H. Crane as Isidore Lechat.
Lechat is represented as the typical parvenu, relentlessly ambitious of financial power and distinction. Harriet O. Dillenbaugh acted Mme. Lechat; Katherine Grey, the daughter Germaine; and J. Wheelock, Jr., the "waster" of a son Xavier. Reviewed in *New York dramatic mirror*, v. 52, Oct. 1, 1904, p. 16, * DA; and in *Theatre magazine*, v. 4, p. 272–273, † NBLA. See also under the name of the play in Warren C. Cawley Collection of about 100,000 clippings on plays, box Bit-By, MWE.

Mr. Benjamin Disraeli and Viscount Palmerston [a dialogue]. (Punch's imaginary conversations.) (Punch. London, 1857. 4°. v. 33, p. 237–238.) * DX
Reprinted in *Albion*, New York, 1858, v. 36, p. 5, * A.

MITCHELL, A. *See* sub-entry under DE LA RAMÉE, LOUISE.

MITCHELL, LANGDON ELWYN. *See* sub-entry under MOSENTHAL, SALOMON HERMANN, RITTER VON.

THE JEW IN ENGLISH DRAMA 93

Individual Plays — 1838–1914, continued

MOLNÁR, FERENC. The guardsman; a comedy in three acts, by Franz Molnar, translation by Grace I. Colbron and Hans Bartsch, acting version by Philip Moeller, foreword by Theresa Helburn. The Theater Guild version, with three illustrations from photographs of the Theater Guild production. New York: Boni and Liveright [cop. 1924]. xv p., 3 l., 23–189 p. front., plates. 12°. NWF
Reprinted in his *Plays*, with an introduction by L. Rittenberg, New York [1929], p. 144–182, *NWF*.
The original Hungarian was staged at Budapest, Nov. 19, 1910. The Theatre Guild version was produced at the Garrick Theatre, New York, Oct. 13, 1924, with Philip Loeb as the creditor (called Rosenzweig in the English text). Reviewed by G. J. Nathan in *American mercury*, New York, 1924, v. 3, p. 501–502, * *DA;* by J. W. Krutch in *Nation*, New York, v. 119, p. 501–502, * *DA;* and in *Town and country*, New York, v. 81, Nov. 1, 1924, p. 46, * *DA.* See also *Collection of newspaper clippings of dramatic criticism, 1924–1925*, v. F–L, † *NBL.*
Produced at the St. James's Theatre, London, June 20, 1925, with Willie Warde as the creditor. Reviewed in *Era*, London, v. 88, June 27, 1925, p. 1, † *NAFA;* *Illustrated London news*, v. 166, p. 1316, * *DA;* by Ashley Dukes in *Illustrated sporting and dramatic news*, London, v. 107, p. 856, * *DA;* by J. T. Grein in *The Sketch*, London, v. 131, p. 664, * *DA;* and in *Truth*, London, v. 98, p. 20, * *DA.*
Playing with fire, an adaptation of the author's *A testőr*, was produced at the Comedy Theatre, London, April 29, 1911. Reviewed in *Illustrated London news*, London, 1911, v. 138, p. 666, * *DA;* and in *Truth*, London, v. 69, p. 1141, * *DA.*
Where ignorance is bliss, a translation of the author's *A testőr* by Philip Littell, was produced by Harrison G. Fiske, at the Lyceum Theatre, New York, Sept. 3, 1913, with Kevitt Manton as the bill collector. Reviewed in *New York dramatic mirror*, v. 70, Sept. 10, 1913, p. 6, * *T–* DA;* and (with illus.) in *Theatre magazine*, New York, 1913, v. 18, p. 115, † *NBLA.*

—— Liliom; a legend in seven scenes and a prologue, by Franz Molnar; English text and introduction by Benjamin F. Glazer. New York: Boni and Liveright [cop. 1921]. 2 p.l., vii–xiv p., 2 l., 185 p. 12°.
Reprinted in his *Plays*, with an introduction by L. Rittenberg, New York [1929], p. 94–143, *NWF;* in S. M. Tucker, editor, *Modern continental plays*, New York, 1929, p. 563–601, *NAFH;* in T. H. Dickinson, editor, *Chief contemporary dramatists; third series*, Boston [1930], p. 527–568, *NAFH;* in M. J. Moses, editor, *Dramas of modernism and their forerunners*, Boston, 1931, p. 327–369, *NAFH;* in S. M. Tucker, editor, *Twenty-five modern plays*, New York [cop. 1931], p. 593–631, *NAFH;* in G. H. Leverton, editor, *Plays for the college theater*, New York, 1932, p. 481–511, *NAFH;* and in *Theatre Guild anthology*, New York [cop. 1936], p. 111–172, *NAFH.*
Numerous extracts, with a running synopsis, are given in *Best plays of 1920–21*, Boston [cop. 1921], p. 162–195, *NAFH.*
Produced by the Theatre Guild, at the Garrick Theatre, New York, April 20, 1921, with Henry Travers as Wolf Berkowitz (the Wolf Beifeld in the printed text), W. Bowman as Linzman, the hold-up victim, and Edgar Stehli as Dr. Reich, the richly dressed man in the scene in the Beyond. For reviews see *Collection of newspaper clippings of dramatic criticism, 1920–1921*, v. G–L, † *NBL.*

Shillingford, Osmond, and A. E. Ellis. The daisy; a legend of the roundabouts, founded on the original of Molnar, was produced at the Kingsway Theatre, London, Sept. 14, 1920.
Reviewed in *Era*, London, v. 84, Sept. 22, 1920, p. 12, † *NAFA.*
A new version by the same adaptors, under the title of *Liliom*, was produced at the King's Theatre, Southsea, Nov. 29, 1926, and at the Duke of York's Theatre, London, Dec. 23, 1926, with W. Kendall as Wolf, and D. Burbidge as Linz. See J. E. Agate, *The Contemporary theatre, 1926*, London, 1927, p. 83–87, *NAFA.*

Stragnell, Gregory. A psychopathological study of Franz Molnar's Liliom. (Psychoanalytic review. New York, 1922. 4°. v. 9, p. 40–49.) YEA

MONTEFIORE, CLAUDE JOSEPH GOLDMID. Concerning forms, a [dramatic] dialogue. (Jewish chronicle. London, 1890. f°. Nov. 7, 1890, p. 16–17.) * PBE
The speakers are Charles Moss arguing for Reformed, and Jacob Emmett for Orthodox, Judaism.

MONTGOMERY, JAMES. "Ready money"; a comedy in three acts. Rev., 1920... New York: S. French [etc.], cop. 1920. 113 p. 12°. (French's standard library edition.) NBL p.v.114
A play about criminals. Produced at Maxine Elliott's Theatre, New York, Aug. 19, 1912, with Leo Donnelly as Sidney Rosenbaum, of "the Equality Insurance Co." In the printed text his name is given as Rosenthal. Reviewed in *Dramatist*, Easton, Pa., v. 4, p. 286–287, *NAFA;* and in *New York dramatic mirror*, v. 68, Aug. 21, 1912, p. 10, * *T–* DA.* A synopsis is given in *Green book album*, Chicago, v. 8, p. 899–900, and a novelization of the play by Marie L. Gannon, ibid., p. 1086–1104, *NAFA.*
See also D. H. Wallace, "Writing a successful play," James Montgomery reveals the secret of his craft," in *New York dramatic mirror*, v. 68, Oct. 2, 1912, p. 3, 10, * *T–* DA.*
Produced at the New Theatre, London, Aug. 12, 1912, with A. E. Benedict as Sydney Rosenthal. Reviewed by Egan Mew in *Academy*, London, 1912, v. 83, p. 213–214, * *DA;* *The Athenæum*, London, 1912, v. 140, p. 172, * *DA;* with illus. in *Illustrated sporting and dramatic news*, London, v. 77, p. 1184, 1234, 1245, * *DA;* and in *The Queen*, London, v. 132, p. 363, * *DA.*
"Oh, look!" a musical comedy in two acts, with lyrics by Joseph McCarthy, suggested by the author's *Ready money*, was staged at the Vanderbilt Theatre, New York, March 7, 1918. George Sidney played Sidney Rosenthal; Alfred Kappeler, Sam Welch. For reviews see *Collection of newspaper clippings of dramatic criticism, 1917–1918*, vol. H–O, † *NBL.*

MOORE, BERNARD FRANCIS. Belle the typewriter girl; or, The vampires of Chicago. A play in five acts... Boston: Walter H. Baker & Co., 1908. 44 p. 12°.
Contains a Jewish comic part.

MOORE, FRANK FRANKFORT. The discoverer; a drama in five acts. (In his: The discoverer and In the queen's room. London, 1910. 12°. p. 5–145.) NCR
The discoverer is Columbus. Luis de Torres and Rodrigo Sanchez figure as sailors on the first voyage on the *Santa Maria*.

MOORE, REGINALD. *See* sub-entry under MOSENTHAL, SALOMON HERMANN, RITTER VON.

MOOS, H. M. Mortara; or, The Pope and his inquisitors. A drama [in five acts]. Together with choice poems. Cincinnati: Bloch & Co., 1860. 171 p. 16°. NBM
Based on the notable case of the forcible abduction of the Jewish child Edgar Mortara, in Bologna, on June 23, 1858, by the papal guards of the Holy Office.
Choice poems, p. 147–171.
Noticed in *Jewish chronicle*, London, June 1, 1860, p. 2, * *PBE.*

MORDAUNT, JOHN. *See* sub-entry under DICKENS, CHARLES.

Individual Plays — 1838-1914, continued

MORRIS, EDWIN B. The arctic architects; a farce in two acts... Philadelphia: Penn Pub. Co., 1915. 34 p. 12°. NBL p.v.47, no.16
Olmstein and Weissenpimpfle, two "Hebrew architects," discover the North Pole; have it stolen from them, but recover it and turn it into profit. The directions give the make-up for the two architects to fit either a German or a Jewish character.

MORTON, VICTORIA. The yellow ticket, from the play of the same name by Michael Morton... New York: Grosset & Dunlap [cop. 1914]. 2 p.l., 313 p. illus. (front.) 8°.
Extracts from the text of the play are given in *Hearst's magazine*, New York, 1914, v. 25, p. 424–435, * DA.
A play, the scene of which is in the capital of czaristic Russia. Produced at the Eltinge Theatre, New York, Jan. 20, 1914, with Florence Reed as Marya Varenka, the Jewish girl with the yellow passport. Reviewed in *Dramatist*, Easton, Pa., 1915, v. 6, p. 536–538, *NAFA*; *New York dramatic mirror*, v. 71, Jan. 28, 1914, p. 6, * *T-* *DA*; and (with illus.) in *Theatre magazine*, New York, 1914, v. 19, p. 64, 94–95, 112–113, 129, 251, *NBLA*.
Produced in London, at the Playhouse, Sept. 12, 1917, with Gladys Cooper as Marya Varenka. Reviewed in *Era*, London, v. 81, Sept. 19, 1917, p. 1, † *NAFA*; *Illustrated London news*, 1917, v. 151, p. 346, * *DA*; and in *The Times*, London, Sept. 13, 1917, p. 9, col. 5, * *A*. Illustrations are given in *Graphic*, London, 1917, v. 105, p. 432, * *DA*.

MOSENTHAL, SALOMON HERMANN, RITTER VON. Deborah... As performed by Fanny Janauschek and her company of German artists. New York: Academy of Music [1867?]. 37 p. 8°. NGB p.v.178
t. p. missing.
On cover: Classic dramas as performed by Fanny Janauschek.
German and English texts in parallel columns.
The author intended the play as an appeal for the religious and civil emancipation of the Jews. The action of the piece is laid in Styria in 1780. "There is a strong Jewish interest throughout the play which, in its way, is an epic of the wandering and persecuted Jew, and the villain of the piece is an apostate, Nathan." *Landa, p. 190*.
The first German production took place at the Hamburger Stadttheater, Jan. 15, 1849. In Berlin it was produced at the Hoftheater in 1850, with Bertha Thomas in the title rôle. Fanny Janauschek played it in Frankfurt-am-Main, and on the German stage in New York City. In Mosenthal's native Vienna it was not seen till June 28, 1864, at the Burgtheater.
It was first seen in New York in the original German at the Olympic Theatre, March 21, 1852, when only one scene was staged, with Caroline Lindemann as Deborah and Herrmann as Ruben. On Feb. 11, 1853, the full play was given, again in German, under the title *Deborah; die edle Jüdin Ungarns*, at the Deutsches National Theater, New York.

—— Deborah. A drama in four acts by S. B. [sic] Mosenthal... The Italian translation by Sig. Gaetano Cerri. New York: Sanford, Harroun & Co., 1866. 45 p. 8°. * PSQ
Italian and English texts.
On the occasion of its production at Her Majesty's Theatre, London, July 4, 1863, with Mme. Ristori in the title rôle, Henry Morley in his *Journal of a London playgoer from 1851 to 1866*, London, 1866, p. 300–308, 316–318, *NCOM*, gives a résumé of the play, places the acting of Mme. Ristori far above that of Kate Bateman in Daly's *Leah*, and concludes: "The charm of the pastoral play has been all trampled out by the hoof of the American adapter [Daly]."
See Daly's version *infra*.

Cheltnam, Charles Smith. Deborah; or, The Jewish maiden's wrong! A drama, in three acts ... London: T. H. Lacy [186–?]. 38 p. nar. 12°. (Lacy's acting edition of plays. v. 63.)
NCO (Lacy)
The Library also has a prompter's copy with ms. notes, *NCOF*.

—— ...Deborah <Leah>; or, The Jewish maiden's wrong. A drama, in three acts... as first performed at the Royal Victoria Theatre, London...on Tuesday, July 12, 1864. New York: R. M. De Witt [186–?]. 33 p. (incl. plans.) 12°. (De Witt's acting plays. no. 58.)
NCO p.v.526
Julia Seaman acted Deborah; Basil Potter, Nathan the apostate; and R. Marchant, Reuben "an emigrant Jew." Reviewed in *Era*, London, v. 26, July 24, 1864, p. 10, † *NAFA*.
A recitation, styled a *Dramatic pathos romance monologue for a woman*, is printed in *Werner's readings and recitations*, New York, 1913, no. 53, p. 101–103, *NACG - W. R.*

Conquest, George Augustus. Deborah; or, The Jewish outcast, a new version of Mosenthal's drama, in four acts, was produced at the Grecian Theatre, London, Feb. 15, 1864.
This version is closer to the original than Daly's. Edith Heraud acted Deborah; and J. B. Steele, Nathan the schoolmaster. Reviewed in *Athenæum*, London, 1864, v. 43, p. 271, * *DA*, "Every sentence for religious toleration was loudly applauded"; and in *Era*, London, v. 26, Feb. 21, 1864, p. 10, † *NAFA*.

Courtney, John. Leah and Nathan was produced at the City of London Theatre, London, June 24, 1848.
It had been licensed with the Lord Chamberlain as *Leah the Jewess of Constantine; or, The Arab's sacrifice*.

Daly, Augustin. Leah the forsaken; a play in five acts... Arranged from the "Deborah" of Mosenthal, expressly for Miss Bateman... [New York:] Printed for the author, 1863. 33 l., 16 p. 8°.
Text of play on recto of each leaf.
16 p., at end, Memoir of Miss Bateman.

—— —— London: S. French [1872?]. 44 p. 12°. (French's acting edition.) NCO p.v.686
The Library also has a prompter's copy, with interleaved notes, *NCOF*.

—— —— New York, London: S. French [1895–1910?]. 44 p. 12°. (French's standard drama, the acting edition. no. 398.) NBL p.v.110
Scene 3 of act IV is reprinted in Frank H. Fenno, *The Speaker's favorite*, Philadelphia, 1893, part 2, p. 176–180, *NANV*.
Both Cheltnam and Daly have set back the action of their versions to the early part of the eighteenth century. Daly's version was first staged at the Howard Athenæum, Boston, Dec. 8, 1862, with Kate Bateman as Leah (a rôle in which she established her reputation) and Arthur Stirling as Nathan, known as Carl the schoolmaster. Daly's company brought it to New York, at Niblo's Garden, Jan. 19, 1863, with J. W. Wallack, Jr., as Nathan. Subsequently it was seen in nearly every city and town of the United States.
Reviewed in *Albion*, New York, 1863, v. 41, p. 223, * *A*; *Business mirror*, New York, May 9, 16, 30, 1863, p. 3 of each issue, * *A*; by G. W. Curtis in *Harper's weekly*, New York, 1863, v. 7, p. 146, * *DA*; and in *Spirit of the times*, New York, 1863, new series (3), v. 7, p. 352, † *MVA*. For reviews and playbills of the production in 1862–1865 in London and American cities, see *Daly's Theatre scrapbooks*, v. 1, † *NBL*.

THE JEW IN ENGLISH DRAMA 95

Individual Plays — 1838-1914, continued

MOSENTHAL, S. H., RITTER VON, *continued*

See also J. F. Daly, "History of the productions of *Deborah*," in his *The Life of Augustin Daly*, New York, 1917, p. 47–55, *MWES (Daly)*. G. W. Curtis in his review beheld in this play an appeal for the Negro race and an argument for upholding the hands of Lincoln against the critics of his administration.

By the same Daly company it was produced at the Adelphi Theatre, London, Oct. 1, 1863, where it had an unusually long run. To qualify it for London, it was subjected to further revision. Reviewed in *Athenæum*, London, v. 42, p. 472, * *DA;* *Era*, London, v. 26, Oct. 4, 1863, p. 10, † *NAFA;* and in *The Times*, London, Oct. 2, 1863, p. 7, col. 5–6, * *A*. The last review calls it "a play with a purpose." It was revived at the Lyceum Theatre, London, with Miss Bateman again in her celebrated impersonation of the title part, May 18, 1872, and at the Opera Comique, London, April 27, 1897, with Ethel Rayner as Leah.

A version called *Leah, the Jew's daughter*, was seen at the Bowery Theatre, New York, May 9, 1864.

Leah the forsook, a burlesque, in two acts, was seen at Tripler's Hall, New York, July 13, 1863, with Setchell as Leah, "the shrewish maiden," and Sol. Smith, Jr., as Nathan.

Geller, James Jacob. Leah the forsaken. (In his: Grandfather's follies. New York [cop. 1934]. 8°. p. 28–31.)   MWED

Odell, George C. D. Kate Bateman as Leah: Augustin Daly. port. (In his: Annals of the New York stage. New York, 1931. 4°. v. 7, p. 484–486.)   *R–MWED (New York)

The portrait is that of Kate Bateman in the part.

Daly, Augustin. New Leah; Daly's second adaptation of Mosenthal's play "Deborah," was produced at the Fifth Avenue Theatre, New York, Nov. 22, 1875.

Clara Morris played Esther (the Leah of the first version) and Charles Fisher, Nathan the renegade, here named Miguel or Mizael. Reviewed in *Arcadian*, New York, v. 4, Nov. 27, 1875, p. 4, * *DA;* and in *New York tribune*, Nov. 23, 1875, p. 4, col. 6, * *A*. See also *Daly's Theatre scrapbooks*, v. 6, f. 15–19, † *NBL*.

Hagar, the outcast Jewess, a new version of Deborah, was produced at the Britannia Theatre, London, July 5, 1869.

Adelaide Ross played the part of the Jewish maiden; Reynolds, the schoolmaster named Haman in this version; and C. Pitt, Isaac the blind Jew. Reviewed in *Era*, London, v. 31, July 11, 1869, p. 11, † *NAFA*.

Mitchell, Langdon Elwyn. Deborah; a play in five acts was first performed at the St. James Theatre, London, Feb. 22, 1892.

Revived in Bristol in September, 1893, under the title of *The Slave girl*.

Moore, Reginald. Ruth; a version of Mosenthal's Deborah, was produced at the Princess Theatre, London, July 7, 1868.

All that was Jewish in the original was lost in this version. Motive and spirit were eliminated so that "the performance was little more than a travesty." Kate Saville played Ruth (Deborah) and Brandon Ellis, Nathan. The adapter makes the latter commit suicide. Reviewed in *Athenæum*, London, 1868, v. 52, p. 55–56, * *DA;* and in *Era*, London, v. 30, July 12, 1868, p. 11, † *NAFA*.

Naomie, the Jewish maiden; an adaptation was produced at the Worrell Sisters' Theatre, New York, October 21, 1867. Fanny B. Price played the title part. See Brown, II:384.

Pray, Isaac C. Deborah of Steinmark; a version of Leah. Produced at the Winter Garden, New York, May 30, 1863, with Catherine Selden as Deborah and George Jamieson as Nathan.

See Odell, VII:480. Brown, 1:456, records for the present date a *Deborah* at Tripler Hall.

Price, Edward W. Leah [a poem]. (In his: Leah, Ecce homo, and other poems. London, 1864. 12°. p. 1–149.)

The plot of the poem is adapted from the drama, as produced at the Adelphi Theatre in Daly's version.

Rankin, McKee, and M. Ludovici. The Jewess; or, Leah the forsaken, a new version, was produced at the Shaftesbury Theatre, London, June 27, 1899.

It was staged at the Tremont Street Theatre, Boston, Feb. 18, 1904.

According to one reviewer this dramatization was the work of Rankin and W. P. Carleton. Nance O'Neill played Leah; N. McGregor and/or Arbuckle, the apostate Nathan; and W. P. Carleton, the village priest. Reviewed in *Athenæum*, London, 1899, v. 114, p. 44, * *DA; Jewish chronicle*, London, June 30, 1899, p. 27, * *PBD; Sketch*, London, v. 26, p. 478, * *DA;* and in *The Times*, London, June 29, 1899, p. 4, col. 2, * *A*. The popularity with which the *Deborah* plays were welcomed in the sixties had waned by this time, and *The Times* reviewer commented "Fashion or taste has ruled the *Deborah* and plays like it are out of date."

Routledge, William. Leah, a hearty joke in a cab age; a new and original burlesque. (In his: Mrs. Beflat's blunder. [London, 1869.] 12°. p. 27–76.)

In six scenes.

Produced Jan. 23, 1869, at the Royal Gallery of Illustration, London.

Copy: Harvard College Library.

Description of the principal characters: "Abraham — Leah's father, general and unfair dealer, merchant in anything that pays, advocate of the early worn-out clothing movement. Leah — the injured heroine, fiery, flighty, and fanciful. Nathan — the village school master, passing off as a Gentile, but like a second-hand quid, 'a wandering chew.'"

Toube, Teresa S. Leah the forsaken; costume monologue, pantomime or tableaux [*sic*] for a woman. New York: E. S. Werner, cop. 1901. 16 p., 11 ports. 12°. (The reciter's library. v. 4, no. 11.)

Wood, Frank. Leah the forsook; a burlesque in two acts of Leah the forsaken. Produced at Tripler Hall, New York, July 13, 1863. Dan Sitchell played "the shrewish maiden" and Sol Smith, Nathan.

Slobod, Fay. "Leah the forsaken"; the story of a once popular American play dealing with the persecution of the Jews in Europe. illus. (American Hebrew. New York, 1933. 4°. v. 133, p. 114, 124.)   *PBD

MUMFORD, EDWARD WARLOCH. Bargain day at Bloomstein's; an entertainment in one act. Philadelphia: Penn Pub. Co., 1913. 28 p. 12°.
NBL p.v.32, no.5

Another edition was published in 1924.

Isaac Bloomstein, proprietor of the Palace Dry Goods Emporium, makes peace among his bargain hunters.

Individual Plays — 1838–1914, continued

MURRAY, EUSTACE CLARE GRENVILLE. ...Dizziben-Dizzy; or, The orphan of Bagdad... With five full-page and numerous other illustrations. [By E. C. G. Murray.] London: Weldon & Co., 1878. x, 62 p. 8°. (Weldon's Christmas annual. 5th season.)
A satire on Benjamin Disraeli, largely in dialogue form, fashioned after Byron's *Childe Harold.*

MURRAY, WILLIAM HENRY WOOD. *See* subentry under DICKENS, CHARLES.

MUSKERRY, WILLIAM. *See* sub-entry under DU MAURIER, GEORGE LOUIS PALMELLA BUSSON.

NEWBOUND, EDGAR. *See* sub-entry under SEJOUR, VICTOR.

NEWTON, HARRY LEE. Business is business; a comedy [in one act]. Chicago: T. S. Denison & Co. [cop. 1912.] 16 p. 12°. (Denison's little plays.)
Jacob Lowenstein, New York cloak merchant, and his two employees.

—— Izzy's vacation; a summer episode in two scenes... New York [etc.]: M. Witmark & Sons, cop. 1913. 12 p. 12°. (Harry L. Newton's one-act comedy sketches, monologues and dramatic episodes.)

—— The little red school house; a burlesque sketch on education for a singing quartette [in one act]. Chicago: T. S. Denison & Co. [cop. 1908.] 8 p. 12°. (Denison's vaudeville sketches.)
A German teacher and his three pupils; a nice one, a bad one, and Ikey Goldsilver, the Hebrew boy.

—— A special sale; a vaudeville sketch [in one act]. Chicago: T. S. Denison & Co. [cop. 1905.] 9 p. 12°. (Denison's vaudeville sketches.)
Aronson, pawnbroker, sells his friend, Solomon, a coat.

—— The umbrella mender; a character comedy act. Chicago: T. S. Denison & Co. [cop. 1906.] 8 p. 12°. (Denison's vaudeville sketches.)
Ikey Isaacstein as an umbrella mender, in conversation with "an Irish gentleman."

NEWTON, HARRY LEE, AND A. S. HOFFMAN. All about Goldstein; a Hebrew monologue. Chicago and New York: Dramatic Pub. Company, cop. 1902. 6 p. 12°.

—— Glickman the glazier; a vaudeville sketch [in one act]. Chicago: T. S. Denison & Co. [cop. 1904.] 13 p. 12°. (Denison's vaudeville sketches.)   NBL p.v.291
Jacob Glickman the glazier and Charlotte Russe, an actress.

—— The troubles of Rozinski; a Hebrew monologue. Chicago: T. S. Denison & Co. [cop. 1904.] 10 p. 12°. (Denison's vaudeville sketches.)   NBL p.v.291
Moses Rozinski and his plight as a member of the coatmakers' union.

NOBLES, MILTON. The phœnix; a drama in four acts... Chicago: The Dramatic Publishing Co., 1900. 3 p.l., 139 p. 12°.   NBL p.v.14
On cover: Green room edition of copyrighted plays.
The NYPL copy as well as that of the Library of Congress, 128 p., ends with the third act and is incomplete. The fourth act occupies p. 129–139.
"I may claim...that I was the first to place on the stage the modern young American Jew [Moses Solomons, a broker], a jolly up-to-date man about town, and not a villain." — *Preface.*
Under the title *Jim Bludsoe; or, Bohemians and detectives,* it was first produced at Wood's Museum, Philadelphia, Jan. 30, 1875, with William Davidge, Jr., as Moses Solomons, the broker, and at Wood's Museum, New York, May 19, 1875, with George Ketchum in the same rôle.
Under the title, *The Phoenix,* it was produced at the Théâtre Comique, New York, May 29, 1875.

NORDAU, MAX SIMON. A question of honor; a tragedy of the present day. In four acts, by Max Nordau; translated from the German by Mary J. Safford. Boston and London: J. W. Luce and Company, 1907. 169(1) p. 8°.   *PSQ
Reviewed by Max Heller in *American Israelite,* Cincinnati, v. 50, Jan. 14, 1904, p. 1, *PBD; by Horace Traubel in *Conservator,* Philadelphia, 1907, v. 18, p. 93, *DA; *Jewish comment,* Baltimore, 1907, v. 25, p. 287, *PBD; and by Bernard Shillman in *Jewish world,* London, Dec. 26, 1929, p. 6–7, *PBE.
First published in German in 1898 under the title of *Doktor Kohn.* The scene is laid in a university town in central Germany and the time is given as the present, i.e. 1898, when anti-Semitic agitation was widespread. Politically it is a strong appeal to the Jews to reassert their nationality. The plot revolves around the love of a brilliant young Jewish mathematician for a German girl, daughter of a converted Jew. The first English production took place at Mercantile Hall, Philadelphia, Jan. 13, 1909, under the auspices of several Jewish fraternal lodges. Michael Grades played Dr. Kohn and Jacob Teitelbaum, J. C. Moser, ex-Jewish father of the girl. Reviewed in *Jewish exponent,* Philadelphia, v. 48, Jan. 15, 1909, p. 9, *PBD.

NORRIS, FRANK. ...The pit; a story of Chicago. New York: Doubleday, Page & Co., 1903. 5 p.l., (1)4–421 p. 8°.   NBO
Second novel of a trilogy of the epic of wheat. Narrative of a "deal" in the Chicago wheat pit.
Dramatized by Channing Pollock and produced at the Lyric Theatre, New York, Feb. 10, 1904, with Richard Manuel as Hirsch, "a young Jew, pit trader for a small firm in La Salle Street," and George Grey as Grossman, "an insignificant trader." Reviewed in *New York dramatic mirror,* v. 51, Feb. 20, 1904, p. 16, *T-*DA; and in *Theatre magazine,* New York, 1904, v. 4, p. 57–58, †NBLA.

NOSSIG, ALFRED. Abarbanel; the drama of a people. Authorized translation by Abram Lipsky. (Maccabaean. New York, 1907–08. 8°. v. 13, p. 227–234; v. 14, p. 9–16.)   *PBD
A translation of the first act, in eight scenes. The historic Isaac Abravanel and Abraham Senior are among the characters in it. The action takes place in Spain in 1492. The Jews are about to be expelled. The drama of the people centers in the problem where to go after the expulsion. Abravanel deposed from his high office argues as do the Zionists of today. Others propose emigration to more tolerant lands in the diaspora. The original German, in two acts, is abstracted in *The Jewish comment,* Baltimore, v. 23, Aug. 17, 1906, p. 1–2, *PBD.

NUTTALL, EDITH (SMITH), "MRS. HARRY NUTTALL." *See* sub-entry under BEACONSFIELD, BENJAMIN DISRAELI, 1ST EARL OF.

Individual Plays — 1838-1914, continued

OGILVIE, G. STUART. Hypatia; a play in four acts, founded on Charles Kingsley's novel of that name... First performed at the Theatre Royal, Haymarket, London, January 2nd, 1893. London: Chiswick Press, 1894. 69 p., 1 l. 12°.
NCO p.v.335

The scene is Alexandria, 413 A. D., during the reign of Emperor Honorius, and the theme is the conflict of paganism and Christianity. The central character is Issachar, a Jew, a sort of Richelieu or Joseph Süss as Feuchtwanger lately conceived him, whose motives are political domination. In this he is foiled by his erring daughter, who is betrayed by the Roman Orestes. It is founded on Charles Kingsley's novel of the same name, but the plot and the situations are the dramatist's own. Issachar is modelled after Raphael in the novel. Produced at the Haymarket Theatre, London, Jan. 2, 1893, with H. Beerbohm Tree as Issachar, Olga Brandon as his daughter Ruth, and H. Piffard as Jonadab. Reviewed in *Jewish chronicle*, London, Jan. 6, 1893, p. 9, * *PBE*; *Speaker*, London, v. 7, p. 17-18, * *DA*; *Theatre*, London, 1893, new series, v. 21, p. 105-106, * *T-* *DA*; by William Winter in his *Theatrical 'world' of 1893*, London, 1894, p. 9-17, NCOA; *The Times*, London, Jan. 3, 1893, p. 8, col. 3, * *A*; and in *Truth*, London, v. 33, p. 81-82, * *DA*.

Haymarket Theatre, London. Hypatia, by G. Stuart Ogilvie... On Monday, January 2nd, 1893. [London, 1893.] 10½ x 8 in.
Portfolio of 9 portraits of characters and scenes in the play.

OHNET, GEORGES. ...Serge Panine... Paris: Paul Ollendorf, 1883. 2 p.l., 442 p. 85. ed. 12°. (Les battailes de la vie.) NKV

"An original adaptation" in five acts, by Augustin Daly, was staged in New York, Feb. 5, 1883, with Charles Leclercq as baron Abram Herzog, described in the novel as a German Jew, originally from Posen. Another dramatization was produced at the Avenue Theatre, London, June 4, 1891, with Hamilton Knight as Mr. Herzog, which was reviewed in *Theatre*, London, 1891, new series, v. 18, p. 35-36, * *T-* *DA*.

THE (OLD CLOTHES) Merchant of Venice; or, The young judge and Old Jewry. A burlesque sketch [in verse, founded on Shakespeare's "Merchant of Venice"], for the drawing room. New York: De Witt, 1884. 15 p. 8°. (De Witt's acting plays. no. 331.)

Title from British Museum Catalogue, where it is listed under Shakespeare, Merchant of Venice, Travesties.
See Otto Burmeister, *Nachdichtungen und Bühneneinrichtungen von Shakespeare's Merchant of Venice*, Rostock, 1902, p. 90-98, NDD p.v.3.

ORTON, JASON R. Arnold, a play. New York: Partridge & Brittan, 1854. Tarrytown, N. Y.: Reprinted, W. Abbatt, 1931. 94 p. 4°. (The Magazine of history, with notes and queries. Extra number. no. 167 [v. 42, no. 3].) IAG

Reprinted from his *Arnold and other poems*.
In five acts.
In act II, scene 5, Arnold is represented hard pressed for money. A Jew, whom Arnold addresses as Mordecai, comes to have the General's note renewed and to advance more funds.

OUR charge to the Jewry; a pastoral (after the manner of the ancients). illus. (The Man in the moon. London [1847]. 16°. v. 2, no. 10, p. 237-240.) NDF

The speakers are Smouchy, Sheeney, and the man in the moon.

OUR intelligence bureaus. Reported by "Ed." illus. (Judge. New York, 1882. f°. v. 3, no. 103, Oct. 28, 1882, p. 11.) *DX

Ikey, the office clerk.

OUR jurymen. Reported by "Ed." (Judge. New York, 1881. f°. v. 1, Nov. 26, 1881, p. 10.) *DX
Israel Isaacs from Chatham Street is rejected as a juror.

OUR relief societies. Reported by "Ed." (Judge. New York, 1881. f°. v. 1, Dec. 10, 1881, p. 7.) *DX
Rabbi Ben Levi as the representative of the Israelite Society for the Succor of the Poor.

OUR telephones. Reported by "Ed." (Judge. New York, 1881. f°. v. 1, Dec. 17, 1881, p. 7.) *DX
The voice of "Shacob Shacobs, der original clothing bazaar" on the phone.

OXENFORD, JOHN. See sub-entry under DICKENS, CHARLES.

PALMER, T. A. Too late to save; or, Doomed to die. A story of old Paris. Drama in four acts... London, New York: S. French [1876-86?]. 36 p. nar. 12°. (French's acting edition of plays. v. 112.) NCO (Lacy)

First performed at the Theatre Royal, Exeter, 1861. Mr. McGowan as Shadrach, "a Jew money-lender," murdered in the course of the play. Scene: Paris. Period: 1704-05.

PARKER, LEM B. Thorns and orange blossoms; a dramatization in four acts of Bertha M. Clay's novel of the same name, by Lem B. Parker, edited by Charles O'Brien Kennedy... New York, N. Y., Los Angeles, Calif.: S. French, Inc.; London: S. French, Ltd. [etc.], cop. 1935. 97 p., 2 l. diagrs. 12°. (French's standard library edition.) NBL p.v.354

Bertha M. Clay is the pseudonym of Charlotte Monica Braeme. Her novel was published in 1884. See the copy in NYPL. In the *Preface*, the editor states that this melodrama was printed "in view of the ever-increasing demand for the old-time plays for revival purposes." Louis, "a grimly humorous old Jewish pawn-broker," is introduced as a minor character, in a scene located at a country fair.

PARKER, LOUIS NAPOLEON. Disraeli; a play. New York: John Lane Company, 1911. 6 p.l., 11-114 p. front., ports. 12°. NCR

—— —— New York: Dodd, Mead and Company, 1932. 6 p.l., 11-114 p. front., ports. 12°. NCR

Copious extracts from the text, with a running synopsis, are given in *The Best plays of 1909-1919*, New York, 1933, p. 79-117, NAFH.
In a note in the printed text, the author says: "This is not an historical play, but only an attempt to show a picture of the days — not so very long ago — in which Disraeli lived, and some of the racial, social, and political prejudices he fought against and conquered." The action takes place in 1875 and the scenes are at Glastonbury Towers, the British Foreign Office, and Hughendon Manor, the home of Lord Beaconsfield. The play centers about Disraeli's famous Suez Canal coup, and the intrigues that beset him. Refused financial assistance by the Governor of the Bank of England he turns to Hugh Meyers, Jewish financier — presumably the Rothschilds — and secures the necessary capital. It was staged with great success both here and in England. Mrs. Noel Travers and Foljambe, foreign spies, were represented as Russians in the first

Individual Plays — 1838-1914, continued

PARKER, LOUIS NAPOLEON, *continued*
production in 1911 but became Germans when the play was brought to London during the Great War in 1916.
Produced at the Princess Theatre, Montreal, Jan. 23, 1911; at the Grand Opera House, Chicago, Feb. 13, 1911, and at Wallack's Theatre, New York, Sept. 18, 1911, with George Arliss as Disraeli. Reviewed by Louis Lipsky in *American Hebrew*, New York, v. 89, p. 629–630, * PBD; *New York dramatic mirror*, v. 66, Sept. 20, 1911, p. 11 (illus., Oct. 18, p. 2, and Oct. 25, p. 9), * *T-* DA; and in *Theatre magazine*, New York, v. 14, Nov., 1911, p. xiii–xiv (illus., v. 13, p. 205), † *NBLA*. A synopsis with many extracts from the text is given in *Current literature*, New York, v. 51, p. 663–669, * DA. The Philadelphia production of Feb., 1913 was reviewed in *Jewish exponent*, Philadelphia, v. 56, Feb. 21, 1913, p. 13, * PBD.
First English production at the Royalty Theatre, London, April 4, 1916, with Dennis Eadie as Disraeli and Vincent Sternroup as Hugh Meyers. Reviewed in *The Athenæum*, London, v. 147, p. 207, * DA; *Illustrated London news*, London, v. 148, p. 506, * DA; by A. Croom-Johnson in *Review of reviews*, London, v. 53, p. 437–438, * DA; by Arthur A. Baumann in *Saturday review*, London, v. 121, p. 415, * DA; and in *The Times*, London, April 5, 1916, p. 11, col. 4, * A. Illustrations of the production appeared in *Graphic*, London, v. 93, p. 494, 646; v. 94, p. 658, * DA; *Illustrated sporting and dramatic news*, London, v. 85, p. 207, 211, * DA; and in *Play pictorial*, London, v. 28, no. 168, p. 33–48, † *NCOA*. An interview with L. N. Parker as to how and why he wrote this play was printed in *Jewish chronicle*, London, April 7, 1916, p. 14, * PBE (reprinted in *Jewish exponent*, Philadelphia, v. 63, May 5, 1916, p. 15, * PBD). The early stage history of the play is given by George Arliss in his *Up the years from Bloomsbury*, Boston, 1927, p. 232–263, *MWES (Arliss).*

Krauskopf, Joseph. Disraeli: two discourses, at Temple Keneseth Israel... March 9th and March 16, 1913. (In his: Sunday discourses. Philadelphia, 1913. 8°. series 26, p. 81–105.)
* PLM
Abstracted in *Jewish exponent*, Philadelphia, v. 56, March 14, 1913, p. 9, and March 21, p. 2, * PBD.

PARKER, LOUIS NAPOLEON. The York pageant, July 26, 27, 28, 29, 30, 31, 1909. Invented and arranged by Louis N. Parker. York: Cooper & Swann [1909]. 128 p. sq. 8°.
The pageant is in seven episodes covering the history of York from B.C. 800 to 1644 A.D. Scene 4 in episode 5, p. 76–80, is dated A.D. 1190, and deals with the historic massacre of the Jews of York. Josias, a Jew; Anna, his wife, their five children and a Rabbi, fleeing from the mob, seek shelter at the home of Tooke Flower, the mayor, and his wife Smimeria. An illustration from the pageant, "The rabbi's blessing" coincident with the York massacre, is given in *Sphere*, London, 1909, v. 38, July 24, Supplement, p. iv, * DA.
For a complete description of the pageant see *The Book of the York pageant*, York, 1909.

PARKER, W. COLEMAN. The bank cashier; a sensational melodrama in four acts... Chicago: T. S. Denison and Company [cop. 1903]. 57 p. diagrs. 12°. (Alta series.)
Ichabod Slick, called Ikey or Ike, member of Sharp & Slick, lawyers, detectives and collectors. Speaks in dialect.

PARSONS, JAMES FRANKLIN. Bernstein and Firestein, a musical sketch in one act, with words and music of the song "Oh, my! von't ve make der money!" New York: Dick & Fitzgerald, 1904. 14 p. illus. (music.) 12°.
A vaudeville sketch for "a couple of 'Irishmen' trying to turn an honest penny into a nickel."

PEAKE, RICHARD BRINSLEY. HB.; a dramatic caricature sketched in one act... Correctly printed from the prompter's copy... London: Sherwood, Gilbert and Piper [18—?]. iv, (1)6–24 p. front. 12°. (In: B. N. Webster, editor, The acting national drama. v. 8 [no. 88].)
H. B. are the initials of two fellow lodgers; Humphrey Bobus, proprietor of a provincial paper, and Henry Belasquez, a Jewish dandy. Produced at the Adelphi Theatre, London, Dec. 9, 1839, with Yates as Belasquez. Reviewed in *Spectator*, London, 1839, v. 12, p. 1183, * DA.

PENNIE, JOHN FITZGERALD. The Varangian; or, Masonic honour. A tragedy [in five acts]. (In his: Britain's historical drama; a second series of national tragedies. London, 1839. 8°. p. 257–460.)
Notes to The Varangian: p. 419–436.
Dissertation on the origin, antiquity, and descent of Free-masonry: p. 437–460.
Time: the eleventh century. The dramatis personae are twelve Normans, among whom William the Conqueror is one; seven Saxons, including Harold and Edgar, heir to the English throne; and the following Jews: Ben Zadoc (slave merchant), his wife Tabitha, his steward Tobias, and Hexulph, chief of his rovers. Ben Zadoc is represented as having come from Spain to prey upon the English and enslave them. He saves the Saxon Hereward de Wake, Lord of Brunne, and is in turn saved by him, upon their recognition of one another as brother Masons.

PEREZ, ISAAC LOEB. After burial. Translated by Henry Goodman. (East and West. New York, 1916. 4°. v. 1, p. 347–348.) * PBD
"Tells the inmost thoughts and reaction of a young widow, following the funeral of her husband."

—— After the funeral. (In: Etta Block, translator, One-act plays from the Yiddish; second series. New York, 1929. 12°. p. 45–52.)
* PTP (Block)
This is another translation of the preceding.

—— Bride and groom. [In one act.] (Observer. Chicago, 1930. 8°. v. 20, May 1, 1930, p. 116–118.)
Reprinted in a volume called *Social orientation*, Chicago, 1930, p. 105–107. Originally appeared in Hebrew in *Achiasaf*, Warsaw, 1902, p. 482–486, * PBA.
Presented as a part of the Jewish Folk Lore Revue by the Institute Players Guild at the Majestic Theatre, Chicago, May 26, 1929.

—— Champagne. (In: Etta Block, translator, One-act plays from the Yiddish. Cincinnati [cop. 1923]. 12°. p. 1–15.) * PTP
Three pitiful, ironic results of a mother's overanxious care.

—— He and she; a prologue. Translated by H. Champvert. (East and West. New York, 1915. 4°. v. 1, p. 149.) * PBD
In a garden, summer.

—— Of an early morning, drama. (In: Etta Block, translator, One-act plays from the Yiddish: second series. New York, 1929. 12°. p. 81–91.) * PTP
"Describes the struggle of a whole family in poverty and hardships."

—— The sewing of the wedding gown (picture of life in Warsaw); dramatic poem in one act. (In: B. F. White, translator, Nine one-act plays

Individual Plays—1838-1914, continued

from the Yiddish. Boston [cop. 1932]. 8°.
p. 119-139.) *PTP
Title in the original: Bei dem fremden Chuppahkleid.
A gorgeous wedding gown being made ready by a group of very poor seamstresses. Accompanying music is outlined.

—— The sisters, comedy. (In: Etta Block, translator, One-act plays from the Yiddish: second series. New York, 1929. 12°. p. 93-123.) *PTP

—— Three sisters. Translated by H. Champvert. (East and West. New York, 1915. 4°. v. 1, p. 164-171.) *PBD
A drama in eight scenes.
Same as the preceding, in another translation.
"Depicts the conflict among sisters as a result of their struggle in misery and poverty to retain their selfrespect and virtue."
After the funeral, Of an early morning, and *Three sisters* were staged at a Perez evening in 1915, by the Neighborhood Playhouse, at the Grand Street Theatre, New York. See *Zukunft*, New York, 1915, v. 20, p. 573-574, *PBB.

PERTWEE, GUY. See sub-entry under DICKENS, CHARLES.

PETRISCHEV, A. His first examination; a play in one act. (Jewish comment. Baltimore, 1912. f°. v. 38, p. 247-249.) *PBD
A Jewish domestic scene. The discrimination against Jewish students in Russian public schools is its theme.

PHELPS, PAULINE. A Shakespearian conference. New York: Edgar S. Werner & Company [cop. 1901]. 15 p. 12°.
Cover-title.
On cover: Pauline Phelps' pieces.
A number of Shakespeare's characters, with Shylock among them, hold a conference to discuss "the unpopularity of Shakespeare's plays and the remedy for it."

PHILLIPS, JONAS B. See sub-entry under AINSWORTH, WILLIAM HARRISON.

PHILLIPS, WATTS. Theodora: actress and empress. An original historical drama, in five acts ... London: T. H. Lacy [1866?]. 64 p. nar. 12°. (Lacy's acting edition of plays. v. 74.)
NCO (Lacy)
Another edition was published by Samuel French.
The action is assigned to the years 522-541 A. D., during the reign of Justinian, husband of Theodora, and the scene of action is chiefly in Byzantium. First performed at the Surrey Theatre, London, April 9, 1866. Miss G. Pauncefort as Miriam, a young Jewess, and Miss Clifton as Zilpah, a Jewish slave girl, handmaid to Theodora. Reviewed in *The Athenæum*, London, 1866, v. 47, p. 504-505, *DA; and in *Era*, London, v. 28, April 15, 1866, p. 10, † NAFA.

PILGRIM, JAMES. Yankee Jack; or, The buccaneer of the Gulf...a nautical drama in three acts. [New York? 1852?] 30, 22, 29 f. 3 pamphlets. 4°. † NCOF
Prompter's copy made by E. S. Bowles.
Produced at the Chatham Theatre, New York, Feb. 9, 1852. In subsequent years it was produced, in varying versions, under the titles *Beacon of death*, or *Floating beacon*. See Odell, VI, Index. The scene is at the dock section of New Orleans. The Jewish character is Kizer, a tavern keeper.

PINERO, SIR ARTHUR WING. The cabinet minister; a farce in four acts. New York: J. W. Lovell Company [cop. 1891]. 3 p.l., 188 p. 12°.

—— —— New York: United States Book Co. [1892.] 3 p.l., 188 p. 16°. NCO p.v.505
Imprint on cover: W. H. Baker & Co., as publisher.

—— —— Boston: Walter H. Baker Co. [cop. 1892.] x, 188 p. 16°. NCR
Introductory note, p. ix-x, by Malcolm A. Salaman.

—— —— London: William Heinemann, 1892. x p., 2 l., 188 p. 16°. NCR
Introductory note, p. ix-x, by Malcolm A. Salaman.

—— ...The cabinet minister; a farce in four acts... Mit Anmerkungen zum Schulgebrauch, hrsg. von Dr. Engelbert Hertel... Bielefeld and Leipzig: Velhagen & Klasing, 1928. ix, 120, 16 p. 12°. (Velhagen & Klasings Sammlung französischer u. englischer Schulausgaben. English authors. Bd. 181.)
First produced at the Court Theatre, London, April 23, 1890. Weedon Grossmith as Joseph Lebanon, a new type of money-lender; Rosina Filippi as his sister, Mrs. Gaylustre, "a widow or something." The latter is the extremely rare type on the stage of an objectionable Jewess. Reviewed by C. S. in *Illustrated London news*, London, 1890, v. 96, p. 550, *DA. "It is marvellous...how many Jews of different types and idiosyncracies can be seen on the stage"; *Illustrated sporting and dramatic news*, London, v. 33, p. 202, *DA; *Truth*, London, v. 27, p. 880, *DA; and *The Times*, London, April 24, 1890, p. 5, col. 6, *A.
Produced at Daly's Theatre, New York, Jan. 11, 1892, with Sidney Herbert as Lebanon and Edith Crane as Mrs. Gaylustre. Reviewed in *New York clipper*, 1892, v. 39, p. 763, col. 3-4, *T-† MVA; *New York dramatic mirror*, v. 27, Jan. 23, 1892, p. 2, *T-* DA; and in *Spirit of the times*, New York, v. 123, p. 20, † MVA.

—— Iris; a drama in five acts... London: William Heinemann, 1902. 4 p.l., 224 p. 16°.
Another issue, 1924. NCR

—— —— New York: R. H. Russell, 1902. 3 p.l., 224 p. 12°. NCR

—— —— Boston: W. H. Baker & Co. [1925?] 3 p.l., 224 p. 12°.
Reprinted in his *Social plays*, edited with a critical preface by Clayton Hamilton, New York, 1918, [v. 2], p. 221-423, NCR; and in R. A. Cordell, editor, *Representative modern plays, British and American, from Robertson to O'Neill*, New York, 1929, p. 150-205, NCO.
Reviewed in *The Athenæum*, London, 1905, v. 126, p. 219, *DA.
The scene is London and Italy. The author has more than suggested that Maldonado should be represented as a Jew, and the character was so played. First produced at the Garrick Theatre, London, Sept. 21, 1901, with Oscar Asche as Maldonado, described as "handsome according to the Jewish type, somewhat ebullient in manner." Reviewed by W. L. Courtney in *Fortnightly review*, London, 1901, v. 76 [new series, v. 70], p. 902-910, *DA; *The Times*, London, Sept. 23, 1901, p. 5, col. 4, *A; and by Agnes E. Platt, in her *The stage in 1902*, London, 1903, p. 24-41, NCOM.
A notable revival took place at the Adelphi Theatre, London, March 21, 1925, which ran 152 times, with Henry Ainley as Maldonado. Reviewed in *Illustrated London news*, London, 1925, v. 166, p. 560, *DA; and by Ivor Brown in *Saturday review*, London, v. 139, p. 325-326, *DA. See illus. in *Graphic*, London, 1925, v. 111, p. 763, *DA.
First staged at the Euclid Avenue Opera House, Cleveland, Sept. 15, 1902, and brought to New York, at the Criterion Theatre, Sept. 23, 1902, with Oscar Asche as Maldonado. Reviewed in *New York clipper*, New York, 1902, v. 50, p. 700, *T-† MVA; *New York dramatic mirror*, New York, v. 48, Oct. 4, 1902, p. 16, *T-* DA; *Spirit of the times*, New York, v. 144,

Individual Plays, 1838–1914, continued

PINERO, SIR ARTHUR WING, *continued*

p. 232, † *MVA;* (with illus.) in *Theatre magazine,* New York, v. 2, Nov., 1902, p. 1, 5–6, † *NBLA;* and in *Town topics,* New York, v. 48, Sept. 25, 1902, p. 13, * *DA.*

—— Letty; an original drama, in four acts and an epilogue... London: William Heinemann, 1904. 3 p.l., 247 p. 12°. NCR

—— —— Boston: W. H. Baker & Co. [etc.], 1905. 225 p. 12°.
Reviewed in *The Athenæum,* London, 1905, v. 126, p. 219, * *DA.*
Reprinted in his *Social plays,* edited with a critical preface by Clayton Hamilton, New York, 1919, [v. 3], p. 9–239, *NCR.*
Produced at the Duke of York's Theatre, London, Oct. 8, 1903, with Fred Kerr as Bernard Mandeville. Reviewed in *Illustrated sporting and dramatic news,* London, 1903, v. 60, p. 260–261 (illus. on p. 256), * *DA; The Queen,* London, v. 114, p. 617 (illus. on p. 590), * *DA;* and by Max Beerbohm in *Saturday review,* London, v. 96, p. 511–512, * *DA.*
It was first seen in America, at the Hudson Theatre, New York, Sept. 12, 1904, with Arthur Playfair as Mandeville. Reviewed in *New York dramatic mirror,* v. 52, Sept. 24, 1904, p. 16, * *T–* DA.* Illus. is given in *Theatre magazine,* New York, 1904, v. 4, p. 244, † *NBLA.*

—— ...The "Mind the paint" girl. A comedy, in four acts. London: Printed at the Chiswick Press, 1912. 121(1) p. 8°.
At head of title: Printed for use in the theatre, not for circulation.

—— —— London: William Heinemann, 1913. 4 p.l., 234 p., 1 l. 12°. NCR
First produced at the Duke of York's Theatre, London, Feb. 17, 1912, with Nigel Playfair as Sam de Castro, the genial "bounder," with a pathetic passion for the green room. He is described as "a stout, coarse, but genial looking gentleman of forty, of marked Jewish appearance, speaking with a lisp." Reviewed in *Academy,* London, 1912, v. 82, p. 275–277, * *DA;* by S. O. in *English review,* London, v. 11, p. 155–157, * *DA;* by J. M. B. in *Graphic,* London, v. 85, p. 254 (illus. on p. 333), * *DA; Illustrated London news,* London, v. 140, p. 302, * *DA;* by John Palmer in *Saturday review,* London, v. 113, p. 235–236, * *DA;* and in *The Times,* London, Feb. 19, 1912, p. 11, col. 4–5, * *A.* An abstract of several London reviews is printed in *Literary digest,* New York, v. 44, p. 534–535, * *DA.*
First American production at the Lyceum Theatre, New York, Sept. 9, 1912, with Leo Cooper as Sam de Castro. Reviewed by Arthur Ruhl in *Collier's,* New York, v. 50, Oct. 5, 1912, p. 28, * *DA; Everybody's magazine,* New York, v. 27, p. 668–670, * *DA;* by J. S. Metcalfe in *Life,* New York, v. 60, p. 1812–1813, * *DA;* by Willa Sibert Cather (with illus.) in *McClure's magazine,* New York, v. 40, March, 1913, p. 63–64, 67, * *DA;* by Matthew White, Jr., in *Munsey's magazine,* New York, v. 48, p. 349–350, * *DA; New York dramatic mirror,* v. 68, Sept. 11, 1912, p. 6, * *T–* DA;* and (with illus.) in *Theatre magazine,* New York, v. 16, p. 98–99, † *NBLA.* A synopsis of the play with numerous illustrations is given in *Green book album,* Chicago, v. 8, p. 740–743, 772, *NAFA.* More illustrations and an interview with Pinero by L. V. De Foe appear ibid., p. 761–770, *NAFA.* Illustrations are also found in *Harper's weekly,* New York, v. 56, Aug. 24, 1912, p. 16, and Oct. 19, p. 19, * *DA.*

—— Trelawny of the "Wells"; a comedietta in four acts. New York: The De Witt Publishing House [etc.], 1898. 4 p.l., 215 p. 12°. (Green-room edition of copyrighted plays.)

—— —— Chicago: The Dramatic Pub. Co., cop. 1898. 3 p.l., 215 p. 12°. (Sergel's acting drama. no. 573.)

—— —— New York: R. H. Russell, 1899. 4 p.l., 215 p. col'd front., illus. 8°.

—— —— London: W. Heinemann, 1899. 4 p.l., 215 p. 12°. NCR

—— —— London: William Heinemann, Ltd., 1930. 4 p.l., 215 p. 12°. (The plays of Arthur W. Pinero.)
Reprinted in J. W. Marriott, compiler, *Great modern British plays,* London [1929], p. 129–202, *NCO.*
An extract from act I is printed in Allardyce Nicoll, editor, *Readings from British drama,* New York [1928], p. 407–410, * *R–NCO.*
First produced at the Court Theatre, London, Jan. 20, 1898. A play of theatrical life. *The Wells* has been identified as Sadler's Wells. The date of the action is assigned to the early sixties of the last century. Mrs. Mossop, "a portly, middle-aged Jewish lady, elaborately attired," keeper of a shabby theatrical rooming-house, was played by Miss Le Thiere. Reviewed by George Bernard Shaw in *Saturday review,* London, 1898, v. 85, p. 170–172, * *DA; The Times,* London, Jan. 21, 1898, p. 4, col. 6, * *A;* and (with illustrations, one of which is that of Mrs. Mossop) in *To-day,* London, v. 18, p. 18–19, * *DA.*
It was first produced in this country at the Lyceum Theatre, New York, Nov. 22, 1898, with Mrs. Thomas Whiffen as Mrs. Mossop. Reviewed in *New York dramatic mirror,* v. 40, Dec. 3, 1898, p. 16, * *T–* DA.* Mrs. Whiffen, in an all-star cast revival and in her last stage appearance, played the same part at the New Amsterdam Theatre, New York, Jan. 31, 1927.

Salaman, Malcolm C. The Royal Court Theatre. Souvenir Trelawney of the "Wells." London: Marion & Co. [1898.] 12 l. ports., illus. f°.
Cover-title.

PINK, WAL. *See* sub-entry under DICKENS, CHARLES.

PINSKI, DAVID. A dollar! Symbolic comedy in one act. Authorized translation from the Yiddish by Joseph Michael. (Stratford journal. Boston, 1917. 8°. v. 1, June, 1917, p. 25–41.)
* DA

—— A dollar; a comedy in one act... Translated by Isaac Goldberg. New York [etc.]: Samuel French [1932]. 3 p.l., 3–24 p. 12°.
This translation was previously printed in his *Ten plays,* Isaac Goldberg, translator, New York, 1920, p. 51–73, * *PTP;* and in B. Roland Lewis, *Contemporary one-act plays,* New York [1922], p. 321–341, *NAFH (Lewis).* The original Yiddish appeared in *Zukunft,* New York, 1914, v. 19, p. 344–351, * *PBB.*
Seven stranded actors find a dollar and quarrel over it. Meanwhile it is stolen from them.
Staged by the Little Theatre of Temple Israel, Boston, Dec. 10, 1930. See *Jewish advocate,* Boston, v. 58, Dec. 5, 1930, p. 1, 5, * *PBD.*

—— The dumb messiah; a drama in three acts. <1911.> (In his: Three plays, translated by Isaac Goldberg. New York, 1918. 12°. p. 167–234.)
* PTP
The action takes place in the year 1306, during the time of a great expulsion of the Jews from Illyria. Although the persons in the drama and the scene of its action are fictitious, the year 1306 mentioned above identifies the play as being based upon the events occurring during the banishment of all Jews from France in the reign of Philip the Fair. Certain historical episodes of that event form the basis of the present drama.

—— Forgotten souls; a drama in one act... Translated by Isaac Goldberg. New York [etc.]: S. French [1932]. 2 p.l., 3–20 p. 12°.
* PSQ p.v.5
Repr.: Frank Shay and P. Loving, editors, *Fifty con-*

Individual Plays — 1838–1914, continued
temporary one-act plays, Cincinnati [cop. 1920], p. 545–552, *NAFH (Shay)*.
The original title is *Glücks-Vergessene*, i.e. those who have been forgotten, or overlooked, by happiness. The theme is that of one self-sacrificing sister for another. The scene is laid in a Russian provincial town.

—— געװיסען. [In one act.] (צוקונפט.) New York, 1913. 4°. v. 18, p. 493–496.) * PBB
Under the title *Conquest*, Hedwig Reichert appeared in the main part at the Majestic Theatre, Milwaukee, April 15, 1913.

—— Isaac Sheftel; a drama in three acts. (In his: Three plays. New York, 1918. 12°. p. 1–79.) * PTP
Written in 1899 and first published in a German translation by Martin Buber, in Berlin, 1904. The original Yiddish was first printed by A. M. Evalenko, in 1907. The action takes place in a large city of the Russian Pale, in the early nineties of the nineteenth century. "The chief character was suggested to the dramatist by the strange figure of a Warsaw workingman who was gifted with inventive talent, yet sold his contrivances to his employer for a mere pittance, in order always to be near his beloved brain children."

—— The last Jew; a tragedy in four acts. (In his: Three plays, translated by Isaac Goldberg. New York, 1918. 12°. p. 81–166.) * PTP
Reviewed by M. C. D. in *The Nation*, New York, 1918, v. 107, p. 210, * *DA*.
Written in 1903–04, and known in Yiddish and other languages as *Die Familie Zwie*. As such it was produced, in a German translation, at the Schiller Theatre, Berlin, and in many continental cities where Jewish theatres exist. In New York, it was produced in Russian at the Orlenoff Lyceum, Dec. 7, 1905, with Paul Orlenoff in the leading rôle of Reb Moshe Zwie. Reviewed in *New York dramatic mirror*, New York, v. 54, Dec. 9, 1905, p. 16, * *T–* DA*.
The author in his foreword says: "This is not a pogrom-tragedy, but the tragedy of a sole survivor, the tragedy of a moribund religion, of a crumbling world-philosophy. Who can say this is exclusively Jewish?"

—— Sorrows. (In: B. F. White, translator, Nine one-act plays from the Yiddish. Boston [cop. 1932]. 8°. p. 195–218.) * PTP
"A sensitive study of the Jew in relation to the early revolutionary movement in Russia." Said to be Pinski's first play, with the exception of a juvenile attempt at the age of ten.

—— The stranger (or, "The eternal Jew"); a legend-drama in one act. Authorized translation from the Yiddish by Isaac Goldberg, with an introductory appreciation by the translator: David Pinski, master dramatist. (Menorah journal. New York, 1918. 4°. v. 4, p. 214–227.)
* PBD
The original first appeared in *Der Arbeiter*, New York, Dec. 8, 15, 22, 29, 1906, * *PBB*.
Time: 70 A. D., in the city of Beris Arva.
The story is based on a legend from Midrash Eicha Rabothi, the text of which is given as comment on Lamentations 1:16.
Reprinted in Isaac Goldberg, translator, *Six plays of the Yiddish theatre; second series*, Boston [1918], p. 25–69, * *PTP*; and in the author's *Ten plays*, New York, 1920, p. 177–209, * *PTP*.
Produced by the Pathfinders-Reviewers, San Francisco, May 23, 1929.

—— The treasure; a drama in four acts; translated by Ludwig Lewisohn. New York: B. W. Huebsch, 1915. 8 p., 1 l., 9–194 p. 16°. * PTP
Reviewed in *Drama*, Chicago, 1916, v. 6, p. 154–155,

NAFA; and in *Independent*, New York, 1915, v. 84, p. 478, * *DA*.
The scene is in a village in the Russian Pale, on the edge of a cemetery, in and about the house of the cemetery caretaker. A few coins are unearthed and a discovered treasure is imagined. The caretaker's family and the whole town are seized by the spell of greed. "The first play of the modern Jewish theatre to be offered to an English reading audience."
It first appeared in a German translation by F. Frisch, in 1910 or 1911.
Reinhardt staged it, under its German title *Der Schatz*, at the Deutsches Theater, Berlin, Feb. 2, 1911, with Victor Arnold as Chone the gravedigger, and Frl. Eibenschütz as his daughter Tille. Produced by the Theatre Guild, at the Garrick Theatre, New York, Oct. 4, 1920, with Dudley Digges as Chone, Celia Adler as Tille, and Helen Westley as Jachne Braine, Chone's wife. Reviewed by O. W. Firkins in *Review*, New York, 1920, v. 3, p. 354–356, * *DA*. For other reviews see *Collection of newspaper clippings of dramatic criticism, 1920–1921*, v. S–Z, † *NBL*.
Produced by the Jewish Drama League, for the first time in London, June 12, 1932, with Abraham Sofaer as Chone the gravedigger, Doris Gilmour as Tille, and Reginald Jarman as parnass of the congregation. Reviewed in *Jewish chronicle*, London, June 17, 1932, p. 32, * *PBE*.

—— With triumphant banners [a comedy in one act]. Translated by H. Goodman. (East and West. New York, 1916. 4°. v. 1, p. 291–296.)
* PBD

PLACE aux dames; or, The ladies speak at last. New York: Fitzgerald Publishing Corporation, n.d. 18 p. 12°.
Contains a character from *The Merchant of Venice*.

PLANCHÉ, JAMES ROBINSON. An old offender; a comic drama in two acts... London: T. H. Lacy [186–?]. 40 p. nar. 12°. (Lacy's acting edition of plays. v. 41.) NCO (Lacy)

—— —— London, New York: S. French [1859–76?]. 40 p. 12°. (French's acting edition. [no. 615.]) NCO p.v.507
First performed at the Adelphi Theatre, London, July 21, 1859. Period: 1724, "when Jack Sheppard was abroad." Ben Isaacs, played by Manley, appears towards the end of the play, without speaking. Reviewed in *Era*, London, July 24, 1859, p. 11, col. 3, † *NAFA*.

POTTER, PAUL MEREDITH. *See* sub-entries under DE LA RAMÉE, LOUISE; DU MAURIER, GEORGE LOUIS PALMELLA BUSSON.

PRAED, ROSA CAROLINE (MURRAY-PRIOR), "MRS. CAMPBELL PRAED." Ariane; or, The bond of wedlock, a tale of London life... London: George Routledge and Sons, 1888. 2 p.l., 278 p. 12°.
Dramatized by the authoress, with the assistance of Richard Lee, and produced at the Opera Comique, London, Feb. 8, 1888, with Leonard Bayne as Sir Leopold D'Acosta, wealthy suitor. Reviewed in *Theatre*, London, 1888, series 4, v. 11, p. 154–156, *NCOA*.

Burnand, Francis Cowley. "Airey" Annie; travesty on Mrs. Campbell Praed's play of "Ariane"... London: Bradbury, Agnew & Co. [1888.] 24 p. 8°.
From British Museum catalogue.
Produced at the Strand Theatre, London, April 4, 1888, with Albert Chevalier as Sir Leopold. Reviewed by Percy FitzGerald in *Theatre*, London, 1888, series 4, v. 11, p. 267–271, *NCOA*.

PRAY, ISAAC C. *See* sub-entry under MOSENTHAL, SALOMON HERMANN, RITTER VON.

Individual Plays — 1838–1914, continued

PRICE, EDWARD W. *See* sub-entry under MOSENTHAL, SALOMON HERMANN, RITTER VON.

PROCTER, BRYAN WALLER. A Jew's use for riches. [Dramatic fragment, no.] 68. (In his: English songs and other small poems. London, 1844. 24°. p. 257–258.) NCM

—— —— (In: same. Boston, 1851. 12°. p. 352.) NCM

PUNCH'S essence of parliament. [In three scenes.] (Punch. London, 1860. 4°. v. 38, p. 43–44.) *DX
Reprinted in *Albion*, New York, 1860, v. 38, p. 94, *A.
Disraeli, one of the characters.

THE PURSUIT of Peruna. As presented by the University Triangle Club. (Princeton tiger. Princeton, N. J., 1913. 4°. v. 24, Dec., 1913, p. 10–11.) STG
Peruna, "a Yiddish heiress."

QUIRE, HARRY S. Wall Street in Paradise: an original and musical extravaganza. New-York: G. F. Nesbitt & Co., 1869. 28 p. 12°. NBF p.v.35
Jew-Peter, head-centre of Olympus; no Jewish interest, except the pun on the name.

THE RABBI of York; a tragedy in five acts. London: Baily Bros., 1852. 3 p.l., 73 p. 8°.
The characters are three Christians, among whom one is the governor of York Castle, and five Jews, among whom are Elam Asshur, rabbi of York, and his granddaughter Esther. "The coronation of Richard I. of England was ushered in by an almost general massacre of the Jews... This historical event is the subject of the present tragedy, in which the author has endeavoured to elevate the character of the Jews, as he has equally sought to delineate the perversion of Christianity at the period of the Crusades." — Preface.

RALEIGH, CECIL. ...Hearts are trumps; original drama in four acts... London: J. Miles & Co., 1899. 143 p. 8°. NCO p.v.469
At head of title: Printed, not published.
A melodrama produced at Drury Lane, London, Sept. 16, 1899, with Dagnall as Leopold Kolditz, villainous financier and would-be murderer. Reviewed in *The Athenæum*, London, 1899, v. 114, p. 427–428, *DA*; by W. M. Thomas in *Graphic*, 1899, v. 60, p. 418, *DA*; and in *Illustrated sporting and dramatic news*, 1899, v. 52, p. 113, *DA.*

RANKIN, MCKEE, AND M. LUDOVICI. *See* sub-entry under MOSENTHAL, SALOMON HERMANN, RITTER VON.

RAPPAPORT, SOLOMON. Father and son; a play in one act, by S. Ansky [pseud.]... Translated by Bessie F. White. Boston: W. H. Baker Co. [cop. 1932.] 28 p. 12°. (Baker's royalty plays.)
First appeared in Russian in *Voskhod, Knizhki Voskhoda*, St. Petersburg, 1906, v. 26, p. 35–58, *PBI.

RAVOLD, JOHN. *See* sub-entry under DICKENS, CHARLES.

RAYMOND, GEORGE LANSING. Columbus the discoverer; a drama, by Walter Warren [pseud.]. Boston: Arena Publishing Company, 1893. vi, 164 p. 8°.
Published under the author's name, with the title *Columbus*, in five acts, in his *The Aztec god and other dramas*, New York, 1900, p. 127–149, NBM. The Library has a second edition, 1908, with omitted passages printed in footnotes, and a still later edition, 1916, p. 133–307, differing further from the 1900 and 1908 editions.
Luis de St. Angel and Roderigo Sanchez, two Marrano Jews, are among the characters. Sanchez of Segovia, described here as the inspector-general of Columbus's expedition, was one of the several Jews on Columbus's first voyage. He is said to have joined the expedition at the special command of Queen Isabella.

READE, CHARLES. Gold!; a drama, in five acts ... London: T. H. Lacy [185–?]. 48 p. nar. 12°. (Lacy's acting edition of plays. [no. 152.] v. 11.) NCO (Lacy)
The action of the play passes in England, 1847, and Australia, 1848. First produced at the Drury Lane, London, Jan. 10, 1853, with Edward Stirling as Isaac Levi, the kindly Jewish moneylender who outwits the "Christian" usurer Meadows, the villain of the play. F. Cooke acted the small part of Nathan, "a young Jew." The *Era* reviewer wrote: "There is a novel feature in the introduction of a Jew of some feeling and honesty; and we compliment the author upon his courage in doing so much justice to a class among whom there are many excellent people." On the basis of *Gold* Reade wrote his novel *It's never too late to mend*, on which play he founded his well-known drama, similarly entitled.
Reviewed in *Athenæum*, London, 1853, v. 26, p. 87, *DA; Era*, London, v. 15, Jan. 16, 1853, p. 10, † *NAFA*; and in *The Times*, London, Jan. 11, 1853, p. 8, col. 4, *A.

—— It's never too late to mend. Drama in five acts... London: Williams and Strahan [1872–73?]. 97(1) p. 8°.
Title from Michael Sadleir's *Excursions in Victorian bibliography*, p. 174–175. It is also stated, ibid., that the reissue of this play by W. Spearing, London, 1890, varies considerably in text from the present edition.

—— —— Drama in four acts. London: W. Spearing, 1890. 2 p.l., (1)6–76 p. 8°.
At head of title: For private use only, not for circulation.
Interleaved ms. copy. Prompter's copy of W. S. Hartford.
Written in 1864 and produced at the Princes Theatre, London, Oct. 4, 1865, with Tom Mead as Isaac Levi. Reviewed in *Era*, London, Oct. 8, 1865, p. 11, † *NAFA*; and in *The Times*, London, Oct. 5, 1865, p. 12, * A.
In America it was first produced at Wallack's Theatre, New York, May 7, 1866, with John Gilbert as Isaac Levi. See *New York Daily Tribune*, May 8, 1866, p. 5, col. 5, * A.

Hazlewood, Colin Henry. Never too late to mend; a drama of real life in four acts. Founded on Mr. Charles Reade's popular novel... London: T. H. Lacy [185–?]. 65 p. 12°.
Also issued as no. 370 of French's standard drama. The acting edition.
Performed at the Royal Marylebone Theatre, 1859. H. Forrester played Isaac Levi, "a Jew and money lender, but whose actions and sentiments are worthy of any Christian."
"Reade was rightly furious at the unauthorized issue of this version and hastened to prepare one of his own."
A new version, called *Never too late to mend*, by Cyril Searle, was first produced at the Booth Theatre, New York, March 26, 1883, with H. A. Weaver as Isaac Levi. Reviewed in *New York dramatic mirror*, v. 9, March 31, 1883, p. 2, col. 2–3, * T–* DA.

Individual Plays — 1838–1914, continued

REEVE, WYBERT. Won at last! An original comedy-drama, in three acts... London: T. H. Lacy [1857–73?]. 40 p. nar. 12°. (Lacy's acting edition of plays. v. 87.)   NCO (Lacy)
Also issued as no. 1298 of French's acting edition of plays.
First produced at the Charing Cross Theatre, Oct. 30, 1869, with Philip Day as Adolphus Buchanan, owner of "Wolff & Co.," moneylenders, the villain of the piece, and J. Wallace as Mr. Wolff, his clerk. Reviewed in *The Athenæum*, London, 1869, v. 54, p. 601, * *DA*; and in *Era*, London, v. 32, Nov. 14, 1869, p. 10, † *NAFA*.

REISEN, ABRAHAM. Brothers, a play. Translated from the Yiddish by Etta Block. (In: Frank Shay, editor, Fifty more contemporary one-act plays. New York [1928]. 8°. p. 405–412.)   NAFH
Original title, Jolly brothers. In three scenes. "Comedy of good-natured fellowship and generosity among those who have nothing to give."

—— —— (In: Etta Block, translator, One-act plays from the Yiddish; second series. New York, 1929. 12°. p. 53–69.)   * PTP

—— Captives two. [In one act.] Translated from the Yiddish, by David J. Galter. (Review. Philadelphia, 1917. 12°. v. 12, Feb., 1917, p. 24–30.)
Scene is in Rome, after the destruction of the second temple. The characters are two Roman soldiers, and a captive youth and maiden, children of the high priest. Based on a legend told in *Gittin*, 58a.

REYNOLDSON, THOMAS H. The rich man of Frankfort; or, The poisoned crown. An historical drama in three acts... Printed from the acting copy, with remarks biographical and critical by D.-G. [i.e. George Daniel]... As performed at the metropolitan minor theatres ... London: J. Cumberland, n. d. 55 p. incl. front. 24°. (Cumberland's minor theatre. v. 14.)   NCO (Cumberland)

—— —— As performed at the Theatres Royal, London... London: G. H. Davidson [1849–55?]. 55 p. incl. front. 24°. (Cumberland's minor theatre. no. 129.)
The action of the play is placed in the year 1519, when Charles the Fifth became emperor. Place: Frankfort. It is, according to G. Daniel, an adaptation of the French play *Samuel le marchand*. Produced at the Surrey Theatre, London, Nov. 12, 1838. The rich man of Frankfort is Isaac Ben-Samuel, "known under the name of Master Didier the Lombard," and the rôle was acted by Cooper. Mrs. H. Vining played the part of his daughter, Esther, and E. F. Saville, Emanuel. Nicoll gives Oct. 31, as the date of first production.

RICHARD, HENRY, PSEUD. *See* sub-entry under DUMAS, ALEXANDRE, THE ELDER.

ROBERTS, MORLEY. Lady Penelope... Illustrated by Arthur William Brown. Boston: L. C. Page & Company, 1905. 3 p.l., 362 p., front., 8 pl. 8°.   NCW

Vachell, Horace Annesley. "Pen," a comedy in three acts, dramatized from Morley Roberts' *Lady Penelope*, was produced at St. James' Theatre, London, May 3, 1916.
Warwick Ward played the part of Isidore de Vere, born Cohen, a poet and one of four admirers of Lady Penelope. Reviewed in *Era*, London, v. 79, May 10, 1916, p. 13, † *NAFA*; *Graphic*, London, v. 93, p. 652, * *DA*; *Illustrated London news*, v. 148, p. 632, * *DA*; and in *The Times*, London, May 4, 1916, p. 11, col. 3, * *A*.

ROBERTSON, THOMAS WILLIAM. Society; a comedy in three acts...· London: T. H. Lacy [186–?]. 65(1) p. diagrams. nar. 12°. (Lacy's acting edition of plays. v. 71.)   NCO (Lacy)
The Library has another edition in *NCO p.v.642*.
Also issued as no. 1060 of French's acting edition of plays.

—— —— (In his: Society and Caste. Edited by T. Edgar Pemberton. Boston and London [cop. 1905]. 16°. p. 1–101.) (The belles lettres series. Section III. The English drama.)   NCR
See Introduction, p. ix–xxxv(i), and the editor's comment about Moses Aaron as the comic stage Jew, p. xxix.
"The original ms., dated Aug. 12, 1864, [is] now in the Shakespeare Memorial Library at Stratford-on-Avon, as a gift of the editor."
Reprinted in his *Principal dramatic works*, London, 1889, v. 2, p. 683–742, *NCR*; in Alfred Bates, editor, *The Drama*, London, 1903, v. 16, p. 257–320, *NAF*; and in H. F. Rubinstein, editor, *Great English plays*, New York and London, 1928 (another edition, London, 1928), p. 1023–1061, *NCO*.
Produced at the Prince of Wales Theatre, Liverpool, May 8, 1865, with Mr. Davidge in the rôle of Moses Aaron (a bailiff) and at the Prince of Wales Theatre, London, Nov. 11, 1865, with G. Atkins as Moses Aaron. Reviewed in *The Athenæum*, London, 1865, v. 46, p. 697, * *DA*; *Era*, v. 27, May 21, 1865, p. 13, col. 2, and Nov. 19, p. 15, † *NAFA*; and in *The Times*, London, Nov. 14, 1865, p. 7, col. 5, * *A*.
First American production took place at the Wallack Theatre, New York, Feb. 22, 1866, with G. F. Browne as Moses Aaron.

ROBINSON, MARVIN G. *See* sub-entry under DICKENS, CHARLES.

ROBINSON, RAYMOND M. A thief in the house; a comedy in one act. Boston: W. H. Baker Company [cop. 1909]. 29 p. 12°. (Baker's edition of plays.)   NBL p.v.202
A detective in disguise of a Jewish peddler.

ROBINSON, W. BEVAN. *See* sub-entry under ERCKMANN, ÉMILE, AND ALEXANDRE CHATRIAN.

ROBY, BERNARD SOANE. *See* sub-entry under DICKENS, CHARLES.

ROESSLER, CARL. The five Frankforters; a comedy in three acts, by Carl Roessler; authorized English version, by J. Fuchs; with a preface by the translator "Concerning the Jews of Frankfort." New York: The H. K. Fly Company [cop. 1913]. 2 p.l., 9–127 p. front., plates. 8°.   NGE

—— The five Frankforters; translated by Gertrude Einson. (International. New York, 1912. 4°. v. 6, p. 82–84.)   * DA
A translation of the greater part of the last act.
Reprinted in *Jewish exponent*, Philadelphia, v. 55, Oct. 4, 1912, p. 8, * *PBD*.
The play deals with an episode in the early career of the Rothschilds when they were first created barons. The five Frankforters are the five Rothschild brothers at five European centers. A sympathetic treatment of high Frankfort Jewry. Zangwill in his *Shylock and other stage Jews* states that it is not true to its period.
The translation for the stage was made by Basil Hood and it was first produced at the Lyric Theatre, London, May 7, 1912, with Henrietta Watson as Frau Naomi,

Individual Plays — 1838-1914, continued

ROESSLER, CARL, *continued*

Gladys Guy as the granddaughter Rachel and Henry Ainley as the son David. In the later American production these are named Frau Gudula, Charlotte and Jacob respectively. Reviewed by J. M. B. (with illus.) in *Graphic*, London, v. 85, p. 714, 738, * *DA; Truth*, London, v. 71, p. 1243, * *DA;* and in *The Times*, London, May 8, 1912, p. 7, col. 3, * *A.* Illustrations are given in *Illustrated sporting and dramatic news*, London, v. 77, p. 567, * *DA.*

Produted in New York at the 39th Street Theatre, March 3, 1913, with Mathilde Cottrelly as grandmother Gudula, Alma Belwin as Charlotte, and Pedro de Cordoba as Jacob. Reviewed in *American playwright*, New York, v. 2, p. 111–113, *NAFA;* by Clayton Hamilton (with illus.) in *Bookman*, New York, v. 37, p. 308–310, * *DA;* by Arthur Ruhl (with illus.) in *Collier's weekly*, New York, v. 51, April 5, 1913, p. 26, * *DA;* by Fanny Cannon in *Editor*, Ridgewood, N. J., v. 37, p. 355–356, *NARA;* by Channing Pollock (with illus.) in *Green book album*, Chicago, v. 9, p. 740–742, 810–811 and v. 10, p. 22–23, *NAFA;* by J. S. Metcalfe in *Life*, New York, v. 61, p. 532, * *DA;* by Matthew White, Jr., in *Munsey's magazine*, New York, v. 49, p. 285–289, * *DA; New York dramatic mirror*, v. 69, March 5, 1913, p. 6-7, * *DA; Theatre magazine*, New York, v. 17, p. 98–99, † *NBLA;* and (with illus.) by Hillel Rogoff in *Zukunft*, New York, 1913, v. 18, p. 511–515, * *PBB.* More illustrations are in *Harper's weekly*, New York, v. 57, March 15, 1913, p. 24, * *DA.* Detailed synopses are printed, by Wilson D. Busch (with illus.) in *American citizen*, New York, v. 2, p. 199–201, * *PBD; American Hebrew*, New York, v. 90, p. 366, * *PBD;* with extracts in *Current opinion*, New York, v. 55, p. 25–29, * *DA;* and (with illus.) in *Hearst's magazine*, New York, v. 24, p. 474–486, * *DA.* A novelization by Edgar Bruno of the B. Hood translation appeared in *Green book album*, Chicago, v. 10, p. 168–184, *NAFA.*

Produced at the Little Theatre of Temple Israel, Boston, May 19, 1931, with Pauline L. Freedman as old mother Gudula, and Eunice Cabot as the granddaughter Charlotte. For comment and illustrations see *Jewish advocate*, Boston, May 12, 1931, p. 5, and May 15, part 1, p. 6, * *PBD.*

ROGERS, HARRISON W. The dawn of eternity; a spectacular drama in five acts and nine epochs. [New York? cop. 1910.] 80 p. f°. † NBM

On cover: Presented to Mr. David Belasco.
The first epoch is laid in 1906 B.C., and the ninth in the Millennium. Epoch the seventh, in the third act, is labelled the Congress of Religions, in Jerusalem in 1950, where the representatives of the great powers vote to sell Palestine to the Jews as a homeland. Much intriguing on the part of the Russian delegate takes place before that is accomplished. The Jewish representative at the Congress is named Dr. Darius.

ROMAN, RONETTI. ...Manasse; drama in 4 acte. Piatra-N: Editura D. Samsony, 1912. 122 p. 12°. NQYD

Leonard, Oscar. New lamps and old; a play in four acts. Adapted and translated by Oscar Leonard.

It was produced for the first time on the English stage, at the Suburban Garden, St. Louis, Mo., July 18, 1909. Wilton Lackaye played the part of Manasse the grandfather; Wilbur Higby, his son Nisim Cohanovici; Frances Neilson, the granddaughter Lelie; King Baggott, Mater Frunza, the Christian wooer; and George S. Spencer, Zelig Schorr, the comedian matchmaker of the play. For a synopsis of the plot, critiques, reviews of the production by R. D. Saunders, and illustrations, see *St. Louis Post-Dispatch*, July 11, 1909, part 2, p. 12; July 18, part 1, p. 4, and July 19, p. 4, * *A.* For a further discussion of the play and a biographical sketch of Roman see Oscar Leonard in *Jewish American*, Detroit, v. 15, April 3, 1908, p. 7-8, * *PBD.*

ROSE, EDWARD. *See* sub-entry under AUGIER, GUILLAUME VICTOR ÉMILE, AND JULES SANDEAU.

ROSENER, GEORGE M. Cohen's divorce; a vaudeville sketch in one act, for "straight" and Jew comedy. Boston: W. H. Baker & Company [cop. 1911]. 9 p. 12°.

Cohen wants a divorce but changes his mind, when he finds out how expensive it is.

—— The Goldstein wedding; Yiddish comedy drama in one act... New York: Wetzel, Rosener & James, 1912. 14 p. 24°.

See United States. — Copyright Office, *Dramatic compositions copyrighted in the United States, 1870 to 1916*, item 17031.

—— *See also* sub-entry under DICKENS, CHARLES.

ROSENFELD, SIDNEY. *See* sub-entry under ERCKMANN, ÉMILE, AND ALEXANDRE CHATRIAN.

ROTH, SAMUEL. ...The broomstick brigade; a play of Palestine [in two acts]. New York: Bloch Pub. Company [cop. 1914]. 15(1) p. 16°.

At head of title: To my friends in the Maccabean Zion Association.
A juvenile play. Scene: Herzl Street, Jerusalem.

ROUTLEDGE, WILLIAM. *See* sub-entry under MOSENTHAL, SALOMON HERMANN, RITTER VON.

ROWE, GEORGE FAWCETT. *See* sub-entry under ERCKMANN, ÉMILE, AND ALEXANDRE CHATRIAN.

RUSSELL, LIVINGSTON. *See* sub-entry under ERCKMANN, ÉMILE, AND ALEXANDRE CHATRIAN.

RYAN, JAMES. *See* sub-entry under ELIOT, GEORGE, PSEUD.

SARGENT, FREDERICK LEROY. Omar and the Rabbi; Fitzgerald's translation of the Rubaiyat of Omar Khayyam, and Browning's Rabbi Ben Ezra, arranged in dramatic form. Cambridge: Harvard Coöperative Society, 1909. 28 p. 16°.
NBL p.v.12

—— —— Boston: The Four Seas Co., 1919. 2 p.l., 3–30 p. 3. ed. 16°. NBF p.v.15

The two main characters are those given in the title. A public performance of this dramatic poem was given by the senior class of Emerson College, at Chickering Hall, Boston, April 11, 1910.

SAVOIR, ALFRED. In Manchuria. [A one-act play from the French.] (Tales. New York, 1905. 8°. Aug., 1905, p. 74–83.) NAL

One of the characters is a Jew.
Time: Russian-Japanese war.

SCHEFFAUER, HERMAN GEORGE. Der neue Shylock; ein Schauspiel in vier Akten... Autorisierte Übertragung aus dem englischen von L. Leonhard. Berlin: Berliner Theater-Verlag [cop. 1913]. 84 p. 12°.

This American ghetto comedy was first performed at the Lyric Theatre, London, Oct. 29, 1914, with Louis Calvert as Simon Ehrlich and Madge Titheradge as his daughter Rebecca.
"It is the story of one Simon Ehrlich and his family. But, though he lent money, he was no Shylock but a

THE JEW IN ENGLISH DRAMA 105

Individual Plays — 1838–1914, continued

'big baby'; his daughter ran away with a Christian, who in the end offered to become a Jew, and his son, whom he wanted to be a rabbi, became a rather shady business-man. But, even he improved in the end. The title-part was well performed by Calvert. The play, however, has no Shakespearean merit, and as the *Times* said a *New Shylock* has still to be written." — Extract from a letter to the compiler by Elkan N. Adler, London. Reviewed in *The Athenæum*, London, 1914, v. 144, p. 486, * *DA; Era,* London, v. 78, Nov. 4, 1914, p. 8, † *NAFA; Illustrated London news,* 1914, v. 145, p. 626, * *DA; The Times,* London, Oct. 30, 1914, p. 10, * *A;* and in *Truth,* London, 1914, v. 76, p. 860, * *DA.* Illustrations are given in *Illustrated sporting and dramatic news,* London, 1914, v. 82, p. 285, 302, * *DA.*

Under the title *The Bargain,* with the name of the Ehrlich family changed to that of Lusskin, it was produced at the Comedy Theatre, New York, Oct. 6, 1915. See review and illustrations in *New York dramatic mirror,* v. 74, Oct. 16, 1915, p. 8; Oct. 23, p. 2, 4, * *T–* *DA.*

SCHNITZLER, ARTHUR. ...The anti-Semites <Professor Bernhardi: a play>... Girard, Kansas: Haldeman-Julius Co. [19—?]. 63 p. 24°. (Little blue book. no. 226.) NAC (Little)

—— Professor Bernhardi; a comedy, by Arthur Schnitzler; an adaptation in English, by Mrs. Emil Pohli. San Francisco: P. Elder and Company [cop. 1913]. 3 p.l., v–ix, 64 p., 1 l. 8°. NCo
Reprinted in Leo W. Schwarz, editor, *A Golden treasury of Jewish literature,* New York [cop. 1937], p. 468–504, * *PSY.*
This is a "pure problem" play. It raises in an arresting form the problem of whether it is better to die *in* peace (in the ordinary sense) or *at* peace (in the theological). Professor Bernhardi, the director of a hospital, refuses on one occasion to allow the priest to approach the bedside of a dying girl; and for this refusal he is subsequently prosecuted for 'sacrilege' and imprisoned. He is a Jew, but it is in no sense as a Jew that he has acted, or even as a scientist, but simply as a man doing in a specific instance what he deems to be best. Was he right, was he wrong? See H. B. Samuel, *Modernities,* New York, 1914, p. 188–191, *NABO.*
The characters are fourteen physicians and a nurse; the action takes place in Vienna in 1900. The incident upon which it is founded occurred in Vienna. Prof. Bernhardi and Dr. Schreimann, a baptized Jew, are the Jewish characters. "I am told that Prof. Bernhardi in the play of the same name must be regarded as a pretty faithful portrait of the elder Schnitzler." — E. F. Walbridge, in his *Drames à clef,* quoting Edwin Björkman's introduction to *The Lonely way.*
The play was first performed, under the management of Barnowsky, at the Kleine Theater, Berlin, Nov. 28, 1912. It has since been produced in the majority of the larger German and Austrian cities, generally under severe censorship restrictions. In this country, it was given by the German Repertory Company, at the Irving Place Theatre, New York, Jan. 21, 1914, with Rudolf Christians in the title rôle. Reviewed (with illus.) in *Current opinion,* New York, 1914, v. 56, p. 193–194, * *DA;* and by J. B. Rethy in *International,* New York, v. 8, p. 92, * *DA.*

—— Professor Bernhardi; a comedy in five acts... Translated by Hetty Landstone. London: Faber & Gwyer [1927]. 160 p. 12°.
In this translation it was produced by the Jewish Drama League, at the Phoenix Theatre, London, March 22, 1931, with Abraham Sofaer in the title rôle. See *Jewish chronicle,* London, March 27, 1931, p. 48, * *PBE.*

—— Professor Bernhardi; a play in three acts. English version by Louis Borell and Ronald Adam. London: Victor Gollancz, Ltd., 1936. 110 p. 12°.
Reprinted in *Famous plays of 1936,* London, 1936, p. 9–118, *NAFH.*
In this translation, and under the direction of Heinrich Schnitzler, son of the author, it was staged anew at the Embassy Theatre, London, June 15, 1936, and transferred to the Phoenix Theatre, July 14, 1936, with Abraham Sofaer in the title rôle. See *Jewish chronicle,* London, June 19, 1936, p. 46–47; July 17, p. 47, * *PBE.*

Naumburg, Bernard. Schnitzler's "Professor Bernhardi." (Judaeans. Judaean addresses. New York, 1917. 8°. v. 2, p. 119–126.) * PBL

THE SÉANCE [in one scene]. (Vanity fair. London, 1884. f°. v. 32, p. 314–315.) * DA
Gladstone visits a medium. The ghost of his predecessor, Lord Beaconsfield, speaks to him.

SEARLE, CYRIL. *See* sub-entry under DICKENS, CHARLES.

SEJOUR, VICTOR. La tireuse de cartes; drame en cinq actes et un prologue en prose. Paris: Michel Lévy frères, 1860. 131 p. 12°.
Copy in the Schomburg collection at the 135th Street Branch.
The Library also has a Portuguese translation published at Lisbon, 1861, *NQM p.v.82.*

—— The fortune teller. (Occident. Philadelphia, 1860. 4°. v. 17, p. 301–302, 307–308.)
Signed: S. Bloch. * PBD
This is a synopsis of, with copious extracts from, Sejour's *La Tireuse de cartes,* produced at the Théâtre Porte-Saint-Martin, Paris, in 1859 and published in 1860. This synopsis by S. Bloch originally appeared in *L'Univers israélite,* Paris, 1860, année 15, p. 289–298, * *PBF,* and was here translated by an American lady. The play was inspired by the Mortara incident of June 23, 1858, where a Jewish child was forcibly abducted by the Papal guards in Bologna. In Sejour's play the action is laid in Genoa, at the beginning of the seventeenth century, and the parents are named Gideon and Gemea. A Catholic servant in the house baptizes their infant daughter Naomi, and turns her over to the Duchess Bianca. The larger part of the play is concerned with the struggle of the mother to regain the daughter and the refusal of the great lady, who had adopted her, to make the surrender.

Coyne, Joseph Stirling. The woman in red; a drama in a prologue and three acts... London: T. H. Lacy [18—?]. 56 p. nar. 12°. (Lacy's acting edition of plays. v. 92.) NCO (Lacy)
Adapted and altered from Sejour's piece.
Performed at the St. James's Theatre, London, April 13, 1868, with Mme. Celeste in the title rôle as Miriam and Rudiga.
The story of a child separated from her mother and brought up as a Christian. The place is France, 1670, and Geneva and Venice, 1686–87.

Heron, Matilda. Gamea; or, The Jewish mother, an adaptation from the French. Produced at Niblo's Garden, New York, Sept. 29, 1863, with Mlle. Vestvali in the title rôle.
Reviewed in *Albion,* New York, 1863, v. 41, p. 475, 487, * *A.* "A clumsy play, designed to illustrate the vital endurance of Judaism, and the ardent devotion of a mother's love."

Newbound, Edgar. Gemea; a drama in a prologue and three acts, was produced at the Britannia Theatre, London, March 29, 1880.
Information from *Era almanack,* 1881, p. 79.

Individual Plays — 1838–1914, continued

SELBY, CHARLES. Paris and pleasure; or, Home and happiness. A drame fantastique, or tale of diablerie, in four acts, by Charles Selby, comedian... London: T. H. Lacy [1859–73?]. iv, (1)6–55 p. nar. 12°. (Lacy's acting edition of plays. [no. 725.] v. 49.)   NCO (Lacy)
Based on a Parisian piece, *Les Enfers de Paris*, by MM. Roger de Beauvoir and Lambert Thiboust, which was first staged at the Théâtre des Variétés, Paris, Sept. 16, 1853. Selby's adaptation was produced at the Lyceum Theatre, London, Nov. 28, 1859. In the French original, the nationality of Jacobus, a usurer, is not given; in the English version he is identified as a Jew. The part was acted by James Vining. Reviewed in *The Athenæum*, London, 1859, v. 34, p. 745, * *DA;* and in *Era*, London, v. 22, Dec. 4, 1859, p. 10, † *NAFA*.

SELWYN, EDGAR. The country boy; a comedy in four acts... New York: S. French [etc.], cop. 1917. 101 p. 8°. (French's standard library edition.)   NBM
First produced at the Liberty Theatre, New York, Aug. 30, 1910, with Arthur Shaw as Joe Weinstein, a theatre ticket speculator, "quick, impulsive, but warm-hearted." Reviewed in *New York dramatic mirror*, v. 64, Sept. 10, 1910, p. 7, * *T–* DA*. Illustrations are given in *Green book album*, Chicago, 1911, v. 5, p. 1150–1152, *NAFA*. A novelization of the play by Charles De Forrest is given, ibid., p. 1153–1178.

SHALOM ALECHEM, PSEUD. OF SHALOM RABINOWITZ. Gymnazie; a monologue. (In: B. F. White, translator, Nine one-act plays from the Yiddish. Boston [cop. 1932]. 8°. p. 219–235.)   * PTP

—— שװער צו זײן א איד [a comedy in four acts, with a prologue and epilogue]. (צוקונפט. New York, 1921. 8°. v. 26, p. 555–567, 627–639, 674–686.)   * PBB
Reprinted in his פון צװײ װעלטען, New York, 1923, p. 7–164, * *PTL*.
Written in 1914.
A gentile student in Russia takes the place of his Jewish friend to find out what it is really like to be a Jew in Czarist Russia.
In an English translation by Tamara Berkowitz in three acts, it was staged at the Ambassador Theatre, New York, Sept. 24, 1931, with Edward Leiter as the Russian, Harry Mervis as the Jewish student, and Maurice Schwartz as David Shapiro. For reviews see *Collection of newspaper clippings of dramatic criticism, 1931–32*, v. I–L, † *NBL*. See also *Zukunft*, New York, 1931, v. 36, p. 722, * *PBB*.
With Robert Speaight and Victor Lewisohn in the parts of the two students, it was produced at the Shaftesbury Theatre, London, June 15, 1933. Reviewed in *Era*, London, v. 96, June 21, 1933, p. 12, † *NAFA;* with illus. in *Jewish chronicle*, London, June 23, 1933, p. 41, * *PBE;* and in *Theatre world*, London, 1933, v. 20, p. 18, *MWA*.

—— It's a lie (a dialogue in Galicia). Translated by Bernard G. Richards. (Maccabaean. New York, 1915. 4°. v. 26, p. 45–46.)   * PBD

—— "Liars!" a comedy. By F. Bimko [sic!]. (In: Etta Block, translator, One-act plays from the Yiddish; second series. New York, 1929. 12°. p. 71–79.)   * PTP
Reprinted in Frank Shay, editor, *Fifty more contemporary one-act plays*, New York [cop. 1928], p. 3–5, *NAFH* (Shay).
Conversation takes place on board a train en route between Kolomea, a Galician town, and the Russian frontier. The Galician professes disbelief in the malevolent gossip he himself narrates.

—— She must marry a doctor; sketch in one act. By Solomon J. Rabinowitsch. (In: I. Goldberg, translator, Six plays of the Yiddish theatre. Boston [1916]. 12°. p. 91–118.)   * PSQ
Title in the original Yiddish, "A doctor for a bridegroom"; first published 1887. A professional matchmaker is the central character. Produced by the Young Women Union Players at Philadelphia, Feb. 18, 1917.

—— When a broom looms large. From the Yiddish of Sholom Aleichem, by Oscar Leonard. (American Hebrew. New York, 1917. 4°. v. 100, p. 681.)   * PBD
In one act.
The characters are Jewish food dishes.
In the original: What should one eat on Passover.

SHAW, BERNARD. The doctor's dilemma, with a preface on doctors. New York: Brentano's, 1913. 1 p.l., v–xcii, 116 p. 12°.
A tragedy, in four acts.

—— —— New York: Brentano's, 1915. 1 p.l., v–xcii, 116 p. 12°.
Also printed in his *The Doctor's dilemma, Getting married and The Showing up of Blanco Posnet*, New York, 1916, p. v–xcii, 1–116, *NCR;* in his *The Doctor's dilemma and The Dark lady of the sonnets*, Leipzig, n.d., p. 9–224; and, without Preface, in his *Complete plays*, London [1931], p. 503–546, *NCR*.
Reviewed by Horace Traubel in *Conservator*, Philadelphia, 1911, v. 22, p. 89–91, * *DA;* by Temple Scott in *Forum*, New York, v. 45, p. 343–346, * *DA;* and in *Spectator*, London, v. 106, p. 360–361, * *DA*. A review, with copious extracts, is printed in *Current literature*, New York, 1911, v. 50, p. 419–424, * *DA*.
A satire on doctors. First produced at the Court Theatre, London, Nov. 20, 1906. Michael Sherbrooke played Dr. Schutzmacher, the Jewish physician in the group. He is described as having made a fortune in the East End by selling advice and drugs for six pence, under the sign "cure guaranteed." Reviewed in *Academy*, London, 1906, v. 71, p. 527, * *DA;* by Desmond McCarthy in *Speaker*, London, new series, v. 15, p. 226–227, and again, p. 255–256, * *DA;* by J. M. B. in *Sphere*, London, v. 27, p. 176, * *DA; The Times*, London, Nov. 21, 1906, p. 11, col. 1–2, * *A;* and in *Truth*, London, v. 60, p. 1301–1302, * *DA*. Illustrations can be seen in *Illustrated sporting and dramatic news*, London, v. 66, p. 573, * *DA*.
First produced in America, at Wallack's Theatre, New York, March 26, 1915, with Wright Kramer as Dr. Schutzmacher. Reviewed by Ethellyn B. De Foe in *Green book magazine*, Chicago, 1915, v. 13, p. 1146–1147, *NAFA;* by F. in *Nation*, New York, v. 100, p. 364, * *DA;* by Francis Hackett in *New republic*, New York, v. 2, p. 264, * *DA; New York clipper*, New York, v. 63, April 3, 1915, p. 6, * *T–* MVA;* by F. S. in *New York dramatic mirror*, v. 73, March 31, 1915, p. 8, * *T–* DA;* and in *Theatre magazine*, New York, v. 21, p. 229, † *NBLA*. A synopsis of the plot is printed in *Dramatist*, Easton, Pa., 1913, v. 4, p. 335, *NAFA*.
A notable revival was staged by the Theatre Guild, at the Guild Theatre, New York, Nov. 21, 1927, with Morris Carnovsky as Dr. Schutzmacher. For reviews see *Collection of newspaper clippings of dramatic criticism, 1927–1928*, v. D–G, † *NBL*.

—— Der Arzt am Scheideweg; Komödie in fünf Akten... Berlin: S. Fischer, 1914. 127(1) p. 4. Auf. 12°.
A French translation by Augustin and Henriette Hamon was published in 1921 in *Revue de Paris*, année 28, tome 5, p. 673–705; tome 6, p. 59–97, 316–338, * *DM*.

Walkley, Arthur Bingham. The doctor's dilemma. (In his: Drama and life. New York, 1908. 12°. p. 239–244.)   NAFD
Originally appeared in the *The Times*, London, Nov. 21, 1906 and reprinted by J. E. Agate in his *The English dramatic critics; an anthology*, London [1932], p. 261–265, *NCOM*.

Individual Plays — 1838-1914, continued

SHAW, BERNARD. Man and superman; a comedy and a philosophy... London: Constable & Co., Ltd., 1903. xxxvii p., 2 l., 244 p. 12°. 8–NCR
Contents: Man and superman. The revolutionist's handbook. Maxims for revolutionists.
Reviewed by William Barry in *Bookman,* London, 1903, v. 25, p. 45–46, * *GDD.*
Published in New York by Brentano's, 1904, *NCR,* 1905, *NCR,* 1907, 1913, and 1914, *NCR;* and by Bernhard Tauchnitz at Leipzig [1913] (Collection of British and American authors, v. 4436).
Reprinted, without Preface, in his *Complete plays,* London [1931], p. 332–405, *NCR.*
In an interpolated scene, omitted from the stage productions, Shaw introduced Mendoza, chief of brigands, a Jew and a would-be Zionist. Produced at the Court Theatre, London, May 23, 1905. Reviewed by Reginald Farrer in *Speaker,* London, 1905, new series, v. 12, p. 232–233, * *DA; Truth,* London, v. 57, p. 1393–1394, * *DA;* and by William Archer in *World,* London, 1905, p. 914–915, * *DA.* See also A. B. Walkley in his *Drama and life,* New York, 1908, p. 224–232, *NAFD.*
Produced at the Hudson Theatre, New York, Sept. 5, 1905. Reviewed in *New York dramatic mirror,* v. 54, Sept. 16, 1905, p. 2, * *T-* DA;* and in *Theatre magazine,* New York, v. 5, p. 238–239, † *NBLA.*
See Bessie D. Katzenberg, "Shaw's treatment of religious subjects," in *Review,* Philadelphia, v. 6, March, 1911, p. 20–26.

——— ...Mensch und Übermensch. [Eine Komödie und eine Philosophie. Deutsch von Siegfried Trebitsch.] Berlin: S. Fischer [1927]. 4 p.l., 11–338 p., 1 l. 12°.

Gauger, Rudolf. Man and superman. (In his: Amerikanergestalten in der englischen Literatur der Gegenwart. Bochum, 1933. 8°. p. 35–40.) NAC p.v.349

SHELLAND, HARRY E. Fun in a school room; a farciful sketch in one act. New York: Fitzgerald Pub. Corp., cop. 1908. 13 p. 12°.
Herr Spitznoodle, the teacher, and Isaac Cohen, one of his three pupils.

——— The great libel case, a mock trial... New York: Dick & Fitzgerald, cop. 1900. 31 p. 12°. (Dick's American edition.) NBL p.v.109, no.8
Another issue was published by the Fitzgerald Pub. Co., 1900.
Theodore Rosenvelt, "Jew peddler," one of twelve jurors. A take-off of a backwoods court in Kentucky.

——— Two wandering Jews; a vaudeville sketch [in one act]. New York: Fitzgerald Pub. Corp., cop. 1904. 10 p. 16°.
"Abe Cohen and Julius Simpson try to insult each other, but it's impossible."

SHERWOOD, CLARA HARRIOT. The cable car; an Howellian burlesque, in two acts... New York: T. H. French; London: S. French, cop. 1891. 13 p. nar. 12°. (French's acting edition of plays. [no. 1995.] v. 133.) NCO (Lacy)
"A Jew," one of the characters.

SHILLINGFORD, OSMOND, AND A. E. ELLIS. *See* sub-entry under MOLNAR, FERENC.

SHOULD we pray in Hebrew or English? (Israel. London, 1900. 4°. v. 4, p. 141–143.)
A dialogue between George Merton and Mordecai Levin.
Copy: Library of the American Jewish Historical Society.

SIMONS, SARAH EMMA, AND C. I. ORR. Tales of a wayside inn [dramatized]. (In their: Dramatization... Third year. Chicago, New York [cop. 1913]. 12°. p. 42–58.) SSD p.v.80
The Spanish Jew of Longfellow's poem.

SKEEN, W. H. *See* sub-entry under DICKENS, CHARLES.

STEPHENS, HENRY POTTINGER, AND W. YARDLEY. *See* sub-entry under AINSWORTH, WILLIAM HARRISON.

STEELL, WILLIS. A bride from home; a vaudeville sketch in one act... Boston: W. H. Baker & Co. [cop. 1912.] 11 p. 12°. (The vaudeville stage.)
The scene is Division Street, New York City. All the four characters are given Jewish names. Maxoff, a young merchant, sends for a bride from the old country.

STEINER, RUDOLPH. Four mystery plays... Translated and edited... by H. Collison... S. M. K. Gandell... and R. T. Gladstone... New York and London: G. P. Putnam's Sons, 1920. 2 v. 12°. NGE
The four plays are The portal of initiation, The soul's probation, The guardian of the threshold, and The soul's awakening. They are described in the introduction as Christian mystery plays, showing the progress of the soul through its several incarnations.
In the second play, Prof. Capesius has a vision of the fourteenth century, in which are seen the former incarnations of several characters of the play, among them that of Simon the Jew, a physician regarded as a sorcerer, the former incarnation of Dr. Strader. Written and produced in Munich, in 1910, 1911, 1912 and 1913, in August of each year.

STEVENSON, AUGUSTA. The treason of Benedict Arnold [in five acts]. illus. (In her: Children's classics in dramatic form. Book five. Boston [etc., cop. 1912.] 8°. p. 261–303.)
"Based on authentic records."
Time: Sept. 20–30, 1780. Place: the Hudson River valley.
Major Franks is represented as one of two aides to General Arnold. The Franks here alluded to is David Saulsbury Franks. See A. S. W. Rosenbach, "Documents relative to Major David S. Franks while aide-de-camp to General Arnold," in American Jewish Historical Society, *Publications* [Baltimore], 1897, no. 5, p. 157–190, * *PXX.*

STIRLING, EDWARD. The anchor of hope; or, The seaman's star! A drama in two acts... London, New York: S. French [1869–76?]. 31 p. 12°. (French's acting edition of plays. [no. 1657.] v. 111.) NCO (Lacy)
First produced at the Surrey Theatre, London, April 19, 1847, with Edward Stirling, the author, as Abraham Moses, a pedlar, who falls among smugglers. Speaks in dialect. Scene: Cornwall, England.
Produced at the National Theatre, New York, March 26, 1852.

——— The Jew's daughter; an original drama, in two acts... London: T. H. Lacy [1857]. 18 p. nar. 12°. (Lacy's acting edition of plays. v. 29.) NCO (Lacy)
Also issued as no. 430 of French's acting edition of plays.
Scene: Padua, Italy. Produced at the Strand Theatre, London, Jan. 5, 1857, wth Kate Percy in the title rôle. Reviewed in *The Times,* London, Jan. 11, 1857, p. 11, * *A.* The reviewer states that the play was written to combat prejudice against the Jews by showing that "a Jewess may be possessed of as many of the finest traits of womanhood as those of another belief."

Individual Plays — 1838-1914, continued

STIRLING, EDWARD. The mendicant's son! or, The Jew of Southwark; a drama in three acts ... By permission from the prompter's book ... As performed at the London theatres... London: John Duncombe [184–?]. 48 p. incl. front. 16°. (Duncombe's edition:)
Copy: Harvard College Library.
Produced at the Surrey Theatre, London, Dec. 26, 1845, with Henry Hughes as Ishmael Lyons, dealer in cast-off garments in Southwark, and Mrs. H. Vining as his daughter Rachel. The mendicant's son turns out to be the rightful heir. The Jew helps him to foil the bogus son, and he is rewarded by the marriage of his daughter to the rich heir and her entry into Society as a "lady." Reviewed in *The Times*, London, Dec. 27, 1845, p. 5, col. 4, * A.
Produced at the New Bowery Theatre, New York, under the title *The Jew of Southwark*, Oct. 31, 1863. Reviewed in *Sunday mercury*, New York, Nov. 8, 1863, p. 4, col. 7, * A.

—— *See also* sub-entry under DICKENS, CHARLES.

STRICKLAND, SIR WALTER WILLIAM. A slight misunderstanding; or, Sono cose che succedono — in Russia. (In his: Three trilogies; or, Nine dramas in prose and verse. New York, 1929. 12°. p. 304–332.) NCR
Published 1905 in a volume called *Dramatic pieces*.
"How a head of the police mistook the live Banker of an Empress for her dead poodle, and what happened in consequence." A political farce, in one act. Scene: St. Petersburg, at the time of Catherine the Great. Sunderland is described as "a Jewish London banker, City type." The author in a note states that this farce is historical and given in the memoirs of Comte de Ségur.

STRUNSKY, HYMAN. Zalmen the powerful; a drama of Russian life in one act. (Jewish comment. Baltimore, 1908. f°. v. 28, p. 65–69.)
* PBD
An episode of self-defense and martyrdom during a massacre.

SULIVAN, ROBERT. Elopements in high life; a comedy in five acts... London: T. H. Lacy [185–?]. 54 p. nar. 12°. (Lacy's acting edition of plays. v. 10.) NCO (Lacy)
Produced at Haymarket Theatre, London, April 7, 1853, with Braid as Mr. Abraham, ex-partner and executor of the deceased gentile Lovelock, who had amassed a fortune as a moneylender. Reviewed in *Era*, London, v. 15, April 10, 1853, p. 11, † *NAFA*; and in *Spectator*, 1853, v. 26, p. 344, * *DA*.

SUTER, HENRY CHARLES. *See* sub-entry under DICKENS, CHARLES.

SWAN, HOWARD. Paul and Joseph; or, God and Mammon in Transvaal... An unfinished drama. London: Samuel Baxter [1899?]. 23 p. 8°. NCO p.v.338
In a prologue and two acts.
Deals with the Boer war of 1899–1902. Paul and Joseph refer to Paul Kruger and Joseph Chamberlain, Great Britain's colonial secretary during 1895–1900. There is a great deal in it about Jews, but it is difficult to say what it is all about. Among the characters are General Jewbear, Baron Roughchild, Abe Goldstein, and Moses Angel. Swan was also the author of *South Africa up to date, the manifesto of peace... being the letter to "the people across the river" — the "Hebrews" of to-day* [London, 1899], BNY p.v.2, no.16.

SWANWICK, CATHERINE. The Jew doctor; a drama [in five acts]. (In her: Three dramas. London: F. Pitman, 1866. 12°. p. 101–160.)
Action passes in England at an undeterminable period. Morland, the rightful Lord Glenville, supposedly drowned, returns to his estate. In disguise of a Jewish doctor he saves his daughter, by means of an elixir, from being buried alive and regains his title from his villainous brother.

TAG, RALPH W. Handy Solomon; a farce in one act... New York: Fitzgerald Pub. Corp., cop. 1914. 14 p. 12°.
Solomon Sofransky, an old clothes dealer. Everyone mistakes him for someone else.

TALFOURD, FRANCIS. The merchant of Venice travestie; a burlesque in one act... Oxford: E. T. Spiers, 1849. 33 p. 12°.

—— Shylock; or, The merchant of Venice preserved. An entirely new reading of Shakespeare. From an edition hitherto undiscovered by modern authorities, and which it is hoped may be received as the stray leaves of a Jerusalem hearty-joke... London: T. H. Lacy [185–?]. 30 p. 12°. (Lacy's acting edition of plays. v. 11.) NCO (Lacy)

—— Shylock; or, The merchant of Venice preserved... As performed in the London and American theatres. New York: S. French [187–?]. 30 p. 12°. (Minor drama. no. 132.)
In five scenes.
The Lacy and French editions differ not only in title page but in the stage directions and lists of casts given. Both editions are an expansion of the author's earlier travesty, published in 1849, but not performed then.
First produced at the Royal Olympic Theatre, London, July 4, 1853 with Frederick Robson as Shylock, "a Jew who does not on this occasion conduct himself as a Gentile-man", and Miss E. Turner as Jessica, Shylock's "one fair daughter and — something more." W. D. Adams calls it the first burlesque of *The Merchant of Venice*. Cf. *Dictionary of national biography*, under Thomas Frederick Robson. Reviewed in *The Athenæum*, London, 1853, p. 832, * *DA*; in *Era*, v. 15, July 10, 1853, p. 10, † *NAFA;* in *Examiner*, London, 1853, p. 439, * *DA;* and in *Spectator*, London, 1853, v. 26, p. 654, * *DA*.
Produced at Burton's Theatre, New York, Oct. 29, 1853, with T. B. Johnston as Shylock and Mrs. W. E. Burton as Jessica. It was again produced at Wallack's Theatre, New York, July 27, 1857, with John Wood who "made a great hit as Shylock." Port. of Wood in the part is reproduced by Odell in v. 7, facing p. 534. Odell also quotes from the *New York Tribune* of July 28.
Under its sub-title, *Merchant of Venice preserved*, it was revived at the Fifth Avenue Theatre, New York, Sept. 28, 1868, with M. W. Leffingwell as Shylock and Lina Edwin as Jessica. See Brown II:400.

TAYLOR, SIR HENRY. The virgin widow. A play. London: Longman, Brown, Green, and Longmans, 1850. viii, 192 p. 12°.
Reprinted in his *Works*, London, 1878, v. 3, p. 1–131, NCG.
Haggai, Sadoc and Shallum.
"In labelling his brigands as Jews, he has travelled beyond the confines of actual knowledge and experience." — *Mabon, The Jews in English poetry and drama*, p. 425.

Individual Plays — 1838-1914, continued

TAYLOR, THOMAS PROCLUS. The tower of London; or, Queen Mary... London: J. Dicks [18—?]. 16 p. 12°. (Dicks' standard drama. no. 612.)
"The Tower of London [by W. H. Ainsworth], together with Marie Tudor by Dumas was turned into a play, The Tower of London; or, Queen Mary, by J. [sic] P. Taylor (Adelphi, Nov. 30, 1840), in which Barnabas, a Jew of Antwerp, played by Maynard [is one of the characters]." — Landa, p. 169. It is reviewed in Literary gazette, London, 1840, p. 788, * DA; and in The Times, London, Dec. 1, 1840, p. 3, col. 4, * A. The part of the Jew was minor.
On Dec. 21, 1840, it was staged at the Adelphi again, under the title The Tower of London; or, Og, Gog and Magog. See Nicoll, p. 534.

TAYLOR, TOM. Going to the bad; an original comedy, in two acts... London: T. H. Lacy [185–?]. 71(1) p. 12°. (Lacy's acting edition of plays. v. 37.) NCO (Lacy)
First produced at the Olympic Theatre, London, for the benefit of Robson, June 5, 1858, with two Jewish bailiffs, Moss (H. Cooper) and Davis. Among the dramatis personae is one curiously called Bevis Marks, the name of the Spanish and Portuguese synagogue of London. He is a broker and uncle to Potts, hero of the play who started out "going to the bad." Judging from this relationship he was probably not represented as a Jew. His rôle was acted by G. Cooke. Reviewed in The Athenæum, London, 1858, v. 31, p. 760, * DA; Era, London [v. 20], June 13, 1858, p. 11, † NAFA; Literary gazette, London, 1858, p. 572, * DA; and in The Times, London, June 7, 1858, p. 9, col. 2-3, * A.
Produced at Wallack's Theatre, New York, Nov. 12, 1858, with Levere as Moss and C. Bernard as Davis. Reviewed in Spirit of the times, New York, 1858, new series, v. 5, p. 192, † MVA.

—— Helping hands. A domestic drama, in two acts... Boston: W. V. Spencer [1856?]. 48 p. 12°. (Spencer's Boston theatre. [v. 12,] no. 69 [i.e. 89].)
Copy: University of Michigan.

—— —— London, New York: Samuel French [1885-1910?]. 52 p. 12°. (Lacy's acting edition of plays. v. 22.) NCO (Lacy)
Also issued as no. 278 of French's standard drama. Produced at the Adelphi Theatre, London, June 20, 1855. The plot centers around a lost Stradivarius. C. Selby played Isaac Wolff, a rascally broker, and C. J. Smith, Lazarus Solomon, a dishonest appraiser and valuer who, in league with the villain, sets a low price on the violin. Reviewed in The Athenæum, London, 1855, v. 28, p. 738, * DA; Examiner, London, 1855, p. 390, * DA; and in Era, London, v. 17, June 24, 1855, p. 10, † NAFA.
Produced at Burton's Theatre, New York, March 10, 1856, with Mr. Moore as Isaac Wolff and Mr. Gourley as Lazarus Solomon.

—— Our clerks; or, No. 3, Fig Tree Court, Temple. An original farce in 1 act... London: T. H. Lacy [1852?]. 26 p., 1 l. nar. 12°. (Lacy's acting edition of plays. v. 6.) NCO (Lacy)
Also issued as no. 80 of French's acting edition. First performed at the Princess' Theatre, London, March 6, 1852, with F. Cooke as Mr. Levi Abrahams "of Cursitor Street," a writ-server. Reviewed in The Athenæum, London, 1852, v. 25, p. 306, * DA.
Produced at Burton's Theatre, New York, April 23, 1852. On April 26, 1852, it was staged at the National Theatre, New York, as Lawyer's clerks.

—— "Payable on demand"; an original domestic drama, in two acts... London: T. H. Lacy [186–?]. 53 p. 12°. (Lacy's acting edition of plays. v. 41.) NCO (Lacy)
Also issued as no. 614 of French's acting edition. Based on an incident in the rise of the Rothschild fortunes. Meyer Rothschild is here named Goldsched and the Landgrave of Hesse, the Marquis de St. Cast. Goldsched, acted by Robson, is in this play not the honest financier he is accepted to have been; that rôle was by Taylor given to his gentile wife. Act I takes place on Oct. 22, 1792, during the occupation of Frankfort by the French troops; act II, on April 4, 1814, in Goldsched's house, London. It was first presented at the Olympic Theatre, London, July 11, 1859, with Miss Wyndham as Lina, Reuben's wife, later as his daughter Lina, whom our author marries off to the son of the Marquis St. Cast. G. Cooke played Jonadab ben Manasseh. Reviewed in The Athenæum, London, 1859, v. 34, p. 89, * DA; Era, London, v. 21, July 17, 1859, p. 11, † NAFA; Literary gazette, London, new series, v. 3, p. 72-73, * DA; and in The Times, London, July 12, 1859, p. 5, col. 5, * A.

—— The ticket-of-leave man. A drama, in four acts. Founded on a French dramatic tale, "Le retour de Melun," included in "Les drames de la vie," by M. M. Brisebarre and Nuz... London: T. H. Lacy [186–?]. (1)4-84 p. nar. 12°. (Lacy's acting edition of plays. v. 59.) NCO (Lacy)

—— —— New York: J. Polhemus [186–?]. 64 p. 8°. NCO p.v.749

—— —— New-York: S. French [1876-86?]. 56 p. 12°. (French's standard drama. The acting edition. no. 329.) NCO p.v.557
The Library also has two prompter's copies, one with interleaved ms. notes, the other with mounted clippings and port., NCOF.

—— —— Clyde, Ohio: A. D. Ames [187–?]. 54 p. 12°. (Ames' series of standard and minor drama. no. 201.)

—— —— Philadelphia: The Penn Publishing Company, 1904. 64 p. 12°.
Reprinted with an introduction in M. J. Moses, editor, Representative British dramas, Victorian and modern, Boston, 1918 (a new and rev. ed., 1931), p. 217-267, NCO (Moses).
"All credit for the invention of the story [of this play] belongs to MM. Brisebarre and Nuz, the authors of both of 'Les drames de la vie' and of the drama of 'Leonard.' " — Tom Taylor.
Written under the influence of Victor Hugo's Les Misérables. Robert Brierly is the Jean Valjean of the play and Melter Moss, counterfeiter, thieves' agent, and one of the most obnoxious Jewish characters in English nineteenth century drama, is his evil genius. This play, first produced at the Olympic Theatre, London, May 27, 1863, with G. Vincent as Moss, was very successful on the stage and bred many imitations. Reviewed in The Athenæum, London, 1863, v. 41, p. 753, * DA; Era, London, v. 25, May 31, 1863, p. 10, † NAFA; and in The Times, London, May 28, 1863, p. 11, col. 1, * A. See Landa, p. 186-189.
It was put on at the Winter Garden, New York, Nov. 30, 1863, with Humphrey Bland as Melter Moss, and ran continuously till March 26, 1864. During the same period it was seen also at the New Bowery, Brooklyn Park, and Barnum's Museum. Reviewed in Albion, New York, 1863, v. 41, p. 583, * A. Odell, VII:555, quotes in part a review by James Otis. See the Herald, New York, Feb. 15, 1864, p. 7, col. 3, * A.
A revival of this favorite was put on at the Palm Garden Music Hall, New York, June 24, 1934, with Harry Cooke as Moss.

Geller, James Jacob. The ticket of leave man. (In his: Grandfather's follies. New York [cop. 1934]. 8°. p. 32-35.) MWED

Individual Plays—1838-1914, continued

THACHER, GEORGE HORNELL. Hypatia; an historical tragedy, in three acts. With an apostrophe. [Albany,] cop. 1913. 1 p.l., 141 p. sq. 12°.
Alexandria, 415 A. D. The plot is taken largely from Kingsley's historical novel of the same name. In the struggle for supremacy between the Christians and the Romans in the Alexandria of that time, the Jews, in the person of Rafael and his sister, Doria, are represented as the adherents of the Roman side.

THOMAS, AUGUSTUS. As a man thinks; a play in four acts. New York: Duffield & Company, 1911. 213 p. front. (port.) 8°.   NBM
—— New York, London: Samuel French, cop. 1911. 213 p. 12°.
Reprinted in G. P. Baker, editor, *Modern American plays*, New York, 1920, p. 1–100, NBL.
The author deals with the dual moral standard for the two sexes and the problem of intermarriages arising out of race prejudice. The reviewers have pointed out that the circumstances surrounding his plot and the character of his Jewish dramatis personae weakened greatly the thesis of his problem and rendered his solution inconclusive.
A synopsis of the play, with copious extracts from the text, is given in *Current literature*, New York, v. 50, p. 529–536, * DA. Mr. Thomas explains his conception of the Jewish character in his *The Print of my remembrance*, New York, 1922, p. 450–453, MWES (Thomas). See comment in *Jewish exponent*, Philadelphia, v. 71, Dec. 22, 1922, p. 4, * PBE.
Prior to its production, it was announced and advertised as *The Jew*. See *American Hebrew*, New York, 1910, v. 87, p. 263, * PBD; and William Winter in *Harper's weekly*, New York, v. 54, Oct. 8, 1910, p. 3, * DA.
Produced at Nazimova's 39th Street Theatre, March 13, 1911, with John Mason as Dr. Seelig, Amelia Gardner as Mrs. Seelig, Charlotte Ives as their daughter Vedah, and Walter Hale as Benjamin DeLota. Reviewed by Louis Lipsky in *American Hebrew*, New York, v. 89, p. 9, * PBD; Dramatist, Easton, Pa., v. 2, p. 142–143, NAFA; *New York dramatic mirror*, v. 65, March 15, 1911, p. 7, * T-* DA; and (with illus.) in *Theatre magazine*, v. 13, April, 1911, p. 107–108, ix–x, † NBLA.
A review of the Baltimore production of Jan., 1912, is given in *Jewish comment*, Baltimore, v. 38, p. 213, * PBD.

Schulman, Samuel. The Jewish features of Mr. Thomas's play. (American Hebrew. New York, 1911. 4°. v. 89, p. 61–62.)   * PBD
Discourse delivered on Sunday, April 23, 1911, at Temple Beth-El.

THORNE, DAVID. *See* sub-entry under WILDE, OSCAR.

TIBBALS, SEYMOUR SELDEN. Izzy's troubles. [A monologue.] Franklin, Ohio: Eldridge Entertainment House, Inc. [1914?] 4 p. 12°.
Cover-title.

TILTON, DWIGHT, PSEUD. OF G. T. RICHARDSON AND W. D. QUINT. Meyer & son; a novel, by Dwight Tilton...based upon the three-act play of the same name by Thomas Addison. Boston, Mass.: The C. M. Clark Publishing Company, 1908. 2 p.l., 323 p., front., 7 pl. 12°.   NBO

Addison, Thomas. Meyer and son; a drama in three acts, was produced at Plainfield, N. J., on Feb. 27, 1909 and at the Garden Theatre, New York, March 1, 1909.
An intermarriage problem play. The college educated son of a Jewish banker is in love with the daughter of his father's rival. William Humphrey played Nathan Meyer, the father; Franklin Richie, his son Max; and H. G. Carlton, Jacob Strauss, a clerk at Meyer's, who spoke his lines in dialect and provided the comic rôle. Reviewed by Louis Lipsky in *American Hebrew*, New York, 1909, v. 84, p. 475, * PBD; *New York clipper*, v. 57, p. 117, * T-† MVA; *New York dramatic mirror*, v. 61, March 13, 1909, p. 3, * DA; and in *Theatre magazine*, New York, v. 9, April, 1909, p. xi–xii, † NBLA.

TOBIAS, MRS. LILY. AND L. LEWISOHN. *See* sub-entry under ELIOT, GEORGE, PSEUD.

TOLSTOĬ, ALEKSEĬ KONSTANTIONOVICH, GRAF. The death of Ivan the Terrible; a drama in verse...rendered into English verse by Alfred Hayes. With a preface by C. Nabakoff... London: K. Paul, Trench, Trubner & Co., Ltd., 1926. viii, 185 p. front. (port.) 12°.   ** QDK
In a translation by George Rapall Noyes it was included in G. R. Noyes, compiler, *Masterpieces of the Russian drama*, New York, 1933, p. 457–546, ** QDK.
In a translation by Mrs. S. R. de Meissner, it was first produced on the American stage by Richard Mansfield at the New Amsterdam Theatre, New York, March 1, 1904, with Kingdon as Roman Eleazerych Jakoby, one of two physicians called in to minister to the Czar. Reviewed in *New York dramatic mirror*, v. 51, March 12, 1904, p. 16, * T-* DA; and in *Theatre magazine*, New York, 1904, v. 4, p. 83–84, † NBLA.
Queen Elizabeth sent a doctor, believed to be a Jew, named Jacob, to the Czar of Russia. That Ivan may have been ministered to by a Jewish physician is not without likelihood. See S. L. Lee in New Shakspere Society, *Transactions*, series 1, no. 12, p. 158, * NCK, who bases his opinion on Wm. Munk, *The Roll of the Royal College of Physicians of London*, London, 1878, v. 1, p. 88, Ref. Cat. 276.

TOLSTOĬ, LEV NIKOLAYEVICH, GRAF. The fruits of culture; a comedy in four acts, by Count Leo Tolstoĭ. Translated by George Schumm. Boston: B. R. Tucker, 1891. 185 p. 8°.   ** QDK
Grossman: "of Jewish type, very lively, nervous: he talks very loud."

—— —— (In his: Plays. Translated by Louise and Aylmer Maude. London, 1914. 8°. p. 121–227.)   ** QDK

—— The fruits of enlightenment, a comedy in four acts by Lyof Tolstoy. Translated from the Russian by E. J. Dillon, with an introduction by Arthur W. Pinero. London: William Heinemann, 1891. viii, 276 p., front. (port.) 12°.

—— —— Authorized ed. New York: United States Book Company [cop. 1891]. 149 p. 12°. (Lovell's Westminster series. no. 27.)

—— —— Boston: Walter H. Baker & Company, 1901. 149 p. 12°.   ** QDK

—— —— Boston: J. W. Luce & Co. [1911.] 149 p. 8°.

—— —— [Translated by Isabel F. Hapgood and N. H. Dole.] (In his: Novels and other works. New York, 1902. 8°. v. 16, p. 338–455.)
                                      ** QDB

—— The fruits of enlightenment. (In his: Dramatic works. Translated by Nathan Haskell Dole. New York [cop. 1923]. 12°. p. 131–249.)
                                      ** QDK
In an adaptation by Jack R. Crawford it was staged by the Yale Dramatic Association, during the season of 1912–13, at New Haven. See MWEZ n.c.326.
Produced, on the occasion of the centennial of the author's birth, by the Arts Theatre Club, in conjunction with the Tolstoy Society, London, Nov. 2, 1928, with Frederick de Lara as Grossman. Reviewed by Francis Birrell in *Nation & Athenæum*, London, 1928, v. 44, p. 208, * DA; and by Richard Jennings in *Spectator*, London, v. 141, p. 687–688, * DA.

Individual Plays — 1838-1914, continued

TOTTEN, JOSEPH BYRON. *See* sub-entry under KAUFFMAN, REGINALD WRIGHT.

TOUBE, TERESA S. *See* sub-entry under MOSENTHAL, SALOMON HERMANN, RITTER VON.

TOWNSEND, CHARLES. The iron hand; a drama in four acts. Chicago: T. S. Denison & Co. [cop. 1897.] 39 p. 12°. (Alta series.)
"Old Ikey, der most honestest man," accomplice of the villain Montford.

—— The jail bird; a drama in five acts... Author's edition. New York: Dick & Fitzgerald, cop. 1893. 46 p. diagrs. 12°.
Place: New York City.
Solomon Isaacs, a Jewish "crook."
A cast of characters is given for a production in which E. A. Bills played Isaacs.

—— Perils of a great city; a melodrama, in four acts. Philadelphia: Penn Pub. Co., 1911. 47 p. 12°.　　　　　　　　　NBL p.v.42, no.3
Another ed. was published in 1917.
Jacobs, villainous but laughable. Very loud and much jewelry.

TOWNSEND, WILLIAM THOMPSON. ...Whitefriars; a drama in three acts... The only edition, correctly marked, by permission, from the prompter's book... As performed at the London theatres... London: J. Duncombe [1844?]. 44 p. incl. front. 16°. (Duncombe's edition.)　　　　　　　　　NCO p.v.732
Frontispiece missing.

—— Whitefriars; or, The days of Claude du Val. A drama in three acts, from the celebrated romantic novel of the same title... London: T. H. Lacy [1857-73?]. 48 p., 1 pl. nar. 12°. (Lacy's acting edition of plays. v. 40.)
　　　　　　　　　　　　　　NCO (Lacy)
The novel referred to is Emma Robinson, *Whitefriars; or, The days of Charles the Second*, London, 1844, 3 v.
Also issued with the imprint of Samuel French of New York as no. 598 of Lacy's acting edition.
The period of the play is 1660-1685. First produced at the Surrey Theatre, London, April 8, 1844, with R. Honner as Elkanah, "a Jew mediciner or poisoner," who is made to do the "dirty work" of the piece. Reviewed in *The Times*, London, April 9, 1844, p. 5, col. 2, * A.

Newton, Henry Chance. A most daring drama of treason. (In his: Crime and the drama; or, Dark deeds dramatized. London [1927]. 8°. p. 225–229.)　　　　　　　　　　　　NAF

TRAILL, HENRY DUFF. The third age. (In his: Number twenty; fables and fantasies. London [1892]. 12°. p. 39–59.)
Contains a strange and contrary outcome, in dramatic form, to the trial scene of *The Merchant of Venice*. See "A Comedy transformed" in *American Hebrew*, 1892, v. 51, p. 630–631, * PBD.

THE TROUBLES of the millionaire. (Maccabaean. New York, 1905. 8°. v. 9, p. 142–143.) * PBD
The characters are M. De Witte (Russian ambassador at the Russo-Japanese Portsmouth Peace Conference) and a perplexed Jewish millionaire.

TULLIDGE, EDWARD WHEELOCK. Ben Israel; or, From under the curse. A Jewish play in 5 acts ...Salt Lake City: J. C. Graham, 1875. v(i), (1)8–52 p. music inserted. 8°.　　ZZMG p.v.20

—— —— Salt Lake City: Star Publishing Co., 1887. 53 p. 8°.
The author dedicates his play "to the Jews of America," to commemorate the return of their forbears to England, after four hundred years' banishment. He deplores the commonly accepted picture of the Jews on the stage, as exemplified by Shylock and Fagin. The action of the play passes in London, 1660–1685. King Charles II is one of the characters.
First performed at the Grand Opera House, New York, March 6, 1876, with J. H. Vinson in the title rôle, and Amelia Waugh as Rachel. It ran only twice.
Reviewed in *New York dramatic news*, v. 1, March 11, 1876, p. 2, † *NBL*; and in *Spirit of the times*, New York, 1876, v. 91, p. 115, † *MVA*.

ULRICH, CHARLES KENMORE. The Hebrew; a dramatic sketch [in one act]. Chicago: T. S. Denison & Co. [cop. 1910]. 17 p. diagr. 16°.
　　　　　　　　　　　　　NBM (Ulrich) p.v.1
Isadore Finkelstein, "a merchant prince of the ghetto," embarks on a railroad venture in Montana. With him is his daughter, Rachel. He is described as "genial, good-natured, and uneducated. The dominating traits of his character should be love for his child and charity for the oppressed." Produced by the Dickerman School of Acting, Omaha, Neb., March 3, 1910.

—— The high school freshman; a comedy for boys, in three acts... Chicago: T. S. Denison & Company [cop. 1909]. 54 p. 16°. (Alta series.)　　　　　　　　　NBM (Ulrich) p.v.1
Julius Cohen, "a freshman from the ghetto," at a country high school.

—— The town marshall; a comedy drama of the rural Northwest [in four acts]... Chicago: T. S. Denison & Company [cop. 1910]. 68 p. 16°. (Alta series.)　　　NBM (Ulrich) p.v.1
Scene: South Dakota. Ikey Levinsky, a Jewish peddler.

VACHELL, HORACE ANNESLEY. *See* sub-entry under ROBERTS, MORLEY.

VANCE, DAISY MELVILLE. *See* sub-entry under DICKENS, CHARLES.

VAN NOPPEN, LEONARD C. Who is Bashti Beki? From [the advance sheets of] "Armageddon." In verse. [Lynchburg, Va.: Brown-Morrison Co., 1912.] 32 p. 8°.　　　　NBL p.v.26
Cover-title.
A dramatic poem.
A satire on Theodore Roosevelt, during his Progressive campaign of 1912. "Bashti-Beki will be found ...to fit the career of a prominent American politician and publicist. Few will fail to recognize his portrait... It pictures modern Philistines in ancient Philistia." Accordingly there are introduced as speakers a 1st, 2nd and 3rd Hebrew, and a female named Bas-Beya.

VICKERS, GEORGE MORLEY. Petruchio's widow; a Shakesperian travesty, in one act. (In his: Ideal entertainments. Philadelphia, 1888. 8°. p. 181–193.)　　　　　　　　　　NANV
Mr. Moses Shylock, a pawnbroker. Mrs. Jessica Lorenzo, an ungrateful daughter.

VOGL, MRS. VIRGINIE DOUGLASS (HYDE-). Love and lovers [in four acts]. (In her: Echoes and prophecies. Westwood, Mass., 1909. 12°. p. 3–69.)　　　　　　　　　　　　　　NBM
Rabbi Nazimova and his children, friends of their non-Jewish high-school mates.

Individual Plays — 1838-1914, continued

WALLACE, LEWIS. The prince of India; or, Why Constantinople fell, by Lew Wallace... New York: Harper & Brothers, 1893. 2 v. 12°. NBO

The plot is placed in the Byzantine Empire in the 15th century. Dramatized into five acts and a prologue by J. I. C. Clarke and produced at the Broadway Theatre, New York, Sept. 24, 1906, with Emmett Corrigan in the title rôle, Averill Harris as Uel, and Julie Herne as Lael, daughter of Uel. The legend of the Wandering Jew runs throughout the plot. For a criticism from a Jewish point of view, see Jacob Voorsanger in *The Sun*, New York, Jan. 6, 1894, p. 9, * *A*, reprinted from the *San Francisco Chronicle*. Reviewed in *New York dramatic mirror*, v. 56, Oct. 6, 1906, p. 2–3, * *T–* *DA*; and in *Theatre magazine*, New York, 1906, v. 6, p. 285–286, † *NBLA*.

WALLACE, SARAH AGNES. *See* sub-entry under DICKENS, CHARLES.

WALLACE, WILLIAM ROSS. *See* sub-entry under BULWER-LYTTON, EDWARD GEORGE EARLE LYTTON, 1ST BARON LYTTON.

WARE, J. REDDING. *See* sub-entry under ERCKMANN, ÉMILE, AND ALEXANDRE CHATRIAN.

WATKINS, HARRY. *See* sub-entry under DE LA RAMÉE, LOUISE.

WEBSTER, BENJAMIN NOTTINGHAM. *See* sub-entry under DUMAS, ALEXANDRE, THE ELDER.

WEEVER, EDWIN. Uncle Zeberiah; or, Just plain folks. A rural comedy-drama in four acts... Clyde, Ohio: Ames Publishing Co., cop. 1909. 35 p. 12°. (Ames' series of standard and minor drama. no. 487.)

"Isaac Lovinsky, a polished smuggler, and his wife Rachel are tiptop Jew characters."

WHARTON, MRS. EDITH NEWBOLD (JONES). The house of mirth, by Edith Wharton; with illustrations by A. B. Wenzell. New York: C. Scribner's Sons, 1905. 4 p.l., 3–532 p., 1 l. front., 7 pl. 8°. NBO

Wharton, Mrs. Edith Newbold (Jones), and Clyde Fitch. The house of mirth, dramatized into a play of four acts and produced at the Savoy Theatre, New York, Oct. 22, 1906.

Albert Bruening played the part of Simon Rosendale, a Jew, who having made his fortune attempts to break into society. In the play he is represented as in love with Lily, the heroine. The rôle of Rosendale was by the critics considered the central one in the play and the best acted. Reviewed in *New York dramatic mirror*, v. 56, Nov. 3, 1906, p. 3, * *T–* *DA*; and in *Theatre magazine*, New York, v. 6, Dec., 1906, p. 320, xix, † *NBLA*.

WHAT is a Jew? (Israel. London, 1901. 4°. v. 4, p. 168–169.)

Philip Rosenheim, Jewish nationalist, and Harry Marchmont, "very English in his ideas," discuss this question.

Copy: Library of the American Jewish Historical Society.

WHITE, C. V. The Peace Conference, a poem... Boston: R. G. Badger, 1905. 46 p. 12°. NBI

A dramatic poem on the International Peace Conference, The Hague, 1899, with a prophet of Israel as one of the characters.

WHITE, GRACE (MILLER). Rachel Goldstein; or, Struggles of a poor girl in New York. From Theodor Kremer's play. New York: J. S. Ogilvie Publishing Company, 1904. 112 p. 12°.

Kremer, Theodor. Rachel Goldstein; melodrama in four acts. Produced at the Grand Opera House, New York, Sept. 21, 1903.

A sensational melodrama about an immigrant Jewish girl, her gun-toting father and villains of all sorts. The scenes are placed on board an incoming steamer, and in New York City at the Hotel Savoy and on Hester street. Louise Beaton acted the title rôle and E. L. Walton, her father. Reviewed in *New York clipper*, New York, v. 51, p. 733, col. 4, * *T–*† *MVA*; and in *New York dramatic mirror*, v. 50, Oct. 3, 1903, p. 18, * *T–* *DA*.

WHYTE, H., AND R. BALMAIN. *See* sub-entry under DICKENS, CHARLES.

WILDE, OSCAR. The picture of Dorian Gray. (Lippincott's magazine. Philadelphia, 1890. 8°. v. 46, p. 1–100.) *DA

An unnamed Jewish character appears in this story. He introduces Sybil Vane to Dorian, and is referred to as the "horrid old Jew," "hideous Jew."

Lounsbery, Grace C. A dramatization by Grace C. Lounsbery into a play of three acts was staged at the Vaudeville Theatre, London, Aug. 28, 1913, with Ivan Berlyn as Mr. Isaacs, manager of an East End theatre. Reviewed in *Era*, London, v. 77, Sept. 3, 1913, p. 19, † *NAFA*.

Mercet, S. Dorian Gray; drame en un prologue et cinq actes. Tiré du roman Le portrait de Dorian Gray d'Oscar Wilde. Paris: Eugène Figuière [1922]. 168 p., 1 l. 3. ed. 8°. NKP

Illustrated cover, by Kit.

In this French dramatic version of the novel the Jew is called M. Isaac. See act II, scenes 5 and 7.

Miller, Marion Mills. The picture of Dorian Gray, from the novel of that name by Oscar Wilde, dramatized by Marion Mills Miller... New York: Henry Harrison, 1931. 1 p.l., 5–98 p. 8°. NBM

A previous dramatization of Wilde's story by this author was produced on the vaudeville stage. The present version, in emphasizing the murder of Basil, is rendered into a melodrama, depicting the detection and punishment of a strange crime. Other characters, not in the original story, are introduced. The Jew is represented as the manager of a theatre, and is named Abraham Schaumann.

Thorne, David. Dorian Gray, a dramatization in a prologue and three acts, was produced by the Oscaria Theatre Company at the Biltmore Theatre, New York, May 21, 1928.

Reviewed in *Billboard*, Cincinnati, v. 40, June 2, 1928, p. 7, † *MZA*; *Theatre magazine*, New York, v. 48, July, 1928, p. 38, † *NBLA*; and in *Variety*, New York, v. 91, May 23, 1928, p. 58, † *NAFA*. See also *Collection of newspaper clippings of dramatic criticism, 1927–1928*, v. D–G, † *NBL*.

Fehr, Bernhard. Das gelbe Buch in Oscar Wildes Dorian Gray. (Englische Studien. Leipzig, 1921. 8°. Bd. 55, p. 237–256.) RNA

Fischer, Walter. "The poisonous book" in Oskar Wildes Dorian Gray. (Englische Studien. Leipzig, 1917. 8°. Bd. 51, p. 37–47.) RNA

Individual Plays — 1838-1914, continued

Gargiles, Lady. Petit essai sur le "Portrait de Dorian Gray" d'Oscar Wilde; lettres à un ami ... Paris: Librairie mutuelle des auteurs et éditeurs réunis [1917]. 24 p. 16°. NCI p.v.101

WILLIAMS, HENRY LLEWELLYN. *See* sub-entry under BOUCICAULT, DION.

WILLIAMS, JESSE LYNCH. The day dreamer; being the full narrative of "The stolen story" ... New York: C. Scribner's Sons, 1906. 4 p.l., 326 p. 12°. NBO
In magazine form "The Day dreamer" was called "News and the man," and the first chapter in the series, entitled "The Stolen story," appeared in *Scribner's magazine*, New York, 1897, v. 22, p. 232–244, * *DA*. The whole is a novelization of a play called *The Stolen story*, which was produced at the Garden Theatre, New York, Oct. 2, 1906, with Stephen Wright as Jake Shayne and Charles Nevil as Sam Nordheimer, "a couple of grafters." Reviewed in *New York dramatic mirror*, v. 56, Oct. 13, 1906, p. 3, * *T*–* *DA*; and (with illus.) in *Theatre magazine*, New York, 1906, v. 6, p. 189, 268, † *NBLA*.

WILLIAMS, THOMAS JOHN. *See* sub-entry under ELIOT, GEORGE, PSEUD.

WILLS, ANTHONY E. Benjamin, Benny and Ben; a farce in one act... New York: Dick & Fitzgerald [cop. 1906]. 37 p. 12°.

—— A football romance; a college play in four acts... New York: Fitzgerald Publishing Corporation, cop. 1912. 74 p. 12°.
Place: Rogers College, near Chicago, Ill. Mr. Harris, a hard-bargaining money-lender.

—— Taking chances; a comedy in three acts... New York [etc.]: Samuel French, cop. 1930. 104 p., 1 l. diagr. 12°. (French's international copyrighted ... ed. of the works of the best authors. no. 678.) NBL p.v.229
First published 1906.
Mr. Marx, a loan broker, "shrewd, sharp-eyed business man ... by no means to be a caricature, but a distinct type of the present-day, hard-bargaining, Americanized Hebrew."

WILSON, HUNTINGTON. Stultitia; a nightmare and an awakening, in four discussions. February, 1913. [Binghamton and New York: Printed by Vail-Ballou Co., cop. 1914.] 180 p. incl. front. 12°.
Copy: Library of Congress.

—— —— New York: F. A. Stokes Company [1915]. viii, 180 p. front. (plate.) 12°. NBM
A play about preparedness and one hundred per cent Americanism; against Socialists and labor leaders. Mr. Goldstein is the international banker. He is represented as being bought by the German ambassador to oppose the President's policy of national defense. Also published under the title *Save America*, *VWZW*.

WILSON, RANDOLPH C. The schoolboy's nightmare [in one scene]. (English journal. Chicago, 1912. 8°. v. 1, p. 619–624.) RNA
Jacob Keslowitz, struggling in the classroom with Wordsworth's *Daffodils*.

WOOD, FRANK. *See* sub-entry under MOSENTHAL, SALOMON HERMANN, RITTER VON.

YOUNG, MRS. RIDA (JOHNSON). Brown of Harvard, a play in four acts. New York: S. French, cop. 1909. 2 p.l., 3–85 p. 8°. (French's standard library edition.)
Novelized by the author and Gilbert P. Coleman under the same title, and published by Putnam's in 1907 and 1908.
A play of student life at Harvard College. First produced at the Princess Theatre, New York, Feb. 26, 1906, with Louis La Bay as an old clothes man. Reviewed in *New York dramatic mirror*, v. 55, March 10, 1906, p. 3, * *T*–* *DA*. "The old clothes man ... greeted with welcoming cheers on the opening night." Max Keezer, Harvard Square clothing merchant, is mentioned in the dialogue. In the published play, a cast is given with the heading "First produced at the Princess Theatre, New York, May 22, 1906."

ZAMETKIN, MICHAEL. A Russian Shylock; a play in four acts. New York, 1906. 135(1) p. 12°. NBL p.v.8
On cover: Published by the author at ... Brooklyn, New York.
Solomon Isaacovitch Herzfarb, the Shylock of Eusk, Russia.
Reviewed by Joel Enteen in *Zukunft*, New York, 1906, v. 5, p. 508–509, * *PBB*.

ZANGWILL, ISRAEL. Children of the ghetto. Being pictures of a peculiar people ... Philadelphia: Jewish Publication Society of America, 1892. 2 v. 12°.
Several episodes of this novel of London ghetto life were dramatized by the author into a play of four acts, designated "The letter of the law," "The spirit of love," "The letter and the spirit," and "Love and law" respectively.
Staged for copyright purpose, at Oddfellows' Hall, Deal, England, July 26, 1899. First professional production at the New National Theatre, Washington, D. C., Sept. 18, 1899, with Wilton Lackaye as Reb Shemuel, Blanche Bates as Hannah Jacobs, Frank Worthing as David Brandon, William Norris as Melchitsedek Pinchas, Mme. Cottrelly as Mrs. Belcovich, and Mabel Taliaferro as Esther Ansell. Reviewed in *American Hebrew*, New York, 1899, v. 65, p. 610, * *PBD*; by Herbert Friedenwald in *Jewish comment*, Baltimore, v. 9, Sept. 22, 1899, p. 1–2, * *PBD*; and by J. T. Warde, in *New York dramatic mirror*, New York, v. 42, Sept. 23, 1899, p. 12, * *T*–* *DA*.
Produced at the Herald Square Theatre, New York, Oct. 16, 1899, with the original cast. Reviewed by John D. Barry in *Collier's weekly*, New York, v. 24, Oct. 28, 1899, p. 22–23, * *DA*; by George S. Hellman in *East & West*, New York, 1900, v. 1, p. 98–99, * *DA*; by Richard Gottheil in *Jewish chronicle*, London, Nov. 3, 1899, p. 12, * *PBE*; by J. S. Metcalfe in *Life*, New York, 1899, v. 34, p. 332, * *DA*; by *New York dramatic mirror*, v. 42, Oct. 21, 1899, p. 16, * *T*–* *DA*; and by Joseph W. Herbert, in *New York Herald*, Oct. 29, 1899, section 4, p. 12, * *A*.
Produced with the original cast at Ford's Grand Opera House, Baltimore, Sept. 25, 1899, and at the Walnut Street Theatre, Philadelphia, Oct. 2, 1899. Abstracts of six reviews of the Philadelphia production are given in *Jewish exponent*, Philadelphia, v. 29, Oct. 6, 1899, p. 8, * *PBD*.
Produced at the Adelphi Theatre, London, Dec. 11, 1899, with Robert Edeson as David and Rosabel Morrison as Hannah. Reviewed in *Academy*, London, 1899, v. 57, p. 726, * *DA*; *The Athenæum*, London, 1899, v. 114, p. 844, * *DA*; by W. M. T. in *Graphic*, London, 1899, v. 60, p. 819, * *DA*; by *Illustrated sporting and dramatic news*, London, 1899, v. 52, p. 591, * *DA*; by Israel Abrahams in *Jewish chronicle*, London, Dec. 15, 1899, p. 12–13, * *PBE*; by Y. B. in *Outlook*, London, 1899, v. 4, p. 648–649, * *DA*; *Queen*, London, 1899, v. 106, p. 1020, * *DA*; unfavorably by Max Beerbohm in *Saturday review*, London, 1899, v. 88, p. 763–764, * *DA*; by Clement Scott in *Sketch*, London, 1899, v. 28, p. 292–293, * *DA*; anonymously, ibid., v. 28, p. 330, * *DA*; by P. C. in *Speaker*, London, 1899, new series, v. 1, p. 285, * *DA*; by D. S. in *To-day*, London, 1899, v. 25, p. 660, * *DA*; *Truth*,

Individual Plays, 1838–1914, continued

ZANGWILL, ISRAEL, *continued*

London, 1899, v. 46, p. 1478–1479, * *DA;* and *Young Israel,* London, 1899, v. 3, p. 193, * *PBE.*

Illustrations of the various stagings are to be found in *American Hebrew,* New York, 1899, v. 65, p. 528–530, 738–739, * *PBD; Collier's weekly,* New York, v. 24, Oct. 28, 1899, p. 22–23, * *DA; Dramatic magazine,* Chicago, 1899, v. 8, p. 195–209 (together with a synopsis of the play and copious extracts from the text); *Harper's weekly,* New York, 1899, v. 43, p. 1011, * *DA; Jewish chronicle,* London, Nov. 3, 1899, p. 12 and Dec. 15, p. 12–13, * *PBE; Jewish comment,* Baltimore, v. 9, Sept. 22, 1899, p. 1–2, * *PBD;* and *Sketch,* London, 1899, v. 28, p. 292–293, * *DA.* More illustrations, together with numerous clipped reviews, are in *Robinson Locke collection of dramatic scrap books,* v. 43, Blanche Bates, and v. 308, Wilton Lackaye, † *NAFR.*

Interviews are given on various phases of the play, with Blanche Bates, the leading lady, in *Jewish exponent,* Philadelphia, v. 29, Oct. 13, 1899, p. 5, * *PBD;* George Clarke, the production manager, in *Jewish chronicle,* London, Dec. 8, 1899, p. 17, * *PBE;* and Israel Zangwill, the author, ibid., Nov. 3, p. 13, * *PBE.*

A prologue to the play, presented to the audience at the first New York performance, is printed in *Jewish chronicle,* London, Nov. 3, 1899, p. 12, * *PBE;* a poem, "The opinion of a Chillicothe Rube" by John O'Callahan, in *American Hebrew,* New York, 1899, v. 66, p. 89, * *PBD.* See two letters by Thos. L. James and J. H. Hollander, ibid., v. 65, p. 774. Zangwill's answer to Clement Scott's criticism is given in *Jewish exponent,* Philadelphia, v. 30, Oct. 27, 1899, p. 8, * *PBD.* Arthur D. Hall writes about make-up effected by some of the actors in *Popular magazine,* New York, v. 2, June, 1904, p. 191–193, * *DA.*

The literary, dramatic, and Jewish implications of the play are discussed by Abraham Cahan in *Forum,* New York, 1899, v. 28, p. 503–512, * *DA;* John Corbin in *Harper's weekly,* New York, 1899, v. 43, p. 1011, * *DA;* by Maurice H. Harris in *American Hebrew,* New York, 1899, v. 65, p. 738–739, * *PBD;* by Charles I. Hoffman in *Jewish exponent,* Philadelphia, v. 29, Oct. 6, 1899, p. 4, * *PBD;* by William Rosenau, ibid., v. 29, Oct. 13, p. 9, * *PBD;* by Henrietta Szold, ibid., v. 30, Oct. 20, p. 9, * *PBD;* and by Walter E. Weyl, under title of "An autobiographical criticism," ibid., v. 29, Sept. 29, p. 1–2, * *PBD.* See also *American Hebrew,* New York, 1899, v. 64, p. 276, v. 65, p. 528–530, and v. 66, p. 104–105, * *PBD.*

The validity in Jewish law of the mock-marriage of Hannah and David, the main episode of the play, is argued for and against by Israel Abrahams in *Jewish chronicle,* London, Nov. 10, 1899, p. 11, * *PBE;* by Gotthard Deutsch in *American Hebrew,* New York, 1899, v. 66, p. 82–83, * *PBD;* by a Talmud Chacham [pseud.], ibid., v. 65, p. 810, * *PBD.* Cf. also letters by Lewis N. Dembitz, Morris Mandel, Frederick de Sola Mendes, Julius Silberfeld, and Gertrude Veld, ibid., v. 66, p. 12–13, * *PBD.*

Deutsch, Gotthard. Zangwills Ghettokinder auf der Bühne. (Allgemeine Zeitung des Judenthums. Berlin, 1900. 4°. Jahrg. 64, p. 152–153.)
* PBC

Harris, Maurice Henry. Zangwill's "Children of the ghetto." (American Hebrew. New York, 1899. 4°. v. 66, p. 77–79.) * PBD
Sermon delivered Oct. 12, 1899.

Schulman, Samuel. Zangwill's "Children of the ghetto" — an incomplete picture of Jews and Judaism... [New York? 1900?] 12 p. 8°.
Caption-title. * PBM p.v.72

ZANGWILL, ISRAEL. The king of the schnorrers; grotesques and fantasies... with ninety-eight illustrations by Phil May, George Hutchinson, P. H. Townsend, and others. London: William Heinemann, 1894. x p., 1 l., 400 p. illus. 8°.

The author dramatized his novel into a "historic farce," and as such it was produced by the Jewish Drama League at the New Scala, London, Nov. 1, 1925. The play deals with the period (end of the eighteenth century) when the Spanish-Portuguese Jews ruled the world of Jewry in London and the German Jews were considered as inferior immigrants. Lewin Mannering played Manasseh da Costa (the title rôle); Alexander Field, the Chancellor of the Mahamad; Geoffrey Wilkinson, Yankele. Reviewed by G. J. in *Jewish chronicle,* London, Nov. 6, 1925, p. 35, * *PBE.* The League revived this farce with largely the same cast, in August, 1930. See illus. of the production in *Jewish world,* London, Aug. 28, 1930, p. 12, * *PBE.*

Turned into a musical comedy, with the music by J. Brody, it was produced, with Jacob P. Adler in the title rôle, at the Grand Theatre, New York, April 20, 1905. See *New York dramatic mirror,* v. 53, April 29, 1905, p. 16, * *T-* *DA.*

—— The melting-pot; drama in four acts. New York: The Macmillan Company, 1909. ix, 200 p. 12°.

Reviewed by Albert S. Henry in *Book news monthly,* Philadelphia, 1909, v. 28, p. 203–204, * *DA;* in *Dramatist,* Easton, Pa., 1910, v. 1, p. 23–24, *NAFA;* by Clayton Hamilton in *Forum,* New York, 1909, v. 42, p. 434–435, * *DA;* by David de Sola Pool in *Hebrew standard,* New York, v. 55, Oct. 1, 1909, p. 7, * *PBD;* in *Independent,* New York, 1909, v. 67, p. 931–932, * *DA;* by Horace Traubel in *Conservator,* Philadelphia, 1910, v. 21, p. 44, * *DA.*

—— —— New York: Macmillan Co., 1911. ix, 200 p. 12°. NCR

—— —— London: William Heinemann, 1914. 5 p.l., 215(1) p. 8°.

—— —— New York: The Macmillan Company, 1917. ix, 215(1) p. new and rev. ed. 12°.

—— —— London: William Heinemann, Ltd., 1928. 4 p.l., 215(1) p. 8°.

The first revised edition, 1914, and the subsequent ones contain five appendices on the persecution of the Jews in Russia, an *Afterword,* in defence of the play against the published criticisms, and a *Dedication* to Theodore Roosevelt, who had witnessed the original production in Washington and had praised its "message." The 1914 edition was reviewed by Wilfred Whitten, in *Bookman,* London, 1914, v. 45, p. 315, †* *GDD.*

A synopsis of the play with copious extracts is printed in *Current literature,* New York, 1909, v. 47, p. 189–196, * *DA.*

A selection translated into German by A. Hoelper ("Der Schmelztiegel, Israel Zangwills prophetische Vision der Zukunft Amerikas") is to be found in *Deutsche Vorkaempfer,* New York, Jahrg. 3, Aug., 1909, p. 6–8, * *DA.*

First privately staged at the Terminus House, Littlehampton, England, Aug. 21, 1908. Produced at the Columbia Theatre, Washington, D. C., Oct. 5, 1908, with Walker Whiteside as David Quixano, Sheridan Block as his father Mendel, Louise Muldener as his grandmother, and Chrystal Herne as Vera Revandal. Reviewed by B. G. Richards in *American Hebrew,* New York, 1908, v. 83, p. 557–558, * *PBD;* in *Current literature,* New York, 1908, v. 45, p. 671–673, * *DA;* by A. D. Albert in *Jewish exponent,* Philadelphia, v. 47, Oct. 9, 1908, p. 2, * *PBD* (reprinted there from the *Washington Times*); by Charles W. Collins (with illus.) in *Theatre magazine,* New York, 1909, v. 9, p. 58, 60, † *NBLA.* A scene from the play is given in *Bookman,* New York, 1909, v. 28, p. 582, * *DA.* See also a letter by Oscar S. Straus in *American Hebrew,* New York, 1908, v. 83, p. 610, * *PBD;* and one by Jacob H. Schiff, ibid., v. 84, p. 10, * *PBD.*

Produced at the Comedy Theatre, New York, Sept. 6, 1909, with the same cast as that of the Washington

Individual Plays — 1838-1914, continued

production. Reviewed by Joseph Jacobs (with illustrations) in *American Hebrew*, New York, 1909, v. 85, p. 467–468, * *PBD;* by Leo Mielziner, ibid., p. 505, * *PBD;* by Augustus Thomas, ibid., v. 86, p. 192, * *PBD;* in *Bookman*, New York, 1909, v. 30, p. 324–327, * *DA;* by Channing Pollock in *Green book album*, Chicago, 1909, v. 2, p. 1013, *NAFA;* in *Hampton's magazine*, New York, 1909, v. 23, p. 696–699, * *DA;* by J. S. Metcalfe in *Life*, New York, 1909, v. 54, p. 378, * *DA;* in *The Nation*, New York, 1909, v. 89, p. 240, * *DA;* in *New York dramatic mirror*, v. 62, Sept. 18, 1909, p. 5–6, * *T—* *DA;* by Rudolph Klauber in *New York Times*, New York, Sept. 12, 1909, part 6, p. 10, * *A;* and in *Theatre magazine*, New York, 1909, v. 10, p. 106–107, † *NBLA.* A review (with illus.) is given in *American magazine*, New York, 1910, v. 69, p. 409, 411–412, * *DA;* and a scene from the play (with illus.) is given in *Theatre magazine*, New York, 1909, v. 10, p. 132, † *NBLA.*
Produced at the Adelphi Theatre, Philadelphia, Jan. 24, 1910. For an abstract of reviews printed in the Philadelphia dailies of Jan. 25, 1910, see *Jewish exponent*, Philadelphia, v. 50, Jan. 28, 1910, p. 13, * *PBD.*
Also produced by the Dramatic Club of Mount Holyoke College, Dec. 10, 1912, with Marguerite Houston as David Quixano. Reviewed in *Mount Holyoke*, South Hadley, Mass., 1913, v. 22, p. 290–291, *STG.*
Produced at the Court Theatre, London, Jan. 25, 1914 and transferred to Queen's Theatre, Feb. 7, 1914, with Harold Chapin, later Walker Whiteside, as David Quixano; Inez Bensusan as the grandmother, and Phyllis Relph as Vera. It ran 120 times. Reviewed by Egan Mew in *Academy*, London, 1914, v. 86, p. 151–152, and again p. 217, * *DA;* in *The Athenæum*, London, 1914, v. 143, p. 171, * *DA;* unfavorably by J. E. H. Terry in *British review*, London, 1914, v. 6, p. 306–311, * *DA;* by S. O. in *English review*, London, 1914, v. 17, p. 130–132, * *DA;* in *Era*, London, v. 77, Jan. 28, 1914, p. 13, † *NAFA;* by A. Croom-Johnson in *Review of reviews*, London, 1914, v. 49, p. 227–228, * *DA;* by John Palmer in *Saturday review*, London, 1914, v. 117, p. 628–629, * *DA;* and in *Sphere*, London, 1914, v. 57, p. 123, * *DA.* Illustrations are to be found in *Graphic*, London, 1914, v. 89, p. 344, 874, * *DA.*
Revived on March 17, 1932, by the Rosh Pinah players at Everyman Theatre, Hampstead. For a review see *Jewish chronicle*, London, March 25, 1932, p. 31, * *PBE.*
The political and sociological implications of the author's "melting-pot" gospel are discussed by G. K. Chesterton in *Illustrated London news*, London, 1914, v. 144, p. 322, * *DA* (reprinted in *Jewish exponent*, Philadelphia, v. 59, May 8, 1914, p. 2, * *PBD*); by Rudolph I. Coffee in *Jewish criterion*, Pittsburgh, v. 30, March 11, 1910, p. 3–4, * *PBD* (cf. letter by M. Mazer, ibid., p. 4, 13); by J. J. Lieberman in *Jewish outlook*, Denver, v. 7, Jan. 14, 1910, p. 61, 63, 65–66, * *PBD;* by Abram Lipsky in *Maccabaean*, New York, 1913, v. 23, p. 12–15, * *PBD;* by Louis J. Rosenberg, in his *Scraps and bits*, New York [cop. 1916], p. 45–49, *NBQ* (reprint of a letter which appeared in the *Detroit Free Press*, on March 20, 1910); and in *Current literature*, New York, 1908, v. 45, p. 671–673, * *DA.*

Block, Sheridan. The drama; logical, psychological, Hebra-ological. (Review. Philadelphia, 1910. 8°. v. 5, April, 1910, p. 18–20.)
The author of the above played the part of Mendel Quixano in the Washington, D. C., production.

Burrows, Herbert. Zangwill's play. (Jewish world. London, 1914. 4°. June 10, 1914, p. 28–30.) * *PBE*

Dietrich, John Hassler. "The melting pot." A plea for the unborn children of America. A sermon delivered in the St. Mark's Memorial Reformed Church... Pittsburgh, Pa., Sunday, May 8, 1910. Stenographically reported by Katherine A. Moorhead. [Pittsburgh:] Published by members of the congregation [1910]. 15 p. 8°. * *PSQ* p.v.1

Magnes, Judah Leon. The melting pot. (Emanu-El pulpit. New York, 1909. 8°. v. 3, no. 1, p. 1–10.) * *PLM*
Reprinted in *American Hebrew*, New York, 1909, v. 85, p. 619–620, * *PBD.*
A sermon delivered at Temple Emanu-El, New York, Oct. 9, 1909.

Zangwill, Israel. The war god; a tragedy in five acts. London: W. Heinemann, 1911. xi, 163(1) p. 8°. NCR
Another copy autographed: To Austin Harrison with gratitude for his sympathy, Israel Zangwill, belongs to the compiler of this list.

—— —— New York: The Macmillan Company, 1912. ix, 163(1) p., 1 l. 12°.
Reviewed in *The Athenæum*, London, v. 139, p. 23, * *DA;* by Albert S. Henry in *Book news monthly*, Philadelphia, v. 31, p. 288, * *DA;* by Frederick G. Bettany in *Bookman*, London, v. 41, p. 267, †* *GDD;* *Bookman*, New York, v. 35, p. 25, * *DA;* and in *The Nation*, New York, v. 94, p. 501, * *DA.*
A pacifist play about militarism and imperialism, world politics and statecraft, Christianity and Hebraism. The chief characters are Count Frithiof, modelled after and made to look like on the stage, L. N. Tolstoi, and Count Torgrim patented after Bismarck. The Jewish character played by Gerald Lawrence is Karl Blum, a converted Jew, secretary to Torgrim. Blum, behind a mask of loyal service, determines to show up his master. Later he becomes a follower of Frithiof, the apostle of peace.
First produced at His Majesty's Theatre, London, Nov. 8, 1911, but never brought to this country. The critics condemned the play from the point of view of the stage. See Landa, p. 223–228. Reviewed in *Academy*, London, v. 81, p. 636–637, * *DA; American Hebrew*, New York, v. 90, p. 137, * *PBD; The Athenæum*, London, v. 138, p. 603, * *DA;* (with illus.) in *Graphic*, London, v. 84, p. 766, * *DA;* (with illus.) in *Illustrated London news*, London, v. 139, p. 842, 844, * *DA;* by P. P. H. in *Outlook*, London, v. 28, p. 657, * *DA;* by John Palmer, unfavorably, in *Saturday review*, London, v. 112, p. 638–639, * *DA; The Times*, London, Nov. 9, 1911, p. 14, * *A;* and in *Truth*, London, v. 70, p. 1156–1157, * *DA.* More illustrations are in *Graphic*, London, v. 84, p. 693, * *DA;* and in *Illustrated sporting and dramatic news*, London, v. 76, p. 485, * *DA.*

Zola, Émile. ...Les héritiers Rabourdin; comédie en trois actes...avec une préface. Paris: Charpentier et cie, 1874. 2 p.l., xix, 128 p. 12°. NKM p.v.647
First produced at the Théâtre de Cluny, Paris, Nov. 3, 1874.
In an English translation, named *The Heirs of Rabourdin*, by A. Teixeira de Mattos it was produced at the Opera Comique, London, Feb. 23, 1894, with F. Norreys Connell as Isaac, moneylender. See W. Archer, *Theatrical 'world' of 1894*, London, 1895, p. 65–68, 375, *NCOA.*

Zolotkoff, Leon. The dream of Bath-Zion; a symbolic play for Jewish children [in one act of five scenes]. (Maccabaean. New York, 1910. 8°. v. 18, p. 80–85.) * *PBD*
Reprinted in *Young Judaean*, New York, v. 2, Oct., 1911, p. 20–22, Nov., p. 20–23 (copy at Dropsie College).
A symbolic playlet on the history of the Jews since their expulsion, 70 A. D. Bath-Zion is the personification of Palestine. Among the other characters are Bezalel, the Biblical master builder, Judah ha-Levi, fl. 12th century, Sultan Saladin, 1137–1193, Sabbathai Zebi, 1626–1676, and Columbia, representing the United States.

Individual Plays — 1915–1938

A., H. Alexander in Babylon; a tragedy in five acts. (Open court. Chicago, 1920. 8°. v. 34, p. 403–422, 478–493, 533–551.) *DA
Rachel, a Jewish slave, servant to Roxana, wife of Alexander.

ABBOTT, GEORGE, AND JAMES GLEASON. The fall guy; a comedy in three acts. New York: S. French; London: S. French, Ltd., cop. 1928. 97(1) p. plates, diagr. 12°. (French's standard library edition.) NBL p.v.195
Printed in the form of a running story, with many extracts from the dialogue, in *The Best plays of 1924–25*, Boston [cop. 1925], p. 266–302, *NAFH*.
First staged at the Davidson Theatre, Milwaukee, July 14, 1924, and at the Eltinge Theatre, New York, March 10, 1925. Mrs. Bercowich, a neighbor, is heard off stage. For reviews see *Collection of newspaper clippings of dramatic criticism, 1924–1925*, v. F–L, † *NBL*.
Produced at the Apollo Theatre, London, Sept. 20, 1926. It ran till Oct. 30.

ABDULLAH, ACHMED. Black tents. New York: H. Liveright, 1930. 218 p. 12°. NBM
In seven scenes.
A desert story told in dramatic form. The hero is Daoud, a young Bedouin. In scene 3, the bazaar of the Saharan traders, are introduced Rebecca Tordeman, a beautiful Jewess, to whom Daoud makes love, and a Fowl Seller who hawks his wares in the bazaar.
Reviewed in *New York Times book review*, v. 35, Nov. 30, 1930, p. 9, † *NAA*.

ABDULLAH, ACHMED, AND W. A. WOLFF. Broadway interlude... [New York? 1934?] 46, 44, 29 f. 4°. † NCOF
Reproduced from typewritten copy.
A comedy of three acts produced at the Forrest Theatre, New York, April 19, 1934. R. E. Keane played the part of Grant Thompson, by the reviewers accepted to have been a satirical or libelous presentation of the late theatrical producer, David Belasco. The relations of Abdullah and Belasco are set forth in the former's autobiography, *The Cat had nine lives*. Hans Hansen had the rôle of Ben Levi, Belasco's chief factotum. See *Collection of newspaper clippings of dramatic criticism, 1933–34*, v. A–B, † *NBL*.
It was dramatized from the novel of the same name by Achmed Abdullah and Faith Baldwin, New York, 1929.

ABELES, EDWIN V. I. One of the bravest [in three scenes]. New York: New York Theatre League [1936?]. 13 f. 4°.
Cover-title.
Mimeographed.
Based on a happening in a Nazi concentration camp, from a story in *New masses*, New York, v. 13, Nov. 6, 1934, p. 13, * *DA*.

ABELSON, ALTER. The Messiah people. (A historical drama in one act — five scenes.) (Jewish forum. New York, 1919. 8°. v. 2, p. 881–887, 1001–1016.) *PBD
Scene 1 is a synagogue in Spain on Simchath Torah. The succeeding scenes take place around the palace of the king. The time is prior to the expulsion of the Jews from Spain. The chief characters are Don Isaac Abravanel and Torquemada, the chief inquisitor.

ABELSON, ANNA GOLDINA. Love in the deeps [in three acts]. (Jewish forum. New York, 1922. 8°. v. 5, p. 308–311, 319, 396–399.) *PBD
A story of the devotion of a husband and wife, during the sinking of a liner in mid-ocean. Based on the incident of the drowning of Mr. and Mrs. Isidor Straus during the Titanic disaster in 1912. The couple are here called Mr. and Mrs. Noble.

ADKINS, FRANCIS JAMES. Education, a medley in four acts... London: G. Allen & Unwin, Ltd. [1924.] 128 p. 12°. NCR
Each of the first three acts records the founding of a lectureship at Cambridge University. In the first act, laid in 1297, the Jewish characters are Isaac of Lincoln, creditor of the House of Holderness, and Melchior, his secretary. The lectureship founded, in this act, by an abbot, is in memory of St. Thomas Aquinas, the mediaeval authority on the subject of usury. The dialogue develops several of the current and conflicting views on university education.

AGATE, JAMES EVERSHED. Blessed are the rich; episodes in the life of Oliver Sheldon. London: L. Parsons [1924]. 320 p. 12°.
This novel was dramatized by the author and C. E. Openshaw into a comedy of the same title in three acts, and produced at the Vaudeville Theatre, London, Aug. 27, 1925, with Michael Sherbrooke as Mr. Loo Cohen, a lawyer's managing clerk.

AKINS, ZOË. Daddy's gone a-hunting [in three acts]. (In her: Déclassée, Daddy's gone a-hunting, and Greatness. New York, 1924. 12°. p. 103–198.) NBL
Produced at the Plymouth Theatre, New York, Aug. 31, 1921, with Olga Olonova as Olga, described on p. 142 as one of "plain Russian-Jewess business sense." For reviews see *Collection of newspaper clippings of dramatic criticism, 1921–1922*, v. A–D, † *NBL*.

—— Déclassée. (In her: Déclassée; Daddy's gone a-hunting; and Greatness — a comedy. New York, 1924. 12°. p. 1–102.) NBM
In three acts.
Lengthy extracts, with a running descriptive synopsis, are given in *Best plays of 1919–20*, Boston [1920], p. 95–119, *NAFH*.
One of the experiences of Lady Haden (Ethel Barrymore) is her encounter with Rudolph Solomon, millionaire. Produced at the Empire Theatre, New York, Oct. 7, 1919, with Claude King as Solomon. For reviews see *Collection of newspaper clippings of dramatic criticism, 1919–1920*, v. A–E, † *NBL*.

ALDERMAN, JOSEPH S. The net [in two scenes]. (Yale Sheffield monthly. New Haven, 1915. 8°. v. 22, p. 5–14.) OA
Passover night in an Orthodox home on New York's East Side.

ALDIS, MRS. MARY (REYNOLDS). An heir at large; a play in seven scenes, from the cartoon story of John T. McCutcheon. Chicago: Old Tower Press, Ltd. [cop. 1926.] 115 p. front., illus., plates. 12°. NBL p.v.157
"The play...is based on the cartoon-story...published weekly in the *Chicago Tribune* during the year 1921–1922. On Monday mornings for fifty-two weeks a black and white drawing, with a short chapter underneath narrating the adventures of Harry L. Rasher, alias Harry L. Bacon, appeared on the first page." First produced at the Goodman Memorial Theatre, Chicago, Dec. 17, 1925, with Bernard Ostertag in the minor rôle of Mrs. Levinsky, housewife.

ALEXANDER, CECILE. The night of the eighth candle...a one-act play suitable for production by mixed groups ranging in age from 12 to 16. New York: Hebrew Pub. Co., 1935. 29 p. 12°.
Scene: Home of the Bernsteins, in the Bensonhurst section of Brooklyn, N. Y.

Individual Plays — 1915-1938, continued

ALEXANDER, CECILE. A Purimbridge birthday ...a one-act play suitable for production by children (preferably girl groups) ranging in age from 10 to 16. New York: Hebrew Pub. Co., 1935. 32 p. 12°.
Scene: Cannon Street, on the lower East Side of New York City, on the eve of Purim.

ANDERSON, FREDERICK O. How Mr. Smith dropped the hint. (Life. New York, 1932. 4°. v. 99, June, 1932, p. 6, 8.) *DA
A phase in Al Smith's political career. Miss Markowitz, on the present occasion, is his confidential private secretary.

ANDERSON, MAXWELL. Winterset; a play in three acts... Washington: Anderson House, 1935. xi p., 2 l., 3-134 p. 12°. NBM
It appeared in story form, with extracts from the dialogue, in *Best plays of 1935-36*, New York, 1936, p. 32-66, *NAFH*.
A condemnation of capital punishment. It was produced at the Martin Beck Theatre, New York, Sept. 25, 1935, with Anatole Winogradoff as Esdras, a philosopher. For reviews see *Collection of newspaper clippings of dramatic criticism, 1935-36*, v. Tev-Z, † *NBL*.

ANDERSON, MAXWELL, AND HAROLD HICKERSON. Gods of the lightning [in three acts]. (In their: Gods of the lightning [and] Outside looking in. London, 1928. 8°. p. 1-106.) NBM
A re-creation of the Sacco-Vanzetti case. The two defendants are here named Macready and Capraro. The administrative and judicial agents who tried and condemned the two are represented as the tools of an oppressive capitalist system. Produced at the Little Theatre, New York, Oct. 24, 1928, with John R. Hamilton as Glickstein, attorney for the defense, and Sam Silverbush as Ike, a minor rôle. Reviewed by Gilbert V. Seldes in *Dial*, New York, 1929, v. 86, p. 80-82, * *DA;* and (with illus.) by Robert Littell in *Theatre arts monthly*, New York, v. 13, p. 10-17, *NBLA.* See also *Collection of newspaper clippings of dramatic criticism, 1928-1929*, v. E-G, † *NBL*.

ANDERSON, MAXWELL, AND LEONARD STALLINGS. What price glory; a play in three acts. (In their: Three American plays. New York [cop. 1926]. 8°. p. 1-89.) NBM
Reprinted in F. W. Chandler and R. A. Cordell, editors, *Twentieth century plays*, New York, 1934, v. 2, p. 1-34, *NCO (Chandler).*
Printed in the form of a running story, with many extracts from the dialogue, in *The Best plays of 1924-25*, Boston [cop. 1925], p. 30-55, *NAFH.*
Produced at the Plymouth Theatre, New York, Sept. 3, 1924, with Sydney Elliott as Private Louis Lewisohn. Reviewed by G. J. Nathan in *American mercury*, New York, 1924, v. 3, p. 372-373, * *DA;* and by J. W. Krutch in *Nation*, New York, v. 119, p. 316-317, * *DA.* See also *Collection of newspaper clippings of dramatic criticism, 1924-1925*, v. S-Z, † *NBL*.

ANDRASHNIK, A. "Fruition of an ideal"; a skit for YCLA presentation. illus. (Call of youth. New York, 1937. 4°. v. 5, Jan., 1937, p. 9-11.) †* PYO
Four members of the Aarons family are the speakers.

ANDREAS, EULALIE. Yes, yes! go on; a comedy in three acts, by Eulalie Andreas [and] Jane Hurrle; staged by Albert Lang... Boston: Walter H. Baker Co., cop. 1928. 122 p. diagr. 12°. (Baker's royalty plays.) NBL p.v.198
Moses Kraft, a dealer in ready-made dresses, New York City.

ANDREWS, CHARLTON. He got the job; a comedy in one act... New York [etc.]: S. French, Inc., cop. 1935. 16 p., 1 l. diagr. 12°. NBL p.v.390
A business man has advertised for an office-helper. Among the applicants is Harry, "sportily dressed, sleek, swaggering, self-satisfied."

APPLEGARTH, MARGARET TYSON. Color blind; a missionary play in three acts... New York: G. H. Doran [cop. 1923]. 17-32 p. 12°.
Cover-title. NBL p.v.104
Repr.: Short missionary plays, ZKVC.
In the cast, among the children, are Issy, a little girl, and her younger brother, Jaky.

—— Empty stockings, in one act. (In her: More short missionary plays. New York [cop. 1923]. 12°. p. 17-30.) ZKVC
Mrs. Einstein and her little daughter, Becky.

—— Strictly private; or, The lady-who-hoarded-Easter. In one act. (In her: More short missionary plays. New York [cop. 1923]. 12°. p. 47-61.) ZKVC
One of the characters, a Polish Jewess, rejoices in the building of the Christian Centre, "for I ain't so thick on Jews as I was."

ARONIN, BEN. Bialik's last Chanuka; a skit [in one act]. illus. (Haboneh. New York, 1936. 4°. v. 2, Dec., 1936, p. 6-7, 20.)
Scene: house of Bialik, eminent Hebrew poet, 1873-1934. Among the speakers are Joshua H. Rawnitzki, chief rabbi Abraham I. Kook, Saul Tchernichowski, and Henrietta Szold.

—— The partition of the Homentasch. illus. (Haboneh. New York, 1938. 4°. v. 3, Feb., 1938, p. 7-9.)

ARONIN, BEN, AND S. M. BLUMENFIELD. A rabbi's son — a Chanukah play [in four scenes]. (Opinion. New York, 1937. 4°. v. 8, Dec., 1937, p. 8-10.) *PBD
The time is during the years 1936-37.

ARUNDEL, LOUIS. The light of the East... A drama in prologue, epilogue, and three acts... [London:] Cecil Palmer [cop. 1924]. 126 p. 12°. NCR
Marmaduke Brice, newspaper-owner and financier, is a Jew, not known as such, who aims at domination for his race over the gentiles; Rosaline, his daughter; and Jabez Isaacs, a member of Brice's family, socialist leader. The time is "in the coming age of the republics." The prologue and epilogue take place in China.

ASCH, SHALOM. Kiddush Ha-Shem; an epic of 1648, by Sholom Ash, translated by Rufus Learsi [pseud.]. Philadelphia: The Jewish Publication Society of America, 1926. 4 p.l., 227 p. 12°. *PTR
Its first stage presentation took place at the Yiddish Art Theatre, New York, Sept. 20, 1928, with Maurice Schwartz as the "little tailor." Reviewed in *Variety*, New York, v. 94, March 6, 1929, p. 56, † *NAFA.* See also *Collection of newspaper clippings of dramatic criticism, 1928-29*, v. H-K, † *NBL*.
In an adaptation into three acts, as translated by Ben Aronin, it was staged by the Sisterhood of Congregation Anshe Emet, Chicago, on March 11, 1934, with Mrs. Seymour W. Schiff as the young wife, Ted Sills as the ever-hopeful tailor, and Dr. Joseph Gordon as Mendel, the inn-keeper. Reviewed by Lucy Katz in the *Bulletin of the Anshe Emet*, Chicago, 1934, v. 5, no. 24, p. 4, * *PXY.*
In a dramatized version by Mrs. H. H. Rubenovitz, entitled *The Golden slipper*, it was produced by the Boston chapter of the Hadassah, Hotel Statler, Boston, Jan. 7, 1935, with Pauline L. Friedman in the rôle of Mendel. See *Jewish advocate*, Boston, v. 74, Jan. 4, 1935, section 1, p. 1, * *PBD.*

Individual Plays — 1915-1938, continued

ASKOWITH, DORA. A pageant dedicated to the women of Israel throughout the ages. [New York, 1933.] 14 l. incl. cover-title (col'd.). f°.
In nine tableaux or "treks."
The first six sections are Biblical; the last three, modern. The ninth is called "The motherheart of Israel," and the scene is an orphan asylum, in 1830, with Mrs. Rebekah Kohut as the mother of Israel.
Given by the College Division of the Women's Association of the American Jewish Congress at the 44th Street Theatre, New York, April 9, 1933.

AVERILL, MRS. ESTHER (CUNNINGHAM), AND L. A. AVERILL. ...The spirit of Massachusetts; a pageant of the Massachusetts Bay tercentenary... [Boston? 1930.] 11 p. 8°.
At head of title: The Commonwealth of Massachusetts, Department of Education.
In a prologue, five episodes, and a finale.
Scene 1 of episode v is styled The procession of the nations, 1880-1930. The "Jewish race" is one of the foreign groups.

BACON, EVA M. The try outs; a novel entertainment [in one scene]. New York: Fitzgerald Pub. Corp., cop. 1929. 28 p. 12°.
Abie Levinsky, proprietor of a vaudeville agency, and the applicants who put on a show.

BAER, MAX. The trial of Jacob Finklebottom. (A. Z. A. monthly program. Omaha, Neb., 1937. 4°. v. 10, no. 2, p. 6-20.)   * PBD
A B'nai B'rith playlet.

BALDERSTON, JOHN LLOYD, AND J. E. HOARE. Red planet, a play in three acts... New York, N. Y., Los Angeles, Calif.: S. French, Inc.; London: S. French, Ltd. [etc.], 1933. 99 p., 5 l. illus. (plans). 12°. (French's standard library edition.)   NBL p.v.296
A scientist learns from the Red Planet that Christ is about to visit our own planet. The stock market is thrown into a panic. Count de Reinach, "Belgian Jewish financier," attempts to cash in before the big crash. Produced at the Cort Theatre, New York, Dec. 18, 1932, with Walter Armin as de Reinach. Reviewed by R. D. Skinner in *Commonweal*, New York, 1933, v. 17, p. 271, * DA; and by J. W. Krutch in *Nation*, New York, v. 136, p. 27-28, * DA. See also *Collection of newspaper clippings of dramatic criticism, 1932-1933*, v. R-S, † NBL.

BALLARD, FREDERICK. Young America; a play in three acts... (suggested by Pearl Franklin's "Mrs. Doray" stories)... New York: S. French [etc.], cop. 1917. 120 p. diagrs. 8°. (French's standard library edition.)   NBM
Produced at the Astor Theatre, New York, Aug. 28, 1915, with Joseph Berger as Isaac Slavensky, complainant in court against one of young America. Reviewed in *New York dramatic mirror*, v. 74, Sept. 1, 1915, p. 8, * T-* DA.

BALLARD, FREDERICK, AND PEARL FRANKLIN. Young America; play in one act... New York: S. French, Inc. [cop. 1925.] (1) 38-53 p. 12°.
A one-act version of the preceding longer play.
Repr.: One-act plays for stage and study, second series, New York [1925], *NCO (One)*.

BALTIMORE HEBREW CONGREGATION, BALTIMORE. Followers of the light; an epic of the synagogue, by Dorothy Rose Cahn, Adolph D. Cohn, Pauline H. Lazaron, Amy F. Greif, Lillian Greif, Arthur Kaufman, Helen D. Oppenheim, Robert Frank Skutch [and] Rita Gans Solmson. [In a prologue, seven episodes, and an epilogue.] (In: Baltimore Hebrew Congregation. The one hundredth anniversary of the Baltimore Hebrew Congregation...5690-1930. [Baltimore: Lord Baltimore Press, 1930.] f°. p. 9-31.)
A pageant depicting the one hundred years' history of the Congregation, 1830-1930.

BARCLAY, SIR THOMAS. Gambetta and Dr. Stresemann. (Fortnightly review. London, 1923. 8°. v. 120 [new series, v. 114], p. 766-773.)   * DA
The speakers are Gustav Stresemann, Frau Stresemann and the shade of Gambetta. Frau Stresemann, née Kleefeld, of Jewish descent.

—— Gambetta and Monsieur Poincaré. (Fortnightly review. London, 1923. 8°. v. 120, p. 1-7.)   * DA
A one-act playlet. The dramatis personae are Gambetta's shade, M. Raymond Poincare, and Pierre, M. Poincaré's servant. Gambetta urges upon the French premier a policy of conciliation towards Germany. The *New international encyclopaedia* (v. 8, 1904), and some other authorities state that Léon Gambetta, 1838-1882, French statesman, was of Jewish origin.

BARISH, MILDRED. Light; a play in one act. A powerful and romantic episode of the German tragedy. (American Hebrew. New York, 1933. 4°. v. 133, p. 266, 283-284.)   * PBD

BARKER, EDWIN LINCOLN, AND A. BARKER. The man on stilts; a comedy of the great American gah-gah in three acts... New York, Los Angeles: S. French, Inc.; London: S. French, Ltd., cop. 1934. 95(1) p., 3 l. music. 12°.   NBL p.v.387
Poking fun at the American fad of hero-worshipping the so-called Firsts to perform some feat. Produced at the Plymouth Theatre, New York, Sept. 9, 1931, with Mel Tyler as A. L. Fishel, "a Jewish gentleman from the movies." For reviews see *Collection of newspaper clippings of dramatic criticism, 1931-32*, v. M-O, † NBL.

—— Middletown; a play in three acts... [New York, 1934.] 68, 39, 20, 33 f. 4°.   † NCOF
Reproduced from typewritten copy.
"What happens in a small town when it is overtaken by a 'crime of the century.'" It was composed with the Hauptmann case supposedly in mind. Under the title *American holiday* it was produced at the Manhattan Theatre, New York, Feb. 21, 1936, with Alfred Allegro as Mr. Epstein. For reviews see *Collection of newspaper clippings of dramatic criticism, 1935-36*, v. A-B, † NBL.

BARRY, PHILIP. Hotel universe, a play. New York, Los Angeles: S. French; London, S. French, Ltd., 1930. 5 p.l., 3-166 p. 12°.   NBM
Reprinted in G. H. Leverson, editor, *Plays for the college theatre*, New York, 1932, p. 547-578, *NAFH*; and in Theatre Guild, Inc., New York, *Theatre Guild anthology*, New York [cop. 1936], p. 691-754, *NAFH*.
The action of the play is continuous and takes place in the course of about two hours, upon the terrace of a house in the south of France, near Toulon. The time is an evening in early July. Produced at the Martin Beck Theatre, New York, by the Theatre Guild, April 14, 1930, with Earl Larrimore as Norman Rose, the Jewish banker, who rose from peddling on the New York East Side. Reviewed by E. Van R. Wyatt in *Catholic world*, New York, 1930, v. 131, p. 337-338, * DA; by Stark Young in *New republic*, New York, v. 62, p. 326-328, * DA; by O. D. C. in *Outlook*, New York, v. 154, p. 711, * DA; and in *Theatre arts monthly*, New York, v. 14, p. 462, NBLA. See also B. H. Clark, "Philip Barry; the development of a distinguished dramatic talent," in *Theatre Guild magazine*, New York, v. 7, May, 1930, p. 20-26, 60-61, 64, NBLA, and, for further reviews, *Collection of newspaper clippings of dramatic criticism, 1929-1930*, v. D-H, † NBL.

Individual Plays — 1915–1938, continued

BARRY, TOM. Courage, a comedy. New York, Los Angeles: S. French; London: S. French, Ltd., 1929. 5 p.l., 3–119 p. plates. 12°.   NBM
Produced at the Ritz Theatre, New York, Oct. 8, 1928, with Robert Conness as Mr. Rudlin. Reviewed by P. Maxwell in *Theatre magazine*, New York, v. 48, Dec., 1928, p. 47, 78, † *NBLA*; and in *Variety*, New York, v. 93, Oct. 17, 1928, p. 52, † *NAFA*. See also *Collection of newspaper clippings of dramatic criticism, 1928–1929*, v. C–D, † *NBL*.

BASSEN, HAYIM. Back to God; a play of Jewish life in New York, by Hayim ben Bass-Yoh. New York [:H. Bassen, pref. 1924]. 4 p.l., xii p., 25–186 p. 12°.   NBM
A translation from the Yiddish, published 1923, under the title *Zurich zu sich*.
The action of the play takes place in New York, 1915–1919.
"American Jewry! Behold, I show you here the image of thyself — look in it and be proud... In this play, for the first time, the Jews are shown without fear or favor, as they are; with their good and bad traits as I know them." In these words, the author who describes himself as a workingman, introduces his play. He further quotes the following from Dr. A. Coralnik as the greatest truth ever uttered "The non-Jews hate us because we have bound them to the law, to an ethical code, to which they are inwardly opposed, curtailing, as it does to some extent, their barbaric instincts."

BASSHE, EMANUEL JO. The centuries, portrait of a tenement house... A New Playwrights Theatre production. New York: The Macaulay Company [cop. 1927]. 227 p. 12°.   NBM
In five acts.
Jewish immigrants in the American melting pot. The characters, with few minor exceptions, are all Jewish. Setting: tenement house on a street on the East Side of New York. First produced at the New Playwrights' Theatre, New York, Nov. 29, 1927. Reviewed by Stark Young in *New republic*, New York, 1927, v. 53, p. 139–140, * *DA*. See also *Collection of newspaper clippings of dramatic criticism, 1927–28*, v. A–C, † *NBL*.

BATES, HERBERT. The king's English; a phantasy. (In: George A. Goldstone, compiler, One-act plays. Boston [cop. 1926]. 12°. p. 71–109.)
NAFH (Goldstone)
The scene is the lawn of O'Rannigan's home on the tropical island of Karra Wanga. The Jewish character is Morris Perlheimer, who "ain't got no use for Inklish."

BAUM, VICKI. ...Grand Hotel; translated by Basil Creighton. Garden City, N. Y.: Doubleday, Doran & Company, Inc., 1931. 3 p.l., 309 p. 8°   8–NGL
Translated from her novel *Menschen im Hotel*, which deals with the hypothetical happenings during thirty-six hours at a Berlin hotel, and dramatized into a play of three acts and eighteen scenes. Produced at the National Theatre, New York, Nov. 14, 1930, with Henry Hanlon in the part of Gerstenkorn. Reviewed in *Nation*, New York, 1930, v. 131, p. 634, * *DA;* and by G. J. Nathan in *New freeman*, New York, v. 2, p. 280, * *DA*. See also *Collection of newspaper clippings of dramatic criticism, 1930–1931*, v. D–H, † *NBL*.
A running synopsis with excerpts from the high lights of the dialogue, in a translation by W. A. Drake, is given in *Best plays of 1930–31*, New York, 1931, p. 355–391, *NAFH*.
In an adaptation by Edward Knoblock was produced at the Adelphi Theatre, London, Sept. 3, 1931, with Cyril Fairlie as Gerstenkorn. Reviewed in *Era*, London, v. 95, Sept. 9, 1931, p. 9, † *NAFA*; by J. T. Grein in *Illustrated London news*, 1931, v. 179, p. 410, * *DA; Jewish chronicle*, London, Sept. 11, 1931, p. 41, * *PBE;* and by G. Wakefield in *Saturday review*,

London, 1931, v. 152, p. 325, * *DA*. Stage illustrations are given in *Theatre world*, London, 1931, v. 16, p. 175–186, *MWA*.

BAUM, VICKI, AND JOHN GOLDEN. Divine drudge, a play in three acts. New York, N. Y., Los Angeles, Calif.: S. French, Inc.; London: S. French, Ltd. [etc.], cop. 1934. 2 p.l., 3–98 p. diagr. 12°. (French's standard library edition.)
NBL p.v.342
Dramatized from Vicki Baum's novel *Zwischenfall in Lohwinckel*, Berlin, 1930, *NGL*, a translation of which exists under the title *And life goes on*, New York, 1931.
First staged at the Cape Play House, Dennis, Mass., July 3, 1933, and produced at the Royale Theatre, New York, Oct. 26, 1933, with Ralf Belmont as Markus. For reviews see *Collection of newspaper clippings of dramatic criticism, 1933–1934*, v. C–E, † *NBL*.

BECK, EDITH S. ...The old order. [In one act.] New York: Jewish Welfare Board [cop. 1926]. 22 p. 8°. (Jewish Welfare Board publications.)
* PSQ (Jewish)
A comedy based on the shadchan (match maker) theme. Second prize play in the J. W. B. play contest of 1924–1925. First produced by the Washington Heights, New York City, Y. M. H. A. dramatic group at the Forty-ninth Street Theatre, Nov. 29, 1925.

BECKER, CHARLES SAXE. Greater than love; a play in one act... Boston: Walter H. Baker Company [cop. 1933]. 31 p. 12°. (Baker's royalty plays.)
A play about Spinoza, dealing with the episode of his excommunication, Amsterdam, 1656.
Produced by the Little Theatre of Temple Israel, Boston, March 14, 1933, with Leon Rubin as Baruch Espinosa and Irma Lowenstein as his mother. See *Jewish advocate*, Boston, v. 67, March 10, 1933, p. 3, * *PBD*.

BEEBE, HELEN (RICKER). Young Mr. Disraeli; a play in three acts, by Elswyth Thane [pseud.]. London: S. French, Ltd.; New York: S. French, Inc., cop. 1935. 95(1) p. diagrs. 12°. (French's acting edition. no. 681.)
Produced at the Kingsway Theatre, London, Nov. 12, 1934, with Stanley Lathbury as Isaac Disraeli, Selma vaz Dias as Sarah, his daughter, and Derrick de Marney as her brother Benjamin. The play embraces the years 1826 to 1839, when Benjamin was 35 years of age. Reviewed in *Jewish chronicle*, London, Nov. 16, 1934, p. 43, * *PBE*.
Produced in New York, at the Fulton Theatre, Nov. 10, 1937, with Derrick de Marney as Disraeli. See *Collection of newspaper clippings of dramatic criticism, 1937–1938*, v. Y, † *NBL*.

BEHRMAN, SAMUEL NATHANIEL. ...Rain from heaven; a play in three acts... New York: Random House [cop. 1935]. 250 p. 12°.   NBM
Reprinted in Theatre Guild, Inc., New York, *Theatre Guild anthology*, New York [cop. 1936], p. 895–961, *NAFH*.
An extract from act II, scene 1, under the title *That speck*, is reprinted in Leo W. Schwarz, editor, *A Golden treasury of Jewish literature*, New York [cop. 1937], p. 537–541, * *PSY*.
The author of this play has been inspired by the controversy between Alfred Kerr, noted dramatic critic, who had been expelled from Germany on account of his part-Jewishness and Gerhardt Hauptmann whom Kerr had championed as a dramatist. See *Prefatory note* in the present play, p. 7–13.
It was produced by the Theatre Guild at the Golden Theatre, New York, Dec. 24, 1934, with John Halliday as Hugo Willens (Alfred Kerr). Reviewed by Stark Young in *New republic*, New York, 1935, v. 81, p. 308, * *DA*. See also *Collection of newspaper clippings of dramatic criticism, 1934–1935*, v. R, † *NBL*.

Individual Plays — 1915-1938, continued

BEHRMAN, SAMUEL NATHANIEL. Serena Blandish; or, The difficulty of getting married. (Adapted from the novel of the title by "A lady of quality"). (In his: Three plays. New York [cop. 1934]. 12°. p. 1–105.)
In two acts of four and six scenes respectively.
First produced at the Morosco Theatre, New York, Jan. 24, 1929. Clarence Derwent played Sigmund Traub, a rich jeweler of Bond street. Reviewed by R. D. Skinner in *Commonweal*, New York, 1929, v. 9, p. 430–431, * *DA;* by Padraic Colum in *Dial*, New York, v. 86, p. 351, * *DA;* by Stark Young in *New republic,* New York, v. 57, p. 346–347, * *DA;* and by Robert Littell in *Theatre arts magazine*, New York, v. 13, p. 249–250, *NBLA*. See also *Collection of newspaper clippings of dramatic criticism, 1928-1929,* v. S, † *NBL.*
An amateur production, by the Resident Theatre Players at the Y. M.-Y. W. H. A. Auditorium, Kansas City, Mo., was given on March 28, 1933, with Margaret Graham in the title rôle and T. B. Dunn as Sigmund Traub. See *Kansas City Jewish news*, v. 3, March 24, 1933, p. 1.

BENDER, OSCAR G. Susskind von Trimberg [in one act]. (Review. Philadelphia, 1915. 12°. v. 10, Jan., 1915, p. 42–52.)
Copy: Library of the Jewish Theological Seminary of America.
A fictitious incident in the life of the historical Süsskind, a German Jewish minnesinger, native of Trimberg in Franconia, who flourished in the thirteenth century. The date given in this playlet is 1253.

BENGAL, BEN. Plant in the sun. (One act play magazine. New York, 1937. 4°. v. 1, p. 713–741.)
The shipping room of a candy factory, scene of a sit-down strike. Izzie, one of the strikers.

BENNER, LOUIS DANIEL. The golden days; a play instructive and humorous, with two appropriate songs, for the intermission. In two acts. For five young men and eight young women, and two pages... Cleveland: Central Publishing House, cop. 1930. 20 p. 12°.
Which is the golden age in history? Eight amateur performers, speaking before three judges, represent eight ages of history, for each of which the title is respectively claimed. One of the eight, named Daniel, pleads for the golden age of the Jews.

BENNETT, ARNOLD, AND EDWARD KNOBLOCK. London life; a play in three acts and nine scenes. London: Chatto & Windus, 1924. 167(1) p. 12°. NCR

―――― New York: George H. Doran Company [cop. 1924]. 171 p. 8°. NCR
The theme of the play is indicated in its name. Produced at the Drury Lane, London, June 3, 1924, with Frank Cochrane as Sir Howard Nathan, the villain of the play. Reviewed by Horace Shipp in *English review*, London, 1924, v. 39, p. 141–142, * *DA;* *Era*, London, v. 87, June 11, 1924, p. 6, † *NAFA;* (with illus.) in *Graphic*, London, v. 109, p. 1074, * *DA;* by J. T. Grein (with illus.) in *Illustrated London news*, v. 164, p. 1185, * *DA;* by Francis Birrell in *Nation and Athenæum*, v. 35, p. 352–353, * *DA;* by Edward Shanks in *Outlook*, London, v. 53, p. 411, * *DA;* and by Ivor Brown in *Saturday review*, London, v. 137, p. 608, * *DA.* Further illustrations are given in *Illustrated sporting and dramatic news*, London, v. 103, p. 756–757, * *DA.*
No record of an American production has been found.

Drury Lane Theatre, London. Programme and news sheet of London life... London: Drury Lane, 1924. 14 1. ports., facsim., illus. 8°.
Partial contents: Writing for Drury Lane, Arnold Bennett. Fragments of history, H. C. Newton. London life [a poem], W. R. T.

BENNETT, CHARLES. The last hour; a melodrama in three acts... London: Rich & Cowan, Ltd. [1934.] 114 p., 1 l. 12°. NCO p.v.704
The action of the play is laid in a hostelry in a fishing village on the south coast of Devon. The time is ten years after the Great War. Carol Blumfeldt, alias Dr. Hoyt Logan, is one of the main villains of the piece.

BENTON, RITA. The liberty bell. [In one act] (In her: The elf of discontent, and other plays. New York [cop. 1927]. 12°. p. 301–320.) NASH
The scene is a tenement room where representatives of all the American immigrant races foregather to recount their respective contributions to the making of America. Among them is a Jew. George Washington pointing to the Liberty Bell formulates the creed of true Americanism.

BERKOWITZ, ISAAC DOB. Landsleit; a comedy. (In: B. F. White, translator, Nine one-act plays from the Yiddish. Boston [cop. 1932]. 12°. p. 141–172.) * PTP
The original appeared in *Zukunft*, New York, 1921, v. 26, p. 78–86, * *PBB.*

BERMAN, HENRY. The faith of the fathers; a play in three acts. New York: N. L. Brown, 1922. 228 p. 12°. NBM
Slip pasted over imprint of Library's copy reads: W. F. Ottarson.

BERNARD, BARUCH. A Jewish tragedy; drama in three acts... New York: Bloch Publishing Co., 1934. 160 p. 12°.
Reviewed in *Jewish chronicle*, London, Nov. 16, 1934, p. 22, * *PBE*; B. B. St. in *Jüdische Rundschau*, Berlin, Jahrg. 41, Jan. 24, 1936, p. 7, * *PBC.*

Winograd, David. A Jewish tragedy; its social meaning. [New York, 1935.] 8 p. 8°.
Repr.: Jewish forum, New York, 1935, v. 18, p. 2, 5, 28, 33, * *PBD.*

BERRY, LUCILE BLACKBURN. The melting pot; or, The Americanization of the stranger within our gates... Lebanon, Ohio: March Brothers [cop. 1919]. 16 p. 16°.
An American schoolroom. Alien boys of many nationalities display their respective flags, but finally the Stars and Stripes envelops them all. Among them is a Jewish boy.

BINYON, LAURENCE. ...Bombastes in the shades; a play in one act... Oxford: University Press [1915]. 28 p. 12°. BTZE p.v.160
At head of title: Oxford pamphlets, 1914–15.
An anti-German war play. Heine, one of the characters, descants on the spirit of the Germany of 1914.

BLACK, LEOTA HULSE. Beach nuts. Sioux City, Iowa: Wetmore Declamation Bureau, cop. 1935. 3 l. 4°.
Caption-title.
Mimeographed.
A dramatic reading.

Individual Plays — 1915–1938, continued

BLACK, PEARL. Something different; a playlet of Jewish life in three scenes. New York: Bloch Pub. Co., 1927. 10 p. 12°.
Time: Present. Place: Any modern Jewish home. The dialogue is in English and in Yiddish, in English spelling.

BLACKMORE, MADELINE. "I am over forty," a comedy in one act. New York, N. Y., Los Angeles, Calif.: S. French, Inc..; London: S. French, Ltd. [etc., cop. 1933.] 2 p.l., 18 p. diagr. 12°. NBL p.v.352
Bruno Hauser, "German or of Jewish origin," an actress's manager

BLANKFORT, MICHAEL, AND M. GOLD. ..."Battle hymn;" a play in three acts... [New York:] S. French, 1936. [114] f. 4°.
Variously paged.
"As presented by the Experimental Theatre of the Federal Theatre Project, New York, 1936."

—— —— New York [etc.]: S. French, cop. 1936. 108 p. illus., diagrams. 12°.
A play about John Brown, the abolitionist. Produced at Daly's 63rd Street Theatre, New York, May 22, 1936, with Mony Ash as August Bondi (1833–1907), one of his associates at Harper's Ferry. For reviews see *Collection of newspaper clippings of dramatic criticism, 1935–36*, v. A–B, † *NBL*.
As to Bondi, see his own "With John Brown at Kansas" in Kansas State Historical Society, *Transactions*, v. 8, p. 275–289, *IAA;* and Leon Huhner in American Jewish Historical Society, *Publications*, no. 23, p. 55–78, *IAA*.

BLATT, WILLIAM MOSES. A Jewish word; a play in one act... Boston: W. H. Baker Co. [cop. 1933.] 13 p. 12°. (Baker's edition of plays.)
Produced by the West End Community Theatre, Boston, Mass., March 31, 1936, with Helen Zelman as Betty Chandler.

—— Oi, such a family! a monologue. Chicago: T. S. Denison & Co. [cop. 1925.] 12 p. 12°. (Denison's monologues.)
Mrs. Levine and the cares of her family, including her luckless husband.

—— The quality of mercy; a sixth act to "The merchant of Venice." (In his: After the curtain falls. Boston, 1924. 12°. p. 5–19.)
Repr. *Menorah journal*, New York, 1915, v. 1, p. 96–105, * *PBD*.
A revery following the reading of Shakespeare's play.
Performed at the Temple Playhouse, San Francisco, Dec. 16, 1928.

—— The voice of the ages; a drama in one act... Boston: W. H. Baker Company [cop. 1933]. 18 p. 12°. (Baker's all star series.)
Produced at the Little Theatre of Temple Israel, Boston, Oct. 24, 1933. See *Jewish advocate*, Boston, v. 69, Oct. 20, 1933, section 2, p. 1, * *PBD*.

BLOCK, MAXINE. Eyes; a tragedy in one act... New York, N. Y., Los Angeles, Calif.: Samuel French, cop. 1930. 4 p.l., 5–34 p. 12°. (National little theatre tournament plays.) NBL p.v.258
A dumb and paralytic grandmother, whose only power is in her eyes, and her granddaughter, in a New York tenement house, on a Jewish sabbath eve. Produced by the Morse Players of St. Louis, Mo., at the Waldorf Theatre, New York, May 9, 1930, where it won the Samuel French prize in the 1930 National Little Theatre tournament. Therese M. Wittler acted as the old lady and Alice M. Galleher as the young girl. See *Collection of newspaper clippings of dramatic criticism, 1929–30*, v. I–L (under Little Theatre), † *NBL*.

BLOOM, IRVING MORTIMER. A nation's gratitude. [In one act.] (In: Noah Benevolent Society, N. Y. Eighty-fifth anniversary, 1849–1934. [New York,] 1934. 4°. p. 45–46, 50.)
The scene is the American consulate at Tunis, North Africa, in 1814, where Mordecai M. Noah, 1785–1851, was consul at the time. Noah receives the news of his dismissal. "This," says Commodore Stephen Decatur, "is a nation's gratitude."

BLOOM, LENORE. To Palestine and peace [in two acts]. (Young Judaean. New York, 1934. 4°. v. 21, March, 1934, p. 3.) * PBD
Scene: Jewish home in Germany, in 1934.

BOGEN, JESSIE B. The call; a war relief playlet [in one act. New York, 1920]. 5 l. 8°.
"Dedicated to Greater New York appeal for Jewish war sufferers, May 2–11," 1920.
Copy: Library of the Jewish Theological Seminary of America.
A pageant, the characters of which are three modern girls, the Spirit of Judea, and seven Biblical heroines.

BOLITHO, WILLIAM. ...Overture — 1920, a play, foreword by Gabriel Beer-Hofmann. New York: Simon and Schuster, 1931. ix p., 1 l., 136 p., 1 l. front. (port.) 8°. NCR

—— Overture; a drama in three acts... New York: S. French [etc.], cop. 1931. 98 p., 1 l. plates, plan. 12°. (French's standard library edition.)
A synopsis, with many extracts from the dialogue, is printed in *The Best plays of 1930–31*, New York, 1931, p. 286–316, *NAFH*.
The prototype of Levy may have been any of the following or a composite of all of them: Kurt Eisner, 1867–1919; Gustav Landauer, 1870–1919; Eugen Leviné, d. 1919; Max Levin; Erich Muehsam, the "Edelanarchist"; Ernst Toller, the dramatist. They were all among the leaders of the Communist uprisings of Munich in 1918–1919. Information from Mr. A. Berger of The New York Public Library Jewish Division.
Produced at the Longacre Theatre, New York, Dec. 8, 1930. It tells the story of an abortive Communist revolution in the mythical German city of Herfeld in 1920. Maurice Cass played the part of Dr. Levy, editor of a radical periodical. For reviews see *Collection of newspaper clippings of dramatic criticism, 1930–1931*, v. N–R, † *NBL*.
Produced at the Little Theatre, London, April 24, 1933. Reviewed by John Pollock in *Saturday review*, London, 1933, v. 155, p. 412, * *DA;* and in *The Times*, London, April 25, 1933, p. 12, col. 3, and April 26, p. 14, col. 3, * *A*.

BOLTON, GUY REGINALD. Polly preferred; a comedy, in three acts... New York, London: S. French, cop. 1923. 103 p., 3 l. incl. diagrs., plates. 12°. NBL p.v.199
Published the same year as a novel, under the title of *Polly preferred; a comedy romance of faith and salesmanship.*
A straight comedy centering around theatrical life. Produced at the Little Theatre, New York, Jan. 11, 1923 (pre-view at Cleveland, Dec., 1922), with Harold Walbridge as Morris, an office boy, and Richard Malchien as Harold Nathan, an advertising man. Reviewed in *Theatre magazine*, New York, v. 37, March, 1923, p. 19, † *NBLA;* and in *Variety*, New York, v. 69, Jan. 19, 1923, p. 18–19, † *NAFA*. See also *Collection of newspaper clippings of dramatic criticism, 1923–1924*, v. N–P, † *NBL*.
Produced in London, at the Royalty Theatre, April 5, 1924, with Nathan Natoff as Harold Nathan. Reviewed in *Era*, London, v. 87, April 9, 1924, p. 8, † *NAFA*.

Individual Plays — 1915–1938, continued

BOLTON, GUY REGINALD, AND GEORGE MIDDLETON. The light of the world; a modern drama. New York: H. Holt and Company, 1920. 4 p.l., 3–205 p. front., plates. 12°.　　　　　NBM
In three acts.
The action takes place in the Bavarian village of Oberammergau, before and during the rehearsal of the decennial Passion Play. The characters are the participants in the play, and Nathan, the only Jew in the village and friend of Anton, the Christus of the play. Into the home of Anton (Pedro de Cordoba) comes a young Magdalene (Clara Joel). Produced at the Lyric Theatre, New York, Jan. 6, 1920. Fuller Mellish played the part of Nathan, the scorned Jew. Reviewed in *New York clipper*, New York, v. 67, Jan. 14, 1920, p. 25, * T–† *MVA;* and in *New York dramatic mirror*, v. 81, p. 51, * T–* *DA.* See also *Collection of newspaper clippings of dramatic criticism, 1919–1920,* v. L–P, † *NBL.*
The reviewers ascribed this play to Paul Saissons.

BOOTHE, CLARE. The women; a play [in three acts]... New York: Random House [cop. 1937]. xvi p., 2 l., 3–215 p. 8°.　　　　　NBM
Extracts from the dialogue, with running synopses, are given in *Best plays of 1936–37*, New York, 1937, p. 218–256, *NAFH.*
Produced at the Ethel Barrymore Theatre, New York, Dec. 26, 1936, with Audrey Christie as Miriam Aarons, one of "the women" vacationing in Reno. For reviews see *Collection of newspaper clippings of dramatic criticism, 1936–37,* v. To–Z, † *NBL.*

BORSOOK, HENRY. Three weddings of a hunchback; a comedy. (In: Vincent Massey, editor, Canadian plays from Hart House Theatre. Toronto, 1926. 12°. v. 1, p. 93–124.)
　　　　　NCO (Massey)
A Jewish wedding in the Russian Pale.
Produced at the Hart House Theatre, Toronto, in April, 1924.

BOWER, SHERMAN. "Preferred stock;" a play in three acts. (Jewish forum. New York, 1929. 8°. v. 12, p. 231–234.)　　　　　* PBD
Reuben Rosenberg, salesman. Deals humorously with the discrimination against Jewish employees.

BOYD, ERNEST AUGUSTUS. Some of my best friends are Gentiles. (American spectator. New York, 1933. f°. v. 1, March, 1933, p. 3.)
Scene: a committee room in the Morris Sholom Aleichem Club, Sharon-on-Hudson. Four members, Mayer, Kaplan, Schlupinsky and Ippik, of this exclusive club are met to discuss the admission of a new member, Mr. O'Malley. A satire on the other way around. Mr. Boyd's Hebrew vocabulary must have been supplied to him by one of his numerous Jewish friends.

BRADLEY, E. WARNER, AND J. R. REEVES. The old country store; a farce of rural humorosities in one act. New York: Samuel French, cop. 1927. 20 p. 12°. (French's international copyrighted...edition of the works of the best authors. no. 590.)　　　　　NBL p.v.171, no.5
"Does der doggie bite?" sung by Moses Ikenstine.

BRADLEY, MRS. TRIMBLE, AND G. H. BROADHURST. *See* sub-entry under CHESTER, GEORGE RANDOLPH.

BRANDON, DOROTHY. The outsider; a play in three acts. London: S. French, Ltd.; New York: S. French, cop. 1926. 88 p. plates, diagrs. 8°. (French's standard library edition.)
　　　　　NCO p.v.539
Produced at the Pleasure Gardens, Folkestone, England, April 30, 1923, and at the St. James Theatre, London, May 31, 1923. Ragatzy is the outsider. Sir Israel Nathan, played by Randolph McLeod, eminent physician and member of F. R. C. S. is one of those who are pitted against the outsider. Reviewed in *Era*, London, v. 86, June 6, 1923, p. 11, † *NAFA,* and in *Graphic*, London, 1923, v. 107, p. 900, * *DA.*
Produced at the Forty-ninth Street Theatre, New York, March 3, 1924, with John Blair as Sir Israel Nathan. For reviews see *Collection of newspaper clippings of dramatic criticism, 1923–1924,* v. N–P, † *NBL.*

BRAUN, WILBUR. Absent-minded Judy; a buoyant comedy in three flights... New York [etc.]: Samuel French, cop. 1932. 106 p., 1 l. plan. 12°. (French's international copyrighted ...edition of the works of the best authors. no. 709.)　　　　　NBL p.v.280
Dr. Ira Marks, physician.

—— "The closed door"; a comedy drama in three acts... Minneapolis, Minn.: The Northwestern Press, cop. 1932. 92 p. plan. 12°.
The scene is laid in Jamaica, L. I. Izzy Cohen, the practical business man, "out to make a dollar," provides the comedy relief.

BRENT, ROMNEY. The mad Hopes, a comedy in three acts... New York, N. Y., Los Angeles, Calif.: S. French, Inc.; London [etc.]: S. French, Ltd., cop. 1933. 117(1) p. diagr. 12°. (French's standard library edition.)
　　　　　NCO p.v.677
In August, 1932, it was staged at Magnolia, Mass., under the title *The Widow's might*, and, in Boston, in November, 1932, as *No money to guide her*. Under its present title it was produced in New York, at the Broadhurst Theatre, Dec. 1, 1932, with Pierre Watkin as Maurice Klein, "a pleasant, businesslike, Jewish gentleman in his middle forties." The entire action takes place at the Chateau Sans-Souci in Nice. Reviewed in *Theatre arts monthly*, New York, 1933, v. 17, p. 112, 115, *NBLA.* See also *Collection of newspaper clippings of dramatic criticism, 1932–1933,* v. I–Man, † *NBL.*

BREWSTER, SADIE B. ...America's making... Dansville, N. Y.: F. A. Owen Publishing Company [cop. 1926]. 31 p. 8°.　　　　　NAC p.v.151
At head of title: Instructor entertainment series.
On cover: A patriotic pageant.
"Dances and music": p. 16–31.
Representatives of various races, one of whom is Jewish, address America.

BRIGHOUSE, HAROLD. Mary's John; a comedy in three acts. London: S. French, Ltd.; New York: S. French, cop. 1925. 65 p. illus. 8°. (French's standard library ed.)　　NCO p.v.521
Max Abrahams, business man. His Jewishness is once referred to — "You have an Oriental talent for intrigue," act III, sc. 1.
First produced by the Liverpool Repertory Theatre Co., at the Playhouse, Liverpool, Sept. 30, 1924. It was revived in London, at the Royal Academy of Dramatic Art, Oct. 2, 1927.
In this country, it was staged at the Copley Theatre, Boston, March 23, 1925, with C. W. Hulse as Abrahams.

BRIL, ISAAC LEEP. Everyjew; a Jewish morality play [in one scene]. (Young Judaean. New York, 1915. 8°. v. 5, May, 1915, p. 18–20, 29.)
Theodor Herzl, "the true modern Jew," one of the characters.

BRILLIANT, NATHAN, AND L. L. BRAVERMAN. Moses Maimonides; a pageant of his life [in five scenes]. (Jewish teacher. Cincinnati, 1935. 4°. v. 3, April, 1935, p. 24–27.)　　　　　* PYW

Individual Plays — 1915–1938, continued

BRINIG, MYRON. Fear God and take your own part. [A dramatic sketch.] Sioux City, Iowa: Wetmore Declamation Bureau [1925?]. 4 1. f°
Typewritten.
Based on the author's short story of the same title in *Pictorial review*, New York, v. 26, June, 1925, p. 5–7, 49–50, 55–56, *SNA*.
Hailing from Rumania and settled in Montana, Jacob Western, inspired to patriotism by Theodore Roosevelt, sends his unwilling son, who had preferred a musical career, to enlist in the World war. The boy is killed overseas. Jacob later meets Roosevelt and is cheered by the sympathy of one who too has lost a son in the war.

BRODIE, MRS. A. HARRY. Hadassah's call. [In five tableaux. New York: Hadassah, 1931?] 5 f. 4°
Caption-title.
Mimeographed.
Call to service in Hadassah's major activity of health protection in Palestine.

BRODY, ALTER. A house of mourning; a one act play. (In his: Lamentations. New York, 1928. 8°. p. 67–89.) NBM
Though its characters are three in number, its dramatic poem is largely a soliloquy, during the week of mourning, of a mother bewailing the futile and wasted life of her dead daughter.

—— Lowing in the night. An invisible play. (In: American caravan. New York, 1927. 8°. p. 74–81.) NBL (American)
Part of a series of American-Yiddish plays in which the author is attempting to transplant and naturalize the spirit and rhythm of Yiddish into English. The scene is a bedroom, back of a candy store in The Bronx. The lights are out; a man's and a woman's voices are heard.
Reprinted in his *Lamentations; four folk-plays of the American Jew*, New York, 1928, p. 1–15, *NBM*.

—— Rapunzel; a play in one act. (Theatre arts monthly. New York, 1925. 8°. v. 9, p. 257–266.) NBLA
Sholem Sorel, his wife Rifkah, and their daughter Malkah, a girl of fourteen. Scene: In the kitchen of a Harlem flat.
Reprinted in his *Lamentations*, New York, 1928, p. 39–65, *NBM*; and in Edith J. R. Isaacs, compiler, *Plays of American life and fantasy*, New York, 1929, p. 193–212, *NBL*.
Produced by the Menorah societies of Harvard and Radcliffe colleges at the Agassiz Theatre, Cambridge, May 5, 1928, with A. I. M. Abramson as Sholem Sorel.

—— Recess for memorials; a folk-play [in one act]. (Reflex. New York, 1928. 4°. v. 2, Feb., 1928, p. 31–38.) * PBD
Reprinted in his *Lamentations*, New York, 1928, p. 17–38, *NBM*; and in *Canadian Jewish chronicle*, Montreal, v. 20, Sept. 30, 1932, p. 13, 88–90, * *PBD*.
This play is largely a conversation between two old immigrant Jewish mothers at the synagogue during recess in the services on Atonement Day, concerning the vagaries and rebelliousness of their American-born children.

BROSIUS, NANCY BANCROFT. A little learning; a one-act play. (In: Tournament plays. New York [etc.], 1937. 12°. p. 33–47.) NCO
Home of the Epsteins. A letter comes to two devoted sisters from their brother in jail. How the mother learns about the contents of the letter.

BROWN, ALBERT M. Sunday morning; a one-act comedy of American Jewish life... New York: Bloch Publishing Company, 1935. 20 p. incl. cover-title. 12°.
Revolves around the choice of occupations for the children.

BROWN, ARTHUR M. A dramatist in search of a love scene; a one-act skit. (In his: Plays, skits and playlets. Boston [cop. 1931]. 12°. p. 73–79.) NBM
Rifke and Abie, "the Jewish couple."

BROWN, FORMAN GEORGE. Mister Noah [in three scenes]. (In his: The pie-eyed piper and other impertinent plays for puppets. New York [cop. 1933]. 8°. p. 87–116.) NBM
Albert Einstein, famous scientist, is a stowaway on Noah's ship. He hides to avoid detection at Ellis Island by the "militant ladies." He sings a song, p. 112–113, and is off for Pasadena.

BROWN, WALTER M. Reunion on Grand Street; a one-act play for men... Boston, Mass., Los Angeles, Calif. [W. H. Baker Company, cop. 1936.] 19 p. 12°. (Baker's plays.) NBL p.v.391
Reunion at Hershkowitz's candy store on Grand Street, New York City, of those who came years ago as fellow-passengers and steerage immigrants.

BROWNSON, MARY WILSON, AND V. E. KERST. Victory through conflict. Written and presented by Mary W. Brownson and Vanda E. Kerst. The music written or arranged by Walter Wild. The dances directed by Marion Gifford. Illustrated by Woodman Thompson. The pageant given on the college campus [Pennsylvania College for Women], June 8–9, 1920, during the fiftieth anniversary celebration. [Pittsburgh, Pa., cop. 1920.] xvii, 42 p. front., illus. 8°. NBL p.v.78
Words only.
Episode 1 and interlude 1, in Part 1, are from ancient Jewish history.

BRUGGER, FLORENCE. What makes an American? [In one scene.] (In: Rachel D. DuBois, A school and community project in developing sympathetic attitudes toward other races and nations. New York, cop. 1934. 8°. p. 25–28.)
Among the boy speakers is a Jewish boy.

BUCK, EUGENE EDWARD. Amateur night [in one act]. By Gene Buck. (In: Kenyon Nicholson, editor, Revues; a book of short sketches. New York, 1931. 12°. p. 1–15.) 8–NBL
"A more or less authentic representation of a typical amateur night program of the good old days at Miner's Bowery Theatre." It was included by the late Florenz Ziegfeld in his *Follies of 1923*. In the cast was Fanny Brice.

BURNET, DANA, AND GEORGE ABBOTT. Four walls; a play in three acts...copyright, 1924 (under the title of "The prisoner"). Rewritten and revised 1927... New York, London: S. French, cop. 1928. 109 p. plates. 12°. (French's standard library edition.) NBL p.v.182
The principal character in the play is Benny Horowitz, an ex-convict. "He finds freedom from the four walls of prison and the four walls of his own mind." Produced at the John Golden Theatre, New York, Sept. 19, 1927, with Muni Weisenfrend as Benny and Clara Langsner as his mother. Reviewed by Euphemia Van R. Wyatt in *Catholic world*, New York, 1927, v. 26, p. 242–243, * *DA*; by J. W. Krutch in *Nation*, New York, v. 125, p. 343–344, * *DA*; by Lillian Krieger in *Reflex*, New York, v. 1, Nov., 1927, p. 111, * *PBD*; by J. M. Brown in *Theatre arts magazine*, New York, v. 11, p. 819–820, *NBLA*; and by Milton Danley in *Vanguard*, New York, v. 2, May, 1928, p. 57, * *PBD*. See also *Collection of newspaper clippings of dramatic criticism, 1927–1928*, v. D–G, † *NBL*.

Individual Plays — 1915-1938, continued

BURRILL, BERTHA Y. Rich man, poor man; a farce in one act...preface by Theodore B. Hinckley. New York: S. French; London: S. French, Ltd., cop. 1925. v(i), 35 p. 12°. (Playshop plays.)
    Library has an ed., cop. 1927, *NBL p.v.166.*
    Yetta Goldenstein, a little girl, comes to the rummage sale to get a "vatch" for her father.

BURSTEIN, ABRAHAM. The escape from Cordova; a dramatic incident [in one act] in the boyhood of Maimonides... New York: Bloch Publishing Company, 1935. 12 p. incl. cover-title. 12°.

BURSTEIN, ABRAHAM, AND J. BACHER. Haman of today; a Purim play [in one act] about a play... New York: Bloch Pub. Co., 1930. 12 p. 12°. * PSQ p.v.5

BUTTIMER, EDNA, AND A. RADKE. A fair exchange; a comedy in three acts... San Francisco: Banner Play Bureau, Inc., cop. 1930. 68 p. 12°.

BYERS, ALBERT F. Abie eats; a farce comedy [in one act]. Franklin, Ohio [etc.]: Eldridge Entertainment House, Inc., cop. 1927. 8 p. 12°. (Eldridge popular plays.)
    Abie and Izzy at the restaurant, while the waiter prepares the order.

CAIN, JAMES MALLAHAN. The postman always rings twice... New York: A. A. Knopf, 1934. 4 p.l., 3–187(1) p. 12°. 8–NBO
    Dramatized by the author and produced at the Lyceum Theatre, New York, Feb. 25, 1936, with Charles Halton as Manny Katz, unscrupulous lawyer. See *Collection of newspaper clippings of dramatic criticism, 1935–1936,* v. Nin–Pos, † *NBL.*

CALDWELL, JOHN MILTON. The fraternal bond; an original short play. illus. (Stage. New York, 1936. 4°. v. 13, June, 1936, p. 81–84.) NBLA
    Reprinted in Stage, *Forty-minute prize plays,* New York, 1936, p. 67–92, *NBL.*
    A critique of the social fraternity system in the American colleges. Sol Goldberg is the "outside" Jewish student.

CALISCH, EDITH (LINDEMAN). The Jews who stood by Washington; a play in one act. Cincinnati: Department of Synagogue and School Extension of the Union of American Hebrew Congregations, 1932. 24 p. 12°. * PSQ p.v.2
    The historical characters are Mordecai Sheftall of Georgia and Capt. Isaac Franks, 1759–1822, two Jewish Revolutionary patriots. Embodied in the playlet is a simplified version of the letter written by Washington to the Newport, R. I., congregation.

CARB, DAVID, AND W. P. EATON. Queen Victoria; a play in seven episodes. New York: E. P. Dutton & Company [1922]. 3 p.l., 213 p. 8°. NBM
    Reviewed by L. B. in *Freeman,* New York, 1924, v. 8, p. 455, * *DA.*
    Produced at the Forty-eighth Street Theatre, New York, Nov. 15, 1923, with Clarence Derwent as Disraeli. Reviewed by Stark Young in *New republic,* New York, 1923, v. 37, p. 18–19, * *DA;* and (with illus.) in *Outlook,* New York, v. 135, p. 666, * *DA.* For further reviews see *Collection of newspaper clippings of dramatic criticism, 1923–1924,* v. Q–S, † *NBL.*

CARROLL, ARMOND. A pageant and masque for the Shakespeare Tercentenary... Produced under the direction of the Executive Committee of the Atlanta Center of the Drama League of America, in Piedmont Park, Atlanta, May, nineteen hundred sixteen. [Atlanta:] Atlanta Center, Drama League of America, 1916. 79 p. nar. f°. †* NCLF
    Shylock and Jessica.

CARROLL, EARL. Business is business. [In one act.] (In: Kenyon Nicholson, editor, Revues; a book of short sketches. New York, 1931. 12°. p. 137–141.) 8–NBL
    Morris Goldstein on his death bed. This "snapshot" was played in the 1926 edition of Earl Carroll's *Vanities.*

CASEY, ARTEN. "Com'ny 'tention!" a foolish skit for five soldiers. (In his: "Intermission specialties." Minneapolis, Minn., cop. 1933. 12°. p. 69–77.)
    Cohen, a Jewish buck private.

CASPER, JAY. Salesmanship; a different monologue for Hebrew comedian. (Casper's encore. New York, 1929. 8°. series 30, p. 8–10.)

CASSEL, CAROLA. The choice. (Young Israel. Cincinnati, 1934. 4°. v. 26, June, 1934, p. 7.)
    Time: 1492. * PBD

CECIL, MARY. The "ladies from Friday" in a Turkish bath. [A monologue.] (In her: Breezy episodes. New York, 1932. 12°. p. 110–114.) NBM
    Mrs. Rosen is speaking. "This is played with a low-comedy feeling."

——— "Whatcha come to Paris for anyway?" (In her: Breezy episodes. New York, 1932. 12°. p. 74–77.) NBM
    "Published by the N. Y. Paris Herald."
    The scene is Champs-Élysées, Paris. Two fat women are speaking.

CHANCE, W. A. Winkle versus Fitz-Ailwyn; a mock trial, a comedy of a costermonger's donkey barrow damaged by an aristocrat's motor car... London: Samuel French, Ltd., cop. 1931. 38 p. incl. diagrs. 12°. (French's acting ed. no. 1428.) NCO p.v.634
    One of the defendant's seven witnesses is Moses Isaacstein, moneylender.

CHAPLIN, MRS. ALICE LOUISE (WILLIAMS). School days; third entertainment. (In her: Six rehearsal-less entertainments. Boston [cop. 1921]. 12°. p. 31–48.) NBL p.v.254
    "Soloman, the Jewish lad."

CHARM, ANNA B. Business is business; a play in one act... Edited by Bessie F. White. Boston: W. H. Baker Company [cop. 1932]. 2 p.l., 3–13 p. 12°. (Baker's edition of plays.)
    The supposedly Irish Mary Kane turns out to be Mary Kanevsky, scion of a famous rabbi, and her marriage to Joe, her employer's son, is not objected to. First presented by the Little Theatre of Temple Israel, Boston, April 2, 1931.

Individual Plays — 1915-1938, continued

CHEKHOV, ANTON PAVLOVICH. That worthless fellow Platanov... Translated from the Russian by John Cournos. New York: E. P. Dutton & Co., Inc. [cop. 1930.] 279 p. 12°. ** QDK
Also published in London by J. M. Dent & Sons, Ltd. [1930.]
First published posthumously, under the title *Neizdannaya p'esa*, Moscow, 1923. The milieu is that of Russian provincial society before the Revolution. Among the characters are Abraham Abrahamovich Vengerovich, a wealthy Jew, and his son, Isaac Abrahamovich.

CHESTER, GEORGE RANDOLPH. Isidor Iskovitch presents. illus. (Saturday evening post. Philadelphia, 1923. f°. v. 196, Sept. 8, 1923, p. 25–27, 82, 85–86, 88, 93–94.) * DA

Bradley, Mrs. Trimble, and G. H. Broadhurst. Izzy, a comedy in a prologue and three acts, based on G. R. Chester's Iskovitch stories, was produced at the Broadhurst Theatre, New York, Sept. 16, 1924.
Chronicles the rise of the Iskoviches in the film business. Jimmy Hussey played the title rôle and Robert Leonard, Isaac Iskovich. Reviewed in *Jewish tribune*, New York, Oct. 3, 1924, p. 13, * PBD; *Theatre magazine*, New York, v. 40, Nov., 1924, p. 70, † NBLA; and by David Carb in *Vogue*, New York, v. 64, Nov. 15, 1924, p. 116, * DA. See also *Collection of newspaper clippings of dramatic criticism, 1924-1925*, v. F-L, † NBL.
A pre-view of it was seen at the Stamford Theatre, Stamford, Conn., Aug. 20, 1924.

CHESTERTON, ADA ELIZABETH (JONES), AND RALPH NEALE. The man who was Thursday, adapted from the novel of G. K. Chesterton, by Mrs. Cecil Chesterton and Ralph Neale; with a foreword by G. K. Chesterton. London: E. Benn, Limited, 1926. 2 p.l., 3–100 p., 1 l. 12°. (Contemporary British dramatists. v. 34.)
NCO (Contemporary)
Produced at the Everyman Theatre, London, Jan. 20, 1926, with Guy Le Feuvre in the rôle of Wednesday, who is described in dramatis personae as "He might be a Jew." Reviewed in *Curtain*, London, 1926, v. 5, p. 21, NAFA; and by J. E. Agate in his *Contemporary theatre, 1926*, London, 1927, p. 165–169, NAFA. Stage illus. is given in *Illustrated London news*, 1926, v. 168, p. 170, * DA.

CHLUMBERG, HANS. ...Miracle at Verdun, eight scenes by Hans Chlumberg; translated from the German by Julian Leigh. New York: Brentano's, 1931. 5 p.l., 3–161 p. front. (port.) 12°. NGE
At head of title: A Theatre Guild play.
Reprinted in F. W. Chandler and R. A. Cordell, editors, *Twentieth century plays*, New York, 1934, v. 3, p. 79–113, NCO (Chandler).
A symbolic, sociological drama. The dead millions of the World war come back to earth and the manner in which they are received. Produced at the Martin Beck Theatre, New York, March 16, 1931, with Sidney Starvo as chief rabbi Dr. Sorgenreich. Reviewed by E. Van R. Wyatt in *Catholic world*, New York, 1931, v. 133, p. 209–210, * DA; and by E. Wilson in *New republic*, New York, v. 66, p. 182–183, * DA. See also *Collection of newspaper clippings of dramatic criticism, 1930-1931*, v. I-M, † NBL.

—— ...Miracle at Verdun. Translated by Edward Crankshaw. London: Victor Gollancz, Ltd., 1932. 128 p. 8°.
In thirteen scenes.
Reprinted in *Famous plays of 1932-33*, London, 1933, p. 105–232, NAFH.
Produced at the Embassy Theatre, London, Sept.

21, 1932, with Abraham Sofaer as Dr. Forbach, chief rabbi. Reviewed in *Era*, London, v. 96, Sept. 28, 1932, p. 9, † NAFA; by C. B. Purdom in *Everyman*, 1932, v. 8, p. 296, * DA; *Jewish chronicle*, London, Sept. 23, 1932, p. 27, and Oct. 28, p. 33–34, * PBD; and in *New statesman*, London, new series, v. 4, p. 345, * DA.

Epstein, Mordecai. Reflections on a play. (Jewish chronicle. London, 1932. f°. Oct. 14, 1932, p. 12.) * PBD
Letters of Benammi. no. 675.

CHODOROV, EDWARD. Kind lady...adapted from a story [The silver mask] by Hugh Walpole. New York, Los Angeles: S. French; London: S. French, Ltd., 1936. 5 p.l., 3–135 p., 2 l. front., plates, diagrs. 12°. NCR
A melodrama, the scene of which is London. First produced at the Booth Theatre, New York, April 23, 1935, with Jules Epailly as Gustav Rosenberg, French art expert of the firm Bernstein et fils, Paris. For reviews see *Collection of newspaper clippings of dramatic criticism, 1934-35*, v. K-L, † NBL. Walpole's short story, upon which it is based, is included in his *All souls' night*, London, 1933, 8–NCW. No such character as Rosenberg appears in the story.

CITRON, SAMUEL J. The luminary (a play in 3 acts, based on the life of Moses Maimonides) ... New York: The Jewish Forum, cop. 1935. 24 p. 16°.
Repr.: *Jewish forum*, New York, 1935-36, v. 18, p. 255–256, v. 19, p. 23–25, 241–242, * PBD.

—— Ost-Yude; a play for adults, in one act... New York: Education Department, Zionist Organization of America, 1937. 16 p. 8°.
Cover-title.
German Jewish pioneers in present-day Palestine. Reviewed by Leo Shpall in *Jewish ledger*, New Orleans, v. 76, Nov. 19, 1937, p. 4, * PBD.

CLANCY, JOSEPH P. Christmas in the tenements; a one-act play by Rev. Father Joseph P. Clancy... Franklin, Ohio: Eldridge Entertainment House, Inc., cop. 1934. 14 p. 12°. (Eldridge Christmas material.)
Children and grown-ups of many types and nationalities. Among them is Izzy, a Jewish boy.

CLARKE, HAROLD A., AND M. NURNBERG. Chalk dust; a play in three acts... New York [etc.]: S. French, cop. 1937. 48 p., 10 l. illus., diagrs. 12°.
"The story of a large, metropolitan high school."
Produced by the Experimental Theatre of the WPA at Daly's 63rd Street Theatre, New York, March 4, 1936, with Shimen Ruskin as Kaplan, "favorite pupil, eager for knowledge sensitive and proud."
For reviews see *Collection of newspaper clippings of dramatic criticism, 1935-1936*, v. C-Dea, † NBL.

CLEMENTS, FLORENCE (RYERSON), AND C. C. CLEMENTS. The loop, an experiment in light and shadows. [In one act.] By Florence Ryerson and Colin Clements. (Emerson quarterly. Boston, 1930. 4°. v. 10, Jan., 1930, p. 15–17.)
† NANA
Reprinted in Theodore Johnson, editor, *Diminutive comedies*, Boston [cop. 1931], p. 5–17.
A thriller involving the quick solving of a murder mystery, Uncle Izzy, pawnshop proprietor.

CLEWS, HENRY, JR. Mumbo jumbo. New York: Boni and Liveright [cop. 1923]. 5 p.l., 275(1) p. 8°. NBM

—— —— London: G. Richards, Limited, 1923. 279 p. 12°.
The play is intended to expose the machinations of modern art dealers and the gullibility of modern art

Individual Plays — 1915–1938, continued

CLEWS, HENRY, JR., *continued*
patrons. It consists of sixty pages of introduction, sixty-five pages descriptive of the dramatis personae, and four acts of satirical comedy. Among the numerous characters are Isaac Kougelman, Joseph Rosengarten, Moses Stein, and Samuel Van Rensselaer-Levineson, art dealers and critics, and the Duchess of Mandelieu, society leader, born "in a New York pawn shop" of Jewish parents.
Reviewed in *Dial*, New York, 1923, v. 75, p. 302, * *DA*; by H. M. in *New statesman*, London, v. 20, p. 698, * *DA*; *Saturday review*, London, v. 135, p. 776–777, * *DA*; and in *Spectator*, London, v. 130, p. 852–853, * *DA*.

COAKLEY, THOMAS FRANCIS. The discovery of America; a pageant by Thos. F. Coakley, D. D.; illustrations by J. Woodman Thompson. [New York: Printed by Frank Meany Co., cop. 1917.] 59(1) p. plates. 8°. NBM
In three episodes.
"Introduction," p. 3, by Joyce Kilmer.
One of the characters is Santangel, described on p. 7 as "the Church treasurer."

COBB, ELIZABETH, AND MARGARET C. MORGAN. The murder of the night-club crooner. (In their: Murder in your home. New York, 1932. 8°. p. 161–167.)
Ida Gordon, a night-club hostess, is one of three characters.

COGHLAN, JAMES J. Oh, teacher! a blithe act for four males. (Coghlan's jester. Jersey City, N. J., 1922. 8°. no. 2, p. 47–51.)
The characters: Hebrew, sissy, tough, and Italian.

—— A wedding, a monologue for Hebrew comedian. (Coghlan's jester. Jersey City, N. J., 1922. 8°. no. 2, p. 6–7.)

COHEN, IRVING. Music for musicians [a play characterization, in three acts]. Character — the word and the gesture. (Community messenger. Trenton, N. J., 1928. 4°. v. 5, Oct., 1928, p. 19–20, 37–40.)
Copy: Library of the American Jewish Historical Society.

COHEN, ISIDOR. Jewish provincialism in a growing community; a one-act playlet. (Jewish unity. Miami, Fla., 1929. f°. v. 2, June 21, 1929, p. 3, 7.) * PBD

COHN, EMIL BERNHARD. Das reissende Lamm; Drama in fünf Akten, von Emil Bernhard. Berlin: Volksbühnen-Verlag, 1926. 70 p. 12°.
The theme is pacifism during the World war. The scene is a Siberian prisoners' camp, in 1917.
Translated by Alexander Berkman, and under the title, *The Prisoner*, produced at the Provincetown Theatre, New York, Dec. 28, 1927, with Jacob Sandler as the Jew (*Judel Leibowicz*, in the original). Reviewed in *Billboard*, New York, v. 40, Jan. 7, 1928, p. 11, † *MZA*; *Theatre magazine*, v. 47, March, 1928, p. 62, † *NBLA*. See also *Collection of newspaper clippings of dramatic criticism, 1927–1928*, v. M–P, † *NBL*.

COHON, SAMUEL SOLOMON. Every-mother; a morality in three episodes. Cincinnati: Dept. of Synagog and School Extension of the Union of American Hebrew Congregations [cop. 1926]. 30 p. 12°. * PSQ p.v.3
Presented by the Women's Society of Zion Temple, Chicago, at the conference day of the Chicago Jewish Women's Organization, Feb. 15, 1916.

COLEBY, WILFRED T. "Dizzy"; a dramatic comedy in a prologue and three acts. By T. Pellatt (W. T. Coleby)... London: Macmillan & Co., Limited, 1932. vi, 122 p., 1 l. 12°.
NCO p.v.640
The prologue takes place in July, 1836; the remainder in 1878.
Produced at the Westminster Theatre, London, Oct. 5, 1932, with Ernest Milton as Disraeli. Reviewed in *Era*, London, v. 96, Oct. 12, 1932, p. 9, † *NAFA*; by C. B. Purdom (with illus.) in *Everyman*, London, v. 8, p. 364, * *DA*; and in *Jewish chronicle*, London, Oct. 7, 1932, p. 29, * *PBE*.

COLUM, PADRAIC. Balloon; a comedy in four acts. New York: The Macmillan Company, 1929. 4 p.l., 123 p. 8°. NCR
"Mr. Colum presupposes for his dramatic setting a fabulously sumptuous hotel...representing the 'unbuilt-on earth'. There is a landing field on the roof and a balloon is about to ascend from it." Among the characters are Mark Franks, a financier; Cohen Muldoon, a prize fighter; and Leila Pomerants, a cinema star. Reviewed by W. P. Eaton in *Books*, v. 5, July 14, 1929, p. 14, † *NAA*; by H. Clurman in *New republic*, New York, v. 59, p. 266–267, * *DA*; and by Jane Dransfield in *Saturday review of literature*, New York, v. 6, p. 75, † *NAA*.

CONWAY, OLIVE, pseud. OF HAROLD BRIGHOUSE AND J. WALTON. Dux; a tragic satire. (In: The best one-act plays of 1936, selected by J. W. Marriott. London [1937]. 12°. p. 161–178.)
Countess Bretza as a potential Judith and Dux (presumably Hitler) as a possible Holofernes. "A smashing satire on dictatorships."

COOKE, JAMES FRANCIS. Scenes from the life of Richard Wagner [in three acts]. (In: R. H. Schauffler, and A. P. Sanford, editors, Plays for our American holidays. New York, 1928. 12°. [v. 4,] p. 277–287.) NASH (Schauffler)
Among the characters is the composer Meyerbeer.

CORMACK, BARTLETT. The racket; a play. New York City: S. French; London: S. French, Ltd. [cop. 1928.] vii p., 2 l., 3–134 p. 12°. NBM
In three acts.
A synopsis, with copious extracts from the text, is printed in *The Best plays of 1927–28*, New York, 1928, p. 313–349, *NAFH*.
A play of the Chicago underworld. Produced at the Ambassador Theatre, New York, Nov. 22, 1927, with Ralph Adams as Sam Meyer of the legal firm of Reilly, Platka and Cohn. Reviewed by G. M. Leland in *Billboard*, Cincinnati, v. 39, Dec. 3, 1927, p. 10, † *MZA*. See also *Collection of newspaper clippings of dramatic criticism, 1927–1928*, v. Q–S, † *NBL*.

CORNFIELD, MAURICE. Palestine versus Diaspora; a play in three acts, designed for children... Louisville, Ky., 1935. 30 p. 12°.
Time: the present. Place: the first two acts in Germany; the third in Palestine.

The COSTLY party. [In three acts.] By a seventh grade in Louisville, Kentucky. (In: Grace T. Hallock, Dramatizing child health. New York, 1925. 8°. p. 130–164.) NASH
Mr. Solomon is attorney for defendant in a case where health regulations were violated during the "flu" epidemic in 1918.

COURNOS, JOHN. Shylock's choice [in one act]. (Fortnightly review. London, 1925. 8°. v. 124, p. 728–732.) *DA
Reprinted in *Reflex*, New York, v. 2, May, 1928, p. 11–14, * *PBD*; in *Imagist anthology 1930*, New York [1930], p. 67–76, *NCI*; and in Leo W. Schwarz,

Individual Plays — 1915-1938, continued

editor, *A Golden treasury of Jewish literature*, New York [cop. 1937], p. 436–441, * PSY.
Shylock and Tubal, the evening before the trial in Shakespeare's *The Merchant of Venice*. Shylock portrays his intended revenge on Antonio — a different and more subtle form of revenge than is given in the play. Cf. Morris Joseph, "A New Shylock," in *Jewish guardian*, London, v. 7, Dec. 25, 1925, p. 9, * PBE (reprinted in *Jewish exponent*, Philadelphia, Jan. 29, 1926, p. 14, * PBD).

—— Sport of gods, a play in three acts with prologue and epilogue. Founded on an episode from the author's "Babel". London: E. Benn, Ltd., 1925. 99(1) p. 12°. (Contemporary British dramatists. v. 33.) NCO (Contemporary)
Time: autumn-winter, 1913–1914; place: London. The prologue in a Russian country crossroads, about 1890.

COWARD, NOEL PIERCE. ...Design for living, a comedy in three acts. Garden City, N. Y.: Doubleday, Doran and Company, Inc., 1933. 6 p.l., 3–139 p. 12°. NCR

—— —— London: William Heinemann, Ltd. [1933.] 4 p.l., 122 p. 12°.
Reprinted in his *Play parade*, New York, 1933, p. 1–111, NCR.
A synopsis of the story, with copious extracts from the dialogue, is given in *The Best plays of 1932-33*, New York, 1933, p. 134–171, NAFH.
Produced at the Ethel Barrymore Theatre, New York, Jan. 24, 1933, with Campbell Gullan as Ernest Friedman, bourgeois art dealer. Reviewed by E. Van R. Wyatt in *Catholic world*, New York, 1933, v. 136, p. 715–716, * DA; by Stark Young in *New republic*, New York, v. 73, p. 350–352, * DA; and by Barclay McCarty in *Theatre arts monthly*, New York, v. 17, p. 257–258, NBLA. See also *Collection of newspaper clippings of dramatic criticism, 1932–1933*, v. C–D, † NBL.

COWEN, SADA. Auf wiedersehen... New York [etc.]: S. French [cop. 1937]. 2 p.l., 341–358 p., 1 l. incl. illus. diagr. 12°.
Repr.: M. G. Mayorga, ed., *Twenty short plays on a royalty holiday*, New York, 1937, p. 339–358, NBL.
A play of Nazi Germany.

CRANMER-BYNG, LANCELOT ALFRED. Salma; a play in three acts... London: John Murray, 1923. xiii, 110 p. 16°. NCR
It was staged, with incidental music by Granville Bantlock, by the Birmingham University Dramatic Society, at the Midland Institute, Birmingham, Eng., March 2, 1926, with S. M. Kirk in the part of Simeon ben Zachariah, "a Jew chronicler of Abu'l Fath."

CRAWFORD, BOB. On vit de dance; a semi-musical act... Boston: Walter H. Baker Company [cop. 1932]. 16 p. 12°. (Baker's specialties.)
Jake Kaplan directs his daughter Lottie's new singing and dancing act. Becky, Jake's wife.

CREASMAN, MRS. MYRTLE R. How home missions came home to Helen. (In her: Plays and pageants. Nashville, Tenn. [cop. 1930.] 8°. p. 131–145.) NAFM
In one act.
A playlet inculcating the lesson of home missions. Rachel, a Jewish playmate, is one of the characters.

CROCKER, BOSWORTH, PSEUD. The baby carriage; a play. (In: Frank Shay and Pierre Loving, editors, Fifty contemporary one-act plays. Cincinnati [cop. 1920]. 12°. p. 119–131.) NAFH (Shay)
By Mary Arnold (Crocker) Lewisohn.
Reprinted in her *Humble folk*, Cincinnati [cop. 1923], p. 45–83, NBM.
Comedy-drama concerning the poverty-stricken wife of a little Jewish tailor whose stifled desire for beauty almost brings her to petty larceny.
Produced by the Provincetown Players of New York, Feb. 14, 1919, with Dorothy Miller as Mrs. Lezinsky, the tailor's wife.

—— Coquine... New York [etc.]: S. French [cop. 1937]. 3 p.l., 21–42 p., 1 l. incl. illus. diagr. 12°.
Repr.: M. G. Mayorga, ed., *Twenty short plays on a royalty holiday*, New York, 1937, p. 19–42, NBL.
Place: home of Heinrich Heine in Paris, during the second quarter of the 19th century. The main characters are Heine, his friend Alexandre Weill (1811–1898), and Matilda Mirat, Heine's wife.

CROTHERS, RACHEL. The importance of being married; a play in one act. (In her: Six one-act plays. Boston, 1925. 12°. p. 43–66.) NBM
Rosenbaum, business manager of a musical comedy star.

—— A little journey; a comedy in three acts ... New York: S. French; London: S. French, Ltd., cop. 1923. 2 p.l., 199–297 p. 12°. (French's standard library edition.)
Reprinted from her *Mary the third*, "Old lady 31," *A Little journey*, New York [cop. 1923], NBM.
The greater part of the action takes place on a railroad train. Produced at the Little Theatre, New York, Dec. 26, 1918, with Paul E. Burns as Leo Stern, a traveling clothing salesman. A pre-view of it was given at the Shubert Theatre, New Haven, Dec. 19, 1918. For reviews see *Collection of newspaper clippings of dramatic criticism, 1918–1919*, v. G–L, † NBL.

CUNNINGHAM, MARY. Doggone! a farce in one act... Chicago: Dramatic Publishing Company [cop. 1933]. 21 p. diagr. 12°.
Mr. Lundowitz, a Jewish tailor, owner of the Lundowitz Lucky Cleaners and Renovatory.

CURTIS, GEORGE F. The love life of Irene [a monologue]. (In his: Monologues that win. New York, cop. 1930. 16°. p. 44–47.) NBM
The speaker is a snappy, young Jewish girl in the flapper stage.

—— Tea at Mrs. Sinsheimer's. [A monologue.] (In his: Monologues that win. New York, cop. 1930. 16°. p. 12–17.) NBM
A Jewish parvenue who strives to create a social impression.

D., B. C. ...The saving sign; a play [in six scenes]. London: Society for Promoting Christian Knowledge [1930]. 61 p. 12°. (Parish plays. no. 32.) NCO p.v.606
A play of early Christian missions. The scene is Rome and the Saxon court of England, 585–597. Scene I is the marketplace at Rome, A. D. 585, and a Jew is introduced as buying a youth from a slave dealer.

DAINOW, DAVID. Holding aloof, a play in one act. [Johannesburg, S. A.: Central News Agency, Ltd., 1929.] 31 p. 12°.

Individual Plays — 1915–1938, continued

DAIXEL, SAMUEL. After midnight; a fantasy. (In: B. F. White, translator. Nine one-act plays from the Yiddish. Boston [cop. 1932]. 12°. p. 83–117.) *PTP
First appeared in his *10 Ein-akters,* New York, 1925, under title of *Nach zwölf beinacht.*

DAMROSCH, GRETCHEN. The passing present; a play in three acts... New York, N. Y., Los Angeles, Calif.: S. French, Inc.; London: S. French, Ltd., cop. 1932. 2 p.l., 3–95(1) p. plates, diagr. 12°. (French's standard library edition.) NBL p.v.294
"Copyright 1930 (under title, 'Sidelight') by Gretchen Damrosch Finletter."
The disintegration of a New York family of social distinction. Produced at the Ethel Barrymore Theatre, New York, Dec. 8, 1931, with Louis La Bey as Mr. Lerner, "a Jewish realtor, prosperous, agreeable, smooth," who comes to buy the French property. Reviewed by R. D. Skinner in *Commonweal,* New York, 1931, v. 15, p. 245, *DA;* and by J. Hutchens in *Theatre arts monthly,* New York, 1932, v. 16, p. 98–100, *NBLA.* See also *Collection of newspaper clippings of dramatic criticism, 1931–1932,* v. P-S, † *NBL.*

DANNENBAUM, RAYMOND. Samuel Ibn-Nagdela. [In three acts.] (Emanu-El. San Francisco, 1933. 4°. v. 74, Jan. 6, 1933, p. 2, 9; Jan. 13, p. 2; Jan. 27, p. 2, 8; Feb. 3, p. 2.) *PBD
Samuel Ibn-Nagdela (Samuel ha-Nagid), statesman, poet, grammarian and Talmudist, 993–1055, served as Vizier to King Habus, at Granada, Moorish Spain. The scene is the palace of the Vizier, and the time is 1025. Deals with certain alleged episodes in his life, testifying to his wisdom and magnanimity.

—— "Thunder on the left." (Emanu-El. San Francisco, 1933. 4°. v. 74, March 17, 1933, p. 3.) *PBD
Christopher Morley discourses with three Californians on Jews and Jewish authors.

DASEKING, EDITH. Schoolin'. [In one act.] (Theatre and school. Berkeley, Calif., 1929. 8°. v. 7, Jan., 1929, p. 18–28.) MWA
The Mission District of San Francisco; interior of a grocery store. Mrs. Fishbein, "a fat, genial, untidy Jewess," a customer.

DAVAGE, GEORGE. The man tamer; a comedy sketch. (McNally's bulletin. New York, 1919. 8°. no. 5, p. 111–116.) NAC p.v.29

DAVENPORT, SAMUEL R. I am a Jew. [A dramatic reading in one act.] Sioux City, Iowa: Wetmore Declamation Bureau, cop. 1933. 3 f. 4°
Typewritten.
Deals with the anti-Semitic situation in Germany in 1933. The characters are Hitler, a young officer, an old Jewish professor, and his son-in-law.

DAVIDSON, JOSEPH ELIAS. Stamps and their Jewish interest. (Jewish forum. New York, 1935–37. v. 18–20.) *PBD
The following dramatic sketches, based on historical or legendary material, illustrated by stamp issues, are given: Richard I and Maimonides, 1191 (v. 18, p. 85–86, 91); King John III (Sobieski) at the trial of the Jew Bezalel (v. 18, p. 103); Goethe visits the Mendelssohns, 1821 (v. 18, p. 116, 135); The Two Czars discuss the Jew [Isaac Baer] Levensohn, 1825 (v. 18, p. 161–162); Rembrandt and Menasseh ben Israel, 1655 (v. 18, p. 194); Alfieri the poet and Salomon the Florentine Jew, 1778, based on Walter S. Landor's imaginary conversation of the same title (v. 18, p. 222, 252); Trajan and rabbi Akiba ben Joseph (v. 19, p. 93); The Martyrs of Posen, 1399 (v. 20, p. 2); Prince Henry the Navigator and Judah Cresques, the map Jew, 1419 (v. 20, p. 68).

DAVIS, ALLAN. Victims; a picture of an American family against a certain background. In three views... n. p., cop. 1926. 46, 36, 32 f. 4°.
Typewritten. NBL p.v.213
The action takes place in western Pennsylvania, in one of the smaller industrial cities adjoining Pittsburgh. Harry Goldberg, the Jewish character, is described as "a dark...serious-looking young man... the type of successful American merchant of Jewish blood and high principles."

—— Wolves; a play of the great hunger, in one act... [New York,] cop. 1922. 27 f. 4°.
Typewritten. NBL p.v.212

—— —— New York, London: S. French, cop. 1925. 31 p. 12°. (French's international copyrighted edition. no. 518.) NBL p.v.142
Scene: a village in the Ukraine on the Russian border. The action takes place in Feb., 1922, during the wars of the Whites and the Reds. First produced at Syria Mosque, Pittsburgh, Feb. 26, 1922.

DAVIS, EDWARD. The iron cross; a little page from history [in one act]. (Review. Philadelphia, 1915. 12°. v. 10, no. 8, p. 54–58.)
An incident during the European War, in Russian Poland.

DAVIS, JOHN. Lincoln and his Jewish chiropodist. "The head and feet of the nation." (Jewish exponent. Philadelphia, 1933. f°. v. 91, Feb. 10, 1933, p. 1, 9.) *PBD
Scene: a room in the White House in 1863. President Lincoln is receiving a treatment from his Jewish chiropodist, Dr. Issachar Zacharie. Concludes with an historical note on Lincoln and Dr. Zacharie.

DAVIS, OWEN. The detour; a play. Boston: Little, Brown, and Company, 1922. x, 122 p. 12°.
NBM

—— —— New York: S. French; London: S. French, Ltd., cop. 1922. x, 122 p. plates, plans. 12°. (French's standard library edition.)
Foreword signed: Montrose J. Moses.
In three acts.
Reprinted in M. J. Moses, editor, *Representative American dramas, national and local,* Boston, 1925, p. 495–526, *NBL (Moses).*
This is the story of an elderly, toil-worn wife of a farmer. In her drudgery and youthful dreams of life in a great city, the critics have compared her to Robert Mayo in Eugene O'Neill's *Beyond the horizon.* Produced at the Astor Theatre, New York, Aug. 23, 1921, with James R. Waters as Weinstein, an old-furniture dealer, and Chester Herman as his son Jake. For reviews see *Collection of newspaper clippings of dramatic criticism, 1921–1922,* v. A-D, † *NBL.*

DAWN, ISABEL, AND B. DE GAW. "Marathon;" a new comedy drama in three acts... [New York, 1933.] [120] f. 4°. † NCOF
Various foliation.
Reproduced from typewritten copy.
Prompter's book.
A play about Marathon dance contests.
Produced at the Mansfield Theatre, New York, Jan. 28, 1933, with Ivan Triesault as Luis Borkofski (Luis Levinski in the text), one of the dance contestants. See *Collection of newspaper clippings of dramatic criticism, 1932–33,* v. Mar-P, † *NBL.*

Individual Plays — 1915–1938, continued

DEARMER, GEOFFREY. The man with a cane; a comedy in one act. London: H. F. Deane & Sons, the Year Book Press, Ltd. [1930.] 15 p. 12°. (The Y. B. P. series of plays.)
A play of public school life in England. "Ike" Mowenstein, a pupil, and Mrs. Mowenstein, his mother.

DECKER, HERMANN T. The jack in the box; a farce-comedy in four acts... Chicago: T. S. Denison & Company [cop. 1928]. 83 p. diagrs. 12°. (Denison's miscellaneous plays.)
NBL (Denison's)
The action takes place in and about Hollywood, California. Spindler is a partner in the Spindler-Johnson Superfilm.

DEDDENS, MAXINE. The court decides for safety. [In one act.] diagr. (Safety education. New York, 1928. 4°. v. 8, no. 1, Sept., 1928, p. 8–10.)
SPA
A juvenile play worked out by the Junior Safety Council of the Nicholas Finzer School, Louisville, Ky. The defendant in the play, on a charge of hit-and-run, is here named Harry Goldberg. He is found guilty.

DEITCH, JOSEPH. Hurrah for Cheshvan [in one act]. illus. (Young Maccabee. New York, 1934. 4°. v. 1, no. 3, p. 8–10.) *PBD
Cheshvan is the Hebrew month corresponding generally to October.

—— Welcome home [in one act]. illus. (Young Maccabee. New York, 1934. 4°. v. 1, no. 4, p. 3–6.) *PBD

DEMBO, LEON HASKINS. The first baby (a mellow drama in eleven scenes, showing why most insane asylums contain a goodly number of pediatricians). (Phi Delta Epsilon news. New York, 1926. 8°. v. 15, May, 1926, p. 8–12.) SSY

—— Mrs. Feitlebaum and ward C (with apologies to Milt Gross). (Phi Delta Epsilon news. New York, 1926. 8°. v. 15, Oct., 1926, p. 9–10.) SSY

DICKERSON, PENELOPE. The cross word puzzle. [A dramatic reading, in one act.] Sioux City, Iowa: Wetmore Declamation Bureau, cop. 1929. 3 f. 4°.
Typewritten.
Isaacstein, "a Jewish merchant," and other patients in a doctor's outside office.

DICKMAN, ADOLPH. The baron of Budapest; a melodrama in 3 acts. (In his: The baron of Budapest and Rosenbaum and son. Los Angeles, Cal. [1932.] 12°. p. 1–37.) NAFH p.v.117
A melodrama which deals with a modern, newly rich family in Budapest, 1900–1918, whose financial aspirations meet with disaster.

—— Rosenbaum and son; a play in 3 acts. (In his: The baron of Budapest and Rosenbaum and son. Los Angeles, Cal. [1932.] 12°. p. 39–64.) NAFH p.v.117
A scene of American-Jewish life. Much of the dialogue is in Yiddish.
Place: a midwestern city. Time: 1928–1931.

A DIVINE comedy. (Harvard lampoon. Cambridge, 1922. 4°. v. 84, p. 63.) STG
Simmie, the spirit of a prominent Boston "Semitic" ex-banker, offering a big sum for admittance into Heaven, and the Swob, spirit of the widows and orphans of Boston, who were robbed by the banker to the tune of three million dollars, as a fellow applicant, are the two main speakers. There is no contemporary factual warrant for this skit. Let it be put down, therefore, to the *Lampoon* echo of the Harvard anti-Semitism fashionable at that period.

DIXON, THOMAS. A man of the people; a drama of Abraham Lincoln. New York, London: D. Appleton and Company, 1920. xiii, 155(1) p. 12°. NBM
In a prologue, three acts, and an epilogue. One of the characters, in act III, is Judah P. Benjamin, 1811–1884, U. S. senator from Louisiana, Attorney-General, Secretary of War, and Secretary of State of the Confederacy, 1861–1865.
Produced at the Bijou Theatre, New York, Sept. 7, 1920. Reviewed in *New York clipper*, v. 68, Sept. 15, 1920, p. 19, *T–† MVA; *New York dramatic mirror*, 1920, v. 82, p. 464, *T–* DA; by O. W. Firkins in *Review*, New York, 1920, v. 3, p. 255–256, *DA; and in *Theatre magazine*, New York, 1920, v. 32, p. 280, † NBLA.
The first part of act III, where Benjamin appears, was omitted in some of the stage productions.

DONCHIAN, PETER. I object, your honor! a mock trial... New York, Los Angeles: S. French, Inc.; London: S. French, Ltd., cop. 1935. 62 p., 1 l. 12°. NBL p.v.380
Sue de Ruyter, née Rosie Glutz, sues Beau Brummel for breach of promise. Isadore Guinsberg, amateur house detective, testifies in dialect.

DONNEZ MOI, PSEUD. The search, a play by play report [in three acts]. illus. (Bunk. New York, 1932. 4°. v. 2, Oct., 1932, p. 12, 34.)
The characters are the seer, Rowbuck; Izzy A. Bierstein, and Frank Statement.

DORAN, MARIE. The education of Doris; a comedy in three acts... New York, N. Y., Los Angeles, Calif.: S. French, Inc.; London: S. French, Ltd., cop. 1932. 90 p., 1 l. diagrs. 12°. NBL p.v.295
The action throughout occurs at Miss Fraser's fashionable school, where Rachel Stern, girl of wealthy parents, is one of the pupils. In the masquerade party in the last act, she appears as *Rebecca at the well*.

—— The gay co-eds, a comedy in three acts... New York, N. Y., Los Angeles, Calif., S. French, Inc.; London: S. French, Ltd. [etc.] cop. 1933. 85(1) p. diagr. 12°. NBL p.v.322
A play of school life. The characters are a principal and ten pupils. One of the latter is here called Benjamin Stern.

DOS PASSOS, JOHN. Airways, Inc. [In three acts.] New York: Macaulay Company [cop. 1928]. 148 p. 12°. NBM
Reprinted in his *Three plays*, New York [cop. 1934], p. 79–159, NBM.
Airways, Inc. is an enterprise of a group of go-getting business men. With it is linked the story of a factory strike and the framing of the leader by the police. Most of the dramatis personae are given Jewish names. Produced at the Playwright's Theatre, New York, Feb. 20, 1929. Reviewed by W. J. Riley in *Billboard*, New York, v. 41, March 2, 1929, p. 49, † MZA; by Padraic Colum in *Dial*, New York, v. 86, p. 442–443, * DA; *New Palestine*, New York, v. 16, p. 97–98, * PXL; and by Edmund Wilson in *New republic*, New York, v. 58, p. 256–257, * DA. See also *Collection of newspaper clippings of dramatic criticism, 1928–1929*, v. A–B, † NBL.

—— Fortune heights [in three acts]. (In his: Three plays. New York [cop. 1934]. 8°. p. 161–298.) NBM
Act I is captioned The bull market; act II, The great depression; and act III, The new deal.

Individual Plays — 1915–1938, continued

DOUGLAS, NORMAN. South wind... New York: Dodd, Mead and Co., 1926. 413 p. 8°. NCW
First published in London by Martin Secker [1917].

Douglas, Norman, and Isabel C. Tippett. "South wind"; a play in a prologue and two acts. Suggested by Norman Douglas' book of the same name.
Produced by the Repertory Players at the Kingsway Theatre, London, April 29 and 30, 1923. The Jewish character in the novel, Edgar Marten, mineralogist, is omitted in the dramatization.

DRAPKIN, CHARLES. The dictator; a play in one act. (In: Sydney Needoff, editor, Five one-act plays of Jewish interest. [Manchester, Eng., 1937.] 8°. p. 55–64.)
A play of Nazi Germany.

DREISER, THEODORE. The hand of the potter; a tragedy in four acts. New York: Boni and Liveright [cop. 1918]. 5 p.l., 15–209 p. 8°.
8–NBM
Reviewed in *Dial*, New York, 1919, v. 67, p. 276, * *DA*; *Nation*, New York, 1919, v. 109, p. 340, * *DA*; by Jesse L. Bennett in *New republic*, v. 20, p. 297–298, * *DA*; and by G. J. Nathan in *Smart set*, v. 60, Oct., 1919, p. 131–133, 8–*NBA*.
A study in abnormal psychology. The hand of the potter slipped when it created Isidore Berschansky, Jack-the-ripper son of respectable immigrant Jewish parents. The scene is the East Side of New York and the characters are all Jewish, except an officer of the law. Produced at the Provincetown Playhouse, New York, Dec. 5, 1921, with J. Paul Jones as Isidore and Nathaniel Freyer and Dosha Rubinstein as his parents. Reviewed by Ludwig Lewisohn in *Nation*, New York, 1921, v. 113, p. 762–763, * *DA*. See also *Collection of newspaper clippings of dramatic criticism, 1921–1922*, v. E–L, † *NBL*.

The Hand of the potter; a 10-page booklet. Undated. Issued by Boni and Liveright in 1918 for advertising purposes. Contains reviews, letters and excerpts.
In November, 1927, *The Hand of the potter* was published in a revised edition by Boni and Liveright. The revisions were made by the author in the last few pages of the last act.

DUKER, SAMUEL. Concessions! concessions! (Avukah bulletin. New York, 1936. 4°. April, 1936, p. 5, 8.)

DUMONT, FRANK. The night riders; a melodrama in three acts... Philadelphia: Penn Pub. Co., 1916. 62 p. 12°. NBL p.v.46, no.15
Another edition published in 1919.
Ikey Bloomingall, a country peddler, way down South.

—— With the Stars and Stripes in France; a melodrama in three acts... Philadelphia: Penn Pub. Co., 1918. 61 p. diagrs. 12°.
Another issue published in 1920. BTZE p.v.356
"Jacob Stitch, a tailor, may be played by a Jew or Swede."

DUNBAR, ALICE RUTH (MOORE). Mine eyes have seen. illus. (Crisis; a record of the darker races. New York, 1918. 8°. v. 15, p. 271–275.)
IEC
Reprinted in her *Dunbar speaker and entertainer*, Naperville, Ill. [cop. 1920], p. 171–181, *NANV*.
Time: 1918. A patriotic war-play. Jake, a Jewish boy; the other characters are mostly Negroes.

DUNNING, PHILIP HART. Night hostess; a dramatic comedy [in three acts]... New York: Samuel French, 1928. 5 p.l., 3–164 p., 4 plates incl. front. 12°. NBM
A play centering about a night club. Produced at the Martin Beck Theatre, New York, Sept. 12, 1928, with Maurice Freeman as Abe Fischer, proprietor of the "Little Casino," and an "honest" gambler. Reviewed by B. H. Clark in *Drama*, 1928, v. 19, p. 44, *NAFA*; and by J. W. Krutch in *Nation*, New York, v. 127, p. 327–328, * *DA*. See also *Collection of newspaper clippings of dramatic criticism, 1928–1929*, v. N–R, † *NBL*.

DURLACHER, AUGUST JAMES. A tale of Biscay Bay [in one act]. (In his: Off trail echoes. New York [cop. 1933]. 12°. p. 117–134.) NBI
Scene: aboard a U. S. destroyer in the Bay of Biscay, November, 1917. Alex Cohn, renowned on the stage, volunteers during the Great war as a mess cook, where he is known as Jew Davis. He dies in the storm at sea.

EATON, WALTER PRICHARD. Grandfather's chair; a comedy in one act... New York [etc.]: Samuel French [cop. 1930]. 3 p.l., 26 p., 1 l. 12°. NBL p.v.234
A comedy about the hobby of collecting antiques. An antique dealer, "with an accent which suggests the East Side. You find him nowadays setting up shop beside state highways...and you distrust both his knowledge and his word."

EBER, MOTTE ABRAHAM. Messiah, trilogy... [Chicago: The Norman Paul Publishing Company, cop. 1934.] 116 p. 8°. * PSY

ECKHOUSE, L. R. Council's every girl; a playlet [in 4 scenes]. [Newark, N. J.?] Council of Jewish Women, 1922. 26 p. 24°. * PBM p.v.142
A morality play, with the social work of the Council among young girls as its theme.

—— "Dust"; a play [in one act]. New York: National Council of Jewish Women, Dept. of Farm and Rural Work [1927?]. 10 f. 4°.
Mimeographed. NBF p.v.107
The day before the New Year, in an American farmhouse kitchen.

EDITORIAL conference (with wine). (American spectator. New York, 1933. f°. v. 1, Sept., 1933, p. 1.) * DA
Reprinted in part in *Jewish criterion*, Pittsburgh, v. 82, Sept. 8, 1933, p. 4, 20, * *PBD*.
The five editors of *The American spectator*, including George J. Nathan who does most of the talking, make merry about the Jews. See *Jewish exponent*, Philadelphia, v. 92, Sept. 1, 1933, p. 4, * *PBD*; and A. Coralnik, "A Symposium on stilts," in *The Day*, New York, Sept. 23, 1933, p. 10, 12, * *PBD*; and Hayim Fineman, "While sipping wine," in *Der Yiddisher Kaempfer*, New York, v. 13, Sept. 15, 1933, p. 7–8, * *PBB*.

EFROS, ISRAEL ISAAC. The bloody jest; a drama in four acts. Boston: R. G. Badger [cop. 1922]. 89 p. 8°. NBM
Time: 1587. Place: Rome.
"The source of the plot is to be found in Gregorio Leti's *Life of Sixtus V*, where Seche — in this play, Antonio — claims a pound of flesh from a Roman Jew, named Samson Cenada, as the result of a wager." — *Foreword*.

EHRLICH, IDA LUBLINSKI. The still small voice [in one act]. (Young Israel. Cincinnati, 1930. 4°. v. 22, Feb., 1930, p. 14–17.) * PBD
A juvenile morality play.

Individual Plays — 1915–1938, continued

EINSTEIN, IRVING. What's in a name? a dramatic playlet in one act... New York: Metropolitan League of Jewish Community Associations [cop. 1931]. 17 f. 4°.
Cover-title.
Typewritten.
Its theme is the alleged discrimination against Jewish employees by some Gentile firms.

ELDER, ELEANOR. Official announcement; a play in one act... London: S. French [cop. 1937]. 40 p. 12°. (French's acting edition. no. 2065.)
It was produced in England by the Arts League Travelling Theatre. The play deals with modern Nazi Germany and the problems that confront those who have any kind of Jewish connection.

ELDRIDGE, FLORENCE M. The growth of a nation [in a prologue and four tableaux]. (In: R. H. Schauffler, and A. P. Sanford, editors, Plays for our American holidays. New York, 1928. 12°. [v. 3,] p. 237–254.) NASH (Schauffler)
Jews, as one of the component peoples of America, appear with the Reader telling of their entry into this country.

ELDRIDGE, PAUL. His peers [a dramatic sketch]. (Pagan magazine. New York, 1917. 8°. v. 2, Oct./Nov., 1917, p. 16–23.) *DA
Scene: a court room. Various representatives of the religions and great ideas of the world, among whom is a rabbi, examine "a man without a label," who belongs to no party and to no creed.

ELLIS, ELSWORTH, AND EVERETT ELLIS. The sacrifice, a tragic drama... Baltimore: Saulsbury Pub. Co. [1918.] 3 p.l., 3–57 p. 12°. NBM
John Rosenthal, M.D., his wife and their little daughter.

ELSTEIN, NOAH. Israel in the kitchen. A play in three acts... [Preface by J. T. Grein.] London: Sidgwick & Jackson, Ltd., 1928. 4 p.l., 90 p. 12°. NCR
Reviewed in *The Times literary supplement*, London, 1928, v. 27, p. 81, † *NAA*.
Deals with Jewish life in a slum section of an industrial English city of to-day. This play was awarded first prize by the Jewish Drama League of London, and was produced by the League at the London Pavilion, Dec. 5, 1926. Hector Abbas played the rôle of Mr. Israel; Mme. Fanny Waxman, Mrs. Israel; George Owen, Peretz; and Delia Dellvina, Ray Israel. Reviewed by J. E. Agate, who was one of the judges of the play-contest, in his *Contemporary theatre, 1926*, London, 1927, p. 133–138, *NAFA*; and in *Nation*, London, 1926, v. 40, p. 386, * *DA*.
Produced at the Neighborhood Playhouse, New York, May 17, 1929, with Jo Cubert, Gertrude Laitman, H. Birnberg, and Ruth Haimowitz in the respective rôles enumerated above. For reviews see *Collection of newspaper clippings of dramatic criticism, 1928–1929*, v. H–K, † *NBL*.

EMERSON, EDWIN. Benedict Arnold, a drama of the American revolution, in three acts and a prelude. New York: Printed for private distribution by Vail-Ballou Press, Inc. [cop. 1924.] 142 p. 12°. NBM
Major David S. Franks, and his sister Rebecca, figure prominently in this play. Rebecca is represented as loyal to the American cause, although she is the friend of Peggy Arnold and of Major André.
"The Jewish characteristics of Major Franks and his sister should be conveyed in mere hints of a livelier temperament, particularly in the case of the romantic, young Rebecca." — *Preface.*
As to Rebecca, see Max J. Kohler, *Rebecca Franks, an American Jewish belle of the last century*, New York, 1894, * *PWZ p.v.5.*

EMERSON, JOHN, AND ANITA LOOS. The whole town's talking; a farce in 3 acts. New York: Longmans, Green & Co., 1925. 2 p.l., 120 p. 12°. (Longmans' play series.) NBL p.v.132
Adapted from a German play by Francis Arnold and Ernest Bach. The action is laid in Sandusky (in the acted version, Toledo), Ohio. A boob pretends intimacy with a vamp; this rumor makes him popular; the rivalry wins him a wife. A preview of it was given at Hempstead, L. I., Nov. 13, 1922. Produced at the Bijou Theatre, New York, Aug. 29, 1923, with Jeanne Green as Sadie Bloom. Reviewed in *Dramatist*, Easton, Pa., 1923, v. 14, p. 1168–1169, *NAFA*; and (with illus.) in *Metropolitan magazine*, New York, v. 58, Dec., 1923, p. 38–39, 98–99, * *DA;* by L. Lewisohn in *Nation*, New York, v. 117, p. 304, * *DA;* and by Arthur Hornblow in *Theatre magazine*, New York, v. 38, Oct., 1923, p. 66, † *NBLA*. See also *Collection of newspaper clippings of dramatic criticism, 1923–1924*, v. T–Z, † *NBL*.
It was first staged at the Opera House, Leicester, Eng., Aug. 23, 1926, and brought to the Strand Theatre, London, Sept. 7, 1926, with Sheila Courtenay as Sadie Bloom.

EPSTEIN, MRS. MOSES P. A quiet morning in the life of any Hadassah chapter president. [In one act. New York: Hadassah, 1931.] 4 f. f°.
Caption-title.
Mimeographed.
The characters are the members of the president's family and Amanda, colored maid.

ERMATINGER, GERTRUDE L., AND ALMIRA K. DONALDSON. The spirit of the American constitution. [In two scenes.] (Normal instructor and primary plans. Dansville, N. Y., 1925. f°. v. 34, Sept., 1925, p. 74, 76.) † SSA
Among the characters are a monk, a Quaker and a Hebrew, representing a group seeking religious freedom.

ERVINE, ST. JOHN GREER. The lady of Belmont, a play in five acts. London: G. Allen & Unwin, Ltd. [1923.] 95 p. 12°.

———— New York: The Macmillan Company, 1924. 95 p. 12°.
Reviewed by S. R. Golding in *Jewish chronicle*, London, 1925, supplement, Feb., p. iv–vi, * *PBD;* by V. Sackville-West in *Nation*, London, 1924, v. 34, p. 740–741, * *DA; The Times literary supplement,* London, v. 23, p. 73, † *NAA;* and by R. L. P. in *Yale literary magazine*, New Haven, v. 89, p. 196–197, *STG*. A detailed outline is given by Clarence I. Freed in *American Hebrew*, New York, 1924, v. 114, p. 599, * *PBD.*
The scene of this play, which is a sequel to *The Merchant of Venice*, is laid at the home of Portia and Bassanio in Belmont, exactly ten years after the date of Antonio's trial in Shakespeare's play. The entire action takes place in less than twenty-four hours.
First presented by the Dramatic Centre Repertory, Mary Ward Settlement, London, May 31, 1924. Produced by the Arts Theatre Club, London, May 6, 1927, with Brember Wills as Shylock and Ellen Hare as Jessica. Reviewed in *Era*, London, v. 90, May 11, 1927, p. 1, † *NAFA;* by Horace Horsnell in *Outlook*, London, v. 59, p. 626, * *DA;* and by Ivor Brown in *Saturday review*, London, v. 143, p. 742–743, * *DA.*
It was staged by the Jewish Drama League at the Cambridge Theatre, London, March 26, 1933, with Ernest Milton as Shylock and Lydia Sherwood as Jessica. Reviewed by G. J. in *Jewish chronicle*, London, March 31, 1933, p. 53, * *PBE.*
An outline, and stage illustrations of the production, as given by the Minnesota Masquers of the University of Minnesota, is printed in *Drama*, Chicago, 1926, v. 16, p. 226, 229, *NAFA*.

Individual Plays — 1915–1938, continued

EUREKA HIGH SCHOOL, EUREKA, CAL. — HISTORY CLASS. Pageant of ancient civilization [in a prologue and one act]. Written and staged by the History Class, under the direction of Miss Frances Ahl. (Historical outlook. Philadelphia, 1923. 4°. v. 14, p. 182–185.) BAA
Among the characters is a Hebrew.

FAGIN, M. Room 226. [A play in 1 act.] (Poet lore. Boston, 1925. 8°. v. 36, p. 610–614.) *DA
The scene is room 226 at Ellis Island, New York Harbor, quarter of the "disorderly women warrant cases." Mattie, a Jewish unmarried girl, with her sick baby, is detained there together with three other girls, Italian, Polish, and English.

FALLENBERG, ESTHER. Rip Van Winkle. (Jewish teacher. Cincinnati, 1935. 4°. v. 4, Nov., 1935, p. 16–18.) *PYW
In a prologue and one act.

FANNIE finds the way; a community center incident. (Our Jewish neighbors. New York, 1925. 8°. v. 4, March, 1925, p. 28–30.) *PGI
Fannie is a little Jewish girl who finds her way to the mission house and to Jesus.

FARQUHAR, ROBERT. Portia pulls a pinch play; a Shakespearean burlesque... Franklin, Ohio: Farquhar Play Bureau, cop. 1930. 16 p. 12°.

FARQUHAR, Ross. Nothing ever happens; a comedy in two acts... Franklin, Ohio: Farquhar Play Bureau, cop. 1929. 36 p. 12°.
David Genswert, "a big-hearted Hebrew. Possesses the well-known characteristics of his race; economy, shrewdness, worry over money, yet, withal a heart of gold."

FAUCHOIS, RENÉ CHARLES ANDRÉ. ...Prenez garde à la peinture; comédie en trois actes... [Paris: Imp. de l'Illustration,] 1932. 38 p., 1 l. *(La Petite Illustration...23 avril 1932. Théâtre [nouv. série,] no. 299.)* † NKM

Howard, Sidney Coe. The late Christopher Bean, founded upon Prenez garde à la peinture, by René Fauchois. New York, Los Angeles: S. French; London: S. French, Ltd., 1933. 6 p.l., 3–187 p. 12°. NBM
"Copyright 1932, by Sidney Howard under the title of 'Muse of all work.'"

—— —— New York City, N. Y., Los Angeles, Calif.: Samuel French, Inc.; London: Samuel French, Ltd., cop. 1933. 138 p., 1 l. plates, diagrs. 12°. (French's standard library edition.)
Many extracts from the dialogue, with a running synopsis, are printed in *The Best plays of 1932–33,* New York, 1933, p. 238–270, *NAFH.*
Deals with the tricky gentry who hang around the fringes of the art world. Rosen is the comparatively honest one in the lot.
Produced at Henry Miller's Theatre, New York, Oct. 31, 1932, with Clarence Derwent as Rosen, art dealer. Reviewed by R. D. Skinner in *Commonweal,* New York, 1932, v. 17, p. 75, *DA;* and by J. W. Krutch in *Nation,* New York, v. 135, p. 484–485, *DA.* See also *Collection of newspaper clippings of dramatic criticism, 1932–1933,* v. I–Man, † *NBL.*

Williams, Emlyn. The late Christopher Bean; a comedy. An English adaptation of René Fauchois' Prenez garde à la peinture! London: Victor Gollancz, Ltd., 1933. 128 p. 12°. NCR
Reprinted in *Famous plays of 1933,* London, 1933, p. 9–136, *NAFH.*

—— —— London: S. French, Ltd. [etc.], cop. 1935. 102 p. illus. 8°. (French's acting edition. no. 732.)
Produced at the St. James's Theatre, London, May 15, 1933, with Clarence Derwent as Rosen. Reviewed by Ivor Brown in *Drama,* London, 1933, v. 11, p. 145, and by Herbert Farjeon, ibid., p. 161, *NAFA; Jewish chronicle,* London, May 26, 1933, p. 40, * *PBE;* and by G. C. P. in *Saturday review,* London, v. 155, p. 493, * *DA.* Illustrations are given in *Theatre world,* London, 1933, v. 20, p. 19–30, *MWA.*

FEINSTEIN, JACOB. His eyes; a one-act drama. New York: Metropolitan League of Jewish Community Associations [cop. 1931]. 10 f. 4°.
Cover-title.
Mimeographed.
The eyes of a blind man. Time: February, 1930. Place: "East Side," Philadelphia.

FELTON, MRS. CARL. ...Goose money; a one act play. Madison: Extension Service of the College of Agriculture, The University of Wisconsin [1928]. 23 p. illus. 12°. NBL p.v.198
Cover-title.
At head of title: Special circular. June, 1928.
Abe, the Jewish poultry dealer of the village.

FERBER, EDNA. The eldest; a drama of American life. New York, London: D. Appleton and Company, 1925. 3 p.l., 21(1) p. diagr. 12°. (Appleton short plays. no. 14.) NBL p.v.136
Reprinted in Kenyon Nicholson, editor, *The Appleton book of short plays, second series,* New York, 1927, p. 1–25; and in B. H. Clark and Kenyon Nicholson, editors, *The American scene,* New York and London, 1930, p. 389–405, *NBL.*
Produced by the Provincetown Players, Macdougall Street, New York, in January, 1920, with S. K. Powell as Henry Selz.

FERBER, EDNA, AND G. S. KAUFMAN. Stage door; a play [in three acts]... Garden City, N. Y.: Doubleday, Doran & Company, Inc., 1936. ix, 230 p. front. 8°. NBM
Extracts from the dialogue, with running synopses, are given in *Best plays of 1936–37,* New York, 1937, p. 182–217, *NAFH.*
A play about stage folks. The scene is the Footlights Club, home for aspiring actresses. Produced at the Music Box Theatre, New York, Oct. 22, 1936, with Ralph Locke as Adolph Gretzl, a movie magnate, Edmund Dorsay as Lou Milhauser, and Richard Kendrick as Keith Burgess, the young radical playwright who forsakes the theatre for Hollywood, a character said to have had Clifford Odets as its prototype. For reviews see *Collection of newspaper clippings of dramatic criticism, 1936–37,* v. S–Ti, † *NBL.*

FERBER, EDNA, AND N. LEVY. $1200 a year; a comedy in three acts... Garden City, N. Y.: Doubleday, Page & Company, 1920. 5 p.l., 3–173(1) p. 12°. NBM
A young economics professor earning twelve hundred dollars a year decides to become a thirty-dollars-a-week mill hand. Among the characters in the play is Isadore Slotkin, a tailor.
Reviewed by L. B. in *Freeman,* New York, 1920, v. 2, p. 94, *DA;* by Adelaide E. Morey in *Survey,* New York, v. 45, p. 137, *SHA;* and in *Theatre arts magazine,* New York, 1921, v. 5, p. 86, *NBLA.* See also *Booklist,* New York, 1920, v. 17, p. 61, *R– *GBO.*

FEUCHTWANGER, LION. ...Jud Süss: Schauspiel in drei Akten (vier Bildern). München: Georg Müller, 1918. 142 p., 1 l. 12°.

Individual Plays — 1915-1938, continued

Dukes, Ashley. Jew Süss, a tragic comedy in five scenes by Ashley Dukes; based upon the romance of Lion Feuchtwanger. London: M. Secker, 1929. 99(1) p. 12°. NCR
First published in the *Evening standard*, London, Nov. 2-16, 1929.

—— Jew Süss, a drama in five acts based upon Power, the historical romance of Lion Feuchtwanger, by Ashley Dukes. New York: The Viking Press, 1930. 178 p., 1 l. 12°.
First produced at the Opera House, Blackpool, England, July 29, 1929, and at the Duke of York's Theatre, London, Sept. 19, 1929. Matheson Lang in the title rôle (Jew Süss is Joseph Süss Oppenheimer, German financier, 1698-1738); Peggy Ashcroft as his daughter Naemi. Reviewed by G. W. B. in *Era*, London, v. 93, Sept. 25, 1929, p. 1, 6, † *NAFA*; *Jewish chronicle*, London, Oct. 4, 1929, p. 37, * *PBE*; *Jewish guardian*, London, Sept. 27, 1929, p. 10, * *PBE*; illus., in *Theatre arts monthly*, New York, v. 14, Jan., 1930, p. 25-26, *NBLA*. See also Charles Morgan in *New York Times*, Oct. 6, 1929, section 9, p. 1, * *A*.
* Produced at the Erlanger Theatre, New York, Jan. 20, 1930, with Maurice Moscovitch in the title rôle. Reviewed by D. J. Galter, in *Jewish exponent*, Philadelphia, v. 85, Feb. 21, 1930, p. 7, * *PBD*; by Stark Young, in *New republic*, New York, 1930, v. 61, p. 301-302, * *DA*. See also *Collection of newspaper clippings of dramatic criticism, 1929-1930*, v. I-L, † *NBL*.
Produced by the Menorah societies of Harvard and Radcliffe at the Agassiz Theatre, Cambridge, Mass., April 9, 1931, with Lee Srole as Joseph Süss; Sara Horlick as Naemi.

Betts, Ernest, editor. Jew Süss, from the novel by Lion Feuchtwanger; directed by Lothar Mendes; produced by the Gaumont-British Corporation, Ltd. Edited with an introduction by Ernest Betts. London: Methuen & Co., Ltd. [1935.] xviii, 174 p., 8 plates incl. front. (port.) 12°.
This is a scenario in dramatic form of the film shown in England and America, in which Conrad Veidt played Joseph Süss, and Pamela Ostrer, his daughter Naemi.

Feuchtwanger, Lion. 1918; a dramatic novel [in three "books"]. (In his: Three plays. New York, 1934. 8°. p. 79-227.) NGE
Also published in London.
Translated by Emma D. Ashton.
Written in 1918, and published in München, 1920, under the title *Thomas Wendt*. It deals with the German revolution of 1918, and was never permitted to be staged in Germany. One of the extreme proponents of the Revolution is designated as "the East European Jewess."
Reviewed in *The Times literary supplement*, London, 1935, v. 34, p. 19, † *NAA*.

—— The ugly duchess, translated by Willa and Edwin Muir. New York: The Viking Press, 1928. 4 p.l., 3-335 p. 8°. 8-NGL

Beringer, Vera. The ugly duchess: a play in three acts, adapted from Feuchtwanger's novel, was produced at the Arts Theatre Club, London, May 15, 1930.
Philip Brandon played Mendel Hirsch, a Jewish merchant. Reviewed by G. W. Bishop in *Era*, London, v. 93, May 21, 1930, p. 1, † *NAFA*; and in *Jewish chronicle*, London, May 23, 1930, p. 29, * *PBD*.

Field, Rachael Lyman. The fifteenth candle. (In: C. S. Thomas, editor, Atlantic book of junior plays. Boston [cop. 1924]. 12°. p. 126-143.) NAFH (Thomas)
Goldstein, who acts supposedly as the labor agent in a factory. "Performed in Boston and other cities during 1921, 1922, 1923."

Fisher, Mrs. Blanche (Steerman). An evening in Palestine. [In one act. New York: Hadassah, 1934.] 2 f. f°.
Caption-title.
Mimeographed.

—— Women in Israel — a tableau. [New York: Hadassah, 1930.] 3 f. f°.
Caption-title.
Mimeographed.
Scenes depicting women in the Bible and in modern Palestine.
Produced by the Washington, D. C., chapter of Hadassah.

Fitzgerald, Francis Scott Key. The great Gatsby. New York: C. Scribner's Sons, 1925. 3 p.l., 218 p. 12°. NBO

Davis, Owen. The great Gatsby; a drama in a prologue and three acts, dramatized from the novel of the same name by F. S. Fitzgerald. Produced at the Ambassador Theatre, New York, Feb. 2, 1926.
It tells the story of the rise and fall of a super-bootlegger. The prologue takes place in 1917, just before his embarkation with the American army for France; the remainder of the play, a few years after the World war. Charles Dickson played Meyer Wolfsheim, a cautiously loyal, Jewish professional gambler, friend of the hero. For the identification of Wolfsheim with the notorious gambler Arnold Rothstein, see *New republic*, New York, 1937, v. 89, p. 326, * *DA*. Reviewed in *Theatre magazine*, New York, v. 43, April, 1926, p. 64, 66, † *NBLA*. See also *Collection of newspaper clippings of dramatic criticism, 1925-1926*, v. E-J, † *NBL*.

Flattery, M. Douglas. The subterfuge; a comedy drama [in 4 acts]. (In his: Three plays. Boston [cop. 1921]. 12°. p. 149-211.) NBM
Abraham Steiner, "a Hebrew real-estate speculator," and money-lender of the sinister type.

Flavin, Martin A. Amaco, by Martin Flavin, with a letter from Lincoln Steffens. New York, Los Angeles: S. French; London: S. French, Ltd., 1933. 7 p.l., 3-141 p. 12°. NBM
A play in seven episodes, dated 1907 to 1932, dealing with the struggle between capital and labor. Most prominent of the group representing capital is Mr. Loeb, banker and industrialist, of Nathan Loeb & Co., described as "a man of fifty with Semitic features ...and a cold, shrewd, calculating face." No record of its production has been found.

—— The criminal code; with nine stage designs by Albert R. Johnson. New York: H. Liveright [cop. 1929]. 5 p.l., (1)4-200 p. front., plates. 12°. NBM
Copious extracts from the text, with a running synopsis, are printed in *The Best plays of 1929-30*, New York, 1930, p. 71-107, *NAFH*.
A prison play. The action is laid within the walls of the prison. Produced at the National Theatre, New York, Oct. 2, 1929, with Walter Kingsford as Dr. Rinewulf, prison physician. For reviews see *Collection of newspaper clippings of dramatic criticism, 1929-1930*, v. A-C, † *NBL*.

Individual Plays — 1915–1938, continued

FLAVIN, MARTIN A. Lady of the rose; a play in three acts. New York: S. French [etc.], cop. 1925. 106 p. front. (port.) 8°. (French's standard library edition.) NBL p.v.137
Produced at the 49th Street Theatre, New York, May 19, 1925, with Edwin Maxwell as Max Lubin, "short, stout, middle-aged Jew; shrewd, unctuous, voluble and bustling." For reviews see *Collection of newspaper clippings of dramatic criticism, 1924–1925,* v. F–L, † *NBL.*

FLECKER, JAMES ELROY. Hassan: the story of Hassan of Bagdad and how he came to make the golden journey to Samarkand. A play in five acts... London: William Heinemann, 1922. 3 p.l., 182 p., 1 l. 12°. NCR

—— —— New York: A. A. Knopf, 1926. 3 p.l., 168 p., 1 l. 12°. NCR
Also published in London [1935].
In an arrangement by Basil Dean, it was produced at His Majesty's Theatre, London, Sept. 20, 1923, with Tarver Penna as the Principal Jew. It ran 281 times.
Produced at the Knickerbocker Theatre, New York, Sept. 22, 1924, with Henry Morrell as the Principal Jew. For reviews see *Collection of newspaper clippings of dramatic criticism, 1924–25,* v. F–L, † *NBL.*

FLEG, EDMOND. ....Le marchand de Paris; comédie en trois actes... [Paris: Impr. de l'Illustration,] cop. 1929. 30 p., 1 l. f°. (La Petite illustration...no. 429, 4 mai 1929. Théâtre [nouv. série,] no. 229.) † NKM (Petite)
First produced at the Comédie-Française, Paris, March 5, 1929, with Maurice de Féraudy as Samuel Brizach.

Ames, Winthrop. Mr. Samuel, an adaptation by Winthrop Ames, with the scene changed to New York City, was produced at the Little Theatre, New York, Nov. 10, 1930, with Edward G. Robinson as Mr. Samuel, the Samuel Brizach in the French original.
For reviews see *Collection of newspaper clippings of dramatic criticism, 1930–31,* v. I–M, † *NBL.*

FLINT, EVA KAY, AND M. MADISON. Subway express [in three acts]... [New York, 1929.] 45, 32, 34 f. 4°. † NCOF
Reproduced from typewritten copy.
In three acts.
A murder mystery on the subway. The Zlotniks — four of them — are among the passengers. Produced by Edward A. Blatt at the Liberty Theatre, New York, Sept. 24, 1929. See *Collection of newspaper clippings of dramatic criticism, 1929–30,* v. R–S, † *NBL.*

FOSTER, GLADYS. Want; a one-act play for eight women... New York [etc.]: S. French, Inc., cop. 1935. 28 p., 1 l. diagr. 12°. NBL p.v.392
The action takes place in a department store. Mrs. Seligman is described as "an overdressed, nervous, thin, highly excitable, disagreeable woman." *Want* won first place in the New Jersey Women's Clubs Little Theatre Tournament for 1935, "because of its emotional appeal."

FOX, LILLIAN. Abraham Lincoln and the Jewish soldier. Dramatized from the story by Lillian Fox. (In: Jewish Education Committee, Chicago, Programs for Jewish youth clubs. American Jewish history. Chicago, 1929. 3 f. 4°.) * PBM p.v.173
In two scenes.
Mimeographed.
Based on an incident related by Simon Wolf in his *Presidents I have known,* Washington, 1918. p. 5–7, *AGZ.* The characters are a Jewish soldier, his mother, Thomas Corwin, 1794–1865 (Representative from Ohio, 1858–1861, and U. S. Minister to Mexico, 1861–1864); John Hay, 1838–1905, secretary to President Lincoln; and Simon Wolf, 1836–1923, Jewish communal worker, resident at Washington during the Civil War.

FRANK, FLORENCE (KIPER). The faith of their fathers; a play in one act. (Menorah journal. New York, 1925. 4°. v. 11, p. 377–381.) * PBD
A comic sketch. Produced by the Religious School Students' Association of Temple Emanu-El, at the Temple Playhouse, San Francisco, April 13, 1929.

FRANK, MAUDE MORRISON. When Heine was twenty-one. (In her: Short plays about famous authors. New York, 1915. 12°. p. 33–64.) NBM
In one act.
At Hamburg, 1821. The poet, his uncle Salomon, and the latter's daughter Molly (Amelia) figure in the play. The incidents, and the story of the unrequited love of the poet for his cousin Amelia, tally with the biographical facts of Heine's life.

FRANKEN, MRS. ROSE. Another language, a comedy drama in three acts. New York, Los Angeles: S. French; London: S. French, Ltd., 1932. 5 p.l., 3–163 p. 12°. NBM
"Copyright, 1929, by Rose Franken, under the title of 'Hallam wives'; revised and rewritten, 1932."
A running synopsis, with excerpts from the high lights of the dialogue, is given in *Best plays of 1931–1932,* New York, 1932, p. 267–299, *NAFH.*
The characters are eleven Hallams, — a father and mother, four sons and their four wives, and a grandson. Scene: West Side of New York City. Although the name chosen is not distinctly Jewish, the discerning theatre goers who saw it and the critics who reviewed it recognized it as a picture of New York Jewish family life. It was produced at the Booth Theatre, New York, April 25, 1932. Reviewed by Stark Young in *New republic,* New York, 1932, v. 70, p. 351–352, * *DA.* See also *Collection of newspaper clippings of dramatic criticism, 1931–1932,* v. A–B, † *NBL.*
It was staged in London, at the Lyric Theatre, Dec. 1, 1932. Reviewed in *Drama,* London, 1933, v. 11, p. 49, *NAFA;* and (with illus.) in *Illustrated London news,* 1932, v. 181, p. 956, 1012, * *DA.* Further stage illustrations are given in *Theatre world,* London, 1933, v. 19, p. 19–30, *MWA.*
J. T. Grein wrote: "The transference of 'Another language' from its natural Jewish *milieu* to that of London suburbia has robbed the play of much that made the original convincing and amusing."

FREDERICK, JOHN TOWNER. Twelfth night at Fisher's Crossing. (Midland. Iowa City, Iowa, 1916. 8°. v. 2, Jan., 1916, p. 18–24.) * DA
In one act.
Liebmann, a Jewish peddler, sympathetically drawn, in a pathetic scene.

FREED, CLARENCE I. The heart of Solomon; a comedy in one act. (American Hebrew. New York, 1923. f°. v. 113, p. 218, 230.) * PBD
A comedy on the match-making theme.

FREEDMAN, DAVID. Mendel Marantz...illustrations by M. Leone Bracker. New York: The Langdon Publishing Company, Inc., 1926. 301 p. col'd front., plates. 12°.
Originally appeared under varying titles in *Pictorial review,* New York, v. 23–24, in the issues for April, June, August and October, 1922. * *DA.* Adapted by the author into a comedy of three acts, entitled *Mendel, Inc.,* and produced at the Sam H. Harris Theatre, New York, Nov. 25, 1929, with Alexander Carr as Mendel, Lisa Silbert as his wife Zelde, Joe Smith as Bernard Schnapps, Charles Dale as Sam Shtrudel, and Anna Chandler as Bessie Bloom. Reviewed in *Billboard,* Cincinnati, v. 41, Dec. 7, 1929. p. 76, † *MZA;* by Robert Benchley in *New Yorker,* New York, v. 5, Dec. 7, 1929, p. 42, * *DA;* and in *Theatre magazine,* New York, v. 51, Feb., 1930, p. 67–68, † *NBLA.* See also *Collection of newspaper clippings of dramatic criticism, 1929–30,* v. M–Q, † *NBL.*

Individual Plays — 1915-1938, continued

FRIEDMAN, MRS. HENRY A. ..."The Jewish woman in America;" dramatic episodes... [New York:] National Council of Jewish Women [1936?]. [11] f. f°.
Multigraphed.
Prologue: 1645 (should be 1654), Jewish immigrants on the shores of New Amsterdam; scene 1: 1785, the widow of Haym Salomon, Revolutionary patriot; scene 2: 1867, Rebecca Gratz at Philadelphia; scene 3: 1886, Emma Lazarus and her composition of *The New colossus;* scene 4: 1893, Henrietta Szold, Hannah Solomon and Sadie American, during the first year of the National Council of Jewish Women; epilogue: symbolic representation of the Council.

FRIEDMAN, STANLEY S. "The great god Frosh." A one act play — in one act. (Zeta Beta Tau quarterly. New York, 1930. 4°. v. 14, no. 2, p. 27–29.) SSY
"Dedicated to the Bacardi brothers of Cuba."

GAER, YOSSEF. A song unto the Lord [in one act]. (Jewish forum. New York, 1928. 4°. v. 11, p. 452–457.) * PBD
The devotion and childless loneliness of an old couple, in the hour preceding the wife's death.

GAFFNEY, THOMAS J. ...Birds of a feather; a play in four acts. Boston: The Gorham Press [etc., cop. 1915]. 110 p. 12°. (American dramatists series.) NBM
Morris Goldmann, landlord of a tenement house on Rivington Street, East Side of New York, an unsavory figure.

GALSWORTHY, JOHN. Loyalties; a drama in three acts. London: Duckworth and Co. [1922.] 118 p. incl. plans. 16°. NCR

—— —— Illustrated by S. Van Abbé... London: Duckworth, 1930. 5 p.l., (1)12-104 p., 8 pl. incl. front. 4°.

—— —— New York: Charles Scribner's Sons, 1932. 5 p.l., 3–110 p. 12°.
Reprinted in his *Plays; fifth series*, London [1922], 118 p., *NCR;* his *A Family man and other plays* Leipzig [1923], p. 111–210; his *Representative plays*, ed. by G. P. Baker, New York [1924], p. 387–469, *NCR;* his *Works* (Manatan edition), New York, 1924, v. 21, p. 129–257, * *KL;* and in his *Plays*, New York and London, 1928, p. 429–464, *NCR.* Included also in R. W. Pence, editor, *Dramas by present-day writers*, New York [1927], p. 59–148, *NCO (Pence).*
Synopses of the play, with numerous extracts and illustrations, are given, by Morris Fishbein in *B'nai B'rith news*, Mount Morris, Ill., v. 15, Dec. 1922, p. 4, 14, * *PYP; Current opinion*, New York, 1922, v. 73, p. 750–762, * *DA; Everybody's magazine*, New York, v. 48, Feb., 1923, p. 96–103, * *DA; Hearst's international*, New York, v. 42, Dec., 1922, p. 85–87, 146–147, * *DA;* and in *Theatre magazine*, New York, v. 37, Jan., 1923, p. 28, 30, 32, † *NBLA.*
Extracts from the high-lights of the text, with a running synopsis, are given in *Best plays of 1922–23*, Boston [1923], p. 116–139, *NAFH.*
Reviewed in *Dramatist*, Easton, Pa., 1922, v. 13, p. 1134–1135, *NAFA;* by S. O. in *English review*, London, 1922, v. 34, p. 386, * *DA;* by Robert A. Parker in *Independent*, New York, 1923, v. 110, p. 32–34, * *DA;* and by J. Ranken Towse in *Literary review of the New York Evening Post*, Dec. 2, 1922, p. 260, * *A.*
First produced at the St. Martin's Theatre, London, March 8, 1922, with Ernest Milton as Ferdinand De Levis. Reviewed in *Era*, London, v. 85, March 15, 1922, p. 9, † *NAFA;* by John Pollock in *Fortnightly review*, New York, 1922, v. 118, p. 349–352, * *DA;* in *Jewish chronicle*, London, March 17, 1922, p. 35, * *PBE;* by W. J. Turner in *London mercury*, London,

1922, v. 6, p. 90, * *DA; Queen*, London, 1922, v. 151, p. 329, * *DA;* by Tarn, pseud., in *Spectator*, London, 1922, v. 128, p. 398, * *DA;* in *The Times*, London, March 9, 1922, p. 10, * *A;* and in *Truth*, London, 1922, v. 91, p. 448–449, * *DA.* Illustrations are given in *Graphic*, London, 1922, v. 105, p. 399, * *DA;* in *Illustrated London news*, London, 1922, v. 160, p. 386, 478, * *DA;* and in *Sketch*, London, 1922, v. 117, p. 517, 519, * *DA.*
Produced at the Gaiety Theatre, New York, Sept. 27, 1922, with James Dale as De Levis. Reviewed by Gustav Blum in *American Hebrew*, New York, 1922, v. 111, p. 562, 568, * *PBD;* in *Billboard*, New York, v. 34, Oct. 14, 1922, p. 25, † *MZA;* by Walter Prichard Eaton in the *Freeman*, New York, 1922, v. 6, p. 281–282, * *DA; Jewish forum*, New York, 1922, v. 5, p. 394–395, * *PBD;* by Robert C. Benchley in *Life*, New York, v. 80, Oct. 19, 1922, p. 18, * *DA;* by Ludwig Lewisohn in *Nation*, New York, 1922, v. 115, p. 420, * *DA;* by Stark Young in *New republic*, New York, 1922, v. 32, p. 277–278, * *DA;* in *New York clipper*, v. 70, Oct. 4, 1922, p. 21, † *MVA;* by Arthur Hornblow (with illus.) in *Theatre magazine*, New York, 1922, v. 36, p. 370–372, † *NBLA;* in *Town and country*, New York, v. 79, Nov. 1, 1922, p. 36, 72, * *DA;* in *Town topics*, New York, v. 88, Oct. 5, 1922, p. 13, * *DA;* and in *Variety*, New York, v. 68, Oct. 13, 1922, p. 16–17, † *NAFA.* See also *Collection of newspaper clippings of dramatic criticism, 1922–1923*, v. G–L, † *NBL.*
Loyalties was successfully shown as a motion picture in London, May, 1933. Basil Rathbone had the part of De Levis. See *Jewish chronicle*, London, May 26, 1933, p. 43, * *PBD.*
General discussion of the loyalty theme and the author's conception of the Jewish character, De Levis, are taken up by James E. Agate in his *At half-past eight*, New York, 1923, p. 134–138, *NAFD;* by Leon Schalit in his *John Galsworthy; a survey*, New York, 1929, p. 294–303, *NCC (Galsworthy);* by Charles A. Bennett in *Bookman*, New York, 1926, v. 63, p. 161–165, * *DA;* by Mary C. Canfield in *Forum*, New York, 1922, v. 68, p. 1039–1041, * *DA;* by Abraham A. Neuman and Harry Felix in *Jewish exponent*, Philadelphia, v. 73, Oct. 19, 1922, p. 12, * *PBD;* by Edward Shanks in *London mercury*, London, 1923, v. 8, p. 397–398, * *DA;* and by R. D. Stocker in *Standard*, New York, 1923, v. 10, p. 57–61, *YFA.*

—— —— Loyalität (Loyalties); Schauspiel in drei Akten (sieben Szenen) von John Galsworthy; autorisierte Übersetzung aus dem Englischen von Leon Schalit (L. Leonhard). Berlin [etc.]: P. Zsolnay, 1924. 122 p., 2 l., illus. (plans.) 8°.

—— —— Gesellschaft (Loyalties); Schauspiel in drei Akten... Autorisierte Übersetzung aus dem Englischen von Leon Schalit. Berlin [etc.]: Paul Zsolnay Verlag, 1928. 120 p., 1 l. 12°.

—— —— Loyautés, pièce en trois actes. (Revue de Paris. Paris, 1926. 8°. année 33, tome 1, p. 481–507, 794–836.) * DM
Translated by Léonie Jean Proix.

—— —— לאיאליטעט (דראמע אין 3 אקטן 7 סצענעס). יידיש: ב. שטיפט. ווארשע: "בזשאזא", 1928. Warsaw: Bzhoza, 1928. 156 p. 8°.

Edelman, Maurice. A study in loyalties; a tribute to the memory of John Galsworthy. (Jewish chronicle. London, 1934. 4°. supplement 153, p. v–vi.) * PBE

Ettelson, Harry W. An unconscious anti-Semite. Jewish phases of Galsworthy's "Loyalties." (Jewish exponent. Philadelphia, 1923. f°. v. 73, Oct. 26, 1923, p. 1, 12.) * PBD

Individual Plays — 1915-1938, continued

GALSWORTHY, JOHN, *continued*

Feldman, Abraham J. Jews by grace of the enemy. An analysis of Galsworthy's "Loyalties." (Jewish exponent. Philadelphia, 1923. f°. v. 71, Jan. 5, 1923, p. 1, 10.)   *PBD

Schapiro, Eva.

היהודי על במת העולם. (ספר היובל של הדאר.) New York, 1927. 8°. p. 260–261.)   *PBA

GAMBLE, E. L. The lady or the tiger; a burlesque in one act... San Francisco: Banner Play Bureau, cop. 1926. 8 p. 12°.
Izzy Smart, "a Jewish gentleman."

—— Oi, vhat a bargain; a vaudeville act for two male comedians... San Francisco: Banner Play Bureau, 1925. 7 p. 12°.

—— Oi, vot a business! a Hebrew monologue. illus. (In his: Vaudeville gambols; a dozen dashes of variety humor. Chicago [cop. 1922]. 12°. p. 18–28.)

GAMORAN, MAMIE G. Another day. [In one act. New York: Hadassah, 1932?] 4 f. f°.
Caption-title.
Mimeographed.
A sketch of an infant welfare station.

—— Pennies do add up; box collection skit. [New York: Hadassah, 1932?] 2 f. f°.
Caption-title.
Mimeographed.
"Radio sketch."

—— What price Hadassah? [In two scenes. New York: Hadassah, 1934.] 6 f. f°.
Cover-title.
Mimeographed.
Scene I, the husbands. Scene II, the ladies.

GARD, JANICE. Lookin' lovely; a comedy in three acts. Chicago: Dramatic Pub. Company [cop. 1930]. 80 p. plan. 12°. (Sergel's acting drama.)   NBL p.v.246
Moe Dubrowski, theatrical producer and live wire, "well dressed but a little too loud, clever and intelligent, with a slight Jewish accent."

GARDNER, FLORA CLARK, AND M. F. GARDNER. Abraham advertises. (In their: Up-to-date ten-minute plays. Lebanon, Ohio [cop. 1931]. 12°. p. 14–19.)
Abraham Levi advertises his "Jungle-land show."

—— The melting pot minstrel. (In their: Up-to-date ten-minute plays. Lebanon, Ohio [cop. 1931]. 12°. p. 56–65.)
Hebrew, among the other nationalities.

GARVEY, ROBERT. Heroes, old and new [in three scenes]. (Young Judaean. New York, 1935. 4°. v. 23, June, 1935, p. 2–4, 19–20.)   *PBD
Biblical heroes and modern ones in Palestine.

GEORGE, CHARLES. "Abie's license." (In his: "Ten novelty skits." Minneapolis, cop. 1933. 12°. p. 43–46.)   NBL p.v.319
Abie Rosenthal and Julius Muffson.

—— Just pals; a three-act comedy... Franklin, Ohio, and Denver, Colo.: Eldridge Entertainment House, cop. 1929. 89(1) p., 1 l. music. 12°. (Eldridge royalty plays.)
Julius Greenbaum, "a young Jewish music publisher, very breezy and not to be overplayed or made offensive.

He is the modern young Jewish business man with just a trace of accent."

—— Murder in the ferris-wheel; a murder-mystery play in one act... Boston, Los Angeles, Cal.: Baker's Plays [cop. 1936]. 31 p. 12°.   NBL p.v.414
Scene: Coney Island, N. Y. The proprietor of the ferris-wheel company is Sam Glick, "coarse, rough-spoken, typical carnival man."

—— The spite fence; a three-act comedy-drama of charm... Franklin, Ohio [etc.]: Eldridge Entertainment House, Inc., cop. 1930. 98 p. diagr. 12°. (Eldridge hi-test non-royalty plays.)
Place: a farmhouse near a village in the Blue Ridge Mountains. Mrs. Theodore Dreyfus, a social climber.

GERAGHTY, TOM J. A pound of flesh [in one act]. (In: Kenyon Nicholson, editor, Hollywood plays. New York, 1930. 12°. p. 105–126.)   NBL (Nicholson)
J. Skeffington Walpole, manager of the Globe Theatre, rebukes Shakespeare for "taking a crack at a Jew character" and for conceiving Shylock as he did. Produced by the Writers' Club of Hollywood, June 13, 1928.

GERSON, EMILY GOLDSMITH. The seder. [In two scenes.] (Jewish exponent. Philadelphia, 1915. f°. v. 60, March 26, 1915, p. 5.)   †*PBD
When Passover and Good Friday fall on the same day, there is a lesson in toleration and understanding for little Jacob and James, as well as for the Rev. Smith.

GIBBS, ALICE ZARA. Run queeck, Rosie. [A dialogue in dialect.] Chicago: Dramatic Pub. Company [cop. 1929]. 4 f. 4°. (Sergel's manuscript readings.)
Mimeographed.
"Mommer and Rosie" at the tenement house window.

—— Sarah's birthday gift. [A dialogue in dialect.] Chicago: Dramatic Pub. Company [cop. 1929]. 4 f. 4°. (Sergel's manuscript readings.)
Mimeographed.
"Ikey and Sarah discuss the (almost) new car."

—— Von leetle minute. [A dialogue in dialect.] Chicago: Dramatic Pub. Company [cop. 1929]. 4 f. 4°. (Sergel's manuscript readings.)
Mimeographed.
Rosie and Ikey at the theatre ticket window.

GIBSON, E. M. Hot water. [In two scenes.] (In her: English-class plays for new Americans. New York [cop. 1927]. 8°. p. 62–68.)   NBM
Minsky, the landlord, is haled into court by his Jewish and Italian tenants for not supplying hot water.

GINSBURG, ELIAS. Ferdinand Lassalle; an historical drama in four acts. (Vanguard. New York, 1929–30. 8°. v. 4, Nov., 1929, p. 25–36; Dec., 1929, p. 36–45, 64; Feb., 1930, p. 36–45, 63; v. 5, March, 1930, p. 28–41.)   *PBD
Freely translated from his own Yiddish which appeared in *Zukunft*, 1925, v. 30, p. 549–558, 648–652, 687–693, *PBB. For an historical note, see this list under Elbert Hubbard, *Ferdinand Lassalle*.

—— We never die; a dramatic scene in one act ... New York: Metropolitan League of Jewish Community Associations [cop. 1931]. 11 f. 4°.
Cover-title.
Mimeographed.
The action takes place in Jerusalem during an Arab anti-Jewish riot. Spirit of self-sacrificing devotion of the halutzim (pioneers). Among the defenders is an American Jewish tourist.

Individual Plays — 1915–1938, continued

GLASS, MONTAGUE MARSDEN. Present company excepted; a sort of a play, in two acts or thereabouts... [Detroit: Joseph Mack Ptg. House, Inc., cop. 1922.] 4 p.l., 11–48 p. 12°.   NBM
"This play especially written and produced for the eighth annual meeting of Dodge Brothers dealers in the Pennsylvania Hotel, New York City, Jan. 10, 1922." Potash and Perlmutter in the automobile-sales business.

GLASS, MONTAGUE MARSDEN, AND O. M. CARTER. Wall Street; a comedy in three acts. Illustrations by John Desvignes. (Jewish tribune. New York, 1924–25. f°. v. 43, Sept. 26, 1924, p. 12–13, 44, 48, 53, 73; Nov. 7, 1924, p. 20, 22, 44–45, 49; Dec. 5, 1924, p. 27–29, 32; v. 44, Jan. 2, 1925, p. 26, 28, 30–32.)   * PBD

GLEASON, JAMES. The Shannons of Broadway; a comedy in three acts. New York: S. French; London: S. French, Ltd., cop. 1928. 2 p.l., 3–117(1) p. plates, diagr. 12°. (French's standard library edition.)   NBL p.v.183
A comedy of theatrical folks. Produced at the Martin Beck Theatre, Sept. 26, 1927, with Matthew Zeltner as Jake, one of the four Melody boys. For reviews see *Collection of newspaper clippings of dramatic criticism, 1927–1928*, v. Q–S, † NBL.

GLICKMAN, ABRAHAM JACOB. The truth, a drama from life in four acts. Boston: The Christopher Publishing House [cop. 1933]. 160 p. 8°.   8–NBM
A drama by a physician, designed to teach parents and their grown-up children the need of sexual education and the terrible consequences of its ignorance. A teacher in a private school and his wife are here named Mr. and Mrs. Rosen; a physician, Dr. Lieberman. "Most of the characters in the play...have been taken from real life."

GLOVER, HALCOTT. The king's Jewry; a play. London: The Bloomsbury Press [cop. 1921]. 77(1) p. 8°.   NCO p.v.473
Reviewed by A. E. S. in *Jewish guardian*, London, v. 2, Sept. 16, 1921, p. 7, * PBE.

—— —— (In his: Wat Tyler, and other plays. New York, 1927. 12°. p. 121–237.)
"The King's Jewry remains substantially as first conceived... [The original edition is] regarded by the author as cancelled". — *p. 1, 4.*
Reprinted in S. M. Tucker, compiler, *Modern American and British plays*, New York [cop. 1931], p. 419–453, NCO.
Reviewed in *Jewish guardian*, London, v. 8, June 10, 1927, p. 4, * PBD; and in *The Times literary supplement*, London, 1925, v. 24, p. 894, † NAA.
In a prologue and one act.
The scene is in a street in London Jewry, in 1290, the year when the Jews were expelled by Edward I from England. "Founded upon actual conditions and events... is both an attempt at the embodiment of an universal truth — the unchanging character and life-philosophy of the Jewish race as a whole, and the attitude of the Christian towards the Jew, set forth in terms of drama, with dignity and without prejudice."
The author ascribes the immediate cause of the expulsion to the conversion in 1275 of Robert de Reddinge, a Dominican monk, to Judaism.
First produced in Huddersfield, England, in 1928.

GOETZ, AUSTIN. Hillbilly courtship; a farce in three acts... Chicago: T. S. Denison & Company [cop. 1936]. 117 p. 12°. (Denison's red letter series.)
Scene: a cabin in the Ozark Mountains.
Sol Silverstein, "with a likable, if aggressive personality," manager of radio's hillbilly sensation, in quest of more hillbilly entertainers.

—— —— Soup to nuts; a futuristic farce in three acts... New York [etc.]: S. French, cop. 1936. 108 p., 1 l. diagr. 12°.
The hero of this farce is "Doctor Manny Pilski, a progressive, Hebrew health specialist, [who] has conceived the happy idea of opening a dietetic sanitarium ...where meals are served in the form of concentrated pellets."

GOLD, MICHAEL. Money; a play in one act. New York: S. French [cop. 1929]. 2 p.l., 30 p. 12°.   NBL p.v.234
An incident about the loss of a sum of money by one of a group of Jewish peddlers, and the discussion to which it leads.
Printed also in B. H. Clark and Kenyon Nicholson, editors, *The American scene*, New York, London, 1930, p. 125–149, NBL (Clark).
It was staged, as the work of Irwin Granich, named., by the Provincetown Players, New York, in January, 1920, with Remo Bufanu as Moisha, the loser of the money.

GOLDBERG, ISAAC. The better son, a domestic drama, in one act. (The Stratford journal. Boston, 1918. 8°. v. 3, p. 169–180.)   * DA
Scene: in the dining room of the Rubin household. The characters are Mrs. Rubin, a widow; Joseph, her favorite son; and Isaac, his brother.

GOLDBERG, ISRAEL. The ancient fortress. [In one act.] New York: Young Judaea [1919?]. 5 l. f°.
Mimeographed.
A war play. On the Russo-German border on the eve of Succoth, during the great war.

—— —— Bar Giora; a one act play, by Rufus Learsi [pseud.]. [New York:] Zionist Organization of America, cop. 1938. 10 f. 4°.
Mimeographed.
Based on Josephus, Wars of the Jews, VII, 2.

—— —— Brothers; a play in two acts. By Rufus Learsi [pseud.]. New York: Mizpah Pub. Co., 1917. 22 p. 8°.   NBL p.v.194
The meeting of two long-separated brothers, and the effect it has upon the family of one of them.

—— —— "The capture"; a one act play from Chanukah by Rufus Learsi [pseud.]. New York: Department of Education, Zionist Organization of America, cop. 1918. 7 f. 4°.
Time: the present. Place: Russia.
Black Vasily, an agent provocateur and pogrom-organizer, is one of the characters. He is captured by a girl.

—— —— New York: Jewish Welfare Board [1928?]. 7 f. 4°.   * PBM p.v.173

—— —— The eternal bond; a play in one act. By Rufus Learsi [pseud.]. [New York: Young Judaea,] 1919. 1 p.l., 12 l. 4°.
Mimeographed.
During the eighties of the last century, in a Jewish colony, near Jaffa. The devotion of the Bilu settlers to the land is the motif. A translation of this in Hebrew has been made by K. Whiteman.

—— —— The great deliverance; a play in one act. By Rufus Learsi [pseud.]. New York: Department of Education, Zionist Organization of America, 1919. 15 l. 4°.
Mimeographed.

—— —— הישועה הגדולה [Translated into Hebrew, by Kalmen Whiteman. New York, 1919.] 13 f. 4°.
Caption-title.
Mimeographed.
Melodrama of a conflict of the German forces with Palestinian colonists, saved by the Jewish Legion while fighting with the British forces in 1917.

Individual Plays — 1915–1938, continued

GOLDBERG, ISRAEL. ...His children. [In one act.] By Rufus Learsi [pseud.]. New York: Jewish Welfare Board [cop. 1925]. 24 p. 12°. (Jewish Welfare Board publications.)
* PSQ (Jewish)
First prize play in the J. W. B. play contest of 1924–1925. First produced by the Bronx, New York City, Y. M. H. A. dramatic group at the Forty-ninth Street Theatre, Nov. 29, 1925. "The theme of the play is the chasm between the older, and younger generations. It is a study of the estrangement between a stern but loving Orthodox Jew and his children who realize, after his death, his inner character." Reviewed in *Collection of newspaper clippings of dramatic criticism, 1925–1926*, v. L (Little Theatre), † *NBL*.

—— The invader; a comedy in two acts... New York: Jewish Welfare Board [1925]. 30 f. 4°
Reproduced from typewritten copy.
For a statement of the committee of judges on the merits of the present play, the preceding *His children* and Edith B. Beck's *The Old order* (supra) see *Jewish center*, New York, v. 3, March, 1925, p. 2–3, * *PYR*.

GOLDING, LOUIS. Magnolia street... New York: Farrar & Rinehart, Incorporated [cop. 1932]. 4 p.l., 3–526 p. 8°. 8–NCW
The novel is reviewed by John H. Holmes in *Opinion*, New York, 1932, v. 2, no. 9, p. 7–8, * *PBD*; and by Charles Landstone in *Jewish chronicle*, London, Jan. 15, 1932, p. 12, * *PBE*.
The story of a whole neighborhood and its people through many years — Jews in one section and Gentiles in another. Dramatized by the author and A. R. Rawlinson into a drama of three acts and produced at the Adelphi Theatre, London, March 8, 1934. Reviewed in *Jewish chronicle*, London, March 16, 1934, p. 54, * *PBE*; and by J. F. D. in *Theatre world*, London, 1934, v. 21, p. 170, *MWA*.

GOLDMAN, MRS. ROSE. Life begins anew. [In two acts. New York: Hadassah, 1934.] 6 f. f°.
Caption-title.
Mimeographed.
A membership or propaganda play.

GOLDSMITH, MILTON. A prior right [in one act]. (Review. Philadelphia, 1917. 12°. v. 12, May, 1917, p. 22–35.)
Copy: Library of the Jewish Theological Seminary of America.
A domestic scene involving a husband, wedded unknowingly to two wives.

GOLDSTEIN, FANNY. Shabbas cheer; a playlet for children. music. (Pilgrim elementary teacher. Boston, 1935. 8°. v. 19, p. 7–8.)
In one act.

GOLDSTEIN, MRS. ROSE B. Aunt Fan rises to the defense. [In three scenes. New York: Hadassah, 1933.] 7 f. f°.
Caption-title.
Mimeographed.
A sophisticated American girl's romance in Palestine.

GOLLER, ISAK. ..."Cohen & Son"; the play on which the author based his famous novel, "The five books of Mr. Moses" in 3 acts, 10 scenes and a melody. [London: The Ghetto Press, 1932.] 61(1) p., 1 l. port., music. 4°.
Text in double columns.
Cartoon on cover, by the author.
A play of polemics and comedy, with a theme akin to B. Jacobs' and M. Goldsmith's *Rabbi and priest*. Produced as printed at the Royal Court Theatre,

Liverpool, March 6, 1933. A shortened version of the play (act I, scene 3, act II, scenes 1 and 3 and act III, scene 1) was first produced at the Regent Theatre, London, Oct. 3, 1932. On that occasion it was announced as a dramatization of the author's novel. Sema Vas Diaz played Sarah Cohen; Alexander Sarna, her husband Barnett; and Victor Lewisohn, Mr. Moses. Reviewed in *Era*, London, v. 96, Oct. 5, 1932, p. 11, † *NAFA*; *Jewish chronicle*, London, Oct. 7, 1932, p. 28, * *PBD*; by John Pollock in *Saturday review*, London, v. 154, p. 376, * *DA*; and in *The Times*, London, Oct. 4, 1932, p. 12, col. 3, * *A*.

GOODMAN, MRS. A. V. All for the good [in two scenes]. (Jewish teacher. Cincinnati, 1937. 4°. v. 5, Jan., 1937, p. 24–29.) * PYW
A playlet centering around the optimist Nahum of Gimso, tanna of the second century, whose motto was Gam zu l'tobah (this, too, will be for the best).

GOODMAN, KENNETH S., AND BEN HECHT. An idyll of the shops; a play [in one act]. (In their: The wonder hat and other one-act plays. New York, 1925. 12°. p. 81–115.) NBM
A love episode in a Chicago West Side garment factory. Reviewed by Martin Golde in *Jewish exponent*, Philadelphia, v. 77, Nov. 13, 1925, p. 9, * *PBD*. Produced by the Menorah societies of Harvard and Radcliffe colleges, at the Agassiz House, Cambridge, April 9, 1927, with R. M. Cushing and Dorothy Waterman in the leading rôles of the two lovers.
See illustration in *Young Israel*, Cincinnati, v. 25, Nov., 1932, p. 5, * *PBD*.

GORDON, ALBERT I. "This month in history" [a programme in one act]. (Jewish youth journal. New York, 1937. 4°. v. 1, no. 1, p. 4, 7.)
Details the anniversaries of certain events in Jewish history.

GORDON, LEON, AND R. A. PALMER. The piker ... Boston: The Four Seas Company, 1928. 8°.
Title from Ina T. E. Firkins, *Index to plays supplement*, New York, 1935.

GORDON, SAMUEL. The resting place. [In one act.] (In: H. Zimmerman, compiler, Plays of Jewish life. [London, 1931.] 12°. p. 9–29.)
NCO (Zimmerman)
First produced by the Victoria & Chelsea Jewish Literary Society, London, Dec. 9, 1928. The action takes place in pre-war Russia. The parts of the grandmother, granddaughter and Dr. Hermanson were taken by Marion Price, Hilda Nelson and Harry Zimmerman, respectively.

GORSKY, J. ARTHUR. Kislev. (In: H. Zimmerman, compiler, Plays of Jewish life. [London, 1931.] 12°. p. 75–89.) NCO (Zimmerman)
Produced by the Habimah Players Guild of the London Young Mizrachi Society at King George's Hall, London, Dec. 4, 1926. The time of the plot is early in December (Kislev, the Hebrew month).

GOUDVIS, BERTHE. A husband for Rachel. (A scene from Jewish life.) (In her: The way the money goes, and other plays. Johannesburg, So. Africa [1925]. 12°. p. 74–88.) NCO p.v.534
In one act.
Based on the "Shadchan" theme.

GOULD, ALICE. The merchant of Venice; a burlesque operatic version ... Boston: W. H. Baker Company [cop. 1929]. 22 p. 12°. (Baker's edition of plays.)
In five acts.

GOULD, ERNEST M. On the sight-seeing car; a comedy sketch in one act... Philadelphia: Penn Pub. Co., 1915. 18 p. 12°. NBL p.v.43, no.9

Individual Plays — 1915–1938, continued

GRAHAM, CARROLL, AND GARRETT GRAHAM. Queer people. New York: The Vanguard Press [cop. 1930]. 5 p.l., 9–276 p. 8°.

Dramatized into a comedy of three acts and produced at the National Theatre, New York, Feb. 15, 1934, with Lawrence Keating as Milton Hoffberger and Herbert Heywood as Sol Snifkin. It purports to be an indictment of the motion picture business as conducted in Hollywood. For reviews see *Collection of newspaper clippings of dramatic criticism, 1933–34*, v. P–Se, † *NBL.*

GRANVILLE-BARKER, HARLEY GRANVILLE. The secret life; a play, in three acts. Boston: Little, Brown, and Company, 1923. 3 p.l., (1)4–125 p. 12°. NCR

Also published at London by Chatto & Windus, 1923. vii, 160 p. 12°.

A play of present-day England, replete with political and moral discussion. The publisher's jacket describes it in the words of one of the characters as a play depicting "the conflict between the inner life of the soul and the generation of the flesh." The first and second acts take place in England; the third in England and in Massachusetts. Sir Geoffrey Salomons, K.C.B., is described "You would know he was a Jew, but mainly because he seems a little conscious of the racial difference himself. Irony is his main conversational key."

Reviewed by W. J. Turner in *London mercury*, 1923, v. 8, p. 651, * *DA;* and by Martin Armstrong in *Spectator*, London, v. 131, p. 743, * *DA.* See also Karl Arns in *Englische Studien*, Leipzig, 1925, Bd. 59, p. 65–68, *RNA.*

GREEN, PAUL. Johnny Johnson; the biography of a common man, in three acts... Music by Kurt Weill. New York [etc.]: S. French, 1937. 7 p.l., 3–175 p. illus. 12°. NBM

Extracts from the dialogue, with running synopses, are given in *Best plays of 1936–37*, New York, 1937, p. 96–141, *NAFH.*

A medley of caricature, melodrama and social polemic, with the World war of 1914–18 as the background. Presented by the Group Theatre at the 44th Street Theatre, New York, Nov. 19, 1936, with Will Lee as Private Abie Goldberger, "a little, squabby Jew," a member of Johnson's squad in France. For reviews see *Collection of newspaper clippings of dramatic criticism, 1936–1937*, v. His–L, † *NBL.*

GREENE, B. M. The God-intoxicated man; a play in 3 acts. (Menorah journal. New York, 1922. 4°. v. 8, p. 298–308, 368–382.) * PBD

Time: 1650 in Amsterdam.

Characters: Spinoza, young Uriel Acosta, Prof. Van der Ende, Clara Maria, the latter's daughter, and others.

Reprinted in his *Woman the masterpiece* [and] *God-intoxicated man*, Toronto, Canada, 1923.

GRIBBLE, GEORGE DUNNING. The masque of Venice; an entertainment in three acts... [London:] Ernest Benn, Limited, 1924. 130 p., 1 l. 12°. (Contemporary British dramatists. v. 11.) NCO (Contemporary)

Another impression published at London [1928].

It was produced at the Mansfield Theatre, New York, March 2, 1926. For reviews see *Collection of newspaper clippings of dramatic criticism, 1925–1926*, v. K–N, † *NBL.* In London, it was staged at the Savoy Theatre, Jan. 25, 1928.

Greatly altered and renamed *The Artist and the shadow*, this play was produced at the Kingsway Theatre, London, March 15, 1930, with Lyn Harding as Abel Klein, an unscrupulous American picture dealer "of Jewish origin." See *Era*, London, v. 93, March 19, 1930, p. 1, 5, † *NAFA;* and *New York Times*, April 6, 1930, section 9, p. 2, * *A.*

—— The translation of Nathaniel Bendersnap, a triptych. London: E. Benn, Limited, 1925. 82 p., 1 l. 12°. (Contemporary British dramatists. v. 21.) NCO (Contemporary)

Heine (Henry in the play) is one of the characters; described as "a slight pale gentleman, with a Van Dyck beard, and delicate, Semitic feature." Produced by the Interlude Theatre Guild, at the Arts Theatre, London, Dec. 3, 1927. The character of Heine was omitted in the acted version.

GRIFFIN, CHESTER A. The Hicksville bungler; a farce in one scene. Chicago: T. S. Denison & Co. [cop. 1920]. 18 p. 12°. (Amateur series.)

A small town newspaper farce. Finkelstein, "a Hebrew tailor."

GRIFFITH, HUBERT FREELING. Red Sunday; a play in three acts... With a preface on the censorship. London: G. Richards and H. Toulmin, 1929. xxvii, 89 p. 12°. NCR

Jan. 9 (old style 22), 1905 is known in modern Russian history as Red Sunday. The attempt on the life of Lenin was made by Dora Kaplan on Sept. 3, 1918. The action of the play is spread over the years 1906–1920. Both episodes are treated in the play. It was produced at the Arts Theatre, London, June 27, 1929, with John Gielgud as Bronshtein (Trotski) and Lydia Sherwood as Olga [sic] Kaplan. Reviewed in *Nation & Athenæum*, London, 1929, v. 45, p. 476–477, * *DA.* Illus. are given in *The Sphere*, London, v. 118, p. 36, * *DA.*

GROPPER, MILTON HERBERT, AND MAX SIEGEL. We Americans, a new play [in three acts]... New York, London: S. French, cop. 1928. 99 p., 2 l. plates. 12°. (French's standard library edition.) NBL p.v.183

A comedy dealing with the problem of maladjustment between immigrant Jewish parents and their American-born children. Produced at the Sam H. Harris Theatre, New York, Oct. 12, 1926. Paul Muni and Clara Langsner played the parts of Mr. and Mrs. Levine, the parents of the family; Luther Adler and Ailsa Lawson, their son and daughter. For reviews see *Collection of newspaper clippings of dramatic criticism, 1926–1927*, v. T–Y, † *NBL.* See also Morris Teller in *Jewish times*, Baltimore, v. 17, Sept. 23, 1927, p. 36, * *PBD.* The printed text is reviewed in *American Hebrew*, New York, 1929, v. 124, p. 371, * *PBD.*

A pre-view of it was seen at the Bronx Opera House, New York, May 24, 1926.

GROSS, LAURENCE, AND E. C. CARPENTER. Whistling in the dark, a play in three acts... New York, N. Y., Los Angeles, Calif.: S. French, Inc.; London: S. French, Ltd. [etc.], cop. 1933. 109 p., 1 l. plates, diagrs. 12°. (French's standard library ed.) NBL p.v.297

"Copyright, 1930 (under title, 'Melodrama') by Laurence Gross; copyright, 1931 (under title, 'The perfect crime'), by Laurence Gross and Edward Childs Carpenter."

Produced at the Ethel Barrymore Theatre, New York, Jan. 19, 1932, with Charles Halton as Herman Lefkowitz, "a dapper Jew, about thirty, swell dresser ...the Boss's hottest dope peddler." He goes by the name of Herman Lewis, "but who believes him?" Reviewed in *Nation*, New York, 1932, v. 134, p. 152, * *DA;* and (with illus.) in *Theatre Guild magazine*, New York, v. 9, March, 1932, p. 32–34, *NBLA.* See also *Collection of newspaper clippings of dramatic criticism, 1931–1932*, v. T–Z, † *NBL.* It was revived at the Waldorf Theatre, New York, Nov. 7, 1932, with Arthur S. Ross as Lefkowitz.

Produced at the Garrick Theatre, London, Oct. 29, 1933, and transferred to the Comedy Theatre, Dec. 5, 1933, with Finlay Currie as Lefkowitz. Reviewed in *Theatre world*, London, 1934, v. 21, p. 14, *MWA.*

Individual Plays — 1915–1938, continued

GROSSMAN, SAMUEL S. The Beduin fight. A little play for Jewish boys. [New York:] Bureau of Education, n. d. 5 l. 4°. (In his: [Holiday and other plays for Jewish children.])
Mimeographed. NASH
In a Hebrew school in modern Palestine.

—— The land of the Aleph Bes; a wonder play for Jewish children in nine scenes. Philadelphia, Pa.: J. H. Greenstone, 1918. 102 p. front., plates. 8°. * PSQ

—— The masque of the new land. An allegorical masque in one act and two scenes. [New York: Young Judaea,] n. d. 19 l. 4°. (In his: [Holiday and other plays for Jewish children.])
Mimeographed. NASH

—— Tree pantomime. [In one act. New York: Hadassha, 1931?] 3 f. f°.
Caption-title.
Mimeographed.

—— The two angels; a phantasy [in one act] about the angel of death and the angel of dreams. (Young Judaean. New York, 1922. 8°. v. 12, p. 155–158, 182.) * PBD

—— ...Two goyim. [In one act.]... New York: Jewish Welfare Board [cop. 1926]. 24 p. 12°. (Jewish Welfare Board publications.)
* PSQ p.v.1
A comedy on the shadchan (match maker) theme, and a satire on the tendency of some Jewish young men and women to conceal their racial origin.

—— "What to be proud of." (A poem made into a dolly dialogue for Jewish children to act.) (Jewish child. New York, 1917. 4°. v. 5, Aug. 24, 1917, p. 3.) * PBD
The characters are a mother-doll and four other dolls. Among others, Emma Lazarus, 1849–1887, is mentioned by one of the dolls as one "to be proud of."

GROSSWALD, BERNARD. Wings on their backs [a playlet]. (Young Zionist. London, 1933. 4°. v. 7, Aug., 1933, p. 6.) * PZX
Outside the admission bureau of the gates of heaven. The principal speakers are a Jew and a German Fascist.

GUNN, JOHN A. Spinoza; the maker of lenses, a play in three acts. London: George Allen & Unwin, Ltd. [cop. 1932.] 99(1) p. 12°. NCR
"Written and published in celebration of the tercentenary of his birth. Its aim is to present the philosopher in the environment of time and place in which he lived and to convey in small measure the charm of his personality." The scene is laid in Amsterdam, Rijnsburg, and The Hague, during the years 1656–1672.
Reviewed in *The Times literary supplement*, London, 1932, v. 31, p. 461, † *NAA*; and by M. J. W. in *Views*, London, v. 2, January, 1933, * *PBE*.

GUNN, W. E. Scott of Abbotsford; or, The moving hand. A dramatic presentation of the man (in three acts, with prologue)... London: Constable & Co., Ltd., 1932. ix, 66 p. 12°.
NCO p.v.652
In act III, scene 2, in Edinburgh, 1826, appears a clerk to the Jewish firm of Abud & Co., creditors of Sir Walter, and demands 2000 pounds due his firm. This incident has no basis in historical fact. It was staged at the Little Theatre, London, March 29, 1933, with Harold Mortlake as "the Jew."

GUTTMAN, ETHEL FLEMING. Bridge at Upper Montclair. (Opinion. New York, 1937. 4°. v. 7, Jan., 1937, p. 10.) * PBD
Conversation during a bridge game.

HADASSAH. — COLUMBUS, OHIO, CHAPTER. Jigsaw skit for senior-junior meeting. [In one act. New York: Hadassah, 1935.] 7 f. f°.
Caption-title.
Mimeographed.

HADASSAH. — MINNEAPOLIS JUNIOR SECTION. Money talks; a Jewish National Fund skit [in three scenes. New York: Hadassah, 1933?] 3 f. 8°.
Caption-title.
Mimeographed.

HALL, P. P. More money than brains; a comedy in 2 acts... New York: Fitzgerald Pub. Corp., cop. 1919. 22 p. 12°. NBL p.v.70, no.5
Samuel Cohen, "a Second Avenue credit clothier."

HALPER, LEIVICK. The golem...a dramatic poem in eight scenes. Authorized translation from the Yiddish by J. G. Augenlicht. (Poet lore. Boston, 1928. 8°. v. 39, p. 159–289.) * DA
Written in 1917–1920, and translated from the original which was published in Warsaw, 1922.
The first two scenes are translated anew by Bessie F. White in her *Nine one-act plays from the Yiddish*, Boston [cop. 1932], p. 1–35, * *PTP*.

HALYS, NEVIN. Mrs. Witch; a Whitechapel episode [in one act]. (In his: The hut above the tarn, and other plays. London [1930]. 16°. p. 203–239.) NCR
The time is November, 1908, in the kitchen below Moses Solomon's shop. The cast is all Jewish.

HAMILTON, COSMO. Caste... New York, London: G. P. Putnam's Sons, 1927. 1 p.l., 347 p. 12°.
A novel about intermarriage picturing the attitude towards Jews of the "Four Hundred" of American "Society."
Dramatized by the author into a play of three acts and produced at the Mansfield Theatre, New York, Dec. 23, 1927, with Horace Braham as Max Lorberstein, the young Jewish pianist in love with the daughter of Colonel Erskine Delbeatie Farquhar (Reginald Mason), and Albert Bruning as Jacob J. Lorberstein, father of Max. For reviews see *Collection of newspaper clippings of dramatic criticism, 1927–1928*, v. A–C, † *NBL*.

Schechter, Frank Isaac. Golden and other ghettos in recent fiction. (In: The Judaeans, Judaean addresses, selected. New York, 1933. 8°. v. 4, p. 70–78.) * PBL
Deals largely with the present play.

HANANI, YOSEF. Fighting boy of Vienna [in three acts]. (English by Tuvim.) illus. (Haboneh. New York 1938. 4°. v. 3, April, 1938, p. 7–10.)

HARBOUR, J. L. The rummage sale. [Chicago: E. Means Dramatic Service, cop. 1930.] 2 f. f°.
Caption-title.
Mimeographed.

Individual Plays — 1915–1938, continued

HARDY, BERNICE. Miss Ruddy cashes in. (In her: Mono-dramas; the new platform art. Boston [cop. 1930]. 12°. p. 13–25.) NBM
Mr. Frankel, director of revues, and Miss Ruddy, head cashier.

—— Monday morning on "Thoid" avenue. (In her: Mono-dramas; the new platform art. Boston [cop. 1930]. 12°. p. 99–107.) NBM
Poppa, the shopkeeper, and his wife. Scene: a "hole-in-the-wall" sample hat shop, Third Avenue, New York City.

HARE, WALTER BEN. Aboard a slow train in Mizzoury; a farcical entertainment in three acts... Boston: Walter H. Baker & Co., 1920. 52 p. 12°. (Baker's edition of plays.)
Moe Slibitksy, "who sells you almost for nothing." Also published in Boston [cop. 1919] as a number of "Baker's specialties."

—— Am I your vife? (In his: Readings and monologues à la mode. Chicago [cop. 1921]. 12°. p. 83–85.)

—— The cornfed cut-ups; a novelty white-face minstrel show... Boston: W. H. Baker Company, 1921. 1 p.l., 66–82 p. music. 12°.
Jakie Goldfish, "a Hebrew peddler."

—— A country boy scout; a comedy drama for boys, in three acts. Chicago: T. S. Denison & Co. [cop. 1916.] 63 p. 12°. (Alta series.) NASH p.v.1
Moe Skinsky, "a Hebrew crook from the City." In a later edition, in the series "Denison's scout and camp-fire plays," this character is omitted, and Jess Skinnum, a loan shark "from the City," is substituted.

—— Yiddisha love. (In his: Readings and monologues à la mode. Chicago [cop. 1921]. 12°. p. 27–30.)

HARRIS, CLAUDIA LUCAS. It's spring, a fantasy. (Drama. Mt. Morris, 1921. 4°. v. 11, p. 245–250.) NAFA
An old clothes man, plying his trade among unusual folks.

—— Paging John Smith; a comedy in three acts for male characters... Boston: W. H. Baker Company [cop. 1935]. 84 p. 12°. (Baker's edition of plays.) NBL p.v.373
Benny Hirsch, "typical Jewish lad...a bit extravagant as to dress, full of good-will toward everyone. No dialect, simply an accent..."

HARRIS, FRANK. Isaac & Rebecca. [A play in 1 act.] (In his: The yellow ticket, and other stories. New York [cop. 1920]. 8°. p. 113–138.)
Time: 1904. A long way from Scott's Isaac and Rebecca. Here is a gold-digging daughter, and a conniving father in an unsavoury theme, à la Frank Harris.

HARRIS, MAURICE HENRY. The story of the Jew; a play in six acts... New York: Bloch Pub. Company, 1921. 32 p. 12°.
The first act, the discovery of America; the second, the Colonial period — New York, 1654; the third, the Revolutionary War — Boston harbor, 1775; the fourth, Noah's Ark, Niagara Falls, 1825; the fifth, the immigrants at the gate — Ellis Island, N. Y., 1882; the sixth act, in the nineteenth century, is local and applicable only to Temple Israel, New York.
The speakers are, besides other historical characters, in the first act Columbus and his sailors; in the second, Peter Stuyvesant and Asser Levy; in the third, Haym Salomon and Gershom Mendes Seixas; in the fourth, Mordecai M. Noah, Uriah P. Levy, and Judah Touro; in the fifth, Emma Lazarus, Isaac M. Wise, Jacob H. Schiff, Nathan Straus, and others welcoming the new immigration to America. This play was written for Temple Israel's fiftieth anniversary and was produced by the pupils of its Sunday schools.

HARRISON, HARRY A. A modern Esther. [In three acts.] (Light of Israel. Brooklyn, 1923. 4°. v. 1, no. 16, p. 4–6; no. 18, p. 5–6; no. 19, p. 6–7; no. 20, p. 7–8; no. 22, p. 5–6.) †* PBD

HART, MOSS, AND G. S. KAUFMAN. Once in a lifetime, a comedy. New York: Farrar & Rinehart, Incorporated [cop. 1930]. vi p., 2 l., 3–236 p. 12°. NBM

—— —— London: Victor Gollancz, Ltd., 1932. 248 p. 12°.

—— —— New York [etc.]: S. French, Inc., cop. 1933. 144 p., 3 l. illus. (plates), diagrs. 12°. (French's standard library edition.) NBL p.v.299
Reprinted in *Famous plays of 1932*, London, 1932, p. 521–654, NAFH. A synopsis of the play, with copious extracts from the text, is printed in *The Best plays of 1930–31*, New York, 1931, p. 110–146, NAFH.
Extracts are printed, with illustrations from the play, in *Theatre magazine*, New York, Dec., 1930, p. 35–37, 66, 68–69, † NBLA.
A satire on the motion picture industry. Produced at the Music Box Theatre, New York, Sept. 24, 1930, with Charles Halton as Herman Glogauer, the motion picture magnate. For reviews see *Collection of newspaper clippings of dramatic criticism, 1930–1931*, v. N–R, † NBL.
It was produced at the Queen's Theatre, London, Feb. 23, 1933, with Charles Victor as Glogauer. Reviewed in *Theatre magazine*, London, 1933, v. 19, p. 169–170, MWA; and (with illus.) in *The Times*, London, Feb. 24, 1933, p. 12, 18, * A.

HARWOOD, HAROLD MARSH. These mortals; a scrapbook of history... From notes by Homer and R. F. Gore-Browne. London: W. Heinemann, Ltd. [1937.] xxv, 119 p. 8°. NCR
A play in seven scenes.
Disraeli is one of the characters.

HASTINGS, BASIL MACDONALD. Advertisement; a play in four acts. New York: S. French [etc.], cop. 1915. 114 p., 3 l. plans. 12°. (French's acting edition. no. 2530.) NCO p.v.391
"We have...Luke Sufan first as an 'advertisement king', one of the vulgar rich, who used to be a fiddler, then as a pious Jew who married a 'goy' wife, and feels he is justly punished by their not getting on together." — *The Times, London, April 16, 1915, p. 11*, * A. Landa, p. 239–241, says: "Here is an engrossing dramatic thesis, a real problem, that of the child of intermarriage." Time of action: before, during and after the Great war.
Produced at the Kingsway Theatre, London, April 15, 1915, with Sydney Valentine as Luke Sufan. Reviewed in *Academy*, London, 1915, v. 88, p. 284, * DA; *The Athenæum*, London, v. 145, p. 389–390, * DA; *Graphic*, London, v. 91, p. 514 (illus., p. 606), * DA; *Illustrated London news*, London, v. 146, p. 518, * DA; and by William Archer in *Nation*, New York, v. 100, p. 576, * DA.

Individual Plays — 1915-1938, continued

HATTON, FREDERIC, AND MRS. F. C. L. HATTON. Lombardi, Ltd.; a comedy in three acts. New York: S. French; London: S. French, Ltd., cop. 1928. 172 p., 1 l. plates, diagrs. 12°. (French's standard library edition.) NBL p.v.184
Produced at the Morosco Theatre, New York, Sept. 24, 1917, with Harold Russell as Max Strohm, theatrical manager. Reviewed in *New York dramatic mirror,* v. 77, Oct. 6, 1917, p. 5, * *T-* DA.* See also *Collection of newspaper clippings of dramatic criticism, 1917-18,* v. H-O, † *NBL.* It was revived in New York, at the Cohan Theatre, on June 6, 1927, with Arthur Ross as Strohm.

HAUSER, MRS. ERMINIA (ARBIB). The man without a necktie; a play in three [sic] acts and a prologue. Translated [from the Italian] by Doris K. Thompson. New York: Dickens Publishing Co., 1929. 6 p.l., 15-172 p. 8°.
In four (not three) acts. The action is laid in Brazil, 1914, and Paris, 1922. It was published the same year as a novel, and relates the adventures of Mocair, who goes through life refusing to wear a necktie, "the band that separates the heart from the brain." Preaches solidarity and universal peace. The Jewish characters are Dr. Samuel Kramer, photographer, and "the man without a hat," a young Russian-Jewish student. Reviewed in *Books,* New York, v. 6, Jan. 12, 1930, p. 14, † *NAA;* and in *New York Times book review,* v. 35, Jan. 26, 1930, p. 8, † *NAA.*

HAWKRIDGE, WINIFRED. The price of orchids; a sentimental comedy. (Smart set magazine. New York, 1915. 8°. v. 47, Oct., 1915, p. 103-119.) 8-NBA
Slovsky is the middle-aged Jewish proprietor of the shop. It was acted for the first time by the Harvard Dramatic Club at Cambridge and Boston, April 6-8, 1915.

—— The florist shop; one act comedy. (In: Harvard University Dramatic Club. Plays... New York: Brentano's, 1918. 12°. [Series 1], p. 1-28.) NBL (Harvard)
Same as the preceding *The Price of orchids,* in a slightly varying text.

—— Boston: Walter H. Baker Company, cop. 1926. 1 p.l., 28 p. 12°.
Reprinted with comments in E. Van B. Knickerbocker, editor, *Short plays,* New York [cop. 1931], p. 83-106, 479-481, NCO.

HAYWARD, H. RICHARD, AND A. RISH. The Jew's fiddle; a play in one act... Dublin: The Talbot Press; London: T. Fisher Unwin, 1921. 27 p. 12°.
Produced at the Gaiety Theatre, Dublin, by the Ulsters Players, Dec. 18, 1920, with J. G. Abbey as Isaac Perleman, an elderly Jewish dealer in violins.

HEALD, JOHN P. Open house; a tabloid musicomedy in one act... Boston: Walter H. Baker Company [cop. 1931]. 24 p. 12°. (Baker's specialties.)
Scene: the revelers' club house. Abe Rozenbaum, a comical character.

HECHT, BEN, AND GENE FOWLER. The great magoo; a love-sick charade in three acts and something like eight scenes, recounting the didoes of two young and amorous souls, who nigh perished when they weren't in the hay together. This simple and slightly uncouth saga is the work of Messrs. Ben Hecht & Gene Fowler; illustrated by Herman Rosse. New York: Covici-Friede [cop. 1933]. 7 p.l., 3-208 p. col'd illus. 8°. NBM
In three acts.
Produced at the Selwyn Theatre, New York, Dec. 2, 1932, with Harry Green as Moe Weber, a cheap orchestra leader, "one of those Semitic fledglings who seem all beak and ego." In the text he is called Joe; later he becomes Sacha Weber. Joseph Greenwald played the part of Harry Aarons, theatrical agent, "fat, squat Jewish gentleman." The action takes place in and about the boardwalk at Coney Island, and the flea circus. Reviewed by J. W. Krutch in *Nation,* New York, 1932, v. 135, p. 625-626, * *DA;* and by Morton Eustis in *Theatre arts monthly,* New York, 1933, v. 17, p. 112, *NBLA.* See also *Collection of newspaper clippings of dramatic criticism, 1932-1933,* v. E-H, † *NBL.*

HECHT, BEN, & C. G. MACARTHUR. The front page; introduction by Jed Harris. New York: Covici-Friede, 1928. 7 p.l., 189 p. 8°. NBM

—— —— London: G. Richards & H. Toumlin, 1929. 7 p.l., 189 p., 1 l. 12°.
The last leaf consists of an epilogue which is not contained in the American edition.
Extracts from the dialogue, with a running synopsis, are printed in *The Best plays of 1928-29,* New York, 1929, p. 152-194, NAFH.
A newspaper play. The action is laid in the reporter's room of the Criminal Court Building, Chicago. Produced at the Times Square Theatre, New York, Aug. 14, 1928. Reviewed by G. J. Nathan in *American mercury,* New York, 1928, v. 15, p. 251, * *DA;* by G. V. Seldes in *Dial,* New York, v. 85, p. 446, and v. 86, p. 82-83, * *DA;* by J. W. Krutch in *Nation,* New York, v. 125, p. 554, * *DA;* and by R. M. Lovett in *New republic,* New York, v. 56, p. 73-74, * *DA.* See also *Collection of newspaper clippings of dramatic criticism, 1928-1929,* v. E-G, † *NBL.*

HELLER, NACHMAN. A celestial conference. (In his: Facts and fiction; a collection of stories and tales... [New York, cop. 1916.] 12°. p. 8-16.) * PST
"The amateur performers are the following: United States, chairman; England, France, Germany, Russia, Austria, Italy, Japan, Turkey and Spain, delegates: Cherubim, Seraphim, etc." The conference takes place shortly after the Russo-Japanese war. Russia and its Czar are taken to account and their doom foretold. The United States is glorified.

HEPENSTALL, WILLIAM DANIEL, AND RALPH CULLINAN. The call of the banshee, a mystery-farce in three acts, by W. D. Hepenstall and Ralph Culliman[!] a reproduction of the original professional performance by Nathaniel Edward Reeid... New York: Longmans, Green and Co., 1929. vi, 125 p. 12°. (Longmans' play series.) NBL p.v.208
Players' promptbook.
An Irish mystery play, the scene of which is laid in America. Produced as *The Banshee* at Daly's 63rd Street Theatre, Dec. 5, 1927. Conway Wingfield as Dr. Morrison (Markovich in the text), a physician who foils the villain's designs. See reviews in *Collection of newspaper clippings of dramatic criticism, 1927-1928,* v. A-C, † *NBL.*

HEVESH, MARY. The return; a one-act comedy drama. (Jewish forum. New York, 1921. 8°. v. 4, p. 951-956, 1007-1013.) * PBD
Pearl Conheim emancipates herself from the influence of her ambitious, pinochle-playing mother and marries an immigrant Zionist, with the approval of grandmother Conheim.

Individual Plays — 1915–1938, continued

HEYMANS, MARTIN J. Gilded youth; a comedy drama for mixed characters, in four acts. Brooten, Minn.: Catholic Dramatic Company, 1926. 105 p. 16°. (Library of Catholic plays. [no. 44.]) NAC p.v.325
Goldstein, a middle-aged Jewish grocery merchant.

HIBBERT, FRANCIS AIDAN. England's greatness; a play [in three scenes] which tells how the first missionaries came to the English... London: Society for Promoting Christian Knowledge, 1924. 24 p. 12°. NCO p.v.504
In scene 1, at the market place in Rome, 585 A. D., a Jewish slave dealer is represented as leading English boy-captives for sale.

HIGHT, MARY. A Shakespearean fantasy... Costume illustrations by Maude I. G. Oliver. Chicago: Dramatic Pub. Company [cop. 1927]. 48 p. illus. 12°. (Sergel's acting drama. no. 667.)
The characters are all from Shakespeare's plays. Among them are Portia and Shylock.

HILLYER, ROBERT. The masquerade; a comedy. [Hartford, Conn.: The Haylofters Company, cop. 1928.] 31(1) p. 12°. NBL p.v.203
In one act.
The characters are from ancient and modern history. Disraeli, Lord Beaconsfield, is one of them.

HIPSHON, I. The miracle of Lodz; a play in one act, by Alan Peters [pseud.]. (In: Sydney Needoff, editor, Five one-act plays of Jewish interest. [Manchester, Eng., 1937.] 8°. p. 25–38.)
The plot is woven around an interesting and pathetic Jewish superstition. The basic story is similar to that of Mark Schweid's *Borrowed years* (q.v. in this list). The BBC broadcasted this play in 1937. Letters protesting the broadcast by M. J. G., S. A. Polka, and I. J. Levy were printed in *Jewish chronicle*, London, May 28, 1937, p. 48, and in its defense by Stella Richman and the author, ibid., June 4, p. 52, * PBE.
Produced by the Leeds Jewish Institute, at the 9th annual Jewish Drama Festival, Manchester, Eng., March 14, 1936, with Lionel Poyser as the Zadik. The time is 1850. See *Jewish chronicle*, London, March 20, 1936, p. 45, * PBE.

HIRSCHBEIN, PEREZ. Bebele, idyll. (In: Etta Block, translator, One-act plays from the Yiddish: second series. New York, 1929. 12°. p. 1–25.) * PTP
The story of a mother's devotion to her only surviving child.
The original appeared in *Zukunft*, New York, 1915, v. 20, p. 778–785, * PBB.

—— Green fields... translated by Samuel S. Grossman. [New York, n. d.] 15, 14, 14 p. 4°.
Multigraphed.
In three acts.
In the original Yiddish it appeared in *Zukunft*, New York, 1917, v. 22, p. 25–30, 94–98, 153–158, * PBB, and as such produced at the Jewish Art Theatre, New York, May 30, 1919. See review by Hillel Rogoff, in *Forward*, New York, June 6, 1919, p. 6, * PBB.
In the present English translation it was staged by the Anglo-Jewish Players of New York, during the season 1926–1927, and by amateur groups throughout the country.

—— On the threshold. (In: Isaac Goldberg, translator, Six plays of the Yiddish theatre; 2nd ser. Boston [1918]. 12°. p. 73–110.) * PTP
Scene is laid in Russia. The old man who is dying tries to force his daughter to marry according to his wishes. She refuses and is left out, together with her mother, from his will.

—— Raisin and almonds. [In one act.] Translated from the Yiddish by Leah W. Leonard. (American Hebrew. New York, 1918. 4°. v. 102, p. 611–618.) * PBD

—— The snowstorm. Once upon a time Jews made merry! (In: Etta Block, translator, One-act plays from the Yiddish. Cincinnati [cop. 1923]. 12°. p. 83–111.) * PTP
A wild, rollicking farce.
First appeared in *Zukunft*, New York, 1916, v. 21, p. 29–35, * PBB.

—— The stranger. (In: Etta Block, translator, One-act plays from the Yiddish. Cincinnati [cop. 1923]. 12°. p. 49–82.) * PTP
A symbolic playlet. The original title in the Yiddish, *Raisins and nuts*, is taken from the folk slumber song which Fraidele sings to her brother — "Father will buy nuts and raisins for you." It first appeared in *Zukunft*, New York, 1915, v. 20, p. 1002–1010, * PBB.
Produced by the East and West Players, New York City, Jan. 18, 1917. See *American Hebrew*, New York, 1917, v. 100, p. 391, * PBD.

—— When the dew falleth. (In: Etta Block, translator, One-act plays from the Yiddish. Cincinnati [cop. 1923]. 12°. p. 113–138.) * PTP
"An idyl of love and youth and age."

HOBBS, BERTRAM. Hot headlines; a melodrama in 1 act... New York[etc.]: S. French, Inc., cop. 1935. 26 p., 1 l. diagr. 12°. NBL p.v.398
A "crook" play. One of the main characters, Francis Xavier Cohalahan, assumes the disguise and the "speech" of a Jew.

HOFFE, MONCKTON. Cristilinda; a play in four acts... New York: S. French; London: S. French, Ltd., cop. 1926. 63, 5 p. plates, diagrs. 8°. (French's standard library edition.) NCO p.v.539
The characters are divided into two groups, respectable and disreputable. Sir Julius Samoon (Sir Joseph Duveen is here alluded to), "the great art dealer, rather elderly, Jewish but elegant, and very well turned out," is placed in the first class. Iky-Mo, "a Jewish gentleman of the Whitechapel type, quite tidily dressed," belongs to the second group. Under the title *The Painted lady* it was given a preview at the Alvin Theatre, Pittsburgh, Nov., 1922. Under the title *Lady Cristilinda*, it was produced at the Broadhurst Theatre, New York, Dec. 25, 1922, with Eugene Powers as Sir Julius and Ferdinand Gottschalk as Iky-Mo. Reviewed by Arthur Hornblow in *Theatre magazine*, New York, v. 37, Feb., 1923, p. 15, † NBLA. See also *Collection of newspaper clippings of dramatic criticism, 1922–1923*, v. G–L, † NBL.
Produced at the Garrick Theatre, London, Oct. 21, 1925, with Hector Abbas as Sir Julius and C. D. Warren as Iky-Mo. Reviewed in *Era*, London, v. 89, Oct. 24, 1925, p. 4, † NAFA; and by J. E. Agate in his *Contemporary theatre, 1925*, London, 1926, p. 194–198, NAFA.

HOFFMAN, AARON. Give and take. New York: S. French; London: S. French, Ltd., cop. 1926. 2 p.l., 3–100 p. plates. 12°. (French's standard library edition.) NBL p.v.153

—— Two blocks away; a play in three acts. New York: S. French [etc.], cop. 1925. 134 p. plates. 12°. (French's standard library edition.) NBL p.v.134
Nathaniel Pomerantz, played by Barney Bernard, suddenly becoming rich, moves two blocks away from

Individual Plays — 1915–1938, continued

HOFFMAN, AARON, *continued*

Second Avenue, New York, to a "residential" district. The time is July, 1920. The attempt is made to show the effect of wealth upon a group of East Side characters, Jews and Irish. "Uncle Nate" returns to his former station of poverty where all the virtues reside. Tried out at the Apollo Theatre, Atlantic City, N. J., May 23, 1921. Reviewed in *New York dramatic mirror*, 1921, v. 83, p. 965, * *T–* *DA*. Brought to New York, at the George M. Cohan Theatre, Aug. 30, 1921. Reviewed in *New York clipper*, v. 69, Sept. 7, 1921, p. 20, * *T–†* *MVA*; and in *Theatre magazine*, New York, v. 34, p. 344, † *NBLA*. See also *Collection of newspaper clippings of dramatic criticism, 1921–1922*, v. S–Z, † *NBL*.

——— The Cohens and Kellys; a story of Eastside-West-side New York, based on the play "Two blocks away," by Aaron Hoffman, with illustrations produced and filmed by Universal Pictures Corporation... New York: Jacobsen-Hodgkinson-Corporation [cop. 1925]. 1 p.l., 5–135 p. incl. plates. 8°. (Popular plays and screen library.)

——— Welcome stranger; a comedy in four acts. New York: S. French; London: S. French, Ltd., cop. 1926. 111 p., 2 l. plates, diagrs. 12°. (French's standard library ed.)   NBL p.v.154

Long extracts from the play, with a running synopsis by Gustav Blum, are given in *American Hebrew*, New York, 1921, v. 108, p. 234, 236, 249, * *PBD*.

Isidor Solomon comes to live in a New Hampshire town. He is accorded a hostile reception. His chief opponent is the Jewish mayor who hides his racial identity under the name of Ichabod Whitson. He transforms the sleepy and intolerant town into a bustling and flourishing community, and becomes its leading citizen.

Produced at the Cohan and Harris Theatre, New York, Sept. 13, 1920, with George Sidney as "the stranger," and Edmund Breese as Whitson. Reviewed in *Dramatist*, Easton, Pa., 1922, v. 13, p. 1110–1111, *NAFA*; by B. F. in *Jewish forum*, New York, 1920, v. 3, p. 630–632, * *PBD*; and by O. W. Firkins in *Weekly review*, New York, v. 3, p. 354–356, * *DA*. See also *Collection of newspaper clippings of dramatic criticism, 1920–1921*, v. S–Z, † *NBL*.

Produced at the Lyric Theatre, London, Oct. 19, 1921, with Harry Green as Isidor Solomon and Frank E. Petley as Ichabod Whitson. Reviewed in *Era*, London, v. 84, Oct. 26, 1921, p. 9, † *NAFA*; and in *The Times*, London, Oct. 20, 1921, p. 8, * *A*.

HOFFMAN, REBEKAH B. Judah's new deliverer; a Purim allegory [in three scenes]. (Jewish exponent. Philadelphia, 1918. f°. v. 66, Feb. 22, 1918, p. 1, 9.)   †* PBD

An allegorical playlet. Race prejudice and commercialism overthrown, and Zionism enthroned.

HOKKA chynik [in three acts]. (Jewish press. Omaha, Neb., 1933. f°. v. 9, Sept. 20, 1933, section D, p. 14.)

The title is a Yiddish idiom, meaning *to talk too much*.

HOLBROOK, MARION. Angel aware; a comedy in one act... New York [etc.]: S. French, Inc. [cop. 1936.] 3 p.l., 31(1) p. diagr. 12°.

Gustave Meyerbeer, art connoisseur.   NBL p.v.395

HOLDSWORTH, GLADYS BRONWYN (STERN). The matriarch, a play in a prologue and three acts, by G. B. Stern... London: S. French, Ltd.; New York: S. French, Inc., cop. 1931. 84 p. plates. 8°. (French's acting edition. no. 1778.)

"Miss G. B. Stern gratefully acknowledges the collaboration of Mr. Frank Vernon on the scenario of the play." — *t.-p.*

A dramatization of her novel *The Tents of Israel*, relating the fortunes of the international Rakonitz family. The action covers the years 1902–1927. First produced at the Royalty Theatre, London, May 8, 1929, with Mrs. Patrick Campbell as Anastasia, the matriarch of the family, Inez Bensusan as Wanda, and Beatrix Thomson as Toni. Reviewed in *Era*, London, v. 92, May 15, 1929, p. 8, † *NAFA*; by A. G. Macdonell in *London mercury*, v. 20, p. 194–195, * *DA*; and in *Nation*, London, v. 45, p. 239, * *DA*.

Produced at the Longacre Theatre, New York, March 18, 1930, with Constance Collier as Anastasia and the others of the cast the same as those in the London production. Reviewed by Mildred E. Fisher in *American Hebrew*, v. 126, p. 764, 828, * *PBD*; by F. R. Bellamy in *Outlook*, New York, v. 54, p. 550, * *DA*; and by John Hutchens in *Theatre arts monthly*, v. 14, p. 465, *NBLA*. See also *Collection of newspaper clippings of dramatic criticism, 1929–30*, v. M–Q, † *NBL*. Reviewed also by Hannah Moriarta in *Jewish tribune*, New York, July 24, 1925, p. 18, * *PBD*.

It was staged by the Little Theatre of Temple Israel, Boston, May 17, 1932, with Mrs. Robert Freedman as Wanda Rakonitz.

Newman, S. A study in non-Jewishness. illus. (Jewish guardian. London, 1929. f°. v. 10, May 24, 1929, p. 4.)   * PBE

HOLMES, NAT FOSTER. ...The pride of Yosakis [in three acts]... Syracuse, N. Y.: Willis N. Bugbee Co., cop. 1935. 72 p. 12°. (Bugbee's popular plays.)

The scene is the town of Yosakis, "in the great wheat belt region." Samuel Feltman, a Jewish business man, who "feels that he can make more substantial money in a small town than he could in a large city."

HOMER, FRANCES. A prince to order; a comedy in three acts... Boston: Walter H. Baker Company [cop. 1929]. 136 p. 12°. (Baker's royalty plays.)

Abe Silverstein, president of the Silversheet Film Company, "typical movie magnate."

HOROWITZ, ISAAC. The snow man [in one act]. (Young Israel. Cincinnati, 1926. f°. v. 19, no. 4, p. 8–10.)   * PBD

A juvenile playlet, translated from the Yiddish by Jack Greenberg. It was printed in the original as no. 13 of Arbeiter Ring Kinder-Bibliothek, New York, 1928.

HOROWITZ, NATHAN. Souls in exile. A play in four acts. London: Printed by I. Narodiczky, 1928. 52 p. port. 8°.

Erasures and corrections throughout in author's handwriting.

Scene: a Russian-Jewish village, and London. Time: 1900 and 1914. Produced, June, 1928, at the Gaiety Theatre, Manchester, Eng.

HOUSMAN, LAURENCE. His favourite flower; a political myth explained [in one act]. (In his: Angels & ministers. London [1921]. 8°. p. 45–59.)   NCR

Also in the New York edition of *Angels & ministers*, 1922, p. 43–57, *NCR*.

The allusion is to the primrose, Beaconsfield's favorite. Reprinted (with illus.) and dated 1881, the year of the statesman's death, in his *Victoria regina*, London [1934], p. 359–371, *NCR*.

——— The Queen: God bless her! (a scene from home-life in the Highlands) [in one act]. (In his: Angels & ministers. London [1921]. 8°. p. 13–43.)   NCR

Also in the New York edition of *Angels & ministers*, 1922, p. 9–41, *NCR*.

THE JEW IN ENGLISH DRAMA 145

Individual Plays — 1915–1938, continued

Reprinted (with illus.) in his *Victoria regina*, London [1934], p. 333–358, *NCR.*
The main characters are Queen Victoria and Lord Beaconsfield.
Produced by Nigel Playfair at the Arts Theatre Club, London, May, 1929, with Clarke-Smith as Disraeli. Reviewed in *Nation & Athenæum*, London, 1929, v. 45, p. 239, * *DA.* Produced again by the Players' Theatre, London, March 26, 1931, with T. Haslewood as Lord Beaconsfield. Reviewed in *Era*, London, v. 94, April 1, 1931, p. 23, † *NAFA.*

—— Royal favour. [In one act.] (In his: The queen's progress; palace plays, second series. London [1932]. 12°. p. 75–97.) NCR
One of nine plays in a volume depicting the life of Queen Victoria in dramatic form. This one, dated 1859, is laid at Windsor Castle, with the Queen's favorite, Disraeli, Lord Beaconsfield, as the minister in attendance.
Reprinted (with illus.) in his *Victoria regina*, London [1934], p. 269–291, *NCR.*

—— Victoria regina; a dramatic biography... illustrated by Ernest H. Shepard. London: J. Cape [1934]. 469(1) p. 8°. NCR
Made up of plays which have previously appeared in his *Angels and ministers, Palace plays, The Queen's progress,* and *Victoria and Albert.*
Reprinted in part, with running synopses, in *Best plays of 1935–36*, New York, 1936, p. 169–203, *NAFH.*
Produced at the Gate Theatre, London, May 1, 1935, wth V. C. Clinton-Baddeley as Lord Beaconsfield. See *Jewish chronicle*, London, May 3, 1935, p. 40, * *PBE*; at the Broadhurst Theatre, New York, Dec. 26, 1935, with George Zucco in the same rôle. See *Collection of newspaper clippings of dramatic criticism, 1935–36*, v. Ten-Z, † *NBL.*

HOWARD, FLORENCE. On the banks of the river Styx; a play in one act... New York [etc.]: Samuel French; cop. 1926. 25 p. 12°. (French's international copyrighted...ed. of the works of the best authors. no. 576.) NBL p.v.180, no.5
On the banks of the river Styx, outside of a mythical town called Acheron. The cast consists of twelve Biblical and twelve modern women. Miss Lotz, opposite Lot's wife, is the realtor. Miss Saphrinsky, opposite Sapphira, is the press and publicity agent.

HOWARD, SIDNEY COE. Half gods... New York, London: Charles Scribner's Sons, 1930. 7 p.l., 3–203 p. 12°. NBM
In nine scenes.
Reviewed by Norman Marshall in *Drama*, London, 1930, v. 8, p. 126, *NAFA.*
First produced at the Plymouth Theatre, New York, Dec. 21, 1929, with Edward Reese as Dr. Mannering, psychoanalyst. "He has not quite got rid of his last traces of Jewish accent." He is a bit satirized in the play. For reviews see *Collection of newspaper clippings of dramatic criticism, 1929–1930*, v. D–H, † *NBL.*

—— Paths of glory, a play, adapted by Sidney Howard from the novel by Humphrey Cobb. With a foreword for college theatres by Sidney Howard. New York, Los Angeles: Samuel French; London: S. French, Limited, 1935. xvii p., 3 l., 3–174 p. 12°. NBM
An episode of the French army during the Great war. First produced at the Shubert Theatre, New Haven, Conn., Sept. 18, 1935, and at the Plymouth Theatre, New York, Sept. 26, 1935, with George Tobias as Meyer, one of six privates of the 181st Infantry of the French army. Meyer is described as a "soldier of Jewish race and Marseille gestures"; again, as the "Jew fishmonger from Marseille." For reviews see *Collection of newspaper clippings of dramatic criticism, 1935–1936*, v. Nin-Pos, † *NBL.*

HOWARD, SIDNEY COE, AND P. H. DE KRUIF. Yellow Jack; a history...in collaboration with Paul De Kruif; with illustrations by Jo Mielziner. New York: Harcourt, Brace and Company [cop. 1934]. xi, 152 p. plates. 8°. NBM
"Based on the dramatic 'Walter Reed' chapter of Paul De Kruif's *Microbe hunters* [New York, 1926, *AB*]...this play deals with man's struggle against, and final victory over, the dread yellow fever." — *Publisher's announcement.*
Private Levi P. Busch is described as "a city chap of Jewish extraction and intensity"; "a Jewish orphan boy from Chicago." He is one of four American soldiers who, during the summer and fall of 1900, performed heroic service for the American Yellow Fever Commission in Cuba. The true name was Levi E. Folk (see *Note*, p. [v]).
It was produced at the Martin Beck Theatre, New York, March 6, 1934, with Samuel Levene as Busch. Reviewed by John Corbin (with illus.) in *Saturday review of literature*, 1934, v. 10, p. 569–570, † *NAA; Stage* (with illus.), v. 11, March, 1934, p. 13, *NBLA*; and by E. J. R. Isaacs (with illus.) in *Theatre arts monthly*, 1934, v. 18, p. 326–329, † *NBLA.* For further reviews see *Collection of newspaper clippings of dramatic criticism, 1933–1934*, v. U–Z, † *NBL.*

HOYT, ELLA M. Hello Zentral! a Jewish monologue... Dayton, Ohio: Paine Publishing Company [cop. 1928]. 5 p. 12°. (Paine's monologues.)

—— Isaac, he ain't so dumb [a monologue]. Sioux City, Iowa: Wetmore Declamation Bureau, cop. 1930. 1 f. 4°.
Typewritten.

HUDSON, HOLLAND. Action! a melodramatic farce. (In: Frank Shay, editor, A treasury of plays for men. Boston, 1923. 8°. p. 117–131.) NAFH (Shay)
Young George Max comes back from the Palestinian front after the World war with a Zionist bride, whom he had kidnapped from an Arab sheik. Desiring a position "full of action," he gets it in his father's silk business, in New York City.

HURST, FANNIE. The gold in fish; a new story. Illustrations by R. F. Schabelitz. (Hearst's international cosmopolitan. New York, 1925. 4°. v. 79, Aug., 1925, p. 28–31, 185–194.) * *DA*
Reprinted in her *The Song of life,* 1927.
The Goldfishes move from Division Street, Manhattan, to West End Avenue.
Dramatized under the title *It is to laugh* and produced at the Eltinge Theatre, New York, Dec. 26, 1927, with I. Honigman as old father Goldfish, John Davidson as the snobbish son Morris, and Edna Hibbard as the hoydenish daughter Birdie. For reviews see *Collection of newspaper clippings of dramatic criticism, 1927–1928*, v. H–L, † *NBL.*

—— Humoresque. Illustrated by T. D. Skidmore. (Cosmopolitan magazine. New York, 1919. 4°. v. 66, March, 1919, p. 32–39, 94, 96–100.) * *DA*

—— Humoresque; a laugh on life with a tear behind it. [Photoplay ed.] New York and London: Harper & Brothers [cop. 1920]. 5 p.l., 43(1) p. front., plates. 12°.
Based on the author's story and film scenario, it was dramatized into a comedy drama of three acts and produced at the Vanderbilt Theatre, New York, Feb. 27, 1923. The story is that of a Jewish mother and her boy violinist. Laurette Taylor played the mother, Sarah Kantor; Sam Sidman, the husband Abraham; and Alfred Little and Luther Adler, the son Leon. For reviews see *Collection of newspaper clippings of dramatic criticism, 1922–1923*, v. G–L, † *NBL.*
A preview of it was seen at the Montauk Theatre, Brooklyn, N. Y., Jan. 29, 1923.

Individual Plays — 1915-1938, continued

HURST, MONT. ...The family budget; a Hebrew play in one act... Syracuse, N. Y.: W. N. Bugbee Co., cop. 1929. 8 p. 12°. (Bugbee's popular plays.)
Pa Lipsky resists the ambitions of his family, suddenly become rich.

HURWITZ, BERTHA. The adopted son; a play in four acts... Boston: The Stratford Company, 1920. 3 p.l., 90 p. 12°.   NBM
"A historical play in allegorical form. Relates the progress of Judah, how he is hounded from one country to another by Prejudice, becomes the dupe of Assimilation, a beautiful girl. Finally he returns to Palestine, his own mother, where no Prejudice can enter." — *From cover advertisement.*

HURWITZ, ISRAEL. Colleagues. [In one act.] By Zalmon Libin [pseud.]. Translated by Gustav Blum. (East and West. New York, 1915. 4°. v. 1, p. 226-229.)   * PBD
Translated anew by Bessie F. White in her *Nine one-act plays from the Yiddish,* Boston [cop. 1932], p. 173-194, * PTP.
A comic treatment of the sad attempts of Yiddish playwrights trying to break into the English-speaking stage.

IRWIN, WALLACE. Capitol fun. [In two acts.] (Collier's. New York, 1930. f°. v. 85, March 22, 1930, p. 22, 38.)   * DA
A Prohibition skit. Scene: House of Representatives, Washington. William I. Sirovich, M.D., representative from New York, is one of the speakers.

ISH-KISHOR, JUDITH. "Can he do it?" A Succos fantasy in two scenes and an epilogue. [New York: Young Judaea, 1917?] 15 f. 4°.
Mimeographed.
The Feinstein family in a dream of Russia, dream of Spain, and dream of Palestine.

—— Yigael; a play of the settlers of Marchavia in one act. Based on the story "Yigael," by M. Bernstein & Nellie Straus. [New York: Young Judaea, n. d.] 8 f. 4°.
Mimeographed.
A melodrama involving conflict between Arabs and Jewish settlers in Palestine. The story appeared in *Maccabaean,* 1916, v. 28, p. 103-106, 132-135, illus., * PBD; and in *Young Judaean,* New York, v. 25, April, 1937, p. 1-2, 23, * PBD.

JACKSON, F. "Shylock returns." [In 2 scenes.] (Shakespearean quarterly. Sydney, Australia, 1923. 8°. v. 2, April, 1923, p. 25-32.)   * NCK
Ten years after the trial scene in *The Merchant of Venice.* Antonio is now dead. Jessica returns to her father. First performed on April 23, 1923, at the Australian Hall, Sydney, at the birthday celebration of the Shakespeare Society of New South Wales, with Neville Mayman as Shylock and Miss Beryl Alexander as Jessica.

JACKSON, MRS. HARRY L. The quest. [In a prologue and one act. New York: Hadassah, 1933.] 6 f. f°.
Caption-title.
Mimeographed.

JACOB, NAOMI ELLINGTON. Jacob Ussher... London: Thornton Butterworth, Ltd. [1925.] 318 p. 12°.
Reviewed in *Jewish guardian,* London, v. 7, Nov. 13, 1925, p. 14, * PBE.
This is a novelization of Esmond's play listed below, which London and New York saw under different titles.

See letter by Eva Moore in *Jewish guardian,* London, v. 7, Dec. 11, 1925, p. 8, * PBD.
The play in question is *Birds of a feather,* by Henry V. Esmond, which was produced at the Globe Theatre, London, April 9, 1920. A crusty old father, a willful daughter, and a very disagreeable aunt form the main dramatis personae. An intermarriage theme is a secondary thread in the play. Esmond himself played Jacob Ussher the father, and Marie Löhr, his daughter Constance. Reviewed in *Era,* London, v. 83, April 14, 1920, p. 12, † *NAFA.*
As *The House of Ussher* it was produced at the Fifth Avenue Theatre, New York, Jan. 13, 1926, with Clarence Derwent as Jacob Ussher and Rosalind Fuller as his daughter. For reviews see *Collection of newspaper clippings of dramatic criticism, 1925–1926,* v. E-J, † *NBL.* See also *American Hebrew,* New York, 1926, v. 119, p. 83, * PBD.

JACOBS, BERTRAM. The man with the puckel, a comedy in four scenes. (In: H. Zimmerman, compiler, Plays of Jewish life. [London, 1931.] 12°. p. 43-73.)   NCO (Zimmerman)
A comedy. The action takes place in a poor tenement home, in the East End of London. First produced by the University of London Jewish Students' Union at University College, London, March 29, 1930, with I. H. Jacob as the hump-backed Mr. Greenstein. Reviewed by F. H. S. in *Jewish chronicle,* London, April 4, 1930, p. 60, * PBE.

JACOBS, DAVID. The prayers of a people. illus. (Jewish tribune. New York, 1923. f°. May 11, 1923, p. 3, 25.)   * PBD
Dramatization of the leading prayers in the Hebrew ritual, for presentation by the pupils of a religious school.

JACOBS, H. A. George Washington meets his bicentennial press agent. (Life. New York, 1932. 4°. v. 99, July, 1932, p. 23-24.)   * DA
In five scenes.
The press agent is Representative Sol Bloom, chairman of the United States George Washington Bicentennial Commission.

JACOBS, NELLIE CECILIA. America's garden; a making-America pageant. n. p. [1921?] 6 l. illus. 8°.   NAC p.v.76
Cover-title.
In five episodes. The Jews, as one of the races contributing to American progress.

JAMES, GRACE. Robert and Louisa; a play for five boys... London: S. French, Ltd.; New York: S. French, Inc., cop. 1931. 24 p. 12°. (French's plays for boys. no. 19.)
Mr. Nabob, in memory of the story of Naboth's vineyard, is thought to be a rich Jew who has come to force the sale of the cottage.

JASSPON, ETHEL REED, AND B. BECKER. Friendship ceremony. [A pageant in one scene.] (In their: Ritual and dramatized folkways. New York [cop. 1925]. 8°. p. 3-16.)   NASH
Among the children of all peoples is listed a Jewish child.

—— The gate of the West; a dramatization of [R. H. Schauffler's poem] Scum o' the earth. [In one scene.] (In their: Ritual and dramatized folkways. New York [cop. 1925]. 8°. p. 83-91.)   NASH
"A plea to respect the individuality of the immigrant." Among the characters is "a Hebrew man" with a heavy pack.

THE JEW IN ENGLISH DRAMA 147

Individual Plays — 1915-1938, continued

JOHNSON, FREDERICK GREEN. Abie's confessions; a Hebrew monologue... Wilkes-Barre, Pa.: The author [cop. 1925]. 7 p. 12°. (Broadway vaudeville.)
Abie Cohen, "a henpecked Hebrew"; he has just returned from his mother-in-law's funeral.

—— Mrs. Goldblitz on matrimony; a Hebrew monologue... Wilkes-Barre, Pa.: The author [cop. 1929]. 6 p. 12°. (Broadway vaudeville.)

—— Such ignorance! a vaudeville sketch [in one act]. Chicago: T. S. Denison & Co. [cop. 1918.] 9 p. 12°. (Denison's vaudeville sketches.)
A vaudeville sketch for straight and "Hebrew character" comedians.

JOHNSON, THEODORE. Dr. Dobbs' assistant; a comic sketch for six males. (In his: Baker's stunt and game book. Boston [cop. 1928]. 12°. p. 38-46.) MV p.v.116
One of the six is "Ikey, a Jew."

JONES, ELLIS O. Real antiques; farce comedy in one act. New York [etc.]: Samuel French, cop. 1929. 2 p.l., 16 p. 12°. NAFH p.v.50
A burlesque on the popular fad of collecting antiques. Schneider, proprietor of a second-hand store which aspires to be an antique shop.

JORDAN, VIOLA. Bridges. col'd illus. (In: Mount Holyoke College. — Department of English Literature and Drama, Playshop laboratory plays, first series. [Northampton, Mass.,] 1932. 8°. p. 63-96.)
In two "bridges." Both deal with the Jewish insistence against intermarriage. In "bridge" I, in ancient Jerusalem, the old father has his way and forces his son, Jediah, to renounce his love for a Moabite girl. In "bridge" II, in modern Brooklyn, in the shadow of the Brooklyn bridge, the old immigrant mother and the rabbi fail to dissuade young David from his love for the gentile girl.
Produced by the Playshop Laboratory Players of Mount Holyoke College, South Hadley, Mass., April 8 and 9, 1931. The players in the second episode were: Catherine Thornburg, Mrs. Strauss, the mother; Sadie Johnson, David, her son; and Leslie G. Burgevin, Dr. Bashlow, the rabbi.

JOSEPH, LEON. In self-defense only. (Young Judaean. New York, 1937. 4°. v. 25, Jan., 1937, p. 9.) †* PBD
Place: Jewish village in Palestine. Time: recent (1936) riots in Palestine.

JOYCE, JAMES. [Ulysses. Chapter xv.] (In his: Ulysses. Paris, 1922. 8°. p. 408-565.) ***
A chapter in Joyce's novel, cast in dramatic form. The scene is Mabbot Street, Dublin, and the red light district, from 10.30 to 12 P.M. Bloom is there as well as Stephen Daedalus, Bella Cohen, and the ghost of Rudy Bloom. Cf. Paul J. Smith, *A Key to Ulysses of James Joyce*, Chicago, 1927, p. 45-46.

Samuel, Maurice. Bloom of Bloomesalem. (Reflex. Chicago, 1929. 8°. v. 4, Jan., 1929, p. 11-20; Feb., 1929, p. 10-16.) * PBD

KAISER, GEORG. From morn to midnight; a modern mystery in seven scenes. Translated from the German by Ashley Dukes. (Poet lore. Boston, 1920. 8°. v. 31, p. 317-363.) * DA

—— From morn to midnight; a play in seven scenes... Translated from the German by Ashley Dukes. London: Henderson [1920]. viii, 58 p. 12°. NGB p.v.176

—— From morn to midnight; a play in seven scenes... translated from the German by Ashley Dukes (the Theatre Guild version) with eight illustrations from photographs of the Theatre Guild production. New York: Brentano's [cop. 1922]. 8 p.l., 3-154 p. front., plates. 12°.
Reprinted in T. H. Dickinson, *Chief contemporary dramatists: third series*, Boston [1930], p. 229-259, NAFH; and in M. J. Moses, editor, *Dramas of modernism*, Boston, 1931, p. 131-165, NAFH.
An expressionist drama in a series of tableaux. The principal character is a bank cashier who, on a sudden impulse, absconds with a large sum of money and sets out to see what money can buy. In the course of his one day's experience he comes across five Jewish sporting men at a cycle race meeting. The first German production was at the Kammerspiele, Munich, April 28, 1917. The Incorporated Stage Society produced it at the Lyric Theatre, Hammersmith, London, March 28, 1920. Reviewed in *Era*, London, v. 83, March 31, 1920, p. 13, † NAFA; and by Frank Swinnerton in *Nation*, London, v. 27, p. 13-14, * DA.
Produced by the Theatre Guild at the Garrick Theatre, New York, May 21, 1922. For reviews see *Collection of newspaper clippings of dramatic criticism, 1921-1922*, v. E-L, † NBL.

KANDEL, ABEN. The anti-hill. [In one scene.] (Reflex. New York, 1928. 8°. v. 2, Jan., 1928, p. 80-83.) * PBD
Scene: at an asylum for the preservation of the mentally single-tracked. Among various kinds of antis are an anti-Semite and an anti-Gentile.

KANE, EDITH. In thy radiance we see which light; a drama of voices in Columbia University, 1935. (Barnard quarterly. New York, 1935. 4°. v. 9, no. 3, p. 10-13.) STG (Barnard)
The "voices" are those of Cartaphillus, the Wandering Jew, a communist, a poet, and Miriam, "the recorder."

KAPLAN, BERNARD M. The strange melody; a drama in three acts... Foreword by Mrs. Rebekah Kohut... New York: Behrman's Jewish Book House, 1937. 32 p. 8°.
A drama of the Spanish Inquisition, when Gabriel Sanchez was treasurer of Aragon.

KAPLAN, LEAH. Abie and his Martian rose; a play in two acts. (Avukah annual, 1928. New York, 1928. 8°. p. 15-18, 26, 31.) * PZX
The action takes place on Mars. The Jews are admitted there, and expelled forty years later.

KASER, ARTHUR LEROY. And the cow was painted red; a mock trial. (In his: Ten easy acts for men. Chicago [cop. 1930]. 12°. p. 5-28.) NBL p.v.270
Izzy Cohen who was speeding at ten miles per hour.

—— Bargains. (In: Ward Morley, pseud., Headliner monologues for men. Boston, cop. 1927. 12°. p. 9-12.)
Izzy speaking.

—— Casey meets Cohen; a talking act for a Hebrew and an Irishman... Boston: Walter H. Baker Company [cop. 1930]. 11 p. 12°. (Baker's edition of plays.)

Individual Plays — 1915–1938, continued

KASER, ARTHUR LEROY. Did you heard about me? a Jewish monologue. (In his: Snappy plays and monologues for men. Dayton, Ohio [cop. 1931]. 12°. p. 87–93.)

—— Ding, dong, dumb bell; a one-act farcical specialty, by Sidney Steele [pseud.]. Chicago: T. S. Denison & Co. [cop. 1927.] 19 p. 12°. (Denison's specialties.) NBL p.v.274, no.16
School-room farce, with Abie as the Jewish pupil.

—— Dot loafer bum Levi; a monologue. (In his: A world of fun. Dayton, O. [cop. 1928.] 12°. p. 21–22.)

—— Dot vedding skeremony; a Yiddish monologue. By Vance Clifford [pseud.]. Chicago: T. S. Denison and Co. [cop. 1928.] 6 p. 12°. (Denison's vaudeville sketches.)
Jakey tells of the mishaps that befell him at his brother's wedding.

—— The filming of "Uncle Tom's cabin"; a classical comicality in one act... Chicago: T. S. Denison & Co. [cop. 1922.] 15 p. 12°. (Denison's vaudeville sketches.)
"A regular slam-bang travesty on the making of movies. Levi Shootzum, a Jew director who vants de punch." — *From advertisement.*

—— Fresh fish and local color; Hebrew monologue. (In his: Dialect monologues, readings and plays. Dayton, O. [cop. 1928.] 12°. p. 175–178.)

—— The goddess of dancing [a play in one act]. (In his: Dialect monologues, readings and plays. Dayton, O. [cop. 1928.] 12°. p. 26–45.)
An episode in the Cohen home.

—— Gumbummer and his class of poopils; a burlesque school act... New York: Fitzgerald Publishing Corporation [cop. 1931]. 16 p. 12°. (Playhouse plays.)
Abie, one of the pupils.

—— Hands up, sponges and can openers; a farce in one act for male characters... Boston: W. H. Baker Company [cop. 1929]. 19 p. 12°. (Baker's edition of plays.)
Interior of a small-town railroad station. Jake Cohen, "selling waterproof sponges and can openers."

—— Hey! teacher! a humorous entertainment [in two acts]. Chicago: Dramatic Pub. Company [cop. 1928]. 20 p. 12°. (Sergel's acting drama. no. 000142.) NBL p.v.204
The scene is in a burlesqued school room. Izzy is the Jewish pupil.

—— ...Hi times in Judge Sapp's court... Syracuse, N. Y.: Willis N. Bugbee Co., cop. 1935. 36 p. 12°. (Bugbee's novelty entertainments.)
In one act.
Abraham Finkelstein, "typical stage Jew."

—— I'll tell the world; a radio monologue. Chicago: T. S. Denison & Company [cop. 1928]. 8 p. 12°. (Denison's vaudeville sketches.)
Izzy Cohen, "the celebrated Irish tenor."

—— In an airplane passenger station; a one-act comedy... Dayton, O.: Paine Publishing Company [cop. 1928]. 20 p. 16°. (Paine's popular plays.)
Izzy Goldstein, "stage Jew," a passenger on the airplane.

—— In the delicatessen shop. [A monologue] for a Jewish lady. (In his: Dialect monologues, readings and plays. Dayton, O. [cop. 1928.] 12°. p. 146–147.)

—— In der street car; a Jewish monologue. (In his: Vaudeville turns. Boston [cop. 1923]. 12°. p. 14–17.)
Morris Vinestein speaking.

—— Inkelheim on de telephone; a Jewish monologue... San Francisco: Banner Play Bureau, cop. 1927. 6 p. 12°.

—— Isaac Fikelbaum; trouble laden. Jewish monologue. (In his: "Character impersonations." Minneapolis, cop. 1932. 12°. p. 69–73.) NBL p.v.273

—— It vas like dis; a Jewish monologue. (In his: Vaudeville turns. Boston [cop. 1923]. 12°. p. 11–13.)
Morris tells it.

—— Izzybloom's school of acting; a comedy in two acts... Dayton, Ohio: Paine Publishing Company [cop. 1928]. 32 p. 12°. (Paine's popular plays.)
Izzy Izzybloom is the proprietor of the school.

—— Jake the candidate. (In his: Eight snappy vaudeville monologues. Boston [cop. 1926]. 12°. p. 23–29.)

—— Jake and his family. (In his: Sure-fire acts for amateur vaudeville. Boston [cop. 1929]. 12°. p. 49–55.)
The speakers, Blane and Jake, straight and Hebrew.

—— ...Jootenant Levinski up for court martial; a burlesque military trial for nine men... Boston: W. H. Baker Company [cop. 1933]. 15 p. 12°. (Baker's burlesque trials.)
The case against Lieutenant Levinski "in the matter of a bum watch, without the works."

—— The lady minstrels from Dixie; a two-act entertainment... Chicago: T. S. Denison & Company [cop. 1928]. 36 p. music. 12°. (Denison's specialties.) NBL p.v.274
Mrs. Becky Kloffenstein, one of the members of the "Ladies' Aid and Minstrel Semicircle."

—— Levi Beginski telephones; a Yiddish monologue. By Vance Clifford [pseud.]. Chicago: T. S. Denison & Co., cop. 1927. 6 p. 12°. (Denison's vaudeville sketches.) NBL p.v.274, no.1
He speaks to the wrong party.

—— Levi goes a-hunting; a one-act skit. (In his: Top-liners for stunt nights and vod-vil. Boston [cop. 1924]. 12°. p. 25–29.)
The speakers are Levi and Hiram, in a wood or meadow.

—— Levi in the baggage room [in one scene]. (In his: Vaudeville varieties for stage, school, home and church. Boston [cop. 1925]. 12°. p. 59–69.)
"An Irish-Jewish talking act"; Mike, the baggage-master, and Levi "after his beneggage."

Individual Plays—1915–1938, continued

KASER, ARTHUR LEROY. Levi's troubles; a Hebrew monologue... Chicago: T. S. Denison & Co. [cop. 1922.] 6 p. 12°. (Denison's vaudeville sketches.)
Levi recounts his domestic troubles.

—— Levi's view on marriage; Hebrew monologue. (In his: Dialect monologues, readings and plays. Dayton, O. [cop. 1928.] 12°. p. 184–188.)

—— Loose nuts; a farcical sketch, by Sidney Steele [pseud.]. Chicago: T. S. Denison & Co. [cop. 1927.] 13 p. 12°. (Denison's vaudeville sketches.)   NBL p.v.274, no.18
In one act.
Joe Shortlongburg and Jake Longshortsky, hotel guests.

—— Mine friend, Levi Cohen; Jewish monologue. (In his: Right over the footlights; a book of monologues. Chicago [cop. 1927]. 12°. p. 99–106.)   NBL p.v.179

—— Mine frient, Morris. [A monologue.] (In his: Top-liners for stunt nights and vod-vil. Boston [cop. 1924]. 12°. p. 11–13.)

—— Mine gracious! (In his: Talking acts for two; a book of sketches for two players. Chicago [cop. 1927]. 12°. p. 52–58.)
Morris and Jake.

—— Monday morning in Maloney's court. (In his: Half a dozen mock trials. Boston [cop. 1933]. 12°. p. 7–21.)
Izzy Cohen, "typical stage Jew," arrested for speeding.

—— Musical eggs; a singing travesty for six men. (In his: Top-liner acts for amateurs. Minneapolis, cop. 1932. 12°. p. 29–42.)   NBL p.v.287
Among the six are Abraham Steinberg, "vit a grouch," and Izzy, his sixteen-year-old son.

—— The nonsense school; a burlesque school act for male quartet. (In his: Vaudeville turns. Boston [cop. 1923]. 12°. p. 33–42.)
Levi is the Jewish pupil.

—— Object: matrimony; a burlesque entertainment. By Vance Clifford [pseud.]... Chicago: T. S. Denison & Co. [cop. 1927.] 19 p. 12°. (Denison's specialties.)   NBL p.v.176
In one act.
Morris Chairinski's matrimonial bureau and a dozen of its clients. "Mates matched to suit or money refunded."

—— Oi, such a nice vidow voman! a Jewish monologue. By Vance Clifford [pseud.]. Chicago: T. S. Denison & Co. [cop. 1929.] 7 p. 12°. (Denison's vaudeville sketches.)
"Mistair Goldberg," a susceptible bachelor.

—— On the P. D. Q., for a rube and a Jewish comedian. (In his: Talking acts for two; a book of sketches for two players. Chicago [cop. 1927]. 12°. p. 59–66.)
Jim, a station agent de luxe, and Levi, a traveling salesman, at a rural station waiting room.

—— One on Inkel; a brief musical comedy [in one act]. (In his: Amateur acts and monologues. Dayton, Ohio [cop. 1928]. 12°. p. 22–36.)
Morris Inkel, proprietor of Inkel's Department Store, his daughter Mary, and Joe Marcus, the latter's sweetheart.

—— One swaller, one dollar. The acme of nonsense for ten men in one spasm of fifty minutes duration... Boston: Walter H. Baker Company [cop. 1928]. 24 p. 12°. (Baker's edition of plays.)
The scene is a doctor's office. Among the patients is Isadore Shutsky, "Oy! such a sick man."

—— Over the big puddle; a doughboy singing act. (In his: Ten easy acts for men. Chicago [cop. 1930]. 12°. p. 81–84.)   NBL p.v.270
Izzy, one of four buck privates, "over there."

—— Oy! Oy! und den some; monologue for Jewish comedian. (In his: Headliner monologues. Dayton, Ohio [cop. 1929]. 12°. p. 105–110.)   NBF p.v.115

—— A pain in de head; Hebrew talking act. (In his: Amateur acts and monologues. Dayton, Ohio [cop. 1928]. 12°. p. 41–44.)
Jake and Levi are speaking.

—— Poor Izzy! for two Jewish comedians. (In his: Talking acts for two; a book of sketches for two players. Chicago [cop. 1927]. 12°. p. 93–100.)
Benny, an insurance agent, and Izzy, a victim of hard luck.

—— Prof. Dummelhead's class; a school act for 8 men. (In his: Ten easy acts for men. Chicago [cop. 1930]. 12°. p. 93–103.)   NBL p.v.270
Izzy Finkel, a member of the class.

—— Professor Sniderschmultze's pupils; a burlesque school act. (In his: Top-liner acts for amateurs. Minneapolis, cop. 1932. 12°. p. 3–17.)   NBL p.v.287
Izzy is the Jewish pupil.

—— Rachael, her Abie and Izzy. (In his: Humorous monologues for women. Boston [cop. 1933]. 12°. p. 70–75.)   NBF p.v.148
Monologue for "Hebrew lady."

—— The school at Cantaloupe Center. [In three acts.]... Dayton, Ohio: Paine Publishing Company [cop. 1928]. 36 p. 16°. (Paine's popular plays.)
Time: long ago. Place: a country school.
Abie Cornwhiskey is one of four composing the school board, and his son, Izzy, is one of the scholars.

—— ...School days a la foolish... Syracuse, N. Y.: Willis N. Bugbee Co., cop. 1931. 12 p. 12°. (Bugbee's popular plays.)
In one act.
Izzy Ikelbloom, "a Jewish boy," one of the class.

—— Shoot, brother, shoot; a vaudeville sketch ... Chicago: T. S. Denison & Co. [cop. 1934.] 14 p. 12°. (Denison's vaudeville sketches.)
Daniel Boom and David Cricket, "such big game hunters!"

—— Some class; a burlesque schoolroom act. (In his: Sure-fire acts for amateur vaudeville. Boston [cop. 1929]. 12°. p. 11–22.)
Abie Izzybloom, one of three scholars.

Individual Plays—1915-1938, continued

KASER, ARTHUR LEROY. Stranded strangers; one-act farcical specialty. Chicago: T. S. Denison & Co. [cop. 1926.] 17 p. 12°. (Denison's specialties.) NBL p.v.152
Levi, at a small-town railroad station, in a hurry to get to Springfield.

—— Such a nice doggie; Hebrew monologue for male. (In his: Headliner monologues. Dayton, Ohio [cop. 1929]. 12°. p. 133–136.) NBF p.v.115

—— Such a tightness! Jewish monologue. (In his: Right over the footlights; a book of monologues. Chicago [cop. 1927]. 12°. p. 28–32.) NBL p.v.179
Sol Kappelstein describes Morris Klofzonski.

—— Them actors from Tater Vine; a farcical specialty for ten male characters... Boston: W. H. Baker Company [cop. 1931]. 24 p. 12°. (Baker's specialties.) NBL p.v.272
Isadore Epstein, one of the actors, renders "Paul Revere's ride."

—— Vait a minute; talking act. Chicago: T. S. Denison & Co. [cop. 1920.] 8 p. 16°. (Denison's vaudeville sketches.)
Abie and Ikey, two friends.

—— Vell! Vell! Vell! a Jewish monologue. (In his: Amateur acts and monologues. Dayton, Ohio [cop. 1928]. 12°. p. 11–13.)

—— When the school bell rings; a schoolroom sketch in one act... Boston: Walter H. Baker Company [cop. 1926]. 12 p. 12°. (Baker's novelty plays.)
One of the pupils is Ikey.

KATAYEV, VALENTIN PETROVICH. Squaring the circle; a comedy in three acts...translated from the Russian by N. Goold-Verschoyle and adapted for English performance. [London:] Wishart and Co., 1934. 110 p. 12°. **QDK

—— Squaring the circle; a jest in three acts ...translated from the Russian by Charles Malamuth and Eugene Lyons. (In: Eugene Lyons, editor, Six Soviet plays. Boston and New York, 1934. 8°. p. 85–154.) **QDK
Written in 1927–28 and first produced in Moscow in 1928 by the "Small Stage" of the Moscow Art Theatre. "The play pokes fun at petit-bourgeois notions of marriage and the family. At the same time it caricatures no less gently silly attempts to discount love as a mere bourgeois prejudice." The characters are members of the League of Communist Youth, among them Abram or Abramchik.
There is a Jewish character in it called Abram. It was first produced in English at the Mercury Theatre, London, Feb. 27, 1934. In New York it was produced at Carnegie Hall, by the Chamber Theatre, March 6, 1935, and at the Lyceum Theatre, Oct. 3, 1935, with Eric Dressler as Abram. For reviews see *Collection of newspaper clippings of dramatic criticism, 1934–35*, v. Se–Sy, and *1935–36*, v. Sec–Ten, † NBL.

KATZ, FRANCES. But we go on forever...! [In one act.] (The Shofar [of Temple Emanu-El]. Montreal, 1933. 8°. v. 4, no. 3, p. 21–23.)
The scene is Hitler's office. The United States is one of the characters.

KAUFMAN, GEORGE S. The butter and egg man; a comedy in three acts. New York: Boni and Liveright [cop. 1926]. 223 p. 12°. NBM

—— —— New York, N. Y., Los Angeles, Cal.: S. French, Inc.; London: S. French, Ltd., cop. 1930. 109 p., 1 l. plates, diagrs. 12°. (French's standard library edition.)
Reprinted in G. H. Leverton, editor, *Plays for the college theater*, New York, 1932, p. 363–395, NAFH.
Extracts from the text, with a running synopsis, are printed in *The Best plays of 1925–26*, New York, 1926, p. 339–377, NAFH.
Produced at the Longacre Theatre, New York, Sept. 23, 1925, with Robert Middlemas as Joseph Lehman, the shoestring Broadway producer, and Lucille Webster as his wife Fannie. Reviewed by G. J. Nathan in *American mercury*, New York, 1925, v. 6, p. 378, * DA; and in *Town & country*, New York, v. 81, Oct. 15, 1925, p. 50, * DA. See also *Collection of newspaper clippings of dramatic criticism, 1925–1926*, v. A–D, † NBL.
First staged at the Playhouse, Cardiff, Aug. 22, 1927, and brought to the Garrick Theatre, London, Aug. 30, 1927, with Robert Middlemas as Joe Lehman and Jane Oaker as Fanny Lehman. Reviewed by Herbert Farjeon (with illus.) in *Graphic*, London, 1927, v. 117, p. 440–441, * DA. Four illustrations are given in *Sketch*, London, v. 139, p. 414, * DA.

—— ...Le gentleman de l'Ohio; comédie en trois actes. Tr. de l'anglais par Louis Thomas ... [Paris: Impr. de l'Illustration,] cop. 1927. 32 p. f°. (La Petite illustration...no. 351, 24 septembre 1927. Théâtre, [nouv. série] no. 190.) † NKM (Petite)
A translation of *The Butter and egg man.*

KAUFMAN, GEORGE S., AND M. C. CONNELLY. Merton of the movies, in four acts; a dramatization of Harry Leon Wilson's story of the same name, by George S. Kaufman and Marc Connelly... New York: S. French [etc.], cop. 1925. 112 p., 3 l. plates, diagrs. 8°. (French's standard library edition.) NBL p.v.120
Reprinted in R. W. Pence, editor, *Dramas by present-day writers*, New York [cop. 1927], p. 465–565, NCO.
Copious extracts, with a running synopsis, are given in *The Best plays of 1922–23*, Boston [cop. 1923], p. 257–303, NAFH.
Produced at the Cort Theatre, New York, Nov. 13, 1922, with Edwin Maxwell as Sigmund Rosenblatt, a movie director, "a Semitic-appearing young man, rather crude." For reviews see *Collection of newspaper clippings of dramatic criticism, 1922–1923*, v. M–R, † NBL.
Staged at the Shaftesbury Theatre, London, April 17, 1923. Reviewed in *Era*, London, v. 86, April 25, 1923, p. 19, † *NAFA*; and in *Truth*, London, 1923, v. 93, p. 754, * DA.

KAUFMAN, GEORGE S., AND EDNA FERBER. Dinner at eight, a play. Garden City, N. Y.: Doubleday, Doran & Company, Inc., 1932. 7 p.l., 3–259 p. 8°. NBM

—— —— London: William Heinemann, Ltd. [1933.] 5 p.l., 3–156 p. 12°.

—— —— New York, N. Y., Los Angeles, Cal.: S. French, Inc.; London: S. French, Ltd. [etc.], cop. 1935. 2 p.l., 3–163(1) p., 3 l. plates, diagrs. 12°. (French's standard library edition.) NBL p.v.346
Many extracts from the dialogue, with a running synopsis, are given in *The Best plays of 1932–33*, New York, 1933, p. 61–104, NAFH.
First produced at the Music Box Theatre, New York, Oct. 27, 1932, with Samuel Levene as Max Kane. He is described as "swarthy, neat and very Broadway...unmistakably Jewish, but he does not talk with an accent." Reviewed by Benjamin De

Individual Plays — 1915–1938, continued

Casseres in *Arts & decoration*, New York, v. 38, Dec., 1932, p. 50–51, *MAA;* and by J. W. Krutch in *Nation*, New York, v. 135, p. 464–465, * *DA.* See also *Collection of newspaper clippings of dramatic criticism, 1932–1933,* v. C–D, † *NBL.*
Produced at the Palace Theatre, London, Jan. 6, 1933, with Dave Burns as Max Kane. Reviewed by Percy Allen in *Drama*, London, 1933, v. 11, p. 65, *NAFA;* by Leslie Rees in *Era*, London, Jan. 11, 1933, p. 9, *NAFA;* by J. T. Grein (with illus.) in *Illustrated London news*, v. 182, p. 90, * *DA; Jewish chronicle*, London, Jan. 13, 1933, p. 36, * *PBE;* by Charles Hemington in *London mercury*, v. 27, p. 358, * *DA;* and by John Pollock in *Saturday review*, London, v. 155, p. 38, * *DA.*

——— …Lundi huit heures; pièce en trois actes d'après G. S. Kaufman et Edna Ferber… [Paris: L'Illustration,] cop. 1933. 42 p., 1 l. f°. (La Petite illustration…no. 635, 29 juillet 1933. Théâtre [nouv. série], no. 329.) † NKM
In this French translation, by Jacques Deval, it was produced at the Théâtre des Ambassadeurs, Paris, April 21, 1933.

——— The royal family; a comedy in three acts. Garden City, N. Y.: Doubleday, Doran & Company, Inc., 1928. 7 p.l., 3–280 p. 12°. 8–NBM

——— The acting edition of The royal family, a comedy in three acts. New York: S. French; London: S. French, Ltd., cop. 1929. 171 p., 1 l. plates, diagrs. 12°. (French's standard library edition.)
Reviewed by W. H. Blumenthal in *American Hebrew*, New York, 1929, v. 125, p. 247, * *PBD.*
A lengthy synopsis, with many extracts from the text, is printed in *The Best plays of 1927–28,* New York, 1928, p. 78–121, *NAFH.*
"The printed text…is a shade fuller than the acting version."
The action passes in the East Fifties, New York, on a November afternoon. Produced at the Selwyn Theatre, Dec. 28, 1927, with Jefferson de Angelis as Oscar Wolfe, theatrical entrepreneur. See *Collection of newspaper clippings of dramatic criticism, 1927–28,* v. Q–S, † *NBL.* Reviewed also in *Jewish exponent*, Philadelphia, v. 82, April 6, 1928, p. 9, * *PBD.*

KAUFMAN, GEORGE S., AND MOSS HART. Merrily we roll along; a play [in three acts]… New York: Random House [cop. 1934]. vii, 211 p. 8°. NBM
Reprinted in part, with running synopses, in *Best plays of 1934–35,* New York, 1935, p. 203–235, *NAFH.*
A play, the action of which goes backward from 1934 to 1916. Produced at the Music Box Theatre, New York, Sept. 29, 1934, with Charles Halton as Mr. Simon Weintraub, inventor of cello-paper in 1922 and as Cyrus Wunthrop, millionaire and art connoisseur in 1934. Other characters intended to be cast as Jewish are Mr. and Mrs. Murney and Sam Frankel, the composer. For reviews see *Collection of newspaper clippings of dramatic criticism, 1934–35,* v. M–O, † *NBL.*

KAUFMAN, GEORGE S., AND H. J. MANKIEWICZ. The good fellow, a play in three acts. New York, N. Y., Los Angeles, Cal.: S. French, Inc.; London: S. French, Ltd., cop. 1931. 111(1) p. plates, diagr. 12°. (French's standard library edition.) NBL p.v.241
A burlesque on the American habit of lodge-joining. The scene is laid in Wilkesbarre, Pa., at the home of such an enthusiast. Produced at the Playhouse Theatre, New York, Oct. 5, 1926, with Jacob Kingsbury as Saul Rabinowitz, fellow townsman and lodge member. Reviewed in *Variety*, New York, v. 84, Oct. 13, 1926, p. 48, † *NAFA.* See also *Collection of newspaper clippings of dramatic criticism, 1926–1927,* v. D–H, † *NBL.*

KAUFMAN, GEORGE S., AND MORRIE RYSKIND. Let 'em eat cake, a sequel to "Of thee I sing," a musical play, by George S. Kaufman and Morrie Ryskind; lyrics by Ira Gershwin; illustrated by Donald McKay. New York: A. A. Knopf, 1933. 6 p.l., 3–241 (i.e. 245), (1) p. illus., plates. 12°. * MZ (Gershwin)
Produced at the Imperial Theatre, New York, Oct. 21, 1933, with Abe Reynolds as Louis Lippman and Grenna Sloan as Mrs. Lippman. For illus. of the staging see *Theatre Guild quarterly*, New York, v. 11, Nov., 1933, p. 15–21, † *NBLA.* For reviews see *Collection of newspaper clippings of dramatic criticism, 1933–1934,* v. I–L, † *NBL.*

——— …Of thee I sing, a musical play, by George S. Kaufman and Morrie Ryskind; lyrics by Ira Gershwin, with a foreword by George Jean Nathan. New York: A. A. Knopf, 1932. 7 p.l., 3–214 p., 1 l. front., plates (1 double). 12°. (The theatre of today, ed. by G. J. Nathan.)

——— ——— New York: A. A. Knopf, 1933. 7 p.l., 3–214 p., 1 l. front., plates (1 double). 8°. (The theatre of today, ed. by G. J. Nathan.)
* MZ (Gershwin)

——— …Of thee I sing. Music by George Gershwin. Lyrics by Ira Gershwin. Book by George S. Kaufman & Morrie Ryskind… New York: New World Music Corp., cop. 1932. Publ. pl. no. N. W. 107–198. 198 p. f°. * MS
Vocal score. English words.
At head of title: Sam H. Harris presents.

——— …Of thee I sing; a musical play. Lyrics by Ira Gershwin. With a foreword by George Jean Nathan. London: Victor Gollancz, Ltd., 1933. 126 p. 12°. * MG p.v.122
Reprinted in *Famous plays of 1933,* London, 1933, p. 577–702, *NAFH;* and in K. H. C. and W. H. Cordell, *The Pulitzer prize plays,* New York [1935], p. 693–743, *NBL.* Synopsis, with extracts, printed in *The Best plays of 1931–32,* New York, 1932, p. 29–64, *NAFH.*
A satire on American political life. First produced, to the music of George Gershwin, at the Music Box, New York, Dec. 26, 1931. Sam Mann acted Louis Lippman, member of the National Campaign Committee. In the mouth of the French ambassador the librettist put the words: "A vous toot du vrh, a vous?" Reviewed by F. Fergusson in *Bookman*, New York, 1932, v. 74, p. 561–562, * *DA;* by E. Van R. Wyatt in *Catholic world*, New York, 1932, v. 134, p. 587–588, * *DA;* by Stark Young in *New republic*, New York, 1932, v. 70, p. 97–98, * *DA;* (with illus.) in *Stage*, New York, v. 9, Feb., 1932, p. 4, 17–20, *NBLA;* and by J. Hutchens in *Theatre arts monthly*, New York, 1932, v. 16, p. 196, 448, *NBLA.* See also *Collection of newspaper clippings of dramatic criticism, 1931–1932,* v. M–O, † *NBL.*

KAVANAUGH, KATHARINE. Hero-by-the-hour; a comedy in three acts… Chicago: Dramatic Publishing Company [cop. 1930]. 83 p. diagr. 12°. (Sergel's acting drama.)
Wolf and Ruby ("Mr. and Mrs. Ganef"), two jewel thieves.

——— Rose of the East Side; a comedy in three acts… Chicago: T. S. Denison & Company [cop. 1928]. 96 p. 12°. (Denison's select plays.) NBL p.v.200
The Schlagenheimer family and what happens to it, while becoming suddenly wealthy and later poor again.

Individual Plays — 1915-1938, continued

KAVANAUGH, KATHARINE. A thriving business; a farce in one act for seven men. Chicago: Dramatic Publishing Company [cop. 1932]. 21 p. 12°. (Sergel's acting drama.)
Place: interior of a women's clothing store in a small town.
Ike and Moe, "two Jewish gentlemen," speak in dialect.

——— You're the doctor! a farce in three acts... Chicago: Dramatic Publishing Company [cop. 1933]. 96 p. 12°.
Moe Rosenberg, the tricky lawyer of the villain.

KAYE, DONALD, AND W. MCNALLY. We, us & company; a farce comedy and burlesque [in one act]. (McNally's bulletin. New York, 1930. 8°. no. 16, p. 64–69.)
Mr. Jacob, the boss, to be personated by "a Hebrew comedian."

KEARNEY, PATRICK. Elmer Gantry; a drama in three acts. From the novel of the same name by Sinclair Lewis. Produced at the Playhouse, New York, Aug. 9, 1928.
Leo Cooper played the part of Rabbi Bernard Amos, associated with the Rev. Gantry in the latter's local Committee on Public Morals. Reviewed in *Billboard*, Cincinnati, v. 40, Aug. 18, 1928, p. 7, † *MZA*; *Variety*, New York, v. 92, Aug. 15, 1928, p. 48, † *NAFA*; and in *Collection of newspaper clippings of dramatic criticism, 1928–1929*, v. E-G, † *NBL*.

KELLEY, JESSIE A. The rummage sale; an entertainment for four men and ten women [in one act]. Chicago: T. S. Denison & Co. [cop. 1916.] 25 p. 16°. (Denison's specialties.)   NBL p.v.57
Mrs. Rusacow "who is arrested," and Mr. Goldman "who wants to be a dude," among the customers at the sale.

KENNEDY, MARGARET, AND BASIL DEAN. The constant nymph; a play in three acts from the novel of Margaret Kennedy. Garden City, N. Y.: Doubleday, Page & Company, 1926. 5 p.l., 271 p. 12°.   NCR

——— ——— London: William Heinemann, Ltd. [1926.] 5 p.l., 128 p. 8°.

——— ——— London: S. French, Ltd.; New York: S. French, Inc., cop. 1930. 105 p. plates. 12°. (French's acting edition. no. 864.)
Produced at the New Theatre, London, Sept. 14, 1926, with Keneth Kent as Jacob Birnbaum, the "fat, little" but understanding impresario, who marries Tony Sanger, sister to Tessa, the constant nymph. Reviewed by J. E. Agate in his *Contemporary theatre, 1926*, London, 1927, p. 155–164, *NAFA*; and by Milton Waldman in *London mercury*, v. 15, p. 83–85, * *DA*. Stage illustrations are given in *Play pictorial*, London, 1927, v. 50, p. 33–52, † *NCOA*.
Produced at the Selwyn Theatre, New York, Dec. 9, 1926, with Louis Sorin as Birnbaum. Reviewed by G. J. Nathan in *American mercury*, New York, 1927, v. 10, p. 246–248, * *DA*; by Stark Young in *New republic*, New York, 1926, v. 49, p. 160–161, * *DA*; and by J. M. Brown in *Theatre arts monthly*, New York, 1927, v. 11, p. 100, *NBLA*. See also *Collection of newspaper clippings of dramatic criticism, 1926–1927*, v. A-C, † *NBL*.

KENNEL, RUTH E., AND J. N. WASHBURNE. They all come to Moscow; a comedy... [New York: G. Morse, 1933.] [129] f. 4°.   † NCOF
Various paging.
Reproduced from typewritten copy.
In a prologue and three acts.
Presented by the Players Theatre at the Lyceum Theatre, New York, May 11, 1933, with Marshalov as Lebetz, a Russian-American engineer, and Aileen Poe as Molly Mintz, his secretary. The scene is Moscow. For reviews see *Collection of newspaper clippings of dramatic criticism, 1932–33*, v. T-Y, † *NBL*.

KENYON, DORIS MARGARET. A sidewalk controversy in the Ghetto [in one scene]. (In her: Humorous monologues. New York, 1921. 16°. p. 33–37.)   NBL p.v.83
Mrs. Einstein speaking.

KERR, SOPHIE. Tigers is only cats [a dramatic reading, in one act]. Sioux City, Iowa: Wetmore Declamation Bureau, cop. 1931. 3 f. f°. Typewritten.
Mr. Goldmark, theatrical manager, and Aunt Kate with her "man-eating" tiger.

KILIK, MRS. DAVID, AND MRS. P. S. BIRNBAUM. "Do you know?" [New York, 1937.] 4 f. 4°.
Caption-title.
Reproduced from typewritten copy.
A one-act skit for chapters of the National Council of Jewish Women. It was first staged at the Essex House, New York City, March 22, 1937.

KINGSLEY, SIDNEY. ...Dead end; a play in three acts. New York: Random House [cop. 1936]. 155 p., 1 l. illus. 12°.   NBM
Reprinted in part, with running synopses, in *Best plays of 1935–36*, New York, 1936, p. 239–276, *NAFH*.
A play of boy-life in the New York East River slum neighborhoods. Produced at the Belasco Theatre, New York, Oct. 28, 1935, with B. Punsly as Milty Schwartz, one of the gang. For reviews see *Collection of newspaper clippings of dramatic criticism, 1935–36*, v. C-Dea, † *NBL*.

——— ...Men in white, a play in three acts. New York: Covici Friede [cop. 1933]. 137 p., 1 l. front., plates. 8°.   NBM

——— ——— London: Victor Gollancz, Ltd., 1934. 116 p., 2 l. nar. 8°.
Presented in the form of a running story, with the high-spots reproduced in actual dialogue from the text, in *Best plays of 1933–34*, New York, 1934, p. 76–114, *NAFH*.
The chief characters are surgeons in a hospital. Produced with success by the Group Theatre at the Broadhurst Theatre, New York, Sept. 26, 1933, with Morris Carnovsky as Dr. Levine. For reviews see *Collection of newspaper clippings of dramatic criticism, 1933–1934*, v. M-O, † *NBL*.
Reprinted in *Famous plays of 1934*, London, 1934, p. 137–255, *NAFH*.
In an Anglicized version by Merton Hodge it was produced at the Lyric Theatre, London, June 28, 1934. Reviewed (with illus.) by B. W. M. in *Theatre world*, London, 1934, v. 22, p. 65, 130–131, *MWA*.
In Budapest, in a translation by Zsolto Harsanyi, it was presented at the Vigszinhaz Theatre, March 21, 1934.
In a German translation it was produced by the Arbeitsgemeinschaft des Breslauer Kulturbands, November, 1936. See *Central-Verein-Zeitung*, Berlin, 1936, Jahrg. 15, Beiblatt, Dec. 3, p. 1.

——— Люди в белых халатах; пьеса в 4-х действиях и 7 картинах. (Октябрь. Москва, 1935. 8°. Feb., 1935, p. 35–73.)   * QCA
Translated into Russian by Ilya Rubinstein.

KIRSCHNER, HERBERT. Shylock's son: a play in one act. (Emanu-El. San Francisco, 1923. v. 56, Sept. 7, 1923 p. 96–98.)
An episode of racial prejudice taking place in the editor's office of a local newspaper.

Individual Plays — 1915–1938, continued

KLEAGLEMAN, HAROLD, PSEUD. Dredging dad. (Zeta Beta Tau quarterly. New York, 1926. 4°. v. 11, no. 1, p. 12–13.) SSY
"A dramatization of a philosophical tract dictated by Mohamet to Peter the Great while in a state of coma."

KLEIMAN, BLANCHE P. Abarbanel; a sketch in four scenes. (Jewish teacher. Cincinnati, 1937. 4°. v. 5, March, 1937, f. 26–32.) *PYW
Time: 1492. Among the characters are Columbus, Don Isaac Abravanel (1437–1508), whose 500th birthday anniversary was observed in 1937, and (l'avdil) the grand inquisitor, Torquemada.
Produced by the Students' Circle of the Shearith Israel School of Kansas City, Mo.

KLEIN, YETTA, AND FLORINE SCHWARZ. All America's children [in one scene]. (In their: Plays for school children. Boston [cop. 1930]. 12°. p. 133–138.) NAFH p.v.69
A Jewish girl is among them.
Played by the children of Public School 188, Manhattan, New York City.

KLONSKY, MILTON, AND T. BRANFMAN. Peace: the twenty years. (Shofer. Washington, D. C., 1938. 12°. v. 14, no. 3, p. 12–17.) *PYP
A peace play, in one act.

KNOBLOCK, EDWARD, AND BEVERLEY NICHOLS. Evensong; a play in three acts. Adapted from the novel of Beverley Nichols... London: S. French, Ltd.; New York: S. French, Inc., cop. 1932. 90 p., 3 pl. 8°. (French's acting edition. no. 1357.)
The plot centers around a prima donna, who had lost her hold upon the public and is attempting a final season in London.
Produced at the Queen's Theatre, London, June 30, 1932, with Reginald Tate as Julius Rosenberg, impresario, described as "an intelligent-looking Jew of an international type." Reviewed in *Theatre world*, London, 1932, v. 18, p. 65–66, MWA. For stage illustrations see ibid., p. 71–82.
Produced at the Selwyn Theatre, New York, Jan. 31, 1933, with Walter Armin as Rosenberg. See *Collection of newspaper clippings of dramatic criticism, 1932–1933*, v. E–H, † NBL.

KOBER, ARTHUR. "Having wonderful time"... Foreword by Marc Connelly. New York: Random House [cop. 1937]. xiii p., 1 l., 17–203 p. 8°. NBM
In three acts. Deals with the vacationists from the Bronx at Camp Kare-Free in the Berkshires. Produced at the Lyceum Theatre, New York, Feb. 20, 1937. For reviews see *Collection of newspaper clippings of dramatic criticism, 1936–1937*, v. E–Hir, † NBL. See also Joseph Kaye in *Brooklyn Jewish Center review*, Brooklyn, N. Y., v. 17, April, 1937, p. 10, 18, 22, * PBD.

KOBRIN, LEON. The black sheep. (In: Isaac Goldberg, Six plays of the Yiddish theatre: second series. Boston [1918]. 12°. p. 149–180.) *PTP
The black sheep is the white-slaver son of a learned and pious father and brother of a cultured sister.
Produced by the Young Men's and Young Women's Hebrew Association of Philadelphia, Dec. 19, 1926.

—— The eternal mystery. [A prologue to a drama.] (American Hebrew. New York, 1916. 4°. v. 99, p. 654, 656.) *PBD

—— The secret of life. (In: Isaac Goldberg, translator, Six plays of the Yiddish theatre: second series. Boston [1918]. 12°. p. 181–197.) *PTP
The above two titles are two different translations of the same one-act morality, which appeared in the original in *Zukunft*, New York, 1917, v. 22, p. 85–87, * PBB. The speakers are an old man, a woman spirit, and a poet.

KOHLER, MRS. A. S. When? a playlet [in five scenes. New York: National Council of Jewish Women, Dept. of Peace, 1928?]. 2 p.l., 6 l. 4°.
Mimeographed.
A peace play. The characters are Uncle Sam, preparedness, disarmament, a weary pilgrim in search of peace, etc.

KOTTLER, ESTHER, AND ANNA DREXLER. Hadassah on trial. [In one act. New York: Hadassah, 1933?] 5 f. f°.
Caption-title.
Mimeographed.

KRAFT, IRMA. Ambition in Whitechapel. (In her: The power of Purim, and other plays. Philadelphia, 1915. 12°. p. 133–162.) *PSQ

—— Because he loved David so! (In her: The power of Purim, and other plays. Philadelphia, 1915. 12°. p. 163–189.) *PSQ
The characters in this play, and in the preceding *Ambition in Whitechapel*, are school children.

—— The power of Purim. (In her: The power of Purim, and other plays. Philadelphia, 1915. 12°. p. 9–54.) *PSQ
Time: beginning of the present century. Place: the outskirts of a small village, Hatzfeld, in southern Germany. In memory of what happened on Purim, the Siegel children play a game of deliverance from a band of kidnapping gipsies.
It was staged by the Religious School of Congregation Emanu-El, New York, March 19, 1916. See *Emanu-El review*, New York, v. 1, April, 1916, p. 9, * PXY.

—— To save his country. (In her: The power of Purim, and other plays. Philadelphia, 1915. 12°. p. 93–132.) *PSQ
How a 16-year-old French boy, who followed Napoleon to Elba and returned to Paris to fight for his Emperor, comes back to his parents on Passover eve, 1816, in Rochefort, France.

KRAFT, LOUIS. A daughter of her people [in one act]. New York: Jewish Welfare Board [1927]. 7 f. 4°.
Cover-title.
Multigraphed copy.
Scene is laid in Poland, during the feast of Purim where a modern Esther intervenes on behalf of her people.

KREIMER, MILDRED WEINBERG. Mother of exiles; a play in three acts, a prologue and an epilogue. Cincinnati: Department of Synagogue and School Extension of the Union of American Hebrew Congregations [cop. 1931]. 31 p. 12°. *PSQ p.v.2
"Principal bibliography," p. 30.
Prize play, Pennsylvania Federation of Temple Sisterhoods, 1928–29.
Scene: Barcelona, Spain, 1492. Columbus and Luis de Santangel, treasurer of Aragon, are among the characters. The prologue and the epilogue, in modern America.

Individual Plays — 1915-1938, continued

KREYMBORG, A. Brother Bill; a little play from Harlem. illus. (Theatre arts monthly. New York, 1927. 4°. v. 11, p. 299-306.) † NBLA
Reprinted in *One act plays for stage and study, fourth series*, New York, 1928, p. 213-221, NCO; in Edith J. R. Isaacs, compiler, *Plays of American life and fantasy*, New York, 1929, p. 183-192, NBL; and in the author's *How do you do, Sir? and other plays*, New York, 1934, p. 83-93.
"A syncopated study in modern adolescence whose action takes place in a Harlem apartment. Bennie and Jennie are arguing. They have argued before; they will argue again."

—— Frank and Mr. Frankenstein (a play upon the dollar). (In his: How do you do Sir? and other short plays. New York, 1934. 12°. p. 67-73.)
A complete scene, in sonnet form, out of a three-act play in preparation.
A tragic satire on the depression. Frank is the employee, and Mr. Frankenstein is the bank president.

—— I'm not complaining; a kaffeeklatsch. illus. (Theatre arts monthly. New York, 1931. 4°. v. 15, p. 493-498.) NBLA
Mrs. K. and Mrs. B. discuss their children. The scene "might have been in Brooklyn or the Bronx, or midway between, on Manhattan."
Reprinted in *New plays for women and girls*, New York, 1932, p. 245-255, NBL; and in the author's *How do you do, Sir? and other short plays*, New York, 1934, p. 1-14.

KRIMSKY, JOSEPH. The refugee [in one act]. (Menorah journal. New York, 1924. 4°. v. 10, p. 147-154.) *PBD
Reprinted in his *Revisits and revisions*, New York, 1924, p. 131-148, BCK.
The scene is the Rumanian-Russian frontier and Bedloe's Island, New York harbor. The author, an American relief worker in post-war Europe, terms his play "a substantially true story." It concerns the immigration question and was published as "a human document," when agitation for further restriction of immigration was pending in Congress.

KUGEL, HARRY JACOB. Souvenir of the family reunion, in honor of Rebekah Kohut; held at her home, April thirteenth, nineteen twenty. [New York, 1920.] 16 p. 16°.
A playlet in one scene. The speakers are the members of the Kohut family.

KUHN, SAMUEL O. The shadow of war [in one act]. (Review. Philadelphia, 1916. 12°. v. 11, Feb., 1916, p. 37-43.)
An episode during the Civil war, some time in 1864, somewhere in the South, involving the encounter of two Jewish officers, Union and Confederate.

KUMMER, MRS. CLARE (BEECHER). The rescuing angel; a comedy in three acts. New York: S. French [etc.], cop. 1923. 100 p. 12°. (French's standard library ed.) NBL p.v.98
It was produced at the Hudson Theatre, New York, Oct. 8, 1917, with Robert McWade as Meyer Kolinsky, a lawyer who acts as matchmaker to the heroine. For reviews see *Collection of newspaper clippings of dramatic criticism, 1917-1918*, v. P-Y, † NBL.

KYNE, PETER BERNARD. The go-getter. (Golden book magazine. New York, 1927. 8°. v. 5, p. 149-163.) *DA
Under the title *The Blue vase* it was produced by the Pacific Gas and Electric Company in San Francisco in February, 1932. See *Journal of electricity, power and gas*, San Francisco, 1932, v. 68, p. 181, † VGA.
B. Cohen of Cohen's Art Shop is the owner of a blue vase which has been set as a challenge to, and prize for, excelling salesmanship.

KYTE, JOHN. One good turn; a comedy-drama in four acts... Milwaukee, Wis.: Catholic Dramatic Movement, 1933. 3 p.l., 97 p. 12°. ([Library of Catholic plays.]) NAFH p.v.127
"The good turn" was done by Max Webber, gunman, who had saved his officer's life in the World war. In the play, the two are a prisoner and a prosecuting district attorney. Solomon Blume, "hoodlum," is Webber's associate in crime and fellow prisoner.

LAMERS, WILLIAM MATHIAS. The hired ghost; comedy in three acts... Briggsville, Wis.: Catholic Dramatic Movement, cop. 1931. 51 p. 12°. ([Library of Catholic plays.]) NBL p.v.279
Mr. and Mrs. Finkbaum, hotel guests of the newly rich type.

LANDA, GERTRUDE, AND M. J. LANDA. For all eternity. [In one act.] (In: H. Zimmerman, compiler, Plays of Jewish life. [London, 1931.] 12°. p. 31-41.) NCO (Zimmerman)
A war playlet, showing the respective loyalties of two Jewish soldiers: one, a German; the other, a Russian. First produced at the Empire Theatre, Hackney, Eng., April 15, 1915, with Maurice Cowan as the German soldier, and again as part of an "all-Jewish matinée" at the Pavillion Theatre, London, June 15, 1916. Reviewed in *Era*, London, v. 78, April 21, 1915, p. 16, † NAFA. See also Landa, p. 298-301.

LANDAU, JUDAH LEO. Conflicting worlds, a drama of present day Jewish life...translated from the original Hebrew by D. Mierowsky (Ben Eliezer). New York: Bloch Publishing Company, 1933. xii p., 1 l., 201 p. 12°. *PSH
In four acts.
"First published in [Jerusalem] 1921, under the title of 'Lefanim o Leachor' (Forward or backward). It is a modern problem play and gives expression to the deep sense of unrest that exists in Jewry."
The preface is largely a biography of the author by the translator.
Reviewed in *American Hebrew*, New York, 1933, v. 133, p. 200, *PBD; by Louis Cournos in *B'nai B'rith magazine*, Cincinnati, 1934, v. 48, p. 166, *PYP; *Jewish chronicle*, London, Jan. 12, 1934, p. 18-19, *PBE; *Jewish quarterly review*, Philadelphia, 1933, new series, v. 24, p. 206, *PBE; *Jewish standard*, London, v. 1, July 28, 1933, p. 21, *PBE; and in *Temple bulletin* (The Temple), Cleveland, v. 20, Oct. 22, 1933, p. 5-6.

LANG, MRS. LEON S. Disease takes a holiday. [In a prologue and two acts. New York: Hadassah, 1933.] 5 f. f°.
Caption-title.
Mimeographed.

—— The voice within; a playlet for sisterhoods [in one act]. (Women's League outlook. New York, 1936. 4°. v. 6, no. 3, p. 6-7.)
Six characters: mother, daughter, boy, and three voices.

LANGDON, WILLIAM CHAUNCY. In honor of Shakespeare; a dramatic tribute for the Shakespeare tercentenary celebration of Indiana University, at Bloomington, Indiana, April twenty sixth, nineteen sixteen. Bloomington: Indiana University, 1916. 24 p. 8°. *NCV p.v.11
Shylock is one of the characters, among the others of Shakespeare's creations, who appear before their author.

Individual Plays — 1915–1938, continued

LANHAM, CEORA B. Mrs. Schuster on the radio. [Chicago: E. Means Dramatic Service, cop. 1926.] 2 l. 8°.
Caption-title.

LANHAM, FRITZ GARLAND. The pedler. (In: Billie Oneal, compiler, Prize-winning one act plays, book 1. Dallas, Texas [cop. 1930]. 12°. p. 51–78.) NBL
Harold Glenn, one of two suitors, disguises himself as Jake Arrabolinski, a peddler, to gain the hand of Ethel Lane.

LARDNER, RING W., AND G. S. KAUFMAN. June moon; a comedy in a prologue and three acts. New York, London: C. Scribner's Sons, 1930. vi p., 4 l., 3–187 p. 8°. NBM

—— —— New York City, N. Y., Los Angeles, Cal.: S. French, Inc.; London: S. French, Ltd., cop. 1931. 104 p., 3 l. plates, diagrs., music. 12°. (French's standard library edition.)
Reviewed by Walter Prichard Eaton in *Books*, New York, v. 6, June 29, 1930, p. 17, † *NAA*.
Copious extracts from the text, with a running synopsis, are printed in *The Best plays of 1929–30*, New York, 1930, p. 236–271, *NAFH*. Also, with illus., in *Theatre magazine*, New York, v. 51, Feb., 1930, p. 32–35, 58, † *NBLA*.
A satire on song writers and Tin Pan Alley, based on R. W. Lardner's short story *Some like them cold* in his volume *Round up*, New York, 1929. First produced at the Broadhurst Theatre, New York, Oct. 9, 1929, with Florence D. Rice as Goldie (Miss Goldberg), H. Rosenthal as Maxie Schwartz, and Philip Loeb as Benny Fox. For reviews see *Collection of newspaper clippings of dramatic criticism, 1929–1930*, v. I–L, † *NBL*.

LARRIMORE, LIDA. Last tag! a play in one act... Boston: Walter H. Baker Company, cop. 1927. 16 p. 12°. (Baker's edition of plays.)
Swartz, "speaking with a strong Jewish accent," installment collector for a furniture store.

LASSER, FLORENCE. The story of the I. L. G. W. U.; a radio play in six episodes... New York: International Ladies' Garment Workers' Union, Educational Department [1936]. [67] f. 4°.
Various paging.
Multigraphed copy.
Originally presented over WEVD.
The six episodes featured are as follows: 1. Arriving in the land of liberty, Ellis Island, in 1886; 2. Dawn and birth of the International, 1890; 3. The shirtwaist workers, 1909; 4. The cloakmakers' strike of 1910; 5. The Triangle factory fire, 1911; 6. The blue eagle, under the NRA, 1933.

The LAST round-up; or, The shooting of Gasoline Gus. (Petroleum world. Los Angeles, Cal., 1934. 4°. v. 31, Jan., 1934, p. 23–24, 26.) † VHYA
Staged by the California Oil and Gas Association, at the Los Angeles Biltmore, Dec. 20, 1933, as a satire on the NRA price control system. Among the characters is one Rosenblatt (Dan Hogan), an oil buyer.

LAWSON, JOHN HOWARD. Gentlewoman. (In his: With a reckless preface; two plays. New York [cop. 1934]. 8°. p. 113–221.) NBM
A play about the love of a woman of the upper class for a roughneck. Produced at the Cort Theatre, New York, March 22, 1934, with Morris Carnovsky as Dr. Lewis Golden. For reviews see *Collection of newspaper clippings of dramatic criticism, 1933–34*, v. F–H, † *NBL*.

—— —— Processional; a jazz symphony of American life, in four acts; the Theatre Guild version, with eight illustrations from photographs of the Theatre Guild production. New York: T. Seltzer, 1925. xii p., 2 l., 3–218 p. front., plates. 12°. NBM
Reprinted in E. B. Watson and W. B. Pressey, compilers, *Contemporary dramas: American plays*, New York [cop. 1931], v. 1, p. 181–289, *NBL (Watson)*.
"I have endeavored in the present play... to reflect to some extent the color and movement of the American processional as it streams about us." — Preface.
From a Jewish point of view, the play is a study of the disintegrating forces of Jewish life in the smaller American cities. Produced at the Garrick Theatre, New York, Jan. 12, 1925, with Philip Loeb as Isaac Cohen and June Walker as his daughter, Sadie. The scene is in a large town in the West Virginia coal fields during a strike. Reviewed by G. J. Nathan in *American mercury*, 1925, v. 4, p. 372–373, * *DA*; and by G. V. Seldes, in *Dial*, v. 78, p. 341–344, * *DA*. Illustrations are given in *Drama*, Mt. Morris, Ill., v. 15, p. 101, 103, 109, *NAFA*. See also *Collection of newspaper clippings of dramatic criticism, 1924–1925*, v. M-R, † *NBL*.

—— —— Success story, a play. New York: Farrar & Rinehart, Incorporated [cop. 1932]. 6 p.l., 3–245 p. 8°. NBM
Produced at Maxine Elliott's Theatre, New York, Sept. 26, 1932, with Luther Adler as Sol Ginsberg, the hero of the play, and Stella Adler as Sarah Glassman, secretary. Reviewed by N. H. Adlerblum in *Jewish forum*, New York, 1932, v. 15, p. 329–330, * *PBD*; by J. W. Krutch in *Nation*, New York, v. 135, p. 336–337, * *DA*; by Stark Young in *New republic*, New York, v. 72, p. 233–235, * *DA*; by E. K. W. in *Opinion*, New York, v. 3, Nov., 1932, p. 39, * *PBD*; and by Creighton Peet in *Theatre arts monthly*, New York, v. 16, p. 955–957, *NBLA*. See also *Collection of newspaper clippings of dramatic criticism, 1932–1933*, v. R–S, † *NBL*.
In England it was first seen at the Shilling Theatre, Fulham, Jan. 1, 1934, and brought to London, at the Cambridge Theatre, Feb. 15, 1934, with Esmé Percy as Ginsburg and Beatrix Lehman as Sarah Glassman. See *Jewish chronicle*, London, Feb. 23, 1934, p. 42, * *PBE*.

LAZARON, PAULINE H. Fraternity; a play [in one act]. Written for the Baltimore Hebrew Congregation Sisterhood. New York: Bloch Pub. Company, 1921. 19 p. 12°.
Place: Arrowmore College.
A modern college play. Theme based on racial discrimination in student fraternal organizations.

LEE, HENRY WASHINGTON. El Cid Compeador; an opera in three acts, eight scenes; Spain, latter part of the eleventh century... Chicago: Ritzmann, Brookes & Co. [cop. 1917.] 4 p.l., 11–34 p. 12°. NBM
An operatic libretto the plot of which is based on *Gesta Roderici*, a Latin chronicle, and the poem of the Cid. Rachel and Vidas are two Jewish moneylenders.

LEVEGOOD, LYNNE LORENTUS. ...Comedy mock trial; "A landlord and his tenants"; or "Dispensing (with) justice"... New York: Elco Printing Co., cop. 1927. 32 p. 8°. NAFH p.v.17
Cover-title.
Schmulowitz, landlord, vs. McSwatt, tenant.
Produced by the Victoria Men's League, Jamaica, L. I., N. Y.

LEVENBERG, MORRIS. Empty victory; an original one act play. (A. Z. A. monthly program. Omaha, Neb., 1938. 4°. v. 10, no. 8, p. 17–25.)
A play of Nazi Germany. * PBD

Individual Plays — 1915-1938, continued

LEVIN, MEYER. Yehuda. New York: J. Cape & H. Smith [cop. 1931]. 2 p.l., 374 p. 12°. NBO

Feinberg, Adolph, and D. Polish. Yehuda; a dramatization in three acts, from the novel of the same name by M. Levin, was staged at the Wise Center, Cincinnati, Ohio, Feb. 21, 1933.
The production was a part of the festivities of the fifth annual Chamisha Oser be-Shevat celebration by the Cincinnati Young Judaea Organization. Leonard Berman acted the violinist chalutz Yehuda; Beatrice Goldman, Yocheved, daughter of a Chassidic family; Gerald Touff, Yossef Brenner; and Morton Keller, Paley, an American Jew. The scene of action is the colony Carmel, on the banks of the river Kishon, in Palestine. The play deals with the physical and spiritual life of the young Jewish pioneers. See *American Israelite*, Cincinnati, v. 79, Feb. 16, 1933, p. 3, * *PBD;* and *Every Friday*, Cincinnati, v. 12, Feb. 17, 1933, p. 1, * *PBD.*

LEVIN, ZEBULLON. The doctor's first operation; a comedy. (In: Bessie F. White, translator, Nine one-act plays from the Yiddish. Boston [cop. 1932]. 8°. p. 59–81.) * PTP
A comedy based on the "matchmaking" theme.

—— Poetry and prose. (In: Isaac Goldberg, translator, Six plays of the Yiddish theatre: second series. Boston [1918]. 12°. p. 113–143.)
* PTP
Prize play, in 1918, of the I. L. Perez Writers' Club. Produced by the Menorah societies of Harvard and Radcliffe colleges at the Agassiz House, Cambridge, April 10, 1926, with Fay Goell as Anna and L. Huberman as Grubin.

LEVINGER, ELMA C. (EHRLICH). At the gates; a one act modern play. Cincinnati: Dept. of Synagog and School Extension of the Union of American Hebrew Congregations [cop. 1925]. 29 p. 12°. * PSQ p.v.4
Repr.: *American Hebrew*, New York, 1919, v. 104, p. 316, 336, * *PBD.*
Early in the twentieth century, at Ellis Island, N. Y. A father who is refused admission and his children who remain in this country.

—— The burden, a play in one act. Boston: W. H. Baker & Co., 1918. 32 p. 12°. (Baker's acting plays.) NBL p.v.126
First prize play of the Sinai Center, Chicago, which produced it, Oct. 3, 1917. Its theme is the problem of immigrant parents and their American children. S. Bloom played the father Mendel; Earl Ludgin, his son Isadore; and Helen Reinsberg, the daughter Sarah. The scene is laid in a tenement house on the East Side of New York. See *Reform advocate*, Chicago, 1917, v. 53, p. 182, * *PBD.*

—— "Eight o'clock sharp"; a too familiar scene. (Jewish criterion. Pittsburgh, 1920. f°. v. 54, March 5, 1920, p. 5, 25.) * PBD
A take-off on the management of Jewish public meetings and "affaires."

—— The great hope; a modern play. (Stratford journal. Boston, 1919. 8°. v. 5, p. 230–235.) * DA
The great hope is the Jewish Messianic ideal. The time is during the World war, in a country in eastern Europe.

—— The heathen who stood on one foot. [In one scene.] (In her: Entertaining programs for the assembly. Cincinnati [cop. 1930]. 8°. p. 94–97.) * PSY
The characters are Hillel, Shammai, and Gaius, a young heathen. Based on a Talmudic legend.

—— How Succoth came to Chayim, a modern play in one act. Cincinnati, O.: Department of Synagog and School Extension of the Union of American Hebrew Congregations [cop. 1923]. 16 p. 12°. * PSQ p.v.4
Reprinted in her *Jewish festivals in the religious school*, Cincinnati, 1923, p. 263–278, * *PSY.*
Time: the present. Place: a farmhouse in northern Minnesota. How a foreign-born boy influences an American family to observe Succoth.
Produced at the Temple Emanu-El, San Francisco, Oct. 9, 1927. See *Temple chronicle of Temple Emanu-El*, San Francisco, 1927, v. 4, no. 8, p. 2, * *PXY.*

—— ...In the night watches; a drama in one act, for youth clubs... Cincinnati: Dept. of Synagog and School Extension [1932]. 9 f. 4°. (Dramatics. series III, no. 1.)
Cover-title.
Mimeographed.
Repr.: American Hebrew, New York, 1921, v. 109, p. 471–472, * *PBD.*
On board the *Santa Maria* just before dawn, Oct. 12, 1492, when land is sighted by Columbus's crew. Alonzo the pilot, Bernal the ship's physician, and Luis de Torres, interpreter, reveal themselves to one another as Marrano Jews. They speak of their trials in old Spain and dare to hope that the newly discovered land might prove a haven for the children of Israel.

—— It is time; a peace play in one act... Boston: Baker's Plays [cop. 1936]. 31 p. 12°.
NBL p.v.397

—— "Let there be light"...a pageant for religious schools [in seven episodes. New York, 1919?]. 27 p. incl. cover-title. 8°.

—— —— Cincinnati: Department of Synagog and School Extension of the Union of American Hebrew Congregations [cop. 1923]. 32 p., 2 l. illus. 12°. * PSQ p.v.4
Reprinted in her *Jewish festivals in the religious school*, Cincinnati, 1923, p. 517–549, * *PSY.*
Time: episodes depicting Jewish history from Abraham to modern life in America.

—— The magic circle, a series of pictures to illustrate how Thanksgiving came to be. [In one scene.] (In her: Entertaining programs for the assembly. Cincinnati [cop. 1930]. 8°. p. 51–56.) * PSY
Among the historical characters are Moses and Elder Brewster.

—— Pilgrims to Palestine; a travelogue in pictures to music and poetry. (In her: Entertaining programs for the assembly. Cincinnati [cop. 1930]. 8°. p. 73–78.) * PSY
Among the characters are Judah ha-Levi, Nachmanides, Joseph Caro, Moses Montefiore, and Theodor Herzl.

—— The poor student. (A story of the boy Hillel.) (Jewish child. New York, 1918. f°. v. 6, no. 43, p. 1, 4.) * PBD
Reprinted in her *Entertaining programs for the assembly*, Cincinnati [cop. 1930], p. 91–94, * *PSY.*
The playlet is based on a legendary episode in the life of Hillel, a doctor of the law in Jerusalem in the time of King Herod. The story tells of the great zeal of young Hillel for learning, and the scene is a lecture room in an academy at Jerusalem.

—— The priest people. [In one act.] (Review. Philadelphia, 1916. 12°. v. 12, Nov., 1916, p. 3–18.)

Individual Plays — 1915–1938, continued

LEVINGER, ELMA C. (EHRLICH). The Purim robe; a little episode of mediaeval Jewry [in one act]. illus. (American Hebrew. New York, 1920. f°. v. 106, p. 458, 488–489.) *PBD
Love story of a Jewish maiden and a Christian humanist, in the Judengasse of a German city, about 1500. The incident takes place on Purim eve.

—— The tenth man. (Drama. Mount Morris, Ill., 1929. f°. v. 19, p. 204–206, 220–221.) NAFA

—— The tenth man; a play in one act. Boston: W. H. Baker Company [cop. 1931]. 32 p. illus. 12°. (Baker's royalty plays.)
"A word or so on producing 'The tenth man,'" by Charles Freeman, p. 8–10.
An incident among the mystic group of Chassidim, on the eve of Atonement Day, in a Galician village. Originally produced by the Institute Players of the Jewish People's Institute, Chicago.
Translated by Marta N. Bernstein, under title "Manca il decimo," in *Rassegna mensile di Israel*, Roma, 1936, v. 11, p. 128–141, *PBH.

—— The unlighted Menorah; a Chanukah fantasy of the time of Felix Mendelssohn, in one act. Cincinnati, O.: Department of Synagog and School Extension of the Union of American Hebrew Congregations [cop. 1923]. 12 p. 12°. *PBM p.v.98
Also printed in her *Jewish festivals in the religious school*, Cincinnati, 1923, p. 305–316, *PSY.
The characters are Felix Mendelssohn-Bartholdy, his parents, and his grandfather Moses Mendelssohn (seen in a dream). The time is a November evening in the year 1835.

—— The wall between; a one-act play... Chicago: T. S. Denison & Company [cop. 1935]. 20 p. 12°. (Denison's one-act plays.)
The scene is a mountain camp in New York state, and the characters are mostly young people. The wall between is the wall separating non-Jews and Jews as regards marriage.

LEVINSON, HERMAN D. Ideals. [In one act.] (Review. Philadelphia, 1917. 12°. v. 12, April, 1917, p. 22–35.)
When loyalties to abstract ideals and to personalities clash.

—— "Riley"; a comedy [in one act]. New York: Bloch Pub. Company, 1922. 14 p. 12°. Repr.: Review, Philadelphia, v. 11, Dec., 1915, p. 32–46.
A skit about snobbishness, pride of race, and a "good" Jew, with an Irish name.

—— To save a life [in one act]. (Review. Philadelphia, 1915. 12°. v. 10, March, 1915, p. 46–55.)
"To save a life" jeopardized by the charge of murder, as viewed by the mother of the accused and by two outsiders, one of whom is a rabbi.

LEVINSON, SAMUEL J. Oil for the lamps of Israel; a Chanukah playlet. (Southwestern Jewish review. San Diego, Cal., 1937. 4°. v. 23, Dec. 2, 1937, p. 22–23.)
"Nine bridge-playing women get religion."

LEVY, BENN WOLF, AND JOHN VAN DRUTEN. Hollywood holiday, an extravagant comedy. London: M. Secker, 1931. 3 p.l., 9–139(1) p. 12°. NCR
In a prologue, three acts, and an epilogue.
Produced at the New Theatre, London, Oct. 15, 1931, with Arthur Finn as Mike Le Mosenthal and Sydney Keith as Lou Katz. Reviewed in *Era*, London, v. 95, Oct. 21, 1931, p. 9, †*NAFA*; by G. J. in *Jewish chronicle*, London, Oct. 23, 1931, p. 35, *PBE; and by Gilbert Wakefield in *Saturday review*, London, v. 152, p. 527, *DA.

LEVY, EMMANUEL. ...Altar-piece; a play in one act... London: H. F. W. Deane & Sons; Boston: The Baker International Play Bureau [cop. 1933]. 23 p. 12°.
At head of title: The year book press series of plays.
Reviewed in *Jewish chronicle*, London, Nov. 9, 1934, p. 29, *PBE.
An episode in the Florence ghetto of the fifteenth century. Presented by the Great Synagogue Literary Society at the fifth annual Drama Festival of the Manchester, Eng., Union of Jewish Literary Societies, Feb. 13, 1932, with S. M. Phillips as Judah, the supposed master Andrea Venecci, and Kathleen Lizar as Hadassah. See *Jewish chronicle*, London, Feb. 19, 1932, p. 27, *PBE; M. P. Pariser in *Unit magazine*, Manchester, 1932, v. 1, no. 8, p. 19–21, and L. Leiwow, ibid., p. 22–23.
In this country it was staged at the Little Theatre of Temple Israel, Boston, Jan. 27, 1935.

—— I believe (I believe with a perfect faith that the Messiah will come...) a play in one act. (In: Sydney Needoff, editor, Five one-act plays of Jewish interest. [Manchester, Eng. 1937.] 8°. p. 65–80.)
Produced by the Great Synagogue Literary and Social Society, Manchester, Eng., at the 7th annual Jewish Drama Festival, March 24, 1934. See *Jewish chronicle*, London, April 13, 1934, p. 40, *PBE; and *Unit magazine*, Manchester, Eng., 1934, v. 2, no. 2, p. 4–6.

LEVY, MELVIN P. Gold eagle Guy; a play... [New York? 1934?] 149 l. 4°. †NCOF
Cover-title.
Reproduced from typewritten copy.

—— —— New York: Random House [cop. 1935]. 188 p. 12°. NBM
The San Francisco waterfront from 1862 to 1906, the year of the earthquake, is the background for the rise, progress and fall of Guy Button. One of the main characters is Adah Isaacs Menken whom Button meets in the first act, when she is at the height of her fame, through the succeeding decades. Produced at the Morosco Theatre, New York, Nov. 28, 1934, with Stella Adler as Menken, "the divine Jewess."
For reviews see *Collection of newspaper clippings of dramatic criticism, 1934–1935*, v. E-G, †*NBL*.
As to Adah Isaacs Menken see *Dictionary of American biography*, v. 12, p. 536–537, *R–AGZ; Bernard Falk, *The Naked lady; or, Storm over Adah*, London [1934], *MWES (Menken)*; and A. Lesser in American Jewish Historical Society, *Publications*, 1937, no. 34, p. 143–147, *IAA*.

LEVY, NEWMAN. Ridiculously old-fashioned. (American Hebrew. New York, 1924. f°. v. 114, p. 694.) *PBD
Scene: Meshumed country, Westchester county, New York.

LEWIS, SINCLAIR, AND S. C. HOWARD. Sinclair Lewis's Dodsworth, dramatized by Sidney Howard. With comments by Sidney Howard and Sinclair Lewis on the art of dramatization ... New York: Harcourt, Brace and Company [cop. 1934]. lxxii, 162 p. plates. 12°. NBM
p. xxi–lix are numbered 315–353 to correspond to the pagination in the standard American edition of the novel, and the text of that part of the novel is reproduced to show the difference between play and novel technique.

—— Sinclair Lewis' Dodsworth... [New York, 1934?] 49, 53, 40 f. 4°. †NCOF
Reproduced from typewritten copy.
Presented in the form of a running story, with the

Individual Plays — 1915-1938, continued

LEWIS, SINCLAIR, AND S. C. HOWARD, *cont'd*
high-spots reproduced in actual dialogue from the text, in *Best Plays of 1933-34*, New York, 1934, p. 115-158, *NAFH*.
Produced at the Shubert Theatre, New York, Feb. 24, 1934, with Frederick Worlock as Arnold Israel, "international financier." See *Collection of newspaper clippings of dramatic criticism, 1933-34*, v. C-E, † *NBL*.
Produced at the Palace Theatre, London, February, 1938. See *Jewish chronicle*, London, Feb. 25, 1938, p. 40, * *PBE*.

LEWISOHN, LUDWIG. Adam; a dramatic history in a prologue, seven scenes and an epilogue. New York and London: Harper & Brothers, 1929. ix, 99(1) p. 8°. NBM
Reviewed by W. P. Eaton in *Books*, New York, v. 6, March 9, 1930, p. 13, † *NAA;* by C. Castelbolognesi in *Israel, La rassegna mensile*, Milano, 1934, v. 9, p. 103-104, * *PBH; Jewish quarterly review*, Philadelphia, 1931, new series, v. 21, p. 351, * *PBE;* by Lionel Trilling in *Menorah journal*, 1930, v. 18, p. 380-381, * *PBD;* and by Isabel Paterson in *New York Herald Tribune*, Dec. 20, 1929, p. 25, * *A*.
Prologue; Jabneh, Judaea, 70 A. D.; seven scenes, Europe and New York; epilogue, a Jewish colony in modern Palestine. Dedicated "to the memory of our martyrs in Eretz Israel in the year 5689."
First staged by the Menorah societies of Harvard and Radcliffe at Agassiz Hall, Cambridge, April 21, 1930. The souvenir programme for the occasion contains "notes" on Adam by H. T. Schnittkind and Isaac Goldberg. See *Jewish advocate*, Boston, v. 55, April 18, 1930, part 2, p. 3, * *PBD*. Produced also by the Temple Players of the Rodeph Sholom League, New York, Feb. 28, 1931. Reviewed by Judah Aryeh in *New York Jewish tribune*, v. 1, March 6, 1931, p. 20-21, * *PBD*.

—— Adam, récit dramatique... texte français de Maxime Piha, suivi du Testament d'Elhar, document inédit recueilli par Ludwig Lewisohn et Maxime Piha. Paris: Éditions Excelsior, 1933. 154 p., 2 l. 8°.

LIEBERMAN, ELIAS. At the Yiddish theatre. [In one act.] (American Hebrew. New York, 1918. 4°. v. 102, p. 572.) * PBD
The scene is at the box office, on a Saturday afternoon.

—— A cottage for two. (American Hebrew. New York, 1918. 4°. v. 103, p. 288-289.) * PBD
In one act.

—— Two in one. [In three scenes.] (American Hebrew. New York, 1919. f°. v. 105, p. 246, 260.) * PBD

—— Wanted: a doctor. (American Hebrew. New York, 1918. 4°. v. 103, p. 509-510.)
In one act. * PBD

LIEBOVITZ, DAVID. La comédie juive. Atonement; a play in one act. (Menorah journal. New York, 1922. 4°. v. 8, no. 2, p. 90-99.)
* PBD
Modern time. Atonement Day, in the basement of a *Schul* in Arverne, Long Island.

—— La comédie juive. "Matches," a play in one act. (Menorah journal. New York, 1922. 4°. v. 8, p. 23-32.) * PBD
Place: shipping room of a New York, presumably Jewish, firm. Produced by the Menorah societies of Harvard and Radcliffe colleges at the Agassiz Theatre, Cambridge, April 9, 1927, with L. W. Schwartz as Posserl.

LIKE Lincoln. [A sketch for children.] New York: Jewish Welfare Board [1931]. 2 f. 4°.
Caption-title.
Mimeographed.

LINDSAY, HOWARD. She loves me not; dramatized from Edward Hope's novel... [New York, 1933.] [124] f. diagr., plans. 4°. † NCOF
Various paging.
Reproduced from typewritten copy.
Promptbook.

—— She loves me not; a comedy in two acts dramatized from Edward Hope's novel [of the same title]... New York, Los Angeles: S. French; London: S. French, Ltd., cop. 1935. 145(1) p., 1 l. illus., diagrs. 12°. NBL p.v.388
"What happened at Princeton, when four seniors chivalrously give refuge to a pretty night-club hoofer, who is wanted by the police as a witness to a murder." Produced at the Forty-sixth Street Theatre, New York, Nov. 20, 1933, with H. P. Flick as Abram Liebowitz. For reviews see *Collection of newspaper clippings of dramatic criticism, 1933-34*, v. Sh-T, † *NBL*.
Produced at the Adelphi Theatre, London, May 1, 1934. Reviewed in *Jewish chronicle*, London, May 4, 1934, p. 46, * *PBD;* and in *Theatre world*, London, 1934, v. 21, p. 273, *MWA*.

Glazer, Benjamin Floyer. She loves me not. Release dialogue script... [Hollywood?] 1934. [92] f. f°. MFLM (She loves)
Cover-title.
Reproduced from typewritten copy.

LINSKY, FANNIE BARNETT. America and the Jew; a pageant for Thanksgiving day... Cincinnati, O.: Department of Synagog and School Extension of the Union of American Hebrew Congregations [cop. 1923]. 20 p. 12°.
NBL p.v.107, no.8
Foreword by Harry Levi, p. 5.
The characters are allegorical or symbolic. It was written for, and produced by the Sunday School pupils of Temple Israel, Boston, October, 1922.

—— Happy new year; a play in one act, a prologue and an epilogue... Cincinnati: Dept. of Synagogue and School Extension of the Union of American Hebrew Congregations [cop. 1929]. 19 p. 12°. * PSQ p.v.2
Foreword by Harry Levi, p. 3-4.
Different from her playlet, similarly entitled, which had appeared in *Young Israel*, Cincinnati, 1925, v. 18, no. 1, p. 7, * *PBD*.

—— Sundown; play in one act... Boston: Walter H. Baker Company [cop. 1935]. 27 p. 12°. (Baker's edition of plays.) NBL p.v.371
An intermarriage comedy-drama.

—— Three score years and ten. [Boston, 1924?] 13 f. 4°. * PXY
Caption-title.
Typewritten.
A pageant in nine episodes.
Presented at the Temple Israel, Boston, for its seventieth anniversary, 1854-1924, Sunday, Dec. 7, 1924. See *Jewish advocate*, Boston, v. 44, Dec. 4, 1924, p. 1, 3, and Dec. 11, p. 5, 7, * *PBD*.

LOMAS, B. A. Miriam; a tragedy in five acts. (In his: Romantic dramas. New York [cop. 1915]. 16°. p. 131-215.) NBM
Action passes at Byzantium, 320 A. D. Among the characters is Aspar, "a Jewish priest."

THE JEW IN ENGLISH DRAMA 159

Individual Plays — 1915–1938, continued

LONSDALE, FREDERICK. The street singers; a musical play in three acts. The play by Frederick Lonsdale; the lyrics by Percy Greenbank; the music by Harold Fraser-Simson; additional numbers by Ivy St. Helier... London: S. French, Ltd.; New York: S. French, Inc., 1929. 75 p., 1 l. plates, diagrs. 8°. (French's acting edition. no. 562.)
  Produced at the Prince of Wales's Theatre, Birmingham, Eng., Feb. 4, 1924, and at the Lyric Theatre, London, June 27, 1924, with Alfred Beers as Levy, "picture dealer."

LOOS, ANITA, AND J. EMERSON. "Gentlemen prefer blondes"; a comedy in three acts. Based on the book of the same title by Anita Loos. Produced at the Times Square Theatre, New York, Sept. 28, 1926.
  Arthur S. Ross played Gus Eisman, the big button king of Chicago who sends Lorelei on an educational tour to Europe. Reviewed by Edmund Wilson in *New republic*, New York, 1926, v. 48, p. 245–246, * *DA;* by P. Reniers (with illus.) in *Sportsman*, Boston, v. 1, Jan., 1927, p. 50–51, † *MVA;* and by Arthur Hornblow in *Theatre magazine*, New York, v. 44, Dec., 1926, p. 16, *NBLA*. For further reviews see *Collection of newspaper clippings of dramatic criticism, 1926–1927*, v. D–H, † *NBL*.
  Produced at the Prince of Wales's Theatre, London, April 2, 1928, with Nick Adams as Gus Eisman. Reviewed in *Curtain*, London, 1928, v. 7, p. 57, *NAFA;* and in *Era*, London, v. 91, April 4, 1928, p. 4, † *NAFA*.

LOVING, BOYCE. Swappers; a comedy in three acts... New York [etc.]: S. French, Inc., cop. 1934. 102 p., 1 l. diagrs. 12°.
  A farmer and a city clerk swap their jobs. A Mrs. Hefflebaum figures in this farce.

LUKE, PSEUD. The class war in heaven; a drama of future judgment, by Luke. Boston: Richard G. Badger [cop. 1926]. 102 p. 12°.   NBM
  Simon Lebansky, member of the executive committee of the International Brotherhood of Toil.

LYNDON, BARRÉ. The amazing Dr. Clitterhouse. (In: Four plays of 1936. [London, 1936.] 12°. p. 315–516.)   NCO
  A "crook" play, in three acts. First produced at the Haymarket Theatre, London, Aug. 6, 1936, with Charles Mortimer as Benny Kellerman, London's cleverest fence.
  It was brought to New York, at the Hudson Theatre, March 2, 1937, with Clarence Derwent as Kellerman. For reviews see *Collection of newspaper clippings of dramatic criticism, 1936–1937*, v. A–Br, † *NBL*.

LYONS, JIMMY. Mrs. Cohen and her neighbors [a monologue]. (In his: Encyclopedia of stage material. Boston, 1925. 12°. p. 73–75.)

MJK. We're off to —; a short sketch [in one act]. (Young Judaean. New York, 1936. 4°. v. 24, Feb., 1936, p. 5–6.)   * PBD

MCBURNEY, VENITA RICH. Underweight. [A monologue in dialect.] Chicago: Dramatic Pub. Company [cop. 1929]. 3 f. 4°. (Sergel's manuscript readings.)

MACCARTHY, JOHN BERNARD. The grain of the wood; a comedy in three acts... Dublin: M. H. Gill and Son, Ltd. [1931.] 2 p.l., 108 p. 12°.
  NCO p.v.640
  Octavius B. Cohen, a hustling American lawyer from Nebraska, on a visit to Ireland to locate the heirs of one J. J. Ryan, who died intestate in America.

MCCOMAS, EDITH. Brass tacks; a comedy-drama in three acts. Franklin, Ohio [etc.]: Eldridge Entertainment House, Inc., cop. 1928. 1 p.l., 44 p. diagr. 12°. (Eldridge popular plays.)
  Arnold Slovinsky, village doctor, is the villain of the piece.

MACDONALD, DORA MARY. "The contest." (In her: Purpose plays for high school assemblies. Minneapolis, Minn., cop. 1932. 12°. [v. 1,] p. 5–15.)   NBL
  "A one-act play to be used to sell the school paper to an assembly of students."
  Mr. Ogg, merchant, comes to insert an ad. "He might have some of the characteristics of a Jewish salesman."

—— "In the principal's office." (In her: Purpose plays for high school assemblies. Minneapolis, Minn., cop. 1934. 12°. v. 3, p. 27–51.)
  NBL
  A parents-teachers-pupils meeting. Israel Goldberg, one of the pupils.

MCEVOY, JOSEPH PATRICK. In the vernacular. And that, boys and girls, is how I became a producer. (World. New York, 1928. f°. Sept. 23, 1928, metropolitan section, p. 3.)   * A
  Scene: the office of the president of the Thimble Theatre, Inc.

—— Simon and Schuster present Show girl ... [New York: Simon and Schuster, Inc., cop. 1928.] 4 p.l., 215 p. 12°.   8–NBO
  Appeared serially in *New York Telegram*, Sept.–Dec., 1928.
  "Kibbitzer & Eppus: Broadway producers — 'Par nobile fratrum.'"

MCGEE, JOHN. Jefferson Davis; a play in three acts... [New York: Works Progress Administration, Federal Theatre Project, 1936.] [85] f. 4°.
  Reproduced from typewritten copy.
  Contains also an Epilogue.
  Time: Dec. 27, 1860 to April 2, 1865. The Epilogue is dated May 31, 1893, at the Hollywood Cemetery, Richmond, Va.
  Presented by the Federal Theatre Project at the Biltmore Theatre, New York, Feb. 18, 1936, with Harry Golson as Judah P. Benjamin, Confederate statesman. For reviews see *Collection of newspaper clippings of dramatic criticism, 1935–1936*, v. Io–L, † *NBL*.

MACKAYE, HAZEL. ...The quest of youth; a pageant for schools. Washington: Gov. Print. Off., 1924. vi, 102 p. 8°. ([United States] Bureau of Education. Bulletin. 1924, no. 33.)
  STF (U. S.)
  "The theme or story of the pageant is Youth's search for a school," down through the ages. Part 1, action 3, is entitled Early Hebrew education, from 1095 B.C. (the prophet Samuel) to 458 B.C. (Ezra's death).

MCKNIGHT, TOM, AND D. HOBART. ...Double dummy; a new farce-satire... [New York, 1936.] [104] f. 4°.   † NCOF
  At head of title: Mark Hellinger and James R. Ullman present.
  In two acts.
  Reproduced from typewritten copy.
  Adapted from *Poop deck*, by Doty Hobart.
  Deals with an up-to-date bridge game racket. Part of the action is laid in a prison. About six of the characters are given distinctly Jewish names. Produced at the Golden Theatre, New York, Nov. 11, 1936. See *Collection of newspaper clippings of dramatic criticism, 1936–1937*, v. Bu–D, † *NBL*.

Individual Plays — 1915–1938, continued

McMEEKIN, MRS. ISABELLA (MCLENNAN). The goblin and the princess; a play in two acts. New York [etc.]: Samuel French [cop. 1929]. 5 p.l., 3–15 p. 12°. (Junior League plays.)
NBL p.v.226
Based on Talmudic legend of rabbi Simeon ben Yohai (Tanna of the second century) and the demon, Ben Temalion (Me'ilah 17b). The present version is taken from *Jewish fairy book*, edited and translated by Gerald Friedlander, New York, 1920.

McMILLAN, VIRGINIA. A tourist's romance. A comedy in three acts. Philadelphia: Penn Publishing Co., 1928. 42 p. 12°.
As vacation tourists at Raymond Centre, come Moses Aronson (cloaks and suits), and his large family.

McNALLY, WILLIAM. Abe and Jake in politics; a new act for two Hebrew comedians. (McNally's bulletin. New York, 1924. 8°. no. 10, p. 55–57.)

—— Abie's European trip; a roaring Hebrew monologue. (McNally's bulletin. New York, 1927. 8°. no. 13, p. 28–30.)

—— Abraham Cohen, M. V.; Hebrew monologue. (McNally's bulletin. New York, 1925. 8°. no. 11, p. 28–29.)

—— After the revolution; act for two Hebrew comedians. (McNally's bulletin. New York, 1921. 8°. no. 7, p. 64–66.)
NAFA

—— Agency employment; a typical Hebrew monologue. (McNally's bulletin. New York, 1928. 8°. no. 14, p. 29–31.)

—— And say! Hebrew monologue. (McNally's bulletin. New York, 1928. 8°. no. 14, p. 31–32.)

—— As things are; Hebrew and soubrette act. (McNally's bulletin. New York, 1919. 8°. no. 5, p. 92–94.)
NAC p.v.29

—— At the ball game; a new monologue for Hebrew comedian. (McNally's bulletin. New York, 1936. 8°. no. 20, p. 19–20.)

—— Avernsky by the seasky; a typical Hebrew monologue. (McNally's bulletin. New York, 1926. 8°. no. 12, p. 35–36.)

—— Beautiful Sadie; Hebrew monologue. (McNally's bulletin. New York, 1924. 8°. no. 10, p. 21–22.)

—— Believe me; a new monologue for Hebrew comedian. (McNally's bulletin. New York, 1924. 8°. no. 10, p. 22–24.)

—— Blind dates; an act for soubrette and Hebrew comedian. (McNally's bulletin. New York, 1931. 8°. no. 17, p. 50–51.)

—— Business and more trouble; Hebrew monologue. (McNally's bulletin. New York, 1917. 8°. no. 3, p. 13–14.)

—— Clever stuff; straight and Hebrew act. (Dialect.) (McNally's bulletin. New York, 1916. 8°. no. 2, p. 56–59.)

—— Cohen's intended; straight and Hebrew. (Mack's vaudeville guide. New York, 1920. 8°. p. 25–27.)

—— Cohn and Levi in windy planes; a good act for two Hebrew, two Dutch or two wop comedians. (McNally's bulletin. New York, 1930. 8°. no. 16, p. 37–39.)

—— Dirt cheap; straight and Hebrew comedy skit [for two males]. (McNally's bulletin. New York, 1918. 8°. no. 4, p. 52–55.)

—— A dog's life; an act for two Hebrew comedians. (McNally's bulletin. New York, 1925. 8°. no. 11, p. 66–68.)

—— Dummaxes; a monologue for Hebrew or Dutch comedian. (McNally's bulletin. New York, 1930. 8°. no. 16, p. 11–12.)

—— The emigrant; comedy skit for soubrette and Hebrew. (McNally's bulletin. New York, 1918. 8°. no. 4, p. 114–115.)

—— Enough is enough; two male act for two Hebrews. (Dialect.) (McNally's bulletin. New York, 1916. 8°. no. 2, p. 46–48.)

—— Enough is too much; Hebrew monologue. (McNally's bulletin. New York, 1917. 8°. no. 3, p. 14–16.)

—— Even if I mention it myself; a monologue especially written for Hebrew comedian. (McNally's bulletin. New York, 1930. 8°. no. 16, p. 12–13.)

—— Everything; a monologue suitable for Dutch or Hebrew comedian. (McNally's bulletin. New York, 1929. 8°. no. 15, p. 20–21.)

—— Fall fashions; Hebrew monologue. (McNally's bulletin. New York, 1921. 8°. no. 7, p. 28–29.)

—— Family troubles; Hebrew monologue. (Mack's vaudeville guide. New York, 1920. 8°. p. 13–14.)

—— A fool there was; soubrette and Hebrew. (McNally's bulletin. New York, 1918. 8°. no. 4, p. 116–117.)

—— Four of a kind; quartette act for four males. (McNally's bulletin. New York, 1917. 8°. no. 3, p. 123–125.)
Cohen, Hebrew comedian.

—— Friendship; a new Hebrew monologue. (McNally's bulletin. New York, 1925. 8°. no. 11, p. 31–32.)

—— From no place to nowhere on the Ha-ha line; monologue for Hebrew comedian. (McNally's bulletin. New York, 1925. 8°. no. 11, p. 32–34.)

—— Garlic; a Hebrew monologue. (McNally's bulletin. New York, 1916. 8°. no. 2, p. 14–15.)

Individual Plays — 1915–1938, continued

MCNALLY, WILLIAM. Goldberg and Silverstein; act for two Hebrew comedians. (McNally's bulletin. New York, 1934. 8°. no. 19, p. 28–30.)

—— Goldstein's son; Hebrew monologue. (McNally's bulletin. New York, 1918. 8°. no. 4, p. 22–24.)

—— Goldstein's wedding; act for two Hebrew comedians. (McNally's bulletin. New York, 1918. 8°. no. 4, p. 56–58.)

—— A hard explanation; straight and Hebrew act. (McNally's bulletin. New York, 1918. 8°. no. 4, p. 50–52.)

—— Have one on me; act for straight and Hebrew comedian. (McNally's bulletin. New York, 1921. 8°. no. 7, p. 59–62.)

—— Help wanted; a timely act for soubrette and tramp. (McNally's bulletin. New York, 1932. 8°. no. 18, p. 45–46.)
"Hebrew may substitute tramp character."

—— The high cost of kissing; male act for Hebrew and straight. (McNally's bulletin. New York, 1918. 8°. no. 4, p. 78–80.)

—— Horsepistols and sicknesses; a roaring Hebrew monologue. (McNally's bulletin. New York, 1926. 8°. no. 12, p. 33–35.)

—— I see by the newspapers; monologue for Hebrew comedian. (McNally's bulletin. New York, 1931. 8°. no. 17, p. 19–20.)

—— I tell you! a new Hebrew monologue. (McNally's bulletin. New York, 1925. 8°. no. 11, p. 26–27.)

—— Indigestion; act for two Hebrews. (McNally's bulletin. New York, 1918. 8°. no. 4, p. 59–61.)

—— Irving Lipshits the salesman; a typical Hebrew monologue. (McNally's bulletin. New York, 1931. 8°. no. 17, p. 22–23.)

—— It can't be done; Hebrew monologue. (McNally's bulletin. New York, 1917. 8°. no. 3, p. 17–19.)

—— Jake explains; an act for soubrette and Hebrew comedian. (McNally's bulletin. New York, 1936. 8°. no. 20, p. 46–47.)

—— Jake the playwriter; a comical act for straight and Hebrew comedian. (McNally's bulletin. New York, 1928. 8°. no. 14, p. 63–65.)

—— Jake, you are a fake; act for two Hebrew comedians. (McNally's bulletin. New York, 1917. 8°. no. 3, p. 61–63.)

—— Jake's social affairs; a Hebrew monologue. (McNally's bulletin. New York, 1932. 8°. no. 18, p. 19–20.)

—— Just friends; act for two Hebrews. (McNally's bulletin. New York, 1919. 8°. no. 5, p. 66–68.) NAC p.v.29

—— Just the same; straight and Hebrew act. (McNally's bulletin. New York, 1916. 8°. no. 2, p. 52–55.)

—— Keeping a wife; a hot-shot act for straight and Hebrew, or Irish and Hebrew. (McNally's bulletin. New York, 1927. 8°. no. 13, p. 58–60.)

—— Let's do acting? a comedy act for soubrette and blackface. (McNally's bulletin. New York, 1932. 8°. no. 18, p. 47–49.)
"Also suitable for Hebrew."

—— Levi and Cohn, in a new Hebrew act. (McNally's bulletin. New York, 1929. 8°. no. 15, p. 51–53.)

—— Levinsky and daughter; a new act for soubrette and Hebrew comedian. (McNally's bulletin. New York, 1925. 8°. no. 11, p. 95–97.)

—— Levinsky and son; an act for two Hebrew comedians. (McNally's bulletin. New York, 1924. 8°. no. 10, p. 57–59.)

—— Lost in a pullman; Hebrew monologue. (McNally's bulletin. New York, 1918. 8°. no. 4, p. 20–22.)

—— Love and money; act for Hebrew comedian and soubrette. (McNally's bulletin. New York, 1917. 8°. no. 3, p. 96–98.)

—— Marriage and other gambles; an act for soubrette and Hebrew comedian. (McNally's bulletin. New York, 1930. 8°. no. 16, p. 50–51.)

—— Matrimonial harmony; a Hebrew monologue. (McNally's bulletin. New York, 1916. 8°. no. 2, p. 11–13.)

—— Meet the wife; act for straight and Hebrew comedian. (McNally's bulletin. New York, 1930. 8°. no. 16, p. 36–37.)

—— Mine daughter, Rebecca; a Hebrew monologue. (McNally's bulletin. New York, 1916. 8°. no. 2, p. 16–17.)

—— Mine family; Hebrew monologue. (McNally's bulletin. New York, 1917. 8°. no. 3, p. 11–12.)

—— My boy's wedding; Hebrew monologue. (McNally's bulletin. New York, 1919. 8°. no. 5, p. 14–16.) NAC p.v.29

—— My friend, Goldstein; a new monologue. (McNally's bulletin. New York, 1916. 8°. no. 2, p. 18–20.)

—— My wife; an act for Hebrew and soubrette. (McNally's bulletin. New York, 1928. 8°. no. 14, p. 90–92.)

—— My wife's in-laws; a laugh-getting Hebrew monologue. (McNally's bulletin. New York, 1927. 8°. no. 13, p. 27–28.)

Individual Plays — 1915-1938, continued

McNally, William. The new female custom inspector; a different act for Hebrew and soubrette. (McNally's bulletin. New York, 1927. 8°. no. 13, p. 88–90.)

—— The night before the morning; a laugh-getting Hebrew monologue. (McNally's bulletin. New York, 1934. 8°. no. 19, p. 15–16.)

—— Noodle soup and appetites; act for two Hebrew comedians. (McNally's bulletin. New York, 1927. 8°. no. 13, p. 56–58.)

—— Oh! lady, lady! Hebrew monologue. (McNally's bulletin. New York, 1919. 8°. no. 5, p. 16–18.) NAC p.v.29

—— Oh! Polly! Quartette act for two males and two females. (McNally's bulletin. New York, 1921. 8°. no. 7, p. 108–110.)
Levi and Rosie, Hebrew comedians.

—— "Over the counter"; Hebrew monologue. (McNally's bulletin. New York, 1926. 8°. no. 12, p. 37–38.)

—— Papa and Isaac; a bright act for straight and Hebrew comedians. (McNally's bulletin. New York, 1925. 8°. no. 11, p. 63–66.)

—— Politics on a dry platform; Hebrew monologue. (McNally's bulletin. New York, 1921. 8°. no. 7, p. 26–27.)

—— "Preparedness"; Hebrew monologue. (McNally's bulletin. New York, 1918. 8°. no. 4, p. 24–25.)

—— Professor Bolshushki's school; farce comedy and burlesque. (McNally's bulletin. New York, 1929. 8°. no. 15, p. 91–96.)

—— Profiteering landlords; act for two Hebrew comedians. (McNally's bulletin. New York, 1921. 8°. no. 7, p. 62–64.)

—— The radio dentist; a sparkling Hebrew monologue. (McNally's bulletin. New York, 1925. 8°. no. 11, p. 29–30.)

—— Rain insurance; an act for two Dutch or Hebrew comedians. (McNally's bulletin. New York, 1931. 8°. no. 17, p. 41–42.)

—— Rebecca's beau; Hebrew monologue. (McNally's bulletin. New York, 1919. 8°. no. 5, p. 18–20.) NAC p.v.29

—— Rosensky's insurance policy; act for two Hebrew comedians. (McNally's bulletin. New York, 1918. 8°. no. 4, p. 62–64.)

—— 'Round the world; act for Hebrew and straight comedians. (McNally's bulletin. New York, 1917. 8°. no. 3, p. 54–56.)

—— The safest way; act for Hebrew comedian and soubrette. (McNally's bulletin. New York, 1917. 8°. no. 3, p. 98–100.)

—— Say! don't I know? an original act for soubrette and Hebrew. (McNally's bulletin. New York, 1932. 8°. no. 18, p. 51–52.)

—— Say! mister; a clever act for straight and Hebrew comedian. (McNally's bulletin. New York, 1932. 8°. no. 18, p. 38–39.)

—— Selma the flirt; act for soubrette and Hebrew comedian. (McNally's bulletin. New York, 1921. 8°. no. 7, p. 99–101.)

—— Settled; a trio act for three males. (McNally's bulletin. New York, 1918. 8°. no. 4, p. 125–126.)
Abraham, Hebrew comedian.

—— S'sure as I am alive; a funny Hebrew monologue. (McNally's bulletin. New York, 1936. 8°. no. 20, p. 20–21.)

—— The stagehand and the star; an act for two comedians. Suitable for two Hebrews, or straight and Hebrew. (McNally's bulletin. New York, 1932. 8°. no. 18, p. 28–30.)

—— "The star boarder"; Hebrew monologue. (McNally's bulletin. New York, 1918. 8°. no. 4, p. 18–20.)

—— Station N-U-T; broadcasting straight and Hebrew comedians, speaking in an up-to-the-second act. (McNally's bulletin. New York, 1926. 8°. no. 12, p. 70–72.)

—— "Such a woman"; Hebrew monologue. (McNally's bulletin. New York, 1918. 8°. no. 4, p. 16–18.)

—— Summering at a summer resort. Hebrew monologue. (McNally's bulletin. New York, 1919. 8°. no. 5, p. 11–13.) NAC p.v.29

—— Tell me! a real Hebrew monologue. (McNally's bulletin. New York, 1928. 8°. no. 14, p. 33–34.)

—— Temperament; act for two Hebrews. (McNally's bulletin. New York, 1919. 8°. no. 5, p. 68–70.) NAC p.v.29

—— That's that! a new act for soubrette and Hebrew comedians. (McNally's bulletin. New York, 1924. 8°. no. 10, p. 93–95.)

—— There ain't no Santa Claus; a side-splitting act for two Hebrew comedians. (McNally's bulletin. New York, 1926. 8°. no. 12, p. 72–74.)

—— This and that; quartette act for four males. (McNally's bulletin. New York, 1919. 8°. no. 5, p. 107–108.) NAC p.v.29
Goldstein — Hebrew comedian.

—— This, that and something else; act for Hebrew and straight comedians. (McNally's bulletin. New York, 1917. 8°. no. 3, p. 51–53.)

—— This way out; act for Hebrew and straight comedians. (McNally's bulletin. New York, 1917. 8°. no. 3, p. 56–58.)

THE JEW IN ENGLISH DRAMA 163

Individual Plays — 1915-1938, continued

McNally, William. Tillie Tickletoe; or, The un-human vampire. Farce comedy and burlesque. (McNally's bulletin. New York, 1921. 8°. no. 7, p. 114–117.)
The Levinskys, father, mother, and son.

—— Tips, and more tips; straight and Hebrew act. (McNally's bulletin. New York, 1919. 8°. no. 5, p. 61–63.) NAC p.v.29

—— Trial marriages; an up-to-the-split-second Hebrew monologue. (McNally's bulletin. New York, 1929. 8°. no. 15, p. 22–23.)

—— The vamp; a farcical comedy and burlesque. (McNally's bulletin. New York, 1924. 8°. no. 10, p. 113–116.)

—— Waiting for the 5:15; Hebrew and soubrette act. (McNally's bulletin. New York, 1919. 8°. no. 5, p. 95–97.) NAC p.v.29

—— The waiting waiter; a new Hebrew monologue. (McNally's bulletin. New York, 1934. 8°. no. 19, p. 14–15.)

—— Ward 23; a farce comedy and burlesque version of a day's happenings in a busy doctor's office. (McNally's bulletin. New York, 1931. 8°. no. 17, p. 65–71.)
"Solomon Moses, a Hebrew gent, also in bad health."

—— The weeper sex; a funny monologue for Hebrew comedian. (McNally's bulletin. New York, 1931. 8°. no. 17, p. 21–22.)

—— What d'yer mean? Act for straight and Hebrew comedians. (McNally's bulletin. New York, 1919. 8°. no. 5, p. 59–61.) NAC p.v.29

—— Wise and not wise; an act for two Hebrew comedians [or] Hebrew and straight. (McNally's bulletin. New York, 1936. 8°. no. 20, p. 38–39.)

—— "Women! Women!" A new Hebrew monologue. (McNally's bulletin. New York, 1918. 8°. no. 4, p. 14–16.)

—— You can't fool Isaac! act for two Hebrew comedians. (McNally's bulletin. New York, 1926. 8°. no. 12, p. 74–76.)

—— You win; act for Hebrew and straight. (McNally's bulletin. New York, 1919. 8°. no. 5, p. 64–66.) NAC p.v.29

—— You're mine friend; act for two Hebrew comedians. (McNally's bulletin. New York, 1917. 8°. no. 3, p. 59–61.)

McNary, Herbert L. Junior sees it through; a comedy in three acts... Chicago: Dramatic Publishing Company [cop. 1931]. 96 p. 12°. (Sergel's acting drama.) NBL p.v.271
Morris Shulerman, a shrewd, bargaining business man.

Madison, James. A jolly farce entitled A pretty kettle of fish. (Madison's budget. New York, 1921. 4°. no. 18, p. 53–68.) † NBW
Ikey Levi, an obliging man, comedian.

Maibaum, Richard. Birthright, a play of the Nazi regime... New York, N. Y., Los Angeles, Cal.: S. French, Inc.; London: S. French, Ltd. [etc.], cop. 1934. 94 p. plates, diagr. 12°. (French's standard library ed.) NBL p.v.346
A play of the plight of the Jews in Germany during the early part of Hitler's regime. Produced at the Forty-ninth Street Theatre, New York, Nov. 21, 1933, with Sylvia Field as Clara Eisner and Montagu Love as Jakob Eisner. For reviews see *Collection of newspaper clippings of dramatic criticism, 1933-1934*, v. A–B, † *NBL*.
Staged in London, at the Cambridge Theatre, Dec. 16, 1934.

Manley, William Ford. Wild waves; a comedy in three acts... New York: Samuel French, Inc., cop. 1932. 166 p. plans. 12°. (French's standard library edition.) NBL p.v.284
A satire on radio broadcasting. Produced at the Times Square Theatre, New York, Feb. 20, 1932, with Stuart Brown as Bogelman, the announcer, and Joseph King as Edward Reiss. Reviewed by R. D. Skinner in *Commonweal*, New York, 1932, v. 15, p. 525, * *DA*; and by John Hutchens in *Theatre arts monthly*, New York, 1932, v. 16, p. 277–278, † *NBLA*. See also *Collection of newspaper clippings of dramatic criticism, 1931-1932*, v. T–Z, † *NBL*.

Mann, Heinrich. Berlin interlude. In this brief [one-act] play is an illuminating analysis of Nazi psychology. (Jewish standard. Toronto, Canada, 1934. f°. v. 9, March 30, 1934, p. 6.)
* PBE

Manning, Jacolyn. The man who begat six daughters; a comedy of the Chicago ghetto. (In his: The law in Death Valley [and three other one-act plays]. Pasadena, Cal., 1931. 12°. p. 39–48.) NBL p.v.268
Scene: tenement house on Maxwell street, Chicago. "The first author's reading of the play was given by invitation in...Vista del Arroyo Hotel, Pasadena, on the evening of October 26th, 1927, to a group of professional men and women. It is adapted to production by hospital aid societies, nurses and doctors."

Mansfield, H. E. ...Santa Claus and the madonna. Chicago: Dramatic Publishing Company [cop. 1935]. 36 p. diagr. 12°.
At head of title: A Christmas play in one act.
The scene is a department store in Bethlehem, Pa., and the street in front of the store. Mr. Ginsberg, owner of a store, "speaks with a very slight Jewish accent; his part is not played for comedy."

Mantel, Beatrice T. Rebecca Gratz. Winner of the second prize in play contest conducted under the auspices of the Department of Religion and Religious Education of the National Council of Jewish Women. New York: National Council of Jewish Women [1929]. 15 p. 24°. * C p.v.2213
A one-act historical playlet. The characters are Rebecca Gratz, 1781–1869, reputed to be the prototype of Scott's Rebecca in *Ivanhoe*, friend of Washington Irving, philanthropist, and founder of the first Jewish religious school in this country; her elder sister Frances, who in 1792 married Reuben Etting; her younger sister Rachel, 1783–1823; and a fictitious Beatrix Lamonde, a French neighbor. The time is in the early eighteen hundreds, presumably in Philadelphia. See Rebecca Gratz, *Letters*, ed. by D. Philipson, Philadelphia, 1929, *NBV*, and American Jewish Historical Society, *Publications*, Index to numbers 1–20, 1914 (under Gratz), * *PXX*.

Individual Plays — 1915–1938, continued

MARCH of stirring events in founding of Republic. (A. Z. A. monthly program. Omaha, Neb., 1937. 4°. v. 10, no. 1, p. 13–21.) * PBD

A series of dramatic episodes, in which Jewish worthies of Revolutionary fame figure.

MARCIN, MAX. Cheating cheaters; a comic melodrama in four acts... New York, N. Y., Los Angeles, Cal.: S. French, Inc.; London: S. French, Ltd., cop. 1916. 120 p., 2 l. illus. (ports.), plans. 12°. (French's standard library edition.) NBL p.v.296

A preview of it was shown at Atlantic City, N. J., July 31, 1916, which was noted in *New York dramatic mirror*, v. 76, Aug. 12, 1916, p. 14, * T–* DA. Produced at the Eltinge Theatre, New York, Aug. 9, 1916, with Frank Monroe as Ira Lazarre, crooked lawyer and bail getter who "played for safety." Reviewed by Clayton Hamilton in *Bookman*, New York, 1916, v.* 44, p. 198–201, * DA; with illus. in *Green book album*, Chicago, v. 16, p. 417 (a synopsis given ibid., p. 793–795), *NAFA*; by Kathleen Hills (with illus.) in *Leslie's weekly*, New York, v. 123, p. 428, 443, * DA; *Munsey's magazine*, New York, v. 58, p. 693, * DA; by S. W. in *Nation*, New York, v. 103, p. 161, * DA; *New York dramatic mirror*, New York, v. 76, Aug. 19, 1916, p. 8, * T–* DA; and by Arthur Hornblow (with illus.) in *Theatre magazine*, New York, v. 24, p. 137–138, 149, † NBLA.

Produced at the Strand Theatre, London, Feb. 4, 1918, with George Elton as Ira Lazarre. Reviewed in *Era*, London, v. 81, Feb. 6, 1918, p. 1, † *NAFA*; and in *Graphic*, London, v. 97, p. 190, * DA.

MARION, FRANCES. The cup of life [in one scene]. (In: Kenyon Nicholson, editor, Hollywood plays. New York, 1930. 12°. p. 127–150.) NBL (Nicholson)

The scene is in a garden of an insane asylum. There are seven inmates, each one of whom speaks his muddled mind. Among them is Nathan Witzel, ex-tailor. Produced by the Hollywood Writers' Club, at its Little Theatre, Nov. 13, 1925, with Snitz Edwards as the tailor.

MARSCHALL, PHYLLIS. Another man without a country; Benedict Arnold [in seven scenes]. (In: A. P. Sanford, editor, American patriotic plays. New York, 1937. 12°. p. 187–246.) NBL

Major [David S.] Franks is one of the characters.

MARTINESCU, SANDOR. The Jews of Hodos; a play in one act. Translated from the Roumanian by Winifred Katzin and Milda Robin. (In: Winifred Katzin, compiler, Short plays from twelve countries. London [cop. 1937]. 8°. p. 159–203.)

Based on an actual incident which happened in Ismail in 1872. Place: a small town on the Hungarian-Rumanian border, in the household of a Hassidic rabbi. Time: 1912.

For the facts of the Ismail case see Societatea romana pentru ameliorarea situatiunei Israelitor, *Processul de la Ismail inaintea juratilorou din Buzeu*, Bucuresci, 1872, x, 53 p., * PXM.

MASHIOFF, HAROLD H. "Sunday morning's children"; a Hanukah play for children (in three acts and two scenes). (Jewish forum. New York, 1937. 4°. v. 20, p. 142–143.) * PBD

The setting is modern American. Suitable for Hanukkah or any other occasion.

MASON, REDFERN. The girl who knows how... San Francisco, Cal.: Harr Wagner Publishing Company [cop. 1931]. vi, 29 p. 8°. NBM

A comedy in one act, the subject of which is the spirit of San Francisco. The characters, with the exception of Miss San Francisco, are men about town. "The author has insinuated penetrating criticism of the artistic life of the city." It was presented at the Elks Club, 28th and 29th of January, 1931; J. Harold Weiss as Herbert Fleishhacker, one of four bankers and patrons of the western metropolis.

MATTHEWS, ADELAIDE, AND L. SAWYER. Sunset glow; a comedy drama in three acts... Boston: Walter H. Baker Company [cop. 1929]. 148 p. 12°. (Baker's royalty plays.)

Mrs. Epstein, "a Jewess of the superdreadnaught type," is one of the neighbors of the Stebbinses, the main characters in the play.

MAVOR, OSBORNE HENRY. The black eye; a comedy, by James Bridie [pseud.]. London: Constable & Co., Ltd. [1936.] viii, 95(1) p. 12°. NCO p.v.772

Produced at the Shaftesbury Theatre, London, October 11, 1935, with Ralph Roberts as Samuel Samuels, an adventurer. Reviewed in *Jewish chronicle*, London, Oct. 18, 1935, p. 47, * PBE.

MAXFIELD, MINA, AND L. EGGLESTON. The wet parade dramatized...from the novel of Upton Sinclair. Washington, D. C.: Board of Temperance, Prohibition and Public Morals, M. E. Church [cop. 1932]. 5 p.l., 5–55 p. 12°. In four scenes. NAC p.v.326

"The play is a valuable instrument for use in the campaign against the repeal of the eighteenth amendment." The action is laid in the years 1918–1931. First produced in the First Methodist Church of Pasadena, Cal., May 15, 1932. Abe Schilling, speaking in "Russian Jew dialect," is represented as the "buy" man, who secures the evidence for prosecution under the Volstead law. Izzy Einstein, well-known prohibition agent in the early twenties, is the probable prototype.

MAZO, FRANCES. Figs for tea. (To be acted by puppets.) illus. (Young Israel. Cincinnati, 1934. 4°. v. 26, March, 1934, p. 12–14, 22.) * PBD

MEIROVITZ, JOSEPH MOSES. The new generation, a drama in three acts... Boston: Four Seas Company [cop. 1927]. 39 p. 12°. NBL p.v.176

An intermarriage play. The action is laid in New York State, outside of New York City. The author dedicates it to "the men and women who think." "*Herbert*: A fine fellow, that Jacob!... He loved that girl and no one could dissuade him from marrying her. This is the spirit of the new generation." "*Olga*: It is great to live in a new generation." — *p. 39*.

MEISS, EDWIN R. The customer is always right; a comedy for men in one act... New York: Fitzgerald Publishing Corporation [cop. 1933]. 28 p. 12°. (Playhouse plays.)

Wolf, return clerk, in the office of Light & Thomas, wholesalers of men's clothing.

——— "Three of us," a play in one act, seven episodes, dealing with a generation of Americans... New York: Cooperative Publishers, cop. 1936. 48 p. 8°.

Three veterans of the World war, a Catholic, a Jew, and a Protestant and their experiences with religious intolerance in their native America.

MELVILLE, RICHARD L. Sir Ronald Neville, Bart.; a drawing-room comedy in one act... San Francisco: Banner Play Bureau, cop. 1929. 24 p. 12°.

Galinski, a lawyer, who specializes in the arrangement of international marriages.

Individual Plays — 1915–1938, continued

MEREDITH, BURGESS. The adventures of Mr. Bean. (One act play magazine. New York, 1937. 4°. v. 1, p. 675–684.)
Scene: New York motion picture studio. Saul Goldbin is the owner and Gompers his casting director.

MERRYMAN, MILDRED P. Jeroosalem. (In: Encores and extras. New York, cop. 1920. 8°. p. 9–10.)

MEYER, MABEL H. The peace party [in one act]... New York: Young Judaea, 1933. 7 p. 16°.
The characters are the countries of Europe, the United States, and Dr. Palestine.

MEYERSTEIN, EDWARD HARRY WILLIAM. The witches' Sabbath. [A dramatic poem.] (In his: The witches' Sabbath. Oxford, 1917. 12°. p. 7–40.) NCI (Adventurers)
"Adventurers all" series. no. 11.
A Jew is one of the interlocutors.

MIDDLEMASS, ROBERT MIDDLEMASS. The budget ... [New York: Longmans, Green & Co.,] cop. 1932. 25, 39, 24 f. 4°. † NCOF
Reproduced from typewritten copy.
In three acts.
Described on the programme as "a comedy of our times," i.e. the depression period. The scene is Beverly, N. J. Produced at the Hudson Theatre, New York, Sept. 20, 1932, with N. Adams and Grace Fox as Mr. and Mrs. Kaplan. See *Collection of newspaper clippings of dramatic criticism, 1932–33*, v. A–B, † *NBL*.

MIELE, ELIZABETH. ...Anybody's game, a comedy in three acts. Boston: Walter H. Baker Company [cop. 1933]. 139 p. illus. (plan.) 12°. (Baker's professional plays.) NBL p.v.316
How a boy makes good in the advertising business. When first staged, Paul Barton was named as the author and Miss Miele as the producer. First seen at the Bijou Theatre, New York, Dec. 21, 1932, with Louis Sorin in the Jewish comedy part of Sid Lewis of the Nifty-bilt Clothes Store, "a prosperous looking fellow." For reviews see *Collection of newspaper clippings of dramatic criticism, 1932–1933*, v. A–B, † *NBL*.

—— ...Did I say — No? A play in three acts ... Boston: Walter H. Baker Company [cop. 1934]. 127 p. 12°. (Baker's professional plays.)
Produced at the 48th Street Theatre, New York, Sept. 22, 1931, with Maurice Freeman as Judge Louis Levine, Miriam Stuart as Sophia Greenberg, and Anna Appel as her mother, Rebecca. For reviews see *Collection of newspaper clippings of dramatic criticism, 1931–1932*, v. C–E, † *NBL*.

MILLER, FRANCESCA FALK. ...Making Rosie a cook. [In one act.] Chicago: Dramatic Pub. Company [cop. 1929]. 23 p. 12°. (Sergel's playwright series.)
Foreword by Alice Gerstenberg, p. 3.
In a small apartment, Mott street, New York. Mrs. Levinson, the mother, gives up her reputation as a cook, for the sake of her son and daughter-in-law, Rosie.

MILLER, L. Mr. Man; a play in four acts and eight scenes. Translated from the Yiddish by S. K. Padover and Chasye Cooperman. (Poet lore. Boston, 1929. 8°. v. 40, p. 475–543.) * DA

MILLIKEN, FORBES. Get off the track; a comedy sketch for a singing quartet. Chicago: T. S. Denison & Co. [cop. 1928.] 11 p. 12°. (Denison's vaudeville sketches.) NBL p.v.274
In one act.
Abie who "von't" do what the Irish section boss tells him to.

—— Mine fat vife's poor husband; a Hebrew monologue. Chicago: T. S. Denison & Company [cop. 1931). 9 p. 12°. (Denison's vaudeville sketches.)
Abraham Gowitz, "with a vife and other troubles."

—— Says Cohen to Casey; a talking act... Chicago: T. S. Denison & Co. [cop. 1929.] 9 p. 12°. (Denison's vaudeville sketches.)
Cohen, book agent, in an attempt to sell an encyclopedia to an Irish customer.

MILNE, ALAN ALEXANDER. Michael and Mary; a play. London: Chatto & Windus, 1930. xxiv, 96 p. 12°. NCR

—— —— New York, Los Angeles: S. French; London: S. French, Ltd., cop. 1932. 73 p. illus. (plates.) 8°. (French's standard library edition.) NCO p.v.659
Reprinted in his *Four plays*, New York, 1932, p. xiii–xxiv, 1–87, *NCR*.
Presented in form of a running story, with the high-spots reproduced in actual dialogue from the text, in *Best plays of 1929–30*, New York, 1930, p. 272–309, *NAFH*.
It was first staged at the Charles Hopkins Theatre, New York, Dec. 13, 1929, with Vernon Kelso as Harry Price, "Mary's uncle." Reviewed in *American mercury*, New York, 1930, v. 19, p. 246–247, * *DA*; and in *Theatre arts monthly*, New York, 1930, v. 14, p. 109–111, *NBLA*. See also *Collection of newspaper clippings of dramatic criticism, 1929–30*, v. M–Q, † *NBL*.
Produced at the St. James's Theatre, London, Feb. 1, 1930, with D. A. Clarke-Smith as Price.

MR. Isaacstein at the telephone; humorous Hebrew-dialect monologue for man. (In: Werner's readings and recitations. New York, 1915. 12°. no. 56, p. 142–143.) NACG

MITCHISON, NAOMI (HALDANE), AND L. E. GIELGUD. The price of freedom; a play in three acts... London: Jonathan Cape [1931]. 158 p. 12°. NCR
The scene is the Roman camp of Emmaus, 70 A. D., just after the destruction of Jerusalem by Titus. "There are three groups of people, the Roman governor and his family, the broken Jews keeping still a flame of hope, and the first generation of Jewish Christians ... The play, like life, is sometimes tragedy and sometimes farce."
Reviewed in *The Times literary supplement*, London, 1931, v. 30, p. 319, † *NAA*.

MOBILE, ALA. — MURPHY HIGH SCHOOL: MODERN ALCHEMISTS' CLUB. Life of William Henry Perkin [in four scenes]. (Science leaflet. Lancaster, Pa., 1934. 8°. v. 7, p. 1016–1024.) PKA
Deals with the choice of a career for W. H. Perkin, the discoverer of coal tar products. Among the speakers are Prof. Paul Friedlaender, 1857–1923, and Prof. Raphael Meldola, 1849–1915, noted Austrian and English chemists. They appear in the third scene, in 1906, at the 50th anniversary of Perkin's discovery, at the Royal Institute of London.
Written and presented by the Club.

Individual Plays — 1915-1938, continued

MOELLER, PHILIP. Madame Sand; a biographical comedy; with a foreword by Mrs. Fiske and an introduction by Arthur Hopkins... New York: A. A. Knopf, 1917. 167 p. 8°. NBM

—— —— London: William Heinemann, 1920. 198 p., 1 l. 12°. NBM
Reprinted in S. M. Tucker, compiler, *Modern American and British plays*, New York [cop. 1931], p. 455–501, NCO.
Heine, Alfred de Musset, Chopin, and Franz Liszt are among the characters. First tried out at the Academy Theatre, Baltimore, Oct. 28, 1917. Reviewed in *New York dramatic mirror*, v. 77, Nov. 3, 1917, p. 32, * T–* DA. Produced at the Criterion Theatre, New York, Nov. 19, 1917, with Ferdinand Gottschalk as Heinrich Heine. Reviewed by J. S. Metcalfe in *Life*, New York, v. 70, p. 1011, * DA; New York dramatic mirror, v. 77, Dec. 1, 1917, p. 5, * T–* DA. See also *Collection of newspaper clippings of dramatic criticism, 1917–1918*, v. H–O, † NBL.
Produced at the Duke of York's Theatre, London, June 3, 1920, with Frank Collier as Heinrich Heine.

MOLNÁR, FERENC. ...The play's the thing, adapted from the Hungarian by P. G. Wodehouse. New York: Brentano's [cop. 1927]. 4 p.l., 3–139 p. 12°. NWF
Reprinted in his *Plays*, New York [cop. 1929], p. 728–777, NWF.
A synopsis, with extracts from the text, is printed in *The Best plays of 1926–27*, New York, 1927, p. 193–219, NAFH.
"Mansky, the pessimistic collaborator in the play is said to be Emmerich Kalman, the composer of Countess Maritza... Albert Adam, the young composer, is based upon Victor Jacoby... Sandor Turai is Molnar himself. That much of the gossip he frankly admits." — A. W. Pezet, in the *New York Sun*, Nov. 6, 1926, p. 6.
The play is known as *Játèka Kastélyban* in the original Hungarian, and as *Spiel im Schloss* in its German translation.
For the first time in any language, it was staged at the Great Neck Playhouse, Great Neck, L. I., N. Y., Oct. 21, 1926, and brought to the Henry Miller Theatre, New York, Nov. 3, 1926, with Holbrook Blinn as Sandor Turai, Hubert Bruce as Mansky, and Edward Crandall as Albert Adam. Reviewed by Benjamin De Casseres in *Arts & decoration*, New York, v. 26, Jan, 1927, p. 68, MAA; by Gilbert Seldes in *Dial*, New York, v. 82, p. 76–77, * DA; and by B. H. Clark in *Drama*, Chicago, v. 17, p. 105, NAFA. See also *Collection of newspaper clippings of dramatic criticism, 1926–1927*, v. N–Q, † NBL.
The Theatre Guild version was staged at the St. James's Theatre, London, Dec. 4, 1928, with Edmond Breon as Mansky, Gerald Du Maurier as Turai, and Henry Forbes-Robertson as Adam. Reviewed in *Nation & Athenæum*, London, 1928, v. 44, p. 413, * DA; and by David Baxter in *The Queen*, London, v. 164, Dec. 12, 1928, p. 33, * DA.

MOMENT, CORINNE R. The last will. [In two scenes. New York: Hadassah, 1933.] 10 f. 4°.
Caption-title.
Mimeographed.

MORGAN, VAUGHAN. Friar Bacon [a play]. (In his: Poems and plays. [Abertillery: "South Wales Gazette," Ltd., 1917.] sq. 32°. p. 51–60.) NCM
Scene: Oxford, beginning of the reign of Edward I. A Jew and his daughter seeking shelter at the monastery from a pursuing mob.

MORLEY, CHRISTOPHER DARLINGTON. Walt; a one act portrait. With a sketch by Jo Mielziner. port. (Bookman. Concord, N. H., 1924. 8°. v. 59, p. 646–662.) *DA
Horace Traubel is one of the characters. As to Traubel's Jewishness, see *Conservator*, v. 22, p. 124–125, * DA.

MORRIS, ESTHER. The conscript. [A play in one act.] (In her: Tears and laughter. London, 1926. 12°. p. 9–19.) NCR
Interior of a Russian cottage. Early autumn in the year 1900.

—— The matchmakers. [A play in one act.] (In her: Tears and laughter. London, 1926. 12°. p. 21–40.) NCR
Scene in England at the present time.

MORRIS, FRED J. ...Love at second sight; a farce [in one act]... Manchester, Eng.: Abel Heywood & Son, Ltd. [1924?] 18 p. 12°. (Abel Heywood & Son's original dramas. [no. 221.])
Cover-title.
Mosey, "a Jew money-lender."

MORRISON, ANNE, AND J. P. TOOHEY. Jonesy, a comedy in three acts... (based on a series of short stories by Mr. Toohey) (published in the Pictorial review)... New York: S. French; London: S. French, Ltd., cop. 1929. 123(1) p. plates, diagr. 12°. (French's standard library edition.) NBL p.v.209
Produced at the Bijou Theatre, New York, April 9, 1929, with Selden Bennett as Mr. Silverberg. For reviews see *Collection of newspaper clippings of dramatic criticism, 1928–1929*, v. H–K, † NBL.

MORTIMER, LILLIAN. Headstrong Joan; a comedy-drama in three acts... Chicago: T. S. Denison & Co. [cop. 1927.] 97 p. 12°. (Denison's select plays.) NBL p.v.176, no.7
A country village, near Boston. Among the characters are Abie the peddler, his son Ike, and the latter's sweetheart, Rosie.

—— A Manhattan honeymoon, a comedy-drama in three acts... Chicago: T. S. Denison & Company [cop. 1929]. 99 p. 12°. (Denison's select plays.)
The chief characters are the members of the Cohen family, in a Bronx flat.
Produced by the Kenesset Israel Players, Indianapolis, Ind., Dec. 4, 1932. See *Indiana Jewish chronicle*, Indianapolis, 1932, v. 19, no. 11, p. 1.

MULLALLY, DON HIRAM. The camels are coming, a comedy in three acts... New York, N. Y., Los Angeles, Cal.: S. French, Inc.; London: S. French, Ltd., cop. 1932. 98 p. plates, diagrs. 12°. (French's standard library edition.) NBL p.v.265
"Copyright, 1931...under title, 'De solt'n from Toikey.'"
Deals with the theatre "angel" problem. Produced at the President Theatre, New York, Oct. 2, 1931, with Joseph Greenwald as Milton Markowitz, the angel, and Gita Zucker as his daughter, Sylvia. For reviews see *Collection of newspaper clippings of dramatic criticism, 1931–1932*, v. C–E, † NBL.

MUMFORD, EDWARD WARLOCH. The traffic cop; an entertainment in one act... Philadelphia: Penn Publishing Company [cop. 1920]. 30 p. 12°.
The place is a street intersection in a big city. "Ikey Bamberger, bundle messenger for a shirt manufacturer."

MUSIC, A. LEROY. Park Avenue. (In: The Yearbook of short plays; first series. Evanston, Ill. [cop. 1931.] 12°. p. 129–147.)
In one act. NBL (Yearbook)
Mr. and Mrs. Seligman, tenants in an exclusive Park Avenue apartment hotel.

Individual Plays — 1915-1938, continued

NATHAN, THEODORE R. The rod of Aaron; a play in one act. illus. (Viewpoint. New York, 1936. 4°. v. 2, no. 2, p. 5–8.)
Scene: a railroad signal tower. Dr. Israel, a rabbi, and Roger Harris, president of the railroad, as the chief characters.

NATIONAL COUNCIL OF JEWISH WOMEN. [The Council lends a hand; a play in one scene. New York: National Council of Jewish Women, 1928.] 15 f. f°.   * C p.v.2019
Mimeographed.
Regarding the activities of the Council's Department of Immigrant Aid.

NEISULER, DOROTHY. The builders; a one-act play of Palestine, for reading and stage. [New York: Hadassah, 1932?] 5 f. f°.
Caption-title.
Mimeographed.

NELSON, WELLES B. The last day! a one-act play. illus. (10 story book. Chicago, 1928. v. 26, Aug., 1928, p. 9–13, 46.)
An "end of the world" farce. Among the characters are two bargaining Jews.

NERTZ, LOUIS, AND ARMAND FRIEDMANN. Go ahead; a comedy of Jewish life, in three acts ... Adapted from the Viennese by Nathaniel Edward Reeid. Acting edition... New York: Longmans, Green and Co., 1930. 3 p.l., 3–107 p. 12°. (Longmans' play series.)   NBL p.v.227
Produced under the title *The Booster* at the Nora Bayes Theatre, New York, Oct. 24, 1929, with Lester Bernard as Maurice Koppler, Beatrice Miller as his daughter, and Sam Wright as Jacob Stieglitz. For reviews see *Collection of newspaper clippings of dramatic criticism, 1929–1930*, v. A–C, † NBL.

NEUMAN, SARA. The old order, a play in one act. (Drama. Chicago, 1921. 4°. v. 11, p. 147–150.)   NAFA
The uncompromising immigrant Orthodox parents and their Americanized children.

NEWMAN, LOUIS ISRAEL. The emperor, the blacksmith and the cobbler; a legend of days gone by [in one scene]. [New York, 1936.] 8 f. 4°.
Caption-title.
Multigraphed.
Based on two humorous stories told by Jacob Richman in his *Laughs from Jewish lore*, New York, 1926, p. 64–70, * PSW.

—— "The miracle of the scrolls;" or, "The Purim of Saragossa." In three acts with prologue and epilogue... New York, 1936. [2], 13 f. 4°.
Mimeographed.
Based on an incident of deliverance, alleged to have happened to the Jews of Saragossa in 1420, the commemoration of which was celebrated by reading of the scrolls, after the manner of Purim. See "Alphons V. von Aragonien und die Juden in Saragossa" in *Jahrbücher für jüdische Geschichte und Literatur*, Frankfurt a. M., 1885, Jahrg. 7, p. 37–40, * PBC.

—— The triumph of the trees; a play of Palestine today [in three scenes]. [New York, 1936.] ii, 23 f. 4°.
Caption-title.
Mimeographed.
Motivated by the ruthless destruction of vineyards and trees by the Arabs, during the Palestinian riots of 1936.

NEWTON, HENRY LEE. Abie Cohen's wedding. (In his: Some vaudeville monologues. Chicago [cop. 1917]. 12°. p. 41–46.)

—— The customs inspector; a comedy skit in one act. (In his: Vaudevillainies. Boston [cop. 1915]. 12°. p. 11–17.)
Pat Malone and Abie Goldstein, a Hebrew tourist.

NICHOLS, ANNE. Abie's Irish Rose; a comedy in three acts. New York City, cop. 1924. 43 p. 8°.

—— —— New York [etc.]: Samuel French, 1937. 3 p.l., 123(1) p., 1 l., 3 pl. diagrs. 12°.
It was first staged at Stamford, Conn., and brought to the Fulton Theatre, New York, May 23, 1922, where it ran for over five years. R. B. Williams played Abie; Alfred Weisman, his father Solomon Levy; and Marie Carroll, Rosemary Murphy, the Irish girl. Reviewed in *Dramatist*, Easton, Pa., v. 15, p. 1214–1215, NAFA; by Gilbert Seldes in *Dial*, New York, v. 78, p. 432, * DA; by Robert Benchley in *Life*, New York, v. 85, May 21, 1925, p. 20, and June 25, p. 18, * DA; by Robert Littell in *New republic*, New York, v. 42, p. 98–99, * DA; *New York clipper*, New York, v. 70, May 31, 1922, p. 20, * T–† MVA; and in *Theatre magazine*, New York, v. 36, p. 95, † NBLA. See also *Collection of newspaper clippings of dramatic criticism, 1921–1922*, v. A–D, † NBL.
Produced in England at the Prince's Theatre, Manchester, March 28, 1927, and at the Apollo Theatre, London, April 11, 1927, with Joseph Greenwald as Solomon Levy, Russell Morgan as Abie, and Katharine Revner as Rosemary Murphy. Reviewed in *Jewish guardian*, London, v. 8, June 3, 1927, p. 15, * PBE; and (with illus.) in *Illustrated sporting and dramatic news*, London, v. 115, p. 272–273, * DA. See also digest of several London reviews in *Literary digest*, New York, v. 93, May 14, 1927, p. 27, * DA.
The history of this unusually successful play is told by Mary B. Mullett in *American magazine*, New York, v. 98, Aug., 1924, p. 18–19, 170, 172, * DA; by Robert L. Duffus in *Collier's*, Springfield, O., v. 74, July 26, 1924, p. 5, 30, * DA; by John E. Drewry in *National magazine*, Boston, v. 55, p. 12, 44, * DA; by Karl Schmidt in *Ladies' home journal*, Philadelphia, v. 41, Sept., 1924, p. 32, 134, 137, * DA; by the author, Anne Nichols, in *Theatre magazine*, New York, v. 39, July, 1924, p. 19, 54, † NBLA; and by Donald Freeman in *Vanity fair*, New York, v. 26, May, 1926, p. 52, 130, † VSM.
Revived at the Little Theatre, New York, May 12, 1937, and lasted 39 performances. See *Collection of newspaper clippings of dramatic criticism, 1936–1937*, v. A–Br, † NBL.

Seldes, Gilbert. Outlines of a preface [for a proposed novelization of the play]. (New republic. New York, 1927. f°. v. 51, p. 18–19.)   * DA

NICHOLSON, KENYON. Wanderlust; a play in one act... Boston: W. H. Baker Company [cop. 1926]. 2 p.l., 43–60 p. 12°. (Baker's royalty plays.)
A picture of the cheap and the tawdry in a Bronx flat, and Mr. Pollant the elder in the midst of it.
Printed also in L. Phillips and T. Johnson, compilers, *Types of modern dramatic composition*, Boston [1927], p. 41–60, *NCO (Phillips)*; and under the pseud. of Paul Halvey in B. H. Clark and Kenyon Nicholson, editors, *The American scene*, New York, London, 1930, p. 167–187, *NBL (Clark)*.

NORTON, FRANKLIN PIERCE. Abraham Lincoln; or, The rebellion [a play in five acts]. (In his: Six dramas of American romance and history. New York, 1915. 4°. p. 78–107.)   NBM
Judah P. Benjamin, Confederate statesman, one of the characters.

Individual Plays — 1915–1938, continued

NORTON, FRANKLIN PIERCE. Financier of New York. [A play in four acts.] (In his: Six dramas of American romance and history. New York, 1915. 4°. p. 45–77.) NBM
Trebals, a pawnbroker; Mak, his clerk; Esther, his daughter; Isidore Goldstone, a rich merchant. Trebals fashioned after Shylock. Scene: New York City.

NUSBAUM, JULIA K. Golden gifts; a playlet... New York: Bloch Pub. Co., 1922. 6 p. 16°.
Modern juvenile playlet, with some of the characters from the Bible.

O'BRIEN, FARLEY. Fixin' aunt Fanny; a farce in three acts... Franklin, Ohio: Eldridge Entertainment House, Inc., cop. 1935. 94 p. diagrs. 12°. (Eldridge royalty plays.)
Isadore Eisenheimer, collector "who remembers that business is business regardless of who is getting married, or why."

O'BRIEN, FLORENCE ROMA MUIR WILSON. The social climbers; a Russian middle-class tragedy in four acts, seen through western eyes, by Romer Wilson [pseud.]. London: E. Benn, Limited, 1927. vi, 7–79(1) p. 12°. (Benn's yellow books.) NCO p.v.559
Mikhail Abramski, "a middle-class capitalist of Jewish descent," his wife and their daughter. Scene: Russia, 1915–1921.

ODETS, CLIFFORD. "Awake and sing;" a play in three acts... [New York,] cop. 1933. [96] f. 4°. † NCOF
Reproduced from typewritten copy.
Various paging.

—— —— New York: Covici-Friede [cop. 1935]. xi, 15–114 p. front. 12°.
Copyrighted in 1933 under the title *I got the blues*.
Reprinted, with introduction by Harold Clurman, in his *Three plays*, New York [cop. 1935], p. vii–xi, 15–114, NBM.
Reprinted in part, with running synopses, in *Best plays of 1934–35*, New York, 1935, p. 236–261, NAFH; and in *Famous plays of 1935–36*, London, 1936, p. 521–605, NAFH.
A study of the Berger family in the Bronx section of New York City. All the characters are Jewish. Produced at the Belasco Theatre, New York, Feb. 19, 1935. See reviews in *Collection of newspaper clippings of dramatic criticism, 1934–35*, v. A–B, † NBL.
Produced by the Stage Society, London, Feb. 20, 1938. See *Jewish chronicle*, London, Feb. 25, 1938, p. 40, * PBE.

Levy, Henry W. A new playwright; young Philadelphian wins plaudits for play. (Jewish exponent. Philadelphia, 1935. f°. v. 95, March 1, 1935, p. 1, 7.) * PBD

ODETS, CLIFFORD. I can't sleep; a monologue. illus. (New theatre. New York, 1936. 4°. v. 3, Feb., 1936, p. 8–9.) † NBLA
The speaker is "a Russian Jew" accosted by a tramp.
Produced by the New Theatre League, during National theatre week, at the Longacre Theatre, May 26, 1935, with Morris Carnovsky as the speaker. See *Collection of newspaper clippings of dramatic criticism, 1934–1935*, v. H–J, † NBL.

—— Paradise lost; a play in three acts... New York: Random House [cop. 1936]. xiii, 204 p. 12°. NBM
The Gordons and the Katzes, two "liberal, middle-class, American families." Produced by the Group Theatre at the Longacre Theatre, New York, Dec. 9, 1935, with Morris Carnovsky as Leo Gordon and Luther Adler as Marcus Katz. For reviews see *Collection of newspaper clippings of dramatic criticism, 1935–1936*, v. Nin–Pos, † NBL.

Gessner, John W. "Paradise lost" and the theatre of frustration. (New theatre. New York, 1936. 4°. v. 3, Jan., 1936, p. 8–10, 39.) † NBLA

ODETS, CLIFFORD. Till the day I die [in seven scenes]. 74 p. (In his: Three plays. New York [cop. 1935]. 12°.) NBM
Reprinted in Percival Wilde, editor, *Contemporary one-act plays from nine countries*, Boston, 1936, p. 71–124, NAFH; and in *Famous plays of 1936*, London, 1936, p. 503–568, NAFH.
Deals with the persecutions of the Communists by the German Nazis. This one-act piece was "suggested by a letter from Germany in the *New masses*." Produced at the Longacre Theatre, New York, March 26, 1935. For reviews see *Collection of newspaper clippings of dramatic criticism, 1934–1935*, v. T–Y, † NBL.

—— Waiting for Lefty [in six episodes]. 54 p. (In his: Three plays. New York [cop. 1935]. 12°.) NBM
Repr.: New theatre, New York, v. 2, Feb., 1935, p. 13–20, illus.
Deals with the New York taxi strike of 1934. Produced at the Longacre Theatre, New York, March 26, 1935. For reviews see *Collection of newspaper clippings of dramatic criticism, 1934–1935*, v. T–Y, † NBL. The author acted therein the part of Dr. Benjamin.

O'HANLON, EDWIN. The club night night club; a novel amateur revue entertainment with optional music... New York: Fitzgerald Publishing Corporation [cop. 1935]. 62 p. 12°.
Herman Meyer, proprietor of Meyer's Model Wholesale Cloaks and Suits, and Rosita Meyer, his daughter and dress designer.

OLD scenes re-staged. "Macbeth." [Act I, scene 1.] illus. (Truth. London, 1928. f°. v. 104, no. 2725, Dec. 25, 1928, p. 19–21.) * DA
Spirit of Disraeli as the first apparition.

ONE, JUST N. E., PSEUD. Landsleit, a comedy of parents and children [in three scenes]. (Jewish forum. New York, 1928. 8°. v. 11, p. 401–408.) * PBD
In present-day America.

ORNITZ, SAMUEL BADISCH, AND V. CASPARY. Geraniums in my window; a comedy in three acts... [New York, 1934?] 46, 34, 38 l. 4°.
Reproduced from typewritten copy. † NCOF
In three acts.
Staged at the Longacre Theatre, New York, Oct. 26, 1934, with Robert Leonard as Weinstein, "a solid businessman," the Jewish restaurant employer of the two main characters. For reviews see *Collection of newspaper clippings of dramatic criticism, 1934–1935*, v. E–G, † NBL.

ORNITZ, SAMUEL BADISCH, AND DONALD DAVIS. Haunch, paunch and jowl; an anonymous autobiography. New York: Boni and Liveright [1924]. 2 p.l., 7–300 p. 8°. NBO
First edition, 1923.
Story of a young Jewish lawyer rising to fame in New York City by way of graft and corruption. It was dramatized by the author and Donald Davis and produced by the Artef group at the 48th Street Theatre, New York, Dec. 26, 1935. For reviews see *Collection of newspaper clippings of dramatic criticism, 1935–1936*, v. G–Il, † NBL.

Individual Plays — 1915-1938, continued

OSGOOD, ERASTUS. A whiff of evidence; a comedy drama [in three acts]. Franklin, Ohio [etc.]: Eldridge Entertainment House, Inc., cop. 1927. 63 p. 12°. (Eldridge popular plays.)
A rural mystery play. Nathan Weisberg, a peddler. He claims "the world is full of thieves."

OSTERWEIS, ROLLIN GUSTAV. A pageant [in a prologue and seven episodes. New Haven, 1935]. 7 f. 4°.
Reproduced from typewritten copy.
"Depicting the early history of the Jews in New Haven and commemorating the ninety-fifth anniversary of the Congregation Mishkan Israel."

PACKSCHER, HAZEL G. Book friends (playlet in two acts)... Cincinnati, Ohio: Department of Synagogue and School Extension [1935]. 1, 8 f. 4°.
Mimeographed.
"Experimental edition."
The characters are Lord Byron, Robert Browning, the four subjects of four historical fiction books, and a publisher.

—— Real people; a playlet for Jewish book week, in two acts. [Boston, 1936.] 3 f. 4°.
Caption-title.
Mimeographed.

PAIKOFF, SARAH. The calendar comes to life. (Jewish teacher. Cincinnati, 1935. 4°. v. 4, Nov., 1935, p. 19–23.) * PYW

PARFENOFF, STEPHEN S. Inside the great conflict. Epic on the World's war, politics and love. Boston: The Stratford Co., 1920. 8 p.l., 123 p. 12°. BTZI
A play dealing with the European war of 1914–1918 and the Russian Revolution of 1917. It begins with the birth of Wilhelm II, late German Kaiser, and ends with "Trotzky's greed."

PARSONS, JAMES FRANKLIN. Fun in a vaudeville agency; a humorous entertainment, in one scene. Chicago: T. S. Denison & Co. [cop. 1920.] 16 p. 12°. (Denison's specialties.)
Levi Goldstein, cornet player, applies for the position which pays the most.

PARSONS, MRS. MARGARET COLBY (GETCHELL). Life as it ain't; the noble landlord. (In her: Almost rehearsal-less plays; stunts and novelty programs. Boston [cop. 1931]. 12°. p. 26–28.) NBL p.v.272
Mr. Goldscheimer, the landlord, cares little whether or not he gets his rent.

PARSONS, MRS. MARGARET COLBY (GETCHELL), AND MADELEINE POOL. The rummage sale; a one act play for a cast of all women. Chicago: Dramatic Pub. Company [cop. 1927]. 26 p. 12°.
A sale in a vacant store. The women customers are native and foreign. Among the latter is included a Jewess.

PEIXOTTO, EUSTACE MADURO. Political promises [in two scenes]. (In his: Ten boys' farces. Boston, 1916. 12°. p. 67–76.) NASH p.v.1, no.7
Isidore Cohenstein promises the Jewish vote to the mayoralty candidate.

PELÉE, MRS. LILLIAN SUTTON. The trigger; a mystery farce in three acts... New York: Fitzgerald Pub. Corporation, cop. 1927. 64 p. 12°. NBL p.v.171
Mr. Jake Little, motion picture producer and real estate man. "He has coarse, black hair...wears flashy clothes. Very autocratic." The scene is laid in Hollywood, Cal.

PEMBERTON, MURDOCK, AND D. BOEHM. Sing high, sing low; a comedy in two acts and six scenes... New York, N. Y., Los Angeles, Cal.: S. French, Inc.; London: S. French, Ltd., cop. 1932. 2 p.l., 3–99(1) p., 2 l. plates, diagrs. 12°. (French's standard library edition.)
NBL p.v.293
Satirizing the activities and scandals of the Metropolitan Opera Company. Produced at the Sam H. Harris Theatre, New York, Nov. 13, 1931, with Con MacSunday as Weiner, "a loud-voiced, aggressive, middle-aged claque leader." For reviews see *Collection of newspaper clippings of dramatic criticism, 1931–1932*, v. P–S, † NBL.

PEPLE, EDWARD HENRY. The jury of our peers; a comedy in three acts. New York: S. French [etc.], cop. 1925. 120 p. 12°. (French's standard library edition.) NBL p.v.118
Mrs. Rosa Lichtenstein, "a dealer in clothing," member of a jury of all women.

The PERILS of Pauline. [In four scenes. New York: Hadassah, 1933?] 3 f. 8°.
Caption-title.
Mimeographed.

PERLMAN, DAVID H. A war-time Channukah [in one act]. (Review. Philadelphia, 1915. 12°. v. 11, Nov., 1915, p. 32–51.)

—— —— [New York: Jewish Welfare Board, 1915?] 9 f. 4°.
Mimeographed.
The play is staged in the sitting room of an inn in any of the countries at war in Europe.

PERLSTEIN, JENNIE. Getting a contribution. [In one act. New York: Hadassah, 1933?] 5 f. 8°.
Caption-title.
Mimeographed.

PERMANENT values. [In one act. New York: Hadassah, 1933?] 5 f. f°.
Caption-title.
Mimeographed.

PERTWEE, ROLAND. Honours easy; a play in three acts... London: S. French, Ltd.; New York: S. French, Inc., cop. 1932. 70 p., 1 l., 1 pl. 8°. (French's acting edition. no. 121.)
Two Jewish characters, a father and a son, in a struggle with a hard and unscrupulous Gentile who, in revenge for a thirty years old slight, is prepared to foul a blow at the father by besmirching the honor of the son. First produced at the St. Martin's Theatre, London, Feb. 7, 1930, with Allan Aynesworth as Sir Henry Markham, formerly Markheim, the father, and Robert Holmes as his son Henry. Reviewed in *Era*, London, v. 93, Feb. 12, 1930, p. 1, 5, † *NAFA*; *Jewish chronicle*, London, Feb. 14, 1930, p. 35, * *PBE*; and in *Jewish guardian*, London, v. 11, Feb. 7, 1930, p. 5, and Feb. 14, p. 10, * *PBE*.

Individual Plays — 1915–1938, continued

PHELPS, FRANKLIN. Hooligan at the bat; a vaudeville act [for two men]. Chicago: T. S. Denison & Company [cop. 1930]. 11 p. 12°. (Denison's vaudeville sketches.)
Homerun Hooligan fires Stayhome Steinberg off the baseball team.

—— Judge Applesauce presides; a burlesque trial... Chicago: T. S. Denison & Company [cop. 1930]. 22 p. 12°. (Denison's specialties.)
At the trial of Morris Mowitz, plaintiff, who rents a store to Oscar Hummerspitzenheimer, barber.

PHELPS, PAULINE. Pawnshop Granny; a play in one act... New York, N. Y., Los Angeles, Cal.: S. French, Inc.; London: S. French, Ltd. [etc.], cop. 1935. 31(1) p. diagr. 12°.
NBL p.v.357
Mrs. Beckanstin, the kindly landlady of the Irish Pawnshop Granny Riordan.

—— Uncle Peter and the D. D. S.; a one-act farce comedy... New York, N. Y., Los Angeles, Cal.: S. French, Inc.; London: S. French, Ltd. [etc.], cop. 1935. 32 p. diagr. 12°.
NBL p.v.357
Dr. Oswald Warburg, a dentist, with the aid of his mother, performs a dental operation upon Uncle Peter, his prospective father-in-law.

PHILLIPS, DAVID GRAHAM. ...Susan Lenox, her fall and rise...with a portrait of the author. New York [etc.]: D. Appleton and Company, 1917. 2 v. fronts. (ports.) 12°.   8–NBO
A play in four acts by George V. Hobart, entitled *The Fall and rise of Susan Lenox*, based on this novel, was produced at the Forty-fourth Street Theatre, New York, June 10, 1920. Several minor Jewish characters appear in it. See *Collection of newspaper clippings of dramatic criticism, 1919–1920*, v. R–Z, † NBL.

PHILLIPS, H. I. The great club sandwich inquiry [in one scene]. (New York Sun. New York, 1930. f°. May 8, 1930, p. 30.)   * A
Representative Sol Bloom of New York, one of the speakers. House of Representatives, U. S.

PHILLIPS, JOSEPH. The Alexanders; a play in four acts... London: A. H. Stockwell, 1919. 80 p. 12°.   NCR
The scene throughout is the home of an English Jewish family.

PIERCE, CARL WEBSTER. Alicia perks up; a comedy in three acts. Boston: W. H. Baker Company, 1924. 58 p. 12°. (Baker's edition of plays.)
A farcical comedy about Alicia who refuses to grow older. Reba Goldstein, whose motto is "business first."

—— Alley scene; or, The poet and the peasant. Ten minutes of nonsense for three men. (In his: Lucky numbers; thirteen stunts, sketches and monologues. Chicago [cop. 1931]. 12°. p. 131–138.)
A poet, a peasant, and a Jewish "sandwich man."

—— Be an optimist; a comedy in three acts. By Adam Applebud [pseud.]. Boston: W. H. Baker Company [cop. 1926]. 99 p. diagr. 12°. (Baker's royalty plays.)
Isaac Golditch, antiquer, of the Golditch Art Shop, and his daughter Becky. In the directions he is described as "a Hebrew gentleman. Should not be played as a burlesque stage Jew. We know he is a Jew mainly on account of his racial characteristics of gesture and speech."

—— Hixville to Hollywood, a farce comedy in three acts, by Adam Applebud [pseud.] (Carl Pierce)... Boston: Walter H. Baker Company [cop. 1929]. 141 p. incl. diagram. 12°.
Isidore Katz, "world's greatest moving-picture producer."

PINCUS, JOSEPH B. Haman the bully; one act comedy for Purim. illus. (Young Maccabee. New York, 1935. 4°. v. 1, March, 1935, p. 6–7.)
* PBD

PINSKI, DAVID. The beautiful nun; a drama in one act. <Written in June, 1919.> (In his: Ten plays. Isaac Goldberg, translator. New York, 1920. 12°. p. 149–160.)   * PTP
The action takes place in time of war. Two soldiers and four women inmates of a nunnery.

—— Cripples; a comedy in one act... Translated by Isaac Goldberg. New York [etc.]: Samuel French [1932]. 2 p.l., 3–12 p. 12°.
* PSQ p.v.5
Also in his *Ten plays*, New York, 1920, p. 75–86, * PTP.
Beggars squabbling for position on the church steps. Time and place: when and where you please.
Produced by the Menorah societies of Harvard and Radcliffe colleges, at the Agassiz House, Cambridge, Mass., April 10, 1926, and revived by them May 5, 1928. See *Jewish advocate*, Boston, v. 47, April 8, 1926, p. 2, p. 7, * PBD.
The original appeared in *Zukunft*, New York, 1919, v. 24, p. 417–419, * PBB.

—— Diplomacy; a satire. (In his: Ten plays. Isaac Goldberg, translator. New York, 1920. 12°. p. 111–134.)   * PTP
On the manner in which powerful interests work up war hysteria.
Time and place: of a fairy tale.

—— The God of the newly rich wool merchant. (In his: Ten plays. Isaac Goldberg, translator. New York, 1920. 12°. p. 35–49.)   * PTP
A tragi-comedy.
Scene: a vast temple-like hall in the home of a wool merchant. The wool merchant's apotheosis of the woolen deity who blessed him with prosperity.

—— The inventor and the king's daughter. (In his: Ten plays. Isaac Goldberg, translator. New York, 1920. 12°. p. 87–110.)   * PTP
The original appeared in *Zukunft*, New York, 1919, v. 24, p. 4–9, * PBB.
Banquet hall of a palace. An inventor offers to a king the secret of human happiness, in return for his daughter. He is refused and the secret dies with him. Should the princess have placed her love above the eternal happiness of mankind?
Presented at the David Lewis Theatre, Liverpool, by the University Jewish Students' Society, May 19, 1927.

—— Laid off; a tragedy in one act, by David Pinski; translated by Anna K. Pinski. (In: One-act plays for stage and study, seventh series. New York City, 1932. 8°. p. 157–168.)
"Laid off" from employment.   NCO

—— Little heroes; war episode in one act. Authorized translation from the Yiddish by Isaac Goldberg. (Stratford journal. Boston, 1917. 8°. v. 1, June, 1917, p. 15–24.)   * DA
Reprinted in his *Ten plays*, New York, 1920, p. 135–147, * PTP; and in Isaac Goldberg, translator, *Six*

Individual Plays — 1915-1938, continued

plays of the Yiddish theatre, second series, Boston [1918], p. 5-24, * *PTP*.
The original appeared in *Zukunft*, New York, 1916, v. 21, p. 991-994, * *PBB*.
The time is during the World war, in a ruined village of an invaded country. The persons are six youngsters, ranging in age from ten to fourteen. They talk of bold plans of resistance, but succumb to hunger and fright.

—— The phonograph; a comedy. (In his: Ten plays. Isaac Goldberg, translator. New York, 1920. 12°. p. 1-33.) * *PTP*
"The action takes place in a remote Russo-Yiddish town, where the Jews lived upon miracles." The comedy of a man who returned from America to a Russo-Jewish city with a phonograph and American ideas.

—— Poland — 1919, "A scene out of terrible days." Authorized translation from the Yiddish by Isaac Goldberg. (Menorah journal. New York, 1919. 4°. v. 5, p. 179-184.) * *PBD*
"Translator's note," p. 179.
A symbolic play. In a cellar, where a group of Jews, in fear of a massacre, are hiding.
Reprinted in his *Ten plays*, Isaac Goldberg, translator, New York, 1920, p. 161-175, * *PTP*.
Presented at the David Lewis Theatre, Liverpool, by the University Jewish Students' Society, May 19, 1927. Reviewed in *Jewish chronicle*, London, May 27, 1927, p. 35, * *PBE*.

PLUME, N. B., PSEUD. Cinder Eller; a one act play. (Review. Philadelphia, 1921. 16°. v. 13, Nov., 1921, p. 49-57.)
Copy: The Dropsie College, Philadelphia.

POLLOCK, CHANNING. The fool; a play in four acts... New York, London: Brentano's [cop. 1923]. 176 p. 12°. NBM
A synopsis of the play, with many extracts from the dialogue, is given in *The Best plays of 1922-23*, Boston [cop. 1923], p. 215-256, *NAFH*.
The hero of the play is the fool who defies both capital and labor, on behalf of his Christlike ideals. Produced at the Times Square Theatre, New York, Oct. 23, 1922, with Frank Sylvester as the poor man, and Wanda Laurence as Miss Levinson. For reviews see *Collection of newspaper clippings of dramatic criticism, 1922-1923*, v. A-F, † *NBL*.
Produced at the Apollo Theatre, London, Sept. 18, 1924. Reviewed in *Era*, London, v. 88, Sept. 24, 1924, p. 8, † *NAFA*.

POLLOCK, JOHN. For Russia! A legend of Russian history. (In his: Twelve one-acters. Kensington, 1926. 8°. p. 263-282.) NCR
Produced at the London Coliseum, Jan. 4, 1915. The action takes place outside of Moscow during Napoleon's invasion of Russia. As befits the year of its production, when Russia was Great Britain's ally, the play is a glorification of Russian patriotism and the villain is a German officer in the Russian army. Another villain is Moritz Mondstein, "contractor to the Russian army." The part was played by P. R. Goodyer. Reviewed in *Era*, London, v. 78, Jan. 6, 1915, p. 14, † *NAFA*.

POOL, TAMAR (HIRSCHENSOHN). "Lest we forget"; a play in three acts with a prologue, to recall the spirit of 1776. (Jewish forum. New York, 1932. 8°. v. 15, p. 197-200, 232-236, 266-268.) * *PBD*
The characters, with three exceptions, are Jewish historical figures of the Revolutionary period. Among them are the Seixases, the Gomezes, the Frankses, the Phillipses, Major Benjamin Nones, Isaac Moses, etc. The scene is New York and Philadelphia, July 8, 1776 — Thanksgiving Day, 1782.

PORAH, URVA, PSEUD. Thinking aloud. [In two scenes.] (B'nai B'rith magazine. Chicago, 1927. 4°. p. 41, p. 492.) * *PYP*
Jewish father and mother are turned away from an exclusive Adirondack hotel. Daughter undergoes a severe plastic operation for removing the Jewishness of her nose. "Forever we suffer, on account of our religion."

—— Thinking aloud. (B'nai B'rith magazine. Chicago, 1928. 4°. v. 42, p. 252.) * *PYP*
Dialogue between members of a Reformed congregation and their rabbi.

—— Thinking aloud. (B'nai B'rith magazine. Chicago, 1928. 4°. v. 42, p. 364.) * *PYP*
Dialogue between members of two congregations, one Reformed and the other Orthodox.

PORTER, ARTHUR KINGSLEY. The Virgin and the clerk. Boston: Marshall Jones Company, 1929. 2 p.l., 96 p., 1 l. 8°. NBM

—— —— London: Williams & Norgate, Ltd. [cop. 1929.] NBM
The scene is placed in Adana, Cilicia. The Bishop Coadjutor had signed a contract with a Jew for the sale of his soul in return for "success to be delivered" by the Jew. The promised success is about to be delivered, but the bishop refuses to go through with it. The Virgin voids the contract and surrenders it back to the bishop.

POWELL, HERBERT PRESTON. A nose for news; a comedy in three acts... New York: S. French, Inc.; London: S. French, Ltd., cop. 1935. 81(1) p. 12°. NBL p.v.412
How a crime wave is solved in the business office of a newspaper.
Rudy Birnbaum, "a Jew, loud, over-bearing and crafty...decidedly of the lower strata of his race," proprietor of an army and navy goods store.

—— That reminds me; a revue of good stories [in ten scenes]. (In his: The world's best book of minstrelsy. Philadelphia, 1926. 8°. p. 305-319.) MWF
One of the characters in the tenth scene is "the Jew."

PRESTON, EFFA E. Santa Claus on the air; a one-act Christmas comedy. Chicago: T. S. Denison & Company [cop. 1930]. 28 p. 12°. (Denison's Christmas plays.) NAFH p.v.70
Among the characters are Gideon Goldmark, president of the Northern Fur Traders' Association, and his wife — "straight" parts.

PRICE, OLIVE M. The gateway of tomorrow; an Americanization play in four scenes... St. Paul, Minn.: Scott-Mitchell Publishing Co. [cop. 1929.] 48 p. 12°. NBL p.v.256
America as the land of opportunity. The Kharkof family in Russia and in the Chicago ghetto.

PROVENCE, JEAN. At the gates. (In: Quick comedies; a collection of short comedy sketches by various authors. New York [cop. 1935]. 12°. p. 116-122.)
Characters: Mose Cohn, St. Peter, and Jewish angels, at the Pearly Gates.

—— Wedded bliss. (In her: Knockout blackouts. Franklin, Ohio, 1935. 12°. p. 45-47.)
One of the characters is Bullblatt of Bullblatt Brothers Greater Furniture Mart.

Individual Plays — 1915–1938, continued

QUACKENBUSH, CLARENCE EARL. Her busy day; a one act comedy. Edmeston, N. Y.: The author, cop. 1929. 28 p. 8°.   NBL p.v.225
A farcical sketch. "A Jew peddler," one of the characters.

—— The only way; a play in three acts... [Edmeston, N. Y.: The author,] cop. 1929. 80 p. 8°.   NBL p.v.225
Albert Levine, lawyer, "harsh and unscrupulous."

QUAIFE, ELISE WEST, AND ERNEST NEHRING. The trade. (In their: Monologues of every day. New York [cop. 1931]. 12°. p. 29–32.)
NBL p.v.268
Mrs. Weinberg in a crowded grocery store on the West Side of New York City.

—— Tricks of the trade. (In their: Monologues of every day. New York [cop. 1931]. 12°. p. 33–39.)   NBL p.v.268
The same Mrs. Weinberg, and her little Augustus, at the market.

QUINN, HUGH. Collecting the rent. [In one act.] (In his: Mrs. McConaghy's money, A quiet twelfth, Collecting the rent. London, 1932. 12°. p. 109–129.)   NCR
Time: "As the late troubles in Ireland are dying away." Ikey, a Jewish peddler, in company with his Irish friends and women customers, speaks in dialect.

RABINOWITZ, HENRY. The meturgeman. (Hebrew Union College monthly. Cincinnati, 1937. f°. v. 25, no. 2, p. 11.)   * PBD

RABINOWITZ, MOSHEH, PSEUD. The labor government of Palestine [in one act]. illus. (Haboneh. New York, 1935. 4°. v. 1, no. 1, f. 13–17.)

—— The man of labor [in one act], based on the life of Aleph Daled Gordon. (Haboneh. New York, 1936. 4°. v. 1, Jan., 1936, f. 5–6.)
Aaron David Gordon, 1856–1922, a Palestinian labor leader, is one of the prophets of the Poalei Zion movement.

—— The mishpat. (Haboneh. New York, 1935. 4°. v. 1, May, 1935, f. 8–12.)
A one-act sketch, dealing with pioneer life in Jewish Palestine.

—— Purim carnival in Tel Aviv; a comedy. [In one act.] (Haboneh. New York, 1936. 4°. v. 1, Feb., 1936, f. 6–9.)
A one-act playlet.

RAPHAELSON, SAMSON. The jazz singer... (based on his story, "The day of atonement," in Everybody's magazine, January, 1922). New York: Brentano's [cop. 1925]. 10 p., 2 l., 17–153 p. 12°.   NBM

—— —— New York, Los Angeles: S. French; London: S. French, Ltd., 1935. x p., 1 l., 17–158 p., 2 l. diagrs. 12°.
In three acts.
"I have used a Jewish youth as my protagonist because the Jews are determining the nature and scope of jazz more than any other race — more than the negroes, from whom they have stolen jazz and given it a new color and meaning. Jazz is Irving Berlin, Al Jolson, George Gershwin, Sophie Tucker. These are Jews with their roots in the synagogue. And these are expressing in evangelical terms the nature of our chaos today." — *Preface.*
A Jewish youth is faced with the question of choosing between success as an actor on the musical comedy stage and returning to his people to take his father's place as a cantor in an East Side synagogue. He chooses the latter course.
Scene: East Side, New York: and back stage, Fulton Theatre. First produced at the Fulton Theatre, New York, Sept. 15, 1925, with George Jessel as Jake Rubin or Jakie Rabinowitz, and Howard Lang as his father, the cantor. For reviews see *Collection of newspaper clippings of dramatic criticism, 1925–1926,* v. E–J, † *NBL.* See also C. I. Freed in *American Hebrew,* New York, 1926, v. 118, p. 262, 279, * *PBD.*

De Haas, Arline. The jazz singer; a story of pathos and laughter, novelized by Arline De Haas from the play by Samson Raphaelson; illustrated with scenes from the photoplay, a Warner Bros. production, directed by Alan Crosland, starring Al Jolson. New York: Grosset & Dunlap [cop. 1927]. 3 p.l., 248 p. front., plates. 12°.

Gross, Louis Daniel. "The jazz singer" [a sermon]. New York: A. Yokel [1925?]. 15(1) p. nar. 8°.
Cover-title.
Delivered at the Union Temple, Brooklyn, N. Y.

RAPP, WILLIAM JOURDAN. Osman Pasha; a play in four acts... New York, London: Century Co. [cop. 1925.] x, 145 p. front. 12°. NBM
Foreword by Charles V. Vickrey, p. vii–x.
A missionary play, the action of which is laid in Turkey in 1922–23. It deals with the relations of Turkey as a renascent power to the world problems confronting it. Ranking third in the councils of the Young Turk movement is Said Nouri Bey of Dönmeh sect (crypto-Jews descendants of the followers of Sabbatai Zevi) who advises the adoption of the "religion of Jesus of Nazareth" as the Turkish state policy. He is accordingly the exponent of the author's purpose in writing this play.

RAPPAPORT, SOLOMON. The dybbuk; a play in four acts, by S. Ansky [pseud.] translated from the original Yiddish by Henry G. Alsberg and Winifred Katzin, introduction by Gilbert W. Gabriel and a note on Chassidism by Chaim Zhitlowsky. New York: Boni & Liveright, 1926. 145 p., 1 l. front., plates. 12°.   * PTP
Reviewed in *The Times literary supplement,* London, 1927, v. 26, p. 350, † *NAA.*
Reprinted in T. H. Dickinson, editor, *Chief contemporary dramatists; third series,* Boston [1930], p. 605–638, *NAFH.*
Extracts from the text, together with a running synopsis, are given in *The Best plays of 1925–26,* New York, 1926, p. 160–197, *NAFH.*
The trial scene at the exorcizing of the Dybbuk, is reprinted, under the title *The Trial,* in Leo W. Schwarz, editor, *A Golden treasury of Jewish literature,* New York [cop. 1937], p. 457–468, * *PSY.*
First produced Dec. 9, 1920, the thirtieth day after the death of the author, at the Elyseum Theatre, Warsaw, by the Vilna Troupe, with Miriam Orleska as Leah, Elijah Stein as Chonnon, and Noah Nachbush as the itinerant preacher.
First produced in English at the Neighborhood Playhouse, New York, Dec. 15, 1925, with Mary Ellis as Leah and Albert Carroll as Chonnon. Reviewed (with illus.) by Henry G. Alsberg in *B'nai B'rith magazine,* Chicago, 1926, v. 40, p. 120–121, 133, * *PYP;* by A. McC. S. in *Catholic world,* New York, v. 122, p. 665–667, * *DA;* by Helen Walker in *Commonweal,* New York, v. 3, p. 215–216, * *DA;* by Robert Stone in *Jewish exponent,* Philadelphia, v. 77, March 12, 1926, p. 8, * *PBD;* and (with illus.) by Anne Morrow Lindbergh in *Woman citizen,* New York, v. 10, Feb.,

THE JEW IN ENGLISH DRAMA 173

Individual Plays — 1915-1938, continued
1926, p. 16, 39, *SNA*. For additional reviews see *Collection of newspaper clippings of dramatic criticism, 1925-1926*, v. A-D, † *NBL*, containing sixteen newspaper clippings and twenty-three references to other reviews. For additional illustrations see *Arts & decoration*, New York, 1926, v. 24, no. 4, p. 66, 82, *MAA*; *L'Illustration*, Paris, 1926, v. 167, p. 608–609, * *DM*, containing 6 illustrations, three of which are colored, of the Habimah Players' production in Paris, 1926.
A Hebrew version, prepared by Ch. N. Byalik, was staged by the Habimah players of Moscow, at the Mansfield Theatre, New York, Dec. 13, 1926, with Benjamin Zemach and L. Warshawsky as Chonon and Anna Rovina as Leah. For reviews see *Collection of newspaper clippings of dramatic criticism, 1926–1927*, v. D-H, † *NBL*.
First produced in England, by Edith Craig, at the Leeds Civic Playhouse, March 7, 1927, with Laura Earle as Leah and Sydney Mathewman as Chonnon. Reviewed by J. N. in *Jewish chronicle*, London, March 11, 1927, p. 44, * *PBE*.
Produced by the Forum Theatre Guild at the Royalty Theatre, London, April 4, 1927, with Jean Forbes-Robertson as Leah and Ernest Milton as Chonnon. Reviewed in *Country life*, London, 1927, v. 61, p. 610–611, † *MVA*; by Horace Shipp in *English review*, London, v. 44, p. 632–634, * *DA*; *Era*, London, v. 90, April 13, 1927, p. 9, † *NAFA*; by Huntly Carter in *Jewish chronicle*, London, April 8, 1927, v. 43, * *PBD*; (with illus.) in *Jewish guardian*, London, v. 8, April 8, 1927, p. 9, 20 and April 15, p. 3, * *PBE*; by Milton Waldman in *London mercury*, London, v. 16, p. 83–84, * *DA*; by Desmond MacCarthy in *New statesman*, London, v. 28, p. 797–798, * *DA*; by Horace Hornsell in *Outlook*, London, v. 59, p. 407–408, * *DA*; by Ivor Brown in *Saturday review*, London, v. 143, p. 559–560, * *DA*; and in *The Times*, London, April 5, 1927, p. 14, col. 2, * *A*, "The play is a greater one than it appears to be in the present production and there is inherent in it a consistent power now absent." More illustrations are found in *Illustrated sporting and dramatic news*, London, 1927, v. 115, p. 136, * *DA*.

RAPPAPORT, SOLOMON. . . . Le dibbouk; légende dramatique en 3 actes, par An-ski [pseud.]. Version française de Marie-Thérèse Koerner. Paris: Rieder, 1927. 140 p. 12°. (Judaïsme; œuvres... [v.] 6.) * PTP

Cohen, Mortimer J. "The Dybbuk" — its social message. (Jewish exponent. Philadelphia, 1926. f°. v. 78, May 14, 1926, p. 11.) * PBD

Coralnik, Abraham. Fairy-tale to myth. (New Palestine. New York, 1926. f°. v. 11, p. 440–441.) * PXL

Glassman, Leo M. The apocalypse of the ghetto. (Jewish forum. New York, 1927. 8°. v. 10, p. 295–296.) * PBD

Powys, John Cowper. A modern mystery play. (Menorah journal. New York, 1927. 4°. v. 13, p. 361–365.) * PBD

Recht, Charles. The Hebrew theatre in Moscow. illus. (Menorah journal. New York, 1923. 4°. v. 9, p. 124–127.) * PBD

Samuel, Maurice. The dybbuk, in three languages and four dimensions. (Menorah journal. New York, 1927. 4°. v. 13, p. 63–67.) * PBD

Shillman, Bernard. Two great Jewish plays. (Jewish world. London, 1929. f°. Dec. 26, 1929, p. 6–7.) * PBE

RATCLIFFE, DOROTHY UNA (CLOUGH). Nathaniel Baddeley, bookman, a play for the fireside in one act... Illustrated by Fred Lawson. Leeds: At the Swan Press, 1924. 50 p., 1 l. front., illus. 8°. NCO p.v.526
One of the characters is a Mr. Vosenach, undoubtedly meant to be Dr. A. S. W. Rosenbach of Philadelphia, who is represented as a buyer for an American firm, come to Yorkshire, England, to bid for a rare Marvell item.

RAZOVSKY, CECILIA. At Ellis Island, a play in two scenes. New York: General Committee of Immigrant Aid at Ellis Island, cop. 1922. 23 l. 8°.
Typewritten.
Presented before the National Conference of Social Work at Providence, R. I., June 27, 1922, for the purpose of visualizing the human aspect of social work on Ellis Island. The characters are Jewish and other immigrants; and government officials at the Island.

—— I-19; or, The Council lends a hand. A one-act sketch. [New York: Dept. of Immigrant Aid of the National Council of Jewish Women,] 1926. 23 l. 8°.
Typewritten.
Illustrates, in dramatic form, a phase of the activities of the Council, caused by the exigencies of the existing American immigration laws, in uniting the separated members of an immigrant Jewish family.

READE, LESLIE. The shattered lamp. [New York,] cop. 1933. 39, 32, 23 f. f°. † NCOF
Reproduced from typewritten copy.
A play about Nazi Germany.
Under the title *Take heed!* it was produced by the Progressive Players at the Piccadilly Theatre, London, Jan. 28, 1934, with Selma Vas Diaz as the Jewish wife of a German professor. See *Jewish chronicle*, London, Feb. 2, 1934, p. 35, * *PBE*, and again, under the present title, at the same theatre, in July, 1934. See ibid., July 20, 1934, p. 39.
It was first seen in this country, at Maxine Elliott's Theatre, New York, March 21, 1934, with Effie Shannon in the star Jewish part. For reviews see *Collection of newspaper clippings of dramatic criticism, 1933–1934*, v. Sh-T, † *NBL*.

REED, HOWARD. Funny Phinnie; a farce in three acts... Chicago: Dramatic Publishing Company [cop. 1932]. 93 p. diagrs. 12°.
Mr. Glucksman.

—— Right about faces; a farce in one act... Chicago: The Dramatic Publishing Company [cop. 1934]. 31 p. 12°.
Mrs. Goldstein, one of the customers at a beauty shop.

REELY, MARY KATHARINE. To be dealt with accordingly; a play of social adjustment in one act... Boston: W. H. Baker Co. [cop. 1928.] 24 p. 12°. (Baker's edition of plays.)
The conflict is between two mothers, one of old American stock and the other an immigrant Jewish woman, whose children have been brought to court for delinquent conduct. Each blames the other.
This play was produced by the Little Theatre of Temple Israel, Boston.

REISEN, ABRAHAM. Three girls. [In one act.] Translated by Jacob Robbins. (East and West. New York, 1915. 4°. v. 1, p. 44–46.) * PBD
During the World war, Lemberg, Galicia. The feared Russian soldiers have just entered the city.

Individual Plays — 1915-1938, continued

REISS, ISAAC. From "Success"; a play by Moishe Nadir [pseud.]. (The Pagan. New York, 1919. 8°. v. 3, no. 2, March, 1919, p. 37–38.)
* DA
Scene: at a banquet tendered to Ashkenazi, a poverty-stricken Jewish writer, in honor of his fifteen years of literary activity.

REYNOLDS, GERTRUDE M. (ROBINS). The daughter pays. By Mrs. Baillie Reynolds... New York: George H. Doran Company [1916]. 6 p.l., 9–377 p. 8° NCW
Adapted by Miles Malleson into a play of three acts, under the title *The Bargain*, and produced at the Pier Theatre, Eastbourne, England, June 14, 1926, with Frank Lacy as Rosenberg, and Charles Hickman as his son, Gerald.

REZNIKOFF, CHARLES. The black death. [In five scenes.] (In his: Chatterton, The black death, and Meriwether Lewis. [New York, cop. 1922.] 12°. p. 27–37.) NBL p.v.86
Reprinted in *Menorah journal*, New York, 1924, v. 10, p. 381–385, * PBD; and in his *Nine plays*, New York [cop. 1927], p. 74–84, NBM.
In a town in western Europe, 1348–1351, during the black death epidemic. The Jews were blamed as the cause of it.

—— In memoriam: 1933... New York: The Objectivist Press [cop. 1934]. 4 p.l., 54 p. 8°. NBI
Repr.: *Menorah journal*, New York, 1934, v. 22, p. 103–133, * PBD.
A dramatic poem, in seven parts, captioned as follows: Samaria fallen, 722 B.C.E.; Babylon, 539 B.C.E.; The Academy at Jamnia, anno 70; the Synagogue defeated, anno 1096; Spain, anno 1492; Poland, anno 1700; Russia, anno 1905.
Reviewed by Babette Deutsch in *Jewish frontier*, New York, v. 2, March, 1935, p. 25–26, * PBD.

REZNIKOFF, CHARLES. Rashi. (New Palestine. New York, 1925. 4°. v. 8, p. 356–357.) * PXL
The Library also has this issue of the periodical as a separate: New Palestine; Hebrew university issue, * PYX.
In one scene.
Reprinted in his *Nine plays*, New York [cop. 1927], p. 98–103, NBM.
Rashi, 1040–1105, eminent Biblical and Talmudic commentator; Der Spervogel, fl. 1180, one of the German Minnesingers; and Rashi's students are the speakers. The emphasis is laid upon the spirit of learning, embodied by Rashi, as the "inheritance of Israel."

—— Uriel Acosta. [A play in ten scenes.] (In his: Uriel Acosta, and a fourth group of verse. New York [cop. 1921]. 16°. p. 1–42.) NBL p.v.83
Reprinted in abridged form in *Menorah journal*, New York, 1925, v. 11, p. 35–42, * PBD; and in his *Nine plays*, New York [cop. 1927], p. 1–19, NBM.
The three versions differ somewhat in the arrangement of the scenes. The 1927 edition is in nine scenes.
Reprinted in Leo W. Schwarz, editor, *A Golden treasury of Jewish literature*, New York [cop. 1937], p. 441–457, * PSY.
Based on certain historical episodes in the life of Uriel Acosta, 1590?–1647. Place: the home of the Acostas in Portugal; and later, Amsterdam, Holland. Baruch Spinoza, 1632–1677, is represented as a youngster, one of a gang of boys, throwing stones at his uncle, the heretic Acosta.

RICE, ELMER L. Counsellor-at-law, a play in three acts. New York, Los Angeles: S. French; London: S. French, Ltd., 1931. 5 p.l., 3–298 p. plates. 12°. NBM
Reprinted in his *Plays*, London, 1933, p. 297–447, NBM; and in *Famous plays of 1932-33*, London, 1933, p. 575–727, NAFH.
It chronicles the rise of an East Sider to the position of the "most eminent lawyer in New York." Produced at the Plymouth Theatre, New York, Nov. 6, 1931, with Paul Muni in the title rôle as George Simon, and Jennie Moscowitz as his mother. It was revived the following season on Sept. 12, 1932, at the same theatre. Reviewed by L. I. Newman in *Jewish exponent*, Philadelphia, v. 91, Jan. 27, 1933, p. 1, 7, * PBD; by Stark Young in *New republic*, New York, 1932, v. 69, p. 69–70, * DA; and by Meyer Levin, with a general appreciation of the dramatist, in *Theatre arts magazine*, New York, 1932, v. 16, p. 54–63, NBLA. See also *Collection of newspaper clippings of dramatic criticism, 1931–1932*, v. C-E, and *1932–1933*, v. C-D, † NBL.
In London, it was seen at the Piccadilly Theatre, April 3, 1934. Reviewed in *Jewish chronicle*, London, April 13, 1934, p. 50–51, * PBD; and in *Theatre world*, London, 1934, v. 21, p. 224, MWA.

—— The left bank, a play in three acts. New York, Los Angeles: S. French; London: S. French, Ltd., 1931. 4 p.l., 3–225 p. front. 12°. NBM
A synopsis of the plot, with copious extracts from the text, is given in *The Best plays of 1931-32*, New York, 1932, p. 208–235, NAFH.
Deals with life among Americans on the left bank of the Seine, Paris. Produced at the Little Theatre, New York, Oct. 5, 1931, with Murray Alper as Joe Klein described as "an Americanized Russian Jew, small and dark." Reviewed by Stark Young in *New republic*, New York, 1931, v. 68, p. 264–265, * DA; and in *Theatre Guild magazine*, New York, v. 9, Nov., 1931, p. 6–7, NBLA. See also *Collection of newspaper clippings of dramatic criticism, 1931–1932*, v. I-L, † NBL.
Produced at the Ambassador Theatre, London, Sept. 26, 1932, with Denier Warren as Joe Klein. Reviewed by Leslie Rees in *Era*, London, v. 96, Sept. 28, 1932, p. 9, † NAFA; *Jewish chronicle*, London, Sept. 30, 1932, p. 57, * PBE; and in *The Times*, London, Sept. 27, 1932, p. 12, col. 2, and Sept. 28, p. 10, col. 2, * A.

—— Street scene, a play in three acts. New York, Los Angeles: S. French; London: S. French, Ltd., 1929. 4 p.l., 3–239 p. front., plates. 12°. NBM

—— —— London: Victor Gollancz, Ltd., 1930. 126 p. 12°.
Reprinted in his *Plays*, London, 1933, p. 79–202, NBM; in *Six plays*, London, 1930, p. 113–238, NCO; and in F. W. Chandler and R. A. Cordell, editors, *Twentieth century plays*, New York, 1934, v. 2, p. 81–128, NCO.
Extracts from the dialogue, with a running synopsis, are given in *The Best plays of 1928-29*, New York, 1929, p. 26–53, NAFH.
Produced at the Playhouse, New York, Jan. 10, 1929, with Horace Braham as Samuel Kaplan; Leo Bulgakov as his father, Abraham; and Anna Kostant as Shirley Kaplan. Reviewed by Wm. Z. Spiegelman in *B'nai B'rith magazine*, Cincinnati, 1929, v. 43, p. 167–168, * PYP; *Dramatist*, Easton, Pa., 1929, v. 20, p. 1394–1395, NAFA; and by Stark Young in *New republic*, New York, 1929, v. 57, p. 296, * DA. See also *Collection of newspaper clippings of dramatic criticism, 1928–1929*, v. S, † NBL.
Produced at the Globe Theatre, London, Sept. 9, 1930, with Abraham Sofaer as Abraham Kaplan and Mary Grew as Shirley Kaplan. Reviewed in *Era*, London, v. 94, Sept. 17, 1930, p. 1, 5, † NAFA; by G. J. in *Jewish chronicle*, London, Sept. 19, 1930, p. 65, 67, * PBE; by A. G. Macdonell in *London mercury*, v. 23, p. 176–177, * DA; and by Gilbert Wakefield in *Saturday review*, London, v. 150, p. 339, * DA.

Individual Plays — 1915-1938, continued

RICE, ELMER L. La calle (Street scene); drama en tres actos, traducción castellana de Juan Chabas... dibujos de Merlo. Madrid, 1930. 87 p. 16°. (La Farsa. año 4, núm. 168.)
NBL p.v.243
Produced at the Teatro Español, Madrid, Nov. 14, 1930, by the Compañía de Margarita Xirgu.

—— ... We, the people, a play in twenty scenes. New York: Coward-McCann, Inc. [cop. 1933.] ix, 253 p. front. 12°. NBM
Scene 15 of the play, captioned *Fate of Jew and liberal on college faculty*, is reprinted with illus. in *B'nai B'rith magazine*, Cincinnati, 1933, v. 47, p. 232, 253-254, * PYP.
A synopsis of the story, with copious extracts from the text, is printed in *The Best plays of 1932-33*, New York, 1933, p. 271-310, NAFH.
What the present social system is doing to all classes of people. Produced at the Empire Theatre, New York, Jan. 23, 1933, with David Leonard as Morris Hirschbein, a Jewish instructor. Reviewed in *Christian century*, Chicago, 1933, v. 50, p. 231, † ZEA; by A. E. Smith in *New outlook*, New York, v. 161, March, 1933, p. 10, * DA; by Stark Young in *New republic*, New York, v. 74, p. 18-19, * DA; and by Kenneth McKean (with illus.) in *Theatre Guild quarterly*, New York, v. 10, March, 1933, p. 20-21, NBLA. See further reviews in *Collection of newspaper clippings of dramatic criticism, 1933-1934*, v. T-Y, † NBL.

RIEGELMAN, HAROLD. Pledging dad; a one act dialogue. (Jewish tribune. New York, 1925. f°. v. 44, June 5, 1925, p. 4-5.) * PBD
Jephtha David, Jewish fraternity man of Darnell University, explains it all to his father.

RILEY, ALICE CUSHING (DONALDSON). Uplifting Sadie. (In: New plays for women & girls. New York, 1932. 8°. p. 155-173.) NBL
In one act.
Place: directors' room, any woman's club in the U. S. A. Miss Blum is "chairman of table-decorations."

RILEY, EDNA, AND E. P. RILEY. Before morning; a mystery-drama in three acts... Chicago: The Dramatic Publishing Co. [1934.] 77 p. incl. diagrs. 12°. NBL p.v.360

—— —— Before morning; a melodrama... [New York, 1933?] 36, 36, 26, 3 f. plan. 4°. † NCOF
A murder thriller. Produced at the Ritz Theatre, New York, Feb. 9, 1933, with Clyde Fillmore as Leo Bergman, "a man-about-town." See *Collection of newspaper clippings of dramatic criticism, 1932-33*, v. A-B, † NBL.

ROBBIN, EDWARD. Bitter herbs; a play in one act. (Menorah journal. New York, 1928. 4°. v. 15, p. 147-157.) * PBD
The scene is laid in "a village at the far end of Czechoslovakia."

ROHMAN, RICHARD. Power of the press; a contemporary play [in three acts]. [New York,] cop. 1935. 75 f. 4°. † NCOF
Various paging.
With ms. and typewritten additions.
Deals with the organized effort of newspaper men to unionize and the publishers' resistance to collective bargaining. Produced at the Civic Repertory Theatre, New York, April 5, 1936. One of the striking reporters on the *Express* is here called Levy. For reviews see *Collection of newspaper clippings of dramatic criticism, 1935-1936*, v. Pow-Sea, † NBL.

ROMANO, ALBERTO. Match-making in a tavern [in one scene]. From the Judeo-Spanish of G. Buki Romano; translated by N. B. Jopson. (Slavonic review. London, 1930. 8°. v. 9, p. 297-302.) * DA
Reprinted in Joseph Leftwich, editor, *Yisröel; the first Jewish omnibus*, London [1933], p. 1050-1055, * PST.
A translation of "In la lokanda," in the *Sarajevo Jevrejski Glas*, a Serbian Jewish weekly.

ROMONEK, MRS. LEA LIPSEY. Love cannot make the dead dance. [Omaha, Neb., 1931.] [4], 25 f. 4°.
In one act.
Mimeographed.
"Story of the revolt of the individual against destiny." The place is a village in Russia near the German border, fifty years ago.
First produced by the University of Nebraska Players, at Lincoln, Neb., May 14, 1931, and as the second prize play in the Temple Israel of Boston play contest, by the Little Theatre of Temple Israel, Oct., 1932.

—— Passport. [In one act. Omaha, Neb., 1931.] [4], 24 f. 4°.
Mimeographed.
"The forces of enlightenment arrayed against the ugly forces of waste, war and conscription." Time and place: same as in the preceding *Love cannot make the dead dance*.
First staged by the University of Nebraska Players at Lincoln, Neb., May 27, 1931, and by the Little Theatre of Temple Israel, Boston, Oct. 24, 1933.

"ROOSHIAN" tea, fish-balls and marbles. (In: Werner's readings and recitations. New York, 1916. 12°. no. 58, p. 174-175.) NACG
A monologue for a Russian-Jewish woman.

ROSE, EDWARD EVERETT. Penrod; a comedy in four acts, adapted for the stage from Booth Tarkington's Penrod stories, by Edward E. Rose... New York: S. French [etc.], cop. 1921. 126 p. plates. 12°. (French's standard library edition.) NBL p.v.84
A tale of juvenile detectives and love-making villains. First staged at Apollo Theatre, Atlantic City, N. J., May 20, 1918. Reviewed in *New York dramatic mirror*, v. 78, p. 766, * T-* DA. Produced with mostly juvenile actors at the Globe Theatre, New York, Sept. 3, 1918, with Henry Quinn as Maurice Levy "of heroic digestion," one of the gang. Reviewed by C. C. Savage in *Forum*, New York, v. 60, p. 622-623, * DA; by Channing Pollock in *Green book magazine*, Chicago, v. 20, p. 779, 784-786 (with illus.), NAFA; *Independent*, New York, v. 95, p. 338, * DA; and *Theatre magazine*, New York, v. 28, p. 195, 205, 211 (with illus.), † NBLA. See also *Collection of newspaper clippings of dramatic criticism, 1918-1919*, v. M-R, † NBL.

—— Rose of the Ghetto; comedy drama in four acts. New York: S. French; London: S. French, Ltd., cop. 1927. 98 p. 12°. (French's standard library edition.) NBL p.v.174
The action takes place on Halsted St., the Jewish ghetto of Chicago, and at Westchester, N. Y.

ROSENFIELD, JONAS A. Gordon versus Gordon; a mock trial playlet [in one act] for purpose of Zionist propaganda. Dallas, Tex. [cop. 1917.] 32 p. 8°.
The domestic troubles of an enthusiastic Zionist, caused by his work for his ideal and the consequent neglect of his family duties.

Individual Plays — 1915–1938, continued

ROTH, SAMUEL. Herzl; a play in seven scenes and an epilogue. (Jewish tribune. New York, 1924. f°. v. 43, April 18, 1924, p. 10–11, 33–34; May 2, p. 14, 33; June 6, p. 10, 21, 23.) * PBD
The characters are Theodor Herzl, 1860–1904, founder of the modern Zionist movement, Émile Zola, the German Kaiser, Herzl's wife Julia, and others.

—— Mr. Edmund Gosse entertains on the occasion of his seventieth birthday. An imaginary conversation. (Menorah journal. New York, 1922. 4°. v. 8, p. 171–178.) * PBD
The speakers are Sir Edmund Gosse, G. K. Chesterton, Hilaire Belloc, George Moore, Israel Zangwill, and a servant.

RUBIN, WILLIAM BENJAMIN. The Bolshevists; a comedy drama [in four acts]... Boston: Cornhill Co. [cop. 1921.] 6 p.l., (1) 4–87 p. 12°. NBM
Louis Mendel, one of the committee of employees. An anti-red play. "Americans, take heed. Bolshevism is at our door..."

RUBINSTEIN, HAROLD FREDERICK. Britania calling. [In four acts.] (In his: Plays out of time. London and New York [1930]. 12°. p. 89–175.) NCR
Describes an imaginary adventure in Roman Britain, about 300 A. D., viewed in modern perspective. A group of Romans at the mercy of the Druids and Manasseh, "a Hebrew magnate."
Reviewed in *The Times literary supplement*, London, 1930, v. 29, p. 858, † *NAA*.

—— The deacon and the Jewess; a play in one act... London [etc.]: Samuel French, Ltd., cop. 1935. 28 p. 16°. (French's acting edition. no. 1638.)
Reprinted in his *Israel set free*, London [1936], p. 13–52, *NCR*, and in J. W. Marriott, editor, *Best one-act plays of 1935*, London [1936].
The scene is Oxford, England, 1221. Based on the celebrated case of Robert of Reading who embraced Judaism for the love of a Jewish girl. For the history of this case see *The Deacon and the Jewess; or, Apostacy at common law*, by W. F. Maitland, reprinted with a Prefatory note by Israel Abrahams in *Jewish Historical Society of England, Transactions*, 1912, v. 6, p. 254–276, * *PXQ*. In this playlet the Jewish girl is represented as the daughter of Benedict le Puncteur, noted mediaeval Jewish exegete and grammarian in England. Benedict is identified as Berechiah ben Natronai Krespia ha-Nakdan. See the latter name in *Jewish encyclopedia*, v. 3, p. 53–55. Reviewed in *Jewish chronicle*, London, Feb. 28, 1936, p. 26, * *PBE*.

—— Jew Dyte; an historical comedy in one act. (In his: On the father's side. London, New York, cop. 1933. 12°. p. 5–29.) NCO p.v.681
"Historical footnote," p. 27–29.
Reprinted in his *Israel set free*, London [1936], p. 85–116, *NCR*. See "Apropos Jew Dyte," ibid., p. 112–116.
The action centers about the events on the evening of May 16, 1800, when Moses David Dyte, one of the early English ancestors of the author, helped to save the life of King George III, who was shot at by Hadfield, an ex-soldier, during a performance at the Drury Lane Theatre. Cf. James Picciotto, *Sketches of Anglo-Jewish history*, London, 1875, p. 277–278, * *PXQ*. See also C. Roth in *Jewish chronicle*, London, Oct. 6, 1933, p. 23, * *PBE*.
Produced by the Little Theatre of Temple Israel, Boston, March 5, 1935.

—— They went forth; a memorial. (In his: On the father's side. London, New York, cop. 1933. 12°. p. 31–56.) NCO p.v.681
In one act.
The scene is in Mitau, Russian Courland, in the winter of 1832–33. In the incident on which it is based, the escape of a young Jewish recruit from the Russian army into England, one of the author's forbears (on his father's side) is involved as the chief abettor of the escape.
Reprinted in Constance M. Martin, editor, *Fifty one-act plays*, London, 1934, p. 263–283, *NAFH*; and in the author's *Israel set free*, London [1936], p. 117–150, *NCR*. See "Apropos They went forth," ibid., p. 147–150.

—— To the poets of Australia; a play in one act. (In his: Israel set free. London [1936]. 12°. p. 151–186.) NCR
"Apropos To the poets of Australia," p. 185–186.
The scene is Sydney, New South Wales, 1835, and the main characters are the two brothers Barnett and Isaac Levey, and their young nephew, Jacob Marks, recent Australian immigrants from Whitechapel, London. The title refers to a prize offered by B. Levey, proprietor of the Theatre Royal, Sydney, in 1832 for an opening address to be spoken at the initial performance in the Theatre.
The author of this play is a grandson of the above-mentioned Jacob Marks.

—— Whitehall, 1656; a play in one act. London: The Favil Press, 1934. 23 p. 12°.
Reprinted in his *Israel set free*, London [1936], p. 53–83, *NCR*.
Reviewed in *Jewish chronicle*, London, Feb. 1, 1935, p. 20, * *PBE*.
A national conference was summoned by Oliver Cromwell to pass on the legality of the re-admission of the Jews in England. It met at the Whitehall Palace in 1655–1656. The characters are the Protector, his wife and daughter, Menasseh ben Israel, the prime mover in seeking re-admission, and the maranno Samuel Dias, son of Don Antonio ("Hunter" in the play). Cromwell is represented as fully in sympathy with the Jews but urging "gradualness" in face of the likely opposition.

RUTHENBURG, GRACE DORCAS. Hans Bulow's last puppet. [In one act.] (In: G. P. Baker, editor, Yale one-act plays. New York, 1930. 8°. p. 43–68.) NBL (Baker)
Besides the puppetmaker, his daughter Tilda, and the herald of the Markgraf of Munich, an old clothesman is introduced. "This may be played by genuine puppets or by human actors." First produced by the Yale University Department of Drama at the University Theatre, Nov. 6–10, 1928.

SACKLER, HARRY. Due east. [A dramatic episode in one act.] (Jewish tribune. New York, 1927. f°. March 4, 1927, p. 6, 33, 35.) * PBD
An attempt at a psychological portrait of an event in the life of Nahman of Bratzlav, 1770–1811, founder of the sect of Bratzlaver Hasidim, at the moment, in 1798, when he decided to make a pilgrimage to the Holy Land.

—— The seer looks at his bride. (Reflex. New York, 1927. 4°. v. 1, no. 1, p. 49–58.) * PBD

—— —— A play [in three scenes]. Boston: W. H. Baker Company [cop. 1932]. 29 p. 12°. (Baker's royalty plays.)
Based on a Hasidic story believed to have happened with the historic Reb Yaakov Yitzhak Horowitz (Itzikl), b. 1745, and Reb Elimelech, tzaddik of Lizansk, both of whom are among the characters in this play. "The principal episodes were culled from 'Ma'assay Norah.'"
Reprinted in Leo W. Schwarz, editor, *A Golden*

Individual Plays — 1915-1938, continued

treasury of Jewish literature, New York [cop. 1937], p. 514–528, * PSY.
    Produced by the Pathfinders-Reviewers at the Temple Playhouse, San Francisco, Nov. 10, 1929, with Lloyd Silverstein as the seer and Consuelo T. Bley as the bride. Reviewed in Congregation Emanu-El, San Francisco, *Temple chronicle,* Nov. 15, 1929, v. 6, no. 14, * PXY.

—— The tsadik's journey. [In four acts. Translated by the author from his original Yiddish.] (Reflex. New York, 1927. 4°. v. 1, Nov., 1927, p. 71–102.)   * PBD
    Originally appeared in his *Dramen,* New York, 1925, v. 1, p. 129–217, * PTP.
    "This play is an attempt to catch a fleeting glimpse of the milieu in which Hasidism had its rise. The episode around which the tale is spun is typical of the more primitive phase of the movement... Not a record of men and events but an attempt to imprison the exotic shadows of a remote generation." — *Preface.*
Its theme is the struggle between powers of light and darkness for the possession of the soul of a young man named Heshel. The antagonists are a Hasidic saint and an old gipsy, who is Satan incarnate. Place: in the Carpathian mountains. Time: dawn of the last century.
    It was staged by the Yiddish Art Theatre at the Norah Bayes Theatre, Jan. 21, 1926, with Maurice Schwartz as the saint. An illustration is given in *Theatre arts monthly,* New York, 1926, v. 10, on front. facing p. 283, *NBLA.* See also M. Hurwitz, "A Son of his people," in *Jewish tribune,* New York, Oct. 1, 1926, p. 14, 20, 24, * PBD.

ST. CLAIR, ROBERT. "The ghost in the glass;" a mystery comedy in three acts... Minneapolis, Minn.: Northwestern Press, cop. 1934. 80 p. 12°.   NBL p.v.317
    Locality: the Adirondack mountains.
    Herbert Sachs, described as "a personable young man with a ready grin and a nice friendly personality," is one of the characters.

SALANT, PAULINE, AND G. SHADDUCK. Saving the country... a play in one act, 3 scenes. [Katonah, N. Y.: Brookwood Labor College, 1934?] [1], 9 f. 4°.   † NCOF p.v.20
    The scene is a furnished room, on the lower East Side of New York, tenanted by a Jewish orthodox family. Time: during the depression of 1929–1933.

SAMPTER, JESSIE ETHEL. The new apostacy; a play in one act... New York: Young Judaea, cop. 1917. 13 f. 4°.
    Cover-title.
    Mimeographed.
    A nationalist play of modern American Jewish life.

—— The servant girl; a comedy in dialogue. (Opinion. New York, 1938. 4°. v. 8, March, 1938, p. 13–16.)   * PBD

SAMUEL, MAURICE. David's fiancee, a futile conversation [in one scene]. (Reflex. Chicago, 1929. 8°. v. 4, p. 42–47.)   * PBD

SAMUELS, MAURICE VICTOR. A pageant of the strong... [In a prelude and five scenes.] New York: Jarvis-Maxwell Publishing Co., 1923. 58 p. 8°.   NBL p.v.125
    "'A Pageant of the strong' is a revelation of Jewish idealism" as exemplified in five episodes of Jewish history. Scenes 3 and 4 relate to modern history in Europe, and scene 5 to modern America. Presented for the first time at the Hotel Astor, New York, on the evenings of Dec. 26, 27, 28, 1921.

SAUNDERS, LILLIAN. Sob sister, dramatized... from the story of the same name by Fannie Hurst. (Drama. Mt. Morris, Ill., 1921. 4°. v. 11, p. 354–357.)   NAFA
    Max Zincas, of the Zincas Importing Company, breaking away from his lady friend.

SAVAGE, GEORGE. A small down payment; a farce. (In: Glenn Hughes, editor, Short plays for modern players. New York, 1931. 8°. p. 105–121.)   NBL (Hughes)
    The Laskys are harassed by the installment collectors, one of whom is timid Jacobs.

SCHACHTEL, HYMAN JUDAH. The eternal people; a dramatic portrayal of Israel [in two acts and twenty scenes]. New York: Behrman Jewish Book House, 1935. 48 p. illus. 8°.
    Jewish history from the earliest days to the present. Act II, scenes 1 to 4, portray incidents in American Jewish history and introduce Judah Touro, Rebecca Gratz, Isaac Leeser, Penina Moise, and Isaac M. Wise.

SCHIFFER, MRS. ALICE WALLER. Ruth makes a convert [in three scenes. New York: Hadassah, 1933?]. 6 f. f°.
    Caption-title.
    Mimeographed.

SCHIMMEL, ROBERT C. When Irish eyes are smiling; a comedy in three acts... New York: Fitzgerald Publishing Corporation [cop. 1933]. 108 p. 12°. (Playhouse plays.)
    Mrs. Feinberg, the landlady, among her Irish tenants and friends. She too has her troubles but it all comes out well.

SCHOFIELD, STEPHEN. The bruiser's election; a political farce in one act. London: The Labour Publishing Company, Limited [1925]. v, 7–24 p. 12°. (Plays for the people.) NCO p.v.523
    One of the characters is Sir Archibald Ponsonby-Goldman, a candidate for Parliament, described as "a very rich-looking, oily-voiced, middle-aged man."

SCHULMAN, SAMUEL, AND S. MILLER. The spirit of Judaism; a pageant [in eight parts]. Cincinnati, Ohio: Dept. of Synagogue and School Extension of the Union of American Hebrew Congregations [cop. 1926]. 35 p. 8°.
    * PSQ p.v.2
    Parts 7 and 8 of this pageant are entitled "The new world and the new hope" and "The synagogue in America" respectively.
    It was presented at the golden jubilee of Congregation Beth-El, New York, in 1924.

SCHWEID, MARK. Borrowed years; a play in eight scenes. Translated by Samuel S. Grossman. (Jewish tribune. New York, 1925. f°. v. 44, March 6, 1925, p. 10, 12; April 3, p. 8, 10, 47; July 3, p. 12, 14.)   * PBD
    An eminent rabbi is dying. To save his life, others must donate portions of their own. Many donate short periods, but it is not sufficient. Thereupon, Dvoreh, the sexton's young daughter, gives her entire life away, and she accordingly dies. The rabbi recovers and enters upon the long life which would have been Dvoreh's. The remainder of the play consists of episodic visions which the rabbi imagines about his savior, as the might-have-been bride, wife and mother. This popular folk-tale is the subject of two well-known poems, *The Sexton's daughter,* by S. G. Frug, and *The Gift,* by David Frischman.

Individual Plays — 1915–1938, continued

SCHWEIZER, JUSTUS. Domitian; or, The end of the Flavians, a historical drama for male characters, in five acts... Brooten, Minn.: Catholic Dramatic Company, cop. 1926. 80 p. 16°.
Time: Sept. 17th and 18th, A. D. 96. Place: Rome. Elymas, a villainous Jewish magician.

SCOTT, MRS. AGGIE DEAN. The early settlement of Georgia as told in historical playlets... Athens, Ga.: The author [cop. 1932]. 64 p. 8°.
Issued on the occasion of the Georgia bicentennial, 1733–1933. The eighth episode, in two scenes, is named *The Coming of the Israelites.* It is dated July 7, 1733, Savannah, and among the historical characters are Minis, Dr. Nunis, De Lyon and Sheftall. See Leon Huehner, "The Jews of Georgia in colonial times," in American Jewish Historical Society, *Publications,* no. 10, p. 65–95, * PXY.

SEGAL, ALFRED. As I see it; a contribution to a gridiron [in one scene]. (Every Friday. Cincinnati, 1930. 4°. v. 6, March 14, 1930, p. 8, 31.) * PBD
Four ladies at a bridge game, discussing Jewish problems.

SEGAL, HYMAN. East Side, West Side; a play [in three acts]. New York: Langdon Publishing Company, Inc., 1926. 83 p. 12°.
East Side of Manhattan, New York City, about the year 1913.

SEGAL, SAMUEL MICHAEL. The convert [in two acts]. illus. (Young Judaean. New York, 1935. 4°. v. 23, May, 1935, p. 1.) * PBD
"In this playlet we find expressed the traditional reverence of the Jew for learning."

—— Hitlerites and Chanukah lights... New York: Behrman's Jewish Book House, 1933. 2 p.l., 12 p. 12°. * PSQ p.v.5
In the year 2000. Eight surviving Hitlerites are shown the folly and futility of anti-Semitism.

—— The light, the coin and the feast [in four scenes]. New York: Behrman's Jewish Book House, cop. 1934. 20 p. 12°.
Among the characters are Judah ha-Levi, fl. 12th century, and Chayyim Nachman Byalik, 1873–1934, noted Hebrew poets. The occasion is the feast of the Maccabees.

—— One Chanukah morning. New York: Hebrew Publishing Company, 1935. 16 p. 12°.
In one act.
"Characters: Mr. and Mrs. A. L. Werben, and their children, Rhoda and Morty."

—— One Chanukah night. illus. (Young Judaean. New York, 1934. 4°. v. 22, Dec., 1934, p. 2–3, 16.) * PBD
Scene: the interior of a synagogue. "Midnight brings mystery and adventure to the boys... as strange figures appear and vanish..."

—— Treasure Chanukah; a fantasy [in one act]. New York: Hebrew Publishing Company, 1935. 16 p. music. 12°.
Characters: a teacher and her fourteen pupils.

—— Young Maimonides "lost and found"; a fantasy [in one act]... New York: Hebrew Publishing Company, 1935. 16 p. 8°.
Staged by the Junior Guild of Congregation Beth Israel, Richmond Hill, L. I., N. Y., May 5, 1935.

SELIGMAN, ESTHER. Snowball and fair play; a dialogue. (American Hebrew. New York, 1918. 4°. v. 102, p. 406.) * PBD

SEXTON, ETHELYN. Bernstein tries 'em out; entertainment in one act. New York [etc.]: Samuel French, cop. 1925. 20 p. 12°. (French's international copyrighted... edition of the works of the best authors. no. 524.)
NBL p.v.142, no.8
A farcical sketch showing the efforts of vaudeville aspirants to get jobs in Julius Bernstein's de luxe entertainment company.

SHAW, MRS. HENRIETTA OTIS. For freedom; a play [in one act]... Experimental edition. Cincinnati: Dept. of Synagogue and School Extension of the Union of American Hebrew Congregations [1935]. 1, 19 f. 4°.
Typewritten.
An episode of Czarist anti-revolutionary suppression, in the Russian Pale, in 1885.
Produced at the Temple Israel Little Theatre, Boston, Dec. 13, 1932. Described in *Jewish advocate,* Boston, v. 66, Dec. 9, 1932, part 1, p. 6, * PBD.

SHAW, IRWIN. Bury the dead... New York: Random House [cop. 1936]. 107 p. 8°. NBM
It was first printed, under the title *"Bury the dead,"* a play about the war that is to begin tomorrow night, with illustrations, in *New theatre,* New York, v. 3, April, 1936, p. 15–30, † *NBLA.*
Reprinted in *Famous plays of 1936,* London, 1936, p. 327–389, *NAFH.*
The dead of the Great war refuse to be buried. Its theme is very much like that of Hans Chlumberg's *Miracle at Verdun,* q.v. The fifth corpse is that of Private Levy. A discussion about the play, at a public reading of it, on March 29, 1936, at the Hollywood Women's Club, is given in *New theatre,* New York, v. 3, May, 1936, p. 6–8, 34, † *NBLA.* It was staged at the 46th Street Theatre, New York, March 14, 1936, and at the Ethel Barrymore Theatre, April 18, 1936, with Bertram Thorn as Private Levy. For reviews see *Collection of newspaper clippings of dramatic criticism, 1935–1936,* v. A–B, † *NBL.*

—— Second mortgage; a play in one act. (One act play magazine. New York, 1938. 4°. v. 2, May, 1938, p. 47–57.) NAFA
A dramatization of his short story of the same title which had appeared in *New republic,* New York, 1937, v. 92, p. 367–368, * DA.
Pitiable Mrs. Shapiro comes to collect on her second mortgage.

SHERIDAN, DON. Morris and his troubles; Hebrew monologue. (In his: Acts for between acts. Chicago [cop. 1931]. 12°. p. 69–71.)
NBL p.v.332
"Morris Hipinski, who runs a book shop" on the troubles of selling secondhand books.

—— Talking and singing things over; an act for a singing quartet. (In his: On the variety bill. Chicago [cop. 1931]. 12°. p. 47–56.)
NBL p.v.271
Levy Rosenbaum, who owns the village store, "a typical stage Hebrew," and three of his old village cronies.

SHERIDAN, MAHLON B. "Be yourself," a plotless playlet in one act. (Women's wear daily. New York, 1928. f°. v. 37, Sept. 28, 1928, section 1, p. 8, 11.) 3–† VLA
Presented to the delegates at the banquet of the Sales Promotion Division of the National Retail Dry Goods Association, Cincinnati, Sept., 1928. Eddie Silverstein "merchandise manager"; Isaac Thimble, store owner.

Individual Plays — 1915–1938, continued

SHERMAN, ROBERT J. Madam the boss; a comedy-drama in three acts. Chicago: T. S. Denison & Company [cop. 1927]. 85 p. plan. 12°. (Denison's select plays.) NBL p.v.176, no.7
Scene: a middle western city. Sammy Bright, the shrewd and slangy publicity man.

SHERWOOD, ROBERT EMMET. This is New York, a play in three acts. New York: C. Scribner's Sons, 1931. xviii p., 4 l., 7–177 p. 8°. NBM
New York City as seen by one from the hinterland. Produced at the Plymouth Theatre, New York, Nov. 29, 1930, with Robert Barrat as Harry Glassman described, in the stage direction, as "an urbane gorilla." Reviewed by H. H. in *Nation*, New York, 1930, v. 131, p. 716, *DA*; and in *Variety*, New York, v. 100, Dec. 3, 1930, p. 63, † *NAFA*. See also *Collection of newspaper clippings of dramatic criticism, 1930–1931*, v. S–Z, † *NBL*.

SHIFFRIN, ABRAHAM B. Allah be praised! A pointed playlet in one engaging act. illus. (*American Hebrew*. New York, 1925. f°. v. 116, p. 686, 726–727.) *PBD
The Smittys and Mr. Blumberg at a summer hotel.

—— Return at sunset; a play [in one act]. [New York:] New Theatre League [cop. 1937]. 39 p. 12°.
A play of contemporary American Jewish life in New York City. Produced in New York, January, 1936.

—— Wanted a bookkeeper; a play in one act. illus. (*American Hebrew*. New York, 1924. f°. v. 114, p. 813, 826.) *PBD
The theme is that of racial discrimination in mercantile houses.

SHIPMAN, SAMUEL, AND V. VICTOR. The unwritten chapter; a play dealing with Haym Salomon, the Jew who financed the American Revolution. (*American Hebrew*. New York, 1920. f°. v. 107, p. 740–741.) *PBD
The text of the end of the second act is herewith given. Introduction by Elias Lieberman.
This play, in a prologue, three acts and an epilogue, was produced at the Astor Theatre, New York, Oct. 11, 1920. Its title implies an omitted chapter in American history. The characters are mostly historical. Louis Mann played Haym Salomon, 1740–1785, who helped to finance the Revolution; Herman Gerold, Gershom Mendes Seixas, 1745–1816, "the patriot rabbi of the Revolution," who was one of the fourteen clergymen present at the inauguration of Washington; Paul Irving, Isaac Moses, 1742–1818, distinguished merchant and patriot; and Howard Lang, David Franks, a Philadelphia Loyalist. Other historical characters are also introduced. In the prologue and the epilogue appears a "fighting Jew" of the World war, who aims to turn race prejudice into sympathy and understanding. For reviews see *Collection of newspaper clippings of dramatic criticism, 1920–1921*, v. S–Z, † *NBL*.
Originally copyrighted in 1916 under the title *Haym Salomon*.
See United States. — Copyright Office, *Dramatic compositions copyrighted in the United States, 1870 to 1916*, no. 53880.

SHORE, MRS. VIOLA (BROTHERS). The queen's bracelet; a one-act play in which is dramatically presented a new angle of the relationship between Gentile and Jew in America. (*American Hebrew*. New York, 1923. f°. v. 113, p. 369, 408–409.) *PBD

SIFTON, PAUL. The belt; a New Playwrights' Theatre production. New York: The Macaulay Company [cop. 1927]. 193 p. 12°. NBM
Reviewed by F. F. in *Curtain*, London, 1928, v. 7, p. 90, *NAFA*.
The play is "a savage cartoon of life in a factory town," in spirit akin to Toller's *Massemensch*. First presented by the New Playwrights' Theatre, at their playhouse, 40 Commerce St., New York, October 19, 1927, with Benjamin Osipow as Aaronson, secretary of the union. Reviewed by G. V. Seldes in *Dial*, New York, 1928, v. 84, p. 78–80, *DA*; by J. W. Krutch in *Nation*, New York, 1927, v. 125, p. 554, *DA*; by Stark Young in *New republic*, New York, 1927, v. 52, p. 285–286, *DA*; and by J. M. Brown, in *Theatre arts monthly*, New York, 1927, v. 11, p. 904–905, *NBLA*. See also *Collection of newspaper clippings of dramatic criticism, 1927–1928*, v. A–C, † *NBL*.

SIMON, CAROLYN. The under-dog; a one-act play... New York: Jewish Welfare Board, 1925. 12 f. 4°. † NCOF
Reproduced from typewritten copy.
"Awarded honorable mention in Jewish play contest conducted by the Jewish Welfare Board."
Deals with anti-Jewish discrimination in an American college community.
See Edward D. Coleman, *The Bible in English drama*, New York, 1931, p. 160, *NCOD*, where it is listed among the Purim plays.

SIMON, ESTHER JANETT, AND A. M. HUNTER. "The spirit of the South" (an historical pageant of Alabama in sixteen episodes). (In: Peter A. Brannon, editor, The pageant book. Montgomery, Ala., 1926. 4°. p. 7–21.)
Pageant presented in Montgomery, Ala., in celebration of Alabama Home Coming Week, May 5–6, 1926. Episode 6 is dated 1785. In it is introduced "Abram Mordecai, a Jew who comes, in '83, and settles west of Line Creek, bringing the cotton gin to cotton growers." Mordecai was an Indian trader who, after serving in the Revolutionary war, came from Pennsylvania to Montgomery county, Ala., and there erected the first cotton gin. See "Alabama's first industry," ibid., p. 70. See also A. J. Messing, " 'Old Mordecai' — the founder of the city of Montgomery," in American Jewish Historical Society. *Publications*, [Baltimore], 1905, no. 13, p. 71–81, *PXX*.

SIMONS, EVELYN. ...The daughters of Rebekah, by Marie Irish [pseud.]... Syracuse, N. Y.: Willis N. Bugbee Co., cop. 1923. 8 p. 12°. (Bugbee's popular plays.)
The characters of the first part are Biblical figures. The second part is a morality teaching patriotism and mutual understanding.

SIMONS, EVELYN, AND O. BURT. Solomon Levi. (In their: Dandy drills and dances. Syracuse, N. Y. [cop. 1929.] 12°. p. 25–29.)

SINGER, ISRAEL JOSHUA. The sinner (Yoshe Kalb); translated by Maurice Samuel. New York: Liveright, Inc. [cop. 1933.] 3 p.l., 3–314 p. 12°. *PTR
A fantastic story of the Hasidic, wonder-working rabbis of the Austrian-Russian border. Reviewed in *New republic*, New York, 1933, v. 76, p. 55, *DA*.
The original appeared in *Jewish Daily Forward*, New York, June 4 – July 19, 1932. It was first produced at the Yiddish Art Theatre, New York, Oct. 2, 1932, with Maurice Schwartz as rabbi Melech, leader of a Hasidic group in Poland. For reviews see *Collection of newspaper clippings of dramatic criticism, 1932–1933*, v. T–Y, † *NBL*.
In an adaptation into a play of two acts and twenty-eight scenes by Fritz Blocki, it was staged at the

Individual Plays — 1915–1938, continued

SINGER, ISRAEL JOSHUA, *continued*
National Theatre, New York, Nov. 28, 1933, with Fritz Leiber as the wonder rabbi and Erin O'Brien Moore as Malkele. In this English version it lasted only a few nights. For illustration of stage settings see *Theatre arts monthly*, New York, 1933, v. 17, p. 472–473, *NBLA*. For reviews see *Collection of newspaper clippings of dramatic criticism, 1933–1934*, v. U–Z, † *NBL*.

Samuel, Maurice. Yoshe Kalb among the Nordics. Should we try to get ourselves "understood"? (Philadelphia Jewish times. Philadelphia, 1933. f°. v. 15, Feb. 17, 1933, p. 4.)
* PBD

Yiddish Art Theatre, New York. Maurice Schwartz's production of I. J. Singer's play "Yoshe Kalb"... [New York: Trio Press, 1932.] 8 l. ports., facsim., illus., music. 4°.
Synopsis, by Maximilian Hurwitz; criticisms, by various authors.

SISSMAN, PAUL R. A doctor to be. [In one act.] (In: University of Michigan. — English Department. University of Michigan plays. Ann Arbor, Mich., 1932. 12°. book 3, p. 207–250.)
NBL (Michigan)
An incident in the ambition of Jewish parents and two sisters for the son and brother to be admitted to a medical school and "be a doctor."

SKUTCH, ROBERT FRANK. "Spinoza"; a play in four acts. (Jewish comment. Baltimore, 1917. f°. v. 48, p. 537–539.) * PBD
Extracts are given from each of the four acts. Among the characters, besides Spinoza, are his Hebrew teacher, Saul Morteira, 1596–1660, and Clara Van dem Emden, his supposed sweetheart. Produced by the Baltimore section of the Council of Jewish Women, March 27, 1917. For a review of the production, see ibid., v. 49, p. 16.

SLOANE, ROBERT, AND L. PELLÉTIER, JR. Howdy stranger; a comedy in three acts... copyright 1936 (under title "Git along, little dogie")... New York [etc.]: S. French, cop. 1937. 112 p., 1 l. illus., diagrs. 12°. (French's standard library edition.)
Produced at the Longacre Theatre, New York, Jan. 14, 1937, with Louis Sorin as Roy Chadwick, theatrical agent, "a very ebullient, driving, 42nd Street New Yorker. He is obviously Jewish in appearance and speech." For reviews see *Collection of newspaper clippings of dramatic criticism, 1936–1937*, v. His–L, † *NBL*.

SLOANE, WILLIAM M. Art for art's sake [in three acts]. By William M. Sloane III... Boston: Walter H. Baker Company [cop. 1934]. 130 p. illus., diagrs. 12°. (Baker's royalty plays.) NBL p.v.360
Byron Wertheimer, famous art dealer.

SMITH, HARRY JAMES. A tailor-made man; a comedy in four acts... New York: Samuel French [etc.], cop. 1919. 121 p. diagrs., plates. 12°. (French's standard library edition.)
NBL p.v.131
An outline, with many extracts from the text, is printed in *Current opinion*, New York, v. 63, p. 311–314, * *DA*; and in *Hearst's magazine*, New York, v. 32, p. 378–380, 390 (with illus.), * *DA*.
The plot is taken from the German play *The Well-fitting dress coat*, by Gabriel Dregley. The hero "starts out as a tailor's assistant and ends as a power in the world of great affairs." First produced at the Cohan & Harris Theatre, New York, Aug. 27, 1917, with Frank Burbeck as Abraham Nathan, "a distinguished and authoritative financier of the Jewish race." Reviewed by Channing Pollock in *Green book magazine*, Chicago, 1917, v. 18, p. 778–782 (with illus.), *NAFA*; by J. S. Metcalfe in *Life*, New York, v. 70, p. 424, * *DA*; *New York dramatic mirror*, v. 77, Sept. 8, 1917, p. 8 (illus. in Nov. 17, p. 4 and Dec. 22, p. 5), * *T*–* *DA*; and in *Theatre magazine*, New York, v. 26, p. 209, 242, 255 (with illus.), † *NBLA*.

SMITH, WINCHELL, AND J. E. HAZZARD. Turn to the right; a comedy in a prologue and three acts. New York: S. French [etc.], cop. 1916. 140 p. 4°. (French's standard library edition.)
NBL p.v.100
A play about potential and redeemed crooks and an old-fashioned mother. The Jewish characters, both incidental, are Isadore, a pawnbroker, and Moses, an old tailor. They are described as Polish Jews and their rôles were acted by Al Sincoff and George Spelvin. Produced at the Gaiety Theatre, New York, Aug. 17, 1916. Reviewed (with illus.) in *Current opinion*, New York, v. 61, p. 240–244, * *DA*; and in *New York dramatic mirror*, v. 76, Aug. 26, 1916, p. 8, * *T*–* *DA*.
A pre-view of this comedy was seen at Parson's Theatre, Hartford, Conn., May 1, 1916, under the title *Like mother made*.

SNYDER, KATHRYN. The Jewish saleslady; a monologue. Chicago: T. S. Denison & Co. [cop. 1925.] 7 p. 12°. (Denison's monologues.)
A credulous customer is jollied and fooled.

SNYDER, SARA. Election in foodland; a one-act Purim comedy in verse... New York: Bloch Publishing Company, 1938. 10 p. 12°.
Cover-title.

SOIFER, MARGARET K. A dramatization of the sessions of the Royal Commission. Education Dep't., Zionist Organization of America, 1937. 23 f. 4°.
Cover-title.
Mimeographed.
Education Dep't., Z. O. A., no. 23.

—— Dramatization of XX Zionist Congress ... New York: Education Dep't, Zionist Organization of America, 1937. 19 f. ports. 4°.
Cover-title.
Mimeographed.
On cover: No. 44.
Deals with the discussions on the proposed partition of Palestine, at the Congress, August 4–11, 1937.

SORSKY, JOHN. The king of kings; a dramatic episode, in one act, based upon an incident in the life of Sir Moses Montefiore. (American Hebrew. New York, 1934. 4°. v. 135, p. 390, 409.)
* PBD
The characters are Sir Moses, Count Potocki, and a servant. The scene is Vilna, Poland, in 1837.

SPENDER, STEPHEN. ...Trial of a judge; a tragedy in five acts. London: Faber and Faber, Limited [1938]. 115 p. 8°. NCR
A poetic drama based on the struggle between liberalism and autocracy in Nazi Germany. The theme is struggle of conscience. In the last act is a Jewish doctor as a prisoner driven mad. The five acts are named: Illusion and uncertainty, The small scene, The large scene, The trial, and The three cells. Written for the Group Theatre, London, and first produced there.
Reviewed in *Jewish quarterly review*, Philadelphia, 1938, new series, v. 29, p. 224, * *PBE*.

Individual Plays — 1915–1938, continued

SPEWACK, BELLA (COHEN), AND SAMUEL SPEWACK. Clear all wires! A play in three acts; with a note by Herman Shumlin. New York, Los Angeles: S. French; London: S. French, Ltd., 1932. vii p., 2 l., 3–246 p. 12°. NBM
Concerns an American newspaper man in Moscow. Produced at the Times Square Theatre, New York, Sept. 14, 1932, with J. Neradoff in the rôle of Rubinstein, assistant censor of the Russian foreign ministry. Reviewed by J. W. Krutch in *Nation*, New York, 1932, v. 135, p. 290–291, *DA*. See also *Collection of newspaper clippings of dramatic criticism, 1932–1933*, v. C–D, † *NBL*.
Produced at the Piccadilly Theatre, London, April 30, 1933, with Charles Cameron as Rubinstein, and transferred to the Garrick Theatre, June 6, 1933. Reviewed by D. C. F. in *Theatre world*, London, 1933, v. 20, p. 14, *MWA;* and in *The Times*, London, June 7, 1933, p. 10, col. 2, * *A*.

SPEWACK, BELLA (COHEN), & SAMUEL SPEWACK. Poppa; a comedy in three acts. New York: S. French; London: S. French, Ltd. [cop. 1929.] 107 p. 12°. (French's standard library edition.) NBL p.v.207
"Copyright...1927...under the title of 'Pincus' or 'Hizzoner.'"
A story of New York ghetto life. Produced at the Biltmore Theatre, New York, Dec. 24, 1928, with J. Goldsmith as father Schwitzky, an East Side shiftless politician, and Anna Apple as his wife. Reviewed in *Billboard*, Cincinnati, v. 41, Jan. 5, 1929, p. 46, † *MZA;* and in *Variety*, New York, v. 93, Jan. 2, 1929, p. 20, † *NAFA*. See also *Collection of newspaper clippings of dramatic criticism, 1928–1929*, v. N–R, † *NBL;* and W. Zuckerman in *B'nai B'rith magazine*, Cincinnati, 1929, v. 43, p. 143–144, * *PYP*.

—— "Spring song" [in three acts]... [New York? 1934.] [130] f. 4°. † NCOF
Cover-title.
Reproduced from typewritten copy.
Each act has separate pagination.
A drama of the New York ghetto. The plot situation is similar to that of *Kreutzer sonata*. Produced at the Morosco Theatre, New York, Oct. 1, 1934, with Francine Larrimore as the central character Florrie Solomon, Helen Zelinskaya as her mother, and Norman Stuart as Sidney Kurtz. The comic part is provided by Joseph Greenwald as Freiberg. For reviews see *Collection of newspaper clippings of dramatic criticism, 1934–1935*, v. Se–Sy, † *NBL*.

THE SPIRIT of Federation. (Jewish tribune. New York, 1928. f°. v. 93, Nov. 2, 1928, p. 9.) * PBD
A playlet about the work of the Federation for the Support of Jewish Philanthropic Societies of New York City, staged by S. L. Rothafel at the Commodore Hotel, New York, Oct. 21, 1928.

SPIVACK, MORRIS JOSEPH. Broken melody; a drama for the talking screen... New York: The Talking Picture Publishing Co. [cop. 1930.] 158 p. 8°. MFLK

SPRAGUE, MRS. BESSE (TOULOUSE), AND W. SPRAGUE. Blarney street; a farce comedy in three acts. Franklin, Ohio [etc.]: Eldridge Entertainment House, Inc., cop. 1931. 78 p. diagr. 12°. (Eldridge royalty plays.)
The scheming Levi Levinsky, in an Irish dialect play of the bickerings and troubles of two Irish families living in the same duplex.

SPRITZ, CHARLES S. Minutes of the jolly twelve. (In his: Poems by a septuagenarian. Boston [cop. 1931]. 12°. p. 105–136.) NBI
"The jolly twelve" are the card-playing ladies, Mrs. Gottlieb, Mrs. Levy, etc., with their male escorts, their antics and behavior.

STANGE, HUGH STANISLAUS. False dreams, farewell!... [New York: Century Play Co., Inc., 1934?] [93] f. 4°. † NCOF
In three acts.
Various paging.
Reproduced from typewritten copy.
The scene is aboard the S. S. *Atlanta*, England-bound on her maiden voyage. Produced at the Little Theatre, New York, Jan. 15, 1934, with D. Leonard as Murray Fineman and Henry Lase as Irving Silvers, movie agents and producers. See *Collection of newspaper clippings of dramatic criticism, 1933–1934*, v. F–H, † *NBL*.

STAR dust. [A playlet in four scenes.] (Our Jewish neighbors. New York, 1925. 8°. v. 4, June, 1925, p. 26–29.) * PGI
Sam, a Jewish boy, is converted to Jesus at the camp of the Community Center.

STAYTON, GRACIA. Guggenstein and his "green anchel." Sioux City, Iowa: Wetmore Declamation Bureau, 1928. 3 f. 4°.
Mimeographed.
Caption-title.

—— Mr. Mishkowsky und de "younk leddy." Sioux City, Iowa: Wetmore Declamation Bureau, cop. 1928. 3 l. 4°.
Caption-title.
Mimeographed.
"A humorous reading."
Reprinted in Peggy Reece, *Twenty dialect monologues*, Boston [cop. 1938], p. 75–82.

—— Mrs. Dinkelspiel and the P. T. A. [Chicago: E. Means Dramatic Service, cop. 1931.] 3 f. 4°.
Caption-title.
Mimeographed.

—— Mrs. Schnickelfritz und der four o'clock train. Sioux City, Iowa: Wetmore Declamation Bureau, 1928. 2 f. 4°.
Mimeographed.
Caption-title.
Reprinted in Peggy Reece, compiler, *Twenty dialect monologues*, Boston [cop. 1928], p. 68–74.

—— Mrs. Schnickelfritz und der visecrackers. Sioux City, Iowa: Wetmore Declamation Bureau, 1930. 3 f. 4°.
Caption-title.
Mimeographed.

STEEN, EVA. Escaped; a one-act play. New York: Metropolitan League of Jewish Community Associations [cop. 1931]. 20 f. 4°.
Cover-title.
Mimeographed.
A domestic tragedy in a poor home in a small town in modern Russia.

STEVENS, HENRY BAILEY. City rubes; a play in one act with an introduction, A plea for a new attitude toward rural drama. Durham, N. H.: The University of New Hampshire Extension Service [cop. 1924]. 28 p. 8°.
Text on p. 3 of cover. NBL p.v.123
The author in his introduction declares that "The

Individual Plays — 1915-1938, continued

STEVENS, HENRY BAILEY, *continued*

Rube myth has got to go. It is as stale as was the Knight myth in the time of Cervantes." His plan is to use "reverse English" by poking fun at the metropolitan rubes, Isidore Konowitz, a timorous New Yorker, and Patrick James Murphy, a bold Bostonian. Originally produced at the University of New Hampshire, Durham, N. H., Aug. 17, 1922, with H. H. Scudder as Isidore.

STINSON, H. H. The ace is trumped. [A one act play.] (In: Kenyon Nicholson, editor, Hollywood plays. New York, 1930. 12°. p. 1–27.)
NBL (Nicholson)

A final episode in a gangster's career. Produced by the Hollywood Writers' Club, March 12, 1929, with Walter Long as big ace Jacobs.

STONE, IRVING. The white life; a play in one act. Based on the life of Baruch Spinoza. New York: Metropolitan League of Jewish Community Associations [1932]. 19 f. 4°.
Cover-title. † NAC p.v.358
Mimeographed.
Time: July 27, 1656. Place: Sephardic synagog of Amsterdam.

STORM, JUDE. Woman's might, a play in one act... New York, N. Y., Los Angeles, Cal.: S. French, Inc.; London: S. French, Ltd. [etc.], cop. 1934. 25(1) p. diagr. 12°. NBL p.v.353

The locale of the play is a small farm belonging to a widow, about to be foreclosed, in the autumn of 1932. Mr. Marcus is the agent of the foreclosing company.

STRAUS, ROBERT LEE. Westward the course of Israel (a pageant). Written for the one hundredth anniversary of Congregation Bene Israel. (In: Congregation Bene Israel, Cincinnati, One hundredth anniversary, 1824–1924. Cincinnati [1924]. 4°. p. 75–111.)

In seven prologues and seven scenes. Organization of the Congregation, Jan. 1, 1824. Dedication of the first synagogue, Sept. 9, 1836. Presentation of the Tyler Davidson Fountain, Oct. 6, 1871. The installation of the Rev. Dr. David Philipson, Nov. 3, 1888. Dedication of the Rockdale Avenue Temple, Sept. 14, 1906. 25th anniversary of the service of the Rev. Dr. David Philipson, Nov. 2, 1913. The present, 1924.

STREET, JULIAN LEONARD. Rita Coventry. Garden City, N. Y.: Doubleday, Page & Company, 1922. 4 p.l., 306 p. 12°. NBO

Dramatized by Hubert Osborne into a comedy, and produced at the Bijou Theatre, New York, Feb. 20, 1923, with Eugene Powers as Herman Krauss, Jewish banker and patron of music. See *Collection of newspaper clippings of dramatic criticism, 1922–1923*, v. M–R, † *NBL*.

STUART, AIMEE MCHARDY, AND PHILIP STUART. Her shop, a play in three acts. London: E. Benn, Limited, 1929. 4 p.l., 11–119(1) p. 12°. (Contemporary British dramatists. v. 70.)
NCO (Contemporary)

Produced at the Criterion Theatre, London, Feb. 7, 1929, with A. V. Edwards as Mr. McDonald, a Jew, and E. K. Bruce as Mr. Jacob, a Scotsman, partners in a London shop, who overreach themselves in their traditional shrewdness. Lady Mary gets the best of both. Reviewed by Herbert Farjeon in *Graphic*, London, 1929, v. 123, p. 242, * *DA*; *Nation & Athenæum*, London, v. 44, p. 687–688, * *DA*. Illustrations are given in *Sphere*, London, v. 116, p. 387, 508, * *DA*.

Its American premiere took place at the Community Playhouse, Pasadena, Cal., Jan. 22, 1931, with Thurston Vaughn as Mr. McDonald.

ŠUBERT, FRANTIŠEK ADOLF. The great freeholder. A three act drama. Translated from the Bohemian by Beatrice M. Mekota. (Poet lore. Boston, 1924. 8°. v. 35, p. 317–319.) * DA

Aaron Lewi, a money lender; small, corpulent, fashionably attired.

SULLIVAN, FRANK. Defendant fails to show up in ticker tape scandal trial. [In one scene.] (The World. New York, 1928. f°. May 20, 1928, metropolitan section, p. 1.) * A

David Belasco is one of the characters.

SWERLING, JOSEPH, AND E. G. ROBINSON. Kibitzer; a comedy... New York, Los Angeles: Samuel French, Ltd., 1929. 4 p.l., 3–168 p. front., plates. 12°. NBM

In three acts.
Reviewed in *Jewish quarterly review*, Philadelphia, 1930, new series, v. 20, p. 403, * *PBE*; by W. H. Blumenthal, in *American Hebrew*, New York, 1929, v. 125, p. 510, 514, * *PBD*.
Copious extracts (with illus.) are given in *Theatre magazine*, New York, v. 49, May, 1929, p. 26–27, 76–78, † *NBLA*.
A farce of Jewish life in New York centering around good-natured, quarrelling neighborhood pinochle players and their futile race for wealth. Produced at the Royale Theatre, New York, Feb. 18, 1929, with E. G. Robinson in the title rôle. Reviewed by R. Littell in *Theatre arts monthly*, New York, 1929, v. 13, p. 333–334, *NBLA*. See also *Collection of newspaper clippings of dramatic criticism, 1928–1929*, v. H–K, † *NBL*.

SYMONS, ARTHUR. Outlaws of life; a play. (Two worlds. New York, 1925. 8°. v. 1, p. 5–28.) ***

A night tavern near the Docks, London, where the "outlaws of life" foregather. Among them are Judith, reminiscent of her namesake in the Holofernes story, and a young Jew called Isaacs.

TAGGART, TOM. Sold. (In: Easy blackouts; a collection of short comedy sketches by various authors. New York [cop. 1934]. 12°. p. 92–93.)
NBL p.v.363

Characters: Cohen, Feinburg, and a burglar.

TAGGER, THEODOR. Races, a drama by Ferdinand Bruckner [pseud.] translated from the German for the first time by Ruth Langner. New York: A. A. Knopf, 1934. 5 p.l., 3–138 p., 1 l. 12°. NGE

"Originally published as *Die Rassen*," in Zürich, 1933.
Reviewed by E. D. Bramson in *Friday*, Cleveland, v. 1, Sept. 1, 1934, p. 35–36, * *PBD*.
"Portrays what befell the Jews of Germany in March and April, 1933." It was produced by the New York Theatre Guild at Philadelphia, March 19, 1934. It was staged in New York, at the Heckscher Auditorium, May 10, 1935, with Virginia Stevens as Helene Marx, the Jewish girl beloved by a German Aryan medical student. For reviews see *Collection of newspaper clippings of dramatic criticism, 1934–1935*, v. R–Sa, † *NBL*.

Individual Plays — 1915–1938, continued

TALBOT, ALFRED JULIAN. All Fools' eve; a fantasia in Parliament Square, in one act... London: S. French, Ltd.; New York: S. French, Inc., 1934. 29 p. incl. diagr. illus. 12°. (French's acting edition. no. 2240.) NCO p.v.754

The statues of Abraham Lincoln, Disraeli, and Sir Robert Peel in conversation, "March 31st, one of these years." Scene: by Lincoln's statue at Parliament Square, London.

—— One evening at Nero's; or, Shall Agrippina drown? (In: Eight new one-act plays of 1936. London [1936]. 12°. p. 11–38.)
 NCO (Eight)

One of the characters is Poppaea Sabina, Nero's favorite. She had a certain predilection for Judaism, and is known to have interceded for them when needed.

TARKINGTON, BOOTH. Poldekin; the drama of the man who found America. illus. (McClure's magazine. New York, 1920. 4°. v. 52, March/April, 1920, p. 8–11, 91; May, p. 21–23, 51–52, 54; June, p. 30–32, 38, 43; July, p. 31–33, 36, 41.) *DA

In four acts.
A satire on Bolshevism.
A running synopsis, together with copious extracts from the text and illustrations of the production, is printed in *Current opinion*, New York, 1920, v. 69, p. 481–488, * DA.
Produced at the Park Theatre, New York, Sept. 9, 1920, with George Arliss in the title rôle and E. G. Robinson as Pinsky. For reviews see *Collection of newspaper clippings of dramatic criticism, 1920–1921*, v. M–R, † NBL.

TARKINGTON, BOOTH, AND H. L. WILSON. The Gibson upright. Garden City, New York: Doubleday, Page & Company, 1919. 4 p.l., 3–117(1) p. 12°. NBM

Reprinted in J. P. Webber and H. H. Webster, editors, *Typical plays for secondary schools*, Boston [etc., cop. 1929], p. 146–212, NAFH.
Reviewed in *Dial*, 1919, v. 67, p. 115, * DA; *Dramatist*, v. 10, p. 973–974, NAFA; *Nation*, New York, v. 110, p. 79, * DA; and in *Theatre arts magazine*, New York, 1919, v. 4, p. 84–85, NBLA.
First appeared in *Saturday evening post*, July 12, 19, 26, 1919. A factory owner abdicates; his employees run rampant; they welcome his return. Frankel, "Hebraic type," is one of the leaders of the factory strike. It was staged at the Murat Theatre, Indianapolis, Ind., July 14, 1919, with George Somnes as Frankel. It never reached the New York stage.

TARLEAU, LISA YSAYO. Musa Ibn Maimon; a play in verse [in three acts]. Prepared for the Maimonides Octocentennial Committee. New York, 1935. cover-title, 21 f. 4°.

Mimeographed.
On the occasion of the 800th anniversary of the birth of Moses Maimonides, 1135–1204.
Reprinted in part (with illus.) in *Young Judaean*, New York, v. 23, April, 1935, p. 8–9, 19–20, * PBD.

TATROE, RUTH. Mrs. Cohen at the amusement park. Sioux City, Iowa: Wetmore Declamation Bureau, 1929. 2 f. 4°.

Mimeographed.
Caption-title.

TAYLOR, MRS. H. Hadassah women go on a spree. [In one act. New York: Hadassah, 1934.] 3 f. f°.

Caption-title.
Mimeographed.
Scene: a night court.

TAYLOR, REX. Appearances; a comedy. (In: Kenyon Nicholson, editor, Appleton book of short plays: second series. New York, London: D. Appleton and Co., 1927. 8°. p. 215–250.)

Rosentahl, a junk man, misses fifty thousand dollars hidden in an old clock which he had bought.

TAYLOR, RICA BROMLEY. Benny proposes! (In her: Four Jewish sketches. London, New York, cop. 1927. 12°. p. 5–18.)

—— The boomerang! (In her: Four Jewish sketches. London, New York, cop. 1927. 12°. p. 19–31.)

—— Damages — two hundred! (In her: Four Jewish sketches. London, New York, cop. 1927. 12°. p. 33–49.)

—— Paul robs Peter! (In her: Four Jewish sketches. London, New York, cop 1927. 12°. p. 51–64.)

THORNE, ANTHONY. Thirteen o'clock; a play in three acts... London: E. Benn, Limited, 1929. 69(1) p. 12°. (Contemporary British dramatists. v. 71.) NCO (Contemporary)

Jo and Isaac Lorberg, business men.

TITUS, HAROLD. The candle in the window (a story of the Christmas spirit in man) [a dramatic reading in one act]. Sioux City, Iowa: Wetmore Declamation Bureau, n. d. 3 f. f°.

Typewritten.
Goldberg, the peddler, lost in the storm, is guided to shelter by a candle in the window. From his wares he brings joy to the children on Christmas morning.
Based on the author's story of the same title, in *Delineator*, New York, v. 101, Dec., 1922, p. 11–12, 82, † VSA.

TOLLER, ERNST. Brokenbrow, a tragedy by Ernst Toller, translated by Vera Mendel; with drawings by Georg Grosz. London: The Nonesuch Press [1926]. 1 p.l., 5–50 p. plates. 8°.
 * KP (Nonesuch)

Reprinted, under the title *Hinkemann*, in his *Seven plays*, London [1935], p. 155–193, NGE. Printed also in *Two worlds monthly*, New York, 1926, v. 1, p. 321–352, ***.
In three acts.
The story of a war cripple in a merciless world, in a play of pessimism, irony and pity for man as a victim of blind fate and his own stupidity. In the third act a first and a second Jew are introduced. Written in prison in 1921–1922 and published in 1922 under the title *Der Deutsche Hinkemann*. "In 1923 an incomplete translation into English appeared with the title 'Hobbleman' in a periodical publication called 'Germinal.'" Under the title *Bloody laughter* it was produced by the Yiddish Art Theatre, New York, Feb. 27, 1924. See synopsis by M. Hurwitz, in Yiddish Art Theatre, *Programs*, * PTP. See also Lydia Walker in *Theatre Guild magazine*, New York, v. 7, Oct., 1929, p. 30–33, 52, NBLA; and B. H. Clark in *Theatre magazine*, v. 39, June, 1924, p. 22, 48, 50, 52, NBLA.
It was also produced at the Gate Theatre, London, Feb. 3, 1933.

—— Transfiguration; a play [in a prologue and six "stations"] translated by Edward Crankshaw. (In his: Seven plays. London [1935]. 8°. p. 55–106.) NGE

Written in 1917–18.
Published in the original German as *Wandlung; das Ringen eines Menschen*, Potsdam, 1920.
Friedrich, the hero, achieves regeneration through

Individual Plays — 1915-1938, continued

TOLLER, ERNST, *continued*
the gospel of Revolution. The regeneration is a psychological revolt against reality. In scene 1, opening during the Christmas season, he soliloquizes thus: — "I, a Jew, outcast, far from the old and farther from the new."

Freed, Clarence I. Ernst Toller — spirit of revolt, whose plays and poems lay bare the soul of suffering humanity. port. (American Hebrew. New York, 1924. f°. v. 114, p. 668, 737.) * PBD

TORREY, ADELA. The grouch; a comedy drama in three acts... New York, Los Angeles, Cal.: S. French, Inc.; London [etc.]: S. French, Ltd., cop. 1934. 83(1) p. diagr. 12°. NBL p.v.356
Aaron Levin, "a travelling merchant," speaks in dialect.

TUBIASH, NANCY. By bread alone; a drama in one act. Boston: W. H. Baker Company, cop. 1937. 16 p. 12°. (Baker's plays for amateurs.)
Title from p. [1.]
The story concerns a girl, who sacrifices her future for the sake of her family. The milieu is Jewish, but the family might be of any nationality.

TULLY, JIM. Jarnegan. New York: A. & C. Boni, 1926. 4 p.l., 7–265 p. 12°.   8–NBO

Beahan, Charles, and G. Fort. Jarnegan, a play in three acts, based on Jim Tully's novel of the same name, was produced at the Longacre Theatre, New York, Sept. 24, 1928.
A drama of Hollywood life. James R. Waters played Jacob Isaacs, movie producer. Reviewed by Benjamin De Casseres in *Arts & decoration*, New York, v. 30, Dec., 1928, p. 118, *MAA;* and by Joseph W. Krutch in *Nation*, New York, v. 127, p. 382–383, * *DA.* See also *Collection of newspaper clippings of dramatic criticism, 1928–1929*, v. H–K, † *NBL.*

TUPPER, WILBUR S. What price America? a farce in one act... New York: Fitzgerald Pub. Corp. [cop. 1933.] 22 p. 12°. (Playhouse plays.)
"Goldstein gives Isabella a hundred grand for her royal jewels." That is how Columbus happened to discover America.

TURNER, JOHN HASTINGS. The spot on the sun; a comedy in three acts. London: S. French, Ltd.; New York: S. French, cop. 1928. 69 p., 1 l. 1 illus., diagr. 8°. (French's acting edition. no. 759.)   NCO p.v.573
Deals with English upper-class folks at Monte Carlo. Produced at the Ambassador Theatre, London, June 28, 1927, with Frank Cellier as Barrington Woolfe, the outsider in the circle. "His nationality difficult to guess, overdressed, uses his hands too much." He is made to describe himself as "my father was a Macedonian Pole, my mother came from Smyrna." However, Macedonian Poles, when Anglicized, usually do not adopt the surname Woolfe, and the author's intentions are quite obvious. Reviewed in *Era*, London, v. 90, July 6, 1927, p. 1, † *NAFA.*

TURNER, LEWIS MCKENZIE. The midwinter night's dreams of the first Hollywood Christmas festival, 1929–1930... A trial marriage of stage and screen. Baltimore, Md.: Salt House Press, 1929. 7 l. 8°.   NBL p.v.223
Printed on one side of leaf only.
Intended to "spoof Hollywood." John Barrymore as Al Jolson, one of the players, and a General Sam Cohn, one of the queen's royal guard, are introduced.

TURNER, WALTER JAMES REDFERN. The man who ate the popomack; a tragedy-comedy of love in four acts. Oxford: B. Blackwell, 1922. 6 p.l., 90 p., 2 l. 12°. (The British Drama League library of modern British drama. no. 2.)
    NCO (British)

—— —— New York: Brentano's, 1923. 6 p.l., 90 p., 2 l. 12°. (The British Drama League library of modern British drama. no. 2.)
Printed in Great Britain.
The popomack, in this satire, is a rare Chinese fruit of unique effectiveness. Produced by the British Drama League at the Savoy Theatre, London, June 12, 1923, with Frank Royde as Sir Solomon Raub, "millionaire Jewish financier, head of Raub Bros., China & East India merchants," and Isabel Jeans as his daughter Muriel. Reviewed in *Spectator*, London, 1923, v. 130, p. 1042–1043, * *DA*.
Produced at the Cherry Lane Playhouse, New York, March 24, 1924, with Dennis Cleugh as Sir Solomon. For reviews see *Collection of newspaper clippings of dramatic criticism, 1923–1924*, v. M, † *NBL.*

—— The man who ate the popomack; a tragi-comedy of love, in two acts. [Revised edition.] London: Chatto & Windus, 1929. xii, 92 p., 2 l. 12°.
In this revised form it was produced at the Festival Theatre, Cambridge, Eng., Nov. 29, 1926, with John Thatcher as Sir Solomon.

THE TWENTY-THIRD philippic. [A skit in one scene.] illus. (Harvard lampoon. Cambridge, 1920. 4°. v. 78, p. 408.)   STG
Philip Catiline Laski [Harold Joseph Laski, tutor in the Division of History, Government & Economics, Harvard College, 1919–1920], senator from Semitia, one of the characters. Part of the *Lampoon* issue of Jan. 16, 1920, purporting to expose the alleged Bolshevist propaganda of Dr. Laski during the Boston police strike.

UNTERMEYER, LOUIS. Shylock, Christian (from "The merchant of Venice," act VI). (In his: Selected poems and parodies. New York [cop. 1935]. 8°. p. 233–236.)   NBI
Shylock, after his so-called conversion, and his former friend Tubal are the speakers.

VICTOR, VICTOR. Brother against brother; a scene on the European battlefield [in one act]. (American Hebrew. New York, 1917. 4°. v. 101, p. 468.)   * PBD

VIGRAN, BERTHA. Who shall judge? A play for youth clubs. [In two scenes.] Cincinnati: Dept. of Synagog and School Extension [1932]. 11 f. 4°. (Dramatics. series III, no. 2.)
Cover-title.
Mimeographed.
On social prejudices among Jewish college fraternity students. The first scene, at college; the second, ten years later.

VILAS, FAITH VAN VALKENBURGH. The maker of souls, an oriental phantasy in two acts and a prologue, with musical concurrence. [Scarsdale? N. Y., cop. 1924.] 49 p. 8°.

—— —— New York: L. E. Hogan [cop. 1927]. 2 p.l., 52 p. front., plates. 12°.   NBM

THE JEW IN ENGLISH DRAMA

Individual Plays — 1915–1938, continued

VOLLMER, LULA. Moonshine and honeysuckle, a play in three acts. New York, N. Y., Los Angeles, Cal.: S. French, Inc.; London: S. French, Ltd. [etc.], cop. 1934. 99(1) p. diagr. 12°.   NBL p.v.324
"Broadcasted from station WEAF for three years."
Scene: somewhere in the Southern mountains. One of the characters is the peddler, "a fine-looking Jew in his middle thirties, trim, dressed in city clothes."

WALINSKY, LOUIS. Heil Hitler! a play [in three acts] of the National Socialist revolution ... New York: Pilgrim House, 1936. vii p., 2 l., 3–122 p. 12°.   NBM
The characters are mostly historical. The Jewish family — son and parents — is named Marcus.

WALKER, ALICE JOHNSTONE. Christopher Columbus; a play in four acts. (In her: La Fayette; Christopher Columbus; The long knives of Illinois. Brief plays for the young. New York, 1919. 12°. p. 71–149.)   NBM
Santangel, and his twelve-year-old grandson José.

WALKER, KENT. De troubles of Jakey Cohen; a Jewish monologue... Dayton, O.: Paine Publishing Company [cop. 1929]. 6 p. 16°. (Paine's monologues.)

WALLACE, EDGAR. The ringer; a play in four acts... London: Samuel French, Ltd., 1926. 79 p. plates. 8°. (French's acting edition. no. 2305.)   NCO p.v.595
Produced at Wyndham's Theatre, London, May 1, 1926, with Franklin Dyall as Maurice Meister, a solicitor, friend and adviser of all the crooks in London. Reviewed in *Era*, London, v. 89, May 19, 1926, p. 7, † *NAFA*. Illus. appears in *Sphere*, London, v. 105, p. 229, * *DA*.

WALLACE, EMMA GARY, AND A. B. MEAD. ...Why photographers go mad; a short play [in one act]. Syracuse, N. Y.: Willis N. Bugbee Co., cop. 1925. 14 p. 12°. (Bugbee's popular plays.)
Mr. Suffern-Katz, the photographer.

WALLACE, LEW BARRINGTON. The doctor comes from Moscow; a drama in one act... Boston, Los Angeles, Cal.: Baker's plays [cop. 1936]. 17 p. 12°. (Baker's plays for amateurs.)   NBL p.v.414
Scene: the imperial palace, near St. Petersburg, on the night of Nov. 1, 1894, when Czar Alexander III died. The Czar is represented as having prepared a massacre of 500 Jews, and his consort, Maria Feodorovna, as striving to avoid it. A doctor is brought from Moscow, and he, of Jewish origin, poisons him. No part of this melodrama has any historical basis.

WALLACH, SIDNEY W. Imaginary conversations. Heinrich Heine and Benjamin D'Israeli discourse on Jewish proclivities to humor. illus. (B'nai B'rith magazine. Chicago, 1925. 4°. v. 39, p. 234–235.)   * PYP

WARREN, EDWARD H. Shakespeare in Wall Street. Boston and New York: Houghton Mifflin Company [cop. 1929]. 4 p.l., 36 p. 12°.   NBM
A burlesque in the form of a Shakespearean tragedy, celebrating the stock market crash. The scene is laid in New York and New Jersey. Among the characters are Shakespeare, Mrs. Shakespeare, and Shylock, as a modern stock broker.

WAYNE, KATHRYN. It's the fashion; a farce in three acts... Franklin, Ohio: Eldridge Entertainment House, Inc., cop. 1935. 95 p. diagrs. 12°. (Eldridge hi-test non-royalty plays.)
Morris Finklebaum, "a German-Jewish gentleman in the 'wholesale silk' business...not as mean as he would seem."
Scene: the display room of a gown shop.

WEIHL, ELSA. A Jew visits America A.C.E. 2000. (American Israelite. Cincinnati, 1924. f°. v. 71, Aug. 28, 1924, p. 1.)   * PBD
In one act.
The visitor is Sir Alfred Stearns, the Jewish ambassador from Great Britain. The scene is laid in the White House. Sir Alfred, the president of the United States, and the members of his cabinet are the characters.

—— Let down the bars. [In one act.] (American Hebrew. New York, 1924. 4°. v. 114, p. 680, 721, 732.)   * PBD
A satire against barring the Jews from certain exclusive places.

WEINBERG, ROSE D. "Pioneers." [In one act. New York: Hadassah, 1934.] 3 f. f°.
Caption-title.
Mimeographed.

WEINSTEIN, LEWIS H. So let 'em foreclose! or, Temple Olov Hasholom, Inc.; a merry, modern, musical mirrorscope of American Jewish community life. Boston: Walter H. Baker Company [cop. 1934]. 101 p. 12°.
Produced by the Brotherhood and Sisterhood of Temple Kehillath Israel, Boston, at the Repertory Theatre, Boston, March 19 and 20, 1934. See *Jewish advocate*, Boston, v. 71, March 2, 1934, part 2, p. 4, * *PBD*.

WEISSBLATT, HARRY A. A bunch of bones; a play in one act. (Community messenger. Trenton, N. J., 1928. 4°. v. 4, May, 1928, p. 11–12.)
The scene is in a cemetery.
Copy: Library of the American Jewish Historical Society.

WEITZENKORN, LOUIS. Five star final, a melodrama in three acts; preface by Herbert Bayard Swope. New York, Los Angeles: S. French; London: S. French, Ltd., 1931. viii p., 2 l., 3–165 p. 12°.   NBM
Copious extracts from the dialogue, with a running synopsis, are given in *The Best plays of 1930–31*, New York, 1931, p. 254–285, *NAFH*.
An attempt to expose the ways of the tabloid press. The action takes place in New York. Produced at the Cort Theatre, New York, Dec. 30, 1930, with Allen Jenkins as Ziggie Feinstein, one of the reporters of the *Evening Gazette*. For reviews see *Collection of newspaper clippings of dramatic criticism, 1930–1931*, v. D–H, † *NBL*.
Produced, under the title *Late star final*, at the Phoenix Theatre, London, June 25, 1931, with Allen Jenkins as Feinstein. For illustrations of this staging see *Theatre world*, London, 1931, v. 16, p. 73–84, *MWA*.

WELLMAN, RITA. The Gentile wife; a play in four acts. New York: Moffat, Yard & Company, 1919. 128 p. 12°.   * PSQ
The theme is intermarriage. Produced at the Vanderbilt Theatre, New York, Dec. 25, 1918, with Emily Stevens in the title rôle, D. Powell as David Davis, the Jewish husband, and Vera Gordon as David's mother. For reviews see *Collection of newspaper clippings of dramatic criticism, 1918–1919*, v. G–L, † *NBL*.
Under the title *The Wife*, it was presented at the Temple Israel Meeting House, Boston, Mass., May 24, 1933.

Individual Plays — 1915-1938, continued

WELLS, WILLIAM H. Brotherhood. [In one act.] (In: Harvard University. 47 Workshop. Plays. New York, 1925. 12°. fourth series, p. 97–121.) NBL (Harvard)
Friedman, the Jewish member of à gang of striking longshoremen, at the New York waterfront. Produced by the Harvard Dramatic Club, at the Agassiz House Theatre, Jan. 25 and 26, 1924.

WERFEL, FRANZ V. The eternal road; a drama in four acts... English version by Ludwig Lewisohn. New York: The Viking Press, 1936. xi, 144 p. 8°. NGE

——... The eternal road; a new play, by Franz Werfel: music by Kurt Weill... [New York,] cop. 1935. [120] f. 4°. † NCOF
Various paging.
Without music.
In selected episodes, this drama tells the story of the Old Testament, from Abraham to the prophets, against a background of modern persecution. It was staged at the Manhattan Opera House, New York, Jan. 7, 1937. For reviews see *Collection of newspaper clippings of dramatic criticism, 1936–1937,* v. E–Hir, † NBL. References are given ibid. to reviews in periodicals.

WERFEL, FRANZ V. Goat song (Bocksgesang); a drama in five acts by Franz Werfel, translated by Ruth Langner. The Theatre Guild version. Garden City, N. Y.: Published for the Theatre Guild by Doubleday, Page & Company, 1926. viii p., 1 l., 161 p. 12°. NGE
Reprinted in Theatre Guild, Inc., New York, *Theatre Guild anthology,* New York [cop. 1936], p. 387–438, NAFH.
"It is a play of terror, in the purest sense, tragic; the outward action illustrative of profound universal conflicts; the solution, the eternal tragic solution of salvation through vicarious suffering." The scene is laid in Serbia, at about 1790. The plot is based on a newspaper story. Produced at the Guild Theatre, New York, Jan. 25, 1926, with Edward G. Robinson as Reb Feivel, a Jewish revolutionary. Reviewed by R. D. Skinner in *Commonweal,* New York, 1926, v. 3, p. 384–385, * DA; and by A. Coralnik in *Theatre Guild quarterly,* New York, 1926, v. 3, p. 13, 16–17, 24 (illus. on p. 5, 12), † NBLA. See also *Collection of newspaper clippings of dramatic criticism, 1925–1926,* v. E–J, † NBL.

Krass, Nathan. "Goat song"; discourse delivered... Sunday, Feb. 21, 1926, at Temple Emanu-El, New York. Being a revised stenographic report. [New York, 1926.] 28 p., 1 l. 16°. NGB p.v.235

WERFEL, FRANZ V. Juarez and Maximilian; a dramatic history in three phases and thirteen pictures, by Franz Werfel, translated by Ruth Langner, with a note on the play by Gilbert W. Gabriel. The Theatre Guild version. New York: Published for the Theatre Guild, Inc., by Simon and Schuster, 1926. xiii, 160 p. front., plates. 12°.
Produced by the Theatre Guild at the Guild Theatre, New York, Oct. 11, 1926, with Albert Bruning as Doctor Basch, Jewish physician to Maximilian. Reviewed by Larry Barretto in *Bookman,* New York, 1927, v. 64, p. 618, * DA; *Drama calendar,* New York, v. 9, Oct. 18, 1926, p. 3–5, NBL; and by Stark Young in *New republic,* 1926, v. 48, p. 271–272, * DA. See also *Collection of newspaper clippings of dramatic criticism, 1926–1927,* v. I–M, † NBL; and

E. Goldbeck in *Reflex,* New York, v. 2, March, 1928, p. 36–37, * PBD.
The Guild version was produced by the Stage Society, London, Feb. 7, 1932, with Graveley Edwards as Doctor Basch. Reviewed in *Era,* London, v. 95, Feb. 10, 1932, p. 8, † NAFA; and by G. J. in *Jewish chronicle,* London, Feb. 12, 1932, p. 32, * PBE.

WEST, MAE. ...Diamond Lil... New York: The Macaulay Company [cop. 1932]. 256 p. 12°.
This study of life of what was the Bowery, New York City, in the gay nineties, was originally staged as a melodrama in three acts at the Royale Theatre, New York, April 9, 1928, with the author in the title rôle and Louis Nusbaum as Isaac Jacobson. Reviewed by G. V. Seldes in *Dial,* New York, 1928, v. 84, p. 531–532, * DA; and by Stark Young in *New republic,* 1928, v. 55, p. 145–146, * DA. See also *Collection of newspaper clippings of dramatic criticism, 1927–1928,* v. D–G, † NBL.

WEXLEY, JOHN. They shall not die; a play [in three acts]... New York: A. A. Knopf, 1934. 7 p.l., 3–191(1) p. 12°. 8–NBM
Presented in form of a running story, with the high-spots reproduced in actual dialogue from the text, in *Best plays of 1933–34,* New York, 1934, p. 203–255, NAFH.
"Dramatic brief for the nine colored boys twice convicted of the crime of rape in Scottsboro, Alabama." The presence of Samuel S. Leibowitz as counsel for the defense gave one of the prosecuting attorneys an opportunity to indulge in anti-Jewish statements during the summation.
Produced by the Theatre Guild at the Royale Theatre, New York, Feb. 21, 1934, with Claude Raines as Nathan G. Rubin (S. S. Leibowitz), lawyer for the defendants. For reviews see *Collection of newspaper clippings of dramatic criticism, 1933–1934,* v. Sh–T, † NBL.

WHARTON, MRS. EDITH NEWBOLD (JONES). The age of innocence... New York [etc.]: D. Appleton and Company, 1920. 3 p.l., 364 p., 1 l. 12°. NBO

Barnes, Margaret Ayer. The age of innocence, a dramatization in five scenes of Edith N. Wharton's novel of the same name, was produced at the Empire Theatre, New York, Nov. 27, 1928.
Arnold Korff played Julius Beaufort, a courtly Austrian Jewish financier. The plot deals with New York "high society" in the seventies of the last century. Reviewed by G. J. Nathan in *American mercury,* New York, 1929, v. 16, p. 249–250, * DA; by Euphemia Van R. Wyatt in *Catholic world,* New York, v. 128, p. 590–591, * DA; and by Padraic Colum in *Dial,* New York, v. 86, p. 172–173, * DA. See also *Collection of newspaper clippings of dramatic criticism, 1928–1929,* v. A–B, † NBL.

WHEN is the News coming out? (Columbia news. New York, 1921. 8°. v. 34, Dec., 1921, p. 9–10.) STGR
Place: the office of the Columbia news, organ of the Columbia Grammar School, New York.
The speakers are the pupils of the school, engaged in getting out the school paper.

WHITE, MRS. BESSIE (FELSTINER). Brotherhood of man; a short drama of Jewish life in three episodes... New York, cop. 1936. 1, 19 f. 4°.
Reproduced from typewritten copy.
Second prize play of the Young Circle League of the Workmen's Circle, New York, play contest.

—— By any other name; a one-act comedy... New York, Los Angeles, Cal.: S. French, Inc.;

THE JEW IN ENGLISH DRAMA

Individual Plays — 1915–1938, continued

London: S. French, Ltd., cop. 1935. 22 p., 1 l. diagr. 12°. NBL p.v.391
How Mrs. Minnevich, eager at first to change her name, is induced to be known as she is.
Produced by the Drama Group of Temple Kehillath Israel, Boston, April 6, 1937, with Ethel Stern as Mrs. Minnevitch.

—— Family; comedy in one act... New York City, N. Y., Los Angeles, Cal.: S. French, Inc.; London: S. French, Ltd. [cop. 1932.] 229–254 p. 12°.
Repr.: One-act plays for stage and study, New York, 1932, 7th series, p. 229–254, NCO (One).
It satirizes family snobbery of certain Jewish circles. The scene is a girls' college dormitory.

—— Fools' paradise; a play of Jewish life in one act... Boston: Walter H. Baker Company [cop. 1934]. 25 p. 12°. (Baker's royalty plays.)

—— Money in the bank; a comedy in one act ... Boston: W. H. Baker Company [cop. 1934]. 26 p. 12°.
The characters are four Jewish women, and the place is New York City.
Staged at the Little Theatre of Temple Israel, Boston, Nov. 27, 1934.

WHITE, MRS. BESSIE (FELSTINER). Sinners; a drama in one act... Boston: Walter H. Baker Company [cop. 1934]. 22 p. 16°. (Baker's all star series.)

—— A tooth for a tooth; a comedy in one act ... Boston: Walter H. Baker Company [cop. 1934]. 23 p. 12°. (Baker's royalty plays.)
Staged at the Little Theatre of Temple Israel, Boston, Jan. 27, 1935.

—— "Where there's smoke..."; a prize winning Jewish comedy in one act... Boston: Walter H. Baker Company [cop. 1934]. 24 p. 12°.
"The Old Homestead Inn [in Maine] is agog with excitement because of a rumor that some Jews are stopping there...until it is proved that the rumor is based on an error. But then one couple appear... and declare themselves to be the Jews."
Produced by the Temple Israel (Boston) Little Theatre, Feb. 25, 1934, with A. J. Krulee as Gordon, and Pauline Freedman as Mrs. Treadwell. See *Jewish advocate*, Boston, v. 71, Feb. 23, 1934, part 1, p. 2, * PBD.

WHITE, E. MICHAEL. Five out of nine have it; some satirical comments [in one act] on the Supreme Court and poultry. (Common sense. New York, 1935. 4°. v. 4, Sept., 1935, p. 12–14.) *DA
Abridged in *Current thought*, Springfield, Mass., 1935, v. 1, p. 283–284; and reprinted in *Call of youth*, New York, 1936, v. 4, no. 6, p. 8–9, †* PYO.
A take-off on the U. S. Supreme Court's decision in the Schechter poultry case which declared the NRA unconstitutional. Among the speakers are Justices Brandeis and Cardozo.

WHITE, KATE ALICE. Samuel Snickerwitz's Hallowe'en; a stunt for Hallowe'en... Franklin, Ohio: Eldridge Entertainment House, Inc., cop. 1927. 8 p. 12°. (Eldridge special day material.)

WHITEHOUSE, JOSEPHINE HENRY. Jeremiad; a play in one act. New York [etc.]: Samuel French, cop. 1926. 22 p. 12°. (French's international copyrighted...edition of the works of the best authors. no. 561.)
A sketch of the female branch of the West End Avenue, New York, Braunsteins. This play won the cup in the 1926 Westchester County Little Theatre Tournament, at the Westchester Women's Club, Mount Vernon, N. Y., April 17 and 19, 1926.

WICKSER, JOSEPHINE WILHELM. The romance of Buffalo; a pageant in honor of 100 years of growth and progress of a great city of a great nation. (In: Buffalo Centennial Committee, 100 years of Buffalo in ten daily chapters. Buffalo, N. Y., 1932. 4°. p. 14–28.)
A pageant in three parts and twenty-five episodes held in Buffalo July 1st to 10th, 1932, to commemorate the Buffalo centennial, 1832–1932. Episode eight of part two depicts the laying of the cornerstone of the City of Ararat, originally planned by Mordecai Manuel Noah, in Sept., 1825, as a refuge for the Jews. See text on p. 22. For a history of this effort see Max J. Kohler, "Some early American Zionist projects," in American Jewish Historical Society, *Publications*, no. 8, p. 75–118, * PXX.

WIERNIK, BERTHA. When Satan interferes; a comedy [in two scenes]. (Jewish exponent. Philadelphia, 1919. f°. v. 69, Aug. 8, 1919, p. 1, 11.) †* PBD
A comedy involving a suspicious husband and an innocent wife.

WILCOX, C. E., AND HELEN M. WILCOX. The Boomville band concert; a comic entertainment [in one act] for band organizations. Chicago: T. S. Denison & Company [cop. 1931]. 26 p. 12°. (Denison's specialties.)
Ikey, "the Hebrew member" of Professor Atta Boy's band.

WILCOX, CONSTANCE GRENELLE. Egypt's eyes; a three act play with an epilogue. New York: S. French [etc.], cop. 1924. 94 p. plates. 8°. (French's standard library ed.) NBL p.v.118
A fantastic play laid in a modern museum, a modern apartment, and in Egypt before the tomb of Neferet in the year 2000 B. C. Produced by the Playbarn Workshop, New York, July 21, 1924. Jack Williams as Jimmie Greenberg, "a neat little Jew, with a general air of Broadway well-being."

WILDER, SOPHIA CORNELL (HANKS). Strings; an original comedy in three acts, by Mrs. Marshall P. Wilder. [Atlantic City, N. J., 1918?] 42 f. 8°. † NCOF
Reproduced from typewritten copy.
Scene: settlement house on the lower East Side of New York.
Mrs. Epstein and Mrs. Polensky, two middle-aged Russian Jewesses, visitors of the settlement. They are made to speak here in the Russian-Jewish dialect.

WILDER, THORNTON NIVEN. And the sea shall give up its dead. (S 4 N. Northampton, Mass., 1923. 16°. 4th year, Jan./Feb., 1923, p. [7–11.]) *DA
Judgment day, several miles below the surface of the North Atlantic. Horatio Nissem, in life a theatrical producer, "very proud of his race." Reprinted, with slight difference of text, in the author's *The Angel that troubled the waters, and other plays*, New York, 1928, p. 97–103, NBM.

Individual Plays — 1915–1938, continued

WILLARD, CLARK. Polishing papa; a domestic comedy in three acts... Chicago: Dramatic Publishing Company [cop. 1930]. 94 p. diagr. 12°. (Sergel's acting drama.)
Scene: a small town in the Middle West. Samuel Karmen, an advertising solicitor. "This part may be played as a Hebrew part with good effect, if desired."

WILLETS, JEANETTE. The story books before the judge. illus. (Wilson bulletin. New York, 1931. 8°. v. 6, p. 127–130.) *HA
A one-act playlet by an eighth-grade pupil. Adam is the judge, and among the books which present their claim for excellence is Scott's *Ivanhoe*.

WILLIAMS, IDA SAUL. Sabbath lights. [In one act.] (Review. Philadelphia, 1917. 12°. v. 12, Jan., 1917, p. 8–17.)
Copy: Library of the Jewish Theological Seminary of America.

WILLIAMS, LAURA M. On the jury. (In her: Twenty funny monologues. Franklin, Ohio, cop. 1924. 12°. p. 62–69.) NBL p.v.272
Rachel Kolinsky, one of the jurors, pleads for the defendant.

WILLIAMSON, HUGH ROSS. ...Mr. Gladstone; a play in three acts. London: Constable [1937]. vii(i) p., 1 l., 94 p. 12°.
The scenes are set over the period 1876–1894.
Produced at the Gate Theatre Studio, London, Oct., 1937, with Alan Wheatly as Disraeli. See *Jewish chronicle*, London, Oct. 8, 1937, p. 41, * PBD.

WILLMORE, EDWARD. Cromwell, the Protector; a play. London: The Puma Publishing Co., 1923. xxii, 157 p. 12°. NCR
In five acts and an epilogue.
Reviewed in *Jewish chronicle*, London, Sept. 7, 1923, p. 23, * PBD.
Time: 1628–1655.
"Two sections of this play 'Cromwell' have already been printed in the collection of my poems entitled 'Puma passage,' published in the spring of 1921." — *Preface*.
Manasseh b. Joseph b. Israel, 1604–1657, pleading successfully before Cromwell for the readmission of the Jews into England, is one of the characters.

WILSON, EDNA ERLE. Thanksgiving through the ages; a schoolroom pageant. (In her: Good things for harvest time. Chicago [cop. 1924]. 12°. p. 89–94.) MV p.v.67
History presents Ceres, Demeter, and a Jewess as the ancient celebrants of Thanksgiving Day.

WILSON, ELLA M., AND ANNA W. FIELD. A Christmas play [in one act]. (American schoolmaster. Ypsilanti, Mich., 1917. 8°. v. 11, p. 391–399.)
A modern play. Among the characters is a Jewish girl. "Tolstoy's Where love is, there God is also and Mary Antin's Promised land form the basis of this play." It was produced by the children of the Training School of the Michigan State Normal College.

WILSON, GENEVIEVE C. Which are foreign? a world friendship activity. (Sierra educational news. San Francisco, 1932. 8°. v. 28, Oct., 1932, p. 42–43.)
Presented May 18, 1932, by the pupils of Los Angeles city schools, in celebration of the National Good Will Day, sponsored by the World Friendship Committee. Among the children of various nationalities is one from Palestine.

WISE, ERNEST GEORGE. ...Belle; a play [in three acts]. London: Victor Gollancz, Ltd., 1929. 128 p. 12°. NCR
Reprinted, under the title Down our street, in *Six plays*, London, 1930, p. 349–459, NCO.
Under the title *Belle; or, What's the bother*, it was produced by the Incorporated Stage Society, London, Oct. 20, 1929, with Millie Wolf as Tessie Bernstein "from the London East End," and Milton Rosmer as Sam. Reviewed in *Era*, London, v. 93, Oct. 23, 1929, p. 6, † *NAFA*; *Nation & Athenæum*, London, v. 46, p. 140, * *DA*; and by Ivor Brown in *Saturday review*, London, v. 148, p. 475, * *DA*.

WOLF, FRIEDRICH. ...Doktor Mamlocks Ausweg; Tragödie der westlichen Demokratie. Zürich: Oprecht & Helbling, 1935. 80 p., 1 l. 12°. NGB p.v.451
Adapted and translated by Anne Bromberger, under the title *Professor Mamlock*, and produced by the Jewish Unit of the Federal Theatre Project at Daly's 63rd Street Theatre, New York, April 13, 1937, with Morris Strassberg in the title rôle. It deals with the treatment of a German Jewish surgeon by Nazi Germany. For reviews see *Collection of newspaper clippings of dramatic criticism, 1936–1937*, v. P–R, † *NBL*.

WOLFROM, ANNA. The marriage certificate, a one-act play. (In her: Human wisps. Boston, 1917. 12°. p. 1–20.) NBM
The widowed Mrs. Alinsky is aided by her co-religionist Mr. Waldstein. Scene: town on the Missouri river.

WOLFSON, MIRIAM. The spirit of Hadassah; a one-act play. New York: Bloch Publishing Co., 1927. 14 p. 12°.
A review of the achievements of the Zionist movement from the time of Leo Pinsker to our own day. Among the characters are Capt. Dreyfus, Earl Balfour, Dr. Ch. Weitzman, and Henrietta Szold. See *Daily Jewish courier*, Chicago, June 27, 1927, p. 8, * *PBB*.

WOLFSON, VICTOR. Excursion; a play in three acts... New York: Random House [cop. 1937]. 6 p.l., 3–186 p. 8°. NBM
Excerpts from the dialogue, with a running synopsis of the play, are given in *Best plays of 1936–37*, New York, 1937, p. 328–356, *NAFH*.
A fanciful play about a Coney Island excursion boat that puts out to the southern seas. It was produced at the Vanderbilt Theatre, New York, April 9, 1937, with James R. Waters and Jennie Moscowitz as Mr. and Mrs. Fitchel, proprietors of a laundry shop in The Bronx, and passengers on the adventurous boat. For reviews see *Collection of newspaper clippings of dramatic criticism, 1936–1937*, v. E–Hir, † *NBL*.

WOOD, CORNELIUS A. The last Gepuire; a play in one act... Boston [etc.]: Baker's Plays [cop. 1937]. 1 p.l., 68 p., 1 pl. 12°. (Baker's royalty plays.)
The action takes place during the British-Sinn Fein armistice in 1921, in an Irish village, in the home of a lace-making family. Ginsberg, an American lace importer, comes to the cottage to buy the famed Gepuire lace. It was first produced, at Amherst, Mass., under the auspices of the Massachusetts State College, July 28, 1936, with R. P. Baldwin as Ginsberg.

WOODBURY, DAVID O. Hung jury; a play in one act... Boston, Mass., Los Angeles, Cal.: W. H. Baker Company [cop. 1936]. 46 p. 12°. NBL p.v.393
Fischer, a "Jewish meat-market proprietor," one of the jurors. "He speaks exaggerated Jewish English."

Individual Plays — 1915–1938, continued

WOODMAN, NED. Cominski complains; a Jewish telephone monologue... Chicago: T. S. Denison & Co. [cop. 1930.] 10 p. 12°. (Denison's vaudeville sketches.)
Cominski has a claim for damages.

WRIGHT, FRED, AND S. JONAS. ...Shop strife; a play [in three scenes] about the garment industry [in New York City]... Katonah, N. Y.: Brookwood Labor College, 1934. [1], 10 f. 4°. † NCOF p.v.20

WYCKOFF, S. ROBERT. "The western wall"; a one-act play about Tisha b'ab... Brooklyn, N. Y. [1932.] 3, 9 f. 4°. * PBM p.v.193
Typewritten copy.
Dramatized from E. E. Levinger's story of the same name in her *Jewish holiday stories*, New York, 1918, p. 179–192, * PSY.
Scene: Jerusalem before the Wailing Wall, before the World war.
First performed at Camp Delawaxen, Lackawaxen, Pa., Aug. 10, 1932.

WYLIE, IDA ALENA ROSS. Witches Sabbath. Sioux City, Iowa: Wetmore Declamation Bureau, cop. 1934. 4 l. 4°.
Caption-title.
Mimeographed.
A dramatic reading, dealing with persecution of Jews in a small German town, as reflected in the life of a young boy.
Based upon the author's short story of the same title in *Good housekeeping*, New York, v. 99, Oct., 1934, p. 22–25, 240–244, 247–252, *VSA*.

YAFFLE, PSEUD. Foiling the Reds; or, The heart of a labourer. A review in one or more scenes by Yaffle [pseud.]. Illustrations by Flambo. London: Labour Publishing Co., Ltd. [1926.] 48 p. illus. 12°. NCR
An anti-communist play. Trotski, burlesque imitation of the real one, whose mission, in his own words, is to "destroy the Vestern Vorld."

YOFFA, ANNIE. Revenge; or, The comedy of letters; a five act drama. New York: The Martin Press, 1929. 3 p.l., 121 p. 8°.
Reviewed in *Jewish quarterly review*, Philadelphia, 1930, new series, v. 20, p. 296, * PBE.

ZANGWILL, ISRAEL. The cockpit: romantic drama in three acts... New York: The Macmillan Co., 1921. 5 p.l., 263(1) p. 12°. NCR

—— —— London: William Heinemann, 1921. 4 p.l., 257(1) p. 8°.
Reviewed by Elias Lieberman in *American Hebrew*, New York, 1922, v. 110, p. 404, 415, * PBD; by L. B. in *Freeman*, New York, v. 4, p. 622, * DA; by Armin Blau in *Jeschurun*, Berlin, 1928, Bd. 15, p. 49–61, * PBC; *Jewish chronicle*, London, Nov. 18, 1921, p. 32, * PBE; *Saturday review*, London, v. 132, p. 692, * DA; and in *Spectator*, London, v. 127, p. 867, * DA.
A topical play, never produced, which deals with Old World racial frictions. Baron Gripstein, conventional Jewish financier, newspaper and cinema owner, ostentatious in his embrace of the dominant faith and his flamboyant patriotism to the country of his adoption.

—— The forcing house; or, The cockpit continued. Tragi-comedy in four acts. New York: Macmillan Co., 1923. xxiv, 278 p. 12°. NCR
In "To Maurice Maeterlinck," p. v–xx, the author expounds his theory of drama.
Deals with capitalism and communism in Valdania, mythical Balkan state. Gripstein, ex-Jewish financier carried over from Zangwill's earlier *The Cockpit*, threatened with death under the Revolution, returns to his ancestral faith. Reviewed by Alfred Sutro in *Jewish chronicle*, London, March 2, 1923, p. 37, * PBD (reprinted in *Jewish exponent*, Philadelphia, v. 71, March 16, 1923, p. 8, * PBD); *Nation*, London, 1923, v. 32, p. 957–958, * DA; *New York Times book review*, v. 28, Feb. 11, 1923, p. 12, † NAA; and in *Saturday review*, London, 1922, v. 134, p. 839, * DA.

ZAHAJKIEWICZ, SZCZESNY. Zydowskie swaty; obrazek dramatyczny ze spiewami. Napisał Szczesny Zahajkiewicz; muzyka Maryanna S. Rozyckiego. Chicago: W. H. Sajewski, 1915. 40 p. 16°.
Words only.
See United States. — Copyright Office, *Dramatic compositions copyrighted in the United States, 1870 to 1916*, item 56057.

ZECKHAUSER, IOLA, AND J. CASSLEV. Before the wall [Jewish drama in one act]... Boston: Walter H. Baker Company [cop. 1935]. 18 p. 12°.
An episode in the shadow of the Wailing Wall, Jerusalem, during the period following the Arab outbreak against the Jews, in August, 1929.

ZEVE, LEAH. In the balance. Winner of the first prize in play contest conducted under the auspices of the Department of Religion and Religious Education of the National Council of Jewish Women. New York: National Council of Jewish Women [1929]. 23 p. 24°.
* C p.v.2213
A morality playlet, in one act. "Place: in the court of Public Opinion. Time: not the present, but a premonitory vision of what may be," — Faith and Humanity, by the office of Love, Loyalty, and Service.

ZIMMERMAN, HARRY. David's barmitzvah. [In one act.] (In his: Plays of Jewish life. [London, 1931.] 12°. p. 91–105.)
NCO (Zimmerman)
First produced by the Victoria & Chelsea Jewish Literary Society, London, Dec. 9, 1928, with H. Horowitz, Yonne Pass, and Cyril Adler in the parts of father, mother, and son. The scene is the East End of London.

INDEXES

INDEX OF AUTHORS

Numbers refer to pages in the main text of the bibliography.

A

A., H.:
  Alexander in Babylon, 116.
Abbott, George, joint author. *See* Burnet, Dana, and George Abbott.
Abbott, George, and James Gleason:
  The fall guy, 116.
Abdullah, Achmed:
  Black tents, 116.
Abdullah, Achmed, and W. A. Wolff:
  Broadway interlude, 116.
Abel, W. H.:
  Under two flags, 67.
Abeles, Edwin V. I.:
  One of the bravest, 116.
Abelson, Alter:
  The Messiah people, 116.
Abelson, Anna G.:
  Love in the deeps, 116.
Abrahams, Israel:
  Guarini and Luzzatto, 31.
  Jews and the theatre, 2.
  Lessing's first Jewish play, 27.
Acklam, F. Elva:
  Drama, 1.
Adams, O. F.:
  The merchant of Venice, 53.
Adams, Mrs. Sarah F. (F.):
  Vivia Perpetua, 53.
Addison, Thomas:
  Meyer and Son, 110.
Adkins, F. J.:
  Education, 116.
Adler, E. N.:
  Modern London Jews in drama, 2.
Agate, J. E.:
  Blessed are the rich, 116.
Agg, H., joint author. *See* Johnson, Philip, and H. Agg.
Aguilar, Grace:
  The vale of cedars, 53.
Ainsworth, W. H.:
  Jack Sheppard, 53.
Akers, D.:
  A project in stage design for Jew of Malta, 35.
Akins, Zoë:
  Daddy's gone a-hunting, 116.
  Déclassée, 116.
Alderman, J. S.:
  The net, 116.
Aldis, Mrs. Mary (R.):
  An heir at large, 116.
Alexander, Cecile:
  The night of the eighth candle, 116.
  A Purimbridge birthday, 117.
Allary, J.:
  The dramas of Henry Bernstein and the worship of strength, 59, 60.
Allen, Horace:
  Bells of the sleigh, 74.
Allingham, J. T.:
  Transformation, 8.
  Who wins? *See* Charlemagne, Armand, The uncle's will, 10.
Almar, George:
  Jack Ketch, 53.
  Oliver Twist, 68.
Ames, Winthrop:
  Mr. Samuel, 134.
Amherst, J. H.:
  Napoleon Buonaparte's invasion of Russia, 8.
  Will Watch, 8.

Anderson, F. O.:
  How Mr. Smith dropped the hint, 117.
Anderson, Maxwell:
  Winterset, 117.
Anderson, Maxwell, and Harold Hickerson:
  Gods of the lightning, 117.
Anderson, Maxwell, and Leonard Stallings:
  What price glory, 117.
Andrashnik, A.:
  "Fruition of an ideal," 117.
Andreas, Eulalie:
  Yes, yes! go on, 117.
Andrews, Charlton:
  He got the job, 117.
Andrews, M. P.:
  Dissipation, 8.
Andreyev, L. N.:
  Anathema, 55.
  To the stars, 55.
Ansky, S., pseud. *See* Rappaport, Solomon.
Anzengruber, Ludwig:
  The farmer forsworn, 55.
Apollo Theatre, New York:
  Opinions of Frank Crane and other prominent men and women [on Shalom Asch's The God of vengeance], 56.
Applegarth, Margaret T.:
  Color blind, 117.
  Empty stockings, 117.
  Strictly private, 117.
Archer, Thomas:
  The three red men, 55.
Arnold, S. J.:
  The maid and the magpye, 32.
Arnstein, Mark:
  The eternal song, 55.
Aronin, Ben:
  Bialik's last Chanuka, 117.
  The partition of the Homentasch, 117.
Aronin, Ben, and S. M. Blumenfield:
  A rabbi's son, 117.
Arundel, Louis:
  The light of the East, 117.
Asch, Shalom:
  The God of vengeance, 56.
  Kiddush Ha-Shem, 117.
  Night, 56.
  Sabbatai Zevi, 56.
  The sinner, 56.
  Winter, 56.
  With the current, 56.
Askowith, Dora:
  A pageant dedicated to the women of Israel throughout the ages, 118.
Augier, G. V. E., and Jules Sandeau:
  Monsieur Poirier's son-in-law, 56.
Averill, Mrs. Esther (C.), and L. A. Averill:
  The spirit of Massachusetts, 118.
Aymar, Benjamin, and J. R. Blake:
  Ivanhoe, 42.

B

B., C.:
  The advancement of the stage Jew, 68.
B., J. H.:
  Patriots, 57.
Baar, Herman:
  Dialogue on cooking, 57.
  Dialogue on prizes, 57.
  Fashion, 57.
  Visitors, 57.

Bacher, J., joint author. *See* Burstein, Abraham, and J. Bacher.
Bacon, Eva M.:
  The try outs, 118.
Badt-Strauss, Bertha:
  Disraeli und Palästina, 58.
Baer, Max:
  The trial of Jacob Finklebottom, 118.
Baillie, Joanna:
  The siege, 8.
Baker, G. M.:
  Conjuration, 57.
  The peddler of Very Nice, 57.
Baker, Thomas:
  An act at Oxford, 8.
  Hampstead Heath, 8.
Baker, W. G., and J. C. Arnold:
  Jack Sheppard, 54.
Baker, Walter H., and Company:
  Plays for Jewish groups, 1.
Balderston, J. L., and J. E. Hoare:
  Red planet, 118.
Ballard, Frederick:
  Young America, 118.
Ballard, Frederick, and Pearl Franklin:
  Young America, 118.
Balmain, R., joint author. *See* Whyte, H., and R. Balmain.
Baltimore Hebrew Congregation, Baltimore:
  Followers of the light, 118.
Banks, C. E.:
  An American woman, 57.
Barber, James:
  Which is the thief? 33.
Barclay, Sir Thomas:
  Gambetta and Dr. Stresemann, 118.
  Gambetta and Monsieur Poincaré, 118.
Barish, Mildred:
  Light, 118.
Barker, E. L., and A. Barker:
  The man on stilts, 118.
  Middletown, 118.
Barnes, Margaret A.:
  The age of innocence, 186.
Barnett, C. Z.:
  Dream of fate, 57.
  The mariner's dream, 57.
  Oliver Twist, 68.
  The rise of the Rotheschildes, 9.
Barns, Florence E.:
  The background and sources of the Croxton play of the sacrament, 24.
Barrett, A. W.:
  The Jew of Prague, 57.
Barrett, E. S.:
  The school for profligacy, 9.
Barrett, Wilson, and R. S. Hichens:
  The daughters of Babylon, 57.
Barry, Philip:
  Hotel universe, 118.
Barry, Tom:
  Courage, 119.
Bassen, Hayim:
  Back to God, 119.
Basshe, E. J.:
  The centuries, 119.
Baswitz, Charles:
  Jakey Einstein, 58.
Bates, Herbert:
  The king's English, 119.
Bates, William:
  Gil Blas, 9.
Baum, Vicki:
  Grand Hotel, 119.
Baum, Vicki, and John Golden:
  Divine drudge, 119.
Bauman, J. H.:
  The country squire, 58.

Beaconsfield, Benjamin Disraeli, 1st earl of:
  Tancred, 58.
  The wondrous tale of Alroy, 9.
Beahan, Charles, and G. Fort:
  Jarnegan, 184.
Beazley, Samuel:
  Ivanhoe, 42.
Beck, Edith S.:
  The old order, 119.
Becker, B., joint author. *See* Jasspon, Ethel R., and B. Becker.
Becker, C. S.:
  Greater than love, 119.
Beckett, Dan:
  The thief maker, 68.
Beddoes, T. L.:
  The second brother, 58.
Beebe, Helen (R.):
  Young Mr. Disraeli, 119.
Beebe, M. N.:
  The all America eleven, 58.
  Wanted — a pitcher, 58.
Behn, Mrs. Aphra (A.):
  The second part of The rover, 9.
Behrman, S. N.:
  Rain from heaven, 119.
  Serena Blandish, 120.
Belasco, David, joint author. *See* De Mille, H. C., and David Belasco.
Belden, Mary M.:
  The dramatic works of Samuel Foote, 2.
Beljame, A.:
  Les premières oeuvres dramatiques de Shakespeare, 35.
Bell, Kenneth:
  Anti-clericalism in France, 58.
Ben-Zion, Benedix:
  A varumglücktes Auto-da-fé, 45.
Benavente y Martinez, Jacinto:
  Saturday night, 58.
  The smile of Mona Lisa, 58.
Bender, O. G.:
  Susskind von Trimberg, 120.
Benedict, George:
  The masterpiece, 58.
Bengal, Ben:
  Plant in the sun, 120.
Benjamin, pseud.:
  Between ourselves, 59.
Benner, L. D.:
  The golden days, 120.
Bennett, Arnold:
  The great adventure, 59.
Bennett, Arnold, and Edward Knoblock:
  London life, 120.
Bennett, Charles:
  The last hour, 120.
Benson, N. P.:
  A study in character delineation, 35.
Benton, Rita:
  The liberty bell, 120.
Bergstrøm, Hjalmar:
  Lynggaard & Co., 59.
Beringer, Vera:
  The ugly duchess, 133.
Berkowitz, I. D.:
  Landsleit, 120.
Berlyn, Ivan:
  Fagin, 68.
Berman, Henry:
  The faith of the fathers, 120.
Bernard, Baruch:
  A Jewish tragedy, 120.
  See also Carr, Alexander, and B. Bernard.
Bernard, W. B.:
  The philosophers of Berlin, 59.

INDEX OF AUTHORS

Bernstein, Henry:
  Israël, 59.
  Samson, 60.
Berry, Lucile B.:
  The melting pot, 120.
Betts, Ernest, editor:
  Jew Süss, 133.
Biben, Augusta C.:
  The Jew in English literature, 2.
Bienenstok, Montefiore:
  The Hebrew comedian, 2.
Biesecker, C. E.:
  A comparison of The Jew and the Merchant of Venice, 24.
Billings, M. H.:
  The rabbi's spell. *See* Cumberland, S. C. The rabbi's spell, 66.
Binyon, Laurence:
  Bombastes in the shades, 120.
Bird, C. S.:
  Peck vs. Peck, 60.
Birnbaum, Mrs. P. S., joint author. *See* Kilik, Mrs. David, and Mrs. P. S. Birnbaum.
Bisson, A. C. A., and P. Gérard:
  Disparu!!! 60.
Bitney, Mayme R.:
  Cohen's views on business, 60.
Bixby, F. L.:
  The little boss, 60.
Black, Leota H.:
  Beach nuts, 120.
Black, Pearl:
  Something different, 121.
Blackmore, Madeline:
  "I am over forty," 121.
Blake, J. R., joint author. *See* Aymar, Benjamin, and J. R. Blake.
Blaney, C. E.:
  The child slaves of New York, 60.
  Old Isaacs from the Bowery, 60.
Blankfort, Michael, and M. Gold:
  "Battle hymn," 121.
Blass, J. L.:
  Die Entwickelung der Figur des gedungenen Mörders im älteren englischen Drama, 20.
Blathwayt, Raymond:
  Bella donna; the authors, the play and the players, 83.
Blatt, W. M.:
  A Jewish word, 121.
  Oi, such a family! 121.
  The quality of mercy, 121.
  The voice of the ages, 121.
Bloch Publishing Company:
  List of English plays, 1.
Block, Etta, translator:
  One-act plays from the Yiddish, 6.
  One-act plays from the Yiddish: second series, 6.
Block, Maxine:
  Eyes, 121.
Block, Sheridan:
  The drama; logical, psychological, Hebra-ological, 115.
Bloom, I. M.:
  A nation's gratitude, 121.
Bloom, Lenore:
  To Palestine and peace, 121.
Blumenfield, S. M., joint author. *See* Aronin, Ben, and S. M. Blumenfield.
Blunt, W. S.:
  The bride of the Nile, 60.
Boehm, D., joint author. *See* Pemberton, Murdock, and D. Boehm.
Bogen, Jessie B.:
  The call, 121.
Boggs, Robert:
  A stepdaughter of Israel, 60.

Bolitho, William:
  Overture — 1920, 121.
Bolton, G. R.:
  Polly preferred, 121.
Bolton, G. R., and George Middleton:
  The light of the world, 122.
Booth, W. S.:
  [Francis Bacon and the Jew of Malta,] 35.
Boothe, Clare:
  The women, 122.
Borsook, Henry:
  Three weddings of a hunchback, 122.
Boucicault, Dion:
  After dark, 60–61.
  Flying scud, 61.
  London assurance, 61.
  The queen of spades, 62.
Bouilly, J. N.:
  Une folie, 9.
Bourchier, Arthur:
  All alive, oh! *See* Bisson, A. C. A., and P. Gérard, Disparu!!! 60.
  The Jew in drama, 2.
Bower, Sherman:
  "Preferred stock," 122.
Boyd, E. A.:
  Some of my best friends are Gentiles, 122.
Boyer, C. V.:
  Marlowe and the Machiavellian villain-hero, 35.
Bradfield, Thomas:
  Lessing's story of the three rings, 29.
Bradley, E. W., and J. R. Reeves:
  The old country store, 122.
Bradley, Katherine H. *See* Field, Michael, pseud. of Katherine H. Bradley and Edith E. Cooper.
Bradley, Mrs. Trimble, and G. H. Broadhurst:
  Izzy, 125.
Brand, Oswald:
  Oliver Twist, 68.
Brandon, Dorothy:
  The outsider, 122.
Branfman, T., joint author. *See* Klonsky, Milton, and T. Branfman.
Braun, Wilbur:
  Absent-minded Judy, 122.
  "The closed door," 122.
Braverman, L. L., joint author. *See* Brilliant, Nathan, and L. L. Braverman.
Brent, Romney:
  The mad Hopes, 122.
Brereton, Austin:
  The School for scandal, 49.
Brewster, Sadie B.:
  America's making, 122.
Brighouse, Harold:
  Mary's John, 122.
  See also Conway, Olive, pseud. of Harold Brighouse and J. Walton.
Bril, I. L.:
  Everyjew, 122.
Bril, Joseph:
  קטיגור וסניגור, 15.
Brilliant, Nathan, and L. L. Braverman:
  Moses Maimonides, 122.
Brinig, Myron:
  Fear God and take your own part, 123.
Brion, Marcel:
  Robert Greene, 20.
Broadhurst, G. H., joint author. *See* Bradley, Mrs. Trimble, and G. H. Broadhurst.
Brodie, Mrs. A. H.:
  Hadassah's call, 123.
Brody, Alter:
  A house of mourning, 123.
  Lamentations, 7.
  Lowing in the night, 123.
  Rapunzel, 123.
  Recess for memorials, 123.

Bromberger, Anne:
  Professor Mamlock. See Wolf, Friedrich. Doktor Mamlocks Ausweg, 188.
Brome, Richard:
  The Jewish gentleman, 9.
Brooke, C. F. T.:
  Marlowe's versification and style, 35.
  The prototype of Marlowe's Jew of Malta, 35.
Brookfield, C. H. E., and W. Yardley:
  Model Trilby, 71.
Brooks, Shirley:
  The creole, 62.
Brosius, Nancy B.:
  A little learning, 123.
Brough, R. B.:
  The overland journey to Constantinople, 62.
Brough, R. W., and W. Brough:
  The last edition of Ivanhoe, 43.
Brougham, John:
  Columbus el filibustero! 62.
  The great tragic revival, 62.
  The lottery of life, 62.
  Much ado about a merchant of Venice, 62.
Broughton, James:
  The Jew of Malta, 36.
Brown, Albert M.:
  Sunday morning, 123.
Brown, Arthur M.:
  A dramatist in search of a love scene, 123.
Brown, F. G.:
  Mister Noah, 123.
Brown, Muriel:
  Ivanhoe, 43.
Brown, W. M.:
  Reunion on Grand Street, 123.
Brownson, Mary W., and V. E. Kerst:
  Victory through conflict, 123.
Bruckner, Ferdinand, pseud. See Tagger, Theodor.
Brugger, Florence:
  What makes an American? 123.
Buchanan, R. W., and F. Horner:
  The struggle for life, 67.
Buchheim, K. A.:
  Introduction [to Nathan the Wise], 29.
Buck, E. E.:
  Amateur night, 123.
Buckingham, L. S.:
  Belphegor, 63.
Buckstone, J. B.:
  Jack Shepherd, 53.
  Luke the labourer, 10.
  The stone jug, 53.
Buechner, Georg:
  Wozzeck, 63.
Buland, Mable:
  [Its time element,] 20.
  [Time element in the Jew of Malta,] 36.
Bulwer-Lytton, E. G. E. Lytton, 1st baron Lytton:
  Leila, 63.
Bump, C. R.:
  Cumberland's drama of "The Jew," 15.
Bung-your-eye, Solomon, pseud.:
  The informers outwitted, 10.
Bunn, Alfred:
  Ivanhoe, 43.
Burgess, Amy V.:
  An analysis of the female characters of Grillparzer's dramas, 79.
Burnand, F. C.:
  "Airey" Annie, 101.
  Paul Zegers, 74.
Burnet, Dana, and George Abbott:
  Four walls, 123.
Burrill, Bertha Y.:
  Rich man, poor man, 124.
Burroughs, Watkins:
  The Jewess, 46.
Burrows, Herbert:
  Zangwill's play, 115.
Burstein, Abraham:
  The escape from Cordova, 124.
Burstein, Abraham, and J. Bacher:
  Haman of today, 124.
Burt, O., joint author. See Simons, Evelyn, and O. Burt.
Burton, H. B.:
  The battle of the lords, 63.
Bush, Thomas:
  Santiago, 63.
Butler, A. G.:
  Harold, 63.
Butler, R. W., and H. C. Newton:
  Monte Christo, Jr., 71.
Buttimer, Edna, and A. Radke:
  A fair exchange, 124.
Byers, A. F.:
  Abie eats, 124.
Byron, H. J.:
  Ivanhoe, 43.
  The maid and the magpie, 33.

C

C., J.:
  A note on Cervantes and Beaumont and Fletcher, 19.
Cain, J. M.:
  The postman always rings twice, 124.
Caine, Sir Hall:
  The Christian, 63.
  The Jew in literature, 2.
Caldwell, J. M.:
  The fraternal bond, 124.
Calisch, E. N.:
  "The house next door," 91.
  The Jew in English literature, 2.
  A list of non-Jewish authors who have written on or about the Jews, 1.
Calisch, Edith (L.):
  The Jews who stood by Washington, 124.
Calkins, Raymond:
  "Nathan der Weise"; poem or play? 29.
Callahan, C. E.:
  Oliver Twist, 68.
Calmus, P. H.:
  The Jew of Zemplin, 64.
Campbell, A. L. V.:
  The forest oracle, 10.
Campbell, B. T.:
  "Siberia," 64.
Carb, David:
  The racial theatre, 3.
  The voice of the people, 64.
Carb, David, and W. P. Eaton:
  Queen Victoria, 124.
Cardot, Louis:
  The bells, 74.
Cardozo, J. L.:
  A Christian turn'd Turk (1612), 16.
  The contemporary Jew in the Elizabethan drama, 3.
Carlos, pseud.:
  Observations and strictures on the characters of Shylock and Sheva, 15.
Carnarvon, H. J. G. Herbert, 3d earl of:
  Don Pedro, king of Castile, 10.
Caro, Josef:
  Bernard Shaw, 3.
Carpenter, E. C.:
  The tongues of men, 64.
  See also Gross, Laurence, and E. C. Carpenter.
Carr, Alexander, and B. Bernard:
  The humor of the Jewish characters, 78.
Carr, J. W. C.:
  Oliver Twist, 68.

INDEX OF AUTHORS

Carroll, Armand:
　A pageant and masque for the Shakespeare Tercentenary, 124.
Carroll, Earl:
　Business is business, 124.
Carruth, W. H.:
　Lessing's treatment of the story of the ring and its teaching, 29.
Carter, L. H., joint author. See Gall, Ellen M., and L. H. Carter.
Carter, O. M., joint author. See Glass, M. M., and O. M. Carter.
Casey, Arten:
　"Com'ny 'tention!" 124.
Caspary, V., joint author. See Ornitz, S. B., and V. Caspary.
Casper, Jay:
　Salesmanship, 124.
Cassel, Carola:
　The choice, 124.
Casslev, J., joint author. See Zeckhauser, Iola, and J. Casslev.
Cattell, W. F.:
　A receipt for 10,000 dollars, 64.
Cecil, Mary:
　The "ladies from Friday" in a Turkish bath, 124.
　"Whatcha come to Paris for anyway?" 124.
Chance, W. A.:
　Winkle versus Fitz-Ailwyn, 124.
Chang, Y. Z.:
　The Jew in the drama of the English renaissance, 3.
Chaplin, Mrs. Alice L. (W.):
　School days, 124.
Chapman, W., joint author. See Hay, Frederick, and W. Chapman.
Charlemagne, Armand:
　The uncle's will, who wins? 10.
Charm, Anna B.:
　Business is business, 124.
Chase, F. E.:
　The great umbrella case, 64.
　In the trenches, 64.
　A ready-made suit, 64.
Chatrian, Alexandre, joint author. See Erckmann, Émile, and Alexandre Chatrian.
Chekhov, A. P.:
　Ivanoff, 65.
　That worthless fellow Platanov, 125.
Cheltnam, C. S.:
　Deborah, 94.
　The ticket-of-leave man's wife, 65.
Cherbuliez, Victor:
　Samuel Brohl and Company, 65.
Chester, G. R.:
　Isidor Iskovitch presents, 125.
Chesterton, Ada E. (J.), and Ralph Neale:
　The man who was Thursday, 125.
Chiarini, Giuseppe:
　Il giudeo nell' antico teatro inglese, 36.
Chirikov, Y. N.:
　The chosen people, 65.
　The Jews, 65.
Chlumberg, Hans:
　Miracle at Verdun, 125.
Chodorov, Edward:
　Kind lady, 125.
Cibber, Theophilus:
　The harlot's progress, 21.
Citron, S. J.:
　The luminary, 125.
　Ost-Yude, 125.
Clancy, J. P.:
　Christmas in the tenements, 125.
Clark, A. M.:
　The Jew of Malta, 36.
Clark, B. H.:
　The Yiddish drama, 1.

Clark, W. M.:
　A queer fit, 65.
Clarke, H. A., and M. Nurnberg:
　Chalk dust, 125.
Clements, Florence (R.), and C. C. Clements:
　The loop, an experiment in light and shadows, 125.
Clempert, John:
　Jedorka, 46.
Clews, Henry, jr.:
　Mumbo jumbo, 125.
Coakley, T. F.:
　The discovery of America, 126.
Cobb, Elizabeth, and Margaret C. Morgan:
　The murder of the night-club crooner, 126.
Cobb, James:
　A house to be sold, 11.
Coghlan, J. J.:
　Oh, teacher! 126.
　A wedding, 126.
Cohen, A.:
　Some precursors of Anglo-Jewish emancipation, 52.
Cohen, Irving:
　Music for musicians, 126.
Cohen, Isidor:
　Jewish provincialism in a growing community, 126.
Cohen, M. J.:
　"The Dybbuk" — its social message, 173.
Cohen, Rachel:
　Emma Lazarus, 88.
Cohen, Rose:
　Nathan the Wise, 29.
Cohn, E. B.:
　Das reissende Lamm, 126.
Cohon, S. S.:
　Every-mother, 126.
Cole, J. W.:
　Ivanhoe, 43.
Coleby, W. T.:
　"Dizzy," 126.
Coleman, E. D.:
　The Bible in English drama, 1.
　Plays of Jewish interest on the American stage, 1752–1821, 3.
Collier, J. P.:
　Jews in our early plays, 51.
Collingham, George:
　Oliver Twist, 69.
Collins, C. W.:
　The drama of the Jew, 3.
Colman, George, 1732–1794:
　Man and wife, 11.
　Prologue [and] epilogue [to O'Keeffe's The Young Quaker], 41.
Colman, George, 1762–1836:
　Love laughs at locksmiths, 9.
Colum, Padraic:
　Balloon, 126.
Connelly, M. C., joint author. See Kaufman, G. S., and M. C. Connelly.
Conquest, G. A.:
　Deborah, 94.
Conway, Olive, pseud. of Harold Brighouse and J. Walton:
　Dux, 126.
Cook, S. L.:
　Looking back at the "School for scandal," 49.
Cooke, J. F.:
　Scenes from the life of Richard Wagner, 126.
Cooper, Edith E. See Field, Michael, pseud. of Katherine H. Bradley and Edith E. Cooper.
Cooper, F. F.:
　Hercules, king of clubs! 11.
　Ivanhoe, 43.
Coralnik, Abraham:
　Fairy-tale to myth, 173.
　Red snow, 65.

Corbin, John:
   Drama and the Jew, 3.
   Husband, 66.
   The Jew as a dramatic problem, 3.
   The new plays, 3.
Corelli, Marie:
   "Temporal power," 66.
Cormack, Bartlett:
   The racket, 126.
Cornfield, Maurice:
   Palestine versus Diaspora, 126.
Cosulich, Gilbert:
   Three Jewish fathers, 3.
Cournos, John:
   Shylock's choice, 126.
   Sport of gods, 127.
Courtney, John:
   Leah and Nathan, 94.
   The soldier's progress, 66.
Courtney, W. L.:
   [Imitations of passages from Marlowe's play in Shakespeare's Merchant of Venice,] 36.
Coward, N. P.:
   Design for living, 127.
Cowen, Sada:
   Auf wiedersehen, 127.
Cowie, R.:
   Ivanhoe, 43.
Cowley, Mrs. Hannah (P.):
   The belle's stratagem, 11–13.
Coyne, J. S.:
   Oliver Twist, 69.
   This house to be sold, 66.
   The woman in red, 105.
Crabos, P. G.:
   Le Juif dans le théâtre de M. Bernstein, 59, 60.
   Le sémitisme au théâtre, 3.
Cranmer-Byng, L. A.:
   Salma, 127.
Craven, H. T.:
   Philomel, 66.
Crawford, Alice:
   Rebecca and Rowena, 43.
Crawford, Bob:
   On vit de dance, 127.
Creasman, Mrs. Myrtle R.:
   How home missions came home to Helen, 127.
Crocker, Bosworth, pseud.:
   The baby carriage, 127.
   Coquine, 127.
Croker, T. F. D.:
   The stage Israelite, 3.
Cross, J. C.:
   The false friend, 13.
Crothers, Rachel:
   The importance of being married, 127.
   A little journey, 127.
Crowne, John:
   Caligula, 13.
Cullinan, Ralph, joint author. See Hepenstall, W. D., and Ralph Cullinan.
Cumberland, Richard:
   The fashionable lover, 13.
   The generous Jew, 15.
   The Jew, 14.
   The Jew of Mogadore, 16.
   Der Jud Menachem, 15.
   Der Jude, 15.
   The note of hand, 16.
   Zid, 15.
   איש יהודי. עברית יוסף בריליל, 15.
   Один изъ нашихъ или рѣдкій еврей, 15.
Cumberland, S. C.:
   The rabbi's spell, 66.

Cunningham, Mary:
   Doggone! 127.
Curtis, G. F.:
   The love life of Irene, 127.
   Tea at Mrs. Sinsheimer's, 127.

D

D., B. C.:
   The saving sign, 127.
D., O.:
   [A passage in act III, scene 1, of Massinger's Duke of Milan,] 38.
D., W.:
   Marlow's Jew of Malta, 36.
Daborne, Robert:
   A Christian turn'd Turke, 16.
Dainow, David:
   Holding aloof, 127.
Daixel, Samuel:
   After midnight, 128.
Dalrymple, C. Leona:
   A white shawl, 66.
Daly, Augustin:
   The last word, 66.
   Leah the forsaken, 94.
   New Leah, 95.
Damrosch, Gretchen:
   The passing present, 128.
Daniel, P. A.:
   Locrine and Selimus, 20.
Dannenbaum, Raymond:
   Samuel Ibn-Nagdela, 128.
   "Thunder on the left," 128.
Daseking, Edith:
   Schoolin', 128.
Daudet, Alphonse:
   The battle of love, 66.
   La lutte pour la vie, 66.
Davage, George:
   The man tamer, 128.
Davenport, S. R.:
   I am a Jew, 128.
Daventry, G.:
   Under two flags, 67.
Davidson, Israel:
   Shylock and Barabas, 36.
   היהודי בספרות האנגלית, 36.
Davidson, J. E.:
   Stamps and their Jewish interest, 128.
Davis, Allan:
   Gloomy Fanny, 67.
   The iron door, 67.
   The promised land, 67.
   Victims, 128.
   Wolves, 128.
Davis, Donald, joint author. See Ornitz, S. B., and Donald Davis.
Davis, Edward:
   The iron cross, 128.
Davis, John:
   Lincoln and his Jewish chiropodist, 128.
Davis, Owen:
   The detour, 128.
   The great Gatsby, 133.
   Jack Sheppard, 54.
Davis, P. P.:
   An amateur triumph, 67.
Davis, R. H.:
   Peace manoeuvres, 67.
Davis, W. W.:
   Lessing's unfairness in "Nathan the Wise," 29.
Dawn, Isabel, and B. De Graw:
   "Marathon," 128.
Day, John:
   The Travailes of the three English brothers, 16.
Dean, Basil, joint author. See Kennedy, Margaret, and Basil Dean.

INDEX OF AUTHORS 199

Dearmer, Geoffrey:
  The man with a cane, 129.
Decker, H. T.:
  The jack in the box, 129.
Deddens, Maxine:
  The court decides for safety, 129.
Deering, R. W.:
  Lessing's Nathan the Wise, 29.
De Graw, B., joint author. See Dawn, Isabel, and B. De Graw.
De Haas, Arline:
  The jazz singer, 172.
Deighton, Kenneth:
  [Conjectural readings of Webster's The Devil's law-case,] 52.
Deitch, Joseph:
  Hurrah for Cheshvan, 129.
  Welcome home, 129.
Dejob, Charles:
  Le Juif dans le comédie au XVIIIe siècle, 3.
De Kruif, P. H., joint author. See Howard, S. C., and P. H. De Kruif.
De la Ramée, Louise:
  Under two flags, 67.
Delavigne, J. F. C.:
  The monastery of St. Just, 16.
Dembo, L. H.:
  The first baby, 129.
  Mrs. Feitlebaum and ward C, 129.
De Mille, H. C., and David Belasco:
  "Men and women," 67.
Denison, T. S.:
  A dude in a cyclone, 68.
De Noie, Vera, and A. D. Hall:
  The Dreyfus affair, 68.
Deutsch, Gotthard:
  Israel Bruna, 68.
  Zangwills Ghettokinder auf der Bühne, 114.
De Vere, Aubrey:
  Alexander the Great, 68.
Dexter, Walter, and F. T. Harry:
  Oliver Twist, 69.
Dibdin, T. J.:
  Family quarrels, 17.
  Ferdinand, Count Fathom. See Smollett, T. G., The adventures of Ferdinand, Count Fathom, 50.
  Humphrey Clinker, 17.
  Ivanhoe, 43.
  The Jew and the doctor, 17.
  The school for prejudice, 17.
Dickens, Charles:
  Oliver Twist, 68.
Dickerson, Penelope:
  The cross word puzzle, 129.
Dickman, Adolph:
  The baron of Budapest, 129.
  Rosenbaum and son, 129.
Dieckhoff, T. J. C.:
  Introduction [to Nathan the Wise], 29.
Dietrich, J. H.:
  "The melting pot," 115.
Dingman, Mrs. W. B.:
  Our own beloved America, 70.
Dixon, Thomas:
  A man of the people, 129.
Dobsevage, I. G.:
  Drama, 1.
Dodds, Madeleine H.:
  'Lovers' vows,' 26.
Dodsley, Robert:
  Rex et pontifex, 18.
Donaldson, Almira K., joint author. See Ermatinger, Gertrude L., and Almira K. Donaldson.
Donchian, Peter:
  I object, your honor! 129.
Donnay, M. C.:
  Le retour de Jérusalem, 70.

Donnez moi, pseud.:
  The search, 129.
Doran, Marie:
  The education of Doris, 129.
  The gay co-eds, 129.
Dorée, Nadage:
  Gilta, 71.
Doroshevich, V. M.:
  A dream of a Russian subject, 71.
Dos Passos, John:
  Airways, Inc., 129.
  Fortune heights, 129.
Doughty, G. H.:
  Oliver Twist, 69.
Douglas, Norman:
  South wind, 130.
Douglas, Norman, and Isabel C. Tippett:
  "South wind," 130.
Downing, H. F.:
  The shuttlecock, 71.
Drama League of America:
  Shakespeare festival in honor of the poet's birthday, 71.
Drapkin, Charles:
  The dictator, 130.
Dreiser, Theodore:
  The hand of the potter, 130.
Drexler, Anna, joint author. See Kottler, Esther, and Anna Drexler.
Dreyfus, Abraham:
  Le Juif au théâtre, 3.
Drovin, G. A.:
  In Hades, 71.
Drury Lane Theatre, London:
  Programme and news sheet of London life, 120.
Dryden, John:
  Love triumphant, 18.
Duker, Samuel:
  Concessions! concessions! 130.
Dukes, Ashley:
  Jew Süss, 133.
Dumas, Alexandre, the elder:
  Monte-Cristo, 71.
Du Maurier, G. L. P. B.:
  Trilby, 71.
Dumont, Frank:
  The depot lunch counter, 72.
  The district convention, 72.
  The girl from "L Triangle" ranch, 72.
  A gunner in the navy, 72.
  Mock trial of the great kidnapping and breach of promise case, 72.
  The night riders, 72, 130.
  The old New Hampshire home, 72.
  Sky-lark, 72.
  With the Stars and Stripes in France, 130.
Dunbar, Alice R. (M.):
  Mine eyes have seen, 130.
Dunning, P. H.:
  Night hostess, 130.
Dunstan, A. C.:
  E. C.'s drama and "The Duke of Milan," 38.
Durlacher, A. J.:
  A tale of Biscay Bay, 130.
Durning-Lawrence, Sir Edwin:
  The Jew in drama, 3.

E

Eaton, W. P.:
  Drama: a bond of fellowship, 3.
  Grandfather's chair, 130.
  "Israel" and the happy ending, 60.
  See also Carb, David, and W. P. Eaton.
Eber, M. A.:
  Messiah, 130.
Eckhardt, Eduard:
  Die Juden: äussere Merkmale, 3.

Eckhouse, L. R.:
　Council's every girl, 130.
　"Dust," 130.
Edelman, Maurice:
　A study in loyalties, 135.
Edgar, R. H.:
　Ivanhoe, 43.
Efros, I. I.:
　The bloody jest, 130.
Eggleston, L., joint author. *See* Maxfield, Mina, and L. Eggleston.
Ehrke, Karl:
　Selimus, 20.
Ehrlich, Ida L.:
　The still small voice, 130.
Einstein, Irving:
　What's in a name? 131.
Eisenbett, I. G.:
　"Евреи" въ драмѣ г. Чирикова, 65.
Elder, Eleanor:
　Official announcement, 131.
Eldridge, Florence M.:
　The growth of a nation, 131.
Eldridge, Paul:
　His peers, 131.
Eliot, George, pseud.:
　Daniel Deronda, 72.
　The Spanish gypsy, 73.
Ellis, A. E., joint author. *See* Shillingford, Osmond, and A. E. Ellis.
Ellis, Ellsworth, and Everett Ellis:
　The sacrifice, 131.
Ellis, S. M.:
　Jack Sheppard: the youth; the book and the play, 55.
　Jack Sheppard in literature and drama, 55.
Ellison, James:
　The American captive, 18.
Elsner, E.:
　Under two flags, 67.
Elstein, Noah:
　Israel in the kitchen, 131.
Emerson, Edwin:
　Benedict Arnold, 131.
Emerson, John, and Anita Loos:
　The whole town's talking, 131.
Emery, S.:
　The Polish Jew, 74.
Enelow, H. G.:
　"The Jew of Malta," 36.
Epstein, Mrs. M. P.:
　A quiet morning in the life of any Hadassah chapter president, 131.
Epstein, Mordecai:
　Reflections on a play, 125.
Erckmann, Émile, and Alexandre Chatrian:
　The bells, 73.
　Friend Fritz, 73.
　Le juif polonais, 73.
　The Polish Jew, 73.
Ermatinger, Gertrude L., and Almira K. Donaldson:
　The spirit of the American constitution, 131.
Ervine, St. John G.:
　The lady of Belmont, 131.
Esmond, H. V.:
　Birds of a feather. *See* Jacob, Naomi E. Jacob Ussher, 146.
　When we were twenty-one, 74.
Estabrook, H. D.:
　The joust, 43.
Étienne, Louis:
　Un retour du réalisme à la poésie, 73.
Ettelson, H. W.:
　An unconscious anti-Semite. Jewish phases of Galsworthy's "Loyalties," 135.
Eureka High School, Eureka, Cal. — History Class:
　Pageant of ancient civilization, 132.

F

Fagan, J. B.:
　Bella donna, 83.
Fagin, M.:
　Room 226, 132.
Falconer, Edmund, pseud. of Edmund O'Rourke:
　Chrystabelle, 74.
Fallenberg, Esther:
　Rip Van Winkle, 132.
Farquhar, Robert:
　Portia pulls a pinch play, 132.
Farquhar, Ross:
　Nothing ever happens, 132.
Fauchois, R. C. A.:
　Prenez garde à la peinture, 132.
Fehler, Kurt:
　The Jew, 15.
Fehr, Bernhard:
　Das gelbe Buch in Oscar Wildes Dorian Gray, 112.
Feinberg, Adolph, and D. Polish:
　Yehuda, 156.
Feinstein, Jacob:
　His eyes, 132.
Feldman, A. J.:
　Jews by grace of the enemy, 136.
Felton, Mrs. Carl:
　Goose money, 132.
Fenwick, John:
　The Indian, 18.
Feraru, Leon:
　Henri Bernstein and "Israel," 60.
Ferber, Edna:
　The eldest, 132.
　Roast beef medium served hot, 75.
　See also Hobart, G. V., and Edna Ferber; Kaufman, G. S., and Edna Ferber.
Ferber, Edna, and G. S. Kaufman:
　Stage door, 132.
Ferber, Edna, and N. Levy:
　$1200 a year, 132.
Fernow, Hans:
　The three lords and three ladies of London, 51.
Feuchtwanger, Lion:
　Jud Süss, 132.
　1918, 133.
　The ugly duchess, 133.
Field, Anna W., joint author. *See* Wilson, Ella M., and Anna W. Field.
Field, Michael, pseud. of Katherine H. Bradley and Edith E. Cooper:
　A messiah, 75.
Field, Rachel L.:
　The fifteenth candle, 133.
Fielding, Henry:
　Miss Lucy in town, 18.
Findlay, Maud I.:
　Scott's Ivanhoe dramatised for school use, 43.
Fink, M. R.:
　The dramas of Jacob Gordin, 3.
Fischer, Rudolf:
　[Marlowe's Jew of Malta,] 36.
Fischer, Walter:
　The "poisonous book" in Oskar Wildes Dorian Gray, 112.
Fisher, Mrs. Blanche (S.):
　An evening in Palestine, 133.
　Women in Israel, 133.
Fitch, Clyde:
　Beau Brummel, 75.
　The woman in the case, 75.
　See also Wharton, Mrs. Edith N. (J.), and Clyde Fitch.
Fitzball, Edward:
　Azael, the prodigal, 75.
　Ninetta, 33.
Fitzgerald, F. S. K.:
　The great Gatsby, 133.

INDEX OF AUTHORS

Fitz-Gerald, S. J. A.:
"Oliver Twist," 70.
Fitz-Hugh, Alexander:
The Jew of Malta and the Jew of Venice, 36.
Fitzsimons, Simon:
"The Christian" and the critics, 64.
Flattery, M. D.:
The conspirators, 75.
The subterfuge, 133.
Flavin, M. A.:
Amaco, 133.
The criminal code, 133.
Lady of the rose, 134.
Flecker, J. E.:
The golden journey to Samarkand, 75.
Hassan, 134.
Fleg, Edmond:
Le marchand de Paris, 134.
Fletcher, Beaumont:
Trilby as a play, 72.
Fletcher, John, and Philip Massinger:
The custom of the country, 18.
Flint, Eva K., and M. Madison:
Subway express, 134.
Foote, Samuel:
The cozeners, 19.
The devil upon two sticks, 19.
The nabob, 19.
Forbes, James:
The show shop, 75.
Ford, A. H.:
Oliver Twist, 69.
Forman, H. B.:
Thomas Wade: the poet and his surroundings, 52.
Forster, Joseph:
Lessing, 29.
Fort, G., joint author. See Beahan, Charles, and G. Fort.
Foster, Gladys:
Want, 134.
Foster, J. C.:
Harlequin Jack Sheppard, 54.
Fowler, Gene, joint author. See Hecht, Ben, and Gene Fowler.
Fox, A. W.:
Tragedy as it was written, 20.
Fox, Lillian:
Abraham Lincoln and the Jewish soldier, 134.
Fraenkel, J.:
Esther Guiladi, 76.
Frank, Ethel:
Gossip, 76.
Frank, Florence (K.):
The faith of their fathers, 134.
The Jew as Jewish artist, 3.
Frank, Maude M.:
When Heine was twenty-one, 134.
Frankau, Mrs. Julia (D.):
The heart of a child, 76.
Franken, Mrs. Rose:
Another language, 134.
Franklin, Andrew:
The wandering Jew, 19.
Franklin, Pearl, joint author. See Ballard, Frederick, and Pearl Franklin.
Fraser, F. J.:
A burlesque extravaganza entitled "The merry Merchant of Venice," 76.
Frazer, Helen:
A glimpse of the seventeenth century Jew in the drama, 36.
Frederick, J. T.:
Twelfth night at Fisher's Crossing, 134.
Freed, C. I.:
Ernst Toller — spirit of revolt, 184.
The heart of Solomon, 134.
A knock at the door, 82.

Freedman, David:
Mendel Marantz, 134.
Freytag, Gustav:
Die Journalisten, 76.
The journalists, 76.
Friedlander, Gerald:
A Jew in post-Shakespearian drama, 29.
A Jew in pre-Shakespearian drama, 51.
Friedman, Mrs. H. A.:
"The Jewish woman in America," 135.
Friedman, Helen M.:
Yiddish drama, 1.
Friedman, S. S.:
"The great god Frosh," 135.
Friedmann, Armand, joint author. See Nertz, Louis, and Armand Friedmann.
Friel, Thornton:
The case against Casey, 76.
Frischmann, David:
"For Messiah, King," 76.

G

Gabriel, G. W.:
Are we like that? 3.
The Jew in falseface, 3.
Gaer, Yossef:
A song unto the Lord, 135.
Gaffney, T. J.:
Birds of a feather, 135.
Gall, Ellen M., and L. H. Carter:
[Jewish make-up for the stage,] 4.
Gallatin, Alberta:
A dramatization of Sir Walter Scott's novel "Ivanhoe," 44.
Galsworthy, John:
Gesellschaft (Loyalties), 135.
Loyalität, 135.
Loyalties, 135.
Loyautés, 135.
לאיאליטעט. יודיש ב. שטיפט. 135
Gamble, E. L.:
The lady or the tiger, 136.
Oi, vhat a bargain, 136.
Oi, vot a business! 136.
Gamoran, Mamie G.:
Another day, 136.
Pennies do add up, 136.
What price Hadassah? 136.
Gard, Janice:
Lookin' lovely, 136.
Gardner, Flora C., and M. F. Gardner:
Abraham advertises, 136.
The melting pot minstrel, 136.
Gargiles, Lady:
Petit essai sur le "Portrait de Dorian Gray" d'Oscar Wilde, 113.
Garrick, David:
Garrick's vagary, 20.
The jubilee, 20.
Garvey, Robert:
Heroes, old and new, 136.
Gauger, Rudolf:
Man and superman, 107.
Geller, J. J.:
Leah the forsaken, 95.
Siberia, 64.
The ticket of leave man, 109.
"Trilby," 72.
George, Charles:
"Abie's license," 136.
Just pals, 136.
Murder in the ferris-wheel, 136.
The spite fence, 136.
Geraghty, T. J.:
A pound of flesh, 136.
Gérard, P., joint author. See Bisson, A. C. A., and P. Gérard.

Gerhardt, Erich:
　Massinger's "The duke of Milan" und seine Quellen, 38.
Gerson, Emily G.:
　The seder, 136.
Gersoni:
　A dignified and honorable interview, 76.
Gessner, J. W.:
　"Paradise lost" and the theatre of frustration, 168.
Gherardi del Testa, Tommasso, conte:
　La gazza ladra, 33.
Gibbs, Alice Z.:
　Run queeck, Rosie, 136.
　Sarah's birthday gift, 136.
　Von leetle minute, 136.
Gibson, E. M.:
　Hot water, 136.
Gielgud, L. E., joint author. See Mitchison, Naomi (H.), and L. E. Gielgud.
Gilbert, Hugo:
　Robert Greene's Selimus, 20.
Gilbert, Sir W. S.:
　Creatures of impulse, 76.
　An old score, 76.
Ginsburg, Elias:
　Ferdinand Lassalle, 136.
　We never die, 136.
Ginzburg, Simon:
　Dramas and lyrical poems [of Luzzatto], 31.
Glascock, W. N.:
　Land sharks and sea gulls, 77.
Glass, Montague M.:
　Object: matrimony, 77.
　Potash and Perlmutter, 77.
　Present company excepted, 137.
Glass, M. M., and O. M. Carter:
　Wall Street, 137.
Glass, M. M., and J. E. Goodman:
　Business before pleasure, 77.
　His Honor Abe Potash, 77.
　Partners again, 77.
　Potash and Perlmutter, detectives, 77.
Glass, M. M., and R. C. Megrue:
　Abe and Mawruss, 78.
　Potash and Perlmutter in society, 78.
Glassman, L. M.:
　The apocalypse of the ghetto, 173.
Glazer, B. F.:
　She loves me not, 158.
Gleason, James:
　The Shannons of Broadway, 137.
　See also Abbott, George, and James Gleason.
Glickman, A. J.:
　The truth, 137.
Glover, Halcott:
　The king's Jewry, 137.
Goetz, Austin:
　Hillbilly courtship, 137.
　Soup to nuts, 137.
Goffe, Thomas:
　The raging Turke, 20.
Goitein, E. D.:
　The stage Jew of the XVI century, 4, 51.
Gold, Michael:
　Gold, 137.
　See also Blankfort, Michael, and M. Gold.
Goldberg, Isaac:
　The better son, 137.
　David Pinski, 1.
　The dramatic art of David Pinski, 4.
　Perez Hirschbein, 1.
　The Yiddish theatre, 4.
Goldberg, Isaac, editor and translator:
　Six plays of the Yiddish theatre, 7.
　Six plays of the Yiddish theatre: second series, 7.

Goldberg, Israel:
　The ancient fortress, 137.
　Bar Giora, 137.
　Brothers, 137.
　"The capture," 137.
　The eternal bond, 137.
　The great deliverance, 137.
　His children, 138.
　The invader, 138.
　הישועה הגדולה, 137.
Goldberg, Sarah:
　David Pinski: dramatist of depth and vision, 4.
Golden, John, joint author. See Baum, Vicki, and John Golden.
Golding, Louis:
　Magnolia street, 138.
Goldman, Mrs. Rose:
　Life begins anew, 138.
Goldsmith, Milton:
　A prior right, 138.
Goldstein, Fanny:
　Drama, 1.
　Shabbas cheer, 138.
Goldstein, Mrs. Rose B.:
　Aunt Fan rises to the defense, 138.
Goller, Isak:
　"Cohen & Son," 138.
Goodman, Mrs. A. V.:
　All for the good, 138.
Goodman, Henry:
　Perez the playwright, 4.
Goodman, J. E., joint author. See Glass, M. M., and J. E. Goodman.
Goodman, K. S., and Ben Hecht:
　An idyll of the shops, 138.
Gordin, Jacob:
　Captain Dreyfus, 78.
　Gott, Mensch und der Teufel, 78.
　The Jewish King Lear, 78.
　The Kreutzer sonata, 78.
　A new prologue in heaven, 78.
Gordon, A. I.:
　"This month in history," 138.
Gordon, Leon, and R. A. Palmer:
　The piker, 138.
Gordon, Samuel:
　Daughters of Shem, 79.
　The resting place, 138.
Gorsky, J. A.:
　Kislev, 138.
Goudvis, Berthe:
　A husband for Rachel, 138.
Gould, Alice:
　The merchant of Venice, 138.
Gould, E. M.:
　On the sight-seeing car, 79, 138.
Gourvitch, I.:
　Robert Wilson: "The elder" and "the younger," 51.
Grack, Walter:
　Studien über die dramatische Behandlung der Geschichte von Herodes und Mariamne, 38.
Graham, Carroll, and Garrett Graham:
　Queer people, 139.
Granville-Barker, H. G.:
　The secret life, 139.
Green, Paul:
　Johnny Johnson, 139.
Greene, B. M.:
　The God-intoxicated man, 139.
Greene, Robert:
　Selimus, 20.
Greenwood, Thomas:
　"Boz's" Oliver Twist, 69.
　Jack Sheppard, 53.
Greg, W. W.:
　Massinger's autograph corrections in 'The Duke of Milan', 38.

INDEX OF AUTHORS

Greville, Lady Violet:
  An aristocratic alliance, 57.
Gribble, G. D.:
  The masque of Venice, 139.
  The translation of Nathaniel Bendersnap, 139.
Griffin, C. A.:
  The Hicksville bungler, 139.
Griffith, H. F.:
  Red Sunday, 139.
Grillparzer, Franz:
  The Jewess of Toledo, 79.
Gropper, M. H., and Max Siegel:
  We Americans, 139.
Gross, L. D.:
  "The jazz singer," 172.
Gross, Laurence, and E. C. Carpenter:
  Whistling in the dark, 139.
Grossman, Rudolph:
  Shylock and Nathan the Wise, 29.
Grossman, S. S.:
  The Beduin fight, 140.
  "The jewels of God," 79.
  The land of the Aleph Bes, 140.
  The masque of the new land, 140.
  Tree pantomime, 140.
  The trusted jewels, 79.
  The two angels, 140.
  Two goyim, 140.
  "What to be proud of," 140.
Grosswald, Bernard:
  Wings on their backs, 140.
Gruener, Gustav:
  The genesis of the characters in Lessing's 'Nathan der Weise,' 29.
Grundy, Sydney:
  "A bunch of violets," 79.
  Business is business, 92.
  An old Jew, 79.
  A son of Israel, 79.
Grusd, E. E.:
  Lessing; friend of the Jews, 30.
Gubalke, vicar:
  Must Lessing's 'Nathan' be a Jew? 30.
Guest, Carmel H. (G.):
  'The proselyte,' 80.
Gunn, J. A.:
  Spinoza: the maker of lenses, 140.
Gunn, W. E.:
  Scott of Abbotsford, 140.
Gunnison, Binney:
  The baron and the Jew, 44.
  The suffering of Nehushta, 80.
Guttman, Ethel F.:
  Bridge at Upper Montclair, 140.
Gutzkow, K. F.:
  Uriel Acosta, 80.

H

Hadassah. — Columbus, Ohio, Chapter:
  Jigsaw skit for senior-junior meeting, 140.
Hadassah. — Minneapolis Junior Section:
  Money talks, 140.
Hageman, Maurice:
  Hector, 80.
Haines, J. T.:
  Elizabeth Lazarus. See Glascock, W. N. Land sharks and sea gulls, 77.
  Jack Sheppard, 54.
  The life of a woman, 21.
  Ruth, 80.
Hall, A. D., joint author. See De Noie, Vera, and A. D. Hall.
Hall, P. P.:
  More money than brains, 140.
Halliday, Andrew:
  The great city, 80.
  Rebecca, 44.

Halper, Leivick:
  The golem, 140.
Halpern, Jonathan:
  Mother and son, 80.
Halys, Nevin:
  Mrs. Witch: a Whitechapel episode, 140.
Hamilton, Cosmo:
  Caste, 140.
Hanani, Yosef:
  Fighting boy of Vienna, 140.
Hancock, C. W.:
  Down on the farm, 80.
Handasyde, Elizabeth:
  'The Jew of Venice,' 27.
Hannan, Charles:
  A cigarette maker's romance, 80.
Harbour, J. L.:
  The rummage sale, 140.
Harding, T. W.:
  Nina Balatka, 81.
Hardy, Bernice:
  Miss Ruddy cashes in, 141.
  Monday morning on "Thoid" avenue, 141.
Hare, W. B.:
  Aboard a slow train in Mizzoury, 141.
  Am I your vife? 141.
  The cornfed cut-ups, 141.
  A country boy scout, 141.
  Yiddisha love, 141.
Harper, Olive:
  Jack Sheppard, 54.
Harris, A. G.:
  The avalanche, 81.
Harris, Claudia L.:
  It's spring, 141.
  Paging John Smith, 141.
Harris, Frank:
  Isaac & Rebecca, 141.
Harris, George:
  Two bad boys, 81.
Harris, M. H.:
  The story of the Jew, 141.
  Zangwill's "Children of the ghetto," 114.
Harrison, Charles:
  [Jewish make-up for the stage,] 4.
Harrison, H. A.:
  A modern Esther, 141.
Harrison, Thomas:
  Belteshazzar, 21.
Harry, F. T., joint author. See Dexter, Walter, and F. T. Harry.
Hart, Moss, joint author. See Kaufman, G. S., and Moss Hart.
Hart, Moss, and G. S. Kaufman:
  Once in a lifetime, 141.
Hartmann, Hermann:
  Sheridan's School for scandal, 49.
Harwood, H. M.:
  These mortals, 141.
Hase, K. A. von:
  Hans Sachs and Lessing's "Nathan," 30.
Hastings, B. M.:
  Advertisement, 141.
Hastings, E. E.:
  Comparative study of The Jew of Malta and The Merchant of Venice, 36.
Hatton, Frederic, and Mrs. F. C. L. Hatton:
  Lombardi, Ltd., 142.
Hatton, Joseph:
  By order of the czar, 81.
  Jack Sheppard, 54.
Hauenstein, Conrad:
  David Cohn, der New Yorker Heiratsvermittler, 81.
  Samuel Wolf, 81.
Hauptmann, Gerhart:
  The conflagration, 81.
  Florian Geyer, 81.
  Gabriel Schilling's flight, 81.

Hauser, Mrs. Erminia (A.):
   The man without a necktie, 142.
Hawkins, Frederick:
   The first production of The bells, 74.
   Shylock and other stage Jews, 4.
Hawkridge, Winifred:
   The florist shop, 142.
   The price of orchids, 142.
Hay, Frederick, and W. Chapman:
   The deep red rover, 81.
Hayman, Philip, and E. Solomon:
   All my eye-vanhoe, 44.
Haymarket Theatre, London:
   Hypatia, by G. Stuart Ogilvie, 97.
Hayward, H. R., and A. Rish:
   The Jew's fiddle, 142.
Hazlewood, C. H.:
   The bells in the storm, 74.
   Capitola, 81.
   Never too late to mend, 102.
   The stolen Jewess, 81.
Hazlitt, William:
   The school for scandal, 49.
Hazzard, J. E., joint author. See Smith, Winchell, and J. E. Hazzard.
Heald, J. P.:
   Open house, 142.
Hearn, James, and Paul Rubens:
   A Trilby triflet, 71.
Hearn, Lafcadio:
   The Jew upon the stage, 4.
Hebbel, C. F.:
   Der Diamant, 82.
Hecht, Ben, joint author. See Goodman, K. S., and Ben Hecht.
Hecht, Ben, and Gene Fowler:
   The great magoo, 142.
Hecht, Ben, and C. G. MacArthur:
   The front page, 142.
Heermans, Forbes:
   Down the black cañon, 82.
Heijermans, Herman:
   Ahasverus, 82.
   The ghetto, 82.
   The wandering Jew, 82.
Heilperin, Falk:
   Parents, 82.
Heller, Nachman:
   A celestial conference, 142.
Hellstern, Sadie:
   Teachings of "Nathan the Wise," 30.
Helps, Sir Arthur:
   Oulita, the serf, 82.
Henry, Mrs. Re (H.):
   Past, present, and future, 82.
Hepenstall, W. D., and Ralph Cullinan:
   The call of the banshee, 142.
Herbach, Joseph:
   The rehearsal, 82.
Herbert, J. N.:
   Thrilby, 71.
Herford, C. H.:
   Lessing['s Nathan the Wise], 30.
Heron, Matilda:
   Gamea, 105.
Herzberg, Sigmund:
   Jewess of Spain. See Aguilar, Grace, The vale of cedars, 53.
Herzl, Theodor:
   Das neue Ghetto, 82.
Hevesh, Mary:
   The return, 142.
Hewson, J. J.:
   Under the canopy, 81.
Heydemann, Lillian P.:
   The American idea, 83.
Heymans, M. J.:
   Gilded youth, 143.

Hibbert, F. A.:
   England's greatness, 143.
Hichens, R. S.:
   Bella donna, 83.
   Business is business, 92.
   See also Barrett, Wilson, and R. S. Hichens.
Hickerson, Harold, joint author. See Anderson, Maxwell, and Harold Hickerson.
Hight, Mary:
   A Shakespearean fantasy, 143.
Hiland, F. E.:
   Who caught the count, 83.
Hill, Aaron:
   The walking statue, 21.
Hill, Roland:
   Christopher Columbus, 83.
Hillyer, Robert:
   The masquerade, 143.
Hind, Lewis:
   A souvenir of "Ivanhoe," 45.
Hipshon, I.:
   The miracle of Lodz, 143.
Hirschbein, Perez:
   Bebele, 143.
   Elijah the prophet, 83.
   Green fields, 143.
   The haunted inn, 83.
   In the dark, 83.
   Lone worlds! 83.
   On the threshold, 143.
   Raisin and almonds, 143.
   The snowstorm, 143.
   The stranger, 143.
   When the dew falleth, 143.
Hirschfeld, Georg:
   The mothers, 83.
His Majesty's Theatre, London:
   "Oliver Twist" portfolio, 69.
Hoare, J. E., joint author. See Balderston, J. L., and J. E. Hoare.
Hobart, D., joint author. See McKnight, Tom, and D. Hobart.
Hobart, G. V.:
   The fall and rise of Susan Lenox. See Phillips, D. G. Susan Lenox, her rise and fall, 170.
Hobart, G. V., and Edna Ferber:
   Our Mrs. McChesney, 75.
Hobbs, Bertram:
   Hot headlines, 143.
Hodges, Horace, and T. W. Percyval:
   Grumpy, 83.
Hoffe, Monckton:
   Cristilinda, 143.
Hoffman, A. S., joint author. See Newton, H. L., and A. S. Hoffman.
Hoffman, Aaron:
   The Cohens and Kellys, 144.
   Give and take, 143.
   Two blocks away, 143.
   Welcome stranger, 144.
Hoffman, Rebekah B.:
   Judah's new deliverer, 144.
Hoggan-Armadale, E.:
   Sleigh bells, 74.
Holberg, Ludvig, baron:
   Captain Bombastes Thunderton, 21.
   Ulysses von Ithacia, 21.
Holbrook, Marion:
   Angel aware, 144.
Holcroft, Thomas:
   Hear both sides, 22.
   The vindictive man, 22.
Holdsworth, Gladys B. (S.):
   The matriarch, 144.
Holford, Mrs. Margaret (W.):
   Neither's the man, 22.

Hollstein, Ernst:
  Verhältnis von Ben Jonson's "The Devil is an ass" und John Wilson's "Belphegor," 52.
Holmes, N. F.:
  The pride of Yosakis, 144.
Homer, Frances:
  A prince to order, 144.
Hook, T. E.:
  The invisible girl, 22.
Horne, R. H.:
  Laura Dibalzo, 84.
Horner, F., joint author. *See* Buchanan, R. W., and F. Horner.
Horniman, Roy:
  Idols, 89.
Horowitz, Isaac:
  The snow man, 144.
Horowitz, Nathan:
  Souls in exile, 144.
Housman, Laurence:
  Angels & ministers, 7.
  His favourite flower, 144.
  The Queen: God bless her! 144.
  Royal favour, 145.
  Victoria regina, 145.
Howard, Florence:
  On the banks of the river Styx, 145.
Howard, S. C.:
  Half gods, 145.
  The late Christopher Bean, 132.
  Paths of glory, 145.
  See also Lewis, Sinclair, and S. C. Howard.
Howard, S. C., and P. H. De Kruif:
  Yellow Jack, 145.
Howe, Julia (W.):
  The world's own, 84.
Hoyt, Ella M.:
  Hello Zentral! 145.
  Isaac, he ain't so dumb, 145.
Hubbard, Elbert:
  Ferdinand Lassalle & Helene von Donniges, 84.
Hudson, Holland:
  Action! 145.
Hughes, Rupert:
  Excuse me, 84.
Hugo, V. M., comte:
  Cromwell, 22.
  Mary Tudor, 22–23.
  Torquemada, 84.
Hunter, A. M., joint author. *See* Simon, Esther J., and A. M. Hunter.
Hurd, St. Clair:
  Counsel for the plaintiff, 84.
Hurst, Fannie:
  The gold in fish, 145.
  Humoresque, 145.
Hurst, Mont:
  The family budget, 146.
Hurwitz, Bertha:
  The adopted son, 146.
Hurwitz, Israel:
  Colleagues, 146.
  The thief, 84.
Hyamson, A. M.:
  The Jew in English drama, 4.

I

Iffland, A. W.:
  Antwort... über die Schauspiel Der Jude, 15.
  Crime from ambition, 23.
Iliowizi, Henry:
  Shylock and Nathan, 30.
Irwin, Wallace:
  Capitol fun, 146.
Ish-Kishor, Judith:
  "Can he do it?" 146.
  Yigael, 146.

J

Jackson, F.:
  "Shylock returns," 146.
Jackson, Mrs. H. L.:
  The quest, 146.
Jackson, John P.:
  The Templar and the Jewess, 44.
Jacob, Naomi E.:
  Jacob Ussher, 146.
Jacobs, Bertram:
  The man with the puckel, 146.
Jacobs, David:
  The prayers of a people, 146.
Jacobs, H. A.:
  George Washington meets his bicentennial press agent, 146.
Jacobs, Nellie C.:
  America's garden, 146.
James, C. S.:
  Jonathan Wild, 54.
James, Grace:
  Robert and Louisa, 146.
James, Henry, Jr.:
  Daniel Deronda, 72.
Jasspon, Ethel R., and B. Becker:
  Friendship ceremony, 146.
  The gate of the West, 146.
Jay, Harriet:
  Złoty wiek rycerstwa, 84.
Jephson, Robert:
  Julia, 23.
Jerome, J. K.:
  Der Fremde, 85.
  Le locataire du troisième sur la cour, 85.
  The passing of the third floor back, 85.
Jerrold, D. W.:
  The painter of Ghent, 23.
  The prisoners of war, 85.
Jessop, G. H.:
  Samuel of Posen, 85.
Jewish Welfare Board:
  English plays of Jewish interest translated from the Yiddish, 1.
  English plays of Jewish interest in two or more acts, 1.
  List of plays of Jewish interest for juniors and intermediates, 1.
  Selected list of English plays of Jewish interest, 1.
Johnson, F. G.:
  Abie's confessions, 147.
  Mrs. Goldblitz on matrimony, 147.
  Such ignorance! 147.
Johnson, Owen:
  Return from Jerusalem, 71.
Johnson, Philip, and H. Agg:
  The new school for scandal, 49.
Johnson, Theodore:
  Dr. Dobbs' assistant, 147.
Johnstone, J. B.:
  Oliver Twist, 69.
Jonas, S., joint author. *See* Wright, Fred, and S. Jonas.
Jones, E. O.:
  Real antiques, 147.
Jones, F. L.:
  Echoes of Shakspere in later Elizabethan drama, 23.
Jones, George:
  Tecumseh and the prophet of the West, 86.
Jones, H. A.:
  Judah, 86.
Jordan, Viola:
  Bridges, 147.
Joseph, Leon:
  In self-defense only, 147.
Joyce, James:
  Ulysses, 147.

K

K., E. E.:
  Barrabas and Shylock compared, 36.
Kaaplander, M. H.:
  The convert, 86.
Kaiser, Georg:
  From morn to midnight, 147.
Kampf, Leopold:
  On the eve, 86.
Kandel, Aben:
  The anti-hill, 147.
Kane, Edith:
  In thy radiance we see which light, 147.
Kane, J. N.:
  The Jew on the modern English stage, 4.
Kaplan, B. M.:
  The strange melody, 147.
Kaplan, Leah:
  Abie and his Martian rose, 147.
Kaser, A. L.:
  And the cow was painted red, 147.
  Bargains, 147.
  Casey meets Cohen, 147.
  Did you heard about me? 148.
  Ding, dong, dumb bell, 148.
  Dot loafer bum Levi, 148.
  Dot vedding skeremony, 148.
  The filming of "Uncle Tom's cabin," 148.
  Fresh fish and local color, 148.
  The goddess of dancing, 148.
  Gumbummer and his class of poopils, 148.
  Hands up, sponges and can openers, 148.
  Hey! teacher! 148.
  Hi times in Judge Sapp's court, 148.
  I'll tell the world, 148.
  In an airplane passenger station, 148.
  In the delicatessen shop, 148.
  In der street car, 148.
  Inkelheim on de telephone, 148.
  Isaac Fikelbaum, 148.
  It vas like dis, 148.
  Izzybloom's school of acting, 148.
  Jake the candidate, 148.
  Jake and his family, 148.
  Jootenant Levinski up for court martial, 148.
  The lady minstrels from Dixie, 148.
  Levi Beginski telephones, 148.
  Levi goes a-hunting, 148.
  Levi in the baggage room, 148.
  Levi's troubles, 149.
  Levi's view on marriage, 149.
  Loose nuts, 149.
  Mine friend, Levi Cohen, 149.
  Mine frient, Morris, 149.
  Mine gracious! 149.
  Monday morning in Maloney's court, 149.
  Musical eggs, 149.
  The nonsense school, 149.
  Object: matrimony, 149.
  Oi, such a nice vidow voman! 149.
  On the P. D. Q., 149.
  One on Inkel, 149.
  One swaller, one dollar, 149.
  Over the big puddle, 149.
  Oy! Oy! und den some, 149.
  A pain in de head, 149.
  Poor Izzy! 149.
  Prof. Dummelhead's class, 149.
  Professor Sniderschmultze's pupils, 149.
  Rachael, her Abie and Izzy, 149.
  The school at Cantaloupe Center, 149.
  School days a la foolish, 149.
  Shoot, brother, shoot, 149.
  Some class, 149.
  Stranded strangers, 150.
  Such a nice doggie, 150.
  Such a tightness! 150.

Kaser, A. L., continued
  Them actors from Tater Vine, 150.
  Vait a minute, 150.
  Vell! Vell! Vell! 150.
  When the school bell rings, 150.
Katayev, V. P.:
  Squaring the circle, 150.
Katz, Frances:
  But we go on forever, 150.
Kauffman, R. W.:
  The house of bondage, 87.
Kaufman, G. S.:
  The butter and egg man, 150.
  Le gentleman de l'Ohio, 150.
  See also Ferber, Edna, and G. S. Kaufman; Hart, Moss, and G. S. Kaufman; Lardner, R. W., and G. S. Kaufman.
Kaufman, G. S., and M. C. Connelly:
  Merton of the movies, 150.
Kaufman, G. S., and Edna Ferber:
  Dinner at eight, 150.
  Lundi huit heures, 151.
  The royal family, 151.
Kaufman, G. S., and Moss Hart:
  Merrily we roll along, 151.
Kaufman, G. S., and H. J. Mankiewicz:
  The good fellow, 151.
Kaufman, G. S., and Morrie Ryskind:
  Let 'em eat cake, 151.
  Of thee I sing, 151.
Kavanaugh, Katharine:
  Hero-by-the-hour, 151.
  Rose of the East Side, 151.
  A thriving business, 152.
  You're the doctor! 152.
Kaye, Donald, and W. McNally:
  We, us & company, 152.
Kearney, Patrick:
  Elmer Gantry, 152.
Kelley, Jessie A.:
  The pedlers' parade, 87.
  The rummage sale, 152.
Kellner, Leon:
  Die Quelle von Marlowe's "Jew of Malta," 36.
Kelsall, Charles:
  The first sitting of the committee on the proposed monument to Shakspeare, 24.
Kennedy, H. C.:
  Siberia, 64.
Kennedy, James:
  Ella Rosenberg, 24–25.
Kennedy, Margaret, and Basil Dean:
  The constant nymph, 152.
Kennel, Ruth E., and J. N. Washburne:
  They all come to Moscow, 152.
Kenrick, William:
  The duellist, 25.
Kenyon, Doris M.:
  A sidewalk controversy in the Ghetto, 152.
Kerr, Sophie:
  Tigers is only cats, 152.
Kerst, V. E., joint author. See Brownson, Mary W., and V. E. Kerst.
Kies, P. P.:
  Lessing's relation to early English sentimental comedy, 27.
  The sources of Lessing's Die Judin, 27.
Kilik, Mrs. David, and Mrs. P. S. Birnbaum:
  "Do you know?" 152.
Killigrew, Thomas:
  Thomaso, 25.
Kingsley, Sidney:
  Dead end, 152.
  Men in white, 152.

  Люди в белых халатах, 152.
Kirschner, Herbert:
  Shylock's son, 152.

INDEX OF AUTHORS

Kitchel, Mary E.:
  A literary reception, 87.
Kleagleman, Harold, pseud.:
  Dredging dad, 153.
Kleiman, Blanche P.:
  Abarbanel, 153.
Klein, Charles:
  Maggie Pepper, 87.
  The third degree, 87.
Klein, J. L.:
  The Jew of Malta, 36.
Klein, Joe:
  Hard luck Cohen, 87.
Klein, Yetta, and Florine Schwarz:
  All America's children, 153.
Klonsky, Milton, and T. Branfman:
  Peace: the twenty years, 153.
Knipe, Charles:
  A city ramble, 25.
Knoblock, Edward:
  "The faun," 87.
Knoblock, Edward, and Beverley Nichols:
  Evensong, 153.
Knowles, J. S.:
  The maid of Mariendorpt, 87.
Kober, Arthur:
  "Having wonderful time," 153.
Kobrin, Leon:
  The black sheep, 153.
  The eternal mystery, 153.
  The secret of life, 153.
Koeppel, Emil:
  Konfessionelle Strömungen in der dramatischen Dichtung des Zeitalters der beiden ersten Stuart-Könige, 4.
Kohler, Mrs. A. S.:
  When? 153.
Kohler, M. J.:
  The Jew in pre-Shakespearean literature, 4.
Kohut, Adolph:
  Lessing and "Nathan the Wise," 30.
Kohut, G. A.:
  Victor Hugo and the Jews, 22.
Kohut, G. A., editor:
  A Hebrew anthology, 7.
Kopald, L. J.:
  The friendship of Lessing and Mendelssohn, 30.
Kornfeld, Muriel G.:
  Drama and the Jew, 4.
Kottler, Esther, and Anna Drexler:
  Hadassah on trial, 153.
Kotzebue, A. F. F. von:
  Family distress, 25.
  Self immolation, 25.
  Lovers' vows, 26.
  The natural son, 26.
Kraemer, Georg:
  [Characterization of Barabas in The Jew of Malta,] 36.
Kraft, Irma:
  Ambition in Whitechapel, 153.
  Because he loved David so! 153.
  Borderlands, 88.
  The power of Purim, 153.
  The power of Purim, and other plays, 7.
  To save his country, 153.
Kraft, Louis:
  A daughter of her people, 153.
Krasiński, Zygmunt, hrabia:
  The undivine comedy, 26.
Krass, Nathan:
  "Goat song," 186.
Krauskopf, Joseph:
  Disraeli, 98.
  Nathan the Wise, the historic Jew, 30.
Kreimer, Mildred W.:
  Mother of exiles, 153.

Kremer, Theodor:
  Rachel Goldstein, 112.
Kreymborg, A.:
  Brother Bill, 154.
  Frank and Mr. Frankenstein, 154.
  I'm not complaining, 154.
Krimsky, Joseph:
  The refugee, 154.
Krohn, Mrs. H. N.:
  The Jew in present day drama, 4.
Kugel, H. J.:
  Souvenir of the family reunion, 154.
Kuhn, S. O.:
  The shadow of war, 154.
Kummer, Clare (B.):
  The rescuing angel, 154.
Kunitz, Joshua:
  [Chirikov's Jewish play,] 65.
Kupsch, Walther:
  Wozzeck. Ein Beitrag zum Schaffen Georg Büchners, 63.
Kyne, P. B.:
  The go-getter, 154.
Kyte, John:
  One good turn, 154.

L

Lacy, M. R.:
  The maid of Judah, 44.
Lacy, T. H.:
  The Jewess, 46.
Lammers, W. M.:
  The hired ghost, 154.
Landa, Gertrude, and M. J. Landa:
  For all eternity, 154.
Landa, M. J.:
  Do Jews lisp? 4.
  Index of plays, 2.
  "The Jew of Arragon," 52.
  The Jew in drama, 4.
  The Jew and the [English] drama, 4.
  Marlowe's Jew, 36.
  Marlowe's "Jew of Malta," 36.
  The name "Moss," 4.
  Nathan the neglected, 30.
  New ghetto, 82.
  The original of Fagin, 70.
Landau, J. L.:
  Conflicting worlds, 154.
Landman, Isaac:
  Jews and present-day dramatic art, 4.
Landstone, Charles:
  The future of Anglo-Jewish drama, 5.
Lang, Mrs. L. S.:
  Disease takes a holiday, 154.
  The voice within, 154.
Langdon, W. C.:
  The chapel masque of Christmas, 88.
  In honor of Shakespeare, 154.
Lanham, Ceora B.:
  Mrs. Schuster on the radio, 155.
Lanham, F. G.:
  The pedler, 155.
Lansdowne, G. G., baron:
  The Jew of Venice, 27.
Lardner, R. W., and G. S. Kaufman:
  June moon, 155.
The Larks, pseud.:
  The Shakespeare watercure, 88.
Larrimore, Lida:
  Last tag! 155.
Lasher-Schlitt, Mrs. Dorothy:
  Grillparzer's attitude toward the Jews, 79.
Lasser, Florence:
  The story of the I. L. G. W. U., 155.

La Touche, H. N. D., and O. Savini:
    The eagle, 88.
Laujon, Pierre:
    Le Juif bienfaisant, 15.
Laurent, Madame, and W. H. Oxberry:
    The Truand chief! 27.
Lavedan, H. L. E.:
    The Prince d'Aurec, 88.
Lawson, J. H.:
    Gentlewoman, 155.
    Processional, 155.
    Success story, 155.
Lazaron, Pauline H.:
    Fraternity, 155.
Lazarus, Emma:
    The dance to death, 88.
Learsi, Rufus, pseud. See Goldberg, Israel.
Leavitt, Ezekiel:
    Ghetto silhouettes, 88.
    The "pleasures" of the Czar, 88.
    "Professor" Getzel, 88.
    Stomachs and hearts, 88.
Leckie, Mrs.:
    The Hebrew boy, 88.
Lederer, Moritz:
    Der Jude in Drama, 5.
Lee, H. W.:
    El Cid Compeador, 155.
Lee, Nelson:
    The maid and the magpie, 33.
Lee, Sir S. L.:
    Elizabethan England and the Jews, 5.
    Shylock and his predecessors, 51.
Leiser, Joseph:
    The development of the Jew in the drama, 5.
    The genesis of religious tolerance, 30.
Lenz, J. R.:
    Das Gericht der Templar, 45.
Leo, Mrs.:
    Salomme and Eleazer, 27.
Leonard, Oscar:
    New lamps and old, 104.
Leroy-Denis, Jeanne:
    Ivanhoé, 45.
Lessing, G. E.:
    The Jews, 27.
    Nathan the Wise, 28–29.
    The three rings, 29.
Levegood, L. L.:
    Comedy mock trial; "A landlord and his tenants," 155.
Levenberg, Morris.:
    Empty victory, 155.
Levey, Sivori:
    Mahmud, the Sultan, 89.
Levi, Harry:
    "The dance to death," Emma Lazarus, 88.
    "The duenna," 47.
    "The Jew," 15.
    "The Jew of Malta," 36.
    Jewish characters in fiction, 5.
Levin, L. H.:
    Breadth and culture, 89.
    Clean, 89.
    Desertion, 89.
    Jewish missionaries, 89.
    The melting pot, 89.
    Not needed, 89.
    The only language, 89.
    Saving Judaism, 89.
    The two reforms, 89.
Levin, Meyer:
    Yehuda, 156.
Levin, Zebullon:
    The doctor's first operation, 156.
    Poetry and prose, 156.

Levinger, Elma C. (E.):
    At the gates, 156.
    The burden, 156.
    "Eight o'clock sharp," 156.
    "False jewels," 89.
    God's fool, 89.
    The great hope, 156.
    The heathen who stood on one foot, 156.
    How Succoth came to Chayim, 156.
    In the night watches, 156.
    It is time, 156.
    "Let there be light," 156.
    List of plays suitable for Jewish groups, 2.
    The magic circle, 156.
    Pilgrims to Palestine, 156.
    The poor student, 156.
    The priest people, 156.
    The Purim robe, 157.
    The sad jester, 89.
    A selective play-list for a Jewish dramatic group, 2.
    The tenth man, 157.
    The unlighted Menorah, 157.
    The wall between, 157.
    Why no Jewish plays? 5.
Levinson, H. D.:
    Ideals, 157.
    "Riley," 157.
    To save a life, 157.
Levinson, S. J.:
    Oil for the lamps of Israel, 157.
Levy, B. W., and John Van Druten:
    Hollywood holiday, 157.
Levy, Emmanuel:
    Altar-piece, 157.
    I believe, 157.
Levy, H. W.:
    A new playwright, 168.
Levy, M. P.:
    Gold eagle Guy, 157.
Levy, Newman:
    Ridiculously old-fashioned, 157.
    See also Ferber, Edna, and N. Levy.
Lewis, L. D.:
    The bells, 74.
Lewis, Sinclair, and S. C. Howard:
    Dodsworth, 157.
Lewisohn, Ludwig:
    Adam, 158.
    See also Tobias, Mrs. Lily, and L. Lewisohn.
Lieberman, Elias:
    At the Yiddish theatre, 158.
    A cottage for two, 158.
    Two in one, 158.
    Wanted: a doctor, 158.
Liebovitz, David:
    Atonement, 158.
    "Matches," 158.
Lindau, Paul:
    Maria and Magdalena, 89.
Lindsay, Howard:
    She loves me not, 158.
Lindsey, Theophilus:
    Divisione della Polonia, 31.
    Le partage de la Pologne, 31.
    The Polish partition, illustrated, 30.
    Die Theilung von Pohlen, 31.
    De verdeeling van Polen, 31.
Linsky, Fannie B.:
    America and the Jew, 158.
    Happy new year, 158.
    Sundown, 158.
    Three score years and ten, 158.
Lipsky, Louis:
    In the forest, 89.
    In shofar, 89.
Locke, W. J.:
    Idols, 89.

INDEX OF AUTHORS

Loeb, Oscar:
  Up to the minute, 89.
Lomas, B. A.:
  Miriam, 158.
London, Walter:
  Hebrew monologues, 90.
Lonsdale, Frederick:
  The street singers, 159.
Loos, Anita, and J. Emerson:
  "Gentlemen prefer blondes," 159.
Lord, Alice E.:
  A vision's quest, 90.
Lord, W. W.:
  André, 90.
Lounsbery, Grace C.:
  A dramatization of Oscar Wilde's Picture of Dorian Gray, 112.
Loving, Boyce:
  Swappers, 159.
Loyson, P. H.:
  The apostle, 90.
Lucas, W. J.:
  Traitor's gate, 31.
Ludovici, M., joint author. See Rankin, McKee, and M. Ludovici.
Luke, pseud.:
  The class war in heaven, 159.
Luzzatto, M. H.:
  Lah-y' shaw-riem tehilaw ("Praise for righteousness"), 31.
  [Migdol Oz,] 31.
Lyndon, Barré:
  The amazing Dr. Clitterhouse, 159.
Lyons, Jimmy:
  Mrs. Cohen and her neighbors, 159.
Lyons, Mabel:
  Chanuka in camp, 90.
  Some recent plays of Jewish interest, 5.

M

M., H.:
  Jew of Malta — Marlow, 36.
MJK:
  We're off to —, 159.
Mabon, C. B.:
  The Jew in English poetry and drama, 5.
MacArthur, C. G., joint author. See Hecht, Ben, and C. G. MacArthur.
Macauley, Elizabeth W.:
  The duke of Milan, 38.
McBurney, Venita R.:
  Underweight, 159.
MacCarthy, J. B.:
  The grain of the wood, 159.
McComas, Edith:
  Brass tacks, 159.
Macdonald, Dora M.:
  "The contest," 159.
  "In the principal's office," 159.
McEvoy, J. P.:
  In the vernacular, 159.
  Simon and Schuster present Show girl, 159.
Macfarren, George:
  Malvina, 31.
McGee, John:
  Jefferson Davis, 159.
McIntyre, J. T.:
  The Bowery night school, 90.
MacKaye, Hazel:
  The quest of youth, 159.
Macklin, Charles:
  Love a-la-mode, 31–32.
McKnight, Tom, and D. Hobart:
  Double dummy, 159.

Maclarin, Archibald:
  Britons to arms! 32.
  The ways of London, 32.
McMeekin, Mrs. Isabella (M.):
  The goblin and the princess, 160.
McMillan, Virginia:
  A tourist's romance, 160.
McNally, William:
  Abe and Jake in politics, 160.
  Abie's European trip, 160.
  Abraham Cohen, M. V., 160.
  After the revolution, 160.
  Agency employment, 160.
  And say! 160.
  As things are, 160.
  At the ball game, 160.
  Avernsky by the seasky, 160.
  Beautiful Sadie, 160.
  Believe me, 160.
  Blind dates, 160.
  Business and more trouble, 160.
  Clever stuff, 160.
  Cohen's intended, 160.
  Cohn and Levi in windy planes, 160.
  Dirt cheap, 160.
  A dog's life, 160.
  Dummaxes, 160.
  The emigrant, 160.
  Enough is enough, 160.
  Enough is too much, 160.
  Even if I mention it myself, 160.
  Everything, 160.
  Fall fashions, 160.
  Family troubles, 160.
  A fool there was, 160.
  Four of a kind, 160.
  Friendship, 160.
  From no place to nowhere on the Ha-ha line, 160.
  Garlic, 160.
  Goldberg and Silverstein, 161.
  Goldstein's son, 161.
  Goldstein's wedding, 161.
  A hard explanation, 161.
  Have one on me, 161.
  Help wanted, 161.
  The high cost of kissing, 161.
  Horsepistols and sicknesses, 161.
  I see by the newspapers, 161.
  I tell you! 161.
  Indigestion, 161.
  Irving Lipshits the salesman, 161.
  It can't be done, 161.
  Jake explains, 161.
  Jake the playwright, 161.
  Jake, you are a fake, 161.
  Jake's social affairs, 161.
  Just friends, 161.
  Just the same, 161.
  Keeping a wife, 161.
  Let's do acting? 161.
  Levi and Cohn, 161.
  Levinsky and daughter, 161.
  Levinsky and son, 161.
  Lost in a pullman, 161.
  Love and money, 161.
  Marriage and other gambles, 161.
  Matrimonial harmony, 161.
  Meet the wife, 161.
  Mine daughter, Rebecca, 161.
  Mine family, 161.
  My boy's wedding, 161.
  My friend, Goldstein, 161.
  My wife, 161.
  My wife's in-laws, 161.
  The new female custom inspector, 162.
  The night before the morning, 162.
  Noodle soup and appetites, 162.

McNally, William, *continued*
  Oh! lady, lady! 162.
  Oh! Polly! 162.
  "Over the counter," 162.
  Papa and Isaac, 162.
  Politics on a dry platform, 162.
  "Preparedness," 162.
  Professor Bolshushki's school, 162.
  Profiteering landlords, 162.
  The radio dentist, 162.
  Rain insurance, 162.
  Rebecca's beau, 162.
  Rosensky's insurance policy, 162.
  'Round the world, 162.
  The safest way, 162.
  Say! don't I know? 162.
  Say! mister, 162.
  Selma the flirt, 162.
  Settled, 162.
  S'sure as I am alive, 162.
  The stagehand and the star, 162.
  "The star boarder," 162.
  Station N-U-T, 162.
  "Such a woman," 162.
  Summering at a summer resort, 162.
  Tell me! 162.
  Temperament, 162.
  That's that! 162.
  There ain't no Santa Claus, 162.
  This and that, 162.
  This, that and something else, 162.
  This way out, 162.
  Tillie Tickletoe, 163.
  Tips, and more tips, 163.
  Trial marriages, 163.
  The vamp, 163.
  Waiting for the 5:15, 163.
  The waiting waiter, 163.
  Ward 23, 163.
  The weeper sex, 163.
  What d'yer mean? 163.
  Wise and not wise, 163.
  "Women! Women!" 163.
  You can't fool Isaac! 163.
  You win, 163.
  You're mine friend, 163.
  See also Kaye, Donald, and William McNally.
McNary, H. L.:
  Junior sees it through, 163.
Madison, Charles A.:
  David Pinski, the dramatist, 5.
  The Yiddish theatre, 5.
Madison, James:
  General Breakdown, U. S. A., 90.
  Getting his goat, 90.
  Ghetto get-backs between Cohen and Levi, 90.
  He would be a cop, 90.
  I'm your friend, 90.
  More tribulations of Cohen & Levi, 90.
  A pretty kettle of fish, 163.
  Two Hebrew sports, 90.
Madison, M., joint author. *See* Flint, Eva K., and M. Madison.
Magnes, J. L.:
  The melting pot, 115.
Maibaum, Richard:
  Birthright, 163.
Major, A. S.:
  A gallant Jew, 34.
Malbim, M. L.:
  [Extract from the first act of Mashel uMelitzah,] 90.
Malleson, Miles:
  The bargain. *See* Reynolds, Gertrude M. (R.) The daughter pays, 174.
Malone, Walter:
  Inez, 90.
Mankiewicz, H. J., joint author. *See* Kaufman, G. S., and H. J. Mankiewicz.

Manley, W. F.:
  Wild waves, 163.
Mann, Heinrich:
  Berlin interlude, 163.
Manners, J. H.:
  The house next door, 90.
Manning, Jacolyn:
  The man who begat six daughters, 163.
Mansfield, H. E.:
  Santa Claus and the madonna, 163.
Mantel, Beatrice T.:
  Rebecca Graz, 163.
Mapu, Abraham:
  The shepherd prince, 91.
Marcin, Max:
  Cheating cheaters, 164.
Marcus, Joseph:
  Luzzatto's Sefer ha-Mahzot, 31.
Marcus, Michael:
  Lessing's Nathan der Weise, 30.
Marion, Frances:
  The cup of life, 164.
Marks, Milton, and others:
  God is one, 91.
Marlowe, Christopher:
  The Jew of Malta, 34–35.
Marschall, Phyllis:
  Another man without a country: Benedict Arnold, 164.
Martel de Janville, Sibylle G. M. A. de Riquetti de Mirabeau, comtesse de:
  Le Friquet, 91.
Martinescu, Sandor:
  The Jews of Hodos, 164.
Mary Agnes, Sister:
  At the court of Isabella, 91.
Mashioff, H. H.:
  "Sunday morning's children," 164.
Mason, Redfern:
  The girl who knows how, 164.
Massinger, Philip:
  The Duke of Milan, 38.
  See also Fletcher, John, and Philip Massinger.
Mathews, C. J.:
  Patter versus Clatter, 91.
Matthews, Adelaide, and L. Sawyer:
  Sunset glow, 164.
Matthews, W.:
  The piracies of Macklin's love à-la-mode, 32.
Maugham, W. S.:
  Lady Frederick, 91.
  Smith, 91.
Mavor, O. H.:
  The black eye, 164.
Maxfield, Mina, and L. Eggleston:
  The wet parade dramatized, 164.
Mayer, Eli:
  Shakespeare, Lessing and the Jew, 30.
Mayhew, Henry, and A. S. Mayhew:
  Jubilee, 92.
  Passport, 92.
  Watchman, 92.
Mayo, Margaret:
  Polly at the circus, 92.
  Under two flags, 67.
Mazo, Frances:
  Figs for tea, 164.
Mead, A. B., joint author. *See* Wallace, Emma G., and A. B. Mead.
Medoff, Joseph:
  The Jew in the world's drama, 5.
Megrue, R. C., joint author. *See* Glass, M. M., and R. C. Megrue.
Meirovitz, J. M.:
  The new generation, 164.
Meiss, E. R.:
  The customer is always right, 164.
  "Three of us," 164.

INDEX OF AUTHORS

Mels, Edgar:
The Jew in modern drama, 2.
The Jews as portrayed in stage fiction, 2.
Melville, R. L.:
Sir Ronald Neville, Bart., 164.
Melville, Walter:
Ivanhoe, 44.
Mercet, S.:
Dorian Gray, 112.
Meredith, Burgess:
The adventures of Mr. Bean, 165.
Merryman, Mildred P.:
Jeroosalem, 165.
Mersand, Joseph:
Jewish dramatists and the American drama, 5.
Lessing and the Jews, 27.
Mew, James:
Yiddish literature and drama, 5.
Meyer, E. S.:
[Machiavelli and the Jew of Malta,] 36.
Meyer, Felix:
Dialogue of the dead, 92.
Meyer, Mabel H.:
The peace party, 165.
Meyer, Wilhelm:
Der Wandel des jüdischen Typus in der englischen Literatur, 5.
Meyerstein, E. H. W.:
The witches' Sabbath, 165.
Michelson, H.:
The Jew in early English literature, 5.
Marlowe's Jew of Malta, 36.
Middlemass, R. M.:
The budget, 165.
Middleton, George, joint author. See Bolton, G. R., and George Middleton.
Middleton, Jessie A.:
Red Sefchen, 92.
Middleton, Thomas:
The triumphs of honour and industry, 39.
Miele, Elizabeth:
Anybody's game, 165.
Did I say — No? 165.
Miller, Francesca F.:
Making Rosie a cook, 165.
Miller, L.:
Mr. Man, 165.
Miller, Marion M.:
The picture of Dorian Gray, 112.
Miller, S., joint author. See Schulman, Samuel, and S. Miller.
Miller, W. L.:
Life of Columbus, 92.
Milliken, Forbes:
Get off the track, 165.
Mine fat vife's poor husband, 165.
Says Cohen to Casey, 165.
Millingen, J. G.:
The miser's daughter, 39.
Mills, J. W.:
The repulsiveness of The Duke of Milan, 38.
Mills, S. A.:
Judith, 92.
Milne, A. A.:
Michael and Mary, 165.
Milner, H. M.:
The Jew of Lubeck, 39.
The Moorish page. See Chantilly, 10.
Miner, C. S., and others:
Merchant of Venice, 92.
Mirbeau, Octave:
Les affaires sont les affaires, 92.
Mitchell, A.:
Under two flags, 67.
Mitchell, L. E.:
Deborah, 95.
Mitchison, Naomi (H.), and L. E. Gielgud:
The price of freedom, 165.

Mobile, Ala. — Murphy High School: Modern Alchemists' Club:
Life of William Henry Perkin, 165.
Moeller, Philip:
Madame Sand, 166.
Mogadoriensis, pseud.:
[A letter to the editor,] 16.
Molnár, Ferenc:
The guardsman, 93.
Liliom, 93.
The play's the thing, 166.
Moment, Corinne R.:
The last will, 166.
Moncrieff, W. T.:
The heart of London, 39.
Ivanhoe! 44.
Jack Sheppard, 54.
The Jewess, 46.
Rochester, 39.
Van Diemen's Land, 39.
Montefiore, C. J. G.:
Concerning forms, 93.
Montgomery, James:
"Ready money," 93.
Moore, B. F.:
Belle the typewriter girl, 93.
Moore, F. F.:
The discoverer, 93.
Moore, Reginald:
Ruth, 95.
Moos, H. M.:
Mortara, 93.
Mordaunt, John:
Oliver Twist, 69.
Morgan, Margaret C., joint author. See Cobb, Elizabeth, and Margaret C. Morgan.
Morgan, Vaughan:
Friar Bacon, 166.
Morley, C. D.:
Walt, 166.
Morosco, Oliver, and G. V. Hobart:
Letty Pepper. See Klein, Charles. Maggie Pepper, 87.
Morris, E. B.:
The arctic architects, 94.
Morris, Esther:
The conscript, 166.
The matchmakers, 166.
Morris, F. J.:
Love at second sight, 166.
Morrison, Anne, and J. P. Toohey:
Jonesy, 166.
Mortimer, Lillian:
Headstrong Joan, 166.
A Manhattan honeymoon, 166.
Morton, Thomas:
Zorinski, 40.
Morton, Victoria:
The yellow ticket, 94.
Mory, E.:
Marlowes Jude von Malta und Shakespeares Kaufmann von Venedig, 36.
Moser, Joseph:
The bubbles, 40.
Mosenthal, S. H., Ritter von:
Deborah, 94.
Mullally, D. H.:
The camels are coming, 166.
Mumford, E. W.:
Bargain day at Bloomstein's, 95.
The traffic cop, 166.
Murphy, Arthur:
The temple of Laverna, 40.
Murray, E. C. G.:
Dizzi-ben-Dizzi, 96.
Murray, W. H. W.:
Ivanhoe, 44.
Jack Sheppard, 54.
Oliver Twist, 69.

Music, A. L.:
  Park Avenue, 166.
Muskerry, William:
  "Thrillby," 71.

N

Nathan, T. R.:
  The rod of Aaron, 167.
National Council of Jewish Women:
  The Council lends a hand, 167.
Naumburg, Bernard:
  Schnitzler's "Professor Bernhardi," 105.
Neale, Ralph, joint author. See Chesterton, Ada E. (J.), and Ralph Neale.
Needoff, Sydney, editor:
  Five one-act plays of Jewish interest, 7.
Nehring, Ernest, joint author. See Quaife, Elise W., and Ernest Nehring.
Neisuler, Dorothy:
  The builders, 167.
Nelson, W. B.:
  The last day! 167.
Nertz, Louis, and Armand Friedmann:
  Go ahead, 167.
Nettleton, G. H.:
  The first editions of The School for scandal, 49.
Neuman, Sara:
  The old order, 167.
Neustadt, Bernhard:
  Ben David, der Knabenräuber. See Spindler, Karl. The Jew, 50.
New York (state). — Courts: Supreme Court:
  The people of the state of New York, respondents, against Harry Weinberger [and others], 56.
New York Public Library:
  List of dramas relating to the Jews, 2.
Newbery, Francis:
  Epilogue to Love a-la-mode, 32.
Newbound, Edgar:
  Gemea, 105.
Newman, L. I.:
  The emperor, the blacksmith and the cobbler, 167.
  "The miracle of the scrolls," 167.
  Richard Cumberland, critic and friend of the Jews, 15.
  The triumph of the trees, 167.
Newman, S.:
  A study in non-Jewishness, 144.
Newton, H. C.:
  All the Jack Sheppards, 55.
  A most daring drama of treason, 111.
  See also Butler, R. W., and H. C. Newton.
Newton, H. L.:
  Abie Cohen's wedding, 167.
  Business is business, 96.
  The customs inspector, 167.
  Izzy's vacation, 96.
  The little red school house, 96.
  A special sale, 96.
  The umbrella mender, 96.
Newton, H. L., and A. S. Hoffman:
  All about Goldstein, 96.
  Glickman the glazier, 96.
  The troubles of Rozinski, 96.
Nichols, Anne:
  Abie's Irish rose, 167.
Nichols, Beverley, joint author. See Knoblock, Edward, and Beverley Nichols.
Nicholson, Kenyon:
  Wanderlust, 167.
Nobles, Milton:
  The phœnix, 96.
Nordau, M. S.:
  A question of honor, 96.
Norman, Hilda L.:
  The sons of Turcaret, 60, 88.

Norris, C. G.:
  Ivanhoe, 44.
Norris, Frank:
  The pit, 96.
Norton, F. P.:
  Abraham Lincoln, 167.
  Financier of New York, 168.
Nossig, Alfred:
  Abarbanel, 96.
Nurnberg, M., joint author. See Clarke, H. A., and M. Nurnberg:
Nusbaum, Julia K.:
  Golden gifts, 168.
Nuttall, Edith (S.):
  Tancred, 58.

O

O'Brien, Farley:
  Fixin' Aunt Fanny, 168.
O'Brien, Florence R. M. W.:
  The social climbers, 168.
O'Brien, J. F.:
  A character study of Barabas, 37.
Odell, G. C. D.:
  Kate Bateman as Leah, 95.
Odets, Clifford:
  "Awake and sing," 168.
  I can't sleep, 168.
  Paradise lost, 168.
  Till the day I die, 168.
  Waiting for Lefty, 168.
Odgers, J. C.:
  Some expressions of opinions and a sermon on "The passing of third floor back," 85.
Ogilvie, C. S.:
  Hypatia, 97.
O'Hanlon, Edwin:
  The club night night club, 168.
O'Hara, Julie C.:
  Christopher Marlowe's Jew of Malta, 37.
Ohnet, Georges:
  Serge Panine, 97.
O'Keeffe, John:
  Cunning Isaac's escape, 48.
  The fair American, 41.
  The little hunch-back, 40.
  The London hermit, 40.
  Peeping Tom of Coventry, 41.
  The young Quaker, 41.
One, Just N. E., pseud.:
  Landsleit, 168.
Ornitz, S. B., and V. Caspary:
  Geraniums in my window, 168.
Ornitz, S. B., and Donald Davis:
  Haunch, paunch and jowl, 168.
O'Rourke, Edmund. See Falconer, Edmund, pseud.
Orr, C. I., joint author. See Simons, Sarah E., and C. I. Orr.
Orton, J. R.:
  Arnold, 97.
Osgood, Erastus:
  A whiff of evidence, 169.
Osterweis, R. G.:
  A pageant, 169.
Oxberry, W. H., joint author. See Laurent, Madame, and W. H. Oxberry.
Oxenford, John:
  Old London, 54.
  Oliver Twist, 69.

P

Pace, William:
  Lydia, 41.
Packscher, Hazel G.:
  Book friends, 169.
  Real people, 169.

INDEX OF AUTHORS

Paikoff, Sarah:
  The calendar comes to life, 169.
Palmer, R. A., joint author. *See* Gordon, Leon, and R. A. Palmer.
Palmer, T. A.:
  Too late to save, 97.
Palmer, William:
  Ivanhoe, 44.
Parfenoff, S. S.:
  Inside the great conflict, 169.
Parker, L. B.:
  Thorns and orange blossoms, 97.
Parker, L. N.:
  Disraeli, 97.
  The York pageant, 98.
Parker, W. C.:
  The bank cashier, 98.
Parsons, J. F.:
  Bernstein and Firestein, 98.
  Fun in a vaudeville agency, 169.
Parsons, Mrs. Margaret C. (G.):
  Life as it ain't, 169.
Parsons, Mrs. Margaret C. (G.), and Madeleine Pool:
  The rummage sale, 169.
Pasquin, P. P.:
  Jewish conversion, 41.
Passmann, Hanns:
  Der Typus der Kurtisane im elisabethanischen Drama, 37.
Paul, Howard:
  The genesis of London assurance, 61.
Pavey, C. C.:
  The stories of "the three rings," 30.
Payne, J. H.:
  Trial without jury, 33.
Peake, R. B.:
  The bottle imp, 42.
  HB, 98.
Peixotto, E. M.:
  Political promises, 169.
Pelée, Mrs. Lillian S.:
  The trigger, 169.
Pelletier, L., jr., joint author. *See* Sloane, Robert, and L. Pelletier, jr.
Pellico, Silvio:
  Esther of Engaddi, 42.
Pemberton, Murdock, and D. Boehm:
  Sing high, sing low, 169.
Pennie, J. F.:
  The Varangian, 98.
Peple, E. H.:
  The jury of our peers, 169.
Percyval, T. W., joint author. *See* Hodges, Horace, and T. W. Percyval.
Perez, I. L.:
  After burial, 98.
  After the funeral, 98.
  Bride and groom, 98.
  Champagne, 98.
  He and she, 98.
  Of an early morning, 98.
  The sewing of the wedding gown, 98.
  The sisters, 99.
  Three sisters, 99.
Perlman, D. H.:
  A war-time Channukah, 169.
Perlstein, Jennie:
  Getting a contribution, 169.
Pertwee, Guy, editor:
  Oliver Twist in Fagin's den, 69.
Pertwee, Roland:
  Honours easy, 169.
Petrischev, A.:
  His first examination, 99.

Pfitzner, Käthe:
  Die Ausländertypen im englischen Drama der Restorationszeit, 5.
  Die Juden; ässere Merkmale, 9.
Pflaum, Heinz:
  Les scènes de Juifs dans la littérature dramatique du moyen-âge, 5.
Phelps, Franklin:
  Hooligan at the bat, 170.
  Judge Applesauce presides, 170.
Phelps, Pauline:
  Pawnshop Granny, 170.
  A Shakespearian conference, 99.
  Uncle Peter and the D. D. S., 170.
Philipson, David:
  [Abstract of] a lecture, 37.
  Cumberland's "The Jew," 16.
  The Jew in English fiction, 5.
  Marlowe's Jew of Malta, 37.
Phillips, D. G.:
  Susan Lennox, her rise and fall, 170.
Phillips, Frederick:
  Cromwell, 22.
Phillips, H. I.:
  The great club sandwich inquiry, 170.
Phillips, J. B.:
  Jack Sheppard, 54.
Phillips, Joseph:
  The Alexanders, 170.
Phillips, P. D.:
  The Jew in English literature, 5.
Phillips, Watts:
  Theodora: actress and empress, 99.
Pierce, C. W.:
  Alicia perks up, 170.
  Alley scene, 170.
  Be an optimist, 170.
  Hixville to Hollywood, 170.
Pietzker, Annemarie:
  Der Kaufmann in der elisabethanischen Literatur, 37.
Pilgrim, James:
  Yankee Jack, 99.
Pincus, J. B.:
  Haman the bully, 170.
Pinero, Sir A. W.:
  The cabinet minister, 99.
  Iris, 99.
  Letty, 100.
  The "Mind the paint" girl, 100.
  Trelawny of the "Wells," 100.
Pink, Wal:
  Oliver twisted, 69.
Pinski, David:
  The beautiful nun, 170.
  Cripples, 170.
  Diplomacy, 170.
  A dollar! 100.
  The dumb messiah, 100.
  Forgotten souls, 100.
  The God of the newly rich wool merchant, 170.
  The inventor and the king's daughter, 170.
  Isaac Sheftel, 101.
  Laid off, 170.
  The last Jew, 101.
  Little heroes, 170.
  The phonograph, 171.
  Poland — 1919, "A scene out of terrible days," 171.
  Sorrows, 101.
  The stranger, 101.
  Ten plays, 7.
  Three plays, 7.
  The treasure, 101.
  With triumphant banners, 101.
  געװיסען, 101.

Planché, J. R.:
　He's Jack Sheppard, 54.
　The Jewess, 46.
　An old offender, 101.
Plowman, T. F.:
　Isaac abroad, 45.
　Isaac of York, 45.
Plume, N. B., pseud.:
　Cinder Eller, 171.
Pocock, Isaac:
　The magpie, or the maid? 33.
Poel, William:
　Shakespeare's Jew and Marlowe's Christians, 37.
Polish, D., joint author. See Feinberg, Adolph, and D. Polish.
Pollock, Channing:
　The fool, 171.
Pollock, John:
　For Russia! 171.
Pool, Madeleine, joint author. See Parsons, Mrs. Margaret C. (G.), and Madeleine Pool.
Pool, Tamar (H.):
　"Lest we forget," 171.
Poole, J. F.:
　Blueskin, 54.
　Jerry Ledrew, 54.
Porah, Urva, pseud.:
　Thinking aloud, 171.
Porter, A. K.:
　The Virgin and the clerk, 171.
Possolo Hogan, Alfredo:
　Ivanhoe, 46.
Potter, P. M.:
　Trilby, 72.
　Under two flags, 67.
Powell, H. P.:
　A nose for news, 171.
　That reminds me, 171.
Powys, J. C.:
　A modern mystery play, 173.
Praed, Rosa C. (M.-P.):
　Ariane, 101.
Pray, I. C.:
　Deborah of Steinmark, 95.
Preston, Effa E.:
　Santa Claus on the air, 171.
Price, E. W.:
　Leah, 95.
Price, Olive M.:
　The gateway of tomorrow, 171.
Price, Samuel:
　Lessing the Christian liberal, 30.
Primer, Sylvester:
　Lessing's religious development, 30.
Procter, B. W.:
　A Jew's use for riches, 102.
Provence, Jean:
　At the gates, 171.
　Wedded bliss, 171.

Q

Quackenbush, C. E.:
　Her busy day, 172.
　The only way, 172.
Quaife, Elise W., and Ernest Nehring:
　The trade, 172.
　Tricks of the trade, 172.
Quinn, Hugh:
　Collecting the rent, 172.
Quint, W. D. See Tilton, Dwight, pseud. of G. T. Richardson and W. D. Quint.
Quire, H. S.:
　Wall Street in Paradise, 102.

R

Rabinowitz, Henry:
　The meturgeman, 172.
Rabinowitz, Mosheh, pseud.:
　The labor government of Palestine, 172.
　The man of labor, 172.
　The mishpat, 172.
　Purim carnival in Tel Aviv, 172.
Rabinowitz, Shalom. See Shalom Alechem, pseud.
Radke, A., joint author. See Buttimer, Edna, and A. Radke.
Raleigh, Cecil:
　Hearts are trumps, 102.
Rands, W. B.:
　George Eliot as a poet, 73.
Rankin, McKee, and M. Ludovici:
　The Jewess, 95.
Raphaelson, Samson:
　The jazz singer, 172.
Rapp, W. J.:
　Osman Pasha, 172.
Rappaport, Solomon:
　Le dibbouk, 173.
　The dybbuk, 172.
　Father and son, 102.
Ratcliffe, Dorothy U. (C.):
　Nathaniel Baddeley, bookman, 173.
Ravold, John:
　Oliver Twist, 69.
Raymond, G. L.:
　Columbus the discoverer, 102.
Razovsky, Cecilia:
　At Ellis Island, 173.
　I-19, 173.
Reade, Charles:
　Gold! 102.
　It's never too late to mend, 102.
Reade, Leslie:
　The shattered lamp, 173.
Recht, Charles:
　The Hebrew theatre in Moscow, 173.
Rede, W. L.:
　The skeleton witness, 42.
Reed, Howard:
　Funny Phinnie, 173.
　Right about faces, 173.
Reely, Mary K.:
　To be dealt with accordingly, 173.
Reeve, Wybert:
　Won at last! 103.
Reeves, J. R., joint author. See Bradley, E. W., and J. R. Reeves.
Reinicke, Walter:
　Der Wucherer im älteren englischen Drama, 5.
Reisen, Abraham:
　Brothers, 103.
　Captives two, 103.
　Three girls, 173.
Reiss, Isaac:
　"Success," 174.
Reitzel, William:
　Mansfield Park and Lovers' vows, 26.
Reynolds, Gertrude M. (R.):
　The daughter pays, 174.
Reynoldson, T. H.:
　The rich man of Frankfort, 103.
Reznikoff, Charles:
　The black death, 174.
　In memoriam: 1933, 174.
　Nine plays, 7.
　Rashi, 174.
　Uriel Acosta, 174.
Rhodes, R. C.:
　Belle's stratagem, 13.
　Bibliography of The Duenna, 48.
　The genuine and piratical texts [of the School for scandal], 49.

INDEX OF AUTHORS 215

Rhodes, R. C., *continued*
  Sheridan; a study in theatrical bibliography, 48, 49.
  Some aspects of Sheridan bibliography, 49.
Rice, E. L.:
  La calle, 175.
  Counsellor-at-law, 174.
  The left bank, 174.
  Street scene, 174.
  We, the people, 175.
Richardson, G. T. *See* Tilton, Dwight, pseud. of G. T. Richardson and W. D. Quint.
Riegelman, Harold:
  Pledging dad, 175.
Riley, Edna, and E. P. Riley:
  Before morning, 175.
Rish, A., joint author. *See* Hayward, H. R., and A. Rish.
Robbin, Edward:
  Bitter herbs, 175.
Roberts, Morley:
  Lady Penelope, 103.
Roberts, R. A.:
  Jack Sheppard, 54.
Roberts, W.:
  Jack Sheppard in literature, 55.
Robertson, T. W.:
  Society, 103.
Robinson, E. G., joint author. *See* Swerling, Joseph, and E. G. Robinson.
Robinson, M. G.:
  Oliver Twist, 69.
Robinson, R. M.:
  A thief in the house, 103.
Robinson, W. B.:
  Bells across the snow, 74.
Roby, B. S.:
  Bill Sykes, 70.
Rodenberg, Julius:
  The Jews in England, 5.
Roessler, Carl:
  The five Frankforters, 103.
Rogers, H. W.:
  The dawn of eternity, 104.
Rogoff, Hillel:
  אידישע פיעסען אויף דער ענגלישער ביהנע, 5.
Rohman, Richard:
  Power of the press, 175.
Roman, Ronetti:
  Manasse, 104.
Romano, Alberto:
  Match-making in a tavern, 175.
Romonek, Mrs. Lea L.:
  Love cannot make the dead dance, 175.
  Passport, 175.
Rose, E. E.:
  Penrod, 175.
  Rose of the Ghetto, 175.
Rose, Edward:
  Equals, 57.
Rosener, G. M.:
  Cohen's divorce, 104.
  The Goldstein wedding, 104.
  Under London, 70.
Rosenfeld, Sidney:
  Those bells, 74.
Rosenfield, J. A.:
  Gordon versus Gordon, 175.
Ross, Crystal R.:
  The Machiavellian man in Elizabethan drama, 20, 37.
Roth, Samuel:
  The broomstick brigade, 104.
  Herzl, 176.
  Mr. Edmund Gosse entertains on the occasion of his seventieth birthday, 176.
Routledge, William:
  Leah, a hearty joke in a cab age, 95.

Rowe, G. F.:
  The sleigh bells, 74.
Rowson, Susanna H.:
  Slaves in Algiers, 42.
Rubenovitz, Mrs. H. H.:
  The Golden slipper. *See* Asch, Shalom. Kiddush Ha-Shem, 117.
Rubens, Paul, joint author. *See* Hearn, James, and Paul Rubens.
Rubin, W. B.:
  The Bolshevists, 176.
Rubinstein, H. F.:
  Britania calling, 176.
  The deacon and the Jewess, 176.
  Israel set free, 7.
  Jew Dyte, 176.
  They went forth, 176.
  To the poets of Australia, 176.
  Whitehall, 1656, 176.
Russell, Livingston:
  The death dream, 74.
Ruthenburg, Grace D.:
  Hans Bulow's last puppet, 176.
Ryan, James:
  Daniel Deronda, 72.
Ryskind, Morrie, joint author. *See* Kaufman, G. S., and Morrie Ryskind.

S

Sabatzky, Kurt:
  Der Jude in der dramatischen Gestaltung, 5.
Sackler, Harry:
  Due east, 176.
  The seer looks at his bride, 176.
  The tsadik's journey, 177.
St. Clair, Robert:
  "The ghost in the glass," 177.
Salaman, M. C.:
  The Royal Court Theatre. Souvenir. Trelawney of the "Welles," 100.
Salant, Pauline, and G. Shadduck:
  Saving the country, 177.
Sampter, Jessie E.:
  The new apostacy, 177.
  The servant girl, 177.
Samuel, Maurice:
  Bloom of Bloomesalem, 147.
  David's fiancee, 177.
  The dybbuk, in three languages and four dimensions, 173.
  Yoshe Kalb among the Nordics, 180.
Samuels, M. V.:
  A pageant of the strong, 177.
Sandeau, Jules, joint author. *See* Augier, G. V. E., and Jules Sandeau.
Sargent, F. L.:
  Omar and the rabbi, 104.
Saunders, Lillian:
  Sob sister, 177.
Savage, George:
  A small down payment, 177.
Savini, O., joint author. *See* La Touche, H. N. D., and O. Savini.
Savoir, Alfred:
  In Manchuria, 104.
Sawyer, L., joint author. *See* Matthews, Adelaide, and L. Sawyer.
Schachtel, H. J.:
  The eternal people, 177.
Schapiro, Eva:
  היהודי על במת העולם, 136.
Schau, Kurt:
  Sprache und Grammatik der Dramen Marlowes, 37.

Schechter, F. I.:
   Golden and other ghettos in recent fiction, 140.
Scheffauer, H. G.:
   Der neue Shylock, 104.
Schick, J.:
   Christopher Marlowe, 37.
Schiffer, Mrs. Alice W.:
   Ruth makes a convert, 177.
Schimmel, R. C.:
   When Irish eyes are smiling, 177.
Schipper, Jacobus:
   De versu Marlovii, 37.
Schneider, R. K.:
   Der Mönch in der englischen Dichtung, 37.
Schnitzler, Arthur:
   The anti-Semites, 105.
   Professor Bernhardi, 105.
Schofield, Stephen:
   The bruiser's election, 177.
Schulman, Samuel:
   The Jewish features of Mr. Thomas's play, 110.
   Zangwill's "Children of the ghetto" — an incomplete picture of Jews and Judaism, 114.
Schulman, Samuel, and S. Miller:
   The spirit of Judaism, 177.
Schwarz, Florine, joint author. See Klein, Yetta, and Florine Schwarz.
Schweid, Mark:
   Borrowed years, 177.
Schweizer, Justus:
   Domitian, 178.
A Scotsman's remarks on the farce of Love a la mode, 32.
Scott, Mrs. Aggie D.:
   The early settlement of Georgia, 178.
Scott, Sir Walter:
   Scene from "Ivanhoe," 45.
Scribe, A. E.:
   La Juive, 46.
Searle, Cyril:
   Nancy Sikes, 70.
   Never too late to mend. See Hazlewood, H. C. Never too late to mend, 102.
Seaton, Ethel:
   Fresh sources for Marlowe, 37.
Segal, Alfred:
   As I see it, 178.
Segal, Hyman:
   East Side, West Side, 178.
Segal, S. M.:
   The convert, 178.
   Hitlerites and Chanukah lights, 178.
   The light, the coin and the feast, 178.
   One Chanukah morning, 178.
   One Chanukah night, 178.
   Treasure Chanukah, 178.
   Young Maimonides "lost and found," 178.
Sejour, Victor:
   The fortune teller, 105.
   La tireuse de cartes, 105.
Selby, Charles:
   Paris and pleasure, 106.
Seldes, Gilbert:
   Jewish plays and Jew-plays in New York, 5.
   Outlines of a preface [for a novelization of Abie's Irish rose], 167.
Seligman, Esther:
   Snowball and fair play, 178.
Selwyn, Edgar:
   The country boy, 106.
Sessa, K. B. A.:
   The ways of our tribe, 46.
Sexton, Ethelyn:
   Bernstein tries 'em out, 178.
Shadduck, G., joint author. See Salant, Pauline, and G. Shadduck.

Shalom Alechem, pseud. of Shalom Rabinowitz:
   Gymnazie, 106.
   It's a lie, 106.
   "Liars!" 106.
   She must marry a doctor, 106.
   When a broom looms large, 106.
   שׁװער צו זיין א איד, 106.
Shaw, Bernard:
   Der Arzt am Scheideweg, 106.
   The doctor's dilemma, 106.
   Man and superman, 107.
   Mensch und Übermensch, 107.
Shaw, Mrs. Henrietta O.:
   For freedom, 178.
Shaw, Irwin:
   Bury the dead, 178.
   Second mortgage, 178.
Shelland, H. E.:
   Fun in a school room, 107.
   The great libel case, a mock trial, 107.
   Two wandering Jews, 107.
Shelley, P. B.:
   Œdipus tyrannus, 47.
Sheridan, Don:
   Morris and his troubles, 178.
   Talking and singing things over, 178.
Sheridan, M. B.:
   "Be yourself," 178.
Sheridan, R. B. B.:
   La duègne, 47.
   The duenna, 47.
   An ode to scandal, 49.
   The school for scandal, 48–49.
Sherman, R. J.:
   Madam the boss, 179.
Sherwood, Clara H.:
   The cable car, 107.
Sherwood, R. E.:
   This is New York, 179.
Shiel:
   The passing of the bill, 50.
Shiffrin, A. B.:
   Allah be praised! 179.
   Return at sunset, 179.
   Wanted a bookkeeper, 179.
Shillingford, Osmond, and A. E. Ellis:
   The daisy, 93.
Shillman, Bernard:
   Legends of the Jew in English literature, 6.
   Two great Jewish plays, 173
Shipman, Samuel, and V. Victor:
   The unwritten chapter, 179.
Shirley, Arthur, and W. M. Tilson:
   Old London bridge in the days of Jack Sheppard and Jonathan Wild, 54.
Shore, Mrs. Viola (B.):
   The queen's bracelet, 179.
Shostac, P. B.:
   The modern Yiddish stage, 6.
Siegel, Max, joint author. See Gropper, M. H., and Max Siegel.
Sifton, Paul:
   The belt, 179.
Silbermann, A. M.:
   Untersuchungen über die Quellen des Dramas "The true Tragedy of Herod and Antipater with the death of faire Marriam," 38.
Silverman, Joseph:
   Nathan the Wise, 30.
Simon, Abram:
   Prejudice and literature, 6.
Simon, Carolyn:
   The under-dog, 179.
Simon, Esther J., and A. M. Hunter:
   "The spirit of the South," 179.
Simons, Evelyn:
   The daughters of Rebekah, 179.

INDEX OF AUTHORS

Simons, Evelyn, and O. Burt:
  Solomon Levi, 179.
Simons, Sarah E., and C. I. Orr:
  Ivanhoe, 45.
  Tales of a wayside inn, 107.
Singer, I. J.:
  The sinner, 179.
Sissman, P. R.:
  A doctor to be, 180.
Skeen, W. H.:
  Oliver Twist, 70.
Skutch, R. F.:
  "Spinoza," 180.
Sloane, Robert, and L. Pelletier, jr.:
  Howdy stranger, 180.
Sloane, W. M.:
  Art for art's sake, 180.
Slobod, Fay:
  "Leah the forsaken;" the story of a once popular play, 95.
Small, S. A.:
  'The Jew,' 24.
Smith, H. J.:
  A tailor-made man, 180.
Smith, J. S.:
  The siege of Algiers, 50.
Smith, Winchell, and J. E. Hazzard:
  Turn to the right, 180.
Smollett, T. G.:
  The adventures of Ferdinand, Count Fathom, 50.
Snyder, Kathryn:
  The Jewish saleslady, 180.
Snyder, Sara:
  Election in foodland, 180.
Soane, George:
  The Hebrew, 45.
Soifer, Margaret K.:
  A dramatization of the sessions of the Royal Commission, 180.
  Dramatization of XX Zionist Congress, 180.
Solomon, E., joint author. See Hayman, Philip, and E. Solomon.
Sorsky, John:
  The king of kings, 180.
Southerne, Thomas:
  Money the mistress, 50.
Spencer, Hazelton:
  Granville's The Jew of Venice, 27.
  Marlowe's rice "with a powder," 37.
Spender, Stephen:
  Trial of a judge, 180.
Spewack, Bella (C.), and Samuel Spewack:
  Clear all wires! 181.
  Poppa, 181.
  "Spring song," 181.
Spindler, Karl:
  The Jew, 50.
Spivack, M. J.:
  Broken melody, 181.
Sprague, Mrs. Bessie (T.), and W. Sprague:
  Blarney street, 181.
Spritz, C. S.:
  Minutes of the jolly twelve, 181.
Stallings, Leonard, joint author. See Anderson, Maxwell, and Leonard Stallings.
Stange, H. S.:
  False dreams, farewell! 181.
Stayton, Gracia:
  Guggenstein and his "green anchel," 181.
  Mr. Mishkowsky und de "younk leddy," 181.
  Mrs. Dinkelspiel and the P. T. A., 181.
  Mrs. Schnickelfritz und der four o'clock train, 181.
  Mrs. Schnickelfritz und der visecrackers, 181.
Steell, Willis:
  A bride from home, 107.
Steen, Eva:
  Escaped, 181.

Steiner, Rudolph:
  Four mystery plays, 107.
Stephens, H. P., and W. Yardley:
  Little Jack Sheppard, 54.
Stephenson, Edgar:
  Henry Bernstein — France's new high-pressure playwright, 60.
Stern, Miss G. B. See Holdsworth, Gladys B. (S.)
Stevens, Ernest:
  Ivanhoe, 45.
Stevens, H. B.:
  City rubes, 181.
Stevenson, Augusta:
  Ivanhoe, 45.
  The treason of Benedict Arnold, 107.
Stinson, H. H.:
  The ace is trumped, 182.
Stirling, Edward:
  The anchor of hope, 107.
  The Jew's daughter, 107.
  The mendicant's son! 108.
  Oliver Twist, 70.
Stockley, W. F. P.:
  The Jews of Marlowe and Shakespeare, 37.
Stoecker, Wilhelm:
  Pinero's Dramen, 6.
Stokes, H. P.:
  The Jew in English literature, 2.
Stone, Dalton:
  Ivanhoe a la carte, 45.
Stone, Irving:
  The white life, 182.
Stonex, A. B.:
  The usurer in Elizabethan drama, 6.
Storm, Jude:
  Woman's might, 182.
Straus, R. L.:
  Westward the course of Israel, 182.
Street, J. L.:
  Rita Coventry, 182.
Strickland, Sir W. W.:
  A slight misunderstanding, 108.
Strunsky, Hyman:
  Zalmen the powerful, 108.
Stuart, Aimee McH., and Philip Stuart:
  Her shop, 182.
Stuart, Charles:
  The distress'd baronet, 50.
Sturge, L. J.:
  Webster and the law: a parallel, 52.
Sturgis, J. R.:
  Ivanhoe, 45.
Stragnell, Gregory:
  A psychopathological study of Franz Molnar's Liliom, 93.
Subert, F. A.:
  The great freeholder, 182.
Sulivan, Robert:
  Elopements in high life, 108.
Sullivan, Frank:
  Defendant fails to show up in ticker tape scandal trial, 182.
Suter, H. C.:
  Fagin's last night alive, 70.
Swan, Arthur:
  "The Jew that Marlowe drew," 37.
Swan, Howard:
  Paul and Joseph, 108.
Swanwick, Catherine:
  The Jew doctor, 108.
Swerling, Joseph, and E. G. Robinson:
  Kibitzer, 182.
Symonds, J. A.:
  [Transfigured avarice,] 37.
Symons, Arthur:
  Outlaws of life, 182.

T

Tag, R. W.:
  Handy Solomon, 108.
Taggart, Tom:
  Sold, 182.
Tagger, Theodor:
  Races, 182.
Talbot, A. J.:
  All Fools' eve, 183.
  One evening at Nero's, 183.
Talfourd, Francis:
  The merchant of Venice travestie, 108.
  Shylock, 108.
Tarkington, Booth:
  Poldekin, 183.
Tarkington, Booth, and H. L. Wilson:
  The Gibson upright, 183.
Tarleau, Lisa Y.:
  Musa Ibn Maimon, 183.
Tarnawski, Władysław:
  [A critique,] 37.
Tatroe, Ruth:
  Mrs. Cohen at the amusement park, 183.
Taylor, Mrs. H.:
  Hadassah women go on a spree, 183.
Taylor, Sir Henry:
  The virgin widow, 108.
Taylor, Rex:
  Appearances, 183.
Taylor, Rica B.:
  Benny proposes! 183.
  The boomerang! 183.
  Damages — two hundred! 183.
  Four Jewish sketches, 7.
  Paul robs Peter! 183.
Taylor, T. P.:
  The tower of London, 109.
Taylor, Tom:
  Going to the bad, 109.
  Helping hands, 109.
  Our clerks, 109.
  "Payable on demand," 109.
  The ticket-of-leave man, 109.
Thacher, G. H.:
  Hypatia, 110.
Thimme, Margarete:
  Marlowes "Jew of Malta," 37.
Thomas, Augustus:
  As a man thinks, 110.
Thomson, O. R. H.:
  Andreyev's "Anathema" and the Faust legend, 55.
Thorne, Anthony:
  Thirteen o'clock, 183.
Thorne, David:
  Dorian Gray, 112.
Throckmorton, Cleon:
  After dark; or, Neither wife, maid nor widow. See Boucicault, Dion, After dark, 61.
Tibbals, S. S.:
  Izzy's troubles, 110.
Tilbury, W. H.:
  The German Jew, 51.
Tilton, Dwight, pseud. of G. T. Richardson and W. D. Quint:
  Mayer & son, 110.
Tippett, Isabel C., joint author. See Douglas, Norman, and Isabel C. Tippett.
Titus, Harold:
  The candle in the window, 183.
Tobias, Mrs. Lily, and L. Lewisohn:
  Daniel Deronda, 73.
Tobin, John:
  The faro table, 51.
  The fisherman, 51.
Toller, Ernst:
  Brokenbrow, 183.
  Transfiguration, 183.
Tolstoĭ, A. K., graf:
  The death of Ivan the Terrible, 110.
Tolstoi, L. N., graf:
  The fruits of culture, 110.
  The fruits of enlightenment, 110.
Tomlinson, W. E.:
  "The Duke of Milan" von Philip Massinger, 38.
Toohey, J. P., joint author. See Morrison, Anne, and J. P. Toohey:
Torrey, Adela:
  The grouch, 184.
Totten, J. B.:
  The house of bondage, 87.
Toube, Teresa S.:
  Leah the forsaken, 95.
Townsend, Charles:
  The iron hand, 111.
  The jail bird, 111.
  Perils of a great city, 111.
Townsend, W. T.:
  Whitefriars, 111.
Traill, H. D.:
  The third age, 111.
Tree, Sir H. B.:
  A souvenir of "Trilby" by Paul M. Potter, 72.
Truth, pseud.:
  Mr. Morton's Zorinski and Brooke's Gustavus Vasa compared, 40.
Tubiash, Nancy:
  By bread alone, 184.
Tullidge, E. W.:
  Ben Israel, 111.
Tully, Jim:
  Jarnegan, 184.
Tupper, W. S.:
  What price America? 184.
Turner, J. H.:
  The spot on the sun, 184.
Turner, L. McK.:
  The midwinter night's dreams, 184.
Turner, W. J. R.:
  The man who ate the popomack, 184.

U

Ulrich, C. K.:
  The Hebrew, 111.
  The high school freshman, 111.
  The town marshall, 111.
Union of American Hebrew Congregations. — Department of Synagogue and School Extension:
  Plays, 2.
United States. — Works Progress Administration: Federal Theatre Project, New York:
  Anglo-Jewish plays in English and Yiddish, 2.
  Anti-war plays, 2.
  Jewish non-royalty plays and pageants, 2.
Untermeyer, Louis:
  Shylock, Christian, 184.
Uvarov, S.:
  [A critical study,] 37.

V

Vachell, H. A.:
  "Pen," 103.
Vance, Daisy M.:
  A lamb among wolves, 70.
  Vengeance, 70.
Van Druten, John, joint author. See Levy, B. W., and John Van Druten.
Van Noppen, L. C.:
  Who is Bashti Beki? 111.
Veen, H. R. S. van der:
  Jewish characters in eighteenth century English fiction and drama, 6.

INDEX OF AUTHORS 219

Vickers, G. M.:
 Petruchio's widow, 111.
Victor, Victor:
 Brother against brother, 184.
 See also Shipman, Samuel, and V. Victor.
Vigran, Bertha:
 Who shall judge? 184.
Vilas, Faith Van V.:
 The maker of souls, 184.
Vogl, Mrs. Virginie D. (H.):
 Love and lovers, 111.
Vollmer, Lula:
 Moonshine and honeysuckle, 185.

W

W., W. R.:
 "An old Jew," 79.
Wade, Thomas:
 The Jew of Arragon, 52.
Wagener, E. A.:
 The Jew of Lessing and of Shakespeare, 30.
Walinsky, Louis:
 Heil Hitler! 185.
Walker, Alice J.:
 Christopher Columbus, 185.
Walker, Kent:
 De troubles of Jakey Cohen, 185.
Walkley, A. B.:
 The doctor's dilemma, 106.
Wallace, Edgar:
 The ringer, 185.
Wallace, Eglantine (M.), lady:
 The ton, 52.
Wallace, Emma G., and A. B. Mead:
 Why photographers go mad, 185.
Wallace, Lew B.:
 The doctor comes from Moscow, 185.
Wallace, Lewis:
 The prince of India, 112.
Wallace, Sarah A.:
 Scenes from "Oliver Twist," 70.
Wallace, W. R.:
 Leila, 63.
Wallach, S. W.:
 Imaginary conversations, 185.
Walton, J. *See* Conway, Olive, pseud. of Harold Brighouse and J. Walton.
Wann, Louis:
 The Oriental in Elizabethan drama, 6.
Ward, A. W.:
 [Marlowe's Jew of Malta and its resemblance to Shakespeare's Merchant of Venice,] 37.
Ware, J. R.:
 The Polish Jew, 74.
Warren, E. H.:
 Shakespeare in Wall Street, 185.
Washburne, J. N., joint author. *See* Kennel, Ruth E., and J. N. Washburne.
Watchman, pseud.:
 The stage, the Jew, and the Jewish Drama League, 6.
Watkins, Harry:
 Under two flags, 67.
Wayne, Kathryn:
 It's the fashion, 185.
Webster, B. N.:
 Monte Cristo, 71.
Webster, John:
 Des Teufels Rechtshandel, 52.
 The Deuils Law-case, 52.
Weever, Edwin:
 Uncle Zeberiah, 112.
Weihl, Elsa:
 A Jew visits America, 185.
 Let down the bars, 185.

Weinberg, Rose D.:
 "Pioneers," 185.
Weinman, Nettie C.:
 Companionship of Mendelssohn and Lessing, 30.
Weinstein, L. H.:
 So let 'em foreclose! 185.
Weiss, Kurt.:
 Richard Brinsley Sheridan als Lustspieldichter, 48, 49.
Weissblatt, H. A.:
 A bunch of bones, 185.
Weitzenkorn, Louis:
 Five star final, 185.
Wellman, Rita:
 The Gentile wife, 185.
Wells, W. H.:
 Brotherhood, 186.
Werfel, F. V.:
 The eternal road, 186.
 Goat song, 186.
 Juarez and Maximilian, 186.
Werne, Isaac:
 6, היהודי בגיא החזיון.
West, Mae:
 Diamond Lil, 186.
Wexley, John:
 They shall not die, 186.
Wharton, Mrs. Edith N. (J.):
 The age of innocence, 186.
 The house of mirth, 112.
Wharton, Mrs. Edith N. (J.), and Clyde Fitch:
 The house of mirth, 112.
White, Mrs. Bessie (F.):
 Brotherhood of man, 186.
 By any other name, 186.
 Family, 187.
 Fools' paradise, 187.
 Money in the bank, 187.
 Sinners, 187.
 A tooth for a tooth, 187.
 "Where there's smoke," 187.
White, Bessie (W.), translator:
 Nine one-act plays from the Yiddish, 8.
White, C. V.:
 The Peace Conference, 112.
White, E. M.:
 Five out of nine have it, 187.
White, Grace (M.):
 Rachel Goldstein, 112.
White, H. A.:
 [The dramatizations of Scott's Ivanhoe,] 46.
White, Kate A.:
 Samuel Snickerwitz's Hallowe'en, 187.
White, N. I.:
 Shelley's Swell-foot the tyrant in relation to contemporary political satires, 47.
Whitehouse, Josephine H.:
 Jeremiad, 187.
Whyte, H., and R. Balmain:
 Oliver Twist, 70.
Wickser, Josephine W.:
 The romance of Buffalo, 187.
Wiernik, Bertha:
 Satan interferes, 187.
Wilcox, C. E., and Helen M. Wilcox:
 The Boomville band concert, 187.
Wilcox, Constance G.:
 Egypt's eyes, 187.
Wilde, Oscar:
 The picture of Dorian Gray, 112.
Wilder, Sophia C. (H.):
 Strings, 187.
Wilder, T. N.:
 And the sea shall give up its dead, 187.
Wilkinson, Matt:
 Jack Sheppard, 54.

Wilks, T. E.:
 Rinaldo Rinaldini, 52.
Willard, Clark:
 Polishing papa, 188.
Willets, Jeanette:
 The story books before the judge, 188.
Williams, Emlyn:
 The late Christopher Bean, 132.
Williams, H. L.:
 After dark, 61.
Williams, Ida S.:
 Sabbath lights, 188.
Williams, J. L.:
 The day dreamer, 113.
Williams, Laura M.:
 On the jury, 188.
Williams, T. J.:
 A silent protector, 73.
Williamson, H. R.:
 Mr. Gladstone, 188.
Willmore, Edward:
 Cromwell, the Protector, 188.
Wills, A. E.:
 Benjamin, Benny and Ben, 113.
 A football romance, 113.
 Taking chances, 113.
Wilson, Edna E.:
 Thanksgiving through the ages, 188.
Wilson, Ella M., and Anna W. Field:
 A Christmas play, 188.
Wilson, Genevieve C.:
 Which are foreign? 188.
Wilson, H. L., joint author. See Tarkington, Booth, and H. L. Wilson.
Wilson, Huntington:
 Stultitia, 113.
Wilson, J. H.:
 Granville's "stock-jobbing Jew," 27.
Wilson, John:
 Belphegor, 52.
Wilson, R. C.:
 The schoolboy's nightmare, 113.
Wilstach, Paul:
 Dramatisations of Scott, 46.
Winograd, David:
 A Jewish tragedy; its social meaning, 120.
Winter, William:
 Edward S. Willard in The Middleman and Judah, 86.
Wise, E. G.:
 Belle, 188.
Wohlbrück, W. A.:
 Tempelherren og Jødinden, 46.
 Der Templer und die Jüdin, 46.
Wolf, Friedrich:
 Doktor Mamlocks Ausweg, 188.
Wolff, W. A., joint author. See Abdullah, Achmed, and W. A. Wolff.
Wolfrom, Anna:
 The marriage certificate, 188.
Wolfson, Miriam:
 The spirit of Hadassah, 188.
Wolfson, Victor:
 Excursion, 188.
Wolheim, Louis, and I. Goldberg:
 The idle inn, 83.
Wollman, Maurice:
 The governess, 48.
 The Jews in G. B. Shaw's plays, 6.
 Some notes on Sheridan, "The Duenna," and Isaac Mendoza, 48.

Wood, C. A.:
 The last Gepuire, 188.
Wood, F. T.:
 The Merchant of Venice in the eighteenth century, 27.
Wood, Frank:
 Leah the forsook, 95.
Woodbury, D. O.:
 Hung jury, 188.
Woodman, Ned:
 Cominski complains, 189.
Wright, Fred, and S. Jonas:
 Shop strife, 189.
Wyckoff, S. R.:
 "The western wall," 189.
Wylie, Ida A. R.:
 Witches Sabbath, 189.
Wynne, Arnold:
 [The Jew of Malta,] 37.

Y

Yaffle, pseud.:
 Foiling the Reds, 189.
Yardley, W., joint author. See Stephens, H. P., and W. Yardley; Brookfield, C. H. E., and W. Yardley.
Yiddish Art Theatre, New York:
 Maurice Schwartz's production of I. J. Singer's play "Yoshe Kalb," 180.
Yoffa, Annie:
 Revenge, 189.
Young, Mrs. H.:
 Jonathan Wild, 54.
Young, Henry:
 Jonathan Wild, 54.
Young, Mrs. Rida (J.):
 Brown of Harvard, 113.

Z

Zahajkiewicz, Szczesny:
 Zydowskie swaty, 189.
Zametkin, Michael:
 A Russian Shylock, 113.
Zangwill, Israel:
 Children of the ghetto, 113.
 The cockpit, 189.
 The forcing house, 189.
 The Jew in drama and in life, 6.
 The king of the schnorrers, 114.
 The melting-pot, 114.
 Richard Cumberland centenary memorial paper, 16.
 Shylock and other stage Jews, 6.
 Two unjewish Jewish plays, 30.
 The war god, 115.
Zeckhauser, Iola, and J. Casslev:
 Before the wall, 189.
Zeve, Leah:
 In the balance, 189.
Zimmerman, Harry:
 David's barmitzvah, 189.
Zimmerman, Harry, compiler:
 Plays of Jewish life, 8.
Zinnecker, W. D.:
 Lessing the dramatist, 27, 30.
Zola, Émile:
 Les héritiers Rabourdin, 115.
Zolotkoff, Leon:
 The dream of Bath-Zion, 115.

INDEX OF TITLES

Numbers refer to pages in the main text of the bibliography.
Cross references are given for some alternative titles mentioned in the notes.

A

Abarbanel, Blanche P. Kleiman, 153.
Abarbanel, Alfred Nossig, 96.
Abe and Jake in politics, William McNally, 160.
Abe and Mawruss, M. M. Glass and R. C. Megrue, 78.
Abie Cohen's wedding, H. L. Newton, 167.
Abie eats, A. F. Byers, 124.
Abie and his Martian rose, Leah Kaplan, 147.
Abie's confessions, F. G. Johnson, 147.
Abie's European trip, William McNally, 160.
Abie's Irish Rose, Anne Nichols, 167.
"Abie's license," Charles George, 136.
Aboard a slow train in Mizzoury, W. B. Hare, 141.
Abraham advertises, Flora C. Gardner and M. F. Gardner, 136.
Abraham Cohen, M. V., William McNally, 160.
Abraham Lincoln, F. P. Norton, 167.
Abraham Lincoln and the Jewish soldier, Lillian Fox, 134.
Absent-minded Judy, Wilbur Braun, 122.
The Ace is trumped, H. H. Stinson, 182.
An Act at Oxford, Thomas Baker, 8.
Action! Holland Hudson, 145.
Adam, Ludwig Lewisohn, 158.
The Adopted son, Bertha Hurwitz, 146.
The Adventures of Mr. Bean, Burgess Meredith, 165.
Advertisement, B. M. Hastings, 141.
Les Affaires sont les affaires, Octave Mirbeau, 92.
After burial, I. L. Perez, 98.
After dark, Dion Boucicault, 60–61.
After the funeral, I. L. Perez, 98.
After midnight, Samuel Daixel, 128.
After the revolution, William McNally, 160.
The Age of innocence, Margaret A. Barnes, 186.
The Age of innocence, Mrs. Edith N. (J.) Wharton, 186.
Agency employment, William McNally, 160.
Ahasverus, Herman Heijermans, 82.
"Airey" Annie, F. C. Burnand, 101.
Airways, Inc., John Dos Passos, 129.
Alexander in Babylon, H. A., 116.
Alexander the Great, Aubrey De Vere, 68.
The Alexanders, Joseph Phillips, 170.
Alicia perks up, C. W. Pierce, 170.
All about Goldstein, H. L. Newton and A. S. Hoffman, 96.
All alive, oh! Arthur Bourchier. See Disparu!!! A. C. A. Bisson and P. Gérard, 60.
The All America eleven, M. N. Beebe, 58.
All America's children, Yetta Klein and Florine Schwarz, 153.
All Fools' eve, A. J. Talbot, 183.
All for the good, Mrs. A. V. Goodman, 138.
All my eye-vanhoe, Philip Hayman and E. Solomon, 44.
Allah be praised! A. B. Shiffrin, 179.
Alley scene, C. W. Pierce, 170.
Altar-piece, Emmanuel Levy, 157.
Am I your vife? W. B. Hare, 141.
Amaco, M. A. Flavin, 133.
Amateur night, E. E. Buck, 123.
An Amateur triumph, P. P. Davis, 67.
The Amazing Dr. Clitterhouse, Barré Lyndon, 159.
Ambition in Whitechapel, Irma Kraft, 153.
America and the Jew, Fannie B. Linsky, 158.
America's garden, Nellie C. Jacobs, 146.
America's making, Sadie B. Brewster, 122.
The American captive, James Ellison, 18.
American holiday, E. L. Barker and A. Barker. See their Middletown, 118.

The American idea, Lillian P. Heydemann, 83.
An American woman, C. E. Banks, 57.
Among the musicians, anon., 55.
Anathema, L. N. Andreyev, 55.
The Anchor of hope, Edward Stirling, 107.
The Ancient fortress, Israel Goldberg, 137.
And the cow was painted red, A. L. Kaser, 147.
And say! William McNally, 160.
And the sea shall give up its dead, T. N. Wilder, 187.
André, W. W. Lord, 90.
Angel aware, Marion Holbrook, 144.
Another day, Mamie G. Gamoran, 136.
Another language, Mrs. Rose Franken, 134.
Another maid and another magpie, anon. See Trial without jury, J. H. Payne, 33.
Another man without a country: Benedict Arnold, Phyllis Marschall, 164.
Anti-clericalism in France, Kenneth Bell, 58.
The Anti-hill, Aben Kandel, 147.
The Anti-Semites, Arthur Schnitzler, 105.
Anybody's game, Elizabeth Miele, 165.
The Apostle, P. H. Loyson, 90.
Appearances, Rex Taylor, 183.
The Arctic architects, E. B. Morris, 94.
Ariane, Rosa C. (M.-P.) Praed, 101.
An Aristocratic alliance, Lady Violet Greville, 57.
Arnold, J. R. Orton, 97.
Art for art's sake, W. M. Sloane, 180.
The Artist and the shadow, G. D. Gribble. See his The Masque of Venice, 139.
Der Arzt am Scheideweg, Bernard Shaw, 106.
As I see it, Alfred Segal, 178.
As a man thinks, Augustus Thomas, 110.
As things are, William McNally, 160.
At the ball game, William McNally, 160.
At the court of Isabella, Sister Mary Agnes, 91.
At Ellis Island, Cecilia Razovsky, 173.
At the gates, Elma C. (E.) Levinger, 156.
At the gates, Jean Provence, 171.
At the Yiddish theatre, Elias Lieberman, 158.
Atonement, David Liebovitz, 158.
Auf wiedersehen, Sada Cowen, 127.
Aunt Fan rises to the defense, Mrs. Rose B. Goldstein, 138.
The Avalanche, A. G. Harris, 81.
Avernsky by the seasky, William McNally, 160.
"Awake and sing," Clifford Odets, 168.
Azael, the prodigal, Edward Fitzball, 75.

B

The Baby carriage, Bosworth Crocker, pseud., 127.
Back to God, Hayim Bassen, 119.
Balloon, Padraic Colum, 126.
The Bank cashier, W. C. Parker, 98.
The Banshee, W. D. Hepenstall and Ralph Cullinan. See their The Call of the banshee, 142.
Bar Giora, Israel Goldberg, 137.
The Bargain, Miles Malleson. See The Daughter pays, Gertrude M. (R.) Reynolds, 174.
The Bargain, H. G. Scheffauer. See his Der neue Shylock, 104.
Bargain day at Bloomstein's, E. W. Mumford, 95.
Bargains, A. L. Kaser, 147.
The Baron of Budapest, Adolph Dickman, 129.
The Baron and the Jew, Binney Gunnison, 44.
"Battle hymn," Michael Blankfort and M. Gold, 121.
The Battle of the lords, H. B. Burton, 63.
The Battle of love, Alphonse Daudet, 66.
Be an optimist, C. W. Pierce, 170.

"Be yourself," M. B. Sheridan, 178.
Beach nuts, Leota H. Black, 120.
Beacon of death, James Pilgrim. *See* his Yankee Jack, 99.
Beau Brummel, Clyde Fitch, 75.
The Beautiful nun, David Pinski, 170.
Beautiful Sadie, William McNally, 160.
Bebele, Perez Hirschbein, 143.
Because he loved David so! Irma Kraft, 153.
The Beduin fight, S. S. Grossman, 140.
Before morning, Edna Riley and E. P. Riley, 175.
Before the wall, Iola Zeckhauser and J. Casslev, 189.
Believe me, William McNally, 160.
Bella donna, J. B. Fagan, 83.
Bella donna, R. S. Hichens, 83.
Belle, E. G. Wise, 188.
Belle the typewriter girl, B. F. Moore, 93.
The Belle's stratagem, Mrs. Hannah P. Cowley, 11–13.
The Bells, Louis Cardot, 74.
The Bells, Émile Erckmann and Alexandre Chatrian, 73.
The Bells, L. D. Lewis, 74.
Bells across the snow, W. B. Robinson, 74.
Bells bell-esqued and the Polish Jew polished off, anon., 74.
Bells of the sleigh, Horace Allen, 74.
The Bells in the storm, C. H. Hazlewood, 74.
Belphegor, L. S. Buckingham, 63.
Belphegor, John Wilson, 52.
The Belt, Paul Sifton, 179.
Belteshazzar, Thomas Harrison, 21.
Ben David, der Knabenräuber; oder, Der Christ und der Jude, Bernhard Neustadt. *See* The Jew, Karl Spindler, 50.
Ben Israel, E. W. Tullidge, 111.
Beneberak, the Spanish Jew, Robert Boggs. *See* his A Stepdaughter of Israel, 60.
Benedict Arnold, Edwin Emerson, 131.
Benevolent Jew, anon., 15.
Benjamin, Benny and Ben, A. E. Wills, 113.
Benny proposes! Rica B. Taylor, 183.
Berlin interlude, Heinrich Mann, 163.
Bernstein and Firestein, J. F. Parsons, 98.
Bernstein tries 'em out, Ethelyn Sexton, 178.
The Better son, Isaac Goldberg, 137.
Between ourselves, Benjamin, pseud., 59.
Bialik's last Chanuka, Ben Aronin, 117.
Bill Sykes, B. S. Roby, 70.
Birds of a feather, H. V. Esmond. *See* Jacob Ussher, Naomi E. Jacob, 146.
Birds of a feather, T. J. Gaffney, 135.
Birthright, Richard Maibaum, 163.
Bitter herbs, Edward Robbin, 175.
The Black death, Charles Reznikoff, 174.
The Black eye, O. H. Mavor, 164.
Black sheep, Leon Kobrin, 153.
Black tents, Achmed Abdullah, 116.
Blarney street, Mrs. Besse (T.) Sprague and W. Sprague, 181.
Blessed are the rich, J. E. Agate, 116.
Blind dates, William McNally, 160.
The Bloody jest, I. I. Efros, 130.
Bloody laughter, Ernst Toller. *See* his Brokenbrow, 183.
Bloom of Bloomesalem, Maurice Samuel, 147.
The Blue vase, P. B. Kyne. *See* his The Go-getter, 154.
Blueskin; or, Jack and his pals, J. F. Poole, 54.
The Bolshevists, W. B. Rubin, 176.
Bombastes in the shades, Laurence Binyon, 120.
Book friends, Hazel G. Packscher, 169.
The Boomerang! Rica B. Taylor, 183.
The Boomville band concert, C. E. Wilcox and Helen M. Wilcox, 187.
The Booster, Louis Nertz and Armand Friedmann. *See their* Go ahead, 167.

Borderlands, Irma Kraft, 88.
Borrowed years, Mark Schweid, 177.
The Bottle imp, R. B. Peake, 42.
The Bowery night school, J. T. McIntyre, 90.
"Boz's" Oliver Twist, Thomas Greenwood, 69.
Brass tacks, Edith McComas, 159.
Breadth and culture, L. H. Levin, 89.
Bride and groom, I. L. Perez, 98.
A Bride from home. Willis Steell, 107.
The Bride of the Nile, W. S. Blunt, 60.
Bridge at Upper Montclair, Ethel F. Guttman, 140.
Bridges, Viola Jordan, 147.
Britannia calling, H. F. Rubinstein, 176.
Britons to arms! Archibald Maclarin, 32.
Broadway interlude, Achmed Abdullah and W. A. Wolff, 116.
Broken melody, M. J. Spivack, 181.
Brokenbrow, Ernst Toller, 183.
The Broomstick brigade, Samuel Roth, 104.
Brother against brother, Victor Victor, 184.
Brother Bill, A. Kreymborg, 154.
Brotherhood, W. H. Wells, 186.
Brotherhood of man, Mrs. Bessie (F.) White, 186.
Brothers, Israel Goldberg, 137.
Brothers, Abraham Reisen, 103.
Brown of Harvard, Mrs. Rida (J.) Young, 113.
The Bruiser's election, Stephen Schofield, 177.
The Bubbles, Joseph Moser, 40.
The Budget, R. M. Middlemass, 165.
The Builders, Dorothy Neisuler, 167.
A Bunch of bones, H. A. Weissblatt, 185.
"A Bunch of violets," Sydney Grundy, 79.
The Burden, Elma C. (E.) Levinger, 156.
Bury the dead, Irwin Shaw, 178.
Business before pleasure, M. M. Glass and J. E. Goodman, 77.
Business is business, Earl Carroll, 124.
Business is business, Anna B. Charm, 124.
Business is business, Sydney Grundy, 92.
Business is business, R. S. Hichens, 92.
Business is business, H. L. Newton, 96.
Business and more trouble, William McNally, 160.
But we go on forever, Frances Katz, 150.
The Butter and egg man, G. S. Kaufman, 150.
By any other name, Mrs. Bessie (F.) White, 186.
By bread alone, Nancy Tubiash, 184.
By order of the czar, Joseph Hatton, 81.

C

The Cabinet minister, Sir A. W. Pinero, 99.
The Cable car, Clara H. Sherwood, 107.
The Calendar comes to life, Sarah Paikoff, 169.
Caligula, John Crowne, 13.
The Caliph's buffoon, anon., 10.
Capitola, C. H. Hazlewood, 81.
The Call, Jessie B. Bogen, 121.
The Call of the banshee, W. D. Hepenstall and Ralph Cullinan, 142.
La Calle, E. L. Rice, 175.
The Camels are coming, D. H. Mullally, 166.
"Can he do it?" Judith Ish-Kishor, 146.
The Candle in the window, Harold Titus, 183.
Capitol fun, Wallace Irwin, 146.
Captain Bombastes Thunderton, Ludvig, baron Holberg, 21.
Captain Dreyfus, Jacob Gordin, 78.
Captives two, Abraham Reisen, 103.
"The Capture," Israel Goldberg, 137.
The Case against Casey, Thornton Friel, 76.
Casey meets Cohen, A. L. Kaser, 147.
Caste, Cosmo Hamilton, 140.
Caught in a corner, W. J. Shaw. *See* Samuel of Posen, G. H. Jessop, 85.

INDEX OF TITLES 223

A Celestial conference, Nachman Heller, 142.
The Centuries, Emanuel J. Basshe, 119.
Chalk dust, H. A. Clarke and M. Nurnberg, 125.
Champagne, I. L. Perez, 98.
Chantilly, anon., 10.
Chanuka in camp, Mabel Lyons, 90.
The Chapel masque of Christmas, W. C. Langdon, 88.
Cheating cheaters, Max Marcin, 164.
The Child slaves of New York, C. E. Blaney, 60.
Children of the ghetto, Israel Zangwill, 113.
The Choice, Carola Cassel, 124.
The Chosen people, Y. N. Chirikov, 65.
The Christian, Sir Hall Caine, 63.
A Christian turn'd Turke, Robert Daborne, 16.
A Christmas play, Ella M. Wilson and Anna W. Field, 188.
Christmas in the tenements, J. P. Clancy, 125.
Christopher Columbus, Roland Hill, 83.
Christopher Columbus, Alice J. Walker, 185.
Chrystabelle, Edmund Falconer, pseud. of Edmund O'Rourke, 74.
El Cid Compeador, H. W. Lee, 155.
A Cigarette maker's romance, Charles Hannan, 80.
Cinder Eller, N. B. Plume, pseud., 171.
A City ramble, Charles Knipe, 25.
City rubes, H. B. Stevens, 181.
The Class war in heaven, Luke, pseud., 159.
Clean, L. H. Levin, 89.
Clear all wires! Bella (C.) Spewack and Samuel Spewack, 181.
Clever stuff, William McNally, 160.
"The Closed door," Wilbur Braun, 122.
The Club night night club, Edwin O'Hanlon, 168.
The Cockpit, Israel Zangwill, 189.
"Cohen & Son," Isak Goller, 138.
Cohen's divorce, G. M. Rosener, 104.
Cohen's intended, William McNally, 160.
Cohen's views on business, Mayme R. Bitney, 60.
The Cohens and Kellys, Aaron Hoffman, 144.
Cohn and Levi in windy planes, William McNally, 160.
Colleagues, Israel Hurwitz, 146.
Collecting the rent, Hugh Quinn, 172.
Color blind, Margaret T. Applegarth, 117.
Columbus the discoverer, G. L. Raymond, 102.
Columbus el filibustero! John Brougham, 62.
Cominski complains, Ned Woodman, 189.
"Com'ny 'tention!" Arten Casey, 189.
Comoedia genannt Dass wohl gesprochene Uhrtheil eynes weiblichen Studenten, 11.
Concerning forms, C. J. G. Montefiore, 93.
Concessions! concessions! Samuel Duker, 130.
The Conflagration, Gerhart Hauptmann, 81.
Conflicting worlds, J. L. Landau, 154.
Conjuration, G. M. Baker, 6.
The Conscript, Esther Morris, 166.
The Conspirators, M. D. Flattery, 75.
The Constant nymph, Margaret Kennedy and Basil Dean, 152.
"The Contest," Dora M. Macdonald, 159.
The Convert, M. H. Kaaplander, 86.
The Convert, S. M. Segal, 178.
Coquine, Bosworth Crocker, pseud., 127.
The Cornfed cut-ups, W. B. Hare, 141.
The Costly party, anon., 126.
A Cottage for two, Elias Lieberman, 158.
The Council lends a hand, National Council of Jewish Women, 167.
Council's every girl, L. R. Eckhouse, 130.
Counsel for the plaintiff, St. Clair Hurd, 84.
Counsellor-at-law, E. L. Rice, 174.
The Country boy, Edgar Selwyn, 106.
A Country boy scout, W. B. Hare, 141.
The Country mad-cap in London, Henry Fielding. See his Miss Lucy in town, 18.
The Country squire, J. H. Bauman, 58.
Courage, Tom Barry, 119.
The Court decides for safety, Maxine Deddens, 129.

The Cozeners, Samuel Foote, 19.
Creatures of impulse, Sir W. S. Gilbert, 76.
The Creole, Shirley Brooks, 62.
Crime from ambition, A. W. Iffland, 23.
The Criminal code, M. A. Flavin, 133.
Cripples, David Pinski, 170.
Cristilinda, Monckton Hoffe, 143.
Cromwell, V. M., comte Hugo, 22.
Cromwell, Frederick Phillips, 22.
Cromwell, the Protector, Edward Willmore, 188.
The Cross word puzzle, Penelope Dickerson, 129.
Cunning Isaac's escape, John O'Keeffe, 48.
The Cup of life, Frances Marion, 164.
The Custom of the country, John Fletcher and Philip Massinger, 18.
The Customer is always right, E. R. Meiss, 164.
The Customs inspector, H. L. Newton, 167.

D

Daddy's gone a-hunting, Zoë Akins, 116.
The Daisy, Osmond Shillingford and A. E. Ellis, 93.
Damages — two hundred! Rica B. Taylor, 183.
The Dance to death, Emma Lazarus, 88.
Daniel Deronda, George Eliot, 72.
Daniel Deronda, Henry James, Jr., 72.
Daniel Deronda, James Ryan, 72.
Daniel Deronda, Mrs. Lily Tobias and L. Lewisohn, 73.
A Daughter of her people, Louis Kraft, 153.
The Daughter pays, Gertrude M. (R.) Reynolds, 174.
The Daughters of Babylon, Wilson Barrett, 57.
The Daughters of Rebekah, Evelyn Simons, 179.
Daughters of Shem, Samuel Gordon, 79.
David Cohn, der New Yorker Heiratsvermittler, Conrad Hauenstein, 81.
David's barmitzvah, Harry Zimmerman, 189.
David's fiancee, Maurice Samuel, 177.
The Dawn of eternity, H. W. Rogers, 104.
The Day dreamer, J. L. Williams, 113.
The Deacon and the Jewess, H. F. Rubinstein, 176.
Dead end, Sidney Kingsley, 152.
The Death dream, Livingston Russell, 74.
The Death of Ivan the Terrible, graf A. K. Tolstoi, 110.
Deborah, C. S. Cheltnam, 94.
Deborah, G. A. Conquest, 94.
Deborah, L. E. Mitchell, 95.
Deborah, S. H., Ritter von Mosenthal, 94.
Deborah of Steinmark, I. C. Pray, 95.
Déclassée, Zoë Akins, 116.
The Deep red rover, Frederick Hay and W. Chapman, 81.
Defendant fails to show up in ticker tape scandal trial, Frank Sullivan, 182.
The Depot lunch counter, Frank Dumont, 72.
Deronda and his mother, anon., 72.
Des Teufels Rechtshandel, John Webster, 52.
Desertion, L. H. Levin, 89.
Design for living, N. P. Coward, 127.
The Detour, Owen Davis, 128.
The Devil upon two sticks, Samuel Foote, 19.
Devil's Island. See The Dreyfus affair, Vera De Noie and A. D. Hall, 68.
The Devils law-case, John Webster, 52.
Dialogue on cooking, Herman Baar, 57.
Dialogue of the dead, Felix Meyer, 92.
Dialogue on prizes, Herman Baar, 57.
Der Diamant, C. F. Hebbel, 82.
Diamond Lil, Mae West, 186.
Le Dibbouk, Solomon Rappaport, 173.
The Dictator, Charles Drapkin, 130.
Did I say — No? Elizabeth Miele, 165.
Did you heard about me? A. L. Kaser, 148.
Die von Hochsattel, L. W. Stein and Ludwig Heller. See The House next door, J. H. Manners, 90.

A Dignified and honorable interview, Gersoni, 76.
Ding, dong, dumb bell, A. L. Kaser, 148.
Dinner at eight, G. S. Kaufman and Edna Ferber, 150.
Diplomacy, David Pinski, 170.
Dirt cheap, William McNally, 160.
The Discoverer, F. F. Moore, 93.
The Discovery of America, T. F. Coakley, 126.
Disease takes a holiday, Mrs. L. S. Lang, 154.
Disparu!!! A. C. A. Bisson and P. Gérard, 60.
Disraeli, L. N. Parker, 97.
Dissipation, M. P. Andrews, 8.
The Distress'd baronet, Charles Stuart, 50.
The District convention, Frank Dumont, 72.
A Divine comedy, anon., 129.
Divine drudge, Vicki Baum and John Golden, 119.
Divisione della Polonia, Theophilus Lindsey, 31.
Dizzi-ben-Dizzy, E. C. G. Murray, 96.
"Dizzy," W. T. Coleby, 126.
"Do you know?" Mrs. David Kilik and Mrs. P. S. Birnbaum, 152.
The Doctor comes from Moscow, L. B. Wallace, 185.
Dr. Dobb's assistant, Theodore Johnson, 147.
A Doctor to be, P. R. Sissman, 180.
The Doctor's dilemma, Bernard Shaw, 106.
The Doctor's first operation, Zebullon Levin, 156.
Dodsworth, Sinclair Lewis and S. C. Howard, 157.
A Dog's life, William McNally, 160.
Doggone! Mary Cunningham, 127.
Doktor Kohn, M. S. Nordau. See his A Question of honor, 96.
Doktor Mamlocks Ausweg, Friedrich Wolf, 188.
A Dollar! David Pinski, 100.
Domitian, Justus Schweizer, 178.
Don Adrian, anon., 70.
Don Juan of Austria, J. F. C. Delavigne. See his The Monastery of St. Just, 16.
Don Pedro, king of Castile, H. J. G. Herbert, 3rd earl of Carnarvon, 10.
Dorian Gray, S. Mercet, 112.
Dorian Gray, David Thorne, 112.
Dot loafer bum Levi, A. L. Kaser, 148.
Dot vedding skeremony, A. L. Kaser, 148.
Double dummy, Tom McKnight and D. Hobart, 159.
Down the black cañon, Forbes Heermans, 82.
Down on the farm, C. W. Hancock, 80.
Down our street, E. G. Wise. See his Belle, 188.
Down stream, Shalom Asch. See his With the current, 56.
A Dramatist in search of a love scene, A. M. Brown, 123.
A Dramatization of the sessions of the Royal Commission, Margaret K. Soifer, 180.
A Dramatization of Sir Walter Scott's novel "Ivanhoe," Alberta Gallatin, 44.
Dramatization of XX Zionist Congress, Margaret K. Soifer, 180.
The Dream of Bath-Zion, Leon Zolotkoff, 115.
Dream of fate, C. Z. Barnett, 57.
A Dream of a Russian subject, V. M. Doroshevich, 71.
Dredging dad, Harold Kleagleman, pseud., 153.
The Dreyfus affair, Vera De Noie and A. D. Hall, 68.
The Drummer, M. B. Curtis. See Samuel of Posen, G. H. Jessop, 85.
The Drummer from Posen, M. B. Curtis. See Samuel of Posen, G. H. Jessop, 85.
A Dude in a cyclone, T. S. Denison, 68.
Due east, Harry Sackler, 176.
La Duègne, R. B. B. Sheridan, 47.
The Duellist, William Kenrick, 25.
The Duenna, R. B. B. Sheridan, 47.
The Duke of Milan, Philip Massinger, 38.
The Dumb messiah, David Pinski, 100.
Dummaxes, William McNally, 160.
"Dust," L. R. Eckhouse, 130.
Dux, Olive Conway, pseud., 126.
The Dybbuk, Solomon Rappaport, 172.

E

The Eagle, H. N. D. La Touche and O. Savini, 88.
The Early settlement of Georgia, Mrs. Aggie D. Scott, 178.
East Side, West Side, Hyman Segal, 178.
L'Ebreo, anon., 63.
Edelmuth und Schlechtsinn, L. T. H. W. Wichmann. See The Ways of our tribe, K. B. A. Sessa, 46.
Editorial conference (with wine), anon., 130.
Education, F. J. Adkins, 116.
The Education of Doris, Marie Doran, 129.
Egypt's eyes, Constance G. Wilcox, 187.
"Eight o'clock sharp," Elma C. (E.) Levinger, 156.
The Eldest, Edna Ferber, 132.
Election in foodland, Sara Snyder, 180.
Elijah the prophet, Perez Hirschbein, 83.
Elizabeth Lazarus, J. T. Haines. See Land sharks and sea gulls, W. N. Glascock, 77.
Ella Rosenberg, James Kenney, 24–25.
Elmer Gantry, Patrick Kearney, 152.
Elopements in high life, Robert Sulivan, 108.
The Emigrant, William McNally, 160.
L'Émigré à Londres, anon., 18.
The Emperor, the blacksmith and the cobbler, L. I. Newman, 167.
Empty stockings, Margaret T. Applegarth, 117.
Empty victory, Morris Levenberg, 155.
England's greatness, F. A. Hibbert, 143.
Enough is enough, William McNally, 160.
Enough is too much, William McNally, 160.
Epilogue to Love a-la-mode, Francis Newbery, 32.
Equals, Edward Rose, 57.
The Escape from Cordova, Abraham Burstein, 124.
Escaped, Eva Steen, 181.
Esther of Engaddi, Silvio Pellico, 42.
Esther Guiladi, J. Fraenkel, 76.
The Eternal bond, Israel Goldberg, 137.
The Eternal Jew, David Pinski. See his The Stranger, 101.
The Eternal mystery, Leon Kobrin, 153.
The Eternal people, H. J. Schachtel, 177.
The Eternal road, F. V. Werfel, 186.
The Eternal song, Mark Arnstein, 55.
Euer Verkehr, Julius von Voss. See The Ways of our tribe, K. B. A. Sessa, 46.
Even if I mention it myself, William McNally, 160.
An Evening in Palestine, Mrs. Blanche (S.) Fisher, 133.
Evensong, Edward Knoblock and Beverley Nichols, 153.
Every-mother, S. S. Cohon, 126.
Everyjew, I. L. Bril, 122.
Everything, William McNally, 160.
Excursion, Victor Wolfson, 188.
Excuse me, Rupert Hughes, 84.
Eyes, Maxine Block, 121.

F

Fagin, Ivan Berlyn, 68.
Fagin's last night alive, H. C. Suter, 70.
The Fair American, John O'Keeffe, 41.
A Fair exchange, Edna Buttimer and A. Radke, 124.
The Faith of the fathers, Henry Berman, 120.
Faith Mather, M. D. Flattery. See his The Conspirators, 75.
The Faith of their fathers, Florence (K.) Frank, 134.
Fall fashions, William McNally, 160.
The Fall guy, George Abbott and James Gleason, 116.
The Fall of Haman, anon., 75.
The Fall and rise of Susan Lenox, G. V. Hobart. See Susan Lenox, her fall and rise, D. G. Phillips, 170.
False dreams, farewell! H. S. Stange, 181.
The False friend, J. C. Cross, 13.
"False jewels," Elma C. E. Levinger, 89.
La Fameuse tragédie du riche Juif de Malte, Christopher Marlowe, 35.

INDEX OF TITLES 225

Die Familie Zwie, David Pinski. *See his* The Last Jew, 101.
Family, Mrs. Bessie (F.) White, 187.
The Family budget, Mont Hurst, 146.
Family distress, A. F. F. von Kotzebue, 25.
Family quarrels, T. J. Dibdin, 17.
Family troubles, William McNally, 160.
Fannie finds the way, anon., 132.
The Farmer forsworn, Ludwig Anzengruber, 55.
The Faro table, John Tobin, 51.
Fashion, Herman Baar, 57.
The Fashionable lover, Richard Cumberland, 13.
Father and son, Solomon Rappaport, 102.
"The Faun," Edward Knoblock, 87.
Fear God and take your own part, Myron Brinig, 123.
The Felon's last dream; or, Jack Sheppard in France, anon., 54.
Ferdinand, Count Fathom, T. J. Dibdin. *See* The Adventures of Ferdinand, Count Fathom, T. G. Smollett, 50.
Ferdinand Lassalle, Elias Ginsburg, 136.
Ferdinand Lassalle & Helene von Donniges, Elbert Hubbard, 84.
The Fifteenth candle, Rachael L. Field, 133.
Fighting boy of Vienna, Yosef Hanani, 140.
Figs for tea, Frances Mazo, 164.
The Filming of "Uncle Tom's cabin," A. L. Kaser, 148.
Financier of New York, F. P. Norton, 168.
Find the woman, Charles Klein. *See his* The Third degree, 87.
The First baby, L. H. Dembo, 129.
The First sitting of the committee on the proposed monument to Shakspeare, Charles Kelsall, 24.
The Fisherman, John Tobin, 51.
The Fisherman's hut, John Tobin. *See his* The Fisherman, 51.
The Five Frankforters, Carl Roessler, 103.
Five out of nine have it, E. M. White, 187.
Five star final, Louis Weitzenkorn, 185.
Fixin' Aunt Fanny, Farley O'Brien, 168.
Floating beacon, James Pilgrim. *See his* Yankee Jack, 99.
Florian Geyer, Gerhart Hauptmann, 81.
The Florist shop, Winifred Hawkridge, 142.
Flying scud, Dion Boucicault, 61.
Foiling the Reds, Yaffle, pseud., 189.
Une Folie, J. N. Bouilly, 9.
Followers of the light, Baltimore Hebrew Congregation, Baltimore, Md., 118.
The Fool, Channing Pollock, 171.
A Fool there was, William McNally, 160.
Fools' paradise, Mrs. Bessie (F.) White, 187.
A Football romance, A. E. Wills, 113.
For all eternity, Gertrude Landa and M. J. Landa, 154.
For freedom, Mrs. Henrietta O. Shaw, 178.
"For Messiah, King," David Frischmann, 76.
For Russia! John Pollock, 171.
The Forcing house, Israel Zangwill, 189.
The Forest oracle, A. L. V. Campbell, 10.
Forgotten souls, David Pinski, 100.
Fortune heights, John Dos Passos, 129.
The Fortune teller, Victor Sejour, 105.
Four of a kind, William McNally, 160.
Four mystery plays, Rudolph Steiner, 107.
Four walls, Dana Burnet and George Abbott, 123.
Frank and Mr. Frankenstein, A. Kreymborg, 154.
The Fraternal bond, J. M. Caldwell, 124.
Fraternity, Pauline H. Lazaron, 155.
Der Fremde, J. K. Jerome, 85.
Fresh fish and local color, A. L. Kaser, 148.
Friar Bacon, Vaughan Morgan, 166.
Friend Fritz, Émile Erckmann and Alexandre Chatrian, 73.
Friendship, William McNally, 160.
Friendship ceremony, Ethel R. Jasspon and B. Becker, 146.

Le Friquet, Sibylle G. M. A. de R. de Mirabeau, comtesse de Martel de Janville, 91.
From morn to midnight, Georg Kaiser, 147.
From no place to nowhere on the Ha-ha line, William McNally, 160.
The Front page, Ben Hecht and C. G. MacArthur, 142.
"Fruition of an ideal," A. Andrashnik, 117.
The Fruits of culture, graf L. N. Tolstoi, 110.
The Fruits of enlightenment, graf L. N. Tolstoi, 110.
Fun in a school room, H. E. Shelland, 107.
Fun in a vaudeville agency, J. F. Parsons, 169.
Funny Phinnie, Howard Reed, 173.

G

Gabriel Schilling's flight, Gerhart Hauptmann, 81.
A Gallant Jew, S. Major, 34.
Gambetta and Dr. Stresemann, Sir Thomas Barclay, 118.
Gambetta and Monsieur Poincaré, Sir Thomas Barclay, 118.
Gamea, Matilda Heron, 105.
Garlic, William McNally, 160.
Garrick's vagary, David Garrick, 20.
The Gate of the West, Ethel R. Jasspon and B. Becker, 146.
The Gateway of tomorrow, Olive M. Price, 171.
The Gay co-eds, Marie Doran, 129.
La Gazza ladra, conte Tommasso Gherardi del Testa, 33.
Gelta; or, The Czar and the songstress, Nadage Dorée. *See her* Gilta, 71.
Gemea, Edgar Newbound, 105.
General Breakdown, U. S. A., James Madison, 90.
The Generous Jew, Richard Cumberland, 15.
The Gentile wife, Rita Wellman, 185.
Le Gentleman de l'Ohio, G. S. Kaufman, 150.
"Gentlemen prefer blondes," Anita Loos and J. Emerson, 159.
Gentlewoman, J. H. Lawson, 155.
George Washington meets his bicentennial press agent, H. A. Jacobs, 146.
Geraniums in my window, S. B. Ornitz and V. Caspary, 146.
Das Gericht der Templar, J. R. Lenz, 45.
The German Jew, W. H. Tilbury, 51.
Gesellschaft, John Galsworthy, 135.
Get off the track, Forbes Milliken, 165.
Getting a contribution, Jennie Perlstein, 169.
Getting his goat, James Madison, 90.
The Ghetto, Herman Heijermans, 82.
Ghetto get-backs between Cohen and Levi, James Madison, 90.
Ghetto silhouettes, Ezekiel Leavitt, 88.
"The Ghost in the glass," Robert St. Clair, 177.
The Gibson upright, Booth Tarkington and H. L. Wilson, 183.
Gil Blas, William Bates, 9.
Gilded youth, M. J. Heymans, 143.
Gilta, Nadage Dorée, 71.
The Girl from "L triangle" ranch, Frank Dumont, 72.
The Girl who knows how, Redfern Mason, 164.
Give and take, Aaron Hoffman, 143.
Gladstone and the House of Lords, anon., 76.
Glickman the glazier, H. L. Newton and A. S. Hoffman, 96.
Gloomy Fanny, Allan Davis, 67.
Glücks-Vergessene, David Pinski. *See his* Forgotten souls, 100.
Go ahead, Louis Nertz and Armand Friedmann, 167.
The Go-getter, P. B. Kyne, 154.
Goat song, F. V. Werfel, 186.
The Goblin and the princess, Mrs. Isabella (McL.) McMeekin, 160.

The God-intoxicated man, B. M. Greene, 139.
God is one, Milton Marks and others, 91.
The God of the newly rich wool merchant, David Pinski, 170.
The God of vengeance, Shalom Asch, 56.
God's fool, Elma C. E. Levinger, 89.
The Goddess of dancing, A. L. Kaser, 148.
Gods of the lightning, Maxwell Anderson and Harold Hickerson, 117.
Going to the bad, Tom Taylor, 109.
Gold! Charles Reade, 102.
Gold eagle Guy, M. P. Levy, 157.
The Gold in fish, Fannie Hurst, 145.
Goldberg and Silverstein, William McNally, 161.
The Golden days, L. D. Benner, 120.
Golden gifts, Julia K. Nusbaum, 168.
The Golden journey to Samarkand, J. E. Flecker, 75.
The Golden slipper, Mrs. H. H. Rubenovitz. See Kiddush Ha-Shem, Shalom Asch, 117.
The Goldstein wedding, G. M. Rosener, 104.
Goldstein's son, William McNally, 161.
Goldstein's wedding, William McNally, 161.
The Golem, Levick Halper, 140.
The Good fellow, G. S. Kaufman and H. J. Mankiewicz, 151.
Goose money, Mrs. Carl Felton, 132.
Gordon versus Gordon, J. A. Rosenfield, 175.
Gossip, Ethel Frank, 76.
Gott, Mensch und der Teufel, Jacob Gordin, 78.
The Governess, R. B. B. Sheridan, 48.
The Grain of the wood, J. B. MacCarthy, 159.
Grand Hotel, Vicki Baum, 119.
Grandfather's chair, W. P. Eaton, 130.
The Great adventure, Arnold Bennett, 59.
The Great city, Andrew Halliday, 80.
The Great club sandwich inquiry, H. I. Phillips, 170.
The Great deliverance, Israel Goldberg, 137.
The Great freeholder, F. A. Subert, 182.
The Great Gatsby, Owen Davis, 133.
The Great Gatsby, F. S. K. Fitzgerald, 133.
"The Great god Frosh," S. S. Friedman, 135.
The Great hope, Elma C. (E.) Levinger, 156.
The Great libel case, H. E. Shelland, 107.
The Great magoo, Ben Hecht and Gene Fowler, 142.
The Great tragic revival, John Brougham, 62.
The Great umbrella case, F. E. Chase, 64.
Greater than love, C. S. Becker, 119.
Green fields, Perez Hirschbein, 143.
The Greenhorn from Breslau, H. H. Winslow. See Samuel of Posen, G. H. Jessop, 85.
The Grouch, Adela Torrey, 184.
The Growth of a nation, Florence M. Eldridge, 131.
Grumpy, Horace Hodges and T. W. Percyval, 83.
The Guardian of the threshold, Rudolph Steiner, 107.
Guardians, John Tobin. See his The Faro table, 51.
The Guardsman, Ferenc Molnár, 93.
Guggenstein and his "green anchel," Gracia Stayton, 181.
Gumbummer and his class of poopils, A. L. Kaser, 148.
A Gunner in the navy, Frank Dumont, 72.
Gymnazie, Shalom Alechem, pseud., 106.

H

HB., R. B. Peake, 98.
Hadassah on trial, Esther Kottler and Anna Drexler, 153.
Hadassah women go on a spree, Mrs. H. Taylor, 183.
Hadassah's call, Mrs. A. H. Brodie, 123.
Hagar, the outcast Jewess, anon., 95.
Half gods, S. C. Howard, 145.
Haman the bully, J. B. Pincus, 170.
Haman of today, Abraham Burstein and J. Bacher, 124.
Hampstead Heath, Thomas Baker, 8.
The Hand of the potter, Theodore Dreiser, 130.

Hands up, sponges and can openers, A. L. Kaser, 148.
Handy Solomon, R. W. Tag, 108.
Hans Bulow's last puppet, Grace D. Ruthenburg, 176.
Happy new year, Fannie B. Linsky, 158.
A Hard explanation, William McNally, 161.
Hard luck Cohen, Joe Klein, 87.
Harlequin Jack Sheppard; or, All right, my covey, J. C. Foster, 54.
Harlequin Jack Sheppard; or, The blossom of Tyburn Tree, anon., 54.
The Harlot's progress, Theophilus Cibber, 21.
Harold, A. G. Butler, 63.
Hassan: the story of Hassan of Bagdad and how he came to make the golden journey to Samarkand, J. E. Flecker, 134.
Haunch, paunch and jowl, S. B. Ornitz and Donald Davis, 168.
The Haunted inn, Perez Hirschbein, 83.
Have one on me, William McNally, 161.
"Having wonderful time," Arthur Kober, 153.
Haym Salomon, Samuel Shipman and V. Victor. See their The Unwritten chapter, 179.
He got the job, Charlton Andrews, 117.
He and she, I. L. Perez, 98.
He would be a cop, James Madison, 90.
He's Jack Sheppard, J. R. Planché, 54.
Headstrong, Joan, Lillian Mortimer, 166.
Hear both sides, Thomas Holcroft, 22.
The Heart of a child, Mrs. Julia D. Frankau, 76.
The Heart of London, W. T. Moncrieff, 39.
The Heart of Solomon, C. I. Freed, 134.
Hearts are trumps, Cecil Raleigh, 102.
Hearts and stomachs, Ezekiel Leavitt. See his Stomachs and hearts, 88.
The Heathen who stood on one foot, Elma C. (E.) Levinger, 156.
The Hebrew, George Soane, 45.
The Hebrew, C. K. Ulrich, 111.
The Hebrew boy, Mrs. Leckie, 88.
Hebrew monologues, Walter London, 90.
Hector, Maurice Hageman, 80.
Heil Hitler! Louis Walinsky, 185.
An Heir at large, Mrs. Mary (R.) Aldis, 116.
The Heirs of Rabourdin, Émile Zola. See his Les Héritiers Rabourdin, 115.
Hello Zentral! Ella M. Hoyt, 145.
Help wanted, William McNally, 161.
Helping hands, Tom Taylor, 109.
Her busy day, C. E. Quackenbush, 172.
Her shop, Aimee McH. Stuart and Philip Stuart, 182.
Hercules, king of clubs! F. F. Cooper, 11.
Les Héritiers Rabourdin, Émile Zola, 115.
Hero-by-the-hour, Katharine Kavanaugh, 151.
Heroes, old and new, Robert Garvey, 136.
Herzl, Samuel Roth, 176.
Hey! teacher! A. L. Kaser, 148.
Hi times in Judge Sapp's court, A. L. Kaser, 148.
The Hicksville bungler, C. A. Griffin, 139.
The High cost of kissing, William McNally, 161.
The High school freshman, C. K. Ulrich, 111.
Hillbilly courtship, Austin Goetz, 137.
Hinkemann, Ernst Toller. See his Brokenbrow, 183.
The Hired ghost, W. M. Lamers, 154.
His children, Israel Goldberg, 138.
His eyes, Jacob Feinstein, 132.
His favourite flower, Laurence Housman, 144.
His first examination, A. Petrischev, 99.
His Honor Abe Potash, M. M. Glass and J. E. Goodman, 77.
His peers, Paul Eldridge, 131.
Hitlerites and Chanukah lights, S. M. Segal, 178.
Hixville to Hollywood, C. W. Pierce, 170.
Hobbleman, Ernst Toller. See his Brokenbrow, 183.
Hokka chynik, anon., 144.
Holding aloof, David Dainow, 127.
Hollywood holiday, B. W. Levy and John Van Druten, 157.

INDEX OF TITLES 227

Honours easy, Roland Pertwee, 169.
Hooligan at the bat, Franklin Phelps, 170.
Horsepistols and sicknesses, William McNally, 161.
Hot headlines, Bertram Hobbs, 143.
Hot water, E. M. Gibson, 136.
Hotel universe, Philip Barry, 118.
The House of bondage, R. W. Kauffman, 87.
The House of bondage, J. B. Totten, 87.
The House of mirth, Mrs. Edith N. (J.) Wharton and Clyde Fitch, 112.
A House of mourning, Alter Brody, 123.
The House next door, J. H. Manners, 90.
A House to be sold, John Baylis. *See* A House to be sold, James Cobb, 11.
A House to be sold, James Cobb, 11.
The House of Ussher, H. V. Esmond. *See* Jacob Ussher, Naomi E. Jacob, 146.
How home missions came home to Helen, Mrs. Myrtle R. Creasman, 127.
How Mr. Smith dropped the hint, F. O. Anderson, 117.
How Succoth came to Chayim, Elma C. (E.) Levinger, 156.
Howdy stranger, Robert Sloane and L. Pelletier, jr., 180.
Humoresque, Fannie Hurst, 145.
Humphrey Clinker, T. J. Dibdin, 17.
A Hundred years hence, anon., 84.
Hung jury, D. O. Woodbury, 188.
Hurrah for Cheshvan, Joseph Deitch, 129.
Husband, John Corbin, 66.
A Husband for Rachel, Berthe Goudvis, 138.
Hypatia, G. S. Ogilvie, 97.
Hypatia, G. H. Thacher, 110.

I

I am a Jew, S. R. Davenport, 128.
"I am over forty," Madeline Blackmore, 121.
I believe, Emmanuel Levy, 157.
I can't sleep, Clifford Odets, 168.
I object, your honor! Peter Donchian, 129.
I see by the newspapers, William McNally, 161.
I tell you! William McNally, 161.
I–19, Cecilia Razovsky, 173.
Ideals, H. D. Levinson, 157.
The Idle apprentice; or, The two roads of life, anon., 54.
The Idle inn, Louis Wolheim and I. Goldberg, 83.
Idols, Roy Horniman, 89.
Idols, W. J. Locke, 89.
An Idyll of the shops, K. S. Goodman and Ben Hecht, 138.
I'll tell the world, A. L. Kaser, 148.
I'm not complaining, A. Kreymborg, 154.
I'm your friend, James Madison, 90.
Imaginary conversation, anon., 84.
Imaginary conversations, S. W. Wallach, 185.
The Importance of being married, Rachel Crothers, 127.
In an airplane passenger station, A. L. Kaser, 148.
In the balance, Leah Zeve, 189.
In the dark, Perez Hirschbein, 83.
In the delicatessen shop, A. L. Kaser, 148.
In the forest, Louis Lipsky, 89.
In Hades, G. A. Drovin, 71.
In honor of Shakespeare, W. C. Langdon, 154.
In Manchuria, Alfred Savoir, 154.
In memoriam: 1933, Charles Reznikoff, 174.
In the night watches, Elma C. (E.) Levinger, 156.
"In the principal's office," Dora M. Macdonald, 159.
In self-defense only, Leon Joseph, 147.
In der street car, A. L. Kaser, 148.
In thy radiance we see which light, Edith Kane, 147.

In the trenches, F. E. Chase, 64.
In the vernacular, J. P. McEvoy, 159.
The Indian, John Fenwick, 18.
Indigestion, William McNally, 161.
Inez, Walter Malone, 90.
The Informers outwitted, Solomon Bung-your-eye, pseud., 10.
Inkelheim on de telephone, A. L. Kaser, 148.
Der Innocent Drummer, M. B. Curtis. *See* Samuel of Posen, G. H. Jessop, 85.
Inside the great conflict, S. S. Parfenoff, 169.
The Invader, Israel Goldberg, 138.
The Inventor and the king's daughter, David Pinski, 170.
Investigate, anon., 84.
The Invisible girl, T. E. Hook, 22.
Iris, Sir A. W. Pinero, 99.
The Iron cross, Edward Davis, 128.
The Iron door, Allan Davis, 67.
The Iron hand, Charles Townsend, 111.
Irving Lipshits the salesman, William McNally, 161.
Isaac abroad, T. F. Plowman, 45.
Isaac Fikelbaum: trouble laden, A. L. Kaser, 148.
Isaac, he ain't so dumb, Ella M. Hoyt, 145.
Isaac & Rebecca, Frank Harris, 141.
Isaac Sheftel, David Pinski, 101.
Isaac of York, T. F. Plowman, 45.
Isidor Iskovitch presents, G. R. Chester, 125.
Isidore, Samuel of Posen's brother, M. B. Curtis. *See* Samuel of Posen, G. H. Jessop, 85.
Israel, Henry Bernstein, 59.
Israel Bruna, Gotthard Deutsch, 68.
Israel in the kitchen, Noah Elstein, 131.
The Israelites, anon., 23.
The Israelites amid Philistines, T. L. Beddoes. *See his* The second brother, 58.
It can't be done, William McNally, 161.
It is time, Elma C. (E.) Levinger, 156.
It is to laugh, Fannie Hurst. *See her* The Gold in fish, 145.
It vas like dis, A. L. Kaser, 148.
It's the fashion, Kathryn Wayne, 185.
It's a lie, Shalom Alechem, pseud., 106.
It's never too late to mend, Charles Reade, 102.
It's spring, Claudia L. Harris, 141.
Ivanhoe, Benjamin Aymar and J. R. Blake, 42.
Ivanhoe, Samuel Beazley, 42.
Ivanhoe, Muriel Brown, 43.
Ivanhoe, Alfred Bunn, 43.
Ivanhoe, J. W. Cole, 43.
Ivanhoe, F. F. Cooper, 43.
Ivanhoe, R. Cowie, 43.
Ivanhoe, T. J. Dibdin, 43.
Ivanhoe, R. H. Edgar, 43.
Ivanhoé, Jeanne Leroy-Denis, 45.
Ivanhoe, Walter Melville, 44.
Ivanhoe! W. T. Moncrieff, 44.
Ivanhoe, W. H. W. Murray, 44.
Ivanhoe, C. G. Norris, 44.
Ivanhoe, William Palmer, 44.
Ivanhoe, Alfredo Possolo Hogan, 46.
Ivanhoe, Sarah E. Simons and C. I. Orr, 45.
Ivanhoe, Ernest Stevens, 45.
Ivanhoe, Augusta Stevenson, 45.
Ivanhoe, J. R. Sturgis, 45.
Ivanhoe; or, The Jew of York, anon., 44.
Ivanhoe; or, The Saxon chief, anon., 44.
Ivanhoe a la carte, Dalton Stone, 45.
Ivanhoe, in accordance with the spirit of the times, H. J. Byron, 43.
Ivanoff, A. P. Chekhov, 65.
Izzy, Mrs. Trimble Bradley and G. H. Broadhurst, 125.
Izzy's troubles, S. S. Tibbals, 110.
Izzy's vacation, H. L. Newton, 96.
Izzybloom's school of acting, A. L. Kaser, 148.

J

Jack Drum's entertainment, anon., 23.
The Jack in the box, H. T. Decker, 129.
Jack Ketch, George Almar, 53.
Jack Shepherd, J. B. Buckstone, 53.
Jack Sheppard, Owen Davis, 54.
Jack Sheppard, Thomas Greenwood, 53.
Jack Sheppard, J. T. Haines, 54.
Jack Sheppard, Olive Harper, 54.
Jack Sheppard, Joseph Hatton, 54.
Jack Sheppard, W. H. W. Murray, 54.
Jack Sheppard, J. B. Phillips, 54.
Jack Sheppard, R. A. Roberts, 54.
Jack Sheppard, Matt Wilkinson, 54.
Jack Sheppard; or, Newgate routed, W. G. Baker and J. C. Arnold, 54.
Jack Sheppard; or, The progress of crime, W. T. Moncrieff, 54.
Jack Sheppard and his dog, anon., 54.
Jack Sheppard on horseback, anon., 54.
Jacob Ussher, Naomi E. Jacob, 146.
The Jail bird, Charles Townsend, 111.
Jake the candidate, A. L. Kaser, 148.
Jake explains, William McNally, 161.
Jake and his family, A. L. Kaser, 148.
Jake the playwriter, William McNally, 161.
Jake, you are a fake, William McNally, 161.
Jake's social affairs, William McNally, 161.
Jakey Einstein, Charles Baswitz, 58.
Jakey and old Jacob, anon., 84.
Jarnegan, Charles Beahan and G. Fort, 184.
Jarnegan, Jim Tully, 184.
The Jazz singer, Arline De Haas, 172.
The Jazz singer, Samson Raphaelson, 172.
Jedorka (the Jewess), John Clempert, 46.
Jefferson Davis, John McGee, 159.
Jeremiad, Josephine H. Whitehouse, 187.
Jeroosalem, Mildred P. Merryman, 165.
Jerry Ledrew; or, The American Jack Sheppard, J. F. Poole, 54.
The Jerusalem infirmary, anon., 23.
The Jew, anon., 24.
The Jew, Richard Cumberland, 14.
The Jew, Karl Spindler, 50.
The Jew of Arragon, Thomas Wade, 52.
The Jew decoy'd, anon., 21.
The Jew doctor, Catherine Swanwick, 108.
The Jew and the doctor, T. J. Dibdin, 17.
Jew Dyte, H. F. Rubinstein, 176.
The Jew of Lubeck, H. M. Milner, 39.
The Jew of Malta, Christopher Marlowe, 34.
The Jew of Mogadore, Richard Cumberland, 16.
The Jew of Prague, A. W. Barrett, 57.
The Jew of Southwark, Edward Stirling. See his The Mendicant's son! 108.
Jew Süss, Ernest Betts, 133.
Jew Süss, Ashley Dukes, 133.
The Jew of Venice, George Granville, baron Lansdowne, 27.
A Jew visits America A.C.E. 2000, Elsa Weihl, 185.
The Jew of Zemplin, P. H. Calmus, 64.
The Jew's daughter, Edward Stirling, 107.
The Jew's fiddle, H. R. Hayward and A. Rish, 142.
A Jew's use for riches, B. W. Procter, 102.
"The Jewels of God," S. S. Grossman, 79.
The Jewess, Watkins Burroughs, 46.
The Jewess, T. H. Lacy, 46.
The Jewess, W. T. Moncrieff, 46.
The Jewess, J. R. Planché, 46.
The Jewess, McKee Rankin and M. Ludovici, 95.
The Jewess, or, The cardinal's daughter, anon., 46.
Jewess of Spain, Sigmund Herzberg. See The Vale of cedars, Grace Aguilar, 53.
The Jewess of Toledo, Franz Grillparzer, 79.
Jewish conversion, P. P. Pasquin, 41.
The Jewish gentleman, Richard Brome, 9.
The Jewish King Lear, Jacob Gordin, 78.
Jewish missionaries, L. H. Levin, 89.
Jewish provincialism in a growing community, Isidor Cohen, 126.
The Jewish saleslady, Kathryn Snyder, 180.
A Jewish tragedy, Baruch Bernard, 120.
"The Jewish women in America," Mrs. H. A. Friedman, 135.
A Jewish word, W. M. Blatt, 121.
The Jews, Y. N. Chirikov, 65.
The Jews, G. E. Lessing, 27.
The Jews of Hodos, Sandor Martinescu, 164.
Jews in Russia, Y. N. Chirikov. See his The Chosen people, 65.
The Jews who stood by Washington, Edith (L.) Calisch, 124.
Jigsaw skit for senior-junior meeting, Hadassah. — Columbus, Ohio, Chapter, 140.
Jim Bludsoe; or, Bohemians and detectives, Milton Nobles. See his The Phœnix, 96.
Johnny Johnson, Paul Green, 139.
Jolly brothers, Abraham Reisen. See his Brothers, 103.
Jonathan Wild, C. S. James, 54.
Jonathan Wild, Henry Young, 54.
Jonathan Wild; or, The storm on the Thames, Mrs. H. Young, 54.
Jonathas the Jew (miracle play), 24.
Jonesy, Anne Morrison and J. P. Toohey, 166.
Jootenant Levinski up for court martial, A. L. Kaser, 148.
Joseph and his brethren, anon., 86.
The Journalists, Gustav Freytag, 76.
The Joust, H. D. Estabrook, 43.
Juarez and Maximilian, F. V. Werfel, 186.
The Jubilee, David Garrick, 20.
Jubilee, Henry and A. S. Mayhew, 92.
Der Jud Menachem, Richard Cumberland, 15.
Jud Süss, Lion Feuchtwanger, 132.
Judah, H. A. Jones, 86.
Judah's new deliverer, Rebekah B. Hoffman, 144.
Der Jude, Richard Cumberland, 15.
Der Jude von Malta, Christopher Marlowe, 35.
Judge Applesauce presides, Franklin Phelps, 170.
Judith, S. A. Mills, 92.
Le Juif bienfaisant, Pierre Laujon, 15.
Le Juif de Malte, Christopher Marlowe, 35.
Le Juif polonais, Émile Erckmann and Alexandre Chatrian, 73.
La Juive, A. E. Scribe, 46.
Julia, Robert Jephson, 23.
June moon, R. W. Lardner and G. S. Kaufman, 155.
Junior sees it through, H. L. McNary, 163.
The Jury of our peers, E. H. Peple, 169.
Just friends, William McNally, 161.
Just pals, Charles George, 136.
Just the same, William McNally, 161.

K

Keeping a wife, William McNally, 161.
Kibitzer, Joseph Swerling and E. G. Robinson, 182.
Kiddush Ha-Shem, Shalom Asch, 117.
Kind lady, Edward Chodorov, 125.
The King of kings, John Sorsky, 180.
The King of the schnorrers, Israel Zangwill, 114.
The King's English, Herbert Bates, 119.
The King's Jewry, Halcott Glover, 137.
Kislev, J. A. Gorsky, 138.
Knights of the mist, anon., 54.
A Knock at the door, C. I. Freed, 82.
The Kreutzer sonata, Jacob Gordin, 78.

INDEX OF TITLES

L

The Labor government of Palestine, Mosheh Rabinowitz, pseud., 172.
The "Ladies from Friday" in a Turkish bath, Mary Cecil, 124.
The Lady of Belmont, St. John G. Ervine, 131.
Lady Cristilinda, Monckton Hoffe. See his Cristilinda, 143.
Lady Frederick, W. S. Maugham, 91.
The Lady minstrels from Dixie, A. L. Kaser, 148.
Lady Penelope, Morley Roberts, 103.
Lady of the rose, M. A. Flavin, 134.
Lady Teazle, J. K. Bangs and R. C. Penfield. See The School for scandal, R. B. B. Sheridan, 48.
The Lady or the tiger, E. L. Gamble, 136.
Lah-y' shaw-riem tehilaw, M. H. Luzzatto, 31.
Laid off, David Pinski, 170.
A Lamb among wolves, Daisy M. Vance, 70.
The Land of the Aleph Bes, S. S. Grossman, 140.
Land sharks and sea gulls, W. N. Glascock, 77.
A Landlord and his tenants, L. L. Levegood, 155.
Landsleit, I. D. Berkowitz, 120.
Landsleit, J. N. E. One, pseud., 168.
The Last day! W. B. Nelson, 167.
The Last edition of Ivanhoe, R. B. and W. Brough, 43.
The Last Gepuire, C. A. Wood, 188.
The Last hour, Charles Bennett, 120.
The Last Jew, David Pinski, 101.
The Last round-up, anon., 155.
Last tag! Lida Larrimore, 155.
The Last will, Corinne R. Moment, 166.
The Last word, Augustin Daly, 66.
The Late Christopher Bean, S. C. Howard, 132.
The Late Christopher Bean, Emlyn Williams, 132.
Late star final, Louis Weitzenkorn. See his Five star final, 185.
Laura Dibalzo, R. H. Horne, 84.
The Lawyer, the Jew and the Yorkshireman, T. J. Dibdin. See his The School for prejudice, 17.
Lawyer's clerks, Tom Taylor. See his Our clerks, 109.
Leah, E. W. Price, 95.
Leah the forsaken, Augustin Daly, 94.
Leah the forsaken, Teresa S. Toube, 95.
Leah the forsook, anon. See Leah the forsaken, Augustin Daly, 94.
Leah the forsook, Frank Wood, 95.
Leah, a hearty joke in a cab age, William Routledge, 95.
Leah, the Jew's daughter, anon. See Leah the forsaken, Augustin Daly, 94.
Leah and Nathan, John Courtney, 94.
The Left bank, E. L. Rice, 174.
Leila, E. G. E. L. Bulwer-Lytton, 1st baron Lytton, 63.
Leila, W. R. Wallace, 63.
Leonora, Julia (W.) Howe. See her The World's own, 84.
"Lest we forget," Tamar (H.) Pool, 171.
Let down the bars, Elsa Weihl, 185.
Let 'em eat cake, G. S. Kaufman and Morrie Ryskind, 151.
"Let there be light," Elma C. (E.) Levinger, 156.
Let's do acting? William McNally, 161.
Letty, Sir A. W. Pinero, 100.
Letty Pepper, Oliver Morosco and G. V. Hobart. See Maggie Pepper, Charles Klein, 87.
Levi in the baggage room, A. L. Kaser, 148.
Levi Beginski telephones, A. L. Kaser, 148.
Levi and Cohn, William McNally, 161.
Levi goes a-hunting, A. L. Kaser, 148.
Levi's troubles, A. L. Kaser, 149.
Levi's view on marriage, A. L. Kaser, 149.
Levinsky and daughter, William McNally, 161.
Levinsky and son, William McNally, 161.
"Liars!" Shalom Alechem, pseud., 106.

Liberal opinions, T. J. Dibdin. See his The School for prejudice, 17.
The Liberty bell, Rita Benton, 120.
Life as it ain't, Mrs. Margaret C. (G.) Parsons, 169.
Life begins anew, Mrs. Rose Goldman, 138.
Life of Columbus, W. L. Miller, 92.
The Life and death of Jack Sheppard, anon., 54.
Life of William Henry Perkin, Mobile, Ala. — Murphy High School: Modern Alchemists' Club, 165.
The Life of a woman, J. T. Haines, 21.
Light, Mildred Barish, 118.
The Light, the coin and the feast, S. M. Segal, 178.
The Light of the East, Louis Arundel, 117.
The Light of the world, G. R. Bolton and George Middleton, 122.
Like Lincoln, anon., 158.
Like mother made, Winchell Smith and J. E. Hazzard. See their Turn to the right, 180.
Liliom, Ferenc Molnár, 93.
Lincoln and his Jewish chiropodist, John Davis, 128.
A Literary reception, Mary E. Kitchel, 87.
The Little boss, F. L. Bixby, 60.
Little heroes, David Pinski, 170.
The Little hunch-back, John O'Keeffe, 40.
Little Jack Sheppard, H. P. Stephens and W. Yardley, 54.
A Little journey, Rachel Crothers, 127.
A Little learning, Nancy B. Brosius, 123.
The Little red school house, H. L. Newton, 96.
Le Locataire du troisième sur la cour, J. K. Jerome, 85.
Lombardi, Ltd., Frederic Hatton and Mrs. F. C. L. Hatton, 142.
London assurance, Dion Boucicault, 61.
The London hermit, John O'Keeffe, 40.
London life, Arnold Bennett and Edward Knoblock, 120.
Lone worlds! Perez Hirschbein, 83.
Lookin' lovely, Janice Gard, 136.
The Loop, Florence (R.) Clements and C. C. Clements, 125.
Loose nuts, A. L. Kaser, 149.
Lost in a pullman, William McNally, 161.
The Lottery of life, John Brougham, 62.
Love a-la-mode, Charles Macklin, 31–32.
Love at second sight, F. J. Morris, 166.
Love cannot make the dead dance, Mrs. Lea L. Romonek, 175.
Love in the deeps, Anna G. Abelson, 116.
Love laughs at locksmiths, George Colman, the younger, 9.
The Love life of Irene, G. F. Curtis, 127.
Love and lovers, Mrs. Virginie D. (H.-) Vogl, 111.
Love and money, William McNally, 161.
Love triumphant, John Dryden, 18.
Lovers' vows, A. F. F. von Kotzebue, 26.
Lowing in the night, Alter Brody, 123.
Loyalität, John Galsworthy, 135.
Loyalties, John Galsworthy, 135.
Loyautés, John Galsworthy, 135.
Luke the labourer, J. B. Buckstone, 10.
The Luminary, S. J. Citron, 125.
Lundi huit heures, G. S. Kaufman and Edna Ferber, 151.
La Lutte pour la vie, Alphonse Daudet, 66.
Lydia, William Pace, 41.
Lynggaard & Co., Hjalmar Bergstrøm, 59.

M

The Mad Hopes, Romney Brent, 122.
Madam the boss, R. J. Sherman, 179.
Madame Sand, Philip Moeller, 166.
Maggie Pepper, Charles Klein, 87.
The Magic circle, Elma C. (E.) Levinger, 156.
Magnolia street, Louis Golding, 138.

The Magpie, anon., 33.
The Magpie, or the maid? Isaac Pocock, 33.
Mahmud the Sultan, Sivori Levey, 89.
The Maid of Judah, M. R. Lacy, 44.
The Maid and the magpie, anon., 33.
The Maid and the magpie, H. J. Byron, 33.
The Maid and the magpie, Nelson Lee, 33.
The Maid and the magpie; or, Harlequin and the magic spoon, C. S. Jones. See Trial without jury, J. H. Payne, 33.
The Maid and the magpye, S. J. Arnold, 32.
The Maid of Mariendorpt, J. S. Knowles, 87.
The Maker of souls, Faith Van V. Vilas, 184.
Making Rosie a cook, Francesca F. Miller, 165.
Malvina, George Macfarren, 31.
The Man with a cane, Geoffrey Dearmer, 129.
The Man of labor, Mosheh Rabinowitz, pseud., 172.
A Man of the people, Thomas Dixon, 129.
The Man with the puckel, Bertram Jacobs, 146.
The Man on stilts, E. L. Barker and A. Barker, 118.
Man and superman, Bernard Shaw, 107.
The Man tamer, George Davage, 128.
The Man who ate the popomack, W. J. R. Turner, 184.
The Man who begat six daughters, Jacolyn Manning, 163.
The Man who was Thursday, Ada E. (J.) Chesterton and Ralph Neale, 125.
Man and wife, George Colman, the elder, 11.
The Man without a necktie, Mrs. Erminia (A.) Hauser, 142.
Man and woman, H. C. De Mille and David Belasco. See their "Men and women," 67.
Manasse, Ronetti Roman, 104.
A Manhattan honeymoon, Lillian Mortimer, 166.
"Marathon," Isabel Dawn and B. De Gaw, 128.
The March on London, anon., 91.
March of stirring events in founding of Republic, anon., 164.
Le Marchand de Paris, Edmond Fleg, 134.
Maria and Magdalena, Paul Lindau, 89.
The Mariner's dream, C. Z. Barnett, 57.
The Marriage certificate, Anna Wolfrom, 188.
Marriage and other gambles, William McNally, 161.
Mary Tudor, V. M., comte Hugo, 22–23.
Mary's John, Harold Brighouse, 122.
Mashel uMelitzah, M. L. Malbim, 90.
The Masque of flowers, anon., 37.
The Masque of the new land, S. S. Grossman, 140.
The Masque of Venice, G. D. Gribble, 139.
The Masquerade, Robert Hilliard, 143.
The Masterpiece, George Benedict, 58.
Match-making in a tavern, Alberto Romano, 175.
"Matches," David Liebovitz, 158.
The Matchmakers, Esther Morris, 166.
The Matriarch, Gladys B. (S.) Holdsworth, 144.
Matrimonial harmony, William McNally, 161.
Mayer and son, Thomas Addison, 110.
Meet the wife, William McNally, 161.
The Melting pot, Lucile B. Berry, 120.
The Melting pot, L. H. Levin, 89.
The Melting pot, Israel Zangwill, 114.
The Melting pot minstrel, Flora C. Gardner and M. F. Gardner, 136.
Men in white, Sidney Kingsley, 152.
"Men and women," H. C. De Mille and David Belasco, 67.
Mendel, Inc., David Freedman. See his Mendel Marantz, 134.
Mendel Marantz, David Freedman, 134.
The Mendicant's son! Edward Stirling, 108.
Mensch und Übermensch, Bernard Shaw, 107.
The Merchant of Venice, Alice Gould, 138.
The Merchant of Venice: act vi, O. F. Adams, 53.
Merchant of Venice by William Shakespeare, C. S. Miner and others, 92.

Merchant of Venice preserved, Francis Talfourd. See his Shylock, 108.
The Merchant of Venice travestie, Francis Talfourd, 108.
Merrily we roll along, G. S. Kaufman and Moss Hart, 151.
The Merry merchant of Venice, F. J. Fraser, 76.
Merton of the movies, G. S. Kaufman and M. C. Connelly, 150.
Messiah, M. A. Eber, 130.
A Messiah, Michael Field, pseud., 75.
The Messiah people, Alter Abelson, 116.
The Meturgeman, Henry Rabinowitz, 172.
Meyer & son, Dwight Tilton, pseud., 110.
Michael and Mary, A. A. Milne, 165.
Middletown, E. L. Barker and A. Barker, 118.
The Midwinter night's dreams, L. McK. Turner, 184.
Migdol Oz, M. H. Luzzatto, 31.
The "Mind the paint" girl, Sir A. W. Pinero, 100.
Mine daughter, Rebecca, William McNally, 161.
Mine eyes have seen, Alice R. (M.) Dunbar, 130.
Mine family, William McNally, 161.
Mine fat vife's poor husband, Forbes Milliken, 165.
Mine friend, Levi Cohen, A. L. Kaser, 149.
Mine frient, Morris, A. L. Kaser, 149.
Mine gracious! A. L. Kaser, 149.
Minutes of the jolly twelve, C. S. Spritz, 181.
The Miracle of Lodz, I. Hipshon, 143.
"The Miracle of the scrolls," L. I. Newman, 167.
Miracle at Verdun, Hans Chlumberg, 125.
Miriam, B. A. Lomas, 158.
The Miser's daughter, J. G. Millingen, 39.
The Mishpat, Mosheh Rabinowitz, pseud., 172.
Miss Lucy in town, Henry Fielding, 18.
Miss Ruddy cashes in, Bernice Hardy, 141.
Mr. Benjamin Disraeli and Viscount Palmerston, anon., 92.
Mr. Edmund Gosse entertains on the occasion of his seventieth birthday, Samuel Roth, 176.
Mr. Gladstone, H. R. Williamson, 188.
Mr. Isaacstein at the telephone, anon., 165.
Mr. Man, L. Miller, 165.
Mr. Mishkowsky und de "younk leddy," Gracia Stayton, 181.
Mister Noah, F. G. Brown, 123.
Mr. Samuel, Winthrop Ames, 134.
Mrs. Cohen at the amusement park, Ruth Tatroe, 183.
Mrs. Cohen and her neighbors, Jimmy Lyons, 159.
Mrs. Dinkelspiel and the P. T. A., Gracia Stayton, 181.
Mrs. Feitlebaum and ward C, L. H. Dembo, 129.
Mrs. Goldblitz on matrimony, F. G. Johnson, 147.
Mrs. Schnickelfritz und der four o'clock train, Gracia Stayton, 181.
Mrs. Schnickelfritz und der visecrackers, Gracia Stayton, 181.
Mrs. Schuster on the radio, Ceora B. Lanham, 155.
Mrs. Witch: a Whitechapel episode, Nevin Halys, 140.
Mock trial of the great kidnapping and breach of promise case, Frank Dumont, 72.
Model Trilby, C. H. E. Brookfield and W. Yardley, 71.
A Modern Esther, H. A. Harrison, 141.
The Monastery of St. Just, J. F. C. Delavigne, 6.
Monday morning in Maloney's court, A. L. Kaser, 149.
Monday morning on "Thoid" avenue, Bernice Hardy, 141.
Money, Michael Gold, 137.
Money in the bank, Mrs. Bessie (F.) White, 187.
Money the mistress, Thomas Southerne, 50.
Money talks, Hadassah. — Minneapolis Junior Section, 140.
Monsieur Poirier's son-in-law, G. V. E. Augier and Jules Sandeau, 56.

INDEX OF TITLES 231

Monte-Christo, Jr., R. W. Butler and H. C. Newton, 71.
Monte-Cristo, Alexandre Dumas, the elder, 71.
Monte Cristo, B. N. Webster, 71.
Moonshine and honeysuckle, Lula Vollmer, 185.
The Moorish page, H. M. Milner. *See* Chantilly, 10.
More money than brains, P. P. Hall, 140.
More tribulations of Cohen & Levi, James Madison, 90.
Morris and his troubles, Don Sheridan, 178.
Mortara, H. M. Moos, 93.
Moses Maimonides, Nathan Brilliant and L. L. Braverman, 122.
Mother of exiles, Mildred W. Kreimer, 153.
Mother and son, Jonathan Halpern, 80.
The Mothers, Georg Hirschfeld, 83.
Much ado about a merchant of Venice, John Brougham, 62.
Mumbo jumbo, Henry Clews, jr., 125.
Murder in the ferris-wheel, Charles George, 136.
The Murder of the mount; or, Whitechapel, in 1740, anon. *See* The Skeleton witness, W. L. Rede, 42.
The Murder of the night-club crooner, Elizabeth Cobb and Margaret C. Morgan, 126.
Musa Ibn Maimon, Lisa Y. Tarleau, 183.
Music for musicians, Irving Cohen, 126.
Musical eggs, A. L. Kaser, 149.
My boy's wedding, William McNally, 161.
My friend, Goldstein, William McNally, 161.
My noble son-in-law, G. V. E. Augier and Jules Sandeau. *See their* Monsieur Poirier's son-in-law, 56.
My wife, William McNally, 161.
My wife's in-laws, William McNally, 161.

N

The Nabob, Samuel Foote, 19.
Nancy Sikes, Cyril Searle, 70.
Naomie, the Jewish maiden, anon., 95.
Napoleon Buonaparte's invasion of Russia, J. H. Amherst, 8.
Nathan the Wise, G. E. Lessing, 28–29.
Nathaniel Baddeley, bookman, Dorothy U. (C.) Ratcliffe, 173.
A Nation's gratitude, I. M. Bloom, 121.
The Natural son, A. F. F. von Kotzebue, 26.
Neither's the man, Mrs. Margaret W. Holford, 22.
The Net, J. S. Alderman, 116.
Das Neue Ghetto, Theodor Herzl, 82.
Der Neue Shylock, H. G. Scheffauer, 104.
Never too late to mend, C. H. Hazlewood, 102.
Never too late to mend, Cyril Searle. *See* Never too late to mend, C. H. Hazlewood, 102.
The New apostacy, Jessie E. Sampter, 177.
The New female custom inspector, William McNally, 162.
The New generation, J. M. Meirovitz, 164.
New ghetto, M. J. Landa, 82.
New lamps and old, Oscar Leonard, 104.
A New prologue in heaven, Jacob Gordin, 78.
The New School for scandal, Philip Johnson and H. Agg, 49.
Night, Shalom Asch, 56.
The Night before the morning, William McNally, 162.
The Night of the eighth candle, Cecile Alexander, 116.
Night hostess, P. H. Dunning, 130.
The Night riders, Frank Dumont, 72, 130.
Nina Balatka, T. W. Harding, 81.
1918, Lion Feuchtwanger, 133.
Ninetta, Edward Fitzbal, 33.
No money to guide her, Romney Brent. *See his* The Mad Hopes, 122.
The Nonsense school, A. L. Kaser, 149.
Noodle soup and appetites, William McNally, 162.
A Nose for news, H. P. Powell, 171.
Not needed, L. H. Levin, 89.
The Note of hand, Richard Cumberland, 16.
Nothing ever happens, Ross Farquhar, 132.

O

Object: matrimony, M. M. Glass, 77.
Object: matrimony, A. L. Kaser, 149.
Œdipus tyrannus, P. B. Shelley, 47.
Of an early morning, I. L. Perez, 98.
Of thee I sing, G. S. Kaufman and Morrie Ryskind, 151.
Official announcement, Eleanor Elder, 131.
Oh! lady, lady! William McNally, 162.
"Oh, look!" Joseph McCarthy. *See* "Ready money," James Montgomery, 93.
Oh! Polly! William McNally, 162.
Oh, teacher! J. J. Coghlan, 126.
Oi, such a family! W. M. Blatt, 121.
Oi, such a nice vidow voman! A. L. Kaser, 149.
Oi, vhat a bargain, E. L. Gamble, 136.
Oi, vot a business! E. L. Gamble, 136.
Oil for the lamps of Israel, S. J. Levinson, 157.
The (Old Clothes) Merchant of Venice, anon., 97.
The Old country store, E. W. Bradley and J. R. Reeves, 122.
Old Isaacs from the Bowery, C. E. Blaney, 60.
An Old Jew, Sydney Grundy, 79.
"An Old Jew," W. R. W., 79.
Old London, John Oxenford, 54.
Old London Bridge in the days of Jack Sheppard and Jonathan Wild, Arthur Shirley and W. M. Tilson, 54.
The Old New Hampshire home, Frank Dumont, 72.
An Old offender, J. R. Planché, 101.
The Old order, Edith S. Beck, 119.
The Old order, Sara Neuman, 167.
Old scenes restaged. "Macbeth," anon., 168.
An Old score, Sir W. S. Gilbert, 76.
Oliver Twist, George Almar, 68.
Oliver Twist, C. Z. Barnett, 68.
Oliver Twist, Oswald Brand, 68.
Oliver Twist, C. E. Callahan, 68.
Oliver Twist, J. W. C. Carr, 68.
Oliver Twist, George Collingham, 69.
Oliver Twist, J. S. Coyne, 69.
Oliver Twist, Walter Dexter and F. T. Harry, 69.
Oliver Twist, Charles Dickens, 68.
Oliver Twist, G. H. Doughty, 69.
Oliver Twist, A. H. Ford, 69.
Oliver Twist, J. B. Johnstone, 69.
Oliver Twist, John Mordaunt, 69.
Oliver Twist, W. H. W. Murray, 69.
Oliver Twist, John Oxenford, 69.
Oliver Twist, John Ravold, 69.
Oliver Twist, M. G. Robinson, 69.
Oliver Twist, W. H. Skeen, 70.
Oliver Twist, Edward Stirling, 70.
Oliver Twist, H. Whyte and R. Balmain, 70.
Oliver Twist in Fagin's den, Guy Pertwee, 69.
Oliver twisted, Wal. Pink, 69.
Omar and the rabbi, F. L. Sargent, 104.
On the banks of the river Styx, Florence Howard, 145.
On the eve, Leopold Kampf, 86.
On the jury, Laura M. Williams, 188.
On the P. D. Q., A. L. Kaser, 149.
On the sight-seeing car, E. M. Gould, 79, 138.
On the threshold, Perez Hirschbein, 143.
On vit de dance, Bob Crawford, 127.
Once in a lifetime, Moss Hart and G. S. Kaufman, 141.
One of the bravest, E. V. I. Abeles, 116.
One Chanukah morning, S. M. Segal, 178.
One Chanukah night, S. M. Segal, 178.
One evening at Nero's, A. J. Talbot, 183.
One good turn, John Kyte, 154.
One on Inkel, A. L. Kaser, 149.
One swaller, one dollar, A. L. Kaser, 149.
The Only language, L. H. Levin, 89.
The Only way, C. E. Quackenbush, 172.
Open house, J. P. Heald, 142.
Orval; or, The Fool of time, Earl of Lytton. *See* The Undivine comedy, Zygmunt Krasiński, 26.

Osman Pasha, W. J. Rapp, 172.
Ost-Jude, S. J. Citron, 125.
Oulita, the serf, Sir Arthur Helps, 82.
Our charge to the jury, anon., 97.
Our clerks, Tom Taylor, 109.
Our Hebrew friends, G. H. Jessop. See his Samuel of Posen, 86.
Our intelligence bureaus, anon., 97.
Our jurymen, anon., 97.
Our Mrs. McChesney, G. V. Hobart and Edna Ferber, 75.
Our own beloved America, Mrs. W. B. Dingman, 70.
Our relief societies, anon., 97.
Our telephones, anon., 97.
Outlaws of life, Arthur Symons, 182.
The Outsider, Dorothy Brandon, 122.
Over the big puddle, A. L. Kaser, 149.
"Over the counter," William McNally, 162.
The Overland journey to Constantinople, R. B. Brough, 62.
Overture, William Bolitho, 121.
Oy! Oy! und den some, A. L. Kaser, 149.

P

A Pageant, R. G. Osterweis, 169.
Pageant of ancient civilization, Eureka High School, Eureka, Cal. — History Class, 132.
A Pageant dedicated to the women of Israel throughout the ages, Dora Askowith, 118.
A Pageant and masque for the Shakespeare Tercentenary, Armond Carroll, 124.
A Pageant of the strong, M. V. Samuels, 177.
Paging John Smith, Claudia L. Harris, 141.
A Pain in de head, A. L. Kaser, 149.
The Painted lady, Monckton Hoffe. See his Cristilinda, 143.
The Painter of Ghent, D. W. Jerrold, 23.
Palestine versus Diaspora, Maurice Cornfield, 126.
Papa and Isaac, William McNally, 162.
Paradise lost, Clifford Odets, 168.
Parents, Falk Heilperin, 82.
Paris and pleasure, Charles Selby, 106.
Park Avenue, A. L. Music, 166.
Le Partage de la Pologne, Theophilus Lindsey, 31.
The Partition of the Homentasch, Ben Aronin, 117.
Partners again, M. M. Glass and J. E. Goodman, 77.
The Passing of the bill, Shiel, 50.
The Passing present, Gretchen Damrosch, 128.
The Passing of the third floor back, J. K. Jerome, 85.
Passport, Henry and A. S. Mayhew, 92.
Passport, Mrs. Lea L. Romonek, 175.
Past, present, and future, Mrs. Re H. Henry, 82.
Paths of glory, S. C. Howard, 145.
Patriots, J. H. B., 57.
Patter versus Clatter, C. J. Mathews, 91.
Paul and Joseph, Howard Swan, 108.
Paul robs Peter! Rica B. Taylor, 183.
Paul Zegers, F. C. Burnand, 74.
Pawnshop Granny, Pauline Phelps, 170.
"Payable on demand," Tom Taylor, 109.
The Peace Conference, C. V. White, 112.
Peace manoeuvres, R. H. Davis, 67.
The Peace party, Mabel H. Meyer, 165.
Peace: the twenty years, Milton Klonsky and T. Branfman, 153.
Peck vs. Peck, C. S. Bird, 60.
The Peddler of Very Nice, G. M. Baker, 57.
The Pedler, F. G. Lanham, 155.
The Pedlers' parade, Jessie A. Kelley, 87.
Peeping Tom of Coventry, John O'Keeffe, 41.
"Pen," H. A. Vachell, 103.
Pennies do add up, Mamie G. Gamoran, 136.
Penrod, E. E. Rose, 175.
Perils of a great city, Charles Townsend, 111.
The Perils of Pauline, anon., 169.

Permanent values, anon., 169.
Petruchio's widow, G. M. Vickers, 111.
Philomel, H. T. Craven, 66.
The Philosophers of Berlin, W. B. Bernard, 59.
The Phœnix, Milton Nobles, 96.
The Phonograph, David Pinski, 171.
The Picture of Dorian Gray, Marion M. Miller, 112.
The Picture of Dorian Gray, Oscar Wilde, 112.
The Piker, Leon Gordon and R. A. Palmer, 138.
The Pilgrim from Palestine, George Soane. See his The Hebrew, 45.
Pilgrims to Palestine, Elma C. (E.) Levinger, 156.
"Pioneers," Rose D. Weinberg, 185.
The Pit, Frank Norris, 96.
Place aux dames, anon., 101.
Plant in the sun, Ben Bengal, 120.
A Play, Harry Sackler, 176.
The Play of the sacrament (miracle play), 24.
The Play's the thing, Ferenc Molnár, 166.
Playing with fire, Ferenc Molnár. See his The Guardsman, 93.
The "Pleasures" of the Czar, Ezekiel Leavitt, 88.
Pledging dad, Harold Riegelman, 175.
Poetry and prose, Zebullon Levin, 156.
Poland — 1919, David Pinski, 171.
Poldekin, Booth Tarkington, 183.
The Polish Jew, S. Emery, 74.
The Polish Jew, Émile Erckmann and Alexandre Chatrian, 73.
The Polish Jew, J. R. Ware, 74.
The Polish partition, Theophilus Lindsey, 30.
Polishing papa, Clark Willard, 188.
Political promises, E. M. Peixotto, 169.
Politics on a dry platform, William McNally, 162.
Pollock's characters & scenes in Oliver Twist, 69.
Polly at the circus, Margaret Mayo, 92.
Polly preferred, G. R. Bolton, 121.
Poor Izzy! A. L. Kaser, 149.
The Poor student, Elma C. (E.) Levinger, 156.
Poppa, Bella (S.) Spewack and Samuel Spewack, 181.
The Portal of initiation, Rudolph Steiner, 107.
Portia pulls a pinch play, Robert Farquhar, 132.
The Postman always rings twice, J. M. Cain, 124.
Potash and Perlmutter, M. M. Glass, 77.
Potash and Perlmutter, detectives, M. M. Glass and J. E. Goodman, 77.
Potash and Perlmutter in society, M. M. Glass and R. C. Megrue, 78.
A Pound of flesh, T. J. Geraghty, 136.
Power of the press, Richard Rohman, 175.
The Power of Purim, Irma Kraft, 153.
The Prayers of a people, David Jacobs, 146.
"Preferred stock," Sherman Bower, 122.
Prenez garde à la peinture, R. C. A. Fauchois, 132.
"Preparedness," William McNally, 162.
Present company excepted, M. M. Glass, 137.
A Pretty kettle of fish, James Madison, 163.
The Price of freedom, Naomi (H.) Mitchison and L. E. Gielgud, 165.
The Price of orchids, Winifred Hawkridge, 142.
The Pride of Yasakis, N. F. Holmes, 144.
The Priest people, Elma C. (E.) Levinger, 156.
The Prince d'Aurec, H. L. E. Lavedan, 88.
The Prince of India, Lewis Wallace, 112.
A Prince to order, Frances Homer, 144.
A Prior right, Milton Goldsmith, 138.
Prison thoughts, T. L. Beddoes. See his The Second brother, 58.
The Prisoner, E. B. Cohn. See his Das Reissende Lamm, 126.
Prisoner at war, D. W. Jerrold. See his The Prisoners of war, 85.
The Prisoners of war, D. W. Jerrold, 85.
Processional, J. H. Lawson, 155.
Prof. Dummelhead's class, A. L. Kaser, 149.
Professor Bernhardi, Arthur Schnitzler, 105.
Professor Bolshushki's school, William McNally, 162.

INDEX OF TITLES

"Professor" Getzel, Ezekiel Leavitt, 88.
Professor Mamlock, Friedrich Wolf. See his Doktor Mamlocks Ausweg, 188.
Professor Sniderschmultze's pupils, A. L. Kaser, 149.
Profiteering landlords, William McNally, 162.
The Promised land, Allan Davis, 67.
'The Proselyte,' Carmel H. G. Guest, 80.
Punch's essence of parliament, anon., 102.
Purim carnival in Tel Aviv, Mosheh Rabinowitz, pseud., 172.
The Purim robe, Elma C. (E.) Levinger, 157.
A Purimbridge birthday, Cecile Alexander, 117.
The Pursuit of Peruna, anon., 102.

Q

The Quality of mercy, W. M. Blatt, 121.
The Queen: God bless her! Laurence Housman, 144.
The Queen of spades, Dion Boucicault, 62.
Queen Victoria, David Carb and W. P. Eaton, 124.
The Queen's bracelet, Mrs. Viola (B.) Shore, 179.
A Queer fit, W. M. Clark, 65.
Queer people, Carroll Graham and Garrett Graham, 139.
The Quest, Mrs. H. L. Jackson, 146.
The Quest of youth, Hazel MacKaye, 159.
A Question of honor, M. S. Nordau, 96.
A Quiet morning in the life of any Hadassah chapter president, Mrs. M. P. Epstein, 131.

R

The Rabbi of York, anon., 102.
A Rabbi's son, Ben Aronin and S. M. Blumenfield, 117.
The Rabbi's spell, S. C. Cumberland, 66.
Races, Theodor Tagger, 182.
Rachel Goldstein, Theodor Kremer, 112.
Rachel Goldstein, Grace (M.) White, 112.
Rachel, her Abie and Izzy, A. L. Kaser, 149.
The Racket, Bartlett Cormack, 126.
The Radio dentist, William McNally, 162.
The Raging Tvrke, Thomas Goffe, 20.
Rain from heaven, S. N. Behrman, 119.
Rain insurance, William McNally, 162.
Raisin and almonds, Perez Hirschbein, 143.
Rapunzel, Alter Brody, 123.
Rashi, Charles Reznikoff, 174.
A Ready-made suit, F. E. Chase, 64.
"Ready money," James Montgomery, 93.
Real antiques, E. O. Jones, 147.
Real people, Hazel G. Packscher, 169.
Rebecca, Andrew Halliday, 44.
Rebecca Gratz, Beatrice T. Mantel, 163.
Rebecca and Rowena, Alice Crawford, 43.
Rebecca's beau, William McNally, 162.
A Receipt for 10,000 dollars, W. F. Cattell, 64.
Recess for memorials, Alter Brody, 123.
Red planet, J. L. Balderston and J. E. Hoare, 118.
Red Sefchen, Jessie A. Middleton, 92.
Red snow, Abraham Coralnik, 65.
Red Sunday, H. F. Griffith, 139.
The Refugee, Joseph Krimsky, 154.
The Rehearsal, Joseph Herbach, 82.
Das Reissende Lamm, E. B. Cohn, 126.
The Rescuing angel, Mrs. Clare (B.) Kummer, 154.
The Resting place, Samuel Gordon, 138.
Le Retour de Jérusalem, M. C. Donnay, 70.
The Return, Mary Hevesh, 142.
Return from Jerusalem, Owen Johnson, 71.
Return at sunset, A. B. Shiffrin, 179.
Reunion on Grand Street, W. M. Brown, 123.
Revenge, Annie Yoffa, 189.
Rex et pontifex, Robert Dodsley, 18.

The Rich man of Frankfort, T. H. Reynoldson, 103.
Rich man, poor man, Bertha Y. Burrill, 124.
Ridiculously old-fashioned, Newman Levy, 157.
Right about faces, Howard Reed, 173.
"Riley," H. D. Levinson, 157.
Rinaldo Rinaldini, T. E. Wilks, 52.
The Ringer, Edgar Wallace, 185.
Rip Van Winkle, Esther Fallenberg, 132.
The Rise of the Rotheschildes, C. Z. Barnett, 9.
Rita Coventry, J. L. Street, 182.
Roast beef medium served hot, Edna Ferber, 75.
Robert and Louisa, Grace James, 146.
Rochester, W. T. Moncrieff, 39.
The Rod of Aaron, T. R. Nathan, 167.
The Romance of Buffalo, Josephine W. Wickser, 187.
Room 226, M. Fagin, 132.
"Rooshian" tea, fish-balls and marbles, anon., 175.
Rose of the East Side, Katharine Kavanaugh, 151.
Rose of the Ghetto, E. E. Rose, 175.
Rosenbaum and son, Adolph Dickman, 129.
Rosensky's insurance policy, William McNally, 162.
'Round the world, William McNally, 162.
The Rover, Mrs. Aphra A. Behn, 9.
The Royal family, G. S. Kaufman and Edna Ferber, 151.
Royal favour, Laurence Housman, 145.
The Rummage sale, J. L. Harbour, 140.
The Rummage sale, Jessie A. Kelley, 152.
The Rummage sale, Mrs. Margaret C. (G.) Parsons and Madeleine Pool, 169.
Run queeck, Rosie, Alice Z. Gibbs, 136.
A Russian Sabbath eve, Herman Heijermans. See his Ahasverus, 82.
A Russian Shylock, Michael Zametkin, 113.
Ruth, J. T. Haines, 80.
Ruth, Reginald Moore, 95.
Ruth makes a convert, Mrs. Alice W. Schiffer, 177.

S

Sabbatai Zevi, Shalom Asch, 56.
Sabbath lights, Ida S. Williams, 188.
The Sacrifice, Elsworth Ellis and Everett Ellis, 131.
The Sad jester, Elma C. E. Levinger, 89.
The Safest way, William McNally, 162.
Salesmanship, Jay Casper, 124.
Salma, L. A. Cranmer-Byng, 127.
Salomme and Eleazer, Mrs. Leo, 27.
Samson, Henry Bernstein, 60.
Samuel Brohl and Company, Victor Cherbuliez, 65.
Samuel Ibn-Nagdela, Raymond Dannenbaum, 128.
Samuel of Pilsen, Lester Franklin. See Samuel of Posen, G. H. Jessop, 85.
Samuel of Posen, G. H. Jessop, 85.
Samuel Posen as the drummer on the road, M. B. Curtis. See Samuel of Posen, G. H. Jessop, 85.
Samuel Snickerwitz's Hallowe'en, Kate A. White, 187.
Samuel Wolf, Conrad Hauenstein, 81.
Santa Claus on the air, Effa E. Preston, 171.
Santa Claus and the madonna, H. E. Mansfield, 163.
Santiago, Thomas Bush, 63.
Sarah's birthday gift, Alice Z. Gibbs, 136.
Saturday night, Jacinto Benavente y Martinez, 58.
Save America, Huntington Wilson. See his Stultitia, 113.
Saving the country, Pauline Salant and G. Shadduck, 177.
Saving Judaism, L. H. Levin, 89.
The Saving sign, B. C. D., 127.
Say! don't I know? William McNally, 162.
Say! mister, William McNally, 162.
Says Cohen to Casey, Forbes Milliken, 165.
Scenes from the life of Richard Wagner, J. F. Cooke, 126.

Scenes from "Oliver Twist," Sarah A. Wallace, 70.
Der Schatz, David Pinski. See his The Treasure, 101.
The School at Cantaloupe Center, A. L. Kaser, 149.
School days, Mrs. Alice L. (W.) Chaplin, 124.
School days a la foolish, A. L. Kaser, 149.
The School for prejudice, T. J. Dibdin, 17.
The School for profligacy, E. S. Barrett, 9.
The School for scandal, R. B. B. Sheridan, 48.
The School for scandal; a comedy, anon., 49.
A School for scandal; or, Newspapers, anon., 49.
The School for scandal scandalized, J. P. Kemble. See The School for scandal, R. B. B. Sheridan, 48.
The Schoolboy's nightmare, R. C. Wilson, 113.
Schoolin', Edith Daseking, 128.
Scott of Abbotsford, W. E. Gunn, 140.
Scott's Ivanhoe dramatised for school use, Maud I. Findlay, 43.
The Séance, anon., 105.
The Search, Donnez moi, pseud., 129.
The Second brother, T. L. Beddoes, 58.
Second mortgage, Irwin Shaw, 178.
The Secret life, H. G. Granville-Barker, 139.
The Secret of life, Leon Kobrin, 153.
The Seder, Emily G. Gerson, 136.
The Seer looks at his bride, Harry Sackler, 176.
Self immolation, A. F. F. von Kotzebue, 25.
Selimus, Robert Greene, 20.
Selma the flirt, William McNally, 162.
Serena Blandish, S. N. Behrman, 120.
Serge Panine, Georges Ohnet, 97.
The Servant girl, Jessie E. Sampter, 177.
Settled, William McNally, 162.
The Sewing of the wedding gown, I. L. Perez, 98.
Shabbas cheer, Fanny Goldstein, 138.
The Shadow of war, S. O. Kuhn, 154.
Shakespeare festival in honor of the poet's birthday, Drama League of America, 71.
Shakespeare in Wall Street, E. H. Warren, 185.
The Shakespeare water-cure, The Larks, pseud., 88.
A Shakespearean fantasy, Mary Hight, 143.
A Shakespearian conference, Pauline Phelps, 99.
The Shannons of Broadway, James Gleason, 137.
The Shattered lamp, Leslie Reade, 173.
She loves me not, B. F. Glazer, 158.
She loves me not, Howard Lindsay, 158.
She must marry a doctor, Shalom Alechem, pseud., 106.
The Shepherd prince, Abraham Mapu, 91.
The Shofar, Louis Lipsky, 89.
Shoot, brother, shoot, A. L. Kaser, 149.
Shop strife, Fred Wright and S. Jonas, 189.
Should we pray in Hebrew or English? anon., 107.
The Show shop, James Forbes, 75.
The Shuttlecock, H. F. Downing, 71.
Shylock, Francis Talfourd, 108.
Shylock, Christian, Louis Untermeyer, 184.
"Shylock returns," F. Jackson, 146.
Shylock's choice, John Cournos, 126.
Shylock's son, Herbert Kirschner, 152.
Siberia, B. T. Campbell, 64.
Siberia, H. C. Kennedy, 64.
A Sidewalk controversy in the Ghetto, Doris M. Kenyon, 152.
The Siege, Joanna Baillie, 8.
The Siege of Algiers, J. S. Smith, 50.
A Silent protector, T. J. Williams, 73.
Simon and Schuster present Show girl, J. P. McEvoy, 159.
Sing high, sing low, Murdock Pemberton and D. Boehm, 169.
The Sinner, Shalom Asch, 56.
The Sinner, I. J. Singer, 179.
Sinners, Mrs. Bessie (F.) White, 187.
Sir Ronald Neville, Bart., R. L. Melville, 164.
The Sisters, I. L. Perez, 99.
The Skeleton witness, W. L. Rede, 42.
Sky-lark, Frank Dumont, 72.
The Slave girl, L. E. Mitchell. See his Deborah, 95.

Slaves in Algiers, Susanna H. Rowson, 42.
Sleigh bells, E. Hoggan-Armadale, 74.
The Sleigh bells, G. F. Rowe, 74.
A Slight misunderstanding, Sir W. W. Strickland, 108.
A Small down payment, George Savage, 177.
The Smile of Mona Lisa, Jacinto Benavente y Martinez, 58.
Smith, W. S. Maugham, 91.
The Snow man, Isaac Horowitz, 144.
Snowball and fair play, Esther Seligman, 178.
The Snowstorm, Perez Hirschbein, 143.
So let 'em foreclose! L. H. Weinstein, 185.
Sob sister, Lillian Saunders, 177.
The Social climbers, Florence R. M. W. O'Brien, 168.
Society, T. W. Robertson, 103.
Sold, Tom Taggart, 182.
The Soldier's progress, John Courtney, 66.
Solomon Levi, Evelyn Simons and O. Burt, 179.
Some class, A. L. Kaser, 149.
Some of my best friends are Gentiles, E. A. Boyd, 122.
Something different, Pearl Black, 121.
A Son of Israel, Sydney Grundy, 79.
A Song unto the Lord, Yossef Gaer, 135.
Sorrows, David Pinski, 101.
The Soul's awakening, Rudolph Steiner, 107.
The Soul's probation, Rudolph Steiner, 107.
Souls in exile, Nathan Horowitz, 144.
Soup to nuts, Austin Goetz, 137.
The South Briton, anon., 50.
South wind, Norman Douglas, 130.
"South wind," Norman Douglas and Isabel C. Tippett, 130.
Souvenir of the family reunion, in honor of Rebekah Kohut, H. J. Kugel, 154.
The Spanish gypsy, George Eliot, 73.
A Special sale, H. L. Newton, 96.
"Spinoza," R. F. Skutch, 180.
Spinoza: the maker of lens, J. A. Gunn, 140.
The Spirit of the American constitution, Gertrude L. Ermatinger and Almira K. Donaldson, 131.
The Spirit of Federation, anon., 181.
The Spirit of Hadassah, Miriam Wolfson, 188.
The Spirit of Judaism, Samuel Schulman and S. Miller, 177.
The Spirit of Massachusetts, Mrs. Esther (C.) Averill and L. A. Averill, 118.
"The Spirit of the South," Esther J. Simon and A. M. Hunter, 179.
The Spite fence, Charles George, 136.
Sport of gods, John Cournos, 127.
Spot cash; or, Samuel of Posen on the road, M. B. Curtis and E. Marble. See Samuel of Posen, G. H. Jessop, 85.
The Spot on the sun, J. H. Turner, 184.
"Spring song," Bella (C.) Spewack and Samuel Spewack, 181.
Squaring the circle, V. P. Katayev, 150.
S'sure as I am alive, William McNally, 162.
Stage door, Edna Ferber and G. S. Kaufman, 132.
The Stagehand and the star, William McNally, 162.
The Stallion, anon., 18.
Stamps and their Jewish interest, J. E. Davidson, 128.
"The Star boarder," William McNally, 162.
Star dust, anon., 181.
Station N-U-T, William McNally, 162.
A Stepdaughter of Israel, Robert Boggs, 60.
The Still small voice, Ida L. Ehrlich, 130.
The Stolen Jewess, C. H. Hazlewood, 81.
The Stolen story, J. L. Williams. See his The Day dreamer, 113.
Stomachs and hearts, Ezekiel Leavitt, 88.
The Stone jug, J. B. Buckstone, 53.
The Story books before the judge, Jeanette Willets, 188.
The Story of the I. L. G. W. U., Florence Lasser, 155.
The Story of the Jew, M. H. Harris, 141.
Stranded strangers, A. L. Kaser, 150.
The Strange melody, B. M. Kaplan, 147.

INDEX OF TITLES 235

The Stranger, Perez Hirschbein, 143.
The Stranger, David Pinski, 101.
Street scene, E. L. Rice, 174.
The Street singers, Frederick Lonsdale, 159.
Strictly private, Margaret T. Applegarth, 117.
Strings, Sophia C. (H.) Wilder, 187.
The Struggle for life, R. W. Buchanan and F. Horner, 67.
Stultitia, Huntington Wilson, 113.
The Subterfuge, M. D. Flattery, 133.
Subway express, Eva K. Flint and M. Madison, 134.
"Success," Isaac Reiss, 174.
Success story, J. H. Lawson, 155.
Such ignorance! F. G. Johnson, 147.
Such a nice doggie, A. L. Kaser, 150.
Such a tightness! A. L. Kaser, 150.
"Such a woman," William McNally, 162.
The Suffering of Nehushta, Binney Gunnison, 80.
Summering at a summer resort, William McNally, 162.
Sunday morning, A. M. Brown, 123.
"Sunday morning's children," H. H. Mashioff, 164.
Sundown, Fannie B. Linsky, 158.
Sunset glow, Adelaide Matthews and L. Sawyer, 164.
Susan Lenox, her fall and rise, D. G. Phillips, 170.
Susskind von Trimberg, O. G. Bender, 120.
Swappers, Boyce Loving, 159.

T

A Tailor-made man, H. J. Smith, 180.
Take heed! Leslie Reade. *See his* The Shattered lamp, 173.
Taking chances, A. E. Wills, 113.
A Tale of Biscay Bay, A. J. Durlacher, 130.
Tales of a wayside inn, Sarah E. Simons and C. I. Orr, 107.
Talking and singing things over, Don Sheridan, 178.
Tancred, Edith S. Nuttall, 58.
Tea at Mrs. Sinsheimer's, G. F. Curtis, 127.
Tecumseh and the prophet of the West, George Jones, 86.
Tell me! William McNally, 162.
Tempelherren og Jødinden, W. A. Wohlbrück, 46.
Temperament, William McNally, 162.
The Templar and the Jewess, J. P. Jackson, 44.
The Temple of Laverna, Arthur Murphy, 40.
Der Templer und die Jüdin, W. A. Wohlbrück, 46.
"Temporal power," Marie Corelli, 66.
The Tenth man, Elma C. (E.) Levinger, 157.
Thanksgiving through the ages, Edna E. Wilson, 188.
That reminds me, H. P. Powell, 171.
That worthless fellow Platanov, A. P. Chekhov, 125.
That's that! William McNally, 162.
Die Theilung von Pohlen, Theophilus Lindsey, 31.
Them actors from Tater Vine, A. L. Kaser, 150.
Theodora: actress and empress, Watts Phillips, 99.
There ain't no Santa Claus, William McNally, 162.
These mortals, H. M. Harwood, 141.
They all come to Moscow, Ruth E. Kennel and J. N. Washburne, 152.
They shall not die, John Wexley, 186.
They went forth, H. F. Rubinstein, 176.
The Thief, Israel Hurwitz, 84.
A Thief in the house, R. M. Robinson, 103.
The Thief maker, Dan Beckett, 68.
Thinking aloud, Urva Porah, pseud., 171.
The Third age, H. D. Traill, 111.
The Third degree, Charles Klein, 87.
Thirteen o'clock, Anthony Thorne, 183.
This house to be sold, J. S. Coyne, 66.
This is New York, R. E. Sherwood, 179.
"This month in history," A. I. Gordon, 138.
This and that, William McNally, 162.
This, that and something else, William McNally, 162.
This way out, William McNally, 162.
Thomas Wendt, Lion Feuchtwanger. *See his* 1918, 133.
Thomaso, Thomas Killigrew, 25.

Thorns and orange blossoms, L. B. Parker, 97.
Those bells, Sidney Rosenfeld, 74.
Three blueskins, anon., 54.
Three girls, Abraham Reisen, 173.
The Three ladies of London, anon., 50–51.
The Three red men, Thomas Archer, 55.
The Three rings, G. E. Lessing, 29.
Three score years and ten, Fannie B. Linsky, 158.
Three sisters, I. L. Perez, 99.
"Three of us," E. R. Meiss, 164.
Three weddings of a hunchback, Henry Borsook, 122.
Thrilby, J. N. Herbert, 71.
"Thrillby," William Muskerry, 71.
A Thriving business, Katharine Kavanaugh, 152.
"Thunder on the left," Raymond Dannenbaum, 128.
The Ticket-of-leave man, Tom Taylor, 109.
The Ticket-of-leave man's wife, C. S. Cheltnam, 65.
Tigers is only cats, Sophie Kerr, 152.
Till the day I die, Clifford Odets, 168.
Tillie Tickletoe, William McNally, 163.
Tips, and more tips, William McNally, 163.
La Tireuse de cartes, Victor Sejour, 105.
To be dealt with accordingly, Mary K. Reely, 173.
To Palestine and peace, Lenore Bloom, 121.
To the poets of Australia, H. F. Rubinstein, 176.
To save his country, Irma Kraft, 153.
To save a life, H. D. Levinson, 157.
To the stars, L. N. Andreyev, 55.
The Ton; or, Follies of fashion, Eglantine Maxwell, lady Wallace, 52.
The Tongues of men, E. C. Carpenter, 64.
Too late to save, T. A. Palmer, 97.
A Tooth for a tooth, Mrs. Bessie (F.) White, 187.
Torquemada, V. M., comte Hugo, 84.
A Tourist's romance, Virginia McMillan, 160.
The Tower of London, T. P. Taylor, 109.
The Town marshall, C. K. Ulrich, 111.
The Trade, Elise W. Quaife and Ernest Nehring, 172.
The Traffic cop, E. W. Mumford, 166.
The Tragical reign of Selimus, Robert Greene, 20.
Traitor's gate, W. J. Lucas, 31.
Transfiguration, Ernst Toller, 183.
Transformation, J. T. Allingham, 8.
The Translation of Nathaniel Bendersnap, G. D. Gribble, 139.
The Travailes of three English brothers, John Day, 16.
The Treason of Benedict Arnold, Augusta Stevenson, 107.
The Treasure, David Pinski, 101.
Treasure Chanukah, S. M. Segal, 178.
Tree pantomime, S. S. Grossman, 140.
Trelawny of the "Wells," Sir A. W. Pinero, 100.
The Trial of Jacob Finklebottom, Max Baer, 118.
Trial of a judge, Stephen Spender, 180.
Trial without jury, J. H. Payne, 33.
Trial marriages, William McNally, 163.
Tricks of the trade, Elise W. Quaife and Ernest Nehring, 172.
The Trigger, Mrs. Lillian S. Pelée, 169.
Trilby, G. L. P. B. Du Maurier, 71.
Trilby, P. M. Potter, 72.
A Trilby triflet, James Hearn and Paul Rubens, 71.
The Triumph of the trees, L. I. Newman, 167.
The Triumphs of honour and industry, Thomas Middleton, 39.
De Troubles of Jakey Cohen, Kent Walker, 185.
The Troubles of the millionaire, anon., 111.
The Troubles of Rozinski, H. L. Newton and A. S. Hoffman, 96.
The Truand chief! Madame Laurent and W. H. Oxberry, 27.
The Trusted jewels, S. S. Grossman, 79.
The Truth, A. J. Glickman, 137.
The Try outs, Eva M. Bacon, 118.
The Tsadik's journey, Harry Sackler, 177.
Turn to the right, Winchell Smith and J. E. Hazzard, 180.

Twelfth night at Fisher's Crossing, J. T. Frederick, 134.
$1200 a year, Edna Ferber and N. Levy, 132.
The Twenty-third philippic, anon., 184.
The Two angels, S. S. Grossman, 140.
Two bad boys, George Harris, 81.
Two blocks away, Aaron Hoffman, 143.
Two goyim, S. S. Grossman, 140.
Two Hebrew sports, James Madison, 90.
The Two Jack Sheppards, anon., 54.
Two in one, Elias Lieberman, 158.
The Two reforms, L. H. Levin, 89.
Two wandering Jews, H. E. Shelland, 107.

U

The Ugly duchess, Vera Beringer, 133.
The Ugly duchess, Lion Feuchtwanger, 133.
Ulysses, James Joyce, 147.
Ulysses von Ithacia, Ludvig, baron Holberg, 21.
The Umbrella mender, H. L. Newton, 96.
Uncle Peter and the D. D. S., Pauline Phelps, 170.
Uncle Zeberiah, Edwin Weever, 112.
The Uncle's will, Armand Charlemagne, 10.
Under the canopy, J. J. Hewson, 81.
Under London, G. M. Rosener, 70.
Under two flags, anon., 67.
Under two flags, W. H. Abel, 67.
Under two flags, G. Daventry, 67.
Under two flags, E. Elsner, 67.
Under two flags, Louise de la Ramée, 67.
Under two flags, Margaret Mayo, 67.
Under two flags, A. Mitchell, 67.
Under two flags, P. M. Potter, 67.
Under two flags, Harry Watkins, 67.
The Under-dog, Carolyn Simon, 179.
Underweight, Venita R. McBurney, 159.
The Undivine comedy, Zygmunt, hrabia Krasiński, 26.
The Unlighted Menorah, Elma C. (E.) Levinger, 157.
The Unwritten chapter, Samuel Shipman and V. Victor, 179.
Up to the minute, Oscar Loeb, 89.
Uplifting Sadie, Alice C. (D.) Riley, 175.
Uriel Acosta, K. F. Gutzkow, 80.
Uriel Acosta, Charles Reznikoff, 174.

V

Vait a minute, A. L. Kaser, 150.
The Vale of cedars, Grace Aguilar, 53.
The Vamp, William McNally, 163.
Van Diemen's Land, W. T. Moncrieff, 39.
The Varangian, J. F. Pennie, 98.
A varumglücktes Auto-da-fé, Benedix Ben-Zion, 45.
Vell! Vell! Vell! A. L. Kaser, 150.
Venetian comedy, anon., 51.
Vengeance, Daisy M. Vance, 70.
De Verdeeling van Polen, Theophilus Lindsey, 31.
Victims, Allan Davis, 128.
Victoria regina, Laurence Housman, 145.
Victory through conflict, Mary W. Brownson and V. E. Kerst, 123.
The Vindictive man, Thomas Holcroft, 22.
The Virgin and the clerk, A. K. Porter, 171.
The Virgin widow, Sir Henry Taylor, 108.
A Vision's quest, Alice E. Lord, 90.
Visitors, Herman Baar, 57.
Vivia Perpetua, Mrs. Sarah F. F. Adams, 53.
The Voice of the ages, W. M. Blatt, 121.
The Voice of the people, David Carb, 64.
The Voice within, Mrs. L. S. Lang, 154.
Von leetle minute, Alice Z. Gibbs, 136.

W

Waiting for the 5:15, William McNally, 163.
Waiting for Lefty, Clifford Odets, 168.
The Waiting waiter, William McNally, 163.
The Walking statue, Aaron Hill, 21.
The Wall between, Elma C. (E.) Levinger, 157.
Wall Street, M. M. Glass and O. M. Carter, 137.
Wall Street in Paradise, H. S. Quire, 102.
Walt, C. D. Morley, 166.
The Wandering Jew, Andrew Franklin, 19.
The Wandering Jew, Herman Heijermans, 82.
Wanderlust, Kenyon Nicholson, 167.
Want, Gladys Foster, 134.
Wanted a bookkeeper, A. B. Shiffrin, 179.
Wanted: a doctor, Elias Lieberman, 158.
Wanted — a pitcher, M. N. Beebe, 58.
The War god, Israel Zangwill, 115.
A War-time Chanukah, D. H. Perlman, 169.
Ward 23, William McNally, 163.
Watchman, Henry and A. S. Mayhew, 92.
The Ways of London, Archibald Maclarin, 32.
The Ways of our tribe, K. B. A. Sessa, 46.
We Americans, M. H. Gropper and Max Siegel, 139.
We never die, Elias Ginsburg, 136.
We, the people, E. L. Rice, 175.
We, us & company, Donald Kaye and W. McNally, 152.
Wedded bliss, Jean Provence, 171.
A Wedding, J. J. Coghlan, 126.
The Weeper sex, William McNally, 163.
Welcome home, Joseph Deitch, 129.
Welcome stranger, Aaron Hoffman, 144.
We're off to —, MJK, 159.
"The Western wall," S. R. Wyckoff, 189.
Westward the course of Israel, R. L. Straus, 182.
The Wet parade dramatized, Mina Maxfield and L. Eggleston, 164.
What d'yer mean? William McNally, 163.
What is a Jew? anon., 112.
What makes an American? Florence Brugger, 123.
What price America? W. S. Tupper, 184.
What price glory, Maxwell Anderson and Leonard Stallings, 117.
What price Hadassah? Mamie G. Gamoran, 136.
"What to be proud of," S. S. Grossman, 140.
What's in a name? Irving Einstein, 131.
"Whatcha come to Paris for anyway?" Mary Cecil, 124.
When? Mrs. A. S. Kohler, 153.
When a broom looms large, Shalom Alechem, pseud., 106.
When the dew falleth, Perez Hirschbein, 143.
When Heine was twenty-one, Maude M. Frank, 134.
When Irish eyes are smiling, R. C. Schimmel, 177.
When is the News coming out? anon., 186.
When knights were bold, Harriet Jay. See her Złoty wiek rycerstwa, 84.
When Satan interferes, Bertha Wiernik, 187.
When the school bell rings, A. L. Kaser, 150.
When we were twenty-one, H. V. Esmond, 74.
Where ignorance is bliss, Ferenc Molnár. See his The Guardsman, 93.
"Where there's smoke...," Mrs. Bessie (F.) White, 187.
Which are foreign? Genevieve C. Wilson, 188.
Which is the thief? James Barber, 33.
A Whiff of evidence, Erastus Osgood, 169.
Whistling in the dark, Laurence Gross and E. C. Carpenter, 139.
The White life, Irving Stone, 182.
A White shawl, C. Leona Dalrymple, 66.
Whitefriars, W. T. Townsend, 111.
Whitehall, 1656, H. F. Rubinstein, 176.
Who caught the count, F. E. Hiland, 83.
Who is Bashti Beki? L. C. Van Noppen, 111.

INDEX OF TITLES

Who shall judge? Bertha Vigran, 184.
The Whole town's talking, John Emerson and Anita Loos, 131.
Why photographers go mad, Emma G. Walker and A. B. Mead, 185.
The Widow's might, Romney Brent. *See his* The Mad Hopes, 122.
The Wife, Rita Wellman. *See her* The Gentile wife, 185.
Wild waves, W. F. Manley, 163.
Will Watch, J. H. Amherst, 8.
Wings on their backs, Bernard Grosswald, 140.
Winkle versus Fitz-Ailwyn, W. A. Chance, 124.
Winter, Shalom Asch, 56.
Winterset, Maxwell Anderson, 117.
Wisdom of Doctor Dodypoll, anon., 52–53.
Wise and not wise, William McNally, 163.
Witches Sabbath, Ida A. R. Wylie, 189.
The Witches' Sabbath, E. H. W. Meyerstein, 165.
With the current, Shalom Asch, 56.
With the Stars and Stripes in France, Frank Dumont, 130.
With triumphant banners, David Pinski, 101.
Wolves, Allan Davis, 128.
The Woman in the case, Clyde Fitch, 75.
The Woman in red, J. S. Coyne, 105.
Woman's might, Jude Storm, 182.
The Women, Clare Boothe, 122.
Women in Israel, Mrs. Blanche (S.) Fisher, 133.
"Women! Women!" William McNally, 163.
Won at last! Wybert Reeve, 103.
The Wondrous tale of Alroy, Benjamin Disraeli, 1st earl of Beaconsfield, 9.
The World's own, Julia W. Howe, 84.
Wozzeck, Georg Buechner, 63.

Y

Yankee Jack, James Pilgrim, 99.
Yehuda, Adolph Feinberg and D. Polish, 156.
Yehuda, Meyer Levin, 156.
Yellow Jack, S. C. Howard and P. H. De Kruif, 145.
The Yellow ticket, Victoria Morton, 94.
Yes, yes! go on, Eulalie Andreas, 117.
Yiddisha love, W. B. Hare, 141.
Yigael, Judith Ish-Kishor, 146.
The York pageant, L. N. Parker, 98.
Yoshe Kalb, I. J. Singer. *See his* The Sinner, 179.
You can't fool Isaac! William McNally, 163.
You win, William McNally, 163.
You're the doctor! Katharine Kavanaugh, 152.
You're mine friend, William McNally, 163.
Young America, Frederick Ballard, 118.
Young America, Frederick Ballard and Pearl Franklin, 118.
Young Maimonides "lost and found," S. M. Segal, 178.
Young Mr. Disraeli, Helen (R.) Beebe, 119.
The Young Quaker, John O'Keeffe, 41.

Z

Zalmen the powerful, Hyman Strunsky, 108.
Zid, Richard Cumberland, 15.
Złoty wiek rycerstwa, Harriet Jay, 84.
Zorinski, Thomas Morton, 40.
Zorinski; or, The Salt mine of Cracow, anon. *See* Zorinski, Thomas Morton, 40.
Zydowskie swaty, Szczesny Zahajkiewicz, 189.

* * *

APPENDIX I:

The Jew in Western Drama: A Check List

By Edgar Rosenberg

The point of the following check list is to implement Coleman's exhaustive bibliography by providing a survey of some 500 "Jewish" plays by some of the recognized Western authors of the past four centuries. The hypothetical consumer whom I have had in mind in compiling this roster is someone — ideally, I suppose, a student of comparative literature or of thematics — who may want to undertake a book-length critical study of the subject, and who may find the next few pages convenient in getting started. M. J. Landa's book, *The Jew in Drama*, is so heavily weighted in favor of the English repertory at the expense of the Continental that its very title is misleadingly inclusive; besides, the book falls off sadly once Landa gets past the eighteenth century, when the sheer number of pertinent plays begins to unhinge his sense of seemliness, and intelligent commentary dwindles into perfunctory notation. As a critic, Landa is too often the victim of his righteousness. Like a lot of earlier studies, his book leaves the reader with the unnerving impression that the merits of a given play are somehow in direct proportion to the virtues of its Jewish personnel, and that philo-Semitism is the *sine qua non* to genius. But no amount of special pleading will justify Cumberland's *Jew* to posterity; and, whatever its shortcomings and blatant vulgarities, *The Jew of Malta* will continue to enjoy a better press than *Abie's Irish Rose*. At least I hope it will.

Landa's book has now entered middle age, and by the laws of the academic whirligig his topic is anyhow due to turn up again. Certainly it deserves to. The list I subjoin draws so heavily on Coleman's enormous labors, as well as on Landa's pandect, that I run it here as the shakiest of trailers. My chief excuse for running it at all is to open up a little the area of Coleman's lifelong solicitude by making room for "qualified" non-English playwrights, mainly French and German (some of whom Coleman in fact cites in translated editions). Secondly, to provide a certain critical perspective by limiting the list to reasonably well-known writers and so restore a kind of symmetry which is bound to be absent from a work in which GLASS, MONTAGUE MARSDEN deflects attention from SHAKESPEARE, WILLIAM, and in which a typescript inflicted on The New York Public Library by the Columbus, Ohio chapter of Hadassah shares equal honors with a play that has taxed the assiduity and vigilance of fifteen editors. As a loose principle of selection, therefore, and by way of redressing the balance, I have given rather more weight to the importance of the writer than to the extensiveness in the treatment of Jewish characters, which may range from a single scene (Buechner) to the entire play (Marlowe). The playwrights I list are those who turn up in the standard histories of the national literatures that I cover; but since I have drawn the line beneath, not above, some nationally known second-raters, it is idle to expect that all of the titles will ignite sparks of recognition all round. Professor X (English), who has yet to pick up Count Platen's *Fatal Fork*, will not cast a cool eye on Professor Y (German) for having all along maintained an austere distance from Thomas Goffe's *Raging Turk*.

I have taken certain liberties by sneaking in a number of titles which purists may disallow as irrelevant. Biblical dramas evidently belong into a category of their own, and Coleman devotes a companion-bibliography to them which the publisher is about to re-issue.* The problems they raise are virtually unrelated to the problems provoked by playwrights who treat the Jew as a contemporary or historical actuality. Even so, I have admitted over a hundred plays on Old Testament themes where the reputation of the author acted as a potent stimulus to name-dropping and the play has gained general recognition; their inclusion seemed to me reasonably aboveboard where the author (Hebbel, Kaj Munk) has furnished the repertory with both sorts of Jews — according to Scriptures, according to "life." I have exercised a similar permissiveness by including a few of the anonymous English mysteries which feed into Marlowe and Shakespeare and seem to me of some literary merit in their own right, and in which the portrayal of Judas is handled with a certain weird realism. Lastly it seemed a shame to exclude some good playwrights who manipulate their Jewish figures by (conspicuous) negative reference: either by presenting a non-Jew who assumes the role of a Jew, a strategy which lays bare the preconceptions in back of the act with elementary immediacy (Webster, Dumas Sr.); or by predicating the plot on an event that significantly involves Jews without bringing them physically onstage (Sartre). In a few instances, in which the Jewishness of a character has been generally assumed but queried by authorities like Cardozo, I precede the title with a question mark. I add that the check list displays its lopsidedness in slighting Spanish and Italian drama and may raise eyebrows among the Romance Literature people. My own researches have turned up very little in these areas, and the few specialists whom I have consulted reassure me that there *is* very little. For the rest, I daresay the list can be augmented by as many as two hundred titles of roughly similar importance without losing its equilibrium, but perhaps not more than that.

Since I may as well confess that Coleman's chronological divisions strike me as something short of ideal, I have followed the simpler and leaner method of the annalist, indicating breaks in chronology where literary historians normally put them.

Cornell University
Ithaca, N. Y.

**The Bible in English Drama* (The New York Public Library 1930). A new printing with the addition of "A Survey of Major Recent Plays" (1968) by Isaiah Sheffer will be published jointly by The New York Public Library and Ktav Publishing House, Inc. in 1969.

APPENDIX I

I

?1350-1430 — *York Plays*
No. 26, The Cutlers' Play ("The Conspiracy")
No. 32, The Cooks' Play ("Remorse of Judas")

14th-15th century — *Chester Plays*
No. 15, The Bakers' Play ("Betrayal of Christ")

15th century — *Towneley Plays*
No. 21, "The Conspiracy"
No. 22, "The Buffeting"
No. 23, "The Scourging"

c. 1450 — Jean du Prier, *Le mystère du roy Avenir*

1452 — Arnold Gréban, *Le mystère de la passion*

c. 1460 — Pietro d'Antonio da Lucignano, *Il drama della conversione di S. Paolo*

c. 1461 — *The Croxton Play of the Sacrament: The Conversion of Sir Jonathas the Jew by Miracle of the Blessed Sacrament*

1474 — Hans Folz, *Der Juden und Christen Streit von Kaiser Constantinus*

?c. 1475 — Bernardo Pulci, *Rappresentazione di Barlaam e Josafat* [published 1516]
———, *Rappresentazione di Agnolo Ebreo* [published 1554]
———, *Rappresentazione della Disputa al Tempio* [published 1559]

c. 1480 — Hans Folz, *Fastnachtspiele:*
Die Alt und Neue Ehe, die Sinagog, von Ueberwindung der Juden, etc.
Ein Spiel von dem Herzogen von Burgund
Des Entchrist Fasnacht

16th century — *Towneley Plays*
No. 24, "The Hanging of Judas" [Fragment]

1517 — Pamphilus Gengenbach, *Nollhart*
Gil Vicente, *Auto da barca do inferno*

1519 — Castellano Castellani, *Rappresentazione della cena e passione*

1523 — Gil Vicente, *Farça de Inês Pereira*

1525 — Gil Vicente, *Farça do Juiz da Beira*

c. 1526 — Gil Vicente, *Diálogo sôbre a resurreicão*

1530 — Hans Sachs, *Comedie: Dass Christus der wahre Messias sei*

c. 1530 — Diego Sánchez de Badajoz, *Farsa de los doctores*
———, *Farsa de la iglesia*

1532 — Gil Vicente, *Auto da Lusitânia*

1533-1560 — Hans Sachs [Old Testament Tragedies and Comedies: *Die Opferung Isaac; Absalom mit David; Jael erwuergt Siseram*, etc.]

1538 — John Bale, *A Tragedy or Interlude Manifesting the Chief Promises of God . . . from the Fall of Adam*

APPENDIX I

II

1550	Théodore de Bèze, *Abraham sacrifiant*
1557	Hans Sachs, *Fastnachtspiel: Der Teufel nahm ein altes Weib* ?Nicholas Udall, *Jacob and Esau*
1561	Georg Rollenhagen, *Spiel von Abraham*
1568	Thomas Garter, *The Comedy of the Most Virtuous and Godly Susannah*
1572	Jean de la Taille, *Saül furieux*
1576	Georg Rollenhagen, *Spiel von Tobias*
1577	Arthur Golding, *A Tragedy of Abraham's Sacrifice* [trans. of Théodore de Bèze]
1580	Thomas Le Coq, *Tragédie representant l'odieus et sanglant meurtre commis par le maudit Cain à l'encontre de son frère Abel* Cornelius Schonaeus, *Tobaeus: comoedia sacra et nova*
1581	Cornelius Schonaeus, *Naaman: comoedia sacra et nova*
1583	Robert Garnier, *Sédécie, ou les juives*
1584	Robert Wilson, *The Three Ladies of London*
1589	Christopher Marlowe, *The Jew of Malta*
1591	Thomas Legge, *The Destruction of Jerusalem*
c. 1592	Cornelius Schonaeus, *Saulus* ———, *Nehemias*
1594	Robert Greene, *The First Part of ... Selimus, Emperor of the Turks* Cornelius Schonaeus, *Juditha*
c. 1595	Jakob Ayrer, *Fastnachtspiele:* *Von einem halbnaerrischen Wucherer* *Von einem Juden zu Frankfurt, der einem Dieb will sein gestohlen* *Vom falschen Notarius mit seiner unwahrhaften Beicht*
1596	Cornelius Schonaeus, *Daniel: comoedia sacra et nova* William Shakespeare, *The Merchant of Venice*
1597	Jakob Ayrer, *Comoedie von Nikolaus, dem verlohrenen Sohn Machiavellus*
c. 1598	Jakob Ayrer, *Comoedie vom Soldan von Babylonia*
1599	George Peele, *The Love of King David and Fair Bethsabe*
1600	John Marston, ?*Jack Drum's Entertainment*
c. 1600	Damián Salustio del Poyo, *La vida y muerte de Judas*
1601	Hugo Grotius, *Adamus exul* ———, *Sophomphanaeas* [Joseph and His Brothers] Antoine de Montchrétien, *Aman* ———, *David*

APPENDIX I

1602	Anthony Munday and Thomas Dekker, *Jephtha* Samuel Rowley, *Joshua*
1605	Ben Jonson, John Marston, and George Chapman, ?*Eastward Ho*
1607	John Day, William Rowley, and George Wilkins, *The Travels of the Three English Brothers Sherley*
1608	*Das Wohl Gesprochene Urtheil . . . oder der Jud von Venedig*
1610	Ben Jonson, ?*The Alchemist* Felix Lope de Vega Carpio, *La hermosa Esther*
1612	Robert Daborne, *A Christian Turn'd Turk* Tirso de Molina, *La mujer que manda en casa*
?1612	Tirso de Molina, *La vida y muerte de Herodes*
1613	Lady Elizabeth Carew, *The Tragedy of Mariam, the Fair Queen of Jewry* John Marston and William Barksted, *The Insatiate Countess*
1614	Tirso de Molina, *La mejor Espigadera*
1616	Francis Beaumont and John Fletcher, ?*The Scornful Lady* *Das Endinger Judenspiel*
1617	Lope de Vega, *Las paces de los reyes y Judía de Toledo*
1618	Lope de Vega, *Barlán y Josafa*
1619	Philip Massinger and Nathaniel Field, *The Fatal Dowry*
1620	John Fletcher, ?*Women Pleased* John Fletcher and ?Philip Massinger, *The Custom of the Country* Joost van den Vondel, *Hierusalem Verwoest* [*Jerusalem Laid Waste*]
1622	Gervase Markham and William Sampson, *Herod and Antipater*
1623	Juan Ruiz de Alarcon, *El Anticristo* Philip Massinger, *The Duke of Milan* John Webster, *The Devil's Law Case*
1627	Thomas Goffe, *The Raging Turk*
1635	Antonio Mira de Amescua, *La desgraciada Raquel, y Rei Don Alphonso el Ocho*
1640	Joost van den Vondel, *Gebroeders* ———, *Joseph in Dothan* ———, *Joseph in Egypten*
1648	Andreas Gryphius, *Horribilicribrifax*

III

1654	Thomas Killigrew, *Thomaso, or the Wanderer* Joost van den Vondel, *Lucifer*
1660	Joost van den Vondel, *Koning David in ballingschap* [*King David in Banishment*] ———, *Koning David Hersteld* [*King David Restored*]

APPENDIX I

1662	William Hemminge, *The Jews' Tragedy, or Their Fatal and Final Overthrow by Vespasian and Titus*
1664	Pedro Calderon de la Barca, *La cena del Rey Baltasar* Joost van den Vondel, *Adam in ballingschap*
1667	Juan Bautista Diamante, *La Judía de Toledo* Joost van den Vondel, *Noah*
1671	John Milton, *Samson Agonistes* Jean Racine, *Bérénice*
1677	John Crowne, *The Destruction of Jerusalem* John Dryden, *The State of Innocence and Fall of Man* Thomas Otway, *Titus and Berenice* [adapted from Racine]
1681	Aphra Behn, *The Second Part of the Rover*
1689	Jean Racine, *Esther*
1690	Jean Racine, *Athalie*
1691	John Wilson, *Belphegor, or The Marriage of the Devil*
1694	Roger Boyle, *Herod the Great* John Dryden, *Love Triumphant*
1698	John Crowne, *Caligula*
1701	George Granville, *The Jew of Venice*
1703	Roger Boyle, *The Tragedy of King Saul*
1710	Aaron Hill, *The Walking Statue*
1722	Ludvig Holberg, *Den Politiske Kandestøber* [*The Political Tinker*]
1723	Elijah Fenton, *Mariamne*
1724	Ludvig Holberg. *Diderich Menschenskraek* [*Diderich the Terrible*] ———, *Ulysses von Ithaica* ———, *Det Arabiske Pulver* [*The Arabian Powder*] François Marie Arouet de Voltaire, *Mariamne*
1733	Theophilus Cibber, *The Harlot's Progress, or The Ridotto al Fresco*
c. 1735	Gaspar Fernández y Ávila, *La infancia de Jesu-Christo*
c. 1740	Aaron Hill, *Saul* [published 1760]
1742	Henry Fielding, *Miss Lucy in Town*
1743	Pietro Metastasio, *Isacco, figure del redentore*
1749	Gotthold Ephraim Lessing, *Die Juden* Voltaire, *La femme qui a raison*
1755	Voltaire, *Saul*

APPENDIX I

1757   Friedrich Gottlieb Klopstock, *Der Tod Adams*

1759   Charles Macklin, *Love à la Mode*

1760   Benjamin Stillingfleet, *Moses and Zipporah*
―――, *Joseph*
―――, *David and Bathsheba*

1764   Oliver Goldsmith, *The Captivity*
F. G. Klopstock, *Salomo*

1768   Samuel Foote, *The Devil upon Two Sticks*

1770   Gottlieb Stephanie (der Juengere), *Die Abgedankten Offiziere*

1772   Richard Cumberland, *The Fashionable Lover*
Samuel Foote, *The Nabob*
F. G. Klopstock, *David*

1773   Johann Wolfgang von Goethe, *Das Jahrmarktsfest zu Plundersweilen* [original version]
Christian Gottlob Stephanie (der Aeltere), *Der neue Weiberfeind und die schoene Juedin*

1774   Richard Cumberland, *The Note of Hand*
Samuel Foote, *The Cozeners*
Jakob Michael Reinhold Lenz, *Die Tuerkensklavin*
Joseph Pauersbach, *Der redliche Bauer und der grossmuetige Jude*
Gottlieb Stephanie (d.J.), *Der Eigensinnige*

1775   Carl Martin Pluemicke, *Der Volontair*
Richard Brinsley Sheridan, *The Duenna*
Heinrich Leopold Wagner, *Die Reue nach der Tat*
Francis Godolphin Waldron, *The Contrast, or the Jew and the Married Courtezan*

1776   J. M. R. Lenz, *Die Soldaten*
Pietro Metastasio, *Giuseppe riconosciuto*

1777   Richard Brinsley Sheridan, *The School for Scandal*

1778   Johannes Friedrich (Maler) Mueller, *Fausts Leben*
Vicente Garcia de la Huerta, *La Raquel*

1779   G. E. Lessing, *Nathan der Weise*

1780   Jacob Bischoff, *Der Judenfeind*
Hannah Cowley, *The Belle's Stratagem*
Gottlieb Stephanie (d.J.), *Das Maedchen in der Irre*

1781   Friedrich Schiller, *Die Raeuber*

1782   Hannah More, *Sacred Dramas* ["Belshazzar," "Daniel," etc.]

1783   John O'Keefe, *The Young Quaker*

1784   Vittorio Alfieri, *Saul*
August Wilhelm Iffland, *Verbrechen aus Ehrsucht*

1785   Stéphanie-Félicité Comtesse de Genlis, *Théatre à l'usage de jeunes personnes* ["La mort d'Adam," "Agar dans le désert," "Isaac," "Joseph reconnu par ses frères," "Ruth et Noémie"]

APPENDIX I

The Israelites; or The Pampered Nabob [in H. R. S. van der Veen, *Jewish Characters in Eighteenth-Century English Fiction and Drama*]

1789   Vittorio Alfieri, *Abele*
John O'Keefe, *Little Hunchback; or, A Frolic in Bagdad*

IV

1790   August von Kotzebue, *Das Kind der Liebe*

1791   Gottlieb Stephanie (d.J.), *Grader Sinn und Hinterlist*

1792   Carl Friedrich Hensler, *Das Judenmaedchen aus Prag*

1794   Richard Cumberland, *The Jew*
Susanna Haswell Rawson, *Slaves in Algiers; or, A Struggle for Freedom*

1795   August Wilhelm Iffland, *Dienstpflicht*

1797   Andrew Franklin, *The Wandering Jew; or Love's Masquerade*

1798   Thomas Dibdin, *The School for Prejudice*
August von Kotzebue, *Der Opfertod*

c. 1800   Royall Tyler, *The Origin of the Feast of Purim*
———, *Joseph and His Brethren*
———, *The Judgment of Solomon*

1801   Thomas Dibdin, *The Jew and the Doctor*

1802   Thomas Dibdin, *Family Quarrels*

1803   George Colman, Jr., *Love Laughs at Locksmiths*
William Dunlap, *Bonaparte in England*
Thomas Holcroft, *Hear Both Sides*

1806   Thomas Holcroft, *The Vindictive Man*
Edward Hook, *The Invisible Girl*
Zacharias Werner, *Das Kreuz an der Ostsee*

1807   James Kenney, *Ella Rosenberg*

1808   Richard Cumberland, *The Jew of Mogadore*

1809   Gavriil Romanovich Derzhavin, *Herod and Mariamond*

1810   Alexander Alexandrovich Shakovskoi, *Deborah, or The Triumph of Faith*

1811   Ludwig Achim von Arnim, *Halle und Jerusalem*

1812   James Ellison, *The American Captive; or, Siege of Tripoli*
Theodor Koerner, *Zrinny*

1815   L. C. Caigniez and T. M. T. Baudouin, *La pie voleuse*
Petr Alexandrovich Korsakov, *The Maccabaeans*
Karl Borromaeus Sessa, *Unser Verkehr, oder Die Judenschule*

1817   Tommasso conte Gherardi del Testa, *La gazza ladra* [adapt. from *La pie voleuse*]

APPENDIX I

1818   William Thomas Moncrieff, *Rochester; or King Charles Second's Merry Days*

1819   Joseph Aloys Gleich, *Der Hoelle Zaubergaben*
Henry M. Milner, *The Jew of Lubeck*

1820   Henry Hart Milman, *The Fall of Jerusalem*

1821   George Gordon, Lord Byron, *Cain*
Percy Bysshe Shelley, *Hellas*

1822   Henry Hart Milman, *Belshazzar*

1823   Marc-Antoine-Madeleine Désaugiers, *Le juif*

1826   August von Platèn, *Die Verhaengnisvolle Gabel*

1827   Ernst August Friedrich Klingemann, *Ahasver*
Victor Hugo, *Cromwell*

1828   Thomas Dibdin, *Humphrey Clinker* [adapt. from Smollett's novel]

1830   Mihael Yurevich Lermontov, *The Spaniards*
W. T. Moncrieff, *Van Diemen's Land*
Thomas Wade, *The Jew of Arragon*

1832   Christian Dietrich Grabbe, *Kosciuzko* [fragment]
Frédéric Soulié and Adolphe Bossange, *Clotilde*

1833   Victor Hugo, *Mary Tudor*
Samuel B. H. Judah, *The Maid of Midian*
William Leman Rede, *The Skeleton Witness, or The Murder of the Mount*

1834   Joseph-Philippe Lockroy and Anicet Bourgeois, *L'impératrice et la juive*
Pierre Biarnoy de Merville and Julien de Mallian, *Le juif errant*

1835   Christian Dietrich Grabbe, *Aschenbroedel*
Jean François Casimir Delavigne, *Don Juan d'Autriche*
James Robinson Planché, *The Jewess*
Augustin-Eugène Scribe, *La juive*

1836   Georg Buechner, *Woyzeck*
Douglas Jerrold, *The Painter of Ghent*

1837   Adam Oehlenschlaeger, *Den lille Skuespiller* [*The Little Actor*]

V

1838   Edward Bulwer-Lytton, *Leila*
Sheridan Knowles, *The Maid of Mariendorpt*

1840   Friedrich Hebbel, *Judith*
Nestor Vasilievich Kukolnik, *Prince Daniel Vasilievich Kholmsky*
George Sand, *Les Mississipiens*

1841   Dion Boucicault, *London Assurance*
Karl Gutzkow, *Die Schule der Reichen*
Friedrich Hebbel, *Genoveva*

1842   Annette von Droste-Huelshoff, *Die Judenbuche* [novella; dramatic adapt. 1885]
Douglas Jerrold, *The Prisoners of War*

APPENDIX I

1844	Elizabeth Barrett Browning, *A Drama of Exile*
1846	Théophile Gautier and Noël Parfait, *La juive de Constantine*
1847	Friedrich Hebbel, *Der Diamant*
1848	Alexandre Dumas, Sr., *Monte-Cristo* Karl Gutzkow, *Uriel Acosta*
1849	Arthur Hugh Clough, *The Mystery of the Fall* [published 1869] Friedrich Hebbel, *Herodes und Mariamne* Alfred de Musset and Émile Augier, *L'habit vert*
1850	Salomon Ritter von Mosenthal, *Deborah* Sir Henry Taylor, *The Virgin Widow; or, A Sicilian Summer*
1851	Dion Boucicault, *The Queen of Spades* Ferdinand Dugué, *Salvator Rosa*
1852	Otto Ludwig, *Die Makkabaeer* Harry Quire, *The Rabbi of York*
1853	Roger de Beauvoir and Lambert Thiboust, *Les enfers de Paris* Adrien Decourcelle and Adolphe Jaime, *On demande un gouverneur* Gustav Freytag, *Die Journalisten* Charles Reade, *Gold!*
1854	Ferdinand Dugué, *Le juif de Venise*
1855	Émile Augier and Jules Sandeau, *Le gendre de M. Poirier* Franz Grillparzer, *Die Juedin von Toledo* Tom Taylor, *Helping Hands*
1857	Paolo Giacometti, *Giuditta*
1858	Tom Taylor, *Going to the Bad*
1859	Tom Taylor, *Payable on Demand*
1860	Eugène Labiche, *J'invite le Colonel!*
1861	Franz Grillparzer, *Esther* [fragment] Imre Madach, *Az ember tragédiájá* [*The Tragedy of Man*]
1863	Tom Taylor, *The Ticket-of-Leave Man*
1864	Paul Heyse, *Hans Lange*
1865	Charles Reade, *It's Never Too Late to Mend* Thomas W. Robertson, *Society* Alexei Tolstoi, *The Death of Ivan the Terrible*
1866	Dion Boucicault, *Flying Scud*
1867	Paul Heyse, *Die Gluecklichen Bettler* Ouida, *Under Two Flags* [dramatic adapt. 1870]
1868	Dion Boucicault, *After Dark*
1869	Meir Aron Goldschmidt, *Rabbien og Ridderen* [*The Rabbi and the Knight*]

APPENDIX I

1870   William Schwenck Gilbert, *An Old Score*

1871   Ludwig Anzengruber, *Der Meineidsbauer*
Émile Erckmann and Alexandre Chartrian, *Le juif polonais*
Paul Heyse, *Die Franzosenbraut*
Leopold Lewis, *The Bells* [adapt. from *Le juif polonais*]
Henry Wadsworth Longfellow, *Judas Maccabaeus*
Stéphane Mallarmé, *Hérodiade*

1873   Alexandre Dumas, Jr., *La femme de Claude*
Leopold Lewis, *The Wandering Jew*
Alexis Theofilakhovich Pisemsky, *Baal*

1874   Émile Zola, *Les héritiers Rabourdin*

1876   Louis-Poupart Davyl, *Coq-Hardy*
Erckmann-Chatrian, *L'ami Fritz*

1880   Paul Lindau, *Graefin Lea*

1881   Anton Pavlovich Chekhov, *Platonov*

1882   Victor Hugo, *Torquemada*
Catulle Mendès, *Les mères ennemies*

1883   Achille Torelli, *L'Israelita*

1884   Paul Delair [Michel Salomon], *Les rois en exil* [adapt. from Daudet's novel]

1887   Anton Pavlovich Chekhov, *Ivanov*

1889   Alphonse Daudet, *La lutte pour la vie*
Leo Tolstoi, *The Fruits of Enlightenment*

1890   Henry Arthur Jones, *Judah*
Arthur Wing Pinero, *The Cabinet Minister*

1892   Henri Léon Émile Lavedan, *Le Prince d'Aurec*
Oscar Wilde, *Salomé*

1894   George Du Maurier, *Trilby*
Sydney Grundy, *An Old Jew*
Israel Zangwill, *The King of the Schnorrers* [dramatic adapt. 1925]

1896   Gerhart Hauptmann, *Florian Geyer*

1898   André Gide, *Saul*
Theodor Herzl, *Das Neue Ghetto*
Max Nordau, *Doktor Kohn*
Arthur Wing Pinero, *Trelawney of the "Wells"*
Arthur Symons, "The Lover of the Queen of Sheba" [in *Images of Good and Evil*, 1899]

1899   Herman Heijermans, *Ghetto*
Israel Zangwill, *Children of the Ghetto*

1900   Paul Claudel, *L'échange*

VI

1901	Albert Guinon, *Décadence* Gerhart Hauptmann, *Der Rote Hahn* Arthur Wing Pinero, *Iris* Carl Sternheim, *Judas Ischariot: Die Tragoedie vom Verrat*
1903	Hermann Bahr, *Der Meister* Jacinto Benavente y Martinez, *La noche del sabado* Maurice Donnay, *Le retour de Jerusalem* Octave Mirbeau, *Les affaires sont les affaires* Thomas Sturge Moore, *Absalom* Arthur Wing Pinero, *Letty* George Bernard Shaw, *Man and Superman* Hermann Sudermann, *Der Sturmgeselle Sokrates*
1904	Yevgeni Nikolaevich Chirikov, *The Jews* Catulle Mendès, *Le fils d'Étoile* David Pinski, *The Last Jew*
1905	Richard Beer-Hofmann, *Der Graf von Charolais* Wilhelm von Scholz, *Der Jude von Konstanz*
1906	Carl Hauptmann, *Moses* Gerhart Hauptmann, *Gabriel Schillings Flucht* Bernard Shaw, *The Doctor's Dilemma* Edith Wharton, *The House of Mirth*
1907	Leonid Andreyev, *To the Stars* Shalom Asch, *The God of Vengeance* W. Somerset Maugham, *Lady Frederick* Alfred Savoir and Fernand Nozière, *Le baptême*
1908	Shalom Asch, *Sabbatai Zevi* Henry Bernstein, *Israel* Jerome K. Jerome, *The Passing of the Third Floor Back* Israel Zangwill, *The Melting Pot*
1909	Hjalmar Bergstrøm, *Lynggaard & Co.* W. Somerset Maugham, *Smith* Henri Nathansen, *Daniel Hertz*
1910	Leonid Andreyev, *Anathema* Shalom Asch, *Um Winter* Ferenc Molnar, *A testör* [*The Guardsman*] William Vaughn Moody, *The Death of Eve* [fragment]
1911	Hermann Bahr, *Das Taenzchen* Georg Kaiser, *Die Juedische Witwe* Thomas Sturge Moore, *Judith* ———, *Mariamne* Carl Roessler, *Die Fuenf Frankfurter* Carl Sternheim, *Die Hose* Israel Zangwill, *The War God*
1912	André Gide, *Bethsabé* Henri Nathansen, *Inden for Murene* [*Within the Walls*] Arthur Wing Pinero, *The Mind-the-Paint Girl* Arthur Schnitzler, *Professor Bernhardi*
1913	Arnold Bennett, *The Great Adventure* Edward Knoblock, *The Faun* André Pascal, *Croesus* Arnold Zweig, *Die Sendung Semaels*

APPENDIX I

1914 Richard Harding Davis, *Peace Manoeuvers*
      Frank Wedekind, *Simson, oder Scham und Eifersucht*
      Arnold Zweig, *Die Umkehr*

1915 Shalom Asch, *Jephtha's Daughter*
      Ernst Hardt, *Koenig Salomo*

1916 Georg Kaiser, *Von Morgen bis Mitternacht*
      Louis Parker, *Disraeli*
      Isaac Rosenberg, *Moses: A Play*
      Reinhard Johannes Sorge, *Koenig David*
      Arthur Symons, *Cleopatra in Judaea*

1917 Bernard Shaw, *Annajanska the Bolshevik Empress*

1918 Paul Claudel, *Le pain dur*
      Theodore Dreiser, *The Hand of the Potter*
      Ernst Toller, *Die Wandlung*
      Stefan Zweig, *Jeremias*

VII

1919 Richard Beer-Hofmann, *Jaakobs Traum*
      Arnold Bennett, *Judith*
      Paul Claudel, *Le père humilié*

1920 S. Ansky, *The Dybbuk*

1921 John Masefield, *Esther*
      Ferenc Molnar, *Liliom*
      Carl Sternheim, *Der Entfesselte Zeitgenosse*
      Franz Werfel, *Bockgesang*
      Stefan Zeromski, *Ponad śnieg bielszym się stanę* [*Whiter Than the Snow*]

1922 John Galsworthy, *Loyalties*
      Anne Nichols, *Abie's Irish Rose*
      Bernard Shaw, *Back to Methuselah: A Metabiological Pentateuch*
      Carl Sternheim, *Der Nebbich*
      Ernst Toller, *Hinckemann*

1923 Leonid Andreyev, *Samson in Chains*
      Walther Eidlitz, *Der Berg in der Wueste*
      Jan Fabricius, *Seideravond*
      Harley Granville-Barker, *The Secret Life*
      René Morax, *Le roi David*

1924 Maxwell Anderson and Laurence Stallings, *What Price Glory?*
      Ernst Barlach, *Die Suendflut*
      Arnold Bennett and Edward Knoblock, *London Life*
      St. John Ervine, *The Lady of Belmont*
      Franz Werfel, *Juarez und Maximilian*

1925 F. Scott Fitzgerald, *The Great Gatsby* [dramatic adapt.]
      Ludwig Lewisohn, *Israel*
      Carl Zuckmayer, *Der Froehliche Weinberg*

1926 T. W. Harding, *Nina Balatka* [adapt. from Trollope's novel]
      D. H. Lawrence, *David*
      Anita Loos, *Gentlemen Prefer Blondes*
      Ferenc Molnar, *Játèka Kastélyban* [*The Play's the Thing*]
      Franz Werfel, *Paulus unter den Juden*

APPENDIX I

1927	Karel and Josef Čapek, *Adam stvoritel* [*Adam the Creator*] Karl Schoenherr, *Der Judas von Tirol*
1928	Paul Claudel, *Le soulier de satin* Valentin Petrovich Katayev, *Squaring the Circle* Kaj Munk, *En Idealist* [*King Herod*]
1929	Paul Claudel, *Le pain dur* Padraic Colum, *Balloon* Marc Connelly, *The Green Pastures* John Dos Passos, *Airways, Inc.* Sidney Howard, *Half-Gods* Ring Lardner, *June Moon* A. A. Milne, *Michael and Mary* Elmer Rice, *Street Scene*
1930	Vicky Baum, *Menschen im Hotel* George S. Kaufman, *Once in a Lifetime* Paul Kornfeld, *Jud Suess* [adapt. from Lion Feuchtwanger's novel]
1931	Hans Chlumberg, *Das Wunder um Verdun* Jean Giraudoux, *Judith* Elmer Rice, *Counsellor-at-Law*
1932	Sidney Howard, *The Late Christopher Bean* Else Lasker-Schueler, *Arthur Aronymus und Seine Vaeter* Elmer Rice, *We, the People*
1933	Richard Beer-Hofmann, *Der Junge David* Noel Coward, *Design for Living* Sidney Kingsley, *Men in White* Friedrich Wolf, *Dr. Mamlock*
1934	S. N. Behrman, *Rain from Heaven* George S. Kaufman, *Merrily We Roll Along* Sinclair Lewis and Sidney Howard, *Dodsworth* Clifford Odets, *Waiting for Lefty*
1935	Maxwell Anderson, *Winterset* Laurence Housman, *Victoria Regina* Sidney Kingsley, *Dead End* Clifford Odets, *Awake and Sing* Franz Werfel, *Deg Weg der Verheissung*
1936	Irwin Shaw, *Bury the Dead*
1937	Clifford Odets, *Golden Boy*
1938	James M. Barrie, *The Boy David* S. N. Behrman, *Wine of Choice* Bertolt Brecht, *Furcht und Elend des Dritten Reiches* Kaj Munk, *Han sidder ved Smeltedigden* [*He Sits at the Melting Pot*] Stephen Spender, *Trial of a Judge*
1939	Clair Booth, *Margin for Error* Irwin Shaw, *The Gentle People*
1941	Paul Green and Richard Wright, *Native Son*
1942	Paul Claudel, *L'histoire de Tobie et de Sara*
1943	Jean Giraudoux, *Sodome et Gomorrhe*

APPENDIX I

1944   Paul Claudel and Jean-Louis Barrault, *Le soulier de satin* [full acting version]
Franz Werfel, *Jakobowsky und der Oberst*

1946   Carl Zuckmayer, *Des Teufels General*
Arnold Zweig, *Austreibung, 1744*

1947   Jean Anouilh, *L'invitation au château*

1948   Christopher Fry, *The Firstborn*

1950   Christopher Fry, *Ring Round the Moon* [adapt. from Anouilh's *L'invitation*]
Laurence Housman, *Old Testament Plays*
Nelly Sachs, *Eli*
Carl Zuckmayer, *Der Gesang im Feuerofen*

1951   Christopher Fry, *A Sleep of Prisoners*

1954   Herman Wouk, *The Caine Mutiny Court-Martial*

1955   Francis Goodrich and Albert Hackett, *The Diary of Anne Frank*

1958   Archibald MacLeish, *J. B.*

1959   Jean-Paul Sartre, *Les séquestrés d'Altona*

1962   Paddy Chayefsky, *Gideon*
Rolf Hochhuth, *Der Stellvertreter*

1964   Arthur Miller, *Incident at Vichy*

1965   Peter Weiss, *Die Ermittlung*

APPENDIX II:

Addenda to The Jew in English Drama

By Flola L. Shepard

The following addenda are not intended as a comprehensive supplement to Mr. Coleman's work, but rather are references to plays discovered in the course of research on related topics. I hope they will prove helpful to scholars in the field.

The abbreviation "Ld Ch" signifies plays submitted for licensing to the Lord Chamberlain of England, according to the lists of Allardyce Nicoll, *A History of English Drama, 1660-1900* (Cambridge University Press 1952-1959, 6 vols. rev. eds). "Genest Collection" referred to in the notes is the Genest Collection, Beinecke Rare Book and Manuscript Library, Yale University.

Livingstone College
Salisbury, N. C.

Abarbance the Hebrew; or, Raymond the Betrayer.
Tragedy.
Ld Ch, Aug. 10, 1849.

Aladdin and the Wonderful Lamp; or, New Lamps for Old Ones by Albert Richard Smith, and James Kenney. London: W. S. Johnson [1844] 32 p.   NCO p.v. 892
Burlesque.
First performed at the Theatre Royal Lyceum, London, on Aug. 5, 1844.
Abanazar, in "Jewish costume," sells lamps.

Baron Fitzadern. 8°. 1845.
Tragedy.
Copy in Genest Collection.
Levi, a Jew, and "another Jew."

The Benevolent Jew; or, The Gamester, the Seducer and the Murderer.
Melodrama.
Performed at the Royalty Theatre, London, on Monday, Dec. 17, 1821.

The Blazing Comet: The Mad Lovers; or, The Beauties of the Poets by Samuel Johnson of Cheshire. London: J. Crockatt, 1732. x, 52 p. 12°.   NCO p.v. 1045; NAC p.v. 221
Performed at the Haymarket Theatre, London, March 1732.
"A Wand'ring Jew—Mr. Giles."

Call Again To-morrow by Don T. de Trueba Cosio.   MWEZ 1231
Musical Farce.
Playbill, Royal Olympic Theatre, London, Thursday, August 2, 1832. "Music by Mr. Hawes."
Afterpiece has money-lender, Isaac Percent, who probably used a dialect. Minton played the role.

The Catawba Travellers by [Mark?] Lonsdale.
Performed at Sadler's Wells Theatre, London, in 1797.
Copy in Genest Collection.
Leir Lyon, an English Jew peddler, takes Chicka as his wife. He speaks in Jewish dialect. Chicka is probably Indian.

Conrad, the Robber Chieftain; or, the Benevolent Israelite.
Performed at Sadler's Wells Theatre, London, on Monday, Nov. 10, 1828.
Reviewed in *The Stage or the Theatrical Inquisitor,* vol. 2, pages 165–168.
The Jewish traveller brings about the villain's defeat by helping father and daughter to escape from the cavern.

The Contrast; or, The Jew and the Married Courtezan by Francis Waldron.
Farce.
Performed at Drury Lane Theatre, London, on Friday, May 12, 1775.

The Diamond Ring; or, The Jew Outwitted.
Musical Piece.
Performed at the Royal Grove, London.
Israel played by Mr. D'Castro.
Noted in *The Gazeteer and New Daily Advertiser* of July 30, 1788.

The English Moor; or, The Mock-Marriage by Richard Brome. In *The Dramatic Works of Richard Brome* vol. 2, London, J. Pearson, 1873.   NCP
Performed in London, 1628.
Comedy.
The *Dramatis Personae* does not say that the old usurer is a Jew, but in Act 3, Scene 3, Theophilus's servant says that "the old Jew has lost his wife" and in Act 4, Scene 2, Baneless says, "We came to jear the Jew and he jears us."
British Museum has copy in *Five New Playes,* London, 1659, 8°.

Esther; or, Faith Triumphant by Thomas Brereton. London, 1715.
British Museum has a copy, *Esther, or A Sacred Tragedy* [in verse translated from Racine's *Esther*] 1715, 12°.

Esther, the Royal Jewess; or, The Death of Haman by Elizabeth Polack. London: J. Duncombe & co. [1835?] 30 p.   NCO p.v. 691
Drama.
Performed at the Royal Pavilion Theatre, London, on Monday, March 9, 1835.

The Fairy Lake; or, The Magic Veil by Charles Selby. London: J. Duncombe & co. [1850?] 26 p.   NCO p.v. 959
Burletta.
Performed at the Strand Theatre, London, Monday, May 13, 1839.
According to Nicoll (*A History of English Drama, 1660–1900*), an adaptation of the French opera *Le lac des fées*.
"Issacher, a Jew." He is the stage-type: a dialect-speaking money-lender.

The Fair Refugee, or, The Rival Jews.
Comedy.
Performed at the Haymarket Theatre, London, in 1785.
Catalogue of the Larpent Plays in the Huntington Library (MacMillan), San Marino, California, 1939. Number 651.
This may be a version of *Machiavellus* (see below).

Freebooters of Vienna! or, The Jew and his Family by H. M. Milner.   MWEZ 8710
Playbill for the Royal Coburg Theatre, London, July 19, 1824.
Cast listings include: Jew... Mr. Cobham; Steward to the Jew... Mr. Davidge; Lindor, valet to the Jew... Mr. Blanchard; Rosa, daughter to the Jew... Miss Watson.
This must be a version of *The Jew of Lubeck* (see above, p. 39). The title *The Jew of Lubeck! or The Heart of a Father* is used in a playbill of Jan. 23, 1826 for the Coburg, but the playbill for the Coburg of March 3, 1831 has the title *The Jew of Vienna! or The Heart of a Father* with Cobham as the Jew ("his first appearance this season").

Furibond; or, Harlequin Negro. London: J. Scales [1807?] 26 p.   NCO p.v. 919
Grand Comical Pantomime.
Performed at Drury Lane Theatre, London, on Monday, Dec. 28, 1807.
Catalogue of the Larpent Plays in the Huntington Library. Number 1533.
Published description notes that the Jew Boy was played by Master West. Also, the Old Clothes Man might have been made to seem Jewish in some way.

The Gambler's Life in London; or, Views in the Country and Views in Town by Andrew Leonard Vouillaire Campbell. London, n.d.
Drama.
Performed at Sadler's Wells Theatre, London, on Friday, Dec. 26, 1828.
Published by J. Duncombe & co. Copy in Genest Collection.
The Jewish Clothesman uses dialect when cheating.

The German Jew; or, The Deserter from Orleans by W. H. Tilbury [1830?].
Published by J. Duncombe & co. No copy located.

Gold Dust by G. DeLara or J. Rhymer? [or both?].
Frances Fleetwood, in *Conquest; the Story of a Theatre Family* [London, W. H. Allen 1953] p. 47, writes of the resentment of Jews at having Jew villains in *Gold Dust*.

The Gospel Shop by Richard Hill [c. 1770].
Comedy.
The title page notes that the play was kept from being presented by the demand of some "eminent divines." They may have objected to the character of Mordecai, a Jew and a dealer in "old-cloathes," but, more probably, they objected to Racket, a poor parson, Dr. Scapegoat, a rich covetous Methodist preacher, and Parson Prolix, Dr. Scapegoat's partner.
Copy (London, 1778) in the F. Longe Collection of Plays (vol. 164) in the Rare Book Room of the Library of Congress.

The Gypsy Prince by Thomas Moore.
Musical Entertainment.
Music by Mr. Kelly.
Performed at the Haymarket Theatre, London, on July 24, 1801.
According to Oulton (*A History of the Theatres of London . . .*, vol. III, a disguised Spanish prince, leader of a Gypsy band, rescues a poor Jew from capture by officers of the Inquisition. The play, called a "flimsy production," was "performed a few nights."

Harlequin Hoax; or, A Pantomime Proposed by Thomas John Dibdin. London: Whittingham and Arliss, 1815. 28 p. Second edition. 8°.   NCO p.v. 196
Extravaganza.
Performed at the Lyceum Theatre, London, Aug. 16, 1814.
Shadrach is not listed in the cast as a Jew, but Factotem brings old clothes from him in the first scene and Shadrach comes demanding money. Oxberry plays Shadrach.

Heaster and Asheweros.
Mentioned in Henslowe's *Diary* for June 3, 1594.
Barker's Complete List of Plays . . . To 1803 [J. Barker & Son 1803] suggests that this might be the *Queen Hester*, anon.

The Hebrew by Wilkins.
Performed at the City of London Theatre, London, in Feb. 1852.
The *Era* of Feb. 15, 1852 calls it the "long-promised spectacle," not "great drama."

The Hebrew Diamond; or, The Eye of Light by C. H. Hazlewood.
Drama.
Ld Ch, July 10, 1865.

The Hebrew Family; or, A Traveller's Adventure.
Melodrama.
Performed at Covent Garden Theatre, London, on April 8, 1825.
Ld Ch listing, *The Englishman in Spain.*

The Hebrew Husband; or, The Jew's Revolt by George Dibdin Pitt.
Drama.
Performed at the Royal Coburg Theatre, London, on Jan. 14, 1833.

The Hebrew Maiden; or, Harlequin Prince Leoline and the Fairy of the Chain of Brillaints.
Pantomime.
Ld Ch, City of London Theatre, Dec. 12, 1869.
This may be a pantomime version of the drama, *The Hebrew Maiden; or, The Lost Diamond* (see below).

The Hebrew Maiden; or, The Lost Diamond.
Drama.
Performed at the City of London Theatre, London, in April, 1841.

APPENDIX II

The Hebrew Patriarch; or, The Unknown Knight.
Melodrama.
Performed at the Royalty Theatre, London, on Sept. 9, 1822.

The Hebrew Son; or, The Child of Babylon.
Drama.
Ld Ch, Olympic Theatre, March 7, 1852. According to Nicoll, the license was refused.

The Hebrew's Sacrifice.
Drama.
Ld Ch, City of London Theatre, Jan. 24, 1852. License refused here also, according to Nicoll.

The Hebrew Tribe of Rome; or, The Greek Hero and the Jewish Maiden.
Drama.
Ld Ch, Standard Theatre, Feb. 2, 1852.
The *Era* of Feb. 8, 1852 reports the success of this new drama based on the history of the persecution of the Jews by Romans.

The Hebrew Twins by W. J. Lucas.
Drama.
Performed at the City of London Theatre, London, on Nov. 22, 1847.

Herod and Mariamne by Christopher Bullock.
Droll.
Performed at Southwark Fair, Sept., 1723.

Herod and Mariamne by Samuel Pordage. 1673.
Tragedy.
Copy in University of Chicago Library.
Nicoll, vol. I (1952), p. 424, should be consulted for information on production.

Honour and Shame; or, The Ballet-girl and the Jew.
Drama.
Performed at the Royal Pavilion Theater, London, on Oct. 14, 1849.

Hyram Balthazar; or, The Maniac Jew.
Drama.
Ld Ch, Britannia Theatre, Nov. 3, 1856.

Jacob and Esau. 1568.
Entered on the Stationer's Register, 1557.
Printed for the Malone Society. Oxford, Oxford University Press, 1956. ix p., reprint [56] p. Facsimile from the copy in the Bodleian Library.
The text of 1568 is the earliest that has been found.

The Jamaica Lady; or, The Life of Bavia. London, 1720.
Copy in Yale University Library.
A merchant of Port-Royal is in love with the Jew's wife. With the help of Bavia, she escapes from her husband and flees with her lover.

The Jew and the Gentile; or, The Filial Sacrifice.   MWEZ 8710
Serious Burletta.
Performed at the Olympic Theatre, London, in Jan., 1825.
The playbill for the Jan. 17, 1825 performance advertises the last six nights of Kent's performance at the Olympic Theatre with a Prelude followed by the "serious Burletta."

The Life of King Ahasuerus; or, The Delightful History of Esther.
Droll.
Performed at Punch's Theatre, London, for Easter, 1719.

The Jew and the Gentile; or, No Bottle, No Bird by J. C. Cross. With Songs, Duets, Glees, Chorusses &c. London, 1796.
Burletta.
Performed at the Royal Circus, London, on Sept. 24, 1795.
Copy in Genest Collection.
Mordecai Moses sings (to the tune of "The Dead of Night") of his love for Mistress Solomons, for marriage and children. He and Tim have a duet as they drink Mordecai's wine; each is glad that the other is drunk. Mordecai is somewhat worried about money. The last song before the Finale is for Mordecai, who pronounces further life "in amities" and the end of "sheating play."

The Jewess by John Knowles.
Ld Ch, Manchester, May 7, 1850.

The Jew of Canada.
Burletta.
Performed at the Royal Coburg Theatre, London, on Nov. 9, 1829.
Fleetwood in *Conquest* . . ., p. 29, says that Sloman played the role of Abraham.

Jewish Courtship.
Entertainment.
Performed at Drury Lane Theatre, London, on April 23, 1787.
Mentioned in Nicoll, vol. III (1952), p. 333 and 404, as *A Specimen of Jewish Courtship.*

Jewish Education.
Interlude.
Performed at the Drury Lane Theatre, London, April 19, 1784.
This is probably another name for *Moses and Shadrac* (see below).

The Jew of Capua.
Tragedy.
The *Journal and Musical Intelligence,* no. 13 (March 1840), lists the play as a new tragedy.
The *Theatrical Journal and Stranger's Guide* (Sept. 4, 1841) refers to the title role as a dignified one for the actor.
Played by the Shakespearians at the Italian Opera House.

The Jewish Wars by William Heming.
Tragedy.
Imperfect copy of text of 1662 in the F. Longe Collection of Plays (vol. 211) in the Rare Book Room of the Library of Congress, with title *The Jewish War Tragedy; or, Their Fatal and Final Overthrow by Vespatian and Titus.*

The Jew's Revenge.
Ld Ch, York, May 2, 1844.

Kings in Babylon by Alice Mary Buckton. London: Methuen and co. [1906] 72 p. 12°.
NCO p.v. 584
Drama.

The Lawyers' Panic; or, Westminster Hall in an Uproar by John Dent. London 1785.
Prelude.
Performed at Covent Garden Theatre, London, on May 1, 1785.
Moses Lyons, who speaks dialect, has an important role—that of a German Jew.

Leah, a Travestie by J. W. Boddam. n.p., n.d.
Copy in Yale University Library.
Characters include "Abraham, an ancient Jew, who had been young and foolish . . ., and Leah, an orphan Jewess."

The Mad-House by A Gentleman of the Inner Temple. London, 1787.
Performed at Lincoln's-Inn-Fields.
"A Rehearsal of a New Ballad-Opera Burlesqu'd" precedes the title; "after the Manner of Pasquin" follows the title.
Copy in Yale University Library.
I'm not sure that the noise being "heard without" — which the mad doctor declares is the muttering of Hebrew roots by the Jew — should be called a Jewish character. Although he does not appear on stage, he is called by the name Aaron Circumcision, the rich Jew of Poultry.

The Maid and the Magpie by Isaac Pocock.
See entry in Coleman above, p. 33.
For the Covent Garden performance of Sept. 15, 1815, *The Theatrical Inquisitor and Monthly Mirror*, vol. 7 (1815), p. 227, reported that the part was lengthened for Farley to let him show his "supposed proficiency in the Hebrew dialect." But he wasn't good in the role. The October production at the Royal Pavilion added an "effective scene between the Jew and Grandville."

The Maid of Marienburg. 1798.
From the German of Kratter.
Kratter may possibly be the source of *The Maid of Mariendorpt*.

Malak the Jew; or, The Bandits.
Performed at Sadler's Wells Theatre, London, Nov. 8, 1830.

Moses in the Bulrushes.
Sacred Drama.
Performed in Doncaster in 1703.
This play is taken from a piece of the same title in Mrs. Hannah More's *Sacred Dramas* — all on Old Testament subjects — which were written for plays for the youth.

Moses and Shadrac; or, A Specimen of Jewish Education.
"Petit piece"; one act.
Performed at Drury Lane Theatre, London, April 17, 1780.
Catalogue of the Larpent Plays in the Huntington Library. Number 517.

My Poll and My Partner Joe by John Thomas Haines.
Melodrama.
Performed in Surrey, on March 31, 1835.
A Jewish peddler at the Inn in Portsmouth has a few lines in Act 3, Scene 1.

Nicholas Mendoza by F. Bromley.
Melodrama.
Performed at the Royal Coburg Theatre, London, on Dec. 7, 1829.
The Dramatic Magazine of Jan. 1, 1830 reported "the principal character is a benevolent Jew, which was supported by Dowton with great warmth of feeling, and chasteness of style."

Machiavellus.
Play in Latin.
Performed at St. John's College, Cambridge, on Dec. 9, 1597.
According to William John Lawrence, *Pre-restoration Stage Studies* [Cambridge, Harvard University Press 1927], Machiavellus and Jacuppus are rivals for the love of the daughter of Andronicus. Their actions are in the tradition of high melodrama. Finally the daughter's betrothed, who had been reported dead, returns, and puts an end to the schemes.

The Nondescript; or, Beauty in Ugliness by Henry Archibald Major. [London] Taylor & co. 40 p. NCO p.v. 948
Performed at Lincoln's-Inn-Fields, 187–?.
Solomon Wisdom ("Jew vs Gentile") is represented as an ugly, dialect-speaking, kind-hearted Jew who in the end gives his percentage for the benefit of the blind children.

The Nymph of the Fountain by J. C. Cross.
Pantomime.
Performed at the Royal Circus Theatre, London, on Sept. 18, 1797.
Pilbrow boasts of being able to "take in a Jew," and he does an imitation of "Moses" — probably of Mordecai Moses of *The Jew and the Gentile* (see above), which had a run of some nights and was still being produced in 1797.

Policy; or, Thus Runs the World by Henry Siddons.
Performed at Drury Lane Theatre, London, on Oct. 15, 1814.
According to Oulton, vol. I, one of the characters is "an old Israelite."

The Prophet by Richard Bentley. Airs, Duetts, Trios, Chorusses, &c. London 1788.
Comic Opera.
Performed at Covent Garden Theatre, London, on Dec. 15, 1788.
Copy in Genest Collection.
Lazarus has a scurrilous dialect-song.

The Rabbi's Son; or, The Last Link of the Chain by E. Manuel.
Performed at the Britannia Theatre, London, on April 14, 1879.
This play is announced in Charles Eyre Pascoe's *Dramatic Notes* (NCO p.v. 830) for the spring of 1879.

Robin Hood and His Merry Men; or, Harlequin Ivanhoe, the Knight Templar and the Jewess by Colin Henry Hazlewood.
Performed at the Royal Pavilion Theatre, London, on Dec. 24, 1867.

The Sea Devil; or, The Adventures of Shadrac the Benevolent Jew.
Performed in Surrey, on Sept. 21, 1822.
The production was praised by *The Theatre or Daily Miscellany of Fashion:* "The principal object in the piece is Shadrac, who bears a part in every incident. An unwearied solicitude about his pack of hardware, and a generous sacrifice of his money whenever distress presents itself, are attributes with which the Jew is invested. The character is amusing, and it was ably presented by Mr. Bengough." The heroine was considered adequate and the scenery, good.

Tombo-Chiqui; or, The American Savage by John Cleland. London 1758.
Dramatic Entertainment. Three Acts.
Copy in Genest Collection.
Here, too, is a Jewish peddler.

The Voice of Nature by James Boaden.
Performed at the Haymarket Theatre, London, on July 31, 1802.
From the French of Caigniez, *Le jugement de Salomon*, which is the story of Solomon in the Scripture.

The Wars of the Jews; or, The Fall of Jerusalem.
Spectacle.
Performed at Astley's Amphitheatre, London, in Dec. 1848.

What Will the World Say? by William Gillum. 1787.
Two Acts.
In his *Miscellaneous Poems*, 1787.
Copy in Genest Collection.
Something kept it from being performed.

INDEX TO
THE JEW IN WESTERN DRAMA
AND THE APPENDICES

Note that the page numbers from 1 to 50 in this index refer to the new paging for the introductory essay, "The Jew in Western Drama: An Essay," not to the main text of Coleman's bibliography.

A

Abarbance the Hebrew 255
Abele 247
Die Abgedankten Offiziere 246
Abie's Irish Rose 252
Abraham sacrifiant 243
Absalom 251
Absalom mit David 242
Adam in ballingschap 245
Adam stvoritel 253
Adamus exul 243
Les affaires sont les affaires 251
After Dark 249
Ahasver 248
Airways, Inc. 253
Aladdin and the Wonderful Lamp 255
Alarcon, Juan Ruiz de 244
The Alchemist 244
Alfieri, Vittorio 246, 247
Die Alt und Neue Ehe 242
Aman 243
The American Captive 247
Amescua, Antonio Mira de 244
L'ami Fritz 250
Anathema 251
Anderson, Maxwell 252, 253
Andreyev, Leonid 251, 252
Annajanska the Bolshevik Empress 252
Anouilh, Jean 254
Ansky, S. 252
El Anticristo 244
Anzengruber, Ludwig 250
Det Arabiske Pulver 245
Arnim, Ludwig Achim von 247
Arthur Aronymus und Seine Vaeter 253
Asch, Shalom 251, 252
Aschenbroedel 248
Athalie 245
Augier, Emile 249
Austreibung, 1744 254
Auto da Lusitânia 242
Avila, Gaspar Fernández y 245
Awake and Sing 253
Ayrer, Jakob 243
Az ember tragédiájá 249

B

Baal 250
Back to Methuselah 252
Badajoz, Diego Sánchez de 242
Bahr, Hermann 251
Bale, John 242
Balloon 253
Le baptême 251
Barca, Pedro Calderon de la 245
Barksted, William 244
Barlach, Ernst 252
Barlán y Josafa 244
Baron Fitzadern 255
Barrault, Jean-Louis 254
Barrie, James M. 253
Baudouin, T. M. T. 247
Baum, Vicky 253
Beaumont, Francis 244
Beauvoir, Roger de 249

Beer-Hoffmann, Richard 251, 252, 253
Behn, Aphra 245
Behrman, S. N. 253
The Belle's Stratagem 246
The Bells 250
Belphegor 245
Belshazzar 248
The Benevolent Jew 255
Bennett, Arnold 251, 252
Bentley, Richard 258
Bérénice 245
Der Berg in der Wueste 252
Bergstrøm, Hjalmar 251
Bernstein, Henry 251
Bethsabé 251
de Béze, Théodore 243
The Bible in English Drama 1
Bischoff, Jacob 246
The Blazing Comet 255
Boaden, James 258
Boddam, J. W. 257
Bonaparte in England 247
Bockgesang 252
Booth, Clair 253
Bossange, Adolphe 248
Boucicault, Dion 248, 249
Bourgeois, Anicet 248
The Boy David 253
Boyle, Roger 245
Brecht, Bertolt 48, 253
Brereton, Thomas 256
Brome, Richard 255
Bromley, F. 258
Browning, Elizabeth Barrett 249
Buckton, Alice Mary 257
Buechner, Georg 46, 248
Bullock, Christopher 257
Bulwer-Lytton, Edward 248
Bury the Dead 253

C

The Cabinet Minister 250
Caigniez, L. C. 247
The Caine Mutiny Court-Martial 254
Caligula 245
Call Again To-morrow 255
Campbell, Andrew Leonard Vouillaire 256
Capek, Joseph 253
Capek, Karel 253
The Captivity 246
Carew, Lady Elizabeth 244
Carpio, Felix Lope de Vega 244
Castellani, Castellano 242
The Catawba Travellers 255
La cena del Rey Baltasar 245
Chapman, George 244
Chatrian, Alexandre 250
Chayefsky, Paddy 254
Chekhov, Anton Pavlovich 46-47, 250
Chester Plays: No 15, The Bakers' Play 242
Children of the Ghetto 250
Chirikov, Yevgeni Nikolaevich 251
Chlumberg, Hans 253
A Christian Turn'd Turk 244
Cibber, Colley 17-18

259

Cibber, Theophilus 245
Cinderella 46
Claudel, Paul 250, 252, 253, 254
Cleland, John 258
Cleopatra in Judaea 252
Clotilde 248
Clough, Arthur Hugh 249
Coleman, Edward 1, 2, 239
Colman, George Jr 247
Colum, Padraic 253
Comoedie von Nikolaus 243
The Comedy of the Most Virtuous and Godly Susannah 243
Comoedie vom Soldan von Babylonia 243
Connelly, Marc 253
Conrad, the Robber Chieftan 255
The Contrast 246, 255
Coq-Hardy 250
Cosio, Don T. de Trueba 255
Counsellor-at-Law 253
Coward, Noel 253
Cowley, Hannah 246
The Cozeners 246
Croesus 251
Cromwell 248
Cross, J. C. 257, 258
Crowne, John 245
The Croxton Play of the Sacrament . . . 2-7, 242
Cumberland, Richard 20, 28, 43-44, 45, 239, 246, 247
The Custom of the Country 17, 244

D

Daborne, Robert 244
Daniel 243
Daniel Hertz 251
Dass Christus der wahre Messias sei 242
Daudet, Alphonse 250
David 243, 252
David and Bathsheba 246
Davis, Richard Harding 252
Davyl, Louis-Poupart 250
Day, John 244
Dead End 253
The Death of Eve 251
The Death of Ivan the Terrible 249
Deborah 247, 249
Décadence 251
Decourcelle, Adrien 249
Dekker, Thomas 243
Delair, Paul 250
Delavigne, Jean François Casimir 248
Dent, John 257
Derzhavin, Gavriil Romanovich 247
Désaugiers, Marc-Antoine-Madeleine 248
La desgraciada Raquel 244
Design for Living 253
The Destruction of Jerusalem 243, 245
The Devil upon Two Sticks 246
The Devil's Law-Case 8, 244
Diálogo sôbre a resurreição 242
Der Diamant 46, 248
Diamante, Juan Bautista 245
The Diamond Ring 255
The Diary of Anne Frank 254
Dibdin, Thomas 43-44, 247, 248, 256
Diderich Menschenskraek 8
Dienstpflicht 247
Disraeli, Benjamin 47
Disraeli 252
The Doctor's Dilemma 251
Dodsworth 253
Doktor Kohn 48, 250
Don Juan d'Autriche 248
Donnay, Maurice 251
Dos Passos, John 253

Il drama della conversione di S. Paolo 242
A Drama of Exile 249
Dreiser, Theodore 252
Droste-Huelshoff, Annette von 248
Dryden, John 40, 245
Du Maurier, George 250
The Duenna 24, 246
Dugué, Ferdinand 249
The Duke of Milan 244
Dumas, Alexandre, Jr 41, 250
Dumas, Alexandre, Sr 8, 240, 249
Dunlap, William 247
The Dybbuk 252

E

Eastward Ho 244
L'échange 250
Eidlitz, Walther 252
Der Eigensinnige 246
Êli 254
Eliot, T. S. 19, 23
Ella Rosenberg 247
Ellison, James 247
Das Endinger Judenspiel 244
Les enfers de Paris 249
The English Moor 255
Des Entchrist Fasnacht 242
Der Entfesselte Zeitgenosse 252
Erckmann-Chatrian 250
Erckmann, Emile 250
Die Ermittlung [*The Investigation*] 49, 254
Ervine, St. John 252
Esther 245, 249, 252, 256

F

Fabricius, Jan 252
The Fair Refugee 256
The Fairy Lake 256
The Fall of Jerusalem 248
Falschen Notarius mit seiner unwahrhaften Beicht 243
Family Quarrels 247
Farça de Inês Pereira 242
Farça do Juiz da Beira 242
Farsa de los doctores 242
Farsa de la iglesia 242
Fastnachtspiel 243
Fastnachtspiele [Folz] 242, [Ayrer] 243
The Fatal Dowry 244
The Faun 251
Fausts leben 246
La femme de Claude 41, 250
La femme qui a raison 40, 245
Fenton, Elijah 245
Fielding, Henry 245
Field, Nathaniel 244
Le fils d'Étoile 251
The Firstborn 254
The First Part of . . . Selimus 243
Fitzgerald, F. Scott 252
Fletcher, John 17, 244
Florian Geyer 250
Flying Seud 249
Folz, Hans 242
Foote, Samuel 246
Franklin, Andrew 247
Die Französenbraut 250
Freebooters of Vienna! 256
Freytag, Gustav 46, 249
Der Froehliche Weinberg 252
The Fruits of Enlightenment 40, 250
Fry, Christopher 254
Die Fuenf Frankfurter 251
Furcht und Elend des Dritten Reiches 48, 253
Furibond 256

G

Gabriel Schillings Flucht 48, 251
Galsworthy, John 252
The Gambler's Life in London 256
Garnier, Robert 243
Garter, Thomas 243
Gautier, Théophile 249
La gazza ladra 247
Gebroeders 244
Le gendre de M. Poirier 249
Gengenbach, Pamphilus 242
Genlis, Stéphanie-Félicité Comtesse de 246
Genoveva 248
The Gentle People 253
Gentlemen Prefer Blondes 252
The 'German Jew 256
Gerontion 19
Der Gesang im Feurofen 254
Ghetto 250
Giacometti, Paolo 249
Gide, André 250, 251
Gideon 254
Gil Vicente 242
Gilbert, William Schwenck 250
Gillum, William 258
Giraudoux, Jean 253
Giuditta 249
Gleich, Joseph Aloys 248
Die Gluecklichen Bettler 249
The God of Vengeance 251
Goethe, Johann Wolfgang von 246
Goffe, Thomas 244
Going to the Bad 249
Gold! 249
Gold Dust 256
Golden Boy 253
Golding, Arthur 243
Goldschmidt, Meir Aron 249
Goldsmith, Oliver 246
Goodrich, Francis 254
The Gospel Shop 256
Grabbe, Christian Dietrich 46, 248
Grader Sinn und Hinterlist 247
Graefin Lea 250
Der Graf von Charolais 251
Granville, George 20, 245
Granville-Barker, Harley 252
The Great Adventure 251
The Great Gatsby 252
Gréban, Arnold 242
The Green Pastures 253
Green, Paul 253
Greene, Robert 243
Grillparzer, Franz 48, 249
Grotius, Hugo 243
Grundy, Sydney 250
Gryphius, Andreas 244
Guinon, Albert 251
Guiseppe riconosciuto 246
Gutzkow, Karl 248, 249
The Gypsy Prince 256

H

L'habit vert 249
Hackett, Albert 254
Haines, John Thomas 258
Einem halbnaerrischen Wucherer 243
Half-Gods 253
Halle und Jerusalem 247
Han sidder ved Smeltedigden 253
The Hand of the Potter 252
Hans Lange 249
Harding, T. W. 252
Hardt, Ernst 252
Harlequin Hoax 256
The Harlot's Progress 245

Hauptmann, Carl 251
Hauptmann, Gerhart 48, 250, 251
Hazlewood, Colin Henry 256, 258
Hear Both Sides 247
Heaster and Asheweros 256
Hebbel, Friedrich 46, 240, 248, 249
The Hebrew 256
The Hebrew Diamond 256
The Hebrew Family 256
The Hebrew Husband 256
The Hebrew Maiden 256
The Hebrew Patriarch 257
The Hebrew's Sacrifice 257
The Hebrew Son 257
The Hebrew Tribe of Rome 257
The Hebrew Twins 257
Heijermans, Herman 250
Helping Hands 249
Heming, William 257
Hemminge, William 245
Hensler, Carl Friedrich 247
Les héritiers Rabourdin 27, 250
La hermosa Esther 244
Herod and Antipater 244
Herod and Mariamond 247
Herod and Mariamne 257
Herod the Great 245
Herodes und Mariamne 249
Hérodiade 250
Herzl, Theodor 250
Heyse, Paul 249, 250
Hierusalem Verwoest 244
Hill, Aaron 245
Hill, Richard 256
Hinckemann 252
L'histoire de Tobie et de Sara 253
Hochhuth, Rolf 48, 254
Der Hoelle Zaubergaben 248
Holberg, Ludvig 8, 245
Holcroft, Thomas 247
Honour and Shame 257
Hook, Edward 247
Horribilicribrifax 244
Die Hose 251
The House of Mirth 251
Housman, Laurence 253, 254
Howard, Sidney 253
Huerta, Vicente Garcia de la 246
Hugo, Victor 248, 250
Humphrey Clinker 248
Hyram Balthazar 257

I

En Idealist 253
Iffland, August Wilhelm 246, 247
L'impératrice et la juive 248
Incident at Vichy 254
Inden for Murene 48, 251
La infancia de Jesu-Christo 245
The Insatiate Countess 244
The Investigation 49, 254
The Invisible Girl 247
L'invitation au château 254
Iris 251
Israel 251, 252
It's Never Too Late to Mend 249
Isacco 245
L'Israelita 250
The Israelites 247
Ivanov 250

J

J. B. 254
Jaakobs Traum 252
Jack Drum's Entertainment 243
Jacob and Esau 243, 257
Jael erwuergt Siseram, etc. 242

INDEX TO WESTERN DRAMA AND APPENDICES

Das Jahrmarktsfect zu Plundersweiden 246
Jaime, Adolphe 249
Jakobowsky und der Oberst 254
The Jamaica Lady 257
Játèka Kastélyban 252
Jephtha 243
Jephtha's Daughter 252
Jeremias 252
Jerome, Jerome K. 251
Jerrold, Douglas 248
The Jew 20, 28, 44-45, 239, 247
The Jew and the Doctor 44-46, 247
The Jew in Drama (Landa) 2, 239
The Jew in English Drama 1, 2
The Jew of Arragon 248
The Jew and the Gentile 257
The Jew of Canada 257
The Jew of Capua 257
The Jew of Lubeck 248
The Jew of Malta 15-24, 32-36, 38, 41, 239, 243
The Jew of Mogadore 247
The Jew of Venice 20, 245
The Jewess 248, 257
Jewish Courtship 257
Jewish Education 257
The Jewish Wars 257
The Jews 251
The Jew's Revenge 257
The Jews' Tragedy 245
J'invite le Colonel! 249
Johnson, Samuel 255
Jones, Henry Arthur 250
Jonson, Ben 244
Joseph 246
Joseph and His Brethren 247
Joseph in Dothan 244
Joseph in Egypten 244
Joshua 243
Die Journalisten 46, 249
Juarez und Maximilian 252
Jud Suess 253
Judah 250
Judah, Samuel B. H. 248
Judas Ischariot 251
Judas Maccabaeus 250
Der Judas von Tirol 253
Der Jude von Konstanz 251
Die Juden 20, 245
Der Juden und Christen Streit von Kaiser Constantinus 242
Einem Juden zu Frankfurt 243
Die Judenbuche 248
Der Judenfeind 246
Das Judenmaedchen aus Prag 247
The Judgment of Solomon 247
La Judia de Toledo 245
Judith 248, 251, 252, 253
Juditha 243
Die Juedin von Toledo 48, 249
Die Juedische Witwe 251
Le juif 248
Le juif errant 248
Le juif polonais 250
Le juif de Venise 249
La juive 248
La juive de Constantine 249
June Moon 253
Der Junge David 253

K

Kaiser, Georg 251, 252
Katayev, Valentin Petrovich 253
Kaufman, George S. 253
Kenney, James 247, 255
Killigrew, Thomas 244
Das Kind der Liebe 247
The King of the Schnorrers 250
Kings in Babylon 257

Kingsley, Sidney 253
Klingemann, Ernest August Friedrich 248
Klopstock, Friedrich Gottlieb 246
Knoblock, Edward 251, 252
Knowles, John 257
Knowles, Sheridan 248
Koenig David 252
Koenig Salomo 252
Koerner, Theodor 247
Koning David Hersteld 244
Koning David in ballingschap 244
Kornfeld, Paul 253
Korsakov, Petr Alexandrovich 247
Kosciuzko 248
Kotzebue, August von 27-28, 247
Das Kreuz an der Ostsee 247
Kukolnik, Nestor Vasilievich 248

L

Labiche, Eugène 249
The Lady of Belmont 252
Lady Frederick 251
Landa, M. J. 2, 239
DeLara, G. 256
Lardner, Ring 253
Lasker-Schueler, Else 253
The Last Jew 251
The Late Christopher Bean 253
Lavedan, Henri León Emile 250
Lawrence, D. H. 252
The Lawyers' Panic 257
Leah 257
Le Coq, Thomas 243
Leila 248
Legge, Thomas 243
Lenz, Jakob Michael Reinhold 246
Lermontov, Mihael Yurevich 248
Lessing, Gotthold Ephraim 20, 40, 245, 246
Letty 251
Lewis, Leopold 250
Lewis, Sinclair 253
Lewisohn, Ludwig 252
The Life of King Ahasuerus 257
Liliom 252
Den lille Skuespiller 248
Lindau, Paul 250
Little Hunchback 247
Lockroy, Joseph-Philippe 248
London Assurance 248
London Life 252
Longfellow, Henry Wadsworth 250
Lonsdale [Mark?] 255
Loos, Anita 252
Love à la Mode 246
The Love of King David and Fair Bethsabe 243
Love Laughs at Locksmiths 247
Love Makes a Man 18
Love Triumphant 40, 245
"The Lover of the Queen of Sheba" 250
Loyalties 252
Lucas, W. J. 257
Lucifer 244
Lucignano, Pietro d'Antonio da 242
Ludwig, Otto 249
La lutte pour la vie 250
Lynggard & Co. 251

M

The Maccabaeans 247
Machiavellus 258
Macklin, Charles 246
MacLeish, Archibald 254
Madach, Imre 249
The Mad-House 258
Das Maedchen in der Irre 246
The Maid and the Magpie 258

The Maid of Marienburg 258
The Maid of Mariendorpt 248
The Maid of Midian 248
Die Makkabaeer 249
Malak the Jew 258
Mallarmé, Stéphane 250
Mallian, Julien de 248
Dr. Mamlock 253
Man and Superman 251
Manuel, E. 258
Margin for Error 253
Mariamne 245, 251
Markham, Gervase 244
Marlowe, Christopher 14-24, 32-36, 38, 41, 243
Marston, John 243, 244
Martinez, Jacinto Benavente y 251
Mary Tudor 248
Masefield, John 252
Massinger, Philip 244
Maugham, W. Somerset 48, 251
Der Meineidsbauer 250
Der Meister 251
La mejor Espigadera 244
The Melting Pot 251
Men in White 253
Mendés, Catulle 250, 251
Menschen im Hotel 253
The Merchant of Venice 15-19, 25-26, 29-39, 41-44, 243
Les mères ennemies 250
Merrily We Roll Along 253
Merville, Pierre Biarnoy de 248
Metastasio, Pietro 245, 246
Michael and Mary 253
Miller, Arthur 254
Milton, John 245
Miss Lucy in Town 245
Milman, Henry Hart 248
Milne, A. A. 253
Milner, Henry M. 248, 256
The Mind-the-Paint Girl 251
Mirbeau, Octave 251
Les Mississipiens 248
Molina, Tirso de 244
Molnar, Ferenc 251, 252
Moncrieff, William Thomas 248
Montchrétien, Antoine de 243
Monte-Cristo 8, 249
Moody, William Vaughn 251
Moore, Thomas 256
Moore, Thomas Sturge 251
Morax, René 252
More, Hannah 246
Mosenthal, Salomon Ritter von 249
Moses 251, 252
Moses and Shadrac 258
Moses and Zipporah 246
Moses in the Bulrushes 258
Mueller, Johannes Friedrich (Maler) 246
La mujer que manda en casa 244
Munday, Arthur 243
Munk, Kaj 48, 240, 253
Musset, Alfred de 249
My Poll and My Partner Joe 258
Le mystère du roy Avenir 242
Le mystère de la passion 242
The Mystery of the Fall 249

N

Naaman 243
Nashe, Thomas 9-14
Nathan der Weise 28, 40, 246
Nathansen, Henri 48, 251
Native Son 253
Der Nebbich 252
Nehemias 243
Das Neue Ghetto 250
Der neue Weiberfeind und die schoene Juedin 246

Nicholas Mendoza 258
Nichols, Anne 252
Nina Balatka 252
Noah 245
La noche del sabado 251
Nollhart 242
The Nondescript 258
Nordau, Max 48, 250
The Note of Hand 246
Nozière, Fernand 251
The Nymph of the Fountain 258

O

Odet, Clifford 253
Oehlenschlaeger, Adam 248
O'Keefe, John 246, 247
An Old Jew 250
An Old Score 250
Old Testament Plays 254
On demande un gouverneur 249
Once in a Lifetime 253
Der Opfertod 27-28, 247
Die Opferung Isaac 242
The Origin of the Feast of Purim 247
Otway, Thomas 245
Ouida 249

P

Las paces de los reyes y Judia de Toledo 244
Le pain dur 252, 253
The Painter of Ghent 248
Parfait, Noël 249
Parker, Louis 252
Pascal, André 251
The Passing of the Third Floor Back 251
Pauersbach, Joseph 246
Paulus unter den Juden 252
Payable on Demand 249
Peace Manoeuvers 252
Peele, George 243
Le père humilié 252
La pie voleuse 247
Pinero, Arthur Wing 48, 250, 251
Pinski, David 251
Pisemsky, Alexis Theofilakhovich 250
Pitt, George Dibdin 256
Planché, James Robinson 248
Platen, August von 248
Platonov 46-47, 250
Pluemicke, Carl Martin 246
Pocock, Isaac 258
Policy 258
Den Politiske Kandestøber 245
Ponad śnieg bielszym się stanę 252
Pordage, Samuel 257
Poyo, Damián Salustio del 243
Prier, Jean du 242
Le Prince d'Aurec 250
Prince Daniel Vasilievich Kholmsky 248
The Prisoners of War 248
Professor Bernhardi 48, 251
The Prophet 258
Pulci, Bernardo 242

Q

The Queen of Spades 249
Quire, Harry 249

R

The Rabbi of York 249
Rabbien og Ridderen 249
The Rabbi's Son 258
Racine, Jean 245
Die Raeuber 246
Rain from Heaven 253

INDEX TO WESTERN DRAMA AND APPENDICES

The Raging Turk 244
Rappresentazione della cena e passione 242
Rappresentazione di Agnolo Ebreo 242
Rappresentazione di Barlaam e Josafat 242
Rappresentazione della Disputa al Tempio 242
La Raquel 246
Rawson, Susanna Haswell 247
Reade, Charles 249
Rede, William Leman 248
Der redliche Bauer und der grossmuetige Jude 246
Le retour de Jerusalem 251
Die Reue nach der Tat 28, 246
Rhymer, J. 256
Rice, Elmer 253
Richard III 21
Ring Round the Moon 254
Robertson, Thomas W. 249
Robin Hood and His Merry Men 258
Rochester 248
Roessler, Carl 251
Le roi David 252
Les rois en exil 250
Rollenhagen, Georg 243
Rosenberg, Isaac 252
Der Rote Hahn 251
Rowley, William 244

S

Sabbatai Zevi 251
Sachs, Hans 242, 243
Sachs, Nelly 254
Sacred Dramas 246
Salomé 250
Salomo 246
Salomon, Michel 250
Salvator Rosa 249
Sampson, William 244
Samson Agonistes 245
Samson in Chains 252
Sand, George 248
Sandeau, Jules 249
Sartre, Jean-Paul 48, 240, 254
Saul 245, 246, 250
Saül furieux 243
Saulus 243
Savoir, Alfred 251
Schiller, Friedrich 246
Schnitzler, Arthur 48, 251
Schoenherr, Karl 253
Schonaeus, Cornelius 243
The School for Prejudice 45, 247
The School for Scandal 42, 246
Die Schule der Reichen 248
The Scornful Lady 244
Scribe, Augustin-Eugéne 248
The Sea Devil 258
The Second Part of the Rover 245
The Secret Life 252
Sédécie 243
Seideravond 252
Selby, Charles 256
Die Sendung Semaels 251
Les séquestrés d'Altona 254
Sessa, Karl Borromaeus 247
Shakespeare, William 14-19, 21, 25-26, 29-39, 41-44, 243
Shakovskoi, Alexander Alexandrovich 247
Shaw, George Bernard 251
Shaw, Irwin 253
Sheridan, Richard Brinsley 24, 42, 246
Sholz, Wilhelm von 251
Siddons, Henry 258
Simson 52
The Skele on Witness 248
Slaves in Algiers 247
A Sleep of Prisoners 254
Smith 251
Smith, Albert Richard 255
Society 249
Sodome et Gomorrhe 253

Die Soldaten 246
Sophomphaneas 243
Sorge, Reinhard Johannes 252
Soulie, Frédéric 248
Le soulier de satin 253, 254
The Spaniards 248
Spender, Stephen 253
Spiel von Abraham 243
Ein Spiel von dem Herzogen von Burgund 242
Spiel von Tobias 243
Stallings, Laurence 252
The State of Innocence and Fall of Man 245
Der Stellvertreter 254
Stephanie, Christian Gottlob 246
Stephanie, Gottlieb 246, 247
Sternheim, Carl 251, 252
Stillingfleet, Benjamin 246
Street Scene 253
Der Sturmgeselle Sokrates 251
Sudermann, Hermann 251
Die Suendflut 252
Symons, Arthur 250, 252

T

Das Taenzchen 251
Taille, Jean de la 243
Tancred 47
Taylor, Sir Henry 249
Taylor, Tom 46, 249
Testa, Tommasso conte Gherardi del 247
A testör 251
Der Teufel nahm ein altes Weib 243
Des Teufels General 254
Théatre à l'usage de jeunes personnes 246
Thiboust, Lambert 249
Thomaso, or the Wanderer 244
The Three Ladies of London 8, 243
The Ticket-of-Leave Man 46, 249
Tilbury, W. H. 256
Titus and Berenice 245
Titus Andronicus 21
To the Stars 251
Tobaeus 243
Der Tod Adams 246
Toller, Ernst 252
Tolstoi, Alexei 249
Tolstoi, Leo 40, 250
Tombo-Chiqui 258
Torelli, Achille 250
Torquemada 250
Towneley Plays: No. 21, "The Conspiracy"; No. "The Buffeting"; No. 23, "The Scourging"; 24, "The Hanging of Judas" [Fragment] 24:
Tragédie représentant l'odieus et sanalant meurtre ce mis par le maudit Cain à l'encontre de son fr Abel 243
A Tragedy of Abraham's Sacrifice 243
The Tragedy of King Saul 245
A Tragedy or Interlude Manifesting the Chief Prom of God . . . from the Fall of Adam 242
The Tragedy of Mariam 244
The Travels of the Three English Brothers Sherley 244
Trelawney of the "Wells" 250
Trial of a Judge 253
Trilby 250
Die Tuerkensklavin 246
Tyler, Royall 247

U

Udall, Nicholas 243
Ulysses von Ithaica 245
Um Winter 251
Die Umkehr 251
Under Two Flags 249
The Unfortunate Traveller 9-14
Unser Verkehr 247
Uriel Acosta 249

V

van der Veen, H.R.S.   247
Vega, Lope de   244
Verbrechen aus Ehrsucht   246
Die Verhaengnisvolle Gabel   248
Victoria Regina   253
La vida y muerte de Herodes   244
La vida y muerte de Judas   243
The Vindictive Man   247
The Virgin Widow   249
The Voice of Nature   258
Der Volontair   246
Voltaire, François Marie Arouet de   40, 245
Von Morgen bis Mitternacht   252
Vondel, Joost van den   244, 245

W

Wade, Thomas   248
Wagner, Heinrich Leopold   28, 246
Waiting for Lefty   253
Waldron, Francis Godolphin   246, 255
The Walking Statue   245
The Wandering Jew   247, 250
Die Wandlung   252
The War God   251
The Wars of the Jews   258
We, the People   253
Webster, John   8, 240, 244
Wedekind, Frank   252
Deg Weg der Verheissung   253
Weiss, Peter   49, 254
Werfel, Franz   48, 252, 253, 254
Werner, Zacharias   247
Wharton, Edith   251
What Price Glory?   252
What Will the World Say?   258
Wilde, Oscar   250
Wilkins   256
Wilkins, George   244
Wilson, John   245
Wilson, Robert   8, 243
Wine of Choice   253
Winterset   253
Das Wohl Gesprochene Urtheil . . .   244
Wolf, Friedrich   253
Women Pleased   244
Wouk, Herman   254
Woyzeck   46, 248
Wright, Richard   253
Das Wunder um Verdun   253

Y

York Plays: No. 26, The Cutlers' Play; No. 32, The Cooks' Play   242
The Young Quaker   246

Z

Zangwill, Israel   250, 251
Zeromski, Stefan   252
Zola, Emile   27, 250
Zrinny   247
Zuckmayer, Carl   252, 254
Zweig, Arnold   251, 252, 254
Zweig, Stefan   252